MW00668757

THE

EMPHATIC DIAGLOTT:

CONTAINING THE

Original Greek Text

OF WHAT IS COMMONLY STYLED THE

NEW TESTAMENT,

(According to the Recension of Dr. J. J. Griesbach,)

WITH AN

INTERLINEARY WORD FOR WORD ENGLISH TRANSLATION;

A NEW EMPHATIC VERSION,

BASED ON THE INTERLINEARY TRANSLATION, ON THE RENDERINGS OF EMINENT CRITICS, AND ON THE VARIOUS READINGS OF

THE VATICAN MANUSCRIPT,

No. 1209 in the Vatican Library.

TOGETHER WITH ILLUSTRATIVE AND EXPLANATORY FOOT NOTES AND A COPIOUS SELECTION OF REFERENCES

TO THE WHOLE OF WHICH IS ADDED,

A VALUABLE ALPHABETICAL APPENDIX.

BY BENJAMIN WILSON.

NEW YORK:

FOWLER & WELLS CO., PUBLISHERS,

775 BROADWAY

1891

Part 1

PREFACE.

To trouble the reader with any lengthy remarks on the important advantages to be derived from a new translation of the Sacred Writings, is deemed altogether unnecessary. Much information on this point has been given by others, who have published modern Versions of the New Testament, with the reasons which have induced them to do so. Those reasons will serve in a great measure also for this. It is generally admitted by all critics, that the Authorized or Common version of the Scriptures, absolutely needs revision. Obsolete words, uncouth phrases, bad grammar and punctuation, etc., all require alteration. But this is not all. There are errors of a more serious nature which need correction. The translators of the Common version were circumscribed and trammelled by royal mandate; they were required to retain certain old ecclesiastical words, which accordingly were left untranslated. Thus the minds of many who had no means of knowing the meaning of the original words have been misled and confused. Biblical criticism, however, during the last two hundred years, has done much to open up and elucidate the Word of God, by discovering many things which were unknown to the old translators, making great improvements in the text, detecting numerous interpolations and errors, and suggesting far better renderings of many passages. Many modern versions have availed themselves of this valuable assistance, and it is believed they have thereby been enabled to give the English reader a better understanding of what was originally written.

Without presuming to claim any superiority for this, as a translation of the New Testament, over any other modern version, it is thought that the present Work presents certain valuable features, not to be found elsewhere, and which will be of real practical utility to every one who wishes to read the books of the Evangelists and Apostles, as they were written under the guidance and inspiration of the Holy Spirit. These features are;—An approved Greek text, with the various Readings of the Vatican Manuscript, No. 1209; an Interlineary literal Word for Word English translation; a New Version, with the Signs of Emphasis; a copious selection of References; many appropriate, illustrative, and exegetical Foot-notes; and a valuable Alphabetical Appendix. This combination of important items cannot be found in any other book. The reader will find further remarks on this subject, on the page headed, "Plan of the Work;" and he is also invited to read the pages with the respective captions;—"To the Reader;" "History of the Greek Text;" and "History of English Versions." Also, on another page will be found the "Letters and Pronunciation of the Greek Alphabet," for the special benefit of those who may wish to obtain a rudimentary knowledge of that language.

The intelligent reader will at once perceive the utility and importance of this arrangement. Readers who are familiar with the original tongue, obtain in this Work one of the best Greek Testaments, with important ancient Readings, well worthy of their attention, and, it is presumed, that there are even few Greek scholars, who are so far advanced, but may derive some help from the translation given. Those who have only a little or no knowledge of the Greek, may by careful reading, and a little attention to the Interlineary translation, soon become familiar with it. This Work, in fact, places in the hands of the intelligent English reader the means of knowing and appropriating for his own benefit, with but little labor on his part, what it has cost others years of study and severe toil to acquire.

Scrupulous fidelity has been maintained throughout this version in giving the true rendering of the original text into English; no regard whatever being paid to the prevailing doctrines or prejudices of sects, or the peculiar tenets of theologians. To the Divine authority of the original Scriptures alone has there been the most humble and unbiassed submission.

In the preparation of this Work for the press, all available help to be derived from the labors of great and learned men, has been obtained and appropriated. Lexicons, Grammars, ancient and modern Versions, Commentaries, critical and explanatory, Cyclopedias, Bible and other Dictionaries, etc., have been consulted and culled from. Also, the suggestions, opinions, and criticisms of friends, on words, phrases, and passages, have been duly considered, and sometimes adopted. It is not presumed that this Work is free from faults or errors. Infallibility is left for others to claim. Great care, however, has been exercised to make it as correct as possible.

The Work is now sent forth to the public, to stand or fall on its own merits. True, it cannot boast of being the production of a council of learned men, as King James' version, but let it be remembered that TYNDALE alone, under very disadvantageous circumstances, did far more for the English Bible than that learned body, for they only followed in the wake of his labors.

This Volume, principally designed for the instruction and advantage of others, is now reverently committed to the blessing of our Father in the heavens, with an earnest and sincere desire that many of those who peruse its pages may be led by the knowledge, faith, and obedience inculcated therein, to obtain an inheritance in the aionian kingdom of Jesus the Anointed one.

B. WILSON.

HISTORY OF THE GREEK TEXT.

THE following condensed account of the different editions of the Greek New Testament, will introduce the reader to the history of the Greek Text, and the various steps taken by learned men for the purpose of editing it with greater critical accuracy. The history will commence with the first printed editions.

The first *printed* edition of the whole of the Greek New Testament was that contained in the Complutensian Polyglot; published by Francis XIMENES de CISNEROS. The principal editor of the work was Lopez de Stunica. It was printed in Greek and Latin, and completed January 10th, 1514. In consequence of the delay as to the publication of this edition (from 1514 to 1520) that of ERASMUS was commenced and completed, and was published in 1516, being the *first edition published* of the Greek New Testament. Like the Complutensian edition, this was also in Greek and Latin. The latter part of the book of Revelation being wanting in his MS. he supplied the same by *translating the Latin Vulgate into Greek.*

The Greek Manuscripts used for these two editions were few in number, of little critical value, and therefore do not possess much real authority. In 1535, Erasmus published his fifth edition, which is the basis of the common Text.*

In 1546, and again in 1549, ROBERT STEPHENS printed, at Paris, two beautiful small editions of the Greek New Testament; and in 1550 his folio edition with various readings from several Manuscripts—he collated some 15 MSS., but chiefly followed the Complutensian copy.

BEZA published five editions of the Greek Testament; the first in 1565, the last in 1598.

In 1624, the ELZEVIR, printers at Leyden, published a small and beautiful Greek Testament, the editor of which is wholly unknown. It differs little from Stephens' folio edition. The printers gave to this Text the name of "Textus Receptus."

In WALTON'S POLYGLOT of 1657, the Greek New Testament was given according to the Text of Stephens: and in the last volume there was a collection of various Readings from such MSS. as were then known. These various Readings, with some additions, were given in the Greek Testament, published by Bishop Fell, at Oxford, in 1675.

In 1707, Dr. MILL'S Greek Testament appeared. His Text is simply taken from Stephens' as given in Walton's Polyglot; his collection of various Readings was extensive, and these were made the ground for a critical amendment of the Text.

Dr. EDWARD WELLS published the first *critical revision* in parts at Oxford, between 1709 and 1719, with a translation and paraphrase.

BENGEL followed on in the same work and published his edition in 1734, and in his "Apparatus Criticus" he enlarged the stock of various Readings.

WETSTEIN published his Greek Testament in 1751–2, but only indicates in his inner margin, the few Readings which he preferred to those of the Elzevir edition. But in the collection of critical materials he did more than all his predecessors put together.

GRIESBACH, in critical labors, excels by far any who preceded him. He *used* the materials others had gathered. His first edition was commenced in 1775; his last completed in 1806. He combined the results of the collations of Birch, Matthaei and others, with those of Wetstein. In his Revision he often preferred the testimony of the *older* MSS. to the *mass* of modern copies.

Since the publication of Griesbach's Text, three or four other critical editions have been published, and have received the examination and approval of scholars. Of these, the edition of Scholz, has passed through numerous editions. His fundamental principle of criticism was, that the great majority of copies decide as to the correctness of the Text; hence, those who prefer the more ancient documents, will consider the Text of Griesbach preferable; while those whose judgment would favor the mass of testimonies, would prefer that of Scholz.

In addition to Scholz's collation, Lachmann, Tischendorf, Tregelles, &c., have given to the world the result of their critical labors, and which are acknowledged to be of the highest authority.

The number of MSS. now known, and which have been examined, is nearly 700; thus affording now a far better chance, to obtain a correct Greek Text, than when the authorised version was at first published.

* Erasmus, in his third edition of 1522, inserted, the text, 1 John v. 7, on the authority of a MS. now in Dublin. Tyndale used this edition to revise his English version.

HISTORY OF ENGLISH VERSIONS.

THE first English version of the New Testament was that made by JOHN WICLIF, or WICLIFFE, about the year 1367. It was translated from the Latin Bible, *verbatim*, without any regard to the idiom of the languages. Though this version was first in point of time, no part of it was printed before the year 1731.

TYNDALE'S translation was published in 1526, either at Antwerp or Hamburg. It is commonly said that Tyndale translated from the Greek, but he never published it to be so on any title page of his Testament. One edition, not published by him, has this title—"The Newe Testament, dylygently corrected and compared with the Greke, by Willyam Tyndale, and fynesshed in the yere of oure Lorde God, A. M. D. and xxxiiij. in the moneth of Nouember." It is evident he only translated from the Vulgate Latin.

COVERDALE published the whole Bible in English, in the year 1535. He "followed his interpreters," and adopted Tyndale's version, with the exception of a few alterations.

MATTHEW'S BIBLE was only Tyndale and Coverdale's, published under the feigned name of Thomas Matthews.

HOLLYBUSHE'S NEW TESTAMENT was printed in 1538, "both in Latin and English, after the Vulgate text," to which Coverdale prefixed a dedication to Henry VIII.

THE GREAT BIBLE, published in 1539, purported to be "translated after the veryte of the Hebrue and Greke textes," but it is certain that it was only a revision of Matthew's, with a few small alterations. It was named "the Great Bible," because of its large size.

CRANMER'S BIBLE, published in 1540, was essentially the same as the Great Bible, but took his name on account of a few corrections which he made in it.

THE GENEVA BIBLE was published at Geneva in 1560. The New Testament in 1557. Coverdale was one of the Geneva brethren who issued it.

THE BISHOPS' BIBLE was a revisal of the English Bible, made by the bishops, and compared with the originals. It was published in 1568.

THE DOWAY BIBLE appeared in 1609, and was translated from the *authentical Latin*, or Vulgate.

KING JAMES' BIBLE, or the Authorized Version, was published in 1611. In the year 1604, forty-seven persons learned in the languages, were appointed to revise the translation then in use. They were ordered to use the Bishops' Bible as the basis of the new version, and to alter it as little as the original would allow; but if the prior translations of Tyndale, Coverdale, Matthew, Cranmer or Whitchurch, and the Geneva editors agreed better with the text, to adopt the same. This translation was perhaps the best that could be made at the time, and if it had not been published by *kingly* authority, it would not now be venerated by English and American protestants, as though it had come direct from God. It has been convicted of containing over 20,000 errors. Nearly 700 Greek MSS. are now known, and some of them very ancient; whereas the translators of the common version had only the advantage of some 8 MSS., none of which were earlier than the tenth century.

Since 1611, many translations of both Old and New Testaments, and portions of the same, have been published. The following are some of the most noted.

The Family Expositor: or a Paraphrase and Version of the New Testament, with Critical Notes. By Philip Doddridge. 1756.

The Four Gospels translated from the Greek. By George Campbell. 1790.

A New Literal Translation, from the Original Greek, of the Apostolical Epistles. By James Macknight. 1795.

A Translation of the New Testament. By Gilbert Wakefield. 1795.

A Translation of the New Testament, from the original Greek. Humbly attempted by Nathaniel Scarlett, assisted by men of piety and literature. 1798.

The New Testament in an Improved Version, upon the basis of Archbishop Newcome's New Translation, with a corrected Text. 1808.

The New Testament, in Greek and English; the Greek according to Griesbach; the English upon the basis of the fourth London edition of the Improved Version, with an attempt to further improvement from the translations of Campbell, Wakefield, Scarlett, Macknight, and Thomson. By Abner Kneeland. 1823.

A New Family Bible, and improved Version, from corrected Texts of the Originals, with Notes Critical, &c. By B. Boothroyd. 1823.

The Sacred Writings of the Apostles and Evangelists, translated from the Original, by Campbell, Macknight, and Doddridge, with various Emendations by A. Campbell. 1833.

A New and Corrected Version of the New Testament. By R. Dickinson. 1833.

The Book of the New Covenant, a Critical Revision of the Text and Translation of Common Version, with the aid of most ancient MSS. By Granville Penn. 1836.

The Holy Bible, with 20,000 emendations. By J. T. Conquest. 1841.

The Good News of our Lord Jesus, the Anointed; from the Critical Greek of Tittman. By N. N. Whiting. 1849.

A Translation of the New Testament, from the Syriac. By James Murdock. 1852.

Translation of Paul's Epistles. By Joseph Turnbull. 1854.

The New Testament, translated from Griesbach's Text. By Samuel Sharpe. 1856.

TO THE READER.

THAT "All Scripture, divinely inspired, is profitable for Teaching, for Conviction, for Correction, for THAT Instruction which is in Righteousness," is the truthful testimony of the Sacred Writings about themselves. We rejoice to express our conviction that the Word of God was perfect and infallible as it emanated from those holy men of old, the Prophets and Apostles, who "spoke, being moved by the Holy Spirit." As a revelation of Jehovah's will to the human race, it was requisite that it should be an unerring guide. Amid the ever conflicting strife of human opinions, and the endless diversity of thought, we needed such a standard, to lead us safely through the perplexing problems of life, to counsel us under all circumstances, to reveal the will of our Heavenly Parent, and to lift on high a celestial light, which streaming through the thick darkness that broods around, shall guide the feet of his erring and bewildered children to their loving Father's home. We needed therefore a testimony upon which to repose our faith and hope, free from all error, immutable, and harmonious in all its details—something to tell us how to escape from the evils of the present, and attain to a glorious future. With reverence and joy we acknowledge the Sacred Writings to be such, as they were originally dictated by the Holy Spirit. How important then that they should be correctly read and understood!

But can it be fairly said that such is the case with our present English Version? We opine not. Though freely acknowledging that it is sufficiently plain to teach men the social and religious duties of life, and the path to Immortality, yet it is a notable fact that King James' Translation is far from being a faithful reflection of the mind of the Spirit, as contained in the Original Greek in which the books of the New Testament were written. There are some thousands of words which are either mistranslated, or too obscurely rendered; besides others which are now obsolete, through improvement in the language. Besides this, it has been too highly colored in many places with the party ideas and opinions of those who made it, to be worthy of full and implicit confidence being placed in it as a genuine record. In the words of Dr. Macknight, "it was "made a little too complaisant to the "King, in favoring his notions of predes-"tination, election, witchcraft, familiar "spirits, and kingly rights, and these it "is probable were also the translators' "opinions. That their translation is par-"tial, speaking the language of, and giv-"ing authority to one sect." And according to Dr. Gell, it was wrested and partial, "and only adapted to one sect;" but he imputes this, not to the translators, but to those who employed them, for even some of the translators complained that they could not follow their own judgment in the matter, but were restrained by "reasons of state."

The Version in common use will appear more imperfect still, when the fact is known, that it was not a translation from the Original, but merely a revision of the Versions then in use. This is evident from the following directions given by King James to the translators, viz.: "The Bishops' Bible to be "followed, and altered as little as the Origi-"nal will permit. And these translations to "be used when they agree better with the "text than the Bishops' Bible—namely, Tyn-"dal's, Matthew's, Coverdale's, Whitchurch's, "Geneva." None of these were made from the Original Greek, but *only compared with it*—being all translated from the *Vulgate Latin*. Hence it follows, that the authorized version is simply a revision of the Vulgate. And the Greek Text, with which it was compared, was compiled from Eight MSS. only, all of which were written since the tenth century, and are now considered of comparatively slight authority. The "*Textus Receptus*," or Received Greek Text, was made from these MSS., and is now proved to be the very worst Greek Text extant, in a printed form. And there was only one MS. for the Book of Revelation, and part of that wanting, which was supplied by translating the Latin of the Vulgate into Greek! Since the publication of the "*Textus Receptus*," and the Common Version, some 660 MSS. have been discovered, some of which are very ancient, and very valuable. The best and oldest of these is one marked B., *Cod. Vaticanus*, No. 1209, of the fourth and fifth centuries. The second marked A., *Cod. Alexandrinus*, of the fifth century. The third marked C., *Cod. Ephrem.*, about the fifth century, and the fourth, marked D., *Cod. Cantabrigiensis*, of the seventh century.

Besides valuable assistance from ancient MSS., the DIAGLOTT has obtained material aid from the labors of many eminent Biblical Critics and Translators. Among these may be mentioned,—Mill, Wetstein, Griesbach, Scholz, Lachmann, Tischendorf, Tittman, Tregelles, Doddridge, Macknight, Campbell, Horne, Middleton, Clark, Wakefield, Bloomfield, Thompson, Murdock, Kneeland Boothroyd, Conquest, Sharpe, Gaussen, Turnbull, Trench, &c., &c.

Should any person doubt the propriety of the Translation, in any particular part, let him not hastily censure or condemn till he has compared it carefully with the various authorities on which it is based; and even should he see reason to differ in some respects, a *correct Greek Text* is given, so that the Original may be always appealed to in cases of doubt. However imperfect the Translation may be considered by the Critic, it cannot adulterate the Original.

PLAN OF THE WORK.

1. Greek Text and Interlineary Translation.—The left hand column contains the GREEK TEXT according to Dr. J. J. Griesbach, and interlined with it a LITERAL WORD-FOR-WORD TRANSLATION, wherein the corresponding English is placed directly under each Greek word.

The *Sectional* Divisions are those of the Vatican and Alexandrian MSS. Greek Words enclosed in brackets [thus,] though authorized by Griesbach, are omitted by the Vat. MS.

The advantages to be derived from such an arrangement must be apparent to the Bible Student. The learned have a *Greek Text* acknowledged to be one of the best extant, while the unlearned have almost an equal chance with those acquainted with the Original, by having the meaning and grammatical construction given to each word. This part of the work will be a desideratum by many, but more adapted for criticism than reading. Although by adhering to the arrangement of the Original, the Translation may appear uncouth, yet the strength and beauty of many passages are thereby preserved.

The frequent recurrence of the Greek article of emphasis, and an occasional ellipsis, often interfere with the sense and elegance of a sentence, but this cannot well be avoided in a word-for-word Translation. The advantages, however, accruing to the diligent investigator of the Divine Word by persuing this plan are many, and will be duly appreciated.

2. New Version.—The column on the right hand side of the page is a NEW VERSION for general reading. This rendering is based upon that in the left hand Column, and the labors of many talented Critics and Translators of the Scriptures. The Readings of the oldest Manuscripts now known are sometimes incorporated, and always referred to. In this Column the EMPHATIC SIGNS are introduced, by which the Greek Words of Emphasis are designated. For the use and beauty of this arrangement, the reader is requested to examine the annexed remarks on Signs of Emphasis.

The *Chapters* and *Verses* of the Common Version have been retained, principally for convenience of reference. The reader however, by following the paragraphs in the opposite column, need not be governed by these arbitrary divisions. Chapters and Verses were not introduced till the middle of the 16th century.

3. Foot Notes and References.—The various Readings of the Vatican MS., Notes for the elucidation of the text, and References, are introduced at the bottom of the page. The Notes are critical, illustrative, explanatory, and suggestive. Old Testament quotations are always referred to, and copious parallel passages in the New.

4. Appendix.—It is intended to add an Appendix to the Work, containing all the Geographical and Proper Names found in the New Testament, with Words and Phrases intimately connected with doctrinal subjects, alphabetically arranged. These will be critically examined, and the light of Biblical science thrown upon such as have given rise to sectarian disputes, and the cavils of infidels.

SIGNS OF EMPHASIS.

The Greek article often finds its equivalent in the English definite article *the*, but in the majority of cases it is evidently only a mark of emphasis. It frequently precedes a substantive, an adjective, a verb, an adverb, a participle or a particle, thus pointing out the emphatic words. The Greek article and Emphatic Pronouns exercise a most important influence on the meaning of words, and sometimes throw light on doctrines of the highest interest. The sacred penmen of the New Testament were, in the opinion of many eminent persons, guided by Divine inspiration in the choice of their words: and in the use of the Greek article there was clearly a remarkable discretion displayed. In fact, the Signs of Emphasis are incorporated with the words in such a manner, that the latter cannot be stated without conveying at the same time to the intelligent mind an idea of the very intonation with which the sentence was spoken when it was written down. This peculiarity of the Greek language cannot be properly expressed in English except by the use of typographical signs; such as, Initial Capital letters, *italics*, SMALL CAPITALS, and CAPITALS.

The Common Version of the New Testament fails to give the reader a full conception of the meaning designed to be conveyed by the Greek original, in regard—

1st. To those Words which are connected with the Greek Article;

2d. To those Pronouns Substantive which are intended to carry in themselves a peculiar emphasis; and,

3d. To those Adjectives and Pronouns which obtain a comparative importance, by reason of the position which they occupy in the Greek Text, with reference to some other words.

To remedy these deficiencies, the following System of Noattion is employed in the English column of the DIAGLOTT.

1. Those Words rendered *positively* emphatic by the presence of the *Greek article*, are printed in Small Capitals: as, "The LIFE was the LIGHT of MEN."

2. Those Pronouns Substantive which, in the Greek, are intended to be *positively* emphatic are printed in Black Letter: as, "𝔥𝔢 must increase, but 𝔦 must decrease."

3. Those Adjectives and Pronouns which in the Greek are *comparatively* emphatic, as indicated by their position, are printed with an Initial Capital Letter: as, "One Body, and One Spirit, even as ye are called in One Hope of your CALLING."

4. All Greek Substantives, as being of more importance than other words, are also commenced with a Capital Letter.

By adopting these Signs of Emphasis, it is believed *certainty* and *intensity* are given to passages where they occur, as well as *vivacity* and *earnestness* to the discourses in which they are found; thus rendering the reader, a hearer, as it were, of the life-words of Him "who spoke as never man spoke," or which were enunciated by His inspired apostles.

LETTERS AND PRONUNCIATION OF THE GREEK ALPHABET.

FIGURE.	NAME.	SOUND, OR POWER.
Α α	Alpha	a
Β β	Beta	b
Γ γ	Gamma	g hard, as in be*g*in
Δ δ	Delta	d
Ε ε	Epsilon	e short, as in m*e*t
Ζ ζ	Zeta	z
Η η	Eta	e long, as in k*ee*n
Θ θ	Theta	th
Ι ι	Iota	i
Κ κ	Kappa	k
Λ λ	Lambda	l
Μ μ	Mu	m
Ν ν	Nu	n
Ξ ξ	Xi	x
Ο ο	Omicron	o short, as in l*o*t
Π π	Pi	p
Ρ ρ	Rho	r
Σ σ, final ς	Sigma	s
Τ τ	Tau	t
Υ υ	Upsilon	u
Φ φ	Phi	ph
Χ χ	Chi	ch hard, as in *ch*ord
Ψ ψ	Psi	ps
Ω ω	Omega	o long, as in thr*o*ne.

REMARKS.

*** ACCENTS are said to sometimes assist the reader to discriminate between words which are alike in form, but different in meaning; but as they are by no means necessary, either for the pronouncing or understanding of the Greek language, and as the earliest of all the manuscripts of the Greek Testament is without accents, it has been thought best to omit them in the DIAGLOTT, leaving the sense, in doubtful cases, to be determined by the context. If accents favor a particular sense, it may be an erroneous one, and then they are injurious; and if they do not favor any particular sense, then they are unnecessary.

PRONUNCIATION.—Considerable discrepancy of opinion prevails among the learned concerning the proper sound of some of these letters, and as it is impossible at this distance of time to ascertain the mode of pronunciation among the ancient Greeks, the simplest plan is to consider each Greek letter as corresponding in sound to its correlative letter in our own alphabet, as shown in the Table.

The LETTERS are divided into seven vowels and seventeen consonants.

The VOWELS are ε, ο, short; η, ω, long; and α, ι, υ, doubtful.

DIPHTHONGS are formed of two vowels joined together, and are twelve in number; six proper, αι, αυ, ει, ευ, οι, ου and six improper, ᾳ, ῃ, ῳ, ηυ, ωυ, υι. The little stroke under ᾳ, ῃ, ῳ, standing for *Iota*, called *Iota subscript*, is not sounded, but merely serves to show the derivation.

The LABIALS, (π, β, φ,) the PALATALS, (κ, γ, χ,) and the DENTALS, (τ, δ, θ,) are named according to the organs of articulation employed in pronouncing them. To each of these classes belongs a *double* letter, so called because combining the sound of ς with that of another consonant; thus, the Labials, πς, βς, φς, are equal to ψ, the Palatals, κς, γς, χς, to ξ, and the Dentals, τς, δς, to ζ.

The letter ν can stand only before Dentals; before Labials it becomes μ· before the liquids, (λ, μ, ν, ρ,) assimilation takes place, so that before λ it becomes λ, before ρ it becomes ρ, &c. Before Palatals ν is converted into γ· but observe, that whenever γ is found before another γ, or either of the other Palatals, it is always pronounced like *n*; thus αγγελος (*angel*) is pronounced *an*-gelos, not aggelos.

Every word having a vowel or diphthong for the first letter is, in most printed books, marked at the beginning either with an *aspirate*, or rough breathing, (ʽ), as ἡλιος, (*sun*,) pronounced as if written *h*elios; or with a smooth one, (ʼ), as ἐπι, (upon,) simply read *epi*. The former one of these breathings is only of necessary use, and may be considered as having the force of the English letter *h*. The aspirate is placed over ρ and υ when they stand at the beginning of a word; thus ῥοδον, (*a rose*,) pronounced *rhodon*. In diphthongs the breathing is placed over the second vowel; thus υἱος, (*a son*,) pronounced *why-os*. When ρ is doubled, the last one takes the aspirate, as ἐρρωσο, pronounced *errhoso*.

Words in Greek are of eight kinds, called Parts of Speech; viz., *Article*, *Noun*, *Pronoun*, *Verb*, *Participle*, *Adverb*, *Preposition*, and *Conjunction*.

The Article, Noun, Pronoun, and Participle, are declined with *Gender*, *Number*, and *Case*.

There are three Genders; the *Masculine*, *Feminine* and *Neuter*.

There are two Numbers; the *Singular*, which speaks of *one*, as λογος, *a word;* and the *Plural*, which speaks of *more than one*, as λογοι, *words*.

To these the Greeks added a third number, called the *Dual*, which only sp[illegible]s of *two*, but this number was not much used, and is not found either in the Septuagint, or New Testament.

There are five Cases; the *Nominative*, *Genitive*, *Dative*, *Accusative*, and *Vocative*.

The Article ὁ, ἡ, το, generally answers to the definite article *the* in English. When no article is expressed in Greek, the English indefinite article *a* is signified. Thus ανθρωπος means *a man*, or *man* in general; and ὁ ανθρωπος, *the man*. It is thus declined:

SINGULAR.	*Masc.*	*Fem.*	*Neut.*		PLURAL.	*Masc.*	*Fem.*	*Neut.*	
Nom.	ὁ,	ἡ,	το,	*the.*	Nom.	οἱ,	αἱ,	τα,	*the.*
Gen.	του,	της,	του,	*of the.*	Gen.	των,	των,	των,	*of the.*
Dat.	τῳ,	τῃ,	τῳ,	*to the.*	Dat.	τοις,	ταις,	τοις,	*to the.*
Acc.	τον,	την,	το,	*the.*	Acc.	τους,	τας,	τα,	*the.*

The Article has no vocative; ω, which sometimes precedes a noun in the vocative, is an Interjection.

The Article takes the consonant τ in every Case, except in the nom. sin. masc. and fem. ὁ, ἡ, and in the nom. pl. masc. and fem. οἱ, αἱ, where the τ is superseded by the aspirate (ʽ).

The gen. pl. in all genders and in every declension, ends in ων.

The Personal or Primitive Pronouns are three; εγω, *I*, plural ἡμεις, *we*, of the first person; συ, *thou*, plural ὑμεις, *you*, of the second; Gen. οὑ, *he* or *she*, plural σφεις, *they*, of the third.

The Relative Pronouns are ὁς, ἡ, ὁ, *who*, *which*, and αυτος, αυτη, αυτο, *he*, *she*, *it*, &c., &c., &c.

To those wholly unacquainted with Greek, the foregoing remarks will give some, though perhaps but little satisfaction. If a further knowledge is desired, the reader had better procure a Grammar. A very good book to commence with has been published by Bagster & Sons, London, entitled, "A Practical Guide to the first Study of the Greek Testament," designed for those who have no knowledge of the Greek language.

*[ΕΥΑΓΓΕΛΛΙΟΝ] ΚΑΤΑ ΜΑΤΘΑΙΟΝ.

[GLAD TIDINGS] BY MATTHEW.

ACCORDING TO MATTHEW.

ΚΕΦ. ά. 1.

1 Βιβλος γεννεσεως Ιησου Χριστου, υἱου
A record of descent of Jesus Christ, son of
Δαυιδ, υἱου Αβρααμ. 2 Αβρααμ εγεννησε τον
David, son of Abraam. Abraam begot the
Ισαακ· Ισαακ δε εγεννησε τον Ιακωβ· Ιακωβ
Isaac; Isaac and begot the Jacob; Jacob
δε εγεννησε τον Ιουδαν και τους αδελφους
and begot the Judas and the brothers
αυτου. 3 Ιουδας δε εγεννησε τον Φαρες και τον
of him. Judas and begot the Phares and the
Ζαρα εκ της Θαμαρ. Φαρες δε εγεννησε τον
Zara by the Thamar. Phares and begot the
Εσρωμ· Εσρωμ δε εγεννησε τον Αραμ· 4 Αραμ
Esrom; Esrom and begot the Aram; Aram
δε εγεννησε τον Αμιναδαβ· Αμιναδαβ δε
and begot the Aminadab; Aminadab and
εγεννησε τον Ναασσων· Ναασσων δε εγεννησε
begot the Naasson; Naasson and begot
τον Σαλμων· 5 Σαλμων δε εγεννησε τον Βοοζ
the Salmon. Salmon and begot the Booz
εκ της Ῥαχαβ. Βοοζ δε εγεννησε τον Ωβηδ εκ
by the Rachab. Booz and begot the Obed by
της Ῥουθ. Ωβηδ δε εγεννησε τον Ιεσσαι·
the Ruth. Obed and begot the Jesse;
6 Ιεσσαι δε εγεννησε τον Δαυιδ τον βασιλεα.
Jesse and begot the David the king.
Δαυιδ δε *[ὁ βασιλευς] εγεννησε τον Σολομωνα
David and [the king] begot the Solomon
εκ της του Ουριου. 7 Σολομων δε εγεννησε
by the of the Urias. Solomon and begot
τον Ῥοβοαμ· Ῥοβοαμ δε εγεννησε τον Αβια·
the Roboam; Roboam and begot the Abia;
Αβια δε εγεννησε τον Ασα· 8 Ασα δε εγεννησε
Abia and begot the Asa; Asa and begot
τον Ιωσαφατ· Ιωσαφατ δε εγεννησε τον Ιωραμ·
the Josaphat; Josaphat and begot the Joram,
Ιωραμ δε εγεννησε τον Οζιαν· 9 Οζιας δε εγεν-
Joram and begot the Ozias; Ozias and begot
νησε τον Ιωαθαμ· Ιωαθαμ δε εγεννησε τον Αχαζ·
the Jotham; Jotham and begot the Achaz;
Αχαζ δε εγεννησε τον Εζεκιαν· 10 Εζεκιας δε
Achaz and begot the Ezekias; Ezekias and
εγεννησε τον Μανασση· Μανασσης δε εγεννησε
begot the Manasses; Manasses and begot
τον Αμων· Αμων δε εγεννησε τον Ιωσιαν· 11 Ιωσιας
the Amon; Amon and begot the Josias; Josias
δε εγεννησε τον Ιεχονιαν και τους αδελφους
and begot the Jechonias and the brothers
αυτου, επι της μετοικεσιας Βαβυλωνος.
of him, near the removal Babylonian.

CHAPTER I.

1 A Register of the ‡ Lineage of Jesus Christ, Son of David, Son of Abraham.

2 From ‡ Abraham proceeded ISAAC; from ‡ Isaac, JACOB; from ‡ Jacob, JUDAH and his BROTHERS;

3 from Judah, PHAREZ and ZARAH, by TAMAR; from Pharez, HEZRON; from Hezron, RAM;

4 from Ram, AMMINADAB; from Amminadab, NAHSHON; from Nahshon, SALMON;

5 from Salmon, BOAZ, by RAHAB; from Boaz, OBED, by RUTH; from Obed, JESSE;

6 and from ‡ Jesse, DAVID the KING. David had ‡ SOLOMON by the [WIDOW] of URIAH;

7 Solomon had ‡ REHOBOAM; Rehoboam had ABIJAH; Abijah had ASA;

8 Asa had JEHOSHAPHAT; Jehoshaphat had † JEHORAM; Jehoram had UZZIAH;

9 Uzziah had JOTHAM; Jotham had AHAZ; Ahaz had HEZEKIAH;

10 Hezekiah had MANASSEH; Manesseh had AMON; Amon had JOSIAH;

11 and † Josiah had JECHONIAH and his BROTHERS, near the time of the CARRYING-AWAY to Babylon.

---

* VATICAN MANUSCRIPT—*Title*—According to Matthew. 6. the KING—*omit.*

† 8. By reference to 2 Chron. xxii., and following chapters, it will be seen that the names of *Ahaziah, Joash*, and *Amaziah*, the immediate descendants of Jehoram, are omitted in the text. † 11. Some MSS. read, "Josiah begot Jehoiakim, and Jehoiakim begot Jechoniah," probably inserted to make up fourteen generations, as mentioned in verse 17. Doddridge, Macknight, Clarke, and some others, adopt this reading. It is not found in the oldest MSS.

‡ 1. Luke iii. 23. ‡ 2. Gen. xxi. 2; xxv. 26; xxix. 35. ‡ 6. 1 Sam. xvi. 1; xvii. 12. ‡ 2 Sam. xii. 24. ‡ 7. 1 Chron. iii. 10.

12 Μετα δε την μετοικεσιαν Βαβυλωνος, Ιεχονιας
After and the removal Babylonian, Jechonias
εγεννησε τον Σαλαθιηλ. Σαλαθιηλ δε εγεννησε
begot the Salathiel. Salathiel and begot
τον Ζοροβαβελ· 13 Ζοροβαβελ δε εγεννησε τον
the Zorobabel; Zorobabel and begot the
Αβιουδ· Αβιουδ δε εγεννησε τον Ελιακειμ· Ελια-
Abiud; Abiud and begot the Eliakim; Elia-
κειμ δε εγεννησε τον Αζωρ· 14 Αζωρ δε εγεννησε
kim and begot the Azor; Azor and begot
τον Σαδωκ· Σαδωκ δε εγεννησε τον Αχειμ· Αχειμ
the Sadok; Sadok and begot the Achim; Achim
δε εγεννησε τον Ελιουδ· 15 Ελιουδ δε εγεννησε
and begot the Eliud; Eliud and begot
τον Ελεαζαρ· Ελεαζαρ δε εγεννησε τον Ματθαν·
the Eleazar; Eleazar and begot the Matthan;
Ματθαν δε εγεννησε τον Ιακωβ· 16 Ιακωβ δε
Matthan and begot the Jacob; Jacob and
εγεννησε τον Ιωσηφ, τον ανδρα Μαριας, εκ ἡς
begot the Joseph, the husband of Mary, of whom
εγεννηθη Ιησους, ὁ λεγομενος Χριστος.
was born Jesus, that being named Christ.
17 Πασαι ουν αἱ γενεαι απο Αβρααμ ἑως Δαυιδ,
All then the generations from Abraam till David,
γενεαι δεκατεσσαρες· και απο Δαυιδ ἑως της
generations fourteen; and from David till the
μετοικεσιας Βαβυλωνος, γενεαι δεκατεσσαρες·
removal Babylonian, generations fourteen;
και απο της μετοικεσιας Βαβυλωνος ἑως του
and from the removal Babylonian till the
Χριστου, γενεαι δεκατεσσαρες.
Christ, generations fourteen.
18 Του δε Ιησου Χριστου ἡ γενεσις οὑτως ην.
Of the now Jesus Christ the birth thus was.
Μνηστευθεισης γαρ της μητρος αυτου Μαριας τῳ
Being espoused for the mother of him Mary to the
Ιωσηφ, πριν η συνελθειν αυτους, εὑρεθη εν
Joseph, before either came together them, she was found in
γαστρι εχουσα εκ πνευματος ἁγιου. 19 Ιωσηφ δε
womb having by a spirit holy. Joseph and
ὁ ανηρ αυτης, δικαιος ων και μη θελων αυτην
the husband of her, a just man being and not willing her
παραδειγματισαι, εβουληθη λαθρα απολυσαι
to publicly expose, was inclined secretly to release
αυτην. 20 Ταυτα δε αυτου ενθυμηθεντος, ιδου,
her. These but of him thinking on, lo,
αγγελος κυριου κατ' οναρ εφανη αυτῳ, λεγων·
a messenger of a lord in a dream appeared to him, saying;
Ιωσηφ, υἱος Δαυιδ, μη φοβηθης παραλαβειν Μα-
Joseph, son of David, not thou shouldst fear to take Ma-
ριαμ την γυναικα σου· το γαρ εν αυτῃ γεννηθεν,
ry the wife of thee; that for in her being formed,
εκ πνευματος εστιν ἁγιου· 21 τεξεται δε υἱον, και
by a spirit is holy; she shall bear and a son, and
καλεσεις το ονομα αυτου Ιησουν· αυτος γαρ σωσει
thou shalt call the name of him Jesus; he for shall save

12 And after the CARRYING-AWAY to Babylon, from Jeconiah descended SALATHIEL; from Salathiel, ZERUBBABEL;

13 from Zerubbabel, ABIUD; from Abiud, ELIAKIM; from Eliakim, AZOR;

14 from Azor, ZADOC; from Zadoc, ACHIM; from Achim, ELIUD;

15 from Eliud, ELEAZAR; from Eleazar, MATTHAN; from Matthan, JACOB;

16 and from Jacob, JOSEPH, the HUSBAND of Mary, of whom was born THAT Jesus, who is NAMED Christ.

17 † [All the GENERATIONS, then, from Abraham to David, are fourteen Generations; from David till the CARRYING-AWAY to Babylon, fourteen Generations; and from the CARRYING-AWAY to Babylon till the MESSIAH, fourteen Generations.]

18 Now the ‡ NATIVITY of the *CHRIST Jesus was thus: Mary his MOTHER had been pledged to JOSEPH; but before they united, she was discovered to be pregnant by the holy Spirit.

19 Then Joseph, her affianced HUSBAND, being a just man, and unwilling to expose her, purposed to ‡ divorce her privately.

20 But while he was reflecting on these things, behold! an Angel of the Lord appeared to him in a Dream, saying, "Joseph, Son of David, fear not to take Mary, thy affianced WIFE; for THAT BEING FORMED in her is by the holy Spirit:

21 she will bear a Son, and thou shalt ‡ call his NAME † Jesus; for he will

* VATICAN MANUSCRIPT—18. the CHRIST Jesus.

† 17. Penn omits this verse; Newcome, Pearce, and others regard it as a marginal gloss. † 18. Fifth year before the common *Anno Domini*. † 21. Jesus—Heb. YAHVA-SHUA, i. e., *Yah-shua*, or *Joshua*. YAH, or JAH, *I shall be*; and SHUA, *Powerful*—hence the name signifies, *I shall be the Powerful*. "Thou shalt call his name JESUS," for this reason, "Because HE will save his PEOPLE from their SINS." See Acts vii. 45, Heb. iv. 8, and Appendix, word *Jesus*.

‡ 18. Luke i. 27. ‡ 19. Deut. xxiv. 1. ‡ 21. Luke i. 31; ii. 21.

τον λαον αὐτου απο των ἁμαρτιων αυτων·22(Τουτο
the people of him from the sins of them; This
δε ὁλον γεγονεν, ἱνα πληρωθῃ το ῥηθεν ὑπο
and all was done, so that might be fulfilled the word spoken by
του κυριου δια του προφητου, λεγοντος· 23"Ἰδου,
the lord through the prophet, saying; "Lo,
ἡ παρθενος εν γαστρι ἑξει, και τεξεται υἱον, και
the virgin in womb shall have, and shall bear a son, and
καλεσουσι το ονομα αυτου Εμμανουηλ·" ὁ εστι
they shall call the name of him Emmanuel;" which is
μεθερμηνευομενον, μεθ' ἡμων *[ὁ] θεος.)
being translated, with us [the] God.
24Διεγερθεις δε ὁ Ιωσηφ απο του ὑπνου, εποιησεν
Being aroused and the Joseph from the sleep, he did
ὡς προσεταξεν αυτῳ ὁ αγγελος κυριου· και παρε-
as commanded to him the messenger of a lord; and took
λαβε την γυναικα αὐτου, 25και ουκ εγινωσκεν
the wife of him, but not he knew
αυτην ἑως οὑ ετεκε *[τον] υἱον *[αὐτης τον
her till she brought forth [the] son [of her the
πρωτοτοκον·] και εκαλεσε το ονομα αυτου Ιησουν.
first-born;] and called the name of him Jesus.

ΚΕΦ. β'. 2.

1Του δε Ιησου γεννηθεντος εν Βηθλεεμ της
The and Jesus being born in Bethleem of the
Ιουδαιας, εν ἡμεραις Ἡρωδου του βασιλεως, ιδου,
Judea, in days of Herod the king, lo,
μαγοι απο ανατολων παρεγενοντο εις Ἱεροσολυ-
wise-men from an east country came into Jerusalem,
μα, λεγοντες· 2Που εστιν ὁ τεχθεις βασιλευς των
saying; Where is the new-born king of the
Ιουδαιων; ειδομεν γαρ αυτου τον αστερα εν τῃ
Jews? we saw for of him the star in the
ανατολῃ, και ηλθομεν προσκυνησαι αυτῳ. 3Ακου-
rising, and are come to do homage to him. Having
σας δε Ἡρωδης ὁ βασιλευς εταραχθη, και πασα
heard and Herod the king was alarmed, and all
Ἱεροσολυμα μετ' αυτου· 4και συναγαγων παντας
Jerusalem with him; and having called together all
τους αρχιερεις και γραμματεις του λαου, επυν-
the chief-priests and scribes of the people, he in-
θανετο παρ' αυτων, που ὁ Χριστος γενναται. 5Οἱ
quired of them, where the Anointed should be born. They
δε ειπον αυτῳ· Εν Βηθλεεμ της Ιουδαιας· οὑτω
and said to him; In Bethleem of the Judea; thus
γαρ γεγραπται δια του προφητου· 6"Και συ Βηθ-
for it is written by the prophet "And thou Beth-
λεεμ, γη Ιουδα, ουδαμως ελαχιστη ει εν τοις
leem, land of Juda, by no means least art among the
ἡγεμοσιν Ιουδα· εκ σου γαρ εξελευσεται ἡγουμε-
princes of Juda; out of thee for shall come forth a prince,
νος, ὁστις ποιμανει τον λαον μου, τον Ισραηλ."
who shall govern the people of me, the Israel."
7Τοτε Ἡρωδης λαθρα καλεσας τους μαγους,
Then Herod privately having called the wise-men,

‡ save his PEOPLE from their SINS."

22 (All this occurred, that the WORD SPOKEN by the Lord through the PROPHET, might be verified, saying:

23 ‡ "Behold! the VIRGIN shall conceive, and "bear a Son, and his "NAME shall be called "† Imma-nu-el;" which signifies, God with us.)

24 And JOSEPH, being raised from SLEEP did as the ANGEL of the Lord had commanded him, and took his WIFE;

25 but he knew her not, till ‡ she brought forth a Son, and called his NAME Jesus.

CHAPTER II.

1 And JESUS being born in Bethlehem of JUDÆA, in the Days of Herod, the KING, behold, † Magians from the East, came into Jerusalem; saying:

2 "Where is the NEW-BORN KING of the JEWS? for we saw his STAR at its RISING, and are come to do him homage."

3 Now * Herod, the KING, having heard, was alarmed, and All Jerusalem with him.

4 And having assembled All the CHIEF-PRIESTS and Scribes of the PEOPLE, he inquired of them where the MESSIAH should be born.

5 And THEY answered, "In Bethlehem, of JUDÆA;" for thus it is written by the PROPHET:

6 ‡ "And thou Bethlehem, "Land of JUDAH, art by "no means least as to the "PRINCES of Judah; for out "of thee shall come forth "a Prince, who shall rule "my PEOPLE ISRAEL."

7 Then Herod, having secretly called the MAGIANS,

---

* VATICAN MANUSCRIPT—23. a God. 25. a Son. 25. of her the first-born.—*om.*; so Lachmann and Tischendorf. 3. the KING Herod.

† 23. Heb. IMMA, *with*; NU, *us*; and EL, *God*—the *future* name of Jesus; showing that he will be "*a God with us.*" It is not emphatically "GOD" who will be with his people under the name of Immanuel; but "God," in the same sense in which it is said "The WORD was God."—John i. 1. (See Dr. Middleton on the Greek Article.) 1. A Sect of Philosophers.

‡ 21. Isa. lix. 20; Rom. xi. 26, 27. ‡ 23. Isa. vii. 14. ‡ 25. Luke ii. 7. ‡ 6. Micah v. 2.

ηκριβωσε παρ' αυτων τον χρονον του φαινομενου
learned exactly from them the time of the appearing
αστερος, 8 και πεμψας αυτους εις Βηθλεεμ,
a star, and sending them into Bethlehem,
ειπε· Πορευθεντες, ακριβως εξετασατε περι του
he said; Passing on your way, exactly inquire about the
παιδιου· επαν δε εὑρητε, απαγγειλατε μοι, ὁπως
infant; as soon as and you have found, bring word to me, that
κἀγω ελθων προσκυνησω αυτῳ. 9 Οι δε ακουσαντες
I also going pay homage to him. They and having heard
του βασιλεως επορευθησαν. Και ιδου, ὁ αστηρ,
of the king departed. And lo, the star,
ὁν ειδον εν τῃ ανατολῃ, προηγεν αυτους, ἑως
which they saw in the rising, went before them, till
ελθων εστη επανω οὑ ην το παιδιον. 10 Ιδοντες
going it stood over where was the infant. Seeing
δε τον αστερα, εχαρησαν χαραν μεγαλην σφοδρα·
and the star, they rejoiced a joy very great;
11 και ελθοντες εις την οικιαν, ειδον το παιδιον μετα
and being come into the house, they saw the infant with
Μαριας της μητρος αυτου, και πεσοντες † προσεκυ-
Mary the mother of it, and falling down did homage
νησαν αυτῳ, και ανοιξαντες τους θησαυρους αυτων,
to it, and opening the treasuries of them,
προσηνεγκαν αυτῳ δωρα, χρυσον και λιβανον και
they offered to it gifts, gold and frankincense and
σμυρναν. 12 Και χρηματισθεντες κατ' οναρ, μη
myrrh. And being warned in a dream not
ανακαμψαι προς Ἡρωδην, δι' αλλης ὁδου ανεχω-
to return to Herod, by another way they
ρησαν εις την χωραν αὑτων.
withdrew into the country of them.

13 Αναχωρησαντων δε αυτων, ιδου, αγγελος
Having withdrawn but of them, lo, a messenger
κυριου φαινεται κατ' οναρ τῳ Ιωσηφ, λεγων·
of a lord appears in a dream to the Joseph, saying;
Εγερθεις παραλαβε το παιδιον και την μητερα
Arising take the infant and the mother
αυτου, και φευγε εις Αιγυπτον, και ισθι εκει,
of it, and flee into Egypt, and be thou there,
ἑως αν ειπω σοι· μελλει γαρ Ἡρωδης ζητειν το
till I speak to thee; is about for Herod to seek the
παιδιον, του απολεσαι αυτο. 14 Ὁ δε εγερθεις
infant, to kill it. He then arising
παρελαβε το παιδιον και την μητερα αυτου νυκτος,
took the infant and the mother of it by night,
και ανεχωρησεν εις Αιγυπτον· 15 Και ην εκει ἑως
and went into Egypt; and he was there till
της τελευτης Ἡρωδου· ἱνα πληρωθῃ το ρηθεν
the death of Herod; that might be fulfilled the word spoken
ὑπο του κυριου δια του προφητου, λεγοντος·
by the lord through the prophet, saying;
"Εξ Αιγυπτου εκαλεσα τον υἱον μου."
"Out of Egypt I called the son of me."
16 Τοτε Ἡρωδης ιδων ὁτι ενεπαιχθη ὑπο των
Then Herod seeing that he was mocked by the

ascertained exactly from them the TIME of the STAR'S APPEARING;
8 and sending them to Bethlehem, he said, "Go, search strictly for the CHILD; and as soon as you have found him, bring me Word, that I also may go and pay him reverence."
9 And THEY, having heard the KING, departed; and behold! the STAR which they saw at its RISING, preceded them, till it came and stood over the place where the CHILD was.
10 And seeing the STAR, they rejoiced with very great Joy.
11 And coming into the HOUSE, they saw the CHILD with Mary his MOTHER; and prostrating, they honored him. Then opening their CASKETS, they offered, as Presents to him, Gold, Frankincense, and Myrrh.
12 And being warned in a Dream not to return to Herod, they went HOME by Another Way.
13 But they having *retired into their own COUNTRY, behold! an Angel of the Lord *appeared to JOSEPH in a Dream, saying: "Arise, take the CHILD and his MOTHER, and fly to Egypt; and remain there, till I speak to thee; for Herod is about to seek the CHILD to DESTROY him."
14 Then HE, arising, took the CHILD and his MOTHER, by night, and withdrew to Egypt;
15 and remained there till the DECEASE of Herod; so that the WORD SPOKEN by the *Lord through the PROPHET might be verified, saying: ‡"From Egypt I have called back my SON."
16 Then Herod, perceiving That he had been de-

* VATICAN MANUSCRIPT—13. retired into their own COUNTRY. 13. appeared. 15. Lord.

† 11. The homage of prostration, which is signified by this Greek word, in sacred authors as well as in profane, was throughout all Asia, commonly paid to kings and other superiors, both by Jews and by Pagans. It was paid by Moses to his father-in-law, Exod. xviii. 7, called in the E. T. "obeisance."—*Campbell.*

‡ 15. Hoshea xi. 1.

μαγων, εθυμωθη λιαν· και αποστειλας ανειλε
wise-men, was enraged much; and sending forth he slew
παντας τους †παιδας τους εν Βηθλεεμ και εν
all the boys the in Bethleem and in
πασα τοις ὁριοις αυτης, απο διετους και κατω-
all the borders of her, from two years and under,
τερω, κατα τον χρονον ὁν ηκριβωσε παρα των
according to the time which he exactly learnt from the
μαγων. 17 Τοτε επληρωθη το ῥηθεν ὑπο Ἱερεμιου
wise-men. Then was fulfilled the word spoken by Jeremiah
του προφητου, λεγοντος, 18 "Φωνη εν Ῥαμα
the prophet, saying, "A voice in Rama
ηκουσθη, *[θρηνος και] κλαυθμος και οδυρμος
was heard, [lamentation and] weeping and mourning
πολυς· Ῥαχηλ κλαιουσα τα τεκνα αὑτης· και
great; Rachel bewailing the children of her; and
ουκ ηθελε παρακληθηναι, ὁτι ουκ εισι."
not is willing to be comforted because not they are."

19 Τελευτησαντος δε του Ἡρωδου, ιδου, αγ-
Having died and of the Herod, lo, a
γελος κυριου κατ' οναρ φαινεται τῳ Ιωσηφ εν
messenger of a lord in a dream appears to the Joseph in
Αιγυπτω, λεγων· 20 Εγερθεις παραλαβε το
Egypt, saying; Arising take the
παιδιον και την μητερα αυτου, και πορευου εις
infant and the mother of it, and go thou into
γην Ισραηλ· τεθνηκασι γαρ οἱ ζητουντες την
land Israel; they are dead for the seeking the
ψυχην του παιδιου. 21 Ὁ δε εγερθεις παρελαβε
life of the infant. He and arising took
το παιδιον και την μητερα αυτου, και ηλθεν εις
the infant and the mother of it, and came into
γην Ισραηλ. 22 Ακουσας δε, ὁτι Αρχελαος
land Israel. Hearing and, that Archelaus
βασιλευει επι της Ιουδαιας αντι Ἡρωδου του
was reigning over the Judea instead of Herod the
πατρος αυτου, εφοβηθη εκει απελθειν· χρημα-
father of him, he was afraid there to go; being
τισθεις δε κατ' οναρ, ανεχωρησεν εις τα
warned and in a dream, he withdrew into the
μερη της Γαλιλαιας. 23 Και ελθων κατῳκησεν
region of the Galilee. And coming he dwelt
εις πολιν λεγομενην Ναζαρετ· ὁπως πληρωθη
into a city named Nazareth; that might be fulfilled
το ῥηθεν δια των προφητων, ὁτι Ναζωραιος
the word spoken through the prophets, that a Nazarite
κληθησεται.
he will be called.

ceived by the MAGIANS, was greatly enraged; and despatching emissaries he slew all †THE MALE CHILDREN in Bethlehem and in All its VICINITY, from the age of Two-years and under, according to the TIME which he accurately learnt from the MAGIANS.

17 Then was verified the WORD SPOKEN * through Jeremiah the PROPHET, saying,

18 ‡ "A Voice was "heard †in Ramah, Weep-"ing and great Mourning; "Rachel bemoaning her "CHILDREN, and unwil-"ling to be comforted, Be-"cause they are no more."

19 When HEROD was dead, behold! an Angel of the Lord appears in a Dream to JOSEPH in Egypt, saying:

20 "Arise, take the CHILD and his MOTHER, and go into the Land of Israel; for THEY are dead who SOUGHT the CHILD'S LIFE."

21 Then HE, arising, took the CHILD and his MOTHER, and * entered into the Land of Israel;

22 but hearing That Archelaus was reigning over JUDÆA instead of his FATHER Herod, he was afraid to return there; and being warned in a Dream, retired into the DISTRICT of GALILEE;

23 and coming into a City named †Nazareth, he abode; that the WORD SPOKEN through the PROPHETS might be verified, "That he will be called "† a Nazarite."

---

* 17. through Jeremiah—Lachmann & Tischendorf. VATICAN MANUSCRIPT—18. lamentation and—*omit*. 21. entered into.

† 16. THE MALE-CHILDREN. The Greek article being masculine, it defines the sex. In nine other places in this chapter, infant is in the neuter gender. 18. in Ramah. A city not far from Bethlehem in Judea, on the confines of the territory of Benjamin. Origen and Jerome say that the Hebrew term rendered *in Ramah*, by the LXX, should be translated, *on high*. Matthew, or his translator, followed the Septuagint. 23. Nazareth—A small city of the Zebulonites, in Galilee, about 75 miles north of the city of Jerusalem. 23. a Nazarite. Matthew evidently understood this the same as a Nazarene, or a native of Nazareth. A Nazarite was one under a vow of self-denial. In Judges xiii. 5, Samson is called a Nazarite. The apostle Paul was accused by Turtullus, before Felix, as being "a ringleader of the sect of the Nazarites," Acts xxiv. 5. Some derive the name from Isa. xi. 1, where the promised Messiah is called a *Nazar*, or branch.

‡ 18. Jer. xxxi. 15.

ΚΕΦ. γ. 3.

1 Εν δε ταις ἡμεραις εκειναις παραγινεται
In now the days those comes
Ιωαννης ὁ βαπτιστης, κηρυσσων εν τῃ ερημῳ
John the dipper, proclaiming in the desert
της Ιουδαιας, [και] λεγων· 2 Μετανοειτε·
of the Judea, [and] saying; Reform ye;
ηγγικε γαρ ἡ †βασιλεια των ουρανων. 3 Ουτος
has come nigh for the majesty of the heavens This
γαρ εστιν ὁ ῥηθεις ὑπο Ἡσαιου του προφητου,
for is he spoken of by Esaias the prophet,
λεγοντος· "Φωνη βοωντος εν τῃ ερημῳ·
saying; "A voice crying out in the desert;
ἑτοιμασατε την ὁδον κυριου, ευθειας ποιειτε
make ye ready the way of a lord, straight make ye
τας τριβους αυτου."
the beaten tracks of him."
4 Αυτος δε ὁ Ιωαννης ειχε το ἐνδυμα αὐτου
He and the John had the outer garment of him
απο τριχων καμηλου, και ζωνην δερματινην
from hairs of a camel, and a belt made of skin
περι την οσφυν αὐτου· ἡ δε τροφη αυτου ην
around the loins of him; the and food of him was
ακριδες και μελι αγριον. 5 Τοτε εξεπορευετο
locusts and honey wild. Then went out
προς αυτον Ἱεροσολυμα, και πασα ἡ Ιουδαια,
to him Jerusalem, and all the Judea,
και πασα ἡ περιχωρος του Ιορδανου· 6 και
and all the country about of the Jordan; and
εβαπτιζοντο εν τῳ Ιορδανῃ ὑπ' αυτου, εξομολο-
were dipped in to the Jordan by him, confessing
γουμενοι τας αμαρτιας αὐτων.
the sins of them.
7 Ιδων δε πολλους των Φαρισαιων και Σαδδου-
Seeing and many of the Pharisees and Sadducees
καιων ερχομενους επι το βαπτισμα αὐτου, ειπεν
coming to the dipping of him, he said
αυτοις· Γεννηματα εχιδνων, τις ὑπεδειξεν
to them; O broods of venomous serpents, who pointed out
ὑμιν φυγειν απο της μελλουσης οργης;
to you to flee from the coming wrath?
8 Ποιησατε ουν καρπον αξιον της μετανοιας,
Bring forth then fruit worthy of the reformation,
9 και μη δοξητε λεγειν εν ἑαυτοις· Πατερα
and not think to say in yourselves; A father
εχομεν τον Αβρααμ· λεγω γαρ ὑμιν, ὁτι δυναται
we have the Abraam; I say for to you, that is able
ὁ θεος εκ των λιθων τουτων εγειραι τεκνα τῳ
the God out of the stones these to raise up children to the

CHAPTER III.

1 Now in those DAYS appeared John the IMMERSER, in the †DESERT of JUDÆA, publicly announcing,

2 †"Reform! because the ROYAL MAJESTY of the HEAVENS has approached."

3 For this is HE of whom Isaiah the PROPHET SPOKE, saying: ‡"A Voice "proclaiming in the DES-"ERT, 'Prepare the WAY "'for the Lord, make the "'HIGHWAYS straight for "'him.'"

4 ‡Now JOHN wore a MANTLE of Camel's Hair, with a leathern Girdle encircling his WAIST; and his FOOD was Locusts and wild Honey.

5 Then resorted to him Jerusalem, and All JUDÆA, and All the COUNTRY along the JORDAN;

6 and were immersed by him in the *River JORDAN, confessing their SINS.

7 But seeing many of the PHARISEES and Sadducees coming to *the IMMERSION, he said to them; ‡"O Progeny of Vipers! who has admonished you to fly from the APPROACHING VENGEANCE?

8 Produce, then, Fruit worthy of REFORMATION:

9 and presume not to say to yourselves, 'We have a Father,—ABRAHAM;' for I assure you, That GOD is able out of these STONES to raise up Children to ABRAHAM.

---

* VATICAN MANUSCRIPT—6. the River JORDAN. 7. the IMMERSION.

† 1. DESERT. This does not always mean an uninhabited region, but one comparatively barren, with a sparse population. See Joshua xv. 61, 62, where mention is made of "six cities with their villages," in the wilderness. 2. Reform. The word "repent" does not express the force of the original; which signifies a change of character, a permanent alteration of the dispositions and habits. The same remark may be applied to the noun of the same meaning in verse 8.—*Gannett.* 2. *Basileia* means *kingly power, authority, royal dignity, majesty, &c.*, as well as *kingdom, realm*, or *reign*. The prophet Daniel uses kings and kingdoms synonymously, (Dan. ii. 44); so also the evangelists. See Matt. xxi. 5, 9; Mark xi. 9, 10; Luke xix. 38; and Zech. ix. 9. John's mission was "to go before the face of the Lord, to prepare his ways," (Luke i. 76); and to point out the Messiah. See John i. 6—8, 20—31, 34; Acts xiii. 24, 25. Therefore he called on the people to "Reform, because the Majesty of the heavens (God's Anointed) has come."

‡ 3. Isa. xl. 3. ‡ 7 Luke iii. 7—9.

Αβρααμ. 10 Ηδη δε *[και] ἡ αξινη προς την
Abraam. Now and [even] the axe to the
ῥιζαν των δενδρων κειται· παν ουν δενδρον μη
root of the trees lies; every therefore tree not
ποιουν καρπον καλον, εκκοπτεται, και εις πυρ
bearing fruit good, is cut down, and into a fire
βαλλεται. 11 Εγω μεν βαπτιζω ὑμας εν ὑδατι,
is cast. I indeed dip you in water,
εις μετανοιαν· ὁ δε οπισω μου ερχομενος,
into reformation; he but after of me coming,
ισχυροτερος μου εστιν, ου ουκ ειμι ἱκανος τα
mightier of me is, of whom not I am worthy the
ὑποδηματα βαστασαι· αυτος ὑμας βαπτισει εν
sandals to carry; he you will dip in
πνευματι ἁγιῳ και πυρι. 12 Ου το πτυον εν
spirit holy and fire. Of whom the winnowing shovel in
τῃ χειρι αυτου, και διακαθαριει την ἁλωνα
the hand of him, and he will thoroughly cleanse the threshing floor
αὑτου· και συναξει τον σιτον αὑτου εις την
of him; and he will gather the wheat of him into the
αποθηκην, το δε αχυρον τακαυσει πυρι
storehouse, the but chaff he will burn up in fire
ασβεστῳ.
inextinguishable.
13 Τοτε παραγινεται ὁ Ιησους απο της Γαλι-
Then comes the Jesus from the Galilee
λαιας επι τον Ιορδανην προς τον Ιωαννην, του
to the Jordan to the John, of the
βαπτισθηναι ὑπ' αυτου. 14 Ὁ δε Ιωαννης διεκωλυεν
to be dipped by him; The but John refused
αυτον, λεγων· Εγω χρειαν εχω ὑπο σου βαπτισ-
him saying; I need to have by thee to be
θηναι, και συ ερχῃ προς με; 15 Αποκριθεις δε ὁ
dipped, and thou comest to me? Answering and the
Ιησους ειπε προς αυτον· Αφες αρτι· οὑτω γαρ
Jesus said to him; Permit now; thus for
πρεπον εστιν ἡμιν, πληρωσαι πασαν δικαιοσυνην.
becoming it is to us, to fulfil all righteousness.
Τοτε αφιησιν αυτον. 16 Και βαπτισθεις ὁ Ιησους
Then he suffered him. And having been dipped the Jesus
ανεβη ευθυς απο του ὑδατος· και ιδου, ανεῳχ-
went up immediately from the water; and lo, were
θησαν *[αυτῳ] οἱ ουρανοι, και ειδε το πνευμα
opened [to him] the heavens, and was seen the spirit
του θεου καταβαινον ὡσει περιστεραν, [και]
of the God descending like a dove, [and]
ερχομενον επ' αυτον. 17 Και ιδου, φωνη εκ των
coming on him. And lo, a voice out of the
ουρανων, λεγουσα· Οὑτος εστιν ὁ υἱος μου ὁ
heavens, saying, This is the son of me the
αγαπητος, εν ᾡ ευδοκησα.
beloved, in whom I delight.

10 Even now the AXE lies at the ROOT of the TREES; Every Tree, therefore, not producing good Fruit, is cut down, and cast into a Fire.

11 I, indeed, † immerse you in Water in order to Reformation; but HE who is COMING after me, is more powerful than I, † Whose SANDALS I am not worthy to carry; ‡ he will immerse you in holy Spirit and in Fire.

12 Whose WINNOWING SHOVEL is in his HAND, and he will effectually cleanse his THRESHING-FLOOR; he will gather his WHEAT into * his GRANARY, but the CHAFF he will consume with Fire inextinguishable."

13 Then comes JESUS from GALILEE to the JORDAN, to be IMMERSED by JOHN.

14 But * HE refused him, saying; "I have Need to be immersed by thee, and thou comest to me!"

15 But JESUS answering, said to him; "Permit it now; for thus it is becoming us to establish Every Ordinance." Then John suffered him.

16 And JESUS being immersed, went up from the WATER; and, behold! instantly the HEAVENS were opened, and * the Spirit of God appeared, descending, like a Dove, and ‡ resting on him.

17 And, behold! a Voice from the HEAVENS, saying; ‡ "This is my SON, the BELOVED, in whom I delight."

* VATICAN MANUSCRIPT—10. even—*omit.* 12. his GRANARY. 14. HE refused. 16. to him—*omit.* 16. the Spirit of God. 16. and—*omit.*

† 11. immerse you in Water. *Baptizo,* and its root *Bapto,* signify to dip, to plunge, to immerse, and was rendered by Tertullian, *tingere,* the term used for dyeing cloth, which was by immersion. It is always construed suitably to this meaning. Thus it is *en hudatee en to Iordanee.—Campbell.* 11. Whose SANDALS, &c. The office alluded to, though of a servile description, was performed by disciples for their instructors, as it appears from the Talmudists and Eusebius. 12. The allusion in this passage is to an ancient process in agriculture, by which the chaff was driven towards a fire prepared for burning it, in order that it might not be blown back and mixed again with the wheat.

‡ 11. Acts i. 5; ii. 2—4 xi. 16. ‡ 16. Isa. xi. 2; lxi. 1. ‡ 17. Isa. xlii. 1; Luke ix. 35.

ΚΕΦ. δ'. 4.

1 Τοτε ὁ Ιησους ανηχθη εις την ερημον ὑπο
Then the Jesus was led into the desert by
του πνευματος, πειρασθηναι ὑπο του διαβολου.
the spirit, to be tempted by the accuser.
2 Και νηστευσας ἡμερας τεσσαρακοντα και νυκτας
And fasting days forty and nights
τεσσαρακοντα, ὑστερον επεινασε. 3 Και προσ-
forty, after he was hungry. And coming
ελθων αυτῳ ὁ πειραζων, ειπεν· Ει υἱος ει του
to him the tempter, said; If a son thou be of the
θεου, ειπε, ἱνα οἱ λιθοι οὑτοι αρτοι γενωνται.
God, speak, that the stones these loaves may become.
4 Ὁ δε αποκριθεις ειπε· Γεγραπται· "Ουκ επ'
He but answering said; It is written; "Not by
αρτῳ μονῳ ζησεται ανθρωπος· αλλ' επι παντι
bread alone shall live a man; but by every
ῥηματι εκπορευομενῳ δια στοματος θεου."
word proceeding from mouth of God."
5 Τοτε παραλαμβανει αυτον ὁ διαβολος εις την
Then takes him the accuser into the
ἁγιαν πολιν, και ἱστησιν αυτον επι το πτερυγιον
holy city, and places him on the wing
του ἱερου· 6 και λεγει αυτῳ· Ει υἱος ει του θεου,
of the temple; and says to him; If a son thou be of the God,
βαλε σεαυτον κατω· γεγραπται γαρ· "Ὁτι τοις
cast thyself down; it is written for; "That to the
αγγελοις αὑτου εντελειται περι σου· και επι
messengers of him he will give charge of thee; and on
χειρων αρουσι σε, μηποτε προσκοψῃς προς
hands they shall raise thee, lest thou strike against
λιθον τον ποδα σου." 7 Εφη αυτῳ ὁ Ιησους·
a stone the foot of thee." Said to him the Jesus:
Παλιν γεγραπται· "Ουκ εκπειρασεις κυριον
Again it is written; "Not thou shalt put to the proof Lord
τον θεον σου."
the God of thee."

8 Παλιν παραλαμβανει αυτον ὁ διαβολος εις
Again takes him the accuser into
ορος ὑψηλον λιαν, και δεικνυσιν αυτῳ πασας
a mountain high exceedingly, and shows to him all
τας βασιλειας του κοσμου και την δοξαν αυτων,
the kingdoms of the world and the glory of them,
και λεγει αυτῳ· Ταυτα παντα σοι δωσω, εαν
and says to him: These all to thee I will give, if
πεσων προσκυνησῃς μοι. 10 Τοτε λεγει αυτῳ
falling down thou wilt do homage to me. Then says to him
ὁ Ιησους· Ὑπαγε οπισω μου, σατανα· γεγραπ-
the Jesus: Go thou behind of me, adversary: it is written
ται γαρ· "Κυριον τον θεον σου προσκυνησεις,
for: "Lord the God of thee thou shalt worship,
και αυτῳ μονῳ λατρευσεις." 11 Τοτε αφιησιν
and to him only thou shalt render service." Then leaves
αυτον ὁ διαβολος· και ιδου, αγγελοι προσηλθον
him the accuser: and lo, messengers came
και διηκονουν αυτῳ.
and ministered to him.

CHAP. IV.

1 Then JESUS was conducted by the SPIRIT into the DESERT, to be tempted by the ENEMY.

2 And after fasting forty Days and forty Nights, he was hungry.

3 Then the TEMPTER approaching him, said; "If thou be a Son of GOD, command that these STONES become Loaves."

4 But HE answering, said; "It is written, ‡* 'MAN shall not live by 'Bread only, but by Every 'Word proceeding from 'the Mouth of God.'"

5 Then the ENEMY conducts him into the HOLY City, and places him on the BATTLEMENT of the TEMPLE,

6 and says to him, "If thou be a Son of GOD, cast thyself down; for it is written, ‡ 'He will give 'his ANGELS charge of 'thee; they shall uphold 'thee on their Hands, lest 'thou strike thy FOOT 'against a Stone.'"

7 JESUS answered; "Again, it is written, ‡ 'Thou shalt not try the 'Lord thy GOD.'"

8 Again, the ENEMY takes him to a very high Mountain, and shows him All the KINGDOMS of the † WORLD, and the GLORY of them;

9 and says to him; "All these will I give thee, if prostrating thou wilt worship me."

10 Then Jesus says to him; "Get thee behind me, Adversary; for it is written, ‡ 'Thou shalt 'worship the Lord thy 'GOD, and him only shalt 'thou serve.'"

11 Then the ENEMY leaves him; and behold! Angels came and ministered to him.

* VATICAN MANUSCRIPT—4. MAN.

† 8. WORLD. *Kosmos*, here translated world, may be restricted to the Land of Palestine, as it is in Rom. iv. 13; though in Luke iv. 5, *hee oikoumenee* is found, which may possibly include the Roman empire, in which acceptation it is frequently used.

‡ 4. Deut. viii. 3. ‡ 6. Psa. xci. 11, 12. ‡ 7. Deut. vi. 16. ‡ 10. Deut. vi. 13.

[12]Ακουσας δε ὁ Ιησους, ὁτι Ιωαννης παρεδοθη,
Hearing now the Jesus, that John was delivered up,
ανεχωρησεν εις την Γαλιλαιαν. [13] Και κατα-
he withdrew into the Galilee. And having
λιπων την Ναζαρετ, ελθων κατῳκησεν εις
left the Nazareth. coming dwelt at
Καπερναουμ την παραθαλασσιαν, εν δριοις
Capernaum the by the sea-side, in borders
Ζαβουλων και Νεφθαλειμ· [14] ἱνα πληρωθη το
of Zabulon and Nephthalim; that might be fulfilled the
ῥηθεν δια Ἡσαιου του προφητου, λεγοντος·
word spoken through Esaias the prophet, saying;
[15] "Γη Ζαβουλων και γη Νεφθαλειμ ὁδον
"Land of Zabulon and land Nephthalim way
θαλασσης περαν του Ιορδανου, Γαλιλαια των
of the sea by the Jordan, Galilee of the
εθνων. [16] Ὁ λαος ὁ καθημενος εν σκοτει ειδε φως
nations. The people who are sitting in darkness saw a light
μεγα· και τοις καθημενοις εν χωρᾳ και σκιᾳ
great; and to those sitting in a region even a shade
θανατου, φως ανετειλεν αυτοις."
of death, a light has arisen to them."
[17] Απο τοτε ηρξατο ὁ Ιησους κηρυσσειν, και
From that time began the Jesus to proclaim, and
λεγειν· Μετανοειτε· ηγγικε γαρ ἡ βασιλεια
to say; Reform; has come nigh for the royal dignity
των ουρανων.
of the heavens.
[18] Περιπατων δε παρα την θαλασσαν της
Walking and by the sea of the
Γαλιλαιας, ειδε δυο αδελφους, Σιμωνα τον
Galilee, he saw two brothers, Simon the
λεγομενον Πετρον, και Ανδρεαν τον αδελφον
called Peter, and Andrew the brother
αυτου, βαλλοντας αμφιβληστρον εις την θαλασ-
of him, casting a fishing-net into the sea;
σαν· ησαν γαρ ἁλιεις. [19] Και λεγει αυτοις·
they were for fishers. And he says to them;
Δευτε οπισω μου, και ποιησω ὑμας ἁλιεις
Come behind of me, and I will make you fishers
ανθρωπων. [20] Οἱ δε ευθεως αφεντες τα δικτυα,
of men. They and immediately leaving the nets,
ηκολουθησαν αυτῳ. [21] Και προβας εκειθεν, ειδεν
followed him. And going on from thence, he saw
αλλους δυο αδελφους, Ιακωβον τον του Ζεβε-
other two brothers, James the of the Zebe-
δαιου και Ιωαννην τον αδελφον αυτου, εν τῳ
dee and John the brother of him, in the
πλοιῳ μετα Ζεβεδαιου του πατρος αυτων, καταρ-
ship with Zebedee of the father of them, mend-
τιζοντας τα δικτυα αυτων· και εκαλεσεν αυτους.
ing the nets of them; and he called them.
[22] Οἱ δε ευθεως αφεντες το πλοιον και τον πατερα
They and forthwith leaving the ship and the father
αυτων, ηκολουθησαν αυτῳ
of them, followed him.
[23] Και περιηγεν ὁλην την Γαλιλαιαν ὁ Ιησους,
And went about all the Galilee the Jesus,
διδασκων εν ταις συναγωγαις αυτων, και κηρυσ-
teaching in the synagogues of them, and preach-

12 Now JESUS, hearing That John was imprisoned, retired into GALILEE;
13 and, having left NAZARETH, resided at THAT Capernaum, by the lake, in the Confines of Zebulon and Naphtali;
14 so that the WORD SPOKEN through Isaiah the PROPHET, might be verified, saying;
15 ‡ "Land of Zebulon "and Land of Naphtali, "situate near the lake, on "the JORDAN, Galilee of "the NATIONS;
16 "THAT PEOPLE, "dwelling in Darkness, "saw a great Light; and "to THOSE INHABITING "a Region, even a Shadow "of Death, a Light arose."
17 From that time JESUS began to proclaim, and to say; "Reform; for the ROYAL MAJESTY of the HEAVENS has approached."
18 And walking by the LAKE of GALILEE, he saw Two Brothers, THAT Simon who is SURNAMED Peter, and Andrew his BROTHER, casting a Drag into the LAKE; for they were Fishermen.
19 And he says to them, "Follow me; and I will make you Fishers of Men."
20 And THEY, immediately leaving the NETS, followed him.
21 And going forward from thence, he saw Other Two Brothers, James the son of ZEBEDEE, and John his BROTHER, in the BOAT with Zebedee their FATHER, repairing their NETS; and he called them.
22 And THEY, instantly leaving the BOAT and their FATHER, followed him.
23 And *JESUS journeyed throughout All GALILEE, teaching in their SYNAGOGUES, and proclaiming the GLAD TIDINGS of the KINGDOM,

* VATICAN MANUSCRIPT—23. he went about throughout All.

‡ 15. Isa. ix. 1, 2.

σων το ευαγγελιον της βασιλειας, και θεραπευων
ing the glad tidings of the kingdom, and curing
πασαν νοσον και πασαν μαλακιαν εν τῳ λαῳ.
every disease and every malady among the people.
24 Και απηλθεν ἡ ακοη αυτου εις ὁλην την
And went the report of him into all the
Συριαν· και προσηνεγκαν αυτῳ παντας τους
Syria; and they brought to him all the
κακως εχοντας, ποικιλαις νοσοις και βασανοις
sick having various diseases and torments
συνεχομενους, *[και] δαιμονιζομενους, και σεληνι-
seized with, [and] demoniacs, and lu-
αζομενους, και παραλυτικους· και εθεραπευσεν
natics, and paralytics; and he cured
αυτους. 25 Και ηκολουθησαν αυτῳ οχλοι πολλοι
them. And followed to him crowds great
απο της Γαλιλαιας, και Δεκαπολεως, και Ἱερο-
from the Galilee, and Decapolis, and from
σολυμων, και Ιουδαιας, και περαν του Ιορδανου.
Jerusalem, and Judea, and beyond of the Jordan.

ΚΕΦ. ε. 5.

1 Ιδων δε τους οχλους, ανεβη εις το ορος· και
Seeing and the multitudes, he went up to the mountain; and
καθισαντος αυτου, προσηλθον *[αυτῳ] οἱ μαθη-
having seated himself, came [to him] the disci-
ται αυτου· 2 και ανοιξας το στομα αὐτου, εδι-
ples of him; and opening the mouth of him, he
δασκεν αυτους, λεγων· 3 Μακαριοι οἱ πτωχοι τῳ
taught them, saying; Blessed the poor to the
πνευματι· ὁτι αυτων εστιν ἡ βασιλεια των
spirit; because of them is the kingdom of the
ουρανων. 4 Μακαριοι οἱ πενθουντες· ὁτι αυτοι
heavens. Blessed the mourners; for they
παρακληθησονται. 5 Μακαριοι οἱ πραεις· ὁτι
shall be comforted. Blessed the meek; for
αυτοι κληρονομησουσι την γην. 6 Μακαριοι οἱ
they shall inherit the earth. Blessed the
πεινωντες και διψωντες την δικαιοσυνην· ὁτι
hungering and thirsting the righteousness; for
αυτοι χορτασθησονται. 7 Μακαριοι οἱ ελεημο-
they shall be satisfied. Blessed the merciful;
νες· ὁτι αυτοι ελεηθησονται.
for they shall obtain mercy.
8 Μακαριοι οἱ καθαροι τῃ καρδιᾳ· ὁτι αυτοι
Blessed the clean to the heart; for they
τον θεον οψονται. 9 Μακαριοι οἱ ειρηνοποιοι·
the God shall see. Blessed the peace-makers;
ὁτι αυτοι υἱοι θεου κληθησονται. 10 Μακαριοι οἱ
for they sons of God shall be called. Blessed those

and healing Every kind of Disease and Infirmity among the PEOPLE.

24 And his FAME spread through All SYRIA: and they brought to him All the SICK, having Various Disorders, and arrested by Severe Complaints;—demoniacs, and lunatics, and paralytics;—and he healed them.

25 And great Crowds followed him from GALILEE, and Decapolis, and Jerusalem, and Judæa, and from the vicinity of the Jordan.

CHAPTER V.

1 And beholding the CROWDS, he ascended the †MOUNTAIN, and having sat down, his DISCIPLES *came up:

2 And opening his MOUTH, he taught them, saying:

3 "Happy the ‡POOR (in SPIRIT); for theirs is the KINGDOM of the HEAVENS!

4 Happy the ‡MOURNERS; seeing that they will be consoled!

5 Happy the ‡MEEK; because they will possess the LAND!

6 Happy ‡they who HUNGER and THIRST (for righteousness); since they will be satisfied!

7 Happy the MERCIFUL; because they will receive mercies!

8 Happy the ‡PURE (in heart); for they will behold God!

9 Happy the PEACEMAKERS; because they will be called Sons of God!

* VATICAN MANUSCRIPT—24. and—*omit*. 1. came up. 1. to him—*omit*.

† 1. Some particular mountain in the neighborhood of Capernaum is generally supposed to be here intended, probably Mount Tabor, or an elevation well known in that vicinity.
† 3. Wetstein thinks this phrase ought to be construed—"Happy in the Spirit's account are the poor;" and Geo. Campbell renders it—"Happy the poor who repine not." Both do violence to the original. The former interferes with the arrangement of the words, and the latter paraphrases rather than translates. In Luke vi. 20, we have the sentence just as our Lord uttered it; but here it seems Matthew explains the metaphor, parenthetically, by adding "*in spirit*." So in verses 6 and 8. For a further illustration, see James ii. 5. The article and noun is in the dative case, and conveys the same meaning as our preposition *in*.

‡ 3. Luke vi. 20; James ii. 5. ‡ 4. Isa. lxi. 2, 3. ‡ 5. Psa. xxxvii. 11, 29. ‡ 6. Isa. lv. 1. ‡ 8. 1 John iii. 2, 3.

δεδιωγμενοι ἑνεκεν δικαιοσυνης· ὁτι αυτων εστιν
being persecuted on account of righteousness: for of them is
ἡ βασιλεια των ουρανων. 11 Μακαριοι εστε,
the kingdom of the heavens. Blessed are ye,
ὁταν ονειδισωσιν ὑμας και διωξωσι, και ειπωσι
whenever they reproach you and persecute, and say
παν πονηρον ῥημα καθ' ὑμων, ψευδομενοι, ενεκεν
every evil word against you, speaking falsely, because
εμου. 12 Χαιρετε και αγαλλιασθε· ὁτι ὁ μισθος
of me. Rejoice ye and exult ye, for the reward
ὑμων πολυς εν τοις ουρανοις· οὑτω γαρ εδιωξαν
of you great in the heavens; in this way for they persecuted
τους προφητας τους προ ὑμων. 13 Ὑμεις εστε
the prophets those before you. You are
το ἁλας της γης. Εαν δε το ἁλας μωρανθῃ, εν
the salt of the earth. If but the salt become tasteless, with
τινι ἁλισθησεται; εις ουδεν ισχυει ετι, ει μη
what shall it be salted? for nothing is it of service any more, except
βληθηναι εξω, και καταπατεισθαι ὑπο των
to be cast out, and trodden under foot by the
ανθρωπων.
men.

14 Ὑμεις εστε το φως του κοσμου. Ου δυναται
You are the light of the world. Not possible
πολις κρυβηναι επανω ορους κειμενη· 15 ουδε
a city to hide upon a hill being situated; nor
καιουσι λυχνον, και τιθεασιν αυτον ὑπο τον
they light a lamp, and place him under the
μοδιον, αλλ' επι την λυχνιαν· και λαμπει πασι
measure, but on the lamp-stand, and it gives light to all
τοις εν τῃ οικιᾳ. 16 Οὑτω λαμψατω το φως
those in the house. Thus let it shine the light
ὑμων εμπροσθεν των ανθρωπων, ὁπως ιδωσιν
of you in the presence of the men, that they may see
ὑμων τα καλα εργα, και δοξασωσι τον πατερα
of you the good works, and may praise the father
ὑμων τον εν τοις ουρανοις.
of you that in the heavens.

17 Μη νομισητε, ὁτι ηλθον καταλυσαι τον
Not think ye, that I have come to destroy the
νομον η τους προφητας· ουκ ηλθον καταλυσαι,
law or the prophets; not I have come to destroy
αλλ' πληρωσαι. 18 Αμην γαρ λεγω ὑμιν, ἑως
but to fulfil. Indeed for I say to you, till
αν παρελθῃ ὁ ουρανος και ἡ γη, ιωτα ἑν η μια
pass away the heaven and the earth, iota one or one
κεραια ου μη παρελθῃ απο του νομου, ἑως αν
fine point in no wise pass from the law. till
παντα γενηται. 19 Ὁς εαν ουν λυσῃ μιαν των
all be fulfilled. Whoever therefore breaks one of the

10 Happy the ‡ PERSECUTED on account of Righteousness; for theirs is the KINGDOM of the HEAVENS!

11 Happy are you, when they revile and persecute you, and, on my account, falsely allege, Every kind of Evil against you.

12 Rejoice and exult, Because your ‡ REWARD will be great in the HEAVENS; for thus THOSE PROPHETS who preceded you were persecuted.

13 You are the ‡ SALT of the EARTH. But if the † SALT become insipid, how shall it recover its savor? It is then worthless, except to be cast out and trodden down by MEN.

14 You are the ‡ LIGHT of the WORLD. A city being situated on a hill cannot be concealed:

15 nor is a Lamp lighted to be placed under the † CORN MEASURE, but on the LAMP-STAND; and it gives light to ALL the FAMILY.

16 Thus, let your LIGHT shine before MEN, that they may see your GOOD works, and glorify THAT FATHER of yours in the HEAVENS.

17 Think not, That I have come to subvert the LAW, or the PROPHETS: I have come not to subvert, but to establish.

18 For, indeed, I say to you, Till HEAVEN and EARTH pass away, one Iota or One Tip of a letter shall by no means pass from the LAW, till all be accomplished.

19 Therefore, whoever

† 13. Perhaps allusion is here made to a bituminous and fragrant species of salt, found at the Lake Asphaltites; great quantities of which were thrown by the priests over the sacrifices, to counteract the smell of the burning flesh, and to hasten its consumption. This substance, however, was easily damaged by exposure to the atmosphere; and the portion of it thus rendered unfit for the purpose to which it was ordinarily applied, was strewed upon the pavement of the temple, to prevent slipping in wet weather. Maundrell, in his travels, states that he tasted some that had entirely lost its savor.—*Trollope.* † 15. The *modius* was a measure, both among the Greeks and Romans, containing a little less than a *peck;* but it is clear that nothing here depends upon the capacity of the measure.

‡ 10. 2 Tim. ii. 12; Acts xiv. 22; Rev. iii. 21. ‡ 12. Rom. viii. 18. ‡ 13. Luke xiv. 34, 35. ‡ 14. Phil. ii. 15.

ελαχιστων, και διδαξῃ οὑτω τους ανθρωπους,
least, and teach thus the men,
ελαχιστος κληθησεται εν τῃ βασιλειᾳ των
least he shall be called in the kingdom of the
ουρανων· ὁς δ' αν ποιησῃ και διδαξῃ, οὑτος
heavens; who but ever shall do and teach, the same
μεγας κληθησεται εν τῃ βασιλειᾳ των ουρανων.
great shall be called in the kingdom of the heavens.
20 Λεγω γαρ ὑμιν, ὁτι εαν μη περισσευσῃ ἡ
I say for to you, that except abound the
δικαιοσυνη ὑμων πλειον των γραμματεων και
righteousness of you more of the scribes and
Φαρισαιων, ου μη εισελθητε εις την βασιλειαν
Pharisees, by no means you may enter into the kingdom
των ουρανων.
of the heavens.

21 Ηκουσατε, ὁτι ερρεθη τοις αρχαιοις· "Ου
You have heard, that it was said to the ancients, "Not
φονευσεις· ὁς δ' αν φονευσῃ, ενοχος εσται τῃ
thou shalt kill, who and ever shall kill, liable shall be to the
κρισει." 22 Εγω δε λεγω ὑμιν, ὁτι πας ὁ οργι-
tribunal." I but say to you, that all the being
ζομενος τῳ αδελφῳ αὑτου· *[εικη,] ενοχος εσται
angry to the brother of him; [without cause,] liable shall be
τῃ κρισει· ὁς δ' αν ειπῃ τῳ αδελφῳ αυτου·
to the tribunal; who and ever shall say to the brother of him;
ῥακα, ενοχος εσται τῳ συνεδριῳ· ὁς δ' αν ειπῃ·
vile fellow, liable shall be to the sanhedrim; who and ever shall say;
μωρε, ενοχος εσται εις την γεενναν του πυρος.
O fool, liable shall be to the Gehenna of the fire.
23 Εαν ουν προσφερῃς το δωρον σου επι το
If therefore thou bring the gift of thee to the
θυσιαστηριον, κἀκει μνησθῃς, ὁτι ὁ αδελφος
altar, and there remember, that the brother
σου εχει τι κατα σου· 24 αφες εκει το δωρον
of thee has somewhat against thee; leave there the gift
σου εμπροσθεν του θυσιαστηριου, και ὑπαγε,
of thee before the altar, and go,
πρωτον διαλλαγηθι τῳ αδελφῳ σου, και τοτε
first be thou reconciled to the brother of thee, and then
ελθων προσφερε το δωρον σου. 25 Ισθι ευνοων
coming offer the gift of thee. Be thou willing to agree
τῳ αντιδικῳ σου ταχυ, ἑως ὁτου ει εν τῃ ὁδῳ
with the opponent of thee quickly, while thou art in the way
μετ' αυτου· μηποτε σε παραδῳ ὁ αντιδικος τῳ
with him; lest thee deliver up the opponent to the
κριτῃ, και ὁ κριτης [σε παραδῳ] τῳ ὑπηρετῃ,
judge, and the judge [thee deliver up] to the officer,
και εις φυλακην βληθησῃ. 26 Αμην λεγω σοι,
and into prison thou shalt be cast. Indeed I say to thee,
ου μη εξελθῃς εκειθεν, ἑως αν αποδῳς τον
by no means thou wilt come out thence, till thou hast paid the
εσχατον κοδραντην.
last farthing.

shall violate one of the LEAST of these COMMANDS, and shall teach MEN SO, will be called little in the KINGDOM of the HEAVENS; but whoever shall practise and teach them, will be called great in the KINGDOM of the HEAVENS.

20 For I tell you, that unless your RIGHTEOUSNESS excel that of the SCRIBES and Pharisees, you shall never enter into the KINGDOM of the HEAVENS.

21 You have heard That it was said to the ANCIENTS, ‡ 'Thou shalt not 'kill; and whoever shall 'kill, will be †amenable to 'the JUDGES.'

22 But I say to you, That every one BEING ANGRY with his BROTHER, shall be amenable to the JUDGES: and whoever shall say to his BROTHER, Fool! will be subject to the HIGH COUNCIL; but whoever shall say, Apostate wretch! will be obnoxious to the BURNING of GEHENNA.

23 If, therefore, thou bring thy GIFT to the ALTAR, and there recollect That thy BROTHER has ought against thee,

24 leave there thy GIFT before the altar, and go, first be reconciled to thy BROTHER, then come, and present thy GIFT.

25 Agree quickly with thy PROSECUTOR, while thou art on the ROAD with him; lest the PROSECUTOR deliver thee to the JUDGE, and the JUDGE to the OFFICER, and thou be cast into Prison.

26 Indeed, I say to thee, Thou wilt by no means be released, till thou hast paid the LAST Farthing.

* VATICAN MANUSCRIPT—22. without cause—*omit*. 25. deliver thee—*omit*.

† 21. The Jews had a Common Court consisting of *twenty-three* men, which had power to sentence criminals to death, by beheading or strangling; this was called the *Judgment*, or Court of *Judges*. The Sanhedrim or High Council consisted of *seventy-two* men, being the Court of the Jews, before which the highest crimes were tried. This Court alone had power to punish with death by stoning. This was thought a more terrible death than the former.

27 Ηκουσατε, ὁτι ερρεθη· "Ου μοιχευ-
You have heard, that it was said; "Not thou shalt commit
σεις." 28 Εγω δε λεγω ὑμιν, ὁτι πας ὁ βλεπων
adultery." I but say to you, that all who looking at
γυναικα προς το επιθυμησαι αυτης, ηδη εμοι-
a woman in order to lust after her, already has
χευσεν αυτην εν τῃ καρδιᾳ αυτου. 29 Ει δε ὁ
debauched her in the heart of him. If and the
οφθαλμος σου ὁ δεξιος σκανδαλιζει σε, εξελε
eye of thee the right ensnare thee, tear out
αυτον, και βαλε απο σου· συμφερει γαρ σοι,
it, and cast it from thee; it is profitable for to thee,
ἱνα αποληται ἑν των μελων σου, και μη ὁλον
that should perish one of the members of thee, and not whole
το σωμα σου βληθῃ εις γεενναν. 30 Και ει ἡ
the body of thee should be cast into Gehenna. And if the
δεξια σου χειρ σκανδαλιζει σε, εκκοψον αυτην,
right of thee hand ensnare thee, cut off her,
και βαλε απο σου· συμφερει γαρ σοι ἱνα απο-
and cast from thee; it is profitable for to thee that should
ληται ἑν των μελων σου, και μη ὁλον το σωμα
perish one of the members of thee, and not whole the body
σου βληθῃ εις γεενναν.
of thee should be cast into Gehenna.

31 Ερρεθη δε, "ὁτι ὁς αν απολυσῃ την γυναικα
It was said and, "that whoever shall release the wife
αὑτου, δοτω αυτῃ αποστασιον." 32 Εγω δε
of him, let him give her a bill of divorce." I but
λεγω ὑμιν, ὁτι ὁς αν απολυσῃ την γυναικα αὑ
say to you, that whoever may release the wife
του, παρεκτος λογου πορνειας, ποιει αυτην
him, except on account of fornication, makes her
μοιχασθαι· και ὁς εαν απολελυμενην γαμησῃ,
to commit adultery; and whoever her being divorced may marry,
μοιχαται.
commits adultery.

33 Παλιν ηκουσατε, ὁτι ερρεθη τοις αρχαιοις·
Again you have heard, that it was said to the ancients;
"Ουκ επιορκησεις· αποδωσεις δε τῳ κυριῳ
"Not thou shalt swear falsely; shalt perform but to the Lord
τους ὁρκους σου." 34 Εγω δε λεγω ὑμιν μη ομοσαι
the oaths of thee." I but say to you not swear
ὁλως· μητε εν τῳ ουρανῳ, ὁτι θρονος εστι του
at all; not even by the heaven, for a throne it is of the
θεου· 35 μητε εν τῃ γῃ, ὁτι ὑποποδιον εστι των
God; nor by the earth, for a footstool it is of the
ποδων αυτου· μητε εις Ἱεροσολυμα, ὁτι πολις
feet of him; neither by Jerusalem, for a city
εστι του μεγαλου βασιλεως· 36 μητε εν τῃ
it is of the great king; nor by the

27 You have heard That it was said, ‡'Thou shalt 'not commit adultery;'

28 but I say to you, That every man GAZING AT a Woman, in order to CHERISH IMPURE DESIRE, has already committed lewdness with her in his HEART.

29 Therefore, if thy RIGHT EYE insnare thee, pluck it out, and throw it away: it is better for thee to lose one of thy MEMBERS, than that thy Whole BODY should be cast into Gehenna.

30 And if thy RIGHT Hand insnare thee, cut it off, and throw it away: it is better for thee to lose one of thy MEMBERS, than that thy Whole BODY should * be cast into Gehenna.

31 And it was said, ‡'Whoever shall dismiss 'his WIFE, let him give 'her a Writ of Divorce.'

32 But I say to you, That * EVERY-ONE who DISMISSES his WIFE, except on account of Whoredom, causes her to commit adultery; and * HE who MARRIES the divorced woman, commits adultery.

33 † Again, you have heard That it was said to the ANCIENTS; ‡'Thou 'shalt not perjure thyself, 'but shalt perform to the 'LORD thine OATHS;'

34 but I say to you, ‡Swear not at all; neither by the HEAVEN, for it is GOD'S Throne;

35 nor by the EARTH, because it is a Footstool for his FEET; neither shalt thou swear by Jerusalem,

* VATICAN MANUSCRIPT—30. go away. 32. EVERY-ONE who DIVORCES. 32. HE who MARRIES.

† 33. The morality of the Jews in regard to oaths was truly execrable. They maintained that a man might swear with his lips, and annul it at the same moment in his heart. They also held that oaths are binding only according to the nature of the thing by which a man swears; asserting that the law, which our Savior here cites, referred to those oaths only which were of a binding nature. Instances of this distinction, which they made between oaths that were and were not binding, are expressly cited and condemned by our Lord in Matt. xxiii. 16—22; and the injunction here given against swearing by *Heaven*, by *Jerusalem*, &c., is in relation to a variety of frivolous adjurations which were constantly in their mouths.

‡ 27. Exod. xx. 14. ‡ 31. Deut. xxiv. 1; Matt. xix. 3—9; Mark x. 2—12. ‡ 33. Deut. xxiii. 21—23; Num. xxx. 2. ‡ 34. James v. 12.

κεφαλη σου ομοσης, ὁτι ου δυνασαι μιαν τριχα
head of thee shalt thou swear, for not thou art able one hair
λευκην η μελαιναν ποιησαι. 37 Εστω δε ὁ λογος
white or black to make. Let be but the word
ὑμων· ναι ναι· ου ου· το δε περισσον τουτων,
of you; yes yes; no no; that for over and above of these,
εκ του πονηρου εστιν.
of the evil is.

38 Ηκουσατε, ὁτι ερρεθη· "Οφθαλμον αντι
You have heard, that it was said; An eye for
οφθαλμου, και οδοντα αντι οδοντος." 39 Εγω δε
an eye, and a tooth for a tooth." I but
λεγω ὑμιν, μη αντιστηναι τῳ πονηρῳ· αλλ' ὁστις
say to you, not resist the evil; but whoever
σε ῥαπισει επι την δεξιαν σου σιαγονα, στρεψον
thee shall slap upon the right of thee cheek, turn
αυτῳ και την αλλην· 40 και τῳ θελοντι σοι κρι-
to him also the other; and to the purposing thee to sue
θηναι, και τον χιτωνα σου λαβειν, αφες αυτῳ
at law, and the tunic of thee to take, give up to him
και το ἱματιον· 41 και ὁστις σε αγγαρευσει μιλιον
also the mantle; and whoever thee shall force to go mile
ἑν, ὑπαγε μετ' αυτου δυο. 42 Τῳ αιτουντι σε
one, go with him two. To the asking thee
διδου· και τον θελοντα απο σου δανεισασθαι,
do thou give; and the wishing from thee to borrow money,
μη αποστραφῃς.
not do thou repulse.

43 Ηκουσατε, ὁτι ερρεθη· "Αγαπησεις το
You have heard, that it was said; "Thou shalt love the
πλησιον σου, και μισησεις τον εχθρον σου."
neighbor of thee, and hate the enemy of thee."
44 Εγω δε λεγω ὑμιν, αγαπατε τους εχθρους ὑμων,
I but say to you, love the enemies of you,
*[ευλογειτε τους καταρωμενους ὑμας, καλως
[bless those cursing you, good
ποιειτε τοις μισουσιν ὑμας,] και προσευχεσθε
do to those hating you,] and pray
ὑπερ των [επηρεαζοντων ὑμας και] διωκοντων
for those injuring you and] persecuting
ὑμας· 45 ὁπως γενησθε υἱοι του πατρος ὑμων,
you; that you may be sons of the father of you,
του εν ουρανοις· ὁτι τον ἡλιον αὑτου ανατελλει
of the in heavens: for the sun of him it rises
επι πονηρους και αγαθους, και βρεχει επι δικαι-
on evil and good, and it rains on just
ους και αδικους. 46 Εαν γαρ αγαπησητε τους
and unjust. If for you love those
αγαπωντας ὑμας, τινα μισθον εχετε; ουχι και
loving you, what reward have you? not even
οἱ τελωναι το αυτο ποιουσι; 47 και εαν ασπα-
the tax-gatherers the same do? and if you
σησθε τους αδελφους ὑμων μονον, τι περισσον
salute the brothers of you only, what more

for it is the ‡ city of the GREAT KING;
36 nor by thy HEAD, because thou canst not make One Hair white or black.
37 But let your Yes be yes; and your No, no: for whatever EXCEEDS these, proceeds from EVIL.
38 You have heard That it was said, ‡ 'Eye for 'Eye, and Tooth for 'Tooth;'
39 but I say to you, ‡ oppose not the INJURIOUS PERSON; but if any one strike thee on thy RIGHT Cheek, turn to him also the LEFT;
40 and WHOEVER WILL sue thee for thy COAT, let him have the MANTLE also.
41 And if a man † press thee to go one † Mile with him, go two.
42 ‡ Give to HIM who SOLICITS thee; and HIM, who WOULD borrow from thee, do not reject.
43 You have heard That it was said, ‡ 'Thou shalt 'love thy NEIGHBOR, and 'hate thine ENEMY;'
44 but I say to you, Love your ENEMIES, and pray for THOSE who *PERSECUTE you;
45 that you may resemble THAT FATHER of yours in the HEAVENS, who makes his SUN arise on Bad and Good, and sends rain on Just and Unjust.
46 For if you love THEM only who LOVE you, What Reward can you expect? Do not even the TAX-GATHERERS the SAME?
47 And if you salute your BRETHREN only, in what do you excel? Do

* VATICAN MANUSCRIPT—44. bless THOSE who CURSE you, do good to THOSE who HATE you—*omit*. 44. PERSECUTE: you.

† 41. An allusion to the *Angari*, or couriers of the Persians, who had authority to impress into their service men, horses, and ships, or any thing that came in their way, and which might serve to accelerate their journey. From the Persians this custom passed to the Romans, and it is still retained in the East. † 41. The Roman *milion*, or mile, measured a thousand paces.

‡ 35. Psa. xlviii. 2. ‡ 38. Exod. xxi. 24; Deut. xix. 21. ‡ 39. Prov. xx. 22; xxiv. 29; Rom. xii. 17—19. ‡ 42. Deut. xv. 7—11. ‡ 43. Lev. xix. 18; Deut. xxiii. 6.

ποιειτε; ουχι και οἱ εθνικοι οὑτω ποιουσιν;
do you? not even the Gentiles so do?
48 Εσεσθε ουν ὑμεις τελειοι, ὡσπερ ὁ πατηρ
Shall be therefore you perfect, as the father
ὑμων, ὁ εν τοις ουρανοις, τελειος εστι.
of you, who in the heavens, perfect is.

ΚΕΦ. ϛʹ. 6.

1 Προσεχετε την δικαιοσυνην, ὑμων μη ποιειν
Take heed the righteousness, of you not to do
εμπροσθεν των ανθρωπων, προς το θεαθηναι
in the presence of the men, so as to be exhibited
αυτοις· ει δε μηγε, μισθον ουκ εχετε παρα τῳ
to them; if but otherwise, reward not you have with to the
πατρι ὑμων, τῳ εν τοις ουρανοις. 2 Ὁταν ουν
father of you, to the in the heavens. When then
ποιῃς ελεημοσυνην, μη σαλπισῃς εμπροσθεν
thou doest alms, not sound a trumpet in the presence
σου, ὡσπερ οἱ ὑποκριται ποιουσιν εν ταις συνα-
of thee, like the hypocrites do in the syna-
γωγαις και εν ταις ῥυμαις, ὁπως δοξασθωσιν
gogues and in the streets, that they may have praise
ὑπο των ανθρωπων. Αμην λεγω ὑμιν, απεχουσι
of the men. Indeed I say to you, they obtain
τον μισθον αὑτων. 3 Σου δε ποιουντος ελεημο-
the reward of them. Of thee but doing alms-
συνην, μη γνωτω ἡ αριστερα σου, τι ποιει ἡ
giving, not let it know the left of thee, what does the
δεξια σου· 4 ὁπως ῃ σου ἡ ελεημοσυνη εν τῳ
right of thee; that may be of thee the alms-giving in the
κρυπτῳ· και ὁ πατηρ σου, ὁ βλεπων εν τῳ
secret; and the father of thee, who seeing in the
κρυπτῳ, *[αυτος] αποδωσει σοι *[εν τῳ φανερῳ.]
secret [himself] will give back to thee [in the clear light.)
5 Και ὁταν προσευχῃ, ουκ εσῃ ὡσπερ οἱ
And when thou prayest, not thou shalt be like the
ὑποκριται· ὁτι φιλουσιν εν ταις συναγωγαις και
hypocrites; for they love in the synagogues and
εν ταις γωνιαις των πλατειων ἑστωτες προσευ-
in the corners of the wide places standing to
χεσθαι, ὁπως αν φανωσι τοις ανθρωποις. Αμην
pray, that they may appear to the men. Indeed
λεγω ὑμιν, ὁτι απεχουσι τον μισθον αὑτων.
I say to you, that they have in full the reward of them.
6 Συ δε, ὁταν προσευχῃ, εισελθε εις το ταμι-
Thou but, when thou prayest, enter into the retired
ειον σου, και κλεισας την θυραν σου, προσευξαι
place of thee, and locking the door of thee, pray thou
τῳ πατρι σου, τῳ εν τῳ κρυπτῳ· και ὁ πατηρ
to the father of thee, to the in the secret; and the father
σου, ὁ βλεπων εν τῳ κρυπτῳ, αποδωσει σοι
of thee who seeing in the secret place, will give to thee
*[εν τῳ φανερῳ.] 7 Προσευχομενοι δε μη βατ-
(in the clear light.) Praying but not bab-
τολογησητε, ὡσπερ οἱ εθνικοι· δοκουσι γαρ ὁτι
ble, like the Gentiles; they imagine for that

not even the GENTILES * the SAME.

48 ‡ Be You therefore perfect, even as * your HEAVENLY FATHER is perfect.

CHAPTER VI.

1 Beware, that you perform not your RELIGIOUS DUTIES before MEN, in order to be OBSERVED by them; otherwise, you will obtain no Reward from THAT FATHER of yours in the HEAVENS.

2 When, therefore, thou ‡ givest Alms, proclaim it not by †sound of trumpet, as the HYPOCRITES do, in the ASSEMBLIES and in the STREETS, that they may be extolled by MEN. Indeed, I say to you, They have their REWARD.

3 But thou, when giving Alms, let not thy LEFT hand know what thy RIGHT hand does;

4 so that Thine ALMS may be PRIVATE; and THAT FATHER of thine, who SEES in SECRET, will recompense thee.

5 And when * you pray, you shall not imitate the HYPOCRITES, for they are fond of standing up in the ASSEMBLIES and at the CORNERS of the OPEN SQUARES to pray, so as to be OBSERVED by MEN. Indeed, I say to you, They have their REWARD.

6 But thou, when thou wouldst pray, enter into thy PRIVATE ROOM, and having closed the DOOR, pray to THAT FATHER of thine who is INVISIBLE; and THAT FATHER of thine, who SEES in SECRET, will recompense thee.

7 And in prayer, ‡ use not foolish repetitions, as the * HYPOCRITES; for

* VATICAN MANUSCRIPT—47. the SAME. 48. your HEAVENLY FATHER is perfect. 5. you pray, you shall not. 7. HYPOCRITES.

† 2. The phrase of *sounding a trumpet before them* seems only a figurative expression to represent their doing it in a noisy, ostentatious way.—*Doddridge.* Erasmus and Beza justly observe, that *theathanai* in verse 1 is a theatrical word; that *hypokritai* signifies *disguised players in masks*; and that *sounding a trumpet* may allude to the *music* of the stage.

‡ 48. Luke vi. 36; Eph. v. 1. ‡ 2. Rom. xii. 8. ‡ 7. Eccles. v. 2.

εν τῃ πολυλογιᾳ αὐτων εισακουσθησονται.
in the wordiness of them they shall be heard.
8 Μη ουν ὁμοιωθητε αυτοις· οιδε γαρ ὁ πατηρ
Not therefore you may be like to them; knows for the father
ὑμων, ὡν χρειαν εχετε, προ του ὑμας
of you, of what things need you have, before of the you
αιτησαι αυτον. 9 Οὑτως ουν προσευχεσθε ὑμεις·
ask him. In this way then pray you;
Πατερ ἡμων, ὁ εν τοις ουρανοις, ἁγιασθητω το
Father of us, who in the heavens, reverenced the
ονομα σου· 10 ελθετω ἡ βασιλεια σου· γενηθητω
name of thee; let come the kingdom of thee; let be done
το θελημα σου, ὡς εν ουρανῳ, και επι της γης·
the will of thee, as in heaven, also on the earth;
11 τον αρτον ἡμων τον επιουσιον δος ἡμιν
the bread of us the sufficient give thou to us
σημερον· 12 και αφες ἡμιν τα οφειληματα ἡμων,
to-day; and discharge to us the debts of us,
ὡς και ἡμεις αφιεμεν τοις οφειλεταις ἡμων·
as even we discharge to the debtors of us;
13 και μη εισενεγκῃς ἡμας εις πειρασμον, αλλα
and not bring us into temptation, but
ῥυσαι ἡμας απο του πονηρου. 14 Εαν γαρ αφητε
save us from the evil. If for you forgive
τοις ανθρωποις τα παραπτωματα αυτων, αφησει
to the men the faults of them, will forgive
και ὑμιν ὁ πατηρ ὑμων ὁ ουρανιος· 15 εαν δε μη
also to you the father of you the heavenly; if but not
αφητε τοις ανθρωποις τα παραπτωματα αυτων,
forgive to the men the faults of them,
ουδε ὁ πατηρ ὑμων αφησει τα παραπτωματα
neither the father of you will forgive the faults
ὑμων.
of you.
16 Ὁταν δε νηστευητε, μη γινεσθε, ὡσπερ οἱ
When and you fast, not be, like the
ὑποκριται, σκυθρωποι· αφανιζουσι γαρ τα προσ-
hypocrites, of a sad face; they disfigure for the fa-
ωπα αὐτων, ὁπως φανωσι τοις ανθρωποις
ces of them, so that they may seem to the men
νηστευοντες. Αμην λεγω ὑμιν, ὁτι απεχουσι
to be fasting. Indeed I say to you, that they obtain
τον μισθον αὐτων. 17 Συ δε νηστευων, αλειψαι
the reward of them. Thou but fasting, anoint
σου την κεφαλην, και το προσωπον σου νιψαι·
of thee the head, and the face of thee wash;
18 ὁπως μη φανῃς τοις ανθρωποις νηστευων,
so that not thou mayest seem to the men fasting,
αλλα τῳ πατρι σου, τῳ εν τῳ κρυπτῳ· και ὁ πα-
but to the father of thee, that in the secret; and the fa-
τηρ σου, ὁ βλεπων εν τῳ κρυπτῳ, αποδωσει σοι.
ther of thee, who seeing in the secret, will give to thee.
19 Μη θησαυριζετε ὑμιν θησαυρους επι της γης,
Not lay up to you treasures on the earth,
ὁπου σης και βρωσις αφανιζει, και ὁπου κλεπται
where moth and rust destroys, and where thieves
διορυσσουσι και κλεπτουσι· 20 θησαυριζετε δε
dig through and steal; lay up but

they think that by using MANY WORDS that they will be accepted.

8 Therefore, do not imitate them; for *GOD your FATHER knows your Necessities, before you ASK him.

9 Thus, then, pray you: ‡Our Father, THOU in the HEAVENS, Revered be thy NAME!

10 let thy ‡ KINGDOM come; thy WILL be done upon EARTH, even as in Heaven.

11 Give us This-day our NECESSARY FOOD;

12 and ‡ forgive us our DEBTS, as * we have forgiven our DEBTORS;

13 and ‡ abandon us not to Trial, but ‡ preserve us from EVIL.

14 For if you ‡ forgive MEN their OFFENCES, your HEAVENLY FATHER will also forgive you;

15 but if you ‡ forgive not MEN their OFFENCES, neither will your FATHER forgive your OFFENCES.

16 Moreover, when you ‡ fast, be not as the HYPOCRITES, of a melancholy aspect; for they distort their FEATURES, that they may seem fasting to MEN. Indeed, I say to you, They have their REWARD.

17 But thou, when fasting, anoint thy head, and wash thy face;

18 that thy fasting may not appear to MEN, but to THAT FATHER of thine who is INVISIBLE; and THAT FATHER of thine who SEES in SECRET, will recompense thee.

19 Do not accumulate for yourselves ‡ Treasures upon the EARTH, where Moth and Rust consume, and where Thieves break through and steal;

20 but deposit for yourselves Treasures in Hea-

* VATICAN MANUSCRIPT—8. GOD your FATHER. 12. we have forgiven.

‡ 9. Luke xi. 2. ‡ 10. Dan. ii. 44. ‡ 12. Matt. xviii. 21—35. ‡ 13. 1 Cor. x. 13. ‡ 13. John xvii. 15. ‡ 14. Mark xi. 25, 26. ‡ 15. James ii. 13. ‡ 16. Isa. lviii. 5. ‡ 19. Prov. xxiii. 4; 1 Tim. vi. 10, 17—19.

ὑμιν θησαυρους εν ουρανῳ, ὁπου ουτε σης ουτε
to you treasures in heaven, where neither moth nor
βρωσις αφανιζει, και ὁπου κλεπται ου διορυσ-
rust destroys, and where thieves not dig
σουσιν ουδε κλεπτουσιν. 21 Ὁπου γαρ εστιν ὁ
through nor steal. Where for is the
θησαυρος ὑμων, εκει εσται και ἡ καρδια ὑμων.
treasure of you, there will be also the heart of you.
22 Ὁ λυχνος του σωματος εστιν ὁ οφθαλμος.
The lamp of the body is the eye.
Εαν ουν ὁ οφθαλμος σου ἁπλους ῃ, ὁλον
If therefore the eye of thee sound may be, whole
το σωμα σου φωτεινον εσται. 23 Εαν δε ὁ οφθαλ-
the body of thee enlightened will be. If but the eye
μος σου πονηρος ῃ, ὁλον το σωμα σου σκοτει-
of thee evil may be, whole the body of thee darkness
νον εσται. Ει ουν το φως, το εν σοι, σκοτος
will be. If then the light, that in thee, darkness
εστι, το σκοτος ποσον;
is, the darkness how great?
24 Ουδεις δυναται δυσι κυριοις δουλευειν· η
No one is able two lords to serve; either
γαρ τον ἑνα μισησει, και τον ἑτερον αγαπησει·
for the one he will hate, and the other he will love;
η ἑνος ανθεξεται, και του ἑτερου καταφρονησει.
or one he will cling to, and the other he will slight.
Ου δυνασθε θεῳ δουλευειν και μαμωνᾳ. 25 Δια
Not you are able God to serve and mammon. For
τουτο λεγω ὑμιν· Μη μεριμνατε τῃ ψυχῃ ὑμων,
this I say to you: Not be over careful the life of you,
τι φαγητε, και τι πιητε· μηδε τῳ σωματι
what you may eat, and what you may drink; nor to the body
ὑμων, τι ενδυσησθε. Ουχι ἡ ψυχη πλειον εστι
of you, what you may put on. Not the life more is
της τροφης, και το σωμα του ενδυματος; 26 Εμ-
the food, and the body the clothing? Look
βλεψατε εις τα πετεινα του ουρανου, ὁτι ου
attentively at the birds of the heaven, for not
σπειρουσιν, ουδε θεριζουσιν, ουδε συναγουσιν εις
they sow, nor reap, nor gather into
αποθηκας· και ὁ πατηρ ὑμων ὁ ουρανιος τρεφει
barns; and the father of you the heavenly feeds
αυτα. Ουχ ὑμεις μαλλον διαφερετε αυτων;
them. Not you greatly excel them?
27 Τις δε εξ ὑμων μεριμνων δυναται προσθειναι
Which and of you being over careful is able to add
επι την ἡλικιαν αὑτου πηχυν ἑνα; 28 Και περι
to the age of him span one? And about
ενδυματος τι μεριμνατε; Καταμαθετε τα κρινα
clothing why be over careful? Consider the lilies
του αγρου πως αυξανει· ου κοπια, ουδε νηθει·
of the field how it grows; not it labors, nor spins;
29 Λεγω δε ὑμιν, ὁτι ουδε Σολομων εν παση τῃ
I say but to you, that not even Solomon in all the

ven where neither Moth nor Rust can consume, and where Thieves break not through, nor steal.
21 For where * thy TREASURE is, there * thy HEART will also be.
22 ‡ The LAMP of the BODY is * thine EYE; if, therefore, thine EYE be clear, thy Whole BODY will be enlightened;
23 but if thine EYE be dim, thy Whole BODY will be darkened. If, then, THAT LIGHT which is in thee be Darkness, how great is that DARKNESS!
24 ‡ No man can serve Two Masters; for either he will hate ONE, and love the OTHER; or, at least, he will attend to One, and neglect the OTHER. You cannot serve God and † Mammon.
25 Therefore, I charge you, ‡ Be not anxious about your LIFE, what you shall eat, or what you shall drink; nor about your BODY, what you shall wear. Is not the LIFE of more value than FOOD, and the BODY than RAIMENT?
26 Observe the BIRDS of HEAVEN; they sow not, nor reap, nor gather into Store-houses; ‡ but your HEAVENLY FATHER feeds them. Are not you of greater value than they?
27 Besides, which of you, by being anxious, can prolong his LIFE one Moment?
28 And why are you anxious about Raiment? Mark the † LILIES of the FIELD. How do they grow? They neither labor nor spin;
29 yet I tell you, That not even Solomon in All

* VATICAN MANUSCRIPT—21. thy TREASURE. 21. thy HEART. 22. thine EYE.

† 24. *Mammon* is a Syriac word for *riches*, which our Lord beautifully represents as a person whom the folly of men had deified. † 28. *Syriac*—wild lilies, or lilies of the desert. Supposed by Kitto and Sir J. E. Smith to be the *amaryllis lutea*, a golden liliaceous flower, which grows wild in the Levant, and blooms in Autumn. Dr. Bowring thinks it is the *Martagon lily*, which grows profusely in Galilee, and is of a brilliant red color.

‡ 22. Luke xi. 34. ‡ 24. Luke xvi. 13. ‡ 25. Luke xii. 22; Phil. iv. 6; 1 Pet. v. 7. ‡ 26. Job xxxviii. 41; Psa. cxlvii. 9.

δοξῃ αὑτου περιεβαλετο ὡς ἑν τουτων. 30 Ει
glory of him was clothed like one of these. If
δε τον χορτον του αγρου, σημερον οντα και
then the grass of the field, to-day existing and
αυριον εις κλιβανον βαλλομενον, ὁ θεος οὑτως
to-morrow into an oven is being cast, the God so
αμφιεννυσιν, ου πολλῳ μαλλον ὑμας, ολιγοπισ-
clothes, not much more you, O you of weak
τοι; 31 Μη ουν μεριμνησητε, λεγοντες· Τι
faith? Not therefore you may be over careful, saying; What
φαγωμεν, η τι πιωμεν, η τι περιβαλωμεθα;
may we eat, or what may we drink, or what may we put on?
32 Παντα γαρ ταυτα τα εθνη επιζητει· οιδε γαρ
All for these the Gentiles seeks; knows for
ὁ πατηρ ὑμων ὁ ουρανιος, ὁτι χρῃζετε τουτων
the father of you the heavenly, that you have need of these
ἁπαντων. 33 Ζητειτε δε πρωτον την βασιλειαν
all. Seek you but first the kingdom
του θεου και την δικαιοσυνην αυτου· και ταυτα
of the God and the righteousness of him; and these
παντα προστεθησεται ὑμιν. 34 Μη ουν μεριμ-
all shall be superadded to you. Not therefore be over
νησητε εις την αυριον· ἡ γαρ αυριον μεριμ-
careful for the morrow; the for morrow will be over
νησει *[τα] ἑαυτης. Αρκετον τῃ ἡμερᾳ ἡ κακια
careful [the] of herself. Enough to the day the trouble
αυτης.
of her.

his SPLENDOR, was arrayed like one of these.

30 If, then, GOD so decorate the HERB of the FIELD, (which flourishes To-day, and To-morrow will be cast into a Furnace,) how much more you, O you distrustful!

31 Therefore, be not anxious, saying, What shall we eat? or, What shall we drink? or, With what shall we be clothed?

32 for all the nations require these things; and your HEAVENLY FATHER knows That you have need of all these things.

33 But ‡ seek you first * his RIGHTEOUSNESS and KINGDOM; and all these things shall be superadded to you.

34 Be not anxious, then, about the MORROW; for the MORROW will claim anxiety for itself. Sufficient for each DAY is its own TROUBLE.

ΚΕΦ. ζ.′ 7.

1 Μη κρινετε, ἱνα μη κριθητε. 2 Εν ᾡ γαρ
Not do you judge, that not you may be judged. In what for
κριματι κρινετε, κριθησεσθε· και εν ᾡ μετρῳ
judgment you judge, you shall be judged; and in what measure
μετρειτε, μετρηθησεται ὑμιν. 3 Τι δε βλεπεις
you measure, it shall be measured to you. Why and seest thou
το καρφος, το εν τῳ οφθαλμῳ του αδελφου
the splinter, that in the eye of the brother
σου, την δε εν τῳ σῳ οφθαλμῳ δοκον ου κατα-
of thee, that but in thine-own eye beam not per-
νοεις; 4 η πως ερεις τῳ αδελφῳ σου· Αφες,
ceivest? or how wilt thou say to the brother of thee; Allow me,
εκβαλω το καρφος απο του οφθαλμου σου· και
I can pull the splinter from the eye of thee; and
ιδου, ἡ δοκος εν τῳ οφθαλμῳ σου; 5 Ὑποκριτα,
lo, the beam in the eye of thee? O Hypocrite,
εκβαλε πρωτον την δοκον εκ του οφθαλμου σου,
pull first the beam out of the eye of thee,
και τοτε διαβλεψεις εκβαλειν το καρφος εκ του
and then thou shalt see clearly to pull the splinter out of the
οφθαλμου του αδελφου σου.
eye of the brother of thee.

6 Μη δωτε το αγιον τοις κυσι, μηδε βαλητε
Not you may give the holy to the dogs, neither cast
τους μαργαριτας ὑμων εμπροσθεν των χοιρων·
the pearls of you before the swine;

CHAPTER VII.

1 ‡ Judge not, that you may not be judged;

2 for as you Judge, you will be judged; and ‡ by the Measure you dispense, it will be measured to you.

3 ‡ And why observest thou THAT SPLINTER in thy BROTHER'S EYE, and perceivest not the THORN in THINE-OWN Eye?

4 or, how wilt thou say to thy BROTHER, Let me take the SPLINTER from thine EYE; and, behold, a THORN in thine-own EYE?

5 Hypocrite! first extract the THORN from thine-own EYE, and then thou wilt see clearly to take the SPLINTER from thy BROTHER'S EYE.

6 ‡ Give not SACRED THINGS to DOGS, nor throw your PEARLS before SWINE; lest they tread

* VATICAN MANUSCRIPT—33. his RIGHTEOUSNESS and KINGDOM. 34. the things of—*omit*.

‡ 33. Luke xii. 31. ‡ 1. Luke vi. 37; Rom. ii. 1; xiv. 4; 1 Cor. iv. 5; James iv. 11, 12.
‡ 2. Mark iv. 24. ‡ 3. Luke vi. 41. ‡ 6. Prov. ix. 7, 8; xxiii. 9.

μηποτε καταπατησωσιν αυτους εν τοις ποσιν
lest they should trample them under the feet
αὐτων, και στραφεντες ῥηξωσιν ὑμας.
of them, and turning they should rend you.
7 Αιτειτε, και δοθησεται ὑμιν· ζητειτε, και
Ask, and it shall be given to you: seek, and
εὑρησετε· κρουετε, και ανοιγησεται ὑμιν. 8 Πας
you shall find; knock, and it shall be opened to you. All
γαρ ὁ αιτων λαμβανει· και ὁ ζητων εὑρισκει·
for the asking receives; and the seeking finds,
και τῳ κρουοντι ανοιγησεται. 9 Η τις *[εστιν]
and to the knocking it shall be opened. Or what [is there]
εξ ὑμων ανθρωπος, ὁν εαν αιτηση ὁ υἱος αυτου
of you a man, who if ask the son of him
αρτον, μη λιθον επιδωσει αυτῳ; 10 και εαν ιχθυν
bread, not a stone will give to him? or if a fish
αιτηση, μη οφιν επιδωσει αυτῳ; 11 Ει ουν ὑμεις,
he asks, not a serpent will give to him? If then you,
πονηροι οντες, οιδατε δοματα αγαθα διδοναι τοις
bad ones being, know gifts good to give to the
τεκνοις ὑμων, ποσῳ μαλλον ὁ πατηρ ὑμων, ὁ
children of you, how much more the father of you, that
εν τοις ουρανοις, δωσει αγαθα τοις αιτουσιν
in the heavens, give good to those asking
αυτον; 12 Παντα ουν, ὁσα αν θελητε ἱνα
him? All therefore, as much soever you may will that
ποιωσιν ὑμιν οἱ ανθρωποι, οὑτω και ὑμεις ποιειτε
should do to you the men, even so also you do
αυτοις· οὑτος γαρ εστιν ὁ νομος και οἱ προφηται.
to them; this for is the law and the prophets.
13 Εισελθετε δια της στενης πυλης· ὁτι
Enter you in through the strait gate; for
πλατεια ἡ πυλη, και ευρυχωρος ἡ ὁδος ἡ
wide the gate, and broad the road that
απαγουσα εις την απωλειαν· και πολλοι εισιν
leading into the perdition; and many are
οἱ εισερχομενοι δι᾽ αυτης. 14 Τι στενη ἡ πυλη,
those entering through her. How strait the gate,
και τεθλιμμενη ἡ ὁδος ἡ απαγουσα εις την
and difficult the road that leading into the
ζωην· και ολιγοι εισιν οἱ εὑρισκοντες αυτην.
life; and few are they finding her.
15 Προσεχετε δε απο των ψευδοπροφητων,
Beware ye and of the false prophets,
οἱτινες ερχονται προς ὑμας εν ενδυμασι προβα-
who come to you in clothing of sheep,
των, εσωθεν δε εισι λυκοι ἁρπαγες. 16 Απο
within but they are wolves ravenous. By
των καρπων αυτων επιγνωσεσθε αυτους. Μητι
the fruits of them you shall know them. What
συλλεγουσιν απο ακανθων σταφυλην, η απο
do they gather from thorns a cluster of grapes, or from
τριβολων συκα; 17 Οὑτω παν δενδρον αγαθον
thistles figs? So every tree good
καρπους καλους ποιει· το δε σαπρον δενδρον
fruits good bears; the but corrupt tree
καρπους πονηρους ποιει. 18 Ου δυναται δενδρον
fruits evil bears. Not is possible tree

them under their FEET, or turning again they tear you.

7 ‡ Ask, and it will be given you; seek, and you will find; knock, and it will be opened to you:

8 for ‡ EVERY-ONE who ASKS, receives; and every one who SEEKS, finds; and to HIM who KNOCKS, the door * is opened.

9 Indeed, ‡ What Man among you, who, if his SON request Bread, will offer him a Stone?

10 or, if he ask for a Fish, will give him a Serpent?

11 If you, then, being evil, know how to impart good Gifts to your CHILDREN, how much more will THAT FATHER of yours in the HEAVENS give Good things to THOSE who ASK him?

12 ‡ Whatever you wish that MEN should do to you, do you the same to them; for this is the LAW and the PROPHETS.

13 ‡ Enter in through the NARROW Gate; for wide is the GATE of DESTRUCTION, and broad THAT WAY LEADING thither; and MANY are they who enter through it.

14 How narrow is the GATE of LIFE! how difficult THAT WAY LEADING thither! and how FEW are they who FIND it.

15 ‡ Beware of FALSE TEACHERS, who come to you in the Garb of Sheep, while inwardly they are ravenous Wolves.

16 ‡ By their FRUITS you will discover them. Are Grapes gathered from Thorns, or Figs from Thistles?

17 ‡ Every good Tree yields good Fruit; but the BAD tree produces bad Fruit.

18 A good Tree cannot

* VATICAN MANUSCRIPT—8. is opened. 9. is there—*omit.*

‡ 7. Matt. xxi. 22; Mark xi. 24; Luke xi. 9; John xv. 24; James i. 5. ‡ 8. Prov. viii. 17; Jer. xxix. 12, 13. ‡ 9. Luke xi. 11—13. ‡ 12. Luke vi. 31. ‡ 13. Luke xiii. 24. ‡ 15. 2 Pet. ii. 1—3; 1 John iv. 1; Acts xx. 29—30. ‡ 16. Luke vi. 43. ‡ 17. Matt. xii. 33.

αγαθον καρπους πονηρους ποιειν, ουδε δενδρον
good fruits evil to bear, neither tree
σαπρον καρπους καλους ποιειν. 19 Παν δενδρον,
corrupt fruits good to bear. Every tree,
μη ποιουν καρπον καλον, εκκοπτεται και εις πυρ
not bearing fruit good is cut down and into a fire
βαλλεται. 20 Αραγε απο των καρπων αυτων
is cast. Therefore by the fruits of them
επιγνωσεσθε αυτους.
you shall know them.

21 Ου πας ὁ λεγων μοι· Κυριε, κυριε, εισελευ-
Not all who saying to me; O Lord, O Lord, shall enter
σεται εις την βασιλειαν των ουρανων· αλλ' ὁ
into the kingdom of the heavens; but he
ποιων το θελημα του πατρος μου, του εν ουρανοις.
doing the will of the father of me, of that in heavens.
22 Πολλοι ερουσι μοι εν εκεινῃ τῃ ἡμερᾳ· Κυριε,
Many shall say to me in that the day; O Lord,
κυριε, ου τῳ σῳ ονοματι προεφητευσαμεν, και
O Lord, not to the thy name have we prophesied, and
τῳ σῳ ονοματι δαιμονια εξεβαλομεν, και τῳ
to the thy name demons have we cast out, and to the
σῳ ονοματι δυναμεις πολλας εποιησαμεν; 23 Και
thy name wonders many have we done? And
τοτε ὁμολογησω αυτοις· Ὁτι ουδεποτε εγνων
then I will declare to them; Because never I knew
ὑμας· αποχωρειτε απ' εμου οἱ εργαζομενοι την
you, depart from me those working the
ανομιαν.
lawlessness.

24 Πας ουν ὁστις ακουει μου τους λογους
All therefore whoever hears of me the words
τουτους, και ποιει αυτους, ὁμοιωσω αυτον ανδρι
these, and does them, I will compare him to a man
φρονιμῳ, ὁστις ᾠκοδομησε την οικιαν αὑτου επι
prudent, who built the house of him upon
την πετραν· 25 και κατεβη ἡ βροχη, και ηλθον
the rock; and fell down the rain, and came
οἱ ποταμοι, και επνευσαν οἱ ανεμοι, και προσε-
the floods, and blew the winds, and beat
πεσον τῃ οικιᾳ εκεινῃ· και ουκ επεσε· τεθεμελι-
against the house that; and not it fell; it was founded
ωτο γαρ επι την πετραν.
for on the rock.

26 Και πας ὁ ακουων μου τους λογους τουτους,
And all who hearing of me the words these,
και μη ποιων αυτους, ὁμοιωθησεται ανδρι μωρῳ,
and not doing them, shall be compared to a man foolish,
ὁστις ᾠκοδομησε την οικιαν αὑτου επι την αμμον·
who built the house of him upon the sand;
27 και κατεβη ἡ βροχη, και ηλθον οἱ ποταμοι,
and fell down the rain, and came the floods,
και επνευσαν οἱ ανεμοι, και προσεκοψαν τῃ
and blew the winds, and dashed against the
οικιᾳ εκεινῃ, και επεσε· και ην ἡ πτωσις αυτης
house that, and it fell; and was the fall her
μεγαλη.
great.

yield bad Fruit; nor a bad Tree, good Fruit.

19 ‡ (Every Tree not producing good Fruit, is cut down, and cast into a Fire.)

20 Therefore, by their FRUITS you will discover them.

21 Not EVERY-ONE who SAYS to me, ‡ Master, Master, will enter into the KINGDOM of the HEAVENS; but HE who PERFORMS the WILL of THAT FATHER of mine in * the HEAVENS.

22 Many will say to me in That DAY, Master, Master, have we not taught in THY Name? and in THY Name expelled Demons? and in THY Name performed many Wonders?

23 And then I will plainly declare to them, ‡ I never approved of you. Depart from me, YOU who PRACTISE INIQUITY.

24 ‡ Therefore, whoever hears these PRECEPTS of Mine, and obeys them, * he will be compared to a prudent Man, who built * HIS House on the ROCK;

25 for though the RAIN fell, and the TORRENTS came, and the WINDS blew, and rushed upon that HOUSE, it fell not, because it was founded on the ROCK.

26 But EVERY-ONE who HEARS these PRECEPTS of Mine, and disobeys them, will be compared to a foolish Man, who built * HIS House on the SAND;

27 for when the RAIN fell, and the TORRENTS came, and the WINDS blew, and dashed against that HOUSE, it fell, and great was its RUIN."

* VATICAN MANUSCRIPT—21. the HEAVENS. 24. he will be compared. 24. HIS House. 26. HIS House.

‡ 19. Matt. iii. 10. ‡ 21. Matt. xxv. 11; Luke vi. 46, xiii. 25; Rom. ii. 13; James i. 22. ‡ 23. Luke xiii. 27. ‡ 24. Luke vi. 47—49.

[28] Και εγενετο, ὁτε συνετελεσεν ὁ Ιησους
And it came to pass, when had finished the Jesus
τους λογους τουτους, εξεπλησσοντο οἱ οχλοι
the words these, were astounded the crowds
επι τῃ διδαχῃ αυτου. [29] Ην γαρ διδασκων
at the teaching of him. He was for teaching
αυτους ὡς εξουσιαν εχων, και ουχ ὡς οἱ γραμ-
them as authority having, and not as the scribes.
ματεις.

ΚΕΦ. ή. 8.

[1] Καταβαντι δε αυτῳ απο του ορους, ηκολου-
Coming down and to him from the mountain, followed
θησαν αυτῳ οχλοι πολλοι. [2] Και ιδου, λεπρος
after him crowds great. And lo, a leper
ελθων προσεκυνει αυτῳ, λεγων· Κυριε, εαν
coming prostrated to him, saying; O sir, if
θελῃς, δυνασαι με καθαρισαι. [3] Και εκτεινας
thou wilt, thou art able me to cleanse. And putting forth
την χειρα, ἡψατο αυτου ὁ Ιησους, λεγων· Θελω,
the hand, he touched him the Jesus, saying; I will,
καθαρισθητι. Και ευθεως εκαθαρισθη αυτου ἡ
be thou cleansed. And immediately was cleansed of him the
λεπρα. [4] Και λεγει αυτῳ ὁ Ιησους· Ὁρα μηδενι
leprosy. And says to him the Jesus; See no one
ειπῃς· αλλα ὑπαγε, σεαυτον δειξον τῳ ἱερει,
thou tell; but go, thyself show to the priest,
και προσενεγκε το δωρον, ὁ προσεταξε Μωσης,
and offer the gift, which commanded Moses,
εις μαρτυριον αυτοις.
for a witness to them.
[5] Εισελθοντι δε αυτῳ εις Καπερναουμ, προσ-
Having entered and to him into Capernaum, came
ηλθεν αυτῳ ἑκατονταρχος, παρακαλων αυτον,
to him a centurion, addressing him,
[6] και λεγων· Κυριε, ὁ παις μου βεβληται εν τῃ
and saying; O sir, the boy of me is laid in the
οικιᾳ παραλυτικος, δεινως βασανιζομενος. [7] Και
house a paralytic, greatly being afflicted. And
λεγει αυτῳ ὁ Ιησους· Εγω ελθων θεραπευσω
says to him the Jesus; I coming will heal
αυτον. [8] Και αποκριθεις ὁ ἑκατονταρχος εφη·
him. And answering the centurion said;
Κυριε, ουκ ειμι ἱκανος ἱνα μου ὑπο την στεγην
O sir, not I am fit that of me under the roof
εισελθῃς· αλλα μονον ειπε λογῳ, και ιαθη-
thou shouldst enter; but only speak a word, and will be
σεται ὁ παις μου. [9] Και γαρ εγω ανθρωπος ειμι
healed the boy of me. Even for I a man am

28 And it happened, when JESUS had finished this DISCOURSE, that ‡the PEOPLE were struck with awe at his mode of INSTRUCTION;
29 for he taught them as possessing Authority, and not as *their SCRIBES.

CHAPTER VIII.

1 Being come down from the MOUNTAIN, followed by great Crowds,
2 behold, ‡a Leper coming, prostrated himself, saying, "Sir, if thou wilt, thou canst cleanse me."
3 And JESUS extending his HAND, touched him, saying, "I will; be thou clean:" and instantly he was † purified from His LEPROSY.
4 Then JESUS says to him, "See that thou tell no one; but go, ‡show thyself to the PRIEST, and present the † OBLATION enjoined by Moses, for † Notifying [the cure] to the people."
5 ‡ And having entered Capernaum, a † Centurion came to him, earnestly accosting him,
6 and saying, "Sir, my SERVANT is laid in the HOUSE, seized with palsy, being greatly afflicted."
7 * He says to him, "I am coming, and will cure him."
8 *And the CENTURION answered, "Sir, I am not worthy that thou shouldst come under my ROOF; but only command by word, and my SERVANT will be cured:
9 for even I am a man

* VATICAN MANUSCRIPT—29. their SCRIBES. 7. He says. 8. And the CENTURION.

† 3. By such a sign did Moses convince the house of Israel that God had sent him; and the Jews themselves confess that leprosy is the finger of God, a disease peculiarly of his sending and removing; and that it is not lawful for the physician, or any but the priest directly appointed in his course, so much as to attempt the cure of it.—*Towneon.* † 4. A sin-offering, and a burnt-offering with the meat-offering, and the priest shall make atonement for him.—Lev. xiv. 31. † 4. for notifying [the cure] to the people—so *Geo. Campbell* translates. The oblation could not be an evidence to the priest, as he had the privilege to inspect the man in private, before he was permitted to enter the temple to make an oblation. The ceremony consequent upon obtaining this permission, was the testimony of the priest to the people, that the man's leprosy was removed, and that he was no longer excluded from society. † 5. A Roman officer, who had the command of one hundred soldiers.

‡ 28. Mark i. 22; Luke iv. 32. ‡ 2. Mark i. 40—44; Luke v. 12—14. ‡ 4. Lev. xiv. 2—32. ‡ 5. Luke vii. 1—10.

ὑπο εξουσιαν, εχων ὑπ' εμαυτον στρατιωτας·
under authority, having under myself soldiers;
και λεγω τουτῳ· Πορευθητι, και πορευεται· και
and I say to this; Go, and he goes; and
αλλῳ· Ερχου, και ερχεται· και τῳ δουλῳ μου·
to another; Come, and he comes; and to the slave of me;
Ποιησον τουτο, και ποιει. 10 Ακουσας δε ὁ
Do this, and he does. Hearing and the
Ιησους, εθαυμασε, και ειπε τοις ακολουθουσιν·
Jesus, was astonished, and said to those following;
Αμην λεγω ὑμιν, ουδε εν τῳ Ισραηλ τοσαυτην
Indeed I say to you, not even in the Israel so great
πιστιν εὑρον. 11 Λεγω δε ὑμιν, ὁτι πολλοι απο
faith I have found. I say but to you, that many from
ανατολων και δυσμων ἡξουσι, και ανακλιθησονται
east and west will come, and will lie down
μετα Αβρααμ και Ισαακ και Ιακωβ εν τῃ βασιλ-
with Abraam and Isaac and Jacob in the kingdom
ειᾳ των ουρανων. 12 Οι δε υἱοι της βασιλειας
of the heavens. The but sons of the kingdom
εκβληθησονται εις το σκοτος το εξωτερον· εκει
shall be cast out into the darkness the outer; there
εσται ὁ κλαυθμος και ὁ βρυγμος των οδοντων.
will be the weeping and the gnashing of the teeth.
13 Και ειπεν ὁ Ιησους τῳ ἑκατονταρχῃ· Ὑπαγε,
And said the Jesus to the centurion; Go,
*[και] ὡς επιστευσας γενηθητω σοι. Και ιαθη
[and] as thou hast believed let it be done to thee. And was healed
ὁ παις αυτου εν τῃ ὡρᾳ εκεινῃ.
the boy of him in the hour that.
14 Και ελθων ὁ Ιησους εις την οικιαν Πετρου,
And coming the Jesus into the house of Peter,
ειδε την πενθεραν αυτου βεβλημενην και πυρεσ-
saw the mother-in-law of him being laid down and burning
σουσαν. 15 Και ἡψατο της χειρος αυτης, και
with fever. And he touched the hand of her, and
αφηκεν αυτην ὁ πυρετος· και ηγερθη, και διη-
left her the fever; and arose, and minis-
κονει αυτοις. 16 Οψιας δε γενομενης, προσηνεγ-
tered to them. Evening now being come, they brought
καν αυτῳ δαιμονιζομενους πολλους· και εξεβαλε
to him being possessed many; and he cast out
τα πνευματα λογῳ, και παντας τους κακως
the spirits by a word, and all those sickness
εχοντας εθεραπευσεν· 17 ὁπως πληρωθη το
having he healed; that might be fulfilled the
ῥηθεν δια Ἡσαιου του προφητου, λεγοντος·
word spoken through Esaias the prophet, saying;
"Αυτος τας ασθενειας ἡμων ελαβε, και τας
"Himself the weaknesses of us he took away, and the
νοσους εβαστασεν."
diseases he removed."
18 Ιδων δε ὁ Ιησους πολλους οχλους περι
Seeing and the Jesus great multitudes about

*appointed under Authority, having soldiers under me, say to this one, 'Go,' and he goes; to another, 'Come,' and he comes; and to my SERVANT, 'Do this,' and he does it."

10 And JESUS listening, was astonished, and said to THOSE WALKING with him, "Indeed, I say to you, I have not found So-great Faith *among any in ISRAEL:

11 and I assure you, ‡That many will come from the East and from the West, and will recline with Abraham and Isaac and Jacob, in the KINGDOM of the HEAVENS;

12 ‡but the SONS of the KINGDOM will be driven into the †OUTER DARKNESS, where will be WEEPING and GNASHING of TEETH."

13 Then JESUS said to the CENTURION, "Go; be it done to thee as thou hast believed." And *the SERVANT was IMMEDIATELY restored.

14 ‡Then JESUS entering into Peter's HOUSE, saw his WIFE'S MOTHER lying sick of a fever:

15 and he touched her HAND, and the FEVER left her; and she arose, and entertained *him.

16 ‡Now, in the evening, they brought to him many demoniacs; and he expelled the SPIRITS with a Word, and cured ALL the SICK;

17 that the WORD SPOKEN through Isaiah the PROPHET might be verified, saying, ‡†"He has "himself carried off our "INFIRMITIES, and borne "our DISTRESSES."

18 And JESUS seeing

* VATICAN MANUSCRIPT—9. appointed under. 10. among any in. 13. and—*omit*. 13. the SERVANT. 15. him.

† 12. Our Lord continues the image of a feast: the banqueting room was in the night illuminated with many lamps. He who is driven *out* of it and the house, is in *darkness*, and the further he is *removed*, the grosser the darkness.—*Wetstein*. † 17. "This man beareth away our sins, and for us he is in sorrow."—*Thomson's Septuagint translation of* Isa. liii. 4.

‡ 11. Luke xiii. 29. ‡ 12. Matt. xxi. 43. ‡ 14. Mark i. 29—31; Luke iv. 38. ‡ 16. Mark i. 32; Luke iv. 40. ‡ 17. Isa. liii. 4.

αὑτον, εκελευσεν απελθειν εις το περαν. [19] Και
him, he gave orders to depart to the other side. And
προσελθων εἱς γραμματευς, ειπεν αυτῳ· Διδασ-
coming one scribe, said to him; O teacher,
καλε, ακολουθησω σοι, ὁπου εαν απερχῃ. [20] Και
I will follow thee, where ever thou goest. And
λεγει αυτῳ ὁ Ιησους· Αἱ αλωπεκες φωλεους
says to him the Jesus, The foxes dens
εχουσι, και τα πετεινα του ουρανου κατασκηνω-
they have, and the birds of the heaven nests;
σεις· ὁ δε υἱος του ανθρωπου ουκ εχει, που την
the but son of the man not he has, where the
κεφαλην κλινῃ. [21] Ἑτερος δε των μαθητων
head he may rest. Another and of the disciples
αυτου ειπεν αυτῳ· Κυριε, επιτρεψον μοι πρωτον
of him said to him; O master, permit thou me first
απελθειν, και θαψαι τον πατερα μου. [22] Ὁ δε
to go, and to bury the father of me. The but
Ιησους ειπεν αυτῳ· Ακολουθει μοι, και αφες
Jesus said to him; Follow me, and leave
τους νεκρους θαψαι τους ἑαυτων νεκρους.
the dead ones to bury the of themselves dead ones

[23] Και εμβαντι αυτῳ εις το πλοιον, ηκολουθη-
And entering to him into the ship, followed
σαν αυτῳ οἱ μαθηται αυτου. [24] Και ιδου, σεισμος
to him the disciples of him. And lo, a commotion
μεγας εγενετο εν τῃ θαλασσῃ, ὡστε το πλοιον
great arose in the sea, so as the ship
καλυπτεσθαι ὑπο των κυματων· αυτος δε εκα-
to cover by the waves; he but was
θευδε. [25] Και προσελθοντες οἱ μαθηται ηγειραν
asleep. And coming the disciples awoke
αυτον, λεγοντες· Κυριε, σωσον *[ἡμας,] απολ-
him, saying; O master, do thou save [us.] we
λυμεθα. [26] Και λεγει αυτοις· Τι δειλοι εστε,
perish. And he says to them: How timid you are,
ολιγοπιστοι; Τοτε εγερθεις επετιμησε τοις
O you of weak faith? Then arising he rebuked the
ανεμοις και τῃ θαλλασσῃ· και εγενετο γαληνη
winds and the sea; and there was a calm
μεγαλη. [27] Οἱ δε ανθρωποι εθαυμασαν, λεγοντες·
great. The and men were astonished, saying;
Ποταπος εστιν οὗτος, ὁτι και οἱ ανεμοι και ἡ
What is this, that even the winds and the
θαλασσα ὑπακουουσιν αυτῳ;
sea hearken to him?

[28] Και ελθοντι αυτῳ εις το περαν, εις την
And coming to him to the other side, into the
χωραν των Γεργεσηνων, ὑπηντησαν αυτῳ δυο
country of the Gergesenes, met him two
δαιμονιζομενοι, εκ των μνημειων εξερχομενοι,
being demonized, out of the sepulchres coming forth,
χαλεποι λιαν, ὡστε μη ισχυειν τινα παρελθειν
fierce very, so that not to be able any one to pass along

*a Crowd about him, gave orders to pass to the †OPPOSITE-SIDE.

19 And a certain Scribe approaching, said to him, ‡"Rabbi, I will follow thee wherever thou goest."

20 And JESUS says to him, "The FOXES have Holes, and the BIRDS of HEAVEN places of shelter, but the SON of MAN has not where he may recline his HEAD."

21 And another, one of *the DISCIPLES said to him, ‡"Master, permit me first to go and bury my FATHER."

22 But JESUS *says to him, "Follow me; and leave the DEAD ONES to inter THEIR own Dead."

23 Then going on board *a Boat, his DISCIPLES followed him.

24 ‡And behold, there arose a violent Tempest in the LAKE, so that the BOAT was being covered by the BILLOWS; but he was asleep.

25 And *they came and awoke him, saying, "Save, Master; we perish!"

26 And he says to them, "Why are you afraid, O you distrustful?" Then arising, he rebuked the WINDS and the SEA, and there was a great Calm.

27 And the MEN were astonished, saying, "How great is this man! for even the WINDS and the SEA obey him."

28 ‡And coming to the OPPOSITE-SIDE, into the REGION of the *GADARENES, there met him two Demoniacs, coming forth from the MONUMENTS, so very furious, that no one was able to pass along by that ROAD.

* VATICAN MANUSCRIPT—18. a Crowd. 21. the DISCIPLES. 22. says. 23. a Boat—so Lachmann and Tischendorf. 25. they came. 25. us—*omit*. 28. GADARENES—so Tischendorf; but Lachmann reads GERASENES.

† 18. Opposite side or shore of the Lake Gennesareth. *Crossing* this lake does not always denote sailing from the east side to the west, or inversely; though the river Jordan, both above and below the lake, ran southwards. The lake was of such a form, that, without any impropriety, it might be said to be crossed in other directions, even by those who kept on the same side of the Jordan.—*Campbell.*

‡ 19. Luke ix. 57. ‡ 21. Luke ix. 59. ‡ 24. Mark iv. 37; Luke viii. 23. ‡ 28. Mark v. 1; Luke viii. 26.

δια την ὁδου εκεινης. 29 Και ιδου, εκραξαν
by the way that. And lo, they cried out
λεγοντες· Τι ἡμιν και σοι, υἱε του θεου; Ηλ-
saying; What to us and to thee. O son of the God? Comest
θες ὡδε προ καιρου βασανισαι ἡμας; 30 Ην δε
thou here before a destined time to torment us? There was now
μακραν απ' αυτων αγελη χοιρων πολλων
at some distance from them a herd of swine many
βοσκομενη. 31 Οἱ δε δαιμονες παρεκαλουν αυτον,
feeding. The and demons implored him,
λεγοντες· Ει εκβαλλεις ἡμας, αποστειλον ἡμας
saying: If thou cast out us, send us
εις την αγελην των χοιρων. 32 Και ειπεν αυτοις·
to the herd of the swine. And he said to them;
Ὑπαγετε. Οἱ δε εξελθοντες απηλθον εις τους
Go; They and coming out they went to the
χοιρους. Και ιδου, ὡρμησε πασα ἡ αγελη κατα
swine. And lo, rushed whole the herd down
του κρημνου εις την θαλασσαν, και απεθανον εν
the steep place into the lake, and died in
τοις ὑδασιν. 33 Οἱ δε βοσκοντες εφυγον, και
the waters. They and feeding them fled, and
απελθοντες εις την πολιν, απηγγειλαν παντα,
arriving at the city, related all,
και τα των δαιμονιζομενων. 34 Και ιδου, πασα
and that of those being demonized. And lo, whole
ἡ πολις εξηλθεν εις συναντησιν τῳ Ιησου· και
the city went out to a meeting to the Jesus; and
ιδοντες αυτον, παρεκαλεσαν, ὁπως μεταβῃ
seeing him, they entreated, that he would depart
απο των ὁριων αυτων.
from the coasts of them.

ΚΕΦ. θ'. 9.

1 Και εμβας εις το πλοιον, διεπερασε, και
And stepping into the boat, he passed over, and
ηλθεν εις την ιδιαν πολιν. 2 Και ιδου, προσεφερον
came to the own city. And lo, they brought
αυτῳ, παραλυτικον, επι κλινης βεβλημενον.
to him, a paralytic, upon a bed lying.
Και ιδων ὁ Ιησους την πιστιν αυτων, ειπε τῳ
And seeing the Jesus the faith of them, he said to the
παραλυτικῳ· Θαρσει, τεκνον· αφεωνται *[σοι]
paralytic; Take courage, son; are forgiven [thee]

29 And, behold, they cried out, saying, "What hast thou to do with us, O Son of GOD? Comest thou hither before the appointed Time, to torment us?"

30 Now there was a some distance from them a great Herd of Swine feeding.

31 And the DEMONS implored him, saying, "If thou dismiss us, send us away to the HERD of SWINE."

32 And he said to them, "Go." And THEY, going forth, went away to the SWINE; and behold, the Whole HERD rushed down † the PRECIPICE into the LAKE, and perished in the WATERS.

33 Then the SWINE-HERDS fled, and reaching the CITY, related all this, and the THINGS concerning the DEMONIACS.

34 And presently the Whole CITY came forth to meet JESUS, and seeing him, they entreated that he would retire from their VICINITY.

CHAPTER IX.

1 Then stepping on board *a Boat, he crossed the lake, and came to his ‡ OWN City.

2 And they brought to him a paralytic, lying on a Bed: and JESUS perceiving their FAITH, said to the PARALYTIC, "Son,

* VATICAN MANUSCRIPT—1. a Boat. 2. thee—*omit*

† 32. The following extract from "Hackett's Tour in the Holy Land," will serve as an illustration:—"COUNTRY OF THE GADARENES.—I spent a night, and part of two days, in the vicinity of the Lake of Tiberias. My tent was pitched near the Hot Baths, about a mile south of the town of Tiberias, and, consequently, near the south end of the lake. In looking across the water to the other side, I had before me the country of the Gadarenes, where the swine, impelled by an evil spirit, plunged into the sea. I was struck with a mark of accuracy in the sacred writers, which had never occurred to me till then. They state that 'the swine ran violently down *the* steep place or precipice,' (the article being required by the Greek,) 'and were choked in the waters.' It is implied here, first, the hills in that region approach near the water; and, secondly, that they fall off so abruptly along the shore, that it would be natural for a writer, familiar with that fact, to refer to it as well known. Both these implications are correct. A mass of rocky hills overlook the sea on that side, so near the water, that one sees their dark outline reflected from its surface, while their sides, in general, are so steep, that a person familiar with the scenery would hardly think of speaking of *a* steep place or precipice, where so much of the coast forms but one continuous precipice. Our translators omit the definite article, and show, by this inadvertence, how naturally the more exact knowledge of the Evangelists influenced their language."

‡ 1. Matt iv. 13. ‡ 2. Mark ii. 3; Luke v. 18.

αἱ ἁμαρτιαι σου. 3 Και ιδου, τινες των γραμμα-
the sins of thee. And lo, some of the scribes
τεων ειπον εν ἑαυτοις· Οὑτος βλασφημει. 4 Και
said among themselves; This blasphemes. And
ιδων ὁ Ιησους τας ενθυμησεις αυτων, ειπεν·
knowing the Jesus the thoughts of them, says;
Ἱνατι ὑμεις ενθυμεισθε πονηρα εν ταις καρδιαις
Why you think evils in the hearts
ὑμων; 5 Τι γαρ εστιν ευκοπωτερον; ειπειν·
of you? Which for is easier? to say;
Αφεωνται σου αἱ ἁμαρτιαι; η ειπειν· Εγειραι
Are forgiven of thee the sins? or to say: Arise
και περιπατει; 6 Ἱνα δε ειδητε ὁτι εξουσιαν
and walk? That but you may know that authority
εχει ὁ υἱος του ανθρωπου επι της γης αφιεναι
has the son of the man on the earth to forgive
ἁμαρτιας· (τοτε λεγει τῳ παραλυτικῳ·) Εγερ-
sins; (then he says to the paralytic;) Arising
θεις αρον σου την κλινην, και ὑπαγε εις τον
take up of thee the bed, and go into the
οικον σου. 7 Και εγερθεις απηλθεν εις τον οικον
house of thee. And arising he went to the house
αὑτου. 8 Ιδοντες δε οἱ οχλοι εθαυμασαν, και
of him. Seeing and the crowds wondered, and
εδοξασαν τον θεον, τον δοντα εξουσιαν τοιαυτην
glorified the God, that having given authority so great
τοις ανθρωποις.
to the men.

9 Και παραγων ὁ Ιησους εκειθεν, ειδεν ανθρω-
And passing on the Jesus from thence, he saw a man
πον καθημενον επι το τελωνιον, Ματθαιον
sitting at the custom-house, Matthew
λεγομενον· και λεγει αυτῳ· Ακολουθει μοι.
being named; and he says to him; Follow me.
Και αναστας ηκολουθησεν αυτῳ. 10 Και εγενετο,
And rising up he followed him. And it happened,
αυτου ανακειμενου εν τῃ οικιᾳ, και ιδου, πολλοι
of him reclining at table in the house, and lo, many
τελωναι και ἁμαρτωλοι ελθοντες συνανεκειντο
publicans and sinners coming reclined
τῳ Ιησου και τοις μαθηταις αυτου. 11 Και
with the Jesus and the disciples of him. And
ιδοντες οἱ Φαρισαιοι ειπον τοις μαθηταις αυτου·
seeing the Pharisees said to the disciples of him;
Διατι μετα των τελωνων και ἁμαρτωλων εσθιει
Why with the publicans and sinners eats
ὁ διδασκαλος ὑμων; 12 Ὁ δε Ιησους ακουσας,
the teacher of you? The and Jesus hearing
ειπεν *[αυτοις·] Ου χρειαν εχουσιν οἱ ισχυοντες
says [to them;] No need have those being well
ἰατρου, αλλ᾽ οἱ κακως εχοντες. 13 Πορευθεντες
of a physician, but those sick being. You are going
δε μαθετε, τι εστιν· "Ελεον θελω, και ου
but learn what is; Mercy I wish, and not

take courage; Thy SINS
are forgiven."
3 And behold, some of
the SCRIBES said among
themselves, "This man
blasphemes."
4 But JESUS discerning
their THOUGHTS, said,
"Why do you think evil
[things] in your HEARTS?
5 For, which is easier?
to say, * Thy SINS are forgiven; or to say, [with
effect,] Arise, and walk?
6 But that you may
know that the SON of MAN
has Authority on EARTH
to forgive Sins," (then he
says to the PARALYTIC,)
"Arise, take up Thy BED,
and go to thy HOUSE."
7 And arising, he went
to his HOUSE.
8 And the PEOPLE see-
ing it, *feared and praised
THAT GOD who had GIVEN
such Authority to MEN.

9 ‡ And JESUS, passing
on from thence, saw a
Man, named Matthew,
sitting at the † TAX-OF-
FICE; and he says to him,
"Follow me." And he
arose, and followed him.
10 And it came to pass,
as he was reclining at table in his HOUSE, behold,
‡ Many Tribute-takers
and † Sinners coming,
reclined with JESUS and
his DISCIPLES.
11 And the PHARISEES
observing it, said to his
DISCIPLES, ‡ "Why does
your TEACHER eat with
TRIBUTE TAKERS and
Sinners?"
12 But * HE hearing it,
says, "THEY who are in
HEALTH have no need of
a Physician, but THEY
who are SICK.
13 But go, and learn
what that is, ‡ 'I desire

* VATICAN MANUSCRIPT—5. Thy SINS. 8. feared—so Lach. and Tisch. 12. HE hearing. 12. to them—*omit*.

† 9. Probably an office erected on the side of the lake for collecting toll of passengers, and receiving the customs for goods carried by water. † 10. The word *hamartoolos*, sinner, is generally used in the Gospels, and indeed throughout the N. T., either to signify a Gentile, or such of the Jews who, from their illicit practices, were looked upon in the same light with the Gentiles. See Gal. ii. 15.

‡ 9. Mark ii. 14; Luke v. 27. ‡ 10. Mark ii. 15; Luke v. 29 ‡ 11. Luke xv. 2 ‡ 13. Hos. vi. 6; Matt. xii. 7.

θυσιαν." Ου γαρ ηλθον καλεσαι δικαιους, αλλ'
a sacrifice." Not for I am come to call just persons, but
ἁμαρτωλους.
sinners.
14 Τοτε προσερχονται αυτῳ οἱ μαθηται Ιωαννου,
Then came to him the disciples of John,
λεγοντες· Διατι ἡμεις και οἱ Φαρισαιοι νηστευ-
saying; Why we and the Pharisees fast
ομεν *[πολλα,] οἱ δε μαθηται σου ου νηστευουσι;
[much,] the but disciples of thee not fast?
15 Και ειπεν αυτοις ὁ Ιησους· Μη δυνανται οἱ υἱοι
And says to them the Jesus Not are able the sons
του νυμφωνος πενθειν, εφ' ὁσον μετ' αυτων
of the bridal chamber to mourn in as much with them
εστιν ὁ νυμφιος; Ελευσονται δε ἡμεραι, ὁταν
is the bridegroom? Shall come but days, when
απαρθῃ απ' αυτων ὁ νυμφιος, και τοτε νηστευ-
may be taken from them the bridegroom, and then they shall
σουσιν. 16 Ουδεις δε επιβαλλει επιβλημα ῥακους
fast. No one now puts a patch of cloth
αγναφου επι ἱματιῳ παλαιῳ· αιρει γαρ το πλη-
unfulled on to a mantle old, takes away for the patch
ρωμα αυτου απο του ἱματιου, και χειρον σχισμα
of it from the mantle, and worse a rent
γινεται. 17 Ουδε βαλλουσιν οινον νεον εις
becomes. Nor do they put wine new into
ασκους παλαιους· ει δε μηγε, ῥηγνυνται οἱ ασκοι,
bottles old; if but not, burst the bottles,
και ὁ οινος εκχειται, και οἱ ασκοι απολουνται·
and the wine is spilled, and the bottles are destroyed;
αλλα βαλλουσιν οινον νεον εις ασκους καινους,
but they put wine new into bottles new,
και αμφοτεροι συντηρουνται.
and both are preserved together.
18 Ταυτα αυτου λαλουντος, αυτοις, ιδου, αρχων
These of him speaking, to them, lo, a ruler
εἱς ελθων προσεκυνει αυτῳ, λεγων· Ὁτι ἡ
certain coming prostrated to him, saying; That the
θυγατηρ μου αρτι ετελευτησεν· αλλα ελθων
daughter of me now is dead; but coming
επιθες την χειρα σου επ' αυτην, και ζησεται.
lay the hand of thee upon her, and she shall live.
19 Και εγερθεις ὁ Ιησους ηκολουθησεν αυτῳ,
And arising the Jesus went after him,
και οἱ μαθηται αυτου. 20 Και ιδου, γυνη αἱμορ-
and the disciples of him. And lo, a woman having a
ῥουσα δωδεκα ετη, προσελθουσα οπισθεν,
flow of blood twelve years, approaching behind,
ἡψατο του κρασπεδου του ἱματιου αυτου. 21 Ελ-
touched the tuft of the mantle of him. She
εγε γαρ εν ἑαυτῃ· Εαν μονον ἁψωμαι του ἱματιου
said for within herself; If only I can touch the mantle
αυτου, σωθησομαι. 22 Ὁ δε Ιησους επιστραφεις
of him, I shall be healed. The but Jesus turning

'Compassion, †and not 'a Sacrifice;' for I came not to call Righteous men, but Sinners."

14 Then John's DISCIPLES accosting him, said, ‡"*We* and the PHARISEES fast, why not also thy DISCIPLES?"

15 And JESUS says to them, ‡"Can the BRIDEMEN mourn, while the BRIDEGROOM is with them? But the Time will come, when the BRIDEGROOM will be taken from them, † and then they will fast.

16 No one puts a Piece of undressed Cloth on an old Garment; because the PATCH itself would tear the GARMENT, and a worse Rent be made.

17 Neither do persons put new Wine into old †Skins; for if they do, the SKINS burst, and the WINE is spilled, and the SKINS are destroyed: but they put new Wine into new Skins, and both are preserved."

18 ‡ While he was thus speaking to them, a certain Ruler coming, prostrated to him, saying, "My DAUGHTER is by this time dead; but come, lay thy HAND on her, and she will revive."

19 And JESUS arising, with his DISCIPLES, followed him.

20 ‡ And, behold, a Woman, having been afflicted with an hemorrhage for Twelve Years, coming behind, touched the TUFT of his MANTLE;

21 for she said within herself, "If I can only touch his MANTLE, I shall be cured."

22 JESUS turning, and

* VATICAN MANUSCRIPT—14. much—*omit.*

† 13. "I desire mercy, rather than sacrifice."—*Septuagint.* † 15. The force of our Lord's answer will appear more appropriate from the fact that John was now in prison, so that his followers were fasting in consequence of their master's removal from them. † 17. Skins of the kid were very much used by the ancients for their wine. They were used whole, and the openings for the legs and head were tied up with strings. They were not strong enough to be used a second time for the same purpose.—*Samuel Sharpe.*

‡ 14. Mark ii. 18; Luke v. 33. ‡ 15. John iii. 29. ‡ 18. Mark v. 22; Luke viii. 41. ‡ 20. Mark v. 25; Luke viii. 43.

και ιδων αυτην, ειπε· Θαρσει, θυγατερ· ἡ
and seeing her, said; Take courage, daughter; the
πιστις σου σεσωκε σε. Και εσωθη ἡ γυνη απο
faith of thee has saved thee. And was well the woman from
της ὡρας εκεινης. 23 Και ελθων ὁ Ιησους εις
the hour of that. And coming the Jesus into
την οικιαν του αρχοντος, και ιδων τους αυλητας,
the house of the ruler, and seeing the flute-players,
και τον οχλον θορυβουμενον, 24 λεγει *[αυτοις·]
and the crowd making a noise, says [to them;]
Αναχωρειτε· ου γαρ απεθανε το κορασιον, αλλα
Withdraw; not for is dead the girl, but
καθευδει. Και κατεγελων αυτου. 25 Ὁτε δε
sleeps. And they derided him. When but
εξεβληθη ὁ οχλος, εισελθων εκρατησε της
they put out the crowd, he entering took hold of the
χειρος αυτης· και ηγερθη το κορασιον. 26 Και
hand of her: and was raised the girl. And
εξηλθεν ἡ φημη αὑτη εις ὁλην την γην εκεινην.
went forth the report this into all the land that.

27 Και παραγοντι εκειθεν τῳ Ιησου, ηκολου-
And passing on from there the Jesus, went
θησαν *[αυτῳ] δυο τυφλοι, κραζοντες και
after [him] two blind men, crying out and
λεγοντες· Ελεησον ἡμας, υἱε Δαυιδ. 28 Ελθοντι
saying; Have pity on us, O son of David. Being come
δε εις την οικιαν, προσηλθον αυτῳ οἱ τυφλοι,
and into the house, came to him the blind men,
και λεγει αυτοις ὁ Ιησους· Πιστευετε, ὁτι δυνα-
and says to them the Jesus; Do you believe, that I am
μαι τουτο ποιησαι; Λεγουσιν αυτῳ· Ναι κυριε.
able this to do? They say to him; Yes O master;
29 Τοτε ἡψατο των οφθαλμων αυτων, λεγων·
Then he touched the eyes of them, saying;
Κατα την πιστιν ὑμων γενηθητω ὑμιν. 30 Και
According to the faith of you be it done to you. And
ανεῳχθησαν αυτων οἱ οφθαλμοι. Και ενεβριμη-
were opened of them the eyes And strictly
σατο αυτοις ὁ Ιησους, λεγων· Ὁρατε, μηδεις
charged them the Jesus. saying; See, no one
γινωσκετω. 31 Οἱ δε εξελθοντες διεφημισαν
knows. They but having gone published
αυτον εν ὁλη τη γη εκεινη. 32 Αυτων δε εξερ-
him in all the land that. These and going
χομενων, ιδου, προσηνεγκαν αυτῳ ανθρωπον
away, lo, they brought to him a man
κωφον, δαιμονιζομενον. 33 Και εκβληθεντος του
dumb, being demonized. And having cast out the
δαιμονιου, ελαλησεν ὁ κωφος. Και εθαυμασαν
demon, spoke the dumb. And were astonished
οἱ οχλοι, λεγοντες· Ουδεποτε εφανη οὑτως εν
the crowds, saying; Never was it seen thus in

seeing her, said, "Take courage, Daughter; thy FAITH has cured thee." And the WOMAN was well from that HOUR.

23 ‡ JESUS being come into the RULER'S HOUSE, and seeing the † FLUTE-PLAYERS and the CROWD making lamentation,

24 says to them, "Leave the place; for the GIRL is not dead, but sleeps." And they derided him.

25 But when the COMPANY was excluded, he entering in, grasped her HAND, and the GIRL was raised.

26 And the REPORT of this [miracle] went forth through All that REGION.

27 And JESUS passing from thence, Two Blind men followed, exclaiming, "O Son of David, have compassion on us!"

28 And being come into the HOUSE, the BLIND men came to him; and JESUS says to them, "Do you believe That I can do this?" They reply to him, "Yes, Master."

29 Then he touched their EYES, saying, "Be it done to you according to your FAITH."

30 And Their EYES were opened; and JESUS strictly charged them, saying, "See that you inform no one."

31 But THEY, having departed, spread his fame through All that LAND.

32 Now, as these men were going out, behold, ‡ there was brought to him a Dumb man, being demonized.

33 And the DEMON having been expelled, the DUMB man spoke, and the PEOPLE were astonished, saying, "Never was it thus seen in ISRAEL!"

* VATICAN MANUSCRIPT—24. to them—*omit*. 27. him—*omit*.

† 23. *Servius* on *Virgil* says, "The funerals of the elder sort with the trumpet, and those of the younger with the flute." *Lightfoot* remarks, "On the death of his wife even the poorest Jew will afford not less than two pipes (or flutes,) and one woman to make lamentation." See 2 Chron. xxxv. 25; Eccles. xii. 5; Jer. ix. 17; xlviii. 36.

‡ 23. Mark v. 38; Luke viii. 51. ‡ 32. Matt. xii. 22; Luke xi. 14.

τῳ Ισραηλ. 34 Οἱ δε Φαρισαιοι ελεγον· Εν τῳ
to the Israel. The but Pharisees said; By the
αρχοντι των δαιμονιων εκβαλλει τα δαιμονια.
prince of the demons he casts out the demons.
35 Και περιηγεν ὁ Ιησους τας πολεις πασας
And went about the Jesus the cities all
και τας κωμας, διδασκων εν ταις συναγωγαις
and the villages, teaching in the synagogues
αυτων, και κηρυσσων το ευαγγελιον της βασιλ-
of them, and publishing the glad tidings of the kingdom,
ειας, και θεραπευων πασαν νοσον και πασαν
and healing every disease and every
μαλακιαν.
malady.
36 Ιδων δε τους οχλους, εσπλαγχνισθη περι
Seeing and the crowds, he was moved with pity for
αυτων, ὁτι ησαν εσκυλμενοι και ερριμμενοι,
them, because they were jaded and scattered,
ὡσει προβατα μη εχοντα ποιμενα. 37 Τοτε λεγει
like sheep not having a shepherd. Then he says
τοις μαθηταις αὑτου· Ὁ μεν θερισμος πολυς, οἱ
to the disciples of him; The indeed harvest plenteous, the
δε εργαται ολιγοι. 38 Δεηθητε ουν του κυριου
but laborers few. Implore then the lord
του θερισμου, ὁπως εκβαλῃ εργατας εις τον
of the harvest, that he would send out laborers into the
θερισμον αὑτου. ΚΕΦ. ι. 10. 1 Και προσ-
harvest of him. And having
καλεσαμενος τους δωδεκα μαθητας αὑτου, εδω-
called the twelve disciples of him, he
κεν αυτοις εξουσιαν πνευματων ακαθαρτων, ὡστε
gave to them authority spirits unclean, so as
εκβαλλειν αυτα, και θεραπευειν πασαν νοσον
to cast out them, and to heal every disease
και πασαν μαλακιαν.
and every malady.
2 Των δε δωδεκα αποστολων τα ονοματα
Of the now twelve apostles the names
εστι ταυτα· πρωτος, Σιμων ὁ λεγομενος
are these; first, Simon that being called
Πετρος, και Ανδρεας ὁ αδελφος αυτου· Ιακω-
Peter, and Andrew the brother of him; James
βος ὁ του Ζεβεδαιου, και Ιωαννης ὁ αδελφος
that of the Zebedee, and John the brother
αυτου· 3 Φιλιππος, και Βαρθολομαιος· Θωμας, και
of him; Philip, and Bartholomew; Thomas, and
Ματθαιος ὁ τελωνης· Ιακωβος ὁ του Αλφαιου,
Matthew the tax-gatherer; James that of the Alpheus,
και *[Λεββαιος ὁ επικληθεις] Θαδδαιος· 4 Σιμων
and [Lebbeus that surnamed] Thaddeus; Simon
ὁ κανανιτης, και Ιουδας ὁ Ισκαριωτης, ὁ και
the Canaanite, and Judas that Iscariot, who even
παραδους αυτον.
delivered up him.
5 Τουτους τους δωδεκα απεστειλεν ὁ Ιησους,
These the twelve sent forth the Jesus
παραγγειλας αυτοις, λεγων· Εις ὁδον εθνων μη
commanding them, saying; Into a road of Gentiles not
απελθητε, και εις πολιν Σαμαρειτων μη εισελ-
you may go, and into a city of Samaritans not you may

34 But the PHARISEES said, ‡ "He expels the DEMONS by the PRINCE of the DEMONS."

35 ‡ And JESUS went through all the CITIES and VILLAGES teaching in their SYNAGOGUES, and announcing the GLAD TIDINGS of the KINGDOM, and curing Every Disease and Every Malady.

36 ‡ And beholding the CROWDS, he deeply pitied them, Because they were being harassed and dispersed, as Sheep having no Shepherd.

37 Then he says to his DISCIPLES, ‡ "The HARVEST indeed is great, but the REAPERS are few;

38 beseech, therefore, the LORD of the HARVEST, that he would send Laborers to REAP it."

CHAPTER X.

1 And having summoned his TWELVE Disciples, ‡ he gave them Authority to expel impure Spirits, and to cure Diseases and Maladies of Every kind.

2 Now these are the NAMES of the TWELVE Apostles; The first, THAT Simon, NAMED Peter, and Andrew his BROTHER; THAT James, son of ZEBEDEE, and John his BROTHER;

3 Philip and Bartholomew; Thomas, and Matthew the TRIBUTE TAKER; THAT James, son of ALPHÆUS, and Thaddeus;

4 Simon the Canaanite; and THAT Judas Iscariot, who even delivered him up.

5 These TWELVE JESUS commissioned, instructing them, saying, "Go not Away to the Gentiles, and enter not any city of the Samaritans;

* VATICAN MANUSCRIPT—3. THAT Lebbæus, surnamed—omit.

‡ 34. Mark iii. 22; ‡ 35. Mark vi. 6; Luke xiii. 22. ‡ 36. Mark vi. 34; Ezek. xxxiv. 5; Jer. xxiii. 1—4. ‡ 37. Luke x. 2; John iv. 35. ‡ 1. Mark iii. 13; ix. 1.

θητε. 6 Πορευεσθε δε μαλλον προς τα προβατα
enter. Go you but rather to the sheep
τα απολωλοτα οικου Ισραηλ. 7 Πορευομενοι δε
the perishing house of Israel. Passing on your way and
κηρυσσετε, λεγοντες· Ὅτι ηγγικεν ἡ βασιλεια
preach you, saying; That has come nigh the kingdom
των ουρανων. 8 Ασθενουντας θεραπευετε, νεκ-
of the heavens. Those being sick heal, dead
ρους εγειρετε, λεπρους καθαριζετε, δαιμονια
ones raise up, lepers cleanse, demons
εκβαλλετε· δωρεαν ελαβετε, δωρεαν δοτε.
cast out; freely you have received, freely give.
9 Μη κτυσησθε χρυσον, μηδε αργυρον, μηδε
Not provide gold nor silver, nor
χαλκον εις τας ζωνας ὑμων· 10 μη πηραν εις ὁδον,
copper in the belts of you; not a bag for a journey,
μηδε δυο χιτωνας, μηδε ὑποδηματα, μηδε ῥαβδον.
nor two tunics, nor sandals, nor a staff.
Αξιος γαρ ὁ εργατης της τροφης αὐτου εστιν.
Worthy for the laborer of the food of him is.
11 Εις ἡν δ' αν πολιν η κωμην εισελθητε,
Into what and ever city or country-town you may enter.
εξετασατε, τις εν αυτῃ αξιος εστι· κακει μεινατε,
search out, who in her worthy is; and there abide,
ἑως αν εξελθητε. 12 Εισερχομενοι δε εις την
till you go thence. Entering and into the
οικιαν, ασπασασθε αυτην. 13 Και εαν μεν ῃ
house, salute her. And if indeed may be
ἡ οικια αξια, ελθετω ἡ ειρηνη ὑμων επ' αυτην.
the house worthy, let come the peace of you on her;
εαν δε μη ῃ αξια, ἡ ειρηνη ὑμων προς ὑμας
if but not may be worthy, the peace of you to you
επιστραφητω. 14 Και ὁς εαν μη δεξηται ὑμας,
let it turn. And who if not may receive you,
μηδε ακουσῃ τους λογους ὑμων, εξερχομενοι της
nor hear the words of you, coming out of the
οικιας η της πολεως εκεινης, εκτιναξατε τον
house or of the city that, shake off the
κονιορτον των ποδων ὑμων. 15 Αμην λεγω ὑμιν,
dust of the feet of you. Indeed I say to you,
ανεκτοτερον ἐσται γῃ Σοδομων και Γομορρων εν
more tolerable will be land of Sodom and Gomorrah in
ἡμερᾳ κρισεως, η τῃ πολει εκεινῃ. 16 Ιδου, εγω
a day of trial, than the city that. Lo, I
αποστελλω ὑμας ὡς προβατα εν μεσῳ λυκων.
send you as sheep in midst of wolves.
Γινεσθε ουν φρονιμοι ὡς οἱ οφεις, και ακεραιοι
Be ye therefore wise as the serpents, and artless
ὡς αἱ περιστεραι.
as the doves.
17 Προσεχετε δε απο των ανθρωπων. Παρα-
Take heed and of the men. They will
δωσουσι γαρ ὑμας εις συνεδρια, και εν ταις
hand over for you to sanhedrims, and in the

6 ‡ But go rather to the PERISHING SHEEP of the Stock of Israel.

7 ‡ And as you go, proclaim, saying, 'The KINGDOM of the HEAVENS has approached.'

8 Heal the Sick, †[raise the Dead,] cleanse Lepers, expel Demons; freely you have received, freely give.

9 Provide neither Gold, nor Silver, nor Copper, in your † GIRDLES;

10 carry no Traveling Bag, no spare Clothes, Shoes, or Staff; ‡ for the WORKMAN is worthy of his MAINTENANCE.

11 And whatever City or Village you enter, inquire what worthy person resides there; and remain with him till you leave the place.

12 When you enter the HOUSE, salute the family.

13 And if the FAMILY be worthy, let the PEACE you wish come upon them; but if unworthy, let your PEACE return * upon yourselves.

14 And whoever will not receive you, nor hear your WORDS, in departing from that HOUSE or CITY, shake the DUST off your FEET.

15 Indeed, I say to you, ‡ it will be more endurable for the Land of Sodom and Gomorrah, in a Day of Judgment, than for that CITY.

16 ‡ Behold! I send you forth as Sheep * into the Midst of Wolves; be, therefore, sagacious as SERPENTS, and innocent as DOVES.

17 But beware of these MEN; ‡ for they will deliver you up to High

* VATICAN MANUSCRIPT—13. upon you. 16. into

† 8. [Raise the Dead.] This clause, though found in the Vatican, is wanting in a great number of MSS. Griesbach excluded it from his first edition of the Greek text, but inserted it in subsequent editions, marked as doubtful. Campbell, Wetstein, and Wakefield reject it. Macknight, Whitby, and Doddridge think it better to retain the clause, as it is evident some passages in this discourse refer to events which did not immediately take place. See verses 18, 21, 23. † 9. Their purses were commonly in their girdles.

‡ 6. Isa. liii. 6; Acts xiii. 46. ‡ 7. Mark vi. 8; Luke ix. 3; x. 7. ‡ 10. 1 Tim. v. 18. ‡ 15. Matt. xi. 22, 24. ‡ 16. Luke x. 3. ‡ 17. Matt. xxiv. 9.

συναγωγαις αὑτων μαστιγωσουσιν ὑμας· 18 και
synagogues of them they shall scourge you; and
επι ἡγεμονας δε και βασιλεις αχθησεσθε ἑνεκεν
before governors and also kings you shall be lead on account
εμου, εις μαρτυριον αυτοις και τοις εθνεσιν.
of me, for a witness to them and to the nations.
19 Ὁταν δε παραδιδωσιν ὑμας, μη μεριμνησητε,
When but they shall deliver up you, not you may be anxious,
πως η τι λαλησητε· δοθησεται γαρ ὑμιν εν
how or what you must speak; it shall be given for to you in
εκεινη τη ὡρᾳ, τι λαλησετε. 20 Ου γαρ ὑμεις
that the hour, what you shall speak Not for you
εστε οἱ λαλουντες, αλλα το πνευμα του πατρος
are the speaking, but the spirit of the father
ὑμων, το λαλουν εν ὑμιν. 21 Παραδωσει δε
of you, that is speaking in you. Will give up and
αδελφος αδελφον εις θανατον, και πατηρ τεκνον·
a brother a brother to death, and a father a child;
και επαναστησονται τεκνα επι γονεις, και θανα-
and shall rise up children against parents, and deliver
τωσουσιν αυτους· 22 και εσεσθε μισουμενοι ὑπο
to death them; and you will be being hated by
παντων δια το ονομα μου. Ὁ δε ὑπομεινας εις
all for the name of me. The but persevering to
τελος, οὑτος σωθησεται.
end, the same shall be saved.

23 Ὁταν δε διωκωσιν ὑμας εν τη πολει ταυτη,
When but they persecute you in the city this
φευγετε εις την ἑτεραν· καν εκ ταυτης διωκωσιν
flee into the other, and if out of this they persecute
ὑμας, φευγετε εις την αλλην. Αμην γαρ λεγω
you, flee into the other. Indeed for I say
ὑμιν, ου μη τελεσητε τας πολεις του Ισραηλ,
to you, in no wise you may finish the cities of the Israel,
ἑως αν ελθη ὁ υἱος του ανθρωπου. 24 Ουκ εστι
till may come the son of the man. Not is
μαθητης ὑπερ τον διδασκαλον, ουδε δουλος ὑπερ
a disciple above the teacher, nor a slave above
τον κυριον αὑτου. 25 Αρκετον τῳ μαθητη ἱνα
the lord of him. Sufficient to the disciple that
γενηται ὡς ὁ διδασκαλος αυτου, και ὁ δουλος ὡς
he be as the teacher of him, and the slave as
ὁ κυριος αυτου Ει τον οικοδεσποτην Βεελζεβουλ
the lord of him. If the master of the house Beelzebul
επεκαλεσαν, ποσῳ μαλλον τους οικιακους αυτου;
they have named, how much more the domestics of him?
26 Μη ουν φοβηθητε αυτους. Ουδεν γαρ εστι
Not therefore you may fear them. Nothing for is
κεκαλυμμενον, ὁ ουκ αποκαλυφθησεται· και
having been covered, which not shall be uncovered; and

Councils, and scourge you in their SYNAGOGUES;

18 and they will bring you before Governors and Kings, on my account, to bear Testimony to them and the GENTILES.

19 ‡ But when they deliver you up, be not anxious how, or what you shall speak, because what you should say shall be suggested to you in That MOMENT.

20 For it is not *you* that shall SPEAK; but the SPIRIT of your FATHER is THAT which SPEAKS by you.

21 ‡ Then Brother will deliver up Brother to Death, and a Father his Child; and Children will rise up against Parents, and cause them to die.

22 And you will be hated by all on account of my NAME. But HE who PATIENTLY ENDURES to the End, will be saved.

23 But when they persecute you in this CITY, fly to the OTHER; †[and from that, if they persecute you, take refuge in ANOTHER;] for indeed I declare to you, you will not have gone through the CITIES of *Israel, till the SON of MAN be come.

24 ‡ A Disciple is not above his TEACHER, nor a Servant above his MASTER.

25. It is sufficient for the DISCIPLE that he be as his TEACHER, and the SERVANT as his MASTER. If they have called the HOUSEHOLDER Beelzebul, how much more THOSE of his HOUSEHOLD?

26 ‡ Therefore, fear them not; for there is nothing concealed, which will not be discovered;

---

* VATICAN MANUSCRIPT—23. Israel.

† 23. This sentence is not found in the Vatican MS., though it is approved by Griesbach. Clarke says—"This clause is found in MSS D L, and eight others; the *Armenian*, *Saxon*, all the *Itala* except *three*; *Athan.*, *Theodor.*, *Tertul.*, *August.*, *Ambr.*, *Hilar.*, and *Juvencus*. *Bengel* in his *gnomon*, approves of this reading. On the above authorities, Griesbach has inserted it in his text. It probably made a portion of this gospel as written by Matthew."

‡ 19. Mark xiii. 11; Luke xii. 11. ‡ 21. Luke xxi. 16. ‡ 24. [illegible] John xiii. 16; xv. 20. ‡ 26. Mark iv. 22; Luke viii. 17; xii. 2.

κρυπτον, ὃ ου γνωσθησεται. 27 Ὁ λεγω ὑμιν εν
secret, which not shall be known: What I say to you in
τῃ σκοτιᾳ, ειπατε εν τῳ φωτι· και ὃ εις το ους
the darkness, speak in the light; and what in the ear
ακουετε, κηρυξατε επι των δωματων· 28 Και μη
you hear, preach you on the house-tops. And not
φοβεισθε απο των αποκτενοντων το σωμα, την
be afraid of those killing the body, the
δε ψυχην μη δυναμενων αποκτειναι· φοβηθητε
but life not being able to kill: be afraid
δε μαλλον τον δυναμενον και ψυχην και σωμα
but rather that being able both life and body
απολεσαι εν γεεννῃ. 29 Ουχι δυο στρουθια
to destroy in Gehenna. Not two sparrows
ασσαριου πωλειται; και ἑν εξ αυτων ου πεσει-
an assarius are sold? and one of them not shall
ται επι την γην ανευ του πατρος ὑμων. 30 Ὑμων
fall upon the earth without the father of you. Of you
δε και αἱ τριχες της κεφαλης πασαι ηριθμημεναι
and even the hairs of the head all being numbered
εισι. 31 Μη ουν φοβηθητε· πολλων στρουθιων
are. Not therefore fear you; many sparrows
διαφερετε ὑμεις.
are better you.

32 Πας ουν ὁστις ὁμολογησει εν εμοι εμπροσ-
All therefore whoever shall confess to me in presence
θεν των ανθρωπων, ὁμολογησω καγω εν αυτῳ
of the men, I will confess even I to him
εμπροσθεν του πατρος μου, του εν ουρανοις.
in presence of the father of me, of that in heavens.
33 Ὁστις δ' αν αρνησηται με εμπροσθεν των
Whoever but if may deny me in presence of the
ανθρωπων, αρνησομαι αυτον καγω εμπροσθεν
men, I will deny him even I in presence
του πατρος μου, του εν ουρανοις.
of the father of me, of that in heavens.

34 Μη νομισητε, ὁτι ηλθον βαλειν ειρηνην επι
Not you must suppose that I am come to send peace upon
την γην· ουκ ηλθον βαλειν ειρηνην, αλλα
the earth; not I am come to send peace, but
μαχαιραν. 35 Ηλθον γαρ διχασαι ανθρωπον κατα
a sword. I am come for to set a man against
του πατρος αὑτου, και θυγατερα κατα της μη-
the father of him, and a daughter against the mo-
τρος αὑτης, και νυμφην κατα της πενθερας
ther of her, and a daughter-in-law against the mother-in-law
αυτης· 36 και εχθροι του ανθρωπου, οἱ οικιακοι
of her; and enemies of the man, the household
αυτου.
of him.

37 Ὁ φιλων πατερα η μητερα ὑπερ εμε, ουκ
He loving father or mother above me, not
εστι μου αξιος· και ὁ φιλων υἱον η θυγατερα
is of me worthy; and he loving son or daughter

and hid, which will not be made known.

27 What I tell you in the DARK, publish in the LIGHT; and what is whispered in your EAR, proclaim from the † HOUSE-TOPS.

28 Be not afraid of THOSE who KILL the BODY, but cannot destroy the [future] † LIFE; but rather fear HIM who CAN utterly destroy both Life and Body in † Gehenna.

29 Are not Two Sparrows sold for an † Assarius? Yet neither of them shall fall on the GROUND without †your FATHER.

30 And even the HAIRS of Your HEAD are all numbered.

31 Fear not, then; you are of more value than Many Sparrows.

32 ‡Whoever, therefore, shall acknowledge me before MEN, I also will acknowledge him before THAT FATHER of mine in * the HEAVENS.

33 But whoever shall renounce me before MEN, I also will renounce him before THAT FATHER of mine in * the HEAVENS.

34 ‡ Think not That I am come to send forth Peace on this LAND; I am come not to send Peace, but War.

35 For my coming will set ‡a Man against his FATHER, and a Daughter against her MOTHER, and a Daughter-in-law against her Mother-in-law;

36 so that a MAN's Enemies will be found in his own FAMILY.

37 ‡HE who LOVES Father or Mother more than me, is not worthy of me; and HE who LOVES Son or Daughter more than me, is not worthy of me.

* VATICAN MANUSCRIPT—32. the HEAVENS. 33. the HEAVENS.

† 27. The houses were flat-roofed. Compare Deut. xxii. 8, Josh. ii. 6, Neh. viii. 16, Isa. xv. 3. Jer. xxxii. 29, Acts x. 9. † 28. See Appendix and verse 38. † 29. *Assarion*—in value about one cent and five mills, or three farthings sterling. † 29. Some Greek copies read in this place *tees boulees*—the will of.

‡ 32. Luke xii. 8; ix. 26; Mark viii. 38; Rom. x. 9; 2 Tim. ii. 12. ‡ 34. Luke xii. 51. ‡ 35. Micah vii. 6. ‡ 37. Luke xiv. 26.

ὑπερ εμε, ουκ εστι μου αξιος· [38] και ὁς ου λαμ-
above me, not is of me worthy; and who not takes
βανει τον σταυρον αὑτου, και ακολουθει οπισω
the cross of himself, and follows after
μου, ουκ εστι μου αξιος. [39] Ὁ εὑρων την ψυχην
me, not is of me worthy. He finding the life
αὑτου, απολεσει αυτην· και ὁ απολεσας την
of himself, shall lose her; and he having lost the
ψυχην αὑτου ἑνεκεν εμου, εὑρησει αυτην. [40] Ὁ
life of himself on account of me, shall find her. He
δεχομενος ὑμας, εμε δεχεται· και ὁ εμε δεχομ-
receiving you, me receives; and he me receiv-
ενος, δεχεται τον αποστειλαντα με. [41] Ὁ
ing, receives him sending me. He
δεχομενος προφητην εις ονομα προφητου, μισ-
receiving a prophet in a name of a prophet, a re-
θον προφητου λη̂ψεται· και ὁ δεχομενος
ward of a prophet shall obtain; and he receiving
δικαιον εις ονομα δικαιου, μισθον δικαιου
a just man in a name of a just man, a reward of a just man
λη̂ψεται. [42] Και ὁς εαν ποτιση ἑνα των μικρων
shall obtain. And whoever may give to one of the little-ones
τουτων ποτηριον ψυχρου μονον, εις ονομα μα-
these a cup of cold only, in a name of a
θητου, αμην λεγω ὑμιν, ου μη απολεση τον
disciple, indeed I say to you, not not may lose the
μισθον αὑτου.
reward of himself.

ΚΕΦ. ια'. 11.

[1] Και εγενετο, ὁτε ετελεσεν ὁ Ιησους διατασ-
And it happened, when had finished the Jesus charg-
σων τοις δωδεκα μαθηταις αὑτου, μετεβη
ing to the twelve disciples of himself, he departed
εκειθεν, του διδασκειν και κηρυσσειν εν ταις
thence, of the to teach and to preach in the
πολεσιν αυτων. [2] Ὁ δε Ιωαννης ακουσας εν τῳ
cities of them. The and John having heard in the
δεσμωτηριῳ τα εργα του Χριστου, πεμψας δυο
prison the works of the Anointed, having sent two
μαθητων αὑτου, [3] ειπεν αυτῳ· Συ ει ὁ ερχομενος,
disciples of himself, said to him; Thou art the coming one,
η ἑτερον προσδοκωμεν; [4] Και αποκριθεις ὁ
or another are we to look for? And answering the
Ιησους ειπεν αυτοις· Πορευθεντες απαγγειλατε
Jesus said to them; Going away relate
Ιωαννῃ ἁ ακουετε και βλεπετε· [5] τυφλοι ανα-
to John what you hear and see; blind ones see
βλεπουσι, και χωλοι περιπατουσι, λεπροι
again, and lame ones are walking about, lepers
καθαριζονται, και κωφοι ακουουσι, νεκροι εγει-
are cleansed, and deaf ones are hearing, dead ones are
ρονται, και πτωχοι ευαγγελιζονται· [6] και μακ-
raised up, and poor ones are addressed with joyful news; and blessed
αριος εστιν, ὁς εαν μη σκανδαλισθῃ εν εμοι.
is, whoever not may be offended in me.
[7] Τουτων δε πορευομενων, ηρξατο ὁ Ιησους
These and going away, began the Jesus

38 ‡ And he who does not take his CROSS, and follow me, is not worthy of me.

39 HE who PRESERVES his LIFE shall lose it; but HE who LOSES his LIFE, on my account, will preserve it.

40 ‡ He who RECEIVES you, receives me, and HE who RECEIVES me, receives HIM who SENT me.

41 HE who ENTERTAINS a Prophet, because he is a Prophet, will obtain a Prophet's Reward; and HE who ENTERTAINS a Righteous man, because he is a Righteous man, will obtain a Righteous man's Reward.

42 ‡ And whoever shall give a single Cup of Cold water, to refresh one of these LOWLY ONES, because he is my Disciple, I assure you, that by no means will he lose his REWARD."

CHAPTER XI.

1 And it occurred when JESUS had concluded instructing his TWELVE Disciples, he departed thence to TEACH and to proclaim in their CITIES.

2 ‡ Now JOHN, having heard in PRISON of the WORKS of the MESSIAH; sending * by his DISCIPLES,

3 said to him, ‡ "Art thou the COMING ONE, or are we to expect another?"

4 And JESUS answering, said to them, "Go, tell John what you have heard and seen;

5 ‡ the Blind are made to see, and the Lame to walk; Lepers are cleansed; the Deaf hear; the Dead are raised; and glad tidings are announced to the Poor;

6 And happy is he, who shall not stumble at me."

7 And as they were

* VATICAN MANUSCRIPT.—2. by his DISCIPLES.

‡ 38. Matt. xvi. 24; Mark viii. 34; Luke ix. 23; xvii. 33; John xii. 25. ‡ 40. Luke x. 16; John xiii. 20. ‡ 42. Mark xi. 41. ‡ 2. Luke vii. 18. ‡ 3. Gen. xlix. 10; Dan. ix. 24. ‡ 5. Isa. xxxv. 5; lxi. 1.

λεγειν τοις οχλοις περι Ιωαννου· Τι εξηλθετε
to say to the crowds concerning John; What went you out
εις την ερημον θεασασθαι; καλαμον ὑπο ανεμου
into the desert to see? a reed by wind
σαλευομενον; 8 Αλλα τι εξηλθετε ιδειν; ανθρω-
being shaken? But what went you out to see? a man
πον εν μαλακοις ἱματιοις ημφιεσμενον; Ιδου,
in soft garments having been clothed; Lo,
οἱ τα μαλακα φορουντες, εν τοις οικοις των
those the soft (garments) wearing, in the houses of the
βασιλεων εισιν. 9 Αλλα τι εξηλθετε ιδειν;
kings are. But what went you out to see?
προφητην; Ναι, λεγω ὑμιν, και περισσοτερον
a prophet? Yes, I say to you, and much more
προφητου. 10 Οὑτος *[γαρ] εστι, περι οὑ
of a prophet. This [for] is, concerning whom
γεγραπται· "Ιδου, εγω αποστελλω τον αγγελον
it is written, "Lo, I send the messenger
μου προ προσωπου σου, ὁς κατασκευασει την
of me before the face of thee, who shall prepare the
ὁδον σου εμπροσθεν σου." 11 Αμην λεγω ὑμιν,
way of thee in presence of thee." Indeed I say to you,
ουκ εγηγερται εν γεννητοις γυναικων μειζων,
not has risen among born of woman greater,
Ιωαννου του βαπτιστου· ὁ δε μικροτερος εν τῃ
of John the dipper; the but less in the
βασιλειᾳ των ουρανων, μειζων αυτου εστιν.
kingdom of the heavens greater of him is.
12 Απο δε των ἡμερων Ιωαννου του βαπτιστου ἑως
From and the days of John the dipper till
αρτι, ἡ βασιλεια των ουρανων βιαζεται, και
now, the kingdom of the heavens has been invaded, and
βιασται ἁρπαζουσιν αυτην. 13 Παντες γαρ οἱ
invaders seize on her. All for the
προφηται και ὁ νομος ἑως Ιωαννου, προεφητευ-
prophets and the law till John, prophesied.
σαν. 14 Και ει θελετε δεξασθαι, αυτος εστιν
And if you are willing to receive, this is
Ηλιας, ὁ μελλων ερχεσθαι. 15 Ὁ εχων ωτα
Elias, that being about to come. He having ears
*[ακουειν,] ακουετω.
[to hear,] let him hear.

16 Τινι δε ὁμοιωσω την γενεαν ταυτην; Ὁμοια
To what but shall I compare the generation this? Like
εστι παιδιοις εν αγοραις καθημενοις, και προσ-
it is boys in markets sitting, and call-
φωνουσι τοις ἑταιροις αὐτων, 17 *[και] λεγου-
ing to the companions of them, [and] saying;
σιν· Ηυλησαμεν ὑμιν, και ουκ ωρχησασθε·
We have played on the flute to you; and not you have danced;
εθρηνησαμεν ὑμιν, και ουκ εκοψασθε. 18 Ηλθε
we have mourned to you, and not you have lamented. Came

departing, ‡JESUS proceeded to say to the CROWDS concerning John, *"Why went you out into the DESERT? To see a Reed shaken by the Wind?

8 But why went you out? To see a man robed in Soft Raiment? Behold! THOSE WEARING FINE clothing are in ROYAL PALACES.

9 But why went you out? To see a Prophet? Yes, I tell you, and one more excellent than a Prophet.

10 This is he concerning whom it is written, ‡'Behold! I send my MESSENGER before thy Face, 'who will prepare thy WAY 'before thee!'

11 Indeed, I say to you, Among those born of Women, there has not arisen a greater than John the IMMERSER; yet the LEAST in the KINGDOM of the HEAVENS is superior to him.

12 ‡And from the DAYS of John the IMMERSER till now, the KINGDOM of the HEAVENS has been forcibly assailed, and the violent seize it.

13 †For ALL the PROPHETS and the LAW instructed till John.

14 And if you are disposed to receive it, he is THAT ‡Elijah who is to come.

15 He HAVING Ears, let him hear.

16 But to what shall I compare this GENERATION? It is like Boys sitting in Public Places, and calling to *OTHERS;

17 saying, We have played to you on the flute, but you have not danced; we have sung mournful songs to you, but you have not lamented.

* VATICAN MANUSCRIPT.—7. Why went you out into the DESERT? To see a Reed shaken by the Wind? 8. But why went you out? To see a Man, &c. 9. But why went you out? To see a Prophet? 10. For—*omit.* 15. to hear—*omit.* 16. OTHERS. 17. And—*omit.*

† 13. It was a common saying with the Jews before the birth of Christ, that the prophets prophesied only till the times of the Messiah.

‡ 7. Luke vii. 24. ‡ 10. Mal. iii. 1; Mark i. 2; Luke i. 76. ‡ 12. Luke xvi. 16. ‡ 14. Mal. iv. 5; Matt. xvii. 11. ‡ 16. Luke vii. 31.

γαρ Ιωαννης, μητε εσθιων μητε πινων· και λεγ-
for John, neither eating nor drinking; and they
ουσι· Δαιμονιον εχει. 19 Ηλθεν ὁ υἱος του
say A demon he has. Came the son of the
ανθρωπου, εσθιων και πινων· και λεγουσιν· Ιδου,
man, eating and drinking; and they say; Lo,
ανθρωπος φαγος και οινοποτης, τελωνων φιλος
a man a glutton and a wine drinker, of tax-gatherers a friend
και ἁμαρτωλων. Και εδικαιώθη ἡ σοφια απο των
and sinners. But is justified the wisdom by the
τεκνων αὑτης.
children of her.

20 Τοτε ηρξατο ονειδιζειν τας πολεις, εν αἱς
Then he began to reproach the cities, in which
εγενοντο αἱ πλεισται δυναμεις αυτου, ὁτι ου
were done the most mighty works of him, because not
μετενοησαν· 21 Ουαι σοι, Χοραζιν, ουαι σοι,
they reformed; Woe to thee, Chorazin, woe to thee,
Βηθσαιδαν· ὁτι ει εν Τυρῳ και Σιδωνι εγενοντο
Bethsaida; for if in Tyre and Sidon had been done
αἱ δυναμεις, αἱ γενομεναι εν ὑμιν, παλαι αν
the mighty works, those being performed in you, long ago would
εν σακκῳ και σποδῳ μετενοησαν. 22 Πλην
in sackcloth and ashes they have reformed. But
λεγω ὑμιν· Τυρῳ και Σιδωνι ανεκτοτερον
I say to you, Tyre and Sidon more tolerable
εσται εν ἡμερᾳ κρισεως, η ὑμιν. 23 Και συ,
will be in a day of trial than you. And thou,
Καπερναουμ, ἡ ἑως του ουρανου ὑψωθεισα,
Capernaum, which even to the heaven art being exalted,
ἑως ᾁδου καταβιβασθηση· ὁτι ει εν Σοδομοις
to invisibility shalt be brought down; for if in Sodom
ἐγενοντο αἱ δυναμεις, αἱ γενομεναι εν σοι,
had been done the mighty works, those being done in thee,
εμειναν αν μεχρι της σημερον. 24 Πλην λεγω
it had remained till this day. But I say
ὑμιν, ὁτι γῃ Σοδομων ανεκτοτερον εσται εν
to you, that land of Sodom more tolerable will be in
ἡμερᾳ κρισεως, η σοι.
a day of trial, than thee.

25 Εν εκεινῳ τῳ καιρῳ αποκριθεις ὁ Ιησους
On that the occasion answering the Jesus
ειπεν· Εξομολογουμαι σοι, πατερ, κυριε του
said; I adore thee, O father, O lord of the
ουρανου και της γης, ὁτι απεκρυψας ταυτα απο
heaven and of the earth, because thou hast hid these from
σοφων και συνετων, και απεκαλυψας αυτα
wise men and discerning men, and thou hast revealed them
νηπιοις. 26 Ναι, ὁ πατηρ, ὁτι οὑτως εγενετο
to babes. Yes, the father, for even so it was
ευδοκια εμπροσθεν σου. 27 Παντα μοι παρεδοθη
good in presence of thee. All to me are given

18 For John came abstaining from meat and drink, and they say, He has a Demon;

19 the SON of MAN came partaking of meat and drink, and they say, Behold, a Glutton and a Wine drinker! an Associate of Tribute-takers and Sinners? But WISDOM is vindicated by her CHILDREN.

20 ‡Then he began to censure the CITIES in which MOST of his MIRACLES had been performed, Because they did not reform.

21 Woe to thee Chorazin! woe to thee, Bethsaida! For if THOSE MIRACLES which are BEING PERFORMED in you, had been done in Tyre and Sidon, they would long since have reformed in Sackcloth and Ashes.

22 Therefore, I say to you, it will be more endurable for Tyre and Sidon, in a Day of Judgment, than for you.

23 And thou, Capernaum, THOU which art BEING EXALTED to HEAVEN, ‡wilt be brought down to †Hades; for if THOSE MIRACLES which are BEING PERFORMED in thee, had been done in Sodom, it had remained till THIS DAY.

24 But I say to you, That it will be more endurable for the Land of Sodom, in a Day of Judgment, than for thee."

25 ‡On That OCCASION, JESUS said, "I adore thee O Father, Lord of HEAVEN and EARTH, Because, having concealed these things from the Wise and Intelligent, thou hast revealed them to Babes.

26 Yes, FATHER, For thus it was well pleasing in thy sight."

---

† 23. Hades—from *a*, not, and *idein*, to see; and literally means *hidden, obscure, invisible*. It is found *eleven* times in the New Testament. In the Common Version, it is rendered *grave* in 1 Cor. xv. 55, and in all other places *hell*; but the latter is now universally admitted to be an incorrect translation. See Appendix—word *hades*.

‡ 20. Luke x. 13. ‡ 23. Isa. xiv. 15; Ezek. xxviii. 8. ‡ 25. Luke x. 21.

υπο του πατρος μου· και ουδεις επιγινωσκει τον
by the father of me; and no one knows the
υιον, ει μη ὁ πατηρ· ουδε τον πατερα τις επι-
son, if not the father; neither the father any one
γινωσκει, ει μη ὁ υιος, και ᾧ εαν βουληται
knows, if not the son, and to whom may be willing
ὁ υιος αποκαλυψαι. 28 Δευτε προς με παντες οἱ
the son to reveal. Come to me all the
κοπιωντες και πεφορτισμενοι, καγω αναπαυσω
toiling and being burdened, and I will cause to rest
ὑμας. 29 Αρατε τον ζυγον μου εφ' ὑμας, και
you. Take the yoke of me upon you, and
μαθετε απ' εμου· ὁτι πρᾳος ειμι, και ταπεινος
be informed by me; for meek I am, and humble
τῃ καρδιᾳ· και εὑρησετε αναπαυσιν ταις ψυχαις
to the heart; and you shall find a rest to the lives
ὑμων. 30 Ὁ γαρ ζυγος μου χρηστος, και το
of you. The for yoke of me easy, and the
φορτιον μου ελαφρον εστιν.
burden of me light is.

ΚΕΦ. ιβ'. 12.

1 Εν εκεινῳ τῳ καιρῳ επορευθη ὁ Ιησους τοις
At that the season passed the Jesus to the
σαββασι δια των σποριμων· οἱ δε μαθηται αυτου
sabbath through the corn-fields, the and disciples of him
επεινασαν, και ηρξαντο τιλλειν σταχυας, και
were hungry, and began to pluck ears of corn, and
εσθιειν. 2 Οἱ δε Φαρισαιοι ιδοντες, ειπον αυτῳ·
to eat. The and Pharisees seeing, said to him;
Ιδου, οἱ μαθηται σου ποιουσιν, ὁ ουκ εξεστι
Lo, the disciples of thee are doing, that not is lawful
ποιειν εν σαββατῳ. 3 Ὁ δε ειπεν αυτοις· Ουκ
to do on a sabbath. He but said to them; Not
ανεγνωτε, τι εποιησε Δαυιδ, ὁτε επεινασε, και
have you known, what did David, when he was hungry, and
οἱ μετ' αυτου; 4 πως εισηλθεν εις τον οικον
those with him? how he entered into the house
του θεου, και τους αρτους της προθεσεως εφαγεν,
of the God, and the loaves of the presence did eat,
οὑς ουκ εξον ην αυτῳ φαγειν, ουδε τοις μετ'
which not lawful was to him to eat, neither to those with
αυτου, ει μη τοις ἱερευσι μονοις; 5 Η ουκ
him, except the priests alone? Or not
ανεγνωτε εν τῳ νομῳ, ὁτι τοις σαββασιν οἱ
have you read in the law, that to the sabbaths the
ἱερεις εν τῳ ἱερῳ το σαββατον βεβηλουσι, και
priests in the temple the sabbath violate, and
αναιτιοι εισι; 6 Λεγω δε ὑμιν, ὁτι του ἱερου
blameless are? I say but to you, that of the temple

27 ‡ All things are imparted to me by my FATHER; and no one, but the FATHER, knows the SON; nor does any one know the FATHER, except the SON, and he to whom the SON is pleased to reveal him.

28 Come to me, ALL YOU LABORING and burdened ones, and I will cause you to rest.

29 Take my YOKE on you, and be taught by me; For I am meek and lowly in HEART; and your LIVES will find ‡a Resting-place.

30 ‡ For my YOKE is easy, and my BURDEN is light.

CHAPTER XII.

1 At That TIME ‡JESUS on the †SABBATH went through the FIELDS OF GRAIN; and his DISCIPLES were hungry, and began to pluck off Ears of Grain, and to eat.

2 Now the PHARISEES, observing, said to him, "Behold, thy DISCIPLES are doing what is not lawful to do on a Sabbath."

3 But HE said to them, ‡"Have you not read what David did, when *he was hungry, and THOSE who were with him?

4 how he †entered into the TABERNACLE of GOD, and ate the LOAVES of the PRESENCE, which were not lawful for him to eat, nor for THOSE who were with him, but for the PRIESTS alone?

5 ‡Or, have you not read in the LAW, that †the PRIESTS in the TEMPLE profane the REST to be observed on the SABBATHS and are blameless?

6 But I say to you,

* VATICAN MANUSCRIPT.—3. he was.

† 1. SABBATH—with us, *Saturday*, or rather Friday at sun-set to Saturday at sun-set, for so the Jews reckoned. † 4. By comparing 1 Sam. xxi. 1—6, and Lev. xxiv. 5—9, it will appear that this also transpired on a Sabbath. † 5. From Num. xxviii. 9, it appears that two additional lambs were sacrificed on the Sabbath, by which the ordinary work of the week was doubled. Compare Exod. xxix. 38.

‡ 27. Matt. xxviii. 18; John iii. 25; vi. 46; x. 15. ‡ 29. John xiv. 3; Heb. iv. 9—11. ‡ 30. 1 John v. 3. ‡ 1. Mark ii. 23; Luke vi. 1; Deut. xxiii. 25. ‡ 3. 1 Sam. xxi. 1—6. ‡ 5. Lev. xxiv. 5; Num. xxviii. 9.

μειζων εστιν ὡδε. 7 Ει δε εγνωκειτε, τι εστιν·
greater is here. If but you had known, what is;
"Ελεον θελω, και ου θυσιαν" ουκ αν κατε-
"Mercy I desire, and not a sacrifice," not would you
δικασατε τους αναιτιους. 8 Κυριος γαρ εστι
have condemned the blameless. A lord for is
του σαββατου ὁ υἱος του ανθρωπου.
of the sabbath the son of the man.

Και μεταβας εκειθεν, ηλθεν εις την συνα-
And passing on from thence, he came into the syna-
γωγην αυτων. 10 Και ιδου, ανθρωπος ην την
gogue of them. And lo, a man there was the
χειρα εχων ξηραν. Και επηρωτησαν αυτον,
hand having withered. And they asked him,
λεγοντες· Ει εξεστι τοις σαββασι θεραπευειν;
saying; If it is lawful to the sabbaths to heal?
ἱνα κατηγορησωσιν αυτου. 11 Ὁ δε ειπεν αυτοις·
that they might accuse him. He but said to them;
Τις εσται εξ ὑμων ανθρωπος, ὁς ἑξει προβατον
What shall be among you a man, who shall have sheep
ἑν, και εαν εμπεσῃ τουτο τοις σαββασιν εις
one, and if should fall this to the sabbath into
βοθυνον, ουχι κρατησει αυτο, και εγερει;
a pit, not seize it, and raise it up?
12 Ποσῳ ουν διαφερει ανθρωπος προβατου; Ὡστε
How much then is superior a man of a sheep? So that
εξεστι τοις σαββασι καλως ποιειν. 13 Τοτε
it is lawful to the sabbath good to do. Then
λεγει τῳ ανθρωπῳ· Εκτεινον την χειρα σου.
he says to the man; Stretch out the hand of thee.
Και εξετεινε· και αποκατεσταθη ὑγιης, ὡς
And he stretched it out; and it was restored whole, as
ἡ αλλη.
the other.

14 Οἱ δε Φαρισαιοι συμβουλιον ελαβον κατ'
The then Pharisees a council held against
αυτου εξελθοντες, ὁπως αυτον απολεσωσιν.
him going out, how him they might destroy.
15 Ὁ δε Ιησους γνους ανεχωρησεν εκειθεν· και
The but Jesus knowing withdrew from thence; and
ηκολουθησαν αυτῳ οχλοι πολλοι· και εθερα-
followed him crowds great; and he
πευσεν αυτους παντας, 16 και επετιμησεν
healed them all. and charged
αυτοις, ἱνα μη φανερον αυτον ποιησωσιν· 17 ὁπως
them, that not known him they should make; so that
πληρωθῃ το ῥηθεν δια Ἡσαιου του προ-
it might be fulfilled the word spoken through Esaias the pro-
φητου, λεγοντος· 18 "Ιδου, ὁ παις μου, ὁν
phet saying; "Lo, the servant of me, whom

That one greater than the TEMPLE is here.

7 If, then, you had known what this is; ‡ 'I 'desire Compassion, and 'not a Sacrifice,' you would not have condemned the INNOCENT;

8 for the SON of MAN is Master of the SABBATH."

9 ‡ And having left that place, he went into their SYNAGOGUE;

10 and behold, there was a Man who had * a withered Hand. They asked JESUS, with a design to accuse him, ‡ "Is it lawful to heal on the SABBATH?"

11 And HE answered them, "What Man is there among you, who, having one Sheep, ‡ if it fall into a pit on the SABBATH, will not lay hold on it, and lift it out?

12 Does not a Man greatly surpass a Sheep? Therefore, it is lawful to do good on the SABBATH."

13 Then he says to the MAN, "Stretch out Thine HAND." And he stretched it out; and it was restored to soundness, like the other.

14 Then the PHARISEES, departing, held a Council concerning him, how they might destroy him.

15 But JESUS knowing it, withdrew from them, and * many followed him, and he healed them all;

16 and charged them not to make him known:

17 so that the WORD SPOKEN through Isaiah the PROPHET might be verified, saying;

18 ‡ † "Behold, my SER-

* VATICAN MANUSCRIPT.—10. a withered Hand. 15. many followed.

† 18. The following is from the Septuagint version of Isa. xlii. 1, translated by Thompson:—"Jacob *is* my servant, I will uphold him; Israel *is* my chosen one, my soul hath embraced him. I have put my spirit upon him; he will publish judgment to the nations: he will not cry aloud, nor urge with vehemence, nor will his voice be heard abroad. A bruised reed he will not break, nor will he quench smoking flax, but will bring forth judgment unto truth,—and in his name shall the nations trust (or hope)." The words *Jacob* and *Israel*, added by the authors of the Septuagint, have obscured this prophecy.

‡ 7. Hos. vi. 6; Matt. ix. 13. ‡ 9. Mark iii. 1; Luke vi. 6. ‡ 10. Luke xiii. 14; xiv. 3; John ix. 16. ‡ 11. Exod. xxiii. 4, 5; Deut. xxii. 4. ‡ 18. Isa. xlii. 1.

ᾑρετισα, ὁ αγαπητος μου, εις ὁν ευδοκησεν ἡ
I have chosen, the beloved of me, in whom takes delight the
ψυχη μου· θησω το πνευμα μου επ' αυτον,
soul of me; I will put the spirit of me upon him,
και κρισιν τοις εθνεσιν απαγγελει. [19] Ουκ
and judgment to the nations he shall declare. Not
ερισει, ουδε κραυγασει, ουδε ακουσει τις εν
he shall strive, nor cry out, nor shall hear any one in
ταις πλατειαις την φωνην αυτου· [20] καλαμον
the wide places the voice of him; a reed
συντετριμμενον ου κατεαξει, και λινον τυφομ-
having been bruised not he shall break, and flax smoking
ενον ου σβεσει· ἑως αν εκβαλῃ εις νικος
not he shall quench, till he bring forth to a victory
την κρισιν. [21] Και τῳ ονοματι αυτου εθνη
the judgment. And to the name of him nations
ελπιουσι."
will hope."

[22] Τοτε προσηνεχθη αυτῳ δαιμονιζομενος,
Then was brought to him a demoniac,
τυφλος και κωφος· και εθεραπευσεν αυτον, ὡστε
blind and dumb; and he healed him, so that
τον τυφλον και κωφον και λαλειν και βλεπειν.
the blind and dumb both to speak and to see.
[23] Και εξισταντο παντες οἱ οχλοι, και ελεγον·
And were amazed all the crowds, and said;
Μητι οὑτος εστιν ὁ υἱος Δαυιδ [24] Οἱ δε
Not this is the son David? The and
Φαρισαιοι ακουσαντες, ειπον· Οὑτος ουκ εκ-
Pharisees hearing, said; This not
βαλλει τα δαιμονια, ει μη εν τῳ Βεελζεβουλ,
casts out the demons, if not by the Beelzebul,
αρχοντι των δαιμονιων. [25] Ειδως δε ὁ Ιησους
a prince of the demons. Knowing but the Jesus
τας ενθυμησεις αυτων, ειπεν αυτοις· Πασα βα-
the thoughts of them, said to them; Every
σιλεια μερισθεισα καθ' ἑαυτης, ερημουται· και
kingdom being divided against itself, is laid waste; and
πασα πολις η οικια μερισθεισα καθ' ἑαυτης, ου
every city or house being divided against itself, not
σταθησεται. [26] Και ει ὁ σατανας τον σαταναν
will stand. And if the adversary the adversary
εκβαλλει, εφ' ἑαυτον εμερισθη· πως ουν στα-
casts out, with himself he is at variance, how then
θησεται ἡ βασιλεια αυτου; [27] Και ει εγω εν
will stand the kingdom of him? And if I by
Βεελζεβουλ εκβαλλω τα δαιμονια, οἱ υἱοι ὑμων
Beelzebul cast out the demons, the sons of you
εν τινι εκβαλλουσι; Δια τουτο αυτοι ὑμων
by whom do they cast out? In this they of you
εσονται κριται. [28] Ει δε εν πνευματι θεου εγω
shall be judges. If but by spirit of God I
εκβαλλω τα δαιμονια, αρα εφθασεν εφ'
cast out the demons, then has suddenly come among

"VANT, whom I have cho-
"sen, my BELOVED, in
"whom I take delight: I
"will put my SPIRIT upon
"him, and he shall pro-
"claim Justice to the NA-
"TIONS.
19 "He will not strive
"nor cry out, nor will any
"one hear his VOICE in
"the OPEN SQUARES.
20 "He will not break
"a bruised Reed, and a
"dimly burning Taper he
"will not extinguish, till
"he send forth the JUDG-
"MENT to victory.
21 "The nations also
"will hope in his name."
22 ‡Then *they brought
to him a demoniac, blind
and dumb; and he cured
him, so that *the DUMB
man spake and saw.
23 And All the PEOPLE
with amazement, asked,
"Is this the SON of Da-
vid?"
24 But the PHARISEES
hearing them, said, "This
man could not expel DE-
MONS, except through
Beelzebul, the Prince of
the DEMONS."
25 And *he knowing
their thoughts, said unto
them, "Every Kingdom
being divided against it-
self, is desolated; and No
City or House being di-
vided against itself, can
stand.
26 Now if the ADVER-
SARY expel the ADVER-
SARY, he is at variance
with himself; how then
will his KINGDOM stand?
27 Besides, if I through
Beelzebul expel DEMONS,
through whom do your
SONS expel them? There-
fore, they will be Your
Judges.
28 But, if it be by Di-
vine co-operation that I
cast out DEMONS, then
† GOD'S ROYAL MAJESTY

* VATICAN MANUSCRIPT.—22. they brought. 22. the DUMB man spake and saw. 25. he knowing.

† 28. See note on *Basileia*, Matt. iii. 2. It is not according to fact, to make Jesus say, that "the kingdom of God has come unto you," as rendered in the Common Version, and followed by modern translators. The context shows that our Lord is speaking of himself These miracles were proofs of his Messiahship. See John iii. 2; v. 36; vii. 31.

‡ 22. Luke xi. 14. ‡ 24. Mark iii. 22.

ὑμας ἡ βασιλεια του θεου. [29] Η πως δυναται
you the majesty of the God. Or how is able
τις εισελθειν εις την οικιαν του ισχυρου, και
any one to enter into the house of the strong man, and
τα σκευη αυτου διαρπασαι, εαν μη πρωτον
the household stuff of him to plunder, if not first
δηση τον ισχυρον; και τοτε την οικιαν αυτου
he should bind the strong man? and then the house of him
διαρπασει. [30] Ὁ μη ων μετ' εμου, κατ' εμου
he shall plunder. He not being with me, against me
ἐστι· και ὁ μη συναγων μετ' εμου, σκορπιζει.
is; and he not gathering with me, scatters.
[31] Δια τουτο λεγω ὑμιν· Πασα ἁμαρτια και
Therefore this I say to you; All sin and
βλασφημια αφεθησεται τοις ανθρωποις· ἡ δε
evil-speaking shall be forgiven to the men; the but
του πνευματος βλασφημια ουκ αφεθησεται
of the spirit evil-speaking not shall be forgiven
*[τοις ανθρωποις·] [32] και ὁς αν ειπῃ λογον
[to the men;] and who ever may speak a word
κατα του υἱου του ανθρωπου, αφεθησεται αυτῳ·
against of the son of the man, it shall be forgiven to him;
ὁς δ' αν ειπῃ κατα του πνευματος του ἁγιου,
who but ever may speak against of the spirit of the holy,
ουκ αφεθησεται αυτῳ, ουτε εν τουτῳ τῳ αιωνι,
not it shall be forgiven to him, neither in this the age,
ουτε εν τῳ μελλοντι. [33] Η ποιησατε το δεν-
nor in the coming. Either make you the tree
δρον καλον, και τον καρπον αυτου καλον· η
good, and the fruits of him good; or
ποιησατε το δενδρον σαπρον, και τον καρπον
make you the tree corrupt, and the fruits
αυτου σαπρον· εκ γαρ του καρπου το δενδρον
of him corrupt; by for the fruit the tree
γινωσκεται. [34] Γεννηματα εχιδνων, πως
is known. O broods of venomous serpents, how
δυνασθε αγαθα λαλειν, πονηροι οντες; εκ γαρ
are you able good (things) to speak, evil (men) being; out of for
του περισσευματος της καρδιας το στομα λαλει.
the fulness of the heart the mouth speaks.
[35] Ὁ αγαθος ανθρωπος εκ του αγαθου θησαυρου
The good man out of the good treasure
εκβαλλει τα αγαθα· και ὁ πονηρος ανθρωπος
brings forth the good (things); and the evil man
εκ του πονηρου θησαυρου εκβαλλει πονηρα.
out of the evil treasure brings forth evil (things).
[36] Λεγω δε ὑμιν, ὁτι παν ῥημα αργον, ὁ εαν
I say but to you, that every word idle, which if
λαλησωσιν οἱ ανθρωποι, αποδωσουσι, περι
may speak the men, they shall give account, concerning
αυτου λογον εν ἡμερᾳ κρισεως· [37] Εκ γαρ των
this word in a day of trial. By for the
λογων σου δικαιωθηση, και εκ των λογων σου
words of thee thou shalt be acquitted, and by the words of thee
καταδικασθηση.
thou shalt be condemned.

has unexpectedly appeared among you.

29 Moreover, how can any one enter the STRONG one's HOUSE, and plunder his GOODS, unless he first bind the STRONG ONE? and then indeed he may plunder his HOUSE.

30 HE who IS not with me, is against me; and HE who GATHERS not with me, scatters.

31 ‡ Therefore, I say to you, Though every other Sin and Blasphemy will be forgiven * to YOU MEN; yet the BLASPHEMY of the SPIRIT will not be forgiven.

32 For whoever may speak a Word against the SON of MAN, it * † will be forgiven him; but he who may speak against the HOLY SPIRIT, * it will in no wise be forgiven him, neither in this nor in the coming AGE.

33 ‡ Either call the TREE good, and its FRUIT good; or call the TREE bad, and its FRUIT bad; for we know the TREE by the FRUIT.

34 O Progeny of Vipers! ‡ how can you, being evil, speak good things? for out of the EXUBERANCE of the HEART the mouth speaks.

35 ‡ The GOOD Man out of his GOOD Treasure produces * good things; and the EVIL Man out of his BAD Treasure produces evil things.

36 But I say to you, That for Every pernicious Word which MEN may utter, they shall be Responsible, on a Day of Judgment.

37 For by thy WORDS thou wilt be acquitted; and by thy WORDS thou wilt be condemned."

---

* VATICAN MANUSCRIPT.—31. to YOU MEN. 31. to MEN—*omit*. 32. not be forgiven him. 32. in no wise be forgiven him. 35. of the HEART—*omit*. 35. good things.

† 32. The Vat. MSS. here reads, "it shall *not* be forgiven him," which is contrary to what is stated in verse 31, and the parallel passage in Luke xii. 10. Probably it is an error of the transcriber. For this reason it has not been inserted in the text.

‡ 31. Mark iii. 28; Luke xii. 10; 1 John v. 16. ‡ 33. Matt. vii. 17; Luke vi. 43, 44. ‡ 34. Matt. iii. 7; xxiii. 33. ‡ 35. Luke vi. 45.

38 Τοτε απεκριθησαν τινες των γραμματεων
Then answered some of the scribes
*[και Φαρισαιων,] λεγοντες· Διδασκαλε, θελ-
[and Pharisees,] saying; O teacher, we
ομεν απο σου σημειον ιδειν. 39 Ὁ δε αποκριθεις
wish from thee a sign to see. He but answering
ειπεν αυτοις· Γενεα πονηρα και μοιχαλις ση-
said to them; A generation evil and adulterous a
μειον επιζητει· και σημειον ου δοθησεται αυτῃ,
sign demands; and a sign not shall be given to her,
ει μη το σημειον Ιωνα του προφητου. 40 Ὡσπερ
if not the sign of Jonas, the prophet. Like as
γαρ ην Ιωνας εν τῃ κοιλιᾳ του κητους τρεις
for was Jonas in the belly of the fish three
ἡμερας και τρεις νυκτας· οὑτως εσται ὁ υἱος
days and three nights; so shall be the son
του ανθρωπου εν τῃ καρδιᾳ της γης τρεις ἡμερας
of the man in the heart of the earth three days
και τρεις νυκτας. 41 Ανδρες Νινευιται αναστη-
and three nights. Men Ninevites shall stand
σονται εν τῃ κρισει μετα της γενεας ταυτης,
up in the judgment against the generation of this,
και κατακρινουσιν αυτην· ὁτι μετενοησαν
and shall give judgment against her; for they reformed
εις το κηρυγμα Ιωνα· και ιδου πλειον Ιωνα ὡδε.
at the preaching of Jonas; and lo a greater of Jonas here.
42 Βασιλισσα νοτου εγερθησεται εν τῃ κρισει
Queen of south shall rise up in the judgment
μετα της γενεας ταυτης, και κατακρινει
against the generation of this, and shall give judgment against
αυτην· ὁτι ηλθεν εκ των περατων της γης
her; for she came from the ends of the earth
ακουσαι την σοφιαν Σολομωνος· και ιδου, πλειον
to hear the wisdom of Solomon; and lo, a greater
Σολομωνος ὡδε. 43 Ὁταν δε το ακαθαρτον
of Solomon here. When but the unclean
πνευμα εξελθῃ απο του ανθρωπου, διερχεται
spirit may come out from the man, it wanders about
δι' ανυδρων τοπων ζητουν αναπαυσιν, και ουχ
through dry places seeking a resting-place, and not
εὑρισκει. 44 Τοτε λεγει· Επιστρεψω εις τον
it finds. Then it says; I will return into the
οικον μου, ὁθεν εξηλθον. Και ελθον εὑρισκει
house of me, whence I came. And coming it finds
σχολαζοντα, σεσαρωμενον, και κεκοσμημενον.
it being empty, having been swept, and having been set in order.
45 Τοτε πορευεται, και παραλαμβανει μεθ' ἑαυτου
Then it goes, and takes with itself
ἑπτα ἑτερα πνευματα, πονηροτερα ἑαυτου, και
seven other spirits, more wicked of itself. and
εισελθοντα κατοικει εκει· και γινεται τα
they entering finds an abode there; and becomes the

38 ‡Then some of the SCRIBES *answered him, saying, "Teacher, we desire to witness †a Sign from thee."

39 But HE answering, said to them, ‡"A wicked and faithless Generation demands a Sign; but no Sign will be given it, except the SIGN of Jonah the PROPHET.

40 ‡For as Jonah was Three Days and Three Nights in the STOMACH of the GREAT FISH; so will the SON of MAN be Three Days and Three Nights †in the HEART of the EARTH.

41 The Ninevites will stand up in the JUDGMENT against this GENERATION, and cause it to be condemned; ‡For they reformed at the WARNING of Jonah; and behold, something greater than Jonah is here.

42 ‡The Queen of the †South will rise up at the JUDGMENT against this GENERATION, and cause it to be condemned; for she came from a DISTANT LAND to hear the WISDOM of Solomon; and behold, something greater than Solomon is here.

43 ‡When the IMPURE Spirit is gone out of the MAN, it roves through Parched Deserts, seeking a Place of Rest, and finds it not.

44 Then it says, I will return to my HOUSE, whence I came. And coming, it finds it empty, swept, and furnished.

45 It then departs, and takes with itself Seven Other Spirits, more wicked

* VATICAN MANUSCRIPT.—38. and Pharisees—*omit*. 38. answered him, saying.

† 38. This was a demand often made—see Matt. xvi. 1; Mark viii. 11; Luke xi. 16—and probably founded on the prophecy of Dan. vii. 13, which describes the Son of Man as coming in the clouds of heaven. It was almost a characteristic of the Jews to ask a sign. See 1 Cor. i. 22. They demanded one from *heaven*—some *celestial* phenomenon—which would be the strongest test of Jesus' pretensions.—*Bloomfield*. † 40. That is, simply, *in the earth*. So Tyre is said to be *in the heart of the sea*, Ezek. xxviii. 2, although it was so near the continent, that, when Alexander beseiged it, he carried a causeway from the land to the city.—*Trollope*. † 42. In the Old Testament—*Sheba*.

‡ 38. Luke xi. 29. ‡ 39. Matt. xvi. 4. ‡ 40. Jonah i. 17. ‡ 41. Jonah iii. 5. ‡ 42. 1 Kings x. 1; 2 Chron. ix. 1. ‡ 43. Luke xi. 24

εσχατα του ανθρωπου εκεινου χειρονα των
last (state) of the man that worse of the
πρωτων. Ούτως εσται και τῃ γενεᾳ ταυτῃ
first. Thus will be and the generation this
τῃ πονηρᾳ.
the wicked.

46 Ετι δε αυτου λαλουντος τοις οχλοις, ιδου,
While and he is talking to the crowds, lo,
ἡ μητηρ και οἱ αδελφοι αυτου είστηκεισαν εξω,
the mother and the brothers of him stood without,
ζητουντες αυτῳ λαλησαι *[47 Ειπε δε τις
seeking to him to speak [Said then one
αυτῳ· Ιδου, ἡ μητηρ σου και οἱ αδελφοι σου
to him; Lo, the mother of thee and the brothers of thee
εξω ἑστηκασι, ζητουντες σοι λαλησαι.] 48 Ὁ
without stand, seeking to thee to speak.] He
δε αποκριθεις ειπε τῳ ειποντι αυτῳ· Τις εστιν
but answering said to the man informing him; Who is
ἡ μητηρ μου; και τινες εἰσιν οἱ αδελφοι μου;
the mother of me? and who are the brothers of me?
49 Και εκτεινας την χειρα αὑτου επι τους
And stretching out the hand of him towards the
μαθητας αυτου, ειπεν· Ιδου, ἡ μητηρ μου, και
disciples of him, said; Lo, the mother of me, and
οἱ αδελφοι μου. 50 Ὁστις γαρ αν ποιησῃ το
the brothers of me. Whoever for may do the
θελημα του πατρος μου, του εν ουρανοις, αυτος
will of the father of me, that in heavens, the same
μου αδελφος και αδελφη και μητηρ εστιν.
of me a brother and a sister and a mother is.

ΚΕΦ. ιγ'. 13.

1 Εν δε τῃ ἡμερᾳ εκεινῃ εξελθων ὁ Ιησους απο
In but the day that departing the Jesus from
της οικιας, εκαθητο παρα την θαλασσαν· 2 και
the house, he sat by the sea; and
συνηχθησαν προς αυτον οχλοι πολλοι, ὡστε
were gathered to him crowds great, so that
αυτον εις το πλοιον εμβαντα καθησθαι· και πας
he into the ship entering to be seated; and all
ὁ οχλος επι τον αιγιαλον ειστηκει. 3 Και
the crowd on the shore stood. And
ελαλησεν αυτοις πολλα εν παραβολαις, λεγων·
he spake to them much in parables, saying;
Ιδου, εξηλθεν ὁ σπειρων του σπειρειν. 4 Και
Lo, went out the sower of the (seed) to sow. And
εν τῳ σπειρειν αυτον, ἁ μεν επεσε παρα την
in the sowing it, some indeed fell on the
ὁδον· και ηλθε τα πετεινα, και κατεφαγεν αυτα.
path; and came the birds, and ate them.

than itself, and entering, they abide there; and ‡the LAST state of that MAN IS worse than the FIRST. Thus will it also be with this EVIL GENERATION.

46 While he was yet talking to the CROWDS, ‡behold, his MOTHER and his BROTHERS stood without, desiring to speak to him.

47 *[And one said to him, "Behold, thy MOTHER and thy BROTHERS are standing without, wishing to speak to thee."]

48 But HE answering, said to the PERSON INFORMING him, †"Who is my MOTHER? and who are my BROTHERS?"

49 And extending his HAND towards his DISCIPLES, he said, "Behold my MOTHER, and my BROTHERS!

50 ‡For whoever shall do the WILL of THAT FATHER of mine in the HEAVENS, that one is my Brother, or Sister, or Mother."

CHAPTER XIII.

1 On that DAY, JESUS, having gone out of the HOUSE, ‡sat by the SIDE of the LAKE;

2 but so many People gathered around him, that he entered *a Boat, and sat down; and All the PEOPLE stood on the SHORE.

3 Then he discoursed much to them in Parables, saying; ‡"Behold, the SOWER went forth to SOW.

4 And in SOWING, some seeds fell †by the ROAD; and the BIRDS came and picked them up.

* VATICAN MANUSCRIPT.—47. And one said to him, "Behold, thy MOTHER and thy BROTHERS are standing without, wishing to speak to thee"—*omit*. 2. a Boat. 5. EARTH.

† 48. To suppose that our Lord here intends to put any slight on his mother would be very absurd; he only took the opportunity of expressing his affection to his obedient disciples in a peculiarly endearing manner; which could not but be a great comfort to them, it appears from Luke viii. 2, Susanna, Joanna, Mary Magdalene, and others were then with him. † 4. The ordinary roads or paths in the East lead often along the edge of the fields, which are unenclosed. Hence, as the sower scatters his seed, some of it is liable to fall beyond the ploughed portion, on the hard beaten ground, which forms the way-side.—*Hackett*.

‡ 45. Heb. vi. 4; x. 26; 2 Peter ii. 20—22. ‡ 46. Mark iii. 31; Luke viii. 19. ‡ 50. John xv. 14; Gal. iii. 28: Heb. ii. 11. ‡ 1. Mark iv. 1. ‡ 3. Luke viii. 5.

*Αλλα δε επεσεν επι τα πετρωδη όπου ουκ
Others and fell on the rocky ground, where not
ειχε γην πολλην· και ευθεως εξανετειλε, δια
it had earth much; and immediately sprung up, through
το μη εχειν βαθος γης· 6 ἡλιου δε ανατει-
the not to have a depth of earth; sun and having
λαντος, εκαυματισθη· και δια το μη εχειν
arisen, it was scorched. and through the not to have
ῥιζαν, εξηρανθη. 7 Αλλα δε επεσεν επι τας
a root, was dried up. Others and fell among the
ακανθας· και ανεβησαν αἱ ακανθαι, και απεπνιξαν
thorns; and sprung up the thorns, and choked
αυτα. 8 Αλλα δε επεσεν επι την γην την
them. Others and fell on the ground the
καλην· και εδιδου καρπον, ὁ μεν ἑκατον, ὁ
good, and bore fruit the one a hundred, the
δε ἑξηκοντα, ὁ δε τριακοντα. 9 Ὁ εχων ωτα
other sixty, the other thirty. He having ears
ακουειν, ακουετω. 10 Και προσελθοντες οἱ
to hear, let him hear. And coming the
μαθηται ειπον αυτῳ· Διατι εν παραβολαις
disciples said to him; Why in parables
λαλεις αυτοις. 11 Ὁ δε αποκριθεις ειπεν αυ-
speakest thou to them? He and answering said to
τοις· Ὁτι ὑμιν δεδοται γνωναι τα μυστηρια
them; Because to you it is given to know the secrets
της βασιλειας των ουρανων· εκεινοις δε ου
of the kingdom of the heavens; to them but not
δεδοται. 12 Ὁστις γαρ εχει, δοθησεται αυτῳ,
it is given. Whoever for has, it shall be given to him,
και περισσευθησεται· ὁστις δε ουκ εχει, και
and he will be gifted with abundance; whoever but not has, even
ὁ εχει, αρθησεται απ' αυτου. 13 Δια τουτο
what he has, shall be taken from him. Therefore this
εν παραβολαις αυτοις λαλω, ότι βλεποντες ου
in parables to them I speak, for seeing not
βλεπουσι, και ακουοντες ουκ ακουουσιν, ουδε
they see, and hearing not they hear, neither
συνιουσι. 14 Και αναπληρουται αυτοις ἡ προ-
do they understand. And is fulfilled to them the
φητεια Ἡσαιου, ἡ λεγουσα· "Ακοῃ ακουσετε,
prophecy of Esaias, that saying; "By hearing you shall hear,
και ου μη συνητε· και βλεποντες βλεψετε,
and not not you may understand; and seeing you will see,
και ου μη ιδητε. 15 Επαχυνθη γαρ ἡ καρδια του
and not not you may see. Has grown fat for the heart of the

5 And others fell on ROCKY GROUND, where they had not much Soil; and immediately vegetated, through not HAVING a Depth of * EARTH;
6 † and when the Sun had risen, they were scorched, and HAVING NO Root, they withered.
7 And others fell among †THORNS; and the THORNS choked them.
8 But others fell on GOOD GROUND, and yielded Increase; ONE a hundred, ONE sixty, and ONE thirty.
9 HE HAVING Ears to hear, let him hear.
10 ‡ Then the DISCIPLES approaching, said to him, "Why dost thou speak to them in Parables?"
11 HE answering, said to them, "Because You are permitted to know the SECRETS of the KINGDOM of the HEAVENS; but to them this privilege is not given.
12 For whoever has, to him more will be given, and he shall abound; but whoever has not, from him will be taken even that which he has.
13 For this reason I I speak to them in Parables; Because seeing, they do not perceive; and hearing, they do not understand; nor do they regard.
14 And in them is fulfilled THAT PROPHECY of Isaiah, which says; ‡ 'By 'Hearing you will hear, 'though you may not un-'derstand; and seeing, you 'will see, though you may 'not perceive.
15 'For the UNDER-'STANDING of this PEO-

* VATICAN MANUSCRIPT.—5. EARTH.

† 6. In Palestine, during the seed time, (which is in November,) the sky is generally overspread with clouds. The seed *then* springs up even in *stony* ground; but when the sun dissipates the clouds, having outgrown its strength, it is quickly dried away.—*Rosenmuller*.
† 7. among THORNS—or rather, "upon thorny ground." The field sown may be considered to consist of the different varieties of soil specified; viz., the *rocky*, the *thorny*, and the *good* ground.

‡ 10. Mark iv. 10; Luke viii. 9.
‡ 14. Isa. vi. 9; John xii. 39; Acts xxviii 26; Rom. xi. 8.

λαου τουτου, και τοις ωσι βαρεως ηκουσαν, και
people this, and with the ears heavily they hear, and
τοις οφθαλμους αὐτων εκαμμυσαν, μηποτε
the eyes of them they shut, lest
ιδωσι τοις οφθαλμοις, και τοις ωσιν ακου-
they should see with the eyes, and with the ears they should
σωσι, και τῃ καρδιᾳ συνωσι, και επιστρε-
hear, and with the heart should understand, and they should
ψωσι, και ιασωμαι αυτους." 16 Ὑμων δε
turn, and I should heal them. Of you but
μακαριοι οἱ οφθαλμοι ὁτι βλεπουσι· και τα ωτα
blessed the eyes for they see; and the ears
*[ὑμων,] ὁτι ακουει. 17 Αμην γαρ λεγω ὑμιν,
[of you,] for they hear. Indeed for I say to you,
ὁτι πολλοι προφηται και δικαιοι επεθυμησαν
that many prophets and righteous men have desired
ιδειν, ἁ βλεπετε, και ουκ ειδον· και ακουσαι,
to see what you see, and not saw; and to hear,
ἁ ακουετε, και ουκ ηκουσαν.
what you hear, and not heard.
18 Ὑμεις ουν ακουσατε την παραβολην του
You therefore hear the parable of the
σπειροντος. 19 Παντος ακουοντος τον λογον
sower. Any one hearing the word
της βασιλειας, και μη συνιεντος, ερχεται ὁ
of the kingdom, and not understanding, comes the
πονηρος, και ἁρπαζει το εσπαρμενον εν τῃ καρδιᾳ
wicked (one,) and snatches that having been sown in the heart
αυτου· οὑτος εστιν, ὁ παρα την ὁδον σπαρεις.
of him; this is, that on the path being sown.
20 Ὁ δε επι τα πετρωδη σπαρεις, οὑτος εστιν,
That but on the rocky ground being sown, this is,
ὁ τον λογον ακουων και ευθυς μετα χαρας
who the word hearing and forthwith with joy
λαμβανων αυτον· 21 ουκ εχει δε ῥιζαν εν ἑαυτῳ,
receiving it; not he has but a root in himself,
αλλα προσκαιρος εστι· γενομενης δε θλιψεως η
but transient is; arising and trial or
διωγμου δια τον λογον, ευθυς σκανδαλιζεται.
persecution through the word, immediately he is offended.
22 Ὁ δε εις τας ακανθας σπαρεις, οὑτος εστιν,
That but into the thorns being sown, this is,
ὁ τον λογον ακουων, και ἡ μεριμνα του αιωνος
who the word hearing, and the care of the age
τουτου, και ἡ απατη του πλουτου συμπνιγει
this, and the delusion of the riches chokes
τον λογον· και ακαρπος γινεται. 23 Ὁ δε επι
the word; and unfruitful becomes. That but on
την γην την καλην σπαρεις, οὑτος εστιν, ὁ τον
the ground the good being sown, this is, who the
λογον ακουων, και συνιων· ὁς δη καρποφορει,
word hearing, and understanding; who really bears fruit,

'FLE is stupified; they
'hear heavily with their
'EARS, and their EYES
'they close; lest seeing
'with their EYES, and
'hearing with their EARS,
'and comprehending with
'their MIND, they should
'retrace their steps, and
'I should restore them.'
16 ‡But blessed are
Your EYES, because they
see; and EARS, because
they hear.
17 For indeed I say to
you, ‡That Many Pro-
phets and Righteous men
have desired to see what
you behold, but have not
seen; and to hear what
you hear, but have not
heard.
18 ‡Understand you,
therefore the PARABLE of
the SOWER.
19 When any one hears
the ‡WORD of the KING-
DOM, but considers it not,
the EVIL one comes and
snatches away THAT hav-
ing been sown in his
HEART. This explains
THAT which was SOWN
by the ROAD.
20 THAT which was
sown on ROCKY GROUND,
denotes him, WHO HEAR-
ING the WORD, receives
it immediately with Joy;
21 yet, it having no
Root in his mind, he re-
tains it only a short time;
for when Affliction or Persecution arises, on ac-
count of the WORD, he
instantly stumbles.
22 THAT which was
sown among THORNS, de-
notes THAT HEARER, in
whom the CARES of *the
AGE and the DECEPTIVE-
NESS of RICHES, chok
the WORD, and render it
unproductive.
23 But THAT which was
sown on GOOD SOIL, and
produced fruit, ONE a
hundred, ONE sixty, and
ONE thirty, denotes HIM,
who not only hears and

* VATICAN MANUSCRIPT.—16. your—*omit*. 22. the AGE.

‡ 16. Luke x. 23. ‡ 17. 1 Peter i. 10, 11. ‡ 18. Mark iv. 14; Luke viii. 11. ‡ 19. Matt. iv. 23.

και ποιει, ὁ μεν ἑκατον, ὁ δε ἑξηκοντα, ὁ
and yields, the one a hundred, the other sixty, the
δε τριακοντα.
other thirty.
24 Αλλην παραβολην παρεθηκεν αυτοις, λεγων·
Another parable he proposed to them, saying;
Ὡμοιωθη ἡ βασιλεια των ουρανων ανθρωπῳ
May be compared the kingdom of the heavens to a man
σπειροντι καλον σπερμα εν τῳ αγρῳ αὑτου.
sowing good seed in the field of him.
25 Εν δε τῳ καθευδειν τους ανθρωπους, ηλθεν
In and the to sleep the men, came
αυτου ὁ εχθρος, και εσπειρε ζιζανια ανα μεσον
of him the enemy, and sowed darnel through midst
του σιτου· και απηλθεν. 26 Ὁτε δε εβλαστησεν
of the wheat; and went forth. When and was sprung up
ὁ χορτος και καρπον εποιησε, τοτε εφανη και
the blade and fruit yielded, then appeared also
τα ζιζανια. 27 Προσελθοντες δε οἱ δουλοι του
the darnel. Coming and the slaves of the
οικοδεσποτου, ειπον αυτῳ· Κυριε, ουχι καλον
householder, said to him; O lord, not good
σπερμα εσπειρας εν τῳ σῳ αγρῳ; ποθεν ουν εχει
seed didst thou sow in the thy field? whence then has it
ζιζανια; 28 Ὁ δε εφη αυτοις· Εχθρος ανθρωπος
darnel? He and said to them; An enemy a man
τουτο εποιησεν. Οἱ δε δουλοι ειπον αυτῳ·
this has done. The and slaves said to him;
Θελεις ουν απελθοντες συλλεξωμεν αυτα;
Dost thou wish then going forth we should gather them?
29 Ὁ δε εφη· Ου· μηποτε, συλλεγοντες τα ζιζανια,
He and said; No, lest, gathering the darnel,
εκριζωσητε ἁμα αυτοις τον σιτον. 30 Αφετε
you should root up with them the wheat. Leave them
συναυξανεσθαι αμφοτερα μεχρι του θερισμου·
to grow together both till the harvest;
και εν καιρῳ του θερισμου ερω τοις θερισταις·
and in time of the harvest I will say to the harvesters;
Συλλεξατε πρωτον τα ζιζανια, και δησατε αυτα
Gather you first the darnel, and bind you them
εις δεσμας, προς το κατακαυσαι αυτα· τον δε
into bundles, for the to burn them; the but
σιτον συναγαγετε εις την αποθηκην μου.
wheat bring together into the barn of me.
31 Αλλην παραβολην παρεθηκεν αυτοις, λεγων·
Another parable he proposed to them, saying;
Ὁμοια εστιν ἡ βασιλεια των ουρανων κοκκῳ
Like is the kingdom of the heavens to a grain
σιναπεως, ὁν λαβων ανθρωπος εσπειρεν εν τῳ
of mustard, which taking a man sowed in the

considers, but obeys the WORD.
24 He proposed to them another Parable, saying, The KINGDOM of the HEAVENS may be compared to the FIELD in which the Owner sowed Good Grain:
25 but while the MEN SLEPT, His ENEMY came and sowed † Darnel among the WHEAT, and went away.
26 When the BLADE shot up, and put forth the Ear, then appeared also the DARNEL.
27 And the SERVANTS of the HOUSEHOLDER, coming said to him, Master, thou didst sow Good Seed in THY Field; whence, then, has it Darnel?
28 He replied, an Enemy has done this. * And THEY say to him, Dost thou wish then, that we should weed them out?
29 And HE said, No; lest in weeding out the DARNEL, you also tear up the WHEAT.
30 Let both grow together till the HARVEST; and in the TIME of HARVEST, I will say to the REAPERS, First gather the DARNEL, and bind it in Bundles for BURNING; ‡ then bring together the wheat into my GRANARY."
31 ‡ Another Parable he proposed to them, saying; The KINGDOM of the HEAVENS is like to a Grain of Mustard, which a Man planted in his FIELD;

* VATICAN MANUSCRIPT.—28. And THEY say to him.

† 25. A plant which bears a striking resemblance to wheat. The following remarks by H. B. Hackett, will fully illustrate this:—"In passing through the fertile country of the ancient Philistines, on the south of Palestine, I asked the guide, one day, a native Syrian, if he knew of a plant which was apt to make its appearance among the wheat, and which resembled it so much that it could hardly be distinguished from it He replied that it was very common, and that he would soon show me a specimen of it. Soon after this he pointed out to me some of this grass, growing near our path; and afterwards, having once seen it, I found it in almost every field where I searched for it. Except that the stalk was not so high, it appeared otherwise precisely like wheat, just as the ears begin to show themselves, and the kernels are swelling out into shape. I collected some specimens of this deceitful weed, and have found, on showing them to friends, that they have mistaken them quite invariably for some species of grain, such as wheat or barley."

‡ 30. Matt. iii. 12. ‡ 31. Mark iv. 30; Luke xiii. 18.

αγρῳ αὐτου. 32 Ὁ μικροτερον μεν εστι παντων
field of him. Which less indeed is of all
των σπερματων· ὁταν δε αυξηθῃ, μειζον των
of the seeds; when but it may be grown, a greater of the
λαχανων εστι, και γινεται δενδρον, ὡστε ελθειν
herbs is, and becomes a tree, so that to come
τα πετεινα του ουρανου, και κατασκηνουν εν
the birds of the heaven, and to make nests in
τοις κλαδοις αυτου.
the branches of it.
33 Αλλην παραβολην ελαλησεν αυτοις· Ὁμοια
Another parable he spake to them; Like
εστιν ἡ βασιλεια των ουρανων ζυμῃ, ἡν λαβουσα
is the kingdom of the heavens to leaven, which taking
γυνη ενεκρυψεν εις αλευρου σατα τρια, ἑως οὑ
a woman mixed in of meal measures three, till of it
εζυμωθη ὁλον. 34 Ταυτα παντα ελαλησεν ὁ
was leavened whole. These all spake the
Ιησους εν παραβολαις τοις οχλοις, και χωρις
Jesus in parables to the crowds, and without
παραβολης ουκ ελαλει αυτοις· 35 ὁπως πλη-
a parable not he spake to them; so that it might
ρωθῃ το ῥηθεν δια του προφητου, λεγοντος·
be fulfilled the word spoken through the prophet, saying,
"Ανοιξω εν παραβολαις το στομα μου· ερευ-
'I will open in parables the mouth of me; I will
ξομαι κεκρυμμενα απο καταβολης
openly declare things having been hid from a beginning
*[κοσμου."]
[of the world."]
36 Τοτε αφεις τους οχλους, ηλθεν εις την
Then leaving the crowds, went into the
οικιαν ὁ Ιησους. Και προσηλθον αυτῳ οἱ
house the Jesus. And came to him the
μαθηται αυτου, λεγοντες· Φρασον ἡμιν την
disciples of him, saying; Explain to us the
παραβολην των ζιζανιων του αγρου. 37 Ὁ δε
parable of the darnels of the field. He and
αποκριθεις ειπεν *[αυτοις·] Ὁ σπειρων το
answering said [to them;] He sowing the
καλον σπερμα, εστιν ὁ υἱος του ανθρωπου·
good seed, is the son of the man;
38 ὁ δε αγρος, εστιν ὁ κοσμος· το δε καλον
the and field, is the world; the and good
σπερμα, οὑτοι εισιν οἱ υἱοι της βασιλειας· τα
seed, they are the sons of the kingdom; the
δε ζιζανια, εισιν οἱ υἱοι του πονηρου· 39 ὁ δε
and darnel, are the sons of the wicked (one); the and
εχθρος, ὁ σπειρας αυτα, εστιν ὁ διαβολος· ὁ δε
enemy, he having sown them, is the adversary, the and
θερισμος, συντελεια του αιωνος εστιν· οἱ δε
harvest, end of the age is; the and

32 which indeed is one of the †least of ALL SEEDS; but when grown it is larger than any HERB, †and becomes a Tree, so that the BIRDS of HEAVEN come and build their nests on its BRANCHES.

33 ‡Another Parable he spake to them; "The KINGDOM of the HEAVENS resembles Leaven, which a Woman taking, mingled in three †Measures of Meal, till the whole fermented."

34 All these things JESUS communicated to the CROWDS in Parables, and without a Comparison he taught them not;

35 so that the WORD SPOKEN through the PROPHET might be verified, saying; †‡"I will open "my mouth in parables, "I will openly declare "things having been hid "from the beginning."

36 Then *JESUS leaving the PEOPLE, retired to the HOUSE; and his disciples approached him, saying, "Explain to us the PARABLE of the DARNEL in the FIELD."

37 He answering, said, "He who sows the GOOD Seed is the SON of MAN:

38 the FIELD is the WORLD; the GOOD Seed are the SONS of the KINGDOM; the DARNEL are the SONS of the EVIL one;

39 THAT ENEMY who SOWED them is the ADVERSARY; the HARVEST is the End of the *Age; and the REAPERS are Messengers.

* VATICAN MANUSCRIPT.—35. of the World—*omit*. 36. he left. 37. to them—*omit*. 39. Age.

† 32. That is, of all those seeds with which the people of Judea were then acquainted. Our Lord's words are to be interpreted by popular use. And we learn from Matt. xvii. 20, that *like a grain of mustard seed* was become proverbial for expressing a very small quantity.—*Geo. Campbell.* † 32. *And becomes a tree.* It attains a large size in Judea. Lightfoot says, R. Simeon Ben Chalaphta mentions one "into which he was wont to climb, as men are wont to climb into a fig-tree." Trench quotes a traveler in Chili who had ridden under one. † 33. A measure containing about a peck and a half, wanting a little more than a pint. Three of them made an ephah. † 35. "I will open my mouth in parables: I will utter dark sayings *which have been* from the beginning."—*Sir L. C. L. Brenton's Septuagint translation of* Psa. lxxviii. 2.

‡ 33. Luke xiii. 20. ‡ 35. Psa. lxxviii. 2.

θερισται, αγγελοι εισιν. 40 Ὡσπερ ουν συλ-
reapers, messengers are. As therefore are
λεγεται τα ζιζανια, και πυρι καιεται· οὑτως
gathered the darnel, and in a fire are burned; so
εσται εν τῃ συντελειᾳ του αιωνος τουτου.
will it be in the end of the age this.
41 Αποστελει ὁ υἱος του ανθρωπου τους αγγελους
Will send the son of the man the messengers
αὑτου, και συλλεξουσιν εκ της βασιλειας αυτου
of him, and they will gather out of the kingdom of him
παντα τα σκανδαλα και τους ποιουντας την ανο-
all the seducers and those working the law-
μιαν, 42 και βαλουσιν αυτους εις την καμινον
lessness, and they will cast them into the furnace
του πυρος· εκει εσται ὁ κλαυθμος και ὁ βρυγμος
of the fire; there shall be the weeping and the gnashing
των οδοντων. 43 Τοτε οἱ δικαιοι εκλαμψουσιν,
of the teeth. Then the righteous shall shine,
ὡς ὁ ἡλιος, εν τῃ βασιλειᾳ του πατρος αὑτων.
as the sun, in the kingdom of the father of them.
Ὁ εχων ωτα *[ακουειν,] ακουετω.
He having ears [to hear,] let him hear.
44 *[Παλιν] ὁμοια εστιν ἡ βασιλεια των
[Again] like is the kingdom of the
ουρανων θησαυρῳ κεκρυμμενῳ εν τῳ αγρῳ, ὁν
heavens to a treasure having been hid in the field, which
εὑρων ανθρωπος εκρυψε, και απο της χαρας
finding a man he hides, and from the joy
αυτου ὑπαγει, και παντα ὁσα εχει πωλει, και
of him he goes, and all as much as he has sells, and
αγοραζει τον αγρον εκεινον.
buys the field that.
45 Παλιν ὁμοια εστιν ἡ βασιλεια των ουρανων
Again like is the kingdom of the heavens
*[ανθρωπῳ] εμπορῳ, ζητουντι καλους μαργαρι-
[to a man] a merchant, seeking choice pearls.
τας. 46 Εὑρων δε ἑνα πολυτιμον μαργαριτην,
Finding and one costly pearl,
απελθων πεπρακε παντα ὁσα ειχε, και ηγορα-
going he sold all as much as he had, and bought
σεν αυτον.
it.
47 Παλιν ὁμοια εστιν ἡ βασιλεια των ουρανων
Again like is the kingdom of the heavens
σαγηνῃ, βληθειςῃ εις την θαλασσαν, και εκ
to a drag-net, being cast into the sea, and of
παντος γενους συναγαγουσῃ· 48 ἡν, ὁτε επλη-
every kind bringing together, which, when it is
ρωθη, αναβιβασαντες επι τον αιγιαλον, και
full, drawing to the shore, and
καθισαντες συνελεξαν τα καλα εις αγγεια, τα
sitting down they collected the good into vessels, the
δε σαπρα εξω εβαλον. 49 Οὑτως εσται εν τῃ
but bad away they cast. So it will be in the

40 As therefore the DARNEL is gathered and burned in a Fire, so will it be in the END of *the AGE.

41 The SON of MAN will ‡send forth his MESSENGERS, who will gather out of his KINGDOM All SEDUCERS and INIQUITOUS PERSONS;

42 ‡and will throw them into the FURNACE of FIRE; there will be the WEEPING and the GNASHING of TEETH.

43 ‡Then will the RIGHTEOUS be resplendent as the SUN in the KINGDOM of their FATHER. HE who HAS ears, let him hear.

44 The KINGDOM of the HEAVENS is like a hidden Treasure in a FIELD, which, a Man finding, he covers up, and, from his JOY, he goes and sells all that he has, and buys that FIELD.

45 Again, the KINGDOM of the HEAVENS is like a Pearl of Great value;

46 which †a Merchant, who was seeking Choice Pearls, having found, went and sold all that he had, and bought it.

47 Again, the KINGDOM of the HEAVENS resembles a Drag-net, being cast into the SEA, and enclosing fishes of Every Kind;

48 which, when it is full, they draw to the SHORE, and sitting down, gather the GOOD into vessels, but throw the USELESS away.

49 So will it be at the

* VATICAN MANUSCRIPT.—40. the AGE. 43. to hear—*omit*. 44. Again—*omit*. 45. Man—*omit*.

† 40. To translate *aioon*, by the word *world*, has a tendency to lead the reader astray. No less than thirteen different meanings are attached to this word, in the Common Version. The meaning is *age*, and this rendering can always be understood. The context will determine, generally, what age is referred to—the Jewish, Christian, Messianic, or the endless succession of ages. For further remarks, see Appendix. † 46. Such as those found in the East, who travel about buying or exchanging jewels, pearls, or other valuables.

‡ 41. Matt. xxii 7. ‡ 42. Matt. iii. 12. ‡ 43. Dan. xii. 3.

συντελειᾳ του αιωνος. Ἐξελευσονται οἱ αγγε-
end of the age. Shall go forth the messen-
λοι, και αφοριουσι τους πονηρους εκ μεσου των
gers, and will separate the wicked from among the
δικαιων, 50 και βαλουσιν αυτους εις την καμινον
just, and shall cast them into the furnace
του πυρος· εκει εσται ὁ κλαυθμος και ὁ βρυγμος
of the fire; there will be the weeping and the gnashing
των οδοντων. 51 *[Λεγει αυτοις ὁ Ιησους.]
of the teeth. [Says to them the Jesus.]
Συνηκατε ταυτα παντα; Λεγουσιν αυτῳ·
Have you understood these things all? They say to him;
Ναι [κυριε.] 52 Ὁ δε ειπεν αυτοις· Δια τουτο
Yes [O lord.] He then said to them; Therefore this
πας γραμματευς, μαθητευθεις τη βασιλειᾳ των
every scribe, being instructed to the kingdom of the
ουρανων, ὁμοιος εστιν ανθρωπῳ οικοδεσποτῃ,
heavens, like is to a man an householder,
ὁστις εκβαλλει εκ του θησαυρου αὑτου καινα
who brings out of the treasury of him new
και παλαια.
and old.

53 Και εγενετο, ὁτε ετελεσεν ὁ Ιησους τας
And it came to pass, when had concluded the Jesus the
παραβολας ταυτας, μετηρεν εκειθεν. 54 Και
parables these, he departed thence. And
ελθων εις την πατριδα αὑτου, εδιδασκεν αυτους
coming into the country of him, he taught them
εν τῃ συναγωγῃ αυτων, ὡστε εκπληττεσθαι
in the synagogue of them, so as to astonish
αυτους, και λεγειν· Ποθεν τουτῳ ἡ σοφια
them, and to say. Whence this the wisdom
αὑτη, και αἱ δυναμεις; 55 Ουχ οὑτος εστιν ὁ
this and these powers? Not this is the
του τεκτονος υἱος; ουχι ἡ μητηρ αυτου λεγεται
of the carpenter son? not the mother of him is called
Μαριαμ; και οἱ αδελφοι αυτου Ιακωβος, και
Mary? and the brothers of him James, and
Ιωσης, και Σιμων, και Ιουδας; 56 και αἱ αδελφαι
Joses, and Simon, and Judas? and the sisters
αυτου ουχι πασαι προς ἡμας εισι; ποθεν ουν
of him not all with us are? whence then
τουτῳ ταυτα παντα; 57 Και εσκανδαλιζοντο εν
this these all? And they found a difficulty in
αυτῳ. Ὁ δε Ιησους ειπεν αυτοις· Ουκ εστι
him. The and Jesus said to them; Not is
προφητης ατιμος, ει μη εν τῃ πατριδι αὑτου,
a prophet unhonored, if not in the country of him,
και εν τῃ οικιᾳ αὑτου. 58 Και ουκ εποιησεν
and in the house of him. And not he did do
εκει δυναμεις πολλας, δια την απιστιαν
there mighty works many, because of the unbelief of
αυτων.
them.

END of the AGE. The MESSENGERS will go forth, and will separate the WICKED from among the RIGHTEOUS;

50 and will throw them into the FURNACE of FIRE; there will be the WEEPING and the GNASHING of TEETH.

51 Have you understood all these things?" They answered, "Yes."

52 Then HE said to them, "Every Scribe, therefore, being instructed * in the KINGDOM of the HEAVENS, is like a Householder, who produces from his TREASURY, new things and old."

53 And it occurred, when JESUS had concluded these PARABLES, he departed thence.

54 ‡ And coming into † his OWN CITY he so taught the inhabitants in their SYNAGOGUE, that they were astonished, and said, "Whence has this man, this WISDOM, and these MIRACULOUS POWERS?

55 ‡ Is not this the CARPENTER'S SON? is not his MOTHER called Mary? and do not his BROTHERS, James, and † Joses, and Simon, and Judas,

56 and all his † SISTERS, live with us? Whence, then, has he all these things."

57 And they ‡ stumbled at him. But JESUS said to them, "A Prophet is not without honor, except in his OWN COUNTRY, and in his own FAMILY."

58 ‡ And he did not perform many Miracles there, because of their UNBELIEF.

* VATICAN MANUSCRIPT.—51. JESUS says to them—*omit.* 51. Lord—*omit.* 52. In.

† 54. That is, Nazareth, where he had been brought up; Luke iv. 16, 23. † 55. Joseph—so read Lachmann, Tischendorf, and Tittman. † 56. According to Theophylact, the names of the sisters of Jesus were Mary and Salome.

‡ 54. Matt. ii. 23; Mark vi. 1. ‡ 55. John vi. 42. ‡ 57. Matt. xi. 6; Isa. viii. 14; Rom. ix. 32, 33; 1 Peter ii. 8. ‡ 58. Mark vi. 5, 6.

ΚΕΦ. ιδ'. 14.

1 Εν εκεινῳ τῳ καιρῳ ηκουσεν Ἡρωδης ὁ
At that the time heard Herod the
τετραρχης την ακοην Ιησου, 2 και ειπε τοις
tetrarch the fame of Jesus, and said to the
παισιν αὑτου· Οὑτος εστιν Ιωαννης ὁ βαπτιστης·
servants of him; This is John the dipper;
αυτος ηγερθη απο των νεκρων, και δια τουτο αἱ
he is raised from the dead, and therefore this the
δυναμεις ενεργουσιν εν αυτῳ. 3 Ὁ γαρ Ἡρωδης,
mighty powers work in him. The for Herod,
κρατησας τον Ιωαννην, εδησεν αυτον, και εθετο
seizing the John, had bound him, and put
εν φυλακῃ, δια Ἡρωδιαδα την γυναικα Φιλ-
in prison, on account of Herodias the wife of
ιππου του αδελφου αυτου. 4 Ελεγε γαρ αυτῳ ὁ
Philip the brother of him. Had said for to him the
Ιωαννης· Ουκ εξεστι σοι εχειν αυτην. 5 Και
John; Not it is lawful to thee to have her. And
θελων αυτον αποκτειναι, εφοβηθη τον οχλον,
wishing him to destroy, he feared the people,
ὁτι ὡς προφητην αυτον ειχον. 6 Γενεσιων δε
for as a prophet him they esteemed. Birth-day of but
αγομενων του Ἡρωδου, ωρχησατο ἡ θυγατηρ
was being held of the Herod, danced the daughter
της Ἡρωδιαδος εν τῳ μεσῳ· και ηρεσε τῳ
of the Herodias in the midst; and pleased the
Ἡρωδῃ· 7 ὁθεν μεθ' ὁρκου ὡμολογησεν αυτῃ
Herod; whereupon with an oath he promised to her
δουναι, ὁ εαν αιτησηται. 8 Ἡ δε, προβι-
to give, what soever she might ask. She and, being
βασθεισα ὑπο της μητρος αυτης, Δος μοι,
incited by the mother of her, Give to me,
φησιν, ὡδε επι πινακι την κεφαλην Ιωαννου του
she said, here upon a plate the head of John the
βαπτιστου. 9 Και ελυπηθη ὁ βασιλευς· δια δε
dipper. And was sorry the king; because of but
τους ὁρκους και τους συνανακειμενους, εκε-
the oaths and those reclining at table, he com-
λευσε δοθηναι. 10 Και πεμψας απεκεφαλισε
manded it to be given. And sending he cut off the head of
τον Ιωαννην εν τῃ φυλακῃ· 11 Και ηνεχθη ἡ
the John in the prison. And was brought the
κεφαλη αυτου επι πινακι, και εδοθη τῳ κορα-
head of him on a plate, and it was given to the little
σιῳ· και ηνεγκε τῃ μητρι αὑτης. 12 Και προσ-
girl; and she brought it to the mother of her. And coming
ελθοντες οἱ μαθηται αυτου ηραν το σωμα, και εθ-
the disciples of him took the body, and they
αψαν αυτο· και ελθοντες απηγγειλαν τῳ Ιησου.
buried it; and departing they told it to the Jesus.

CHAPTER XIV.

1 At That TIME, ‡ Her-
od the † TETRARCH, hear-
ing of the FAME of Jesus,
2 said to his SERVANTS,
"This is John the IM-
MERSER; he is raised from
the DEAD; and therefore
MIRACLES are performed
by him."
3 For ‡ HEROD * then
had caused JOHN to be
seized, bound, and put in
* PRISON, on account of
† Herodias, his BROTHER
Philip's WIFE;
4 for John had said to
him, ‡ "It is not lawful
for thee to have her."
5 And wishing to kill
him, he feared the PEO-
PLE, ‡ Because they es-
teemed him as a Prophet.
6 But when HEROD'S
Birth-day was kept, the
† DAUGHTER of HERODI-
AS danced in the MIDST,
and pleased HEROD;
7 whereon he promised
with an Oath to give her
whatever she might re-
quest.
8 And SHE, being insti-
gated by her MOTHER,
said, "Give me here, on a
Platter, the HEAD of JOHN
the IMMERSER."
9 And the * KING, be-
ing sorry on account of the
OATHS and the GUESTS,
commanded that it should
be given her.
10 Accordingly, by his
order, JOHN was behead-
ed in the PRISON.
11 And his HEAD was
brought on a Platter, and
presented to the GIRL;
and she carried it to her
MOTHER.
12 And his DISCIPLES
coming, carried off * the
DEAD-BODY, and buried

* VATICAN MANUSCRIPT.—3. then had. 3. PRISON. 9. KING, being sorry on account of the OATHS and the GUESTS, commanded. 12. the DEAD-BODY.

† 1. Properly, the governor of the fourth part of a country; commonly used as a title inferior to a KING, and denoting chief ruler. The person here spoken of was Antipas, a son of Herod the Great. The name KING is sometimes given to tetrarchs. See verse 9.—*Geo. Campbell.* † 3. He had married a daughter of Aretas, an Arabian prince, whom he put away, after he had induced Herodias to quit her husband; this occasioned a war between Herod and Aretas. † 6. Named Salome, daughter of Herodias by her former husband.—*Josephus*, Ant. xviii. v. 4.

‡ 1. Mark vi. 14; Luke ix. 7. ‡ 3. Mark vi. 17; Luke iii. 19, 20. ‡ 4. Lev. xviii. 16; xx. 21. ‡ 5. Matt. xxi. 26; Luke xx. 6.

13 Και ακουσας ὁ Ιησους, ανεχωρησεν εκειθεν
And having heard the Jesus, withdrew from thence
εν πλοιῳ εις ερημον τοπον κατ' ιδιαν· και ακου-
in a ship into a desert place by himself; and having
σαντες οἱ οχλοι, ηκολουθησαν αυτῳ πεζῃ απο
heard the crowds, they followed him by land from
των πολεων. 14 Και εξελθων ὁ Ιησους ειδε
the cities. And coming out the Jesus saw
πολυν οχλον· και εσπλαγχνισθη επ' αυτοις,
great a crowd; and he was moved with pity towards them;
και εθεραπευσε τους αρρωστους αυτων.
and healed the sick of them.

15 Οψιας δε γενομενης, προσηλθον αυτῳ οἱ
Evening and having come, came to him the
μαθηται αυτου, λεγοντες· Ερημος εστιν ὁ τοπος,
disciples of him, saying; A desert is the place,
και ἡ ὡρα ηδη παρηλθεν· απολυσον τους
and the hour already has passed by; dismiss the
οχλους, ἱνα απελθοντες εις τας κωμας, αγο-
crowds, that going into the villages, they
ρασωσιν ἑαυτοις βρωματα. 16 Ὁ δε Ιησους
may buy themselves victuals. The but Jesus
ειπεν αυτοις· Ου χρειαν εχουσιν απελθειν· δοτε
said to them; No need they have to go away; give
αυτοις ὑμεις φαγειν. 17 Οἱ δε λεγουσιν αυτῳ·
to them you to eat; They and say to him;
Ουκ εχομεν ὡδε, ει μη πεντε αρτους και δυο
Not we have here, except five loaves and two
ιχθυας. 18 Ὁ δε ειπε· Φερετε μοι αυτους ὡδε.
fishes. He and said; Bring to me them here.
19 Και κελευσας τους οχλους ανακλιθηναι επι
And directing the crowds to recline upon
τους χορτους, λαβων τους πεντε αρτους και
the grass, taking the five loaves and
τους δυο ιχθυας, αναβλεψας εις τον ουρανον,
the two fishes, looking up to the heaven,
ευλογησε· και κλασας, εδωκε τοις μαθηταις
he gave praise; and breaking, he gave to the disciples
τους αρτους, οἱ δε μαθηται τοις οχλοις. 20 Και
the loaves, the and disciples to the crowds. And
εφαγον παντες, και εχορτασθησαν· και ηραν
they ate all, and were filled; and they took up
το περισσευον των κλασματων, δωδεκα κοφινους
that over and above of the fragments, twelve baskets
πληρεις. 21 Οἱ δε εσθιοντες ησαν ανδρες ὡσει
full. Those and eating were men about
πεντακισχιλιοι, χωρις γυναικων και παιδιων.
five-thousand. besides women and children.
22 Και ευθεως ηναγκασεν τους μαθητας εμβηναι
And immediately he urged the disciples to enter

it; and departing, told JESUS.

13 ‡ And JESUS having heard, privately withdrew from thence, by Boat, into a Desert Place; of which the PEOPLE being informed, followed him by Land from the CITIES.

14 And * coming out, he saw a Great Crowd; and he had compassion on them, and healed their SICK.

15 ‡ And † Evening having arrived, * the DISCIPLES came to him, saying, "The PLACE is a Desert, and the HOUR is now past; dismiss the crowds, that they may go to the VILLAGES, and buy themselves Provisions."

16 But JESUS said to them, "They need not depart; you supply them."

17 THEY, however, replied to him, "We have here only Five Loaves and Two Fishes."

18 And HE said, "Bring them here to me."

19 And commanding the PEOPLE to recline on the grass, he took the FIVE Loaves and the TWO Fishes, and looking towards HEAVEN, ‡ praised God; then † breaking the LOAVES, he gave them to the DISCIPLES, and the disciples distributed to the CROWDS.

20 And they all ate and were satisfied; and of the REMAINING FRAGMENTS they gathered † Twelve Baskets full.

21 Now THEY who had EATEN, were about five thousand men, besides women and children.

22 And immediately * he constrained the DISCIPLES to enter * a Boat,

* VATICAN MANUSCRIPT.—14. he went. 15. the DISCIPLES. 22. he constrained. 22. a Boat.

† 15. The *first* evening, which commenced at three o'clock. The *second* evening, which began at sunset, is that mentioned in verse 23. † 19. The Jewish loaves were broad, thin, and brittle; so that a knife was not required for dividing them. † 20 These were small wicker baskets, which the Jews carried their victuals in, when from home; and by the number here particularized, it would seem that each apostle filled his own basket.—*Pearce.*

‡ 13. Mark vi. 32; Luke ix. 10; John vi. 1, 2. ‡ 15. Mark vi. 35; Luke ix. 12; John vi. 5. ‡ 19. Matt. xv. 36.

εις το πλοιον, και προαγειν αυτον εις το περαν,
into the ship, and to go before him to the other side,
ἑως οὑ απολυσῃ τους οχλους. 23 Και απο-
while he should dismiss the crowds. And having
λυσας τους οχλους, ανεβη εις το ορος κατ'
sent away the crowds, he went up into the mountain by
ιδιαν προσευξασθαι. Οψιας δε γενομενης, μονος
himself to pray. Evening and having come, alone
ην εκει. 24 Το δε πλοιον ηδη μεσον της
he was there. The and ship now in the midst of the
θαλασσης ην, βασανιζομενον ὑπο των κυματων·
sea was, having been tossed by the waves;
ην γαρ εναντιος ὁ ανεμος. 25 Τεταρτῃ δε φυλακῃ
was for contrary the wind. In fourth and watch
της νυκτος απηλθε προς αυτους, περιπατων επι
of the night he went to them, walking upon
της θαλασσης. 26 Και ιδοντες αυτον οἱ μαθηται
the sea. And seeing him the disciples
επι την θαλασσαν περιπατουντα, εταραχθησαν,
upon the sea walking, they were terrified.
λεγοντες· Ὁτι φαντασμα εστι· και απο του
saying; That an apparition is; and from the
φοβου εκραξαν. 27 Ευθεως δε ελαλησεν αυτοις
fear they cried aloud. Immediately but spake to them
ὁ Ιησους, λεγων· Θαρσειτε, εγω ειμι· μη φο-
the Jesus, saying. Take courage. I am; not be
βεισθε. 28 Αποκριθεις δε αυτῳ ὁ Πετρος ειπε·
afraid. Answering and him the Peter said;
Κυριε, ει συ ει, κελευσον με προς σε ελθειν επι
O lord, if thou art, bid me to thee to come upon
τα ὑδατα. 29 Ὁ δε ειπεν· Ελθε. Και καταβας
the water. He and said; Come. And descending
απο του πλοιου ὁ Πετρος, περιεπατησεν επι τα
from the boat the Peter, he walked upon the
ὑδατα, ελθειν προς τον Ιησουν. 30 Βλεπων δε
water, to come to the Jesus. Seeing but
τον ανεμον ισχυρον, εφοβηθη· και αρξαμενος
the wind strong, he was afraid; and beginning
καταποντιζεσθαι, εκραξε, λεγων· Κυριε, σωσον
to sink, he cried, saying; O lord, save
με. 31 Ευθεως δε ὁ Ιησους εκτεινας την χειρα,
me. Immediately and the Jesus stretching out the hand,
επελαβετο αυτου, και λεγει αυτῳ· Ολιγοπιστε,
took hold of him, and says to him; O distrustful man,
εις τι εδιστασας; 32 Και εμβαντων αυτων εις
for why didst thou doubt? And entering of them into
το πλοιον, εκοπασεν ὁ ανεμος. 33 Οἱ δε εν τῳ
the ship, ceased the wind. They and in the

and precede him to the OTHER SIDE, while he dismissed the CROWDS.

23 ‡ And having dismissed the CROWDS, he privately ascended the MOUNTAIN to pray; and remained there alone till it was Late.

24 By this time the BOAT * was many Furlongs distant from the LAND, tossed by the WAVES; for the WIND was contrary.

25 And in the † Fourth Watch of the NIGHT, he went towards them, walking on the LAKE.

26 And when the DISCIPLES saw him † walking on the LAKE, they were terrified, and exclaimed, "It is an Apparition!" and they cried aloud, through fear.

27 But Jesus immediately spoke to them, saying, "Take courage, it is I; be not afraid."

28 And PETER answering, said to him, "Master, if it be thou, bid me come to thee on the WATER."

29 And JESUS said, "Come." Then * Peter descending from the BOAT, walked on the WATER, * and came to JESUS.

30 But perceiving the WIND strong, he was afraid; and beginning to sink, he exclaimed, "Master, save me!"

31 And JESUS instantly extending his HAND, took hold of him, and said to him, "O distrustful man! why didst thou doubt?"

32 And * going up into the BOAT, the WIND subsided.

33 Then THOSE in the

* VATICAN MANUSCRIPT.—24. many Furlongs distant from the LAND, tossed. 29. Peter. 29. and came to. 32. going up into.

† 25. Between the hours of three and six in the morning. Grotius observes, that this was the Roman division of the night, taken by them from the Greeks; and that the Jews from the time of Pompey, after they were become a dependent people, had adopted this mode of reckoning, instead of their own, which originally consisted of three watches only. † 26. In Job ix. 8, this is a prerogative ascribed to God, and which is freely rendered by the LXX, thus; "Walking upon the sea, as upon a pavement." An Egyptian hieroglyphic for expressing impossibility was, a picture of two feet walking on the sea.

‡ 23. Mark vi. 36; John vi. 16.

πλοιῳ, *[ελθοντες] προσεκυνησαν αυτῳ, λεγ-
ship, [coming] prostrated to him, say-
οντες· Αληθως θεου υἱος ει. 34 Και διαπε-
ing; Certainly of a God a son thou art. And having
ρασαντες, ηλθον εις την γην Γεννησαρετ. 35 Και
passed over, they came to the land Gennesaret. And
επιγνοντες αυτον οἱ ανδρες του τοπου εκεινου,
knowing him the men of the place that,
απεστειλαν εις ὁλην την περιχωρον εκεινην·
they sent into all the country round about that;
και προσηνεγκαν αυτῳ παντας τους κακως
and they brought to him all those disease
εχοντας, 36 και παρεκαλουν αυτον ἱνα μονον
having, and besought him that only
ἁψωνται του κρασπεδου του ἱματιου αυτου·
they might touch the tuft of the mantle of him;
και ὁσοι ἡψαντο, διεσωθησαν.
and as many as touched, were made whole.

BOAT, did homage to him, saying, ‡"Assuredly, thou art God's Son."

34 ‡And having passed over they came *to LAND at Gennesaret.

35 And the MEN of that PLACE recognizing him, sent through ALL that COUNTRY, and brought to him ALL the diseased;

36 and implored him, that they might only touch the TUFT of his MANTLE; and as many as touched, were cured.

ΚΕΦ. ιε΄. 15.

1 Τοτε προσερχονται τῳ Ιησου οἱ απο Ἱερο-
Then came to the Jesus those from Jeru-
σολυμων γραμματεις και Φαρισαιοι, λεγοντες·
salem scribes and Pharisees, saying;
2 Διατι οἱ μαθηται σου παραβαινουσι την παρα-
Why the disciples of thee transgress the tradi-
δοσιν των πρεσβυτερων; ου γαρ νιπτονται τας
tion of the elders? not for they wash the
χειρας αὑτων, ὁταν αρτον εσθιωσιν. 3 Ὁ δε
hands of them, whenever bread they may eat. He but
αποκριθεις ειπεν αυτοις· Διατι και ὑμεις παρα-
answering said to them; Why also you trans-
βαινετε την εντολην του θεου, δια την παρα-
gress the commandment of the God, through the tradi-
δοσιν ὑμων; 4 Ὁ γαρ θεος ενετειλατο, λεγων·
tion of you? The for God has commanded, saying;
"Τιμα τον πατερα και την μητερα·" και· "Ὁ
"Honor the father and the mother;" and; "He
κακολογων πατερα ἠ μητερα, θανατῳ τελευ-
reviling father or mother, death let him
ταεω." 5 Ὑμεις δε λεγετε· Ὁς αν ειπῃ τῳ
die." You but say; Whoever may say to the
πατρι η τῃ μητρι· Δωρον, ὁ εαν εξ εμου
father or the mother; A gift, whatever out of me
ωφεληθῃς· και ου μη τιμησῃ τον πατερα
thou mightest be profited; then not not may honor the father
αὑτου *[η την μητερα αὑτου.] 6 Και ηκυρωσατε
of him [or the mother of him.] And you annul
την εντολην του θεου δια την παραδοσιν ὑμων.
the commandment of the God through the tradition of you.
7 Ὑποκριται, καλως προεφητευσε περι ὑμων
O hypocrites, well prophesied concerning you

CHAPTER XV.

1 ‡Then came to JESUS *Pharisees and Scribes from Jerusalem, saying,

2 "Why do thy DISCIPLES violate the †TRADITIONARY PRECEPT of the ELDERS? for they do not wash *their HANDS before Meals."

3 But HE answering, said to them, "Why do YOU also violate the COMMANDMENT of GOD by your TRADITION?

4 For GOD *said, ‡'Honor FATHER and MOTHER;' and ‡'HE who REVILES Father or Mother, 'shall be punished with 'Death.'

5 But **you** assert, 'If any one say to FATHER or MOTHER, An Offering is that by which thou mightest derive assistance from me;

6 then *he shall by no means honor his FATHER.' Thus, by your TRADITION, you annul the *WORD of GOD.

7 ‡Hypocrites! well did Isaiah prophesy concerning you, saying,

8 ‡'This people †[draw

---

* VATICAN MANUSCRIPT.—34. to LAND at Gennesaret. 1. Pharisees and Scribes from Jerusalem. 2. the HANDS. 4. said, 'Honor ... HER.' 6. He shall by no means honor his FATHER. Thus. 6. or his MOTHER—omit. 6. WORD.

† 2. He that eateth with unwashed hands is guilty of death.—*Rabbi Abiba.* † 8. The words in brackets are found in the prophecy from which they are taken, both in the Hebrew and Septuagint. They are omitted by the Vatican and several other excellent MSS., and by some ancient versions. Erasmus, Mill, Drusius, and Bengel, approve of the omission; and Griesbach has left it out of the text. But as they are found in the place from which they are quoted, it has been thought best to insert them in the text.

‡ 33. Matt. xxvii. 54. ‡ 34. Mark vi. 53. ‡ 1. Mark vii. 1. ‡ 4. Exod. xx. 12; Deut. v. 16; Eph. vi. 2. ‡ 4. Exod. xxi. 17; Lev. xx. 9; Deut. xxvii. 16; Prov. xx. 20. ‡ 7. Mark vii. 6. ‡ 8. Isa. xxix. 13.

Ἡσαιας, λεγων· " Ὁ λαος οὑτος τοις χειλεσι
Esaias, saying; "The people this with the lips
με τιμα· ἡ δε καρδια αυτων πορρω απεχει απ'
me honor; the but heart of them far off is removed from
εμου. 9 Ματην δε σεβονται με, διδασκοντες
me. Without profit but they reverence me, teaching
διδασκαλιας, ενταλματα ανθρωπων." 10 Και
doctrines, commandments of men." And
προσκαλεσαμενος τον οχλον, ειπεν αυτοις·
having called the crowd, he said to them;
Ακουετε και συνιετε. 11 Ου το εισερχομενον εις
Hear you and be instructed Not that entering into
το στομα κοινοι τον ανθρωπον· αλλα το εκπορ-
the mouth pollutes the man; but that proceed-
ευομενον εκ του στοματος τουτο κοινοι τον
ing out of the mouth this pollutes the
ανθρωπον. 12 Τοτε προσελθοντες οἱ μαθηται
man. Then having come the disciples
αυτου, ειπον αυτῳ· Οιδας, ὁτι οἱ Φαρισαιοι,
of him, said to him; Knowest thou, that the Pharisees,
ακουσαντες τον λογον, εσκανδαλισθησαν; 13 Ὁ
hearing that saying, found a difficulty? He
δε αποκριθεις ειπε· Πασα φυτεια, ἡν ουκ εφυ-
but answering said, Every plantation, which not has
τευσεν ὁ πατηρ μου ὁ ουρανιος, εκριζωθησεται.
planted the father of me the heavenly, shall be rooted up.
14 Αφετε αυτους· ὁδηγοι εισι τυφλοι *[τυφλων.]
Let alone them; guides they are blind [of blind.]
Τυφλος δε τυφλον εαν ὁδηγῃ, αμφοτεροι εις
Blind and blind if may lead, both into
βοθυνον πεσουνται. 15 Αποκριθεις δε ὁ Πετρος
a pit will fall. Answering and the Peter
ειπεν αυτῳ· Φρασον ἡμιν την παραβολην ταυτην.
said to him; Explain to us the comparison this.
16 Ὁ δε Ιησους ειπεν· Ακμην και ὑμεις ασυνετοι
The and Jesus said; Yet also you unintelligent
εστε; 17 Ου*[πω] νοειτε, ὁτι παν το εισπορευ-
are? Not [yet] perceive you, that all that enter-
ομενον εις το στομα, εις την κοιλιαν χωρει,
ing into the mouth, into the belly passes,
και εις αφεδρωνα εκβαλλεται; 18 Τα δε εκπορευ-
and into a privy is cast; Those but proceed-
ομενα εκ του στοματος, εκ της καρδιας εξερ-
ing out of the mouth, from the heart issues
χεται, κακεινα κοινοι τον ανθρωπον. 19 Εκ γαρ
forth, and they pollute the man. From for
της καρδιας εξερχονται διαλογισμοι πονηροι·
the heart comes forth purposes evil;
φονοι, μοιχειαι, πορνειαι, κλοπαι, ψευδομαρτυ-
murders, adulteries, fornications, thefts, false testimo-
ριαι, βλασφημιαι. 20 Ταυτα εστι τα κοινουντα
nies, evil speakings. These is the (things) polluting
τον ανθρωπον· το δε ανιπτοις χερσι φαγειν ου
the man; that but with unwashed hands to eat not
κοινοι τον ανθρωπον.
pollutes the man.

'nigh to ME with their 'MOUTH, and] honor Me 'with their LIPS; but 'their heart is far remov- 'ed from me.

9 'But in vain do they 'worship me, teaching as 'Doctrines, the Precepts 'of Men.'"

10 ‡ And having called the CROWD, he said to them, "Hear, and be instructed:

11 Not THAT ENTERING the MOUTH, pollutes the MAN, but THAT PROCEEDING from the MOUTH, pollutes the MAN."

12 Then *the DISCIPLES approaching, say to him, "Didst thou observe That the PHARISEES were offended, when they heard that SAYING?"

13 But HE answering, said, "Every Plantation, which my HEAVENLY FATHER has not planted, shall be extirpated.

14 Leave them; ‡ they are blind Guides; and if the Blind lead the Blind, both will fall into the Pit."

15 ‡ Then PETER replying, said to him, "Explain to us *that SAYING."

16 And *HE said, "Are you also yet without understanding?

17 Do you not perceive, That WHATEVER ENTERS the MOUTH, passes into the BELLY, and is ejected?

18 But ‡ those THINGS PROCEEDING out of the MOUTH, issue from the HEART; and they pollute the MAN.

19 ‡ For out of the HEART proceed iniquitous Designs;—Murders, Adulteries, Fornications, Thefts, false Testimonies, Calumnies.

20 These are the THINGS which POLLUTE the MAN; but to EAT with Unwashed Hands pollutes not the MAN."

---

* VATICAN MANUSCRIPT.—12. the DISCIPLES approaching, say. 14. of the Blind.—*omit.* 15. that SAYING. 16. HE said. 17. yet—*omit.*

‡ 10. Mark vii. 14. ‡ 14. Isa. ix. 16; Mal. ii. 8; Matt. xxiii. 16; Luke vi. 39. ‡ 15. Mark vii. 17. ‡ 18. James iii. 6. ‡ 19. Mark vii. 21.

21 Και εξελθων εκειθεν ὁ Ιησους ανεχωρησεν
And departing thence the Jesus withdrew
εις τα μερη Τυρου και Σιδωνος. 22 Και ιδου,
into the confines of Tyre and Sidon. And lo,
γυνη Χαναναια, απο των ὁριων εκεινων εξελθου-
a woman Canaanitish, of the parts those coming
σα, εκραυγασεν αυτῳ, λεγουσα· Ελεησον με,
out, cried out to him, saying; Pity me,
κυριε, υἱε Δαυιδ· ἡ θυγατηρ μου κακως δαιμονι-
O lord, O son David; the daughter of me sadly is demon-
ζεται. 23 Ὁ δε ουκ απεκριθη αυτῃ λογον. Και
ized. He but not answered her a word. And
προσελθοντες οἱ μαθηται αυτου, ηρωτων αυτον,
coming the disciples of him, besought him,
λεγοντες· Απολυσον αυτην, ὁτι κραζει οπισθεν
saying; Send away her, for she cries at the back
ἡμων. 24 Ὁ δε αποκριθεις ειπεν· Ουκ απεστα-
of us. He but answering said; Not I am
λην, ει μη εις τα προβατα τα απολωλοτα οικου
sent, except to the sheep the perishing house of
Ισραηλ. 25 Ἡ δε ελθουσα προσεκυνει αυτῳ,
Israel. She then coming prostrated to him,
λεγουσα· Κυριε, βοηθει μοι. 26 Ὁ δε αποκριθεις
saying; O lord, give aid to me. He but answering
ειπεν· Ουκ εστι καλον λαβειν τον αρτον των
said; Not it is right to take the bread of the
τεκνων, και βαλειν τοις κυναριοις. 27 Ἡ δε
children, and to throw to the dogs. She but
ειπε. Ναι, κυριε· και γαρ τα κυναρια εσθιει
said; True, O lord; even for the dogs eateth
απο των ψιχιων των πιπτοντων απο της τραπε-
of the crumbs of the falling from the table
ζης των κυριων αὐτων. 28 Τοτε αποκριθεις ὁ
of the masters of them. Then answering the
Ιησους ειπεν αυτῃ· Ω γυναι, μεγαλη σου ἡ
Jesus said to her; O woman, great of thee the
πιστις· γενηθητω σοι, ὡς θελεις. Και ιαθη
faith; let it be to thee, as thou wilt. And was healed
ἡ θυγατηρ αυτης απο της ὡρας ἐκεινης.
the daughter of her from the hour that.
29 Και μεταβας εκειθεν ὁ Ιησους, ηλθε παρα
And departing thence the Jesus, came near
την θαλασσαν της Γαλιλαιας· και αναβας εις
the sea of the Galilee; and ascending into
το ορος, εκαθητο εκει. 30 Και προσηλθον αυτῳ
the mountain, he sat down there. And came to him
οχλοι πολλοι, εχοντες μεθ' ἑαυτων χωλους,
crowds great, having with them lame,
τυφλους, κωφους, κυλλους, και ἑτερους πολλους·
blind, deaf, maimed, and others many;
και ερριψαν αυτους παρα τους ποδας του Ιησου,
and they laid them at the feet of the Jesus,
και εθεραπευσεν αυτους· 31 ὡστε τους οχλους
and he healed them; so that the crowds
θαυμασαι, βλεποντας κωφους λαλουντας, κυλ-
to wonder, beholding deaf speaking, maimed

21 ‡And JESUS departing thence, withdrew into the CONFINES of Tyre and Sidon.

22 And behold, a Canaanitish Woman coming from those PARTS, cried out to him, saying, "Have compassion on me, O Master, Son of David! my DAUGHTER is sadly demonized."

23 But he answered her not a Word. And his disciples coming, entreated him, saying, "Dismiss her; For she cries after us."

24 But HE answering, said, ‡"I am only sent to the PERISHING SHEEP of the Stock of Israel."

25 Yet advancing, SHE prostrated to him, saying, "O Master, help me!"

26 But HE answering, said, "It is not proper to take the CHILDREN'S BREAD, and throw it to †‡the DOGS."

27 But she said, "I beseech thee, Sir; for even the DOGS eat THOSE CRUMBS which FALL from their MASTERS' TABLE."

28 Then Jesus answering, said to her, "O Woman! great is Thy FAITH; be it to thee as thou desirest." And her DAUGHTER was cured from that very MOMENT.

29 ‡And Jesus, having left that place, came to the LAKE of GALILEE; and ascending the MOUNTAIN sat down there.

30 And great Crowds came to him, bringing with them the lame, *the †crippled, the blind, the deaf, and many others, and laid them at *his FEET, and he cured them;

31 so that the CROWDS beheld, with wonder, ‡the Deaf *hearing, the Crippled restored, the Lame

* VATICAN MANUSCRIPT.—30. crippled, blind, deaf, and. 30. his FEET. 31. hearing.

† 26. The Jews likened the heathen nations to dogs.—*Lightfoot.* † 30. The original word *kullos*, properly signifies, one whose hand or arm has been cut off; (see Mark ix. 43.) but it is sometimes applied to those who were only disabled in those parts. To supply a lost limb was a creation, and therefore an astonishing miracle.

‡ 21. Mark vii. 24. ‡ 24. Matt. x. 6; Acts iii. 26; Rom. xv. 8. ‡ 26. Matt. vii. 6 ‡ 29. Mark vii 31. ‡ 31. Isa. xxxv. 5, 6.

λους ὑγιεις, χωλους περιπατουντας, και τυφλους
* sound, lame walking, and blind
βλεποντας· και εδοξασαν τον θεον Ισραηλ. 32 Ὁ
seeing; and they glorified the God of Israel. The
δε Ιησους, προσκαλεσαμενος τους μαθητας αὐ-
then Jesus, having called the disciples of
του, ειπε· Σπλαγχνιζομαι επι τον οχλον, ὁτι
him, said; I have compassion on the crowd, for
*[ηδη] ἡμεραι τρεις, προσμενουσι μοι, και ουκ
[already] days three, they have remained with me, and not
εχουσι τι φαγωσι· και απολυσαι αυτους
they have any thing they may eat; and to send away them
νηστεις ου θελω, μηποτε εκλυθωσιν εν τῃ ὁδῳ.
fasting not I will, lest they may faint in the way.
33 Και λεγουσιν αυτῳ οἱ μαθηται αὐτου· Ποθεν
And they say to him the disciples of him; Whence
ἡμιν εν ερημιᾳ αρτοι τοσουτοι, ὡστε χορτασαι
to us in a desert place loaves so many, so as to satisfy
οχλον τοσουτον; 34 Και λεγει αυτοις ὁ Ιησους·
a crowd so great? And says to them the Jesus;
Ποσους αρτους εχετε; Οἱ δε ειπον· Ἑπτα, και
How many loaves have you? They and said; Seven, and
ολιγα ιχθυδια. 35 Και εκελευσε τοις οχλοις
a few small fishes. And he directed the crowds
αναπεσειν επι την γην. 36 Και λαβων τους
to recline upon the ground. And taking the
ἑπτα αρτους και τους ιχθυας, ευχαριστησας
seven loaves and the fishes, giving thanks
εκλασε και εδωκε τοις μαθηταις αὐτου, οἱ δε
he broke and he gave to the disciples of him, the and
μαθηται τῳ οχλῳ. 37 Και εφαγον παντες, και
disciples to the crowd. And they ate all, and
εχορτασθησαν· και ηραν το περισσευον των
were filled; and they took up that over and above of the
κλασματων, ἑπτα σπυριδας πληρεις. 38 Οἱ δε
fragments, seven large baskets full. They and
εσθιοντες ησαν τετρακισχιλιοι ανδρες, χωρις
eating were four thousand men. besides
γυναικων και παιδιων.
women and children.

39 Και απολυσας τους οχλους, ανεβη εις
And having sent away the crowds, he went into
το πλοιον, και ηλθεν εις τα ὁρια Μαγδαλα.
the ship, and came to the coasts of Magdala.
ΚΕΦ. ις'. 16. 1 Και προσελθοντες οἱ Φαρισαιοι
And coming the Pharisees
και Σαδδουκαιοι, πειραζοντες επηρωτησαν αυτον,
and Sadducees, tempting they asked him,
σημειον εκ του ουρανου επιδειξαι αυτοις. 2 Ὁ
a sign from the heaven to show to them He

walking,* and the Blind seeing; and they glorified the GOD of Israel.

32 ‡Then JESUS having called his DISCIPLES, said. "I have compassion on the CROWD, because they have continued with me three Days, and have nothing to eat; and I do not wish to dismiss them fasting, lest they should faint on the ROAD."

33 And his DISCIPLES say to him, ‡"How can we get so many Loaves in a Desert-place, to satisfy such a Crowd?"

34 And JESUS says to them, "How many Loaves have you?" And THEY said, "Seven, and a Few Small fishes."

35 Then he commanded the PEOPLE to recline on the GROUND;

36 and taking the SEVEN Loaves and the FISHES, ‡he offered thanks, and broke them, and gave to his DISCIPLES, and the DISCIPLES distributed to the CROWD.

37 And they all ate and were satisfied; and of the REMAINING FRAGMENTS they gathered Seven large † Baskets full.

38 Now THEY who had EATEN were * about Four thousand Men, besides Women and Children.

39 ‡ And having dismissed the CROWDS, he went into the BOAT, and came to the † COAST of * Magdala.

CHAPTER XVI.

1 ‡ Then the PHARISEES and SADDUCEES drew near, and tempting asked him to show them a Sign from HEAVEN.

* VATICAN MANUSCRIPT.—32. already—*omit*. 38. about. 39. Magadan—so also Lachmann and Tischendorf.

† 37. Baskets of larger capacity than the wicker baskets mentioned in Chap. xiv. 20—large enough to contain a man's body. See Acts ix. 25. † 39 The modern name is *Ard el-Mejdel*, field or coast of Mejdel. Mejdel, from which the plain takes its name, is a paltry village, about an hour from Tiberias, near where a line of high rocks overhangs the lake. This was the ancient Magdala, called in Mark viii. 10, Dalmanutha; the birth place of that Mary, out of whom were expelled seven demons.

‡ 32. Mark viii. 1. ‡ 33. 2 Kings iv. 43. 36. Matt. xiv. 19; Luke xxii. 19.
‡ 39. Mark viii. 10. ‡ 1. Matt. xii. 38.

δε αποκριθεις ειπεν αυτοις· *[Οψιας γενομενης,
but answering said to them; [Evening coming,
λεγετε· Ευδια· πυρραζει γαρ ὁ ουρανος. 3 Και
you say; Fair weather; reddens for the heaven. And
πρωι· Σημερον χειμων· πυρραζει γαρ στυγ-
in the morning; To-day a storm; is red for low-
ναζων ὁ ουρανος. Ὑποκριται, το μεν προσωπον
ering the heaven. Hypocrites, the truly face
του ουρανου γινωσκετε διακρινειν, τα δε σημεια
of the heaven you know to judge, the but signs
των καιρων ου δυνασθε;] 4 Γενεα πονηρα και
of the times not can you?] A generation evil and
μοιχαλις σημειον επιζητει· και σημειον ου δο-
adulterous a sign seeks; and a sign not shal
θησεται αυτῃ, ει μη το σημειον Ιωνα *[του
be given to her, except the sign of Jonas [the
προφητου.] Και καταλιπων αυτους, απηλθε.
prophet.] And leaving them, he went away.
5 Και ελθοντες οἱ μαθηται αυτου εις το περαν,
And coming the disciples of him to the other side,
επελαθοντο αρτους λαβειν. 6 Ὁ δε Ιησους ειπεν
had forgotten loaves to take. The and Jesus said
αυτοις· Ὁρατε και προσεχετε απο της ζυμης
to them; Look and take heed of the leaven
των Φαρισαιων και Σαδδουκαιων. 7 Οἱ δε διελο-
of the Pharisees and Sadducees. They and rea-
γιζοντο εν ἑαυτοις, λεγοντες· Ὁτι αρτους ουκ
soned among themselves, saying; Because loaves not
ελαβομεν. 8 Γνους δε ὁ Ιησους ειπεν· Τι δια-
we have brought. Knowing and the Jesus said; Why rea-
λογιζεσθε εν ἑαυτοις, ολιγοπιστοι, ὁτι αρτους
son you among yourselves, O you of weak faith, because loaves
ουκ *[ελαβετε;] 9 Ουπω νοειτε, ουδε μνημον-
not [you have brought?] Not yet perceive you, nor remem-
ευετε τους πεντε αρτους των πεντακισχιλιων,
ber you the five loaves of the five-thousand,
και ποσους κοφινους ελαβετε; 10 Ουδε τους
and how many baskets you took up? Nor the
ἑπτα αρτους των τετρακισχιλιων, και ποσας
seven loaves of the four thousand, and how many
σπυριδας ελαβετε; 11 Πως ου νοειτε, ὁτι ου
large baskets you took up? Why not do you perceive, that not
περι αρτου ειπον ὑμιν προσεχειν απο της ζυμης
about bread I spoke to you to take heed of the leaven
των Φαρισαιων και Σαδδουκαιων; 12 Τοτε συ-
of the Pharisees and Sadducees? Then they
νηκαν, ὁτι ουκ ειπε προσεχειν απο της ζυμης
understood, that not he did say beware of the leaven
του αρτου, αλλ' απο της διδαχης των Φαρισαιων
of the bread, but of the doctrine of the Pharisees
και Σαδδουκαιων.
and Sadducees.

2 But he answering, said to them, *["In the Evening, you say, 'It will be Fair weather, for the SKY is red;'

3 and in the Morning, 'There will be a Storm To-day, for the SKY is red and lowering.' Hypocrites! you can correctly judge as to the APPEARANCE of the SKY, but cannot discern the SIGNS of the TIMES.]

4 ‡A wicked and faithless Generation demands a Sign; but no Sign will be given it, except the SIGN of Jonah." And leaving them, he went away.

5 ‡Now, *the DISCIPLES passing to the OTHER SIDE, had forgotten to take Loaves with them.

6 And Jesus said to them, ‡"Observe, and beware of the LEAVEN of the PHARISEES and Sadducees."

7 And THEY reasoned among themselves, saying, "Because we have brought no Loaves."

8 But Jesus knowing it, said, "O you distrustful! Why do you reason among yourselves, Because you have no Bread?

9 Do you not yet perceive, or recollect ‡ the FIVE Loaves of the FIVE-THOUSAND, and How many Baskets you took up?

10 nor ‡the SEVEN Loaves of the FOUR THOUSAND, and How many large Baskets you took up?

11 How is it that you do not comprehend, That I spoke not to you about Bread, *but beware you of the LEAVEN of the PHARISEES and Sadducees?"

12 Then they understood That he did not tell them to beware of the LEAVEN of BREAD, but of the DOCTRINE of the *SADDUCEES and Pharisees.

* VATICAN MANUSCRIPT.—2 and 3—*omit*. 4. the PROPHET—*omit*. 5. the DISCIPLES. 8. brought—*omit*. 11. but beware you of. 12. SADDUCEES and Pharisees.

‡ 4. Matt. xii. 39. ‡ 5. Mark viii. 14. ‡ 6. Luke xii. 1. ‡ 9. Matt. xiv. 17. ‡ 10. Matt. xv. 34.

13 Ἐλθων δε ὁ Ιησους εις τα μερη Καισαρειας
Coming and the Jesus into the parts of Cesarea
της Φιλιππου, ηρωτα τους μαθητας αὑτου, λε-
of the Philip, asked the disciples of him, say-
γων· Τινα με λεγουσιν οἱ ανθρωποι ειναι, τον
ing; Who me say the men to be, the
υἱον του ανθρωπου; 14 Οἱ δε ειπον· Οἱ μεν,
son of the man? They and said; Some,
Ιωαννην τον βαπτιστην· αλλοι δε, Ηλιαν· ἑτεροι
John the dipper; others and, Elias; others
δε, Ἱερεμιαν, η ἑνα των προφητων. 15 Λεγει
and, Jeremias, or one of the prophets. He says
αυτοις· Ὑμεις δε τινα με λεγετε ειναι; 16 Αποκ-
to them; You but who me say to be? Ans-
ριθεις δε Σιμων Πετρος ειπε· Συ ει ὁ Χριστος,
wering the Simon Peter said; Thou art the Anointed,
ὁ υἱος του θεου του ζωντος. 17 Και αποκριθεις
the son of the God the living. And answering
ὁ Ιησους ειπεν αυτῳ· Μακαριος ει, Σιμων βαρ
the Jesus said to him; Blessed art thou, Simon son
Ιωνα· ὁτι σαρξ και αἱμα ουκ απεκαλυψε σοι,
of Jonas; for flesh and blood not it has revealed to thee,
αλλ' ὁ πατηρ μου, ὁ εν τοις ουρανοις. 18 Καγω
but the father of me, that in the heavens. Also I
δε σοι λεγω, ὁτι συ ει Πετρος, και επι ταυτῃ
and to thee say, that thou art a rock, and upon this
τῃ πετρᾳ οικοδομησω μου την εκκλησιαν, και
the rock I will build of me the church, and
πυλαι ἁδου ου κατισχυσουσιν αυτης. 19 Και
gates of hades not shall prevail against her. And
δωσω σοι τας κλεις της βασιλειας των ου-
I will give to thee the keys of the kingdom of the hea-
ρανων· και ὁ εαν δησῃς επι της γης, εσται
vens; and whatever thou mayest bind upon the earth, shall be
δεδεμενον εν τοις ουρανοις· και ὁ εαν λυσῃς
bound in the heavens; and whatever thou mayest loose
επι της γης, εσται λελυμενον εν τοις ουρανοις.
upon the earth, shall be loosed in the heavens.
20 Τοτε διεστειλατο τοις μαθηταις αὑτου, ἱνα
Then he charged the disciples of him, that
μηδενι ειπωσιν ὁτι αυτος εστιν ὁ Χριστος.
no one they should tell that he is the Anointed.

21 Απο τοτε ηρξατο ὁ Ιησους δεικνυειν τοις
From that time began the Jesus to show to the

13 And JESUS coming
into the PARTS of † Cesa-
rea PHILIPPI, questioned
his DISCIPLES, saying,
‡ "Who do MEN say that
* the SON of MAN is?"
14 And THEY replied,
"SOME, John the IMMER-
SER; * SOME, Elijah; and
others, Jeremiah, or one
of the PROPHETS."
15 He says to them,
"But who do you say
that I am?"
16 Simon Peter answer-
ing, said, ‡ "Thou art the
CHRIST, the SON of the
LIVING God."
17 And Jesus answer-
ing, said to him, "Happy
art thou, Simon, son of
Jonah; for Flesh and
Blood has not revealed
this to thee, but THAT
FATHER of mine in the
* Heavens.
18 Moreover, I also say
to thee, That thou art ‡ a
Rock, and on ‡ this ROCK
I will build My CHURCH;
and † the Gates of Hades
shall not triumph over it.
19 And I will give thee
† the KEYS of the KING-
DOM of the HEAVENS;
‡ and whatever thou shalt
bind on the EARTH, shall
be bound in the HEAV-
ENS; and whatever thou
shalt loose on the EARTH,
shall be loosed in the
HEAVENS."
20 ‡ Then he command-
ed * the DISCIPLES that
they should tell no one,
that he is the MESSIAH.
21 From that time, JE-
SUS began to disclose to

* VATICAN MANUSCRIPT.—13. the SON of MAN is? 14. SOME. 17. Heavens. 20. the DISCIPLES.

† 13. This town was near to the spring-head of the Jordan, and was built by Philip, tetrarch of Galilee, in honor of Tiberius Cæsar; and to distinguish it from the sea-port town of Cesarea, mentioned frequently in the Acts of the Apostles, it was called Cesarea Philippi. See *Josephus*, Ant. xviii. 2, 1, and xx. 8, 4. † 18. Parkhurst says, "This expression seems allusive to the form of the Jewish sepulchres, which were large subterraneous caves, with a narrow *mouth* or *entrance*, many of which are to be found in Judea, to this day. The LXX render the corresponding phrase from the Heb. of Isa. xxxviii. 10, *the gates of the sepulchre.* The full meaning of our Lord's promise seems to be, that his church on earth, however persecuted and distressed, should never fail till the consummation of all things, and should then, at *the resurrection of the just,* finally triumph over death and the grave." Compare 1 Cor. xv. 54, 55. † 19. It is said, that when the Jews made a man a doctor of the law, they used to put into his hands the key of the closet in the temple, where the sacred books were deposited, and also tablets to write upon; signifying that they gave him authority to teach and to explain the scriptures and law of God to the people.

‡ 13. Mark viii. 27; Luke ix. 18. ‡ 16. Mark viii. 29; Luke ix 20; John i. 49; vi. 69; xi. 27. ‡ 18. John i. 42. ‡ 18. Eph. ii. 20. ‡ 19. Matt. xviii. 18; John xx. 23. ‡ 20. Matt. xvii. 9; Mark viii. 30; Luke ix. 21.

μαθηταις αὑτου, ὁτι δει αυτον απελθειν εις Ἱερο-
disciples of him, that must he to go to Jeru-
σολυμα, και πολλα παθειν απο των πρεσβυτε-
salem, and many (things) to suffer from the elders
ρων και αρχιερεων και γραμματεων, και αποκ-
and high-priests and scribes, and to be
τανθηναι, και τη τριτη ἡμερᾳ εγερθηναι. 22 Και
killed, and the third day to be raised. And
προσλαβομενος αυτον ὁ Πετρος, ηρξατο επιτιμαν
taking aside him the Peter, began to reprove
αυτῳ, λεγων· Ἱλεως σοι, κυριε· ου μη εσται
him; saying; Be it far from thee, O lord; not not shall be
σοι τουτο. 23 Ὁ δε στραφεις ειπε τῳ Πετρῳ·
to thee this. He but turning said to the Peter;
Ὑπαγε οπισω μου, σατανα· σκανδαλον μου
Go thou behind of me, adversary; a stumbling-block of me
ει· ὁτι ου φρονεις τα του θεου, αλλα τα
thou art; for not thou regardest the (things) of the God, but those
των ανθρωπων. 24 Τοτε ὁ Ιησους ειπε τοις μα-
of the men. Then the Jesus said to the dis-
θηταις αὑτου· Ει τις θελει οπισω μου ελθειν,
ciples of him; If any one wish after me to come,
απαρνησασθω ἑαυτον, και αρατω τον σταυρον
let him deny himself, and let him bear the cross
αὑτου, και ακολουθειτω μοι. 25 Ὁς γαρ αν
of him, and follow me. Whoever for
θελῃ την ψυχην αὑτου σωσαι, απολεσει αυτην·
may wish the life of him to save, shall lose her;
ὁς δ' αν απολεσῃ την ψυχην αὑτου ἑνεκεν
whoever and may lose the life of him on account
εμου, εὑρησει αυτην. 26 Τι γαρ ωφελειται αν-
of me, shall find her. What for is profited a
θρωπος, εαν τον κοσμον ὁλον κερδησῃ, την δε
man, if the world whole he may win, the and
ψυχην αὑτου ζημιωθῃ; η τι δωσει ανθρωπος
life of him he may forfeit? or what shall give a man
ανταλλαγμα της ψυχης αὑτου; 27 Μελλει γαρ
in exchange for the life of him? Is about for
ὁ υἱος του ανθρωπου ερχεσθαι εν τη δοξῃ του
the son of the man to come in the glory of the
πατρος αὑτου, μετα των αγγελων αὑτου, και
father of him, with the messengers of him, and
τοτε αποδωσει ἑκαστῳ κατα την πραξιν
then he will render to each one according to the behavior
αυτου.
of him.
28 Αμην λεγω ὑμιν, εισι τινες των ὡδε ἑστω-
Indeed I say to you, there are some of those here having
των, οἱτινες ου μη γευσωνται θανατου, ἑως αν
stood, who not not shall taste of death, till
ιδωσι τον υἱον του ανθρωπου ερχομενον εν τῃ
they may see the son of the man coming in the
βασιλειᾳ αὑτου. ΚΕΦ. ιζ'. 17. 1 Και μεθ'
royal majesty of him. And after
ἡμερας ἑξ παραλαμβανει ὁ Ιησους τον Πετρον,
days six takes the Jesus the Peter,
και Ιακωβον, και Ιωαννην τον αδελφον αυτου·
and James, and John the brother of him;

his DISCIPLES, ‡ That he must go to Jerusalem, and suffer much from the ELDERS, and High-priests, and Scribes, and be killed, and that on the THIRD Day he must be raised up.

22 And PETER taking him aside, and * rebuking him, said, "Be this far from thee, Master; this shall not be to thee."

23 But HE turning, said to PETER, "Get thee behind me, Adversary; thou art a Stumbling-block to me; for thou regardest not the THINGS of GOD, but THOSE of MEN."

24 Then JESUS said to his DISCIPLES, ‡ "If any one wish to come after me, let him renounce himself, and take up his CROSS, and follow me

25 ‡ For whoever would save his LIFE, shall lose it; and whoever loses his LIFE on my account, shall find it.

26 For what is a Man profited, if he should gain the whole WORLD, and forfeit his LIFE? or what will ‡ a man give in Ransom for his LIFE?

27 ‡ For the SON of MAN is about to come in the GLORY of his FATHER, with his ANGELS; and then he will recompense to each one according to his CONDUCT.

28 ‡ Indeed I say to you, * That there are SOME of those STANDING here, who will not taste of Death, till they see the SON of MAN coming in his ROYAL MAJESTY."

CHAPTER XVII.

1 ‡ And after six days, JESUS took PETER, James, and John the BROTHER of James, and privately con-

* VATICAN MANUSCRIPT.—22. rebuking him, said. 28. That there are.

‡ 21. Matt. xvii. 22; xx. 17; Mark viii. 31; ix. 31; x. 33; Luke ix. 22, 44; xviii. 31; xxiv. 6, 7. ‡ 24. Matt. x. 38; Mark viii. 34; Luke ix. 23; xiv. 27. ‡ 25. Luke xvii 33; John xii. 25. ‡ 26. Psa. xlix. 7, 8. ‡ 27. Matt. xxv. 31—46; Mark viii. 38; Luke ix. 26. ‡ 28. Mark ix. 1; Luke ix. 27. ‡ 1. Mark ix. 2; Luke ix. 28.

και αναφερει αυτους εις ορος ὑψηλον κατ' ἰδιαν.
and leads up them into a mountain high privately.
2 Και μετεμορφωθη εμπροσθεν αυτων, και
And he was transfigured in the presence of them, and
ελαμψε το προσωπον αυτου ὡς ὁ ἡλιος· τα δε
shone the face of him as the sun; the and
ἱματια αυτου εγενετο λευκα ὡς το φως. 3 Και
garments of him became white as the light. And
ἰδου, ωφθησαν αυτοις Μωσης και Ηλιας, μετ'
lo, appeared to them Moses and Elias, with
αυτου συλλαλουντες. 4 Αποκριθεις δε ὁ Πετρος
him talking. Answering and the Peter
ειπε τῳ Ιησου· Κυριε, καλον εστιν ἡμας ὡδε
said to the Jesus; O lord, good it is us here
ειναι· ει θελεις, ποιησωμεν ὡδε τρεις σκηνας,
to be; if thou wilt, we may make here three tents,
σοι μιαν, και Μωσῃ μιαν, και μιαν Ηλιᾳ. 5 Ετι
to thee one, and Moses one, and one Elias. Still
αυτου λαλουντος, ἰδου, νεφελη φωτος επεσ-
of him speaking, lo, a cloud of light over-
κιασεν αυτους· και ἰδου, φωνη εκ της νεφελης,
shadowed them. and lo, a voice out of the cloud,
λεγουσα· "Οὑτος εστιν ὁ υἱος μου ὁ αγαπητος,
saying; "This is the son of me the beloved,
εν 'ῳ ευδοκησα· αυτου ακουετε." 6 Και ακου-
in whom I delight, of him hear you." And having
σαντες οἱ μαθηται, επεσον επι προσωπον αὑτων,
heard the disciples, they fell upon face of them,
και εφοβηθησαν σφοδρα. 7 Και προσελθων ὁ
and were frightened greatly. And coming near the
Ιησους, ἡψατο αυτων, και ειπεν· Εγερθητε, και
Jesus, touched them, and said; Be you raised, and
μη φοβεισθε. 8 Επαραντες δε τους οφθαλμους
not be afraid. Lifting up then the eyes
αὑτων, ουδενα ειδον, ει μη τον Ιησουν μονον.
of them, no one they saw, except the Jesus alone.
9 Και καταβαινοντων αυτων, εκ του ορους,
And descending of them, from the mountain,
ενετειλατο αυτοις ὁ Ιησους, λεγων· Μηδενι ει-
charged them the Jesus, saying; To no one you
πητε το ὁραμα, ἑως οὑ ὁ υἱος του ανθρωπου εκ
may tell the vision, till the son of the man from
νεκρων αναστῃ.
dead (ones) should be raised.
10 Και επηρωτησαν αυτον οἱ μαθηται αυτου,
And asked him the disciples of him,
λεγοντες· Τι ουν οἱ γραμματεις λεγουσιν, ὁτι
saying; Why then the scribes say, that
Ηλιαν δει ελθειν πρωτον; 11 Ὁ δε Ιησους
Elias must to come first? The but Jesus
αποκριθεις ειπεν *[αυτοις·] Ηλιας μεν ερχεται
answering said [to them;] Elias truly comes
πρωτον, και αποκαταστησει παντα· 12 λεγω δε
first, and shall restore all things; I say but
ὑμιν, ὁτι Ηλιας ηδη ηλθε, και ουκ επεγνωσαν
to you, that Elias just now came, and not they knew
αυτον, αλλ' εποιησαν εν αυτῳ ὁσα ηθελησαν·
him, but have done to him as much as they wished;

ducted them up a lofty
Mountain;
2 and he was trans-
formed in their presence,
his FACE shone as the
SUN, and his GARMENTS
became white as the
LIGHT.
3 And behold, Moses
and Elijah appeared to
them, conversing with
him.
4 Then PETER address-
ing JESUS, said, "Master,
it is good for us to be
here; if thou wilt, * I will
make here three Booths;
one for thee, one for Mo-
ses, and one for Elijah."
5 While he was speak-
ing, behold, ‡a Cloud of
light covered them; and
behold, a Voice from the
CLOUD, declaring, ‡"This
is my SON; the BELOVED,
in whom I delight; hear
him!"
6 And the DISCIPLES
having heard it, fell on
their Faces, and were
greatly frightened.
7 And JESUS approach-
ing, ‡touched them, and
said, "Arise, and be not
afraid."
8 Then raising their
EYES, they saw no one,
except JESUS.
9 ‡ And as they were
descending the MOUN-
TAIN, JESUS commanded
them, saying Tell the VI-
SION to no one, till the
SON of MAN be risen from
the Dead.
10 And the DISCIPLES
asked him, saying ‡"Why
then do the SCRIBES say
That Elijah must first
come?"
11 *HE answering, said,
"Elijah indeed * comes,
and will restore all things.
12 But I say to you,
‡ That Elijah has already
come, and they did not
recognize him, but have
done to him whatever
they wished. Thus also

* VATICAN MANUSCRIPT.—4. I will make here three Booths. 11. HE answering
11. comes, and will restore.

‡ 5. 2 Peter i. 17; Matt. iii. 17; Mark i. 11; Luke iii. 22. ‡ 7. Dan. viii. 18; x. 9, 10, 18; Rev. i. 17. ‡ 9. Mark ix. 9. ‡ 10. Mal. iv. 5. ‡ 12. Matt. xi. 14; Mark ix. 12, 13.

οὑτω και ὁ υἱος του ανθρωπου μελλει πασχειν
thus also the son of the man is about to suffer
ὑπ' αυτων. 13 Τοτε συνηκαν οἱ μαθηται, ὁτι
by them. Then understood the disciples, that
περι Ιωαννου του βαπτιστου ειπεν αυτοις.
concerning John the dipper he spoke to them.
14 Και ελθοντων αυτων προς τον οχλον, προσ-
And having come of them to the crowd,
ηλθεν αυτῳ ανθρωπος, γονυπετων αυτον, 15 και
came to him a man, knee-falling him, and
λεγων· Κυριε, ελεησον μου τον υἱον· ὁτι σεληνιαζεται
saying; O lord, have pity on of me the son; for he is
νιαζεται, και κακως πασχει· πολλακις γαρ
moon-struck, and sadly suffers; often for
πιπτει εις το πυρ, και πολλακις εις το ὑδωρ.
he falls into the fire, and often into the water.
16 Και προσηνεγκα αυτον τοις μαθηταις σου, και
And I brought him to the disciples of thee, and
ουκ ηδυνηθησαν αυτον θεραπευσαι. 17 Αποκρι-
not they were able him to heal. Answer-
θεις δε ὁ Ιησους ειπεν· Ω γενεα απιστος και
ing and the Jesus said; O generation unfaithful and
διεστραμμενη· ἑως ποτε εσομαι μεθ' ὑμων;
having been perverted; till when shall I be with you?
ἑως ποτε ανεξομαι ὑμων; φερετε μοι αυτον ὡδε.
till when shall I bear you? bring you to me him here.
18 Και επετιμησεν αυτῳ ὁ Ιησους, και εξηλθεν
And rebuked him the Jesus, and came out
απ' αυτου το δαιμονιον· και εθεραπευθη ὁ παις
of him the demon; and was cured the boy
απο της ὡρας εκεινης. 19 Τοτε προσελθοντες
from the hour that. Then coming
οἱ μαθηται τῳ Ιησου κατ' ιδιαν, ειπον· Διατι
the disciples to the Jesus by himself, said; Why
ἡμεις ουκ ηδυνηθημεν εκβαλειν αυτο; 20 Ὁ δε
we not were able to cast out it? The and
Ιησους ειπεν αυτοις· Δια την απιστιαν ὑμων.
Jesus said to them; On account of the unbelief of you.
Αμην γαρ λεγω ὑμιν, εαν εχητε πιστιν ὡς κοκ-
Indeed for I say to you, if you have faith as a
κον σιναπεως, ερειτε τῳ ορει τουτῳ· Μετα-
grain of mustard, you will say to the mountain; this Be thou
βηθι εντευθεν εκει, και μεταβησεται· και ουδεν
removed from here there, and it will remove; and nothing
αδυνατησει ὑμιν. 21 *[Τουτο δε το γενος ουκ
will be impossible to you. [This but the kind not
εκπορευεται, ει μη εν προσευχῃ και νηστειᾳ.]
goes out, if not in prayer and fasting.]
22 Αναστρεφομενων δε αυτων εν τῃ Γαλιλαιᾳ,
Were traveling and of them in the Galilee,
ειπεν αυτοις ὁ Ιησους· Μελλει ὁ υἱος του αν-
said to them the Jesus; Is about the son of the
θρωπου παραδιδοσθαι εις χειρας ανθρωπων,
man to be delivered up into hands of men,
23 και αποκτενουσιν αυτον· και τῃ τριτῃ ἡμερᾳ
and they will kill him; and the third day
εγερθησεται. Και ελυπηθησαν σφοδρα.
he will be raised. And they were grieved exceedingly.

the SON of MAN is about to suffer by them."

13 Then the DISCIPLES understood That he spoke to them concerning John the IMMERSER.

14 ‡And they having come to the CROWD, a Man came to him, kneeling and saying,

15 "O Sir, have compassion on My SON; for he is a lunatic, and *sickly; for he frequently falls into the FIRE, and frequently into the WATER.

16 And I brought him to thy DISCIPLES, but they could not cure Him."

17 Then JESUS answering said, "O unbelieving and perverse Generation! how long must I be with you? how long must I endure you? bring him here to me."

18 And JESUS rebuked him, and the DEMON came out of him; and the BOY was restored from that HOUR.

19 Then the DISCIPLES coming to JESUS privately, said, "Why were we not able to cast it out?"

20 And *HE says to them, "On account of your *LITTLE-FAITH; For indeed I say to you, ‡If you have Faith, as a Grain of Mustard, you might say to this MOUNTAIN, Remove there from here, and it would remove; and nothing would be impossible to you.

21 *†[This KIND, however, goes not out but by Prayer and Fasting."]

22 ‡Now while they were traveling in GALILEE, JESUS said to them, "The SON of MAN is about to be delivered up into the Hands of Men;

23 and they will kill him, and the THIRD Day he will *rise. And they were exceedingly grieved.

* VATICAN MANUSCRIPT.—15. sickly. 20. HE says. 20. LITTLE-FAITH. 21.—*omit.* 23. rise.

† 21. This verse is wanting in the *Coptic, Ethiopic, Syriac hieros,* and in one *Itala* MSS.

‡ 14. Mark ix. 14; Luke ix. 37. ‡ 20. Matt. xxi. 21; Mark xi. 23; Luke xvii. 6; 1 Cor. xiii. 2. ‡ 22. Matt. xvi. 21; xx. 18; Mark ix. 30, 31; Luke ix. 44.

24 Ελθοντων δε αυτων εις Καπερναουμ,
Having arrived and of them at Capernaum.
προσηλθον οἱ τα διδραχμα λαμβανοντες τῳ
came those the didrachmas receiving to the
Πετρῳ, και ειπον· Ὁ διδασκαλος ὑμων ου τελει
Peter, and said; The teacher of you not pays
τα διδραχμα; 25 Λεγει· Ναι. Και ὁτε εισηλ-
the didrachmas? He says; Yes. And when he was
θεν εις την οικιαν, προεφθασεν αυτον ὁ Ιησους,
come into the house, anticipated him the Jesus,
λεγων· Τι σοι δοκει, Σιμων; Οἱ βασιλεις
saying; Which to thee seems right, Simon? The kings
της γης απο τινων λαμβανουσι τελη η κηνσον;
of the earth from whom do they take taxes or census?
απο των υἱων αὑτων, η απο των αλλοτριων;
from the sons of them, or from the aliens?
26 Λεγει αυτῳ ὁ Πετρος· Απο των αλλοτριων.
Says to him the Peter; From the aliens.
Εφη αυτῳ ὁ Ιησους· Αραγε ελευθεροι εισιν οἱ
Says to him the Jesus, Then exempt are the
υἱοι. 27 Ἱνα δε μη σκανδαλισωμεν αυτους,
sons. That but not we may offend them,
πορευθεις εις την θαλασσαν, βαλε αγκιστρον,
going to the sea, cast thou a hook,
και τον αναβαντα πρωτον ιχθυν αρον· και ανοι-
and the ascending first fish take up; and open-
ξας το στομα αυτου, εὑρησεις στατηρα· εκεινον
ing the mouth of him, thou wilt find a stater; that
λαβων, δος αυτοις αντι εμου και σου.
taking, give to them for me and thee.

ΚΕΦ. ιη'. 18.

1 Εν εκεινῃ τῃ ὡρᾳ προσηλθον οἱ μαθηται τῳ
In that the hour came the disciples to the
Ιησου, λεγοντες· Τις αρα μειζων εστιν εν τῃ
Jesus, saying; Who then greater is in the
βασιλειᾳ των ουρανων; 2 Και προσκαλεσαμενος
kingdom of the heavens? And having called
ὁ Ιησους παιδιον εστησεν αυτο εν μεσῳ αυτων,
the Jesus a little child placed it in midst of them,
3 και ειπεν· Αμην λεγω ὑμιν, εαν μη στραφητε
and said; Indeed I say to you, if not you be changed
και γενησθε ὡς τα παιδια, ου μη εισελθητε εις
and become as the little children, not not you may enter into
την βασιλειαν των ουρανων. 4 Ὁστις ουν
the kingdom of the heavens. Whoever therefore

24 ‡ And having arrived at Capernaum, the COLLECTORS of † DIDRACHMS came to PETER, and said, "Does not your TEACHER pay the DIDRACHMS?"

25 He says, "Yes." And when *they were come into the HOUSE, JESUS anticipated him, saying, "What is thy opinion, Simon? From whom do the KINGS of the EARTH take Tax or Census? from their own SONS, or from OTHERS?"

26 *And when he said, "Of OTHERS," Jesus says, "The SONS then are exempt.

27 But lest we should offend them, go to the LAKE, throw a Hook, and take the first FISH COMING UP, and opening its MOUTH, thou wilt find † a Stater; take That, and give it to them, for me and thee."

CHAPTER XVIII.

1 *And at That TIME the DISCIPLES came to JESUS, saying, ‡ "Who then is greatest in the KINGDOM of the HEAVENS?"

2 And *he having called a Little child, placed him in the Midst of them,

3 and said, "Indeed I say to you, ‡ Unless you be changed, and become as LITTLE CHILDREN, you will never enter the KINGDOM of the HEAVENS.

4 Whoever, therefore,

* VATICAN MANUSCRIPT.—25. they were come. 26. And when he said, "Of OTHERS," Jesus says. 1. And at. 2. he having called.

† 24. A half shekel, in value about 30 cents, or 1s. 3d. It appears from Exodus xxx. 13, 14, that every male among the Jews, of twenty years old and upwards, was commanded to give a certain sum every year, as an offering to the Lord, for the service of the temple at Jerusalem. Scott refers to Jos. Ant. xviii. 9, 1, to show that the Jews continued to send the same sum every year, wherever they lived; which Philo too particularly mentions, de Monarch. ii. 635, ed. col. "Sums of money, on account of the Jews, were carried every year out of Italy and all your provinces to Jerusalem." Cic. pro Flac. 8. "Every Jew, despising the religion of the country in which he lived, sent his donations and tribute to Jerusalem and the temple." Tac. Hist. lib. 5. Josephus (B. J. vii. 27) says, "the Roman emperor Vespasian imposed upon every Jew the same contribution for the Capitol, as they had before paid to the Temple." "Titus imposed on them a yearly tribute of a didrachm to Capitoline Jupiter." Xiphil. Dion. lib. lxvi. These tribute gatherers must have been sent by the superintendents of the Temple, and have acted by the authority of the high priest; for the force of our Lord's argument depends upon this particular.—*Wakefield.* † 27. A shekel, or half an ounce of silver, in value about 60 cents, or 2s. 6d., at 5s. per ounce.

‡ 24. Mark ix. 33. ‡ 1. Mark ix. 33; Luke ix. 46; xxii. 24. ‡ 3. Matt. xix. 14; Mark x. 15; Luke xviii. 17; 1 Cor. xiv 20; 1 Peter ii. 2.

ταπεινωσῃ ἑαυτον ὡς το παιδιον τουτο, οὑτος
may humble himself as the little child this, he
εστιν ὁ μειζων εν τῃ βασιλειᾳ των ουρανων.
is the greater in the kingdom of the heavens.
5 Και ὁς εαν δεξηται παιδιον τοιουτον ἑν επι τῳ
And whoever may receive a little child such one on the
ονοματι μου, εμε δεχεται. 6 Ὁς δ' αν σκανδα-
name of me, me receives. Who but ever may in-
λισῃ ἑνα των μικρων τουτων, των πιστευοντων
snare one of the little-ones these, of the believing
εις εμε, συμφερει αυτῳ, ἱνα κρεμασθῃ μυλος
into me, it is appropriate to him, that should be hung a millstone
ονικος επι τον τραχηλον αυτου, και καταπον-
upper on the neck of him, and he should be
τισθῃ εν τῳ πελαγει της θαλασσης.
sunk in the depth of the sea.

7 Ουαι τῳ κοσμῳ απο των σκανδαλων. Αναγ-
Woe to the world from the snares. Neces-
κη γαρ εστιν ελθειν τα σκανδαλα· πλην ουαι
sary for it is to come the snares; but woe
τῳ ανθρωπῳ εκεινῳ δι' οὑ το σκανδαλον
to the man to that through whom the snare
ερχεται. 8 Ει δε ἡ χειρ σου η ὁ πους σου
comes. If therefore the hand of thee or the foot of thee
σκανδαλιζει σε, εκκοψον αυτα, και βαλε απο
insnares thee, cut off them, and cast from
σου· καλον σοι εστιν εισελθειν εις την ζωην
thee; good to thee it is to enter into the life
χωλον η κυλλον, η δυο χειρας η δυο ποδας
lame or a cripple, than two hands or two feet
εχοντα βληθηναι εις το πυρ το αιωνιον. 9 Και
having to be cast into the fire the age-lasting. And
ει ὁ οφθαλμος σου σκανδαλιζει σε, εξελε αυτον,
if the eye of thee insnares thee, tear out it,
και βαλε απο σου· καλον σοι εστι μονοφθαλμον
and cast from thee; good to thee it is one-eyed
εις την ζωην εισελθειν, η δυο οφθαλμους εχοντα
into the life to enter, than two eyes having
βληθηναι εις την γεενναν του πυρος. 10 Ὁρατε,
to be cast into the Gehenna of the fire. See,
μη καταφρονησητε ἑνος των μικρων τουτων·
not you may despise one of the little-ones these;
λεγω γαρ ὑμιν, ὁτι οἱ αγγελοι αυτων εν ουρα-
I say for to you, that the messengers of them in hea-
νοις διαπαντος βλεπουσι το προσωπον του
vens perpetually see the face of the
πατρος μου, του εν ουρανοις. *[11 Ηλθε γαρ ὁ
father of me, that in heavens. [Is come for the
υἱος του ανθρωπου σωσαι το απολωλος.] 12 Τι
son of the man to save the having been lost.] What

may humble himself like this LITTLE CHILD, he will be the GREATEST in the KINGDOM of the HEAVENS.

5 ‡ And whoever may receive one such Little child in my NAME, receives Me.

6 ‡ But whoever shall insnare one of the LEAST of THESE who BELIEVE in me, it would be better for him that an † upper Mill-stone were hanged about his NECK, and that he were sunk in the DEPTH of the SEA.

7 Alas for the WORLD, because of SNARES! for it must be that SNARES come; but alas for that MAN through whom the SNARE comes.

8 ‡ If, then, thy HAND or thy FOOT insnare thee, cut it off, and throw it away; it is better for thee to enter LIFE * crippled or lame, than having Two Hands or Two Feet, to be cast into the † AIONIAN FIRE.

9 And if thine EYE insnare thee, pluck it out, and throw it away; it is better to enter LIFE one-eyed, than having Two Eyes to be cast into the BURNING of GEHENNA.

10 Take care, that you do not despise one of the LEAST of these; for I assure you, that ‡ their ANGELS in * the HEAVENS continually behold the FACE of THAT FATHER of mine in the Heavens.

11 * † ‡ [For the SON of MAN is come to save THAT which was LOST.]

---

* VATICAN MANUSCRIPT.—8. crippled or lame. 10. the HEAVENS. 11.—*omit.* See also Lachmann and Tischendorf.

† 6. A mill-stone turned by an ass, and consequently much larger than one turned by the hand. The punishment of death by drowning, though not in use by the Jews, was so among the surrounding nations. It seems to have grown into a proverb for dreadful and inevitable ruin. † 8. *Aioonion.* This word is the adjective of *aioon*, age, and as we have no word in English which exactly conveys the idea attached to it in the original, it has been left untranslated. The adjective form of the word, however, cannot rise higher in meaning than the noun from which it is derived, and must always be governed by it. See Note on Matt. xiii. 40, and Appendix. † 11. This verse is omitted in the Vatican and several other MSS., and marked as doubtful by Griesbach. In Boothroyd's translation it is appended to the fourteenth verse, as making a better connection.

‡ 5. Matt. x. 42; Luke ix. 48. ‡ 6. Mark ix. 42; Luke xvii. 1, 2. ‡ 8. Matt. v. 29, 30; Mark ix 43, 45. ‡ 10. Psa. xxxiv. 7; Luke i. 19. ‡ 11. Luke ix. 56; xix. 10; John iii 17; xii. 47

ὑμιν δοκει; εαν γενηται τινι ανθρωπῳ ἑκατον
to you seems right? if should have any man a hundred
προβατα, και πλανηθῃ ἑν εξ αυτων· ουχι αφεις
sheep, and should go astray one from them; not leaving
τα εννενηκονταεννεα επι τα ορη, πορευθεις ζη-
the ninety-nine upon the mountains, going he
τει το πλανωμενον; 13 Και εαν γενηται εὑρειν
seeks that having strayed? And if he should happen to find
αυτο, αμην λεγω ὑμιν, ὁτι χαιρει επ' αυτῳ
it, indeed I say to you, that he rejoices over it
μαλλον, η επι τοις εννενηκονταεννεα, τοις μη
more, than over the ninety-nine, those not
πεπλανημενοις. 14 Οὑτως ουκ εστι θελημα
having been led astray. Thus not it is will
εμπροσθεν του πατρος ὑμων, του εν ουρανοις,
in the presence of the father of you, of that in heavens,
ἱνα αποληται εἱς των μικρων τουτων. 15 Εαν
that should perish one of the little-ones of them. If
δε ἁμαρτησῃ *[εις σε] ὁ αδελφος σου, ὑπαγε,
and should be in error [against thee,] the brother of thee, go,
ελεγξον αυτον μεταξυ σου και αυτου μονου.
test him between thee and him alone.
Εαν σου ακουσῃ, εκερδησας τον αδελφον σου·
If thee he may hear, thou hast won the brother of thee;
16 εαν δε μη ακουσῃ, παραλαβε μετα σου ετι
if but not he may hear, take with thee besides
ἑνα η δυο· ἱνα επι στοματος δυο μαρτυρων η
one or two; that by mouth two of witnesses or
τριων σταθῃ παν ῥημα. 17 Εαν δε πα-
of three may be proved every word. If and he
ρακουσῃ αυτων, ειπε τῃ εκκλησιᾳ· εαν δε
should disregard them, tell thou to the congregation; if and
και της εκκλησιας παρακουσῃ, εστω σοι
also of the congregation he should disregard, let him be to thee
ὡσπερ ὁ εθνικος και ὁ τελωνης. 18 Αμην
as the Gentile and the tax-gatherer. Indeed
λεγω ὑμιν, ὁσα εαν δησητε επι της γης,
I say to you, whatever you may bind on the earth,
εσται δεδεμενα εν τῳ ουρανῳ· και ὁσα εαν
shall be having been bound in the heaven; and whatever
λυσητε επι της γης, εσται λελυμενα εν
you may loose on the earth, shall be having been loosed in
τῳ ουρανῳ.
the heaven.

19 Παλιν λεγω ὑμιν, ὁτι εαν δυο ὑμων συμφω-
Again I say to you, that if two of you may
νησωσιν επι της γης, περι παντος πραγματος,
agree upon the earth, about any matter,
οὑ εαν αιτησωνται, γενησεται αυτοις παρα του
whatever they may ask, it shall be to them from the
πατρος μου, του εν ουρανοις. 20 Οὑ γαρ εισι
father of me, of that in heavens. Where for are
δυο η τρεις συνηγμενοι εις το εμον ονομα, εκει
two or three having come together in the my name, there
ειμι εν μεσῳ αυτων. 21 Τοτε προσελθων αυτῳ
I am in the midst of them. Then coming to him

12 What do you think? ‡If a Man have a Hundred Sheep, and one of them go astray, *will he not leave the NINETY-NINE Sheep on the MOUNTAINS, and go and seek the STRAY ONE?

13 And if he happen to find it, indeed I say to you, that he rejoices more over it, than over THOSE NINETY-NINE which WENT NOT ASTRAY.

14 Thus it is not the Will *of THAT FATHER of mine in the Heavens, that in his presence one of the LEAST of these should be lost.

15 ‡Now, if thy BROTHER be in error, go, convict him, between thee and him alone. ‡If he hear thee, thou hast gained thy BROTHER.

16 But if he hear thee not, take with thee one or two more; ‡that by the Testimony of Two or three Witnesses, Every Thing may be proved

17 But if he disregard them, inform the CONGREGATION, and if he disregard the CONGREGATION also, ‡let him be to thee as a PAGAN and a TRIBUTE-TAKER.

18 Indeed, I say to you, ‡Whatever you may bind on EARTH, will be as having been bound in *Heaven; and whatever you may loose on EARTH will be as having been loosed in Heaven.

19 *Again, indeed, I say to you, That if two of you on EARTH may agree about any thing which they may ask, it will be done for them, by THAT FATHER of mine in the Heavens.

20 For where two or three are assembled in MY Name, I am there in the Midst of them."

* VATICAN MANUSCRIPT.—12. will he not leave the NINETY-NINE Sheep on the MOUNTAINS, and go and seek 14. of THAT FATHER of mine. 15. against thee—omit. 18. Heaven. 18. Heaven. 19. Again, indeed, I say.

‡ Luke xv. 4. ‡ 15. Lev. xix 17; Luke xvii. 3. ‡ 15. James v. 19, 20
‡ 16. Deut. xix. 15; John viii. 17; 2 Cor. xiii. 1, ‡ 17. Rom. xvi. 17; 2 Thess. iii. 6, 14.
‡ 18. Matt. xvi. 19; John xx. 23.

ὁ Πετρος, ειπε· Κυριε, ποσακις ἁμαρτησει εις
the Peter, said; O lord, how often shall sin against
εμε ὁ αδελφος μου, και αφησω αυτῳ; ἑως
me the brother of me, and I shall forgive him? till
ἑπτακις; 22 Λεγει αυτῳ ὁ Ιησους· Ου, λεγω
seven times? Says to him the Jesus; Not, I say
σοι, ἑως ἑπτακις, αλλ' ἑως εβδομηκοντακις
to thee, till seven times, but till seventy times
ἑπτα. 23 Δια τουτο ὡμοιωθη ἡ βασιλεια
seven. Therefore this has been compared the kingdom
των ουρανων ανθρωπῳ βασιλει, ὁς ηθελησε συ-
of the heavens to a man king, who wished to
ναραι λογον μετα των δουλων αὐτου. 24 Αρξα-
settle an account with the slaves of him. Having
μενου δε αυτου συναιρειν, προσηνεχθη αυτῳ εις
begun and of him to settle, they brought to him one
οφειλετης μυριων ταλαντων. 25 Μη εχοντος δε
a debtor of ten thousand talents. Not having but
αυτου αποδουναι, εκελευσεν αυτον ὁ κυριος αυ-
of him to pay, ordered him the lord of
του πραθηναι, και την γυναικα αυτου, και τα
him to be sold, and the wife of him, and the
τεκνα, και παντα ὁσα ειχε, και αποδοθηναι.
children, and all as much as he had, and payment to be made.
26 Πεσων ουν ὁ δουλος προσεκυνει αυτῳ,
Falling down therefore the slave he prostrated to him,
λεγων· *[Κυριε,] μακροθυμησον επ' εμοι, και
saying, [O lord,] have patience with me, and
παντα σοι αποδωσω. 27 Σπλαγχνισθεις δε ὁ
all to thee I will pay. Being moved with pity then the
κυριος του δουλου εκεινου, απελυσεν αυτον, και
lord of the slave of that, loosed him, and
το δανειον αφηκεν αὐτῳ. 28 Εξελθων δε ὁ
the debt remitted to him. Going out but the
δουλος *[εκεινος,] εὑρεν ἑνα των συνδουλων
slave [that,] found one of the fellow-slaves
αὐτου, ὁς ωφειλεν αυτῳ ἑκατον δηναρια· και
of him, who owed to him a hundred denarii; and
κρατησας αυτον επνιγε, λεγων· Αποδος μοι ει
seizing him he choked him, saying; Pay to me if
τι οφειλεις. 29 Πεσων ουν ὁ συνδουλος
any thing thou owest. Falling down therefore the fellow-slave
αυτου, παρεκαλει αυτον, λεγων· Μακροθυμησον
of him, besought him, saying; Have patience
επ' εμοι, και *[παντα] αποδωσω σοι. 30 Ὁ δε
with me, and [all] I will pay to thee. He and
ουκ ηθελεν· αλλ' απελθων εβαλεν αυτον εις
not he would; but going away he cast him into
φυλακην, ἑως οὑ αποδῳ το οφειλομενον. 31 Ιδον-
prison, till he should pay that he was owing. See-
τες δε οἱ συνδουλοι αυτου τα γενομενα, ελυπη-
ing and the fellow-slaves of him that having been done, were
θησαν σφοδρα· και ελθοντες διεσαφησαν τῳ
grieved much; and going they related to the

21 Then Peter coming,
*said to him, ‡"Lord,
how often shall I forgive
my BROTHER, if he re-
peatedly trespass against
me? till seven times?"
22 JESUS says to him,
"I say to thee, Not till
seven times only, but till
seventy times seven.
23 In this, the KING-
DOM of the HEAVENS has
been compared to a King,
who determined to settle
Accounts with his SER-
VANTS.
24 And having begun
to settle, they brought to
him one Debtor of Ten
thousand † Talents.
25 But he not having
means to refund, *the
MASTER, to obtain † pay-
ment, ordered that he,
and his WIFE and CHIL-
DREN, and all that he
had, should be sold.
26 The SERVANT, then,
falling down, prostrated
to him, saying, 'Have pa-
tience with me, and I will
pay thee all.'
27 And the MASTER of
*the SERVANT, being com-
passionate, loosed him,
and remitted the DEBT.
28 But the SERVANT go-
ing out, found one of his
FELLOW-SERVANTS, who
owed him a Hundred † De-
narii; and seizing him he
choked him, saying, 'Pay
* whatever thou owest.'
29 And his FELLOW-
SERVANT falling down,
entreated him, saying,
'Have patience with me
and I will pay thee.'
30 But HE would not;
and departing, committed
him to Prison, till he
should pay the DEBT.
31 *When, therefore,
His FELLOW-SERVANTS
seeing WHAT was DONE,
they were indignant; and

* VATICAN MANUSCRIPT.—21. said to him, "Lord." 25. the MASTER. 26. O lord—*omit*. 27. the SERVANT. 28. that—*omit*. 28. whatever thou owest. 29. all—*omit*. 31. When, therefore, His FELLOW-SERVANTS.

† 24. Of silver; gold is never to be supposed, unless mentioned.—*Bloomfield*. † 25. It was usual among the Jews for the family of the debtor to be sold for the benefit of the creditor. See 2 Kings iv. 1; Neh. v. 8. This bondage, however, only extended to *six* years. † 28. This was a Roman coin worth about 14 cents, or 7d.

‡ 21. Luke xvii. 3. 4.

κυριῳ αὑτων παντα τα γενομενα. 32 Τοτε
lord of them all that having been done. Then
προσκαλεσαμενος αυτον ὁ κυριος αυτου, λεγει
having called him the lord of him, says
αυτῳ· Δουλε πονηρε, πασαν την οφειλην εκεινην
to him; O slave wicked, all the debt that
αφηκα σοι, επει παρεκαλεσας με· 33 ουκ εδει
I remitted to thee, because thou besought me; not was it binding
και σε ελεησαι τον συνδουλον σου, ὡς και εγω
also thee to have pitied the fellow-slave of thee, as also I
σε ηλεησα; 34 Και οργισθεις ὁ κυριος αυτου
thee pitied? And being provoked the lord of him
παρεδωκεν αυτον τοις βασανισταις, ἑως οὑ αποδῳ
delivered him to the jailors, till he may pay
παν το οφειλομενον *[αυτῳ.] 35 Οὑτω και ὁ
all that owing [to him.] So also the
πατηρ μου ὁ επουρανιος ποιησει ὑμιν, εαν μη
father of me the heavenly will do to you, if not
αφητε ἑκαστος τῳ αδελφῳ αὑτου απο των
you forgive each one the brother of him from the
καρδιων ὑμων.
hearts of you.

ΚΕΦ. ιθ'. 19.

1 Και εγενετο, ὁτε ετελεσεν ὁ Ιησους τους
And it came to pass, when ended the Jesus the
λογους τουτους, μετηρεν απο της Γαλιλαιας,
words these, he departed from the Galilee,
και ηλθεν εις τα ὁρια της Ιουδαιας, περαν του
and came into the confines of the Judea, beyond the
Ιορδανου. 2 Και ηκολουθησαν αυτῳ οχλοι
Jordan. And followed him crowds
πολλοι· και εθεραπευσεν αυτους εκει.
great; and he healed them there.
3 Και προσηλθον αυτῳ οἱ Φαρισαιοι, πειρα-
And came to him the Pharisees try-
ζοντες αυτον, και λεγοντες *[αυτῳ·] Ει εξεστιν
ing him, and saying [to him;] If it is lawful
ανθρωπῳ απολυσαι την γυναικα αυτου κατα
to a man to release the wife of him upon
πασαν αιτιαν; 4 Ὁ δε αποκριθεις ειπεν αυτοις·
every cause; He and answering said to them;
Ουκ ανεγνωτε, ὁτι ὁ ποιησας απ' αρχης αρσεν
Not have you read, that the Creator from a beginning a male
και θηλυ εποιησεν αυτους; 5 και ειπεν· "Ἑνεκεν
and a female he made them? and says, "On account
τουτου καταλειψει ανθρωπος τον πατερα και
of this shall leave a man the father and
την μητερα, και προσκολληθησεται τη γυναικι
the mother, and shall be closely united to the wife
αὑτου· και εσονται οἱ δυο εις σαρκα μιαν."
of him; and shall be the two into flesh one."
6 Ὡστε ουκετι εισι δυο, αλλα σαρξ μια. Ὁ
So that no longer they are two, but flesh one. What
ουν ὁ θεος συνεζευξεν, ανθρωπος μη χωριζετω.
then the God has joined together, a man not disunites.
7 Λεγουσιν αυτῳ· Τι ουν Μωσης ενετειλατο
They say to him; Why then Moses did enjoin

going to their MASTER,
they related ALL that had
OCCURRED.
32 Then his MASTER
having called him, said to
him, 'O wicked SERVANT!
All that DEBT I forgave
thee, because thou didst
entreat me;
33 was it not binding
on thee also to have had
pity on thy FELLOW-SER-
VANT, as I also had pity
on thee?'
34 And his MASTER be-
ing provoked, delivered
him to the JAILORS, till
he should discharge the
DEBT.
35 Thus also will my
HEAVENLY FATHER treat
you, unless you from your
HEART, each one ‡forgive
his BROTHER."

CHAPTER XIX.

1 ‡And it happened,
when JESUS ended these
WORDS, he departed from
Galilee, and came into the
CONFINES of JUDEA, be-
yond the JORDAN.
2 And great Crowds fol-
lowed him, and he cured
their sick.
3 And the *Pharisees
came to him, trying him,
and saying, ‡"Is it law-
ful for a man to dismiss
his WIFE for Any Cause?"
4 And He answering,
said to them, "Have you
not read, That the CREA-
TOR, at the first, ‡made a
male and a female;
5 and said, ‡'On ac-
count of this a man shall
leave FATHER and MOTH-
ER, and adhere to his
WIFE; and they TWO shall
become one Flesh?'
6 So that they are no
longer Two, but one Flesh.
What GOD, then, has uni-
ted, let no man sever."
7 They say to him,
‡"Why then did Moses
command to give a Writ

* VATICAN MANUSCRIPT.—34. to him—omit. 3. Pharisees. 3. to him—omit.

‡ 35. Prov. xxi. 13; Matt. vii. 1, 2. ‡ 1. Mark x. 1. ‡ 3. Mark x. 2. ‡ 4. Gen. i. 27; Mal. ii. 15. ‡ 5. Gen. ii. 24, 1 Cor. vi. 16; Eph. v. 31. ‡ 7. Deut. xxiv. 1.

δουναι βιβλιον αποστασιου, και απολυσαι αυτην;
to give a scroll of separation, and to release her?
8 Λεγει αυτοις· Ὁτι Μωσης προς την σκλη-
He says to them; That Moses for the hardness
ροκαρδιαν ὑμων επετρεψεν ὑμιν απολυσαι τας
of heart of you suffered you to release the
γυναικας ὑμων· απ' αρχης δε ου γεγονεν οὑτω.
wives of you; from a beginning but not it was so.
9 Λεγω δε ὑμιν, ὁτι ὁς αν απολυσῃ την γυναικα
I say but to you, that whoever may release the wife
αυτου, μη επι πορνειᾳ, και γαμησῃ αλλην,
of him, except for fornication, and may marry another,
μοιχαται· και ὁ απολελυμενην γαμησας, μοι-
commits adultery; and he her being released marrying, com-
χαται. 10 Λεγουσιν αυτῳ οἱ μαθηται αυτου·
mits adultery. They say to him the disciples of him;
Ει οὑτως εστιν ἡ αιτια του ανθρωπου μετα της
If thus is the case of the man with the
γυναικος, ου συμφερει γαμησαι. 11 Ὁ δε ειπεν
woman, not it is profitable to marry. He but said
αυτοις· Ου παντες χωρουσι τον λογον τουτον,
to them, Not all admit the word this,
αλλ' οἱς δεδοται. 12 Εισι γαρ ευνουχοι,
but to whom it has been given. There are for eunuchs,
οἱτινες εκ κοιλιας μητρος εγεννηθησαν οὑτω·
who from womb of mother were born so;
και εισιν ευνουχοι, οἱτινες ευνουχισθησαν ὑπο
and there are eunuchs, who were made eunuchs by
των ανθρωπων· και εισιν ευνουχοι, οἱτινες ευνου-
the men; and there are eunuchs, who made
χισαν ἑαυτους δια την βασιλειαν των ουρα-
eunuchs themselves on account of the kingdom of the heav-
νων. Ὁ δυναμενος χωρειν, χωρειτω.
ens. He being able to admit, let him admit.

13 Τοτε προσηνεχθη αυτῳ παιδια, ἱνα τας
Then were brought to him little children, that the
χειρας επιθῃ αυτοις, και προσευξηται· οἱ
hands he might lay on them, and he might pray; the
δε μαθηται επετιμησαν αυτοις. 14 Ὁ δε Ιησους
but disciples rebuked them. The and Jesus
ειπεν· Αφετε τα παιδια, και μη κωλυετε αυτα
said; Suffer the little children, and not hinder them
ελθειν προς με· των γαρ τοιουτων εστιν ἡ
to come to me; of the for such like is the
βασιλεια των ουρανων. 15 Και επιθεις αυτοις
kingdom of the heavens. And laying on them
τας χειρας, επορευθη εκειθεν.
the hands, he departed thence.

16 Και ιδου, εἱς προσελθων, ειπεν αυτῳ· Δι-
And lo, one coming, said to him; O
δασκαλε αγαθε, τι αγαθον ποιησω, ἱνα εχω
teacher good, what good must I do, that I may have

of Divorce, and dismiss her?"

8 He says to them, "Moses, indeed, permitted you to divorce your WIVES, on account of your STUBBORN DISPOSITION; but from the Beginning it was not so.

9 ‡ But I say to you, Whoever dismisses his WIFE, except *on Account of Whoredom, causes her to commit adultery; and HE who MARRIES the divorced woman, commits adultery."

10 *The DISCIPLES say to him, "If the CASE of the HUSBAND with his WIFE be thus, it is not good to marry."

11 But HE answered, ‡"None can admit *the WORD, but those to whom it is given.

12 For there are some Eunuchs, by natural constitution; others have been made Eunuchs by MEN; and † ‡ others have made themselves Eunuchs on account of the KINGDOM of the HEAVENS. HE who is ABLE to do this, let him do it."

13 ‡ Then they brought to him Little children, that he might place his HANDS on them, and pray; and the DISCIPLES rebuked them.

14 But Jesus said, "Let the LITTLE CHILDREN alone, and forbid them not to come to me; ‡ because to SUCH AS THESE belongs the KINGDOM of the HEAVENS."

15 And having laid his hands on them, he departed thence.

16 ‡ And behold, one approaching, said *to him,

---

* VATICAN MANUSCRIPT.—9. on Account of Whoredom, causes her to commit adultery; and HE who MARRIES. 10. The DISCIPLES. 11. the WORD. 16. to him, said, "O Teacher!"

† 12. A highly figurative mode of expression, similar to what is found in Matt. v. 29, 30; xviii. 8, 9. The amputation of the desire, not of the member, is here intended, as is evident from the two species of eunuchism previously mentioned. It was so understood by Justin Martyr, Chrysostom, Tertullian, &c., except Origen, who not only interpreted the words *literally*, but is said to have exemplified them upon himself.—See *Analecta Theologica*.

‡ 9. Matt. v. 32; Mark x. 11; Luke xvi. 18; 1 Cor. vii. 10. ‡ 11. 1 Cor. vii. 2, 7, 9, 17. ‡ 12. 1 Cor. vii. 32—34. ‡ 13. Mark x. 13. ‡ 14. Matt. v. 3; xviii. 3. ‡ 16. Mark x. 17; Luke xviii. 18.

ζωην αιωνιον; 17 Ὁ δε ειπεν αυτῳ· Τι με
life age-lasting? He and he said to him; Why me
ερωτᾳς περι του αγαθου; εἷς εστιν ὁ αγαθος.
askest thou concerning the good? one is the good.
Ει δε θελεις εισελθειν εις την ζωην, τηρησον
If but thou wishest to enter into the life, keep strictly
τας εντολας. 18 Λεγει αυτῳ· Ποιας; Ὁ δε
the commandments. He says to him; Which? The and
Ιησους ειπε· Το· "Ου φονευσεις· Ου μοι-
Jesus said; This; Not thou shalt kill; Not thou shalt
χευσεις· Ου κλεψεις· Ου ψευδομαρτυρη-
commit adultery; Not thou shalt steal; Not thou shalt testify
σεις· 19 Τιμα τον πατερα και την μητερα." και·
falsely; Honor the father and the mother;" and;
"Αγαπησεις τον πλησιον σου ὡς σεαυτον."
"Thou shalt love the neighbor of thee as thyself"
20 Λεγει αυτῳ ὁ νεανισκος· Παντα ταυτα εφυ-
Says to him the young man; All these I
λαξαμην *[εκ νεοτητος μου·] τι ετι ὑστερω;
kept [from childhood of me:] what more do I want?
21 Εφη αυτῳ ὁ Ιησους· Ει θελεις τελειος
Said to him the Jesus: If thou wishest perfect
ειναι, ὑπαγε, πωλησον σου τα ὑπαρχοντα, και
to be, go, sell of thee the possessions, and
δος πτωχοις· και ἑξεις θησαυρον εν ουρα-
give to poor· and thou shalt have treasure in hea-
νῳ· και δευρο, ακολουθει μοι. 22 Ακουσας δε ὁ
ven: and hither, follow me. Having heard and the
νεανισκος τον λογον, απηλθε λυπουμενος· ην
young man the word, went away sorrowing: he was
γαρ εχων κτηματα πολλα. 23 Ὁ δε Ιησους
for having possessions many. The and Jesus
ειπε τοις μαθηταις αὑτου· Αμην λεγω ὑμιν, ὁτι
said to the disciples of himself: Indeed I say to you, that
δυσκολως πλουσιος εισελευσονται εις την βασι-
with difficulty a rich man shall enter into the king-
λειαν των ουρανων. 24 Παλιν δε λεγω ὑμιν.
dom of the heavens. Again and I say to you;
ευκοπωτερον εστι καμηλον δια τρυπηματος ῥα-
easier it is a camel through a hole of a
φιδος εισελθειν, η πλουσιον εις την βασιλειαν
needle to pass, than a rich man into the kingdom
του θεου εισελθειν. 25 Ακουσαντες δε οἱ μαθη-
of the God to enter. Having heard and the disci-
ται, εξεπλησσοντο σφοδρα, λεγοντες· Τις αρα
ples, were amazed exceedingly, saying: Who then

"Good Teacher! what good
thing must I do, that I
may obtain aionian Life?"
17 And HE said to him,
* †"Why dost thou call Me
GOOD? GOD alone is good.
If, however, thou desirest
to enter that LIFE, keep
the COMMANDMENTS."
18 He says to him,
"Which?" JESUS answered,
"These; ‡ 'Thou
'shalt not commit murder;
'Thou shalt not commit
'adultery; Thou shalt not
'steal; Thou shalt not
'testify falsely;
19 'Honor thy FATHER
'and thy MOTHER;' and
'‡ 'Thou shalt love thy
'NEIGHBOR as thyself.'"
20 The YOUNG MAN
says to him, "All these
have I kept; what want I
more?"
21 JESUS replied, "If
thou desirest to be perfect,
go, sell thy POSSESSIONS,
and give to the * POOR;
and thou shalt have Treasure
in Heaven; and come,
follow me."
22 But the YOUNG MAN
having heard this WORD,
went away sorrowing; for
he had great * Riches.
23 Then JESUS said to
his DISCIPLES, ‡ "Indeed
I say to you, That it will
be difficult for a Rich man
to enter the KINGDOM of
the HEAVENS.
24 And again I say to
you, † It is easier for a
Camel to pass through a
Needle's Eye than for a
Rich man to enter the
KINGDOM † of GOD."
25 And the DISCIPLES
hearing, were greatly as-

* VATICAN MANUSCRIPT.—17. "Why askest thou Me concerning THAT which is GOOD? One is the GOOD: but if thou wilt." 20. from my childhood—*omit*. 21. POOR. 22. this WORD. 22. Riches.

† 17. The Common reading has been preferred to either Griesbach's text, or the Vatican MS. George Campbell regards the evidence for it from the majority of MSS., to be vastly superior. The versions on both sides nearly balance each other; but the internal evidence arising from the connection of the thoughts, is decisive on the point. Besides it corresponds with both Mark and Luke, who record the same conversation, in nearly the same words, and no different reading is noted. † 24. Rabbins, as well as Arabs, were accustomed, in describing an impossibility, or a high degree of improbability, to say, "It will not happen before a camel, or an elephant, has crept through the eye of a needle."—*Marsh's Translation of Michaelis.* † 24. of HEAVEN.—*Lachmann & Tischendorf.*

‡ 18. Exod. xx. 13; Deut. v. 17. ‡ 19. Lev. xix. 18. ‡ 23. Mark x. 24; Luke xviii. 24; 1 Tim. vi. 9, 10.

δυναται σωθηναι; [26] Εμβλεψας δε ὁ Ιησους
is able to be saved? Looking but the Jesus
ειπεν αυτοις· Παρα ανθρωποις τουτο αδυνατον
said to him: With man this impossible
εστι· παρα δε θεῳ παντα δυνατα.
is: with but God all possible.

[27] Τοτε αποκριθεις ὁ Πετρος ειπεν αυτῳ· Ιδου,
Then answering the Peter said to him; Lo,
ἡμεις αφηκαμεν παντα, και ηκολουθησαμεν σοι·
we left all, and followed thee;
τι αρα εσται ἡμιν; [28] Ὁ δε Ιησους ειπεν αυ-
what then shall be to us? The and Jesus said to
τοις· Αμην λεγω ὑμιν, ὁτι ὑμεις οἱ ακολουθη-
them; Indeed I say to you, that you the having fol-
σαντες μοι, εν τῃ παλιγγενεσιᾳ ὁταν καθισῃ ὁ
lowed me, in the new birth day when may sit the
υἱος του ανθρωπου επι θρονου δοξης αὑτου,
son of the man upon a throne of glory of him,
καθισεσθε και ὑμεις επι δωδεκα θρονους, κρινον-
shall sit also you upon twelve thrones, judg-
τες τας δωδεκα φυλας του Ισραηλ. [29] Και πας
ing the twelve tribes of the Israel And all
ὁς αφηκεν οικιας, η αδελφους, η αδελφας, η
who left houses, or brothers, or sisters, or
πατερα, η μητερα, *[η γυναικα,] η τεκνα, η
father, or mother, [or wife,] or children, or
αγρους, ἑνεκεν του ονοματος μου, ἑκατοντα-
fields, on account of the name of me, a hundred
πλασιονα ληψεται, και ζωην αιωνιον κληρο-
fold shall receive, and life age-lasting shall
νομησει.
inherit.

[30] Πολλοι δε εσονται πρωτοι, εσχατοι· και
Many but shall be first, last; and
εσχατοι, πρωτοι. ΚΕΦ. κ'. 20. [1] Ὁμοια γαρ
last, first. Like for
εστιν ἡ βασιλεια των ουρανων ανθρωπῳ οικοδεσ-
is the kingdom of the heavens to a man a house-
ποτῃ, ὁστις εξηλθεν ἁμα πρωι μισθωσασθαι
holder, who went out with morning to hire
εργατας εις τον αμπελωνα αὑτου. [2] Συμφω-
laborers into the vineyard of him. Having
νησας δε μετα των εργατων εκ δηναριου την
agreed and with the laborers for a denarius the
ἡμεραν, απεστειλεν αυτους εις τον αμπελωνα
day, he sent them into the vineyard
αὑτου. [3] Και εξελθων περι τριτην ὡραν, ειδεν
of him. And going out about third hour, he saw
αλλους ἑστωτας εν τῃ αγορᾳ αργους· [4] κακει-
others standing in the market-place idle: and to
νοις ειπεν· Ὑπαγετε και ὑμεις εις τον αμπελωνα·
them he said: Go also you into the vineyard:

tonished, saying, "Who then can be saved?"

26 JESUS looking at them, answered, "With Men this is impossible; but with God everything is possible."

27 ‡Then PETER replying, said to him, "Behold, ‡we have forsaken all, and followed thee; what, therefore, shall we obtain?"

28 And JESUS said to them, "Indeed, I say to you, That in the RENOVATION, †when the SON of MAN shall sit on the throne of his Glory, ‡you, my FOLLOWERS, shall also sit on Twelve Thrones, judging the TWELVE Tribes of ISRAEL.

29 ‡And whoever has forsaken, *on account of MY Name, Houses, or Brothers, or Sisters, or Father, or Mother, or Wife, or Children, or Lands, shall receive *Manifold, and shall inherit aionian Life.

30 ‡But many shall be first, that are last; and last, that are first.

CHAPTER XX.

1 For the KINGDOM of the HEAVENS resembles a Householder, who went out early in the Morning, to hire Laborers for his VINEYARD.

2 And having agreed with some LABORERS for a †Denarius a DAY, he sent them into his VINEYARD.

3 And going out about the †Third Hour, he saw others standing unemployed in the market-place;

4 and he said to THEM, 'Go YOU also into the

* VATICAN MANUSCRIPT.—29. on account of MY Name. 29. or Wife—*omit.* 29. Manifold.

† 28. That glorious moral, social, political, religious, and physical change which will be introduced by the Messiah, who says, "Behold, I make all things new," Rev. xxi. 5. † 2. A denarius is the eighth part of an ounce—value 14 cents, or 7d. † 3. Nine in the morning.

‡ 27. Mark x. 28; Luke xviii. 28. ‡ 27. Matt. iv. 20; Luke v. 11. ‡ 28. Luke xxii. 30 ‡ 29. Mark x. 29, 30; Luke xviii. 29, 30. ‡ 30. Matt. xx. 16; Luke xiii. 30.

και ὁ εαν ῃ δικαιον, δώσω ὑμιν. Οἱ δε
and whatever may be just, I will give to you. They and
απηλθον. 5 Παλιν εξελθων περι ἑκτην και
went away. Again going out about sixth and
εννατην ὡραν, εποιησεν ὡσαυτως. 6 Περι δε
ninth hour, he did in like manner. About and
την ἑνδεκατην *[ὡραν] εξελθων, εὑρεν αλλους
the eleventh [hour] going out, he found others
ἑστωτας, και λεγει αυτοις· Τι ὡδε ἑστηκατε
standing, and he says to them: Why here stood you
ὁλην την ἡμεραν αργοι; 7 Λεγουσιν αὐτῳ· Ὁτι
all the day idle? They say to him Because
ουδεις ἡμας εμισθωσατο. Λεγει αυτοις· Ὑπα-
no one us hired. He says to them: Go
γετε και ὑμεις εις τον αμπελωνα· *[και ὁ εαν
also you into the vineyard: [and whatever
ῃ δικαιον, ληψεσθε.] 8 Οψιας δε γενο-
may be just, you shall receive.] Evening and having
μενης, λεγει ὁ κυριος του αμπελωνος τῳ
come on, says the lord of the vineyard to the
επιτροπῳ αὐτου· Καλεσον τους εργατας, και
steward of him; Call the laborers, and
αποδος αυτοις τον μισθον, αρξαμενος απο των
give to them the hire, beginning from the
εσχατων, ἑως των πρωτων. 9 Και ελθοντες οἱ
last, till the first. And having come those
περι την ἑνδεκατην ὡραν, ελαβον ανα δηναριον.
about the eleventh hour, received each a denarius.
10 Ελθοντες δε οἱ πρωτοι, ενομισαν, ὁτι πλειονα
Having come then those first, supposed, that more
ληψονται· και ελαβον και αυτοι ανα δηναριον.
they shall receive. and received also they each a denarius.
11 Λαβοντες δε εγογγυζον κατα του οικοδεσποτου,
Having received but they murmured against the householder,
12 λεγοντες· Ὁτι οὑτοι οἱ εσχατοι μιαν ὡραν
saying; That these the last one hour
εποιησαν, και ισους ἡμιν αυτους εποιησας, τοις
worked, and equal to us them thou hast made, to the
βαστασασι το βαρος της ἡμερας, και τον καυ-
having endured the burden of the day, and the burn-
σωνα. 13 Ὁ δε αποκριθεις ειπεν ἑνι αυτων·
ing heat. He but answering said to one of them;
Ἑταιρε, ουκ αδικω σε· ουχι δηναριου συνεφω-
Friend, not I wrong thee; not of a denarius didst thou
νησας μοι; 14 Αρον το σον, και ὑπαγε. Θελω
agree to me? Take the thine, and go. I wish
δε τουτῳ τῳ εσχατῳ δουναι ὡς και σοι. 15 Η
and to this the last to give as also to thee. Or
ουκ εξεστι μοι ποιησαι ὁ θελω εν τοις εμοις;
not is it lawful to me to do what I will with the my own?
η ὁ οφθαλμος σου πονηρος εστιν, ὁτι εγω
or the eye of thee evil is, because I
αγαθος ειμι; 16 Οὑτως εσονται οἱ εσχατοι,
good am? Thus shall be the last,

VINEYARD, and whatever
is reasonable, I will give
you.' And THEY went.
5 Again having gone
out about the †sixth hour,
and about the †ninth, he
did in like manner.
6 And about the †ELEV-
ENTH, going out, he found
others standing, and says
to them, 'Why stood you
here All the day unem-
ployed?'
7 They say to him, 'Be-
cause no one has hired
us." He says to them,
'Go you also into the
VINEYARD.'
8 And Evening having
come on, the OWNER of
the VINEYARD says to his
STEWARD, 'Call the LA-
BORERS, and give them
their WAGES, beginning
with the LAST, and end-
ing with the FIRST.'
9 And THOSE who came
about the ELEVENTH
hour, received each one,
a Denarius.
10 Then THOSE who
came FIRST, expected that
they should receive more;
and they also received,
each one, a Denarius.
11 But having received
it, they murmured against
the HOUSEHOLDER,
12 saying, 'These LAST
have worked One Hour,
and thou hast made them
equal to us, who have EN-
DURED the BURDEN and
the SCORCHING HEAT of
the DAY.'
13 He answering said
to one of them, 'Friend,
I do not injure thee; didst
not thou agree with me
for a Denarius?
14 Take THAT which is
THINE, and go thy way;
*I will give to This LAST,
even as to thee.
15 Is it not lawful for
me to do what I please
with MY OWN? Is thine
EYE envious, Because I
am liberal?'
16 Thus the LAST shall

* VATICAN MANUSCRIPT.—6. hour—*omit*. 7. and whatever may be right, you shall receive.—*omit*. 14. I will.

† 5. Noon. † 5. Three o'clock in the afternoon. † 6. Five o'clock in the afternoon.

πρωτοι· και οἱ πρωτοι, εσχατοι. *[Πολλοι
first; and the first, last. [Many
γαρ εισι κλητοι, ολιγοι δε εκλεκτοι.]
for are called, few but chosen.]

17 Και αναβαινων ὁ Ιησους εις Ἱεροσολυμα,
And going up the Jesus to Jerusalem,
παρελαβε τους δωδεκα μαθητας κατ' ιδιαν εν
he took the twelve disciples privately in
τῃ ὁδῳ, και ειπεν αυτοις· 18 Ιδου, αναβαινομεν
the way, and said to them; Lo, we go up
εις Ἱεροσολυμα, και ὁ υἱος του ανθρωπου παρα-
to Jerusalem, and the son of the man will be
δοθησεται τοις αρχιερευσι και γραμματευσι· και
delivered up to the high-priests and scribes; and
κατακρινουσιν αυτον *[θανατῳ,] 19 και παρα-
they will condemn him [to death,] and they will
δωσουσιν αυτον τοις εθνεσιν εις το εμπαιξαι,
deliver up him to the Gentiles for the to mock,
και μαστιγωσαι, και σταυρωσαι· και τῃ τριτῃ
and to scourge, and to crucify; and in the third
ἡμερᾳ αναστησεται.
day he will stand up.

20 Τοτε προσηλθεν αυτῳ ἡ μητηρ των υἱων
Then came to him the mother of the sons
Ζεβεδαιου, μετα των υἱων αὐτης, προσκυνουσα,
of Zebedee, with the sons of her, prostrating,
και αιτουσα τι παρ' αυτου. 21 Ὁ δε ειπεν
and asking something from him. He and said
αυτῃ· Τι θελεις; Λεγει *[αυτῳ·] Ειπε, ἱνα
to her; What wilt thou? She says [to him;] Say, that
καθισωσιν αὑτοι οἱ δυο υἱοι μου, εἱς εκ δεξιων
may sit these the two sons of me, one at right
σου, και εἱς εξ ευωνυμων σου, εν τῃ βασιλειᾳ
of thee, and one at left of thee, in the kingdom
σου. 22 Αποκριθεις δε ὁ Ιησους ειπεν· Ουκ οι-
of thee. Answering but the Jesus said; Not you
δατε, τι αιτεισθε. Δυνασθε πιειν το ποτηριον,
know, what you ask. Are you able to drink the cup,
ὁ εγω μελλω πινειν; Λεγουσιν αυτῳ· Δυ-
which I am about to drink? They say to him; We
ναμεθα. 23 *[Και] λεγει αυτοις· Το μεν πο-
are able. [And] he says to them; The indeed
τηριον μου πιεσθε· το δε καθισαι εκ δεξιων
cup of me you shall drink; the but to sit at right
μου και εξ ευωνυμων μου, ουκ εστιν εμον δουναι,
of me and at left of me, not is mine to give,
αλλ' οἱς ἡτοιμασται ὑπο του πατρος μου.
but to whom it has been prepared by the father of me.
24 Και ακουσαντες οἱ δεκα, ηγανακτησαν περι
And having heard the ten, were angry on account of
των δυο αδελφων. 25 Ὁ δε Ιησους, προσκαλε-
the two brothers. The but Jesus, having

be ‡ first; and the FIRST, last."

17 ‡ And * when Jesus was about to go up to Jerusalem, he took the TWELVE Disciples privately, * and said to them on the WAY,

18 ‡ "Behold, we go up to Jerusalem; and the SON of MAN will be delivered to the HIGH-PRIESTS and Scribes, and they will condemn him;

19 and will deliver him to the GENTILES, to be MOCKED, and scourged, and crucified, and on the THIRD Day he will rise.

20 ‡ Then the MOTHER of Zebedee's CHILDREN came to him with her SONS, prostrating, and requesting something from him.

21 And HE said to her, "What dost thou wish?" * And SHE said, "Command, that in thy KINGDOM, one of These my TWO Sons may sit at thy Right hand, and the other at thy Left."

22 But Jesus answering, said, "You know not what you request. Can you drink of ‡ the CUP, of which I am about to drink?" They say to him, "We can."

23 He says to them, ‡ "You will, indeed, drink of my CUP; but to sit at my Right hand, and at * the Left, is not mine to give, except for whom it has been prepared by my FATHER."

24 ‡ And the TEN, having heard, were indignant against the TWO Brothers.

25 But JESUS, having called them, said, "You

* VATICAN MANUSCRIPT.—16. For many are called, but few chosen—*omit.* 17. when Jesus was about to go up to Jerusalem, he took. 17. and said to them on the WAY. 18. to Death—*omit.* 21. And SHE said. 21. to him—*omit.* 23. And—*omit.* 23. the Left.

† 23. This was fulfilled, when "Herod killed James, the BROTHER of John, with a sword," Acts xii. 2; and when John was banished to "THAT ISLE which is CALLED Patmos, for the WORD of GOD, and for the TESTIMONY of Jesus Christ," Rev. i. 9.

‡ 16. Matt. xix. 30. ‡ 17. Matt. xvi. 21; Mark x. 32; Luke xviii. 31; John xii. 12. ‡ 20. Matt. iv. 21; Mark x. 35. ‡ 22. Matt. xxvi. 39, 42; Mark xiv. 36; Luke xxii. 42; John xviii. 11. ‡ 23. Acts xii. 2; Rom. viii. 17; 2 Cor. i. 7; Rev. i. 9. ‡ 24. Mark x. 41; Luke xxii. 24.

σαμενος αυτους, ειπεν Οιδατε, ὁτι οἱ αρχοντες
called them, said; You know, that the rulers
των εθνων κατακυριευουσιν αυτων, και οἱ μεγαλοι
of the nations domineer over them, and the great
κατεξουσιαζουσιν αυτων. 26 Ουκ οὑτως εσται
exercise authority over them. Not thus it shall be
εν ὑμιν· αλλ' ὁς εαν θελῃ εν ὑμιν μεγας
among you: but whoever may wish among you great
γενεσθαι, εστω ὑμων διακονος· 27 και ὁς εαν
to become, let him be of you a servant; and whoever
θελῃ εν ὑμιν ειναι πρωτος, εστω ὑμων
may wish among you to be first, let him be of you
δουλος· 28 ὡσπερ ὁ υἱος του ανθρωπου ουκ ηλθε
a slave: even as the son of the man not came
διακονηθηναι αλλα διακονησαι, και δουναι την
to be served but to serve, and to give the
ψυχην αὑτου λυτρον αντι πολλων.
life of him a ransom for many.
29 Και εκπορευομενων αυτων απο Ἱεριχω,
And departing of them from Jericho,
ηκολουθησεν αυτῳ οχλος πολυς. 30 Και ιδου,
followed him a crowd great. And lo,
δυο τυφλοι, καθημενοι παρα την ὁδον, ακουσαν-
two blind (men,) sitting by the way, hear-
τες ὁτι Ιησους παραγει, εκραξαν, λεγοντες·
ing that Jesus passes by, cried out, saying;
Ελεησον ἡμας, κυριε, υἱος Δαυιδ. 31 Ὁ δε οχλος
Pity us, O lord, son of David. The and crowd
επετιμησεν αυτοις, ἱνα σιωπησωσιν. Οἱ δε
reproved them, that they might be silent. They but
μειζον εκραζον, λεγοντες· Ελεησον ἡμας, κυριε,
more did cry out, saying; Pity us, O lord,
υἱος Δαυιδ. 32 Και στας ὁ Ιησους εφω-
son of David. And having stopped the Jesus he
νησεν αυτους, και ειπε· Τι θελετε ποιησω
called them, and said; What do you wish I should do
ὑμιν; 33 Λεγουσιν αυτῳ. Κυριε, ἱνα ανοιχθωσιν
to you? They say to him; O lord, that may be opened
ἡμων οἱ οφθαλμοι. 34 Σπλαγχνισθεις δε ὁ
of us the eyes. Being moved with pity and the
Ιησους, ἡψατο των οφθαλμων αυτων· και ευ-
Jesus, he touched the eyes of them; and im-
θεως ανεβλεψαν αυτων οἱ οφθαλμοι· και ηκο-
mediately saw again of them the eyes: and they
λουθησαν αυτῳ.
followed him.

ΚΕΦ. κα'. 21.

1 Και ὁτε ηγγισαν εις Ἱεροσολυμα, και ηλθον
And when they were nigh to Jerusalem, and had come
εις Βηθφαγη προς το ορος των ελαιων, τοτε ὁ
to Bethphage by the mountain of the olive-trees, then the
Ιησους απεστειλε δυο μαθητας, λεγων αυτοις·
Jesus sent away two disciples, saying to them:
2 Πορευθητε εις την κωμην την απεναντι ὑμων,
You may go to the village the over against you,
και ευθεως εὑρησετε ονον δεδεμενην, και πωλον
and immediately you will find an ass having been bound, and a foal

know That the PRINCES of the NATIONS rule imperiously over them; and the GREAT exercise authority over them.

26 ‡It *is not so among you; but whoever may desire to become great among you, let him be Your Servant;

27 ‡and whoever may desire to be chief, let him be Your Slave;

28 ‡even as the SON of MAN came not to be served, but to serve, and ‡to give his LIFE a Ransom for many."

29 ‡And departing from Jericho, a great Crowd followed him.

30 And behold, Two blind men sitting by the ROAD, hearing That Jesus passed by, cried out, saying, "O Master, Son of David, have pity on us!"

31 And the PEOPLE reproved them, that they might be silent; but THEY cried the louder, saying, "O Master, Son of David, have pity on us!"

32 And JESUS stopping, called them, and said, "What do you wish I should do for you?"

33 They say to him, "Sir, that *our EYES may be opened."

34 And Jesus being moved with compassion, touched *Their EYES; and *they received sight, and followed him.

CHAPTER XXI.

1 ‡And when they were nigh to Jerusalem, and had come to Bethphage, near to the MOUNT of OLIVES, then JESUS sent Two Disciples, saying to them,

2 "Go to THAT VILLAGE which is OVER-AGAINST you, and you will immediately find an Ass

* VATICAN MANUSCRIPT.—26. is not so. 33. our EYES. 34. Their EYES. 34. they received sight.

‡ 26. Matt. xxiii. 11; 1 Pet. v. 3. ‡ 27. Matt. xviii. 4; Mark ix. 35; x. 43. ‡ 28. Luke xxii. 27; John xiii. 4, 14; Phil. ii. 7. ‡ 28. Isa. liii. 10, 11; Dan. ix. 24, 26; Matt. xxvi. 28; 1 Tim. ii. 6; Titus ii. 14; Heb. ix. 28. ‡ 1. Mark xi. 1; Luke xix. 29.

μετ' αυτης· λυσαντες αγαγετε μοι. 3 Και εαν
with her; having loosed bring to me. And if
τις ὑμιν ειπῃ τι, ερειτε· Ὅτι ὁ
any (one) to you should say any (thing,) you shall say; That the
κυριος αυτων χρειαν εχει· ευθεως δε αποσ-
lord of them need has; immediately and he will
τελλει αυτους. 4 Τουτο δε ὁλον γεγονεν, ἱνα
send them. This and all has been done, that
πληρωθῃ το ῥηθεν δια του προφητου,
might be fulfilled the word spoken through the prophet,
λεγοντος· 5 "Ειπατε τῃ θυγατρι Σιων· Ιδου,
saying; "Say to the daughter of Zion; Lo,
ὁ βασιλευς σου ερχεται σοι πραυς, και επιβε-
the king of thee comes to thee meek, and having
βηκως επι ονον, και πωλον υἱον ὑποζυγιου."
been set on an ass, even a foal a son of a beast of burden."
6 Πορευθεντες δε οἱ μαθηται, και ποιησαντες
Having gone and the disciples, and having done
καθως προσεταξεν αυτοις ὁ Ιησους, 7 ηγαγον
as commanded to them the Jesus, they led
την ονον και τον πωλον, και επεθηκαν επανω
the ass and the foal, and they placed upon
αυτων τα ἱματια αυτων· και επεκαθισεν επανω
them the mantles of them; and they caused to sit on (one)
αυτων. 8 Ὁ δε πλειστος οχλος εστρωσαν ἑαυ-
of them. The and greater crowd spread of them-
των τα ἱματια εν τῃ ὁδῳ· αλλοι δε εκοπτον
selves the mantles in the way; others and cut off
κλαδους απο των δενδρων, και εστρωννυον εν
branches from the trees, and scattered in
τῃ ὁδῳ. 9 Οἱ δε οχλοι οἱ προαγοντες και οἱ
the way. The and crowds those going before and those
ακολουθουντες εκραζον, λεγοντες· Ὡσαννα τῳ
following did cry, saying; Hosanna to the
υἱῳ Δαυιδ· ευλογημενος ὁ ερχομενος εν ονοματι
son of David; worthy of blessing he coming in name
κυριου· ὡσαννα εν τοις ὑψιστοις. 10 Και εισελ-
of Lord: hosanna in the highest. And having
θοντος αυτου εις Ἱεροσολυμα, εσεισθη πασα
entered of them into Jerusalem, was moved all
ἡ πολις, λεγουσα· Τις εστιν οὑτος; 11 Οἱ
the city, saying: Who is this? The
δε οχλοι ελεγον· Οὑτος εστιν Ιησους ὁ προφη-
and crowds said: This is Jesus the prophet,

tied, and a Colt with her; loose them, and bring them to me.

3 And if any one questions you, reply, 'That the MASTER wants them;' and he will send them promptly."

4 Now all this was performed, that the WORD SPOKEN through the PROPHET might be verified, saying,

5 ‡"Say to the DAUGHTER of Zion, Behold thy "KING comes to thee, "lowly, †being seated on "an Ass, even *on a Colt "of a Laboring Beast."

6 ‡And the DISCIPLES went, and having done as JESUS directed them,

7 they led the ASS, and the COLT, and ‡put their MANTLES over them, and made him ride.

8 And a GREAT PART of the Crowd spread *Their own GARMENTS on the ROAD; and others cut Branches from the TREES, and scattered them on the ROAD.

9 And THOSE CROWDS *PRECEDING him, and THOSE that FOLLOWED, shouted, saying, †"Hosanna to the SON of David! ‡'Blessed be HE who 'COMES in the Name of 'Jehovah.' Hosanna in the HIGHEST heaven!"

10 ‡And having entered Jerusalem, the Whole CITY was in commotion, asking, "Who is this?"

11 And the CROWDS answered, "This is Jesus, THAT PROPHET who

* VATICAN MANUSCRIPT.—5. on a Colt. 8. Their-own GARMENTS. 9. PRECEDING him, and.

† 5. Christ's triumphant entry into Jerusalem riding on an ass, has been objected to as mean and ridiculous, but it ought to be remembered that this circumstance was an exact fulfillment of Ezek. ix. 9, and exemplified at the same time his strict observance of the divine law. Eastern asses are much larger and more beautiful than ours, and kings and patriarchs did not disdain to ride on them. Compare Gen. xxii. 3; Exod. iv. 20; Num. xxii. 21; Judges v. 10; x. 4; 2 Sam. xvi. 2; xvii. 23; xix. 26; 1 Kings i. 33, 34. When Solomon and succeeding princes multiplied horses they were rebuked by the prophets, and chastised by God for it. See Isa. ii. 6, 7; xxxi. 1; Hos. xiv. 3. Compare also Hos. i. 7; Micah v. 10, 11; Zech. ix. 10. † 9. Hosanna, is a Hebrew word, signifying, "Save, we beseech thee!" and in this place is similar to the French "*vive le roi*," or the English "God save the king." "Hosanna to the SON of David," is equivalant to "God preserve the SON of David."

‡ 5. Isa. lxii. 11; Zech ix. 9; John xii. 15. ‡ 6. Mark xi. 4. ‡ 7. 2 Kings ix. 13; ‡ 9. Psa. cxviii. 26. ‡ 10. Mark xi. 15.

της, ὁ απο Ναζαρετ της Γαλιλαιας. 12 Και
that from Nazareth of the Galilee. And
εισηλθεν ὁ Ιησους εις το ἱερον *[του θεου,]
entered the Jesus into the temple [of the God,]
και εξεβαλε παντας τους πωλουντας και αγορα-
and cast out all the selling and buy-
ζοντας εν τῳ ἱερῳ, και τας τραπεζας των κολλυ-
ing in the temple, and the tables of the money-
βιστων κατεστρεψε, και τας καθεδρας των
changers overturned and the seats of the
πωλουντων τας περιστερας· 13 και λεγει αυ-
selling the doves: and he says to
τοις· Γεγραπται· "Ὁ οικος μου, οικος προσευχης
them: It is written: "The house of me, a house of prayer
κληθησεται· ὑμεις δε αυτον εποιησατε σπηλαιον
shall be called: you but it have made a den
ληστων." 14 Και προσηλθον αυτῳ τυφλοι και
of robbers." And came to him blind and
χωλοι εν τῳ ἱερῳ, και εθεραπευσεν αυτους.
lame in the temple, and he healed them.
15 Ιδοντες δε οἱ αρχιερεις και οἱ γραμματεις τα
Having seen but the high-priests and the scribes the
θαυμασια, ἁ εποιησε, και τους παιδας κρα-
wonders, which he did, and the boys cry-
ζοντας εν τῳ ἱερῳ, και λεγοντας· Ὡσαννα τῳ
ing in the temple, and saying; Hosanna to the
υἱῳ Δαυιδ· ηγανακτησαν, 16 και ειπον αυτῳ·
son of David; they were angry, and said to him;
Ακουεις τι οὑτοι λεγουσιν; Ὁ δε Ιησους
Hearest thou what these are saying? The and Jesus
λεγει αυτοις· Ναι· ουδεποτε ανεγνωτε· "Ὁτι
says to them; Yes; never have you read; "That
εκ στοματος νηπιων και θηλαζοντων κατηρ-
out of mouth of babes and of sucking (ones) thou hast
τισω αινον;" 17 Και καταλιπων αυτους,
perfected praise?" And having left them,
εξηλθεν εξω της πολεως εις Βηθανιαν, και
he went out of the city into Bethany, and
ηυλισθη εκει.
he lodged there.

18 Πρωιας δε, επαναγων εις την πολιν, επει-
Early but, returning into the city, he was
νασε. 19 Και ιδων συκην μιαν επι της ὁδου,
hungry. And seeing a fig-tree one by the way,
ηλθεν επ' αυτην, και ουδεν εὑρεν εν αυτῃ ει μη
he came to her, and nothing found in her except
φυλλα μονον· και λεγει αυτῃ· Μηκετι εκ σου
leaves alone; and he says to her; No more by thee
καρπος γενηται εις τον αιωνα. Και εξη-
fruit may be produced to the age. And with-
ρανθη παραχρημα ἡ συκη. 20 Και ιδοντες οἱ
ered immediately the fig-tree. And seeing the
μαθηται εθαυμασαν, λεγοντες· Πως παραχρημα
disciples wondered, saying: How soon
εξηρανθη ἡ συκη; 21 Αποκριθεις δε ὁ Ιησους
withered the fig-tree? Answering and the Jesus

is from Nazareth in GALILEE."

12 ‡And JESUS went into †the TEMPLE, and expelled ALL THOSE SELLING and buying, and overturned the TABLES of the BANKERS, and the SEATS of the SELLERS of DOVES;

13 and said to them, "It is written, ‡'My 'HOUSE shall be called a 'House of Prayer;' but you *make it a Den of Robbers."

14 And the Blind and Lame came to him in the TEMPLE, and he healed them.

15 But when the HIGH-PRIESTS and SCRIBES saw the WONDERS which he performed, and *THOSE BOYS who were CRYING in the TEMPLE, "Hosanna to the SON of David!" they were exasperated,

16 and said to him, "Dost thou hear what these are saying?" And JESUS says to them, "Yes; have you never read, ‡'Out of the Mouth of Infants and Nurselings thou hast perfected Praise.'"

17 And having left them, he went out of the CITY, ‡to Bethany; and passed the night there.

18 ‡Returning to the CITY, in the Morning, he was hungry;

19 and seeing a single Fig-tree by the ROAD, he went to it; but finding nothing on it, except Leaves, he said, "May no fruit grow on thee to the AGE!" And the FIG-TREE instantly withered.

20 ‡And the DISCIPLES seeing it, were astonished, saying, "How soon is the FIG-TREE withered!"

21 JESUS answering,

* VATICAN MANUSCRIPT.—12. of GOD—*omit*. 13. make it. 15. THOSE BOYS who were CRYING.

† 12. The TEMPLE—*to hieron*. This was not the *naos*, house, or *Temple* strictly so called, including only the vestibule, the sanctuary, and the holy of holies. To this our Lord himself had not access, because not of the posterity of Aaron. The traffic was carried on in the outer courts. These courts the Pharisees did not account holy.

‡ 12. Luke xix. 45; John ii. 15. ‡ 13. Isa. lvi. 7. ‡ 16. Psa. viii. 2. John xi. 18. ‡ 18. Mark ix. 12. ‡ 20. Mark xi. 20.

ειπεν αυτοις· Αμην λεγω ὑμιν, εαν εχητε
said to them: Indeed I say to you, if you may have
πιστιν, και μη διακριθητε, ου μονον το
faith, and not should doubt, not only the (miracle)
της συκης ποιησετε, αλλα καν τῳ ορει τουτῳ
of the fig-tree you shall do, but also if to the mountain this
ειπητε· Αρθητι, και βληθητι εις την
you should say; Be thou lifted up, and be cast into the
θαλασσαν· γενησεται. 22 Και παντα, ὁσα αν
sea; it shall be done. And all, whatever
αιτησητε εν τῃ προσευχῃ, πιστευοντες,
you shall ask in the prayer, believing,
ληψεσθε.
you shall receive.

23 Και ελθοντι αυτῳ εις το ἱερον, προσηλθον
And having come to him into the temple, came
αυτῳ διδασκοντι οἱ αρχιερεις και οἱ πρεσβυτεροι
to him teaching the high-priests and the elders
του λαου, λεγοντες· Εν ποιᾳ εξουσιᾳ ταυτα
of the people, saying; By what authority these (things)
ποιεις; και τις σοι εδωκε την εξουσιαν ταυτην;
doest thou? and who to thee gave the authority this?
24 Αποκριθεις δε ὁ Ιησους ειπεν αυτοις· Ερωτησω
Answering and the Jesus said to them; I will ask
ὑμας καγω λογον ἑνα. ὁν εαν ειπητε μοι,
you also I word one; which if you may say to me,
καγω ὑμιν ερω, εν ποιᾳ εξουσιᾳ ταυτα
also I to you will tell, by what authority these (things)
ποιω· 25 το βαπτισμα Ιωαννου ποθεν ην; εξ
I do; the dipping of John whence was? from
ουρανου, η εξ ανθρωπων; Οἱ δε διελογιζοντο
heaven, or from men? They and reasoned
παρ᾽ ἑαυτοις, λεγοντες· Εαν ειπωμεν, εξ ουρα-
among themselves, saying; If we should say, from hea-
νου· ερει ἡμιν· Διατι ουν ουκ επιστευσατε
ven, he will say to us: Why then not did you believe
αυτῳ; 26 Εαν δε ειπωμεν, εξ ανθρωπων· φοβου-
to him? If but we should say, from men: we
μεθα τον οχλον· παντες γαρ εχουσι τον Ιωαννην
fear the crowd: all for hold the John
ὡς προφητην. 27 Και αποκριθεντες τῳ Ιησου
as a prophet: And they answering to the Jesus
ειπον· Ουκ οιδαμεν. Εφη αυτοις και αυτος·
said: Not we know. Said to them and he:
Ουδε εγω λεγω ὑμιν εν ποιᾳ εξουσιᾳ ταυτα
Neither I say to you by what authority these (things)
ποιω. 28 Τι δε ὑμιν δοκει; Ανθρωπος ειχε
I do. What but to you seems right? A man had
τεκνα δυο· και προσελθων τῳ πρωτῳ, ειπε·
children two: and coming to the first, he said:
Τεκνον, ὑπαγε, σημερον εργαζου εν τῳ αμπελωνι
Son, go, to-day work in the vineyard
μου. 29 Ὁ δε αποκριθεις ειπεν· Ου θελω·
of me. He and answering said: Not I will:
ὑστερον δε μεταμεληθεις, απηλθε. 30 Και
afterward but having changed his mind, he went. And
προσελθων τῳ ἑτερῳ, ειπεν ὡσαυτως. Ὁ δε
coming to the other, he said just the same. He and

said to them, "Indeed, I say to you, ‡ If you have an unshaken Faith, you will not only do THIS miracle of the FIG-TREE, but also, if you should say to this MOUNTAIN, 'Be thou lifted up, and thrown into the SEA,' it will be done."

22 ‡ And whatever you shall ask in PRAYER, believing, you will receive."

23 ‡ And having entered the TEMPLE, the HIGH-PRIESTS and ELDERS of the PEOPLE, came near, as he was teaching, and said, "By What Authority dost thou perform these things? and who EMPOWERED thee."

24 Jesus replying, said to them, "I will also ask you one Question, which if you answer me, I also will inform you by What Authority I do these things.

25 Whence was * THAT IMMERSION which was of John? From Heaven, or from Men?" And THEY reasoned thus among themselves, "If we say, From Heaven, he will retort, Why then did you not believe him?

26 And if we say, From Men, we dread the CROWD; for they all regard JOHN as a Prophet."

27 They, therefore, said to JESUS, in reply, "We cannot tell." And he said to them, "Neither do I tell you by What Authority I perform these things.

28 But what is your opinion of this? A Man had * Two Sons; and coming to the FIRST, he said, 'Son, go work To-day in my VINEYARD.'

29 HE answered, * 'I will, sir,' but went not.

30 And coming to the SECOND, he said the same.

* VATICAN MANUSCRIPT.—25. THAT IMMERSION which was of John. 28. Two Sons. 29. 'I will, sir;' but went not. 30. And coming to the SECOND, he said the same. And HE answering, said, 'I will not;' but afterwards he repented and went.

‡ 21. Matt. xvii. 20; Luke xvii. 6; James i. 6; 1 Cor. xiii. 2. ‡ 22. Matt. vii. 8; Mark xi. 24; James v. 16; 1 John iii. 22; v. 14. ‡ 23. Mark xi. 27; Luke xx. 1.

αποκριθεις ειπεν· Εγω κυριε, και ουκ απηλθε.
answering said; I lord, and not went.
31 Τις εκ των δυο εποιησε το θελημα του πατρος;
Who of the two did the will of the father?
Λεγουσιν *[αυτῳ·] Ὁ πρωτος. Λεγει αυτοις ὁ
They say [to him;] The first. Says to them the
Ιησους· Αμην λεγω ὑμιν, ὁτι οἱ τελωναι και
Jesus; Indeed I say to you, that the tax-gatherers and
αἱ πορναι προαγουσιν ὑμας εις την βασιλειαν
the harlots go before you into the kingdom
του θεου. 32 Ηλθε γαρ προς ὑμας Ιωαννης εν
of the God. Came for to you John in
ὁδῳ δικαιοσυνης, και ουκ επιστευσατε αυτῳ· οἱ
a way of righteousness, and not you believed him; the
δε τελωναι και αἱ πορναι επιστευσαν αυτῳ·
but tax-gatherers and the harlots believed him;
ὑμεις δε ιδοντες ου μετεμεληθητε ὑστερον, του
you and seeing not repented afterwards, of the
πιστευσαι αυτῳ.
to believe him.
33 Αλλην παραβολην ακουσατε· *[Ανθρωπος]
Another parable hear you; [A man]
ην οικοδεσποτης, ὁστις εφυτευσεν αμπελωνα,
was a householder, who planted a vineyard,
και φραγμον αυτῳ περιεθηκε, και ωρυξεν εν
and a hedge to it placed around, and digged in
αυτῳ ληνον, και ῳκοδομησε πυργον· και εξ-
it a wine-press, and built a tower; and let
εδοτο αυτον γεωργοις, και απεδημησεν. 34 Ὁτε
out it to husbandmen, and went abroad. When
δε ηγγισεν ὁ καιρος των καρπων, απεστειλε
and drew near the time of the fruits, he sent
τους δουλους αὑτου, προς τους γεωργους, λα-
the slaves of him, to the husbandmen, to
βειν τους καρπους αυτου. 35 Και λαβοντες οἱ
receive the fruits of it. And having taken the
γεωργοι τους δουλους αυτου, ὁν μεν εδειραν,
husbandmen the slaves of him, him indeed they flayed,
ὁν δε απεκτειναν, ὁν δε ελιθοβολησαν. 36 Παλιν
him and they killed, him and they pelted with stones. Again
απεστειλεν αλλους δουλους, πλειονας των
he sent other slaves, greater the
πρωτων· και εποιησαν αυτοις ὡσαυτως. 37 Ὑσ-
first; and they did to them in like manner. After-
τερον δε απεστειλε προς αυτους τον υἱον αὑτου,
wards and he sent to them the son of him,
λεγων· Εντραπησονται τον υἱον μου. 38 Οἱ
saying; They will regard the son of me. The
δε γεωργοι, ιδοντες τον υἱον, ειπον εν ἑαυτοις·
but husbandmen, seeing the son, said among themselves;
Οὑτος εστιν ὁ κληρονομος· δευτε, αποκτει-
This is the heir; come, we may
νωμεν αυτον, και κατασχωμεν την κληρονομιαν
kill him, and may retain the inheritance

And HE answering, said, 'I will not;' but afterwards repenting, he went.
31 Which of the TWO performed the FATHER'S WILL?" They say, "The *LATTER." JESUS said to them, ‡"Indeed, I say to you, That the TRIBUTE-TAKERS and the HARLOTS precede you into the KINGDOM of GOD.
32 For ‡John came to you in a Way of Righteousness, and you believed him not; but the TRIBUTE-TAKERS and the HARLOTS believed him; yet you, having seen it, did not afterwards repent, SO AS TO BELIEVE him.
33 Hear Another Parable. There was a Householder, ‡who planted a Vineyard, and enclosed it with a Hedge, and digged †a Wine-press in it, and built a Tower, and leased it to Cultivators, and left the country.
34 And when the VINTAGE approached, he sent his SERVANTS to the CULTIVATORS, to receive the FRUITS.
35 But the ‡CULTIVATORS having seized his SERVANTS, severely beat one, and murdered another, and stoned another.
36 Again, he sent Other Servants, more honorable than the FIRST, and they treated them in a similar manner.
37 Finally, ‡he sent his SON to them, saying, 'They will respect my SON.'
38 But the CULTIVATORS seeing the SON, said among themselves, 'This is the HEIR; ‡come, let us kill him, and forcibly hold the INHERITANCE.'

* VATICAN MANUSCRIPT.—31. to him—*omit*. 31. LATTER. 33. A man—*omit*.

† 33. *Leenon*, wine-press, is the word used by Matthew, while *hupoleenion*, wine-vat, is used by Mark, ch. xii. 1. Dr. Robinson saw a wine-press at Hebeh, which was hewn out of a rock, and divided into two parts. The upper and more shallow part was the place where the grapes were put, the lower and deeper one was the place for receiving the liquid pressed out of them. These two places served for both *wine-press* and *wine-vat*. This fact will serve to illustrate the words of Jesus as recorded by the two historians.

‡ 31. Luke vii. 29. ‡ 32. Matt. xi. 18; Luke vii. 33. ‡ 33. Cant. viii. 11; Isa. v. 1 Mark xii. 1; Luke xx. 9. ‡ 35. Heb. xi. 36, 37. ‡ 37. Heb. i. 2; 1 John iv. 9. ‡ 38. Matt. xxvi. 3—4; John xi. 53.

αυτου. [39] Και λαβοντες αυτον, εξεβαλον εξω
of him. And having taken him, they cast out
του αμπελωνος, και απεκτειναν. [40] Ὁταν ουν
of the vineyard, and killed. When therefore
ελθῃ ὁ κυριος του αμπελωνος, τι ποιησει
may come the lord of the vineyard, what will he do
τοις γεωργοις εκεινοις; [41] Λεγουσιν αυτῳ·
to the husbandmen to those? They say to him;
Κακους κακως απολεσει αυτους· και τον αμπε-
Wretches wretchedly destroy them; and the vine-
λωνα εκδωσεται αλλοις γεωργοις, οἱτινες απο-
yard will let out to other husbandmen, who will
δωσουσιν αυτῳ τους καρπους εν τοις καιροις
render to him the fruits in the seasons
αυτων. [42] Λεγει αυτοις ὁ Ιησους· Ουδεποτε
of them. He says to them the Jesus; Never
ανεγνωτε εν ταις γραφαις· "Λιθον ὁν απεδοκι-
have you read in the writings: "A stone which rejec-
μασαν οἱ οικοδομουντες, οὑτος εγενηθη εις
ted they building, the same was made into
κεφαλην γωνιας· παρα κυριου εγενετο αὑτη,
a head of a corner; from Lord was this,
και εστι θαυμαστη εν οφθαλμοις ἡμων;" [43] Δια
and it is wonderful in eyes of us?" On account of
τουτο λεγω ὑμιν, ὁτι αρθησεται αφ' ὑμων ἡ
this I say to you, that shall be taken from you the
βασιλεια του θεου, και δοθησεται εθνει ποιουντι
kingdom of the God, and shall be given to a nation making
τους καρπους αυτης. [44] Και ὁ πεσων ἐπι τον
the fruits of her. And he falling on the
λιθον τουτον, συνθλασθησεται· εφ' ὁν δ' αν
stone this, shall be broken: on whom but
πεσῃ, λικμησει αυτον.
it shall fall, it will crush to pieces him.

[45] Και ακουσαντες οἱ αρχιερεις και οἱ Φαρι-
And having heard the high-priests and the Phari-
σαιοι τας παραβολας αυτου, εγνωσαν, ὁτι περι
sees the parables of him, knew, that about
αυτων λεγει. [46] Και ζητουντες αυτον κρατησαι,
them he says. And seeking him to seize,
εφοβηθησαν τους οχλους· επειδη ὡς προφητην
they feared the crowds: since as a prophet
αυτον ειχον. ΚΕΦ. κβ'. 22. Και αποκριθεις
him they held. And answering
ὁ Ιησους παλιν ειπεν αυτοις εν παραβολαις,
the Jesus again said to them in parables,
λεγων· [2] Ὡμοιωθη ἡ βασιλεια των ουρανων
saying: Has been likened the kingdom of the heavens
ανθρωπῳ βασιλει, ὁστις εποιησε γαμους τῳ
to a man a king, who made marriage-feasts to the
υἱῳ αὑτου, [3] και απεστειλε τους δουλους αὑτου,
son of him, and he sent the slaves of him,

39 Then seizing him, they ‡thrust him out of the VINEYARD and killed him.

40 When, therefore, the OWNER of the VINEYARD comes, what will he do to those OCCUPANTS?"

41 They reply to him, ‡"He will put those wretches to a wretched death, and will lease the VINEYARD to Other Cultivators, who will render him the FRUITS in their SEASONS."

42 JESUS says to them, "Have you never read in the SCRIPTURES, †‡'A 'Stone, which the BUILD-'ERS rejected, the same 'is made the Head-stone 'of the Corner; this Je-'hovah has effected, and 'it is wonderful in our 'Eyes?'

43 Because of this, I tell you, ‡That the KINGDOM of GOD will be taken from you, and given to a People who will produce its proper FRUITS.

44 ‡And HE who FALLS on this STONE, will be bruised; and him, on whom it shall fall, it will crush to pieces."

45 And the HIGH-PRIESTS and PHARISEES having heard his PARABLES, knew that he was speaking about them.

46 And seeking to apprehend him, they feared the CROWDS, for they esteemed him as a Prophet.

CHAPTER XXII.

1 And JESUS continuing to discourse to them in Parables, said,

2 "The KINGDOM of the HEAVENS may be compared to a Royal Person, who prepared a Marriage festival for his SON,

3 and he sent his SER-

† 42. "A Stone, which the BUILDERS rejected." An expression borrowed from masons, who, finding a stone, which being tried in a particular place, and appearing improper for it, is thrown aside, and another taken: however, at last, it may happen that the *very stone* which had been before *rejected*, may be found the most suitable as the *head stone of the corner*.—*Clarke*.

‡ 39. John xix. 17, 18; Heb. xiii. 11—13. ‡ 41. Mark xii. 9; Luke xx. 16. ‡ 42. Psa. cxviii. 22; Acts iv. 11; 1 Pet. ii. 7. ‡ 43. Matt. viii. 12; Luke xiii. 28, 29. ‡ 44. Isa. viii. 14, 15; Dan. ii. 34, 44, 45.

καλεσαι τους κεκλημενους εις τους γαμους·
to call the having been invited to the marriage-feasts
και ουκ ηθελον ελθειν. 4 Παλιν απεστειλεν
and not they would to come. Again he sent
αλλους δουλους, λεγων· Ειπατε τοις κεκλημε-
other slaves, saying; Say to the having been
νοις· Ιδου, το αριστον μου ἡτοιμασα· οἱ ταυροι
called; Lo, the dinner of me I prepared; the bullocks
μου και τα σιτιστα τεθυμενα, και παντα ἑτοιμα·
of me and the fatlings having been killed, and all (things) ready.
δευτε εις τους γαμους. 5 Οἱ δε αμελησαντες,
come to the marriage-feasts. They but neglecting,
απηλθον· ὁ μεν εις τον ιδιον αγρον, ὁ δε εις
went away; he indeed to the own field, he and to
την εμποριαν αὑτου. 6 Οἱ δε λοιποι κρατη-
the traffic of him. The and remainder having
σαντες τους δουλους αυτου, ὑβρισαν και απεκτει-
seized the slaves of him, insulted and killed.
ναν. 7 Ακουσας δε ὁ βασιλευς, ωργισθη· και
Having heard and the king, was wroth: and
πεμψας τα στρατευματα αὑτου, απωλεσε τους
having sent the armies of him, destroyed the
φονεις εκεινους, και την πολιν αυτων ενεπρησε.
murderers those, and the city of them burned.
8 Τοτε λεγει τοις δουλους αυτου· Ὁ μεν
Then he says to the slaves of him: The indeed
γαμος ἑτοιμος εστιν, οἱ δε κεκλημενοι ουκ
marriage-feast ready is, they but having been called not
ησαν αξιοι. 9 Πορευεσθε ουν επι τας διεξοδους
were worthy. Go you therefore to the outlets
των ὁδων, και ὁσους αν ευρητε, καλεσατε εις
of the ways, and whoever you may find, call you to
τους γαμους. 10 Και εξελθοντες οἱ δουλοι
the marriage-feasts. And having gone forth the slaves
εκεινοι εις τας ὁδους, συνηγαγον παντας,
those into the ways, they brought together all,
ὁσους ευρον, πονηρους τε και αγαθους· και
as many as they found, bad ones both and good ones: and
επλησθη ὁ γαμος ανακειμενων. 11 Εισελθων
was filled the marriage-feast of reclining ones. Having entered
δε ὁ βασιλευς θεασασθαι τους ανακειμενους,
and the king to see the reclining ones,
ειδεν εκει ανθρωπον ουκ ενδεδυμενον ενδυμα
saw there a man not having been clothed a garment
γαμου· 12 και λεγει αυτῳ· Ἑταιρε, πως
of marriage: and he says to him: Friend, how
εισηλθες ὡδε, μη εχων ενδυμα γαμου; Ὁ
didst thou enter here, not having a garment of marriage: He
δε εφιμωθη. 13 Τοτε ειπεν ὁ βασιλευς
but was struck speechless. Then said the king
τοις διακονοις· Δησαντες αυτου ποδας και
to the servants: Having bound of him feet and
χειρας, αρατε αυτον, και εκβαλετε εις το σκοτος
hands, take him, and cast into the darkness
το εξωτερον· εκει εσται ὁ κλαυθμος και ὁ
the outer: there shall be the weeping and the

VANTS to call THOSE who
had been INVITED to the
FESTIVITIES; and they
refused to come.
4 Again, he sent Other
Servants, saying, 'Inform
THOSE who are INVITED,
‡ Behold, I have prepared
my ENTERTAINMENT; my
OXEN and FATLINGS are
killed, and all is ready;
come to the FESTIVAL.'
5 But THEY, disregard-
ing it, went away, ONE to
his OWN Farm, and ONE
to his MERCHANDISE;
6 and the REST seizing
his SERVANTS, insulted,
and killed them.
7 * And the KING was
indignant; and having
sent ‡ his MILITARY FOR-
CES, destroyed those MUR-
DERERS, and burned their
CITY.
8 He then says to his
SERVANTS, 'The ENTER-
TAINMENT indeed is rea-
dy, but THOSE who have
been INVITED, were ‡ un-
worthy.
9 Go, therefore, into
the PUBLIC ROADS, and
whoever you may find,
invite to the NUPTIAL-
FEASTS.'
10 And those SERVANTS
went out into the ROADS,
and brought together all
that they met, Good and
Bad; and the FEAST was
well supplied with guests.
11 Now the KING hav-
ing entered to view the
GUESTS, saw there a Man
‡ not clothed with a Wed-
ding Garment;
12 and he says to him,
'Friend, how camest thou
here, not having a Wed-
ding Garment?' And HE
was struck speechless.
13 The KING then said
to the SERVANTS, 'Bind
his Hands and Feet; take
him, and thrust * him
into the OUTER DARK-
NESS;' there will be the
WEEPING and the GNASH-
ING of TEETH.

* VATICAN MANUSCRIPT.—7. And the KING was indignant. 13. him.

‡ 4. Prov. ix. 2. ‡ 7. Dan. ix. 26. ‡ 8. Acts xiii. 46. ‡ 11. 2 Cor. v. 3; Rev. iii. 4; xvi. 15; xix. 8.

βρυγμος των οδοντων. 14Πολλοι γαρ εισι
gnashing of the teeth. Many for are
κλητοι, ολιγοι δε εκλεκτοι·
called, few but picked out.
15Τοτε πορευθεντες οἱ Φαρισαιοι συμβουλιον
Then having gone the Pharisees counsel
λαβον, ὁπως αυτον παγιδευσωσιν εν λογῳ.
took, how him they might insnare in word.
16Και αποστελλουσιν αυτῳ τους μαθητας αὑτων
And they sent away to him the disciples of them
μετα των Ἡρωδιανων, λεγοντες. Διδασκαλε,
with the Herodians, saying, O teacher,
οιδαμεν, ὁτι αληθης ει, και την ὁδον του
we know, that true thou art, and the way of the
θεου εν αληθειᾳ διδασκεις, και ου μελει σοι
God in truth thou teachest, and not there is care to thee
περι ουδενος· ου γαρ βλεπεις εις προσωπον
about no one; not for thou lookest into face
ανθρωπων. 17Ειπε ουν ἡμιν, τι σοι δοκει;
of men. Say therefore to us, what to thee seems right?
εξεστι δουναι κηνσον Καισαρι, η ου; 18Γνους
is it lawful to give tribute to Cesar, or not? Knowing
δε ὁ Ιησους την πονηριαν αυτων, ειπε· Τι με
but the Jesus the wickedness of them, said; Why me
πειραζετε ὑποκριται; 19Επιδειξατε μοι το
tempt you hypocrites? Show you to me the
νομισμα του κηνσου. Οἱ δε προσηνεγκαν αυτῳ
coin of the tribute. They and brought to him
δηναριον. 20Και λεγει αυτοις· Τινος ἡ εικων
a denarius. And he says to them; Of whom the likeness
αὑτη και ἡ επιγραφη; 21Λεγουσιν *[αυτῳ·]
this and the inscription? They say [to him;]
Καισαρος. Τοτε λεγει αυτοις· Αποδοτε ουν
Of Cesar. Then he says to them; Give you back then
τα Καισαρος Καισαρι· και τα του θεου
the (things) of Cesar to Cesar; and the (things) of the God
τῳ θεῳ. 22Και ακουσαντες εθαυμασαν· και
to the God. And having heard they wondered; and
αφεντες αυτον απηλθον.
leaving him they departed.
23Εν εκεινῃ τῃ ἡμερᾳ προσηλθον αυτῳ Σαδ-
In that the day came to him Sad-
δουκαιοι, οἱ λεγοντες, μη ειναι αναστασιν· και
ducees, they saying, not to be a resurrection; and
επηρωτησαν αυτον, 24λεγοντες· Διδασκαλε,
they asked him, saying; O teacher,
Μωσης ειπεν· "Εαν τις αποθανῃ μη εχων
Moses said; "If any one should die not having
τεκνα, επιγαμβρευσει ὁ αδελφος αυτου την
children, shall marry the brother of him the

14 For there are Many invited, but Few selected.

15 ‡Then the PHARISEES having withdrawn, consulted how they might entrap him in Conversation.

16 And they sent to him their DISCIPLES with the HERODIANS, saying, "Teacher, we know That thou art sincere, and teachest the WAY of GOD in Truth, neither carest thou for any one; for thou lookest not to the Appearance of Men.

17 Tell us, therefore, thy opinion; Is it lawful to pay Tax to Cesar, or not?"

18 But JESUS knowing their WICKEDNESS, said, "Hypocrites! why do you try me?

19 Show me the TAX-COIN." And THEY handed him a Denarius.

20 And he says to them, †"Whose LIKENESS and INSCRIPTION is this?"

21 They say, "Cesar's." Then he replies to them, ‡"Render, therefore, the THINGS of Cesar, to Cesar; and the THINGS of GOD, to GOD."

22 And having heard this, they wondered; and leaving him, they went away.

23 ‡On that day, *Sadducees came to him, who say there is no †Resurrection, and asked him,

24 saying, "Teacher, ‡Moses said, †If a man die, having no Children, his BROTHER shall marry his WIDOW, and raise up

* VATICAN MANUSCRIPT.—21. to him—*omit*. 23. Sadducees came to him, who say.

† 20. Dr. Lightfoot tells us that the Jews have a tradition among them, that to admit of the title of any prince on their current coin, was an acknowledgment of subjection to him. Their acceptance of this coin when offered to them in payment, was in effect a confession that they were conquered by the Romans, and that the emperor had a right to their tribute. † 23. This is rendered *future life* by some modern translators; which is, as Dr. Bloomfield very justly observes, "no version at all, but merely an *explanation*." *Anastasis* can only mean *future life*, by implication; its primary signification being a *standing* or *rising up*. If a future life be understood by the term, then it evidently depends upon, and follows a resurrection. † 24. The words of the Law are not quoted *verbatim*, but according to their sense. The intention was that children by the second marriage should be reckoned in the genealogy of the deceased brother, and inherit his property.

‡ 15. Mark xii. 13; Luke xx. 20. ‡ 21. Rom. xiii. 7. ‡ 23. Mark xii. 18; Luke xx. 27; Acts xxiii. 8. ‡ 24. Deut. xxv. 5.

γυναικα αυτου, και αναστησει σπερμα τῳ
wife of him, and shall raise seed to the
αδελφῳ αὑτου." [25] Ησαν δε παρ' ἡμιν ἑπτα
brother of him." There were now with us seven
αδελφοι· και ὁ πρωτος, γαμησας, ετελευτησε·
brothers: and the first, having married, died:
και μη εχων σπερμα, αφηκε την γυναικα αὑτου
and not having seed, left the wife of him
τῳ αδελφῳ αὑτου. [26] Ὁμοιως και ὁ δευτερος,
to the brother of him. Likewise also the second,
και ὁ τριτος, ἑως των ἑπτα. [27] Ὑστερον δε
and the third, till the seven. After and
παντων απεθανε και ἡ γυνη. [28] Εν τη ουν
of all died also the woman. In the therefore
αναστασει, τινος των ἑπτα εσται γυνη; παντες
resurrection, of whom of the seven shall be a wife? all
γαρ εσχον αυτην. [29] Αποκριθεις δε ὁ Ιησους
for had her. Answering and the Jesus
ειπεν αυτοις· Πλανασθε, μη ειδοτες τας γρα-
said to them; You go astray, not knowing the writ-
φας, μηδε την δυναμιν του θεου· [30] Εν γαρ
ings, neither the power of the God. In for
τη αναστασει ουτε γαμουσιν, ουτε εκγαμι-
the resurrection neither they marry, nor are given in
ζονται, αλλ' ὡς αγγελοι *[του θεου] εν
marriage, but as messengers [of the God] in
ουρανῳ εισι. [31] Περι δε της αναστασεως των
heaven are. About but the resurrection of the
νεκρων ουκ ανεγνωτε το ῥηθεν ὑμιν ὑπο
dead (ones) not have you read that having been spoken to you by
του θεου, λεγοντος· [32] "Εγω ειμι ὁ θεος
the God, saying: I am the God
Αβρααμ, και ὁ θεος Ισαακ, και ὁ θεος Ιακωβ;"
of Abraam, and the God of Isaac, and the God of Jacob?"
Ουκ εστιν ὁ θεος, θεος νεκρων, αλλα ζωντων.
Not is the God, a God of dead (ones,) but of living (ones.)
[33] Και ακουσαντες οἱ οχλοι, εξεπλησσοντο επι
And having heard the crowds, were astonished at
τη διδαχῃ αυτου.
the teaching of him.

[34] Οἱ δε Φαρισαιοι, ακουσαντες ὁτι εφιμωσε
The and Pharisees, hearing that he silenced
τους Σαδδουκαιους, συνηχθησαν επι το αυτο·
the Sadducees, were assembled on the same;
[35] και επηρωτησεν εἱς εξ αυτων, νομικος, πειρα-
and asked one out of them, a lawyer, tempt-
ζων αυτον *[και λεγων·] [36] Διδασκαλε, ποια
ing him [and saying;] O teacher, which
εντολη μεγαλη εν τῳ νομῳ; [37] Ὁ δε Ιησους
commandment great in the law? The and Jesus
εφη αυτῳ· "Αγαπησεις κυριον τον θεον σου
said to him; "Thou shalt love Lord the God of thee
εν ὁλῃ τῃ καρδιᾳ σου, και εν ὁλῃ τῃ ψυχῃ σου,
in whole the heart of thee, and in whole the soul of thee,
και εν ὁλῃ τῃ διανοιᾳ σου." [38] Αὑτη εστι πρωτη
and in whole the mind of thee." This is first

Offspring to his BRO-
THER.
25 Now, there were with us Seven Brothers; and the FIRST, having married, died; and having no issue, left his WIFE to his BROTHER.
26 Thus also the SECOND, and the THIRD, even to the SEVENTH.
27 And last of all, the WOMAN also died.
28 At the RESURRECTION, therefore, To which of the SEVEN will she be a WIFE? for they all married her."
29 JESUS answering, said to them, "You err, not knowing the SCRIPTURES, nor the POWER of GOD;
30 for in the RESURRECTION [state], they neither marry, nor are given in marriage, but are as ANGELS in * HEAVEN.
31 But concerning the RESURRECTION of the DEAD, Have you not read the WORD SPOKEN to you by GOD, saying,
32 ‡ 'I am the GOD of 'Abraham, and the GOD 'of Isaac, and the GOD of 'Jacob?' * He is not the GOD of the Dead, but of the Living."
33 And the CROWDS hearing this, were amazed at his TEACHING.
34 ‡ Now the PHARISEES hearing That he had silenced the SADDUCEES, flocked about Him.
35 And one of them, ‡ a Lawyer, trying him, proposed this question;
36 "Teacher, which is the great Commandment in the LAW?"
37 * And HE said to him, ‡ "'Thou shalt love 'Jehovah thy GOD with 'All thy HEART, and with 'All thy SOUL, and with 'All thy MIND.'
38 This is * the GREAT and First Commandment

* VATICAN MANUSCRIPT.—30. of GOD—*omit*. 30. HEAVEN. 32. He is not the GOD
35. and saying—*omit*. 37. And HE said. 38. the GREAT and First Commandment.

‡ 32. Exod. iii. 6; Mark xii. 26; Luke xx. 37; Acts vii. 32; Heb. xi. 16. ‡ 34. Mark xii. 28. ‡ 35. Luke x. 25. ‡ 37. Deut. vi. 5; Luke x. 27.

και μεγαλη εντολη. 39 Δευτερα δε όμοια αυτῃ·
and great commandment. Second and like to it:
* Αγαπησεις τον πλησιον σου, ὡς σεαυτον."
"Thou shalt love the neighbor of thee, as thyself."
40 Εν ταυταις ταις δυσιν εντολαις ὁλος ὁ νομος
In these the two commandments whole the law
και οἱ προφηται κρεμανται.
and the prophets are hung.
41 Συνηγμενων δε των Φαρισαιων, επηρωτησεν
Having been assembled and of the Pharisees, asked
αυτους ὁ Ιησους, 42 λεγων· Τι ὑμιν δοκει περι
them the Jesus, saying, What to you thinks about
του Χριστου; τινος υἱος εστι; Λεγουσιν
the Anointed? of whom a son is he? They say
αυτῳ· Του Δαυιδ. 43 Λεγει αυτοις· Πως ουν
to him; Of the David. He says to them; How then
Δαυιδ εν πνευματι κυριον αυτον καλει; λεγων·
David in spirit Lord of him calls? saying;
44 "Ειπεν ὁ κυριος τῳ κυριῳ μου· Καθου εκ
"Said the Lord to the Lord of me: Sit thou at
δεξιων μου, ἑως αν θω τους εχθρους σου ὑπο-
right of me, till I may place the enemies of thee a foot-
ποδιον των ποδων σου." 45 Ει ουν Δαυιδ καλει
stool of the feet of thee." If then David calls
αυτον κυριον, πως υἱος αυτου εστι; 46 Και ουδεις
him Lord, how a son of him is he; And no one
εδυνατο αυτῳ αποκριθηναι λογον· ουδε ετολμησε
was able to him to answer a word; nor dared
τις απ' εκεινης της ἡμερας επερωτησαι αυτον
any one from that the day to ask him
ουκετι.
any more.

39 *The Second is similar; ‡'Thou shalt love 'thy NEIGHBOR as thy-'self.'

40 ‡On These TWO Commandments *depend the Whole LAW and the PROPHETS."

41 ‡And while the PHARISEES were assembled, JESUS asked them,

42 saying, "What is your opinion about the MESSIAH? Whose Son is he?" They say to him, "DAVID'S."

43 He says to them, "How then does David, by Inspiration, call him his Lord? saying,

44 ‡'JEHOVAH said to my LORD, Sit thou at my 'Right hand, till I *put 'thine ENEMIES under-'neath thy FEET?'

45 If, therefore, David call him Lord, how is he his Son?"

46 And no one was able to answer him a Word; nor did any one from That DAY presume to question him any more.

ΚΕΦ. κγ'. 23.

1 Τοτε ὁ Ιησους ελαλησε τοις οχλοις και
Then the Jesus spoke to the crowds and
τοις μαθηταις αὑτου, 2 λεγων· Επι της Μωσεως
to the disciples of him, saying; Upon the Mosee
καθεδρας εκαθισαν οἱ γραμματεις και οἱ Φαρι-
seat sat the scribes and the Phari-
σαιοι. 3 Παντα ουν, ὁσα αν ειπωσιν ὑμιν
sees. All therefore, whatever they say to you
*[τηρειν·] τηρειτε και ποιειτε· κατα δε τα
[to observe;] observe you and do you; according to but the
εργα αυτων μη ποιειτε· λεγουσι γαρ, και ου
works of them not do you; they say for, and not
ποιουσι. 5 Δεσμευουσι γαρ φορτια βαρεα και
they do. They bind for burdens heavy and
δυσβαστακτα, και επιτιθεασιν επι τους ωμους
oppressive, and place upon the shoulders
των ανθρωπων· τῳ δε δακτυλῳ αυτων ου
of the men: of the and finger of them not
θελουσι κινησαι αυτα. 6 Παντα δε τα εργα
they will to move them. All but the works
αὑτων ποιουσι προς το θεαθηναι τοις ανθρωποις.
of them they do to the to be seen to the men.

CHAPTER XXIII.

1 Then JESUS spoke to the CROWDS, and to his DISCIPLES,

2 saying, "The SCRIBES and PHARISEES sit in the Chair of MOSES;

3 therefore All things whatever they command you, *do and observe; but do not according to their WORKS; for they say and do not perform.

4 *And they prepare heavy and oppressive Burdens, for other MEN'S SHOULDERS, but *they will not move them with their FINGER.

5 And they perform all their WORKS to be OBSERVED by MEN; *for this

* VATICAN MANUSCRIPT.—39. The Second is similar. 40. depends. 44. put thine ENEMIES underneath thy FEET. 3. observe—*omit*. 3. do and observe. 4. And they. 4. they will not move them with their FINGER. 5. for they.

‡ 39. Lev. xix. 18; Mark xii. 31; Luke x. 27; Rom. xiii. 9; Gal. v. 14; Jas. ii. 8. ‡ 40. Matt. vii. 12; 1 Tim. i. 5. ‡ 41. Mark xii. 35; Luke xx. 41. ‡ Psa. cx. 1; Acts ii. 34; Heb. i. 13. ‡ 4. Luke xi. 46; Acts xv. 10.

Πλατυνουσι δε τα φυλακτηρια αὑτων, και
They widen and the phylacteries of them, and
μεγαλυνουσι τα κρασπεδα *[των ἱματιων αὑ-
they enlarge the tufts [of the mantles of
των·] 6 φιλουσι τε την πρωτοκλισιαν εν τοις
them;] they love and the upper couch in the
δειπνοις, και τας πρωτοκαθεδριας εν ταις συνα-
feasts, and the first seats in the syna-
γωγαις, 7 και τους ασπασμους εν ταις αγοραις,
gogues, and the salutations in the markets,
και καλεισθαι ὑπο των ανθρωπων ῥαββι,
and to be called by the men rabbi,
*[ῥαββι.] 8 Ὑμεις δε μη κληθητε ῥαββι· εἱς
[rabbi.] You but not may be called rabbi, one
γαρ εστιν ὑμων ὁ καθηγητης· παντες δε ὑμεις
for is of you the leader; all but you
αδελφοι εστι. 9 Και πατερα μη καλεσητε ὑμων
brethren are: And father not you may call of you
επι της γης· εἱς γαρ εστιν ὁ πατηρ ὑμων, ὁ
on the earth: one for is the father of you, he
εν τοις ουρανοις. 10 Μηδε κληθητε καθηγηται·
in the heavens. Neither be ye called leaders:
εις γαρ ὑμων εστιν ὁ καθηγητης, ὁ χριστος.
one for of you is the leader, the anointed
11 Ὁ δε μειζων ὑμων, εσται ὑμων διακονος.
The but greater of you, shall be of you a servant.
12 Ὁστις δε ὑψωσει ἑαυτον, ταπεινωθησεται·
Who and shall exalt himself, shall be humbled;
και ὁστις ταπεινωσει ἑαυτον, ὑψωθησεται.
and who shall humble himself, shall be exalted.
13 Ουαι δε ὑμιν, γραμματεις και Φαρισαιοι, ὑποκ-
Woe but to you, scribes and Pharisees, hypo-
ριται· ὁτι κατεσθιετε τας οικιας των χηρων,
crites: because you devour the houses of the widows.
και προφασει μακρα προσευχομενοι· δια τουτο
and for a show long are praying through this
ληψεσθε περισσοτερον κριμα.
you shall receive heavier judgment
14 *[Ουαι ὑμιν, γραμματεις και Φαρισαιοι,
[Woe to you, scribes and Pharisees,
ὑποκριται· ὁτι κλειετε την βασιλειαν των
hypocrites. because you shut the kingdom of the
ουρανων εμπροσθεν των ανθρωπων· ὑμεις γαρ
heavens in presence of the men you for
ουκ εισερχεσθε, ουδε τους εισερχομενους αφιετε
not enter, nor the entering you permit
εισελθειν.] 15 Ουαι ὑμιν, γραμματεις και Φαρι-
to enter.] Woe to you. scribes and Phari-
σαιοι, ὑποκριται· ὁτι περιαγετε την θαλασσαν
sees, hypocrites: because you go about the sea
και την ξηραν, ποιησαι ἑνα προσηλυτον· και
and the dry, to make one proselyte: and

they widen ‡their †PHYLACTERIES, and enlarge their TUFTS.

6 ‡and love the UPPER COUCH at FEASTS, and the PRINCIPAL SEATS in the SYNAGOGUES,

7 and SALUTATIONS in the PUBLIC PLACES; and to be called by MEN, 'Rabbi.'

8 ‡But you should not be called Rabbi; because one is Your *TEACHER, and all YOU are Brethren.

9 And style no man on the EARTH your Father; for one *is Your HEAVENLY FATHER.

10 Nor assume the title of Leaders; because one is Your LEADER, the MESSIAH.

11 ‡But let the GREATEST of you, become Your Servant.

12 ‡And he who shall exalt himself, will be humbled; and he who shall humble himself, will be exalted.

13 †Woe to you, Scribes and Pharisees, Hypocrites! Because you plunder the FAMILIES of WIDOWS, and for a Disguise make long Prayers; therefore, you will receive a Heavier Judgment.

14 *[Woe to you, Scribes and Pharisees, Hypocrites! Because you shut the KINGDOM of the HEAVENS against MEN; you neither enter yourselves, nor permit THOSE APPROACHING to enter.]

15 Woe to you, Scribes and Pharisees, Hypocrites! Because you traverse SEA and LAND to make One †Proselyte, and when he is gained, you

---

* VATICAN MANUSCRIPT.—5. of their MANTLES—*omit.* 7. Rabbi—*omit.* 8. TEACHER. 9. is Your HEAVENLY FATHER. 14.—*omit.*

† 5. These were small slips of parchment or vellum, on which certain portions of the law were written. The Jews tied them about their foreheads and arms, for three purposes.—1. To put them in *mind* of those precepts which they should constantly observe. 2. To procure them *reverence* and *respect* in the sight of the *heathen.* And 3. To act as *amulets* or *charms* to drive away evil spirits.—*Clarke.* † 13. Lachmann and Tischendorf omit this verse. † 15. A convert to Judaism.

‡ 5. Num. xv. 38; Deut. vi. 8; xxii. 12. ‡ 6. Mark xii. 38, 39; Luke xi. 43; xx. 46. ‡ 8. James iii. 1. ‡ 11. Matt. xx. 26, 27. ‡ 12. Luke xiv. 11; xviii. 14; James iv. 6; 1 Peter v. 5.

ὅταν γενηται, ποιειτε αυτον υἱον γεεννης
when he becomes, you make him a son of Gehenna
διπλοτερον ὑμων. 16 Ουαι ὑμιν, ὁδηγοι τυφλοι,
double of you: Woe to you, guides blind,
οἱ λεγοντες· Ὁς αν ομοσῃ εν τῳ ναῳ, ουδεν
the saying: Whoever may swear by the temple, nothing
εστιν· ὁς δ' αν ομοσῃ εν τῳ χρυσῳ του ναου,
it is who but ever may swear by the gold of the temple,
οφειλει. 17 Μωροι και τυφλοι· τις γαρ μειζων
he is bound. O fools and blind; which for greater
εστιν; ὁ χρυσος, η ὁ ναος, ὁ ἁγιαζων τον
is? the gold, or the temple, that sanctifying the
χρυσον; 18 Και· Ὁς εαν ομοσῃ εν τῳ θυσιαστηριῳ,
gold? Also; Whoever may swear by the altar,
ουδεν εστιν· ὁς δ' αν ομοσῃ εν τῳ
nothing it is; who but ever may swear by the
δωρῳ τῳ επανω αυτου, οφειλει. 19 Μωροι και
gift that upon it, he is bound. O fools and
τυφλοι· τι γαρ μειζον; το δωρον, η το
blind; which for greater? the gift, or the
θυσιαστηριον, το ἁγιαζον το δωρον; 20 Ὁ ουν
altar, that sanctifying the gift, He then
ομοσας εν τῳ θυσιαστηριῳ, ομνυει εν αυτῳ και
swearing by the altar, swears by it and
εν πασι τοις επανω αυτου· 21 και ὁ ομοσας
by all the (things) upon it; and he swearing
εν τῳ ναῳ, ομνυει εν αυτῳ και εν τῳ κατοικησαντι αυτον·
by the temple, swears by it and by the (one) having inhabited it;
22 και ὁ ομοσας εν τω ουρανω,
and he swearing by the heaven,
ομνυει εν τω θρονω του θεου και εν τω καθημενω επανω αυτου.
swears by the throne of the God and by the (one) sitting upon it.

23 Ουαι ὑμιν, γραμματεις και Φαρισαιοι, ὑποκριται·
Woe to you, scribes and Pharisees, hypocrites;
ὁτι αποδεκατουτε το ἡδυοσμον, και το
because you tithe the mint, and the
ανηθον, και το κυμινον· και αφηκατε τα βαρυτερα
dill, and the cummin; and pass by the weightier
του νομου, την κρισιν, και τον ελεον, και
(things) of the law, the justice, and the mercy, and
την πιστιν. Ταυτα δε εδει ποιησαι, κἀκεινα
the faith. These but it is binding to do, and those
μη αφιεναι. 24 Ὁδηγοι τυφλοι· οἱ διυλιζοντες
not to omit. Guides blind; the straining out
τον κωνωπα την δε καμηλον καταπινοντες.
the gnat the but camel swallowing down.

25 Ουαι ὑμιν, γραμματεις και Φαρισαιοι, ὑποκριται·
Woe to you, scribes and Pharisees, hypocrites;
ὁτι καθαριζετε το εξωθεν του ποτηριου
because you cleanse the outside of the cup

make him a Son of Gehenna doubly more than yourselves.

16 Woe to you, ‡ blind Guides! YOU who SAY, To swear by the TEMPLE, it is nothing; but to swear by the GOLD of the TEMPLE, it is binding.

17 Foolish and Blind! for which is more sacred,—the GOLD, ‡ or THAT TEMPLE * which CONSECRATED the GOLD?

18 And, to swear by the ALTAR, it is nothing; but to swear by THAT OFFERING which is upon it is binding.

19 Foolish and Blind! for which is more sacred,—the OFFERING, ‡ or THAT ALTAR which CONSECRATES the OFFERING?

20 HE therefore who SWEARS by the ALTAR, makes oath by it, and by all things on it;

21 and HE who SWEARS by the TEMPLE, makes oath by it, and by HIM who DWELT in it;

22 and HE who SWEARS by HEAVEN, makes oath by ‡ the THRONE of GOD, and by HIM who sits on it.

23 Woe to you, Scribes and Pharisees, Hypocrites! ‡ Because you pay tithe of MINT, and DILL and CUMMIN, ‡ but neglect the MORE IMPORTANT matters of the LAW,—JUSTICE, COMPASSION, and FAITH. These things you ought to practise and not to omit those.

24 Blind Guides! † who filter out the GNAT, yet swallow the CAMEL.

25 Woe to you, Scribes and Pharisees, Hypocrites! ‡ Because you purify the OUTSIDE of the CUP and the DISH, but

* VATICAN MANUSCRIPT.—17. which CONSECRATED.

† 24. An allusion to the custon of the Jews (also Greeks and Romans) of passing their wines through a strainer. The Jews did it from religious scruples, the Gentiles from cleanliness.

‡ 16. Matt. xv. 14. ‡ 17. Exod. xxx. 29. ‡ 19. Exod. xxix. 37. ‡ 22. Matt v. 34. ‡ 23. Luke xi. 42. ‡ 23. 1 Sam. xv. 22; Micah vi. 8; Matt. xii. 7. ‡ 25 Mark vii. 4; Luke xi. 39.

και της παροψιδος, εσωθεν δε γεμουσιν εξ ἁρ-
and of the dish, within but they are full of ra-
παγης και αδικιας. 26 Φαρισαιε τυφλε, καθαρισον
pine and injustice. O Pharisee blind, cleanse
πρωτον το εντος του ποτηριου και της παροψιδος,
first the inside of the cup and of the dish,
ἱνα γενηται και το εκτος αυτων καθαρον.
that may become also the outside of them clean.

27 Ουαι ὑμιν, γραμματεις και Φαρισαιοι, ὑποκ-
Woe to you, scribes and Pharisees, hypo-
ριται· ὁτι παρομοιαζετε ταφοις κεκονιαμενοις,
crites; because you are like to tombs having been whitened,
οἱτινες εξωθεν μεν φαινονται ὡραιοι, εσωθεν δε
which without indeed appear beautiful, within but
γεμουσιν οστεων νεκρων και πασης ακαθαρσιας.
are full of bones of dead and of all uncleanness.
28 Οὑτω και ὑμεις εξωθεν μεν φαινεσθε τοις
So also you without indeed appear to the
ανθρωποις δικαιοι, εσωθεν δε μεστοι εστε ὑποκ-
men just, within but full are of hy-
ρισεως και ανομιας.
pocrisy and of lawlessness.

29 Ουαι ὑμιν, γραμματεις και Φαρισαιοι, ὑποκ-
Woe to you, scribes and Pharisees, hypo-
ριται· ὁτι οικοδομειτε τους ταφους των προφη-
crites; because you build the tombs of the prophets,
των, και κοσμειτε τα μνημεια των δικαιων,
and adorn the monuments of the just,
30 και λεγετε· Ει ημεθα εν ταις ἡμεραις των
and say; If we had been in the days of the
πατερων ἡμων, ουκ αν ημεθα κοινωνοι αυτων
fathers of us, not we had been partakers of them
εν τῳ αἱματι των προφητων. 31 Ὡστε μαρτυ-
in the blood of the prophets: So that you
ρειτε ἑαυτοις, ὁτι υἱοι εστε των φονευσαντων
testify to yourselves, that sons you are of the having killed
τους προφητας. 32 Και ὑμεις πληρωσατε το
the prophets. And you fill you the
μετρον των πατερων ὑμων. 33 Οφεις, γεννηματα
measure of the fathers of you. O serpents, O broods
εχιδνων· πως φυγητε απο της κρισεως της
of vipers: how can you flee from the judgment of the
γεεννης; 34 Δια τουτο, ιδου, εγω αποστελλω
Gehenna? Because of this, lo, I send
προς ὑμας προφητας, και σοφους, και γραμμα-
to you prophets, and wise men, and scribes
τεις· και εξ αυτων αποκτενειτε και σταυρω-
and out of them you will kill and will cru-
σετε, και εξ αυτων μαστιγωσετε εν ταις
cify, and out of them you will scourge in the
συναγωγαις ὑμων και διωξετε απο πολεως εις
synagogues of you and pursue from city to
πολιν· 35 ὁπως ελθῃ εφ' ὑμας παν αιμα
city: so that may come upon you all blood
δικαιον, εκχυνομενον επι της γης απο του
righteous, being shed upon the earth from the
αἱματος Αβελ του δικαιου ἑως του αἱματος
blood of Abel the just to the blood

within, they are full of Rapine and Injustice.

26 Blind Pharisee! first purify the INSIDE of the CUP and the DISH, that the OUTSIDE of them may also become clean.

27 Woe to you, Scribes and Pharisees, Hypocrites! ‡ Because you resemble whitened Sepulchres, which indeed, outwardly, appear beautiful; but within, are full of the Bones of the Dead, and of All Impurity.

28 Thus also you, indeed, outwardly appear righteous to MEN; but inwardly you are full of Hypocrisy and Iniquity.

29 Woe to you, Scribes and Pharisees, Hypocrites! ‡ Because you build the SEPULCHRES of the PROPHETS, and ornament the MONUMENTS of the JUST,

30 and say, If we had lived in the DAYS of our FATHERS, we would not have been Participators with them in the MURDER of the PROPHETS.

31 Thus you testify against yourselves, ‡ That you are the SONS of THOSE who MURDERED the PROPHETS.

32 ‡ You also will fill up the MEASURE of your FATHERS.

33 Serpents, ‡ Progeny of vipers! how can you escape the JUDGMENT of the GEHENNA.

34 On account of this, ‡ Behold, I send to you Prophets, and Wise men, and Instructors; and some of them you will kill and crucify; and others you will scourge in your SYNAGOGUES, and persecute from City to City;

35 so that All the innocent Blood being shed upon the LAND, may come upon you, from the BLOOD of Abel the JUST,

‡ 27. Luke xi. 44; Acts xxiii. 3. ‡ 29. Luke xi. 47. ‡ 31. Acts vii. 51, 52 1 Thess. ii. 15. ‡ 32. 1 Thess. ii 16. ‡ 33. Matt. iii. 7; xii. 34. ‡ 34. Matt. xxi. 34, 35; Luke xi. 49.

Ζαχαριου υἱου Βαραχιου, ὁν εφονευσατε μεταξυ
of Zecharias a son of Barachias, whom you killed between
του ναου και του θυσιαστηριου. 36 Αμην λεγω
the temple and the altar. Indeed I say
ὑμιν, ὁτι ἡξει ταυτα παντα επι την γενεαν
to you, that shall come these (things) all upon the generation
ταυτην. 37 Ἱερουσαλημ, Ἱερουσαλημ, ἡ αποκ-
this. Jerusalem, Jerusalem, the kill-
τεινουσα τους προφητας, και λιθοβολουσα τους
ing the prophets, and stoning the
απεσταλμενους προς αὐτην· ποσακις ηθελησα
having been sent to her; how often I desired
επισυναγαγειν τα τεκνα σου, ὁν τροπον επισυ-
to gather the children of thee, what manner gathers
ναγει ορνις τα νοσσια ἑαυτης ὑπο τας πτερυγας;
a bird the brood or herself under the wings?
και ουκ ηθελησατε. 38 Ιδου, αφιεται ὑμιν ὁ
and not you were willing. Lo, is left to you the
οικος ὑμων *[ερημος.] 39 Λεγω γαρ ὑμιν· Ου
house of you [a desert.] I say for to you; Not
μη με ιδητε απ᾽ αρτι, ἑως αν ειπητε, Ευλογη-
not me you may see from now, till you may say; Having been
μενος ὁ ερχομενος εν ονοματι κυριου.
blessed he coming in name of Lord.

to the BLOOD of ‡ Zechariah, † Son of Barachiah, whom you will murder between the SANCTUARY and the ALTAR.

36 Indeed, I say to you, That all these things will come upon this GENERATION.

37 ‡O Jerusalem, Jerusalem! DESTROYING the PROPHETS, and stoning THOSE SENT to thee, how often have I desired to assemble thy CHILDREN, as a Bird collects her YOUNG under her WINGS! but you would not.

38 Behold, your HABITATION is left to you;

39 for I tell you, You shall not see me from this time, till you shall say, ‡'Blessed be HE who 'COMES in the Name of 'Jehovah.'"

ΚΕΦ. κδʹ. 24.

1 Και εξελθων ὁ Ιησους εκορευετο απο του
And being come out the Jesus was going from the
ἱερου· και προσηλθον οἱ μαθηται αυτου επιδειξαι
temple; and came the disciples of him to point out
αυτῳ τας οικοδομας του ἱερου. 2 Ὁ δε Ιησους
to him the buildings of the temple. The and Jesus
ειπεν αυτοις· Ου βλεπετε παντα ταυτα; αμην
said to them; Not see you all these; indeed
λεγω ὑμιν, ου μη αφεθῃ ὡδε λιθος επι
I say to you, not not should be left here a stone upon
λιθον, ὁς ου καταλυθησεται.
a stone, which not shall be thrown down.

3 Καθημενου δε αυτου επι του ορους των
Sitting and of him upon the mountain of the

CHAPTER XXIV.

1 ‡ And JESUS being come out was going from the TEMPLE; and his DISCIPLES came to show him the BUILDINGS of the TEMPLE.

2 And *HE answering, said to them, "Do you not see all these things? I assure you, ‡There shall not be left here a Stone upon a Stone; all will be overthrown."

3 And as he was sitting on the MOUNT of OLIVES,

* VATICAN MANUSCRIPT.—38. a desert—omit. 2. HE answering, said.

† 35. There are a variety of opinions among critics, as to who is here meant. Some think it is the Zechariah, son of Jehoiadah, mentioned in 2 Chron. xxiv. 20, 21; but this leaves the Jews innocent of the blood shed during nearly nine centuries of the most scandalous years of their history. Others think reference is here made to "Zechariah, the son of Berechiah and the grandson of Iddo," Zech. i. 1; of whose murder mention is made in the *Targum*, or Chaldee paraphrase of Jonathan Ben-Uziel, (said to be a cotemporary of Jesus Christ.) In reply to this complaint of Jeremiah, (Lam. ii. 20,) "Shall the priest and the prophet be slain in the sanctuary of the Lord?" he says, "Was it well in you to slay a prophet as you did Zechariah, the son of Hiddo, in the House of the Lord's sanctuary, because he endeavored to withdraw you from your evil ways?" This Zechariah lived some 320 years after the one previously mentioned, yet a period of over 500 years of Jewish history is left out. Were not the Jews more responsible for innocent blood shed during the last preceding five centuries of their history, than they could be for blood shed before the deluge? Others are of opinion that Jesus spoke this prophetically of that Zechariah who was massacred "in the middle of the holy place," three years before the final destruction of Jerusalem. Of him, Josephus says, he was a just man. Thus Abel was the *first*, and this Zechariah, the *last* just person, whose blood being spilt upon the land, should be required of that generation. This view agrees with the context, and recorded facts; and in agreement with the same, *ephoneusate*, a word in the first aorist tense, has been thrown into the future, instead of the past.

‡ 35. 2 Chron. xxiv. 20, 21. ‡ 37. Luke xiii. 34. ‡ 39. Psa. cxviii. 26; Matt. xxi. 9.
‡ 1. Mark xiii. 1; Luke xxi. 5. ‡ 2. Luke xix. 44.

ελαιων, προσηλθον αυτῳ οἱ μαθηται κατ' ιδιαν,
olive trees, came to him the disciples privately,
λεγοντες· Ειπε ἡμιν, ποτε ταυτα εσται; και
saying; Tell to us, when these (things) shall be? and
τι το σημειον της σης παρουσιας και της
what the sign of the thy presence and of the
συντελειας του αιωνος; 4 Και αποκριθεις ὁ
end of the age? And answering the
Ιησους ειπεν αυτοις· Βλεπετε, μη τις ὑμας
Jesus said to them; Take heed, not any one you
πλανηση. 5 Πολλοι γαρ ελευσονται επι τῳ
may deceive. Many for shall come in the
ονοματι μου, λεγοντες· Εγω ειμι ὁ Χριστος·
name of me, saying; I am the Anointed;
και πολλους πλανησουσι. 6 Μελλησετε δε
and many they shall deceive You shall be about and
ακουειν πολεμους, και ακοας πολεμων· ὁρατε,
to hear wars, and reports of wars; see,
μη θροεισθε· δει γαρ *[παντα] γενεσθαι·
not you be disturbed; it behoves for [all] to take place;
αλλ' ουπω εστι το τελος. 7 Εγερθησεται γαρ
but not yet is the end. Shall be raised up for
εθνος επι εθνος, και βασιλεια επι βασιλειαν· και
nation against nation, and kingdom against kingdom; and
εσονται λιμοι, *[και λοιμοι,] και σεισμοι κατα
there shall be famines, [and plagues,] and earthquakes in
τοπους. 8 Παντα δε ταυτα αρχη ωδινων.
places. All but these a beginning of sorrows.
9 Τοτε παραδωσουσιν ὑμας εις θλιψιν, και αποκ-
Then they shall deliver up you to affliction, and shall
τενουσιν ὑμας· και εσεσθε μισουμενοι ὑπο
kill you; and you shall be being hated by
παντων των εθνων δια το ονομα μου
all of the nations on account of the name of me.
10 Και τοτε σκανδαλισθησονται πολλοι· και
And then shall be caused to stumble many; and
αλληλους παραδωσουσι, και μισησουσιν αλλη-
each other shall deliver up, and shall hate each
λους. 11 Και πολλοι ψευδοπροφηται εγερθη-
other. And many false-prophets shall be
σονται, και πλανησουσι πολλους· 12 και δια
raised up, and shall deceive many; and because
το πληθυνθηναι την ανομιαν, ψυγησεται ἡ
of the to be increased the lawlessness, will be cooled the
αγαπη των πολλων 13 Ὁ δε ὑπομεινας εις
love of the many. He but holding out to
τελος, οὑτος σωθησεται. 14 Και κηρυχθησεται
end, this shall be saved. And shall be published
τουτο το ευαγγελιον της βασιλειας εν ὁλη τῃ
this the glad tidings of the kingdom in whole the
οικουμενη, εις μαρτυριον πασι τοις εθνεσι· και
habitable, for a testimony to all the nations. and
τοτε ἡξει το τελος. 15 Ὁταν ουν ιδητε το
then shall come the end. When therefore you may see the
βδελυγμα της ερημωσεως, το ῥηθεν
abomination of the desolation, the word having been spoken

the DISCIPLES came to him privately, saying, "Tell us, when these things will be?" and "What will be the SIGN of THY presence, and of the CONSUMMATION of the AGE?"

4 And JESUS replying to them, said, ‡"Beware, that no one deceive you;

5 for many will assume my NAME, saying, 'I am the MESSIAH;' and will deceive many.

6 And you will soon hear of Conflicts, and Reports of Battles; but take care that you be not alarmed; for these things must occur; but the END is not yet.

7 For Nation will rise against Nation, and Kingdom against Kingdom; and there will be in various places, Famines and Earthquakes.

8 Yet these are only a Beginning of Sorrows.

9 ‡Then they will deliver you up to affliction, and will destroy you; and you will be detested by All the NATIONS, on account of my NAME.

10 And then ‡ Many will be ensnared, and will betray their associates, and abhor them.

11 And ‡ Many False Prophets will arise, and will deceive Many;

12 and because VICE will abound, the LOVE of the MANY will cool.

13 ‡ But HE who PATIENTLY ENDURES to the End, will be saved.

14 And These ‡ GLAD TIDINGS of the KINGDOM will be published in the Whole HABITABLE, for a testimony to all the NATIONS; and then will the END come.

15 When, therefore, you shall see, stationed on holy Ground, THAT DESTRUCTIVE ‡ ABOMINA

* VATICAN MANUSCRIPT.—6. all—omit. 7. and plagues—omit.

‡ 4. Eph. v. 6; 1 John iv. 1. ‡ 9. Mark xiii. 9; Luke xxi. 12; John xv. 20. ‡ 10. 2 Tim. i. 15. ‡ 11. Acts xx. 29 2 Pet. ii. 1. ‡ 13. Matt. x. 22. ‡ 14. Matt. iv. 23; Rom. x. 18, x. 35 Col. i. 6, 23. ‡ 15. Dan. ix. 27 xii. 11.

δια Δανιηλ του προφητου, ἑστως εν τοπῳ
through Daniel the prophet, having stood in place
ἁγιῳ· (ὁ αναγινωσκων νοειτω·) 16 τοτε οἱ εν
holy: (he reading let him think:) then they in
τῃ Ιουδαιᾳ, φευγετωσαν επι τα ορη· 17 ὁ
the Judea, let them flee to the mountains: he
επι του δωματος, μη καταβαινετω, αραι τα εκ
upon the roof, not let him go down, to take the out of
της οικιας αὐτου· 18 και ὁ ἐν τῳ αγρῳ, μη
the house of him; and he in the field, not
επιστρεψατω οπισω, ι.·ρει τα ἱματια αὐτου.
let him turn back, to take the mantle of him.
19 Ουαι δε ταις εν γαστρι εχουσαις και ταις
Woe and to the in womb having and to the
θηλαζουσαις εν εκειναις ταις ἡμεραις. 20 Προσ-
giving suck in those the days. Pray
ευχεσθε δε, ἱνα μη γενηται ἡ φυγη ὑμων
you and, that not may be the flight of you
χειμωνος, μηδε σαββατῳ. 21 Εσται γαρ τοτε
of winter, nor in sabbath. Shall be for then
θλιψις μεγαλη, οἱα ου γεγονεν απ' αρχης
affliction great, such as not has been from a beginning
κοσμου ἑως του νυν, ουδ' ου μη γενηται. 22 Και
of world till the now, nor not not may be. And
ει μη εκολοβωθησαν αἱ ἡμεραι εκειναι, ουκ αν
except were shortened the days those, not should
εσωθη πασα σαρξ· δια δε τους εκλεκτους
be saved all flesh; on account of but the chosen
κολοβωθησονται αἱ ἡμεραι εκειναι. 23 Τοτε εαν
shall be shortened the days those. Then if
τις ὑμιν ειπῃ· Ἰδου, ὡδε ὁ χριστος, η ὡδε· μη
any to you should say; Lo, here the anointed, or here; not
πιστευσητε. 24 Εγερθησονται γαρ ψευδοχριστοι
believe you. Shall be raised for false anointed ones
και ψευδοπροφηται, και δωσουσι σημεια μεγαλα
and false prophets, and shall give signs great
και τερατα, ὡστε πλανησαι, ει δυνατον και
and wonders, so as to deceive, if possible even
τους εκλεκτους. 25 Ιδου, προειρηκα ὑμιν. 26 Εαν
the chosen. Lo, I have foretold to you. If
ουν ειπωσιν ὑμιν· Ιδου, εν τῃ ερημῳ εστι· μη
then they should say to you; Lo, in the desert he is; not
εξελθητε· Ιδου, εν τοις ταμειοις· μη πιστευ-
you should go out; Lo, in the retired places. not you should
σετε. 27 Ωσπερ γαρ ἡ αστραπη εξερχεται απο
believe. As for the lightning comes out from
ανατολων, και φαινεται ἑως δυσμων, ουτως
east, and shines to west, so

TION, which is SPOKEN
of through Daniel the
PROPHET," (READER at-
tend!)
16 †"then let THOSE
in JUDÆA escape to the
MOUNTAINS;
17 let not HIM who is
on the ROOF descend to
take the things from his
HOUSE;
18 and let not HIM who
is in the FIELD, return to
take his MANTLE.
19 ‡ But alas for the
PREGNANT and the NURS-
ING WOMEN in Those
DAYS!
20 Pray, therefore, that
your FLIGHT be not in
the Winter, nor on a Sab-
bath;
21 for ‡ then there will
be great Distress, such as
never happened from the
beginning of the world till
NOW, nor, nor ever will be.
22 ‡ And unless those
DAYS were cut short, No
One could survive; but
on account of the CHO-
SEN, those DAYS will be
limited.
23 ‡ If any one should
say to you then, 'Behold!
here is the MESSIAH,' or
'there;' believe it not;
24 because False Mes-
siahs and False Prophets
will arise, who will pro-
pose great Signs and
Prodigies; so as to de-
lude, if possible, even the
CHOSEN.
25 Remember, I have
forewarned you.
26 If, therefore, they
say to you, 'Behold, he is
in the DESERT!' go not
forth; or, 'Behold, he is
in SECRET APARTMENTS!'
believe it not.
27 ‡ For as the LIGHT-
NING emerges from the
East, and shines to the

† 16. Not only the temple, and the mountain on which it stood, but the whole city of Jerusalem, and several furlongs of land round about it, were accounted holy. † 16. Josephus and Eusebius inform us that when the Romans under Costius Gallus made their first advance towards Jerusalem, they suddenly withdrew again, in a most unexpected and indeed impolitic manner; at which Josephus testifies his surprise, since the city might then have been easily taken. By this means they gave as it were a signal to the Christians to retire; which, in regard to this admonition, they did, some to Pella, and others to Mount Libanus, and thereby preserved their lives.—*Doddridge.*

‡ 19. Luke xxiii. 29. ‡ 21. Dan. ix. 26. ‡ 22. Isa. lxvi. 8, 9. ‡ 23. Mark xiii. 21; Luke xvii. 23; xxi. 8. ‡ 27. L ıke xvii. 24.

εσται και ἡ παρουσια του υιου του ανθρωπου.
shall be also the presence of the son of the man.
28 Ὁπου *[γαρ] εαν ῃ το πτωμα, εκει συναχ-
Where [for] ever may be the carcase, there will be
θησονται οἱ αετοι. 29 Ευθεως δε μετα την θλιψιν
gathered the eagles. Immediately but after the affliction
των ἡμερων εκεινων, ὁ ἡλιος σκοτισθησεται,
of the days those, the sun shall be darkened,
και ἡ σεληνη ου δωσει το φεγγος αὑτης, και
and the moon not shall give the light of her, and
οἱ αστερες πεσουνται απο του ουρανου, και αἱ
the stars shall fall from the heaven, and the
δυναμεις των ουρανων σαλευθησονται. 30 Και
powers of the heavens shall be shaken. And
τοτε φανησεται το σημειον του υἱου του
then shall appear the sign of the son of the
ανθρωπου εν τῳ ουρανῳ· και τοτε κοψονται
man in the heaven: and then shall lament
πασαι αἱ φυλαι της γης, και οψονται τον υἱον
all the tribes of the earth, and they shall see the son
του ανθρωπου ερχομενον επι των νεφελων του
of the man coming upon the clouds of the
ουρανου, μετα δυναμεως και δοξης πολλης·
heaven, with power and glory much;
31 και αποστελει τους αγγελους αὑτου μετα
and he will send the messengers of him with
σαλπιγγος φωνης μεγαλης· και επισυναξουσι
of trumpet a voice great; and they shall gather
τους εκλεκτους αυτου εκ των τεσσαρων ανεμων,
the chosen (ones) of him from the four winds,
απ' ακρων ουρανων ἑως ακρων αυτων. 32 Απο
from extremities of heavens to extremities of them From
δε της συκης μαθετε την παραβολην· ὁταν
but the fig-tree learn you the parable; when
ηδη ὁ κλαδος αυτης γενηται ἁπαλος, και τα
already the branch of her may be tender, and the
φυλλα εκφυῃ, γινωσκετε, ὁτι εγγυς το
leaves may put forth, you know, that near the
θερος· 33 Οὑτω και ὑμεις, ὁταν ιδητε παντα
summer; So also you, when you may see all
ταυτα, γινωσκετε, ὁτι εγγυς εστιν επι θυραις.
these, know you, that near it is at doors.
34 Αμην λεγω ὑμιν, ου μη παρελθῃ ἡ γενεα
Indeed I say to you, not not may pass away the generation
αὑτη, ἑως αν παντα ταυτα γενηται. 35 Ὁ
this, till all these may be done. The
ουρανος και ἡ γη παρελευσεται· οἱ δε λογοι
heaven and the earth shall pass away; the but words
μου ου μη παρελθωσι.
of me not not may pass away.

36 Περι δε της ἡμερας εκεινης και ὡρας ουδεις
About and the day that and hour no one
οιδεν, ουδε οἱ αγγελοι των ουρανων, ει μη ὁ
knows, nor the messengers of the heavens, except the
πατηρ μονος. 37 Ὡσπερ δε αι ἡμεραι του Νωε,
father alone. As and the days of the Noe,

West; so will be the PRESENCE of the SON of MAN.

28 Wherever the DEAD CARCASS may be, there the ‡EAGLES will be collected.

29 And speedily after the AFFLICTION of those DAYS, ‡the SUN will be obscured, and the MOON will withhold her LIGHT, and the STARS will fall from HEAVEN, and the POWERS of the HEAVENS will be shaken.

30 And the SIGN of the SON of MAN will then appear in *Heaven; ‡and then All the TRIBES of the LAND will lament; and they will see the SON of MAN coming on the CLOUDS of HEAVEN, with great Majesty and Power.

31 ‡And he will send his MESSENGERS with a loud-sounding Trumpet, and they will assemble his CHOSEN from the FOUR Winds,—from one Extremity of Heaven to the other.

32 Now learn a PARABLE from the FIG-TREE. When its BRANCH is yet tender, and puts forth leaves, you know that SUMMER is near.

33 Thus also, when you shall see All these things, know, That ‡he is nigh at the Doors.

34 Indeed, I say to you, *That this ‡GENERATION will not pass away, till All these things be accomplished.

35 The HEAVEN and the EARTH will fail; but my WORDS cannot fail.

36 ‡ But no one knows concerning that DAY and *Hour; no, not the ANGELS of the HEAVENS, *nor the SON, but the FATHER only.

37 *For as the DAYS

* VATICAN MANUSCRIPT.—28 for—*omit*. 30. Heaven. 34. That this. 36. Hour. 36. nor the SON, but the FATHER only. 37. For as.

‡ 28. Deut. xxviii. 49. ‡ 29. Mark xiii. 24; Luke xxi. 25; Acts ii. 20. ‡ 30. Rev. i. 7. ‡ 31. Matt. xiii. 41; 1 Cor. xv. 52; 1 Thess. iv. 16. ‡ 33. James v. 9. ‡ 34. Matt. xxiii. 36; Mark xiii. 30; Luke xxi. 32. ‡ 36. Acts i. 7.

ούτως εσται *[και] ἡ παρουσια του υἱου του
even so will be [also] the presence of the son of the
ανθρωπου. 38 Ὡσπερ γαρ ησαν εν ταις ἡμεραις
man. As for they were in the days
ταις προ του κατακλυσμου τρωγοντες και
the before the flood eating and
πινοντες, γαμουντες και εκγαμιζοντες, αχρι
drinking, marrying and giving in marriage, till
ἡς ἡμερας εισηλθε Νωε εις την κιβωτον,
of which day entered Noe into the ark,
39 και ουκ εγνωσαν, ἑως ηλθεν ὁ κατακλυσμος
and not they knew, till came the flood
και ηρεν ἁπαντας· ούτως εσται *[και] ἡ
and took away all; even so will be [also] the
παρουσια του υἱου του ανθρωπου. 40 Τοτε δυο
presence of the son of the man. Then two
εσονται εν τῳ αγρῳ· ὁ εἱς παραλαμβανεται,
shall be in the field: the one is taken away,
και ὁ εἱς αφιεται. 41 Δυο αληθουσαι εν τῳ
and the one is left. Two grinding in the
μυλωνι· μια παραλαμβανεται, και μια αφιεται.
mill; one is taken away, and one is left.
42 Γρηγορειτε ουν, ὁτι ουκ οιδατε, ποιᾳ ὡρᾳ
Watch you therefore, because not you know, in what hour
ὁ κυριος ὑμων ερχεται. 43 Εκεινο δε γινωσκετε,
the Lord of you comes. This but know you,
ὁτι ει ηδει ὁ οικοδεσποτης, ποιᾳ φυλακῃ ὁ
that if had known the householder, in what watch the
κλεπτης ερχεται, εγρηγορησεν αν, και ουκ
thief comes, he would have watched, and not
αν ειασε διορυγηναι την οικιαν αὑτου.
he would have allowed to be dug-through the house of him.
44 Δια τουτο και ὑμεις γινεσθε ἑτοιμοι· ὁτι,
On account of this also you be ready; because,
ᾗ ὡρᾳ ου δοκειτε, ὁ υἱος του ανθρωπου
in which hour not you think, the son of the man
ερχεται.
comes.

45 Τις αρα εστιν ὁ πιστος δουλος και φρονιμος,
Who then is the faithful slave and prudent,
ὁν κατεστησεν ὁ κυριος αυτου επι της θερα-
whom placed the lord of him over of the domes-
πειας αὑτου, του δουναι αυτοις την τροφην εν
tics of him, of the to give to them the food in
καιρῳ; 46 Μακαριος ὁ δουλος εκεινος, ὁν ελθων
season? Blessed the slave that, whom coming
ὁ κυριος αυτου εὑρησει ποιουντα οὑτως. 47 Αμην
the lord of him shall find doing so. Indeed
λεγω ὑμιν, ὁτι επι πασι τοις ὑπαρχουσιν αυτου
I say to you, that over all the possessions of him
καταστησει αυτον. 48 Εαν δε ειπῃ ὁ κακος
he will place him. If but should say the bad
δουλος εκεινος εν τῃ καρδιᾳ αυτου· Χρονιζει ὁ
slave that in the heart of him; Delays the
κυριος μου *[ελθειν·] 49 και αρξηται τυπτειν τους
lord of me [to come;] and should begin to strike the

of NOAH, thus will be the PRESENCE of the SON of MAN.

38 ‡ For as in those DAYS, THOSE before the DELUGE, they were eating and drinking, marrying, and pledging in marriage, till the Day that Noah entered the ARK,

39 and understood not, till the DELUGE came, and swept them all away; thus will be the PRESENCE of the SON of MAN.

40 ‡ Two men shall then be in the FIELD; * one will be taken, and the * other left.

41 Two women shall be grinding at the MILL; one will be taken, and the other left.

42 ‡ Watch, therefore, Because, you do not know at what * Day your MASTER will come.

43 But you know this, that if the HOUSEHOLDER knew at What Hour of the night ‡ the THIEF would come, he would watch, and not suffer him to break into his HOUSE.

44 Therefore, be you also prepared; Because the SON of MAN will come at an Hour, when you do not expect him.

45 ‡ Who then is the FAITHFUL and prudent Servant, whom his MASTER has placed over his HOUSEHOLD, to GIVE them FOOD in due Season?

46 Happy that SERVANT, whom his MASTER, on coming, shall find thus employed!

47 ‡ Indeed, I say to you, That he will appoint him over All his POSSESSIONS.

48 But if that Servant should WICKEDLY say in his HEART, 'My MASTER delays;'

49 and should begin to

* VATICAN MANUSCRIPT.—37. also—*omit.* 39. also—*omit.* 40. one. 40. other. 42. Day. 48. to come—*omit.*

‡ 38. Gen. vi. 3—5; vii. 5; Luke xvii. 26; 1 Pet. iii. 20. ‡ 42. Matt. xxv. 13; Mark xiii. 33; Luke xxi. 36. ‡ 43. Luke xii. 39; 1 Thess. v. 2; 2 Pet. iii. 10; Rev. iii. 3; xvi. 15. ‡ 47. Matt. xxv. 21, 23; Luke xxii. 29.

συνδουλος, εσθιῃ δε και πινῃ μετα των μεθυον-
fellow-slaves, may eat and also may drink with those getting

των· 50 ἡξει ὁ κυριος του δουλου εκεινου εν
drunk; shall come the lord of the slave that in

ἡμερᾳ, ᾑ ου προσδοκᾳ, και εν ὡρᾳ, ᾑ ου
a day, in which not he expects, and in an hour, in which not

γινωσκει· 51 και διχοτομησει αυτον, και το
he knows; and shall cut asunder him, and the

μερος αυτου μετα των ὑποκριτων θησει· εκει
part of him with the hypocrites will place; there

εσται ὁ κλαυθμος και ὁ βρυγμος των οδοντων.
will be the weeping and the gnashing of the teeth.

beat his FELLOW-SERVANTS, and should eat and drink with the INTEMPERATE;
50 the MASTER of that SERVANT will come in a Day when he does not expect him, and at an Hour of which he is not aware,
51 and will cut him off, and will appoint his PORTION with the HYPOCRITES; ‡there will be the WEEPING and the GNASHING of TEETH.

ΚΕΦ. κε'. 25.

1 Τοτε ὁμοιωθησεται ἡ βασιλεια των ουρανων
Then will be compared the kingdom of the heavens

δεκα παρθενοις, αἱτινες, λαβουσαι τας λαμπαδας
ten virgins, who, having taken the lamps

αὑτων, εξηλθον εις απαντησιν του νυμφιου.
of them, went out to a meeting of the bridegroom.

2 Πεντε δε ησαν εξ αυτων φρονιμοι, και πεντε
Five and were of them prudent, and five

μωραι. 3 Αἱτινες μωραι, λαβουσαι τας λαμπαδας
foolish. Who foolish, having taken the lamps

αὑτων, ουκ ελαβον μεθ' ἑαυτων ελαιον. 4 Αἱ
of them, not took with themselves oil. The

δε φρονιμοι ελαβον ελαιον εν τοις αγγειοις
but prudent took oil in the vessels

*[αὑτων] μετα των λαμπαδων αὑτων. 5 Χρονι-
[of them] with the lamps of them. Delay-

ζοντος δε του νυμφιου, ενυσταξαν πασαι, και
ing and the bridegroom, nodded all, and

εκαθευδον. 6 Μεσης δε νυκτος κραυγη γεγονεν·
did sleep. Of middle and night a cry was raised;

Ιδου, ὁ νυμφιος *[ερχεται·] εξερχεσθε εις απαν-
Lo, the bridegroom [comes;] go out to a meet-

τησιν αυτου. 7 Τοτε ηγερθησαν πασαι αἱ παρθενοι
ing of him. Then arose all the virgins

εκειναι, και εκοσμησαν τας λαμπαδας αὑτων.
those, and put in order the lamps of them.

CHAPTER XXV.

1 The KINGDOM of the HEAVENS, at that time, may be compared to Ten † Virgins, who, having taken their LAMPS, went out †to meet ‡the BRIDEGROOM.
2 Now five of them were * foolish, and five were prudent.
3 * For the FOOLISH took their LAMPS, but carried no Oil with them.
4 The PRUDENT, however, besides * their own LAMPS, took Oil in the VESSELS.
5 While the BRIDEGROOM delayed, ‡ they all became drowsy, and fell asleep.
6 And at Midnight a Cry was raised, 'Behold, the BRIDEGROOM; go out and *meet him!'
7 Then All those VIRGINS arose, ‡and trimmed their LAMPS in order.

* VATICAN MANUSCRIPT.—2. foolish, and five were prudent. 3. For the FOOLISH. 4. their own. 6. comes—*omit*. 6. to the Meeting.

† 1. *Virgin* signifies a chaste or pure person, and is applied to both sexes in the sacred writings. See Rev. xiv. 4 It has been thought best to retain the word here. † 1. An eye-witness of a Hindoo marriage, gives the following striking illustration of this custom:—"The bride lived at Serampore, to which place the bridegroom was to come by water. After waiting two or three hours, at length, near midnight, it was announced in the very words of Scripture, 'Behold, the bridegroom cometh; go ye out to meet him.' All the persons employed now lighted their lamps, and ran with them in their hands to fill up their stations in the procession; some of them had lost their lights, and were unprepared, but it was then too late to seek them, and the cavalcade moved forward to the house of the bride; at which place the company entered a large and splendidly illuminated area, before the house, covered with an awning, where a great multitude of friends, dressed in their best apparel, were seated upon mats. The bridegroom was carried in the arms of a friend, and placed in a superb seat in the midst of the company, where he sat a short time, and then went into the house, the door of which was immediately shut, and guarded by sepoys. I and others expostulated with the door-keepers, but in vain. Never was I so struck with our Lord's beautiful parable as at this moment—'And the door was shut.'"

‡ 51. Matt. viii. 12; xiii. 42; xxv. 30. ‡ 1. [illegible] 29, 30; Rev. xix 7: xxi. 2, 9
‡ 5. 1 Thess. v. 6. ‡ 7. Luke xii. 35.

Αἱ δε μωραι ταις φρονιμοις ειπον· Δοτε ἡμιν
The but foolish to the prudent said; Give to us
εκ του ελαιου ὑμων, ὁτι αἱ λαμπαδες ἡμων
out of the oil of you, because the lamps of us
σβεννυνται. 9 Απεκριθησαν *[δε] αἱ φρονιμοι,
are extinguished. Answered [but] the prudent,
λεγουσαι· Μηποτε ουκ αρκεσῃ ἡμιν και ὑμιν·
saying; Lest not it might suffice to us and to you;
πορευεσθε μαλλον προς τους πωλουντας, και
go you rather to the selling, and
αγορασατε ἑαυταις. 10 Απερχομενων δε αυτων
buy to yourselves. Going away and of them
αγορασαι, ηλθεν ὁ νυμφιος· και αἱ ἑτοιμοι
to buy, came the bridegroom; and the prepared ones
εισηλθον μετ' αυτου εις τους γαμους· και εκ-
entered with him into the nuptial-feasts; and was
λεισθη ἡ θυρα. 11 Ὑστερον δε ερχονται και
closed the door. Afterwards and came also
αἱ λοιπαι παρθενοι, λεγουσαι· Κυριε, κυριε,
the remaining virgins, saying, O lord, O lord,
ανοιξον ἡμιν. 12 Ὁ δε αποκριθεις ειπεν· Αμην
open to us. He but answering said; Indeed
λεγω ὑμιν, ουκ οιδα ὑμας. 14 Γρηγορειτε ουν,
I say to you, not I know you. Watch you therefore,
ὁτι ουκ οιδατε την ἡμεραν, ουδε την ὡραν.
because not you know the day, nor the hour.
14 Ὡσπερ γαρ ανθρωπος αποδημων εκαλεσε τους
Like for a man going abroad called the
ιδιους δουλους, και παρεδωκεν αυτοις τα ὑπαρ-
own slaves, and delivered to them the goods
χοντα αὑτου· 15 και ᾡ μεν εδωκε πεντε
of him. and to him indeed he gave five
ταλαντα, ᾡ δε δυο, ᾡ δε ἑν· ἑκαστῳ
talents, to him and two, to him and one; to each
κατα την ιδιαν δυναμιν· και απεδημησεν
according to the own power; and went abroad
ευθεως. 16 Πορευθεις *[δε] ὁ τα πεντε
immediately. Going [and] he the five
ταλαντα λαβων, ειργασατο εν αυτοις, και
talents having received, traded with them, and
εποιησεν αλλα πεντε *[ταλαντα.] 17 Ὡσαυ-
made other five [talents.] Like
τως *[και ὁ] τα δυο, εκερδησε και αυτος αλλα
wise [also he] the two, gained also he other
δυο. 18 Ὁ δε το ἑν λαβων απελθων ωρυξεν
two. He but the one having received having retired digged
*[εν] τῃ γῃ, και απεκρυψε το αργυριον του
[in] the earth, and hid the silver of the
κυριου αὑτου. 19 Μετα δε χρονον πολυν ερχεται
lord of him. After but time much comes
ὁ κυριος των δουλων εκεινων, και συναιρει
the lord of the slaves those, and adjusts
μετ' αυτων λογον. 20 Και προσελθων ὁ τα
with them an account. And coming he the

8 And the FOOLISH said to the PRUDENT, 'Give us of your OIL; for our LAMPS are going out.'

9 But the PRUDENT replied, saying, 'Lest there be not enough for us and you, go rather to THOSE who SELL, and buy for yourselves!'

10 And while they were going away to buy, the BRIDEGROOM came; and THEY, who were PREPARED, entered with him to the NUPTIAL-FEASTS; ‡ and the DOOR was shut.

11 Afterwards came also the OTHER Virgins, saying, ‡ 'Master, Master, open it for us!'

12 But HE answering, said, 'Indeed, I say to you, I recognize you not.'

13 ‡ Watch, therefore, because you know neither the DAY nor the HOUR.

14 ‡ Again, [it is] like a Man, who, intending to travel, called his OWN Servants, and delivered to them his GOODS.

15 And to ONE he gave Five † Talents, to ANOTHER two, and to ANOTHER one; ‡ to each according to his RESPECTIVE Capacity; and immediately departed.

16 He who had RECIEVED the FIVE Talents, went and traded with them, and * gained Other five.

17 And in like manner HE who had received the TWO, gained Other two.

18 But HE who had received the ONE, went and digged the EARTH, and hid his MASTER'S MONEY.

19 After a long Time the MASTER of those SERVANTS returned, and reckoned with them.

20 Then HE, who had

* VATICAN MANUSCRIPT.—9. but—*omit*. 16. And—*omit*. 16. gained Other five. 16. Talents—*omit*. 17. he also—*omit*. 18. in—*omit*.

† 15. A talent is estimated by different writers to be in value somewhere between 700 and 2,250 dollars, or £140 and £560.

‡ 10. Luke xiii. 25. ‡ 12. Matt. vii. 21, 22. ‡ 13. Matt. xxiv. 42, 44; Mark xiii. 33, 35. ‡ 14. Luke xix. 12. ‡ 15. Rom. xii. 6; 1 Cor. xii. 7, 11, 29; Eph. iv. 11.

πεντε ταλαντα λαβων, προσηνεγκεν αλλα
five talents having received, brought other

πεντε ταλαντα, λεγων· Κυριε, πεντε ταλαντα
five talents, saying; O lord, five talents

μοι παρεδωκας· ιδε, αλλα πεντε ταλαντα
to me thou deliveredst; see, other five talents

εκερδησα *[επ' αυτοις.] 21 Εφη αυτῳ ὁ κυριος
I gained [upon them.] Said to him the lord

αυτου· Ευ, δουλε αγαθε και πιστε· επι ολιγα
of him; Well, O slave good and faithful; over a few (things)

ης πιστος, επι πολλων σε καταστησω·
thou wast faithful, over many thee I will place:

εισελθε εις την χαραν του κυριου σου.
enter into the joy of the lord of thee.

22 Προσελθων δε και ὁ τα δυο ταλαντα *[λα-
Coming and also he the two talents [having

βων,] ειπε· κυριε, δυο ταλαντα μοι παρεδωκας·
received,] said: O lord, two talents to me thou deliveredst;

ιδε, αλλα δυο ταλαντα εκερδησα *[επ' αυτοις·]
lo, other two talents I gained [upon them:]

23 Εφη αυτῳ ὁ κυριος αυτου· Ευ, δουλε αγαθε
Said to him the lord of him: Well, O slave good

και πιστε· επι ολιγα ης πιστος, επι
and faithful; over a few (things) thou wast faithful, over

πολλων σε καταστησω· εισελθε εις την χαραν
many thee I will place; enter into the joy

του κυριου σου. 24 Προσελθων δε και ὁ το ἑν
of the lord of thee. Coming and also he the one

ταλαντον ειληφως, ειπε· κυριε, εγνων σε, ὁτι
talent having taken, said; O lord, I knew thee, that

σκληρος ει ανθρωπος, θεριζων ὁπου ουκ εσπει-
hard thou art a man, reaping where not thou sow-

ρας, και συναγων ὁθεν ου διεσκορπισας· 25 και
edst, and gathering whence not thou scatteredst; and

φοβηθεις, απελθων εκρυψα το ταλαντον σου εν
being afraid, going away I hid the talent of thee in

τῃ γῃ· ιδε, εχεις το σον. 26 Αποκριθεις δε
the earth; lo, thou hast the thine. Answering and

ὁ κυριος αυτου ειπεν αυτῳ· Πονηρε δουλε και
the lord of him said to him: O wicked slave and

οκνηρε, ῃδεις, ὁτι θεριζω ὁπου ουκ εσπειρα,
slothful, didst thou know, that I reap where not I sowed,

και συναγω ὁθεν ου διεσκορπισα; 27 Εδει ουν
and gather whence not I scattered? It behoved then

σε βαλειν το αργυριον μου τοις τραπεζιταις·
thee to cast the silver of me to the bankers:

και ελθων εγω εκομισαμην αν το εμον συν
and coming I might have received the mine with

τοκῳ. 28 Αρατε ουν απ' αυτου το ταλαντον,
interest. Take you therefore from him the talent,

και δοτε τῳ εχοντι τα δεκα ταλαντα. 29 Τῳ
and give to him having the ten talents. To the

RECEIVED the FIVE Talents, came and presented Five Talents more, saying, 'Sir, thou gavest over to me Five Talents; see, I have gained Five other Talents.'

21 His MASTER said to him, 'Well done, good and faithful Servant! thou hast been faithful in a Few things, ‡ I will appoint thee over Many; partake of thy MASTER'S JOY.'

22 HE also who had the TWO Talents, coming, said, 'Sir, thou gavest over to me Two Talents; see, I have gained Two Other Talents.'

23 His MASTER said to him, 'Well done, good and faithful Servant! thou hast been faithful in a Few things, I will appoint thee over Many; partake of thy MASTER'S JOY.'

24 Then HE who had RECEIVED the SINLGE Talent, approaching, said, 'Sir, I knew thee that thou art a Severe Man, reaping where thou hast not sown, and gathering where thou hast not scattered;

25 and being afraid, I went and hid thy TALENT in the EARTH; see, thou hast THINE own.'

26 His MASTER answering, said to him, 'Wicked and indolent Servant, didst thou know That I reap where I have not sown, and gather where I have not scattered?

27 Thou oughtest then to have given my MONEY to the BANKERS, that at my return, I might have received mine OWN with Interest.

28 Take from him, therefore, the TALENT, and give it to HIM who has the TEN Talents;

29 ‡ for to EVERY ONE

* VATICAN MANUSCRIPT.—20. upon them—*omit*. 22. having received—*omit*. 22. upon them—*omit*.

‡ 21. Matt. xxiv. 47; Luke xii. 44; xix. 17; xxii. 29, 30. ‡ 29. Matt. xiii. 12; Mark iv. 25; Luke viii. 18; xix. 26.

γαρ εχοντι παντι δοθησεται, και περισσευ-
for having all shall be given, and he shall
θησεται· απο δε του μη εχοντας, και ὁ εχει,
abound: from but the not having, even what he has,
αρθησεται απ' αυτου. 30 Και τον αχρειον
shall be taken away from him. And the useless
δουλον εκβαλετε εις το σκοτος το εξωτερον·
slave cast you into the darkness the outer:
εκει εσται ὁ κλαυθμος και ὁ βρυγμος των
there shall be the weeping and the gnashing of the
οδοντων.
teeth.

31 Ὁταν δε ελθῃ ὁ υἱος του ανθρωπου εν τῃ
When and may come the son of the man in the
δοξῃ αὑτου, και παντες οἱ αγγελοι μετ' αυτου,
glory of him, and all the messengers with him,
τοτε καθισει επι θρονου δοξης αυτου, 32 και
then shall he sit on a throne of glory of him, and
συναχθησεται εμπροσθεν αυτου παντα τα εθνη·
will be gathered in presence of him all the nations;
και αφοριει αυτους απ' αλληλων, ὡσπερ ὁ
and he will separate them from each other, as the
ποιμην αφοριζει τα προβατα απο των εριφων·
shepherd separates the sheep from the goats;
33 και στησει τα μεν προβατα εκ δεξιων αὑτου,
and he will place the indeed sheep by right of him,
τα δε εριφια εξ ευωνυμων. 34 Τοτε ερει ὁ
the and goats by left. Then will say the
βασιλευς τοις εκ δεξιων αὑτου· Δευτε οἱ
king to the by right of him, Come the
ευλογημενοι του πατρος μου, κληρονομησατε
having been blessed of the father of me, inherit
την ἡτοιμασμενην ὑμιν βασιλειαν απο κατα-
the having been prepared to you kingdom from a foun-
βολης κοσμου. 35 Επεινασα γαρ, και εδωκατε
dation of world. I hungered for, and you gave
μοι φαγειν· εδιψησα, και εποτισατε με·
to me to eat; I thirsted, and you gave drink to me;
ξενος ἠμην, και συνηγαγετε με· 36 γυμνος,
a stranger I was, and you entertained me; naked,
και περιεβαλετε με· ησθενησα, και επεσκεψασθε
and you clothed me; I was sick, and you visited
με· εν φυλακῃ ημην, και ηλθετε προς με.
me: in prison I was, and you came to me.
37 Τοτε αποκριθησονται αυτῳ οἱ δικαιοι, λεγον-
Then shall answer to him the just ones, saying;
τες· Κυριε, ποτε σε ειδομεν πεινωντα, και
O lord, when thee we saw hungering, and
εθρεψαμεν; η διψωντα, και εποτισαμεν; 38 Ποτε
nourished? or thirsting, and we gave drink? When
δε σε ειδομεν ξενον, και συνηγαγομεν; η
and thee we saw a stranger, and we entertained? or
γυμνον, και περιεβαλομεν; 39 Ποτε δε σε
naked, and we clothed? When and thee
ειδομεν ασθενη, η εν φυλακῃ, και ηλθομεν προς
we saw sick, or in prison, and we came to

who HAS, more shall be given, and he shall abound; but from HIM who HAS not, even that which he has shall be taken away.

30 And thrust the UNPROFITABLE Servant into the OUTER DARKNESS: ‡there shall be the WEEPING and the GNASHING of TEETH.

31 ‡Now when the SON of MAN shall come in his GLORY, and All the ANGELS with him, then will he sit upon his Glorious Throne;

32 ‡and All the NATIONS will be assembled before him; and he will separate them from each other, as a SHEPHERD separates the SHEEP from the GOATS;

33 and he will place the SHEEP at his Right hand, but the GOATS at his Left.

34 Then will the KING say to THOSE at his Right hand, 'Come, you BLESSED ones of my FATHER, inherit the KINGDOM ‡prepared for you from the Formation of the World;

35 for I was hungry, and you gave me food; I was thirsty, and you gave me drink; I was a Stranger, and you entertained me;

36 I was naked, and you clothed me; I was sick, and you assisted me; I was in Prison, and you visited me.'

37 The RIGHTEOUS will then reply, saying, 'Lord, when did we see thee hungry, and feed thee? or thirsty, and give thee drink?

38 And when did we see thee a Stranger, and entertain thee? or naked, and clothe thee?

39 And when did we see thee sick, or in Prison, and came to thee?'

‡ 31. Zech. xiv. 5; Matt. xvi. 27; xix. 28; Mark viii. 38; 1 Thess. iv. 16; 2 Thess. i. 7; Jude 14; Rev. i. 7. ‡ 33. Rom. xiv. 10; 2 Cor. v. 10; Rev. xx. 12. ‡ 34. Matt. xx. 23; Mark x. 40; 1 Cor. ii. 9; Heb. xi. 16.

σε; 40 Και αποκριθεις ὁ βασιλευς ερει αυτοις·
thee? And answering the king will say to them;
Αμην λεγω ὑμιν, εφ' ὁσον εποιησατε ἑνι
Indeed I say to you, in whatever you did to one
τουτων των αδελφων μου των ελαχιστων, εμοι
of these of the brothers of me of the least, to me
εποιησατε.
you did.
41 Τοτε ερει και τοις εξ ευωνυμων· Πορευεσθε
Then he will say also to the of left; Go
απ' εμου οἱ κατηραμενοι εις το πυρ το αιωνιον,
from me the having been cursed into the fire the age-lasting,
το ητοιμασμενον τῳ διαβολῳ και τοις αγγελοις
that having been prepared to the accuser and to the messengers
αυτου. 42 Επεινασα γαρ, και ουκ εδωκατε μοι
of him. I hungered for, and not you gave to me
φαγειν· εδιψησα, και ουκ εποτισατε με·
to eat; I thirsted, and not you gave drink to me,
43 ξενος ημην, και ου συνηγαγετε με· γυμνος, και
a stranger I was, and not you entertained me; naked, and
ου περιεβαλετε με· ασθενης, και εν φυλακῃ,
not you clothed me; sick, and in prison,
και ουκ επεσκεψασθε με. 44 Τοτε αποκριθησον-
and not you visited me. Then will answer
ται και αυτοι, λεγοντες· Κυριε, ποτε σε
and they, saying; O lord, when thee
ειδομεν πεινωντα, η διψωντα, η ξενον, η
we saw hungering, or thirsting, or a stranger, or
γυμνον, η ασθενη, η εν φυλακῃ, και ου διη-
naked, or sick, or in prison, and not we
κονησαμεν σοι; 45 Τοτε αποκριθησεται αυτοις,
served thee; Then he will answer them,
λεγων· Αμην λεγω ὑμιν, εφ' ὁσον ουκ εποιη-
saying: Indeed I say to you, in as much not you
σατε ενι τουτων των ελαχιστων, ουδε εμοι
did to one of these of the least, neither to me
εποιησατε. 46 Και απελευσονται οὗτοι εις
you did. And shall go away these into
κολασιν αιωνιον· οἱ δε δικαιοι εις ζωην
a cutting-off age-lasting: the and just ones into life
αιωνιον.
age-lasting.

ΚΕΦ. κς'. 26.

1 Και εγενετο, ὁτε ετελεσεν ὁ Ιησους παντας
And it happened, when had finished the Jesus all
τους λογους τουτους, ειπε τοις μαθηταις αυτου·
the words these, he said to the disciples of him:
2 Οιδατε, ὁτι μετα δυο ἡμερας το πασχα γινεται·
You know, that after two days the passover comes on:
και ὁ υἱος του ανθρωπου παραδιδοται εις το
and the son of the man is delivered into the

40 And the KING answering, will say to them. ‡'Indeed, I say to you, That since you have done it to one of These the LEAST of my BRETHREN, you have done it to me.'

41 He will then also say to THOSE at his Left hand, ‡'Depart from me, you CURSED ones, into THAT AIONIAN FIRE, which is PREPARED for the ADVERSARY, and his MESSENGERS;

42 for I was hungry, but you gave me no food; I was thirsty, but you gave me no drink;

43 I was a Stranger, but you did not entertain me; naked, but you did not clothe me; sick, and in Prison, but you did not relieve me.'

44 Then will THEY also answer, saying, 'Lord, when did we see thee hungering, or thirsting, or a Stranger, or naked, or sick, or in Prison, and did not assist thee?'

45 Then he will reply to them, saying, 'Indeed, I say to you, That since you did it not to one of the LEAST of These, you did it not to me.'

46 ‡ And these shall go forth to the aionian † cutting-off; but the RIGHTEOUS to aionian Life."

CHAPTER XXVI.

1 ‡ And it happened, when JESUS had finished this DISCOURSE, he said to his DISCIPLES,

2 "You know That Two Days hence comes the PASSOVER; then the SON of MAN will be delivered up to be CRUCIFIED."

† 46. That is, in the fire mentioned in verse 41. The Common Version, and many modern ones, render *kolasin aionioon*, everlasting punishment, conveying the idea, as generally interpreted, of *basinos*, torment. *Kolasin* in its various forms only occurs in three other places in the New Testament,—Acts iv. 21; 2 Peter ii. 9; 1 John iv. 18. It is derived from *kolazoo*, which signifies, 1. *To cut off;* as lopping off branches of trees, to prune. 2. *To restrain, to repress.* The Greeks write,—"The charioteer *(kalazei)* restrains his fiery steeds." 3. *To chastise, to punish.* To cut off an indivdual from life, or society, or even to restrain, is esteemed as *punishment*;—hence has arisen this *third* metaphorical use of the word. The primary signification has been adopted, because it agrees better with the second member of the sentence, thus preserving the force and beauty of the antithesis. The righteous go to *life*, the wicked to the *cutting off* from life, or *death*. See 2 Thess. i. 9.

‡ 40. Mark ix. 41. ‡ 41. Matt. vii. 23; Luke xiii. 27. ‡ 46. Dan. xii. 2; John v. 29; Rom. ii. 7, 8. ‡ 1. Mark xiv. 1; Luke xxii. 1; John xiii. 1.

σταυρωθηναι. 3 Τοτε συνηχθησαν οἱ αρχιερεις,
to be crucified. Then were assembled the high-priests,
και οἱ γραμματεις, και οἱ πρεσβυτεροι του λαου,
and the scribes, and the elders of the people,
εις την αυλην του αρχιερεως, του λεγομενου
into the court of the high-priest, that being called
Καιαφα· 4 και συνεβουλευσαντο, ἱνα τον
Kaiaphas: and they consulted, that the
Ιησουν δολῳ κρατησωσι και αποκτεινωσιν.
Jesus with deceit they might seize and might kill.
5 Ελεγον δε· Μη εν τῃ ἑορτῃ, ἱνα μη θορυβος
They said but; Not in the feast, that not a tumult
γενηται εν τῳ λαῳ.
there should be among the people.

6 Του δε Ιησου γενομενου εν Βηθανιᾳ, εν οικιᾳ
The and Jesus having arrived in Bethany, in a house
Σιμωνος του λεπρου, 7 προσηλθεν αὐτῳ γυνη,
of Simon the leper, came to him a woman,
αλαβαστρον μυρου εχουσα βαρυτιμου, και
an alabaster box of balsam having great value, and
κατεχεεν επι την κεφαλην αυτου ανακειμενου.
she poured upon the head of him being reclined.
8 Ιδοντες δε οἱ μαθηται αυτου, ηγανακτησαν,
Seeing and the disciples of him, were displeased,
λεγοντες· Εις τι ἡ απωλεια αὑτη; 9 Ἠδυ-
saying; On account of what the loss this? She was
νατο γαρ τουτο πραθηναι πολλου, και δοθηναι
able for this to have sold of much, and to have given
πτωχοις. 10 Γνους δε ὁ Ιησους ειπεν αυτοις·
to poor. Knowing and the Jesus said to them;
Τι κοπους παρεχετε τῃ γυναικι; εργον γαρ
Why troubles present you to the woman? a work for
καλον ειργασατο εις εμε. 11 Παντοτε γαρ τους
good she has wrought for me. Always for the
πτωχους εχετε μεθ' ἑαυτων· εμε δε ου παντοτε
poor you have with yourselves: me but not always
εχετε. 12 Βαλουσα γαρ αὑτη το μυρον τουτο
you have. Having cast for she the balsam this
επι του σωματος μου, προς το ενταφιασαι με
upon the body of me, to the to prepare for burial me
εποιησεν. 13 Αμην λεγω ὑμιν, ὁπου εαν κη-
she did. Indeed I say to you, wherever may be
ρυχθη το ευαγγελιον τουτο, εν ολῳ τῳ κοσμῳ,
published the glad tidings this, in whole the world,
λαληθησεται και ὁ εποιησεν αὑτη, εις μνημο-
shall be spoken also what did she, for a memo-
συνον αυτης.
rial of her.

14 Τοτε πορευθεις εἱς των δωδεκα ὁ λεγομενος
Then going one of the twelve he being named
Ιουδας Ισκαριωτης, προς τους αρχιερεις, 15 ειπε·
Judas Iscariot, to the high-priests, said;
Τι θελετε μοι δουναι, καγω ὑμιν παραδωσω
What are you willing to me to give, and I to you will deliver up
αυτον; Οἱ δε εστησαν αυτῳ τριακοντα αρ-
him? They and paid to him thirty pieces

3 ‡About this time, the HIGH-PRIESTS, and the SCRIBES, and the ELDERS of the PEOPLE, were convened in the PALACE of THAT HIGH-PRIEST, NAMED Caiaphas,

4 where they consulted how they might seize JESUS by Stratagem and destroy him.

5 But they said, "Not during the FEAST, lest there should be a Tumult among the PEOPLE."

6 ‡Now while JESUS was at Bethany, in the House of Simon the LEPER,

7 a Woman came to him, having an Alabaster box of Balsam, very valuable, which she poured on his HEAD while reclining at table.

8 ‡And *the DISCIPLES seeing it, were displeased, saying, "Why this EXTRAVAGANCE?

9 For This might have been sold at a great price, and given to the POOR."

10 JESUS knowing it, said to them, "Why do you trouble the WOMAN? She has rendered me a kind Office.

11 For you have the POOR always among you; but Me you have not always.

12 For in pouring this BALSAM on my BODY, she did it to EMBALM me.

13 Indeed, I say to you, Wherever these GLAD TIDINGS may be proclaimed in the whole WORLD, what she has done will also be spoken of to her Remembrance."

14 ‡Then THAT one of the TWELVE, NAMED Judas Iscariot, proceeding to the HIGH-PRIESTS,

15 said, "What are you willing to give me, and I will deliver him up to you?" And THEY paid him Thirty Shekels.

* VATICAN MANUSCRIPT.—8. the DISCIPLES.

‡ 3. John xi. 47; Acts iv. 25. ‡ 6. Mark xiv. 3; John xi. 1, 2; xii. 1—8. ‡ 8. John xii. 4. ‡ 14. Mark xiv. 10; Luke xxii. 3; John xiii. 2, 30.

γυρια. 16 Και απο τοτε εζητει ευκαιριαν, ἱνα
of silver. And from then he did seek opportunity, that
αυτον παραδῳ.
him he might deliver up.

17 Τῃ δε πρωτῃ των αζυμων προσηλθον
The and first of the feasts of unleavened bread came
οἱ μαθηται τῳ Ιησου, λεγοντες *[αυτῳ·] Που
the disciples to the Jesus, saying [to him;] Where
θελεις ετοιμασωμεν σοι φαγειν το πασχα; 18 Ὁ
wilt thou we make ready to thee to eat the passover? He
δε ειπεν· Ὑπαγητε εις την πολιν προς τον
and said; Go you into the city to the
δεινα, και ειπατε αυτῳ· Ὁ διδασκαλος λεγει·
certain one, and say to him; The teacher says;
Ὁ καιρος μου εγγυς εστι· προς σε ποιω το
The season of me nigh is; to thee I will make the
πασχα μετα των μαθητων μου. 19 Και εποιησαν
passover with the disciples of me. And did
οἱ μαθηται ὡς συνεταξεν αυτοις ὁ Ἰησους· και
the disciples as commanded to them the Jesus; and
ἡτοιμασαν το πασχα.
they prepared the passover.

20 Οψιας δε γενομενης ανεκειτο μετα των
Of evening and being come he reclined with the
δωδεκα. 21 Και εσθιοντων αυτων, ειπεν· Αμην
twelve. And of eating of them, he said; Indeed
λεγω ὑμιν, ὁτι εἱς εξ ὑμων παραδωσει με. 22 Και
I say to you, that one of you will deliver up me. And
λυπουμενοι σφοδρα, ηρξαντο λεγειν αυτῳ
being grieved exceedingly, they began to say to him
εκαστος *[αυτων·] Μητι εγω ειμι, κυριε;
each one [of them;] Not I am, O lord?
23 Ὁ δε αποκριθεις ειπεν· Ὁ εμβαψας μετ'
He but answering said; He dipping with
εμου εν τω τρυβλιῳ την χειρα, οὑτος με παρα-
me in the bowl the hand, this me will de-
δωσει. 24 Ὁ μεν υἱος του ανθρωπου ὑπαγει,
liver up. The indeed son of the man goes,
καθως γεγραπται περι αυτου· ουαι δε τῳ
as it has been written about him; woe but to the
ανθρωπῳ εκεινῳ, δι' οὑ ὁ υἱος του ανθρωπου
man that, through whom the son of the man
παραδιδοται· καλον ην αυτῳ, ει ουκ εγεννηθη
is delivered up; good it was to him, if not was born
ὁ ανθρωπος εκεινος. 25 Αποκριθεις δε Ιουδας,
the man that. Answering and Judas,
ὁ παραδιδους αυτον, ειπε· Μητι εγω ειμι,
he delivering up him, said: Not I am,
ῥαββι; Λεγει αυτῳ· Συ ειπας.
rabbi? He says to him: Thou hast said.

26 Εσθιοντων δε αυτων, λαβων ὁ Ιησους τον
Eating and of them, having taken the Jesus the

16 And from that time
he sought a fit Occasion
to deliver him up.
17 ‡ Now on the FIRST
day of the † UNLEAVENED
BREAD, the DISCIPLES
came to JESUS, saying,
"Where dost thou wish
that we prepare for thee
the PASCHAL SUPPER?"
18 HE answered, "Go
into the CITY to a CER-
TAIN person, and say to
him, The TEACHER says,
'My TIME is near; I will
celebrate the PASSOVER
at thy house, with my
DISCIPLES.'"
19 And the DISCIPLES
did as JESUS had ordered
them; and they prepared
the PASSOVER.
20 ‡ Now Evening be-
ing come, he reclined at
table with the TWELVE;
21 and as they were
eating, he said, "Indeed,
I tell you, That one of
you will deliver me up."
22 And being extremely
sorrowful, they began,
each one, to ask him,
"Master, is it I?"
23 And HE answering,
said, ‡ "HE who has been
DIPPING his HAND with
mine in the DISH, this
one will deliver me up.
24 The SON of MAN
indeed goes away [to
death], ‡ as it has been
written concerning him;
but alas for that MAN
through whom the SON
of MAN is delivered up!
‡ Good were it for that
MAN if he were not
born."
25 Then THAT Judas
who delivered him up,
inquired, "Rabbi, is it
I?" He says to him,
"Thou hast said."
26 ‡ And as they were
eating, JESUS taking * a

* VATICAN MANUSCRIPT.—17. to him—*omit*. 22. of them—*omit*. 26. a Loaf.

† 17. The Passover feast began yearly on the fourteenth day of the first moon in the Jewish month Nisan, and it lasted only one day; but it was immediately followed by the days of unleavened bread, which were seven. See Josephus, Ant. iii. 10, 5. So that the whole lasted eight days, and all the eight days are sometimes called, "the feast of the passover," and sometimes "the feast (or days) of unleavened bread." See Luke xxii. 1, 7.

‡ 17. Exod. xii. 6, 18; Mark xiv. 12; Luke xxii. 7. ‡ 20. Mark xiv. 17—21; Luke xxii. 14; John xiii. 21. ‡ 23. Psa. xli. 9; Luke xxii. 21; John xiii. 18. ‡ 24. Psa. xxii; Isa. liii; Dan. ix. 26; Mark ix. 12; Luke xxiv. 25, 26, 46; Acts xvii. 3; xxvi. 22, 23; 1 Cor. xv. 3. ‡ 24. John xvii. 12. ‡ 26. Mark xiv. 22; Luke xxii. 19.

αρτον, και ευλογησας, εκλασε, και εδιδου τοις
loaf, and having blessed, broke, and did give to the
μαθηταις, και ειπε· Λαβετε, φαγετε· τουτο
disciples, and said: Take you, eat you: this
εστι το σωμα μου. 27 Και λαβων το ποτηριον,
is the body of me. And having taken the cup,
και ευχαριστησας, εδωκεν αυτοις, λεγων· Πιετε
and having given thanks, he gave to them, saying; Drink you
εξ αυτου παντες· 28 τουτο γαρ εστι το αιμα
out of it all; this for is the blood
μου, το της καινης διαθηκης, το περι πολλων
of me, that of the new covenant, that about many
εκχυνομενον εις αφεσιν ἁμαρτιων. 29 Λεγω δε
being shed for forgiveness of sins; I say but
ὑμιν, ὁτι ου μη πιω απ' αρτι εκ τουτου του
to you, that not not I will drink from now of this the
γεννηματος της αμπελου, ἑως της ἡμερας
product of the vine, till the day
εκεινης, ὁταν αυτο πινω μεθ' ὑμων καινον εν τῃ
that, when it I drink with you new in the
βασιλειᾳ του πατρος μου. 30 Και ὑμνησαντες,
kingdom of the father of me. And having sung a hymn,
εξηλθον εις το ορος των ελαιων.
they departed to the mountain of the olive-trees.
31 Τοτε λεγει αυτοις ὁ Ιησους· Παντες ὑμεις
Then he says to them the Jesus; All you
σκανδαλισθησεσθε εν εμοι εν τῃ νυκτι ταυτῃ·
will be stumbled at me in the night this;
γεγραπται γαρ· "Παταξω τον ποιμενα, και
it is written for: "I will smite the shepherd, and
διασκορπισθησεται τα προβατα της ποιμνης."
will be scattered the sheep of the fold."
32 Μετα δε το εγερθηναι με, προαξω ὑμας εις
After but the to be raised me, I will go before you to
την Γαλιλαιαν. 33 Αποκριθεις δε ὁ Πετρος
the Galilee. Answering and the Peter
ειπεν αυτῳ· Ει παντες σκανδαλισθησονται εν
said to him: If all shall be stumbled at
σοι, εγω ουδεποτε σκανδαλισθησομαι. 34 Εφη
thee, I never will be stumbled. Said
αυτῳ ὁ Ιησους· Αμην λεγω σοι, ὁτι εν ταυτῃ
to him the Jesus: Indeed I say to thee, that in this
τῃ νυκτι, πριν αλεκτορα φωνησαι, τρις απαρνη-
the night, before a cock to have crowed, thrice thou wilt
σῃ με. 35 Λεγει αυτῳ ὁ Πετρος· Καν δεῃ
deny me. Says to him the Peter: And if it may behove
με συν σοι αποθανειν, ου μη σε απαρνησομαι.
me with thee to die, not not thee I will deny.
Ὁμοιως και παντες οἱ μαθηται ειπον. 36 Τοτε
In like manner also all the disciples said. Then

Loaf, and giving praise, he broke, and gave it to the DISCIPLES, and said, "Take, eat; ‡ this is my BODY."

27 Then taking * a Cup, and giving thanks, he gave it to them, saying ‡ "Drink all of you out of it.

28 for * this is my BLOOD of the COVENANT, THAT which is POURED OUT ‡ for Many, for Forgiveness of Sins.

29 ‡ But I tell you, That I will not henceforth drink of This PRODUCT of the VINE, till that DAY when I drink it new with you in my FATHER'S KINGDOM.

30 And having sung, they departed to the MOUNT of OLIVES.

31 Then JESUS says to them, "You will All stumble on my account, this NIGHT; for it is written, ‡ 'I will smite 'the SHEPHERD, and the 'SHEEP of the FLOCK will 'be dispersed.'

32 But after I am RAISED, ‡ I will precede you to GALILEE."

33 And Peter answering, said to him, "If all should stumble with respect to thee, I never will be made to stumble."

34 JESUS said to him, ‡ "Indeed, I say to thee, That This NIGHT, before † the Cock crow, thou wilt thrice disown me."

35 PETER says to him, "Though doomed to die with thee, I will not disown Thee." And All the DISCIPLES said the same.

* VATICAN MANUSCRIPT.—27. a Cup. 28. this is my BLOOD of the COVENANT, THAT which is POURED OUT.

† 34. That is, "before a watch trumpet will sound," etc. It is well known that no cocks were allowed to remain in Jerusalem during the passover feast. The Romans, who had a strong guard in the castle of Antonia, which overlooked the temple, divided the night into four watches, beginning at six, nine, twelve, and three. Mark xiii. 35, alludes to this division of time. The two last watches were both called cock-crowings. The Romans relieved guard at each watch by sound of trumpet: the trumpet of the third watch was called the first, and that of the fourth the second cock. And when it was said the cock crew, the meaning is, that the trumpet of the third watch sounded; which always happened at midnight.

‡ 26. 1 Cor. x. 16. ‡ 27. Mark xiv. 23. ‡ 28. Exod. xxiv. 8; Lev. xvii. 17; Matt. xx. 28; Heb. ix. 22. ‡ 29. Mark xiv. 25. Luke xxii. 18. ‡ 31. Matt. xi. 6; Mark xiv. 27; John xvi. 32. ‡ 31. Zech. xiii. 7. ‡ 32. Matt. xxviii. 7, 10; Mark xiv. 28. ‡ 34. Mark xiv. 30; Luke xxii. 34; John xiii. 38.

ερχεται μετ' αυτων ὁ Ιησους εις χωριον λεγο-
comes with them the Jesus into a place being
μενον Γεθσημανη, και λεγει τοις μαθηταις·
called Gethsemane, and he says to the disciples:
Καθισατε αυτου, ἑως οὑ απελθων προσευξωμαι
Sit you here, while going away I shall pray
εκει. 37 Και παραλαβων τον Πετρον και τους
there. And having taken the Peter and the
δυο υἱους Ζεβεδαιου, ηρξατο λυπεισθαι και αδη-
two sons of Zebedee, he began to be sorrowful and to be
μονειν. 38 Τοτε λεγει αυτοις· Περιλυπος
in anguish. Then he says to them; Extremely sorrowful
εστιν ἡ ψυχη μου ἑως θανατου· μεινατε ὡδε
is the soul of me to death: remain you here
και γρηγορειτε μετ' εμου. 39 Και προελθων
and watch you with me. And going forward
μικρον, επεσεν επι προσωπον αὑτου, προσευ-
a little, he fell on face of him, pray-
χομενος, και λεγων· Πατερ μου, ει δυνατον
ing, and saying; O father of me, if possible
εστι, παρελθετω απ' εμου το ποτηριον τουτο·
it is, let pass from me the cup this;
πλην ουχ ὡς εγω θελω, αλλ' ὡς συ. 40 Και
but not as I will, but as thou. And
ερχεται προς τους μαθητας, και ευρισκει αυτους
he comes to the disciples, and finds them
καθευδοντας, και λεγει τῳ Πετρῳ· Οὑτως ουκ
sleeping, and he says to the Peter, So not
ισχυσατε μιαν ὡραν γρηγορησαι μετ' εμου;
could you one hour to watch with me?
41 Γρηγορειτε και προσευχεσθε, ἱνα μη εισελ-
Watch you and pray you, that not you may
θητε εις πειρασμον· το μεν πνευμα προθυμον,
enter into temptation; the indeed spirit ready,
ἡ δε σαρξ ασθενης.
the but flesh weak.
42 Παλιν, εκ δευτερου απελθων, προσηυξατο,
Again, a second time going away, he prayed,
*[λεγων·] Πατερ μου, ει ου δυναται τουτο
[saying;] O father of me, if not it is possible this
*[το ποτηριον] παρελθειν *[απ' εμου,] εαν μη
[the cup] to pass [from me,] except
αυτο πιω, γενηθητω το θελημα σου. 43 Και
it I drink, be done the will of thee. And
ελθων ευρισκει αυτους παλιν καθευδοντας·
coming he finds them again sleeping;
(ησαν γαρ αυτων οἱ οφθαλμοι βεβαρημενοι·)
(were for of them the eyes weighed down;)
44 και αφεις αυτους, απελθων παλιν, προσηυξατο
and leaving them, going away again, he prayed
εκ τριτου, τον αυτον λογον ειπων. 45 Τοτε
a third time, the same word speaking; Then
ερχεται προς τους μαθητας αὑτου, και λεγει
he comes to the disciples of him, and says
αυτοις· Καθευδετε το λοιπον και αναπαυεσθε;
to them; Sleep you the remainder and rest you?
ιδου, ηγγικεν ἡ ὡρα, και ὁ υἱος του ανθρωπου
lo, has come nigh the hour, and the son of the man

36 ‡Then comes JESUS with them into a Place called Gethsemane, and says to his DISCIPLES, "Remain here, while I go there and pray."

37 And taking with him PETER, and the ‡TWO Sons of Zebedee, he began to be filled with sorrow and anguish.

38 Then he says to them, ‡"My SOUL is surrounded with a deadly anguish; stay here, and watch with me."

39 And going forward a little, he fell on his Face, ‡supplicating and saying, "O my Father, if it be possible, ‡let this CUP be removed from me! yet not as I will, but as thou wilt."

40 And he returns to the DISCIPLES, and finds them sleeping, and says to PETER, "It is so, then, that you could not keep awake with me a Single Hour?

41 ‡Watch and pray, that you enter not into Trial; the SPIRIT indeed is willing, but the FLESH is weak."

42 A second time returning, he supplicated, "O my Father, if it cannot be that This be removed; if I must drink it,—thy WILL be done."

43 And returning, he finds them still sleeping; (for Their EYES were overpowered.)

44 Again, leaving them, he went and prayed a third time, using *again the SAME Words.

45 He then comes to *the DISCIPLES, and says to them, "Do you Sleep NOW, and take your rest? *for behold, the HOUR is arrived, and the SON of

* VATICAN MANUSCRIPT.—42. saying—*omit.* 42. CUP—*omit.* 42. from me—*omit.* 44. again the SAME Words. 45. the DISCIPLES. 45. for behold.

‡ 36. Mark xiv. 32—35; Luke xxii. 39; John xviii. 1. ‡ 37. Matt. iv. 21. ‡ 38. John xii. 27. ‡ 39. Mark xiv. 36; Luke xxii. 42; Heb. v. 7. ‡ 39. John v. 30; vi. 38; Phil. ii. 8. ‡ 41. Mark xiii. 33; xiv. 38; Luke xxii. 40, 46; Eph. vi. 18.

παραδιδοται εις χειρας ἁμαρτωλων. 46 Εγειρεσθε,
is delivered up into hands of sinners. Arise,
αγωμεν· ιδου, ηγγικεν ὁ παραδιδους με.
let us go; lo, has come nigh he delivering up me.

47 Και ετι αυτου λαλουντος, ιδου, Ιουδας, εἱς
And while of him speaking, lo, Judas, one
των δωδεκα, ηλθε, και μετ' αυτου οχλος πολυς
of the twelve, came, and with him a crowd great
μετα μαχαιρων και ξυλων, απο των αρχιερεων
with swords and clubs, from the high-priests
και πρεσβυτερων του λαου. 48 Ὁ δε παραδιδους
and elders of the people. He and delivering up
αυτον, εδωκεν αυτοις σημειον, λεγων· Ὁν αν
him, gave to them a sign, saying; Who ever
φιλησω, αυτος εστι· κρατησατε αυτον. 49 Και
I may kiss, he it is: seize him. And
ευθεως προσελθων τῳ Ιησου, ειπε· Χαιρε ῥαββι·
immediately approaching to the Jesus, he said; hail rabbi;
και κατεφιλησεν αυτον. 50 Ὁ δε Ιησους ειπεν
and kissed him. The but Jesus said
αυτῳ· Ἑταιρε, εφ' ὁ παρει; Τοτε προσελ-
to him; Companion, for what art thou present? Then coming
θοντες επεβαλον τας χειρας επι τον Ιησουν,
they laid the hands on the Jesus,
και εκρατησαν αυτον. 51 Και ιδου, εἱς των
and they seized him. And lo, one of the
μετα Ιησου, εκτεινας την χειρα, απεσπασε την
with Jesus, stretching the hand, drew out the
μαχαιραν αὑτου· και παταξας τον δουλον του
sword of him: and striking the slave of the
αρχιερεως, αφειλεν αυτου το ωτιον. 52 Τοτε
high-priest, cut off of him the ear. Then
λεγει αυτῳ ὁ Ιησους· Αποστρεψον σου την
says to him the Jesus: Return thee the
μαχαιραν εις τον τοπον αυτης· παντες γαρ οἱ
sword into the place of her: all for the
λαβοντες μαχαιραν, εν μαχαιρᾳ απολουνται.
taking a sword, by a sword shall perish.
53 Η δοκεις, ὁτι ου δυναμαι *[αρτι] παρακα-
Or thinkest thou, that not I am able [now] to en-
λεσαι τον πατερα μου, και παραστησει μοι
treat the father of me, and will furnish to me
πλειους η δωδεκα λεγεωνας αγγελων; 54 Πως
more than twelve legions of messengers? How
ουν πληρωθωσιν αἱ γραφαι, ὁτι οὑτω δει
then should be fulfilled the writings, that thus it must
γενεσθαι.
be done.

55 Εν εκεινῃ τῃ ὡρᾳ ειπεν ὁ Ιησους τοις
In that the hour said the Jesus to the
οχλοις· Ὡς επι λῃστην εξηλθετε μετα μαχαιρων
crowds: As upon a robber came you out with swords
και ξυλων, συλλαβειν με· καθ' ἡμεραν *[προς
and clubs, to take me: every day [with
ὑμας] εκαθεζομην διδασκων εν τῳ ἱερῳ, και ουκ
you] I did sit teaching in the temple, and not
εκρατησατε με· 56 Τουτο δε ὁλον γεγονεν, ἱνα
you seized me. This but all has been done, that

MAN is delivered into the Hands of Sinners."

46 Arise, let us go; behold! HE, who BETRAYS me, has come."

47 Now ‡ while Jesus was speaking, behold, Judas, one of the TWELVE, came, accompanied with a great Crowd, armed with Swords and Clubs, from the HIGH-PRIESTS and Elders of the PEOPLE.

48 And HE, who DELIVERED him up, had given them a Sign, saying, "He it is, whom I may kiss; hold him fast."

49 And immediately approaching JESUS, he said, "Hail, Rabbi!" and repeatedly kissed him.

50 But JESUS said to him, "Companion, for what purpose art thou present?" Then coming, they laid HANDS on JESUS, and secured him.

51 And behold, ‡ one of THOSE who were * with him, laying his HAND on his SWORD, drew it, and striking the SERVANT of the HIGH-PRIEST, cut off His EAR.

52 Then JESUS says to him, "Return Thy SWORD to its PLACE; ‡ for All WHO have RECOURSE to the Sword, shall perish by the Sword.

53 Or, dost thou think That I cannot entreat my FATHER, and he will send to my relief more than Twelve Legions of Angels?

54 But, in that case, how could the SCRIPTURES be verified, ‡ That thus it must be?"

55 JESUS at the same TIME said to the CROWDS, "As in pursuit of a Robber, have you come with Swords and Clubs to take me? I sat teaching in the TEMPLE every day, and you did not arrest me.

56 All this, however, has been done, that the

* VATICAN MANUSCRIPT.—51. with him. 53. now—*omit.*

‡ 47. Mark xiv. 43; Luke xxii. 47; John xviii. 3; Acts i. 16. ‡ 51. John xviii. 10. ‡ 52. Gen. ix. 6; Rev. xiii. 10. ‡ 54. Isa. liii. 7; Luke xxiv. 25, 44, 46.

πληρωθωσιν αἱ γραφαι των προφητων. Τοτε
might be fulfilled the writings of the prophets. Then
οἱ μαθηται παντες, αφεντες αυτον, εφυγον.
the disciples all, leaving him, they fled.
57 Οἱ δε κρατησαντες τον Ιησουν, απηγαγον
They and seizing the Jesus, they led
προς Καιαφαν τον αρχιερεα, ὁπου οἱ γραμματεις
to Caiaphas the high-priest, where the scribes
και οἱ πρεσβυτεροι συνηχθησαν. 58 Ὁ δε
and the elders were assembled. The but
Πετρος ηκολουθει αυτῳ απο μακροθεν, ἑως της
Peter followed him at a distance, to the
αυλης του αρχιερεως· και εισελθων εσω, εκαθητο
palace of the high-priest; and having gone in, sat
μετα των ὑπηρετων, ἰδειν το τελος.
with the attendants, to see the end.
59 Οἱ δε αρχιερεις *[και οἱ πρεσβυτεροι] και
The and high-priests [and the elders] and
το συνεδριον ὁλον εζητουν ψευδομαρτυριαν κατα
the high-council whole sought false testimony against
του Ιησου, ὁπως αυτον θανατωσωσι. 60 Και
the Jesus, so that him they might deliver to death. And
ουχ εὑρον, πολλων ψευδομαρτυρων προσελ-
not they found, many false-witnesses having
θοντων. Ὑστερον δε προσελθοντες δυο *[ψευ-
come. Afterwards but coming two [false-
δομαρτυρες,] 61 ειπον· Οὑτος εφη· Δυναμαι
witnesses,] said; This affirmed; I am able
καταλυσαι τον ναον του θεου, και δια τριων
to destroy the temple of the God, and in three
ἡμερων οικοδομησαι αυτον. 62 Και αναστας ὁ
days to build it. And rising up the
αρχιερευς ειπεν αυτῳ· Ουδεν αποκρινῃ; τι
high-priest said to him; Nothing answerest thou? what
οὑτοι σου καταμαρτυρουσιν; 63 Ὁ δε Ιησους
these of thee testify against? The but Jesus
εσιωπα. Και *[αποκριθεις] ὁ αρχιερευς ειπεν
was silent. And [answering] the high-priest said
αυτῳ· Εξορκιζω σε κατα του θεου του ζωντος,
to him; I adjure thee by the God of the living,
ἱνα ἡμιν ειπῃς, ει συ ει ὁ Χριστος, ὁ υἱος του
that to us thou tell, if thou art the Anointed, the son of the
θεου. 64 Λεγει αυτῳ ὁ Ιησους· Συ ειπας.
God. Says to him the Jesus; Thou hast said.
Πλην λεγω ὑμιν, απ᾽ αρτι οψεσθε τον υἱον του
Besides I say to you, from now you shall see the son of the
ανθρωπου καθημενον εκ δεξιων της δυναμεως,
man sitting at right of the power,
και ερχομενον επι των νεφελων του ουρανου.
and coming upon the clouds of the heaven.
65 Τοτε ὁ αρχιερευς διερρηξε τα ἱματια αὑτου,
Then the high-priest rent the clothes of him,

WRITINGS of the PROPHETS might be verified."
Then all *his DISCIPLES deserting him, fled.
57 ‡And THOSE who APPREHENDED JESUS, conducted him to Caiaphas the HIGH-PRIEST, where the SCRIBES and ELDERS were assembled.
58 But PETER followed him at a distance, to the PALACE of the HIGH-PRIEST; and having entered, sat with the ATTENDANTS to see the RESULT.
59 Now the HIGH-PRIESTS and the whole SANHEDRIM sought False-testimony against JESUS, so that they might deliver him to death;
60 and they did not find it, though ‡Many False-witnesses came. But at last, Two approaching,
61 said, "This man declared, ‡'I can destroy the TEMPLE of GOD, and in Three Days rebuild it.'"
62 And the HIGH-PRIEST answering, said to him, "Answerest thou nothing to what these testify against thee?"
63 ‡But Jesus was silent. And the HIGH-PRIEST said to him, †"I adjure thee BY the LIVING GOD, that thou inform us, whether thou art the MESSIAH, the SON of GOD."
64 JESUS says to him. "Thou hast said; moreover I declare to you, ‡Hereafter you shall see the SON of MAN sitting on the Right hand of POWER, and coming on the CLOUDS of HEAVEN."
65 Then the HIGH-PRIEST rent his CLOTHES,

* VATICAN MANUSCRIPT.—56. his DISCIPLES deserting. 59. and the elders—*omit*; so Lachmann and Tischendorf. 60. false-witnesses—*omit*. 63. answering—*omit*.

† 63. A solemn adjuration, which a Jew was bound to answer. Lev. v. 1. After such an adjuration by a magistrate or superior, the answer returned was an answer upon oath; a false answer was perjury, and even the silence of the person adjured was not deemed innocent. Hence it was that the high-priest had recourse to this measure upon our Lord's disdaining to answer the unfounded accusations which were brought against him, from the conviction that his judges were predetermined, and that every thing he could say would be of no avail.

‡ 57. Mark xiv. 53; Luke xxii. 54; John xviii. 12, 14, 24. ‡ 60. Mark xiv. 56—57. ‡ 61. Matt. xxvii. 40; John ii. 19—22. ‡ 63. Isa. liii. 7. Matt. xxvii. 12, 14. ‡ 64. Dan. vii. 13; Matt. xvi. 27; xxiv. 30; xxv. 31; Luke xxi. 27; John i. 51; 1 Thess. iv 16; Rev. i. 7.

λεγων· Ὁτι εβλασφημησε· τι ετι χρειαν
saying; That he blasphemes; what further need
εχομεν μαρτυρων; ιδε, νυν ηκουσατε την
have we of witnesses? see, now you heard the
βλασφημιαν αυτου. 66 Τι ὑμιν δοκει; οἱ δε
blasphemy of him. What to you thinks? they and
αποκριθεντες ειπον· Ενοχος θανατου εστι.
answering said; Liable to death he is.
67 Τοτε ενεπτυσαν εις το προσωπον αυτου, και
Then they spat into the face of him, and
εκολαφισαν αυτον· οἱ δε ερῤαπισαν,
beat with the fist him; they and struck with palms of their hands,
68 λεγοντες· Προφητευσον ἡμιν, χριστε, τις
saying; Prophesy to us, O anointed, who
εστιν ὁ παισας σε;
is he striking thee?

69 Ὁ δε Πετρος εξω εκαθητο εν τῃ αυλῃ.
The and Peter without sat in the court-yard.
Και προσηλθεν αυτῳ μια παιδισκη, λεγουσα·
And came to him one maid-servant, saying;
Και συ ησθα μετα Ιησου του Γαλιλαιου. 70 Ὁ
Also thou wast with Jesus of the Galilee. He
δε ηρνησατο εμπροσθεν αυτων παντων, λεγων·
but denied in presence of them all, saying;
Ουκ οιδα, τι λεγεις. 71 Εξελθοντα δε αυτον εις
Not I know, what thou sayest. Going out and he into
τον πυλωνα, ειδεν αυτον αλλη, και λεγει τοις
the portico, saw him another, and says to those
εκει· Και οὑτος ην μετα Ιησου του Ναζωραιου.
there; Also this was with Jesus of the Nazareth.
Και παλιν ηρνησατο μεθ᾽ ὁρκου· Ὁτι ουκ οιδα
And again he denied with an oath; That not I know
τον ανθρωπον. 73 Μετα μικρον δε προσελθοντες
the man. After a little and approaching
οἱ εστωτες, ειπον τῳ Πετρῳ· Αληθης και
those having stood by, said to the Peter: Certainly also
συ εξ αυτων ει· και γαρ ἡ λαλια σου δηλον σε
thou of them art: even for the speech of thee manifest thee
ποιει. 74 Τοτε ηρξατο καταθεματιζειν, και
makes: Then he began to curse, and
ομνυειν· Ὁτι ουκ οἰδα τον ανθρωπον. Και
to swear. That not I know the man. And
ευθεως αλεκτωρ εφωνησε. 75 Και εμνησθη ὁ
instantly a cock crew. And remembered the
Πετρος του ῥηματος του Ιησου, ειρηκοτος
Peter of the word of the Jesus, declaring
*[αυτω·] Ὁτι πριν αλεκτορα φωνησαι, τρις
[to him:] That before a cock crows, thrice
απαρνησῃ με. Και εξελθων εξω, εκλαυσε
thou wilt deny me. And going out, he wept
πικρως.
bitterly.

saying, "He has spoken blasphemy; what further Need have we of Witnesses? behold, now you have heard *the BLASPHEMY.

66 ‡ What is your opinion?" And THEY answering, said, "He deserves to Die."

67 ‡ Then they spat in his FACE, and beat him with their fists; and SOME struck him on the cheek with the open hand,

68 saying, † "Divine to us, O Messiah, Who is HE STRIKING thee?"

69 ‡ Now PETER sat without in the COURT-YARD; and a Maid-servant came to him, saying, "Thou also wast with JESUS the GALILEAN."

70 But HE denied it before them all, saying, "I know not what thou sayest."

71 And passing out into the PORTICO, another saw him, and says to THEM, "This person was also there with Jesus the NAZARITE."

72 And again he denied with an Oath, "I know not the MAN."

73 And after a while, THOSE who STOOD BY, approaching, said to PETER, "Certainly, thou also art one of them; for even thy DIALECT makes Thee known."

74 Then he began to curse and to swear, "I know not the MAN." And instantly †a Cock crew.

75 And Peter recollected the DECLARATION of JESUS, ‡"That before a Cock crows, thou wilt thrice disown me." And going out, he wept bitterly.

* VATICAN MANUSCRIPT.—65. the BLASPHEMY. 75. to him—*omit.*

† 68. In this insulting taunt there seems to be an indirect sneer at the popular belief in our Lord's Messiahship; which is rendered still more apparent by the sarcastic use of the word *propheteusin.* This word is sometimes used generally in relation to things unknown, so as to correspond with the English *guess.* It should be remembered that Christ was now blindfolded, as appears from Mark xiv. 65; Luke xxii. 64.—*Kuinoel.* † 74. See Note on verse 34.

‡ 66. Mark xiv. 64. ‡ 67. Isa. l. 6; liii. 3; Luke xxii. 63, 64. ‡ 69. Mark xiv. 66; Luke xxii. 55; John xviii. 16—18, 25—27. ‡ 75. See verse 34; Mark xiv. 30; Luke xxii. 61, 62; John xiii. 38.

ΚΕΦ. κζ'. 27.

[1] Πρωιας δε γενομενης, συμβουλιον ελαβον
Morning and having come, a council held
παντες οἱ αρχιερεις και οἱ πρεσβυτεροι του
all the high-priests and the elders of the
λαου κατα του Ιησου, ὡστε θανατωσαι αυτον.
people against the Jesus, so as to deliver to death him.
[2] Και δησαντες αυτον, απηγαγον, και παρεδωκαν
And binding him, they led, and delivered up
αυτον *[Ποντιῳ] Πιλατῳ τῳ ἡγεμονι.
him [to Pontius] Pilate the governor.
[3] Τοτε ιδων Ιουδας, ὁ παραδιδους αυτον, ὁτι
Then seeing Judas, that betraying him, that
κατεκριθη, μεταμεληθεις απεστρεψε τα τρια-
he was condemned, repenting he returned the thirty
κοντα αργυρια τοις αρχιερευσι και τοις πρεσβυ-
pieces of silver to the high-priests and to the elders,
τεροις, [4] λεγων. Ἡμαρτον, παραδους αἱμα
saying, I sinned, having delivered up blood
αθωον. Οἱ δε ειπον· Τι προς ἡμας; Συ οψει.
innocent. They but said: What to us? Thou wilt see.
[5] Και ῥιψας τα αργυρια εν τῳ ναῳ, ανεχωρησε·
And hurling the pieces of silver in the temple, he withdrew;
και απελθων απηγξατο. [6] Οἱ δε αρχιερεις,
and having gone forth strangled himself. The and high-priests,
λαβοντες τα αργυρια, ειπον· Ουκ εξεστι βαλειν
taking the pieces of silver, said; Not it is lawful to put
αυτα εις τον κορβαναν, επει τιμη αἱματος εστι.
them into the treasury, since price of blood it is.
[7] Συμβουλιον δε λαβοντες, ηγορασαν εξ αυτων
Counsel and taking, they bought with them
τον αγρον του κεραμεως, εις ταφην τοις ξενοις.
the field of the potter, to bury the strangers.
[8] Διο εκληθη ὁ αγρος εκεινος, αγρος αἱματος,
Therefore is called the field that, a field of blood,
ἑως της σημερον. [9] Τοτε επληρωθη το ῥηθεν
to the day. Then was fulfilled the word spoken

CHAPTER XXVII.

1 ‡Now, at the Dawn of
day, All the HIGH-PRIESTS
and the ELDERS of the
PEOPLE, held a Council
against JESUS, in order to
deliver him to death.
2 And binding him, they
led and delivered him up
to Pilate, the GOVERNOR.
3 ‡Then THAT Judas
who DELIVERED him up,
perceiving That he was
condemned, repented; and
returned the THIRTY She-
kels to the HIGH-PRIESTS
and the ELDERS,
4 saying, "I have sin-
ned in betraying innocent
Blood." But THEY said,
"What is that to us?
Thou wilt see to that."
5 And hurling the SHE-
KELS in the TEMPLE, he
withdrew, ‡and having
gone away, strangled him-
self.
6 And the HIGH-PRIESTS
taking the MONEY, said,
"It is not lawful to put it
into the †CORBANAN, see-
ing it is the Price of Blood.
7 And taking Counsel
they bought with it the
†POTTER'S FIELD, as a
burial-place for †STRAN-
GERS.
8 Therefore that FIELD
is called, ‡The field of
Blood, even to THIS-DAY.
9 Then was verified the

* VATICAN MANUSCRIPT.—2. Pontius—*omit*.

† 6. The sacred treasury for the gifts which had been vowed to the temple. It was so named from Corban, *a gift*. See Mark vii. 11. It was a large chest with a hole in the lid, and it stood in the court of the altar, on the right side as you face the house of the Lord. See 2 Kings xii. 9. This chest was out of the reach of those who brought their money to it. They delivered their money to the priest, who placed it in the chest. Hence Judas, when his money was refused, had to throw it on to the ground. The Corbanan, or chest in the court of the altar, must be distinguished from the *gazophulakion*, the treasury, mentioned in Mark xii. 41, and John viii. 20. This was a name given to the court of the women, because therein were placed chests for voluntary gifts to the temple. They were there placed because the crowd was greatest in that court; and it was into these chests that a Jew could drop a gift so privately that his left hand should not know what his right did.—*S. Sharpe.* † 7. It was just without the wall of Jerusalem, south of mount Zion, and was originally called the potter's field, because it furnished a sort of clay suitable for potter's ware. Aceldama, as late as the seventeenth century, was used as a burying-place by the Armenian Christians in Jerusalem. But according to Robinson, it has long been abandoned for sepulchral purposes. It is not fenced in, and the charnel house, now a ruin, is all that remains to point out the site. † 7. The article is significant in the original, though our language will not bear it. For it shows that strangers in general, people of a different country and religion, are not meant; but strange Jews only; Jews who were not natives of Jerusalem, but might come there to worship at the temple, or on other business. Where no such specification is intended, the article is omitted. Eph. ii. 12; Heb. xi. 13.—*Wakefield.*

‡ 1. Mark xv. 1; Luke xxii. 66; John xviii. 28. ‡ 3. Matt. xxvi. 14, 15. ‡ 5. Acts i. 18. ‡ 8. Acts i. 19.

δια Ἰερεμιου του προφητου, λεγοντος· "Και
through Jeremiah the prophet, saying; "And
ελαβον τα τριακοντα αργυρια, την τιμην του
I took the thirty pieces of silver, the price of the
τετιμημενου, ὃν ετιμησαντο απο υἱων Ισραηλ,
having been valued, whom they valued from sons of Israel.
10 και εδωκαν αυτα εις τον αγρον του κεραμεως·
and gave them for the field of the potter;
καθα συνεταξε μοι κυριος."
even as directed me a lord."

11 Ὁ δε Ιησους εστη εμπροσθεν του ἡγεμονος·
The and Jesus stood in presence of the governor;
και επηρωτησεν αυτον ὁ ἡγεμων, λεγων· Συ
and asked him the governor, saying; Thou
ει ὁ βασιλευς των Ιουδαιων; Ὁ δε Ιησους
art the king of the Jews? The and Jesus
εφη αυτῳ· Συ λεγεις.
said to him; Thou sayest.
12 Και εν τῳ κατηγο-
And in the to be ac-
ρεισθαι αυτον ὑπο των αρχιερεων και των
cused him by the high-priests and the
πρεσβυτερων, ουδεν απεκρινατο.
elders, nothing he answered.
13 Τοτε λεγει
Then says
αυτῳ ὁ Πιλατος· Ουκ ακουεις, ποσα σου
to him the Pilate; Not thou hearest, how many things of thee
καταμαρτυρουσι;
they bear witness against?
14 Και ουκ απεκριθη αυτῳ
And not he answered him
προς ουδε ἑν ῥημα· ὡστε θαυμαζειν τον ἡγε-
to not even one word; so as to astonish the gov-
μονα λιαν.
ernor greatly.

15 Κατα δε ἑορτην ειωθει ὁ ἡγεμων απο-
At and a feast was accustomed the governor to
λυειν ἑνα τῳ οχλῳ δεσμιον, ὃν ηθελον.
release one to the crowd prisoner, whom they wished.
16 Ειχον δε τοτε δεσμιον επισημον, λεγομενον
They had and then a prisoner noted, being called
Βαραββαν.
Barabbas.
17 Συνηγμενων ουν αυτων, ειπεν
Having being assembled then of them, said
αυτοις ὁ Πιλατος· Τινα θελετε απολυσω ὑμιν;
to them the Pilate; Which wish you I release to you?

WORD SPOKEN through † Jeremiah the PROPHET, saying, ‡ "And I took "the THIRTY Shekels, (the "price at which they val-"ued the PRECIOUS ONE,) "from the Sons of Israel,
10 "and gave them "for the POTTER'S FIELD, "even as the Lord directed "me."
11 And JESUS stood before the GOVERNOR; and HE asked him, saying, ‡ "Art thou the KING of the JEWS?" And JESUS replied, "Thou sayest."
12 But he made no reply to the accusations of the HIGH-PRIESTS and the ELDERS.
13 Then PILATE says to him, "Dost thou not hear how many things they testify against thee?"
14 And he gave him no answer, not even one Word; so that the GOVERNOR was greatly surprised.
15 ‡ And at each Feast the GOVERNOR was accustomed to release to the CROWD one Prisoner, whom they wished.
16 And they had then a well-known Prisoner, named † Barabbas.
17 Therefore, being assembled, PILATE said to them, "Which do you wish that I release to you?

† 9. This quotation from the prophet has greatly puzzled the critics. The passage is not found in Jeremiah; and only something very like it in Zechariah. Several solutions of the difficulty have been offered. 1. A corruption of the names arising from MS. abbreviations; *e. g.*, some copyist mistaking *Zou*, Zechariah, for *Iou*, Jeremiah. 2. That Matthew simply wrote, *through the prophet*, omitting, as he often did, the *name* of the prophet. The ancient Syrian and Persian versions omit the name, and some Greek MSS., but a large majority of MSS. insert it. 3. Mede and Kidder suppose that Jeremiah in the first instance wrote the chapter from which these words are taken, as well as the two former, and that the Evangelist was influenced by this opinion. 4. Whitby says, "We know, from *Jerome*, that there was still extant in his time, an apocryphal book of the prophet Jeremiah, in which was found every letter of the words quoted by Matthew." Dr. Gaussen, remarks on this:—"We know also that the Second Book of Maccabees (ii. 1—9) relates many of the actions and words of Jeremiah, which are taken from another book than that of his canonical prophecies. Why, then, might not the words quoted by the evangelist have been pronounced really by Jeremiah, and have remained in the memory of the Church to the days of Zechariah, who might then have again given them a place theopneustically in holy Scripture, (as is the case with the unwritten words of Enoch, quoted in the Epistle of Jude, (verses 14 and 15,) or the unwritten words of Jesus Christ, quoted by St. Paul in the Book of Acts? (xx. 35.) What confirms this supposition is, that part only of the words quoted by St. Matthew are found in Zechariah. Besides, it is known that this prophet was fond of recalling the words of Jeremiah. (See Zech. i. 4, and Jer. xviii. 11; Zech. iii. 8, and Jer. xxiii. 5.) † 16. Some very ancient authorities cited by Origen, read "Jesus, the son of Abbas;" which Michaelis says is undoubtedly the original reading. The word "Jesus" was omitted in later copies, in honor to the name.

‡ 9. Zech. xi. 12, 13. ‡ 11. Mark xv. 2; Luke xxiii. 3; John xviii. 33. ‡ 15 Mark xv. 6 Luke xxiii. 17; John xviii. 39.

Βαραββαν, η Ιησου, τον λεγομενον Χριστου;
Barabbas? or Jesus, the being called Christ?
18 Ηιδει γαρ, ὁτι δια φθονον παρεδωκαν αυτον.
He knew for, that through envy they had delivered up him.
19 Καθημενου δε αυτου επι του βηματος, απεσ-
Being seated and of him upon the tribunal, sent
τειλε προς αυτον ἡ γυνη αυτου, λεγουσα·
to him the wife of him, saying;
Μηδεν σοι και τῳ δικαιῳ εκεινῳ· πολλα γαρ
Nothing to thee and to the just one that; many things for
επαθον σημερον κατ' οναρ δι' αυτον. 20 Οἱ
I suffered this day in a dream because of him. The
δε αρχιερεις και οἱ πρεσβυτεροι επεισαν τους
but high-priests and the elders persuaded the
οχλους, ἱνα αιτησωνται τον Βαραββαν, τον δε
crowds, that they should ask the Barabbas, the and
Ιησουν απολεσωσιν. 21 Αποκριθεις δε ὁ ἡγεμων
Jesus they might destroy. Answering and the governor
ειπεν αυτοις· Τινα θελετε απο των δυο απολυσω
said to them; Which wish you of the two I shall release
ὑμιν; Οἱ δε ειπον· Βαραββαν. 22 Λεγει αυ-
to you? They and said; Barabbas. He says to
τοις ὁ Πιλατος· Τι ουν ποιησω Ιησουν, τον
them the Pilate; What then shall I do Jesus, the
λεγομενον Χριστον; Λεγουσιν *[αυτῳ] παντες·
being called Christ? They say [to him] all;
Σταυρωθητω. 23 Ὁ δε ἡγεμων εφη· Τι γαρ
Let him be crucified. The and governor said; What for
κακον εποιησεν; Οἱ δε περισσως εκραζον,
evil has he done? They but vehemently cried,
λεγοντες, Σταυρωθητω.
saying; Let him be crucified.
24 Ιδων δε ὁ Πιλατος ὁτι ουδεν ωφελει,
Seeing and the Pilate that nothing profits,
αλλα μαλλον θορυβος γινεται, λαβων ὑδωρ,
but rather a tumult is made, taking water,
απενιψατο τας χειρας απεναντι του οχλου,
he washed the hands before the crowd,
λεγων· Αθωος ειμι απο του αἱματος *[του
saying: Innocent I am from the blood [of the
δικαιου] τουτου· ὑμεις οψεσθε. 25 Και αποκρι-
just] of this: you shall see. And answer-
θεις πας ὁ λαος ειπε· Το αἱμα αυτου εφ' ἡμας,
ing all the people said: The blood of him upon us,
και επι τα τεκνα ἡμων. 26 Τοτε απελυσεν
and upon the children of us. Then he released
αυτοις τον Βαραββαν, τον δε Ιησουν φραγελ-
to them the Barabbas, the and Jesus having
λωσας παρεδωκεν, ἱνα σταυρωθῃ.
scourged he delivered up, that he might be crucified.
27 Τοτε οἱ στρατιωται του ἡγεμονος παραλα-
Then the soldiers of the governor taking

Barabbas? or THAT Jesus who is named Christ?"
18 For he knew That they had delivered him up through Envy.
19 And while he was sitting on the TRIBUNAL, his WIFE sent to him, saying, "Have nothing to do with that JUST person; for I have suffered much † this-day, in a Dream, because of him."
20 ‡ But the HIGH-PRIESTS and the ELDERS persuaded the CROWDS to ask for BARABBAS, and to destroy JESUS.
21 And the GOVERNOR anwering, said to them, "Which of the TWO do you wish me to release to you?" And they said, * "BARABBAS."
22 PILATE says to them, "What then shall I do to THAT Jesus, who is named Christ?" They all say, "Let him be crucified."
23 And * HE said, (No;) "for what Evil has he done?" But THEY vehemently cried, saying, "Let him be crucified."
24 And Pilate, perceiving that he had no influence, but rather a Tumult was made, ‡ taking Water, he washed his hands before the CROWD, saying, "I am innocent of * this BLOOD; see you to it."
25 And All the PEOPLE answering, said, ‡ "His BLOOD rest on us, and on our CHILDREN."
26 He then released to them BARABBAS; and having scourged JESUS, he delivered him up to be crucified.
27 Then the SOLDIERS of the GOVERNOR having

* VATICAN MANUSCRIPT.—21. BARABBAS. 22. to him—*omit*. 23. HE said. 24. JUST—*omit*. 24. this BLOOD; see.

† 19. It is to be observed, that by *this day* is meant *this night*. This may seem a strange interpretation, till it is considered, that *the day*, according to the reckoning in Judea, began on the evening before Pilate's wife sent this message to her husband; and that therefore *the night* in which she had her dream, was a constituent part of what she meant by *this day*. This is agreeable to what we read in Gen. i. 5; "the evening and the morning were the first day."—*Bishop Pearce*.

‡ 20. Mark xv. 11; Luke xxiii. 18; John xviii. 40; Acts iii. 14. ‡ 24. Deut. xxi. 6. ‡ 25. Deut. xix. 10; Acts v. 28.

βοντες τον Ιησουν εις το πραιτωριον, συνηγα-
the Jesus into the judgment hall, they gathered
γον επ' αυτον όλην την σπειραν. 28 Και εκδυ-
together to him whole the company. And having
σαντες αυτον, περιεθηκαν αυτῳ χλαμυδα κοκκι-
stripped him, they put on to him a soldier's cloak scar-
νην. 29 Και πλεξαντες στεφανον εξ ακανθων,
let. And braiding a crown of thorns,
επεθηκαν επι την κεφαλην αυτου, και καλαμον
placed upon the head of him, and a reed
επι την δεξιαν αυτου· και γονυπετησαντες
on the right of him; and bending the knee
εμπροσθεν αυτου, ενεπαιζον αυτῳ, λεγοντες·
in presence of him, mocked him, saying;
Χαιρε, ὁ βασιλευς των Ιουδαιων. 30 Και εμπτυ-
Hail, the king of the Jews. And spit-
σαντες εις αυτον, ελαβον τον καλαμον, και
ting on him, they took the reed, and
ετυπτον εις την κεφαλην αυτου. 31 Και ὁτε
struck on the head of him. And when
ενεπαιξαν αυτῳ, εξεδυσαν αυτον την χλαμυδα,
they had mocked him, they took off him the soldier's cloak,
και ενεδυσαν αυτον τα ἱματια αυτου· και απη-
and put on him the garments of him; and led
γαγον αυτον εις το σταυρωσαι. 32 Εξερχομενοι
away him into the to be crucified. Going out
δε, εὑρον ανθρωπον Κυρηναιον, ονοματι Σιμωνα·
and, they met a man a Cyrenian, by name Simon;
τουτον ηγγαρευσαν, ἱνα αρῃ τον σταυρον
him they compelled, that he might carry the cross
αυτου. 33 Και ελθοντες εις τοπον λεγομενον
of him. And coming into a place being called
Γολγοθα, ὁ εστι λεγομενον κρανιου τοπος,
Golgotha, which is being called of a skull a place,
34 εδωκαν αυτῳ πιειν οξος μετα χολης μεμιγ-
they gave to him to drink vinegar with gall having been
μενον· και γευσαμενος, ουκ ηθελε πιειν.
mixed; and having tasted, not he would drink.
35 Σταυρωσαντες δε αυτον, διεμερισαντο τα
Crucifying and him, they divided the
ἱματια αυτου, βαλλοντες κληρον. 36 Και καθη-
garments of him, casting a lot. And being
μενοι ετηρουν αυτον εκει. 37 Και επεθηκαν
seated they watched him there. And they placed

led JESUS into the † PRÆTORIUM, gathered together against him the Whole COMPANY.

28 And * clothing him, ‡ they put on him a soldier's † scarlet Cloak.

29 ‡ And wreathing a Crown of Acanthus, they placed it on his HEAD, and put a Reed in his RIGHT hand; and kneeling before him, they mocked him, saying, "Hail, * King of the JEWS!"

30 ‡ And spitting on him, they took the REED, and struck him on the HEAD.

31 And when they had insulted him, they divested him of the SOLDIER'S CLOAK, and clothed him with his own RAIMENT, and led him away to be CRUCIFIED.

32 ‡ And going out, they met a Cyrenian, named Simon; him they compelled to carry his CROSS.

33 And having arrived at a Place called Golgotha, which is called, a Place of a Skull,

34 ‡ they gave him * Wine to drink, mixed with Gall; which, having tasted, he would not drink.

35 ‡ And after nailing him to the cross, they distributed his GARMENTS by Lot. †

36 And sitting down, they watched him there.

37 And over his HEAD

* VATICAN MANUSCRIPT.—28. clothing him, they put on him. 29. King of the JEWS. 34. Wine.

† 27. The palace of the Roman governor was so called. But here the court-yard in front of the Prætorium seems meant. The Roman Prætorium had been Herod's palace. It stood to the west of the temple. The road from the *Prætorium* entered the temple by a bridge over the valley at the south-west corner. † 28. The color distinguished it as suitable for a man of high rank in the army; but in shape the *clamys* was the same for the emperor and for the common soldier. This was put on him to ridicule his pretensions to the title of a king. † 29. It does not appear, that this crown was intended to *torture* his head, but rather to mock his claim to royalty. Dr. Clarke says, "Mark, chap. xv. 17; and John, chap. xix. 5, term it *stephanon akanthinon*, which may very well be translated an *acanthine crown*, or wreath formed out of the branches of the herb *acanthus*, or *bear's foot*. This, however, is a prickly plant, though nothing like thorns, in the common meaning of that word." † 35. The clause found in the Common Version, "that it might be fulfilled which was spoken by the prophet, 'They parted my garments among them, and upon my vesture did they cast lots,'" is found in comparatively few MSS., and has no place in the ancient versions.

‡ 27. Mark xv. 16; John xix. 2. ‡ 28. Luke xxiii. 11. ‡ 29. Psa. lxix 19 ‡ 30. Isa. l. 6. ‡ 32. Mark xv. 21; Luke xxiii. 26. ‡ 34. Psa. lxix. 21. ‡ 35 Psa. xxii. 18; John xix. 23.

επανω της κεφαλης αυτου την αιτιαν αυτου
above the head of him the accusation of him
γεγραμμενην· "Ουτος εστιν Ιησους ὁ βασιλευς
having been written; "This is Jesus the king
των Ιουδαιων."
of the Jews."
38 Τοτε σταυρουνται συν αυτῳ δυο λησται·
Then were crucified with him two robbers;
εἱς εκ δεξιων, και εἱς εξ ευωνυμων. 39 Οἱ
one by right, and one by left. Those
δε παραπορευομενοι εβλασφημουν αυτον,
and passing along reviled him,
κινουντες τας κεφαλας αὑτων, 40 και λεγον-
shaking the heads of them, and say-
τες· Ὁ καταλυων τον ναον, και εν τρισιν
ing; He overthrowing the temple, and in three
ἡμεραις οικοδομων, σωσον σεαυτον· ει υἱος
days building, save thyself: if a son
ει του θεου, καταβηθι απο του σταυρου.
thou art of the God, come down from the cross.
41 Ὁμοιως δε και οἱ αρχιερεις, εμπαιζοντες μετα
Likewise and also the high-priests, mocking with
των γραμματεων και πρεσβυτερων, ελεγον·
the scribes and elders, said;
42 Αλλους ησωσεν, ἑαυτον ου δυναται σωσαι· ει
Others he saved, himself not is able to save. if
βασιλευς Ισραηλ εστι, καταβατω νυν απο του
a king of Israel he is, let him come down now from the
σταυρου, και πιστευσομεν αυτῳ. 43 Πεποιθεν
cross, and we will give credit to him. He trusted
επι τον θεον· ῥυσασθω νυν αυτον, ει θελει
in the God; let him rescue now him, if he wishes
αυτον· ειπε γαρ· Ὁτι θεου ειμι υἱος. 44 Το
him; he said for; That of God I am a son. That
δ' αυτο και οἱ λησται, οἱ συσταυρωθεντες
through it also the robbers, those being crucified
αυτῳ, ωνειδιζον αυτον.
with him, reproached him.
45 Απο δε ἑκτης ὡρας σκοτος εγενετο επι
From now sixth hour darkness was on
πασαν την γην, ἑως ὡρας εννατης. 46 Περι δε
all the land, till hour ninth. About and
την εννατην ὡραν ανεβοησεν ὁ Ιησους φωνῃ
the ninth hour cried out the Jesus with a voice
μεγαλῃ, λεγων· Ηλι, ηλι· λαμα σαβαχθανι;
great, saying; Eli, Eli; lama sabachthani?
τουτ' εστι· Θεε μου, θεε μου· ἱνατι με εγκατε-
that is; O God of me, O God of me: why me hast thou
λιπες; 47 Τινες δε των εκει ἑστωτων, ακου-
forsaken? Some and of those there standing, having
σαντες, ελεγον· Ὁτι Ηλιαν φωνει οὑτος. 48 Και
heard, said; For Elias he cries this. And
ευθεως δραμων εἱς εξ αυτων, και λαβων
immediately running one of them, and taking
σπογγον, πλησας τε οξους, και περιθεις
a sponge, filling and of vinegar, and attaching

‡they placed his ACCUSATION in writing, "This is Jesus, the KING of the JEWS"

38 ‡At the same time, Two Robbers were crucified with him, one at his Right hand, and the other at his Left.

39 ‡Now those passing by, reviled him, shaking their heads,

40 and saying, "DESTROYER of the TEMPLE! and Builder of it in Three Days, save thyself. If thou art a Son of *God come down from the CROSS."

41 In like manner also, the HIGH-PRIESTS with the SCRIBES and Elders, deriding, said,

42 "He saved Others; Himself he cannot save. *Is he the King of Israel? let him now descend from the CROSS, and we will believe *on him.

43 He confided in GOD; let him rescue now, if he delights in him; for he said, 'I am God's Son.'"

44 THOSE ROBBERS also, who were CRUCIFIED with him, reproached him.

45 ‡Now from the Sixth Hour there was †Darkness on All the LAND till the ninth Hour.

46 And about the NINTH Hour, JESUS exclaimed, with a loud Voice, saying, "Eli, Eli, lama sabachthani?" that is, "My God! my God! why hast thou forsaken me?"

47 And some of THOSE STANDING there, hearing him, said, "He calls for Elijah."

48 ‡And immediately one of them ran, and taking a Sponge filled it with Vinegar, and putting it

* VATICAN MANUSCRIPT.—40. God. 42. Is he the King of Israel? 42. on him.

† 45. The darkness which occurred at this time was noticed as a prodigy by the heathens themselves. Tertullian appeals in Apol. c. 21, to the record of it in the Roman archives. It is highly improbable that it extended any further than the land of Judea.

‡ 37. Mark xv. 26, Luke xxiii. 38; John xix. 19. ‡ 38. Isa. liii. 12. ‡ 39. Psa. xxii. 7; cix. 25. ‡ 45. Mark xv. 33; Luke xxiii. 44. ‡ 48. Psa. lxix. 21.

καλαμῳ, εποτιζεν αυτον. 49 Οἱ δε λοιποι
on a reed, gave to drink him. The but others
ελεγον· Αφες· ιδωμεν, ει ερχεται Ηλιας,
said; Leave alone; we may see, if comes Elias,
σωσων αυτον. 50 Ὁ δε Ιησους, παλιν κραξας
will be saving him. The then Jesus, again crying
φωνῃ μεγαλῃ, αφηκε το πνευμα.
with a voice great, resigned the breath.

51 Και ιδου, το καταπετασμα του ναου εσχισθη
And lo, the curtain of the temple was rent
εις δυο, απο ανωθεν ἑως κατω· και ἡ γη εσ-
into two, from above to below; and the earth was
εισθη, και αἱ πετραι εσχισθησαν, 52 και τα
shaken, and the rocks were rent, and the
μνημεια ανεῳχθησαν· και πολλα σωματα των
tombs were opened; and many bodies of the
κεκοιμημενων ἁγιων ηγερθη, 53 και εξελθοντες
having been asleep holy ones were raised, and coming forth
εκ των μνημειων, μετα την εγερσιν αυτου
from the tombs, after the resurrection of him
εισηλθον εις την ἁγιαν πολιν, και ενεφανισθησαν
went into the holy city, and appeared
πολλοις.
to many.

54 Ὁ δε εκατονταρχος και οἱ μετ' αυτου
The and centurion and those with him
τηρουντες τον Ιησουν, ιδοντες τον σεισμον
watching the Jesus, seeing the earthquake
και τα γενομενα, εφοβηθησαν σφοδρα,
and the things being done, they were afraid much,
λεγοντες· Αληθως θεου υἱος ην οὑτος.
saying; Truly of God a son was this.
55 Ησαν δε εκει γυναικες πολλαι απο μακ-
Were and there women many from a dis-
ροθεν θεωρουσαι· αἱτινες ηκολουθησαν τῳ Ιησου
tance beholding; who followed the Jesus
απο της Γαλιλαιας, διακονουσαι αυτῳ· 56 εν
from the Galilee, ministering to him; among
αἱς ην Μαρια ἡ Μαγδαληνη, και Μαρια ἡ του
whom was Mary the Magdalene, and Mary the of the
Ιακωβου και Ιωση μητηρ, και ἡ μητηρ των
James and Joses mother, and the mother of the
υἱων Ζεβεδαιου.
sons of Zebedee.

57 Οψιας δε γενομενης, ηλθεν ανθρωπος
Evening and being come, came a man
πλουσιος απο Αριμαθαιας, τουνομα Ιωσηφ, ὁς
rich from Arimathea, by name Joseph, who

on a Reed, gave him to drink.

49 But OTHERS said, "Let him alone; let us see whether Elijah will come to save *him."

50 ‡ Then JESUS crying out again with a loud Voice, expired.

51 ‡ And, behold, † the VEIL of the TEMPLE was rent in Two from top to bottom; and the EARTH trembled, and the ROCKS were rent;

52 and the TOMBS were opened; and Many Bodies of the SLEEPING SAINTS were raised;

53 and coming forth from the TOMBS, after his RESURRECTION went into the HOLY City, and appeared to Many.

54 ‡ Now the CENTURION and THOSE with him WATCHING JESUS, seeing the EARTHQUAKE, and the EVENTS occurring, were greatly afraid, saying, "This was certainly a Son of God."

55 And many Women were there, † beholding at a distance; these had followed JESUS from GALILEE, ministering to him;

56 among them were Mary of MAGDALA, and Mary the MOTHER of JAMES and Joses, and the MOTHER of the SONS of Zebedee.

57 And Evening being come, a rich Man came from Arimathea, named

* VATICAN MANUSCRIPT.—49. him. And another took a spear, and pierced his SIDE, and there came out Blood and Water.

† 51. In Solomon's Temple the sanctuary was divided from the holy of holies by a wall, beyond which the veil fell; but in Herod's Temple, as Maimonides relates, a second veil, at the distance of a cubit from the first, supplied the place of the wall. That it was the interior veil, belonging to the holy of holies, which was rent at the crucifixion is clearly intimated in Heb. ix. 3; x. 19, as well as by the term which the Evangelist has employed to designate it. † 55. So Mark and Luke; nor are they inconsistent with John xix. 25, where our Lord's mother and the other two women are said to have stood beside the cross. They kept at a distance for a while; and afterwards as the darkness came over, gathered courage, and came so near that Jesus had an opportunity to speak to them before he expired.—*Macknight.*

‡ 50. Mark xv. 37; Luke xxiii. 47. ‡ 51. Exod. xxvi. 31; 2 Chron. iii. 14. ‡ 54. Mark xv. 42; Luke xxiii. 50; John xix. 38.

και αυτος εμαθητευσε τῳ Ιησου. 58 Οὑτος
also himself was discipled to the Jesus. He

προσελθων τῳ Πιλατῳ ητησατο το σωμα του
coming to the Pilate requested the body of the

Ιησου. Τοτε ὁ Πιλατος εκελευσεν αποδοθηναι
Jesus. Then the Pilate ordered to be given

το σωμα. 59 Και λαβων το σωμα ὁ Ιωσηφ,
the body. And taking the body the Joseph,

ενετυλιξεν αυτο σινδονι καθαρᾳ· 60 και εθηκεν
wrapped it fine linen cloth clean; and laid

αυτο εν τῳ καινῳ ἁυτου μνημειῳ, ὁ ελατομη-
it in the new of himself tomb, which he had

σεν εν τῃ πετρᾳ· και προσκυλισας λιθον μεγαν
hewn in the rock; and having rolled a stone great

τῃ θυρᾳ του μνημειου, απηλθεν. 61 Ην δε
to the door of the tomb, he went away. Was and

εκει Μαρια ἡ Μαγδαληνη, και ἡ αλλη Μαρια,
there Mary the Magdalene, and the other Mary,

καθημεναι απεναντι του ταφου.
sitting over against the sepulchre.

62 Τῃ δε επαυριον, ἡτις εστι μετα την παρα-
The now next day, which is after the prepa-

σκευην, συνηχθησαν οἱ αρχιερεις και οἱ Φαρι-
ration, were assembled the high-priests and the Phari-

σαιοι προς Πιλατον, 63 λεγοντες· Κυριε,
sees to Pilate, saying; O sir,

εμνησθημεν, ὁτι εκεινος ὁ πλανος ειπεν ετι
we remember, that that the deceiver said while

ζων· Μετα τρεις ἡμερας εγειρομαι. 64 Κε-
living; After three days I will arise. Do

λευσον ουν ασφαλισθηναι τον ταφον ἑως
thou command therefore to be made fast the tomb till

της τριτης ἡμερας, μηποτε ελθοντες οἱ μαθη-
the third day, lest coming the disci-

ται αυτου, κλεψωσιν αυτον, και ειπωσι τῳ
ples of him, might steal him, and might say to the

λαῳ· Ηγερθη απο των νεκρων· και εσται
people; He has been raised from the dead; and will be

ἡ εσχατη πλανη χειρων της πρωτης. 65 Εφη
the last fraud worse of the first. Said

αυτοις ὁ Πιλατος· Εχετε κουστωδιαν· ὑπαγετε,
to them the Pilate; You have a guard; go you,

ασφαλισασθε, ὡς οιδατε. 66 Οἱ δε πορευθεντες
make fast, as you know. They and going

ησφαλισαντο τον ταφον, σφραγισαντες τον
made fast the tomb, having sealed the

λιθον, μετα της κουστωδιας.
stone, with the guard.

‡ Joseph, who also himself was discipled to JESUS.

58 He going to PILATE requested the BODY of JESUS. Then PILATE ordered * it to be given.

59 And JOSEPH, taking the BODY, wrapped it in pure, fine Linen,

60 ‡ and laid it in his own NEW Tomb, which he had excavated in the ROCK; and having rolled a great Stone to the DOOR of the TOMB, he departed.

61 And MARY of MAGDALA was there, and the OTHER Mary, sitting opposite the TOMB.

62 Now on the MORROW, which is after † the PREPARATION, the HIGH-PRIESTS and PHARISEES convened before Pilate,

63 saying, "Sir, we recollect that that imposter said, while living, ‡ 'After Three Days I will arise.'

64 Command, therefore, the TOMB be made secure till the THIRD Day, lest * the DISCIPLES come and steal him, and say to the PEOPLE, 'He is raised from the dead;' and so the LAST Error would be worse than the FIRST."

65 PILATE said to them, † "You have a Guard; go, make it as secure as you know how."

66 And departing, THEY secured the TOMB with the GUARD, ‡ having sealed the STONE.

* VATICAN MANUSCRIPT.—58. it to be given. 64. the DISCIPLES.

† 62. *Paraskeuee* denoted *the day preceding any sabbath or festival*, as being that on which the *preparation* for its celebration was to be made. † 65. The Jews had a Roman guard appointed them for the security of the temple. It was usually stationed in the castle of Antonio, but removed during festivals to the outer court of the temple, to quell any tumult that might arise in the city. Pilate gave them leave to employ this guard for their present purpose. † 66. A mode of security in use from the earliest times, and which supplied the place of locks. See Dan. vi. 17. It was usual to affix the seal to the extremities of a cord or leathern band, passing over the stone. But how futile were the machinations of his enemies in order to prove him to be an impostor! Let it be remembered that the tomb was new, and excavated out of the rock—was contiguous to Jerusalem—a great stone was placed at the entrance, and was sealed to prevent deception—and a guard to protect the body All these facts are strong presumptive proofs of the reality of the resurrection.

‡ 57. Mark xv. 43; Luke xxiii. 50; John xix. 38. ‡ 60. Isa. liii. 9. ‡ 63. Matt xvi. 21; xvii. 23; xx. 19; xxvi. 61; Mark viii. 31; x. 34; Luke ix. 22; xviii. 33; xxiv. 6, 7. John ii. 19. ‡ 66. Dan. vi. 17.

ΚΕΦ. κη΄. 28.

1 Οψε δε σαββατων, τῃ επιφωσκουσῃ εις
After now sabbath, to the dawning into
μιαν σαββατων, ηλθε Μαρια ἡ Μαγδαληνη,
first of week, came Mary the Magdalene,
και ἡ αλλη Μαρια, θεωρησαι τον ταφον. 2 Και
and the other Mary, to see the tomb. And
ιδου, σεισμος εγενετο μεγας· αγγελος γαρ
lo, a shaking occurred great; a messenger for
κυριου, καταβας εξ ουρανου, προσελθων απεκυ-
of a lord, descending from heaven, approaching rolled
λισε τον λιθον *[απο της θυρας,] και εκαθητο
away the stone [from the door,] and sat
επανω αυτου. 3 Ην δε ἡ ἰδεα αυτου ὡς αστρα-
upon it. Was and the aspect of him like light-
πη, και το ενδυμα αυτου λευκον ὡσει χιων.
ning, and the garments of him white as snow.
4 Απο δε του φοβου αυτου εσεισθησαν οἱ
From and the fear of him shook the
τηρουντες, και εγενοντο ὡσει νεκροι. 5 Αποκ-
keepers, and became as dead (men.) An-
ριθεις δε ὁ αγγελος ειπε ταις γυναιξη· Μη
swering and the messenger said to the women; Not
φοβεισθε ὑμεις· οιδα γαρ, ὁτι Ιησουν τον
be afraid you; I know for, that Jesus that
εσταυρωμενον ζητειτε. 6 Ουκ εστιν ὡδε.
having been crucified you seek. Not he is here;
ἠγερθη γαρ, καθως ειπε. Δευτε, ιδετε
he has been raised for, even as he said. Come, see
τον τοπον, ὁπου εκειτο ὁ κυριος. 7 Και ταχυ
the place, where lay the Lord. And quickly
πορευθεισαι ειπατε τοις μαθηταις αυτου, ὁτι
going tell the disciples of him, that
ηγερθη απο των νεκρων· και ιδου, προαγει
he has been raised from the dead; and lo, he goes before
ὑμας εις την Γαλιλαιαν· εκει αυτον οψεσθε·
you into the Galilee; there him you will see;
ιδου, ειπον ὑμιν.
lo, I told you.
8 Και εξελθουσαι ταχυ απο του μνημειου
And coming out quickly from the tomb
μετα φοβου και χαρας μεγαλης, εδραμον απαγ-
with fear and joy great, they ran to in-
γειλαι τοις μαθηταις αυτου. 9 *[Ὡς δε επορ-
form the disciples of him. [As and they
ευοντο απαγγειλαι τοις μαθηταις αυτου,] και
went to inform the disciples of him,] and
ιδου, ὁ Ιησους απηντησεν αυταις, λεγων·
lo, the Jesus met them, saying;
Χαιρετε. Αἱ δε προσελθουσαι εκρατησαν αυτου
Hail you. They and having approached laid hold of him
τους ποδας, και προσεκυνησαν αυτῳ. 10 Τοτε
the feet, and prostrated to him. Then
λεγει αυταις ὁ Ιησους· Μη φοβεισθε· ὑπαγετε,
says to them the Jesus; Not be afraid; go you,
απαγγειλατε τοις αδελφοις μου, ἱνα απελθωσιν
inform to the brethren of me, so that they may go
εις την Γαλιλαιαν, κακει με οψονται.
into the Galilee, and there me they shall see.

CHAPTER XXVIII.

1 ‡ Now after the Sabbath, as it was DAWNING to the first day of the Week, Mary of MAGDALA, and the OTHER Mary, went to see the TOMB.

2 And, behold, a great Shaking occurred; for an Angel of the Lord descending from Heaven, came and rolled back the STONE; and sat upon it.

3 ‡ And his APPEARANCE was like Lightning, and his VESTMENTS white as Snow;

4 and from FEAR of him the GUARDS trembled, and became as Dead men.

5 And the ANGEL answering, said to the WOMEN, "Be not you afraid; for I know That you seek THAT Jesus who was CRUCIFIED.

6 He is not here; for he has been raised, even as he said. Come, see the PLACE where * he lay.

7 And immediately go and tell his DISCIPLES That he has been raised from the DEAD; and, behold, ‡ he precedes you to GALILEE; there you will see Him; behold, I have told you."

8 And coming out immediately from the TOMB, * with Fear and great Joy, they ran to tell his DISCIPLES.

9 ‡ And, behold, JESUS met them, saying, "Rejoice!" And THEY having approached, clasped his FEET, and prostrated to him.

10 Then JESUS says to them, "Be not afraid; go ‡ inform my brethren, so that they may go to GALILEE, and there they will see Me."

* VATICAN MANUSCRIPT.—2. from the DOOR—*omit*. 6. he lay; so Tischendorf. 9. as they were going to tell his disciples—*omit*: so Lachmann and Tischendorf.

‡ 1. Mark xvi. 1; Luke xxiv. 1; John xx. 1. ‡ 3. Dan x. 6. ‡ 7. Matt. xxvi. 32 Mark xvi. 7. ‡ 9. Mark xvi. 9; John xx. 14. ‡ 10. John xx. 17; Rom. viii. 29.

[11] Πορευομενων δε αυτων, ιδου, τινες της
Going away and of them, lo, some of the
κουστωδιας, ελθοντες εις την πολιν, απηγγειλαν
keepers, coming into the city, told
τοις αρχιερευσιν απαντα τα γενομενα. [12] Και
to the high priests all the (things) having been done. And
συναχθεντες μετα των πρεσβυτερων, συμβου-
being assembled with the elders, counsel
λιον τε λαβοντες, αργυρια ἱκανα εδωκαν τοις
and taking, pieces of silver sufficient they gave to the
στρατιωταις, λεγοντες· [13] Ειπατε, Ὁτι οἱ
soldiers, saying; Say you, That the
μαθηται αυτου, νυκτος ελθοντες, εκλεψαν
disciples of him by night coming, stole
αυτον, ἡμων κοιμωμενων. [14] Και εαν ακουσθη
him, of us being asleep. And if should be reported
τουτο επι του ἡγεμονος, ἡμεις πεισομεν αυτον,
this to the governor, we will persuade him,
και ὑμας αμεριμνους ποιησομεν. [15] Οἱ δε λαβ-
and you free from care we will make. They and having
οντες τα αργυρια, εποιησαν ὡς εδιδαχθησαν.
received the pieces of silver, did as they were taught.
Και διεφημισθη ὁ λογος οὑτος παρα Ιουδαιοις
And is spread abroad the word this among Jews
μεχρι της σημερον.
till the day.

[16] Οι δε ἑνδεκα μαθηται επορευθησαν εις την
The and eleven disciples went to the
Γαλιλαιαν, εις το ορας, ὁυ εταξατο αυτοις ὁ
Galilee, to the mountain, where had appointed them the
Ιησους. [17] Και ιδοντες αυτον, προσεκυνησαν
Jesus. And seeing him, they prostrated
αυτῳ· οἱ δε εδιστασαν. [18] Και προσελθων ὁ
to him; they but doubted. And approaching the
Ιησους, ελαλεσεν αυτοις, λεγων· Εδοθη μοι
Jesus, spoke to them, saying; Has been given to me
πασα εξουσια εν ουρανῳ και επι γης. [19] Πορευ-
all authority in heaven and on earth. Going
θεντες μαθητευσατε παντα τα εθνη, βαπτιζον-
forth disciple you all the nations, immers-
τες αυτους εις το ονομα του πατρος και του
ing them into the name of the father and of the
υἱου και του ἁγιου πνευματος· [20] διχασκοντες
son and of the holy spirit; teaching
αυτους τηρειν παντα, ὁσα ενετειλαμην ὑμιν.
them to observe all, whatever I have charged you.
Και ιδου, εγω μεθ' ὑμων ειμι πασας τας ἡμερας,
And lo. I with you am all the days,
ἑως της συντελειας του αιωνος.
till the end of the age.

11 And as they were going away, some of the GUARD, entering the CITY, told to the HIGH-PRIESTS All the THINGS which had HAPPENED.

12 And being assembled with the ELDERS, and taking Counsel, they gave a good many Shekels to the SOLDIERS,

13 saying, "Say you, 'that His DISCIPLES came by Night, and stole him, while we slept;'

14 and if this should be reported to the GOVERNOR, we will persuade him, and make you safe."

15 And they having received the SHEKELS, did as they were instructed; and this SAYING is currently reported among the Jews to * THIS day.

16 And the ELEVEN Disciples went to GALILEE, to the MOUNTAIN where JESUS had ordered them.

17 And seeing him, they (indeed) prostrated to him; but SOME doubted.

18 And JESUS approaching, spoke to them, saying, ‡ "All Authority has been imparted to me, in Heaven and on Earth.

19 ‡ Go, disciple All the NATIONS, immersing them into the NAME of the FATHER, and of the SON, and of the HOLY Spirit;

20 ‡ teaching them to observe all things which I have enjoined upon you; and, behold, I am with you all the DAYS, till the CONSUMMATION of the AGE."

* ACCORDING TO MATTHEW.

* VATICAN MANUSCRIPT.—15. THIS Day. *Subscription*—ACCORDING TO MATTHEW.

‡ 18. Matt. xi. 27; John iii. 35; v. 22; xiii. 3; xvii. 2; Rom. xiv. 9; 1 Cor. xv. 27; Eph. i. 10, 21; Phil. ii 9, 10; 1 Pet. iii. 22. ‡ 19. Mark xvi. 15; Luke xxvi. 47; Rom. x. 18; Col. i. 23. ‡ 20. Acts ii. 42.

*[ΕΥΑΓΓΕΛΙΟΝ] ΚΑΤΑ ΜΑΡΚΟΝ.
[GLAD TIDINGS] BY MARK.

*ACCORDING TO MARK.

ΚΕΦ. α'. 1.

[1] Αρχη του ευαγγελιου Ιησου Χριστου, υἱου
A beginning of the glad tidings of Jesus Christ, a son
του θεου. [2] † Ὡς γεγραπται εν Ἡσαιᾳ τῳ προ-
of the God. As it is written in Esaias the pro-
φητῃ· "Ιδου, εγω αποστελω τον αγγελον
phet; "Lo, I send the messenger
μου προ προσωπου σου, ὁς κατασκευασει την
of me before face of thee, who will prepare the
ὁδον σου. [3] Φωνη βοωντος εν τῃ ερημῳ· Ἑτοι-
way of thee. A voice crying out in the desert; Make
μασατε την ὁδον κυριου, ευθειας ποιειτε τας
you ready the way of a lord, straight make you the
τριβους αυτου." [4] Εγενετο Ιωαννης βαπτιζων
beaten ways of him;" Was John dipping
εν τῃ ερημῳ, και κηρυσσων βαπτισμα μετα-
in the desert, and publishing a dipping of refor-
νοιας εις αφεσιν ἁμαρτιων. [5] Και εξεπορευετο
mation into forgiveness of sins. And went out
προς αυτον πασα ἡ Ιουδαια χωρα, και οἱ Ἱερο-
to him all the Judea country, and the Jeru-
σολυμιται παντες· και εβαπτιζοντο εν τῳ
salem all; and were dipped in the
Ιορδανῃ ποταμῳ ὑπ' αυτου, εξομολογουμενοι
Jordan river by him, confessing
τας ἁμαρτιας αὑτων. [6] Ην δε Ιωαννης ενδεδυ-
the sins of them. Was now John having been
μενος τριχας καμηλου, και ζωνην δερματινην
clothed hairs of a camel, and a belt made of skin
περι την οσφυν αὑτου, και εσθιων ακριδας και
around the loins of him, and eating locusts and
μελι αγριον. [7] Και εκηρυσσε λεγων· Ερχεται
honey wild. And he cried out saying; Comes
ὁ ισχυροτερος μου οπισω *[μου,] οὑ ουκ
the mightier of me after [me,] of whom not
ειμι ἱκανος κυψας λυσαι τον ἱμαντα των
I am worthy bowed down to loose the string of the
ὑποδηματων αυτου. [8] Εγω *[μεν] εβαπτισα
sandals of him. I [indeed] dipped
ὑμας εν ὑδατι· αυτος δε βαπτισει ὑμας εν
you in water; he but will dip you in
πνευματι ἁγιῳ.
spirit holy.

[9] *[Και] εγενετο εν εκειναις ταις ἡμεραις,
[And] it came to pass in those the days,
ηλθεν Ιησους απο Ναζαρετ της Γαλιλαιας, και
came Jesus from Nazareth of the Galilee, and

CHAPTER I.

1 The Beginning of the GLAD TIDINGS of Jesus Christ, the Son of *God;

2 as it is written *†in the PROPHETS, ‡"Behold, "*I send my MESSENGER "before thy Face, who will "prepare thy WAY.

3 ‡"A Voice proclaim-"ing in the DESERT, 'Pre-"pare the WAY for the "Lord, make the HIGH-"WAYS straight for him."

4 ‡John was immersing in the DESERT, and publishing an Immersion of Reformation for Forgiveness of Sins.

5 ‡And resorted to him All the COUNTRY of JUDEA, and all THOSE of Jerusalem, and were immersed by him in the RIVER JORDAN, confessing their SINS.

6 ‡Now John was clothed in Camel's Hair, with a Leathern Girdle encircling his WAIST; and eating Locusts and Wild Honey.

7 And he proclaimed, saying, ‡"The POWERFUL ONE comes after me; for whom I am not worthy to stoop down and untie the STRINGS of his SANDALS.

8 ‡I immerse you in Water, but he will immerse you in holy Spirit."

9 ‡And it occurred, in Those DAYS, that Jesus came from Nazareth of GALILEE, and was im-

---

* VATICAN MANUSCRIPT.—*Title*—ACCORDING TO MARK. 1. God. 2. ISAIAH the PROPHET. 3. I send. 7. me—*omit*. 8. indeed—*omit*. 9. And—*omit*.

† 2. As the common reading has an immense majority in its favor, and some noted versions; as the quotation is from two different prophecies, Mal. iii. 1, and Isa. xl. 2, 3, of which the nearest is not from Isaiah, but from Malachi; and as the Jews often say, "*As it is written in the Prophets*," yet it is never said in the N. T. *written in a prophet*, but *by* him; there seems to be no just ground for departing from the received text.—*Campbell, Whitby, Lightfoot.*

‡ 2. Mal. iii. 1; Matt. xi. 10; Luke vii. 27. ‡ 3. Isa. xl. 3; Matt. iii. 3; Luke iii. 4; John i. 23. ‡ 4. Matt. iii. 1; Luke iii. 3; John iii. 23. ‡ 5 Matt. iii. 5. ‡ 6 Matt. iii. 4. ‡ 7. Matt. iii. 11; John i. 27; Acts xiii. 25. ‡ 8. Acts i. 5; ii. 4; xi. 16; xix. 4; 1 Cor. xii. 13. ‡ 9. Matt. iii. 13; Luke iii. 21.

εβαπτισθη ὑπο Ιωαννου εις τον Ιορδανην. 10 Και
was dipped by John into the Jordan. And
ευθεως αναβαινων απο του ὑδατος, ειδε σχιζο-
immediately ascending from the water, he saw rend-
μενους τους ουρανους, και το πνευμα, ὡς
ing the heavens, and the spirit, as
περιστεραν, καταβαινον επ' αυτον. 11 Και
a dove, descending upon him. And
φωνη εγενετο εκ των ουρανων· "Συ ει ὁ
a voice came out of the heavens; "Thou art the
υἱος μου ὁ αγαπητος, εν ᾧ ευδοκησα."
son of me the beloved, in whom I delight."
12 Και ευθυς το πνευμα αυτον εκβαλλει εις
And immediately the spirit him casts into
την ερημον. 13 Και ην εν τῃ ερημῳ ἡμερας
the desert. And he was in the desert days
τεσσαρακοντα, πειραζομενος ὑπο του σατανα,
forty, being tempted by the adversary,
και ην μετα των θηριων· και οἱ αγγελοι διη-
and was with the wild beasts; and the messengers min-
κονουν αυτῳ.
istered to him.
14 Μετα δε το παραδοθηναι τον Ιωαννην,
After now the to be delivered up the John,
ηλθεν ὁ Ιησους εις την Γαλιλαιαν, κηρυσσων
came the Jesus into the Galilee, preaching
το ευαγγελιον *[της βασιλειας] του θεου,
the glad tidings [of the kingdom] of the God,
15 και λεγων· Ὁτι πεπληρωται ὁ καιρος, και
and saying; That has been fulfilled the season, and
ηγγικεν ἡ βασιλεια του θεου· μετανοειτε, και
has come nigh the majesty of the God; reform you, and
πιστευετε εν τῳ ευαγγελιῳ. 16 Περιπατων δε
believe you in the good message. Walking and
παρα την θαλασσαν της Γαλιλαιας, ειδε Σιμωνα
by the sea of the Galilee, he saw Simon
και Ανδρεαν τον αδελφον αυτου, αμφιβαλλοντας
and Andrew the brother of him, casting
αμφιβληστρον εν τῃ θαλασσῃ· ησαν γαρ
a fishing net in the sea; they were for
ἁλιεις. 17 Και ειπεν αυτοις ὁ Ιησους· Δευτε
fishers. And said to them the Jesus, Come
οπισω μου, και ποιησω ὑμας γενεσθαι ἁλιεις
after me, and I will make you to be fishers
ανθρωπων. 18 Και ευθεως αφεντες τα δικτυα
of men. And immediately leaving the nets
αυτων, ἠκολουθησαν αυτῳ. 19 Και προβας
of them, they followed him. And going
*[εκειθεν] ολιγον, ειδεν Ιακωβον τον του
[thence] a little, he saw James the of the
Ζεβεδαιου, και Ιωαννην τον αδελφον αυτου,
Zebedee, and John the brother of him,
και αυτους εν τῳ πλοιῳ καταρτιζοντας τα
and themselves in the ship were mending the
δικτυα· 20 και ευθεως εκαλεσεν αυτους. Και
nets; and immediately he called them. And

mersed by John in the JORDAN.

10 ‡ And ascending from the WATER, instantly he saw the HEAVENS opening, and the SPIRIT, like a Dove descending upon him.

11 And a Voice came from the HEAVENS, saying, ‡ "Thou art my SON, the BELOVED; in thee I delight."

12 ‡ And immediately the SPIRIT sent Him forth into the DESERT.

13 And he was in the DESERT forty Days, being tempted by the ADVERSARY; and was among the WILD BEASTS; and the ANGELS served him.

14 ‡ Now after JOHN was imprisoned, JESUS came into GALILEE, publishing the GLAD TIDINGS of GOD,

15 and saying, ‡ "The TIME has been accomplished, and GOD'S ROYAL MAJESTY has approached; ‡ Reform, and believe in the GOOD MESSAGE."

16 ‡ * And as he was passing along by the LAKE of GALILEE, he saw Simon, and Andrew * the BROTHER of Simon, casting a Drag into the LAKE; for they were Fishermen.

17 And JESUS said to them, "Come, follow me, and I will make you Fishers of Men.

18 And instantly ‡ leaving * the NETS, they followed him.

19 ‡ And going forward a little, he saw THAT James who is the son of ZEBEDEE, and John his BROTHER; they also were in the BOAT repairing the NETS;

20 and he immediately

* VATICAN MANUSCRIPT.—11. thee I delight. 14. of the KINGDOM—omit. 16. And as he was passing along by. 16. the BROTHER of Simon, casting. 18. the NETS. 19. thence—omit.

‡ 10. Matt. iii. 16; John i. 32. ‡ 11. Mark ix. 7. ‡ 12. Matt. iv. 1; Luke iv. 1. ‡ 14. Matt. iv. 12, 23. ‡ 15. Dan. ix. 25; Gal. iv. 4; Eph. i. 10. ‡ 15. Matt. iv. 17. ‡ 16. Matt. iv. 18; Luke v. 4. ‡ 18. Matt. xix. 27; Luke v. 11. ‡ 19. Matt. iv. 21.

αφεντες τον πατερα αυτων Ζεβεδαιον εν
leaving the father of them Zebedee in
τῳ πλοιῳ μετα των μισθωτων, απηλθον
the ship with the hirelings, they went
οπισω αυτου.
after him.
21 Και εισπορευονται εις Καπερναουμ· και
And they went into Capernaum; and
ευθεως τοις σαββασιν εισελθων εις την συνα-
immediately to the sabbath going into the syna-
γωγην, εδιδασκε. 22 Και εξεπλησσοντο επι
gogue, he taught. And they were amazed at
τη διδαχη αυτου· ην γαρ διδασκων αυτους ὡς
the teaching of him; he was for teaching them as
εξουσιαν εχων, και ουχ ὡς οἱ γραμματεις.
authority having, and not as the scribes.
23 Και ην εν τη συναγωγῃ αυτων ανθρωπος εν
And was in the synagogue of them a man in
πνευματι ακαθαρτῳ, και ανεκραξε, 24 λεγων·
spirit unclean, and he cried out, saying,
*[Εα,] τι ἡμιν και σοι, Ιησου Ναζαρηνε,
[Let alone,] what to us and to thee, Jesus O Nazarene,
ηλθες απολεσαι ἡμας; οιδα σε τις ει, ὁ
camest thou to destroy us; I know thee who thou art, the
ἁγιος του θεου. 25 Και επετιμησεν αυτῳ ὁ
holy of the God. And rebuked him the
Ιησους, λεγων· Φιμωθητι, και εξελθε εξ αυτου.
Jesus, saying; Be silent, and come out of him.
26 Και σπαραξαν αυτον το πνευμα το ακαθαρτον,
And convulsing him the spirit the unclean,
και κραξαν φωνῃ μεγαλῃ, εξηλθεν εξ αυτου.
and crying a voice great, came out of him.
27 Και εθαμβηθησαν παντες, ὡστε συζητειν
And they were astonished all, so as to reason
προς αὑτους, λεγοντες· Τι εστι τουτο, τις ἡ
among themselves, saying; What is this? what the
διδαχη ἡ καινη αυτη; ὁτι κατ' εξουσιαν και
teaching the new this; that with authority even
τοις πνευμασι τοις ακαθαρτοις επιτασσει και
to the spirits to the unclean he enjoins and
ὑπακουουσιν αυτῳ. 28 Εξηλθε δε ἡ ακοη
they hearken to him. Went out and the report
αυτου ευθυς εις ὁλην την περιχωρον της
of him forthwith into whole the country of the
Γαλιλαιας.
Galilee.
29 Και ευθεως, εκ της συναγωγης εξελθοντες,
And instantly, out of the synagogue being come,
ηλθον εις την οικιαν Σιμωνος και Ανδρεου,
he went into the house of Simon and Andrew.
μετα Ιακωβου και Ιωαννου. 30 Ἡ δε πενθερα
with James and John. The and mother-in-law
Σιμωνος κατεκειτο πυρεσσουσα· και ευθεως
of Simon was laid down having a fever; and immediately
λεγουσιν αυτῳ περι αυτης. 31 Και προσελθων
they spoke to him about her. And coming

called them; and leaving
their FATHER Zebedee in
the BOAT with the HIRED
SERVANTS, they followed
him.
21 ‡ And they went to
Capernaum; and on the
SABBATH, entering the
SYNAGOGUE, he taught
the people;
22 ‡ and they were
struck with awe at his
mode of INSTRUCTION;
for he taught them, as
possessing Authority, and
not as the SCRIBES.
23 ‡ Now there was in
their SYNAGOGUE, a Man
with an impure Spirit;
and he exclaimed,
24 saying, "What hast
thou to do with us, Jesus
Nazarene? Comest thou
to destroy us? I know
thee who thou art, the
HOLY ONE of GOD."
25 And JESUS rebuked
it, saying, ‡ "Be silent,
and come out of him."
26 And the IMPURE
SPIRIT, ‡ having convulsed
him, and having cried
with a loud Voice, came
out of him.
27 And they were all so
astonished, as to reason
* with themselves, saying,
"What is this? * A new
Doctrine? With Author-
ity he commands even the
IMPURE SPIRITS, and they
obey him."
28 And his FAME soon
spread abroad * every-
where throughout the En-
tire REGION of GALILEE.
29 ‡ And being come
out of the SYNAGOGUE,
he immediately went into
the HOUSE of Simon and
Andrew with James and
John.
30 Now Simon's MOTH-
ER-IN-LAW lay sick of a
fever, and forthwith they
spoke to him about her.
31 And approaching, he

* VATICAN MANUSCRIPT.—24. Let alone—*omit*. 27. with themselves. 27. A new Doctrine? With Authority. 28. everywhere throughout.

‡ 21. Matt. iv. 13; Luke iv. 31. ‡ 22. Matt. vii. 28. ‡ 23. Luke iv. 33. ‡ 24. Matt. viii. 29. ‡ 25. ver 34; Mark iii. 12. ‡ 26. Mark ix. 20. ‡ 29. Matt. viii. 14; Luke iv. 38.

ηγειρεν αυτην, κρατησας της χειρος αυτης·
he raised her, having laid hold of the hand of her;

και αφηκεν αυτην ὁ πυρετος *[ευθεως·] και
and left her the fever [immediately;] and

διηκονει αυτοις.
ministered to them.

32 Οψιας δε γενομενης, ὁτε εδυ ὁ ἡλιος,
Evening and being come, when set the sun,

εφερον προς αυτον παντας τους κακως εχοντας,
they brought to him all those sickness having,

και τους δαιμονιζομενους· 33 και ἡ πολις
and those being demonized; and the city

ὁλη επισυνηγμενη ην προς την θυραν. 34 Και
whole having been assembled was at the door. And

εθεραπευσε πολλους κακως εχοντας ποικιλαις
he healed many sick having various

νοσοις· και δαιμονια πολλα εξεβαλε, και ουκ
diseases; and demons many he cast out, and not

ηφιε λαλειν τα δαιμονια, ὁτι ηδεισαν αυτον.
allowed to speak the demons, because they knew him.

35 Και πρωι, εννυχον λιαν, αναστας εξηλθε,
And early, night much, having arisen he went out,

*[και απηλθεν] εις ερημον τοπον, κακει
[and departed] into a desert place, and there

προσηυχετο. 36 Και κατεδιωξαν αυτον ὁ Σιμων
prayed. And eagerly followed him the Simon

και οἱ μετ' αυτου. 37 Και εὑροντες αυτον,
and those with him. And having found him,

λεγουσιν αυτῳ· Ὁτι παντες ζητουσι σε.
they say to him; That all seek thee.

38 Και λεγει αυτοις· Αγωμεν εις τας εχομ-
And he says to them; We must go into the neigh-

ενας κωμοπολεις, ἱνα και εκει κηρυξω· εις
boring towns, that also there I may preach; for

τουτο γαρ εξεληλυθα. 39 Και ην κηρυσσων
this because I have come out. And he was proclaiming

εις τας συναγωγας αυτων, εις ὁλην την Γαλι-
in the synagogues of them, in whole the Gali-

λαιαν, και τα δαιμονια εκβαλλων. 40 Και
lee, and the demons casting out. And

ερχεται προς αυτον λεπρος, παρακαλων αυτον,
comes to him a leper, beseeching him,

*[και γονυπετων αυτον, και] λεγων αυτῳ·
[and kneeling him, and] saying to him;

Ὁτι εαν θελῃς, δυνασαι με καθαρισαι. 41 Ὁ
That if thou wilt, thou art able me to cleanse. The

δε Ιησους σπλαγχνισθεις, εκτεινας την χειρα,
and Jesus being moved with pity, stretching out the hand,

ἡψατο αυτου, και λεγει αυτῳ· Θελω, καθα-
touched of him, and says to him; I will, be thou

ρισθητι. 42 Και *[ειποντος αυτου,] ευθεως
cleansed. And [having said of him,] immediately

απηλθεν απ' αυτου ἡ λεπρα, και εκαθαρισθη.
departed from him the leprosy, and he was cleansed.

43 Και εμβριμησαμενος αυτῳ, ευθεως εξεβαλεν
And having strictly charged him, immediately he sent forth

---

took hold of her HAND, raised her up, and the FEVER left her, and she served them.

32 ‡ And Evening being come, when the SUN was set, they brought to him ALL the SICK, and the DEMONIACS;

33 and the whole CITY assembled at the DOOR.

34 And he cured Many sick of Various Disorders, and expelled many Demons; ‡ and permitted not the DEMONS to speak, because they knew * him to be the Christ.

35 ‡ And having arisen very early in the Morning, he went out into a Desert Place, and there prayed.

36 And * Simon and THOSE with him eagerly followed him.

37 And having found him, they say to him, "All seek thee."

38 And he says to them, ‡ "We must go * elsewhere, into the ADJACENT Towns, that I may proclaim there also; for this I have come forth."

39 ‡ And * he went and proclaimed to them in their SYNAGOGUES throughout All GALILEE, and cast out the DEMONS.

40 ‡ And a Leper comes to him, beseeching him, saying, "If thou wilt, thou canst cleanse Me."

41 And * he, being moved with pity, extending * his HAND, touched him, and says to him, "I will; be thou cleansed."

42 And immediately the LEPROSY departed from him, and he was cleansed.

43 And having strictly charged him, he forthwith sent him away,

---

* VATICAN MANUSCRIPT.—31. immediately—*omit*. 34. him to be the Christ. 35. and departed—*omit*. 36. Simon. 38. elsewhere, into. 39. he went and proclaimed to them in. 40. and kneeling down to him, and—*omit*. 41. he, being moved. 41. his HAND.

‡ 32. Matt. viii. 16; Luke iv. 40. ‡ 34. Mark iii. 12; Luke iv. 41; Acts xvi. 17, 18. ‡ 35. Luke iv. 42. ‡ 38. Luke iv. 43. ‡ 39. Matt. iv. 23; Luke iv. 44. ‡ 40. Matt. viii. 2; Luke v. 12.

αυτον, [44] και λεγει αυτῳ· Ὁρα, μηδενι μηδεν
him, and says to him; See, to no one anything
ειπῃς· αλλ' ὑπαγε, σεαυτον δειξον τῳ ἱερει,
thou tell; but go, thyself show to the priest
και προσενεγκε περι του καθαρισμου σου ἁ
and offer for the purification of thee what
προσεταξε Μωσης, εις μαρτυριον αυτοις. [45] Ὁ
enjoined Moses, for a witness to them. He
δε εξελθων ηρξατο κηρυσσειν πολλα και διαφη-
but going out began to publish many (things) and spread
μιζειν τον λογον, ὡστε μηκετι αυτον δυνασθαι
abroad the word, so as no longer him to be able
φανερως εις πολιν εισελθειν· αλλ' εξω εν
publicly into a city to enter; but without in
ερημοις τοποις ην, και ηρχοντο προς αυτον
desert places he was, and they went to him
πανταχοθεν.
from all parts.

ΚΕΦ. β'. 2.

[1] Και παλιν εισηλθεν εις Καπερναουμ δι'
And again he went into Capernaum after
ἡμερων· και ηκουσθη, ὁτι εις οικον εστι.
days; and it was reported, that into a house he is.
[2] Και *[ευθεως] συνηχθησαν πολλοι, ὡστε
And [immediately] were gathered together many, so as
μηκετι χωρειν μηδε τα προς την θυραν· και
no longer to contain not even the places near the door; and
ελαλει αυτοις τον λογον. [3] Και ερχονται προς
he spake to them the word. And they come to
αυτον παραλυτικον φεροντες, αιρομενον ὑπο
him a paralytic bringing, being carried by
τεσσαρων. [4] Και μη δυναμενοι προσεγγισαι
four. And not being able to come nigh
αυτῳ δια τον οχλον, απεστεγασαν την
to him through the crowd, they uncovered the
στεγην, ὁπου ην· και εξορυξαντες χαλωσι
roof, where he was; and having dug through they let down
τον κραββατον, εφ' ᾡ ὁ παραλυτικος κατε-
the bed, upon which the paralytic was
κειτο. [5] Ιδων δε ὁ Ιησους την πιστιν αυτων,
laid. Seeing and the Jesus the faith of them,
λεγει τῳ παραλυτικῳ· Τεκνον, αφεωνται σου
says to the paralytic; Son, are forgiven of thee
αἱ ἁμαρτιαι. [6] Ησαν δε τινες των γραμματεων
the sins. Were but some of the scribes
εκει καθημενοι και διαλογιζομενοι εν ταις
there sitting and reasoning in the
καρδιαις αὑτων· [7] Τι οὑτος οὑτω λαλει βλασ-
hearts of them; Why this thus speaks blas-
φημιας; τις δυναται αφιεναι ἁμαρτιας, ει μη
phemy? who is able to forgive sins, if not
εἱς ὁ θεος; [8] Και ευθεως επιγνους ὁ Ιησους
one the God? And immediately knowing the Jesus

44 And says to him,
‡"See, that thou say nothing to any one; but go, show Thyself to the PRIEST, and present for thy PURIFICATION, those things which Moses commanded, † for Notifying (the cure) to the people."

45 ‡ But HE going out, began to publicly proclaim and divulge the THING, so that he could no longer openly enter a City, but was without in Desert Places; and they resorted to him from all parts.

CHAPTER II.

1 And after some Days, ‡he again entered Capernaum; and it was reported That he was in a House.

2 And Many were gathered together; so that (the house) could not contain them, nor the PARTS at the DOOR; and he spake the WORD to them.

3 And they come * bringing to him a Paralytic, carried by Four.

4 And being unable to approach him, because of the CROWD, they uncovered the ROOF where he was; and having dug through, they lowered the † COUCH on which the PARALYTIC was laid.

5 Now JESUS perceiving their FAITH, says to the PARALYTIC, "Son, thy SINS are forgiven."

6 But there were some of the SCRIBES sitting, and reasoning in their HEARTS,

7 * "Why thus speaks this man? He blasphemes! Who can forgive Sins, but the One GOD?"

8 And JESUS, immedi-

* VATICAN MANUSCRIPT.—2. immediately—*omit*. 3. bringing to him. 7. That this man thus speaks? He blasphemes! Who can.

† 44. See Notes on Matt. viii. 3, 4. † 4. Eastern beds are light and moveable, consisting of a mattrass and two quilts. Dr. Russell tells us, that their beds consist of a mattrass laid on the floor, and over this a sheet, (in winter a carpet, or some such woolen covering,) the other sheet being sewed to the quilt. A divan cushion often serves for a pillow.

‡ 44. Lev. xiv. 2, 4, 10; Matt. viii. 4; Luke v. 14. ‡ 45. Luke v. 15. ‡ 1. Matt. ix. 1; Luke v. 18.

τῳ πνευματι αὐτου, ὁτι *[οὑτως] αυτοι διαλο-
to the spirit of himself, that [thus] they rea-
γιζονται εν ἑαυτοις, ειπεν αυτοις· Τι ταυτα
soned among themselves, said to them; Why these (things)
διαλογιζεσθε εν ταις καρδιαις ὑμων; 9 Τι
reason you in the hearts of you? Which
εστιν ευκοπωτερον; ειπειν τῳ παραλυτικῳ·
is easier? to say to the paralytic;
Αφεωνται σου αἱ ἁμαρτιαι; η ειπειν· Εγειρε,
Are forgiven of thee the sins; or to say; Arise,
αρον σου τον κραββατον, και περιπατει;
take up of thee the bed, and walk?
10 Ἱνα δε ειδητε, ὁτι εξουσιαν εχει ὁ υἱος του
That but you may know, that authority has the son of the
ανθρωπου επι της γης αφιεναι ἁμαρτιας· (λεγει
man on the earth to forgive sins; (he says
τῳ παραλυτικῳ·) 11 Σοι λεγω· Εγειρε, αρον
to the paralytic;) To thee I say; Arise, take up
τον κραββατον σου, και ὑπαγε εις τον οικον
the bed of thee, and go into the house
σου. 12 Και ηγερθη ευθεως, και αρας τον
of thee. And he was raised immediately, and taking up the
κραββατον, εξηλθεν εναντιον παντων· ὡστε
bed, went out in presence of all; so as
εξιστασθαι παντας, και δοξαζειν τον θεον,
to astonish all, and to glorify the God,
λεγοντας· Ὁτι ουδεποτε οὑτως ειδομεν.
saying; That never thus we saw.

13 Και εξηλθε παλιν παρα την θαλασσαν·
And he went out again by the sea.
και πας ὁ οχλος ηρχετο προς αυτον, και εδι-
and all the crowd came to him, and he
δασκεν αυτους. 14 Και παραγων ειδε Λευιν τον
taught them. And passing on he saw Levi the
του Αλφαιου, καθημενον επι το τελωνιον, και
of the Alpheus, sitting at the custom house, and
λεγει αυτῳ· Ακολουθει μοι. Και αναστας
says to him; Follow me. And rising up
ηκολουθησεν αυτῳ.
he followed him.

15 Και εγενετο εν τῳ κατακεισθαι αυτον εν
And it happened in the to recline at table him in
τη οικιᾳ αυτου, και πολλοι τελωναι και ἁμαρ-
the house of him, and many publicans and sin-
τωλοι συνανεκειντο τῳ Ιησου και τοις μαθηταις
ners reclined with the Jesus and the disciples
αυτου· ησαν γαρ πολλοι, και ηκολουθησαν
of him: they were for many, and they followed
αυτῳ. 16 Και οἱ γραμματεις και οἱ Φαρισαιοι
him. And the scribes * and the Pharisees
ιδοντες αυτον εσθιοντα μετα των τελωνων και
seeing him eating with the publicans and
αμαρτωλων, ελεγον τοις μαθηταις αυτου· *[Τι]
sinners, said to the disciples of him: [Why]
ὁτι μετα των τελωνων και αμαρτωλων εσθιει
that with of the publicans and sinners he eats

ately perceiving in his SPIRIT, that they reasoned among themselves, he says to them, "Why do you reason thus in your HEARTS?

9 ‡ Which is easier? to say to the PARALYTIC, 'Thy SINS are forgiven;' or to say (with effect,) 'Arise, take Thy COUCH, and walk?'

10 But that you may know That the SON of MAN has Authority on EARTH to forgive Sins," (he says to the PARALYTIC,)

11 "I say to thee, Arise, take up thy COUCH, and go to thy HOUSE."

12 And he was raised immediately, and taking up the COUCH, went out in presence of all; so that they were all amazed, and glorified GOD, saying. "We never say anything like this!"

13 And he went out again by the LAKE; and All the CROWD resorted to him, and he taught them.

14 ‡ And passing along, he saw THAT Levi who is the son of ALPHEUS, sitting at the TAX-OFFICE, and says to him, "Follow me." And arising, he followed him.

15 ‡ And it occurred, while he RECLINED AT TABLE in his HOUSE, Many Tribute-takers and Sinners also reclined with JESUS and his DISCIPLES; for they were Many, and they followed him.

16 And the SCRIBES * of the PHARISEES observing him eating with the TRIBUTE-TAKERS and † Sinners, said to his DISCIPLES, "He eats with TRIBUTE-TAKERS and Sinners!"

* VATICAN MANUSCRIPT.—8. thus—*omit.* 8. he says to them. 16. of the PHARISEES saw him eat. 16. Why—*omit.*

† 16. By *amartooloi,* sinners, the Gentiles or heathen are generally understood in the Gospels, for this was a term the Jews never applied to any of themselves.—*Clarke.*

‡ 9. Matt. ix. 5. ‡ 14. Matt. ix. 9; Luke v. 27. ‡ 15. Matt. ix. 10.

*[και πινει;] [17] Και ακουσας ὁ Ιησους λεγει
[and drinks?] And hearing the Jesus says
αυτοις· Ου χρειαν εχουσιν οἱ ισχυοντες
to them; No need have those being well
ιατρου, αλλ' οἱ κακως εχοντες. Ουκ ηλθον
of a physician, but those sick being. Not I came
καλεσαι δικαιους αλλα ἁμαρτωλους.
to call just (ones) but sinners.
[18] Και ησαν οἱ μαθηται Ιωαννου και οἱ Φαρι-
And were the disciples of John and the Phari-
σαιοι νηστευοντες· και ερχονται, και λεγουσιν
sees fasting; and they come, and they say
αυτῳ· Διατι οἱ μαθηται Ιωαννου και οἱ των
to him; Why the disciples of John and those of the
Φαρισαιων νηστευουσιν, οἱ δε σοι μαθηται
Pharisees fast, those but to thee disciples
ου νηστευουσι; [19] Και ειπεν αυτοις ὁ Ιησους·
not fast? And said to them the Jesus;
Μη δυνανται οἱ υἱοι του νυμφωνος, εν ᾡ ὁ
Not are able the sons of the bride-chamber, in which the
νυμφιος μετ' αυτων εστι, νηστευειν; ὁσον
bridegroom with them is, to fast? so long
χρονον μεθ' ἑαυτων εχουσι τον νυμφιον, ου
a time with themselves they have the bridegroom, not
δυνανται νηστευειν. [20] Ελευσονται δε ἡμεραι,
are able to fast. Will come but days,
ὁταν απαρθη απ' αυτων ὁ νυμφιος, και
when may be taken away from them the bridegroom, and
τοτε νηστευσουσιν εν εκεινη τη ἡμερα. [21] Ουδεις
then they will fast in that the day. No one
επιβλημα ῥακους αγναφου επιρραπτει επι
a patch of cloth unfulled sews on
ἱματιῳ παλαιῳ· ει δε μη, αιρει το πληρωμα
a mantle old; if but not, takes away the patch
αυτου το καινον του παλαιου, και χειρον
of itself the new of the old, and worse
σχισμα γινεται. [22] Και ουδεις βαλλει οινον
a rent becomes. And no one puts wine
νεον εις ασκους παλαιους· ει δε μη, ῥησσει ὁ
new into bottles old; if but not, bursts the
οινος ὁ *[νεος] τους ασκους, και ὁ οινος
wine the [new] the bottles, and the wine
εκχειται, και οἱ ασκοι απολουνται· αλλα οινον
is spilled, and the bottles are lost; but wine
νεον εις ασκους καινους βλητεον.
new into bottles new must be put.
[23] Και εγενετο παραπορευεσθαι αυτον εν τοις
And it came to pass to go him in the
σαββασι δια των σποριμων, και ηρξαντο οἱ
sabbath through the corn-fields, and began the
μαθηται αυτου ὁδον ποιειν τιλλοντες τους
disciples of him a way to make plucking the
σταχυας. [24] Και οἱ Φαρισαιοι ελεγον αυτῳ·
ears of corn. And the Pharisees said to him;
Ιδε, τι ποιουσιν εν τοις σαββασιν, ὁ ουκ
See, why do they in the sabbath, what not

17 And JESUS having heard it, says to them, ‡"THEY being in HEALTH have no Need of a Physician, but THEY who are SICK. I came not to call the Righteous, but Sinners."

18 ‡Now the DISCIPLES of John and the PHARISEES were fasting; and they come and say to him, "Why do the DISCIPLES of John, *and the DISCIPLES of the PHARISEES fast, but THINE fast not?"

19 And JESUS replied, "Can the BRIDEMEN fast, while the BRIDEGROOM IS with them? During the time they have the BRIDEGROOM with them, they cannot fast.

20 But the Days will come, when the BRIDEGROOM will be taken from them, and then they will fast in That DAY.

21 No one sews a Piece of undressed Cloth on to an old Garment; if so, the NEW PIECE of itself takes away from the OLD, and a worse Rent is made.

22 And no one puts new Wine into old Skins; if so, the WINE *will burst the SKINS; and the WINE will be lost, and the SKINS; but new Wine into new Skins."

23 ‡And it happened, that he *was passing through the FIELDS OF GRAIN on the SABBATH; and his DISCIPLES began, as they *made their way, to pluck the HEADS of GRAIN.

24 And the PHARISEES said to him, "See, why do they on the SABBATH what is not lawful?"

* VATICAN MANUSCRIPT.—16. and drinks—*omit*. 18. and the DISCIPLES of the PHARISEES fast, but THINE fast not? 22. NEW—*omit*. 22. will burst the SKINS, and the WINE will be lost, and the SKINS; but new Wine into new Skins. 23. was passing through. 23. made their way to pluck.

☞ 22. See Note on Matt. ix. 17.

‡ 17. Matt. ix. 12, 13; Luke v. 31, 32. ‡ 18. Matt. ix. 14; Luke v. 33. ‡ 23. Matt. xii. 1; Luke vi. 1.

εξεστι; 25 Και αυτος ελεγεν αυτοις· Ουδεποτε
is lawful? And he said to them: Never
ανεγνωτε, τι εποιησε Δαυιδ, ὁτε χρειαν εσχε,
have you known, what did David, when need he had,
και επεινασεν, αυτος και οἱ μετ' αυτου;
and was hungry, he and those with him;
26 *[Πως] εισηλθεν εις τον οικον του θεου,
[How] he went into the house of the God,
επι Αβιαθαρ του αρχιερεως, και τους αρτους
to Abiathar of the high-priest, and the loaves
της προθεσεως εφαγεν, οὑς ουκ εξεστι φαγειν
of the presence did eat, which not is lawful to eat
ει μη τοις ἱερευσι, και εδωκε και τοις συν
if not the priests, and he gave also to those with
αυτῳ ουσι; 27 Και ελεγεν αυτοις· Το σαβ-
him being? And he said to them, The sab-
βατον δια τον ανθρωπον εγενετο, ουχ' ὁ
bath because of the man was made, not the
ανθρωπος δια το σαββατον. 28 Ὡστε κυριος
man because of the sabbath. So that a lord
εστιν ὁ υἱος του ανθρωπου και του σαββατου.
is the son of the man even of the sabbath.

ΚΕΦ. γ'. 3.

1 Και εισηλθε παλιν εις την συναγωγην·
And he entered again into the synagogue;
και ην εκει ανθρωπος εξηραμμενην εχων την
and was there a man having been withered having the
χειρα 2 και παρετηρουν αυτον, ει τοις σαβ-
hand; and they closely watched him, if to the sab-
βασι θεραπευσει αυτον, ἱνα κατηγορησωσιν
bath he will heal him, that they might accuse
αυτου. 3 Και λεγει τῳ ανθρωπῳ τῳ εξηραμ-
him. And he says to the man to that having been
μενην εχοντι την χειρα· Εγειρε εις το μεσον.
withered having the hand; Arise in the midst.
4 Και λεγει αυτοις· Εξεστι τοις σαββασιν
And he says to them; Is it lawful to the sabbath
αγαθοποιησαι η κακοποιησαι; ψυχην σωσαι,
to do good or to do evil? a life to save,
η αποκτειναι; Οἱ δε εσιωπων. 5 Και περιβλε-
or to destroy? They but were silent. And looking
ψαμενος αυτους μετ' οργης, συλλυπουμενος επι
round them with anger, being grieved at
τῃ πωρωσει της καρδιας αυτων, λεγει τῳ
the hardness of the hearts of them, he says to the
ανθρωπῳ· Εκτεινον την χειρα σου. Και
man; Stretch out the hand of thee. And
εξετεινε· και απεκατεσταθη ἡ χειρ αυτου.
he stretched it out; and was restored the hand of him.
6 Και εξελθοντες οἱ Φαρισαιοι, ευθεως μετα των
And coming out the Pharisees, immediately with the

25 And * he said to
them, ‡ "Have you never
read what David did, when
he had Need, and was
hungry, he, and THOSE
with him?
26 How † he went into
the TABERNACLE of GOD,
to Abiathar (son) of the
HIGH-PRIEST, and ate † the
LOAVES of the PRESENCE,
‡ which none but the
PRIESTS could lawfully
eat; and he gave also to
THOSE with him."
27 He also said to them,
"The SABBATH was made
for MAN, and not MAN for
the SABBATH;
28 ‡ so that the SON of
MAN is Lord even of the
SABBATH."

CHAPTER III.

1 ‡ And again he enter-
ed into the SYNAGOGUE,
where was a Man who had
a Withered HAND.
2 And they watched him
closely, (to see) if he would
cure him on the SABBATH;
that they might accuse
him.
3 And he says to THAT
MAN HAVING the With-
ered HAND, "Arise in the
MIDST."
4 And he says to them,
"Is it lawful to do good
on the SABBATH, or to do
evil? to save Life, or to
destroy?" But THEY were
silent.
5 And surveying them
with Indignation, being
grieved at the HARDNESS
of their HEARTS, he says
to the MAN, "Stretch out
* thine HAND." And he
stretched it out, and his
HAND was restored.
6 ‡ And the PHARISEES
going out, immediately
* held a Council with † the

* VATICAN MANUSCRIPT.—25. he said. 26. How—*omit.* 5. the HAND. 6. gave Counsel.

† 26. David went to the house of Ahimelech at Nob, with whom the tabernacle then was and the ephod, and other holy things. See 1 Sam. xxi. † 26. These loaves were placed on a table on the north side, and at the right hand of him who entered the tabernacle. Exod xxv 30; Lev. xxiv. 5, 6, 8. † 6. The Herodians were a political party who began to become eminent in the days of Herod the Great, as favoring his claims, and those of his patrons, the Romans, to the sovereignty of Judea.

‡ 25 1 Sam. xxi. 6. ‡ 26 Exod. xxix. 32, 33. ‡ 28. Matt. xii. 8. ‡ 1. Matt xii. 9; Luke vi. 6. ‡ 6. Matt. xii. 14.

6 Ἡρωδιανων συμβουλιον εποιουν κατ' αυτου,
Herodians a council held against him,
ὁπως αυτον απολεσωσι.
how him they might destroy.

7 Και ὁ Ιησους μετα των μαθητων αὑτου
And the Jesus with the disciples of him
ανεχωρησεν εις την θαλασσαν· και πολυ πλη-
withdrew to the sea; and a great multi-
θος απο της Γαλιλαιας ηκολουθησαν αυτῳ· και
tude from the Galilee followed him; and
απο της Ιουδαιας, και απο Ιεροσολυμων, 8 και
from the Judea, and from Jerusalem, and
απο της Ιδουμαιος, και περαν του Ιορδανου, και
from the Idumea, and beyond the Jordan, and
*[οι] περι Τυρον και Σιδωνα, πληθος πολυ,
[those] about Tyre and Sidon, a multitude great,
ακουσαντες ὁσα εποιει, ηλθον προς αυτον.
having heard what things he did, came to him.
9 Και ειπε τοις μαθηταις αυτου, ἱνα πλοιαριον
And he spake to the disciples of him, that a small vessel
σκαρτερῃ αυτῳ, δια τον οχλον, ἱνα μη
should attend him, because of the crowd, that not
θλιβωσιν αυτον. 10 Πολλους γαρ εθεραπευσεν,
they might throng him. Many for he cured,
ὡστε επιπιπτειν αυτῳ, ἱνα αυτου ἁψωνται,
so as to rush to him, that him they might touch,
ὁσοι ειχον μαστιγας. 11 Και τα πνευματα τα
as many as had scourges. And the spirits the
ακαθαρτα, ὁταν αυτον εθεωρει, προσεπιπτεν
unclean, when him gazing on, fell before
αυτῳ, και εκραζε, λεγοντα· Ὁτι συ ει ὁ υἱος
him, and cried, saying; That thou art the son
του θεου. 12 Και πολλα επετιμα αυτοις, ἱνα
of the God. And many times he charged them, that
μη φανερον αυτον ποιησωσι. 13 Και αναβαι-
not known him they should make. And he goes
νει εις το ορος, και προσκαλειται οὑς ηθελεν
up into the mountain, and calls whom would
αυτος· και απηλθον προς αυτον.
he; and they came to him.

14 Και εποιησε δωδεκα, ἱνα ωσι μετ' αυτου,
And he appointed twelve, that they should be with him,
και *[ἱνα] αποστελλῃ αυτους κηρυσσειν, 15 και
and [that] he might send them to preach, and
εχειν εξουσιαν *[θεραπευειν τας νοσους, και]
to have authority [to cure the diseases, and]
εκβαλλειν τα δαιμονια. 16 Και επεθηκε τῳ
to cast out the demons. And he put on to the
Σιμωνι ονομα Πετρον· 17 και Ιακωβον τον του
Simon a name Peter; and James that of the
Ζεβεδαιου, και Ιωαννην τον αδελφον του
Zebedee, and John the brother of the
Ιακωβου· και επεθηκεν αυτοις ονοματα Βοαν-
James; and he put on them names Boan-
εργες, ὁ εστιν, υἱοι βροντης· 18 και Ανδρεαν,
erges, that is, sons of thunder; and Andrew,

Herodians, against him, how they might destroy him.

7 But JESUS with his DISCIPLES retired to the LAKE; and a Great Multitude followed him from GALILEE, ‡and from JUDEA,

8 and from Jerusalem, and from IDUMEA, and from beyond the JORDAN; also a great Company from about Tyre and Sidon, having heard what *he had done, came to him.

9 And he spake to his DISCIPLES, that *a Small boat should attend him because of the CROWD, that they might not press upon him.

10 For he had cured Many; so that as many as had Diseases rushed towards him in order to touch him.

11 ‡ And the IMPURE SPIRITS, when they beheld him, fell before him, and cried, saying, "Thou art the SON of GOD."

12 And he repeatedly charged them, that they should not make Him known.

13 ‡ And he ascended the MOUNTAIN, and called whom he would; and they went to him.

14 And he appointed *twelve, that they should accompany him, and that he might send them forth to proclaim,

15 and to have Authority to expel DEMONS.

16 * Now the TWELVE he appointed, were ‡ SIMON, to whom he gave the Name of PETER;

17 and THAT James, son of ZEBEDEE, and John the brother of JAMES; to whom he gave the Names of Boanerges, that is, Sons of Thunder;

18 and Andrew, and

* VATICAN MANUSCRIPT.—8. THOSE—*omit*. 8. he does. 9. Small vessels. 14. twelve, whom also he named Apostles, that. 14. that—*omit*. 15. to cure DISEASES, and—*omit*. 16. And he appointed TWELVE; both SIMON whom he surnamed PETER.

‡ 7. Luke vi. 17. ‡ 11. Mark i. 32, 34; Luke iv. 41. ‡ 13. Matt. x. 1; Luke vi. 13; ix. 1. ‡ 16. John i. 42.

και Φιλιππον, και Βαρθολομαιον, και Ματθαιον,
and Philip, and Bartholomew, and Matthew,
και Θωμαν, και Ιακωβον τον του Αλφαιου, και
and Thomas, and James that of the Alpheus, and
Θαδδαιον, και Σιμωνα τον κανανιτην, 19 *και*
Thaddeus, and Simon the Canaanite, and
Ιουδαν Ισκαριωτην, ὁς και παρεδωκεν αυτον.
Judas Iscariot, who even delivered up him.
20 *Και ερχονται εις οικον. Και συνερχεται*
And they come into a house. And came together
παλιν οχλος, ὡστε μη δυνασθαι αυτους μητε
again a crowd, so as not to be able them not even
αρτον φαγειν. 21 *Και ακουσαντες οἱ παρ'*
bread to eat. And having heard those with
αυτου, εξηλθον κρατησαι αυτον· ελεγον γαρ·
him, went out to restrain him, they said for;
Ὁτι εξεστη. 22 *Και οἱ γραμματεις, οἱ απο*
That he is out of place. And the scribes, those from
Ἱεροσολυμων καταβαντες, ελεγον· Ὁτι Βεελ-
Jerusalem having come down, said; That Beel-
ζεβουλ εχει· και· Ὁτι εν τῳ αρχοντι των
zebul he has; also; That by the chief of the
δαιμονιων εκβαλλει τα δαιμονια. 23 *Και προσ-*
demons he casts out the demons. And having
καλεσαμενος αυτους, εν παραβολαις ελεγεν
called them, in parables he said
αυτοις· Πως δυναται σατανας σαταναν εκβαλ-
to them; How is able an adversary an adversary to cast
λειν; 24 *Και εαν βασιλεια εφ' ἑαυτην μερισ-*
out? And if a kingdom against herself should be di-
θη, ου δυναται σταθηναι ἡ βασιλεια εκεινη·
vided, not is able to stand the kingdom that;
25 *και εαν οικια εφ' ἑαυτην μερισθη, ου δυναται*
and if a house against herself should be divided, not is able
σταθηναι ἡ οικια εκεινη· 26 *και ει ὁ σατανας*
to stand the house that; and if the adversary
ανεστη εφ' ἑαυτον και μεμερισται, ου δυναται
has risen up against himself and have been divided, not is able
σταθηναι, αλλα τελος εχει. 27 *Ουδεις δυναται*
to stand, but an end he has. No one is able
τα σκευη του ισχυρου, εισελθων εις την
the household goods of the strong man, entering into the
οικιαν αυτου, διαρπασαι, εαν μη πρωτον τον
house of him, to plunder, if not first the
ισχυρον δηση· και τοτε την οικιαν αυτου
strong man he should bind; and then the house of him
διαρπασει. 28 *Αμην λεγω ὑμιν, ὁτι παντα*
he will plunder. Indeed I say to you, that all
αφεθησεται τοις υἱοις των ανθρωπων τα ἁμαρτη-
will be forgiven to the sons of the men the sins,
ματα, και αἱ βλασφημιαι, ὁσας αν βλασφημη-
and the evil speakings, whatever they may

Philip, and Bartholomew, and Matthew, and Thomas, and THAT James, son of ALPHEUS, and Thaddeus, and Simon, the CANNANITE,

19 and Judas Iscariot, who even delivered him up.

20 ‡ And they went into a House. And the Crowd assembled again, so that they could not even eat Bread.

21 And THOSE with him having heard, went out to restrain him; for they said. † "He is transported too far."

22 And THOSE SCRIBES who had COME DOWN from Jerusalem said, ‡ "He has Beelzebul," and, "By the RULER of the DEMONS, he expels the DEMONS."

23 ‡ And having called them, he said to them, "How can an Adversary expel an Adversary?

24 And if a Kingdom is divided against itself, that KINGDOM cannot stand;

25 and if a House is divided against itself, that HOUSE cannot stand;

26 and if the ADVERSARY rises up against himself, and is divided, he cannot stand, but has an end.

27 * But no one can enter the STRONG man's HOUSE, and plunder his GOODS, unless he first bind the STRONG man; and then he may plunder his HOUSE.

28 Indeed, I say to you, That All SINS will be forgiven the SONS of MEN, and the BLASPHEMIES with which they may revile;

---

* VATICAN MANUSCRIPT.—27. but no one.

† 21. Doddridge remarks, "Our manner of rendering these words, *He is besides himself*, or *He is mad*, is very offensive. One can hardly think Christ's friends would speak so contemptibly and impiously of him; and if that sense must necessarily be retained, it would be much more decent to render the clause, *It* (that is, the *multitude*,) *is mad*, thus unseasonably to break in upon him." Schotengen contends, that the *multitude*, and not *Christ* is here intended. Christ was in the house; the multitude, *ochlos*, verse 20, went out, *krateenai auton*, to restrain *it*, (viz. *ochlon*, the multitude.) to prevent them from rushing into the house and disturbing their Master, who was taking some refreshment. This conjecture should not be lightly regarded.—*Clarke*.

‡ 20. Mark vi. 31. ‡ 22. Matt. ix. 34; x. 25; Luke xi. 15; John vii. 20; viii. 48, 52; x. 22. ‡ 23. Matt. xii. 25.

σωσιν· 29 ὁς δ' αν βλασφημηση εις το
who but ever may speak evil to the
πνευμα το ἁγιον, ουκ εχει αφεσιν εις τον
spirit the holy, not has forgivness to the
αιωνα, αλλ' ενοχος εστιν αιωνιου κρισεως.
age, but liable is of age-lasting judgment.
30 Ὁτι ελεγον· Πνευμα ακαθαρτον εχει. 31 Ερ-
Because they said; A spirit unclean he has.
χονται ουν ἡ μητηρ αυτου και οἱ αδελφοι
Comes then the mother of him and the brothers
αυτου· και εξω εστωτες απεστειλαν προς αυτον,
of him; and without standing they sent to him,
φωνουντες αυτον. 32 Και εκαθητο οχλος περι
calling him. And sat a crowd about
αυτον· ειπον δε αυτῳ· Ιδου, ἡ μητηρ σου
him; said and to him; Lo, the mother of thee
και οἱ αδελφοι σου εξω ζητουσι σε. 33 Και
and the brothers of thee without are seeking thee. And
απεκριθη αυτοις, λεγων· Τις εστιν ἡ μητηρ
he answered to them, saying; Who is the mother
μου, η οἱ αδελφοι μου; 34 *[Και] περιβλε-
of me, or the brothers of me? [And] looking
ψαμενος κυκλῳ τους περι αυτον καθημενους,
about round those about him sitting,
λεγει· Ιδε ἡ μητηρ μου, και οἱ αδελφοι μου.
he says; Lo the mother of me, and the brothers of me.
35 Ὁς *[γαρ] αν ποιηση το θελημα του θεου,
Who [for] ever may do the will of the God,
οὑτος αδελφος μου, και αδελφη *[μου,] και
this a brother of me, and a sister [of me,] and
μητηρ εστι.
a mother is.

ΚΕΦ. δ'. 4.

1 Και παλιν ηρξατο διδασκειν παρα την
And again he began to teach by the
θαλασσαν· και συνηχθη προς αυτον οχλος πολυς,
sea; and was assembled to him a crowd great,
ὡστε αυτον εμβαντα εις το πλοιον, καθησθαι
so as him entering into the ship, to sit
εν τη θαλασσῃ· και πας ὁ οχλος προς την
in the sea: and all the crowd by the
θαλασσαν επι της γης ην. 2 Και εδιδασκεν
sea on the land was. And he taught
αυτους εν παραβολαις πολλα, και ελεγεν αυτοις
them in parables many, and said to them
εν τη διδαχῃ αὐτου· 3 Ακουετε· Ιδου, εξηλθεν
in the teaching of him: Hear you: Lo, went out
ὁ σπειρων του σπειραι. 4 Και εγενετο εν τῳ
the sower of the (seed) to sow. And it happened in the

29 ‡ but whoever may blaspheme against the HOLY SPIRIT, has no Forgiveness to the AGE, but is exposed to Aionian * † Judgment."

30 Because they said, "He has an impure Spirit."

31 His MOTHER and BROTHERS then came, and standing without, sent to him, calling him.

32 And a Crowd sat round him, and they said to him, "Behold, thy MOTHER and thy BROTHERS are without seeking thee."

33 And he answered them, saying, "Who is my MOTHER, or my BROTHERS?"

34 And looking about on THOSE sitting round him, he said, "Behold my MOTHER, and my BROTHERS.

35 Whoever shall do the WILL of GOD, this is my Brother, and Sister, and Mother."

CHAPTER IV.

1 ‡ And again he began to teach by the LAKE; and so * very great a Crowd gathered about him, that entering the BOAT, he sat on the LAKE; and All the CROWD was by the LAKE on the LAND.

2 And he taught them many things in Parables, and said to them, in his TEACHING;

3 "Hearken! Behold, the SOWER went forth to * sow.

4 And it happened, in

* VATICAN MANUSCRIPT.—29. Transgression. 34. And—*omit.* 35. For—*omit.* 35. my—*omit.* 1. very. 3. sow.

† 29. The *Vat. MSS.* reads *Transgression*, and Griesbach has placed the word *amarteematos*, sin, or transgression, in the margin, with his mark of strong probability. Grotius, Mill, and Bengel prefer this reading. It is also the reading of the *Coptic*, *Armenian*, *Gothic*, *Vulgate*, and all the *Itala* but two. It is a Hebraism for punishment, the effect of sin. The sin against the Holy Spirit is plainly stated to be, ascribing the miracles of Christ and his apostles to demoniacal agency. They who acted thus, could not be converted to the Christain faith, because they resisted the strongest possible evidence. They remained therefore in the same forlorn state in which Christianity found them; which is expressed by the phrase, "he has not forgiveness."

‡ 29. Matt. xii 31. 32. Luke xii. 10; 1 John v. 16 ‡ 31 Matt xii. 46; Luke viii. 19. ‡ 1. Matt. xiii. 1; Luke viii. 4.

σπειρειν, ὁ μεν επεσε παρα την ὁδον· και
sowing, this indeed fell on the path: and
ηλθε τα πετεινα, και κατεφαγεν αυτο. 5 Αλλο
came the birds, and ate it. Another
δε επεσεν επι το πετρωδες, ὁπου ουκ ειχε γην
and fell on the rocky ground, where not it had earth
πολλην· και ευθεως εξανετειλε, δια το μη
much; and immediately it sprung up, through the not
εχειν βαθος γης. 6 Ηλιου δε ανατειλαντος,
to have a depth of earth. Sun and having arisen,
εκαυματισθη, και δια το μη εχειν ῥιζαν, εξη-
it was scorched, and through the not to have a root, was
ρανθη. 7 Και αλλο επεσεν εις ακανθας· και
dried up. And another fell into thorns; and
ανεβησαν αἱ ακανθαι, και συνεπνιξαν αυτο, και
sprung up the thorns, and choked it, and
καρπον ουκ εδωκε. 8 Και αλλο επεσεν εις·την
fruit not it gave. And another fell into the
γην την καλην· και εδιδου καρπον αναβαινοντα
ground the good; and it bore fruit springing up
και αυξανοντα· και εφερεν ἑν τριακοντα, και
and increasing; and bore one thirty, and
ἑν ἑξηκοντα, και ἑν ἑκατον. 9 Και ελεγεν· Ὁ
one sixty, and one a hundred. And he said; He
εχων ωτα ακουειν, ακουετω.
having ears to hear, let him hear.

10 Ὁτε δε εγενετο καταμονας, ηρωτησαν
When and he was alone, asked
αυτον οἱ περι αυτον, συν τοις δωδεκα, την
him those about him, with the twelve, the
παραβολην. 11 Και ελεγεν αυτοις· Ὑμιν δεδο-
parables. And he said to them; To you it is
ται γνωναι το μυστηριον της βασιλειας του
given to know the secret of the kingdom of the
θεου· εκεινοις δε τοις εξω εν παραβολαις τα
God; to them but to those without in parables the
παντα γινεται· 12 ἱνα βλεποντες βλεπωσι,
all (things) are done; that seeing they may see,
και μη ιδωσι· και ακουοντες ακουωσι, και μη
and not they may see; and hearing they may hear, and not
συνιωσι· μηποτε επιστρεψωσι, και αφεθη
they may hear: lest they should turn, and should be forgiven
αυτοις τα ἁμαρτηματα. 13 Και λεγει αυτοις·
to them the sins. And he says to them:
Ουκ οιδατε την παραβολην ταυτην; και πως
Not know you the parable this? and how
πασας τας παραβολας γνωσεσθε; 14 Ὁ σπειρων,
all the parables will you know? He sowing,
τον λογον σπειρει. 15 Ουτοι δε εισιν οἱ παρα
the word sows. These and are they by
την ὁδον, ὁπου σπειρεται ὁ λογος, και ὁταν
the path, where is sown the word, and when
ακουσωσιν, ευθεως ερχεται ὁ σατανας, και
they may hear, immediately comes the adversary, and

SOWING, some seed fell by the ROAD and the BIRDS came and picked it up.
5 And some fell on the ROCKY GROUND, where it had not much Soil; and immediately it vegetated, because it had no Depth of Soil;
6 * and the SUN having arisen, it was scorched; and because it HAD no Root, it withered.
7 And some fell among Thorns; and the THORNS grew up, and choked it, and it bore no Fruit.
8 And some fell on GOOD GROUND, and yielded Fruit, springing up and increasing; and one bore thirty, and one sixty, and one a hundred."
9 And he said, * "He HAVING Ears to hear, let him hear."
10 ‡ And when he had retired, THOSE about him, with the TWELVE, asked him concerning the * PARABLE.
11 And he said to them, * "To you is given the SECRET of the KINGDOM of GOD; but to ‡ THOSE WITHOUT, ALL things are done in Parables;
12 ‡ that seeing, they may see, and not perceive; and hearing, they may hear, and not understand; lest they should turn, and * it should be forgiven them."
13 And he says to them, "Do you not understand this PARABLE? How then will you know All the PARABLES?
14 ‡ The SOWER SOWS the WORD.
15 And these are THOSE where the WORD is sown by the ROAD; and when they have heard, the ADVERSARY comes immediately, and takes away

* VATICAN MANUSCRIPT.—6. and the SUN having arisen. 9. Who has ears. 10. PARABLES. 11. is given the SECRET. 12. it should be.

‡ 10. Matt. xiii. 10; Luke viii 9. ‡ 11. 1 Cor. v. 12; Col. iv. 5; 2 Thess. iv. 12, 1 Tim. iii. 7. ‡ 12. Isa. vi. 9; Matt. xiii. 14; Luke viii. 10; John xii. 40; Acts xxviii. 26; Rom. xi. 8. ‡ 14. Matt. xiii. 19.

αιρει τον λογον τον εσπαρμενον εν ταις καρδιαις
takes the word that having been sown in the hearts
αυτων. 16 Και οὗτοι εισιν ὁμοιως οἱ επι τα
of them. And these are like those on the
πετρωδη σπειρομενοι, οἱ, ὁταν ακουσωσι τον
rocky ground being sown, who, when they may hear the
λογον, ευθεως μετα χαρας λαμβανουσιν αυτον·
word, immediately with joy they receive it;
17 και ουκ εχουσι ῥιζαν εν ἑαυτοις, αλλα προσ-
and not they have a root in themselves, but for a
καιροι εισιν· ειτα γενομενης θλιψεως η διωγμου
season they are; then occurring trial or persecution
δια τον λογον, ευθεως σκανδαλιζονται. 18 Και
through the word, immediately they are offended. And
αλλοι εισιν οἱ εις τας ακανθας σπειρομενοι·
others are those into the thorns being sown;
οὗτοι εισιν οἱ τον λογον ακουοντες, 17 και αἱ
these are those the word hearing, and the
μεριμναι του αιωνος, και ἡ απατη του πλουτου,
cares of the age, and the delusion of the wealth,
και αἱ περι τα λοιπα επιθυμιαι εισπορευομεναι
and the about the other (things) strong desires entering in
συμπνιγουσι τον λογον· και ακαρπος γινεται.
choke the word; and unfruitful it becomes.
20 Και οὗτοι εισιν οἱ επι την γην την καλην
And these are those upon the ground the good
σπαρεντες, οἱτινες ακουουσι τον λογον, και
being sown, who hear the word, and
παραδεχονται· και καρποφορουσιν, ἑν τριακοντα,
accept, and bear fruit, one thirty,
και ἑν εξηκοντα, και ἑν ἑκατον. 21 Και ελεγεν
and one sixty, and one a hundred. And he said
αυτοις· Μητι ὁ λυχνος ερχεται, ἱνα ὑπο τον
to them; Neither the lamp comes, that under the
μοδιον τεθῃ, η ὑπο την κλινην; ουχ᾽ ἱνα
measure it may be placed, or under the couch? not that
επι την λυχνιαν επιτεθῃ; 22 Ου γαρ εστι
on the lamp-stand it may be placed? Not for is
τι κρυπτον, ὁ εαν μη φανερωθῃ· ουδε
any thing hidden, which if not it may be disclosed; nor
εγενετο αποκρυφον, αλλ᾽ ἱνα εις φανερον ελθῃ.
was stored away, but that into light it may come.
23 Ει τις εχει ωτα ακουειν, ακουετω. 24 Και
If any one has ears to hear, let him hear. And
ελεγεν αυτοις· Βλεπετε, τι ακουετε. Εν ᾧ
he said to them; Consider you, what you hear. In what
μετρῳ μετρειτε, μετρηθησεται ὑμιν. 25 Ὁς γαρ
measure you measure, it shall be measured to you. Who for

THAT WORD which was SOWN * upon them.

16 And these in like manner are THOSE SOWN on the ROCKY GROUND; who, when they hear the WORD, receive it immediately with Joy;

17 And having no Root in themselves, they are but temporary; then Trial or Persecution occurring on account of the WORD, they instantly fall away.

18 And others are THOSE who are SOWN among the THORNS; * these are THEY who have HEARD the WORD;

19 and the CARES of the AGE, ‡ and the DECEITFULNESS of RICHES, and the STRONG DESIRES for OTHER things entering in, choke the WORD, and render it unproductive.

20 And * those are THEY, who are SOWN on the GOOD GROUND, who hear the WORD, and accept it, and bear fruit; one thirty, one sixty, and one a hundred."

21 And he said to them, ‡ "Is a lamp brought, to be put under the CORN-MEASURE, or under the COUCH? so that it may not be placed on the LAMP-STAND?

22 ‡ For * nothing was hidden, except that it should be manifested; nor was it concealed, but that it should come to light.

23 If any one has Ears to hear, let him hear."

24 And he said to them, ‡ "Consider what you hear; by the Measure you dispense, it will be measured to * you, and shall be added to you;

25 ‡ for whoever has, to

* VATICAN MANUSCRIPT.—15. upon them. 18. these are THEY who have HEARD the WORD. 20. those are THEY. 22. nothing was hidden, except that it should be manifested; nor was it concealed, but that it should come to light. 24. you, and shall be added to you.

† 21. By *klineen* must be understood the *couch*, (like our sofa,) which, as Grotius observes, had such a cavity as to admit of a *candelabrum* being put under it; nay, it seems, anything much larger; indeed, by the citations adduced by Wetstein, it appears to have been used by the ancients as a common hiding place.—*Bloomfield.*

‡ 19. 1 Tim. vi. 9, 17. ‡ 21. Matt. v. 15; Luke viii. 16; xi. 33. ‡ 22. Matt. x. 26; Luke xii. 2. ‡ 24. Matt. vii. 2; Luke vi. 38. ‡ 25. Matt. xiii. 12; xxv. 29; Luke viii. 18; xix. 26.

αν εχῃ, δοθησεται αυτῳ· και ὁς ουκ εχει, και
ever may have, it shall be given to him: and who not has, even

ὁ εχει αρθησεται απ' αυτου. 26 Και ελεγεν·
what he has will be taken from him. And he said:

Οὑτως εστιν ἡ βασιλεια του θεου, ὡς εαν αν-
Thus is the kingdom of the God, as if a

θρωπος βαλῃ τον σπορον επι της γης, 27 και
man should cast the seed on the earth, and

καθευδῃ και εγειρηται νυκτα και ἡμεραν, και ὁ
should sleep and wake night and day, and the

σπορος βλαστανῃ και μηκυνηται, ὡς ουκ οιδεν
seed should germinate and grow up, as not knows

αυτος. 28 Αυτοματη *[γαρ] ἡ γη καρποφορει,
he. Of its own accord [for] the earth bears fruit,

πρωτον, χορτον, ειτα σταχυν, ειτα πληρη σιτον
first, a plant, then an ear, then full grain

εν τῳ σταχυι. 29 Ὁταν δε παραδῳ ὁ καρπος,
in the ear. When but may be ripe the fruit,

ευθεως αποστελλει το δρεπανον, ὁτι παρεστηκεν
immediately he sends the sickle, for is ready

ὁ θερισμος. 30 Και ελεγε· Τινι ὁμοιωσωμεν
the harvest. And he said; To what may we compare

την βασιλειαν του θεου; η εν ποιᾳ παραβολῃ
the kingdom of the God? or by what parable

παραβαλωμεν αυτην; 31 Ὡς κοκκον σιναπεως,
may we compare her? As a grain of mustard,

ὁς, ὁταν σπαρῃ επι της γης, μικροτερος παν-
which, when it may be sown on the earth, less of

των των σπερματων εστι των επι της γης·
all of the seeds it is of those on the earth:

32 και ὁταν σπαρῃ, αναβαινει και γινεται παν-
and when it may be sown, it springs up and becomes of

των λαχανων μειζων, και ποιει κλαδους μεγα-
all herbs greater, and produces branches great,

λους, ὡστε δυνασθαι ὑπο την σκιαν αυτου τα
so as to be under the shadow of it the

πετεινα του ουρανου κατασκηνουν. 33 Και τοι-
birds of the heaven to build nests. And such

αυταις παραβολαις πολλαις ελαλει αυτοις τον
like parables many he spoke to them the

λογον, καθως ηδυναντο ακουειν. 34 Χωρις δε
word, even as they were able to hear. Without but

παραβολης ουκ ελαλει αυτοις· κατ' ιδιαν δε
a parable not he spoke to them; privately but

τοις μαθηταις αὑτου επελυε παντα.
to the disciples of himself he explained all.

35 Και λεγει αυτοις εν εκεινῃ τῃ ἡμερᾳ, οψιας
And he says to them in that the day, evening

γενομενης· Διελθωμεν εις το περαν. 36 Και
being come; We may pass over to the other side. And

αφεντες τον οχλον παραλαμβανουσιν αυτον, ὡς
having left the crowd they took him, as

him will be given; and he who has not, even what he has will be taken from him."

26 And he said, ‡ "The KINGDOM of GOD is, as though a Man should cast SEED on the GROUND;

27 and should sleep by Night, and wake by Day, and the SEED should germinate, and grow up, he knows not how.

28 The EARTH produces spontaneously; first the Plant, then the Ear, afterwards the Perfect Grain in the EAR.

29 But when the GRAIN is matured, immediately he sends the SICKLE, Because the HARVEST is ready."

30 And he said, ‡ "To what may we compare the KINGDOM of GOD? or * by What Parable may we illustrate it?

31 It resembles a Grain of Mustard, which, when sown on the EARTH, is the least of All THOSE SEEDS that are on the EARTH;

32 but when it is sown, it grows up, and becomes greater than All other HERBS, and produces great BRANCHES; so that the BIRDS of HEAVEN can build their nests under the SHADOW of it."

33 ‡ And with many Such Parables he spoke the WORD to them, even as they were able to understand.

34 * And without a Parable he did not address them; but privately he explained all things to his OWN Disciples.

35 ‡ And on That DAY, Evening having come, he says to them, "Let us pass over to the OTHER SIDE."

36 And having left the CROWD, they took him as

* VATICAN MANUSCRIPT.—28. For—*omit*. 30. in What Comparison shall we place It? 34. And without.

† 31. See Note on Matt. xiii. 32.

‡ 26. Matt. xiii. 24. ‡ 30. Matt. xiii. 31; Luke xiii. 18. ‡ 33. Matt. xiii. 34; John xvi. 12. ‡ 35. Matt. viii. 18, 23; Luke viii. 22.

ην εν τῳ πλοιῳ· *[και] αλλα δε πλοια ην
he was in the ship; [also] other and ships was
μετ' αυτου. 37 Και γινεται λαιλαψ ανεμου μεγα-
with him. And arose a squall of wind great;
λη· τα δε κυματα επεβαλλεν εις το πλοιον,
the and waves dashed into the ship,
ὡστε αυτο ηδη γεμιζεσθαι. 38 Και ην αυτος εν
so as it now to fill. And was he in
τῃ πρυμνῃ, επι το προσκεφαλαιον καθευδων·
the stern, on the pillow sleeping;
και διεγειρουσιν αυτον, και λεγουσιν αυτῳ·
and they awoke him, and they said to him;
Διδασκαλε, ου μελει σοι, ὁτι απολλυμεθα;
O teacher, not it concerns thee, that we perish?
39 Και διεγερθεις επετιμησε τῳ ανεμῳ, και ειπε
And having arisen he rebuked the wind, and said
τῃ θαλασσῃ· Σιωπα, πεφιμωσο. Και εκοπασεν
to the sea; Be silent, be still. And ceased
ὁ ανεμος, και εγενετο γαληνη μεγαλη. 40 Και
the wind and was a calm great. And
ειπεν αυτοις· Τι δειλοι εστε *[οὑτω;] πως
he said to them; Why timid are you [so?] how
ουκ εχετε πιστιν; 41 Και εφοβηθησαν φοβον
not you have faith? And they feared a fear
μεγαν, και ελεγον προς αλληλους· Τις αρα
great, and said to one another; Who then
οὑτος εστιν, ὁτι και ὁ ανεμος και ἡ θαλασσα
this is, for even the wind and the sea
ὑπακουσιν αυτῳ.
hearken to him.

ΚΕΦ. ε'. 5.

1 Και ηλθον εις το περαν της θαλασσης, εις
And they came to the other side of the sea, into
την χωραν των Γαδαρηνων. 2 Και εξελθοντι
the country of the Gadarenes. And having come
αυτῳ εκ του πλοιου, *[ευθεως] απηντησεν αυτῳ
to him out of the ship, [immediately] met him
εκ των μνημειων ανθρωπος εν πνευματι ακαθαρ-
out of the tombs a man in spirit unclean,
τῳ, 3 ὁς την κατοικησιν ειχεν εν τοις μνημασι·
who the dwelling had in the tombs;
και ουτε ἁλυσεσιν ουδεις ηδυνατο αυτον δησαι,
and not even with chains no one was able him to bind,
4 δια το αυτον πολλακις πεδαις και ἁλυσεσι
for the him many times with fetters and chains
δεδεσθαι, και διεσπασθαι ὑπ' αυτου τας
to have been bound, and to have been burst by him the
ἁλυσεις, και τας πεδας συντετριφθαι· και ουδεις
chains, and the fetters to have been broken; and no one

he was in the BOAT. And Other Boats were with him.

37 And there arose a great Gale of Wind, and the WAVES dashed into the BOAT, so that *the BOAT was now full.

38 And he was in the STERN, asleep on the PILLOW; and they awoke him, and said to him, "Teacher, does it not concern thee That we perish?"

39 And arising, he rebuked the WIND, and said to the SEA, "Be silent! be still!" And the WIND ceased, and there was a great Calm.

40 And he said to them, "Why are you afraid? How distrustful you are!"

41 And they were exceedingly afraid, and said to one another, "Who then is this, That even the WIND and the SEA obey him?"

CHAPTER V.

1 ‡And they came to the other side of the LAKE, into the REGION of the *GERASENES.

2 And having come out of the BOAT, there met him out of the †MONUMENTS, a Man with an impure Spirit,

3 who had his HABITATION in the TOMBS; and no one could bind *him any longer with Chains;

4 for many times he had been BOUND with Fetters and Chains, and the CHAINS had been wrenched off by him, and the FETTERS broken; and no

* VATICAN MANUSCRIPT.—36. also—*omit.* 37. the BOAT was. 40. so—*omit.* 1. GERASENES. 2. immediately—*omit.* 3. him any longer with.

† 2. The sepulchres of the Jews were formerly amongst rocks, mountains, and other unfrequented places, in order that there might be as little danger as possible of that pollution which touching any thing dead produced. They were often as large as a commodious room, and are now often resorted to as places of shelter for the night. Sometimes the wandering Arabs, during the winter season, take up their permanent abode in them. It appears that at a very early period, some of these tombs were used for suc ha purpose; as Isaiah speaks of some, "who remain among the graves, and lodge in the monuments," chap. lxv. 4. Burchhardt reports, that he found many sepulchres in the rocks, at *Um Keis*, (supposed to be the ancient Gadara,) showing how naturally the conditions of this narrative could have been fulfilled in that region.

‡ 1. Matt. viii. 28; Luke viii. 26.

αυτον ισχυε δαμασαι· 5 και διαπαντος, νυκτος
him was able to tame; and always, night
και ἡμερας, εν τοις μνημασι και εν τοις ορεσιν
and day, in the tombs and in the mountains
ην κραζων, και κατακοπτων ἑαυτον λιθοις.
he was crying out, and cutting himself with stones,
6 Ιδων δε τον Ιησουν απο μακροθεν, εδραμε, και
Seeing and the Jesus from a distance, he ran, and
προσεκυνησεν αυτῳ· 7 και κραξας φωνῃ μεγαλῃ,
prostrated to him; and crying out with a voice great,
ειπε, τι εμοι και σοι, Ιησου, υἱε του θεου του
said, what to me and to thee, Jesus, O son of the God of the
ὑψιστου; ὁρκιζω σε τον θεον, μη με βασανι-
highest? I will adjure thee the God, not me thou mayst
σῃς. 8 (Ελεγε γαρ αυτῳ· Εξελθε το πνευμα το
torment. (He had said for to him; Come out the spirit the
ακαθαρτον εκ του ανθρωπου.) 9 Και επηρωτα
unclean out of the man.) And he asked
αυτον· Τι σοι ονομα; και λεγει αυτῳ· Λεγεων
him: What thy name? and he says to him; Legion
ονομα μοι· ὁτι πολλοι εσμεν. 10 Και παρεκαλει
name to me; for many we are. And he besought
αυτον πολλα, ἱνα μη αυτους αποστειλῃ εξω
him many times, that not them he would send out
της χωρας. 11 Ην δε εκει προς τῳ ορει αγελη
of the country. Was and there near to the mountain a herd
χοιρων μεγαλη βοσκομενη. 12 Και παρεκαλεσαν
of swine great feeding. And besought
αυτον οἱ δαιμονες, λεγοντες· Πεμψον ἡμας εις
him the demons, saying; Dismiss us into
τους χοιρους, ἱνα εις αυτους εισελθωμεν. 13 Και
the swine, that into them we may go. And
επετρεψεν αυτοις ευθεως ὁ Ιησους. Και εξελ-
gave leave to them immediately the Jesus. And having
θοντα τα πνευματα τα ακαθαρτα εισηλθον εις
come out the spirits the unclean entered into
τους χοιρους· και ὡρμησεν ἡ αγελη κατα του
the swine; and rushed the herd down the
κρημνου εις την θαλασσαν· *[ησαν δε ὡς δισ-
precipice into the sea; [they were and about two
χιλιοι·] και επνιγοντο εν τῃ θαλασσῃ. 14 Οἱ
thousand;] and were choked in the sea. Those
δε βοσκοντες αυτους εφυγον, και απηγγειλαν
and feeding them fled, and reported
εις την πολιν, και εις τους αγρους. Και εξηλ-
to the city, and to the villages. And they came
θον ιδειν, τι εστι το γεγονος. 15 Και ερχονται
out to see, what is that having been done. And they come
προς τον Ιησουν, και θεωρουσι τον δαιμονιζομε-
to the Jesus, and they behold the being demonized
νον καθημενον *[και] ἱματισμενον, και σωφρο-
sitting [and] having been clothed, and being of
νουντα, τον εσχηκοτα τον λεγεωνα· και
sane mind, the having been possessed by the legion; and
εφοβηθησαν. 16 Και διηγησαντο αυτοις οἱ ιδον-
they were afraid. And related to them those having

one was able to subdue
him.
5 And he was always,
Night and Day, in the
SEPULCHRES and in the
MOUNTAINS, crying out,
and cutting himself with
Stones.
6 And seeing JESUS at
a distance, he ran and
prostrated to him,
7 and crying out with a
loud Voice, * said, "What
hast thou to do with me,
Jesus,—O Son of GOD—
the HIGHEST? I implore
thee—GOD,—torment Me
not."
8 (For he had said to
him, "IMPURE SPIRIT,
Come out of the MAN.")
9 And he asked him,
"What is thy Name?"
And he says to him, "My
Name is Legion; For we
are Many."
10 And he earnestly en-
treated him, that he would
not send them out of the
COUNTRY.
11 Now there was by
the MOUNTAIN, a great
Herd of Swine feeding.
12 And *the DEMONS be-
sought him, saying, "Dis-
miss us to the SWINE, that
we may go into them."
13 And * he gave them
leave. And the IMPURE
SPIRITS having come out
went into the SWINE;
and the HERD rushed down
† the PRECIPICE into the
LAKE, and were drowned
in the LAKE.
14 Then the SWINE-
HERDS fled, and reported
it in the CITY, and in the
villages. And they came
out to see what THAT was
which had been DONE.
15 And they came to
JESUS, and beheld the DE-
MONIAC, HIM HAVING
HAD the LEGION, sitting
down, clothed, and in his
right mind; and they were
afraid.
16 And THOSE SEEING
it, related to them what

* VATICAN MANUSCRIPT.—7. says. 12. they besought. 13. he gave them leave. 13. and they were about Two Thousand—*omit.* 15. and—*omit.*

† 13. See Note on Matt. viii. 32.

τες, πως εγενετο τῳ δαιμονιζομενῳ, και περι
seen, how it happened to the one being demonized, and about
των χοιρων. 17 Και ηρξαντο παρακαλειν αυτον
the swine. And they began to entreat him
απελθειν απο των ὁριων αυτων. 18 Και εμβαν-
to depart from the coasts of them. And entering
τος αυτου εις το πλοιον, παρεκαλει αυτον ὁ
of him into the ship, besought him he
δαιμονισθεις, ἱνα η μετ' αυτου. 19 Και
having been demonized, that he might be with him. And
ουκ αφηκεν αυτον, αλλα λεγει αυτῳ· Ὑπαγε
not he suffered him, but he says to him; Go
εις τον οικον σου προς τους σους, και αναγγει-
into the house of thee to the friends, and relate
λον αυτοις, ὁσα σοι ὁ κυριος πεποιηκε, και
to them, how much to thee the Lord has done, and
ηλεησε σε. 20 Και απηλθε, και ηρξατο κηρυσ-
has pitied thee. And he went, and began to pub-
σειν εν τῃ Δεκαπολει, ὁσα εποιησεν αυτῳ ὁ
lish in the Decapolis, how much had done to him the
Ιησους· και παντες εθαυμαζον.
Jesus; and all were astonished.
21 Και διαπερασαντος του Ιησου εν τῳ πλοιῳ
And having passed over the Jesus in the ship
παλιν εις το περαν, συνηχθη οχλος πολυς επ'
again to the other side, were gathered a crowd great to
αυτον· και ην παρα την θαλασσαν. 22 Και
him, and he was by the sea. And
*[ιδου,] ερχεται εἱς των αρχισυναγωγων, ονο-
(lo,) comes one of the synagogue-rulers, by
ματι Ιαειρος· και ιδων αυτον, πιπτει προς τους
name Jairus; and seeing him, he fell to the
ποδας αυτου, 23 και παρεκαλει αυτον πολλα,
feet of him, and besought him much,
λεγων· Ὁτι το θυγατριον μου εσχατως εχει·
saying; That the little-daughter of me last end is;
ἱνα ελθων επιθῃς αυτῃ τας χειρας, ὁπως
that coming thou mayest put to her the hands, so that
σωθῃ· και ζησεται. 24 Και απηλθε μετ'
she may be saved; and she shall live. And he went with
αυτου· και ηκολουθει αυτῳ οχλος πολυς, και
him; and followed him a crowd great, and
συνεθλιβον αυτον. 25 Και γυνη *[τις] ουσα
pressed on him. And a woman [certain] being
εν ρυσει αἱματος ετη δωδεκα, 26 και πολλα
in a flow of blood years twelve. and many things
παθουσα ὑπο πολλων ιατρων, και δαπανησασα
having suffered under many physicians, and having spent
τα παρ' αυτης παντα, και μηδεν ωφελη-
the things of her all, and nothing having been
θεισα, αλλα μαλλον εις το χειρον ελθουσα,
benefited, but rather into the worse state having come,
27 ακουσασα περι του Ιησου, ελθουσα εν τῳ
having heard about the Jesus, having come in the

had happened to the DEMONIAC, and concerning the SWINE.

17 ‡ And they began to entreat him to depart from their BORDERS.

18 And he having entered the BOAT, ‡ HE who had been a DEMONIAC, entreated him that he might be with him;

19 And yet he did not permit him, but says to him, "Go HOME to thy FRIENDS, and tell them how much the LORD has done for thee, and has had pity on thee."

20 And he went away, and began to proclaim in DECAPOLIS, how much JESUS had done for him; and all were astonished.

21 ‡ And JESUS having again passed over in * a Boat to the OTHER SIDE, a great Crowd gathered to him, and he was by the LAKE.

22 ‡ And one of the SYNAGOGUE-RULERS, named Jairus, came, and seeing him, he fell at his FEET,

23 and earnestly entreated him, saying, "My LITTLE DAUGHTER is at the point of death; come, and put thy HANDS on her that she may be restored, and she will live."

24 And he went with him, and a great Crowd followed him, and pressed on him.

25 And a Woman, ‡ having had a Hemorrhage for twelve Years,

26 and having suffered much under Many Physicians, and having expended ALL her property, and not being benefited, but had rather become WORSE,

27 having heard * the things concerning JESUS, came in the CROWD be-

* VATICAN MANUSCRIPT.—21. a Boat—*omit* 22. lo—*omit.* 25. certain—*omit.* 27. the things concerning JESUS.

‡ 17. Matt. viii. 34; Acts xvi. 39. ‡ 18. Luke viii. 38. ‡ 21. Matt. ix. 1; Luke viii. 40. ‡ 22. Matt. ix. 18; Luke viii. 41. ‡ 25. Lev. xv. 25; Matt. ix. 20.

οχλῳ οπισθεν, ἡψατο του ἱματιου αυτου.
crowd behind, touched the mantle of him.
28 (Ελεγε γαρ· Ὁτι καν των ἱματιων αυτου
She said for; That even if the clothes of him
ἁψωμαι, σωθησομαι.) 29 Και ευθεως εξηρανθη
I may touch, I shall be saved.) And immediately was dried up
ἡ πηγη του αἱματος αυτης· και εγνω τῳ
the source of the blood of her; and knew to the
σωματι, ὁτι ιαται απο της μαστιγος. 30 Και
body, that was saved from the scourge. And
ευθεως ὁ Ιησους επιγνους εν ἑαυτῳ την εξ
immediately the Jesus knowing in himself the out of
αὑτου δυναμιν εξελθουσαν, επιστραφεις εν τῳ
himself power having gone out, having turned round in the
οχλῳ, ελεγε· Τις μου ἡψατο των ἱματιων;
crowd, said, Who of me touched the clothes?
31 Και ελεγον αυτῳ οἱ μαθηται αυτου· Βλεπεις
And said to him the disciples of him; Thou seest
τον οχλον συνθλιβοντα σε· και λεγεις· Τις μου
the crowd pressing on thee; and sayest thou; Who me
ἡψατο; 32 Και περιεβλεπετο ιδειν την τουτο
touched? And he was looking round to see the (woman) this
ποιησασαν. 33 Ἡ δε γυνη, φοβηθεισα και τρεμ-
having done. The but woman, fearing and trem-
ουσα, ειδυια ὁ γενονεν επ' αυτη, ηλθε και
bling, having known what was done on her, came and
προσεπεσεν αυτῳ, και ειπεν αυτῳ πασαν την
fell down to him, and told to him all the
αληθειαν. 34 Ὁ δε ειπεν αυτη· Θυγατερ, ἡ
truth. He but said to her; Daughter, the
πιστις σου σεσωκε σε· ὑπαγε εις ειρηνην, και
faith of thee has saved thee; go in peace, and
ισθι ὑγιης απο της μαστιγος σου. 35 Ετι αυτου
be thou well from the scourge of thee. While of him
λαλουντος, ερχονται απο του αρχισυναγωγου,
speaking, they came from the synagogue-ruler's,
λεγοντες· Ὁτι ἡ θυγατηρ σου απεθανε· τι
saying; That the daughter of thee is dead; why
ετι σκυλλεις τον διδασκαλον; 36 Ὁ δε Ιησους
yet troublest thou the teacher? The but Jesus
ευθεως, ακουσας τον λογον λαλουμενον, λεγει
immediately having heard the word being spoken, says
τῳ αρχισυναγωγῳ· Μη φοβου, μονον πιστευε.
to the synagogue-ruler: Not fear, only believe thou.
37 Και ουκ αφηκεν ουδενα αυτῳ συνακολουθησαι,
And not he suffered no one him to follow,
ει μη Πετρον, και Ιακαβον, και Ιωαννην τον
except Peter, and James, and John the
αδελφον Ιακωβου. 38 Και ερχεται εις τον οικον
brother of James. And he comes into the house
του αρχισυναγωγου, και θεωρει θορυβον, και
of the synagogue-ruler, and he sees a tumult, and
κλαιοντας και αλαλαζοντας πολλα. 39 Και
weeping and wailing much And
εισελθων λεγει αυτοις· Τι θορυβεισθε και
having entered he says to them: Why are you troubled and

hind, and touched his MANTLE.

28 For she said, "If I can but touch his GARMENTS, I shall be cured."

29 And immediately her FLOW of BLOOD was dried up; and she felt in her Body That she was cured of that SCOURGE.

30 And immediately, JESUS knowing in himself ‡ the POWER proceeding from him, having turned round in the CROWD, said, "Who touched My GARMENTS?"

31 And his DISCIPLES said to him, "Thou seest the CROWD pressing on thee, and dost thou say, 'Who touched Me?'"

32 And he was looking round to see HER who had DONE this.

33 Then the WOMAN, being conscious of what was wrought upon her, fearing and trembling, came and fell down before him, and told him All the TRUTH.

34 And HE said to her, ‡ "Daughter, thy FAITH has cured thee; go in peace, and be entirely free from thy DISEASE."

35 While he was still speaking, some came from the SYNAGOGUE-RULER's house, who said, "Thy DAUGHTER is dead; why trouble the TEACHER?"

36 * But JESUS, having heard the WORD that was spoken, immediately said to the SYNAGOGUE-RULER, "Fear not; only believe."

37 And he permitted no one to accompany * him, except Peter, and James, and John the BROTHER of James.

38 And * they come to the HOUSE of the SYNAGOGUE-RULER, and he sees the Confusion, and much weeping and lamenting.

39 And having entered, he says to them, "Why do

* VATICAN MANUSCRIPT.—36. But JESUS, neglecting to hear the WORD which was spoken, says. 37. with him. 38. they come to.

‡ 30. Luke vi. 19; viii. 46. ‡ 34. Matt. ix. 22; Mark x. 52; Acts xiv. 9.

κλαιετε; το παιδιον ουκ απεθανεν, αλλα καθευδει.
do you weep? the child not is dead, but sleeps.
40 Και κατεγελων αυτου. Ὁ δε, εκβαλων παντας,
And they derided him. He but, having sent out all
παραλαμβανει τον πατερα του παιδιου, και την
he takes the father of the child, and the
μητερα, και τους μετ' αυτου, και εισπορευεται,
mother, and those with him, and goes in.
ὁπου ην το παιδιον. 41 Και κρατησας της χειρος
where was the child. And having grasped the hand
του παιδιου, λεγει αυτῃ· Ταλιθα, κουμι· ὁ εστι
of the child. he says to her: Talitha, cumi; which is
μεθερμηνευομενον· Το κορασιον, σοι λεγω,
being translated; The girl, to thee I say.
εγειρε. 42 Και ευθεως ανεστη το κορασιον, και
arise. And immediately arose the girl, and
περιεπατει· ην γαρ ετων δωδεκα. Και εξεσ-
walked about; she was for years twelve. And they were
τησαν εκστασει μεγαλῃ. 43 Και διεστειλατο
astonished with an astonishment great. And he charged
αυτοις πολλα, ἱνα μηδεις γνῳ τουτο· και
them much, that no one might know this; and
ειπε δοθηναι αυτῃ φαγειν.
spake to have given to her to eat.

ΚΕΦ. ς'. 6.

Και εξηλθεν εκειθεν, και ηλθεν εις την πατ-
And he went out thence, and came into the country
ριδα αυτου· και ακολουθουσιν αυτῳ οἱ μαθηται
of himself; and follow him the disciples
αυτου· 2 Και γενομενου σαββατου, ηρξατο εν
of him. And being come sabbath, he began in
τῃ συναγωγῃ διδασκειν. Και πολλοι ακουοντες
the synagogue to teach. And many hearing,
εξεπλησσοντο, λεγοντες· Ποθεν τουτῳ ταυτα;
were astonished, saying; Whence to this these things?
και τις ἡ σοφια ἡ δοθεισα αυτῳ; και δυναμεις
and what the wisdom that being given to him? and miracles
τοιαυται δια των χειρων αυτου γινονται.
so great through the hands of him are done.
3 Ουχ ουτος εστιν ὁ τεκτων, ὁ υἱος Μαριας,
Not this is the carpenter, the son of Mary,
αδελφος δε Ιακωβου, και Ιωση, και Ιουδα, και
brother and of James, and Joses, and Juda, and

you weep and make confusion? the CHILD is not dead, but ‡ sleeps."

40 And they derided him. ‡ But putting † them all out, * he takes the FATHER and the MOTHER of the CHILD, and THOSE with him, and goes in where the CHILD was.

41 And having grasped the HAND of the CHILD, he says to her, "Talitha-cumi," which, being translated, signifies, 'YOUNG MAIDEN, I say to thee, arise.'"

42 And immediately the YOUNG MAIDEN arose and walked about, for she was twelve years old. And they were exceedingly astonished.

43 And ‡ he strictly charged them that no one should know this thing; and directed to give her food.

CHAPTER VI.

1 And ‡ he departed thence, and * comes into his OWN COUNTRY; and his DISCIPLES follow him.

2 And the Sabbath having come, he began to teach in the SYNAGOGUE, and * MANY hearing, were astonished, and said, ‡ "Whence has this man these things? and What is THAT WISDOM which is imparted * to him? and how are such MIRACLES performed through his HANDS?

3 Is not this the CARPENTER? the SON of * MARY, and ‡ Brother of James, and Joses, and Ju-

---

* VATICAN MANUSCRIPT.—40. he takes. 1. comes into. 2. MANY. 2. to him? and such MIRACLES. 3. MARY, and Brother of.

† 40 The persons or crowd here spoken of, were probably a set of people usually hired on these occasions to attend the funeral, and follow the procession with their lamentations. This custom prevailed East. These are the *mourning women* mentioned by Jeremiah, chapter ix. 17—21; and by Amos, chapter v. 16. They were called *Præficæ* by the Romans, because they presided over, and began, the funeral dirge. But men seem to have attended amongst them, as well as women. Dr. Shaw mentions this custom to be still continued in the East; and observes, that the women employed on these occasions, perform their parts with such proper sounds, gestures, and motions, that they rarely fail to work up the assembly to an extraordinary pitch of thoughtfulness and sorrow.—*Wakefield.*

‡ 39. John xi. 11. ‡ 40. Acts ix. 40. ‡ 43. Matt. viii. 4; ix. 30; xii. 16; xvii. 9; Mark iii. 12; Luke v. 14. ‡ 1. Matt. xiii. 54; Luke iv. 16. ‡ 2. John vi. 42. ‡ 3. Matt. xii. 46; Gal. i. 19.

Σιμωνος; και ουκ εισιν αἱ αδελφαι αυτου ὡδε
Simon? and not are the sisters of him here
προς ἡμας; Και εσκανδαλιζοντο εν αυτῳ.
with us? And they were stumbled in him.
4 Ελεγε δε αυτοις ὁ Ιησους· Ὁτι ουκ εστι προ-
Said but to them the Jesus; That not is a pro-
φητης ατιμος, ει μη εν τῃ πατριδι αὑτου,
phet without honor, except in the country of himself,
και εν τοις συγγενεσι, και εν τῃ οικιᾳ αὑτου.
and among the relatives, and in the house of himself.
5 Και ουκ ηδυνατο εκει ουδεμιαν δυναμιν ποιη-
And not was able there no one miracle to
σαι, ει μη ολιγοις αρρωστοις επιθεις τας χειρας,
do, except a few sick having put on the hands,
εθεραπευσε. 6 Και εθαυμαζε δια την απιστιαν
were cured. And he wondered because of the unbelief
αυτων.
of them.

Και περιηγε τας κωμας κυκλῳ, διδασκων.
And went round the villages round about, teaching.
7 Και προσκαλειται τους δωδεκα, και ηρξατο
And he calls the twelve, and he began
αυτους αποστελλειν δυο δυο· και εδιδου αυτοις
them to send two two; and he gave to them
εξουσιαν των πνευματων των ακαθαρτων, 8 και
authority of the spirits of the unclean, and
παρηγγειλεν αυτοις, ἱνα μηδεν αιρωσιν εις
he charged them, that nothing they should take for
ὁδον, ει μη ῥαβδον μονον· μη πηραν, μη αρτον,
a way, except a staff only; no bag, no bread,
μη εις την ζωνην χαλκον· 9 αλλ' ὑποδεδεμενους
not into the belt copper money; but having been shod
σανδαλια· και μη ενδυσησθε δυο χιτωνας. 10 Και
sandals and not you may put on two coats. And
ελεγεν αυτοις· Ὁπου εαν εισελθητε εις οικιαν,
he said to them; Where if you may enter into a house,
εκει μενετε ἑως αν εξελθητε εκειθεν. 11 Και
there remain till you may go away from thence. And
ὁσοι αν μη δεξωνται ὑμας, μηδε ακουσωσιν ὑμων,
whoever not may receive you, nor hear you,
εκπορευομενοι εκειθεν, εκτιναξατε τον χουν τον
going away from thence, shake out the dust that
ὑποκατω των ποδων ὑμων, εις μαρτυριον αυτοις.
under the feet of you, for a witness to them.
12 Και εξελθοντες εκηρυσσον, ἱνα μετανοησωσι·
And having gone out they published, that they should reform;
13 και δαιμονια πολλα εξεβαλλον, και ηλειφον
and demons many they cast out, and anointed
ελαιῳ πολλους αρρωστους, και εθεραπευον.
with oil many sick ones, and they were cured.
14 Και ηκουσεν ὁ βασιλευς Ἡρωδης, (φανερον
And heard the king Herod, (well-known
γαρ εγενετο το ονομα αυτου,) και ελεγεν· Ὁτι
for was the name of him,) and he said; That

das, and Simon? and are not his SISTERS here with us?" And they were perplexed with him.
4 But JESUS said to them, ‡"A Prophet is not without honor, except in his OWN COUNTRY, and among his RELATIVES, and in his OWN FAMILY."
5 ‡And he was unwilling to do any MIRACLES there, except a Few Sick persons he cured by laying his HANDS on them.
6 And he was surprised on account of their UNBELIEF. ‡And he went round the VILLAGES teaching.
7 ‡And he called the TWELVE, and sent Them forth in pairs; and gave them Authority over the IMPURE SPIRITS;
8 and he charged them, that they should take Nothing for the Journey, except a single Staff; *no Bread, no Traveling Bag, no Copper in the GIRDLE;
9 but to wear SANDALS, and not put on Two Coats.
10 And he said to them, "Whatever house you enter, there remain, till you leave the place.
11 And *whatever Place will not receive you, nor hear you, in departing thence, † ‡shake off that DUST which is UNDER your FEET, for a Testimony to them.
12 And having gone forth, they proclaimed that men should reform.
13 And they expelled many Demons, and ‡anointed many sick persons with Oil, and cured them.
14 ‡And Herod the KING heard, (for JESUS had become well-known,) and *he said, "John the

* VATICAN MANUSCRIPT.—8. no Bread, no traveling Bag. 11. whatever Place will not. 14. they said.

† 11. An emblematical action, signifying a renunciation of all further concern with them. It was very usual among the people of the East to express their intentions by external signs. Many singular examples of this species of language occur both in Old and New Testaments. See 1 Kings xi. 29; xxii. 11; 2 Kings xiii. 15.

‡ 4. Matt. xiii 57; John iv. 44. ‡ 5. Matt. xiii. 58; Mark ix. 23. ‡ 6. Matt. ix. 35; Luke xiii. 22. ‡ 7. Matt. x. 1; Mark iii. 13, 14; Luke ix. 1. ‡ 11. Acts xiii. 51; xviii. 6. ‡ 13. James v. 14. ‡ 14. Matt. xiv. 1; Luke ix. 7.

Ιωαννης ὁ βαπτιζων εκ νεκρων ηγερθη, και
John he baptizing out of dead has been raised, and
δια τουτο ενεργουσιν αἱ δυναμεις εν αυτῳ.
through this work the mighty powers in him.
15 Αλλοι ελεγον· Ὁτι Ηλιας εστιν· Αλλοι δε
Others said: That Elias he is; Others and
ελεγον· Ὁτι προφητης εστιν, ὡς εἱς των προ-
said: That a prophet he is, like one of the pro-
φητων. 16 Ακουσας δε ὁ Ηρωδης, ειπεν· Ὁτι
phets, Having heard but the Herod, said; That
ὁν εγω απεκεφαλισα Ιωαννην, οὑτος ηγερθη
whom I beheaded John, he is raised
*[εκ νεκρων.] 17 Αυτος γαρ ὁ Ἡρωδης αποσ-
[from dead.] Himself for the Herod send-
τειλας εκρατησε τον Ιωαννην, και εδησεν αυτον
ing seized the John, and bound him
εν φυλακῃ, δια Ἡρωδιαδα, την γυναικα Φιλιπ-
in prison, through Herodias, the wife of Philip
που του αδελφου αὐτου, ὁτι αυτην εγαμησεν.
of the brother of himself, for her he had married.
18 Ελεγε γαρ ὁ Ιωαννης τῳ Ἡρωδῃ· Ὁτι ουκ εξ-
Said for the John to the Herod; That not it is
εστι σοι εχειν την γυναικα του αδελφου σου.
lawful to thee to have the wife of the brother of thee.
19 Ἡ δε Ἡρωδιας ενειχεν αυτῳ και ηθελεν
The and Herodias had a grudge against him and wished
αυτον αποκτειναι· και ουκ ηδυνατο. 20 Ὁ γαρ
him to destroy; and not was able. The for
Ἡρωδης εφοβειτο τον Ιωαννην, ειδως αυτον αν-
Herod feared the John, knowing him a
δρα δικαιον και ἁγιον· και συνετηρει αυτον· και
man just and holy; and protected him; and
ακουσας αυτου, πολλα εποιει, και ἡδεως αυτου
hearing him, many things he did, and gladly him
ηκουε. 21 Και γενομενης ἡμερας ευκαιρου, ὁτε
he heard. And having come a day convenient, when
Ἡρωδης τοις γενεσιοις αὑτου δειπνον εποιει
Herod to the birthday of himself a feast he made
τοις μεγιστασιν αὑτου, και τοις χιλιαρχοις, και
to the nobles of himself, and to the commanders, and
τοις πρωτοις της Γαλιλαιας· 22 και εισελθουσης
to the chiefs of the Galilee; and having entered
της θυγατρος αυτης της Ἡρωδιαδος, και ορχη-
of the daughter of her of the Herodias, and danc-
σαμενης, και αρεσασης τῳ Ἡρωδῃ και τοις
ing, and having pleased the Herod and those
συνανακειμενοις, ειπεν ὁ βασιλευς τῳ κορασιῳ·
reclining at table, said the king to the little girl;
Αιτησον με, ὁ εαν θελῃς, και δωσω σοι.
Ask me, whatever thou wilt, and I will give to thee.
23 Και ωμοσεν αυτῃ· Ὁτι ὁ εαν με αιτησῃς,
And he swore to her; That whatever me thou mayst ask,
δωσω σοι, ἑως ἡμισους της βασιλειας μου.
I will give to thee, till half of the kingdom of me.

IMMERSER * has arisen from the Dead, and therefore MIRACLES are performed by him."
15 Others said, ‡"He is Elijah;" and others said, "He is a Prophet, like one of the PROPHETS."
16 ‡But HEROD having heard, said, "That John, whom I beheaded; he is raised."
17 For HEROD himself had sent and seized JOHN, and bound him in Prison, on account of Herodias, the WIFE of Philip his BROTHER; for he had married Her.
18 For JOHN had said to HEROD, ‡"It is not lawful for thee to have thy BROTHER'S WIFE."
19 Therefore HERODIAS was incensed against him, and wished to kill him, and could not.
20 For HEROD ‡feared JOHN, knowing that he was a just and holy Man; and protected him; and having heard him, he *did many things, and heard Him gladly.
21 And a convenient Day having come, when Herod, on his BIRTH-DAY, made a Feast for his NOBLES, and for the COMMANDERS and CHIEF men of GALILEE;
22 *the DAUGHTER of this HERODIAS having entered, and danced, *she pleased HEROD and the GUESTS, *and the KING said to the GIRL, "Ask me whatever thou wilt, and I will give it to thee."
23 And he swore to her, ‡"Whatever thou mayst ask Me, I will give to thee, even to the Half of my KINGDOM."

* VATICAN MANUSCRIPT.—14. has arisen. 16. from the dead—*omit.* 20. was much perplexed, and heard. 22. his DAUGHTER Herodias. 22. she pleased. 22. and the KING.

† 21. The custom of celebrating stated solemnities, and the anniversary of the birth-day in particular, was very general in the East, and might be transferred from them to the Greeks and Romans. The solemnization of the birth-day by a festival is frequently mentioned, or alluded to, in ancient authors.—*Wakefield.*

‡ 15. Matt. xvi. 14; Mark viii. 28. ‡ 16. Matt. xiv. 2; Luke iii. 19. ‡ 18. Lev. xviii. 16; xx. 21. ‡ 20. Matt. xiv. 5; xxi. 6. ‡ 23. Esther v. 3, 6; vii. 2.

24 Ἡ δε εξελθουσα, ειπε τη μητρι αὑτης· Τι
The and going out said to the mother of herself; What
αιτησομαι; Ἡ δε ειπε· Την κεφαλην Ιωαννου
shall I ask? She and said; The head of John
του βαπτιστου. Και εισελθουσα ευθεως μετα
the dipper. And coming in immediately with
σπουδης προς τον βασιλεα, ητησατο, λεγουσα·
haste to the king, she asked, saying;
Θελω ἱνα μοι δῳς εξαυτης επι πινακι την
I will. that to me thou wouldst give instantly on a plate the
κεφαλην Ιωαννου του βαπτιστου. 26 Και περι-
head of John the dipper. And very
λυπος γενομενος ὁ βασιλευς, δια τους ὁρκους
sorry having become the king, because of the oaths
και τους συνανακειμενους ουκ ηθελησεν αυτην
and those reclining at table not he would her
αθετησαι. 27 Και ευθεως αποστειλας ὁ βασιλ-
reject. And immediately sending the king
ευς σπεκουλατωρα, επεταξεν ενεχθηναι την
a guardsman, he ordered to be brought the
κεφαλην αυτου. Ὁ δε απελθων απεκεφαλισεν
head of him. He and going forth cut off the head of
αυτον εν τῃ φυλακῃ· 28 και ηνεγκε την κεφαλην
him in the prison; and brought the head
αυτου επι πινακι, και εδωκεν αυτην τῳ κορασιῳ·
of him on a plate, and gave her to the little girl;
και το κορασιον εδωκεν αυτην τῃ μητρι αὑτης.
and the little girl gave her to the mother of herself.
29 Και ακουσαντες οἱ μαθηται αυτου, ηλθον, και
And having heard the disciples of him, came, and
ηραν το πτωμα αυτου, και εθηκαν αυτο εν μνη-
took the dead body of him, and placed it in a
μειῳ.
tomb.

30 Και συναγονται οἱ αποστολοι προς τον
And were assembled the apostles to the
Ιησουν, και απηγγειλαν αυτῳ παντα, και ὁσα
Jesus, and reported to him all, and what
εποιησαν, και ὁσα εδιδαξαν. 31 Και ειπεν αυτοις·
they did, and what they taught. And he said to them;
Δευτε ὑμεις αυτοι κατ' ιδιαν εις ερημον τοπον,
Come you yourselves privately into a desert place,
και αναπαυεσθε ολιγον. Ησαν γαρ οἱ ερχομενοι
and rest you a little; Were for those coming

24 And SHE going out, said to her MOTHER, "What shall I ask?" And she said, "The HEAD of John the IMMERSER."

25 And coming in immediately with Haste to the KING, she asked, saying "I desire that thou wouldst give me instantly, on a Platter, the HEAD of John the IMMERSER."

26 ‡ And the KING, being extremely sorry on account of the OATHS and the GUESTS, would not refuse her.

27 And the KING, immediately sending one of † his Guards, ordered his HEAD to be brought. And HE having gone forth beheaded him in the PRISON;

28 † and brought his HEAD on a Platter, and gave it to the GIRL; and the GIRL gave it to her MOTHER.

29 And his disciples having heard, came and carried off the DEAD-BODY, and placed it in a Tomb.

30 ‡ And the APOSTLES were assembled to Jesus, and related to him all things, both what they had done, and what they had taught.

31 And he *said to them, ‡ "Come you, retire by yourselves into a Desert Place, and rest a little;" ‡ for many were THOSE who were COMING and GO-

* VATICAN MANUSCRIPT.—31. says.

† 27. The term, *spekoulatoora* from the Latin *speculator*, denotes one of the body-guards, who were so called, because their principal duty was that of *sentinels*. They had, however, other confidental duties, and among these, that of acting, like Turkish soldiers of the present day, as executioners. † 28. Note here, that very remarkable seems the providence of God, in avenging the death of this holy man upon Herod, Herodias, and her daughter. For 1st, As the war betwixt Herod and Aretas king of Petrea was caused by Herod's wicked contract with Herodias to reject the daughter of Aretas, his lawful wife, and to marry with Herodias, his brother Philip's wife; so Josephus declares that the Jews looked upon the putting John to death, as the cause of the miscarriage of Herod's army; "God being angry with him for the death of John the Baptist." 2dly, Herodias envying the glory of king Agrippa, who had that honour given him by Caius, prevailed with her husband to go to Rome, and accuse Agrippa; whereupon Caius deprived Herod of his government, and her of her money; and gave them both to Agrippa, banishing Herod and Herodias to Lyons in France: "which (says Josephus) was done in punishment of her envy, and of his readiness to hearken to her solicitations." And 3dly, of her daughter it is related, that she going over the ice in winter, the ice broke, and she slipped in to the head, which at last was severed from her body by the sharpness of the ice, God requiring her head for that of the Baptist's she desired; which, if true, was a wonderful providence.—*Whitby.*

‡ 26. Matt. xiv. 9. ‡ 34. Luke ix. 10. ‡ 31. Matt. xiv. 13; John vi. 1, 2.
‡ 31 Mark iii. 20.

και οἱ ὑπαγοντες πολλοι· και ουδε φαγειν ηυκαι-
and those going many; and not even to eat they had
ρουν. 32 Και απηλθον εις ερημον τοπον τῳ
leisure. And they went into a desert place to the
πλοιῳ κατ' ιδιαν. 33 Και ειδον αυτους ὑπαγοντας·
ship privately. And they saw them going away;
και επεγνωσαν πολλοι· και πεζῃ απο πασων
and knew many; and on foot from all
των πολεων συνεδραμον εκει. 34 Και εξελθων
of the cities they ran together there. And coming out
ειδεν πολυν οχλον, και εσπλαγχνισθη επ'
he saw great a crowd, and was moved with pity towards
αυτοις, ὁτι ησαν ὡς προβατα, μη εχοντα ποι-
them, for they were as sheep, not having a
μενα· και ηρξατο διδασκειν αυτους πολλα.
shepherd; and he began to teach them many things.
35 Και ηδη ὡρας πολλης γενομενης, προσελθον-
And already time much having gone, coming
τες αυτῳ οἱ μαθηται αυτου, λεγουσιν· Ὁτι ερη-
to him the disciples of him, they say; That a
μος εστιν ὁ τοπος, και ηδη ὡρα πολλη· 36 απο-
desert is the place, and already time much: dismiss
λυσον αυτους, ἱνα απελθοντες εις τους κυκλῳ
them, that going into the surrounding
αγρους και κωμας, αγορασωσιν ἑαυτοις αρτους·
country and villages, they may buy themselves loaves;
τι γαρ φαγωσιν ουκ εχουσιν. 37 Ὁ δε αποκρι-
any for they might eat not they have. He but answering
θεις ειπεν αυτοις· Δοτε αυτοις ὑμεις φαγειν.
said to them; Give to them you to eat.
Και λεγουσιν αυτῳ· Απελθοντες αγορασωμεν
And they say to him; Going may we buy
δηναριων διακοσιων αρτους, και δωμεν αυτοις
denarii two hundred loaves, and give to them
φαγειν; 38 Ὁ δε λεγει αυτοις· Ποσους αρτους
to eat? He but says to them: How many loaves
εχετε; ὑπαγετε και ιδετε. Και γνοντες,
have you? go you and see you. And having ascertained,
λεγουσι· Πεντε, και δυο ιχθυας. 39 Και επε-
they say: Five, and two fishes. And he or-
ταξεν αυτοις ανακλιναι παντας, συμποσια
dered them to make recline all, company
συμποσια, επι τῳ χλωρῳ χορτῳ. 40 Και ανε-
company, on the green grass. And they
πεσον πρασιαι πρασιαι, ανα ἑκατον, και ανα
reclined squares squares, by a hundred, and
πεντηκοντα. 41 Και λαβων τους πεντε αρτους
by fifty. And taking the five loaves
και τους δυο ιχθυας, αναβλεψας εις τον ουρανον,
and the two fishes, looking up to the heaven,
ευλογησε, και κατεκλασε τους αρτους, και
he gave praise, and broke the loaves, and
εδιδου τοις μαθηταις αυτου, ἱνα παραθωσιν
gave to the disciples of him, that they might set before
αυτοις· και τους δυο ιχθυας εμερισε πασι.
them: and the two fishes he divided to all.

ING, and they had no leisure, not even to eat.

32 And they went away, by the BOAT, into a Desert Place, ‡ to be by themselves.

33 But they saw them departing, and many knew them; and they ran together there on foot from All the CITIES.

34 ‡ And coming out, he saw a Great Crowd; and he deeply pitied them, Because they were like Sheep having no Shepherd; and ‡ he taught them many things.

35 ‡ And much Time having already gone, his DISCIPLES coming to him, say, * "The PLACE is a Desert, and now much Time has passed;

36 dismiss them, that they may go to the adjacent FARMS and Villages, and buy themselves * what they should eat."

37 But HE answering said to them, "You supply them." And they say to him, "Should we go and for Two hundred Denarii buy Loaves, and give them to eat?"

38 And HE says to them, "How Many Loaves have you? Go and see." And having ascertained, they say, ‡ "Five, and Two Fishes."

39 And he commanded them to make all recline in Companies on the GREEN Grass.

40 And they lay down in Squares, by Hundreds and by Fifties.

41 And taking the FIVE Loaves and the TWO Fishes, and looking towards HEAVEN, he praised God, and broke the LOAVES, and gave to * the DISCIPLES to set before them; and the TWO Fishes he distributed to all.

* VATICAN MANUSCRIPT.—35. The PLACE is a Desert. 36. what they should eat. But HE. 41. the DISCIPLES.

‡ 32. Matt. xiv. 13. ‡ 34. Matt. ix. 36; xiv. 14. ‡ 34. Luke ix. 11. ‡ 35. Matt. xiv. 15; Luke ix. 12. ‡ 38. Matt. xiv. 17; Luke ix. 13; John vi. 9.

42 Και εφαγον παντες, και εχορτασθησαν.
And they ate all, and were filled.
43 Και ηραν κλασματων δωδεκα κοφινους πλη-
And they took up of fragments twelve baskets full,
ρεις, και απο των ιχθυων. 44 Και ησαν οἱ φα-
and of the fishes. And were those having
γοντες τους αρτους, πεντακισχιλιοι ανδρες.
eaten the loaves, five thousand men.
45 Και ευθεως ηναγκασε τους μαθητας αὑτου
And immediately he urged the disciples of himself
εμβηναι εις το πλοιον, και προαγειν εις το πε-
to step into the ship, and to go before to the other
ραν προς Βηθσαιδαν, ἑως αυτος απολυσῃ τον
side to Bethsaida, while he should dismiss the
οχλον. 46 Και αποταξαμενος αυτοις, απηλθεν
crowd. And having sent away them, he went
εις το ορος προσευξασθαι. 47 Και οψιας γενο-
into the mountain to pray. And evening having
μενης, ην το πλοιον εν μεσῳ της θαλασσης·
come, was the ship in middle of the sea;
και αυτος μονος επι της γης. 48 Και ειδεν
and he alone upon the land. And he saw
αυτους βασανιζομενους εν τῳ ελαυνειν· ην γαρ
them tormented in the rowing; was for
ὁ ανεμος εναντιος αυτοις. Και περι τεταρτην
the wind opposite to them. And about fourth
φυλακην της νυκτος ερχεται προς αυτους, περι-
watch of the night comes towards them, walk-
πατων επι της θαλασσης· και ηθελε παρελθειν
ing on the sea; and wished to pass
αυτους. 49 Οἱ δε, ιδοντες αυτον περιπατουντα
them. They but, seeing him walking
επι της θαλασσης, εδοξαν φαντασμα ειναι, και
on the sea, they thought a phantom to be, and
ανεκραξαν. 50 Παντες γαρ αυτον ειδον, και
they cried out. All for him saw, and
εταραχθησαν. Και ευθεως ελαλησε μετ' αυτων,
were terrified. And immediately he spoke with them,
και λεγει αυτοις· Θαρσειτε· εγω ειμι, μη φο-
and says to them; Take courage; I am, not be
βεισθε. 51 Και ανεβη προς αυτους εις το πλοιον·
afraid. And he went up to them into the boat:
και εκοπασεν ὁ ανεμος. Και λιαν *[εκ πε-
and ceased the wind. And greatly [out of mea-
ρισσου] εν ἑαυτοις εξισταντο, *[και εθαυμαζον.]
sure] in themselves they were amazed [and wondered.]
52 Ου γαρ συνηκαν επι τοις αρτοις· ην γαρ ἡ
Not for they understood about the loaves; was for the
καρδια αυτων πεπωρωμενη.
heart of them having been stupified.

53 Και διαπερασαντες ηλθον επι την γην Γεν-
And having passed over they came to the land Gen-
νησαρετ· και προσωρμισθησαν. 54 Και εξελθον-
nesaret: and drew to the shore. And coming out
των αυτων εκ του πλοιου, ευθεως επιγνοντες
of them out of the ship, immediately knowing
αυτον, 55 περιδραμοντες ὁλην την περιχωρον
him, running about whole the adjacent country

42 And they all ate and were satisfied.

43 And they took up Twelve Baskets full of Fragments [of the Bread], and of the FISHES.

44 Now THOSE who ATE of the LOAVES were Five thousand Men.

45 ‡ And immediately he constrained his DISCIPLES to go into the BOAT, and precede him to the OTHER SIDE, towards Bethsaida, while he should send away the CROWD.

46 And having dismissed them, he retired to the MOUNTAIN to pray.

47 And Evening having come, the BOAT was in the Midst of the LAKE, and he was alone on the LAND.

48 And he saw them toiling at the OAR; for the WIND was against them; and about the † Fourth Watch of the NIGHT, he comes towards them walking on the LAKE, and wished to pass by them.

49 But seeing him walking on the LAKE, they thought it was an Apparition, and they cried out;

50 for they all saw him, and were terrified. And immediately he spoke with them, saying, "Take courage, it is I; be not afraid."

51 And he went up to them into the BOAT; and the WIND ceased; and they were exceedingly amazed in themselves.

52 For ‡ they understood not about the LOAVES; because their HEART was stupified.

53 And having passed over, they came to the LAND of Gennessaret, and put to the shore.

54 And coming out of the BOAT, immediately they recognized him,

55 and running through that Whole SURROUNDING

* VATICAN MANUSCRIPT.—51. out of measure—*omit*. 51 and wondered—*omit*.

† 48. See Notes on Matt. xiv. 25, 26.

‡ 45. Matt. xiv. 22; John vi. 17. ‡ 52. Mark viii. 17, 18.

εκεινην, ηρξαντο επι τοις κραββατοις τους
that, they began on the couches those
κακως εχοντας περιφερειν, ὁπου ηκουον, ὁτι
sickness having to carry about, where they heard, that
εκει εστι. 56 Και ὁπου αν εισεπορευετο εις
there he is. And wherever he entered into
κωμας, ἡ πολεις, ἡ αγρους, εν ταις αγοραις
towns, or cities, or villages, in the markets
ετιθουν τους ασθενουντας, και παρεκαλουν
they placed those being sick, and they besought
αυτον, ἱνα καν του κρασπεδου του ἱματιου
him, that if even the tuft of the mantle
αυτου ἁψωνται· και ὁσοι αν ἡπτοντο αυτου,
of him they might touch; and whoever touched him,
εσωζοντο.
were saved.

REGION, carried about the SICK on COUCHES, to where they heard he was.

56 And wherever he entered, into Towns, or Cities, or Villages, they placed the SICK in the MARKETS, and implored him, ‡ that they might but touch the TUFT of his MANTLE; and as many as touched him were cured.

ΚΕΦ. ς. 7.

1 Και συναγονται προς αυτον οἱ Φαρισαιοι,
And were gathered to him the Pharisees,
και τινες των γραμματεων, ελθοντες απο Ἱερο-
and some of the scribes, having come from Jeru-
σολυμων· 2 και ιδοντες τινας των μαθητων
salem; and seeing some of the disciples
αυτου κοιναις χερσι, τουτ' εστιν ανιπτοις,
of him with common hands, that is unwashed,
εσθιοντας αρτους· 3 (οἱ γαρ Φαρισαιοι και παν-
eating loaves; (the for Pharisees and all
τες οἱ Ιουδαιοι, εαν μη πυγμη νιψωνται τας
the Jews, if not with fist they may wash the
χειρας, ουκ εσθιουσι, κρατουντες την παραδοσιν
hands, not they eat, holding the tradition
των πρεσβυτερων· 4 και απο αγορας, εαν μη
of the elders; and from a market, if not
βαπτισωνται, ουκ εσθιουσι· και αλλα πολλα
they might dip, not they eat; and other many things
εστιν, ἁ παρελαβον κρατειν, βαπτισμους ποτη-
is, which they received to hold, dippings of
ριων, και ξεστων, και χαλκιων, *[και κλινων·])
cups, and of pots, and of copper vessels, [and of couches;])
5 επειτα επερωτωσιν αυτον οἱ Φαρισαιοι και οἱ
then asked him the Pharisees and the
γραμματεις· Διατι οἱ μαθηται σου ου περιπα-
scribes: Why the disciples of thee not walk
τουσι κατα την παραδοσιν των πρεσβυτερων,
according to the tradition of the elders,
αλλα κοιναις χερσιν εσθιουσι τον αρτον; 6 Ὁ
but with common hands they eat the loaf? He
*[δε αποκριθεις] ειπεν αυτοις· Ὁτι καλως προε-
[but answering] said to them: That well pro-
φητευσεν Ἡσαιας περι ὑμων των ὑποκριτων, ὡς
phesied Esaias about you the hypocrites, as
γεγραπται· "Οὑτος ὁ λαος τοις χειλεσι με
it is written: "This the people with the lips me

CHAPTER VII.

1 ‡ And the PHARISEES, and some of the SCRIBES, having come from Jerusalem, resorted to him.

2 And observing some of his DISCIPLES eating BREAD with common, that is, with Unwashed Hands;

3 (for the PHARISEES, and All the JEWS holding the TRADITION of the ELDERS, eat not, unless they wash their HANDS with the Fist;

4 and coming from a Market, unless they * immerse themselves, they eat not. And many other things there are which they have received to maintain,—Immersions of Cups, and of Pots, and of Copper vessels;)

5 * both the PHARISEES and the SCRIBES asked him, "Why do not thy DISCIPLES walk according to the TRADITION of the ELDERS, but eat BREAD with common Hands?"

6 HE said to them, "Well did Isaiah prophesy concerning you, HYPOCRITES, as it is written, ‡ 'This 'PEOPLE honor me with 'their LIPS, but their

* VATICAN MANUSCRIPT.—4. besprinkle themselves, they eat not. 4. and of couches—*omit*. 5. both the PHARISEES. 6. but answering—*omit*.

† 3. The Pharisees, (says Josephus,) delivered many doctrines of the people as belonging to the law, which were handed down by the fathers, but not written in the law of Moses; and for this reason, the sect of the Sadducees rejects them; maintaining that those things which are written, ought to be accounted parts of the law, and that such as are only received by tradition from the fathers ought not to be observed.—*Ant.* xiii. 18.

‡ 56. Matt. ix. 20; Mark v. 27, 28; Acts xix. 12. ‡ 1. Matt. xv. 1. ‡ 6. Isa. xxix. 13.

τιμα, ἡ δε καρδια αυτων πορρω απεχει απ'
honor, the but heart of them far off is removed from
εμου. 7 Ματην δε σεβονται με, διδασκοντες
me. In vain but they worship me, teaching
διδασκαλιας, ενταλματα ανθρωπων." 8 Αφεντες
teachings, commandments of men." Leaving
*[γαρ] την εντολην του θεου, κρατειτε την
[for] the commandment of the God, you hold the
παραδοσιν των ανθρωπων, *[βαπτισμους ξεστων
tradition of the men, [dippings of pots
και ποτηριων· και αλλα παρομοια τοιαυτα πολλα
and of cups; and other similar such like many things
ποιειτε.] 9 Και ελεγεν αυτοις, Καλως αθετειτε
you do.] And he said to them, Well you set aside
την εντολην του θεου, ἱνα την παραδοσιν ὑμων
the commandment of the God, that the tradition of you
τηρησητε. 10 Μωσης γαρ ειπε· "Τιμα τον
you may keep Moses for said; "Honor the
πατερα σου και την μητερα σου·" και· "Ὁ
father of thee and the mother of thee;" and; "He
κακολογων πατερα ἡ μητερα, θανατῳ τελευ-
cursing father or mother, a death let him
ταπω." 11 Ὑμεις δε λεγετε· Εαν ειπη ανθρω-
die." You but say; If should say a man
πος τῳ πατρι ἡ τῃ μητρι· Κορβαν (ὁ εστι,
to the father or the mother; Corban (which is,
δωρον,) ὁ εαν εξ εμου ωφεληθης· 12 [και]
a gift,) whatever out of me thou mightest be profited; [and]
ουκετι αφιετε αυτον ουδεν ποιησαι τῳ πατρι
no more you suffer him any thing to do for the father
*[αὑτου,] ἡ τῃ μητρι *[αὑτου,] 13 ακυρουντες
[of himself,] or for the mother [of himself,] making void
τον λογον του θεου τῃ παραδοσει ὑμων, ἡ
the word of the God for the tradition of you, which
παρεδωκατε· και παρομοια τοιαυτα πολλα ποι-
you delivered; and similar such like many things you
ειτε. 14 Και προσκαλεσαμενος παντα τον
do. And having called all the
οχλον, ελεγεν αυτοις· Ακουετε μου παντες,
crowd, he said to them; Hear me all,
και συνιετε. 15 Ουδεν εστιν εξωθεν του ανθρω-
and be instructed. Nothing is outside of the man
που, εισπορευομενον εις αυτον, ὁ δυναται αυτον
entering into him, which is able him
κοινωσαι· αλλα τα εκπορευομενα απ' αυτου,
to make common; but the things proceeding from him,
εκεινα εστι τα κοινουντα τον ανθρωπον. 16 *[Ει
those is the things making common the man. [If

'HEART is far removed
'from me.
7 'But in vain do they
'worship me, teaching as
'Doctrines, the Precepts
'of Men.'
8 Laying aside the COMMANDMENT of GOD, you retain the TRADITION of MEN."
9 And he said to them, "Well do you annul the COMMANDMENT of GOD, that you may keep your own TRADITION.
10 For Moses said, ‡'Honor thy FATHER and thy 'MOTHER;' and ‡HE who 'REVILES Father or Mother, let him be punished 'with Death.'
11 But you assert, 'If a man say to FATHER or MOTHER, ‡Be that Corban, that is, an Offering, †by which thou mightest derive assistance from me;
12 you no more permit him to do any thing for FATHER or MOTHER:
13 making void the WORD of GOD by your TRADITION, which you have delivered; and many such like Things you do."
14 ‡And having *again called All of the CROWD, he said to them, "Let all listen to me, and be instructed.
15 There is nothing from without the MAN, which entering in *POLLUTES him; but the THINGS proceeding from *the MAN, are the THINGS which POLLUTE him.
16 *‡[If any one has

* VATICAN MANUSCRIPT.—8. For—*omit.* 8. dippings of Pots and of Cups; and many other such like things you do—*omit.* 12. And—*omit.* 12. his—*omit.* 12. his—*omit.* 14. again called. 15. POLLUTES him. 15. the MAN, are the THINGS which POLLUTE him. 16. If any one has Ears to hear, let him hear—*omit.*

† 11. A piece of history, delivered in the Talmud, will illustrate this subject, and at the same time exhibit in a clear light the profligacy, superstition, and casuistry of the Jews. A man of Beth-Horon had made a vow, and declared that his father should reap no benefit from his property. Afterwards, on the occasion of his son's marriage, he wished to invite his father to the entertainment; and, to evade the obligation of his vow, he transferred his right and property in the room and feast to a friend, who was engaged to invite his father. This, however, was judged to be unlawful, unless he had transferred entirely and truly this part of his property to his friend, without interposing any condition with respect to the invitation of his father, whom he was bound by all means not to profit. How can we be surprised at the severity with which our Savior rebuked such vile casuistry, such want of natural affection, and such abominable hypocrisy?—*Wakefield.*

‡ 10. Exod. xx. 12; Deut. v. 16; Matt. xv. 4. ‡ 10. Exod. xxi. 17; Lev. xx. 9; Prov. xx. 20. ‡ 11. Matt. xv. 5; xxiii. 18. ‡ 14. Matt. xv. 10. ‡ 16. Matt. xi. 15.

τις εχει ωτα ακουειν, ακουετω.] [17] Και
any one has ears to hear. let him hear.] And
ὁτε εισηλθεν εις οικον απο του οχλου,
when he entered into a house from the crowd,
επηρωτων αυτον οἱ μαθηται αυτου περι της
asked him the disciples of him concerning the
παραβολης. [18] Και λεγει αυτοις· Οὑτω και
parable. And he says to them; Thus also
ὑμεις ασυνετοι εστε; Ου νοειτε, ὁτι παν το
you without understanding are? Not know you, that all that
εξωθεν, εισπορευομενον εις τον ανθρωπον, ου
without, entering into the man, not
δυναται αυτον κοινωσαι; [19] ὁτι ουκ εισπορ-
is able him to make common? that not goes
ευεται αυτου εις την καρδιαν, αλλ' εις την κοι-
of it into the heart, but into the belly;
λιαν· και εις τον αφεδρωνα εκπορευεται,
and into the privy goes out,
καθαριζον παντα τα βρωματα. [20] Ελεγε δε·
cleansing all the foods He said and;
Ὁτι το εκ του ανθρωπου εκπορευομενον, εκεινο
That the out of the man proceeding forth, that
κοινοι τον ανθρωπον· [21] Εσωθεν γαρ εκ της
makes common the man; Within for out of the
καρδιας των ανθρωπων οἱ διαλογισμοι οἱ κακοι
heart of the men the purposes the evil
εκπορευονται· μοιχειαι, πορνειαι, φονοι,
proceeds; adulteries, fornications, murders,
[22] κλοπαι, πλεονεξιαι, πονηριαι, δολος, ασελγεια,
thefts, covetousnesses, villanies, deceit, intemperance,
οφθαλμος πονηρος, βλασφημια, ὑπερηφανια,
eye evil, evil speakings, pride,
αφροσυνη· [23] παντα ταυτα τα πονηρα εσωθεν
folly; all these the things evil within
εκπορευεται, και κοινοι τον ανθρωπον.
comes forth. and makes common the man.
[24] Και εκειθεν αναστας, απηλθεν εις τα μεθ-
And thence arising, he went into the bor-
ορια Τυρου και Σιδωνος· και εισελθων εις την
ders of Tyre and Sidon; and entering into the
οικιαν, ουδενα ηθελε γνωναι· και ουκ ηδυνηθη
house, no one he wished to know: and not he was able
λαθειν. [25] Ακουσασα γαρ γυνη περι αυτου, ἡς
to be concealed. Having heard for a woman about him, of whom
ειχε το θυγατριον αὐτης πνευμα ακαθαρτον,
had the little daughter of herself a spirit unclean,
ελθουσα προσεπεσε προς τους ποδας αυτου·
having come fell down to the feet of him
[26] (ην δε ἡ γυνη Ἑλληνις, Συροφοινικισσα τῳ
(was now the woman a Greek, a Syrophenician to the
γενει·) και ηρωτα αυτον, ἱνα το δαιμονιον εκ-
birth:) and she besought him, that the demon he
βαλη εκ της θυγατρος αὐτης. [27] Ὁ δε Ιησους
would cast out of the daughter of herself. The but Jesus
ειπεν αυτῃ· Αφες πρωτον χορτασθηναι τα τεκνα·
said to her; Let alone first to be filled the children;
ου γαρ καλον εστι, λαβειν τον αρτον των τεκ-
not for good it is, to take the bread of the chil-
νων, και βαλειν τοις κυναριοις. [28] Ἡ δε
dren, and to cast to the dogs. She but

Ears to hear, let him hear."]

17 ‡ And when he went from the CROWD into a House, his DISCIPLES asked him concerning the PARABLE.

18 And he says to them, "Are you also so destitute of understanding? Do you not perceive, that nothing from without, ENTERING INTO the MAN, can pollute Him?

19 because it enters not into the HEART, but into the BELLY, and passes into the SINK, purifying All the FOOD."

20 And he said, "THAT which PROCEEDS OUT OF the MAN, that pollutes the MAN.

21 ‡ For from within, out of the HEART of MEN, emanate EVIL PURPOSES;—Adulteries, Fornications, Murders,

22 Thefts, Covetousness, Villanies, Deceit, Intemperance, Envy, Calumnies, Pride, and Folly;

23 All These EVIL things emanate from within, and pollute the MAN."

24 ‡ And arising thence, he retired into the CONFINES of Tyre and Sidon; and having entered into the HOUSE, he desired no one to know it; but he could not be concealed.

25 For a Woman, whose LITTLE DAUGHTER had an unclean Spirit, * immediately heard of him; and having come fell down at his FEET;

26 (now the WOMAN was † an Hellenist, a NATIVE of Syrophenicia.) and she entreated him to expel the DEMON from her DAUGHTER.

27 * And he said to her, "Let the CHILDREN first be satisfied; for it is not proper to take the CHILDREN'S BREAD, and throw it to the DOGS."

* VATICAN MANUSCRIPT.—25. immediately heard. 27. And he said.
† 26. One who spoke the Greek language.
‡ 17. Matt. xv. 15. ‡ 21. Gen. vi. 5; viii. 21; Matt. xv. 19. ‡ 24. Matt. xv. 21.

απεκριθη, και λεγει αυτῳ· Ναι, κυριε· και γαρ
answered, and says to him; Yes, sir; even for
τα κυναρια ὑποκατω της τραπεζης εσθιει απο
the dogs under the table eatest from
των ψιχιων των παιδιων. 29 Και ειπεν αυτῃ·
of the crumbs of the children. And he said to her;
Δια τουτον τον λογον ὑπαγε· εξεληλυθε το
Through this the word go; has come out the
δαιμονιον εκ της θυγατρος σου. 30 Και απελ-
demon from the daughter of thee. And having
θουσα εις τον οικον αὑτης, εὑρε το δαιμονιον
gone into the house of her, she found the demon
εξεληλυθος, και την θυγατερα βεβλημενην επι
having gone out, and the daughter having been laid upon
της κλινης.
the bed.

31 Και παλιν εξελθων εκ των ὁριων Τυρου και
And again coming out from the borders of Tyre and
Σιδωνος, ηλθεν εις την θαλασσαν της Γαλιλαιας,
Sidon, he came to the sea of the Galilee,
ανα μεσον των ὁριων Δεκαπολεως. 32 Και φερ-
through midst of the borders of Decapolis. And they
ουσιν αυτῳ κωφον μογιλαλον, και παρακαλου-
bring to him a deaf man a stammerer, and they entreat
σιν αυτον ἱνα επιθῃ αυτῳ την χειρα. 33 Και
him that he might place to him the hand. And
απολαβομενος αυτον απο του οχλου κατ' ιδιαν,
having taken him from the crowd privately,
εβαλε τους δακτυλους αὑτου εις τα ωτα αυτου,
he put the fingers of himself into the ears of him,
και πτυσας ἡψατο της γλωσσης αυτου· 34 και
and spitting he touched the tongue of him; and
αναβλεψας εις τον ουρανον, εστεναξε, και
looking up to the heaven, he groaned, and
λεγει αυτῳ· Εφφαθα, ὁ εστι, διανοιχθητι.
says to him: Ephphatha, that is, be opened.
35 Και *[ευθεως] διηνοιχθησαν αυτου αἱ ακοαι·
And [immediately] were opened of him the ears
και ελυθη ὁ δεσμος της γλωσσης αυτου, και
and was loosed the bond of the tongue of him, and
αλαλει ορθως. 36 Και διεστειλατο αυτοις, ἱνα
he spoke plainly. And he charged them, that
μηδενι ειπωσιν· ὁσον δε αυτος αυτοις διεστελ-
no one they should tell; what but he to them charged
λετο, μαλλον περισσοτερον εκηρυσσον 37 Και
more abundantly they published. And
ὑπερπερισσως εξεπλησσοντο, λεγοντες· Καλως
beyond measure they were astonished, saying, Well
παντα πεποιηκε· και τους κωφους ποιει ακου-
all (things) he has done; and the deaf ones he makes to
ειν, και τους αλαλους λαλειν·
hear, and the dumb ones to speak.

28 But she answered, and says to him, "True, Sir; yet even the DOGS under the TABLE eat of the CHILDREN'S CRUMBS."

29 And he said to her, "For This REMARK, go; the DEMON has departed from thy DAUGHTER."

30 And departing to her HOUSE, she found * her DAUGHTER laid upon the BED, and the DEMON expelled.

31 ‡ And again leaving the CONFINES of Tyre, * he came by Sidon to the LAKE of GALILEE, through the Midst of the BORDERS of Decapolis.

32 ‡ And they bring to him a deaf man who stammered, and they entreat him to place his HAND on him.

33 And having privately taken him from the CROWD, † he put his FINGERS into his EARS, and spitting, touched his TONGUE;

34 and looking up to HEAVEN, he groaned, and says to him, "Ephphatha," that is, Be opened.

35 And His EARS were opened, and the CORD of his TONGUE was loosed, and he spoke plainly.

36 ‡ And he charged them that they should tell no one; but the more * he charged them, the more abundantly * they published it.

37 And they were astonished beyond measure, saying, "He has done all things well; he makes both the DEAF to hear, and the * Dumb to speak.

* VATICAN MANUSCRIPT.—30. her DAUGHTER laid upon the BED, and the DEMON expelled. 31. he came by Sidon to. 35. immediately—*omit.* 36. he charged. 36. they published 37. Dumb.

† 33. Doddridge well observes about this miracle, "If any should ask Why our Lord used these actions, when a word alone would have been sufficient; and such means (if they can be called means) could in themselves do nothing at all to answer the end,—I frankly confess I cannot tell, nor am I at all concerned to know. * * * * Had Christ's patients, like Naaman, (2 Kings v. 11, 12,) been too nice in their exceptions on these occasions, I fear they would have lost their cure, and the indulgence of a curious, or a petulant mind, would have been but a poor equivalent for such a loss."

‡ 31. Matt. xv. 29. ‡ 32. Matt. ix. 32; Luke xi. 14. ‡ 36. Mark v. 43; viii. 20.

ΚΕΦ. η'. 8.

1 Εν εκειναις ταις ἡμεραις, παμπολλου οχλου
In those the days, very great crowd
οντος, και μη εχοντων τι φαγωσι, προσ-
being, and not having any thing they could eat, having
καλεσαμενος τους μαθητας αὑτου λεγει αυτοις·
called the disciples of himself he says to them;
2 Σπλαγχνιζομαι επι τον οχλον· ὁτι ηδη ἡμεραι
I have pity on the crowd; because now days
τρεις, προσμενουσι *[μοι,] και ουκ εχουσι τι
three, they continue [with me,] and not they have any thing
φαγωσι. 3 Και εαν απολυσω αυτους νηστεις
they can eat. And if I dismiss them fasting
εις οικον αὑτων, εκλυθησονται εν τῃ ὁδῳ· τινες
into house of themselves, they will faint on the way; some
γαρ αυτων μακροθεν ἡκουσι. 4 Και απεκριθησαν
for of them a great distance have come. And answered
αυτῳ οἱ μαθηται αυτου· Ποθεν τουτους δυνησε-
to him the disciples of him; Whence these will be able
ται τις ὡδε χορτασαι αρτων επ' ερημιας; 5 Και
any one here to satisfy of loaves in a desert place? And
επηρωτα αυτους· Ποσους εχετε αρτους; Οἱ δε
he asked them; How many have you loaves? They and
ειπον· Ἑπτα. 6 Και παρηγγειλε τῳ οχλῳ ανα-
said; Seven. And he gave orders to the crowd to
πεσειν επι της γης· και λαβων τους ἑπτα
recline upon the ground; and taking the seven
αρτους, ευχαριστησας εκλασε, και εδιδου τοις
loaves giving thanks he broke, and gave to the
μαθηταις αὑτου, ἱνα παραθωσι· και παρεθηκαν
disciples of himself, that they might place before; and they placed before
τῳ οχλῳ. 7 Και ειχον ιχθυδια ολιγα· και ευλο-
the crowd. And they had small fishes a few; and giving
γησας, ειπε παραθειναι και αυτα. 8 Εφαγον δε,
praise, he said place before also them. They ate and,
και εχορτασθησαν· και ηραν περισσευματα
and were filled; and they took up over and above
κλασματων, ἑπτα σπυριδας. 9 Ησαν δε οἱ φα-
of fragments, seven large baskets. Were and those hav-
γοντες, ὡς τετρακισχιλιοι· και απελυσεν
ing eaten, about four thousand; and he dismissed
αυτους.
them.

10 Και ευθεως εμβας εις το πλοιον μετα των
And immediately entering into the ship with the
μαθητων αὑτου, ηλθεν εις τα μερη Δαλμανουθα.
disciples of himself, he came into the parts of Dalmanutha.
11 Και εξηλθον οἱ Φαρισαιοι, και ηρξαντο συζη-
And came forth the Pharisees, and began to
τειν αυτῳ, ζητουντες παρ' αυτου σημειον απο
argue with him, seeking of him a sign from

CHAPTER VIII.

1 ‡ In Those DAYS the Crowd * again being great, and having nothing to eat, calling his DISCIPLES, he says to them,

2 "I have compassion on the CROWD, Because now they have continued three Days, and have nothing to eat;

3 and if I dismiss them fasting to their Homes, they will faint on the ROAD; for some of them have come from a great distance."

4 And his DISCIPLES answered him, "Whence will any one be able to satisfy These with Bread here in a Desert place?"

5 ‡ And he asked them, "How Many Loaves have you?" And THEY said, "Seven."

6 And he commanded the CROWD to recline on the GROUND; and taking the SEVEN Loaves, ‡ and having given thanks, he broke them, and gave them to his DISCIPLES for distribution, and they placed them before the CROWD.

7 And they had a few Small fishes; and having offered praise for them, he said, "Place * These also before them."

8 Thus they ate, and were satisfied; and they took up of the remaining Fragments Seven large Baskets full.

9 And * they were about Four thousand; and he dismissed them.

10 ‡ And immediately * he entered into the BOAT with his DISCIPLES, and came into the REGION of † Dalmanutha.

11 ‡ And the PHARISEES came forth, and began to argue with him, seeking

* VATICAN MANUSCRIPT.—1. again being great. 7. These. 9. And they were about. 10. he entered.

† 10. The same as Magdala; see Matt. xv. 39.

‡ 1. Matt. xv. 32. ‡ 5. Matt. xv. 34; Mark vi. 38. ‡ 6. Matt. xiv. 19; Mark vi. 41. ‡ 10. Matt. xv. 39. ‡ 11. Matt. xii. 38; xvi. 1; John vi. 30.

του ουρανου, πειραζοντες αυτον. 12 Και ανα
the heaven, tempting him. And groan-
στεναξας τῳ πνευματι αὑτου, λεγει· Τί ἡ γενεα
ing deeply in the spirit of himself, he says: Why the generation
αὑτη σημειον επιζητει; Αμην λεγω *[ὑμιν] ει
this a sign seeks? Indeed I say [to you,] if
δοθησεται τῃ γενεᾳ ταυτῃ σημειον.
shall be given to the generation this a sign.

13 Και αφεις αυτους, εμβας παλιν *[εις το
And leaving them, entering again [into the
πλοιον,] απηλθεν εις το περαν. 14 Και επελα-
ship,] he departed to the other side. And they
θοντο λαβειν αρτους, και ει μη ἑνα αρτον ουκ
forgot to take loaves, and except one loaf not
ειχον μεθ' ἑαυτων εν τῳ πλοιῳ. 15 Και διεσ-
they had with themselves in the ship. And he
τελλετο αυτοις, λεγων· Ὁρατε, βλεπετε απο
charged them, saying; Look you, beware you of
της ζυμης των Φαρισαιων, και της ζυμης Ἡρω-
the leaven of the Pharisees, and of the leaven of He-
δου. 16 Και διελογιζοντο προς αλληλους, *[λε-
rod. And they reasoned with one another, [say-
γοντες·] Ὁτι αρτους ουκ εχομεν. 17 Και γνους
ing;] Because loaves not we have. And knowing
ὁ Ιησους, λεγει αυτοις· Τι διαλογιζεσθε, ὁτι
the Jesus, he says to them; why reason you, because
αρτους ουκ εχετε; Ουπω νοειτε, ουδε
loaves not you have? Not yet perceive you, neither
συνιετε; *[ετι] πεπωρωμενην εχετε την καρ-
understand you? [yet] having been stupified have you the heart
διαν ὑμων; 18 Οφθαλμους εχοντες ου βλεπετε;
of you? Eyes having not see you?
και ωτα εχοντες ουκ ακουετε; και ου μνημον-
and ears having not hear you? and not remember
ευετε; 19 Ὁτε τους πεντε αρτους εκλασα εις
you? When the five loaves I broke to
τους πεντακισχιλιους, ποσους κοφινους πλη-
the five thousand, how many baskets full
ρεις κλασματων ηρατε; Λεγουσιν αυτῳ·
of fragments took you up? They say to him,
Δωδεκα. 20 Ὁτε δε τους ἑπτα εις τους τετρα-
Twelve. When and the seven to the four
κισχιλιους, ποσων σπυριδων πληρωματα κλασ-
thousand, how many large baskets full of
ματων ηρατε; Οἱ δε ειπον· Ἑπτα. 21 Και
fragments took you up? They and said; Seven, And
ελεγεν αυτοις· Πως ου συνιετε;
he said to them; How is it not you understand?

22 Και ερχεται εις Βηθσαιδαν Και φερουσιν
And he comes to Bethsaida. And they bring

of him a Sign from HEAVEN, trying him.

12 And groaning deeply in his SPIRIT, he says, "Why does this GENERATION seek a Sign? Indeed, I say to you, no Sign shall be given to this GENERATION."

13 And leaving them, re-embarking, he passed to the OTHER SIDE.

14 ‡ Now they forgot to take Bread, and had but One Loaf with them in the BOAT.

15 ‡ And he charged them, saying, "Observe! Beware of the † LEAVEN of the PHARISEES and of the LEAVEN of Herod."

16 And they reasoned with one another, * Because they had no Bread.

17 And * he knew it, and says to them, "Why do you reason, Because you have no Bread? ‡ Do you not yet perceive, nor understand? Is your HEART stupified?

18 Having Eyes do you not see? and having Ears, do you not hear? and do you not recollect?

19 ‡ When I broke the FIVE Loaves among the FIVE THOUSAND, How many Baskets full of Fragments took you up?" They say to him, "Twelve."

20 † "And when the SEVEN among the FOUR THOUSAND, How many large Baskets full of Fragments took you up?" And * they say to him, "Seven."

21 And he said to them, "How is it you do not understand?"

22 And * they come to Bethsaida; and they bring

* VATICAN MANUSCRIPT.—12. to you—*omit.* 13. into the BOAT—*omit.* 16. saying—*omit.* 16. Because they had no Bread. 17. he knew it, and says 17. yet—*omit.* 20. they say to him. 22. they come.

† 15. Matthew joins the *Sadducees* with the Pharisees, and makes no mention of *Herod.* But there is no real discrepancy, since Herod and the Herodians (i. e. his adherents and courtiers) were, no doubt, Sadducees, and there is every reason to think that their doctrines and morals were such as to justify the caution of our Lord. *Zumee,* by a striking metaphor, denotes the *infection* of *false doctrines,* (so Matt. xvi. 12,) as well as corrupt morals.—*Bloomfield.*

‡ 14. Matt. xvi. 5. ‡ 15. Matt. xvi. 6; Luke xii. 1. ‡ 17. Mark vi. 52. ‡ 19. Matt. xiv. 20; Mark vi. 43; Luke ix. 17; John vi. 13. ‡ 20. Matt. xv. 37; Mark viii. 8.

αυτῳ τυφλον και παρακαλουσιν αυτον, ἱνα
to him a blind man and beseech him, that
αυτου ἁψηται. 23 Και επιλαβομενος της
him he would touch. And having taken the
χειρος του τυφλου, εξηγαγεν αυτον εξω της
hand of the blind man, he led him outside of the
κωμης· και πτυσας εις τα ομματα αυτου, επι-
village; and having spit into the eyes of him, having
θεις τας χειρας αυτῳ, επηρωτα αυτον, ει
placed the hands to him, he asked him, if
τι βλεπει. 24 Και αναβλεψας ελεγε· Βλεπω
anything he sees. And looking up he says; I see
τους ανθρωπους, ὡς δενδρα, περιπατουντας.
the men, like trees, walking.
25 Ειτα παλιν επεθηκε τας χειρας επι τους
Then again he placed the hands upon the
οφθαλμους αυτου, και εποιησεν αυτον ανα-
eyes of him, and he made him look
βλεψαι· και αποκατεσταθη, και ενεβλεψε
up; and he was restored, and he saw
τηλαυγως ἁπαντας. 26 Και επεστειλεν αυτον
plainly every one. And he sent him
εις οικον αυτου, λεγων· Μηδε εις την κωμην
to house of him, saying; Neither into the village
εισελθης, *[μηδε ειπης τινι εν τῃ κωμῃ.]
mayest thou enter, [nor mayest thou tell any one in the village.]
27 Και εξηλθεν ὁ Ιησους και οἱ μαθηται αυτου
And departed the Jesus and the disciples of him
εις τας κωμας Καισαρειας της Πιλιππου. Και
into the villages of Cesarea of the Philip. And
εν τῃ ὁδῳ επηρωτα τους μαθητας αὐτου, λεγων
on the way he asked the disciples of himself, saying
αυτοις· Τινα με λεγουσιν οἱ ανθρωποι ειναι;
to them; Who me they say the men to be?
28 Οἱ δε απεκριθησαν· Ιωαννην τον βαπτιστην·
They and answered; John the dipper;
και αλλοι, Ηλιαν· αλλοι δε, ἑνα των προφητων.
and others, Elias; others and, one of the prophets.
29 Και αυτος λεγει αυτοις· Ὑμεις δε τινα με
And he says to them; You but who me
λεγετε ειναι; Αποκριθεις δε ὁ Πετρος λεγει
you say to be? Answering and the Peter says
αυτῳ· Συ ει ὁ Χριστος. 30 Και επετιμησεν
to him; Thou art the Anointed. And he strictly charged
αυτοις, ἱνα μηδενι λεγωσι περι αυτου. 31 Και
them, that no one they should tell about him. And
ηρξατο διδασκειν αυτους, ὁτι δει τον υἱον του
he began to teach them, that must the son of the
ανθρωπου πολλα παθειν, και αποδοκιμασθηναι
man many things to suffer, and to be rejected
απο των πρεσβυτερων και των αρχιερεων και
of the elders and of the high-priests and
των γραμματεων, και αποκτανθηναι, και μετα
of the scribes, and to be killed, and after
τρεις ἡμερας αναστηναι· 32 και παρρησιᾳ τον
three days to stand up; and plainly the

a Blind man to him, and beseech him to touch Him.

23 And taking the HAND of the BLIND man, he conducted him out of the VILLAGE; ‡and having spit on his EYES, and placed his HANDS on him, he asked him whether he saw any thing.

24 And looking up, he said, "I see MEN as Trees, walking."

25 Then he placed his HANDS on his EYES again, and *he saw plainly, and was restored, and saw every object clearly.

26 And he sent him away to his * House, saying, "Go not into the VILLAGE."

27 ‡And JESUS and his DISCIPLES went out to the VILLAGES of Cesarea PHILIPPI; and, on the ROAD, he asked his DISCIPLES, saying to them, "Who do MEN say that I am?"

28 And THEY * spoke to him, saying, ‡"John the IMMERSER; and others, Elijah; and others, One of the PROPHETS."

29 And he * asked them, "Who say you that I am?" And PETER answering, says to him, ‡"Thou art the CHRIST."

30 ‡And he strictly charged them that they should tell no one concerning him.

31 And ‡he began to inform them That the SON of MAN must suffer many things, and be rejected by the ELDERS, and the HIGH-PRIESTS, and the SCRIBES, and be put to death, and after Three Days to rise up.

32 And he spoke this

* VATICAN MANUSCRIPT.—25. he saw plainly, and was restored, and saw every object clearly. 26. House, saying, "Go not into." 26. nor mayest thou tell any one in the VILLAGE—omit. 28 spoke to him, saying, "John the IMMERSER." 29. asked them, saying, "Who say."

‡ 23 Mark vii. 33. ‡ 27 Matt. xvi. 13. Luke ix. 18. ‡ 28. Matt. xiv 2. ‡ 29 Matt xvi. 6; John vi. 69; xi. 27. ‡ 30. Matt. xvi. 20. ‡ 31. Matt. xvi. 21; xvii. 22; Luke ix. 22.

λογον ελαλει. Και προσλαβομενος αυτον ὁ Πε-
word he spoke. And taking aside him the Pe-
τρος, ηρξατο επιτιμαν αυτῳ. 33 Ὁ δε επιστρα-
ter, he began to rebuke him. He but turning
φεις, και ιδων τους μαθητας αὑτου, επετιμησε
round, and seeing the disciples of himself, he rebuked
τῳ Πετρῳ, λεγων· Ὑπαγε οπισω μου, σατανα·
the Peter, saying; Go thou behind me, adversary;
ὁτι ου φρονεις τα του Θεου, αλλα τα
because not thou thinkest the things of the God, but the things
των ανθρωπων. 34 Και προσκαλεσαμενος τον
of the men. And having called the
οχλον συν τοις μαθηταις αὑτου, ειπεν αυτοις·
crowd with the disciples of himself, he said to them;
Ὁστις θελει οπισω μου ακολουθειν, απαρνησασ-
Whoever wishes after me to follow, let him deny
θω ἑαυτον, και αρατω τον σταυρον αὑτου, και
himself, and let him bear the cross of himself, and
ακολουθειτω μοι. 35 Ὁς γαρ αν θελῃ την ψυχην
let him follow me. Who for ever may wish the life
αὑτου σωσαι, απολεσει αυτην· ὁς δ' αν απολεσῃ
of himself to save, shall lose her; who but ever may lose
την ἑαυτου ψυχην ἑνεκεν εμου και του ευαγ-
the of himself life on account of me and of the glad
γελιου, σωσει αυτην. 36 (Τι γαρ ωφελησει
tidings, shall save her. (What for will it profit
ανθρωπον, εαν κερδησῃ τον κοσμον ὁλον, και
a man, if he should win the world whole, and
ζημιωθῃ την ψυχην αὑτου; 37 η τι δωσει
should forfeit the life of himself? or what shall give
ανθρωπος ανταλλαγμα της ψυχης αὑτου;)
a man in exchange for the life of himself?)
38 Ὁς γαρ αν επαισχυνθῃ με και τους εμους
Who for ever may be ashamed me and the my
λογους εν τῃ γενεᾳ ταυτῃ τῃ μοιχαλιδι και
words in the generation this the adulterous and
ἁμαρτωλῳ, και ὁ υἱος του ανθρωπου επαισχυν-
sinful, also the son of the man will be
θησεται αυτον, ὁταν ελθῃ εν τῃ δοξῃ του
ashamed him, when he may come in the glory of the
πατρος αὑτου μετα των αγγελων των ἁγιων.
father of himself with the messengers of the holy ones.

ΚΕΦ. θ'. 9. 1 Και ελεγεν αυτοις· Αμην λεγω
And he said to them; Indeed I say
ὑμιν, ὁτι εισι τινες των ὡδε ἑστηκοτων, οἱτινες
to you, that are some of those here having stood, who
ου μη γευσωνται θανατου, ἑως αν ιδωσι την
not not shall taste of death, till they may see the
βασιλειαν του θεου εληλυθυιαν εν δυναμει.
royal majesty of the God having come in power.

2 Και μεθ' ἡμερας ἑξ παραλαμβανει ὁ Ιησους
And after days six takes the Jesus
τον Πετρον, και τον Ιακωβον, και Ιωαννην, και
the Peter, and the James, and John, and
αναφερει αυτους εις ορος ὑψηλον κατ' ιδιαν
leads up them into a mountain high privately

WORD so plainly, that PETER, taking him aside, began to remonstrate with him.

33 But HE, turning round and looking on his DISCIPLES, rebuked * Peter, and says, "Get behind me, Adversary; for thou regardest not the THINGS of GOD, but THOSE of MEN."

34 And having called the CROWD with his DISCIPLES, he said, * ‡ "If any one wish to come after me, let him renounce himself, and take up his CROSS, and follow me.

35 For ‡ whoever would save his LIFE shall lose it; but whoever may lose his LIFE on my account, and that of the GLAD TIDINGS, shall save it.

36 For what * does it profit a Man to gain the whole WORLD, and forfeit his LIFE?

37 * For what could a MAN give to Redeem his LIFE?

38 ‡ If, therefore, any one shall be ashamed of me, and of these MY Words, among this ADULTEROUS and sinful GENERATION; the SON of MAN will also be ashamed of him, when he comes in the GLORY of his FATHER, with the HOLY ANGELS."

CHAPTER IX.

1 And he said to them, ‡ "Indeed I say to you, That there are some of THOSE STANDING here, who will not taste of Death, till they see GOD'S ROYAL MAJESTY having come with power.

2 ‡ And after six Days, JESUS takes PETER, and JAMES, and John, and privately conducts them, by themselves, to a lofty

* VATICAN MANUSCRIPT.—33. Peter, and says. 34. If any one wish. 36. does it profit a Man to gain. 37. For what could a MAN give.

‡ 34. Matt. x. 38 xvi. 24; Luke ix 23; xiv. 27. ‡ 35. John xii. 25. ‡ 38. Matt. x. 33; Luke ix. 26; xii. 9; Rom. i 16 2 Tim. i. 8; ii, 12. ‡ 1. Matt. xvi. 28; Luke ix, 27. ‡ 2. Matt xvii. 1; Luke ix 28.

μονους· και μετεμορφωθη εμπροσθεν αυτων.
alone; and he was transfigured in the presence of them.
3 Και τα ἱματια αυτου εγενετο στιλβοντα, λευκα
And the garments of him became glittering, white
λιαν *[ὡς χιων,] οἱα γναφευς επι της γης ου
extremely [as snow,] such as a fuller upon the earth not
δυναται λευκαναι. 4 Και ωφθη αυτοις Ηλιας
is able to make white. And appeared to them Elias
συν Μωσει· και ησαν συλλαλουντες τῳ Ιησου.
with Moses; and were talking with the Jesus.
5 Και αποκριθεις ὁ Πετρος λεγει τῳ Ιησου·
And answering the Peter says to the Jesus.
Ῥαββι, καλον εστιν ἡμας ὡδε ειναι· και ποιη-
Rabbi, good it is us here to be; and we may
σωμεν σκηνας τρεις, σοι μιαν, και Μωσει μιαν,
make tents three, to thee one, and Moses one,
και Ηλιᾳ μιαν. 6 Ου γαρ ηδει τι λαλησῃ·
and Elias one. Not for he knew any thing he might say;
ησαν γαρ εκφοβοι. 7 Και εγενετο νεφελη επι-
they were for terrified. And there came a cloud over-
σκιαζουσα αυτοις· και ηλθε φωνη εκ της νεφελης·
shadowing them; and came a voice out of the cloud;
Οὑτος εστιν ὁ υἱος μου ὁ αγαπητος· αυτου
This is the son of me the beloved; him
ακουετε. 8 Και εξαπινα περιβλεψαμενοι, ουκετι
hear you. And suddenly looking round, no longer
ουδενα ειδον, αλλα τον Ιησουν μονον μεθ' ἑαυ-
no one they saw but the Jesus alone with them-
των. 9 Καταβαινοντων δε αυτων απο του ορους,
selves. Coming down and of them from the mountain,
διεστειλατο αυτοις, ἱνα μηδενι διηγησωνται ἁ
he charged them, that to no one they should relate what
ειδον, ει μη ὁταν ὁ υἱος του ανθρωπου εκ νεκρων
they saw except when the son of the man out of dead ones
αναστῃ. 10 Και τον λογον εκρατησαν προς
should be raised. And the word they kept to
ἑαυτοις, συζητουντες, τι εστι το εκ νεκρων
themselves, arguing, what is that out of dead ones
αναστηναι. 11 Και επηρωτων αυτον, λεγοντες·
to be raised. And they asked him, saying;
† Ὁτι λεγουσιν οἱ γραμματεις, ὁτι Ηλιαν δει
That say the scribes, that Elias must
ελθειν πρωτον; 12 Ὁ δε αποκριθεις ειπεν αυτοις·
to come first; He and answering said to them;
Ηλιας μεν ελθων πρωτον, αποκαθιστᾳ παντα·
Elias indeed coming first, restores all things;
και πως γεγραπται επι τον υἱον του ανθρωπου,
and how it is written about the son of the man,

Mountain; and he was transformed in their presence.

3 And his GARMENTS became glittering, exceedingly white; such as no Fuller on the EARTH is able * thus to make white.

4 And there appeared to them Elijah, with Moses; and they were conversing with JESUS.

5 And PETER answering says to JESUS, "Rabbi, it is good for us to be here; and let us make * Three Booths; one for thee, and one for Moses, and one for Elijah."

6 For he knew not what to * say; for they were terrified.

7 And there came a Cloud, covering them; and * there was a Voice came out of the CLOUD, "This is my BELOVED SON; hear him."

8 And suddenly looking round, they saw no one * any longer with themselves, except Jesus only.

9 ‡ And as they were descending from the MOUNTAIN, he commanded them that they should relate to no one what they had seen, till the SON of MAN should have risen from the Dead.

10 And they kept the MATTER to themselves, anxiously inquiring, what THE RISING FROM THE DEAD could mean.

11 And they asked him saying, "Why do the SCRIBES say, That Elijah must first come?"

12 And HE * said to them, "Elijah, indeed, is coming first * to restore all things: † and (as it is written of the SON of

* VATICAN MANUSCRIPT.—3. as snow—*omit*. 3. thus to make white. 5. Three Booths. 6. answer; for. 7. there was a Voice. 8. any longer with themselves, except Jesus only. 12. said to them. 12. to restore.

† 11. It is conjectured by Bloomfield that *hoti* ought to be separated, and to read *ho ti*. He has thus edited his text. † 12. There is considerable ambiguity about the reading of this and following verse, as it stands in the Greek. The critics have all been puzzled, and some have suggested an amendment of the text. If read, however, with the parenthetical clauses, and the transposition of the last clause of verse 13, the passage makes good sense, and agrees with the account in Matthew xvii.

‡ 9. Matt. xvii. 9.

ἱνα πολλα παθῃ, και εξουδενωθῃ. 13 Αλλα
that many things he should suffer, and should be despised. But
λεγω ὑμιν, ὁτι και Ηλιας εληλυθε, και εποιησαν
I say to you, that both Elias has come, and they have done
αυτῳ ὁσα ηθελησαν, καθως γεγραπται επ'
to him whatever they wished, even as it is written about
αυτον. 14 Και ελθων προς τους μαθητας, ειδεν
him. And coming to the disciples, he saw
οχλον πολυν περι αυτους, και γραμματεις συζη-
a crowd great about them, and scribes dis-
τουντας αυτοις. 15 Και ευθεως πας ὁ οχλον,
puting with them; And immediately all the crowd,
ιδων αυτον, εξεθαμβηθη, και προστρεχοντες
seeing him, were awe-struck, and running to
ησπαζοντο αυτον. 16 Και επηρωτησεν αυτους·
saluted him. And he asked them;
Τι συζητειτε προς αυτους; 17 Και αποκριθεις εἱς
What dispute you with them? And answering one
εκ του οχλου ειπε· Διδασκαλε, ηνεγκα τον
out of the crowd said: O Teacher, I brought the
υἱον μου προς σε, εχοντα πνευμα αλαλον. 18 Και
son of me to thee, having a spirit dumb. And
ὁπου αν αυτον καταλαβῃ, ῥησσει αυτον· και
wherever him it may seize, it convulses him; and
αφριζει, και τριζει τους οδοντας αὑτου, και
he foams, and grinds the teeth of him, and
ξηραινεται. Και ειπον τοις μαθηταις σου, ἱνα
pines away. And I spoke to the disciples of thee, that
αυτο εκβαλωσι, και ουκ ισχυσαν. 19 Ὁ δε
it they might cast out, and not they had power. He and
αποκριθεις αυτοις λεγει· Ω γενεα απιστος, ἑως
answering them says: O generation without faith, till
ποτε προς ὑμας εσομαι; ἑως ποτε ανεξομαι
when with you shall I be? till when shall I bear
ὑμων; φερετε αυτον προς με. 20 Και ηνεγκαν
you? Bring you him to me. And they brought
αυτον προς αυτον. Και ιδων αυτον, ευθεως το
him to him. And seeing him, immediately the
πνευμα εσπαραξεν αυτον· και πεσων επι της
spirit convulsed him; and falling upon the
γης, εκυλιετο, αφριζων. 21 Και επηρωτησε τον
ground, he rolled, foaming. And he asked the
πατερα αυτου· Ποσος χρονος εστιν, ὡς τουτο
father of him; How long a time is it, since this
γεγονεν αυτῳ; Ὁ δε ειπε· Παιδιοθεν· και
happened to him? He and said; From a child: and
πολλακις αυτον και εις πυρ εβαλε και εις ὑδατα,
often him both into fire has cast and into waters,
ἱνα απολεσῃ αυτον· αλλ', ει τι δυνασαι,
that it might destroy him, but if any thing thou canst do,
βοηθησον ἡμιν, σπλαγχνισθεις εφ' ἡμας.
give aid to us, having pity on us.

MAN,) that he must suffer much, and be despised.

13 But I say to you, ‡ That Elijah has even come, (as it is written of him,) and they have done to him whatever they pleased."

14 ‡ And * coming to the DISCIPLES, * they saw a great Crowd about them, and the Scribes disputing with them.

15 And immediately All the CROWD seeing him, were struck with awe, and running to him, saluted him.

16 And he asked them, "About what are you disputing with them?"

17 And one of the CROWD * answered him, "Teacher, I have brought to thee my SON, who has † a dumb Spirit.

18 And wherever it seizes him it convulses him; and he foams, and grinds * his TEETH, and becomes emaciated. And I spoke to thy DISCIPLES to expel it, and they could not."

19 And HE answering, says to them, "O unbelieving Generation! how long must I be with you? how long must I endure you? bring him to me."

20 And they brought him to him; and seeing him, ‡ the SPIRIT immediately convulsed him; and falling on the GROUND, he rolled about, foaming.

21 And he asked his FATHER, "How long a time is it since this befell him?" And HE said, "From childhood.

22 And often it has thrown him into Fire and into Waters to destroy him; but if thou canst do any thing, have pity on us, and help us."

---

* VATICAN MANUSCRIPT.—14. they came. 14. they saw. 17. answered him, "Teacher." 18. the TEETH.

† 17. The child was subject to epileptic fits, which were supposed to be brought on by the power of demons.—See *Farmer on Demonology*, p. 107. The particulars described in verses 18, 20 and 22 are, indeed, all symptoms of *epilepsy*. But if we even should suppose the man was an epileptic; it would not follow that the disorder was not induced by demoniacal influence. —*Bloomfield.*

‡ 14. Matt. xvii 14; Luke ix. 37. ‡ 20. Luke ix. 42.

23 Ὁ δε Ιησους ειπεν αυτῳ· Το, ει δυνασαι
The and Jesus said to him; That, if thou art able
πιστευσαι· παντα δυνατα τῳ πιστευοντι.
to believe; all things are possible to the believing.
24 *[Και] ευθεως κραξας ὁ πατηρ του παιδιου,
[And] immediately crying out the father of the child,
*[μετα δακρυων] ελεγε· Πιστευω· βοηθει μου
[with tears] he said; I believe; help thou of me
τῃ απιστιᾳ. 25 Ιδων δε ὁ Ιησους, ὁτι επισυν-
the unbelief. Seeing and the Jesus, that runs to-
τρεχει οχλος, επετιμησε τῳ πνευματι τῳ ακα-
gether a crowd, he rebuked the spirit the un-
θαρτῳ, λεγων αυτῳ· Το πνευμα το αλαλον και
clean, saying to it; The spirit the dumb and
κωφον, εγω σοι επιτασσω· Εξελθε εξ αυτου,
deaf, I to thee command; Come out of him,
και μηκετι εισελθῃς εις αυτον. 26 Και κραξαν,
and no more enter into him. And crying out,
και πολλα σπαραξας, εξηλθε. Και εγενετο
and many times convulsing, it came out. And he became
ὡσει νεκρος, ὡστε πολλους λεγειν, ὁτι απεθανεν.
as dead, so that many to say, that he is dead.
27 Ὁ δε Ιησους κρατησας αυτον της χειρος,
The but Jesus taking him of the hand,
ηγειρεν αυτον· και ανεστη.
raised up him; and he stood up.

28 Και εισελθοντα αυτον εις οικον, οἱ μαθηται
And having come him into a house, the disciples
αυτου επηρωτων αυτον κατ᾽ ιδιαν· Ὁτι ἡμεις
of him asked him privately; That we
ουκ ηδυνηθημεν εκβαλειν αυτο; 29 Και ειπεν
not were able to cast out it? And he said
αυτοις· Τουτο το γενος εν ουδενι δυναται εξελ-
to them; This the kind by nothing is able to go
θειν, ει μη εν προσευχῃ *[και νηστειᾳ.]
out, if not in prayer [and fasting.]

30 Και εκειθεν εξελθοντες, παρεπορευοντο δια
And thence departing, he passed through
της Γαλιλαιας· και ουκ ηθελεν, ἱνα τις γνῳ.
the Galilee; and not was willing, that any one should know.
31 Εδιδασκε γαρ τους μαθητας αὑτου, και ελεγ-
He taught for the disciples of himself, and said
εν *[αυτοις·] Ὁτι ὁ υἱος του ανθρωπου παρα-
[to them; That the son of the man is deli-
διδοται εις χειρας ανθρωπων, και αποκτενουσιν
vered up into hands of men, and they will kill
αυτον· και αποκτανθεις, τῃ τριτῃ ἡμερᾳ ανα-
him; and having been killed, the third day he
στησεται. 32 Οἱ δε ηγνοουν το ῥημα, και
will rise. They but did not understand the word, and
εφοβουντο αυτον επερωτησαι.
were afraid him to ask.

33 Και ηλθεν εις Καπερναουμ· και εν τῃ οικιᾳ
And he came to Capernaum; and in the house

23 And JESUS said to him, * "IF THOU CANST? ‡ All things can for the BELIEVING."

24 The FATHER of the CHILD immediately exclaiming, said, "I do believe; help My UNBELIEF."

25 And JESUS perceiving That the Crowd was running together, he rebuked the IMPURE SPIRIT, saying to it, "DUMB and *DEAF SPIRIT, I command thee; come out of him, and enter him no more."

26 And crying out, and greatly convulsing him, it came out; and he became like one dead, so that many said, "He is dead."

27 But JESUS taking * his HAND, raised him, and he stood up.

28 ‡ And having entered a House, his DISCIPLES asked him privately, "Why could not we cast it out?"

29 And he said to them, "This KIND can go out by nothing, except by Prayer."

30 And departing from that place, they passed through GALILEE, and he desired that no one should know it;

31 for he taught his DISCIPLES; and he said to them, ‡ "The SON of MAN is † being delivered into the Hands of Men, and they will kill him; and having been put to death, * after Three Days he will rise."

32 But THEY did not understand the WORD, and were afraid to ask HIM.

33 And he came to Capernaum; and being in the

---

* VATICAN MANUSCRIPT.—23. "IF THOU CANST? All things." 24. And—*omit.* 24. with tears—*omit.* 25. and DEAF. 27. his HAND. 29. and Fasting.—*omit.* 31. to him—*omit.* 31 after Three Days he will rise.

† 31. The parallel passage in Matt. xvii. 22, reads—"The SON of MAN is about to be delivered into the Hands of Men."

‡ 23. Matt. xvii. 20; Mark xi. 23. Luke xvii. 6; John xi. 40. ‡ 28 Matt. xvii. 19. ‡ 31. Matt. xvii. 22; Luke ix. 44.

γενομενος, επηρωτα αυτους· Τι εν τῃ ὁδῳ
being, he asked them; What on the way
*[προς ἑαυτους] διελογιζεσθε; 34 Οἱ δε εσιω-
[among yourselves] were you disputing? They but were
πων· προς αλληλους γαρ διελεχθησαν εν τῃ
silent; with one another for they had disputed on the
ὁδῳ, τις μειζων. 35 Και καθισας, εφωνησε
way, who greater. And sitting down, he called
τους δωδεκα, και λεγει αυτοις· Ει τις θελει
the twelve, and says to them: If any one desires
πρωτος ειναι, εσται παντων εσχατος, και παν-
first to be, he will be of all last, and of
των διακονος. 36 Και λαβων παιδιον, εστησεν
all a servant. And taking a little child, he placed
αυτο εν μεσῳ αυτων, και εναγκαλισαμενος
it in midst of them, and embracing in his arms
αυτο, ειπεν αυτοις· 37 Ὁς εαν ἑν των τοιουτων
it, he said to them; Whoever one of the such
παιδιων δεξηται επι τῳ ονοματι μου, εμε δεχε-
little children may receive in the name of me, me receives;
ται· και ὁς εαν εμε δεξηται, ουκ εμε δεχεται,
and whoever me may receive, not me receives,
αλλα τον αποστειλαντα με. 38 Απεκριθη δε
but the having sent me. Answered and
αυτῳ Ιωαννης, λεγων· Διδασκαλε, ειδομεν τινα
to him John, saying: O teacher, I saw one
τῳ ονοματι σου εκβαλλοντα δαιμονια· και εκω-
to the name of thee casting out demons: and we
λυσαμεν αυτον, ὁτι ουκ ακολουθει ἡμιν. 39 Ὁ
forbad him, because not he follows us. He
δε Ιησους ειπε· Μη κωλυετε αυτον. Ουδεις γαρ
but Jesus said: Not do you forbid him. No one for
εστιν, ὁς ποιησει δυναμιν επι τῳ ονοματι μου,
is, who will do a mighty work in the name of me,
και δυνησεται ταχυ κακολογησαι με. 40 Ὁς
and will be able readily to speak evil of me. Who
γαρ ουκ εστι καθ' ὑμων, ὑπερ ὑμων εστιν. 41 Ὁς
for not is against you, for you is. Who
γαρ αν ποτισῃ ὑμας ποτηριον ὑδατος, εν
for ever may give drink to you a cup of water, in
ονοματι, ὁτι χριστου εστε, αμην λεγω ὑμιν, ου
name, because of Anointed you are, indeed I say to you, not
μη απολεσῃ τον μισθον αὑτου. 42 Και ὁς αν
not he may lose the reward of himself. And whoever
σκανδαλισῃ ἑνα των μικρων, των πιστευοντων
may insnare one of the little ones, of the believing
εις εμε, καλον εστιν αυτῳ μαλλον, ει περικειται
into me, good it is to him rather, if hangs
λιθος μυλικος περι τον τραχηλον αυτου, και
a stone of a mill around the neck of him, and
βεβληται εις την θαλασσαν. 43 Και εαν σκαν-
has been cast into the sea. And if may
δαλιζῃ σε ἡ χειρ σου, αποκοψον αυτην· καλον
insnare thee the hand of thee, cut thou off her: good

HOUSE, he asked them, ‡"What did you dispute about on the ROAD?"

34 But THEY were silent; for they had disputed with each other, on the ROAD, as to who would be greatest.

35 And sitting down, he called the TWELVE, and says to them; ‡If any one desires to be first, he will be last of all, and a Servant of all."

36 And ‡taking a little Child, he placed it in the Midst of them, and embracing it in his arms, he said to them,

37 "Whoever may receive one SUCH little Child in my NAME, receives Me; ‡and whoever *receives Me, receives not Me, but HIM who SENT me."

38 ‡And John *spoke to him, saying, "Teacher, we saw one expelling Demons in thy NAME, and we forbad him, Because he does not follow us."

39 But JESUS said, "Do not forbid him; ‡for there is no one who will do a Miracle in my NAME, and be able rashly to reproach me.

40 For he who is not against you, is for you.

41 ‡For whoever may give you a Cup of Water to drink in *the NAME, That you are CHRIST'S, indeed I say to you, He shall by no means lose his REWARD.

42 ‡And whoever may insnare one of *THESE LITTLE-ONES BELIEVING in me, it would be better for him if a Millstone should be fastened to his NECK, and he should be thrown into the SEA.

43 ‡And if thy HAND insnare thee, cut it off; it

* VATICAN MANUSCRIPT.—33. among themselves—*omit*. 37. receives Me. 38. spoke to him. 41. the NAME, That you are CHRIST'S. 42. THESE LITTLE-ONES.

‡ 33. Matt. xviii. 1; Luke ix. 46; xxii. 24. ‡ 35. Matt. xx. 26, 27; Mark x. 43. ‡ 36. Matt. xviii. 2; Mark x. 16. ‡ 37. Matt. x. 40; Luke ix. 48. ‡ 38. Luke ix. 49. ‡ 39. 1 Cor. xii. 3. ‡ 41. Matt. x. 42. ‡ 42. Matt. xviii. 6; Luke xvii. 1. ‡ 43. Deut. xii 6; Matt. v. 29; xviii. 8.

σοι εστι κυλλον εις την ζωην εισελθειν, η τας
to thee it is crippled into the life to enter, than the
δυο χειρας εχοντα απελθειν εις την γεενναν,
two hands having to go into the Gehenna,
εις το πυρ το ασβεστον, 44 *[οπου ὁ σκωληξ
into the fire the inextinguishable, [where the worm
αυτων ου τελευτᾳ, και το πυρ ου σβεννυται.]
of them not dies, and the fire not is quenched.]
45 Και εαν ὁ πους σου σκανδαλιζῃ σε, αποκοψον
And if the foot of thee may insnare thee, cut thou off
αυτον· καλον εστι σοι εισελθειν εις την ζωην
him; good it is to thee to enter into the life
χωλον, ἠ τους δυο ποδας εχοντα βληθηναι εις
lame, than the two feet having to be cast into
την γεενναν. *[εις το πυρ το ασβεστον, 46 οπου
the Gehenna, [into the fire the inextinguishable, where
ὁ σκωληξ αυτων ου τελευτᾳ, και το πυρ ου
the worm of them not dies, and the fire not
σβεννυται.] 47 Και εαν ὁ οφθαλμος σου σκαν-
is quenched.] And if the eye of thee may
δαλιζῃ σε, εκβαλε αυτον· καλον σοι εστι μονο-
insnare thee, cast thou out him; good to thee it is one-
φθαλμον εισελθειν εις την βασιλειαν του θεου,
eyed to enter into the kingdom of the God,
ἠ δυο οφθαλμους εχοντα βληθηναι εις την γε-
than two eyes having to be cast into the Ge-
ενναν *[του πυρος,] 48 ὁπου ὁ σκωληξ αυτων
henna [of the fire,] where the worm of them
ου τελευτᾳ, και το πυρ ου σβεννυται. 49 Πας
not dies, and the fire not is quenched. Every one
γαρ πυρι ἁλισθησεται· *[και πασα θυσια
for with fire shall be salted; [and every sacrifice
ἁλι αλισθησεται.] 50 Καλον το ἁλας· εαν δε
with salt shall be salted.] Good the salt; if but
το ἁλας αναλον γενεται, εν τινι αυτο αρτυ-
the salt without taste may become, with what it will you
σετε; Εχετε εν ἑαυτοις ἁλας, και ειρηνευετε
season? Have you in yourselves salt, and be you at peace
εν αλληλοις.
with one another.

ΚΕΦ. ι'. 10.

1 Και εκειθεν αναστας ερχεται εις τα ὁρια
And from thence arising he comes into the borders
της Ιουδαιας, δια του περαν του Ιορδανου· και
of the Judea, by the other side of the Jordan; and
συμπορευονται παλιν οχλοι προς αυτον· και,
come together again crowds to him; and,
ὡς ειωθει, παλιν εδιδασκεν αυτους. 2 Και
as he had been accustomed, again he taught them. And
προσελθοντες Φαρισαιοι επηρωτησαν αυτον· Ει
approaching Pharisees asked him; If
εξεστιν ανδρι γυναικα απολυσαι; πειραζοντες
it is lawful for a man a wife to release? trying

is better for thee to enter
LIFE crippled, than having
TWO Hands to depart to
†GEHENNA, into THAT IN-
EXTINGUISHABLE FIRE;
44 †[where the WORM
dies not, and the FIRE is
not quenched.]
45 And if thy FOOT in-
snare thee, cut it off; it is
better for thee to enter
lame into LIFE, than hav-
ing TWO Feet, to be cast
into GEHENNA, †[into the
UNQUENCHABLE FIRE;
46 where the WORM dies
not, and the FIRE is not
quenched.]
47 And if thine EYE in-
snare thee, pluck it out;
it is better for thee to enter one-eyed into the
KINGDOM of GOD, than
having Two Eyes to be cast
into * Gehenna;
48 ‡ where their WORM
dies not, and the FIRE is
not quenched.
49 For every one shall
be salted with fire; †[and
every Sacrifice shall be
seasoned with Salt.]
50 ‡ SALT is good; but
if the SALT become taste-
less, how will you restore
its saltness? Have Salt in
yourselves, and be at
peace with one another."

CHAPTER X.

1 ‡ And arising from
thence, he comes into the
CONFINES of JUDEA, *even
beyond the JORDAN; and
again Crowds come toge-
ther to him, and again, as
he had been accustomed,
he taught them.
2 ‡ And Pharisees ap-
proaching, asked him, to
try him, "Is it lawful for
a Man to dismiss his
Wife?"

* VATICAN MANUSCRIPT.—44. where the WORM dies not, and the FIRE is not quenched—*omit*. 45 & 46. into the INEXTINGUISHABLE FIRE; where their WORM dies not, and the FIRE is not quenched—*omit*. 47. Gehenna. 47. of FIRE—*omit*. 49. and every Sacrifice shall be seasoned with Salt—*omit*. 1. even beyond the JORDAN.

† 43. A Hebrew term, meaning the valley of the son of Hinnom. For futher remarks see Appendix. † 44, 45, 46, 49. The clauses bracketed in these verses, are not [illegible] in the *Vatican*. They are marked as doubtful by Griesbach, and are expunged by Tischendorf

‡ 48. Isa. lxvi. 24. ‡ 50. Matt. v. 13; Luke xiv. 34. ‡ 1. Matt. xix. 1; John x 40; i. 7 ‡ 2. Matt. xix. 3.

αυτον. [3] Ὁ δε αποκριθεις ειπεν αυτοις· Τι
him. He and answering said to them; What
ὑμιν ενετειλατο Μωσης; [4] Οἱ δε ειπον· Μωσης
to you did enjoin Moses? They and said; Moses
επετρεψε βιβλιον αποστασιου γραψαι, και απο-
allowed a scroll of separation to be written, and to re-
λυσαι. [5] Και *[αποκριθεις] ὁ Ιησους ειπεν
lease. And [answering] the Jesus said
αυτοις· Προς την σκληροκαρδιαν ὑμων εγραψεν
to them, For the hardness-of heart of you he wrote
ὑμιν την εντολην ταυτην. [6] Απο δε αρχης
to you the commandment this. From but a beginning
κτισεως αρσεν και θηλυ εποιησεν αυτους ὁ θεος.
of creation a male and a female he made them the God.
[7] "Ενεκεν τουτου καταλειψει ανθρωπος τον
"On account of this shall leave a man the
πατερα αὑτου και την μητερα, *[και προσκολ-
father of himself and the mother, [and shall be closely
ληθησεται προς την γυναικα αὑτου·] [8] Και
united to the wife of himself,] and
εσονται οἱ δυο εις σαρκα μιαν." Ὡστε ουκετι
shall be the two into flesh one." So that no longer
εισι δυο, αλλα μια σαρξ. [9] Ὁ ουν ὁ θεος συνε-
they are two, but one flesh. What then the God has join-
ζευξεν, ανθρωπος μη χωριζετω. [10] Και εν τῃ
ed together, a man not disunites. And in the
οικιᾳ παλιν οἱ μαθηται αυτου περι του
house again the disciples of him concerning of the
αυτου επηρωτησαν αυτον. [11] Και λεγει
him asked him. And he says
αυτοις· Ὁς εαν απολυσῃ την γυναικα αὑτου,
to them; Whoever may release the wife of himself
και γαμησῃ αλλην, μοιχαται επ' αυτην.
and may marry another, commits adultery with her.
[12] Και εαν γυνη απολυσῃ τον ανδρα αὑτης, και
And if a woman may release the husband of herself, and
γαμηθῃ αλλῳ, μοιχαται. [13] Και προσεφερον
may be married to another, commits adultery. And they brought
αυτῳ παιδια, ἱνα ἁψηται αυτων· οἱ δε μαθηται
to him little children that he might touch them; the but disciples
επετιμων τοις προσφερουσιν. [14] Ιδων δε ὁ
rebuked those bringing. Seeing but the
Ιησους ηγανακτησε, και ειπεν αυτοις· Αφετε
Jesus was displeased, and said to them; Allow
τα παιδια ερχεσθαι προς με, μη κωλυετε αυτα·
the little children to come to me, not hinder them;
των γαρ τοιουτων εστιν ἡ βασιλεια του θεου.
of the for such like is the kingdom of the God.
[15] Αμην λεγω ὑμιν, ὁς εαν μη δεξηται την βασι-
Indeed I say to you, whoever not may receive the king-

3 And HE answering said to them, "What did Moses command You?"

4 And THEY said, ‡ "Moses permitted a Writ of Divorce to be written, and to dismiss her."

5 And JESUS said to them, "Because of your STUBBORN DISPOSITION he wrote you this COMMAND.

6 But from the Beginning of Creation, * he made them Male and Female.

7 ‡ On account of this a Man shall leave his FATHER and MOTHER, * and adhere to his WIFE;

8 and the TWO shall become one Flesh; so that they are no longer Two, but One Flesh.

9 What GOD, then, has united, let no Man sever."

10 And, in the HOUSE, * the DISCIPLES again asked him * concerning this.

11 And he says to them ‡ "Whoever shall dismiss his WIFE, and marry another, commits adultery with her.

12 And if * she who † dismisses her HUSBAND, shall marry another, she commits adultery.

13 ‡ And they brought little Children to him, that he might touch them; and the DISCIPLES rebuked * them.

14 But JESUS seeing it, was displeased, and said to them, "Allow the LITTLE CHILDREN to come to me, and forbid them not; for to SUCH LIKE belongs the KINGDOM of GOD.

15 Indeed I say to you, Whoever does not receive the KINGDOM of GOD, like

* VATICAN MANUSCRIPT.—5. answering—*omit.* 6. he made them. 7. and adhere to his WIFE—*omit.* 10. the DISCIPLES. 10. concerning this. 12. she who dismisses her HUSBAND, shall marry another. 13. them. But.

† 12. Strictly speaking, a Jewish wife could not divorce her husband; therefore, *apolusee* may be considered as used with some license, and perhaps, too, with reference to the customs of the Gentiles rather than the Jews, and intended as a rule to the Apostles for *general* application, and which should put both sexes on the same footing.

‡ 4. Deut. xxiv. 1; Matt. v 31; xix. 7. ‡ 7 Gen. ii. 24; 1 Cor. vi 16; Eph v 31 ‡ 11. Matt. v. 32; xix 9; Luke xvi. 18; Rom. vii. 3; 1 Cor. vii. 10, 11 ‡ 13. Matt. xix 13 Luke xviii. 15.

λειαν του θεου ὡς παιδιον, ου μη εισελθῃ εις
dom of the God like a little child, not not may enter into
αυτην: 16 Και εναγκαλισαμενος αυτα, τιθεις
her. And embracing in his arms them, having placed
τας χειρας επ' αυτα, ηυλογει αυτα.
the hands upon them, he blessed them.

17 Και εκπορευομενου αυτου εις ὁδον, προσ-
And going out of him into a way, run-
δραμων εἱς, και γονυπετησας αυτον, επηρωτα
ning up one, and kneeling before him, he asked
αυτον· Διδασκαλε αγαθε, τι ποιησω, ἱνα ζωην
him; O teacher good, what must I do, that life
αιωνιον κληρονομησω; 18 Ὁ δε Ιησους ειπεν
age-lasting I may inherit? The and Jesus said
αυτῳ· Τι με λεγεις αγαθον; ουδεις αγαθος, ει
to him; Why me callest thou good? no one good, if
μη εἱς, ὁ θεος. 19 Τας εντολας οιδας· "Μη
not one, the God. The commandments thou knowest; "Not
μοιχευσῃς· Μη φονευσῃς· Μη κλεψῃς·
thou must commit adultery; Not thou must kill; Not thou must steal;
Μη ψευδομαρτυρησῃς· *[Μη αποστερησῃς·]
Not thou must testify falsely; [Not thou must defraud.]
Τιμα τον πατερα σου, και την μητερα." 20 Ὁ
Honor the father of thee, and the mother." He
δε *[αποκριθεις] ειπεν αυτῳ· Διδασκαλε, ταυτα
but [answering] said to him, O teacher, these
παντα εφυλαξαμην εκ νεοτητος μου. 21 Ὁ δε
all I kept from childhood of me. He but
Ιησους εμβλεψας αυτῳ, ηγαπησεν αυτον, και
Jesus looking on him, loved him, and
ειπεν αυτῳ· Ἑν σοι ὑστερει· ὑπαγε, ὁσα
said to him: One to thee lacks: go, whatever
εχεις πωλησον, και δος τοις πτωχοις· και
thou hast sell, and give to the poor: and
ἑξεις θησαυρον εν ουρανῳ· και δευρο, ακολ-
thou shalt have treasure in heaven: and hither, fol-
ουθει μοι, *[αρας τον σταυρον.] 22 Ὁ δε στυγ-
low me, [taking up the cross.] He but looking
νασας επι τῳ λογῳ, απηλθε λυπουμενος· ην
sad at the word, went away sorrowing; he was
γαρ εχων κτηματα πολλα. 23 Και περιβλεψα-
for having possessions many. And looking
μενος ὁ Ιησους, λεγει τοις μαθηταις αὑτου·
round the Jesus, says to the disciples of himself:
Πως δυσκολως οἱ τα χρηματα εχοντες εις την
How hardly those the riches having into the
βασιλειαν του θεου εισελευσονται. 24 Οἱ δε
kingdom of the God shall enter. They and
μαθηται εθαμβουντο επι τοις λογοις αυτου. Ὁ
disciples were astonished at the words of him. The
δε Ιησους παλιν αποκριθεις λεγει αυτοις· Τεκνα,
but Jesus again answering says to them: Children,
πως δυσκολον εστι *[τους πεποιθοτας επι τοις
how difficult it is [those having confidence in the
χρημασιν,] εις την βασιλειαν του θεου εισελθειν.
riches,] into the kingdom of the God to enter.

a little Child, he will by no means enter it."

16 And taking them in his arms, and placing his HANDS on them, he blessed them.

17 ‡ And going out into the Road, one running up, and kneeling before him, asked him, "Good Teacher! what must I do, that I may inherit aionian Life."

18 And JESUS said to him, Why dost thou call Me good? No one is good, except one, GOD.

19 Thou knowest the COMMANDMENTS; ‡ *Do not commit murder; Do not commit adultery; Do not steal; Do not testify falsely; Honor thy FATHER and MOTHER."

20 And HE said to him, "Teacher, all these have I kept from my Childhood."

21 And JESUS looking on him, loved him, and said to him, "One thing thou lackest; go, sell whatever thou hast, and give to the *Poor, and thou shalt have ‡ Treasure in Heaven; and come, follow me."

22 But HE was grieved at the WORD, and went away sorrowing; for he had great Possessions."

23 Then JESUS looking round, says to his DISCIPLES, ‡ "With what difficulty will THOSE HAVING RICHES enter the KINGDOM of GOD."

24 And the DISCIPLES were astonished at his WORDS. But JESUS again answering, says to them, ‡ "Children, how difficult it is to enter the KINGDOM of GOD.

* VATICAN MANUSCRIPT.—19. Do not commit murder; Do not commit adultery. 19. Do not defraud—*omit.* 20. answering—*omit.* 21. Poor. 21. taking up the CROSS—*omit.* 24. those having confidence in RICHES—*omit.*

‡ 17. Matt. xix. 16; Luke xviii. 18. ‡ 19. Exod. xx. 13. Rom. xiii. 9. ‡ 21. Matt. vi. 19, 20; xix. 21; Luke xii. 33, xvi. 9. ‡ 23. Matt. xix. 23; Luke xviii. 24. ‡ 24. Job xxxi. 24 25; Psa. lii. 7; lxii. 10; 1 Tim. vi. 17.

25 Ευκοπωτερον εστι καμηλον δια της τρυμα-
Easier it is a camel through the hole
λιας της ῥαφιδος διελθειν, η πλουσιον εις την
of the needle to pass, than a rich man into the
βασιλειαν του θεου εισελθειν. 26 Οἱ δε περισ-
kingdom of the God to enter. They and greatly
σως εξεπλησσοντο, λεγοντες προς ἑαυτους·
were amazed, saying among themselves;
Και τις δυναται σωθηναι; 27 Εμβλεψας δε
And who - is able to be saved? Looking on and
αυτοις ὁ Ιησους, λεγει· Παρα ανθρωποις αδυνα-
them the Jesus, says; With men imposs-
τον αλλ' ου παρα τῳ θεῳ· παντα γαρ δυνατα
ble but not with the God: all for possible
εστι παρα τῳ θεῳ. 28 Ηρξατο ὁ Πετρος λεγειν
is with the God. Began the Peter to say
αυτῳ· Ιδου ἡμεις αφηκαμεν παντα, και ηκολ-
to him: Lo, we left all, and fol-
ουθησαμεν σοι. 29 *[Αποκριθεις] ὁ Ιησους
lowed thee. [Answering] the Jesus
ειπεν· Αμην λεγω ὑμιν, ουδεις εστιν, ὁς αφη-
said: Indeed I say to you, no one is, who has
κεν οικιαν, η αδελφος, η αδελφας, η πατερα, η
left houses, or brothers, or sisters, or father, or
μητερα, *[η γυναικα,] η τεκνα, η αγρους,
mother, [or wife,] or children, or fields,
ἑνεκεν εμου και ἑνεκεν του ευγγελιου, 30 εαν
on account of me and on account of the glad tidings, if
μη λαβῃ ἑκατονταπλασιονα, νυν εν τῳ
not he may receive a hundred fold, now in the
καιρῳ τουτω, οικιας, και αδελφους, και αδελ-
season this, houses, and brothers, and sis-
φας, και μητερας, και τεκνα, και αγρους, μετα
ters, and mothers, and children, and fields, with
διωγμων, και εν τω αιωνι τῳ ερχομενῳ ζωην
persecutions, and in the age to come, life
αιωνιον. 31 Πολλοι δε εσονται πρωτοι, εσχα-
age-lasting. Many but shall be first, last;
τοι· και εσχατοι, πρωτοι. 32 Ησαν δε εν τῃ
and last, first. They were and in the
ὁδῳ αναβαινοντες εις Ἱεροσολυμα· και ην
way going up to Jerusalem: and was
πρυαγων αυτους ὁ Ιησους· και εθαμβουντο,
going before them the Jesus: and they were amazed,
και ακολουθοντες εφοβουντο. Και παραλαβων
and following they were afraid. And taking aside
παλιν τους δωδεκα, ηρξατο αυτοις λεγειν τα
again the twelve, he began to them to tell the things
μελλοντα αὑτῳ συμβαινειν· 33 Ὁτι ιδου, ανα-
being about to him to happen: For lo, we
βαινομεν εις Ἱεροσολυμα, και ὁ υἱος του ανθρω-
go up to Jerusalem, and the son of the man
που παραδοθησεται τοις αρχιερευσι και τοις
will be delivered up to the high-priests and to the
γραμματευσι· και κατακρινουσιν αυτον θανατῳ,
scribes: and they will condemn him to death,
και παραδωσουσιν αυτον τοις εθνεσι, 34 και
and they will deliver up him to the Gentiles, and

25 It is easier for a Camel to pass through the NEEDLE'S EYE, than for a Rich man to enter the KINGDOM of GOD."

26 And they were exceedingly astonished, saying *to him, "Who then can be saved?"

27 And JESUS looking on them, says, "With Men it may be impossible, but not with GOD; for with *God everything is possible."

28 ‡PETER began to say to him, "Behold, we have forsaken all, and followed thee."

29 JESUS said, "Indeed I say to you, There is no one who has left House, or Brothers, or Sisters, or Father, or Mother, *or Wife, or Children, or Lands, on my account, and on account of the GLAD TIDINGS,

30 who will not receive ‡a hundred-fold, now, in this TIME,—Houses, and Brothers, and Sisters, and Mothers, and Children, and Lands,—but with Persecutions; and in the AGE to COME, aionian Life.

31 ‡But many will be first, who are last; and last, who are first."

32 ‡And they were on the ROAD going up to Jerusalem; and JESUS was preceding them; and they were *amazed. And THEY who FOLLOWED him were afraid as ‡he took aside again the TWELVE, and began to tell them the THINGS BEING ABOUT to befall him.

33 "Behold, we are going up to Jerusalem, and the SON of MAN will be delivered up to the HIGH-PRIESTS, and to the SCRIBES; and they will condemn him to death, and will deliver him up to the GENTILES;

* VATICAN MANUSCRIPT.—26. to him, "Who." 27. God. 29. answering—*omit.* 29. or Wife—*omit.* 32. amazed And THEY who FOLLOWED him were afraid, as he took.

† 28. Matt. xix. 27; Luke xviii. 28. ‡ 30. Luke xviii. 30. ‡ 31. Matt. xix. 30; Luke xiii. 30. ‡ 32. Matt. xx. 17; Luke xviii. 30. ‡ 32. Mark viii. 31; ix. 31; Luke ix. 22: xviii. 31.

εμπαιξουσιν αυτῳ, και μαστιγωσουσιν αυτον,
they will mock him, and they will scourge him,
και εμπτυσουσιν αυτῳ, και αποκτενουσιν αυτον·
and they will spit upon him. and they will kill him;
και τῃ τριτῃ ἡμερᾳ αναστησεται. 35 Και προσ-
and the third day he will stand up. And come
πορευονται αυτῳ Ιακωβος και Ιωαννης, οἱ υἱοι
to him James and John, the sons
Ζεβεδαιου, λεγοντες· Διδασκαλε, θελομεν, ἱνα
of Zebedee, saying; O teacher, we wish, that
ὁ εαν αιτησωμεν, ποιησῃς ἡμιν. 36 Ὁ δε ειπεν
whatever we may ask, thou mayest do for us. He but said
αυτοις· Τι θελετε ποιησαι με ὑμιν; Οἱ δε
to them; What do you wish to do me for you? They and
ειπον αυτῳ· Δος ἡμιν, ἱνα εἱς εκ δεξιων σου,
said to him; Give to us, that one at right of thee,
και εἱς εξ ευωνυμων σου καθισωμεν εν τῃ δοξῃ
and one at left of thee we may sit in the glory
σου. 38 Ὁ δε Ιησους ειπεν αυτοις· Ουκ οιδατε,
of thee. The and Jesus said to them; Not you know,
τι αιτεισθε. Δυνασθε πιειν το ποτηριον, ὁ
what you ask. Are you able to drink the cup, which
εγω πινω, και το βαπτισμα, ὁ εγω βαπτιζομαι,
I drink, and the dipping, which I am dipped.
βαπτισθηναι; 39 Οἱ δε ειπον αυτῳ· Δυναμεθα.
to be dipped? They and said to him; We are able.
Ὁ δε Ιησους ειπεν αυτοις· Το *[μεν] ποτη-
The and Jesus said to them; The [indeed] cup,
ριον, ὁ εγω πινω, πιεσθε· και το βαπτισμα,
which I drink, you will drink; and the dipping,
ὁ εγω βαπτιζομαι, βαπτισθησεσθε· 40 το δε
which I am dipped, you will be dipped; the but
καθισαι εκ δεξιων μου και εξ ευωνυμων, ουκ εσ-
to sit at right of me and at left, not it
τιν εμον δουναι, αλλ' οἱς ἡτοιμασται.
is mine to give, but to whom it has been prepared.
41 Και ακουσαντες οἱ δεκα, ηρξαντο αγανακτειν
And having heard the ten, they began to be angry
περι Ιακωβου και Ιωαννου. 42 Ὁ δε Ιησους
about James and John. The but Jesus
προσκαλεσαμενος αυτους, λεγει αυτους· Οιδα-
having called them, he says to them; You know
τε, ὁτι οἱ δοκουντες αρχειν των εθνων, κατακυ-
that those presuming to rule the nations, lord it
ριευουσιν αυτων, και οἱ μεγαλοι αυτων κατεξου-
over them, and the great of them exercise
σιαζουσιν αυτων. 43 Ουχ οὑτω δε εσται εν
authority over them. Not so but it shall be among
ὑμιν· αλλ' ὁς εαν θελῃ γενεσθαι μεγας εν
you; but whoever may wish to become great among
ὑμιν, εσται ὑμων διακονος· 44 και ὁς εαν θελῃ
you, shall be of you a servant; and whoever may wish

34 and they will mock
him, and *spit on him,
and scourge him, and put
him to death, and *after
Three Days he will rise."
35 And James and John,
the *TWO Sons of Zebedee,
come to him, *saying to
him, "O Teacher, we wish
that thou wouldst do for
us whatever we may *ask
thee."
36 And HE said to them,
"What do you desire me
to do for you?"
37 And THEY said to him,
"Grant to us that we may
sit, one at *thy Right
hand, and the other at
*thy Left, in thy GLORY."
38 But JESUS said to
them, "You know not
what you ask. Can you
drink the CUP which I
drink? *or undergo the
IMMERSION with which I
am being overwhelmed!"
39 And THEY said to
him, "We can." And JE-
SUS said to them, You will
drink the CUP which I
drink, and undergo the IM-
MERSION with which I
am being overwhelmed;
40 but to SIT at my
Right hand, *or at the
Left, is not mine to give,
except for whom it is prepared."
41 ‡And the TEN, hav-
ing heard, were indignant
against James and John.
42 *And Jesus, having
called them, he says to
them, ‡"You know That
THOSE presuming to rule
the NATIONS domineer
over them, and their GREAT
ones exercise authority
over them.
43 ‡But *it is not so
among you; but whoever
may desire to become great
among you, shall be Your
Servant;
44 and whoever *among
you may desire to become

* VATICAN MANUSCRIPT.—34. spit on him, and scourge him. 34. after Three Days he. 35. TWO Sons. 35. saying to him, "O Teacher." 35. ask thee. 37. the Right. 37. the Left. 38. or. 39. indeed—*omit*. 40. or at the Left. 42. And JESUS. 43. it is not so among you. 44. among you.

‡ 35. Matt. xx. 20. ‡ 41. Matt. xx. 24. ‡ 42. Luke xxii. 25. ‡ 43. Matt xx. 26, 28; Mark ix. 35; Luke ix. 48.

ὑμων γενεσθαι πρωτος, εσται παντων δουλος·
of you to become first, shall be of all a slave;
45 και γαρ ὁ υἱος του ανθρωπου ουκ ηλθε διακον-
and for the son of the man not came to be
ηθηναι, αλλα διακονησαι, και δουναι την ψυχην
served, but to serve, and to give the life
αὑτου λυτρον αντι πολλων.
of himself a ransom for many.

46 Και ερχονται εις Ἱεριχω· και εκπορευομενου
And they come into Jericho; and going out
αυτου απο Ἱεριχω, και των μαθητων αυτου, και
of him from Jericho, and the disciples of him, and
οχλου ἱκανου, υἱος Τιμαιου, Βαρτιμαιος ὁ τυφ-
a crowd great, a son of Timeus, Bartimeus the blind,
λος, εκαθητο παρα την ὁδον προσαιτων. 47 Και
sat by the way begging. And
ακουσας, ὁτι Ιησους ὁ Ναζωραιος εστιν, ηρξατο
hearing, that Jesus the Nazarite it is, he began
κραζειν και λεγειν· Ὁ υἱος Δαυιδ, Ιησου, ελεη-
to cry out and to say; The son of David, Jesus, have pity
σον με. 48 Και επετιμων αυτῳ πολλοι, ἱνα
on me. And rebuked him many, so that
σιωπηση· ὁ δε πολλῳ μαλλον εκραζειν· Υἱε
he might be silent; he but much more cried out; O son
Δαυιδ, ελεησον με. 49 Και στας ὁ Ιησους,
of David, have pity on me. And stopping the Jesus,
ειπεν αυτον φωνηθηναι· και φωνουσι τον τυφ-
told him to be called; and they called the blind,
λον, λεγοντες αυτῳ· Θαρσει, εγειρε· φωνει
saying to him; Take courage, rise up; he calls
σε. 50 Ὁ δε αποβαλων το ἱματιον αὑτου, αναστ-
thee. He and throwing off the mantle of himself, arising
τας ηλθε προς τον Ιησουν. 51 Και αποκριθεις
came to the Jesus. And answering
λεγει αυτῳ ὁ Ιησους· Τι θελεις ποιησω σοι;
says to him the Jesus; What dost thou wish I may do to thee?
Ὁ δε τυφλος ειπεν αυτῳ· Ῥαββουνι, ἱνα ανα-
The and blind said to him; Rabboni, that I may
βλεψω. 52 Ὁ δε Ιησους ειπεν αυτῳ· Ὑπαγε· ἡ
see again. The and Jesus said to him; Go; the
πιστις σου σεσωκε σε. Και ευθεως ανεβλεψε,
faith of thee has saved thee. And immediately he saw again,
και ηκολουθει αυτῳ εν τῃ ὁδῳ.
and followed him in the way.

ΚΕΦ. ια'. 11.

1 Και ὁτε εγγιζουσιν εις Ἱερουσαλημ, εις
And when they drew near to Jerusalem, to
Βηθφαγη και Βηθανιαν, προς το ορος των ελαι-
Bethphage and Bethany, to the mountain of the olive
ων, αποστελλει δυο των μαθητων αὑτου, και
trees, he sends two of the disciples of himself, and

Chief, shall be the Slave of All.

45 ‡For even the SON of MAN came not to be served, but to serve, and to give his LIFE a Ransom for many."

46 ‡And they came to Jericho. And as he was departing from Jericho with his DISCIPLES, and a great Crowd, *a Blind Beggar, †Bartimeus, (the SON of Timeus,) sat by the ROAD.

47 And hearing That it was Jesus the Nazarite, he began to cry out, and say, *"Jesus, SON of David, have pity on me!"

48 And many charged him to be silent; but HE cried out much more, "Son of David, have pity on me!"

49 And JESUS stopping, *said, "Call him." And they called the BLIND man, saying to him, "Take courage, arise; he calls thee."

50 And HE, throwing off his †MANTLE, *leaping up, came to JESUS.

51 And JESUS addressing him, said, "What dost thou wish I may do for thee?" The BLIND man said to him, †"Rabboni! that I may receive my sight."

52 And JESUS said to him, ‡"Go; thy FAITH has restored thee." And he immediately received sight, and followed *him on the ROAD.

CHAPTER XI.

1 And ‡when they drew near to Jerusalem, to Bethphage, and Bethany, near *the MOUNT of OLIVES, he sends Two of his DISCIPLES,

* VATICAN MANUSCRIPT.—46. Bartimeus, a Blind Beggar, the SON of Timeus, sat by the ROAD. And. 47. Son of David, Jesus, have. 49. said, "Call him." And. 50. leaping up, came. 52. him on the ROAD. 1. THAT MOUNT which is.

† 46. *Bartimeus*, is considered by many to be a *real name*, and not an explication of *ho whyos Timaion*. † 50. Or upper garment. This was of considerable dimensions, and enveloped the whole body. In those hot countries, they threw it aside when they were at work, or ploughing in the field.—*Wakefield.* † 51. *Rabboni*, an intensified signification of *Rabbi*, meaning *My Master;* the highest title of honor in the Jewish schools. It is only used in one other passage in the New Testament—John xx. 16.

‡ 45. Matt. xx. 28. ‡ 46. Matt. xx. 29; Luke xviii. 35. ‡ 52. Matt. ix. 22; Mark v. 34. ‡ 1. Matt. xxi 1; Luke xix. 29; John xii. 14.

λεγει αυτοις· 2 Ὑπαγετε εις την κωμην την
says to them: Go you into the town that
κατεναντι ὑμων· και ευθεως εισπορευομενοι
opposite you; and immediately entering
εις αυτην, εὑρησετε πωλον δεδεμενον, εφ' ὁν
into her, you will find a colt having been tied, upon which
ουδεις ανθρωπων κεκαθικε· λυσαντες αυτον
no one of men has sat; having loosed him
αγαγετε. 3 Και εαν τις ὑμιν ειπῃ· Το ποι-
lead you. And if any one to you should say; Why do
ειτε τουτο; ειπατε· *[Ὁτι] ὁ κυριος αυτου
you this? say you: [That] the master of him
χρειαν εχει· και ευθεως αυτον αποστελλει
need has, and immediately him he will send
ὡδε. 4 Απηλθον δε, και εὑρον πωλον δεδεμενον
here. They went and, and found a colt having been tied
προς την θυραν εξω επι του αμφοδου· και
near the door without in the street; and
λυουσιν αυτον. 5 Και τινες των εκει εστηκο-
they loose him. And some of those there stand-
των ελεγον αυτοις· Τι ποιειτε λυοντες τον
ing said to them; What do you loosing the
πωλον; 6 Οἱ δε ειπον αυτοις καθως ενετειλατο
colt? They and said to them even as commanded
ὁ Ιησους· και αφηκαν αυτους. 7 Και ηγαγον
the Jesus; and they suffered them. And they led
τον πωλον προς τον Ιησουν, και επιβαλλουσιν
the colt to the Jesus, and they threw upon
αυτῳ τα ἱματια αὑτων· και εκαθισεν επ' αυτῳ.
him the mantles of themselves; and he sat upon him.
8 Πολλοι δε τα ἱματια αὑτων εστρωσαν εις την
Many and the mantles of themselves spread in the
ὁδον· αλλοι δε στοιβαδας εκοπτον εκ των
way; others and branches cut off from the
δενδρων, *[και εστρωννυον εις την ὁδον.]
trees, [and scattered in the way.]
9 Και οἱ προαγοντες και οἱ ακολουθουντες
And those going before and those following
εκραζον, *[λεγοντες.] Ὡσαννα· ευλογημενος
did cry, [saying. Hosanna; worthy of blessing
ὁ ερχομενος *[εν ονοματι κυριου·] 10 ευλογη-
he coming [in name of Lord;] worthy of
μενη ἡ ερχομενη βασιλεια του πατρος ἡμων
blessing the coming kingdom of the father of us
Δαυιδ· ὡσαννα εν τοις ὑψιστοις. 11 Και εισηλ-
David; Hosanna in the highest. And en-
θεν εις Ἱεροσολυμα ὁ Ιησους, *[και] εις το
tered into Jerusalem the Jesus, [and] into the
ἱερον· και περιβλεψαμενος παντα, οψιας ηδη
temple; and having looked round on all, evening now
ουσης της ὡρας, εξηλθεν εις Βηθανιαν μετα
being the hour, he went out to Bethany with
των δωδεκα.
the twelve.

12 Και τῃ επαυριον εξελθοντων αυτων απο
And the next day coming out of them from

2 and says to them, "Go to THAT VILLAGE which is OVER AGAINST you, and as soon as you enter it, you will find a Colt tied, on which no Man has *yet sat: loose him, and bring him.

3 And if any one should say to you, 'Why do you this?' say, The MASTER needs it; and he will instantly send it hither."

4 And they went and found a Colt fastened at the DOOR outside, in the STREET; and they loosed it.

5 And some of THOSE STANDING there, said to them, "Why do you untie the COLT?"

6 And THEY said to them as JESUS had *directed; and they allowed them.

7 And they *led the COLT to JESUS, and threw on it their MANTLES; and he sat on it.

8 ‡And many spread their GARMENTS on the ROAD; and others cut *Branches, from the TREES, and scattered them on the ROAD.

9 And THOSE PRECEDING and THOSE FOLLOWING, shouted, "Hosanna!" ‡"'Blessed be HE who COMES in the Name of 'Jehovah!'"

10 "Blessed be the coming KINGDOM of our FATHER David!" ‡"Hosanna in the HIGHEST heaven!"

11 ‡And *JESUS went into Jerusalem, and into the TEMPLE. And having looked round on all things, it now being Evening, he went out to Bethany, with the TWELVE.

12 ‡And the NEXT DAY, as they were coming from Bethany, he was hungry;

* VATICAN MANUSCRIPT.—2. yet sat. 3. That—omit. 6. said; and. 7 bring. 8. Branches, cut down out of the FIELDS. And THEY, 8. and scattered in the WAY—omit. 9. saying—omit. 9. in the name of the Lord—omit. 11. he entered. 11. and—omit.

‡ 8. Matt. xxi. 8. ‡ 9. Psa. cxviii. 26. ‡ 10. Psa. cxlviii. 1. ‡ 11. Matt. xxi. 12. ‡ 12. Matt. xxi. 18.

Βηθανιας, επεινασε· 13 και ιδων συκην μακρο-
Bethany, he was hungry; and seeing a fig tree at a dis-
θεν, εχουσαν φυλλα, ηλθεν, ει αρα εὑρησει
tance, having leaves, he went, if perhaps he will find
τι εν αυτῃ· και ελθων επ' αυτην, ουδεν
any thing on her; and coming to her nothing
εὑρεν ει μη φυλλα· ου γαρ ην καιρος συκων.
he found except leaves: not for it was season of figs.
14 Και αποκριθεις ειπεν αυτῃ· Μηκετι εκ σου
And answering he said to her: No more of thee
εις τον αιωνα μηδεις καρπον φαγοι. Και
to the age no one fruit may eat. And
ηκουον οἱ μαθηται αυτου. 15 Και ερχονται εις
heard the disciples of him. And they come to
Ἱεροσολυμα· και εισελθων εις το ἱερον ηρξατο
Jerusalem: and going into the temple he began
εκβαλλειν τους πωλουντας και αγοραζοντας εν
to cast out those selling and buying in
τῳ ἱερῳ· και τας τραπεζας των κολλυβιστων,
the temple: and the tables the money-changers,
και τας καθεδρας των πωλουντων τας περιστε-
and the seats of those selling the doves
ρας κατεστρεψε· 16 και ουκ ηφιεν, ἱνα τις
he overturned: and not suffered, that any one
διενεγκῃ σκευος δια του ἱερου. 17 Και εδιδασ-
should carry an article through the temple. And he taught,
κε, λεγων *[αυτοις·] Ου γεγραπται· "Ὁτι
saying [to them:] Not is it written: "That
ὁ οικος μου, οικος προσευχης κληθησεται
the house of me, a house of prayer shall be called
πασι τοις εθνεσιν; ὑμεις δε εποιησατε αυτον
for all the nations? you but have made it
σπηλαιον λῃστων." 18 Και ηκουσαν οἱ γραμ-
a den of robbers." And heard the scribes
ματεις και οἱ αρχιερεις, και εζητουν πως αυτον
and the high-priests, and they sought how him
απολεσουσιν· εφοβουντο γαρ αυτον, ὁτι πας ὁ
they might destroy: they feared for him, because all the
οχλος εξεπλησσετο επι τῃ διδαχῃ αυτου. 19 Και
crowd was amazed at the teaching of him. And
ὁτε οψε εγενετο, εξεπορευετο εξω της πολεως.
when evening it became, he went out of the city.
20 Και πρωι παραπορευομενοι, ειδον την
And in the morning passing along, they saw the

13 and observing a Fig-tree, at a distance, having Leaves, he went to search for † fruit on it, (for it was not yet † the *SEASON for Figs.) And having come to it, he found nothing but Leaves.

14 Then he said to it † "Let no one eat Fruit of thee to the AGE!" And his DISCIPLES heard him.

15 ‡ And they came to Jerusalem; and going into the TEMPLE, he drove out THOSE SELLING and buying, and overturned the TABLES of the BANKERS, and the SEATS of THOSE SELLING DOVES;

16 and would not permit any one to carry an Article through the TEMPLE.

17 He also taught * and said, "Is it not written, ‡ 'My HOUSE shall be called a House of Prayer for All NATIONS?' but you have made it a Den of Robbers."

18 ‡ And the *HIGH-PRIESTS and the SCRIBES heard, and sought how they might destroy him; for they feared him, Because All the CROWD was astonished at his TEACHING.

19 And when it was Evening, he went out of the CITY.

20 ‡ And passing along in the Morning, they saw

* VATICAN MANUSCRIPT.—13. SEASON. 17. and said, "Is it not." 17. to them—*omit*. 18. HIGH-PRIESTS and the SCRIBES.

† 13. That Jesus had a right to gather figs from this tree, if there had been any upon it, appears from the law of Moses, mentioned in Deut. xxiii 24, 25. Josephus alluding to this law, mentions ripe fruits in general, not grapes and corn only. His words are—"Let not passengers, (whether natives or strangers,) be hindered from touching the ripe fruits. Let them be permitted to fill themselves with them, but not to carry any away." That some ripe figs might be expected on fig-trees at that time of the year will appear, says *Pearce*, from the following considerations;—"Jesus went up to this fig-tree on the 11th day of the month Nisan, i. e. three days before the Passover, which was always on the 14th day of it. 'On the morrow after the Sabbath' which followed the Passover, the first-fruits were to be offered to God in the temple." Lev. xxiii. 11. The leaves on the tree indicated that summer was nigh, Matt. xxiv. 32, and that fruit might be reasonably expected, especially as the fig-tree shoots forth its fruit before the leaves. If, therefore, the tree bore figs, now was the period to find and eat them. † 13. That is, the season for gathering them. † 14. Some cavillers object to this miracle of our Savior, and ask, What right had he to destroy this fig-tree? In answer, observe, that the tree was evidently barren, and therefore of no use to any one; that it could hardly be private property, for it was on the public road; and that it was made the means of inculcating a great moral truth on the minds of his disciples.

‡ 13. Matt. xxi. 19. ‡ 15. Matt. xxi. 12; Luke xix. 45; John ii. 14. ‡ 17. Isa. lvi. 7. ‡ 18. Matt. xxi. 45, 46 Luke xix. 47. ‡ 20. Matt. xxi. 19.

συκην εξηραμμενην εκ ριζων· 21 Και αναμ-
fig-tree having been withered from roots; And remem-
νησθεις ὁ Πετρος, λεγει αυτῳ· Ῥαββι, ιδε, ἡ
bering the Peter, says to him; Rabbi, lo, the
συκη, ἡν κατηρασω, εξηρανται. 22 Και
fig-tree, which thou didst curse, has been withered. And
αποκριθεις ὁ Ιησους λεγει αυτοις· Εχετε πισ-
answering the Jesus says to them; Have you faith
τιν θεου. 23 Αμην γαρ λεγω ὑμιν, ὁτι ὁς αν
of God. Indeed for I say to you, that whoever
ειπῃ τῳ ορει τουτῳ· Αρθητι, και βληθητι
may say to the mountain this; Be lifted up, and cast
εις την θαλασσαν· και μη διακριθῃ εν τῃ
into the sea; and not should doubt in the
καρδιᾳ αὑτου, αλλα πιστευσῃ ὁτι ἁ λεγει
heart of himself, but should believe that what he says
γινεται· εσται αυτῳ ὁ εαν ειπῃ. 24 Δια τουτο
comes to pass; it shall be to him whatever he may say. Through this
λεγω ὑμιν, παντα ὁσα αν προσευχομενοι αιτεισ-
I say to you, all things whatever praying you desire
θε, πιστευετε ὁτι λαμβανετε, και εσται ὑμιν.
believe you that you receive, and it shall be to you.
25 Και ὁταν στηκητε προσευχομενοι, αφιετε, ει
And when you stand praying, forgive, if
τι εχετε κατα τινος· ἱνα και ὁ πατηρ
any thing you have against any one; that also the father
ὑμων, ὁ εν τοις ουρανοις, αφῃ ὑμιν τα παραπ-
of you, that in the heavens, may forgive you the faults
τωματα ὑμων. 26 Ει δε ὑμεις ουκ αφιετε, ουδε
of you. If but you not forgive, neither
ὁ πατηρ ὑμων, ὁ εν τοις ουρανοις, αφησει τα
the father of you, that in the heavens, will forgive the
παραπτωματα ὑμων. 27 Και ερχονται παλιν
faults of you. And they come again
εις Ἱεροσολυμα. Και εν τῳ ἱερῳ περιπατουν-
to Jerusalem. And in the temple walking
τος αυτου, ερχονται προς αυτον οἱ αρχιερεις
of him, come to him the high-priests
και οἱ γραμματεις και οἱ πρεσβυτεροι, 28 και
and the scribes and the elders, and
λεγουσιν αυτῳ· Εν ποιᾳ εξουσιᾳ ταυτα ποιεις;
they say to him; By what authority these things doest thou?
και τις σοι την εξουσιαν ταυτην εδωκεν, ἱνα
and who to thee the authority this gave, that
ταυτα ποιῃς; 29 Ὁ δε Ιησους *[αποκριθεις]
these things thou mayest do. The but Jesus [answering]
ειπεν αυτοις· Επερωτησω ὑμας *[καγω] ἑνα
said to them; I will ask you [also I] one
λογον· και αποκριθητε μοι, και ερω ὑμιν, εν
word; and answer you to me, and I will tell to you, by
ποιᾳ εξουσιᾳ ταυτα ποιω. 30 Το βαπτισμα
what authority these things I do. The dipping

the FIG-TREE withered away from the Roots.

21 And PETER remembering, says to him, "Rabbi, behold, the FIG-TREE which thou didst curse, is withered away."

22 And JESUS answering says to them, "Have Faith in God.

23 For indeed I say to you, ‡ That whoever should say to this MOUNTAIN, 'Be raised up, and thrown into the SEA;' and should not doubt in his HEART, but believe that * what he says is being done; he shall have it.

24 For this reason I say to you, ‡ All things whatever you * pray for, and desire, believe That you will receive, and you shall have them.

25 ‡ And when you stand praying, forgive, if you have any thing against any one; that also THAT FATHER of yours in the HEAVENS may forgive you your OFFENCES.

26 † [But ‡ if you do not forgive, neither will THAT FATHER of yours in the HEAVENS forgive your OFFENCES."]

27 ‡ And they came again to Jerusalem. And as he was walking about in the TEMPLE, the HIGH-PRIESTS, and the SCRIBES, and the ELDERS, came to him,

28 and * they said to him, "By What Authority doest thou these things? * or who EMPOWERED thee to do them?"

29 And JESUS said to them, "I will ask you One Question; and if you answer me, I also will inform you by What Authority I do these things.

* VATICAN MANUSCRIPT.—23. what he says is being done; he shall have it. For this. 24. pray for, and desire, believe you That you did receive. 28. they said. 28. or who. 29. answering—omit. 29. also I—omit.

† 26. This verse is wanting in Dr. Birch's collation of the Vat. MS., and is omitted by several MSS. and Versions.

‡ 23. Matt. xvii. 20; xxi. 21; Luke xvii. 6. ‡ 24. Matt. vii. 7; Luke xi. 9; John xiv 13; James i. 5, 6. ‡ 25. Matt. vi. 14; Col. iii. 13. ‡ 26. Matt. xviii. 35. ‡ 27. Matt. xxi. 23; Luke xx. 1.

Ιωαννου εξ ουρανου ην, ἡ εξ ανθρωπων; αποκ-
of John from heaven was, or from men? answer
ριθητε μοι. 31 Και ελογιζοντο προς ἑαυτους,
you to me. And they reasoned among themselves,
λεγοντες· Εαν ειπωμεν· Εξ ουρανου, ερει·
saying; If we should say, From heaven, he will say;
Διατι ουν ουκ επιστευσατε αυτῳ; 32 Αλλ' εαν
Why then not did you believe him; But if
ειπωμεν· Εξ ανθρωπων· εφοβουντα τον λαον·
we should say; From men; they feared the people;
άπαντες γαρ ειχον τον Ιωαννην, ὁτι οντως
all for held the John, that really
προφητης ην. 33 Και αποκριθεντες λεγουσι τῳ
a prophet was. And answering they say to the
Ιησου. Ουκ οιδαμεν. Και ὁ Ιησους *[αποκρι-
Jesus. Not we know. And the Jesus [answer-
θεις] λεγει αυτοις· Ουδε εγω λεγω ὑμιν, εν
ing he says to them; Neither I say to you, by
ποιᾳ εξουσιᾳ ταυτα ποιω.
what authority these things I do.

ΚΕΦ. ιβ'. 12.

1 Και ηρξατο αυτοις εν παραβολαις λεγειν·
And he began to them in parables to talk;
Αμπελωνα εφυτευσεν ανθρωπος, και περιεθηκε
A vineyard planted a man, and placed around
φραγμον, και ωρυξεν ὑποληνιον, και ῳκοδομησε
a hedge, and dug a wine-vat, and built
πυργον· και εξεδοτο αυτον γεωργοις, και απεδη-
a tower; and let out it to husbandmen and went
μασε. 2 Και απεστειλε προς τους γεωργους τῳ
abroad. And he sent to the husbandmen in the
καιρῳ δουλον, ἱνα παρα των γεωργων λαβῃ
season a slave, that from the husbandmen, he might receive
απο του καρπου του αμπελωνος. 3 Οἱ δε λαβον-
of the fruit of the vineyard. They but taking
τες αυτον, εδειραν, και απεστειλαν κενον. 4 Και
him, they flayed, and sent away empty. And
παλιν απεστειλε προς αυτους αλλον δουλον·
again he sent to them another slave;
κακεινον λιθοβολησαντες εκεφαλαιωσαν, και
and this pelting with stones they wounded on the head, and
*[απεστειλαν] ητιμωμενον. 5 Και αλλον απε-
[sent away] having dishonored. And another he
στειλε· κακεινον απεκτειναν· και πολλους
sent, and this they killed; and many
αλλους, τους μεν δεροντες, τους δε αποκτεν-
others, some indeed flaying, some but killing.
νοντες. 6 Ετι *[ουν] ἑνα υἱον εχων, αγαπητον
Yet [therefore] one son having, beloved
*[αὑτου,] απεστειλε *[και] αυτον προς αυτους
[of himself,] he sent [and] him to them
εσχατον, λεγων· Ὁτι εντραπησονται τον υἱον
last, saying; That they will regard the son
μου. 7 Εκεινοι δε οἱ γεωργοι ειπον προς ἑαυτους·
of me. Those but the husbandmen said to themselves:

30 Was the IMMERSION of *JOHN from Heaven, or from Men? Answer me."

31 And they reasoned among themselves, saying, "If we should say, From Heaven; he will say, Why then did you not believe him?

32 But *should we say, From Men;"—they feared the PEOPLE; for all maintain that ‡JOHN was really a Prophet.

33 And answering they say to JESUS, "We do not know." And JESUS says to them, "neither do I tell you by What Authority I do these things."

CHAPTER XII.

1 ‡And he began to address them in Parables. "A Man planted a Vineyard, and placed a Hedge about it, and dug a †Wine-vat, and built a Tower, and leased it to CULTIVATORS, and left the country.

2 And he sent a Servant to the CULTIVATORS, at the SEASON, that he might receive from the CULTIVATORS of the *FRUITS of the VINEYARD.

3 But *seizing him, they beat Him, and sent him away empty.

4 And again he sent to them another Servant; and *him they wounded in the head, and disgracefully treated.

5 And he sent Another, and him they killed; and Many Others, beating *some, and killing *some.

6 *Having yet One beloved Son, he sent him last to them, saying, 'They will respect my SON.'

7 But Those CULTIVATORS said among them-

* VATICAN MANUSCRIPT.—30. JOHN. 32. should we say. 33. answering—omit. 2. FRUITS of. 4. him they wounded in the head. 4. sent away—omit. 5. some. 5. some. 6. He had yet one Son, beloved; he sent. 6. therefore—omit. 6. of himself—omit. 6. also—omit.

† 1. See Note on Matt. xxi. 33.

‡ 32. Matt. iii. 5; xiv. 5; Mark vi. 20. ‡ 1. Matt. xxi. 23; Luke xxii. 9; See Isa. v. 1—7.

Ὅτι οὗτος εστιν ὁ κληρονομος· δευτε, αποκ-
That this is the heir; come, we may
τεινωμεν αυτον, και ἡμων εσται ἡ κληρονομια.
kill him, and of us shall be the inheritance.
8 Και λαβοντες αυτον, απεκτειναν, και εξεβα-
And having taken him, they killed, and cast
λον εξω του αμπελωνος. 9 Τι *[ουν] ποιησει
out of the vineyard. What [therefore] will do
ὁ κυριος του αμπελωνος; Ελευσεται και απολε-
the Lord of the vineyard? He will come and destroy
σει τους γεωργους, και δωσει τον αμπελωνα
the husbandmen, and will give the vineyard
αλλοις. 10 Ουδε την γραφην ταυτην ανεγνωτε·
to others. Not even the writing this have you read;
"Λιθον ὁν απεδοκιμασον οἱ οικοδομουντες, οὗτος
"A stone which rejected those building, this
εγενηθη εις κεφαλην γωνιας· 11 παρα κυριου
was made into a head of a corner. by a Lord
εγενετο αὕτη, και εστι θαυμαστη εν οφθαλμαις
was done this, and it is wonderful in eyes
ἡμων;" 12 Και εζητουν αυτον κρατησαι, και
of us?" And they sought him to seize, but
εφοβηθησαν τον οχλον· εγνωσαν γαρ, ὁτι προς
they feared the crowd; they knew for, that to
αυτους την παραβολην ειπε. Και αφεντες
them the parable he spoke. And leaving
αυτον, απηλθον.
him, they went away.

13 Και αποστελλουσι προς αυτον τινας των
And they send to him some of the
Φαρισαιων και των Ἡρωδιανων, ἱνα αυτον αγρευ-
Pharisees and of the Herodians, that him they might
σωσι λογῳ. 14 Οἱ δε ελθοντες λεγουσιν αυτῳ·
catch in word. They and having come they say to him:
Διδασκαλε, οιδαμεν, ὁτι αληθης ει, και ου
O teacher, we know, that true thou art, and not
μελει σοι περι ουδενος· ου γαρ βλεπεις εις
cares thee about no one: not for thou lookest into
προσωπον ανθρωπων, αλλ' επ' αληθειας την ὁδον
face of men, but in truth the way
του θεου διδασκεις· εξεστι κηνσον Καισαρι
of the God thou teachest: is it lawful tribute to Cesar
δουναι, η ου; δωμεν, η μη δωμεν; 15 Ὁ
to give, or not? should we give, or not should we give? He
δε ειδως αυτων την ὑποκρισιν, ειπεν αυτοις· Τι
but knowing of them the hypocrisy, said to them: Why
με πειραζετε; φερετε μοι δηναριον, ἱνα ιδω.
me do you tempt? bring you to me a denarius, that I may see.
16 Οἱ δε ηνεγκαν. Και λεγει αυτοις· Τινος η
They and brought. And he says to them: Of whom the

selves; 'This is the HEIR; come, let us kill him, and the INHERITANCE will be ours.'
8 Then seizing him, they killed him, and cast him out of the VINEYARD.
9 What will the LORD of the VINEYARD do? He will come and destroy those CULTIVATORS, and give the VINEYARD to others.
10 Have you not even read this SCRIPTURE?—
‡'A Stone which the BUILDERS rejected, has become the Head of the Corner;
11 this was performed by Jehovah, and it is wonderful in our Eyes.'"
12 ‡And they sought to apprehend Him, but they feared the CROWD; for they knew that he had spoken the PARABLE respecting them; and leaving him, they went away.
13 ‡Then they send to him some of the PHARISEES, and of the Herodians, that they might ensnare Him in Conversation.
14 And having come, THEY say to him, "Teacher, we know that thou art sincere, and carest for no one; for thou lookest not to the Appearance of Men, but teachest the WAY of GOD in Truth. †Is it lawful to pay Tax to Cesar, or not?
15 Should we pay, or should we not pay?" But HE, knowing their HYPOCRISY, said to them, "Why do you try Me? Bring me a Denarius, that I may see it."
16 And THEY brought one. And he says to them,

* VATICAN MANUSCRIPT.—9. therefore—*omit*.

† 14. The Jews, whose religious system was theocracy, were of opinion, that they could not, consistently with their allegiance to God their king, comply with paying an acknowledgment of subordination to an earthly sovereign. Judas of Galilee was the first who endeavored to persuade the Jews of the unlawfulness of paying tribute to a foreign potentate. See Josephus Ant. xviii. 1. and B. J. ii. 12. The primitive Christians also held a similar opinion, and fondly thought, that their subjection to Jesus Christ exempted them from all allegiance to the power of the magistrate. This idea is the proper clue to lead us to a right understanding of all those passages in the epistolary writings of the New Testament, which relate to civil government.—*Wakefield.*

‡ 10. Psa. cxviii. 22. ‡ 12. Matt. xxi. 45, 46; Mark xi. 18; John vii. 25, 30, 44. ‡ 13. Matt xxii. 15; Luke xx. 20.

εικων αυτη, και ἡ επιγραφη; Οἱ δε ειπον αυτῳ·
likeness this, and the inscription? They and said to him;
Καισαρος. 17 Και *[αποκριθεις] ὁ Ιησους ειπεν
Of Cesar. And [answering] the Jesus said
*[αυτοις·] Αποδοτε τα Καισαρος Καισαρι,
[to them;] Give you back the things of Cesar to Cesar,
και τα του θεου, τῳ θεῳ. Και εθαυμασεν
and the things of the God, to the God. And they wondered
επ' αυτῳ. 18 Και ερχονται Σαδδουκαιοι προς
at him. And come Sadducees to
αυτον, οἱτινες λεγουσιν αναστασιν μη ειναι·
him, who say a resurrection not to be;
και επηρωτησαν αυτον, λεγοντες· 19 Διδασκαλε,
and they asked him, saying; O teacher,
Μωσης εγραψεν ἡμιν, "ὁτι εαν τινος αδελφος
Moses wrote for us, "that if any brother
αποθανῃ, και καταλιπῃ γυναικα, και τεκνα μη
should die, and should leave behind a wife, and children not
αφῃ, ἱνα λαβῃ ὁ αδελφος αυτου την γυναι-
should leave, that should take the brother of him the wife
κα αυτου, και εξαναστησῃ σπερμα, τῳ αδελφῳ
of him, and should raise up seed. to the brother
αὑτου." 20 Ἑπτα αδελφοι ησαν· και ὁ πρωτος
of himself." Seven brothers were; and the first
ελαβε γυναικα, και αποθνησκων ουκ αφηκε
took a wife, and dying not left
σπερμα. 21 Και ὁ δευτερος ελαβεν αυτην,
seed. And the second took her,
και απεθανε, και ουδε αυτος αφηκε σπερμα· και
and died, and neither he left seed: and
ὁ τριτος ὡσαυτως. 22 Και *[ελαβον αυτην]
the third in like manner. And [took her]
οἱ ἑπτα, και ουκ αφηκαν σπερμα. Εσχατη
the seven, and not left seed. Last
παντων απεθανε και ἡ γυνη. 23 Εν τῃ *[ουν]
of all died also the woman. In the [therefore]
αναστασει, *[ὁταν αναστωσι,] τινος αυτων
resurrection, [when they shall rise,] of whom of them
εσται γυνη; οἱ γαρ ἑπτα ασχον αυτην γυναι-
shall be a wife? the for seven had her a wife
κα. 24 Και αποκριθεις ὁ Ιησους ειπεν αυτοις·
And answering the Jesus said to them;
Ου δια τουτο πλανασθε, μη ειδοτες τας γραφας,
Not through this do you err, not knowing the writings,
μηδε την δυναμιν του θεου; 25 Ὁταν γαρ εκ
neither the power of the God? When for out of
νεκρων αναστωσιν, ουτε γαμουσιν, ουτε
dead (ones) they may rise, neither they marry, nor
γαμισκονται, αλλ' εισιν ὡς αγγελοι εν τοις
are given in marriage, but are as messengers in the
ουρανοις. 26 Περι δε των νεκρων, ὁτι εγειρον-
heavens. Concerning but the dead (ones,) that they rise
ται, ουκ ανεγνωτε εν τῃ βιβλῳ Μωσεως, επι
not have you read in the book of Moses, at
του βατου ὡς ειπεν αυτῳ ὁ θεος, λεγων·
the bush as said to him the God, saying;
"Εγω ὁ θεος Αβρααμ, και ὁ θεος Ισαακ, και
I the God of Abraham, and the God of Isaac, and

"Whose LIKENESS and IN-
SCRIPTION is this?" And
THEY said to him, "Ce-
sar's."

17 And JESUS said,
"Render the THINGS of
Cesar, to Cesar; and the
THINGS of GOD, to God."
And they *wondered at
him.

18 ‡Then the Sadducees,
who say there is no Resurrection, came to him, and
asked him, saying,

19 "Teacher, Moses
wrote for us, 'That if one's
'Brother should die, and
'leave a Wife behind, and
'leave no Children, that his
'BROTHER should take his
'WIFE, and raise up Off-
'spring for his BROTHER.'

20 There were Seven
Brothers; and the FIRST
took a Wife, and dying,
left no Child.

21 And the SECOND took
her, and died, *leaving no
Child; and the THIRD in
like manner.

22 And the SEVEN left
no Offspring. Last of all
the WOMAN also died.

23 At the RESURREC-
TION, Whose Wife will she
be of them? for the SEVEN
had her for a Wife."

24 And JESUS answering
said to them, "Do you not
err through this,—not
knowing the SCRIPTURES,
nor the POWER of GOD?

25 For when they shall
rise from the Dead, they
will neither marry, nor be
given in marriage; ‡but
be as *THOSE ANGELS in
the HEAVENS.

26 But concerning the
DEAD, that they will rise,
have you not read in the
BOOK of Moses, at the
BUSH, how GOD spoke to
him, saying, ‡'I am the
'GOD of Abraham, and the
*'God of Isaac, and the
*'God of Jacob?'

* VATICAN MANUSCRIPT.— 17. answering—*omit.* 17. to them—*omit.* 17. greatly wondered at him. 21. leaving no Child. 22. took her—*omit.* 23. therefore—*omit.* 23. when they shall rise—*omit.* 25. THOSE ANGELS. 26. God. 26. God.

‡ 18. Matt. xxii. 23; Luke xx. 27. ‡ 25. 1 Cor. xv 42, 49, 52. ‡ 26 Exod iii 6

ὁ θεος Ιακωβ." 27 Ουκ εστιν ὁ θεος νεκρων,
the God of Jacob." Not is the God of dead (ones,)
αλλα ζωντων. Ὑμεις *[ουν] πολυ πλανασθε.
but of living (ones.) You [therefore] greatly err.
28 Και προσελθων εἷς των γραμματεων, ακουσας
And approaching one of the scribes, having heard
αυτων συζητουντων, ειδως ὁτι καλως αυτοις
them disputing, knowing that well to them
απεκριθη, επηρωτησεν αυτον· Ποια εστι πρωτη
he answered, asked him; Which is first
παντων εντολη; 29 Ὁ *[δε] Ιησους απεκριθη
of all commandment; The [and] Jesus replied
αυτῳ· Ὁτι πρωτη *[παντων εντολη·] "Ακουε
to him; That first [of all commandment;] "Hear thou
Ισραηλ, κυριος, ὁ θεος ἡμων, κυριος εἷς εστι·
Israel, a Lord, the God of us, Lord one is:
30 και αγαπησεις κυριον τον θεον σου εξ ὁλης
and thou shalt love a Lord the God of thee out of whole
της καρδιας σου, και εξ ὁλης της ψυχης σου,
of the heart of thee, and out of whole of the soul of thee,
και εξ ὁλης της διανοιας σου, και εξ ὁλης
and out of whole of the mind of thee, and out of whole
της ισχυος σου." *[Αυτη πρωτη εντολη.]
of the strength of thee." [This first commandment.]
31 Και δευτερα *[ὁμοια,] αὑτη· "Αγαπησεις
And second [like,] this: Thou shalt love
τον πλησιον σου ὡς σεαυτον." Μειζων τουτων
the neighbor of thee as thyself." Greater of these
αλλη εντολη ουκ εστι. 32 *[Και] ειπεν αυτῳ
another commandment not is. [And] said to him
ὁ γραμματευς· Καλως, διδασκαλε, επ᾽ αληθειας
the scribe: Well, O teacher, in truth
ειπας, ὁτι εἷς εστι, και ουκ εστιν αλλος πλην
thou speakest, that one he is, and not is another besides
αυτου· 33 και το αγαπᾳν αυτον εξ ὁλης της
him: and the to love him out of whole of the
καρδιας, και εξ ὁλης της συνεσεως, *[και εξ
heart, and out of whole of the understanding, [and out of
ὁλης της ψυχης,] και εξ ὁλης της ισχυος,
whole of the soul,] and out of whole of the strength,
και το αγαπᾳν τον πλησιον ὡς ἑαυτον, πλειον
and the to love the neighbor as himself, more
εστι παντων των ὁλοκαυτωματων και θυσιων.
is of all of the whole burnt offerings and sacrifices.
34 Και ὁ Ιησους, ιδων αυτον, ὁτι νουνεχως απεκ-
And the Jesus, seeing him, that discreetly he an-
ριθη, ειπεν αυτῳ· Ου μακραν ει απο της βα-
swered, said to him: Not far thou art from the king-
σιλειας του θεου. Και ουδεις ουκετι ετολμα
dom of the God. And no one no longer presumed
αυτον επερωτησαι. 35 Και αποκριθεις ὁ Ιησους
him to ask. And answering the Jesus
ελεγε, διδασκων εν τῳ ἱερῳ· Πως λεγουσιν οἱ
said, teaching in the temple: How say the

27 He is not the * God of the dead, but of the Living; * you do greatly err."

28 ‡ And one of the SCRIBES, having heard them disputing, and perceiving That he had ably answered them, asked him, "Which is the Chief Commandment of all?"

29 JESUS replied to him, "The first * is,—‡ 'Hearken, Israel; Jehovah our 'GOD is one Jehovah;

30 'and thou shalt love 'Jehovah thy God with All 'thy * Heart, and with All 'thy * Soul, and with All 'thy * Mind, and with All 'thy STRENGTH.'

31 And the second, this, —‡ 'Thou shalt love thy 'NEIGHBOR as thyself.' There is no Other Commandment greater than these."

32 The SCRIBE said to him, "Of a truth, Teacher thou hast spoken well; for he is One, ‡ and besides him there is no other;

33 and to LOVE him with All the UNDERSTANDING, and with All the STRENGTH, and to LOVE one's NEIGHBOR as one's self, ‡ is * abundantly more than All the WHOLE BURNT OFFERINGS and * Sacrifices."

34 And JESUS perceiving That he had answered wisely, said to him, "Thou art not far from the KINGDOM of GOD." ‡ And no one presumed to question him any further.

35 ‡ And JESUS said, while teaching in the TEMPLE, "Why do the SCRIBES

* VATICAN MANUSCRIPT.—27. God. 27. therefore—*omit.* 27. you do greatly err. — 29. And—*omit.* 29. Commandment of all—*omit.* 29. is. 30. Heart. 30. Soul. 30. Mind. 30. This the First Commandment—*omit.* 31. like—*omit.* 32. And—*omit.* 33. and with All the SOUL—*omit.* 33. abundantly more. 33. Sacrifices.

‡ 28. Matt. xxii. 35. ‡ 29. Deut. vi. 4; Luke x. 27. ‡ 31. Lev. xix. 18; Matt. xxii. 39; Rom. xiii. 9; Gal. v. 14; James ii. 8. ‡ 32. Deut. iv. 39; Isa. xlv. 6, 14; xlvi. 9. ‡ 33. 1 Sam. xv. 22; Hoshea vi. 6; Micah vi. 6—8. ‡ 34. Matt. xxii. 46. ‡ 35. Matt. xxii. 41; Luke xx. 41.

γραμματεις, ὁτι ὁ Χριστος υἱος εστι Δαυιδ;
scribes, that the Anointed a son is of David?
36 Αυτος γαρ Δαυιδ ειπεν εν πνευματι ἁγιῳ·
Himself for David said by a spirit holy;
"Λεγει ὁ κυριος τῳ κυριῳ μου· Καθου εκ δεξι-
Says the Lord to the Lord of me; Sit thou at right
ων μου, ἑως αν θω τους εχθρους σου ὑποποδιον
of me, till I may place the enemies of thee a footstool
των ποδων σου." 37 Αυτος ουν Δαυιδ λεγει
of the feet of thee." Himself therefore David calls
αυτον κυριον· και ποθεν υἱος αυτου εστι; Και
him Lord; and whence a son of him is he? And
ὁ πολυς οχλος ηκουεν αυτου ἡδεως. 38 Και
the great crowd heard him gladly. And
ελεγεν *[αυτοις] εν τῃ διδαχῃ αὑτου· Βλεπετε
he said [to them] in the teaching of himself; Beware you
απο των γραμματεων, των θελοντων εν στολαις
of the scribes, those desiring in long robes
περιπατειν, και ασπασμους εν ταις αγοραις,
to walk about, and salutations in the markets,
39 και πρωτοκαθεδριας εν ταις συναγωγαις, και
and first seats in the synagogues, and
πρωτοκλισιας εν τοις δειπνοις· 40 οἱ κατεσθιοντες
upper couches at the feasts; those devouring
τας οικιας των χηρων, και προφασει μακρα προσ-
the houses of the widows, and for a show long are
ευχομενοι· οὑτοι ληψονται περισσοτερον κριμα.
praying; these will receive heavier judgment.
41 Και καθισας *[ὁ Ιησους] κατεναντι του
And sitting [the Jesus] over against the
γαζοφυλακιου, εθεωρει πως ὁ οχλος βαλλει
treasury, he beheld how the crowd casts
χαλκον εις το γαζοφυλακιον. Και πολλοι
copper into the treasury. And many
πλουσιοι εβαλλον πολλα. 42 Και ελθουσα μια
rich cast much. And coming one
χηρα πτωχη, εβαλε λεπτα δυο, ὁ εστι κοδ-
widow poor, cast mites two, which is a
ραντης. 43 Και προσκαλεσαμενος τους μαθητας
farthing. And having called the disciples
αὑτου, ειπεν αυτοις· Αμην λεγω ὑμιν, ὁτι ἡ
of himself, he said to them; Indeed I say to you, that the
χηρα αὑτη ἡ πτωχη πλειον παντων βεβληκε
widow this the poor more of all has cast
των βαλοντων εις το γαζοφυλακιον. 44 Παν-
of those casting into the treasury. All
τες γαρ εκ του περισσευοντος αυτοις εβαλον·
for out of the abounding fulness to them have cast;
αὑτη δε εκ της ὑστερησεως αὑτης παντα ὁσα
this but out of the poverty of herself all as much as
ειχεν εβαλεν, ὁλον τον βιον αὑτης.
she had cast, whole the living of herself.

say, That the MESSIAH is a Son of David?

36 For David himself said, by the Holy Spirit, ‡†'Jehovah said to my 'LORD, Sit thou at my 'Right hand, till I put 'thine ENEMIES under-'neath thy FEET.'

37 David himself, therefore, calls him Lord, and how then is he * His Son?" And the GREAT Crowd heard him with pleasure.

38 And he said in his TEACHING, ‡"Beware of THOSE SCRIBES who DESIRE to walk about in †Long robes, and ‡love Salutations in the MARKETS,

39 and the Principal seats in the SYNAGOGUES, and the Upper couch at FEASTS;

40 ‡those PLUNDERING the FAMILIES of WIDOWS, and for a Show make long Prayers; these will receive a Heavier Judgment."

41 ‡And sitting opposite to the TREASURY, he beheld how the CROWD cast Money into ‡the TREASURY; and Many Rich men cast in much.

42 And a poor Widow approaching, cast in two Lepta, that is, a †Farthing.

43 And having called to him his DISCIPLES, he said to them, "Indeed I say to you, ‡That this POOR WIDOW has cast in more than All of THOSE CASTING into the TREASURY;

44 for they All cast in out of their SUPERFLUITY, but SHE out of her POVERTY cast in all that she had,—her Whole LIVING."

* VATICAN MANUSCRIPT.—37. His Son. 38. to them—*omit*. 41. JESUS—*omit*.

† 36. In the original (Psa. cx. 1) it is Jehovah. But the Evangelist has adopted the version of the LXX, who, I suppose, could not venture to translate that word which every Jew regarded with the profoundest reverence, and could not pronounce it without danger of forfeiting his claim to a future state.—*Wakefield*. † 38. The *stoles* was an Oriental garment descending to the ancles, and worn by persons of distinction, as Kings, Priests and honorable persons, and were affected by the Jurists of the Pharisaical sect.—*Bloomfield*. † 42. Or rather three-fourths of a farthing, or four mills. A *kodrantes* (Lat. quadrans,) was a Roman copper coin, equivalent to the fourth part of an *assarion*, or two *Lepta*.

‡ 36. Psa. cx. 1. ‡ 38. Matt. xxiii. 1; Luke xx. 46. ‡ 38. Luke xi. 43. ‡ 40. Matt. xxiii. 14. ‡ 41. Luke xxi. 1. ‡ 41. 2 Kings xii. 9. ‡ 43. 2 Cor. viii. 12.

ΚΕΦ. ιγ΄. 13.

¹ Και εκπορευομενου αυτου εκ του ἱερου,
And departing of him out of the temple,
λεγει αυτῳ εἱς των μαθητων αυτου· Διδασκαλε,
says to him one of the disciples of him; O teacher,
ιδε, ποταποι λιθοι και ποταποι οικοδομαι.
see, what stones and what buildings.
² Και ὁ Ιησους *[αποκριθεις] ειπεν αυτῳ·
And the Jesus [answering] said to him;
Βλεπεις ταυτας τας μεγαλας οικοδομας; ου μη
Seest thou these the great buildings? not not
αφεθῃ λιθος επι λιθῳ, ὁς ου μη καταλυθῃ.
may be left a stone upon a stone, which not not may be thrown down.
³ Και καθημενου αυτου εις το ορος των ελαιων,
And sitting of him on the mountain of the olive trees,
κατεναντι του ἱερου, επηρωτων αυτον κατ᾽ ιδιαν
over against the temple, asked him privately
Πετρος, και Ιακωβος, και Ιωαννης, και Ανδρεας·
Peter, and James, and John, and Andrew;
⁴ Ειπε ἡμιν, ποτε ταυτα εσται, και τι το
Say to us, when these things shall be, and what the
σημειον, ὁταν μελλῃ παντα ταυτα συντελεισ-
sign, when are about all these things to be ended?
θαι. ⁵ Ὁ δε Ιησους *[αποκριθεις αυτοις,] ηρξατο
The and Jesus [answering them,] began
λεγειν· Βλεπετε μη τις ὑμας πλανησῃ.
to say; Take heed not any one you may deceive
⁶ Πολλοι *[γαρ] ελευσονται επι τῳ ονοματι μου,
Many [for] shall come in the name of me,
λεγοντες· Ὁτι εγω ειμι· και πολλους πλανη-
saying; That I am; and many they will
σουσιν. ⁷ Ὁταν δε ακουσητε πολεμους και
deceive. When and you all hear wars and
ακοας πολεμων, μη θροεισθε· δει *[γαρ]
reports of wars, not be disturbed; it behoves [for]
γενεσθαι· αλλ᾽ ουπω το τελος. ⁸ Εγερθησεται
to take place; but not yet the end. Shall be raised up
γαρ εθνος επι εθνος, και βασιλεια επι βασι-
for nation against nation, and kingdom against king-
λιαν· *[και] εσονται σεισμοι κατα τοπους,
dom; [and] shall be earthquakes in places,
*[και] εσονται λιμοι *[και ταραχαι.] Αρχαι
[and] shall be famines (and commotions.) Beginnings

CHAPTER XIII.

1 ‡And as he was going
out of the TEMPLE, one of
his DISCIPLES says to him,
"Teacher, see; †What
Stones! and What Build-
ings!"
2 And JESUS said to
him, "Seest thou These
GREAT Buildings? ‡there
shall not be *left here a
Stone upon a Stone; †all
will be overthrown."
3 And as he was sitting
on †the MOUNT of OLIVES
opposite the TEMPLE, Pe-
ter, and James, and John,
and Andrew asked him
privately,
4 "Tell us, when these
things will be?" and
"What will be the SIGN
when all these things are
about to be accomplished?"
5 And JESUS began to
*say to them, ‡"Beware,
that no one deceive You.
6 Many will come in my
NAME, saying, 'I am he;'
and will deceive Many.
7 And when you shall
hear of Conflicts, and Reports of Battles, be not
alarmed; for these things
must occur; but the END
is not yet.
8 For Nation will rise
against Nation, and King-
dom against Kingdom;
there will be Earthquakes
in various places, and there
will be Famines; these are
the *Beginnings of Sor-
rows.

* VATICAN MANUSCRIPT.—2. answering—*omit*. 2. left here. 5. answering them—*omit*. 5. say to them, "Beware." 6. for—*omit*. 7. for—*omit*. 8. and—*omit*. 8. and—*omit*. 8. and commotions—*omit*. 8. a Beginning of.

† 1. Josephus says that the stones with which Herod built the temple, were "of a white and firm substance," and that "every one of them was about twenty-five cubits in length, eight in heighth, and twelve in breadth." A cubit was nearly twenty-two inches of our measure. † 2. How exactly this prediction was fulfilled may be known from Josephus.—He says, Cæsar ordered the soldiers to dig up the whole city and the temple; but to leave three of the highest turrets standing; and a part of the wall, as a security to the garrison. But they so entirely dug up and levelled all the rest of the city, that none who saw it, would think it to have ever been inhabited." Eleazar, in his animated speech to his countrymen, thus exclaims: "Where is that great city, the metropolis of the Jewish people, defended by such walls and such mighty towers? Where is that city, which was thought to be inhabited by GOD? It is torn up from its foundations; and the only memorial that remains of it, is the camp of its destroyers, which is stationed in the ruins." It is also related in the Taanith of Maimonides, that according to Roman custom, the very foundations of the temple were dug up, and that T. Rufus, a Roman commander, carried a plough over them. † 3. From this spot the whole of Jerusalem was spread before the eye; and its situation, form, buildings, boundaries, and different parts, distinctly and individually seen; more especially Mount Moriah and Solomon's Temple, together with its spacious area.

‡ 1. [illegible] v. 1; Luke xxi. 5. ‡ 2. Luke xix. 44. ‡ 5. Jer. xxix. 8; Eph. v 6; 2 Thess. [illegible]

ωδινων ταυτα. 9 Βλεπετε δε ὑμεις ἑαυτους·
of sorrows these. Take heed but you yourselves:
παραδωσουσι *[γαρ] ὑμας εις συνεδρια, και εις
they will deliver up [for] you to sanhedrims, and into
συναγωγας δαρησεσθε, και επι ἡγεμονων και
synagogues you will be beaten, and before governors and
βασιλεων σταθησεσθε, ἑνεκεν εμου, εις μαρτυριον
kings you will stand. on account of me, for a testimony
αυτοις. 10 Και εις παντα τα εθνη δει,
to them. And among all the nations it behoves.
πρωτον κηρυχθηναι το ευαγγελιον. 11 Ὁταν δε
first to be published the glad tidings. When but
αγωσιν ὑμας παραδιδοντες, μη προμεριμνατε
they may lead you delivering up, not be anxious beforehand
τι λαλησετε, *[μηδε μελετατε·] αλλ' ὁ εαν
what you should speak, [nor be concerned;] but whatever
δοθη ὑμιν εν εκεινη τη ὡρα, τουτο λαλειτε·
may be given to you in that the hour, this speak you;
ου γαρ εστε ὑμεις οἱ λαλουντες, αλλα το πνευμα
not for are you the speaking, but the spirit
το ἁγιον. 12 Παραδωσει δε αδελφος αδελφον
the holy. Will deliver up and a brother a brother
εις θανατον, και πατηρ τεκνον· και επαναστη-
to death, and father a child; and they shall
σονται τεκνα επι γονεις, και θανατωσουσιν
rise up children against parents, and deliver to death
αυτους. 13 Και εσεσθε μισουμενοι ὑπο παντων,
them. And you will be being hated by all,
δια το ονομα μου. Ὁ δε ὑπομεινας εις τελος,
through the name of me. He but persevering to end,
οὑτος σωθησεται. 14 Ὁταν δε ιδητε το βδε-
this will be saved. When but you may see the abomi-
λυγμα της ερημωσεως ἑστως ὁπου ου δει· (ὁ
nation of the desolation having stood where not it ought; (he
αναγινωσκων νοειτω·) τοτε οἱ εν τη Ἰουδαιᾳ,
reading let him think;) then those in the Judea,
φευγετωσαν εις τα ορη· 15 ὁ *[δε] επι του
let them flee to the mountains; he [and] on the
δωματος, μη καταβατω *[εις την οικιαν,] μηδε
roof, not let him go down [into the house,] nor
εισελθετω, αραι τι εκ της οικιας αὑτου·
enter, to take any thing out of the house of himself;
16 και ὁ εις τον αγρον ων, μη επιστρεψατω εις
and he in the field being, not let him turn into
τα οπισω, αραι το ἱματιον αυτου. 17 Ουαι δε
the back, to take the mantle of him. Woe but
ταις εν γαστρι εχουσαις και ταις θηλαζουσαις
to the in womb having and to the giving suck
εν εκειναις ταις ἡμεραις. 18 Προσευχεσθε δε,
in those the days. Pray you but,
ἱνα μη γενηται ἡ φυγη ὑμων χειμωνος.
that not may be the flight of you of winter.

9 But ‡take heed to yourselves. They will deliver you up to High Councils and to Synagogues; and you will be beaten, and will stand before Governors and Kings on my account, for a Testimony to them.

10 ‡And the GLAD TIDINGS must first be published among All the NATIONS.

11 ‡But when they conduct you to deliver you up, be not anxious beforehand what you should speak; but whatever may be given you in That HOUR, this speak; for it is not YOU who will SPEAK, but the HOLY SPIRIT.

12 And ‡Brother will deliver up Brother to Death, and a Father his Child; and Children will rise up against Parents, and cause them to die.

13 ‡And you will be hated by all on account of my NAME; but HE, who PATIENTLY ENDURES to the End, he will be saved.

14 ‡But when you shall see THAT DESTRUCTIVE ABOMINATION, standing where it ought not"—(READER, attend!)—"then let THOSE in Judea ESCAPE to the MOUNTAINS;

15 †let not HIM who is on the ROOF descend, nor enter his HOUSE, to take Anything out of it;

16 and let not HIM who is in the FIELD return BACK to take his MANTLE.

17 ‡But alas for the PREGNANT and NURSING WOMEN in Those DAYS!

18 But pray that *it may not be in Winter;

* VATICAN MANUSCRIPT.—9. for—*omit.* 11. nor be concerned—*omit.* 15. and—*omit.* 15. into the HOUSE—*omit.* 18. it may not be.

† 15. The peculiar construction of Eastern houses is here referred to. They were all of the same heighth, so that a person could walk at the top of a range of buildings, without inconvenience, from one end to the other. In Palestine they are still built on this plan. A staircase is carried on the outside from the top of the house to the bottom. The injunction in this verse is delivered in a figure, expressive of great eagerness and expedition; so that if a man was walking on the roof, he was directed to go straight forwards, till he got out of the city; and not to delay even to go down into the house to take the most necessary articles of food and raiment for his flight.

‡ 9. Matt. x. 17, 18; xxiv. 9; Rev. ii. 10. ‡ 10. Luke xxiv. 14. ‡ 11. Matt. x. 19; Luke xii. 11; xxi. 14. ‡ 12. Matt. x. 21; xxiv. 10; Luke xxi. 16. ‡ 13. Matt. 9; Luke xxi. 17. ‡ 14. Dan. ix. 27; Matt. xxiv. 15; Luke xxi. 20. ‡ 17. Luke xxiii. 29

19 Εσονται γαρ αἱ ἡμεραι εκειναι θλιψις, οἱα
Shall be for the days those affliction, such as
ου γεγονε τοιαυτη απ' αρχης κτισεως, ἡς
not has been so great from a beginning of creation, which
εκτισεν ὁ θεος, ἑως του νυν, και ου μη γενηται.
created the God, till the now, and not not may be.
20 Και ει μη κυριος εκολοβωσε τας ἡμερας, ουκ
And if not a Lord shortened the days, not
αν εσωθη πασα σαρξ· αλλα δια τους εκ-
should be saved all flesh; but on account of the cho-
λεκτους, οὑς εξελεξατο, εκολοβωσε τας ἡμερας.
sen (ones,) whom he has chosen, he has shortened the days.
21 Και τοτε εαν τις ὑμιν ειπῃ· Ιδου, ὡδε ὁ
And then if any one to you should say; Lo, here the
χριστος· η· Ιδου, εκει· μη πιστευετε. 22 Εγερ-
Anointed; or; Lo, here; not believe you. Shall
θησονται γαρ ψευδοχριστοι και ψευδοπροφηται,
be raised for false anointed ones and false prophets
και δωσουσι σημεια και τερατα, προς το απο-
and shall give signs and wonders, to the to de-
πλαναν, ει δυνατον, *[και] τους εκλεκτους.
ceive, if possible, [even] the chosen.
23 Ὑμεις δε βλεπετε· *[ιδου,] προειρηκα ὑμιν
You but take heed; [lo,] I have foretold to you
παντα. 24 Αλλ' εν εκειναις ταις ἡμεραις, μετα
all. But in those the days, after
την θλιψιν εκεινην, ὁ ἡλιος σκοτισθησεται,
the affliction that, the sun shall be darkened,
και ἡ σεληνη ου δωσει τοφεγγος αὑτης·
and the moon not shall give the light of herself;
25 και οἱ αστερος του ουρανου εσονται εκπιπτον-
and the stars of the heaven shall be fal-
τες, και αἱ δυναμεις, αἱ εν τοις ουρανοις,
ling, and the powers, those in the heavens,
σαλευθησονται. 26 Και τοτε οψονται τον υἱον
shall be shaken. And then they shall see the son
του ανθρωπου ερχομενον εν νεφελαις, μετα
of the man coming on clouds, with
δυναμεως πολλης και δοξης. 27 Και τοτε αποσ-
power much and glory. And then he will
τελει τους αγγελους αὑτου, και επισυναξει τους
send the messengers of himself, and he will gather the
εκλεκτους αὑτου εκ των τεσσαρων ανεμων,
chosen (ones) of himself from the four winds,
απ' ακρου γης ἑως ακρου ουρανου. 28 Απο
from an extremity of earth to an extremity of heaven. From
δε της συκης μαθετε την παραβολην· ὁταν
but the fig-tree learn you the parable: when
αυτης ηδη ὁ κλαδος ἁπαλος γενηται, και
of her now the branch tender may become, and
εκφυῃ τα φυλλα, γινωσκετε, ὁτι εγγυς το
may put forth the leaves, you know, that near the

19 for in those DAYS will be Distress, ‡ such as has not been from the Beginning of the Creation, which GOD created, till NOW, nor ever will be.

20 And except the Lord cut short the DAYS, No Person could survive; but on account of the CHOSEN, whom he has selected, he has cut short the DAYS.

21 And then if any one should say to you, 'Behold, the MESSIAH is here!' or 'Behold,—there!' believe it not;

22 because False Messiahs and False Prophets will arise, and exhibit Signs and Wonders, to DECEIVE, if possible, the CHOSEN.

23 ‡ But be you on your guard; I have forewarned you.

24 ‡ But in Those DAYS, after that AFFLICTION, the † the SUN will be obscured, and the MOON will withhold her LIGHT,

25 and * the STARS will fall out of HEAVEN, and THOSE POWERS in the HEAVENS will be shaken.

26 ‡ And then they will see the SON of MAN coming in Clouds, with great Power and Glory.

27 And then he will send forth * the MESSENGERS, and assemble his CHOSEN from the FOUR Winds, from the Extremity of Earth to the utmost bound of Heaven.

28 Now learn a PARABLE from the FIG-TREE. When its BRANCH now becomes tender, and puts forth LEAVES, * it is known That SUMMER is near.

* VATICAN MANUSCRIPT.—22. even—*omit.* 23. lo—*omit.* 25. the STARS will fall out of HEAVEN, and THOSE POWERS. 27. the MESSENGERS. 28. it is known That.

† 24. In Isaiah xiii. 9, 10, 13, when the destruction of Babylon is threatened, it is thus expressed, "the stars of heaven and the constellations thereof shall not give their light; the sun shall be darkened in his going forth, and the moon shall not cause her light to shine. I will shake the heavens, &c." And the reader may find the same eastern manner of speaking in the following places of scripture:—Job xxx. 28; Eccl. xii. 1, 2; Isa. xxiv. 23; xxxiv. 4; lx. 20; Jer. iv. 23; xv. 9; Ezek. xxxii. 7, 8; Dan. viii. 10; Joel ii. 10, 30, 31; iii. 15; Amos v. 20; viii. 9, 2 Pet. iii. 10, 12; Rev. vi. 12—14.

‡ 19. Dan. xii. 1; Matt. xxiv. 21. ‡ 23. 2 Pet. iii. 17. ‡ 24. Matt. xxiv. 29; Luke xxi. 25. ‡ 26. Dan. vii. 13, 14; Matt. xxvi. 64; Mark xiv. 62; Rev. i. 7.

θερος εστιν. 29 Οὑτω και ὑμεις, ὁταν ταυτα
summer is. So also you, when these things
ιδητε γινομενα, γινωσκετε, ὁτι εγγυς εστιν
you may see coming to pass, know you, that near he is
επι θυραις. 30 Αμην λεγω ὑμιν, ὁτι ου μη
at doors. Indeed I say to you, that not not
παρελθη ἡ γενεα αὑτη, μεχρις οὑ παντα
may pass away the generation this, till of whom all
ταυτα γενηται. 31 Ὁ ουρανος και ἡ γη παρε-
these may be done. The heaven and the earth shall
λευσεται· οἱ δε λογοι μου ου μη παρελθωσι.
pass away; the but words of me not not may pass away.

32 Περι δε της ἡμερας εκεινης η της ὡρας
Concerning but the day that or the hour
ουδεις οιδεν, ουδε οἱ αγγελοι, οἱ εν ουρανῳ,
no one knows, nor the messengers, those in heaven,
ουδε ὁ υἱος, ει μη ὁ πατηρ. 33 Βλεπετε, αγ-
nor the son, if not the father. Take heed, watch
ρυπνειτε *[και προσευχεσθε·] ουκ οιδατε γαρ
you [and pray you;] not you know for
ποτε ὁ καιρος εστιν. 34 Ὡς ανθρωπος αποδη-
when the season is. As a man going
μος αφεις την οικιαν αὑτου, και δους τοις
abroad leaving the house of himself, and having given to the
δουλοις αὑτου την εξουσιαν, *[και] ἑκαστῳ
slaves of himself the authority, [and] to each one
το εργον αὑτου και τῳ θυρωρῳ ενετειλατο ἱνα
the work of himself and to the porter he commanded that
γρηγορῃ. 35 Γρηγορειτε ουν· ουκ οιδατε γαρ,
he should watch. Watch you therefore; not you know for,
ποτε ὁ κυριος της οικιας ερχεται, οψε, η
when the lord of the house comes, evening, or
μεσονυκτιου, η αλεκτοροφωνιας, η πρωι· 36 μη
midnight, or cock-crowing, or morning: lest
ελθων εξαιφνης, ευρῃ ὑμας καθευδοντας.
coming suddenly, he may find you sleeping.
37 Ἁ δε ὑμιν λεγω, πασι λεγω· Γρηγορειτε.
What and to you I say, to all I say: Watch you.

ΚΕΦ. ιδ'. 14.

1 Ην δε το πασχα και τα αζυμα μετα δυο
Was now the passover and the unleavened cakes after two
ἡμερας· και εζητουν οἱ αρχιερεις και οἱ γραμ-
days: and sought the high-priests and the scribes.
ματεις, πως αυτον εν δολῳ κρατησαντες αποκ-
how him by deceit seizing they
τεινωσιν. 2 Ελεγον δε· Μη εν τῃ ἑορτῃ,
might kill. They said but; Not in the feast,
μηποτε θορυβος εσται του λαου.
lest a tumult shall be of the people.
3 Και οντος αυτου εν Βηθανιᾳ εν τῃ οικιᾳ
And being of him in Bethany in the house
Σιμωνος του λεπρου, κατακειμενου αυτου, ηλθε
of Simon the leper, reclining of him, came

29 Thus also, when you shall see these things transpiring, know That he is near at the Doors.

30 Indeed, I say to you, That this GENERATION will not pass away, till All these things be accomplished.

31 The HEAVEN and EARTH will fail; but ‡ my WORDS cannot fail.

32 But concerning that DAY, *or HOUR, knows no man; not even an Angel in Heaven, nor the SON, but the FATHER.

33 ‡ Take heed, watch; for you know not when the SEASON is.

34 ‡ As a Man going abroad, leaving his HOUSE, and having given the AUTHORITY to his SERVANTS, to each his WORK, he also commanded the PORTER to watch.

35 Watch, therefore; for you know not when the MASTER of the HOUSE comes; *whether at Evening, or at Midnight, or at Cock-crowing, or in the Morning;

36 lest coming unexpectedly he should find you sleeping.

37 And what I say to you, I say to all, Watch."

CHAPTER XIV.

1 ‡ Now after Two Days was the PASSOVER and the feast of UNLEAVENED BREAD; and the HIGH-PRIESTS and SCRIBES sought him how they might take him by Deception, and kill him.

2 * For they said, "Not during the FEAST, lest there should be a Tumult of the PEOPLE."

3 ‡ And he being at Bethany, in the HOUSE of Simon the LEPER, while he was reclining at table, a

* VATICAN MANUSCRIPT.—32. or HOUR knows no man; not even an Angel in Heaven. 33. and pray—*omit.* 34. and—*omit.* 35. whether at Evening. 2. For they said.

‡ 31. Isa. xl. 8. ‡ 33. Matt. xxiv. 42; xxv. 13; Luke xii. 40; xxi. 31; Rom. xiii. 11; 1 Thess. v. 6. ‡ 34. Matt. xxiv. 45; xxv. 14. ‡ 1. Matt. xxvi. 2; Luke xxii. 1; John xi. 55; xiii. 1. ‡ 3. Matt. xxvi. 6; John xii. 1, 3; See Luke vii. 37.

γυνη εχουσα αλαβαστρον μυρου, ναρδου
a woman having an alabaster box of balsam, of spikenard
πιστικης πολυτελους· *[και] συντριψασα το
genuine very costly: [and] breaking the
αλαβαστρον, κατεχεεν αυτου κατα της κεφαλης.
alabaster box, she poured of it down on the head.
4 Ησαν δε τινες αγανακτουντες προς ἑαυτους,
Were and some being angry to themselves,
*[και λεγοντες·] Εις τι ἡ απωλεια αὑτη του
[and saying;] For what the loss this of the
μυρου γεγονεν; 5 Ηδυνατο γαρ τουτο το μυρον
balsam has been made? Could for this the balsam
πραθηναι επανω τριακοσιων δηναριων, και
to be sold more three hundred denarii, and
δοθηναι τοις πτωχοις. Και ενεβριμωντο αυτῃ.
to be given to the poor. And they censured her.
6 Ὁ δε Ιησους ειπεν· Αφετε αυτην· τι αυτῃ
The but Jesus said; Let alone her; why to her
κοπους παρεχετε; καλον εργον ειργασατο εν
troubles present you? good a work she has wrought in
εμοι. 7 Παντοτε γαρ τους πτωχους εχετε μεθ'
me. Always for the poor you have with
ἑαυτων, και, ὁταν θελητε, δυνασθε αυτους ευ
yourselves, and, when you will, you can them good
ποιησαι· ἐμε δε ου παντοτε εχετε. 8 Ὁ εσχεν
to do; me but not always you have. The having
αὑτη, εποιησε· προελαβε μυρισαι μου το σωμα
this, she has done; beforehand to anoint of me the body
εις τον ενταφιασμον. 9 Αμην λεγω ὑμιν, ὁπου
for the burial. Indeed I say to you, wherever
αν κηρυχθῃ το ευαγγελιον τουτο εις ὁλον τον
may be published the glad tidings this in whole the
κοσμον, και ὁ εποιησεν αὑτη λαληθησεται, εις
world, also what she did this shall be spoken, for
μνημοσυνον αυτης.
a memorial of her.
10 Και ὁ Ιουδας ὁ Ισκαριωτης, εἱς των
And the Judas the Iscariot, one of the
δωδεκα, απηλθε προς τους αρχιερεις, ἱνα
twelve, went to the high-priests, that
παραδῳ αυτον αυτοις· 11 Οἱ δε ακουσαντες
he might deliver up him to them: They and hearing
ἐχαρησαν· και επηγγειλαντο αυτῳ αργυριον
were glad; and promised him silver
δουναι. Και εζητει, πως ευκαιρως αυτον
to give. And he sought, how conveniently him
παραδῳ. 12 Και τῃ πρωτῃ ἡμερᾳ των
he might deliver up. And the first day of the
αζυμων, ὁτε το πασχα εθυον, λεγου-
unleavened cakes, when the paschal lamb were sacrificed, they
σιν αυτῳ οἱ μαθηται αυτου· Που θελεις απελ-
say to him the disciples of him; where wilt thou having
θοντες ἑτοιμασωμεν, ἱνα φαγῃς το πασχα;
gone we make ready, that thou mayest eat the passover?

woman came, having an Alabaster box of Balsam of genuine Spikenard, very costly: and breaking the BOX, she poured it on his HEAD.

4 And some were displeased, saying among themselves, "Why has this LOSS of the BALSAM taken place?

5 For * This BALSAM could have been sold for more than † Three hundred Denarii, and given to the POOR." And they censured her.

6 But JESUS said, "Let her alone; why do you trouble the WOMAN? She has done a Good Work for me.

7 ‡ For you have the POOR always among you, and when you will, you can * do Them good; but Me you have not always.

8 POSSESSING This (Balsam,) she has done it, to anoint my BODY beforehand for the BURIAL.

9 * And indeed I say to you, Wherever these GLAD TIDINGS may be proclaimed in the Whole WORLD, this also which she has done shall be spoken of in Memory of her."

10 ‡ And * THAT Judas Iscariot, who was one of the TWELVE, went to the HIGH-PRIESTS, to deliver Him up to them.

11 And hearing it they rejoiced, and promised to give him Money. And he sought how he might conveniently deliver Him up.

12 ‡ Now on the FIRST Day of UNLEAVENED BREAD, when the PASCHAL LAMBS were sacrificed, his DISCIPLES say to him, "Where dost thou wish that we go and prepare that thou mayest eat the PASSOVER?"

* VATICAN MANUSCRIPT.—3. and—*omit.* 4. and saying—*omit.* 5. This BALSAM could. 7. always do them. 9. And indeed. 10. THAT Judas Iscariot.

† 5. A Denarius being in value about 14 cents, or 7d. English, the value of the box of balsam would be forty-two dollars, or £8. 15s.

‡ 7. Deut. xv. 11. ‡ 10. Matt. xxvi. 14; Luke xxii. 3, 4. ‡ 12. Matt. xxvi. 14; Luke xxii. 7.

13 Και αποστελλει δυο των μαθητων αὑτου, και
And he sends two of the disciples of himself, and
λεγει αυτοις· Ὑπαγετε εις την πολιν· και
he says to them, Go you into the city, and
απαντησει ὑμιν ανθρωπος κεραμιον ὑδατος
will meet you a man a pitcher of water
βασταζων· ακολουθησατε αυτῳ· 14 και ὁπου εαν
carrying; follow him and wherever
εισελθῃ, ειπατε τῳ οικοδεσποτῃ· Ὁτι ὁ
he may enter, say to the householder; That the
διδασκαλος λεγει· Που εστι το καταλυμα,
teacher says; Where is the guest-chamber,
ὁπου το πασχα μετα των μαθητων μου φαγω;
where the passover with the disciples of me I may eat?
15 Και αυτος ὑμιν δειξει αναγαιον μεγα εστρω-
And he to you will show an upper room large having
μενον ετοιμον· εκει ἑτοιμασατε ἡμιν.
been furnished ready, there prepare you for us.
16 Και εξηλθον οἱ μαθηται αυτου, και ηλθον εις
And went forth the disciples of him, and came into
την πολιν, και εὑρον καθως ειπεν αυτοις· και
the city, and found even as he said to them; and
ἡτοιμασαν το πασχα. 17 Και οψιας γενομενης,
they prepared the passover. And evening being come.
ερχεται μετα των δωδεκα. 18 Και ανακειμενων
he comes with the twelve. And reclining
αυτων και εσθιοντων, ειπεν ὁ Ιησους· Αμην
of them and eating, said the Jesus; Indeed
λεγω ὑμιν, ὁτι εἱς εξ ὑμων παραδωσει με, ὁ
I say to you, that one of you will deliver up me, who
εσθιων μετ᾽ εμου. 19 Οἱ *[δε] ηρξαντο λυπεισ-
is eating with me. They [and] began to be sor-
θαι, και λεγειν αυτῳ εἱς καθ᾽ εἱς· Μητι εγω;
rowful, and to say to him one by one; Not I?
*[και αλλος· Μητι εγω;] 20 Ὁ δε *[αποκρι-
and another; Not I?] He but [answer-
θεις] ειπεν αυτοις· Εἱς εκ των δωδεκα, ὁ
ing] said to them; One of the twelve, that
εμβαπτομενος μετ᾽ εμου εις το τρυβλιον. 21 Ὁ
dipping in with me into the bowl. The
μεν υἱος του ανθρωπου ὑπαγει, καθως γεγραπ-
indeed son of the man goes away, even as it has been
ται περι αυτου· ουαι δε τῳ ανθρωπῳ εκεινῳ,
written concerning him; woe but to the man that,
δι᾽ οὑ ὁ υἱος του ανθρωπου παραδιδοται·
through whom the son of the man is delivered up.
καλον ην αυτῳ, ει ουκ εγεννηθη ὁ ανθρωπος
good it was to him, if not was born the man
εκεινος. 22 Και εσθιοντων αυτων, λαβων ὁ
that. And eating of them, taking the
Ιησους αρτον, ευλογησας εκλασε, και εδωκεν
Jesus a loaf, having blessed he broke, and gave
αυτοις, και ειπε· Λαβετε· τουτο εστι το σωμα
to them, and said: Take: this is the body

13 And he sends two of his DISCIPLES, and says to them, "Go into the CITY, and a Man carrying a Pitcher of Water will meet you; follow him;

14 and wherever he may enter, say to the HOUSEHOLDER, The TEACHER says, Where is *the GUEST-CHAMBER, where I may eat the PASSOVER with my DISCIPLES?

15 And he will show you a large Upper-room † furnished ready; *there prepare for us."

16 And *the DISCIPLES went forth, and came into the CITY, and found every thing even as he had said to them; and they prepared the PASSOVER.

17 ‡ And Evening being come, he comes with the TWELVE.

18 And as they were reclining at table, and eating, JESUS said, "Indeed I say to you, That *one of YOU who are EATING with me will deliver me up."

19 And *they began to be sorrowful, and to say to him, one by one, "Is it I?"

20 And HE said to them, "It is THAT ONE of the TWELVE DIPPING in with me into the DISH.

21 *The SON of MAN indeed ‡ goes away [to death,] even as it has been written concerning him; but woe to that MAN through whom the SON of MAN is delivered up! Good were it for that MAN if he had not been born."

22 ‡ And as they were eating, *he took a Loaf, and having given praise, he broke it, and gave to them, and said, "Take; this is my BODY."

---

* VATICAN MANUSCRIPT.—14. my GUEST-CHAMBER. 15. and there prepare. 16. the DISCIPLES. 18. one of YOU who are EATING with me. 19. and—*omit.* 19. they. 19. and another; not I?—*omit.* 20. answering—*omit.* 21. Because the SON. 22. he took.

† 15. Furnished ready, probably alludes to the manner of making the room ready for the celebration of the passover; which was examined in every hole and corner by the light of wax candles, and cleared from the smallest crumb of leaven with a scrupulous nicety.—*Ainsworth.*

‡ 17. Matt. xxvi. 20. ‡ 21. Matt. xxvi. 24; Luke xxii. 22; John vii. 33.

μου. 23 Και λαβων το ποτηριον, ευχαριστησας
of me. And taking the cup, having given thanks
εδωκεν αυτοις· και επιον εξ αυτου παντες.
he gave to them; and they drank out of it all.
24 Και ειπεν *[αυτοις.[Τουτο εστι το αἱμα μου,
And he said [to them.] This is the blood of me,
το της καινης διαθηκης, το περι πολλων
that of the new covenant, that concerning many
εκχυνομενον. 25 Αμην λεγω ὑμιν, ὁτι ουκετι
being shed. Indeed I say to you, that no more
ου μη πιω εκ του γεννηματος της αμπελου, ἑως
not not I will drink of the product the vine, till
της ἡμερας εκεινης, ὁταν αυτο πινω καινον εν
the day that, when it I drink new in
τῃ βασιλειᾳ του θεου. 36 Και ὑμνησαντες,
the kingdom of the God. And having sung a hymn,
εξηλθον εις το ορος των ελαιων.
they departed to the mountain of the olive trees.

27 Και λεγει αυτοις ὁ Ιησους· Ὁτι παντες
And says to them the Jesus; That all
σκανδαλισθησεσθε *[εν εμοι εν τῃ νυκτι ταυτῃ·]
will be stumbled [at me in the night this.]
ὁτι γεγραπται· "Παταξω τον ποιμενα, και
for it is written· I will smite the shepherd, and
διασκορπισθησεται τα προβατα." 28 Αλλα
will be scattered the sheep." But
μετα το εγερθηναι με, προαξω ὑμας εις την
after the to be raised me, I will go before you into the
Γαλιλαιαν. 29 Ὁ δε Πετρος εφη αυτῳ· Και ει
Galilee. The but Peter said to him; Even if
παντες σκανδαλισθησονται, αλλ' ουκ εγω.
all shall be stumbled, yet not I.
30 Και λεγει αυτῳ ὁ Ιησους· Αμην λεγω σοι,
And says to him the Jesus; Indeed I say to thee,
ὁτι συ σημερον εν τῃ νυκτι ταυτῃ, πριν η
that thou this-day in the night this, before
δις αλεκτορα φωνησαι, τρις απαρνησῃ με.
twice a cock to have crowed, thrice thou wilt deny me.
31 Ὁ δε εκ περισσου ελεγε μαλλον· Εαν με
He but with vehemence spoke more; If me
δεῃ συναποθανειν σοι, ου μη σε απαρνησομαι.
must to die with thee, not not thee I will deny.
Ὡσαυτως δε και παντες ελεγον. 32 Και ερχον-
In like manner and also all they said. And they
ται εις χωριον, οὑ το ονομα Γεθσημανη· και
came to a place, of which the name Gethsemane; and
λεγει τοις μαθηταις αὑτου· Καθισατε ὡδε,
he says to the disciples of himself; Sit you here,
ἑως προσευξωμαι. 33 Και παραλαμβανει τον
till I shall pray. And he takes the
Πετρον και Ιακωβον και Ιωαννην μεθ' ἑαυτου·
Peter and James and John with himself;
και ηρξατο εκθαμβεισθαι και αδημονειν. 34 Και
and began to be greatly amazed and to be in anguish. And
λεγει αυτοις· Περιλυπος εστιν ἡ ψυχη μου ἑως
he says to them; Extremely sorrowful is the soul of me even to

23 And taking *a Cup, having given thanks, he gave it to them: and they all drank out of it.

24 And he said, ‡"This is THAT BLOOD of mine which is of the COVENANT, THAT which is POURED OUT for many.

25 Indeed I say to you, * That I will drink of the PRODUCT of the VINE no more, till that DAY when I drink It new in the KINGDOM of GOD."

26 ‡And having sung, they went out to the MOUNT of OLIVES.

27 And JESUS says to them, "You will all be stumbled; because it is written, ‡'I will smite the 'SHEPHERD, and the 'SHEEP will be dispersed.'

28 ‡But after I am RAISED, I will precede you to GALILEE."

29 ‡And PETER said to him, "Even if all shall be stumbled, yet I will not."

30 And JESUS says to him, "Indeed I say to thee, That thou This-day, in This NIGHT, before a Cock crows twice, wilt disown Me thrice."

31 But HE spoke with more vehemence, "If I must die with thee, I will by no means disown Thee." And they all said the same.

32 ‡And they came to a Place named Gethsamane, and he says to his DISCIPLES, "Sit here, while I *go away and pray."

33 And he takes with him PETER, and *JAMES, and JOHN, and began to be greatly amazed and full of Anguish.

34 And he says to them, ‡"My SOUL is encompassed with a deadly An-

* VATICAN MANUSCRIPT.—22. a Cup, 24. to them—omit. 24. THAT BLOOD of mine, which is of the COVENANT, THAT which is POURED OUT. 27. at me in this NIGHT—omit. 32. go away and pray. 33. JAMES, and JOHN.

‡ 24. Luke xxii. 20; 1 Cor: xi. 25. ‡ 26. Matt. xxvi. 30. ‡ 27. Zech. xiii. 7. ‡ 28. Matt. xvi. 7. ‡ 29. Matt. xxvi. 33, 34: Luke xxii. 33, 34, John xiii. 37, 38. ‡ 32. Matt. xxvi. 36; Luke xxii. 39: John xviii. 1. ‡ 34. John xii. 27.

θανατου· μεινατε ὡδε, και γρηγορειτε. 35 Και
death; remain you here, and watch. And
προελθων μικρον, επεσεν επι της γης· και
going forward a little, he fell on the ground; and
προσηυχετο, ἱνα, ει δυνατον εστι, παρελθῃ απ'
prayed, that, if possible it is, might pass from
αυτου ἡ ὡρα. 36 Και ελεγεν· Αββα ὁ πατηρ,
him the hour. And he said, Abba the father,
παντα δυνατα σοι· παρενεγκε το ποτηριον απ'
all (things) possible to thee; take the cup from
ἐμου τουτο. Αλλ' ου, τι εγω θελω, αλλα τι
me this. But not, what I will, but what
συ. 37 Και ερχεται, και εὑρισκει αυτους καθευ-
thou. And he comes, and finds them sleep-
δοντας· και λεγει τῳ Πετρῳ· Σιμων, καθευδεις;
ing: and he says to the Peter: Simon, sleepest thou?
ουκ ισχυσας μιαν ὡραν γρηγορησαι; 38 Γρηγορ-
not couldst thou one hour to watch? Watch
ειτε και προσευχεσθε, ἱνα μη εισελθητε εις
you and pray you, that not you enter into
πειρασμον· το μεν πνευμα προθυμον, ἡ δε
temptation: the indeed spirit ready, the but
σαρξ ασθενης. 39 Και παλιν απελθων προσηυ-
flesh weak. And again going away he prayed.
ξατο, τον αυτον λογον ειπων. 40 Και ὑποστρε-
the same words saying. And having returned
ψας, εὑρεν αυτους παλιν καθευδοντας· ησαν
he found them again sleeping: were
γαρ οἱ οφθαλμοι αυτων βεβαρημενοι και ουκ
for the eyes of them weighed down and not
ηδεισαν, τι αυτῳ αποκριθωσι. 41 Και ερχεται
they knew, what to him they might answer. And he comes
το τριτον, και λεγει αυτοις· Καθευδετε το
the third, and he says to them: Do you sleep the
λοιπον και αναπαυεσθε; απεχει, ηλθεν ἡ ὡρα·
now and rest you? It is enough, is come the hour:
ιδου, παραδιδοται ὁ υἱος του ανθρωπου εις τας
lo, is delivered up the son of the man into the
χειρας των ἁμαρτωλων. 42 Εγειρεσθε, αγωμεν·
hands of the sinners. Arise, let us go:
ιδου, ὁ παραδιδους με ηγγικε.
lo, he delivering up me has come near.
43 Και ευθεως, ετι αυτου λαλουντος, παραγι-
And immediately, while of him speaking, comes
νεται Ιουδας, εἱς ων των δωδεκα, και μετ' αυτου
Judas, one being of the twelve, and with him
οχλος *[πολυς] μετα μαχαιρων και ξυλων,
crowd [great] with swords and clubs,
παρα των αρχιερεων και των γραμματεων και
from the high-priests and the scribes and
των πρεσβυτερων. 44 Δεδωκει δε ὁ παραδιδους
the elders. Had given and he delivering up
αυτον συσσημον αυτοις, λεγων· Ὁν αν φι-
him a signal to them, saying: Whoever I
λησω, αυτος εστι· κρατησατε αυτον και
may kiss, he it is: seize him and
απαγαγετε ασφαλως. 45 Και ελθων, ευθεως
lead away safely. And coming, immediately

guish; stay here and watch."

35 And going forward a little, he fell on the GROUND, and prayed, that if possible the HOUR might pass from him.

36 And he said, "Abba, FATHER, all things are possible with thee; remove this CUP from me; ‡yet not what I will, but what thou wilt."

37 And he comes and finds them sleeping; and he says to PETER, "Simon, sleepest thou? couldst thou not keep awake a Single Hour?

38 Watch and pray, that you *enter not into Trial; the SPIRIT indeed is willing, but the FLESH is weak."

39 And going again, he prayed, speaking the SAME Words.

40 And *again he came and found them sleeping; (for Their EYES were overpowered;) and they knew not what to answer him.

41 And he comes the THIRD time, and says to them, "Do you sleep NOW, and take your rest? It is enough, ‡the HOUR is come; behold the SON of MAN is delivered up into the HANDS of SINNERS.

42 ‡Arise, let us go; behold! HE, who DELIVERS me up, has come."

43 ‡And immediately, while he was yet speaking, comes *JUDAS, being one of the TWELVE, and with him a Crowd, armed with Swords and Clubs, from the HIGH-PRIESTS, and the SCRIBES, and the ELDERS.

44 And the BETRAYER had given them a Signal, saying, "He it is, whom I may kiss; seize him, and lead him away safely."

45 And coming, and immediately approaching

* VATICAN MANUSCRIPT.—38. come into. 40. again he came. 43. JUDAS, being one of the twelve. 43. great—*omit*.

‡ 36. John v. 30; vi. 38. ‡ 41. John xiii. 1. ‡ 42. Matt. xxvi. 46; John xviii. 1, 2. ‡ 43. Matt. xxvi. 47; Luke xxii. 47; John xviii. 3.

προσελθων αυτῳ, λεγει· Ῥαββι, *[ῥαββι·]
approaching to him, he says: Rabbi, [rabbi:]
και κατεφιλησεν αυτον. 46 Οἱ δε επεβαλον επ'
and kissed him. They then laid on
αυτον τας χειρας *[αὐτων,] και εκρατησαν
him the hands [of them,] and seized
αυτον. 47 Εἱς δε τις των παρεστηκοτων,
him. One and a certain of those standing,
σπασαμενος την μαχαιραν, επαισε τον δουλον
drawing the sword, struck the slave
του αρχιερεως, και αφειλεν αυτου το ωτιον.
of the high-priest, and cut off of him the ear.
48 Και αποκριθεις ὁ Ιησους ειπεν αυτοις· Ὡς
And answering the Jesus said to them; As
επι λῃστην εξηλθετε μετα μαχαιρων και
upon a robber came you out with swords and
ξυλων, συλλαβειν με. 49 Καθ' ἡμεραν ημην
clubs, to take me. Every day I was
προς ὑμας εν τῳ ἱερῳ διδασκων, και ουκ
with you in the temple teaching, and not
εκρατησατε με· αλλ', ἱνα πληρωθωσιν αἱ γρα-
you seized me; but, that must be fulfilled the writ-
φαι. 50 Και αφεντες αυτον παντες εφυγον.
ings. And leaving him all they fled.
51 Και εἱς τις νεανισκος ηκολουθει αυτῳ, περι-
And one a certain young man followed him, wrap-
βεβλημενος σινδονα επι γυμνου· και κρατουσιν
ped about a linen cloth on naked, and they seized
αυτον *[οἱ νεανισκοι.] 52 Ὁ δε καταλιπων την
him [the young men.] He but leaving the
σινδονα, γυμνος εφυγεν *[απ' αυτων.]
linen cloth, naked he fled [from them.]
53 Και απηγαγον τον Ιησουν προς τον αρχιε-
And they led the Jesus to the high-
ρεα· και συνερχονται αυτῳ παντες οἱ αρχιερεις,
priest; and came together to him all the high-priests,
και οἱ πρεσβυτεροι, και οἱ γραμματεις. 54 Και
and the elders, and the scribes. And
ὁ Πετρος απο μακροθεν ηκολουθησεν αυτῳ ἑως
the Peter at a distance followed him even
εσω εις την αυλην του αρχιερεως· και ην συγ-
to into the palace of the high-priest; and was sit-
καθημενος μετα των ὑπηρετων, και θερμαινο-
ting in company with the attendants, and warming
μενος προς το φως. 55 Οἱ δε αρχιερεις και
himself to the light. The and high priests and
ὁλον το συνεδριον εζητουν κατα του Ιησου
whole the high council sought against the Jesus
μαρτυριαν εις το θανατωσαι αυτον· και ουχ
testimony for the to put to death him; and not
εὑρισκον. 56 Πολλοι γαρ εψευδομαρτυρουν
they found. Many for testified falsely
κατ' αυτου, και ισαι αἱ μαρτυριαι ουκ ησαν.
against him, but consistent the testimonies not were.
57 Και τινες αναστα̇ντες, εψευδομαρτυρουν κατ'
And some having stood up, testified falsely against
αυτου, λεγοντες· 58 Ὁτι ἡμεις ηκουσαμεν αυτου
him, saying; That we heard him

him, he says, "Rabbi," and repeatedly kissed him.

46 Then THEY laid HANDS on him, and seized him.

47 And one of THOSE STANDING by drew a SWORD, and struck a SERVANT of the HIGH-PRIEST, and cut off His *EAR-TIP.

48 ‡ And JESUS answering said to them, "As in pursuit of a Robber, have you come with Swords and Clubs to take me?

49 I was with you every day in the TEMPLE teaching, and you did not arrest me. ‡ But the SCRIPTURES must be verified."

50 And leaving him, they all fled.

51 And a certain Youth followed him, with a Linen cloth wrapped about his naked body; and they seized him;

52 but leaving the LINEN CLOTH, he fled naked.

53 ‡ And they conducted JESUS to the HIGH-PRIEST; and all the HIGH-PRIESTS, and the ELDERS, and the SCRIBES, came together to him.

54 And PETER followed him at a distance, even into the PALACE of the HIGH-PRIEST; and sat in company with the ATTENDANTS, warming himself before the FIRE.

55 ‡ And the HIGH-PRIESTS and the Whole SANHEDRIM sought testimony against JESUS, in order TO KILL him; but they found none.

56 For many testified falsely against him, but their TESTIMONIES were insufficient.

57 And some standing up, testified falsely against him, saying,

58 "We heard him de-

* VATICAN MANUSCRIPT.—45. rabbi—*omit.* 46. of them—*omit.* 47. EAR-TIP. 51. the young men—*omit.* 52. from them—*omit.*

‡ 48. Matt. xxvi. 55; Luke xxii. 52. ‡ 49. Psa. xxii. 6; Isa. liii. 7; Luke xxii. 37; xxiv. 44. ‡ 53. Matt. xxvi. 57; Luke xxii. 54; John xviii. 13. ‡ 55. Matt. xxvi. 59.

λεγοντος· Ὁτι εγω καταλυσω τον ναον τουτον
saying; That I will destroy the temple this
τον χειροποιητον, και δια τριων ἡμερων αλλον
the made with hands, and in three days another
αχειροποιητον οικοδομησω. 59 Και ουδε οὑτως
made without hands I will build. And not even thus
ιση ην ἡ μαρτυρια αυτων. 60 Και αναστας
consistent was the testimony of them. And arising
ὁ αρχιερευς εις μεσον, επηρωτησε τον Ιησουν,
the high priest in midst, he asked the Jesus,
λεγων· Ουκ αποκρινη ουδεν; τι οὑτοι σου
saying; Not answerest thou nothing? what these of thee
καταμαρτυρουσιν; 61 Ὁ δε εσιωπα, και ουδεν
testify against? He but was silent, and nothing
απεκρινατο. Παλιν ὁ αρχιερευς επηρωτα αυτον
he answered. Again the high-priest asked him
και λεγει αυτῳ· Συ ει ὁ Χριστος, ὁ υἱος του
and says to him, Thou art the Anointed, the son of the
ευλογητου; 62 Ὁ δε Ιησους ειπεν· Εγω ειμι·
blessed? The and Jesus said; I am;
και οψεσθε τον υἱον του ανθρωπου εκ δεξιων
and you shall see the son of the man at right
καθημενον της δυναμεως, και ερχομενον μετα
sitting of the power, and coming with
των νεφελων του ουρανου. 63 Ὁ δε αρχιερευς
the clouds of the heaven. The and high-priest.
διαῤῥηξας τους χιτωνας αὑτου, λεγει· Τι ετι
having rent the clothes of himself, says, What further
χρειαν εχομεν μαρτυρων; 64 Ηκουσατε της
need have we of witnesses? You have heard the
βλασφημιας· τι ὑμιν φαινεται; Οἱ δε παντες
blasphemy: what to you appears? They but all
κατεκριναν αυτον ειναι ενοχον θανατου. 65 Και
condemned him to be deserving of death. And
ηρξαντο τινες εμπτυειν αυτῳ, και περικαλυπτειν
began some to spit upon him, and to cover
το προσωπον αυτου, και κολαφιζειν αυτον,
the face of him, and to beat with the fist him,
και λεγειν αυτῳ· Προφητευσον. Και οἱ ὑπη-
and to say to him; Prophesy. And the at-
ρεται ῥαπισμασιν αυτον εβαλλον. 66 Και οντος
tendants with open hands him beat. And being
του Πετρου εν τῃ αυλῃ κατω, ερχεται μια
the Peter in the court-yard below, comes one
των παιδισκων του αρχιερεως· 67 και ιδουσα
of the maid-servants of the high priest: and seeing
τον Πετρον θερμαινομενον, εμβλεψασα αυτῳ
the Peter warming himself, she looking to him
λεγει· Και συ μετα του Ναζαρηνου Ιησου ησθα.
says: And thou with the Nazarene Jesus wast.
68 Ὁ δε ηρνησατο, λεγων· Ουκ οιδα, ουδε
He but denied, saying: Not I know, nor
επισταμαι τι συ λεγεις. Και εξηλθεν εξω εις
comprehend what thou sayest. And he went out into
το προαυλιον· *[και αλεκτωρ εφωνησε.]
the outer court: [and a cock crew.]

clare, ‡ 'I will destroy THIS TEMPLE MADE WITH HANDS, and in Three Days, I will build Another made without hands.'"

59 But not even thus was their TESTIMONY sufficient.

60 And the HIGH-PRIEST standing up in the MIDST, asked JESUS, saying, "Answerest thou nothing *to what these testify against thee?"

61 ‡ But HE was silent, and answered nothing. And the HIGH-PRIEST asked him, and says to him; "Art thou the MESSIAH, the SON of the BLESSED One?"

62 And JESUS said, "I am; and you shall see the SON of MAN sitting at the Right hand of the MIGHTY One, and coming with the CLOUDS of HEAVEN."

63 And the HIGH-PRIEST having rent his GARMENTS, says, "What further need have we of Witnesses?

64 You have heard the BLASPHEMY; What is your opinion?" And they ALL condemned him as worthy of Death.

65 And some began to spit upon him, and to cover His FACE, and to beat him with the fist, and to say to him, "Divine to us;" and the ATTENDANTS struck Him on the cheek with the Open Hand.

66 ‡ And PETER being below in the COURT-YARD, there comes one of the MAID-SERVANTS of the HIGH-PRIEST;

67 and seeing PETER warming himself, earnestly looking at him, she says, "Thou also wast with the NAZARENE, *JESUS."

68 But HE denied, saying, "I *neither know nor understand what thou sayest." And he went out into the OUTER COURT;

* VATICAN MANUSCRIPT.—60. Because these. 67. JESUS. 67 neither know nor understand. 68. and a Cock crew—*omit.*

‡ 58. Mark xv. 29: John ii. 19. ‡ 60. Matt. xxvi. 62. ‡ 61 Matt. xxiv 30; Matt. xxvi. 64; Luke xxii. 69. ‡ 66. Matt. xxvi. 58, 69; Luke xxii. 55; John xviii 16

69 Και ἡ παιδισκη ιδουσα αυτον *[παλιν] ηρξατο
And the maid-servant seeing him [again] began
λεγειν τοις παρεστηκοσιν· Ὁτι οὑτος εξ αυτων
to say to those having stood by; That this of them
εστιν. 70 Ὁ δε παλιν ηρνειτο. Και μετα
is. He and again denied. And after
μικρον παλιν οἱ παρεστωτες ελεγον τῳ Πετρῳ·
a little again those having stood by said to the Peter;
Αληθως εξ αυτων ει· και γαρ Γαλιλαιος ει,
Truly of them thou art; also for a Galilean thou art,
*[και ἡ λαλια σου ὁμοιαζει.] 71 Ὁ δε ηρξατο
[and the speech of thee is like.] He then began
αναθεματιζειν και ομνυναι· Ὁτι ουκ οιδα τον
to curse and swear; That not I know the
ανθρωπον τουτον, ὁν λεγετε. 72 Και εκ δευ-
man this, of whom you say. And of sec-
τερου αλεκτωρ εφωνησε. Και ανεμνησθη ὁ
ond cock crew. And remembered the
Πετρος του ῥηματος, οὑ ειπεν αυτῳ ὁ Ιησους·
Peter the word, of which said to him the Jesus;
Ὁτι πριν αλεκτορα φωνησαι δις, απαρνησῃ με
That before a cock to have crowed twice, thou wilt deny me
τρις. Και επιβαλων εκλαιε.
thrice. And reflecting he wept.

69 ‡ and the MAID-SERVANT seeing him, * said to THOSE STANDING BY, "This is one of them."
70 And HE denied it again. And after a little, THOSE STANDING BY said again to PETER, "Certainly, thou art one of them; for thou art also a Galilean."
71 Then HE began to curse and swear, "I know not this MAN of whom you speak."
72 ‡ And * immediately for a second time † a Cock crew. And PETER recollected the WORD which JESUS spoke to him, "That before a Cock crows twice, thou wilt disown me thrice." And reflecting on it, he wept.

ΚΕΦ. ιε'. 15.

1 Και ευθεως επι το πρωι συμβουλιον ποιη-
And immediately on the morning a council having
σαντες οἱ αρχιερεις μετα των πρεσβυτερων και
been held the high-priests with the elders and
γραμματεων, και ὁλον το συνεδριον, δησαντες
scribes, even whole the sanhedrim, binding
τον Ιησουν, απηνεγκαν και παρεδωκαν τῳ Πι-
the Jesus, carried and delivered up to the Pi-
λατῳ. 2 Και επηρωτησεν αυτον ὁ Πιλατος·
late. And asked him the Pilate;
Συ ει ὁ βασιλευς των Ιουδαιων; Ὁ δε αποκρι-
Thou art the king of the Jews? He and answer-
θεις ειπεν αυτῳ· Συ λεγεις. 3 Και κατηγορουν
ing said to him; Thou sayest. And accused
αυτου οἱ αρχιερεις πολλα. 4 Ὁ δε Πιλατος
him the high-priests many things. The and Pilate
παλιν επηρωτησεν αυτον, λεγων· Ουκ αποκρινῃ
again asked him, saying; Not answerest thou
ουδεν; ιδε, ποσα σου καταμαρτυρουσιν.
nothing? see, how many things of thee they testify against.
5 Ὁ δε Ιησους ουκετι ουδεν απεκριθη· ὡστε
The but Jesus no longer nothing answered: so as
θαυμαζειν τον Πιλατον. 6 Κατα δε ἑορτην
to surprise the Pilate. At now feast
απελυεν αυτοις ἑνα δεσμιον ὁνπερ ῃτουντο.
he used to released to them one prisoner whoever they asked.

CHAPTER XV.

1 ‡ And immediately in the * Morning, the HIGH-PRIESTS, with the ELDERS and Scribes, even the Whole SANHEDRIM, held a Council; and having bound JESUS, they carried and delivered him up to * Pilate.
2 ‡ And PILATE asked him, "Art thou the KING of the JEWS?" And HE answering, * says to him, "Thou sayest it."
3 And the HIGH-PRIESTS accused him of many things.
4 ‡ Then PILATE asked him again, saying, "Answerest thou nothing? See how many things they * accuse thee of."
5 ‡ But JESUS answered no more, so that PILATE was astonished.
6 ‡ Now at each Feast he used to release to them One Prisoner, whoever they asked.

---

* VATICAN MANUSCRIPT.—69. again—*omit*. 69. said to THOSE. 70. and thy SPEECH is like it—*omit*. 72. immediately for a second. 1. Morning. 1. Pilate. 2. says to him. 4. accuse thee of.

† 72. or a watch-trumpet sounded. See Note on Matt. xxvi. 34.

‡ 69. Matt. xxvi. 71, 73; Luke xxii. 58, 59; John xviii. 25, 26. ‡ 72. Matt. xxvi. 75. ‡ 1. Psa. ii. 2; Matt. xxvii. 1; Luke xxii. 66; xxiii. 1; John xviii. 28; Acts iii. 13; iv. 26. ‡ 2. Matt. xxvii. 11. ‡ 4. Matt. xxvii. 13. ‡ 5. Isa. liii. 7; John xix. 9. ‡ 6. Matt. xxvii. 15; Luke xxiii. 17; John xviii. 39.

7 Ην δε ὁ λεγομενος Βαραββας μετα των συστα-
Was and he being named Barabbas with the insur-
σιαστων δεδεμενος, οἱτινες εν τῃ στασει φονον
gents having been bound, who in the sedition murder
πεποιηκεισαν. 8 Και αναβοησας ὁ οχλος
had committed. And crying out the crowd
ηρξατο αιτεισθαι, καθως αει ἐποιει αυτοις.
began to demand, as always he did to them.
9 Ὁ δε Πιλατος απεκριθη αυτοις, λεγων· Θελε-
The but Pilate answered them, saying; Do you
τε απολυσω ὑμιν τον βασιλεα των Ιουδαιων;
wish I shall release to you the king of the Jews?
10 Εγινωσκε γαρ, ὁτι δια φθονον παραδεδωκεισαν
He knew for, that through envy had delivered up
αυτον οἱ αρχιερεις. 11 Οἱ δε αρχιερεις ανεσει-
him the high-priest. The and high-priests stirred
σαν τον οχλον, ἱνα μαλλον τον Βαραββαν
up the crowd, that rather the Barabbas
απολυσῃ αυτοις. 12 Ὁ δε Πιλατος αποκριθεις
he should release to them. The but Pilate answering
παλιν ειπεν αυτοις· Τι ουν θελετε ποιησω ον
again said to them; What then do you wish I shall do whom
λεγετε βασιλεα των Ιουδαιων; 13 Οἱ δε παλιν
you call a king of the Jews? They but again
εκραξαν· Σταυρωσον αυτον. 14 Ὁ δε Πιλατος
cried out; Crucify him. The and Pilate
ελεγεν αυτοις· Τι γαρ κακον εποιησεν; Οἱ δε
said to them; What for evil has he done? They but
περισσως εκραξαν· Σταυρωσον αυτον. 15 Ὁ
vehemently cried out; Crucify him. The
δε Πιλατος, βουλομενος τῳ οχλῳ το ἱκανον
then Pilate, being willing to the crowd the satisfaction
ποιησαι, απελυσεν αυτοις τον Βαραββαν, και
to make, released to them the Barabbas, and
παρεδωκε τον Ιησουν, φραγελλωσας, ἱνα
delivered up the Jesus, having scourged, that
σταυρωθῃ.
he might be crucified.

16 Οἱ δε στρατιωται απηγαγον αυτον εσω της
The and soldiers led away him within the
αυλης, ὁ εστι πραιτωριον· και συγκαλουσιν
court, which is a judgment hall; and they call together
ὁλην την σπειραν. 17 Και ενδυουσιν αυτον
whole the company. And they clothed him
πορφυραν, και περιτιθεασιν αυτῳ πλεξαντες
purple, and placed it around him braiding
ακανθινον στεφανον. 18 Και ηρξαντο ασπαζεσ-
an acanthine wreath. And they began to salute
θαι αυτον· Χαιρε ὁ βασιλευς των Ιουδαιων.
him: Hail the king of the Jews.
19 Και ετυπτον αυτου την κεφαλην καλαμῳ,
And they struck of him the head with a reed,
και ενεπτυον αυτῳ, και τιθεντες τα γονατα
and spit upon him, and placing the knees

7 And there was HE who was NAMED Barabbas, having been imprisoned with the INSURGENTS, who had committed Murder in the INSURRECTION.

8 And the CROWD * going up began to demand what he was accustomed to grant them.

9 But PILATE answered them, saying, "Do you wish me to release to you the KING of the JEWS?"

10 For he knew That * they had delivered him up from Envy.

11 ‡ But the HIGH-PRIESTS stirred up the CROWD, that he should rather release BARABBAS to them.

12 And PILATE answering again, said to them, "What * then shall I do to him you call the KING of the JEWS?"

13 And THEY again cried out, "Crucify him."

14 And PILATE said to them, "For what? Has he done Evil?" But they vehemently cried out, saying, "Crucify him."

15 ‡ Then PILATE, being willing to GRATIFY the CROWD, released BARABBAS to them; and having scourged JESUS, delivered him up to be crucified.

16 ‡ And the SOLDIERS led him away into the COURT, which is the Prætorium; and they called together the Whole COMPANY.

17 And they arrayed him in a Purple garment, and intertwining an Acanthine Wreath, placed it around his head;

18 and began to salute him,—"Hail, KING of the JEWS!"

19 And they struck his HEAD with a Reed, and spit on him, and KNEELING, did homage to him.

* VATICAN MANUSCRIPT.—8. going up began. 10. they had: 12. then shall I do to him you call the KING of the JEWS?

‡ 11. Matt. xxvii. 20: Acts iii 14. ‡ 15. Matt. xxvii. 26: John xix. 1, 16. ‡ 16. Matt. xxvii. 27.

προσεκυνουν αυτῳ. 20 Και ὁτε ενεπαιξαν αυτῳ,
did homage to him. And when they mocked him,
εξεδυσαν αυτον την πορφυραν, και ενεδυσαν
they took off him the purple, and put on
αυτον τα ἱματια τα ιδια· και εξαγουσιν αυτον,
him the clothes the own; and they led out him,
*[ἱνα σταυρωσωσιν αυτον.] 21 Και αγγαρευουσι
[that they might crucify him.] And they compel
παραγοντα τινα Σιμωνα Κυρηναιον, ερχομενον
passing by one Simon a Cyrenian, coming
απ' αγρου, (τον πατερα Αλεξανδρου και Ῥου-
from country, (the father of Alexander and Ru-
φου,) ἱνα αρῃ τον σταυρον αυτου. 22 Και
fus,) that he might bear the cross of him. And
φερουσιν αυτον επι Γολγοθα τοπον· ὁ εστι
they bring him to Golgotha place; which is
μεθερμηνευομενον, κρανιου τοπος. 23 Και εδιδουν
being translated, of a skull a place. And they gave
αυτῳ *[πιειν] εσμυρνισμενον οινον· ὁ δε
him [to drink] having been mixed with myrrh wine; he but
ουκ ελαβε.
not received.

24 Και σταυρωσαντες αυτον, διαμεριζονται τα
And crucifying him, they divide the
ἱματια αυτου, βαλλοντες κληρον επ' αυτα, τις
clothes of him, casting lots on them, who
τι αρῃ. 25 Ην δε ὡρα τριτη, και εσταυρωσαν
what should take. It was and hour third, and they crucified
αυτον. 26 Και ην ἡ επιγραφη της αιτιας αυτου
him. And was the inscription of the accusation of him
επιγεγραμμενη· "Ὁ βασιλευς των Ιουδαιων."
was written over; The king of the Jews."
27 Και συν αυτῳ σταυρουσι δυο λῃστας· ἑνα εκ
And with him they crucify two robbers; one at
δεξιων, και ἑνα εξ ευωνυμων αυτου. 28 *[Και
right, and one at left of him. [And
επληρωθη ἡ γραφη ἡ λεγουσα· "Και μετα
was fulfilled the writing that saying; And with
ανομων ελογισθη."] 29 Και οἱ παραπορευομενοι
lawless ones he was numbered."] And those passing along
εβλασφημουν αυτον, κινουντες τας κεφαλας
reviled him, shaking the heads
αὑτων, και λεγοντες· Ουα· ὁ καταλυων τον
of them, and saying; Ah; he destroying the
ναον, και εν τρισιν ἡμεραις οικοδομων·
temple, and in three days building;
30 σωσον σεαυτον, και καταβα απο του σταυρου.
save thyself, and come down from the cross.
31 Ὁμοιως και οἱ αρχιερεις, εμπαιξοντες προς
In like manner also the high-priests, mocking to
αλληλους μετα των γραμματεων, ελεγον·
one another with the scribes, said;

20 And when they had mocked him, they stripped him of the PURPLE garment, and put on him * his own CLOTHES, and led him out.

21 ‡ And One Simon, a Cyrenian, the FATHER of † Alexander and Rufus, coming from the Country, was passing by, and they compel him to carry his CROSS.

22 ‡ And they bring him to * GOLGOTHA, which, being translated, is, a Place of a Skull.

23 And they presented him Wine mingled with Myrrh; but * HE did not receive it.

24 And * they nail him to the Cross, ‡ and part his GARMENTS, casting Lots for them, what each should take.

25 And it was the third Hour when they nailed him to the Cross.

26 And the INSCRIPTION of his ACCUSATION was written over him, "The KING of the JEWS."

27 And with him they * crucified Two Robbers; one at his Right hand, and the other at his Left.

28 * † [And THAT SCRIPTURE was verified, which SAYS, ‡ "He was numbered "with LAW-BREAKERS."]

29 And THOSE PASSING ALONG reviled him, ‡ shaking their HEADS, and saying, "Ah! THOU DESTROYER of the TEMPLE, and Builder of it in Three Days,—

30 save thyself, and come down from the CROSS!"

31 In like manner also, the HIGH-PRIESTS deriding him, with the Scribes, said

* VATICAN MANUSCRIPT.—20. his CLOTHES. 20. that they might crucify him—omit. 22. GOLGOTHA. 23. to drink—omit. 23. HE. 24. they nail him to the Cross, and part his GARMENTS. 27. crucified. 28.—omit.

† 21. Persons probably well known, and then living at Rome; since Paul, Rom. xvi. 13, salutes *Rufus* there. † 28. Fritz. and Tischendorf cancel this verse, and Griesbach marks it for omission; yet Bloomfield thinks injudiciously, as it is a remarkable fulfilment of prophecy, and is omitted only by a few MSS.

‡ 21. Matt. xxvii. 32; Luke xxiii. 26. ‡ 22. John xix. 17. ‡ 24. Psa. xxii. 18; Luke xxiii. 34; John xix. 23. ‡ 28. Isa. liii. 12; Luke xxii. 37. ‡ 29. Psa. xxii. 7

Αλλους εσωσεν, ἑαυτον ου δυναται σωσαι;
Others he saved, himself not is able to save?
32 Ὁ Χριστος, ὁ βασιλευς του Ισραηλ, κατα-
The Anointed, the king of the Israel, let him
βατω νυν απο του σταυρου, ἱνα ιδωμεν και
descend now from the cross, that we may see and
πιστευσωμεν. Και οἱ συνεσταυρωμενοι αυτῳ
may believe. And those having been crucified with him
ωνειδιζον αυτον. 33 Γενομενης δε ὡρας ἑκτης,
reproached him. Being come and hour sixth,
σκοτος εγενετο εφ' ὁλην την γην, ἑως ὡρας
darkness was on whole the land, till hour
εννατης. 34 Και τῃ ὡρᾳ τῃ εννατῃ εβοησεν ὁ
ninth. And the hour the ninth cried the
Ιησους φωνῃ μεγαλῃ, *[λεγων·] Ελωι, ελωι·
Jesus with a voice loud, [saying;] Eloi, eloi;
λαμμα σαβαχθανι; ὁ εστι μεθερμηνευομενον·
lamma sabachthani? which is being translated;
Ὁ θεος μου, *[ὁ θεος μου·] εις τι με εγκατε-
The God of me, [the God of me:] to what me hast thou
λιπες; 35 Και τινες των παρεστηκοτων ακου-
left; And some of those standing by hear-
σαντες, ελεγον· Ιδου, Ηλιαν φωνει. 36 Δραμων
ing, said: Lo, Elias he calls. Running
δε εἱς, και γεμισας σπογγον οξους, περιθεις τε
and one, and filling a sponge of vinegar, attaching and
καλαμῳ, εποτιζεν αυτον, λεγων· Αφετε· ιδωμεν,
to a reed, gave to drink him, saying: Let alone: we may see,
ει ερχεται Ηλιας καθελειν αυτον. 37 Ὁ δε
if comes Elias to take down him. The then
Ιησους, αφεις φωνην μεγαλην, εξεπνευσε.
Jesus, uttering a voice loud, breathed out.

38 Και το καταπετασμα του ναου εσχισθη εις
And the curtain of the temple was rent into
δυο, απο ανωθεν ἑως κατω. 39 Ιδων δε ὁ κεντυ-
two, from above to below. Seeing but the centu-
ριων, ὁ παρεστηκως εξ εναντιας αυτου, ὁτι
rion, that having stood by over against him, that
οὑτω *[κραξας] εξεπνευσεν, ειπεν· Αληθως ὁ
thus [having cried] he breathed out, said: Truly the
ανθρωπος οὑτος υἱος ἠν θεου. 40 Ησαν δε και
man this a son was of a god. Were and also
γυναικες απο μακροθεν θεωρουσαι· εν αἱς ην και
women from a distance beholding: among whom was also
Μαρια ἡ Μαγδαληνη, και Μαρια ἡ του Ιακωβου
Mary the Magdalene, and Mary the of the James
του μικρου και Ιωση μητηρ, και Σαλωμη· 41 αἱ
the little and Joses mother, and Salome: who
*[και,] ὁτε ην εν τῃ Γαλιλαιᾳ, ηκολουθουν
[also,] when he was in the Galilee, followed
αυτῳ, και διηκονουν αυτῳ· και αλλαι πολλαι,
him, and served him: and others many,
αἱ συναναβασαι αυτῳ εις Ἱεροσολυμα.
those having come up with him to Jerusalem.

to each other, "He saved others; cannot he save himself?
32 The MESSIAH! the KING of *Israel! let him come down now from the CROSS, that we may see and believe." Even those, ‡who were crucified with him, reproached him.
33 And the sixth Hour being come, there was Darkness over the Whole LAND, till the ninth Hour.
34 And at the *NINTH Hour JESUS cried with a loud Voice, ‡"Eloi, Eloi, lamma sabachthani?" which, being translated, is, "My GOD! to what hast thou surrendered me?"
35 And some of THOSE STANDING BY, hearing this, said, "Behold, he calls Elijah."
36 ‡And one ran, and filled a Sponge with Vinegar, and putting it on a Reed, gave him to drink, saying, "Let him alone; let us see whether Elijah will come to take him down."
37 Then JESUS uttering a loud Voice, expired.
38 ‡And the VEIL of the TEMPLE was rent in Two from top to bottom.
39 And THAT CENTURION who STOOD BY over against him, seeing that thus he expired, said, "Certainly, *This MAN was a Son of God."
40 ‡And Women also were beholding from a distance; among whom was Mary of MAGDALA, and Mary the MOTHER of JAMES the YOUNGER, and *of Joses, and Salome;
41 who when he was in GALILEE, ‡followed him, and ministered to him; and MANY Others, who CAME UP with him to Jerusalem.

* VATICAN MANUSCRIPT.—32. Israel. 34. NINTH Hour. 34. saying—*omit.* 34. my GOD—*omit.* 39. having cried—*omit.* 39. This MAN. 40. the mother of. 41. also—*omit.*

‡ 32. Matt. xxvii. 44; Luke xxiii. 39. ‡ 34. Psa. xxii. 1; Matt. xxvii. 46. ‡ 36. Psa. lxix. 21. ‡ 38. Matt. xxvii. 51; Luke xxiii. 45. ‡ 40. Psa. xxxviii. 11. ‡ 41. Luke viii. 2, 3.

42 Και ηδη οψιας γενομενης, (επει ην παρα-
And now evening being come, (since it was prepa-
σκευη, ὁ εστι προσαββατον,) 43 ηλθεν Ιωσηφ
ration, that is before sabbath,) came Joseph
ὁ απο Αριμαθαιας, ευσχημων βουλευτης, ὁς
that from Arimathea, of rank a senator, who
και αυτος ην προσδεχομενος την βασιλειαν του
also himself was expecting the kingdom of the
θεου, τολμησας εισηλθε προς Πιλατον, και
God, assuming courage went in to Pilate, and
ᾐτησατο το σωμα του Ιησου. 44 Ὁ δε Πιλατος
asked for the body of the Jesus. The and Pilate
εθαυμασεν, ει ηδη τεθνηκε· και προσκαλεσα-
wondered, if already he was dead; and having
μενος τον κεντυριωνα, επηρωτησεν αυτον, ει
called the centurion, he asked him, if
παλαι απεθανε. 45 Και γνους απο του κεντυ-
already he had died. And knowing from the centu-
ριωνος, εδωρησατο το σωμα τῳ Ιωσηφ. 46 Και
rion, he gave the body to Joseph. And
αγορασας σινδονα, *[και] καθελων αυτον,
having bought linen, [and] having taken down him,
ενειλησε τῃ σινδονι· και κατεθηκεν αυτον εν
he wrapped the linen; and laid him in
μνημειῳ, ὁ ην λελατομημενον εκ πετρας· και
a tomb, which was having been hewn out of a rock; and
προσεκυλισε λιθον επι την θυραν του μνημειου.
rolled a stone against the door of the tomb.
47 Ἡ δε Μαρια ἡ Μαγδαληνη και Μαρια Ιωση
The but Mary the Magdalene and Mary of Joses
εθεωρουν, που τιθεται.
beheld, where he was laid.

ΚΕΦ. ιϛ'. 16.

1 Και διαγενομενου του σαββατου, Μαρια ἡ
And being past the sabbath, Mary the
Μαγδαληνη, και Μαρια ἡ του Ιακωβου, και
Magdalene, and Mary that of the James, and
Σαλωμη ηγορασαν αρωματα, ἱνα ελθουσαι
Salome bought aromatics, that coming
αλειψωσιν αυτον. 2 Και λιαν πρωι της μιας
they might anoint him. And very early of the first
σαββατων ερχονται επι το μνημειον, ανατει-
of week they came to the tomb, having
λαντος του ἡλιου. 3 Και ελεγον προς ἑαυτας·
risen the sun. And they said to themselves;
Τις αποκυλισει ἡμιν τον λιθον εκ της θυρας του
Who will roll away for us the stone from the door of the
μνημειου; 4 Και αναβλεψασαι θεωρουσιν, ὁτι
tomb? And looking up they saw, that
αποκεκυλισται ὁ λιθος· ην γαρ μεγας σφοδρα.
had been rolled away the stone; it was for great very.
5 Και εισελθουσαι εις το μνημειον, ειδον νε-
And having entered into the tomb, they saw a

42 ‡ And Evening being now come, (since it was the Preparation, that is, the Day before the Sabbath,)

43 THAT Joseph came, who was of Arimathea, an honorable Senator, who himself also was ‡ expecting the KINGDOM of GOD, taking courage, went to * PILATE, and asked for the BODY of JESUS.

44 And PILATE wondered that he was already dead; and having called the CENTURION, he inquired of him * if he was already dead.

45 And having ascertained from the CENTURION, he gave the * DEAD-BODY to JOSEPH.

46 And having bought Linen, taking him down, he wrapped him in the LINEN, and * put him in a Tomb which was hewn out of the Rock, and rolled a Stone to the ENTRANCE of the TOMB.

47 And Mary of MAGDALA, and * THAT Mary the mother of Joses, saw where he was laid.

CHAPTER XVI.

1 ‡ And the SABBATH being past, Mary of MAGDALA, and THAT Mary the mother of JAMES, and Salome, ‡ bought Aromatics, that they might come and anoint him.

2 And very early on the * first day of the WEEK, (about sunrise,) they came to the TOMB.

3 And they said to themselves, "Who will roll away the STONE for us from the ENTRANCE of the TOMB?"

4 (for it was very large.) And looking up, they saw that the STONE had been rolled away.

5 ‡ And * coming to the

* VATICAN MANUSCRIPT.—43. PILATE. 44. if he was already dead. 45. DEAD BODY. 46. and—*omit.* 46. put him. 47. THAT Mary the mother. 2. first day of the WEEK. 5. coming to.

‡ 42. Matt. xxvii. 57; Luke xxiii. 50; John xix. 38. ‡ 43. Luke ii. 25, 38. ‡ 1. Matt. xxviii. 1; Luke xxiv. 1; John xx. 1. ‡ 1. Luke xxiii. 56. ‡ 5. Luke xxiv. 3; John xx. 11, 12.

ανισκον καθημενον εν τοις δεξιοις, περιβεβλη-
youth sitting on the right, having been
μενον στολην λευκην· και εξεθαμβηθησαν.
clothed a robe white; and they were awe-struck.
6 Ὁ δε λεγει αυταις· Μη εκθαμβεισθε· Ιησουν
He but says to them; Not be you amazed; Jesus
ζητειτε τον Ναζαρηνον, τον εσταυρωμενον·
you seek the Nazarene, the having been crucified;
ηγερθη, ουκ εστιν ὡδε· ιδε ὁ τοπος, ὁπου
he has been raised, not he is here; see the place, where
εθηκαν αυτον. 7 Αλλ' ὑπαγετε, ειπατε τοις
they laid him. But go, say to the
μαθηταις αυτου, και τῳ Πετρῳ, ὁτι προαγει
disciples of him, and to the Peter, that he goes before
ὑμας εις την Γαλιλαιαν· εκει αυτον οψεσθε,
you into the Galilee; there him you will see,
καθως ειπεν ὑμιν. 8 Και εξελθουσαι, εφυγον
as he said to you. And having gone out, they fled
απο του μνημειου· ειχε δε αυτας τρομος και
from the tomb, had seized and them trembling and
εκστασις, και ουδενι ουδεν ειπον· εφοβουντο
astonishment, and to no one nothing they said; they were afraid
γαρ.
for.

9 *[Αναστας δε πρωι πρωτῃ σαββατου εφανη
[Having risen and early first of week he appeared
πρωτον Μαριᾳ τῃ Μαγδαληνῃ, αφ' ἡς εκβεβ-
first to Mary the Magdalene, from whom he had
ληκει ἑπτα δαιμονια. 10 Εκεινη πορευθεισα
cast seven demons. She going
απηγγειλε τοις μετ' αυτου γενομενοις, πεν-
brought back word to those with him having been, mourn-
θουσι και κλαιουσι. 11 Κακεινοι ακουσαντες
ing and weeping. And those having heard
ὁτι ζῃ και εθεαθη ὑπ' αυτης, ηπιστησαν.
that he was alive and had been seen by her, they did not believe.
12 Μετα δε ταυτα δυσιν εξ αυτων περιπατουσιν
After but these things to two of them walking
εφανερωθη εν ἑτερᾳ μορφῃ, πορευομενοις εις
he appeared in another aspect, going into
αγρον. 13 Κακεινοι απελθοντες απηγγειλαν
country. And those having gone brought back word
τοις λοιποις· ουδε εκεινοις επιστευσαν.
to the rest; neither to them did they give credit.
14 Ὑστερον, ανακειμενοις αυτοις τοις ἑνδεκα
Afterwards, reclining with them to the eleven
εφανερωθη· και ωνειδισε την απιστιαν αυτων
he appeared; and reproached the unbelief of them
και σκληροκαρδιαν, ὁτι τοις θεασαμενοις αυτον
and hardness of heart, because to those having seen him
εγηγερμενον ουκ επιστευσαν. 15 Και ειπεν
having been raised not they gave credit. And said

TOMB, they saw a Youth sitting at the RIGHT side, clothed with a white Robe; and they were awe-struck.

6 ‡And HE says to them; "Be not alarmed; you seek Jesus, THAT NAZARENE who was CRUCIFIED. He has been raised; he is not here. See the PLACE where they laid him!

7 But go, say to his DISCIPLES, and to PETER, That he precedes you to GALILEE; there you will see Him, ‡as he said to you."

8 And coming out, they fled from the TOMB; for trembling and astonishment had seized them; and they said nothing to any one, for they were afraid.

9 *[And having risen early on the first day of the Week, ‡he appeared first to Mary of MAGDALA, from whom he had expelled Seven Demons.

10 ‡She went and told THOSE who had BEEN with him, as they were mourning and weeping.

11 And they, having heard that he was alive, and had been seen by her, did not believe it.

12 And after THESE things, he appeared in Another Aspect ‡to two of them, as they were walking, going into the country.

13 And they returning announced it to the OTHER disciples; neither to THEM did they give credit.

14 ‡Afterwards he appeared to the ELEVEN, as they were reclining, and censured their UNBELIEF and OBSTINACY, Because they believed not THOSE who had SEEN him after his resurrection,

* VATICAN MANUSCRIPT.—9—20—*omit.*

† 9. From this verse to the end of the chapter is wanting in the Vat. MS., and in many other ancient copies. Griesbach marks the whole passage of very doubtful authenticity, but retains it in the text. Tischendorf rejects the whole clause. But judging from the evidence with regard to this passage, it is probably an authentic fragment, placed as a completion of the Gospel in very early times; and therefore coming to us with strong claims on our reception and reverence.

‡ 6. Matt. xxviii. 5—7. ‡ 7. Matt. xxvi. 32; Mark xiv. 28. ‡ 9. John xx. 14. ‡ 10. Luke xxiv. 10; John xx. 18. ‡ 12. Luke xxiv. 13. ‡ 14. Luke xxiv. 36; John xx. 19; 1 Cor. xv. 5.

αυτοις· Πορευθεντες εις τον κοσμον ἁπαντα,
to them; Having gone into the world all.
κηρυξατε το ευαγγελιον παση τη κτισει. 16 Ὁ
publish the glad tidings to all the creation. He
πιστευσας και βαπτισθεις, σωθησεται· ὁ δε
having believed and having been dipped, shall be saved; he but
απιστησας, κατακριθησεται. 17 Σημεια δε τοις
not having believed, shall be condemned. Signs and to those
πιστευσασι ταυτα παρακολευθησει· Εν τῳ
having believed these shall attend; In the
ονοματι μου δαιμονια εκβαλουσι· γλωσσαις
name of me demons they shall cast out; with tongues
λαλησουσι καιναις· 18 οφεις αρουσι· καν
they shall speak new: serpents they shall take up; and if
θανασιμον τι πιωσιν, ου μη αυτους βλαψει·
deadly thing they may drink, not not them it may hurt:
επι αρρωστους χειρας επιθησουσι, και καλως
upon sick ones hands they shall place, and well
ἑξουσιν. 19 Ὁ μεν ουν κυριος, μετα το λαλη-
they will be. The indeed then Lord, after the to have
σαι αυτοις, ανεληφθη εις τον ουρανον, και
spoken to them, he was taken up into the heaven, and
εκαθισεν εκ δεξιων του θεου· 20 εκεινοι δε εξελ-
sat at right of the God: those and having
θοντες εκηρυξαν πανταχου, του κυριου συνερ-
gone forth published everywhere, the Lord working
γουντος, και τον λογον βεβαιουντος δια των
with, and the word ratifying through the
επακολουθουντων σημειων.]
accompaying signs.]

15 ‡And he said to
them, "Go into all the
WORLD, and proclaim the
GLAD TIDINGS to the
Whole CREATION.
16 HE who BELIEVES
and is immersed will be
saved; but HE who BE-
LIEVES NOT will be con-
demned.
17 And these Signs will
accompany the BELIEV-
ERS; ‡in my NAME they
will expel Demons; ‡they
will speak in new Lan-
guages;
18 ‡they will take up
Serpents; and if they
should drink any deadly
poison, it will not injure
Them; ‡they will lay
Hands on Sick persons,
and they will be well."
19 Then, indeed, after
the LORD had SPOKEN to
them, ‡he was taken up
into HEAVEN, and sat
down at the Right hand of
GOD.
20 And THOSE having
gone forth, proclaimed
everywhere, ‡the Lord
co-operating, and ratifying
the WORD through the
ACCOMPANYING Signs.

* ACCORDING TO MARK.

* VATICAN MANUSCRIPT.—*Subscription*—ACCORDING TO MARK.

‡ 15. Matt. xxviii. 19; Rom. x. 15—18; Col. i. 23. ‡ 16. Acts ii. 38; viii. 12; xvi. 31—33. ‡ 17. Acts v. 16; viii. 7; xvi. 18. ‡ 17. Acts ii. 4; x. 46; xix. 6. ‡ 18. Acts xxviii. 5. ‡ 18. Acts xxviii. 8; James v. 14, 15. ‡ 19. Luke xxiv. 51; Acts i. 9; ii. 34, 35. ‡ 20. Acts v. 12; xiv. 3; 1 Cor. ii. 4, 5; Heb. ii. 4.

[ΕΥΑΓΓΕΛΙΟΝ] ΚΑΤΑ ΛΟΥΚΑΝ.
[GLAD TIDINGS] BY LUKE.

ACCORDING TO LUKE.

ΚΕΦ. α΄. 1.

1 Επειδηπερ πολλοι επεχειρησαν αναταξασθαι
Since many have undertaken to prepare

διηγησιν περι των πεπληροφορημενων εν ἡμιν
a narrative about those having been fully established among us,

πραγματων, 2 καθως παρεδοσαν ἡμιν οἱ απ᾽
facts. even as delivered to us those from

αρχης αυτοπται και ὑπηρεται γενομενοι του
a beginning eye-witnesses and ministers having been of the

λογου· 3 εδοξε καμοι, παρηκολουθηκοτι ανωθεν
word; it seemed right also to me, having traced from the first

πασιν ακριβως, καθεξης σοι γραψαι, κρα-
all accurately, in an orderly manner to thee to write, O most

τιστε Θεοφιλε, 4 ἱνα επιγνῳς περι ὡν
excellent Theophilus, that thou mayest know concerning which

κατηχηθης λογων την ασφαλειαν.
thou hast been taught of words the certainty.

5 Εγενετο εν ταις ἡμεραις Ἡρωδου, του βασι-
Was in the days of Herod, the king

λεως της Ιουδαιας, ἱερευς τις ονοματι Ζαχαριας,
of the Jews, a priest certain name Zacharias,

εξ εφημεριας Αβια· και ἡ γυνη αυτου εκ των
of course of Abia; and the wife of him of the

θυγατερων Ααρων, και το ονομα αυτης Ελισαβετ.
daughters of Aaron, and the name of her Elisabeth.

6 Ησαν δε δικαιοι αμφοτεροι ενωπιον του θεου,
They were and righteous both in presence of the God,

πορευομενοι εν πασαις ταις εντολαις και δικαι-
walking in all the commandments and ordi-

ωμασι του κυριου αμεμπτοι. 7 Και ουκ ην αυτοις
nances of the Lord blameless. And not was to them

τεκνον, καθοτι ἡ Ελισαβετ ην στειρα, και
a child, because the Elisabeth was barren, and

αμφοτεροι προβεβηκοτες εν ταις ἡμεραις αὑτων
both having been advanced in the days of them

ησαν. 8 Εγενετο δε εν τῳ ἱερατευειν αυτον
were. It happened now in the to perform sacred rites him

εν τῃ ταξει της εφημεριας αυτου εναντι του
in the order of the course of him before of the

θεου, 9 κατα το εθος της ἱερατειας ελαχε
God, according to the custom of the priesthood it fell to his lo

CHAPTER I.

1 Since many have un-
dertaken to prepare a History of those FACTS, which
have been FULLY ESTAB-
LISHED among us,
2 ‡ even as THOSE, who
WERE from the Beginning
Eye-witnesses and Dispen-
sers of the WORD, delivered
them to us;
3 it seemed proper for
me also, having accurately
traced all things from the
first, to write to Thee in
consecutive order, ‡ † Most
excellent Theophilus,
4 that thou mayest know
‡ the CERTAINTY of the
Words, concerning which
thou hast been taught.
5 ‡ In the DAYS of
Herod, * King of JUDEA,
there was a certain Priest
named Zachariah, ‡ of the
Course of Abijah; and his
* Wife was of the DAUGH-
TERS of Aaron, and her
NAME was Elizabeth.
6 And they were both
righteous in the sight of
GOD, walking in all the
COMMANDMENTS and In-
stitutions of the LORD
blameless.
7 And they had no Child,
because * Elizabeth was
barren, and both were far
advanced in YEARS.
8 Now it occurred, while
he was PERFORMING THE
PRIEST'S OFFICE before
GOD, in the ORDER of his
CLASS,
9 † that it fell to him by
lot, according to the cus-

---

* VATICAN MANUSCRIPT.—*Title*—ACCORDING TO LUKE. 5. King. 5. Wife. 7. Elizabeth.

† 3. This epithet proves that Theophilus was a man of Senatorian rank; probably a prefect, or governor; the same Greek title being applied to the Roman governor Felix, in Acts xxiii. 26, and elsewhere. It was equivalent to the Latin title *optimus*, bestowed by the Romans on their principal senators. † 9. Prideaux, referring to Lightfoot's Temple Service, says, that the priests, according to David's institution, were divided into twenty-four courses, that each course attended at Jerusalem its week; and every course being divided into seven classes, each class served its day at the temple; and each priest of that class had his part in the service appointed by lot. And Josephus gives much the same account, adding that the priests entered upon their office on the sabbath-day at noon, and left it at the same time on the sabbath-day following; and that this practice, first settled by David, continued to his own days.—*Pearce.*

‡ 2. Heb. ii. 3; 1 Pet. v. 1; 2 Pet. i. 16; 1 John i. 1; Mark i. 1; John xv. 27. ‡ 3. Acts i. 1. ‡ 4. John xx. 31. ‡ 5. Matt. ii. 1. ‡ 5. 1 Chron. xxiv. 10, 19; Neh. xii. 4, 17.

του θυμιασαι, εισελθων εις τον ναον του κυριου·
of the to burn incense, entering into the temple of the Lord;
10 και παν το πληθος ην του λαου προσευχομενον
and whole the multitude was of the people praying
εξω τῃ ὡρᾳ του θυμιαματος. 11 Ωφθη δε
without to the hour of the incense burning. Appeared and
αυτῳ αγγελος κυριου, ἑστως εκ δεξιων του
to him a messenger of a lord, standing at right of the
θυσιαστηριου του θυμιαματος. 12 Και εταραχθη
altar of the incense. And was troubled
Ζαχαριας ιδων, και φοβος επεπεσεν επ' αυτον.
Zacharias seeing, and fear fell upon him.
13 Ειπε δε προς αυτον ὁ αγγελος· Μη φοβου,
Said but to him the messenger; Not fear,
Ζαχαρια· διοτι εισηκουσθη ἡ δεησις σου, και ἡ
Zacharias; because has been heard the prayer of thee, and the
γυνη σου Ελισαβετ γεννησει ὑιον σοι· και
wife of thee Elisabeth shall bear a son to thee; and
καλεσεις το ονομα αυτου Ιωαννην. 14 Και
thou shalt call the name of him John. And
εσται χαρα σοι και αγαλλιασις, και πολλοι
he shall be a joy to thee and exultation, and many
επι τῃ γενεσει αυτου χαρησονται. 15 Εσται
at the birth of him shall be glad. He shall be
γαρ μεγας ενωπιον κυριου· και οινον και σικερα
for great in sight of a lord; and wine and strong drink
ου μη πιῃ· και πνευματος ἁγιου πλησθησεται
not not he may drink; and a spirit of holy shall be filled
ετι εκ κοιλιας μητρος αὑτου. 16 Και πολλους
yet out o womb of mother of himself. And many
των υἱων Ισραηλ επιστρεψει επι κυριον τον
of the sons of Israel shall he turn to a lord the
θεον αυτων. 17 Και αυτος προελευσεται ενωπιον
God of them. And he shall precede in the sight
αυτου εν πνευματι και δυναμει Ηλιου, επιστρε-
of him in spirit and power of Elias, to
ψαι καρδιας πατερων επι τεκνα, και απειθεις εν
turn hearts of fathers to children, and disobedient by
φρονησει δικαιων, ἑτοιμασαι κυριῳ λαον κατε-
wisdom of just (ones,) to make ready for a lord a people having
σκευασμενον. 18 Και ειπε Ζαχαριας προς τον
been prepared. And said Zacharias to the
αγγελον· Κατα τι γνωσομαι τουτο; εγω γαρ
messenger; By what shall I know this? I for
ειμι πρεσβυτης, και ἡ γυνη μου προβεβηκυια
am an old man, and the wife of me far advanced
εν ταις ἡμεραις αὑτης. 19 Και αποκριθεις ὁ
in the days of herself. And answering the
αγγελος ειπεν αυτῳ· Εγω ειμι Γαβριηλ, ὁ
messenger said to him. I am Gabriel, the

TOM of the PRIESTHOOD, ‡to go into the †SANCTUARY of the LORD to burn INCENSE.

10 ‡And the Whole MULTITUDE of the PEOPLE was praying without, at the HOUR of the INCENSE BURNING.

11 And there appeared to him an Angel of the Lord, standing at the right side of the ALTAR of INCENSE.

12 And Zachariah seeing him, ‡was agitated, and Fear fell on him.

13 But the ANGEL said to him, "Fear not, Zachariah; because thy PRAYER has been heard; and thy WIFE Elizabeth will bear thee a Son, ‡and thou shalt call his NAME John.

14 And he will be to thee a Joy and Exultation; and many will rejoice on account of his BIRTH.

15 For he will be great in the sight of the LORD; and ‡will not partake of Wine and †Strong drink; but he will be filled with holy Spirit, even from his Birth.

16 And many of the SONS of Israel will he turn to the Lord their GOD.

17 ‡And he will come first into his sight in the Spirit and Power of Elijah, to turn the Hearts of Fathers to Children, and the Disobedient, by the Wisdom of the Righteous; to make ready for the Lord a prepared People.

18 And Zachariah said to the ANGEL, ‡"By what shall I know this? for I am old, and my WIFE is far advanced in YEARS."

19 And the ANGEL answering, said to him, ‡"I am THAT Gabriel, ATTEND-

† 9. The holy place where the altar of incense stood, before the veil. Exod. xxx. 1, 6—8; xl. 26. † 15. The original word is derived from a root which signifies *to inebriate;* and denotes wine made from fruits, and particularly from the palm. John was to be a Nazarite. Jerome says, "Any inebriating liquor is called *sicera*, whether made of *corn, apples, honey, dates*, or any other fruits." The English word *cider* comes from the same word.

‡ 9. Exod. xxx. 7, 8; 1 Sam. ii. 28; 1 Chron. xxiii. 13; 2 Chron. xxix. 11. ‡ 10. Lev. xvi. 17. ‡ 11. Dan. x. 8; Luke i. 29; ii. 9; Acts x. 4; Rev. i. 17. ‡ 13. ver. 60, 63. ‡ 15. Num. vi. 3; Judges xiii. 4; Mark vii. 33. ‡ 17. Mal. iv. 5; Matt. xi. 14; Mark ix. 12. ‡ 18. Gen. xvii. 17. ‡ 19. Dan. viii. 16; ix. 21—23; Matt. xviii. 10.

παρεστηκως ενωπιον του θεου· και απεσταλην
having attended in presence of the God; and I am sent
λαλησαι προς σε, και ευαγγελισασθαι σοι
to speak to thee. and to tell glad tidings to thee
ταυτα. 20 Και ιδου, εσῃ σιωπων, και μη
these. And lo, thou shalt be having been dumb, and not
δυναμενος λαλησαι, αχρι ἡς ἡμερας γενηται
being able to speak, till of which day may be done
ταυτα· ανθ' ὡν ουκ επιστευσας τοις λογοις
these; because of which not thou hast believed the words
μου, οἱτινες πληρωθησονται εις τον καιρον
of me, which shall be fulfilled into the season
αὑτων. 21 Και ην ὁ λαος προσδοκων τον Ζαχα-
of them. And was the people waiting for the Zacha-
ριαν· και εθαυμαζον εν τῳ χρονιζειν αυτον εν
rias; and wondering in the to delay him in
τῳ ναῳ. 22 Εξελθων δε ουκ ηδυνατο λαλησαι
the temple. Coming out but not he was able to speak
αυτοις· και επεγνωσαν, ὁτι οπτασιαν ἑωρακεν
to them; and they perceived, that a vision he has seen
εν τῳ ναῳ· και αυτος ην διανευων αυτοις, και
in the temple; and he was making signs to them, and
διεμενε κωφος. 23 Και εγενετο ὡς επλησθησαν
remained dumb. And it happened as were filled
αἱ ἡμεραι της λειτουργιας αυτου, απηλθεν εις
the days of the ministration of him, he went to
τον οικον αὑτου. 24 Μετα δε ταυτας τας ἡμερας
the house of himself. After and these the days
συνελαβεν Ελισαβετ ἡ γυνη αυτου· και περι-
conceived Elisabeth the wife of him; and hid
εκρυβεν ἑαυτην μηνας πεντε, λεγουσα· 25 Ὁτι
herself months five, saying: That
οὑτω μοι πεποιηκεν ὁ κυριος εν ἡμεραις, αἱς
thus to me has done the Lord in days, which
επειδεν αφελειν το ονειδος μου εν ανθρωποις.
he looked on to take away the reproach of me among men.
26 Εν δε τῳ μηνι τῳ ἑκτῳ απεσταλη ὁ
In now the month the sixth was sent the
αγγελος Γαβριηλ ὑπο του θεου εις πολιν της
messenger Gabriel by the God to a city of the
Γαλιλαιας, ᾑ ονομα Ναζαρετ, 27 προς παρ-
Galilee, to which a name Nazareth, to a
θενον μεμνηστευμενην ανδρι, ᾡ ονομα Ιωσηφ,
virgin having been betrothed to a man, to whom a name Joseph.
εξ οικου Δαυιδ· και το ονομα της παρθενου,
of house of David: and the name of the virgin,
Μαριαμ. 28 Και εισελθων ὁ αγγελος προς
Mary. And coming the messenger to
αυτην, ειπε· Χαιρε, κεχαριτωμενη· ὁ κυριος
her, said: Hail, having been favored: the Lord
μετα σου· *[ευλογημενη συ εν γυναιξιν.]
with thee: [having been blessed thou among women.]
29 Ἡ δε επι τῳ λογῳ διεταραχθη, και διελογι-
She but at the word was greatly agitated, and pon-
ζετο, ποταπος ειη ὁ ασπασμος οὑτος. 30 Και
dered, what could be the salutation this. And

ING in the presence of GOD; and I am sent to speak with thee, and to tell thee these glad tidings.

20 And behold, thou shalt be silent, and unable to speak, till the Day when these things are accomplished; because thou hast not believed my WORDS, which will be fulfilled in their SEASON."

21 And the PEOPLE were waiting for ZACHARIAH, and wondered at his CONTINUING so long in the SANCTUARY.

22 And coming out, he could not speak to them; and they perceived That he had seen a Vision in the SANCTUARY; for he made Signs to them, and continued † speechless.

23 And it occurred, when ‡ the DAYS of his PUBLIC SERVICE were completed, he returned to his own HOUSE.

24 And after These DAYS Elizabeth his WIFE conceived, and concealed herself five Months, saying,

25 "Thus has the LORD done for me, in the Days when he regarded me, ‡ to take away my REPROACH among Men."

26 Now, in the SIXTH MONTH, the ANGEL Gabriel was sent by GOD to a City of GALILEE, named Nazareth,

27 to a Virgin ‡ betrothed to a Man whose name was Joseph, of the House of David; and the VIRGIN'S NAME was Mary.

28 And coming in to her, he said, ‡ "Hail, favored one! the LORD is with thee!"

29 But SHE was greatly agitated at the WORD; and she pondered what this SALUTATION could mean.

* VATICAN MANUSCRIPT.—28. blessed art thou among women—*omit*.

† 22. or deaf and dumb, for the original word has this double meaning. That Zachariah was deprived for a time of both these senses is evident from verse 62, where it is said, "they made signs to the father."

‡ 23. 2 Kings xi. 5; 1 Chron. ix. 25. ‡ 25. Gen. xxx. 23; Isa. iv. 1; liv. 1, 4.
‡ 27. Matt. i. 18; Mark ii. 4, 5.

ειπεν ὁ αγγελος αυτῃ· Μη φοβου, Μαριαμ·
said the messenger to her; Not fear, Mary;
εὑρες γαρ χαριν παρα τῳ θεῳ. 31 Και ιδου,
thou hast found for favor with the God. And lo,
συλληψῃ εν γαστρι, και τεξῃ υἱον, και
thou shalt conceive in womb, and shalt bear a son, and
καλεσεις το ὀνομα αυτου Ιησουν. 32 Οὑτος
thou shalt call the name of him Jesus. This
εσται μεγας, και υἱος ὑψιστου κληθησεται· και
shall be word, and a son of highest he shall be called; and
δωσει αυτῳ κυριος ὁ θεος τον θρονον Δαυιδ του
shall give to him a lord the God the throne of David the
πατρος αυτου· 33 και βασιλευσει επι τον οικον
father of him; and he shall reign over the house
Ιακωβ εις τους αιωνας, και της βασιλειας αυτου
of Jacob to the ages, and of the kingdom of him
ουκ εσται τελος. 34 Ειπε δε Μαριαμ προς τον
not shall be an end. Said but Mary to the
αγγελον· Πως εσται τουτο, επει ανδρα ου γι-
messenger; How shall be this, since a man not I
νωσκω; 35 Και αποκριθεις ὁ αγγελος ειπεν αυτῃ·
know? And answering the messenger said to her,
Πνευμα ἁγιον επελευσεται επι σε, και δυναμις
A spirit holy shall come upon thee, and a power
ὑψιστου επισκιασει σοι· διο και το γεννωμενον
of highest shall overshadow thee; therefore and the being begotten
ἁγιον, κληθησεται υἱος θεου. 36 Και ιδου,
holy, shall be called a son of God. And lo,
Ελισαβετ ἡ συγγενης σου, και αυτη συνειλη-
Elizabeth the kinswoman of thee, even she having
φυια υἱον εν γηρει αυτης· και οὑτος μην ἑκτος
conceived a son in old age of her; and this month sixth
εστιν αυτῃ τῃ καλουμενῃ στειρᾳ. 37 Ὁτι ουκ
is to her the being called barren. For not
αδυνατησει παρα τῳ θεῳ παν ῥημα. 38 Ειπε δε
shall be impossible with the God every word. Said and
Μαριαμ· Ιδου, ἡ δουλη κυριου· γενοιτο μοι
Mary: lo, the handmaid of a lord: may it be done to me
κατα το ῥημα σου. Και απελθεν απ' αυτης ὁ
according to the word of thee. And went from her the
αγγελος.
messenger.

39 Αναστασα δε Μαριαμ εν ταις ἡμεραις
Arising and Mary in the days
ταυταις, επορευθη εις την ορεινην μετα
those, she went into the hilly country with
σπουδης, εις πολιν Ιουδα. 40 Και εισηλθεν εις
haste, into a city of Juda. And entered into
τον οικον Ζαχαριου, και ησπασατο την Ελισα-
the house of Zacharias, and saluted the Elisa-
βετ. 41 Και εγενετο, ὡς ηκουσεν ἡ Ελισαβετ
beth. And it happened, as heard the Elisabeth

30 And the ANGEL said
to her, "Fear not, Mary;
for thou hast found Favor
with GOD.
31 ‡And behold, thou
wilt conceive, and bear a
Son, and ‡thou shalt call
his NAME †Jesus.
32 **He** will be great, and
will be called a Son of the
Most High; and ‡the Lord
GOD will give him the
THRONE of David his FA-
THER;
33 and ‡he will reign
over the HOUSE of Jacob to
the AGES; and of his KING-
DOM there will be no End."
34 Then Mary said to
the ANGEL, "How can this
be, since I know not a
Man?"
35 And the ANGEL an-
swering, said to her,
‡"Holy Spirit will come
upon thee, and Power from
the Most High will over-
shadow thee; and there-
fore that BEGOTTEN, BEING
HOLY, will be called a Son
of God.
36 And behold, Eliza-
beth, thy KINSWOMAN,
even **she** has conceived a
Son in her Old age; and
this is the sixth Month
with HER who is CALLED
barren.
37 ‡For *No Declara-
tion is impossible with
GOD."
38 And Mary said, "Be-
hold, the HANDMAID of
the Lord! May it be done
to me according to thy
WORD." And the ANGEL
departed from her.
39 And Mary arising in
those DAYS, went to ‡the
MOUNTAINOUS COUNTRY
with haste, to a City of Judah;
40 and entered into the
HOUSE of Zachariah, and
saluted ELIZABETH.
41 And when ELIZA-

* VATICAN MANUSCRIPT.—37. of God No Declaration is.

† 31. See Note on Matt. i. 21.

‡ 31. Isa. vii. 14; Matt. i. 21. ‡ 31. Luke ii. 21. ‡ 32. 2 Sam. vii. 11, 12; Psa cxxxii. 11; Isa. ix. 6; xvi. 5; Jer. xxiii 5; Acts ii. 30. ‡ 33. Isa. xxiv. 23; Dan. ii. 44; vii. 14, 27; Micah iv. 7; Heb. i. 8. ‡ 35. Matt. i. 20. ‡ 37. Gen. xviii. 14; Jer. xxxii. 17; Matt. xix. 26; Mark x. 27; Luke xviii. 37; Rom. iv. 21. ‡ 39. Josh. xx. 7; xxi. 9—11.

τον ασπασμον της Μαριας, εσκιρτησε το βρε-
the salutation of the Mary, leaped the babe
φος εν τῃ κοιλιᾳ αυτης· και πλησθη πνευματος
in the womb of her; and was filled a spirit
ἁγιου ἡ Ελισαβετ, και ανεφωνησε φωνῃ μεγαλῃ
of holy the Elisabeth, and she cried out with a voice great
και ειπεν· 42 Ευλογημενη συ εν γυναιξι· και
and said; Having been blessed thou among women; and
ευλογημενος ὁ καρπος της κοιλιας σου. 43 Και
having been blessed the fruit of the womb of thee. And
ποθεν μοι τουτο, ἱνα ελθῃ ἡ μητηρ του κυριου
whence to me this, that should come the mother of the Lord
μου προς με; 44 Ιδου γαρ, ὡς εγενετο ἡ φωνη
of me to me? Lo for, as came the voice
του ασπασμου σου εις τα ωτα μου, εσκιρτησε
of the salutation of thee into the ears of me, leaped
το βρεφος εν αγαλλιασει εν τῃ κοιλιᾳ μου.
the babe in exultation in the womb of me.
45 Και μακαρια ἡ πιστευσασα, ὁτι εσται τελειω-
And happy she having believed, that shall be a fulfill-
σις τοις λελαλημενοις αυτῃ παρα κυριου.
ment to those having been told to her from a lord.

46 Και ειπε Μαριαμ· Μεγαλυνει ἡ ψυχη μου
And said Mary; magnifies the soul of me
τον κυριον, 47 και ηγαλλιασε το πνευμα μου επι
the Lord, and has exulted the spirit of me in
τῳ θεῳ τῳ σωτηρι μου· 48 ὁτι επεβλεψεν επι
the God the savior of me; for he looked upon
την ταπεινωσιν της δουλης αὑτου. Ιδου γαρ,
the low state of the handmaid of himself. Lo for,
απο του νυν μακαριουσι με πασαι αἱ γενεαι·
from the now will call happy me all the generations;
49 ὁτι εποιησε μοι μεγαλεια ὁ δυνατος· και
for has done to me great things the mighty one; and
ἁγιον το ονομα αυτου, 50 και το ελεος αυτου
holy the name of him, and the mercy of him
εις γενεας γενεων τοις φοβουμενοις αυτον.
to generations of generations to those fearing him.
51 Εποιησε κρατος εν βραχιονι αὑτου· διεσκορ-
He has showed strength with arm of himself: he has
πισεν ὑπερηφανους διανοιᾳ καρδιας αυτων.
dispersed arrogant ones in thought of hearts of them.
52 Καθειλε δυναστας απο θρονων, και ὑψωσε
He has cast down mighty ones from thrones, and lifted up
ταπεινους. 53 Πεινωντας ενεπλησεν αγαθων,
humble ones. Hungering ones he filled of good things,
και πλουτουντας εξαπεστειλε κενους. 54 Αντε-
and being rich he sent away empty. He
λαβετο Ισραηλ παιδος αὑτου, μνησθηναι ελεους,
aided Israel a child of himself, to remember mercy,
55 (καθως ελαλησε προς τους πατερας ἡμων,)
(as he spoke to the fathers of us,)

BETH heard the SALUTATION of MARY, the BABE leaped in her WOMB; and ELIZABETH was filled with holy Spirit.

42 And she exclaimed with a loud *Voice, and said, "Blessed art thou among Women! and blessed is the FRUIT of thy WOMB!

43 But how happens this to me, that the MOTHER of my LORD should come to me?

44 For behold, when the VOICE of thy SALUTATION came to my EARS, the BABE leaped in my WOMB for Joy.

45 And happy SHE HAVING BELIEVED that there will be a Fulfillment of the WORDS SPOKEN to her by the Lord."

46 And Mary said, ‡"My SOUL extols the LORD,

47 and my SPIRIT exults in GOD my SAVIOR;

48 because he kindly viewed the HUMBLE CONDITION of his HANDMAID; for, behold! from THIS TIME ‡All GENERATIONS will pronounce me happy;

49 for the MIGHTY One has done Wonders for me; ‡and holy is his NAME;

50 ‡and his MERCY extends to Generations of Generations of THOSE who FEAR him.

51 ‡He shows Strength †with his Arm; he disperses those Proud in the Thought of their Hearts.

52 ‡He casts down Potentates from Thrones, and raises up the lowly.

53 He fills the Hungry with good things, and the Rich he sends away empty.

54 He supports Israel, his own Child, remembering Mercy,

55 (‡as he spoke to our

* VATICAN MANUSCRIPT.—42. Cry.

51. Grotius observes, that God's *efficacy* is represented by his *finger*, his *great power* by his *hand*, and his *omnipotence* by his *arm*. The plague of *lice* was the *finger* of God, Exod. vii. 18. The plagues in general were wrought by his *hand*, Exod. iii. 30. And the destruction of Pharoah's host in the Red Sea, is called the act of his *arm*, Exod. xv. 16.

‡ 46. 1 Sam. ii. 1. ‡ 48. Luke xi. 27. ‡ 49. Psa. cxi. 9. ‡ 50. Psa. ciii 17, 18. ‡ 51. Psa. xcviii. 1. ‡ 52 1 Sam. ii. 8; Psa. cxiii. 7. ‡ 55. Gen. xvii 19; Psa. cxxxii. 11.

τῳ Αβρααμ και τῳ σπερματι αυτου ἑως αιωνος.
to the Abraam and to the seed of him even to an age.
56 Εμεινε δε Μαριαμ συν αυτῃ ὡσει μηνας τρεις·
Abode and Mary with her about months three:
και ὑπεστρεψεν εις τον οικον αυτης.
and returned to the house of her.

57 Τῃ δε Ελισαβετ επλησθη ὁ χρονος του
To the now Elisabeth was fulfilled the time of the
τεκειν αυτην· και εγεννησεν υἱον. 58 Και ηκου-
to bear her; and she brought forth a son. And heard
σαν οἱ περιοικοι και οἱ συγγενεις αυτης, ὁτι
the neighbors and the kindred of her, that
εμεγαλυνε κυριος το ελεος αὑτου μετ᾽ αυτης·
had magnified a lord the mercy of himself towards her;
και συνεχαιρον αυτῃ. 59 Και εγενετο, εν τῃ
and they rejoiced with her. And it came to pass, in the
ογδοῃ ἡμερᾳ ηλθον περιτεμειν το παιδιον· και
eighth day they came to circumcise the little child; and
εκαλουν αυτο, επι τῳ ονοματι του πατρος αυτου,
called it, after the name of the father of him,
Ζαχαριαν. 60 Και αποκριθεισα ἡ μητηρ αυτου
Zacharias. And answering the mother of him
ειπεν· Ουχι· αλλα κληθησεται Ιωαννης. 61 Και
said; No; but he shall be called John. And
ειπον προς αυτην· Ὁτι ουδεις εστιν εν τῃ
they said to her; That no one is among the
συγγενειᾳ σου, ὁς καλειται τῳ ονοματι τουτῳ.
kindred of thee, who is called to the name this.
62 Ενενευον δε τῳ πατρι αυτου, το τι αν θελοι
They made signs then to the father of him, the what he would desire
καλεισθαι αυτον. 63 Και αιτησας πινακιδιον,
to be called him. And having requested a tablet,
εγραψε, λεγων· Ιωαννης εστι το ονομα αυτου.
he wrote, saying: John is the name of him.
Και εθαυμασαν παντες. 64 Ανεῳχθη δε το
And they wondered all. Was opened and the
στομα αυτου παραχρημα, και ἡ γλωσσα αυτου·
mouth of him immediately, and the tongue of him;
και ελαλει ευλογων τον θεον. 65 Και εγενετο
and he spoke blessing the God. And came
επι παντας φοβος τους περιοικουντας αυτους·
on all a fear those dwelling around them;
και εν ὁλῃ τῃ ορεινῃ της Ιουδαιας διελαλειτο
and in whole the hilly-country of the Judea talked of throughout
παντα τα ῥηματα ταυτα. 66 Και εθεντο παντες
all the things these. And placed all
οἱ ακουσαντες εν τῃ καρδιᾳ αὑτων, λεγοντες·
those having heard in the hearts of themselves, saying;

FATHERS,) to ABRAHAM, and to his POSTERITY, even to the Age."

56 And Mary remained with her about three Months, and returned to her HOUSE.

57 Now ELIZABETH'S TIME to be DELIVERED was fulfilled; and she brought forth a Son.

58 And her NEIGHBORS and RELATIVES heard That the Lord had magnified his MERCY towards her; and they rejoiced with her.

59 And, on † the EIGHTH Day, ‡ when they came to circumcise the CHILD, they were about to call him Zachariah, after the NAME of his FATHER;

60 but his MOTHER interposing, said, "No; but ‡ he shall be called John."

61 And they said to her, "There is no one among thy RELATIVES, who is called by this NAME."

62 Then they asked his FATHER, by Signs, WHAT HE WISHED HIM TO BE CALLED.

63 And requesting † a TABLET, he wrote, saying, ‡ "His NAME is John." And they all wondered,

64 ‡ for his MOUTH was instantly opened, and his TONGUE loosed; and he spoke, praising GOD.

65 And Fear came on ALL their NEIGHBORS. And All these THINGS were talked of through All the ‡ MOUNTAINOUS COUNTRY of JUDEA.

66 And All THOSE HEARING, pondered them in their HEARTS, saying,

† 59. Not before that day, because the mother was unclean seven days, Lev. xii. 1, 2; and so was the child, by touching her, and therefore he was not then fit to be admitted into covenant. The law appointed no certain place in which circumcision was to be done, nor any certain person to perform it, and therefore it was sometimes done by women, Exod. iv. 25; and here in the house of Elizabeth, as appears by her presence at it, verse 60. The Jews did it sometimes in their schools, for the sake of the number of the witnesses. Then also they *named* the infant; because, when GOD instituted circumcision, he changed the names of Abraham and Sarah.—*Whitby*. Among the Jews, the child was named when it was circumcised, and ordinarily the name of the father was given to the first-born son.—*A. Clarke*.
† 63. A thin board, made out of the pine-tree, smeared over with wax, was used among the ancients, as a writing-tablet.

‡ 59. Gen. xvii. 12; Lev. xii. 3. ‡ 60. ver. 13. ‡ 63. ver. 13. ‡ 64. ver. 20. ‡ 65. ver. 39.

Τι αρα το παιδιον τουτο εσται; Και χειρ
What then the child this will be? And hand
κυριου ην μετ' αυτου.
of Lord was with him.

67 Και Ζαχαριας ὁ πατηρ αυτου επλησθη
And Zacharias the father of him was filled
πνευματος ἁγιου, και προεφητευσε, λεγων·
a spirit of holy, and prophesied, saying;
Ευλογητος κυριος, ὁ θεος του Ισραηλ· ὁτι
Blessed Lord, the God of the Israel; for
επεσκεψατο και εποιησε λυτρωσιν τῳ λαῳ
he has visited and wrought redemption to the people
αὑτου, 69 και ηγειρε κερας σωτηριας ἡμιν εν τῳ
of himself, and raised up a horn of salvation to us in the
οικῳ Δαυιδ του παιδος αὑτου· 70 (καθως ελαλησε
house of David the servant of himself; (even as he spoke
δια στοματος των ἁγιων, των απ' αιωνος,
through mouth of the holy ones, of those from an age,
προφητων αὑτου·) 71 σωτηριαν εξ εχθρων ἡμων,
of prophets of himself;) a salvation from enemies of us,
και εκ χειρος παντων των μισουντων ἡμας·
and from hand of all those hating us:
72 ποιησαι ελεος μετα των πατερων ἡμων, και
to perform mercy with the fathers of us, and
μνησθηναι διαθηκης ἁγιας αὑτου, 73 ὁρκον, ὁν
to remember covenant holy of himself, an oath, which
ωμοσε προς Αβρααμ τον πατερα ἡμων, του
he swore to Abraam the father of us, of the
δουναι ἡμιν, 74 αφοβως, εκ χειρος των εχθρων
to give to us, without fear, from hand of the enemies
ἡμων ρυσθεντας, λατρευειν αυτῳ 75 εν ὁσιοτητι
of us having been rescued, to worship him in holiness
και δικαιοσυνῃ ενωπιον αυτου, πασας τας
and righteousness in presence of him, all the
ἡμερας ἡμων. 76 Και συ, παιδιον, προφητης
days of us. And thou, little child, a prophet
ὑψιστου κληθησῃ· προπορευσῃ γαρ προ *[προ-
of highest shalt be called; thou shalt go for before [face]
σωπου] κυριου, ἑτοιμασαι ὁδους αυτου, 77 του
of a lord, to prepare ways of him, of the
δουναι γνωσιν σωτηριας τῳ λαῳ αυτου, εν αφε-
to give knowledge of salvation to the people of him, in forgive-
σει ἁμαρτιων αυτων, 78 δια σπλαγχνα ελεους
ness of sins of them, on account of tender mercies
θεου ἡμων, εν οἱς επεσκεψατο ἡμας ανατολη εξ
of God of us, by which he has visited us a rising from
ὑψους, 79 επιφαναι τοις εν σκοτει και σκιᾳ
on high, to shine to those in darkness and shade

"What then will this CHILD be?" *And the Hand of the Lord was with him.

67 And Zachariah, his FATHER, was filled with holy Spirit, and prophesied, saying,

68 "Blessed be the Lord, the GOD of ISRAEL, because he has visited and wrought Redemption for his PEOPLE;

69 and ‡has raised up †a Horn of Salvation for us, in the *House of David, his SERVANT;

70 (‡even as he spoke by the Mouth of THOSE HOLY ones, his Prophets of the Age;)

71 a Salvation from our Enemies, and from the Hand of ALL who HATE us;

72 to perform his Mercy with our FATHERS; and to remember his holy Covenant;

73 the Oath which he swore to Abraham, our FATHER,—

74 to permit us, being rescued from the Hand of our ENEMIES, fearlessly to worship him,

75 by Holiness and Righteousness in his sight, All our DAYS.

76 And thou, Child, wilt be called a Prophet of the Most High; for thou shalt go ‡before the Lord to prepare his Ways;

77 to impart a Knowledge of Salvation to his PEOPLE in the forgiveness of their Sins,

78 on account of the tender Compassions of our God, by which he has visited us; a Day-dawn from on high,

79 to Illuminate THOSE SITTING in Darkness and Death-shade; to DIRECT

* VATICAN MANUSCRIPT.—66. For also the Hand. 69. the House of David. 76. face—*omit.*

† 69. A *horn* in Scripture is frequently a symbol of *power* or *principality,* and hence this expression will signify, a *mighty Savior,* or *Prince of Salvation.*

‡ 69. Psa. xviii. 2; cxxxii. 17. ‡ 70. Acts iii. 21; Rom. i. 2. ‡ 73. Gen. xii. 3; xviii. 4; xxii. 16, 17; Heb. vi. 13, 17. ‡ 76. Isa. xl. 3; Mal. iii. 1; iv. 5; Matt. xi. 10; ver. 17.

θανατου καθημενοις, του κατευθυναι τους ποδας
of death sitting, of the to guide the feet
ἡμων εις ὁδον ειρηνης. 80 Το δε παιδιον ηυξανε,
of us into a way of peace. The now little child grew,
και εκραταιουτο πνευματι· και ην εν ταις ερη-
and became strong in spirit; and was in the des-
μοις, ἑως ἡμερας αναδειξεως αυτου προς τον
erts, till day of manifestation of him to the
Ισραηλ.
Israel.

ΚΕΦ. β'. 2.

1 Εγενετο δε εν ταις ἡμεραις εκειναις, εξηλθε
It came to pass and in the days those, went forth
δογμα παρα Καισαρος Αυγουστου, απογραφεσ-
a decree from Cesar Augustus, to register
θαι πασαν την οικουμενην. 2 (Αὑτη ἡ απογραφη
all the habitable. (This the registry
πρωτη εγενετο ἡγεμονευοντος της Συριας
first was made being govenor of the Syria
Κυρηνιου.) 3 Και επορευοντο παντες απογρα-
Cyrenius.) And they went all to be
φεσθαι, ἑκαστος εις την ιδιαν πολιν. 4 Ανεβη
registered, each into the his own city. Went up
δε και Ιωσηφ απο της Γαλιλαιας, εκ πολεως
and also Joseph from the Galilee, out of city
Ναζαρετ, εις την Ιουδαιαν, εις πολιν Δαυιδ,
Nazareth, into the Judea, into a city of David,
ἡτις καλειται Βηθλεεμ, (δια το ειναι αυτον εξ
which is called Bethleem, (because the to be him of
οικου και πατριας Δαυιδ,) 5 απογραψασθαι συν
house and family of David,) to be registered with
Μαριαμ τη μεμνηστευμενη αυτω *[γυναικι,]
Mary the having been espoused to him [a wife,]
ουση εγκυω. 6 Εγενετο δε εν τω ειναι αυτους
being with child. It happened but in the to be them
εκει, επλησθησαν αἱ ἡμεραι του τεκειν αυτην.
there were fulfilled the days of the to bear her.
7 Και ετεκε τον υἱον αὑτης του πρωτοτοκον,
And she brought forth the son of her the first-born,
και εσπαργανωσεν αυτον, και ανεκλινεν αυτον
and swathed him, and laid him
εν τη φατνη· διοτι ουκ ην αυτοις τοπος εν τω
in the manger; because not was to them a place in the
καταλυματι.
guest-chamber.

our FEET into the Way of Peace."

80 Now the CHILD grew, and acquired strength of Mind; and he was in the DESERTS till the Day of his public appearance to ISRAEL.

CHAPTER II.

1 Now it occurred in those DAYS, that an Edict went forth from Cesar Augustus, to register All the † HABITABLE.

2 (‡ This * was the first Registry of Quirinus, Governor of SYRIA.)

3 And they all went to be registered, each into his OWN City.

4 And Joseph also went up from GALILEE, out of the City of Nazareth, into JUDEA, into the ‡ City of David, which is called Bethlehem, (‡ because he WAS of the House and Family of David,)

5 to be registered with Mary, ‡ his BETROTHED, being pregnant.

6 And it came to pass while they WERE there, the DAYS of her DELIVERY were accomplished.

7 ‡ And she brought forth her FIRST-BORN SON, and swathed him, and laid him in * † a Manger; because there was no Place for them in the GUEST-CHAMBER.

* VATICAN MSS.—2. This was the first Registry. 5. Wife—*omit.* 7. a Manger.

† 1. *Oikoumenee* literally means the *inhabited* earth, and is applied in this place, by some recent translators, to the Roman Empire. But as no historian mentions a *general census* at this time, the meaning of the word must be restricted to the *land of Judea,* where this enrollment took place. *Oikoumenee* is used by Luke in chap. xxi. 26, and Acts xi. 28, and applied in this restricted sense. † 7. Wetsein has shown from a multitude of instances, that *phatnee* means not merely the *manger*, but the whole *stable.* The room for guests being already full, Joseph and Mary retired to a more homely receptacle, called a *stabulum,* the middle of which afforded room for cattle, and the sides accommodation for persons. It was not properly a stable, but was formed for the convenient lodging of both men and cattle. Bishop Pearce, however, has a note on this verse, which is worthy of consideration. He says, "Upon the whole, it seems to me probable, that Mary was delivered in a *guest-chamber*, or *lodging-room,* (whether it were in a public house, or that of some friend, is not said,) in some chamber of a house, and not of a stable; and that then, for want of a bed in that *guest-chamber,* wherein to lay her Son JESUS, she made use of one of the *Eastern* mangers, made of coarse cloth, and fastened, like our seamen's hammocks, to some part of the chamber where she was; and there laid him, as having no other place for him. This afforded a circumstance by which the shepherds were directed to find him out, and distinguish this holy babe from all others. See verses 12, 16."

‡ 2. Acts v. 37. ‡ 4. 1 Sam. xvi. 1, 4; John vii. 42. ‡ 4. Matt. i. 16; Luke i 27. ‡ 5. Matt. i. 18; Luke i. 27. ‡ 7. Matt. i. 25.

8 Και ποιμενες ησαν εν τῃ χωρᾳ τῃ αυτῃ
And shepherds were in the country the this
αγραυλουντες, και φυλασσοντες φυλακας της
abiding in the fields, and keeping watches of the
νυκτος επι την ποιμνην αυτων. 9 Και *[ιδου,]
night over the flock of them. And [lo,]
αγγελος κυριου επεστη αυτοις, και δοξα κυριου
a messenger of a lord stood near to them, and glory of a lord
περιελαμψεν αυτους: και εφοβηθησαν φοβον
shone round them; and they feared a fear
μεγαν. 10 Και ειπεν αυτοις ὁ αγγελος· Μη
great. And said to them the messenger; Not
φοβεισθε· ιδου γαρ, ευαγγελιζομαι ὑμιν χαραν
fear you; lo for, I bring glad tidings to you a joy
μεγαλην, ἡτις εσται παντι τῳ λαῳ· 11 ὁτι
great, which shall be to all the people: that
ετεχθη ὑμιν σημερον σωτηρ, ὁς εστι Χριστος
was born to you to-day a savior, who is anointed
κυριος, εν πολει Δαυιδ. 12 Και τουτο ὑμιν το
Lord, in city of David. And this to you the
σημειον· Εὑρησετε βρεφος εσπαργανωμενον
sign; You shall find a babe having been swathed
κειμενον εν φατνῃ. 13 Και εξαιφνης εγενετο
lying in a manger. And suddenly was
συν τῳ αγγελῳ πληθος στρατιας ουρανιου,
with the messenger a multitude of host of heaven,
αινουντων τον θεον, και λεγοντων· 14 "Δοξα
praising the God, and saying; "Glory
εν ὑψιστοις θεῳ, και επι γης ειρηνη· εν ανθρω-
in highest heavens to God, and on earth peace; among men
ποις ευδοκια."
good will."

15 Και εγενετο, ὡς απηλθον απ' αυτων εις τον
And it came to pass, when went from them into the
ουρανου οἱ αγγελοι, και οἱ ανθρωποι, οἱ ποιμε-
heaven the messengers, and the men, the shep-
νες, ειπον προς αλληλους· Διελθωμεν δη ἑως
herds, said to one another; We should go now to
Βηθλεεμ, και ιδωμεν το ῥημα τουτο το γεγονος,
Bethleem, and see the thing this the having been done,
ὁ ὁ κυριος εγνωρισεν ἡμιν. 16 Και ηλθον
which the Lord has made known to us. And they came
σπευσαντες, και ανευρον την τε Μαριαμ και τον
having made haste, and they found the both Mary and the
Ιωσηφ, και το βρεφος κειμενον εν τῃ φατνῃ.
Joseph, and the babe lying in the manger.
17 Ιδοντες δε, διεγνωρισαν *[περι] του ῥηματος
Having seen and, they published [around] the declaration
του λαληθεντος αυτοις περι του παιδιου τουτου.
that having been told to them concerning the little child this.
18 Και παντες οἱ ακουσαντες εθαυμασαν περι
And all those having heard wondered about
των λαληθεντων ὑπο των ποιμενων προς αυτους.
those having been told by the shepherds to them.
19 Ἡ δε Μαριαμ παντα συνετηρει τα ῥηματα
The but Mary all kept the words
*[ταυτα,] συμβαλλουσα εν τῃ καρδιᾳ αυτης.
[these,] pondering in the heart of herself.

8 And there were Shepherds in THAT COUNTRY, residing in the fields, and keeping over their FLOCK the Watches of the NIGHT.

9 And an Angel of the Lord stood by them, and the Glory of the Lord shone round them; and they were greatly afraid.

10 And the ANGEL said to them, "Fear not; for behold, I bring you glad tidings, ‡ which will be a great Joy to All the PEOPLE;

11 ‡ because To-day was born for you, in David's City, a Savior, who is the Lord Messiah.

12 And this will be a * Sign to you; you will find a Babe swathed, lying in a Manger."

13 And suddenly there was with the ANGEL a Multitude of the heavenly Host, praising GOD, and saying,

14 "Glory to God in the highest heavens, on Earth Peace, and among Men Good will."

15 Now it occurred, when the ANGELS departed from them to HEAVEN, the MEN, the SHEPHERDS, said, to one another, "Let us go now to Bethlehem, and see this THING which has transpired, which the LORD has made known to us."

16 And they came in haste, and found both MARY and JOSEPH, and the BABE lying in the MANGER.

17 And having seen it, they published THAT DECLARATION which had been SPOKEN to them about this CHILD.

18 And All THOSE HAVING HEARD, wondered at the THINGS RELATED to them by the SHEPHERDS.

19 But MARY kept All these words, pondering them in her HEART.

* VATICAN MANUSCRIPT.—9. lo—*omit*. 12. Sign. 17. around—*omit*. 19. these—*omit*.

‡ 10. Gen. xii. 3; Psa. lxxii. 17; Jer. iv. 2. ‡ 11. Isa. ix. 6.

20 Και ὑπεστρεψαν οἱ ποιμενες δοξαζοντες και
And returned the shepherds glorifying and
αινουντες τον θεον επι πασιν οἷς ηκουσαν και
praising the God for all which they had heard and
ειδον, καθως ελαληθη προς αυτους.
seen, even as it had been told to them.
21 Και ὁτε επλησθησαν ἡμεραι οκτὼ του
And when were fulfilled days eight of the
περιτεμειν αυτον, και εκληθη το ονομα αυτου
to circumcise him, and he was called the name of him
Ιησους, το κληθεν ὑπο του αγγελου προ του
Jesus, that being called by the messenger before of the
συλληφθηναι αυτον εν τη κοιλιᾳ.
was conceived him in the womb.
22 Και ὁτε επλησθησαν αἱ ἡμεραι του καθαρισ-
And when were fulfilled the days of the purifica-
μου αυτων, κατα τον νομον Μωσεως, ανηγαγον
tion of them, according to the law of Moses, they brought
αυτον εις Ιεροσολυμα, παραστησαι τῷ κυριῳ,
him to Jerusalem, to present to the Lord,
23 (καθως γεγραπται εν νομῳ κυριου· "Ὁτι
(as it is written in law of Lord; That
παν αρσεν διανοιγον μητραν, ἁγιον τῳ κυριῳ
every male opening a womb, holy to the Lord
κληθησεται·") 24 και του δουναι θυσιαν, κατα
shall be called;") and of the to offer a sacrifice, according to
το ειρημενον εν νομῳ κυριου· "Ζευγος τρυγο-
that having been said in law of Lord; "A pair of turtle
νων, η δυο νεοσσους περιστερων."
doves, or two young pigeons."
25 Και ιδου, ην ανθρωπος εν Ἱερουσαλημ, ᾧ
And lo, was a man in Jerusalem, to whom
ονομα Συμεων· και ὁ ανθρωπος οὗτος δικαιος
a name of Simeon; and the man this just
και ευλαβης, προσδεχομενος παρακλησιν του
and pious, waiting for consolation of the
Ισραηλ. Και πνευμα ην ἁγιον επ' αυτον· 26 και
Israel. And a spirit was holy upon him; and
ην αυτῳ κεχρηματισμενον ὑπο του πνευματος
it was to him having been informed by the spirit
του ἁγιου, μη ιδειν θανατον, πριν η ιδῃ
of the holy, not to see death, before he should see
τον Χριστον κυριου. 27 Και ηλθεν εν τῳ πνευ-
the anointed of Lord. And he came by the spirit
ματι εις το ἱερον· και εν τῳ εισαγαγειν τους
into the temple; and in the to bring the
γονεις το παιδιον Ιησουν, του ποιησαι αυτους
parents the little child Jesus, of the to do them
κατα το ειθισμενον του νομου περι
according to that having been instituted of the law concerning
αυτου· 28 και αυτος εδεξατο αυτο εις τας αγκα-
him; also he took it into the arms
λας αὑτου, και ευλογησε τον θεον, και ειπε·
of himself, and blessed the God, and said;

20 And the SHEPHERDS returned, glorifying and praising GOD for all which they had heard and seen, even as it had been declared to them.

21 ‡ And when eight Days were ended, the [time] to CIRCUMCISE him, his NAME was called Jesus, THAT NAME given him by the ANGEL before his CONCEPTION.

22 ‡ And when † the * Days of her Purification were completed, according to the LAW of Moses, they carried him up to Jerusalem, to present him to the LORD;—

23 (even as it is written in the Law of the Lord, that ‡ "Every Male, being a first-born, shall be called holy to the Lord;")

24 and to OFFER a Sacrifice, according to what is enjoined in * the LAW of the Lord,—‡ † "A Pair of Turtle-doves, or Two Young Pigeons."

25 And behold, there was a Man in Jerusalem, whose Name was Simeon; and he was a righteous and pious MAN, expecting the Consolation of ISRAEL; and the holy Spirit was on him.

26 And he was divinely informed by the HOLY SPIRIT, that he would not die, till he should see the Lord's MESSIAH.

27 And he came by the SPIRIT into the TEMPLE; and when the PARENTS BROUGHT IN the CHILD Jesus, † to DO according to the CUSTOM of the LAW concerning him,

28 He also took him in his ARMS, and praised GOD, and said,

* VATICAN MANUSCRIPT.—22. Days of her Purification. 24. the LAW of.

† 22. That is, *thirty-three* days after what was termed the seven days of her uncleanness—forty days in all; the time appointed by the law, after the birth of a male child. See Lev. xii. 2, 6. † 24. *One* for a burnt-offering, and the *other* for a sin-offering; See Lev. xii. 8. These were the offerings of the poorer Jewish mothers. † 27. To present him to the Lord, and then redeem him by paying *five shekels*, Num. xviii. 15, 16.

‡ 21. Luke i. 59. ‡ 21. Matt. i. 25; Luke i. 31. ‡ 22. Lev. xii. 2—6. ‡ 23. Exod. xiii. 2; xxii. 29; xxxiv. 19; Num. iii. 13; viii. 17; xviii. 15. ‡ 24. Lev. xii. 8.

29 Νυν απολυεις τον δουλον σου, δεσποτα,
Now dost thou dismiss the servant of thee, O sovereign,
κατα το ρημα σου, εν ειρηνη· 30 ὁτι ειδον οἱ
according to the word of thee, in peace; for have seen the
οφθαλμοι μου το σωτηριον σου, 31 ὁ ἡτοιμα-
eyes of me the salvation of thee, which thou hast
σας κατα προσωπον παντων των λαων· 32 φως
prepared before face of all the people; a light
εις αποκαλυψιν εθνων, και δοξαν λαου σου
for a revelation of nations, and a glory of people of thee
Ισραηλ. 33 Και ην ὁ πατηρ αυτου και ἡ μητηρ
Israel. And was the father of him and the mother
θαυμαζοντες επι τοις λαλουμενοις περι αυτου.
wondering at those being spoken about him.
34 Και ευλογησεν αυτους Συμεων, και ειπε προς
And blessed them Simeon, and said to
Μαριαμ την μητερα αυτου· Ιδου, οὑτος κειται
Mary the mother of him; Lo, this is placed
εις πτωσιν και αναστασιν πολλων εν τῳ
for a fall and rising of many in the
Ισραηλ, και εις σημειον αντιλεγομενον· 35 (και
Israel, and for a sign being spoken against; (also
σου δε αυτης την ψυχην διελευσεται ῥομφαια·)
of thee and of thyself the soul shall pierce through a sword;)
ὁπως αν αποκαλυφθωσιν εκ πολλων καρδιων
so that may be disclosed of many hearts
διαλογισμοι.
reasonings.
36 Και ην Αννα προφητις, θυγατηρ Φανουηλ,
And was Anna a prophetess, a daughter of Phanuel,
εκ φυλης Ασηρ· αὑτη προβεβηκυια εν ἡμεραις
of tribe of Aser; she having been advanced in days
πολλαις, ζησασα ετη μετα ανδρος ἑπτα απο
many, having lived years with a husband seven from
της παρθενιας αὑτης· 37 και αυτη χηρα ὡς ετων
the virginity of herself; also she a widow about years
ογδοηκοντα τεσσαρων, ἡ ουκ αφιστατο απο του
eighty four, who not withdrew from the
ἱερου, νηστειαις και δεησεσι λατρευουσα νυκτα
temple, fastings and prayers serving night
και ἡμεραν. 38 Και αὑτη, αυτη τῃ ὡρᾳ επισ-
and day. And she, this the hour stand-
τασα, ανθωμολογειτο τῳ κυριῳ, και ελαλει περι
ing by, acknowledged the Lord, and spoke about
αυτου πασι τοις προσδεχομενοις λυτρωσιν εν
him to all those looking for redemption in
Ἰερουσαλημ.
Jerusalem.
39 Και ὡς ετελεσαν ἁπαντα τα κατα τον
And when they finished all the things according to the
νομον κυριου, ὑπεστρεψαν εις την Γαλιλαιαν,
law of Lord, they returned into the Galilee,
εις την πολιν αὑτων, Ναζαρετ. 40 Το δε παιδιον
into the city of themselves, Nazareth. The and little child
ηυξανε, και εκραταιουτο *[πνευματι,] πληρου-
grew, and was strengthened [in spirit,] being
μενον σοφιας· και χαρις θεου ην επ' αυτο.
filled with wisdom; and favor of God was on it.

29 "Now, O sovereign Lord, dismiss thy SERVANT according to thy WORD, in Peace;

30 because my EYES have seen thy SALVATION,

31 which thou hast made ready in the Presence of All the PEOPLE;

32 ‡ a Light of Nations for enlightenment, and a Glory of thy People Israel."

33 And his FATHER and MOTHER were wondering at the WORDS SPOKEN concerning him.

34 And Simeon blessed them, and said to Mary his MOTHER, "Behold, this child is destined for the ‡ Fall and Rising of many in ISRAEL; and for ‡ a Mark of contradiction;—

35 (and indeed, a Sword will pierce through the SOUL of Thee Thyself,) that the Reasonings of Many Hearts may be disclosed."

36 There was also a Prophetess, Anna, Daughter of Phanuel, of the tribe of Asher; she was far advanced in Age, having lived with * a Husband seven Years from her VIRGINITY;

37 she was also a Widow * about eighty-four Years, who departed not from the TEMPLE, but serving God ‡ Night and Day with Fastings and Prayers.

38 And she standing by at THAT very time, praised * GOD, and spoke of him to All THOSE EXPECTING ‡ Deliverance in Jerusalem.

39 And when they had finished all things according to the LAW of the Lord, they returned to GALILEE, to their own City Nazareth.

40 ‡ And the CHILD grew, and became strong, filled with Wisdom, and the Favor of God was on him.

* VATICAN MANUSCRIPT.—36. a HUSBAND. 37. till eighty-four. 38. GOD, and spoke. 40. in Spirit—*omit.*

‡ 32. Isa. xlii. 6; xlix. 6; lx. 1; Acts xiii. 47; xxviii. 28. ‡ 34. Isa. viii. 14; Matt. xxi. 44; Rom. ix. 32; 1 Cor. i. 23, 24; 1 Pet. ii. 7, 8. ‡ 34. Heb. xii. 3. ‡ 37. Acts xxvi. 7; 1 Tim. v. 5. ‡ 38. Luke xxiv. 21. ‡ 40. Luke i. 80. ver. 52.

41 Και επορευοντο οἱ γονεις αυτου κατ' ετος εις
And went the parents of him every year to
Ἱερουσαλημ τῃ ἑορτῃ του πασχα.
Jerusalem of the feast of the passover.
42 Και ὁτε εγενετο ετων δωδεκα, αναβαντων
And when he was years twelve, having gone up
αυτων *[εις Ἱεροσολυμα] κατα το εθος της
of them [to Jerusalem] according to the custom of the
ἑορτης· 43 και τελειωσαντων τας ἡμερας, εν
feast; and having ended the days, in
τῳ ὑποστρεφειν αυτους, ὑπεμεινεν Ιησους ὁ
the to return them, remained Jesus the
παις εν Ἱερουσαλημ· και ουκ εγνω Ιωσηφ και
boy in Jerusalem; and not knew Joseph and
ἡ μητηρ αυτου. 44 Νομισαντες δε αυτον εν
the mother of him. Having supposed and him in
τῃ συνοδιᾳ ειναι, ηλθον ἡμερας ὁδον, και
the company to be, they went of a day a journey, and
ανεζητουν αυτον εν τοις συγγενεσι και τοις
they sought him among the kinsmen and the
γνωστοις. 45 Και μη εὑροντες, ὑπεστρεψαν
acquaintances. And not finding, they returned
εις Ἱερουσαλημ, ζητουντες αυτον. 46 Και
to Jerusalem, seeking him. And
εγενετο, μεθ' ἡμερας τρεις εὑρον αυτον εν τῳ
it happened, after days three they found him in the
ἱερῳ καθεζομενον εν μεσῳ των διδασκαλων,
temple sitting in middle of the teachers,
και ακουοντα αυτων, και επερωτωντα αυτους.
and hearing of them, and asking them.
47 Εξισταντο δε παντες *[οἱ ακουοντες αυτου,]
Were amazed and all [those hearing him,]
επι τῃ συνεσει και ταις αποκρισεσιν αυτου.
upon the understanding and the answers of him.
48 Και ιδοντες αυτον, εξεπλαγησαν· και προς
And seeing him, they were amazed; and to
αυτον ἡ μητηρ αυτου ειπε· Τεκνον, τι εποιη-
him the mother of him said; O child, why hast thou
σας ἡμιν οὑτως; ιδου, ὁ πατηρ σου καγω
done to us thus? lo, the father of thee and I
οδυνωμενοι εζητουμεν σε. 49 Και ειπε προς
being in distress have sought thee. And he said to
αυτους· Τι ὁτι εζητειτε με; ουκ ῃδειτε,
them, Why for did you seek me? not know you,
ὁτι εν τοις του πατρος μου δει ειναι με; 50 Και
that in the of the father of me must to be me? And
αυτοι ου συνηκαν το ῥημα, ὁ ελαλησεν αυτοις.
they not understood the word, which he spoke to them.
51 Και κατεβη μετ' αυτων, και ηλθεν εις Ναζα-
And he went down with them, and came into Naza-
ρετ· και ην ὑποτασσομενος αυτοις. Και ἡ
reth; and was being subject to them. And the

41 And his PARENTS went yearly to Jerusalem to the ‡ FEAST of the PASSOVER.

42 And when he was twelve Years old, † they went up according to the CUSTOM of the FEAST.

43 And having † completed the DAYS, on their RETURN, Jesus, the YOUTH, remained in Jerusalem. And * his PARENTS knew it not.

44 And supposing him to be in the COMPANY, they went a Day's Journey; and they sought him, among their RELATIVES and ACQUAINTANCES.

45 But not finding him, they returned to Jerusalem, seeking him.

46 And it happened, after three Days they found him in the TEMPLE, sitting in † the Midst of the TEACHERS, both hearing them, and asking them questions.

47 And ALL were astonished at his INTELLIGENCE and REPLIES.

48 And seeing him, they were amazed; and his MOTHER said to him, "Child, why hast thou done thus to us? behold thy FATHER and I * seek thee sorrowing."

49 And he said to them, "Why did you seek me? Did you not know that I must be in † the [COURTS] of my FATHER?"

50 And they did not understand the WORD which he spoke to them.

51 And he went down with them, and came to Nazareth, and was subject to them. And his MOTHER

* VATICAN MANUSCRIPT.—42. to Jerusalem—*omit.* 43. his PARENTS knew, 47. those hearing him—*omit.* 48. seek thee.

† 42. All the males were required to attend at the three festivals at Jerusalem; and females, though not commanded, yet used often to attend, especially at the Passover. Children were excused; but the Rabbinical writers say, that the above obligation was thought binding at twelve years of age. † 43. That is, been there eight days, of which the feast of the Passover was one, and the rest were the seven days of unleavened bread. † 46. They sat on benches in a half circle, and their scholars at their feet, Acts xxii. 3. † 49. In the *courts* or *house* of my Father, is now generally admitted as correct. A similar ellipsis occurs in Mark v. 35, and Acts xvi. 40.

‡ 41. Exod. xxiii. 15, 17; xxxiv. 23; Deut. xvi. 1. 16.

μητηρ αυτου διετηρει παντα τα ῥηματα ταυτα
mother of him treasured all the words these
εν τῃ καρδιᾳ αὑτης. 52 Και Ιησους προεκοπτε
in the heart of herself. And Jesus advanced
σοφιᾳ, και ἡλικιᾳ, και χαριτι παρα θεῳ και
in wisdom, and in vigor, and in favor with God and
ανθρωποις.
men.

ΚΕΦ. γ'. 3.

1 Εν ετει δε πεντεκαιδεκατῳ της ἡγεμονιας
In year now fifteenth of the government
Τιβεριου Καισαρος, ἡγεμονευοντος Ποντιου Πι-
of Tiberius Cesar, being governor Pontius Pi-
λατου της Ιουδαιας, και τετραρχουντος της
late of the Judea, and being tetrarch of the
Γαλιλαιας Ἡρωδου, Φιλιππου δε του αδελφου
Galilee Herod, Philip and the brother
αυτου τετραρχουντος της Ιτουραιας και Τραχω-
of him being tetrarch of the Ituria and Tracho-
νιτιδος χωρας, και Λυσανιου της Αβιληνης
nitis region, and Lysanias of the Abilene
τετραρχουντος, 2 επι αρχιερεως Αννα και Και-
being tetrarch, under high priests Annas and Cai-
αφα, εγενετο ῥημα θεου επι Ιωαννην, τον
aphas, came a word of God to John, the
Ζαχαριου υἱον, εν τῃ ερημῳ. 3 Και ηλθεν εις
of Zacharias son, in the desert. And he went into
πασαν την περιχωρον του Ιορδανου, κηρυσσων
all the country about the Jordan preaching
βαπτισμα μετανοιας εις αφεσιν ἁμαρτιων· 4 ὡς
a dipping of reformation into a forgiveness of sins; as
γεγραπται εν βιβλῳ λογων Ἡσαιου του προ-
it is written in a book of words of Esaias the pro-
φητου, *[λεγοντες·] "Φωνη βοωντος εν τῃ
phet, [saying] "A voice crying in the
ερημῳ· Ἑτοιμασατε την ὁδον κυριου, ευθειας
desert; Make you ready the way of a lord, straight
ποιειτε τας τριβους αυτου· 5 Πασα φαραγξ
make you the beaten tracks of him; Every ravine
πληρωθησεται, και παν ορος και βουνος ταπει-
shall be filled up, and every mountain and hill shall be
νωθησεται· και εσται τα σκολια εις ευθειαν,
made low; and shall be the crooked into straight,
και αἱ τραχειαι εις ὁδους λειας· 6 και οψεται
and the rough into ways smooth; and shall see
πασα σαρξ το σωτηριον του θεου." 7 Ελεγεν
all flesh the salvation of the God." He said
ουν τοις εκπορευομενοις οχλοις βαπτισθηναι ὑπ'
then to those coming out of crowds to be dipped by
αυτου· Γεννηματα εχιδνων, τις ὑπεδειξεν ὑμιν
him; O broods of venomous serpents, who pointed out to you

kept All * these THINGS in her HEART.

52 ‡ And Jesus advanced * in WISDOM, and in Manliness, and in Favor with God and Men.

CHAPTER III.

1 Now in the fifteenth
Year of the GOVERNMENT
of Tiberius Cesar, Pontius
Pilate being Governor of
JUDEA, and Herod te-
trarch of GALILEE, and
Philip his BROTHER te-
trarch of ITUREA, and the
Province of Trachonitis,
and Lysanias, the tetrarch
of ABILENE,
2 ‡ in the * High-priest-
hood of † Annas, and Cai-
aphas, a Command from
God came to John, the
SON of Zachariah, in the
DESERT.
3 ‡ And he went into All
the adjacent * Country of
the JORDAN, publishing an
Immersion of Reformation
‡ for Forgiveness of Sins.
4 As it is written in the
Book of the Words of
Isaiah, the PROPHET; ‡ "A
"Voice proclaiming in the
"DESERT, Prepare the WAY
"for the Lord, make the
"HIGHWAYS straight for
"him.
5 "Every Ravine shall
"be filled up, and Every
"Mountain and Hill shall
"be made low; and the
"CROOKED roads shall be-
"come straight, and the
"ROUGH Ways smooth;
6 ‡ "and All Flesh shall
"see the SALVATION of
"GOD."
7 Then he said to the
CROWDS COMING FORTH
to be immersed by him,
‡ "O Progeny of Vipers!
who admonished you to fly

* VATICAN MANUSCRIPT.—51. the SAYINGS. 52. in WISDOM and. 2. High-priest. 3. Country. 4. saying—*omit.*

† 2. Doddridge says, "I cannot suppose, as some have done, that Annas was high-priest the former part of this year, and Caiaphas the latter; much less that Luke knew so little of the Jewish constitution, as to suppose there could be two high-priests properly so called. The easiest solution is, that one was the high-priest, and the other his sagan or deputy, so that the title might, with a very pardonable liberty, be applied to both."

‡ 52. 1 Sam. ii. 26; ver. 40. ‡ 2. John xi. 49, 51; xviii. 13; Acts iv. 6. ‡ 3. Matt. iii. 1; Mark i. 4. ‡ 3. Luke i. 77. ‡ 4. Isa. xl. 3; Matt. iii. 3; Mark i. 3; John i. 23. ‡ 6. Psa. xcviii. 3; Isa. lii. 10; Luke ii. 10. ‡ 7. Matt. iii. 7.

φυγειν απο της μελλουσης οργης; 8 Ποιησατε
to flee from the coming wrath? Bring forth
ουν καρπους αξιους της μετανοιας· και μη
then fruits worthy of the reformation; and not
αρξησθε λεγειν εν ἑαυτοις· Πατερα εχομεν τον
you should begin to say in yourselves; A father we have the
Αβρααμ. Λεγω γαρ ὑμιν, ὁτι δυναται ὁ θεος
Abraam. I say for to you, that is able the God
εκ των λιθων τουτων εγειραι τεκνα τῳ Αβρααμ.
out of the stones of these to raise up children to the Abraam.
9 Ηδη δε και ἡ αξινη προς την ῥιζαν των δενδρων
Now and even the axe to the root of the trees
κειται· παν ουν δενδρον μη ποιουν καρπον
is placed; every therefore tree not bearing fruit
καλον, εκκοπτεται, και εις πυρ βαλλεται.
good, is cut down, and into a fire is cast.
10 Και επηρωτων αυτον οἱ οχλοι, λεγοντες· Τι
And asked him the crowds, saying; What
ουν ποιησομεν; 11 Αποκριθεις δε λεγει αυτοις·
then should we do? Answering and he says to them;
Ὁ εχων δυο χιτωνας, μεταδοτω τῳ μη εχοντι·
He having two tunics, let him share with the not having;
και ὁ εχων βρωματα, ὁμοιως ποιειτω.
and he having meats, in like manner let him do.
12 Ηλθον δε και τελωναι βαπτισθηναι, και
Came and also tax-gatherers to be dipped, and
ειπον προς αυτον· Διδασκαλε, τι ποιησομεν;
said to him; O teacher, what should we do?
13 Ὁ δε ειπε προς αυτους· Μηδεν πλεον παρα
He and said to them; Nothing more from
το διατεταγμενον ὑμιν πρασσετε. 14 Επηρωτων
that having been appointed to you collect you. Asked
δε αυτον και στρατευομενοι, λεγοντες· Και
and him also soldiers, saying; And
ἡμεις τι ποιησομεν; Και ειπε προς αυτους·
we what should we do? And he said to them:
Μηδενα διασεισητε, μηδε συκοφαντησητε· και
No one may you extort from, neither may you accuse wrongfully: and
αρκεισθε τοις οψωνιοις ὑμων.
be you content with the wages of you.
15 Προσδοκωντος δε του λαου, και διαλογιζο-
Expecting and of the people, and reason-
μενων παντων εν ταις καρδιαις αὑτων περι του
ing all in the hearts of them about the
Ιωαννου, μηποτε αυτος ειη ὁ Χριστος, 16 απεκ-
John, whether he were the Anointed, an-
ρινατο ὁ Ιωαννης ἁπασι, λεγων· Εγω μεν
swered the John to all, saying: I indeed
ὑδατι βαπτιζω ὑμας· ερχεται δε ὁ ισχυροτερος
in water dip you: comes but the mightier
μου, ου ουκ ειμι ἱκανος λυσαι τον ἱμαντα των
of me, of whom not I am worthy to loose the strap of the
ὑποδηματων αυτου· αυτος ὑμας βαπτισει εν
sandals of him: he you will dip in
πνευματι ἁγιῳ και πυρι. 17 Ου το πτυον
spirit holy and fire. Of whom the winnowing shovel
εν τῃ χειρι αυτου, και διακαθαριει την
in the hand of him, and he will thoroughly cleanse the

from the APPROACHING VENGEANCE?

8 Produce, therefore, Fruits worthy of REFORMATION; and begin not to say among yourselves, 'We have a Father—ABRAHAM;' for I assure you, That GOD is able from these STONES to raise up CHILDREN to ABRAHAM.

9 And even now the AXE lies at the ROOT of the TREES; ‡Every Tree, therefore, not bearing good Fruit is cut down, and cast into the Fire."

10 And the CROWDS asked him, saying, "What then should we do?"

11 He *answered and said to them, ‡"Let HIM who HAS Two Coats give to HIM who HAS none; and let HIM who HAS Food do the same."

12 ‡And Tribute-takers, also, came to be immersed, and said to him, "Teacher, what should we do?"

13 And HE said to them, "Collect nothing more than WHAT IS APPOINTED for you."

14 And Soldiers, also, asked him, *"What also should WE do?" And he said to them, "Oppress, and falsely accuse, No one; and be satisfied with your WAGES."

15 And the PEOPLE were waiting, and all were reasoning in their HEARTS concerning JOHN, whether HE were not the MESSIAH;

16 JOHN answered all, saying, ‡"I indeed immerse you in Water; but a MIGHTIER than I is coming, for whom I am not fit to untie the STRAP of his SANDALS; HE will immerse you in holy Spirit and Fire.

17 Whose WINNOWING SHOVEL in his HAND will effectually cleanse his

* VATICAN MANUSCRIPT.—11. answered and said. 14. What also should WE do?

‡ 9. Matt. vii. 19. ‡ 11. Luke xi. 41; 2 Cor. viii. 14; James ii. 15, 16; 1 John iii. 17; iv. 20. ‡ 12. Matt. xxi. 32; Luke vii. 29. ‡ 16. Matt. iii. 11; Mark i. 7, 8.

ἁλωνα αὐτου· και συναξει τον σιτον εις την
floor of him: and he will gather the wheat into the
αποθηκην αὑτου, το δε αχυρον κατακαυσει πυρι
storehouse of himself, the but chaff he will burn up in fire
ασβεστῳ. 18 Πολλα μεν ουν και ἑτερα
inextinguishable. Many indeed then also other things
παρακαλων ευηγγελιζετο τον λαον. 19 Ὁ δε
exhorting he preached glad tidings the people. The but
Ἡρωδης ὁ τετραρχης, ελεγχομενος ὑπ' αυτου
Herod the tetrarch, being reproved by him
περι Ἡρωδιαδος της γυναικος του αδελφου
about Herodias of the wife of the brother
αυτου, και περι παντων ὡν εποιησε πονηρων ὁ
of him, and about all of which had done evils the
Ἡρωδης, 20 προσεθηκε και τουτο επι πασι, και
Herod. added also this to all, and
κατεκλεισε τον Ιωαννην εν τη φυλακῃ.
shut up the John in the prison.

21 Εγενετο δε εν τῳ βαπτισθηναι ἁπαντα τον
It occurred and in the to have been dipped all the
λαον, και Ιησου βαπτισθεντος και προσευχο-
people, and Jesus having been dipped and pray-
μενου, ανεῳχθηναι τον ουρανον, 22 και καταβη-
ing, to have been opened the heaven, and to des-
ναι το πνευμα το ἁγιον σωματικῳ ειδει, ὡσει
cend the spirit the holy in a bodily form, like
περιστεραν, επ' αυτον, και φωνην εξ ουρανου
a dove. upon him. and a voice out of heaven
γενεσθαι, *[λεγουσαν·] "Συ ει ὁ υἱος μου ὁ
to have come, [saying;] "Thou art the son of me the
αγαπητος, εν σοι ηυδοκησα."
beloved, in thee I delight.

23 Και αυτος ην ὁ Ιησους ὡσει ετων τριακοντα,
And he was the Jesus about years thirty,
αρχομενος, ων, ὡς ενομιζετο, υἱος Ιωσηφ, του
beginning, being, as was allowed, a son of Joseph, of the
Ἡλι, 24 του Ματθατ, του Λευι, του Μελχι,
Heli, of the Matthat, of the Levi, of the Melchi,
του Ιαννα, του Ιωσηφ, 25 του Ματταθιου, του
of the Janna, of the Joseph, of the Mattathias, of the
Αμως, του Ναουμ, του Εσλι, του Ναγγαι, 26 του
Amos, of the Naoum, of the Esli, of the Naggai, of the
Μααθ, του Ματταθιου, του Σεμει, του Ιωσηφ,
Maath, of the Mattathias, of the Semei, of the Joseph,
του Ιουδα, 27 του Ιωαννα, του Ῥησα, του Ζορο-
of the Juda, of the Joanna, of the Rhesa, of the Zoro-
βαβελ,
babel,

*THRESHING-FLOOR; ‡he
will gather the WHEAT into
his GRANARY, but the
CHAFF he will consume
with an inextinguishable
Fire."
18 And exhorting many
other things, he proclaimed
glad tidings to the PEOPLE.
19 ‡But HEROD the
TETRARCH being reproved
by him on account of He-
rodias, his BROTHER'S
WIFE, and about all the
Crimes which Herod had
done,
20 added also this to all,
—he shut up John in
*Prison.
21 And it occurred, when
All the PEOPLE were IM-
MERSED, ‡Jesus also hav-
ing been immersed, and
praying, the HEAVEN was
opened,
22 and the HOLY SPIRIT,
in a Bodily Form like a
Dove, descended upon him,
and there came a Voice
from Heaven, saying,
"Thou art my SON, the
BELOVED; in thee I de-
light."
23 And he, JESUS, was
about ‡thirty years old,
when he began [his work,]
being, ‡as was allowed, a
*Son of JOSEPH, the †son
of ELI,
24 the son of MATTHAT,
the son of LEVI, the son of
MELCHI, the son of JAN-
NAI, the son of JOSEPH,
25 the son of MATTA-
THIAH, the son of AMOS,
the son of NAHUM, the son
of ESLI, the son of NAG-
GAI,
26 the son of MAATH,
the son of MATTATHIAH,
the son of SHIMEI, the son
of JOSEPH, the son of JU-
DAH,
27 the son of JOHANAH,
the son of RESA, the son
of ZERUBBABEL, the son

* VATICAN MANUSCRIPT.—17. to thoroughly cleanse his THRESHING-FLOOR, and to gather. 20. Prison. 22. saying—*omit.* 23. a Son (as was allowed) of JOSEPH.

† 23. or *son-in-law* of Eli, the father of Mary. Luke gives Mary's ancestry, and Matthew that of Joseph. See Appendix.

‡ 17. Micah vi. 13; Matt. xiii. 30. ‡ 19. Matt. xiv. 3; Mark vi. 17. ‡ 21. Matt. iii. 13; Mark i. 9; John i. 32. ‡ 23. See Num. iv. 3. 35. 39. 43. 47. ‡ 23. Matt. xiii. 55; John vi. 42.

του Σαλαθιηλ, του Νηρι, [28] του Μελχι, του
of the Salathiel, of the Neri, of the Melchi, of the
Αδδι, του Κωσαμ, του Ελμωδαμ, του Ηρ, [29] του
Addi, of the Cosam, of the Elmodam, of the Er, of the
Ιωση, του Ελιεζερ, του Ιωρειμ, του Ματθατ,
Jose, of the Eliezer, of the Jorem, of the Matthat,
του Λευι, [30] του Συμεων, του Ιουδα, του Ιωσηφ,
of the Levi, of the Simeon, of the Juda, of the Joseph,
του Ιωναν, του Ελιακειμ, [31] του Μελεα, του
of the Jonan, of the Eliakim, of the Melea, of the
Μαιναν, του Ματταθα,
Mainan, of the Mattatha,

του Ναθαν, του Δαυιδ, [32] του Ιεσσαι, του
of the Nathan, of the David, of the Jesse, of the
Ωβηδ, του Βοοζ, του Σαλμων, του Ναασσων,
Obed, of the Booz, of the Salmon, of the Naasson,
[33] του Αμιναδαβ, του Αραμ, του Εσρωμ, του
of the Aminadab, of the Aram, of the Esrom, of the
Φαρες, του Ιουδα, [34] του Ιακωβ, του Ισαακ,
Phares, of the Juda, of the Jacob, of the Israel,

του Αβρααμ, του Θαρα, του Ναχωρ, [35] του
of the Abraam, of the Thara, of the Nachor, of the
Σερουχ, του Ῥαγαυ, του Φαλεκ, του Εβερ, του
Saruch, of the Ragau, of the Phalec, of the Eber, of the
Σαλα, [36] του Καιναν, του Αρφαξαδ, του Σημ,
Sala, of the Cainan, of the Arphaxad, of the Sem,
του Νωε, του Λαμεχ, [37] του Μαθουσαλα, του
of the Noe, of the Lamech, of the Mathusala, of the
Ενωχ, του Ιαρεδ, του Μαλελεηλ, του Καιναν,
Enoch, of the Jared, of the Maleleel, of the Cainan,
[38] του Ενως, του Σηθ, του Αδαμ, του θεου.
of the Enos, of the Seth, of the Adam, of the God.

ΚΕΦ. δ'. 4.

[1] Ιησους δε πνευματος ἁγιου πληρης ὑπεσ-
Jesus and spirit of holy full re-
τρεψεν απο του Ιορδανου· και ηγετο εν τῳ
turned from the Jordan; and was led about by the
πνευματι εις την ερημον, [2] ἡμερας τεσσαρακοντα
spirit into the desert, days forty
πειραζομενος ὑπο του διαβολου. Και ουκ
being tempted by the accuser. And not
εφαγεν ουδεν εν ταις ἡμεραις εκειναις· και
he ate nothing in the days those; and
συντελεσθεισων αυτων, *[ὑστερον] επεινασε.
being ended of them, [afterwards] he was hungry.

of SALATHIEL, the son of NERI,
28 the son of MALCHI, the son of ADDI, the son of KOSAM, the son of ALMODAM, the son of ER,
29 the son of JOSES, the son of ELIEZER, the son of JORAM, the son of MATTATH, the son of LEVI,
30 the son of SIMEON, the son of JUDAH, the son of JOSEPH, the son of JONAN, the son of ELIAKIM,
31 the son of MELIAH, the son of MAINAN, the son of MATTATHAH, the son of NATHAN, the son of DAVID,
32 the son of JESSE, the son of OBED, the son of BOAZ, the son of SALMON, the son of NAHSHON,
33 the son of AMMINADAB, the son of RAM, the son of HEZRON, the son of PHAREZ, the son of JUDAH,
34 the son of JACOB, the son of ISAAC, the son of ABRAHAM, the son of TERAH, the son of NAHOR,
35 the son of SERUG, the son of REU, the son of PELEG, the son of EBER, the son of SALAH,
36 the son of CAINAN, the son of ARPHAXAD, the son of SHEM, the son of NOAH, the son of LAMECH,
37 the son of METHUSELAH, the son of ENOCH, the son of JARED. the son of MAHALALEEL. the son of CAINAN,
38 the son of ENOS, the son of SETH, the son of ADAM, the son of GOD.

CHAPTER IV.

1 And ‡Jesus, full of holy Spirit, returned from the JORDAN, and was carried about by the SPIRIT * in the DESERT
2 forty Days, being tempted by the ENEMY. ‡And he ate nothing in those DAYS; and when they were completed, he was hungry.

* VATICAN MANUSCRIPT.—1. in the DESERT. 2. afterwards—omit.

‡ 1. Matt. iv. 1. Mark i. 12. ‡ 2. Exod. xxxiv. 28; 1 Kings xix. 8.

Και ειπεν αυτῳ ὁ διαβολος· Ει υἱος ει του
And said to him the accuser; If a son thou art of the
θεου, ειπε τῳ λιθῳ τουτῳ, ἱνα γενηται αρτος.
God, say to the stone this, that it may become a loaf.
4 Και απεκριθη Ιησους προς αυτον, *[λεγων·]
And answered Jesus to him, [saying;]
Γεγραπται· "Ὁτι ουκ επ' αρτῳ μονῳ ζησεται
It is written; That not on bread alone shall live
ὁ ανθρωπος, *[αλλ' επι παντι ῥηματι θεου."]
the man, [but on every word of God."]
5 Και αναγαγων αυτον ὁ διαβολος εις ορος
And having led up him the accuser into mountain
ὑψηλον, εδειξεν αυτῳ πασας τας βασιλειας της
high, he showed to him all the kingdoms of the
οικουμενης εν στιγμῃ χρονου. 6 Και ειπεν
habitable in a moment of time. And said
αυτῳ ὁ διαβολος· Σοι δωσω την εξουσιαν ταυ-
to him the accuser; To thee I will give the authority this
την ἁπασαν, και την δοξαν αυτων· ὁτι εμοι
all, and the glory of them; that to me
παραδεδοται, και ᾡ εαν θελω, διδωμι αυτην·
it has been prepared, and to whoever I will, I give her;
7 συ ουν εαν προσκυνησῃς ενωπιον, μου, εσται
thou then if thou wilt do homage before me, shall be
σου παντα. 8 Και αποκριθεις αυτῳ ειπεν ὁ
to thee all. And answering to him said the
Ιησους· Γεγραπται· "Προσκυνησεις κυριον τον
Jesus; It is written; "Thou shalt worship a lord the
θεον σου, και αυτῳ μονῳ λατρευσεις."
God of thee, and to him alone thou shalt render service."
9 Και ηγαγεν αυτον εις Ἱερουσαλημ, και
And he brought him to Jerusalem, and
εστησεν αυτον επι το πτερυγιον του ἱερου· και
placed him on the wing of the temple; and
ειπεν αυτῳ· Ει υἱος ει του θεου, βαλε σεαυτον
said to him; If a son thou art of the God, cast thyself
εντευθεν κατω· 10 γεγραπται γαρ· "Ὁτι τοις
from this place down; it is written for; That to the
αγγελοις αὑτου εντελειται περι σου, του δια-
messengers of himself he will give charge concerning thee, of the to
φυλαξαι σε· 11 και ὁτι επι χειρων αρουσι σε,
guard thee; and that on hands they shall bear thee,
μηποτε προσκοψῃς προς λιθον τον ποδα σου."
lest thou shouldst strike against a stone the foot of thee."
12 Και αποκριθεις ειπεν αυτῳ ὁ Ιησους· Ὁτι
And answering said to him the Jesus; That
ειρηται· "Ουκ εκπειρασεις κυριον τον θεον
it is said; "Not thou shalt tempt a lord the God
σου."
of thee."
13 Και συντελεσας παντα πειρασμον ὁ διαβο-
And having ended every temptation the accu-
λος, απεστη απ' αυτου αχρι καιρου. 14 Και
ser, departed from him for a season. And

3 And the ENEMY said to him, "If thou art a Son of GOD, command this STONE to become Bread."

4 And *JESUS answered him, "It is written, ‡'MAN 'shall not live on Bread 'only.'"

5 And *taking him up, he showed him All the KINGDOMS of the HABITABLE in a Moment of Time.

6 And the ENEMY said to him, "I will give Thee All this AUTHORITY, and the GLORY of these; ‡For it has been delivered to me, and I give it to whom I please.

7 If, then, thou wilt render homage before me, all shall be thine."

8 And *Jesus answering said, to him, ‡"It is written, 'Thou shalt wor-'ship the Lord thy GOD, 'and Him only shalt thou 'serve.'"

9 ‡And he brought him to Jerusalem, and placed him on the †BATTLEMENT of the TEMPLE, and said to him, "If thou art a Son of GOD, cast thyself down from this place;

10 for it is written, ‡'He 'will give his ANGELS 'charge concerning thee, 'to PROTECT thee;

11 'and they will up-'hold thee on their Hands, 'lest thou strike thy FOOT 'against a Stone.'"

12 And JESUS answering, said to him, "It is 'said, ‡'Thou shalt not 'try the Lord thy God.'"

13 And the ENEMY having finished every Temptation, departed from him for a Season.

14 ‡And JESUS returned

* VATICAN MANUSCRIPT.—4. JESUS. 4. saying—*omit*. 4. but on every word of God—*omit*. 5. bringing him onward, he showed. 8. Jesus.

† 9. Probably the middle part of the royal portico, the highest part of the temple, and which could be seen at a distance of many furlongs. Josephus says, "That the pillars of that portico were a hundred cubits high, and the valley below four hundred deep."

‡ 4. Deut. viii. 3. ‡ 6. John xii. 31: xiv. 30. ‡ 8. Deut. vi. 13; x. 20. ‡ 9. Matt. iv. 5. ‡ 10. Psa. xci. 11. ‡ 12. Deut. vi. 16. ‡ 14. Matt. iv. 12; John iv. 43; Acts x. 37.

ὑπεστρεψεν ὁ Ιησους εν τῃ δυναμει του πνευ-
returned the Jesus in the power of the spirit
ματος εις την Γαλιλαιαν· και φημη εξηλθε
into the Galilee: and a report went out
καθ' ὁλης της περιχωρου περι αυτου. 15 Και
through whole the surrounding region about him. And
αυτος εδιδασκεν εν ταις συναγωγαις αυτων,
he taught in the synagogues of them,
δοξαζομενος ὑπο παντων.
being glorified by all.
16 Και ηλθεν εις την Ναζαρετ, οὗ ην
And he came into the Nazareth, where he was
τεθραμμενος· και εισηλθε, κατα το ειωθος
having been brought up: and entered, according to the custom
αυτῳ εν τῃ ἡμερᾳ των σαββατων, εις την
to him in the day of the sabbaths, into the
συναγωγην· και ανεστη αναγνωναι. 17 Και
synagogue: and stood up to read. And
επεδοθη αυτῳ βιβλιον Ἡσαιου του προφητου·
was delivered to him a roll of Esaias the prophet:
και αναπτυξας το βιβλιον, εὑρε τον τοπον,
and having unrolled the roll, he found the place,
οὗ ην γεγραμμενον· 18 "Πνευμα κυριου επ'
where it was having been written: "A spirit of a lord upon
εμε· οὗ εἱνεκεν αχρισε με ευαγγελισασθαι
me: of which on account of he has anointed me to publish glad tidings
πτωχοις, απεσταλκε με κηρυξαι αιχμαλωτοις
to poor ones, he has sent me to publish to captives
αφεσιν, και τυφλοις αναβλεψιν, αποστειλαι
a deliverance, and to blind ones recovery of sight, to send away
τεθραυσμενους εν αφεσει, 19 κηρυξαι ενιαυτον
those having been crushed in freedom, to publish a year
κυριου δεκτον." 20 Και πτυξας το βιβλιον,
of a lord acceptable." And having rolled up the roll,
αποδους τῳ ὑπηρετῃ, εκαθισε· και παντων
having given back to the attendant, he sat down: and of all
εν τῃ συναγωγῃ οἱ οφθαλμοι ησαν ατενιζοντες
in the synagogue the eyes were looking steadily
αυτῳ. 21 Ηρξατο δε λεγειν προς αυτους· Ὁτι
to him. He began and to say to them: That
σημερον πεπληρωται ἡ γραφη αὑτη εν τοις
to-day is fulfilled the writing this in to the
ωσιν ὑμων. 22 Και παντες εμαρτυρουν αυτῳ,
ears of you. And all bore testimony to him,
και εθαυμαζον επι τοις λογοις της χαριτος, τοις
and wondered at the words of the graciousness, those
εκπορευομενοις εκ του στοματος αυτου, και
proceeding out of the mouth of him, and
ελεγον· Ουχ οὑτος εστιν ὁ υἱος Ιωσηφ; 23 Και
said: Not this is the son Joseph? And

in the POWER of the SPIRIT into GALILEE; and a Report concerning him went out through the Whole ADJACENT COUNTRY.

15 And he taught in their SYNAGOGUES, being applauded by all.

16 And he came to ‡NAZARETH, where he had been brought up; and according to his CUSTOM on the SABBATH-DAY, ‡he entered the SYNAGOGUE, and †stood up to read.

17 And the Book of Isaiah the PROPHET was given to him; †and having unrolled the BOOK, he found the PLACE where it was written,

18 ‡"The Spirit of the "Lord is on me, because "he has anointed me to "proclaim glad tidings to "the Poor; he has sent "me †to publish a Release "to the Captives, and Re-"covery of sight to the "Blind; to dispense Free-"dom to the oppressed;

19 "to proclaim an Era "of acceptance with the "Lord."

20 And having rolled up the BOOK, he returned it to the ATTENDANT, and sat down. And the EYES of all who were in the SYNAGOGUE were attentively fixed on him.

21 And he began to say to them, "To-day, this SCRIPTURE, which is now in your EARS, is fulfilled."

22 And all bore testimony to him, and wondered at ‡THOSE WORDS of GRACE PROCEEDING from his MOUTH. And they said, "Is not this the SON of Joseph?"

† 16. The Jewish doctors, in honor of the law and the prophets, invariably *stood up* while they read them; but *sat down* while they taught or commented on them. This was our Lord's custom, as we learn from Matt. xxvi. 55—"I *sat* teaching in the TEMPLE every day." † 17. The Sacred Writings used to this day, in all Jewish Synagogues, are written on skins of basil, parchment, or vellum, pasted end to end, and rolled on two *rollers* beginning at each end; so that in reading from right to left, they roll *off* with the left, while they roll *on* with the right. The place that he opened was probably the section for the day.—*Clarke.* † 18. "To heal the broken in heart," is omitted both by the Vatican MS. and Griesbach, but Bloomfield thinks without sufficient warrant, as it is found in Isa. lxi. 1.

‡ 16. Matt. ii. 23; xiii. 54; Mark vi. 1. ‡ 16. Acts xiii. 14; xvii. 2. ‡ 18. Isa. lxi. 1. ‡ 22. Psa. xlv. 2. ‡ 22. John vi. 42.

ειπε προς αυτους· Παντως ερειτε μοι την παρα-
he said to them: Surely you will say to me the illus-
βολην ταυτην· "Ιατρε, θεραπευσον σεαυτον·"
tration this; "Physician, heal thyself;"
ὁσα ηκουσαμεν γενομενα εις Καπερναουμ,
what things we have heard having been done in Capernaum,
ποιησον και ὡδε εν τῃ πατριδι σου. 24 Ειπε δε·
do thou also here in the country of thee. He said and,
Αμην λεγω ὑμιν, ὁτι ουδεις προφητης δεκτος
Indeed I say to you, that no one a prophet acceptable
εστιν εν τῃ πατριδι αὑτου. 25 Επ' αληθειας δε
is in the country of himself. In truth but
λεγω ὑμιν, πολλαι χηραι ησαν εν ταις ἡμεραις
I say to you, many widows were in the days
Ηλιου εν τῳ Ισραηλ, ὁτε εκλεισθη ὁ ουρανος
of Elias in the Israel, when was shut up the heaven
επι ετη τρια και μηνας ἑξ, ὡς εγενετο λιμος
for years three and months six, so that came a famine
μεγας επι πασαν την γην· 26 και προς ουδεμιαν
great over all the land; and to no one
αυτων επεμφθη Ηλιας, ει μη εις Σαρεπτα της
of them was sent Elias, if not into Sarepta of the
Σιδωνος προς γυναικα χηραν. 27 Και πολλοι
Sidon to a woman a widow And many
λεπροι ησαν επι Ελισσαιου του προφητου εν τῳ
lepers were in of Elisha the prophet in the
Ισραηλ· και ουδεις αυτων εκαθαρισθη, ει μη
Israel; and no one of them were cleansed, if not
Νεεμαν ὁ Συρος. 28 Και επλησθησαν παντες
Naaman the Syrian. And they were filled all
θυμου εν τῃ συναγωγῃ, ακουοντες ταυτα.
of wrath in the synagogue, having heard these things.
29 Και ανασταντες εξεβαλον αυτον εξω της
And rising up they cast out him outside of the
πολεως· και ηγαγον αυτον ἑως οφρυος του
city; and they led him even to a brow of the
ορους, εφ' οὑ ἡ πολις αυτων ῳκοδομητο, ὡστε
mountain, on which the city of them was built, so as
κατακρημνισαι αυτον· 30 αυτος δε διελθων δια
to cast down him; he but passing through
μεσου αὑτων, επορευετο.
midst of them, went away.
31 Και κατηλθεν εις Κεπερναουμ, πολιν της
And he came down into Capernaum, a city of the
Γαλιλαιας· και ην διδασκων αυτους εν τοις
Galilee; and he was teaching them in the
σαββασι. 32 Και εξεπλησσοντο επι τῃ διδαχῃ
sabbaths. And they were astonished on the teaching
αυτου· ὁτι εν εξουσιᾳ ην ὁ λογος αυτου,
of him; for with authority was the word of him.
33 Και εν τῃ συναγωγῃ ην ανθρωπος εχων
And in the synagogue was a man having

23 And he said to them, "You will certainly refer me to this PROVERB, 'Physician, cure thyself; what things we have heard has been done in CAPERNAUM, do also here in thy own COUNTRY.'"
24 But he said, "Indeed I say to you, ‡ That no Prophet is acceptable in his OWN COUNTRY.
25 But in Truth I say to you, ‡ There were Many Widows in ISRAEL, in the days of Elijah, when the HEAVEN was closed three Years and six Months, so that there came a great Famine over All the LAND;
26 and yet to no one of them was Elijah sent, but to a Widow Woman, at Sarepta, of SIDON.
27 ‡ And there were Many Lepers in ISRAEL, in [the days] of Elisha the PROPHET, and yet no one of them were cleansed, but Naaman, the SYRIAN."
28 And all in the SYNAGOGUE hearing these words, were filled with Wrath;
29 and rising up, they drove him out of the CITY, and led him even to the † Brow of the MOUNTAIN on which their CITY was built, to throw him down;
30 but HE, ‡ passing through the Midst of them, went away.
31 ‡ And he came down to Capernaum, a City of GALILEE, and taught them on the SABBATH.
32 And they were struck with awe at his mode of INSTRUCTION; ‡ For his WORD was with Authority.
33 ‡ Now there was a Man in the SYNAGOGUE,

† 29. Behind the Maronite church is a steep precipice, forty or fifty feet high, "on the brow of the hill;" the very one, it may be, over which the people of Nazareth attempted to thrust the Savior, on the Sabbath when they took such offence at his preaching in the synagogue. I observed other rocky ledges, on other parts of the hill, so precipitous that a person could not be thrown over them without almost certain destruction. A worthless tradition has transferred this event to a hill about two miles to the south-east of the town. But there is no evidence that Nazareth ever occupied a different site from the present one; and that a mob so exasperated, whose object was to put to death the object of their rage, should have repaired to so distant a place for that purpose, is entirely incredible.—*Hackett.*

‡ 24. Matt. xiii. 57; Matt. vi. 4; John iv. 44. ‡ 25. 1 Kings xvii. 9; xviii. 1; James v. 17. ‡ 27. 2 Kings v. 14. ‡ 30. John viii. 59; x. 39. ‡ 31. Matt. iv. 13; Mark i. 21. ‡ 32. Matt. vii. 28, 29. ‡ 33. Mark i. 23.

πνευμα δαιμονιου ακαθαρτου, και ανεκραξε
a spirit of a demon unclean, and he cried out
φωνη μεγαλῃ, 34 *[λεγων·] Εα, τι ἡμιν και
with a voice loud, [saying;] Ah, what to us and
σοι, Ιησου Ναζαρηνε; ηλθες απολεσαι ἡμας·
to thee Jesus O Nazarene? comest thou to destroy us;
οιδα σε τις ει, ὁ ἁγιος του θεου. 35 Και
I know thee who thou art, the holy the God. And
επετιμησεν αυτῳ ὁ Ιησους, λεγων· Φιμωθητι,
rebuked him the Jesus, saying; Be silent,
και εξελθε εξ αυτου. Και ῥιψαν αυτον το
and come out of him. And having thrown him the
δαιμονιον εις μεσον, εξηλθεν απ' αυτου, μηδεν
demon into midst, came out of him, nothing
βλαψαν αυτον· 36 Και εγενετο θαμβος επι
hurting him; And came amazement on
παντας· και συνελαλουν προς αλληλους, λεγον-
all; and talked to one another, say-
τες· Τις ὁ λογος οὑτος, ὁτι εν εξουσιᾳ και
ing; What the word this, for with authority and
δυναμει επιτασσει τοις ακαθαρτοις πνευμασι,
power he commands the unclean spirits,
και εξερχονται; 37 Και εξεπορευετο ηχος περι
and they come out? And went forth a report concerning
αυτου εις παντα τοπον της περιχωρου.
him into every place of the country around.

38 Αναστας δε εκ της συναγωγης, εισηλθεν
Having risen up and out of the synagogue, he entered
εις την οικιαν Σιμωνος· πενθερα δε του Σιμωνος
into the house of Simon; mother-in-law and of the Simon
ην συνεχομενη πυρετῳ μεγαλῳ· και ηρωτησαν
was seized with a fever great; and they asked
αυτον περι αυτης. 39 Και επιστας επανω
him about her. And standing above
αυτης, επετιμησε τῳ πυρετῳ· και αφηκεν
her, he rebuked the fever; and it left
αυτην. Παραχρημα δε αναστασα διηκονει
her. Forthwith and rising up she served
αυτοις.
them.

40 Δυνοντος δε του ἡλιου, παντες ὁσοι ειχον
Setting and of the sun, all as many as had
ασθενουντας νοσοις ποικιλαις, ηγαγον αυτους
being afflicted with diseases various, brought them
προς αυτον· ὁ δε ἑνι ἑκαστῳ αυτων τας
to him; he and one by one separately of them the
χειρας επιθεις, εθεραπευσεν αυτους. 41 Εξηρ-
hands having placed, he healed them. Came
χετο δε και δαιμονια απο πολλων, κραζοντα
out and also demons from many, crying out
και λεγοντα· Ὁτι συ ει ὁ υἱος του θεου. Και
and saying; That thou art the son of the God. And
επιτιμων ουκ εια αυτα λαλειν, ὁτι ηδεισαν
rebuking not he permitted them to say, that they knew
τον Χριστον αυτον ειναι.
the Anointed him to be.

having a Spirit of an †impure Demon; and he exclaimed with a loud Voice.

34 "Ah! what hast thou to do with us, Jesus Nazarene? Comest thou to destroy us? I know thee who thou art; ‡ the HOLY ONE of GOD."

35 And JESUS rebuked him, saying, "Be silent, and come out of him." And the DEMON having thrown him into the Midst, departed from him, without hurting him.

36 And amazement came on all, and they spoke to one another, "What WORD is this! For with Authority and Power he commands the IMPURE Spirits, and they come out."

37 And a Report concerning him went forth into Every Part of the SURROUNDING COUNTRY.

38 ‡ And rising up out of the SYNAGOGUE, he entered the HOUSE of Simon. And SIMON'S Mother-in-law was confined with a violent Fever; and they asked him concerning her.

39 And standing over her, he rebuked the FEVER, and it left her; and instantly rising up, she served them.

40 ‡ Now as the SUN was setting, all who had any sick with various Diseases, brought them to him; and HE, placing his HANDS on each one of them, cured them.

41 And Demons also departed from many, crying out and saying, "Thou art the SON of GOD." And rebuking them, he permitted them not to say That they knew him to be the MESSIAH.

† 33. As *demon* was used both in a *good* and *bad* sense before and after the time of the evangelists, the word *unclean* may have been added here by Luke, merely to express the quality of *this* spirit. But it is worthy of remark, that the inspired writers never use the word *demon* in a *good* sense.—*Clarke.*

‡ 34. Psa. xvi. 10; Dan. ix. 24. ‡ 38. Matt. viii. 14; Mark i. 29. ‡ 40. Matt. viii. 16; Mark i. 32.

42 Γενομενης δε ἡμερας, εξελθων επορευθη εις
Being come and day, coming out he went into
ερημον τοπον· και οἱ οχλοι επεζητουν αυτον,
a desert place: and the crowds sought him,
και ηλθων ἑως αυτου, και κατειχον αυτον μη
and came to him, and urged him not
πορευεσθαι απ' αυτων. 43 Ὁ δε ειπε προς
to depart from them. He but said to
αυτους· Ὁτι και ταις ἑτεραις πολεσιν ευαγ-
them; That also to the other cities to publish
γελισασθαι με δει την βασιλειαν του θεου· ὁτι
glad tidings me must the kingdom of the God; because
εις τουτο απεσταλμαι.
for this I have been sent forth.
44 Και ην κηρυσσων εν ταις συναγωγαις της
And he was preaching in the synagogues of the
Γαλιλαιας. ΚΕΦ. ε'. 5. 1 Εγενετο δε εν τῳ
Galilee. It happened but in to the
τον οχλον επικεισθαι αυτῳ του ακουειν τον
the crowd to press him of the to hear the
λογον του θεου, και αυτος ην ἑστως παρα την
word of the God and he was standing by the
λιμνην Γεννησαρετ· 2 και ειδε δυο πλοια
lake Gennesaret; and he saw two ships
ἑστωτα παρα την λιμνην· οἱ δε ἁλιεις αποβαν-
standing by the lake; the but fishermen having
τες απ' αυτων, απεπλυναν τα δικτυα. 3 Εμβας
gone from them, were washing the nets. Entering
δε εις ἑν των πλοιων, ὁ ην του Σιμωνος· ηρω-
and into one of the ships, which was of the Simon; he
τησεν αυτον απο της γης επαναγαγειν ολιγον·
asked him from the land to put off a little;
και καθισας εδιδασκεν εκ τυυ πλοιου τους
and sitting down he taught out of the ship the
οχλους. 4 Ὡς δε επαυσατο λαλων, ειπε προς
crowds. When and he ceased speaking, he said to
τον Σιμωνα· Επαναγαγε εις το βαθος, και
the Simon; Put out into the deep, and
χαλασατε τα δικτυα ὑμων εις αγραν. 5 Και
let down the nets of you for a draught. And
αποκριθεις ὁ Σιμων ειπεν *[αυτῳ·] Επιστατα,
answering the Simon said [to him] O master
δι' ὁλης της νυκτος κοπιασαντες, ουδεν ελα-
through whole of the night having toiled, nothing we
βομεν· επι δε τῳ ῥηματι σου χαλασω το
have taken; at but the word of thee I will let down the
δικτυον. 6 Και τουτο ποιησαντες, συνεκλει-
net. And this having done, they enclo-
σαν πληθος ιχθυων πολυ· διεῤῥηγνυτο δε το
sed a multitude of fishes great; was rending and the
δικτυον αυτων. 7 Και κατενευσαν τοις μετο-
net of them. And they beckoned to the part-
χοις τοις εν τῳ ἑτερῳ πλοιῳ, του ελθοντας
ners to those in the other ship, of the coming
συλλαβεσθαι αυτοις· και ηλθον, και επλησαν
to help them; and they came, and filled

42 And Day having come, he retired to a Desert Place; and the CROWDS sought him, and came to him, and urged him not to leave them.

43 But HE said to them, "I must proclaim the glad tidings of the KINGDOM of GOD to OTHER Cities also; because for this I have been sent."

44 ‡ And he was preaching * in the SYNAGOGUES of GALILEE.

CHAPTER V.

1 ‡ Now it occurred, as the CROWD PRESSED on him to HEAR the WORD of GOD, he was standing by the † LAKE Gennesaret;

2 and he saw * two Boats stationed near the SHORE; but the FISHERMEN having left them, were washing their NETS.

3 And having gone into one of the BOATS, which was SIMON'S, he asked him to put off a little from the LAND; and sitting down, he instructed the CROWDS out of the BOAT.

4 And when he ceased speaking, he said to SIMON, ‡ "Put out into the DEEP, and let down your NETS for a Draught."

5 And * Simon answering, said, "Master, we have labored through the Whole NIGHT, and have caught nothing; yet, at thy WORD, I will let down the * NETS."

6 And having done this, they enclosed a great Multitude of Fishes; and their * NETS were rending.

7 And they beckoned to their PARTNERS in the OTHER Boat, to come and ASSIST them. And they came, and filled Both the

* VATICAN MANUSCRIPT.—44. to the SYNAGOGUES. 2. two Boats. 5. Simon. 5. to him—*omit.* 5. NETS. 6. NETS.

† 1. Called also the sea or lake of Galilee, and the sea of Tiberias. It was anciently called the sea of Chinnereth. It is about five miles wide, and some sixteen or seventeen miles long.

‡ 44. Mark i. 39. ‡ 1. Matt. iv. 18; Mark i. 16. ‡ 4. John xxi. 6.

αμφοτερα τα πλοια, ὡστε βυθιζεσθαι αυτα.
both the ships, so as to sink them.
8 Ιδων δε Σιμων Πετρος, προσεπεσε τοις γονασι
Seeing and Simon Peter, fell down to the knees
του Ιησου, λεγων· Εξελθε απ᾽ εμου, ὁτι ανηρ
of the Jesus, saying; Depart from me, for a man
ἁμαρτωλος ειμι, κυριε. 9 Θαμβος γαρ περι-
a sinner I am, O lord. Amazement for seized
εσχεν αυτον και παντας τους συν αυτῳ, επι τῃ
him and all those with him, at the
αγρᾳ των ιχθυων, ᾑ συνελαβον 10 ὁμοιως
draught of the fishes, which they had taken; in like manner
δε και Ιακωβον και Ιωαννην, υἱους Ζεβεδαιου,
and also James and John, sons of Zebedee,
οἱ ησαν κοινωνοι τῳ Σιμωνι. Και ειπε προς
who were partners with the Simon. And said to
τον Σιμωνα ὁ Ιησους· Μη φοβου· απο του νυν
the Simon the Jesus; Not fear; from of the now
ανθρωπους εσῃ ζωγρων. 11 Και καταγαγοντες
men thou wilt be catching. And having brought
τα πλοια επι την γην, αφεντες ἁπαντα, ηκολου-
the ships to the land, having left all, they fol-
θησαν αυτῳ.
lowed him.

12 Και εγενετο εν τῳ ειναι αυτον εν μιᾳ των
And it happened in to the to be him in one of the
πολεων, και ιδου, ανηρ πληρης λεπρας· και
cities, and lo, a man full of leprosy; and
ιδων τον Ιησουν, πεσων επι προσωπον, εδεηθη
seeing the Jesus, having fallen on face, entreated
αυτου, λεγων· κυριε, εαν θελῃς, δυνασαι με
him, saying; O lord, if thou wilt, thou art able me
καθαρισαι. 13 Και εκτεινας την χειρα, ἡψατο
to cleanse. And stretching out the hand, he touched
αυτου, ειπων· Θελω, καθαρισθητι. Και ευθεως
him, saying; I will, be thou cleansed. And immediately
ἡ λεπρα απηλθεν απ᾽ αυτου. 14 Και αυτος
the leprosy departed from him. And he
παρηγγειλεν αυτῳ μηδενι ειπειν· αλλα απελ-
commanded him no one to tell: but going
θων δειξον σεαυτον τῳ ἱερει, και προσενεγκε
show thyself to the priest, and offer
περι του καθαρισμου σου, καθως προσεταξε
on account of the cleansing of thee, as enjoined
Μωσης, εις μαρτυριον αυτοις.
Moses, for a witness to them.

15 Διηρχετο δε μαλλον ὁ λογος περι αυτου·
Spread abroad but more the word concerning him;
και συνηρχοντο οχλοι πολλοι ακουειν, και
and came together crowds great to hear, and
θεραπευεσθαι *[ὑπ᾽ αυτου] απο των ασθενειων
to be healed [by him] from the weaknesses

BOATS, so that they were sinking.

8 And Simon Peter seeing it, fell down at the KNEES of * Jesus, saying, "Depart from me, O Lord, For I am a sinful Man."

9 For amazement seized him, and ALL who were with him, at the DRAUGHT of FISHES which they had taken;

10 and in like manner also, James and John, Sons of Zebedee, who were Partners with SIMON. And * Jesus said to SIMON, "Fear not; ‡ HENCEFORTH thou wilt catch Men,"

11 And having brought the BOATS to the LAND, ‡ leaving all, they followed him.

12 ‡ And it occurred, when he WAS in one of the CITIES, behold, a Man full of Leprosy, seeing JESUS, fell on his Face, and besought him, saying, "Sir, if thou wilt, thou canst cleanse Me."

13 And extending his HAND, he touched him, saying, "I will; be thou cleansed." And instantly the LEPROSY departed from him.

14 ‡ And he commanded him to tell no one; "but go, [said he] show thyself to the PRIEST, and present an offering on account of thy CLEANSING, ‡ as Moses commanded, for Notifying [the cure] to the people."

15 But the REPORT concerning him spread abroad the more; and great Crowds came together to hear, and be cured of their INFIRMITIES.

* VATICAN MANUSCRIPT.—8. Jesus. 10. Jesus. 15. by him—*omit*.

† 14. This injunction of our Lord upon the man to show himself to the priest, might have had a further meaning than merely a compliance with the direction of the Mosaic law in this case. The Jewish Rabbins thought that the curing of the leprosy would be characteristic of the Messiah. This makes the obstinacy and unbelief of the Jewish rulers and people appear still more inexcusable.

‡ 10. Matt. iv. 19; Mark i. 17. ‡ 11. Matt. iv. 20; xix. 27; Mark i. 18; Luke xviii. 28. ‡ 12. Matt. viii. 2; Mark i. 40. ‡ 14. Matt. viii. 4. ‡ 14. Lev. xiv. 4, 10, 21, 22.

αὐτων· 16 Αυτος δε ην ὑποχωρων εν ταις ερημοις,
of them: He but was retiring in the deserts,
και προσευχομενος.
and praying.
17 Και εγενετο εν μιᾳ των ἡμερων, και αυτος
And it happened in one of the days, and he
ην διδασκων· και ησαν καθημενοι Φαρισαιοι και
was teaching; and were sitting Pharisees and
νομοδιδασκαλοι, οἱ ησαν εληλυθοτες εκ πασης
teachers of the law, they were having come out of all
κωμης της Γαλιλαιας και Ιουδαιας, και Ἱερου-
villages of the Galilee and Judea and Jeru-
σαλημ· και δυναμις κυριου ην εις το ἰασθαι
salem; and power of Lord was into the to heal
αυτους. 18 Και ιδου, ανδρες φεροντες επι
them. And lo, men bringing on
κλινης ανθρωπον, ὁς ην παραλελυμενος· και
a couch a man, who was having been palsied; and
εζητουν αυτον εισενεγκειν, και θειναι ενωπιον
sought him to bring in, and to place in presence
αυτου. 19 Και μη εὑροντες ποιας εισενεγκωσιν
of him. And not finding how they might bring in
αυτον, δια τον οχλον, αναβαντες επι το δωμα,
him, through the crowd, having gone up to the roof,
δια των κεραμων καθηκαν αυτον συν τῳ
through the tiles they let down him with the
κλινιδιῳ εις το μεσον εμπροσθεν του Ιησου.
little bed into the midst in presence of the Jesus.
20 Και ιδων την πιστιν αυτων, ειπεν· Ανθρωπε,
And seeing the faith of them, he said; O man,
αφεωνται σοι αἱ ἁμαρτιαι σου. 21 Και ηρξαντο
have been forgiven to thee the sins of thee. And began
διαλογιζεσθαι οἱ γραμματεις και οἱ Φαρισαιοι,
to reason the scribes and the Pharisees,
λεγοντες· Τις εστιν οὑτος ὁς λαλει βλασφημιας;
saying; Who is this who speaks blasphemies?
τις δυναται αφιεναι ἁμαρτιας, ει μη μονος ὁ
who is able to forgive sins, if not alone the
θεος; 22 Επιγνους δε ὁ Ιησους τους διαλογισμους
God? Knowing but the Jesus the reasonings
αυτων, αποκριθεις ειπε προς αυτους· Τι διαλο-
of them, answering said to them; Why do you
γιζεσθε εν ταις καρδιαις ὑμων; 23 Τι εστιν
reason in the hearts of you? Which is
ευκοπωτερον; ειπειν· Αφεωνται σοι αἱ ἁμαρ-
easier? to say; Have been forgiven to thee the sins
τιαι σου; η ειπειν· Εγειρε και περιπατει;
of thee? or to say; Arise and walk?
24 Ἱνα δε ειδητε, ὁτι εξουσιαν εχει ὁ υἱος του
That but you may know, that authority has the son of the
ανθρωπου επι της γης αφιεναι ἁμαρτιας, (ειπε
man on the earth to forgive sins, (he said
τῳ παραλελυμενῳ·) Σοι λεγω· Εγειρε, και
to the having been palsied;) To thee I say; Arise, and
αρας το κλινιδιον σου, πορευου εις τον
having taken up the little bed of thee, go into the

16 ‡And he retired into solitary places, and prayed.

17 And it occurred on one of the DAYS, he was teaching, and the *PHARISEES and Teachers of the Law were sitting near, having come out of Every Village of Galilee, and of Judea, and from Jerusalem; and the Mighty Power of the Lord was on *him to CURE.

18 ‡ And, behold, Men bringing on a Bed a palsied Man, and they sought to bring him in, and place him in his presence.

19 And not finding how they could bring him in, on account of the CROWD, having ascended to the ROOF, they lowered him, with the LITTLE BED, †through the TILES, into the MIDST before * them all.

20 And perceiving their FAITH, he said, "Man, thy SINS are forgiven thee."

21 ‡ And the SCRIBES and the PHARISEES began to reason, saying, "Who is this that utters Blasphemies? ‡ Who can forgive Sins, except God only?"

22 But JESUS knowing their THOUGHTS, answering, said to them, "Why do you reason in your HEARTS?

23 Which is easier? to say, 'Thy SINS are forgiven thee;' or to say, [with effect,] 'Arise, and walk?'

24 But that you may know that the SON of MAN has AUTHORITY on EARTH to forgive Sins," (he says to the PALSIED MAN,) "I say to thee, 'Arise, and taking up thy LITTLE BED, go to thy HOUSE.'"

* VATICAN MANUSCRIPT.—17. PHARISEES. 17. him to CURE. And. 19. them all.

† 19. Probably through the door in the roof, which being fastened, was forced open. See Mark ii. 4. Because all the roof, except the door, was covered with tiles, it is said, "they lowered him through the tiles;" of course, by means of the stairs leading down into the area or court of the house, where the people were assembled.

‡ 16. Matt. xiv. 23; Mark vi. 46. ‡ 18. Matt. ix. 2; Mark ii. 3. ‡ 21. Matt. ix. 3; Mark ii. 6, 7. ‡ 21. Psa. xxxii. 5; Isa. xliii. 25.

οικον σου. 25 Και παραχρημα αναστας ενωπιον
house of thee. And instantly arising in presence
αυτων, αρας εφ' ῴ κατεκειτο, απηλθεν
of them, having taked up on which he had been laid, went
εις τον οικον αὑτου, δοξαζων τον θεον. 26 Και
into the house of himself, glorifying the God. And
εκστασις ελαβεν ἁπαντας, και εδοξαζον τον
amazement took all, and they glorified the
θεον· και επλησθησαν φοβου, λεγοντες· Ὁτι
God: and were filled of fear, saying: That
ειδομεν παραδοξα σημερον.
we have seen wonderful things to-day.

27 Και μετα ταυτα εξηλθε, και εθεασατο
And after these he went out, and saw
τελωνην, ονοματι Λευιν, καθημενον επι το
a publican, with a name Levi, sitting at the
τελωνιον· και ειπεν αυτῳ· Ακολουθει μοι.
custom-house: and he said to him: Follow me.
28 Και καταλιπων ἁπαντα, αναστας ηκολουθησεν
And forsaking all, rising up he followed
αυτῳ. 29 Και εποιησε δοχην μεγαλην Λευις
him. And made a feast great Levi
αυτῳ εν τη οικιᾳ αὑτου· και ην οχλος τελωνων
to him in the house of himself: and was a crowd of publicans
πολυς, και αλλων, οἱ ησαν μετ' αυτων κατακει-
great, and of others, who were with them reclin-
μενοι. 30 Και εγογγυζον οἱ γραμματεις αυτων
ing. And murmured the scribes of them
και οἱ Φαρισαιοι προς τους μαθητας αυτου,
and the Pharisees to the disciples of him,
λεγοντες· Διατι μετα των τελωνων και ἁμαρ-
saying: Why with the publicans and sin-
τωλων εσθιετε και πινετε; 31 Και αποκριθεις ὁ
ners do you eat and drink? And answering the
Ιησους ειπε προς αυτους· Ου χρειαν εχουσιν
Jesus said to them: No need have
οἱ ὑγιαινοντες ιατρου, αλλ' οἱ κακως εχοντες·
those being in health of a physician, but those sick being:
32 ουκ εληλυθα καλεσαι δικαιους, αλλα αμαρτω-
not I have come to call just (ones,) but sinners
λους εις μετανοιαν.
to reformation.

33 Οἱ δε ειπον προς αυτον· *[Διατι] οἱ
They and said to him: [Why] the
μαθηται Ιωαννου νηστευουσι πυκνα, και δεησεις
disciples of John fast often, and prayers
ποιουνται, ὁμοιως και οἱ των Φαρισαιων· οἱ δε
make, in like manner and those of the Pharisees: those but
σοι εσθιουσι και πινουσιν; 34 Ὁ δε ειπε προς
to thee eat and drink? He and said to
αυτους· Μη δυνασθε τους υἱους του νυμφιος, εν
them: Not you are able the sons of the bridal-chamber, in
ῴ ὁ νυμφιος μετ' αυτων εστι, ποιησαι
which the bridegroom with them is, to make
νηστευειν; 35 Ελευσονται δε ἡμεραι, και ὁταν
to fast? Will come but days, and when
απαρθη απ' αυτων ὁ νυμφιος, τοτε νηστευσου-
may be taken from them the bridegroom, then they will fast

25 And instantly arising in their presence, and taking up that on which he had been lying, he proceeded to his own HOUSE, praising GOD.

26 And astonishment seized all, and they praised GOD, and were filled with Fear, saying, "We have seen wonderful things to-day."

27 ‡ And after this, he went out, and saw a Tribute-taker, named Levi, sitting at the TAX-OFFICE; and he said to him, "Follow me."

28 And forsaking all, he arose, and followed him.

29 ‡ And * Levi made a great Feast for him, in his own HOUSE; and there was a great Crowd of Tribute-takers, and of others, who were reclining with them.

30 And * the PHARISEES and their SCRIBES complained to his DISCIPLES, saying, "Why do you eat and drink with TRIBUTE-TAKERS and Sinners?"

31 And * Jesus answering, said to them, "THOSE who are in HEALTH have no need of a Physician, but THOSE who are SICK.

32 ‡ I have not come to call the Righteous, but Sinners to Repentance."

33 And THEY said to him, ‡ "The DISCIPLES of John frequently fast and Pray; and in like manner THOSE of the PHARISEES; but THINE eat and drink?"

34 And he said to them, "Can the BRIDEMEN fast, while the BRIDEGROOM is with them?

35 But Days will come, when the BRIDEGROOM will be taken from them, and then they will fast in Those DAYS."

* VATICAN MANUSCRIPT.—29. LEVI. 30. the PHARISEES and their SCRIBES. 31 Jesus.

‡ 27 Matt. ix. 9; Mark ii. 13, 14. ‡ 29. Matt. ix. 10; Mark ii. 15. ‡ 32. Matt. ix. 13; 1 Tim. i. 15. ‡ 33. Matt. ix. 14; Mark ii. 18.

νιν εν εκειναις ταις ἡμεραις. 36 Ελεγε δε και
in those the days. He spoke and also
παραβολην προς αυτους· Ὁτι ουδεις επιβλημα
a parable to them; That no one a patch
ἱματιου καινου επιβαλλει επι ἱματιον παλαιον·
of a mantle new sews on to a mantle old:
ει δε μηγε, και το καινον σχιζει, και τῳ παλαιῳ
if but not, and the new it rends, and the old
ου συμφωνει επιβλημα το απο του καινου.
not agrees a patch that from the new.
37 Και ουδεις βαλλει οινον νεον εις ασκους
And no one puts wine new into skins
παλαιους· ει δε μηγε, ῥηξει ὁ νεος οινος τους
old: if but not, will burst the new wine the
ασκους, και αυτος εκχυθησεται, και οἱ ασκοι
skins, and he will be spilt, and the skins
απολουνται· 38 αλλα οινον νεον εις ασκους και-
will be destroyed: but wine new into skins new
νους βλητεον· *[και αμφοτεροι συντηρουνται.]
requires to be put: [and both are preserved.]
39 *[Και] ουδεις πιων παλαιον, *[ευθεως] θελει
[And] no one having drunk old, [immediately] desires
νεον· λεγει γαρ· Ὁ παλαιος χρηστοτερος εστιν.
new: he says for: The old better is.

ΚΕΦ. ϛ'. 6.

1 Εγενετο δε εν σαββατῳ *[δευτεροπρωτῳ]
It happened and in sabbath [second-first]
διαπορευεσθαι αυτον δια των σποριμων· και
to pass him through the grain-fields: and
ετιλλον οἱ μαθηται αυτου τους σταχυας, και
plucked the disciples of him the ears of grain, and
ησθιον, ψωχοντες ταις χερσι. 2 Τινες δε των
ate, rubbing the hands. Some and of the
Φαρισαιων ειπον *[αυτοις·] Τι ποιειτε, ὁ ουκ εξ-
Pharisees said (to them;) Why do you, which not it is
εστι *[ποιειν] εν τοις σαββασι; 3 Και αποκριθεις
lawful [to do] in the sabbaths? And answering
προς αυτους ειπεν ὁ Ιησους· Ουδε τουτο ανεγ-
to them said the Jesus; Not even this have you
νωτε, ὁ εποιησε Δαυιδ, ὁποτε επεινασεν αυτος
read, what did David, when was hungry he
και οἱ μετ' αυτου οντες; 4 ὡς εισηλθεν εις τον
and those with him being? how he entered into the
οικον του θεου, και τους αρτους της προθεσεως
house of the God, and the loaves of the presence
ελαβε, και εφαγε, και εδωκε *[και] τοις
he took, and ate, and gave [also] to those
μετ' αυτου· οὑς ουκ εξεστι φαγειν, ει μη μονος
with him; which not it is lawful to eat, if not alone
τους ἱερεις; 5 Και ελεγεν αυτοις· *[Ὁτι]
the priests? And he said to them, [That]

36 ‡ And he also spoke a Parable to them; "No one puts a Piece * rent from a new Garment on an old; else the NEW also * will make a rent, and THAT Piece from the NEW * will not agree with the OLD.

37 And no one puts new Wine into † old Skins; else the * NEW WINE will burst the SKINS, and itself be spilt, and the SKINS be destroyed.

38 But new Wine must be put into new Skins.

39 No one having drunk old wine desires new; for he says, 'The OLD is * good.'"

CHAPTER VI.

1 ‡ And it occurred on the Sabbath, that he went through the * Grain-fields, and his DISCIPLES plucked the HEADS of GRAIN, and ate, rubbing them in their HANDS.

2 And some of the PHARISEES said, "Why do you ‡ what is not lawful on the SABBATH?"

3 And * Jesus answering them, said, "Have you not even read this, ‡ which David did, when hungry, he and THOSE who * were with him?

4 He went into the TABERNACLE of GOD, and took the LOAVES of the PRESENCE, and ate, and gave to THOSE with him; ‡ which none but the PRIESTS could lawfully eat."

5 And he said to them,

* VATICAN MANUSCRIPT.—36. rent from a new. 36. will make a rent, and the PIECE. 36. will not agree with. 37. NEW WINE. 38. and both are preserved—*omit.* 39. And—*omit.* 39. immediately—*omit.* 1. second-first—*omit.* 1. Grain-fields. 2. to them—*omit.* 2. to do—*omit.* 3. Jesus. 3. were. 4. how—*omit.* 4. also—*omit.* 5. That—*omit.*

† 37. Bottles of skin or leather, which the Jews used for putting their wines in. Skins are used for this purpose now in Spain, Portugal, and the East. New wine, by fermenting would burst such as these, if they were old, and dry. See Josh. ix. 4, and Job xxxii. 19.

‡ 36. Matt. ix. 16, 17; Mark ii. 21, 22. ‡ 1. Matt. xii. 1; Mark ii. 23. ‡ 2. Exod. xx. 10. ‡ 3. 1 Sam. xxi. 6. ‡ 4. Lev. xxiv. 9.

κυριος εστιν ὁ υἱος του ανθρωπου και του σαβ-
a lord is the son of the man also of the sab-
βατου.
bath.
6 Εγενετο δε *[και] εν ἑτερῳ σαββατῳ εισελ-
It happened and [also] in another sabbath to en-
θειν αυτον εις την συναγωγην, και διδασκειν· και
ter him into the synagogue, and to teach; and
ην εκει ανθρωπος, και ἡ χειρ αυτου ἡ δεξια ην
was there a man, and the hand of him the right was
ξηρα. 7 Παρετηρουν δε αυτον οἱ γραμματεις
withered. Watched and him the scribes
και οἱ Φαρισαιοι ει εν τῳ σαββατῳ θεραπευσι,
and the Pharisees if in the sabbath he will heal,
ἱνα εὑρωσι κατηγοριαν αυτου. 8 Αυτος δε
so that they might find an accusation of him. He but
ηδει τους διαλογισμους αυτων, και ειπε τῳ
knew the purposes of them, and said to the
ανθρωπῳ τῳ ξηραν εχοντι την χειρα· Εγειρε,
man the withered having the hand; Arise,
και στηθι εις το μεσον. Ὁ δε αναστας εστη.
and stand into the midst. He and having arisen stood.
9 Ειπεν ουν ὁ Ιησους προς αυτους· Επερωτησω
Said then the Jesus to them; I will ask
ὑμας· Τι εξεστι τοις σαββασιν; αγαθοποιησαι,
you; What is it lawful to the sabbath? to do good,
η κακοποιησαι; ψυχην σωσαι, η αποκτειναι;
or to do evil? a life to save, or to kill?
10 Και περιβλεψαμενος παντας αυτους, ειπεν
And looking around on all them, he said
αυτῳ· Εκτεινον την χειρα σου. Ὁ δε εποιησε·
to him; Stretch out the hand of thee. He and did;
και απεκατεσταθη ἡ χειρ αυτου *[ὡς ἡ αλλη.]
and was restored the hand of him [as the other.]
11 Αυτοι δε επλησθησαν ανοιας, και διελαλουν
They and were filled madness, and they talked
προς αλληλους, τι αν ποιησειαν τῳ Ιησου.
to one another, what they should do to the Jesus.

12 Εγενετο δε εν ταις ἡμεραις ταυταις, εξηλ-
It came to pass and in the days those, he went
θεν εις το ορος προσευξασθαι· και ην διανυκτε-
out into the mountain to pray; and was passing the
ρευων εν τῃ προσευχῃ του θεου. 13 Και ὁτε
night in the place of prayer of the God. And when
εγενετο ἡμερα, προσεφωνησε τους μαθητας
it became day, he called to the disciples
αὑτου· και εκλεξαμενος απ' αυτων δωδεκα, οὑς
of himself: and having chosen from them twelve, whom
και αποστολους ωνομασε· 14 (Σιμωνα, ὁν και
also apostles he named: (Simon, whom also
ωνομασε Πετρον, και Ανδρεαν τον αδελφον
he named Peter, and Andrew the brother
αυτου, Ιακωβον και Ιωαννην, Φιλιππον και
of him, James and John, Philip and

"The SON of MAN is Lord even of the SABBATH."

6 And it occurred on Another Sabbath, that he entered the SYNAGOGUE, and taught. And a Man was there whose RIGHT HAND was withered.

7 And the SCRIBES and PHARISEES watched him closely [to see] if he would cure on the SABBATH; that they might find an Accusation against him.

8 But he knew their PURPOSES, and said to THAT MAN HAVING the withered HAND, "Arise, and stand in the MIDST." And HE arose and stood.

9 Then JESUS said to them, "I ask you, if it is lawful to do good on the SABBATH, or to do evil? to save Life, or to kill?"

10 And looking round on them all, he said to him, "Stretch out thine HAND." And HE did so; and his HAND was restored.

11 And they were filled with madness, and consulted with one another, what they should do to JESUS.

12 ‡ And it came to pass in those DAYS, that he went out to the MOUNTAIN to pray; and he remained, through the night, in †the ORATORY of GOD.

13 And when it was Day he summoned his DISCIPLES; ‡ and having selected from them twelve, whom he also named Apostles;—

14 Simon, ‡ whom he also named Peter, and Andrew his BROTHER, James and John, Philip and Bartholomew,

* VATICAN MANUSCRIPT.—6. also—*omit.* 9. I ask you, if it is lawful. 10. as the other—*omit.* 15. Alpheus.

† 12. Or the place of prayer to God. Nearly all modern critics translate *proseuke* in this passage and Acts xvi. 13, in this manner. A *proseukee* was a large uncovered building, with seats, as in an amphitheatre, and used for worship where there was no synagogue.

‡ 6. Matt. xii. 9; Mark iii. 1; Luke xiii. 14; xiv. 3; John ix. 16. ‡ 12. Matt. xiv. 23 ‡ 13. Matt. x. 1 ‡ 14. John i. 42.

Βαρθολομαιον, 15 Ματθαιον και Θωμαν, Ιακωβον
Bartholomew, Matthew and Thomas, James
τον του Αλφαιου, και Σιμωνα τον καλουμενον
the of the Alpheus, and Simon the being called
ζηλωτην, 16 Ιουδαν Ιακωβου και Ιουδαν Ισκαρι-
Zelotes, Judas of James and Judas Iscar-
ωτην, ὁς *[και] εγενετο προδοτης·) 17 και
iot, who [also] became a traitor;) and
καταβας μετ' αυτων, εστη επι τοπου πεδινου,
descending with them, he stood on a place level,
και οχλος μαθητων αυτου, και πληθος πολυ
and a crowd of disciples of him, and a multitude great
του λαου απο πασης της Ιουδαιας, και Ἱερου-
of the people from all of the Judea, and Jeru-
σαλημ, και της παραλιου Τυρου και Σιδωνος,
salem, and of the sea-coast of Tyre and Sidon,
οἱ ηλθον ακουσαι αυτου, και ιαθηναι απο των
who came to hear him, and to be healed from the
νοσων αὑτων· 18 και οἱ οχλουμενοι απο πνευμα-
diseases of themselves; and those being troubled from spirits
των ακαθαρτων· και εθεραπευοντο. 19 Και πας
unclean; and they were healed. And all
ὁ οχλος εζητει ἁπτεσθαι αυτου· ὁτι δυναμις
the crowd sought to touch him; for a power
παρ' αυτου εξηρχετο, και ιατο παντας.
from him went out, and healed all.
20 Και αυτος επαρας τους οφθαλμους αὑτου
And he having lifted up the eyes of himself
εις τους μαθητας αὑτου, ελεγε· Μακαριοι οἱ
on the disciples of himself, he said; Blessed the
πτωχοι· ὁτι ὑμετερα εστιν ἡ βασιλεια του
poor: for yours is the kingdom of the
θεου. 21 Μακαριοι οἱ πεινωντες νυν· ὁτι χορτασ-
God. Blessed the hungering now: for you shall
θησεσθε. Μακαριοι οἱ κλαιοντες νυν· ὁτι
be satisfied. Blessed the weeping now; for
γελασετε.
you shall laugh.
22 Μακαριοι εστε, ὁταν μισησωσιν ὑμας οἱ
Blessed are you, when may hate you the
ανθρωποι, και ὁταν αφορισωσιν ὑμας, και
men, and when they may separate you, and
ονειδισωσι, και εκβαλωσι το ονομα ὑμων ὡς
they may revile, and may cast out the name of you as
πονηρον, ἑνεκα του υἱου του ανθρωπου. 23 Χα-
evil, on account of the son of the man. Re-
ρητε εν εκεινῃ τῃ ἡμερᾳ, και σκιρτησατε· ιδου
joice you in that the day, and leap you for joy; lo
γαρ, ὁ μισθος ὑμων πολυς εν τῳ ουρανῳ· κατα
for, the reward of you great in the heaven; according to
ταυτα γαρ εποιουν τοις προφηταις οἱ πατερες
these for did to the prophets the fathers
αυτων.
of them.
24 Πλην ουαι ὑμιν τοις πλουσιοις· ὁτι απε-
But woe to you the rich; for you have

15 Matthew and Thomas, THAT James, son of * Alpheus, and THAT Simon who was CALLED the Zealot.

16 Judas ‡ the brother of James, and Judas Iscariot, who became a Traitor;—

17 and coming down with them, he stood on a level Place, with a * Crowd of his Disciples, ‡ and a great Multitude of PEOPLE from All JUDEA and Jerusalem, and the SEA-COAST of Tyre and Sidon, who came to hear him, and to be restored from their DISEASES;

18 and THOSE who were * distressed by unclean Spirits were cured.

19 And All the CROWD sought to touch him, ‡ For a Power went out from him, and healed all.

20 And he, having lifted up his EYES on his DISCIPLES, said; ‡ "Happy, POOR ones! For yours is the KINGDOM of GOD.

21 ‡ Happy now, HUNGERING ones! Since you will be satisfied. ‡ Happy now, WEEPING ones! Because you will laugh.

22 ‡ Happy are you, when MEN may hate you, and separate you, and may revile and cast out your NAMES as evil, on account of the Son of Man.

23 ‡ Rejoice in That DAY, and leap for joy; for behold, your REWARD will be great in HEAVEN; ‡ for thus their FATHERS did to the PROPHETS.

24 ‡ But Woe to YOU, RICH ones; For you have your CONSOLATION.

* VATICAN MANUSCRIPT.—15. Alpheus. 16. also—*omit.* 17. a great Crowd. 18. distressed by unclean Spirits were cured.

‡ 16. Jude 1. ‡ 17. Matt. iv. 25; Mark iii. 7. ‡ 19. Mark v. 30; Luke viii. 46. ‡ 20. Matt. v. 3; xi. 5; James ii. 5. ‡ 21. Matt. v. 6. ‡ 21. Matt. v. 4. ‡ 22. Matt. v. 11; 1 Pet. ii. 19; iii. 14; iv. 14. ‡ 23. Matt. v. 12; Acts v. 41; Col. i. 24; James i. 2. ‡ 23. Acts vii. 51. ‡ 24. James v. 1.

χετε την παρακλησιν ὑμων. 25 Ουαι ὑμιν, οἱ
in full the comfort of you. Woe to you, those
εμπεπλησμενοι· ὁτι πεινασετε· ουαι ὑμιν, οἱ
having been filled; for you shall hunger: Woe to you, those
γελωντες νυν· ὁτι πενθησετε και κλαυσετε.
laughing now: for you shall mourn and you shall weep.
26 Ουαι, ὁταν καλως ὑμας ειπωσιν οἱ ανθρωποι·
Woe, when well you may speak the men:
κατα ταυτα γαρ εποιουν τοις ψευδοπροφηταις
according to these for did to the false-prophets
οἱ πατερες αυτων.
the fathers of them.

27 Αλλ' ὑμιν λεγω τοις ακουουσιν· Αγαπατε
But to you I say to those hearing: Love you
τους εχθρους ὑμων· καλως ποιειτε τοις μισου-
the enemies of you: good do you to those hat-
σιν ὑμας· 28 ευλογειτε τους καταρωμενους ὑμας·
ing you: bless you those cursing you:
προσευχεσθε ὑπερ των επηρεαζοντων ὑμας.
pray you for those traducing you.
29 Τῳ τυπτοντι σε επι την σιαγονα, παρεχε και
To the striking thee on the cheek, offer also
την αλλην· και απο του αιροντος σου το ἱματιον,
the other: and from the taking of thee the mantle,
και τον χιτωνα μη κωλυσῃς.
also the tunic not thou mayest hinder.

30 Παντι δε τῳ αιτουντι σε διδου· και απο του
To all and those asking thee give thou: and from the
αιροντος τα σα, μη απαιτει. 31 Και καθως
taking what is thine, not demand back. And all
θελετε, ἱνα ποιωσιν ὑμιν οἱ ανθρωποι, *[και
you wish, that may do to you the men, [also
ὑμεις] ποιειτε αυτοις ὁμοιως. 32 Και ει αγα-
you] do you to them in like manner. And if you
πατε τους αγαπωντας ὑμας, ποια ὑμιν χαρις
love those loving you, what to you thanks
εστι; και γαρ οἱ αμαρτωλοι τους αγαπωντας
is it? also for the sinners those loving
αυτους αγαπωσι. 33 Και εαν αγαθοποιητε τους
them love. And if you should do good those
αγαθοποιουντας ὑμας, ποια ὑμιν χαρις εστι;
doing good you, what to you thanks is it?
και *[γαρ] οἱ αμαρτωλοι το αυτο ποιουσι.
also [for] the sinners the same do.
34 Και εαν δανειζητε παρ' ὡν ελπιζετε απολα-
And if you should lend from whom you hope to re-
βειν, ποια ὑμιν χαρις εστι, και *[γαρ] οἱ
ceive, what to you thanks is it? also [for] the
ἁμαρτωλοι ἁμαρτωλοις δανειζουσιν, ἱνα απολα-
sinners to sinners lend, that they may
βωσι τα ισα. 35 Πλην αγαπατε τους εχθρους
receive the like things. But love you the enemies
ὑμων, και αγαθοποιειτε και δανειζετε μηδεν
of you, and do you good and lend you nothing

25 Woe to YOU who are * FULL now! Because you will hunger. * Woe to YOU who LAUGH now! For you will mourn and weep.

26 Woe, when MEN may speak well of you! for * thus their FATHERS did to the FALSE-PROPHETS.

27 ‡ But I say to YOU, who HEAR me, Love your ENEMIES; do good to THOSE who HATE you,

28 ‡ bless THOSE who CURSE you, pray for THOSE who INJURE you.

29 ‡ To HIM STRIKING thee on the CHEEK, present the OTHER also; ‡ and from HIM who TAKES AWAY thy MANTLE, withhold not even thy COAT.

30 ‡ Give to EVERY one ASKING thee; and from HIM who TAKES AWAY what is THINE, demand it not.

31 ‡ And as you would that MEN should do to you, do in like manner to them.

32 ‡ And if you love THOSE who LOVE you, What Thanks are due to you? for even SINNERS love THOSE who LOVE them.

33 * And if you do good to THOSE DOING GOOD to you, What thanks are due to you? SINNERS even do the SAME.

34 * And if you lend to those from whom you hope to receive, What Thanks are due to you? SINNERS even lend to Sinners, that they may receive an EQUIVALENT.

35 But love your ENEMIES, and do good and lend, in Nothing despair-

* VATICAN MANUSCRIPT.—25. FULL now. 25. Woe, YOU who LAUGH now. 26. the SAME did they to the FALSE-PROPHETS. 31. you also—*omit.* 33. For if also you do good. 33. for—*omit.* 34. for—*omit.*

‡ 27. Exod. xxiii. 4; Prov. xxv. 21; Matt. v. 44; Rom. xii. 20. ‡ 28. Matt. v. 44; Luke xxiii. 34; Acts vii. 60. ‡ 29. Matt. v. 39. ‡ 29. 1 Cor. vi. 7. ‡ 30. Deut. xv. 7, 8, 10; Prov. xxi. 26; Matt. v. 42. ‡ 31. Matt. vii. 12. ‡ 32. Matt. v. 46. ‡ 34. Matt. v. 42.

απελπιζοντες· και εσται ὁ μισθος ὑμων πολυς,
despairing! and shall be the reward of you great,
και εσεσθε υἱοι ὑψιστου· ὁτι αυτος χρηστος
and you shall be sons of highest; for he kind
εστιν επι τους αχαριστους και πονηρους.
is to the unthankful and evil.
36 Γινεσθε *[ουν] οικτιρμονες, καθως *[και]
Be you [therefore] compassionate, even as [also]
ὁ πατηρ ὑμων οικτιρμων εστι. 37 Και μη
the father of you compassionate is. And not
κρινετε, και ου μη κριθητε· μη καταδικαζετε,
judge you, and not not you may be judged: not condemn you,
και ου μη καταδικασθητε· απολυετε, και απο-
and not not you may be condemned; release you, and you
λυθησεσθε. 38 Διδοτε, και δοθησεται ὑμιν·
shall be released. Give you, and it shall be given to you:
μετρον καλον πεπιεσμενον *[και] σεσαλευ-
measure good having been pressed down [and] having been
μενον *[και] ὑπερεκχυνομενον δωσουσιν εις τον
shaken [and] running over shall be given into the
κολπον ὑμων· τῳ γαρ αυτῳ μετρῳ, ᾡ
bosom of you, by the for same measure, with which
μετρειτε, αντιμετρηθησεται ὑμιν. 39 Ειπε δε
you measure, it shall be measured again to you. He spoke and
παραβολην αυτοις· Μητι δυναται τυφλος τυφλον
a parable to them; Not is able a blind blind
ὁδηγειν; ουχι αμφοτεροι εις βοθυνον πεσουνται;
to lead? not both into a pit will fall?
40 Ουκ εστι μαθητης ὑπερ τον διδασκαλον
Not is a disciple over the teacher
αὑτου· κατηρτισμενος δε πας εσται ὡς ὁ
of himself; having been fully qualified but every one shall be as the
διδασκαλος αυτου. 41 Τι δε βλεπεις το καρφος
teacher of him. Why and seest thou the splinter
το εν τῳ οφθαλμῳ του αδελφου σου, την δε
that in the eye of the brother of thee, the but
δοκον την εν τῳ ιδιῳ οφθαλμῳ ου κατανοεις;
beam that in thine own eye not perceivest?
42 *[η] πως δυνασαι λεγειν τῳ αδελφῳ σου·
[or] how art thou able to say to the brother of thee:
Αδελφε, αφες, εκβαλω το καρφος το εν τῳ
O brother, allow me, I can cast out the splinter that in the
οφθαλμῳ σου· αυτος την εν τῳ οφθαλμῳ σου
eye of thee; thyself the in the eye of thee
δοκον ου βλεπων; Ὑποκριτα, εκβαλε πρωτον
beam not beholding? O hypocrite, cast out first
την δοκον εκ του οφθαλμου σου, και τοτε
the beam out of the eye of thee, and then
διαβλεψεις εκβαλειν το καρφος το εν τῳ οφθαλ-
thou wilt see clearly to cast out the splinter that in the eye
μῳ του αδελφου σου. 43 Ου γαρ εστι δενδρον
of the brother of thee. Not for is a tree
καλον, ποιουν καρπον σαπρον· ουδε δενδρον
good, bearing fruit corrupt; nor a tree

ing; and your REWARD will be great, and ‡you will be Sons of the Most High: for he is kind to the UNTHANKFUL and Evil.

36 ‡ Be you compassionate, as your FATHER is compassionate.

37 ‡ And judge not, and you will not be judged; condemn not, and you will not be condemned; forgive, and you will be forgiven;

38 ‡ give, and it will be given to you; good Measure, pressed down, shaken together, and overflowing, will be given into your LAP. For by the SAME Measure with which you measure, it will be dispensed to you again."

39 And he spoke a Parable to them; ‡"Can a Blind man lead a Blind man? Will not both fall into a Pit?

40 ‡A disciple is not above his TEACHER; but every one fully qualified will be as his TEACHER.

41 ‡But why observest thou THAT SPLINTER in †thy BROTHER'S EYE, and perceivest not THAT THORN in thine OWN Eye?

42 How wilt thou say to thy BROTHER, 'Brother, let me take out THAT SPLINTER in thine EYE;' thyself not seeing the THORN in thine OWN EYE? Hypocrite! first extract the THORN from thine own EYE, and then thou wilt see clearly to extract THAT SPLINTER in thy BROTHER'S EYE.

43 ‡For there is no good Tree which yields bad Fruit; nor *again a bad

* VATICAN MANUSCRIPT.—36. therefore—*omit.* 36. also—*omit.* 38. and—*omit.* 38. and—*omit.* 42. or—*omit.* 43. again.

† 41. In the Talmud are the following proverbs:—"They who say to others, take the small piece of wood out of thy teeth, are answered by, 'take the beam out of thine own eyes.'"—*Hammand and Lightfoot.*

‡ 35. Matt. v. 45. ‡ 36. Matt. v. 48. ‡ 37. Matt. vii. 1. ‡ 38. Prov. xix. 17. ‡ 39. Matt. xv. 14. ‡ 40. Matt. x. 24; John xiii. 16; xv. 20. ‡ 41. Matt. vii. 3. ‡ 43. Matt. vii. 16. 17.

σαπρον, ποιουν καρπον καλον. 44 Ἑκαστον γαρ
corrupt, bearing fruit good. Every for
δενδρον εκ του ιδιου καρπου γινωσκεται· ου γαρ
tree from the own fruit is known; not for
εξ ακανθων συλλεγουσι συκα, ουδε εκ βατου
from thorns do they gather figs, nor from a bramble
τρυγωσι σταφυλην. 45 Ὁ αγαθος ανθρωπος εκ
do they pick a cluster of grapes. The good man out of
του αγαθου θησαυρου της καρδιας αὑτου προ-
the good treasure of the heart of himself brings
φερει το αγαθον· και ὁ πονηρος *[ανθρωπος]
forth the good; and the evil [man]
εκ του πονηρου *[θησαυρου της καρδιας αὑτου]
out of the evil [treasure of the heart of himself]
προφερει το πονηρον· εκ γαρ του περισσευμα-
brings forth the evil; out of for the fulness
τος της καρδιας λαλει το στομα αυτου. 46 Τι
of the heart speaks the mouth of him. Why
δε με καλειτε, κυριε, κυριε· και ου ποιειτε ἁ
and me do you call, O lord, O lord; and not do what
λεγω;
I say?

47 Πας ὁ ερχομενος προς με, και ακουων μου
All the coming to me, and hearing of me
των λογων, και ποιων αυτους, ὑποδειξω ὑμιν,
the words, and doing them, I will show to you,
τινι εστιν ὁμοιος. 48 Ὁμοιος εστιν ανθρωπῳ
to whom he is like. Like he is to a man
οικοδομουντι οικιαν, ὁς εσκαψε και εβαθυνε,
building a house, who dug and went deep,
και εθηκε θεμελιον επι την πετραν· πλημμυρας
and laid a foundation on the rock; of a flood
δε γενομενης, προσερρηξεν ὁ ποταμος τῃ οικιᾳ
and having come, dashed against the stream the house
εκεινῃ, και ουκ ισχυσε σαλευσαι αυτην· τεθε-
that, and not was able to shake her: it was
μελιωτο γαρ επι την πετραν. 49 Ὁ δε ακουσας,
founded for upon the rock. He but having heard,
και μη ποιησας, ὁμοιος εστιν ανθρωπῳ οικοδο-
and not having done, like he is to a man having
μησαντι οικιαν επι την γην χωρις θεμελιου·
built a house on the earth without a foundation:
ᾗ προσερρηξεν ὁ ποταμος· και ευθεως επεσε,
to which dashed against the stream: and immediately it fell,
και εγενετο το ῥηγμα της οικιας εκεινης μεγα.
and became the ruin of the house that great.

ΚΕΦ. ς'. 7.

1 Επει δε επληρωσε παντα τα ῥηματα αυτου
When and he had ended all the words of him
εις τας ακοας του λαου, εισηλθεν εις Καπερ-
in the ears of the people, he entered into Caper-
ναουμ. 2 Ἑκατονταρχου δε τινι δουλος κακως
naum. Of a centurion and certain slave sick
εχων, ημελλε τελευταν, ὁς ην αυτῳ εντιμος.
being, was about to die, who was to him valuable.

Tree which yields good Fruit.

44 For ‡ Every Tree is known by its OWN Fruit. For they do not gather Figs from Thorns, nor do they pick Grapes from Brambles.

45 The GOOD Man out of the GOOD Treasure of of * the HEART produces GOOD; and the BAD Man out of the EVIL produces EVIL; for out of * an Overflowing Heart his MOUTH speaks.

46 ‡ And why do you call Me, 'Master, Master,' and obey not my commands?

47 ‡ EVERY ONE COMING to me, and hearing My WORDS, and obeying them, I will show you whom he is like;

48 he resembles a Man building a House, who dug deep, and laid a foundation on the ROCK; and a Flood having come, the STREAM dashed against that HOUSE, but could not shake it; * because it was WELL-BUILT on the ROCK.

49 But HE who HEARS and obeys not, resembles a Man building a House on the EARTH, without a Foundation; against which the STREAM dashed, and it fell immediately, and great was the RUIN of that HOUSE.'

CHAPTER VII.

1 Now when he had finished All his SAYINGS in the HEARING of the PEOPLE, ‡ he entered Capernaum.

2 And a Centurion's Servant, who was valuable to him, being sick, was about to die.

* VATICAN MANUSCRIPT.—44. the HEART. 45. Man—*omit.* 45. Treasure of his HEART—*omit.* 45. an Overflowing Heart 48. because it was WELL-BUILT on

‡ 44. Matt. xii. 33. ‡ 46. Matt. vii. 21, 25; Luke xiii. 25. ‡ 47. Matt. vii. 24
‡ 1. Matt. viii. 5.

3 Ακουσας δε περι του Ιησου, απεστειλε προς
Having heard and about the Jesus, he sent to
αυτον πρεσβυτερους των Ιουδαιων, ερωτων
him elders of the Jews, asking
αυτον, ὁπως ελθων διασωσῃ τον δουλον αὐτου.
him, that coming he would save the slave of himself.
4 Οἱ δε παραγενομενοι προς τον Ιησουν, παρεκα-
They and having come to the Jesus, they be-
λουν αυτον σπουδαιως, λεγοντες· Ὁτι αξιος
sought him earnestly, saying; That worthy
εστιν, ᾧ παρεξει τουτο· 5 αγαπᾳ γαρ το
he is, for whom thou wilt confer this; he loves for the
εθνος ἡμων, και την συναγωγην αυτος ᾠκοδο-
nation of us, and the synagogue he built
μησεν ἡμιν. 6 Ὁ δε Ιησους επορευετο συν
for us. The and Jesus went with
αυτοις. Ηδη δε αυτου ου μακραν απεχοντος
them. Already and of him not far being distant
απο της οικιας, επεμψε *[προς αυτον] ὁ ἑκα-
from the house, sent [to him] the cen-
τονταρχος φιλους, λεγων αυτῳ· Κυριε, μη
turion friends, saying to him; O sir, not
σκυλλου· ου γαρ ειμι ἱκανος, ἱνα ὑπο την
be thou troubled: not for I am worthy, that under the
στεγην μου εισελθῃς· 7 διο ουδε εμαυτον
roof of me thou shouldst enter: therefore not even myself
ηξιωσα προς σε ελθειν· αλλα ειπε λογῳ, και
I deemed fit to thee to come; but speak a word, and
ιαθησεται ὁ παις μου. 8 Και γαρ εγω ανθρωπος
will be healed the boy of me. Even for I a man
ειμι ὑπο εξουσιαν τασσομενος, εχων ὑπ' εμαυ-
am under authority being set, having under my-
τον στρατιωτας· και λεγω τουτῳ· Πορευθητι,
self soldiers; and I say to this; Go.
και πορευεται· και αλλῳ· Ερχου, και ερχεται·
and he goes and to another; Come, and he comes:
και τῳ δουλῳ μου· Ποιησον τουτο, και ποιει.
and to the slave of me: Do this, and he does.
9 Ακουσας δε ταυτα ὁ Ιησους, εθαυμασεν αυτον·
Hearing and these the Jesus, admired him:
και στραφεις, τῳ ακολουθουντι αυτῳ οχλῳ ειπε·
and turning, to the following him crowd he said:
Λεγω ὑμιν, ουδε εν τῳ Ισραηλ τοσαυτην πιστιν
I say to you, not even in the Israel so great faith
εὑρον. 10 Και ὑποστρεψαντες οἱ πεμφθεντες
I have found. And having returned those having been sent
εις τον οικον, εὑρον τον *[ασθενουντα] δουλον
into the house, they found the [being sick] slave
ὑγιαινοντα.
being well.

11 Και εγενετο εν τῃ ἑξης, επορευετο εις
And it happened in the next, he was going to
πολιν καλουμενην Ναιν· και συνεπορευοντο
a city being called Nain: and were going

3 And having heard concerning JESUS, †he sent Elders of the JEWS to him, soliciting him, that he would come and save his SERVANT.

4 And having come to JESUS, THEY earnestly besought him, saying, "He is worthy for whom thou shouldst do this;

5 for he loves our NATION, and he built our SYNAGOGUE."

6 Then JESUS went with them; and being not far from the HOUSE, the CENTURION sent Friends, saying to him, "Sir, trouble not thyself; for I am not worthy that thou shouldst come under my ROOF;

7 therefore, I did not think myself even worthy to come to thee; but command by Word, and *my SERVANT will be cured.

8 For even I am a Man appointed under Authority, having Soldiers under me, even I say to this one, 'Go,' and he goes; and to another, 'Come,' and he comes; and to my SERVANT, 'Do this,' and he does it."

9 And JESUS hearing these things, admired him, and turning, said to the CROWD following him, "I tell you, I have not found, even in ISRAEL, such great Faith."

10 And THOSE who had been SENT, having returned to the HOUSE, found the SERVANT restored to health.

11 And it occurred on the NEXT day, that he was going to a City called †Nain; and his DISCIPLES

* VATICAN MANUSCRIPT.—6. to him—*omit.* 7. let my SERVANT be healed. 10. being sick—*omit.*

† 3. Either *magistrates* of the place, or *elders* of the synagogue which the centurion had built. In the parallel place in Matthew, he is represented as coming to Jesus himself; but it is a usual form of speech in all nations, to attribute the act to a person, which is done, not by himself, but by his *authority.—Clarke.* † 11. Nain, was a small city of Galilee, in the tribe of Issachar. According to Eusebius, it was two miles from Mount Tabor, southward, and near to Endor.

αυτῳ οἱ μαθηται αυτου *[ἱκανοι,] και οχλος
with him the disciples of him many,] and a crowd
πολυς. 12 Ὡς δε ηγγισε τῃ πυλῃ της πολεως,
great. As and he drew near to the gate of the city,
και ιδου, εξεκομιζετο τεθνηκως, υἱος μονογενης
and lo, was being carried out a dead man, a son only-born
τῃ μητρι αὑτου, και αὑτη χηρα· και οχλος
to the mother of himself, and she a widow; and a crowd
της πολεως ἱκανος ην συν αυτῃ. 13 Και ιδων
of the city great was with her. And seeing
αυτην ὁ κυριος, εσπλαγχνισθη επ' αυτῃ, και
her the lord, he had compassion on her, and
ειπεν αυτῃ· Μη κλαιε. 14 Και προσελθων
said to her; Not weep. And coming up
ἡψατο της σορου· οἱ δε βασταζοντες εστησαν.
he touched the bier; those and bearing stood still.
Και ειπε· Νεανισκε, σοι λεγω, εγερθητι.
And he said; O young man, to thee I say, rise.
15 Και ανεκαθισεν ὁ νεκρος, και ηρξατο λαλειν·
And sat up the dead, and began to speak
και εδωκεν αυτον τῃ μητρι αυτου. 16 Ελαβε δε
and he gave him to the mother of him. Seized and
φοβος παντας, και εδοξαζον τον θεον, λεγοντες·
a fear all, and they glorified the God, saying:
Ὁτι προφητης μεγας εγηγερται εν ἡμιν, και
That a prophet great has risen among us, and
ὁτι επεσκεψατο ὁ θεος τον λαον αὑτου. 17 Και
that has visited the God the people of himself. And
εξηλθεν ὁ λογος οὑτος εν ὁλῃ τῃ Ιουδαιᾳ περι
went out the word this in whole the Judea concerning
αυτου, και *[εν] πασῃ τῃ περιχωρῳ.
him, and [in] all the surrounding country.
18 Και απηγγειλαν Ιωαννῃ οἱ μαθηται αυτου
And told John the disciples of him
περι παντων τουτων. 19 Και προσκαλεσαμε-
about all these. And having called
νος δυο τινας των μαθητων αὑτου ὁ Ιωαννης,
to two certain of the disciples of himself the John,
επεμψε προς τον Ιησουν, λεγων· Συ ει ὁ ερχο-
sent to the Jesus, saying: Thou art the coming
μενος, η αλλον προσδοκωμεν; 20 Παραγενομενοι
one, or another are we to look for? Having come
δε προς αυτον οἱ ανδρες ειπον· Ιωαννης ὁ βαπ-
and to him the men they said: John the dip-
τιστης απεσταλκεν ἡμας προς σε, λεγων· Συ
per has sent us to thee, saying: Thou
ει ὁ ερχομενος, η αλλον προσδοκωμεν; 21 Εν
art the coming one, or another are we to look for? In
αυτῃ δε τῃ ὡρᾳ εθεραπευσε πολλους απο νοσων
this and the hour he delivered many from diseases
και μαστιγων και πνευματων πονηρων, και
and plagues and spirits evil, and

were going with him, and a great Crowd.

12 And as he approached the GATE of the CITY, behold, a dead man was being carried out, an Only Son of his MOTHER, and she was a Widow; and a great Crowd from the CITY was with her.

13 And seeing her, the LORD had pity on her, and said to her, "Weep not."

14 And approaching, he touched the †BIER, and the BEARERS stood still. And he said, "Young man, I say to thee, Arise."

15 Then HE who had been DEAD sat up, and began to speak; and he gave him to his MOTHER.

16 And fear seized all; and they praised GOD, saying, ‡"A great Prophet has risen among us:" and, ‡"GOD has visited his PEOPLE."

17 And this REPORT concerning him pervaded All JUDEA, and All the SURROUNDING COUNTRY.

18 ‡And John's DISCIPLES told him of all these things.

19 And summoning two of his DISCIPLES, JOHN sent to * the LORD, saying, "Art thou the COMING ONE? or are we to expect Another?"

20 And having come to him, the MEN said, "John, the IMMERSER, *sent us to thee, saying, 'Art thou the COMING ONE? or are we to expect Another?'"

21 And in That HOUR he delivered many from Diseases, and Plagues, and evil Spirits; and he gave

* VATICAN MANUSCRIPT.—11. many—*omit*. 17. in—*omit*. 19. the LORD. saying. 20. sent.

† 14. The people of the East bury the dead without coffins; but they carry them to the grave on a bier which is shaped like one.—*Harmer*. "Presently a funeral procession, consisting of men and women, came rapidly from the city, (the cemetery is outside of the present Jerusalem,) and halted at a newly-made grave sunk three or four feet only below the ground. The body was not enclosed in a coffin, but wrapped in a loose garment and laid on a bier carried by hand. My impression is that even the face was partially exposed to view. It was under similar circumstances that the son of the widow at Nain was borne to the grave."—*Hackett*.

‡ 16. Luke xxiv. 19; John iv. 19; vi. 14; ix. 17. ‡ 16. Luke i. 68. ‡ 18. Matt. xi. 2.

τυφλοις πολλοις εχαρισατο το βλεπειν. 22 Και
to blind ones many he gave the to see. And
αποκριθεις ὁ Ιησους ειπεν αυτοις· Πορευθεντες
answering the Jesus said to them; Going away
απαγγειλατε Ιωαννῃ ἁ ειδετε και ηκουσατε·
relate to John what you have seen and heard;
*[ὁτι] τυφλοι αναβλεπουσι, χωλοι περιπατ-
[that] blind ones see again, lame ones are walking
ουσι, λεπροι καθαριζονται, κωφοι ακουουσι,
about, lepers are cleansed, deaf ones are hearing,
νεκροι εγειρονται, πτωχοι ευαγγελιζονται·
dead ones are raised up, poor ones are addressed with glad tidings
23 και μακαριος εστιν, ὁς εαν μη σκανδαλισθῃ
and blessed is, whoever not may be stumbled
εν εμοι.
in me.
24 Απελθοντων δε των αγγελων Ιωαννου,
Having departed and the messengers of John,
ηρξατο λεγειν προς τους οχλους περι Ιωαννου·
he began to say to the crowds concerning John;
Τι εξεληλυθατε εις την ερημον θεασασθαι;
What have you come out into the desert to see?
καλαμον ὑπο ανεμου σαλευομενον; 25 Αλλα τι
a reed by wind being shaken? But what
εξεληλυθατε ιδειν; ανθρωπον εν μαλακοις ἱμα-
have you come out to see? a man in soft gar-
τιοις ημφιεσμενον; Ιδου, οἱ εν ἱματισμῳ
ments having been clothed? Lo, those in clothing
ενδοξῳ και τρυφῃ ὑπαρχοντες, εν τοις βασι-
showy and in luxury living, in the royal
λειοις εισιν. 26 Αλλα τι εξεληλυθατε ιδειν;
palaces are. But what have you come out to see?
προφητην; Ναι λεγω ὑμιν, και περισσοτερον
a prophet? Yes I say to you, and much more
προφητου. 27 Οὑτος εστι, περι οὑ γεγραπ-
of a prophet. This is, concerning whom it is writ-
ται· "Ιδου, εγω αποστελλω τον αγγελον μου
ten; "Lo, I send the messenger of me
προ προσωπου σου, ὁς κατασκευασει την ὁδον
before face of thee, who shall prepare the way
σου εμπροσθεν σου." 28 Λεγω [γαρ] ὑμιν.
of thee in presence of thee." I say [for] to you,
μειζων εν γεννητοις γυναικων *[προφητης]
a greater among offspring of women [prophet]
Ιωαννου *[του βαπτιστου] ουδεις εστιν· ὁ δε
of John [the dipper] not is; the but
μικροτερος εν τῃ βασιλειᾳ του θεου, μειζων
less in the kingdom of the God, greater
αυτου εστι. 29 Και πας ὁ λαος ακουσας, και
of him is. And all the people having heard, and
οἱ τελωναι, εδικαιωσαν τον θεον, βαπτισθεντες
the tax-gatherers, justified the God, having been dipped
το βαπτισμα Ιωαννου. 30 Οἱ δε Φαρισαιοι και
the dipping of John. The but Pharisees and
οἱ νομικοι την βουλην του θεου ηθετησαν εις
the lawyers the purpose of the God set aside for
ἑαυτους, μη βαπτισθεντες ὑπ' αυτου.
themselves, not having been dipped by him.

* sight to many Blind persons.

22 And *Jesus answering, said to them, ‡"Go, tell John what you have seen and heard; the Blind are made to see, the Lame to walk, the Lepers are cleansed, the Deaf hear, the Dead are raised, ‡glad tidings are announced to the Poor;

23 and happy is he who shall not stumble at me."

24 ‡And John's MESSENGERS having departed, he began to say to the CROWDS concerning John, "Why went you out into the DESERT? To see a Reed shaken by the Wind?

25 But why went you out? To see a Man clothed in soft garments? Behold, THOSE robed in SPLENDID APPAREL, and living in luxury, are in ROYAL PALACES.

26 But why went you out? To see a Prophet? Yes, I tell you, and one more excellent than a Prophet.

27 This is he concerning whom it is written, ‡'Behold! *I send my MESSENGER before thy Face, who will prepare thy WAY before thee.'

28 I say to you, Among those born of Women, there is not a greater than John; yet the LEAST in the KINGDOM of GOD is superior to him.

29 And All the PEOPLE having heard, and the TRIBUTE-TAKERS, justified GOD, ‡having been immersed with the IMMERSION of John.

30 But the PHARISEES and LAWYERS set aside the ‡PURPOSE of GOD towards themselves, not having been immersed by him.

* VATICAN MANUSCRIPT.—21. sight. 22. he answering. 22. That—omit. 27. I send. 28. For—omit. 28. prophet—omit. 28. the dipper—omit.

‡ 22. Matt. xi. 5. ‡ 22. Luke iv 18. ‡ 24. Matt. xi. 7. ‡ 27. Mal. iii. 1. ‡ 29. Matt. iii. 5; Luke iii. 12. ‡ 30. Acts xx. 27.

31 Τινι ουν ὁμοιωσω τους ανθρωπους της
To what then shall I compare the men of the
γενεας ταυτης και τινι εισιν ὁμοιοι; 32 Ὁμοι-
generation this? and to what are they like? Like
οι εισι παιδιοις τοις εν αγορᾳ καθημενοις, και
they are boys those in a market sitting, and
προσφωνουσιν αλληλοις, και λεγουσιν· Ηυλη-
calling to one another, and saying; We have played
σαμεν ὑμιν, και ουκ ωρχησασθε· εθρηνησαμεν
the flute for you, and not you have danced; we have mourned
ὑμιν, και ουκ εκλαυσατε. 33 Εληλυθε γαρ
for you, and not you have wept. Has come for
Ιωαννης ὁ βαπτιστης, μητε αρτον εσθιων,
John the dipper, neither bread eating,
μητε οινον πινων· και λεγετε· Δαιμονιον εχει.
nor wine drinking; and you say; A demon he has.
34 Εληλυθεν ὁ υἱος του ανθρωπου, εσθιων και
Has come the son of the man, eating and
πινων· και λεγετε· Ιδου, ανθρωπος φαγος και
drinking; and you say; Lo, a man glutton and
οινοποτης, φιλος τελωνων και ἁμαρτωλων.
a wine-drinker, a friend of tax-gatherers and sinners.
35 Και εδικαιωθη ἡ σοφια απο των τεκνων αὑτης
And is justified the wisdom by the children of herself
παντων.
all.
36 Ηρωτα δε τις αυτον των Φαρισαιων, ἱνα
Asked and one him of the Pharisees, that
φαγῃ μετ' αυτου· και εισηλθων εις την οικιαν
he might eat with him; and entering into the house
του Φαρισαιου, ανεκλιθη. 37 Και ιδου, γυνη
of the Pharisee, he reclined. And lo, a woman
εν τῃ πολει, ἡτις ην ἁμαρτωλος, επιγνουσα ὁτι
in the city, who was a sinner, knowing that
ανακειται εν τῃ οικιᾳ του Φαρισαιου, κομισασα
he reclines in the house of the Pharisee, having brought
αλαβαστρον μυρου, 38 και στασα οπισω παρα
an alabaster-box of balsam, and standing behind at
τους ποδας αυτου, κλαιουσα, ηρξατο βρεχειν
the feet of him, weeping, she began to wet
τους ποδας αυτου τοις δακρυσι· και ταις θριξι
the feet of him with the tears; and with the hairs
της κεφαλης αὑτης εξεμασσε, και κατεφιλει
of the head of herself wiped, and kissed
τους ποδας αυτου, και ηλειφε τῳ μυρῳ. 39 Ιδων
the feet of him, and anointed with the balsam. Seeing
δε ὁ Φαρισαιος ὁ καλεσας αυτον, ειπεν εν ἑαυτῳ,
but the Pharisee that having called him, spoke in himself,
λεγων· Οὑτος ει ην προφητης, εγινωσκεν αν,
saying; This if he was a prophet, would know,

31 ‡ To what then shall I compare the MEN of this GENERATION? and what are they like?

32 They are like THOSE Boys SITTING in a Public place, and calling to one another, and saying, 'We have played for you on the flute, but you have not danced; we have sung mournful songs for you, but you have not lamented.'

33 ‡ For John the IMMERSER has come neither eating Bread nor drinking Wine, and you say, 'He has a Demon.'

34 The SON of MAN has come eating and drinking, and you say, 'Behold a Glutton and a Wine-drinker! an Associate of Tribute-takers and Sinners!'

35 ‡ But WISDOM is vindicated by All her CHILDREN."

36 ‡ And one of the PHARISEES invited him to eat with him. And entering the HOUSE of the PHARISEE, he reclined.

37 And, behold, a † Woman * who was of the CITY, a Sinner, knowing that he reclined in the PHARISEE'S HOUSE, brought an Alabaster box of Balsam,

38 and standing † behind, at his FEET, weeping, she began to wet his FEET with TEARS, and wiped them with the HAIR of her HEAD, and repeatedly kissed his FEET, and anointed them with the BALSAM.

39 But THAT PHARISEE who had INVITED him observing this, spoke within himself, saying, ‡ "This man, if he were a Prophet,

---

* VATICAN MANUSCRIPT.—37. who was in the CITY, a Sinner.

† 37. There is no good reason for concluding that this woman was a *public prostitute*, as many suppose. She was probably only a *Gentile*, and therefore in the estimation of the Pharisee a *sinner*. *Hamartolos*, is often used in the New Testament in this sense. † 38. This is not intelligible, without adverting to the posture in which the ancients took their meals. They placed themselves along the couch on their sides, supported their heads with one arm, bent at the elbow, and resting on the couch; and with the other they took their food, and were supported at the back by cushions. Their feet of course were accessible to one who came *behind* the couch.—*Wakefield.*

‡ 31. Matt. xi. 16. ‡ 33. Matt. iii. 4; Mark i. 6; Luke i. 15. ‡ 35. Matt. xi 19. ‡ 36. Matt. xxvi. 6; Mark xiv. 3; John xi. 2. ‡ 39. Luke xv. 2.

τις και ποταπη ἡ γυνη, ἡτις ἁπτεται αυτου·
who and what the woman, who touches him;

ὁτι ἁμαρτωλος εστι. 40 Και αποκριθεις ὁ Ιησους
that a sinner she is. And answering the Jesus

ειπε προς αυτον· Σιμων, εχω σοι τι ειπειν.
said to him; Simon, I have to thee something to say.

Ὁ δε φησι· Διδασκαλε, ειπε. 41 Δυο χρεωφει-
He and says: O teacher, say. Two debt-

λεται ησαν δανειστῃ τινι· ὁ εἱς ωφειλε δηναρια
ors were to a creditor certain: the one owed denarii

πεντακοσια, ὁ δε ἑτερος πεντηκοντα. 42 Μη
five hundred, the and other fifty. Not

εχοντων *[δε] αυτων αποδουναι, αμφοτεροις
having [and] of them to pay, both

εχαρισατο. Τις ουν αυτων, *[ειπε] πλειον
he forgave. Which then of them, [say] more

αυτον αγαπησει; 43 Αποκριθεις δε ὁ Σιμων ειπεν·
him will love? Answering and the Simon said:

Ὑπολαμβανω, ὁτι ᾡ το πλειον εχαρισατο.
I suppose, that to whom the more he forgave.

Ὁ δε ειπεν αυτῳ· Ορθως εκρινας. 44 Και στρα-
He and said to him: Rightly thou hast judged. And turn-

φεις προς την γυναικα, τῳ Σιμωνι εφη· Βλεπ-
ing to the woman, to the Simon he said: Seest

εις ταυτην την γυναικα; εισηλθον σου εις την
thou this the woman? I came of thee into the

οικιαν· ὑδωρ επι τους ποδας μου ουκ ἐδωκας·
house: water for the feet of me not thou gavest:

αὑτη δε τοις δακρυσιν εβρεξε μου τους ποδας,
she but with the tears she wet of me the feet,

και ταις θριξι αὑτης εξεμαξε. 45 Φιλημα μοι
and with the hairs of herself has wiped. A kiss to me

ουκ εδωκας· αὑτη δε αφ' ἡς εισηλθον, ου δει-
not thou gavest: she but from of her came in, not has

λιπε καταφιλουσα μου τυυς ποδας. 46 Ελαιῳ
ceased kissing of me the feet. With oil

την κεφαλην μου ουκ ηλειψας· αὑτη δε μυρῳ
the head of me not thou didst anoint: she but with balsam

ηλειψε τους ποδας μου. 47 Οὗ χαριν, λεγω
anointed the feet of me. Therefore, I say

σοι, αφεωνται αἱ ἁμαρτιαι αυτης αἱ πολλαι,
to thee, have been forgiven the sins of her the many,

ὁτι ηγαπησε πολυ· ᾡ δε ολιγον αφιεται,
for that she loved much; to whom but little is forgiven,

ολιγον αγαπᾳ. 48 Ειπε δε αυτῃ· Αφεωνται
little he loves. He said and to her; Have been forgiven

σου αἱ ἁμαρτιαι. 49 Και ηρξαντο οἱ συνανακει-
of thee the sins. And began those reclining

μενοι λεγειν εν ἑαυτοις· Τις οὑτος εστιν, ὁς
with to say in themselves; Who this is, who

και ἁμαρτιας αφιησιν; 50 Ειπε δε προς την
even sins forgives? He said and to the

γυναικα· Ἡ πιστις σου σεσωκε σε· πορευου εις
woman; The faith of thee has saved thee; go in

ειρηνην.
peace.

would know who and what the WOMAN is, that touches him; For she is a Sinner."

40 And JESUS answering, said to him, "Simon, I have something to say to thee." And HE said, "Teacher, say it."

41 "A certain Creditor had Two Debtors; ONE owed five hundred † Denarii, and the OTHER fifty.

42 But not having [the means] to pay, he forgave both. Which of them, therefore, will love him most?"

43 And SIMON answering, said, "He, I suppose, to whom he forgave MOST." And HE said to him, "Thou hast judged correctly."

44 And turning to the WOMAN, he said to SIMON, "Thou seest This WOMAN: I came into Thy HOUSE, thou gavest me no Water for my FEET; but she wet My FEET with TEARS, and wiped them with her HAIR.

45 Thou gavest Me no Kiss; but she, since she came in, has not ceased kissing My FEET.

46 Thou didst not ‡ anoint My HEAD with Oil; but she anointed my FEET with Balsam.

47 ‡ Therefore, I say to thee, Her MANY SINS have been forgiven; on this account she loved much; but he to whom little is forgiven, * also loves little."

48 And he said to her, ‡ "Thy SINS have been forgiven."

49 And the GUESTS began to say among themselves; ‡ "Who is this that even forgives Sins?"

50 And he said to the WOMAN, ‡ "Thy FAITH has saved thee; go in Peace."

* VATICAN MANUSCRIPT.—42. and—*omit.* 42. say—*omit.* 47. also loves.

† 41. A Roman coin worth about 14 cents, or 7d.

‡ 46. Psa. xxiii. 5. ‡ 47. 1 Tim. i. 14. ‡ 48. Matt. ix. 2; Mark ii. 5. ‡ 49. Matt. ix. 3; Mark ii. 7. ‡ 50. Matt. ix. 22; Mark v. 34; x. 52; Luke viii. 48; xviii. 42.

ΚΕΦ. η'. 8.

[1] Και εγενετο εν τῳ καθεξης, και αυτος
And it happened in the afterwards, also he
διωδευε κατα πολιν και κωμην, κηρυσσων
traveled through every city and village, publishing
και ευαγγελιζομενος την βασιλειαν του θεου·
and proclaiming the glad tidings the kingdom of the God;
και οἱ δωδεκα συν αυτῳ, [2] και γυναικες τινες,
and the twelve with him, and women certain,
αἱ ησαν τεθεραπευμεναι απο πνευματων πονη-
who were having been healed from spirits evil
ρων και ασθενειων· Μαρια ἡ καλουμενη Μαγδα-
and infirmities; Mary that being called Magda-
ληνη, αφ' ἡς διαμονια ἑπτα εξεληλυθει, [3] και
lene, from whom demons seven had gone out, and
Ιωαννα, γυνη Χουζα επιτροπου Ἡρωδου, και
Joanna, a wife of Chuza a steward of Herod, and
Σουσαννα, και ἑτεραι πολλαι, αἱτινες διηκονουν
Susanna, and others many, who ministered
αυτῳ απο των ὑπαρχοντων αυταις.
to him from the possessions of them.

[4] Συνιοντος δε οχλου πολλου, και των κατα
Was assemblin and a crowd great, and of the every
πολιν επιπορευομενων προς αυτον, ειπε δια
city were coming to him, he said by
παραβολης· [5] Εξηλθεν ὁ σπειρων του σπειραι
a parable; Went out the sower of the to sow
τον σπορον αὑτου· και εν τῳ σπειρειν αυτον, ὁ
the seed of himself; and in the sowing it, this
μεν επεσε παρα την ὁδον· και κατεπατηθη, και
indeed fell by the path: and it was trodden down, and
τα πετεινα του ουρανου κατεφαγεν αυτο. [6] Και
the birds of the heaven ate it. And
ἑτερον επεσεν επι την πετραν· και φυεν
another fell on the rock; and having sprung up
εξηρανθη, δια το μη εχειν ικμαδα. [7] Και
it dried up, through the not to have moisture. And
ἑτερον επεσεν εν μεσῳ των ακανθων· και συμ-
another fell in midst of the thorns; and having
φυεισαι αἱ ακανθαι απεπνιξαν αυτο. [8] Και
sprung up with the thorns they choked it. And
ἑτερον επεσεν εις την γην την αγαθην· και
another fell in the ground the good: and
φυεν εποιησε καρπον ἑκατονταπλασιονα.
having sprung up bore fruit a hundredfold.
Ταυτα λεγων, εφωνει· Ὁ εχων ωτα ακουειν,
These things having said, he cried: He having ears to hear,
ακουετω. [9] Επηρωτων δε αυτον οἱ μαθηται
let him hear. Asked and him the disciples
αυτου, *[λεγοντες,] τις ειη ἡ παραβολη
of him, [saying,] what may be the parable
αὑτη. [10] Ὁ δε ειπεν· Ὑμιν δεδοται γνωναι τα
this. He and said; To you it is given to know the
μυστηρια της βασιλειας του θεου· τοις δε λοι-
secrets of the kingdom of the God; to the but others
ποις εν παραβολαις· ἱνα βλεποντες μη βλεπωσι,
in parables; that seeing not they may see,

CHAPTER VIII.

1 And it occurred AFTERWARDS that he traveled through every City and Village, publishing and proclaiming the glad tidings of the KINGDOM of GOD; and the TWELVE were with him,

2 and ‡ certain Women, who had been delivered from evil Spirits and Infirmities, THAT Mary who was CALLED of MAGDALA, ‡ from whom seven Demons had been expelled,

3 and Joanna, the Wife of Chuza, Herod's Steward, and Susanna, and many others, who assisted him from their POSSESSIONS.

4 ‡ Now when a great Crowd was assembling, and THEY were COMING to him from every City, he spoke by a Parable:

5 "The SOWER went forth to sow his SEED; and in SOWING, part fell by the ROAD; and it was trodden down, or the BIRDS of HEAVEN picked it up.

6 And another part fell on the ROCK; and having sprung up, it withered away, because it HAD NO Moisture.

7 And another part fell in the Midst of the THORNS; and the THORNS springing up with it, choked it.

8 And another part fell into the GOOD GROUND, and having sprung up, yielded Increase, a hundredfold." And having said this, he cried, "HE having Ears to hear, let him hear."

9 ‡ And his DISCIPLES asked him, "What may *This PARABLE mean?"

10 And HE said, "To you it is given to know the SECRETS of the KINGDOM of GOD; but to the OTHERS in Parables; ‡ that seeing they may not see, and hear-

* VATICAN MANUSCRIPT.—9. This PARABLE. 10. saying.—*omit.*

‡ 2. Matt. xxvii. 55, 56. ‡ 2. Mark xvi. 9. ‡ 4. Matt. xiii. 2; Mark iv. 1.
‡ 9. Matt. xiii. 10; Mark iv. 10. ‡ 10. Isa. vi. 9; Mark iv. 12.

και ακουοντες μη συνιωσιν. 11 Εστι δε αὑτη ἡ
and hearing not they may understand. Is now this the
παραβολη· Ὁ σπορος, εστιν ὁ λογος του θεου.
parable; The seed, is the word of the God.
12 Οἱ δε παρα την ὁδον, εισιν οἱ ακουοντες·
Those and by the path, are those hearing:
ειτα ερχεται ὁ διαβολος, και αιρει τον λογον
then comes the accuser, and takes away the word
απο της καρδιας αυτων, ἱνα μη πιστευσαντες
from the heart of them, so that not having believed
σωθωσιν. 13 Οἱ δε επι της πετρας, οἱ, ὁταν
they may be saved. They and on the rock, who, when
ακουσωσι, μετα χαρας δεχονται τον λογον·
they may hear, with joy receives the word;
και οὑτοι ῥιζαν ουκ εχουσιν, οἱ προς καιρον
and these a root not they have, who for a season
πιστευουσι, και εν καιρῳ πειρασμου αφισταν-
will believe, and in a season of temptation fall away.
ται. 14 Το δε εις τας ακανθας πεσον, οὑτοι
That and into the thorns having fallen, these
εισιν οἱ ακουσαντες, και ὑπο μεριμνων και
are they having heard, and by anxious cares and
πλουτου και ἡδονων του βιου πορευομενοι συμ-
riches and pleasures of the life going forth are
πνιγονται, και ου τελεσφορουσι. 15 Το δε εν
choked, and not bear fruit to perfection. That and in
τῃ καλῃ γῃ, οὑτοι εισιν, οἱτινες εν καρδιᾳ
the good ground, these are, who in heart
καλῃ και αγαθῃ ακουσαντες τον λογον, κατε-
good and upright having heard the word, re-
χουσι, και καρποφορουσιν εν ὑπομονῃ. 16 Ου-
tain, and bear fruit with perseverance. No
δεις δε λυχνον ἁψας, καλυπτει αυτον σκευει, η
one and a lamp having lighted, covers him with a vessel, or
ὑποκατω κλινης τιθησιν· αλλ' επι λυχνιας επι-
under a couch places: but upon a lamp-stand pla-
τιθησιν, *[ἱνα οἱ εισπορευομενοι βλεπωσι το
ces, [that those entering may see the
φως.] 17 Ου γαρ εστι κρυπτον, ὁ ου φανερον
light.] Not for is hidden, which not manifest
γενησεται· ουδε αποκρυφον, ὁ ου γνωσθησεται
will become; nor stored away, which not will be known
και εις φανερον ελθῃ. 18 Βλεπετε ουν, πως
and into light may come. Take heed then, how
ακουετε· ὁς γαρ αν εχῃ, δοθησεται αυτῳ· και
you hear; who for ever may have, it will be given to him: and
ὁς αν μη εχῃ, και ὁ δοκει εχειν, αρθησεται
whoever not may have, even what he seems to have, will be taken
απ' αυτου.
from him.
19 Παρεγενοντο δε προς αυτον ἡ μητηρ και
Came and to him the mother and
οἱ αδελφοι αυτου, και ουκ ηδυναντο συντυχειν
and brothers of him, and not was able to get near
αυτῳ δια τον οχλον. 20 Και απηγγελη
to him on account of the crowd. And it was told
αυτῳ, *[λεγοντων·] Ἡ μητηρ σου και οἱ
to him, [saying;] The mother of thee and the

ing they may not understand.

11 ‡Now the PARABLE is this: The SEED is the WORD of GOD.

12 THOSE by the ROAD are THEY who HEAR; then the ENEMY comes, and takes away the WORD from their HEARTS, that they may not believe and be saved.

13 THOSE on the ROCK are they, who, when they hear, receive the WORD with Joy; and yet these have no Root; they believe for a Time, and in a Time of Trial fall away.

14 And THAT having fallen among the THORNS are THEY, who, HAVING HEARD, and going forth are choked by the Anxieties, and Riches, and Pleasures of LIFE, and bring no fruit to maturity,

15 But THAT in the GOOD Ground are those, who, having heard the WORD, retain it in a good and honest Heart, and bear fruit with Perseverance.

16 ‡Now no one having lighted a Lamp, covers it with a Vessel, or puts it under a Couch, but places it on a Lamp-stand, * that THOSE COMING IN may see the LIGHT.

17 ‡For there is nothing hidden, which will not be disclosed, nor concealed, which will not be known, and come to light.

18 Take heed, therefore, how you hear; ‡ for to him who has, more will be given; but from him who has not, will be taken away even that which he has."

19 ‡Now his MOTHER and BROTHERS came towards him, but could not get near him, on account of the CROWD.

20 And it was told him, "Thy MOTHER and thy

* VATICAN MSS.—16. THOSE COMING IN may see the LIGHT—*omit.* 20. saying—*omit.*

‡ 11. Matt. xiii. 18; Mark iv. 14. ‡ 16. Matt. v. 15; Mark iv. 21; Luke xi. 33. ‡ 17. Matt. x. 26; Luke xii. 2. ‡ 18. Matt. xiii. 12; xxv. 29; Luke xix. 26. ‡ 19. Matt xii. 46; Mark iii. 31.

αδελφοι σου εστηκασιν εξω, ιδειν σε θελοντες.
brothers of thee stand without, to see thee desiring.
21 Ὁ δε αποκριθεις ειπε προς αυτους· Μητηρ
He and answering said to them; Mother
μου και αδελφοι μου οὑτοι εισιν, οἱ τον λογον
of me and brothers of me these are, who the word
του θεου ακουοντες και ποιουντες.
of the God hearing and doing.
22 Και εγενετο εν μιᾳ των ἡμερων, και αυτος
And it happened in one of the days, and he
ενεβη εις πλοιον, και οἱ μαθηται αυτου· και
went into a ship, and the disciples of him; and
ειπε προς αυτους· Διελθωμεν εις το περαν της
said to them, We may pass over to the other side of the
λιμνης· και ανηχθησαν. 23 Πλεοντων δε αυτων,
lake; and they put off. Sailing but of them,
αφυπνωσε. Και κατεβη λαιλαψ ανεμου εις την
he fell asleep. And came down a squall of wind on the
λιμνην, και συνεπληρουντο, και εκινδυνευον.
lake, and they were filling, and were in danger.
24 Προσελθοντες δε διηγειραν αυτον, λεγοντες·
Coming to and they awoke him, saying;
Επιστατα, επιστατα, απολλυμεθα. Ὁ δε εγερ-
O master, O master, we are perishing. He and aris-
θεις επετιμησε τῳ ανεμῳ και τῳ κλυδωνι του
ing rebuked the wind and the raging of the
ὑδατος· και επαυσαντο, και εγενετο γαληνη.
water: and they ceased, and there was a calm.
25 Ειπε δε αυτοις· Που εστιν ἡ πιστις ὑμων;
He said and to them: Where is the faith of you?
Φοβηθεντες δε εθαυμασαν, λεγοντες προς
Fearing and they wondered, saying to
αλληλους· Τις αρα οὑτος εστιν, ὁτι και τοις
one another; Who then this is, that even to the
ανεμοις επιτασσει και τῳ ὑδατι, και ὑπακουου-
winds he gives a charge and to the water, and they hearken
σιν αυτῳ; 26 Και κατεπλευσαν εις την χωραν
to him? And they sailed into the country
των Γαδαρηνων, ἡτις εστιν αντιπεραν της
of the Gadarenes, which is over-against the
Γαλιλαιας.
Galilee.
27 Ἐξελθοντι δε αυτῳ επι την γην, ὑπηντη-
Going out and to him on the land, met
σεν αυτῳ ανηρ τις εκ της πολεως, ὁς ειχε
him a man certain out of the city, who had
δαιμονια εκ χρονων ἱκανων, και ἱματιον ουκ
demons from times many, and a mantle not
ενεδιδυσκετο, και εν οικιᾳ ουκ εμενεν, αλλ' εν
he put on, and in a house not he remained, but in

BROTHERS stand without, desiring to see thee."

21 But HE answering, said to them, "My Mother and my Brothers are THESE who HEAR the WORD of GOD, and obey it."

22 ‡ And it came to pass on one of the DAYS, that he went into a Boat with his DISCIPLES; and he said to them, "Let us pass over to the OTHER SIDE of the LAKE." And they set sail.

23 And as they were sailing, he fell asleep; and there came down a Gale of Wind on the LAKE; and they were deluged, and were in danger.

24 And approaching, they awoke him, saying, "Master! Master! we are perishing." Then arising, HE rebuked the WIND and the RAGING of the WATER; and they ceased, and there was a Calm.

25 And he said to them, "Where is your FAITH?" And being afraid, they wondered, saying to one another, "Who then is this that commands even the WINDS and the WATER, * and they obey him."

26 ‡ And they sailed to the REGION of the * † GERASENES, which is opposite to GALILEE.

27 And going out on SHORE, * a Certain Man of the CITY met him, who had * Demons; and for a long Time he wore no Clothes, nor remained in a House, but in the TOMBS.

---

* VATICAN MANUSCRIPT.—25. and they obey him—*omit*. 26. GERASENES. 27. a Certain Man. 27. Demons; and for a long Time he wore.

† 26. "I was afterwards informed by Mr. Thomson of Sidon, who had recently traversed this region, and whose knowledge both of the country and its language gave him great facilities in picking up information, that nearly opposite Mejdel (Magdala,) or just about opposite where we turned south, there is a place called by the natives *Girsa*, which Mr. T. supposes to be a corruption of *Gergesene*. Here there is a sharp sloping precipice of perhaps 2000 feet high. This is the 'steep place' (*kreemnou*) Matt. vii. 33; Mark v. 13; Luke viii. 33. Mark and Luke say it was in the country of the *Gadarenes*, and we know that Gadara (eight miles from Tiberias according to Josephus, Life, 65) must have been farther south. But the term Gadarene may be a wide one, and besides, the reading in Mark and Luke is a very doubtful one; the mass of evidence preponderates in favor of *Gerasene* instead of *Gadarene*."
—*Hackett*.

‡ 22. Matt. viii. 23; Mark iv. 35. ‡ 26. Matt. viii. 28; Mark v. 1.

τοις μνημασιν. 28 Ιδων δε τον Ιησουν, και
the tombs. Seeing and the Jesus, and
ανακραξας, προσεπεσεν αυτῳ, και φωνῃ μεγαλῃ
crying out, he fell down to him, and with a voice loud
ειπε· Τι εμοι και σοι, Ιησου, υἱε του θεου του
he said; What to me and to thee, Jesus, O son of the God of the
ὑψιστου; δεομαι σου, μη με βασανισῃς.
highest? I beseech thee, not me thou mayst torment.
29 (Παρηγγειλε γαρ τῳ πνευματι τῳ ακαθαρτῳ
(He had commanded for the spirit the unclean
εξελθειν απο του ανθρωπου· πολλοις γαρ χρο-
to come out from the man; many for times
νοις συνηρπακει αυτον· και εδεσμειτο ἁλυσεσι
it had seized him; and he was bound with chains
και πεδαις, φυλασσομενος· και διαρρησσων τα
and fetters, being guarded; and breaking the
δεσμα, ηλαυνετο ὑπο του δαιμονος εις τας ερη-
bonds, he was driven by the demon into the des-
μους.) 30 Επηρωτησε δε αυτον ὁ Ιησους,
erts.) Asked and him the Jesus,
*[λεγων·] Τι σοι εστιν ονομα; Ὁ δε ειπε·
[saying;] What to thee is a name? He and said,
Λεγεων· ὁτι δαιμονια πολλα εισηλθεν εις αυτον.
Legion: for demons many had entered into him.
31 Και παρεκαλει αυτον, ἱνα μη επιταξῃ αυτοις
And he besought him, that not he would command them
εις την αβυσσον απελθειν. 32 Ην δε εκει
into the abyss to go. Was and there
αγελη χοιρων ἱκανων βοσκομενων εν τῳ ορει·
a herd of swine many feeding in the mountain:
και παρεκαλουν αυτον, ἱνα επιτρεψῃ αυτοις εις
and they besought him, that he would permit them into
εκεινους εισελθειν. Και επετρεψεν αυτοις.
them to enter. And he permitted them.
33 Εξελθοντα δε τα δαιμονια απο του ανθρωπου,
Having gone out and the demons from the man,
εισηλθεν εις τους χοιρους· και ὡρμησεν ἡ
they entered into the swine: and rushed the
αγελη κατα του κρημνου εις την λιμνην, και
herd down the precipice into the lake, and
απεπνιγη. 34 Ιδοντες δε οἱ βοσκοντες το
were choked. Seeing and those feeding that
γεγονος, εφυγον και απηγγειλαν εις την πολιν
having been done, fled and reported in the city
και εις τους αγρους. 35 Εξηλθον δε ιδειν το
and in the villages. They came out and to see that
γεγονος· και ηλθον προς τον Ιησουν, και
having been done: and came to the Jesus, and
εὑρον καθημενον τον ανθρωπον, αφ' οὑ τα
found sitting the man, from whom the
δαιμονια εξεληλυθει, ἱματισμενον και σωφρο-
demons had gone out, having been clothed and being of
νουντα, παρα τους ποδας του Ιησου· και εφοβη-
sane mind, at the feet of the Jesus; and they
θησαν. 36 Απηγγειλαν δε αυτοις και οἱ ιδοντες,
were afraid. Reported and to them and those having seen

28 And seeing JESUS, he fell down before him, and crying out with a loud Voice, said, "What hast thou to do with me, Jesus,—O Son of GOD—the HIGHEST? I beseech thee, torment me not."

29 (For he had commanded the IMPURE SPIRIT to come out of the MAN. For it had frequently seized him; and he was bound with Chains and Fetters, and guarded; and breaking the BONDS, he was driven by the DEMON into the DESERTS.)

30 And JESUS asked him, "What is thy Name?" And HE said, "Legion;" Because many Demons had entered into him.

31 And he besought him that he would not command them to go out into the ABYSS.

32 Now there was a Herd of many Swine feeding on the MOUNTAIN; and they besought him to permit them to go into them. And he permitted them.

33 Then the DEMONS having come out of the MAN, went into the SWINE; and the HERD rushed down the PRECIPICE into the LAKE, and were † drowned.

34 And the SWINE-HERDS, seeing THAT HAVING BEEN DONE, fled, and reported it in the CITY and in the VILLAGES.

35 And they went out to see THAT HAVING BEEN DONE. And they came to JESUS, and found the MAN from whom the DEMONS had gone out, sitting at the FEET of * Jesus, clothed, and in his right mind; and they were afraid.

36 Then THOSE who SAW it informed them how

* VATICAN MANUSCRIPT.—30. saying—*omit.* 35. Jesus.

† 33. Some sceptics have objected to this transaction, as not conformable to the character of Jesus. Now as the Jews were prohibited by the laws of Hyrcanus from keeping swine, and by the law of Moses from using them as food, this act was a just punishment on these violators of law. The miracle itself served to manifest Christ's own regard to the law of God, while the disposition displayed by the people, in desiring him to depart from them, showed how well they needed correction.

πως εσωθη ὁ δαιμονισθεις. 37 Και ηρωτησαν
how was saved he having been demonized. And asked
αυτον ἁπαν το πληθος της περιχωρου των
him whole the multitude of the surrounding region of the
Γαδαρηνων, απελθειν απ' αυτων· ὁτι φοβῳ
Gadarenes, to go from them; for with a fear
μεγαλῳ συνειχοντο.
great they were seized.

Αυτος δε εμβας εις το πλοιον, ὑπεστρεψεν.
He and having gone into the ship, returned.
38 Εδεετο δε αυτου ὁ ανηρ, αφ' οὑ εξεληλυθει
Begged and of him the man, from whom had gone out
τα δαιμονια, ειναι συν αυτῳ. Απελυσε δε
the demons, to be with him. Sent away but
αυτον ὁ Ιησους, λεγων· 39 Ὑποστρεφε εις τον
him the Jesus, saying; Return to the
οικον σου, και διηγου, ὁσα εποιησε σοι ὁ θεος.
house of thee, and relate, how much has done to thee the God.
Και απηλθε, καθ' ὁλην την πολιν κηρυσσων,
And he went away, through whole the city publishing,
ὁσα εποιησεν αυτῳ ὁ Ιησους.
how much had done to him the Jesus.

40 Εγενετο δε εν τῳ ὑποστρεψαι τον Ιησουν,
It happened and in the to return the Jesus,
απεδεξατο αυτον ὁ οχλος· ησαν γαρ παντες
gladly received him the crowd; they were for all
προσδοκωντες αυτον. 41 Και ιδου, ηλθεν ανηρ,
waiting for him. And lo, came a man,
ᾡ ονομα Ιαειρος, και αυτος αρχων της συνα-
to whom a name Jairus, and he a ruler of the syna-
γωγης ὑπηρχε· και πεσων παρα τους ποδας του
gogue was; and falling at the feet of the
Ιησου, παρεκαλει αυτον εισελθειν εις τον οικον
Jesus, besought him to come into the house
αὑτου· 42 ὁτι θυγατηρ μονογενης ην αυτῳ ὡς
of himself: for a daughter only was to him about
ετων δωδεκα, και αὑτη απεθνησκεν. Εν δε τῳ
years twelve, and she was dying. In and to the
ὑπαγειν αυτον, οἱ οχλοι συνεπνιγον αυτον.
to go him, the crowds pressed him.
43 Και γυνη ουσα εν ῥυσει αἱματος απο ετων
And a woman being in a flow of blood from years
δωδεκα, ἡτις ιατροις προσαναλωσασα ὁλον τον
twelve, who with physicians having expended whole the
βιον, ουκ ισχυσεν ὑπ' ουδενος θεραπευθηναι·
living, not had strength by any one to be cured;
44 προσελθουσα οπισθεν, ἡψατο του κρασπεδου
coming behind, touched the tuft
του ἱματιου αυτου· και παραχρημα εστη ἡ
of the mantle of him: and immediately stopped the
ῥυσις του αἱματος αυτης. 45 Και ειπεν ὁ Ιησους·
flow of the blood of her. And said the Jesus,
Τις ὁ ἁψαμενος μου; Αρνουμενων δε παντων,
Who the having touched me? Denying and all,
ειπεν ὁ Πετρος *[και οἱ συν αυτῳ·] Επιστατα,
said the Peter [and those with him:] O master,

the DEMONIAC was restored.

37 ‡And the Whole MULTITUDE of the SURROUNDING COUNTRY of the *GERASENES ‡desired him to depart from them; For they were seized with great Fear. And having entered the *Boat he returned.

38 Now ‡the MAN from whom the DEMONS had gone out, desired to be with him. But *he dismissed him, saying,

39 "Return to thy HOUSE, and relate how much GOD has done for thee." And he went away, and published through the Whole CITY how much JESUS had done for him.

40 And it occurred, as JESUS RETURNED, the CROWD gladly received him; for they were all waiting for htm.

41 ‡And, behold, there came a Man, whose name was Jairus, and he was a Ruler of the SYNAGOGUE; and falling at the FEET of *Jesus, entreated him to come into his HOUSE;

42 For he had an only Daughter, about twelve Years of Age, and she was dying. And as he WENT the CROWDS pressed on him.

43 ‡And a Woman having had an Hemorrhage for twelve Years, who *had consumed her Whole LIVING on Physicians, and could not be cured by any one,

44 coming up behind, touched the TUFT of his MANTLE; and immediately the FLOW of her BLOOD stopped.

45 And JESUS said, "WHO TOUCHED me?" and all denying it, PETER and THOSE with him said,

* VATICAN MANUSCRIPT.—37. GERASENES. 37. Boat. 38. he dismissed him. 41. Jesus. 43. could not be cured by any one, coming up. 45. and those with him—*omit.*

‡ 37. Matt. viii. 34. ‡ 37. Acts xvi. 39. ‡ 38. Mark v. 18. ‡ 41. Matt. ix. 18; Mark v. 22. ‡ 43. Matt. ix. 20.

οἱ οχλοι συνεχουσι σε και αποθλιβουσι· και
the crowds press on thee and crowd; and
λεγεις· Τις ὁ ἁψαμενος μου; 46 Ὁ δε Ιησους
sayest thou, Who the having touched me? The and Jesus
ειπεν· Ἡψατο μου τις· εγω γαρ εγνων
said; Touched me some one; I for know
δυναμιν εξελθουσαν απ' εμου. 47 Ιδουσα δε ἡ
a power went out from me. Seeing and the
γυνη, ὁτι ουκ ελαθε, τρεμουσα ηλθε, και
woman, that not she was unnoticed, trembling came, and
προσπεσουσα αυτῳ, δι' ἡν αιτιαν ἡψατο αυτου,
falling down to him, through what cause she touched him,
απηγγειλεν *[αυτῳ] ενωπιον παντος του λαου,
related [to him] in presence of all of the people,
και ὡς ιαθη παραχρημα. 48 Ὁ δε ειπεν αυτῃ·
and how she was cured immediately. He and said to her;
*[Θαρσει,] θυγατερ· ἡ πιστις σου σεσωκε σε·
[Take courage,] O daughter; the faith of thee has saved thee:
πορευου εις ειρηνην. 49 Ετι αυτου λαλουντος,
go in peace. While of him speaking,
ερχεται τις παρα του αρχισυναγωγου, λεγων
comes some one from of the synagogue-ruler's, saying
*[αυτῳ·] Ὁτι τεθνηκεν ἡ θυγατηρ σου· μη
[to him;] That is dead the daughter of thee: not
σκυλλε τον διδασκαλον. 50 Ὁ δε Ιησους
trouble thou the teacher. The but Jesus
ακουσας, απεκριθη αυτῳ, *[λεγων·] Μη
having heard, answered him, [saying:] Not
φοβου· μονον πιστευε, και σωθησεται. 51 Ελ-
fear: only believe thou, and she shall be saved. Com-
θων δε εις την οικιαν, ουκ αφηκεν εισελθειν
ing and into the house, not he suffered to enter
ουδενα, ει μη Πετρον και Ιωαννην και Ιακωβον,
no one, except Peter and John and James,
και τον πατερα της παιδος και την μητερα.
and the father of the child and the mother.
52 Εκλαιον δε παντες, και εκοπτοντο αυτην.
Was weeping and all, and lamenting her.
Ὁ δε ειπε· Μη κλαιετε· ουκ απεθανεν, αλλα
He but said: Not weep you: not she is dead, but
καθευδει. 53 Και κατεγελων αυτου, ειδοτες ὁτι
sleeps. And they derided him, knowing that
απεθανεν. 54 Αυτος δε *[εκβαλων εξω παντας,
she was dead. He but [having put out all,
και] κρατησας της χειρος αυτης, εφωνησε,
and] having grasped the hand of her, called out,
λεγων· Ἡ παις, εγειρου. 55 Και επεστρεψε το
saying; The child, arise. And returned the
πνευμα αυτης, και ανεστη παραχρημα· Και
breath of her, and she stood up immediately: And
διεταξεν αυτῃ δοθηναι φαγειν. 56 Και εξεστη-
he commanded to her to be given to eat. And were aston-
σαν οἱ γονεις αυτης. Ὁ δε παρηγγειλεν αυτοις
ished the parents of her. He but charged them
μηδενι ειπειν το γεγονος.
no one to tell that having been done.

"Master, the CROWDS press on and crowd thee, and dost thou say, 'WHO TOUCHED me?'"

46 And Jesus said, "Some one touched me; ‡for I know a Power went out from me."

47 Then the WOMAN, seeing that she was discovered, came trembling, and falling down, related to him in presence of All the PEOPLE, why she had touched him, and how she was immediately cured.

48 And he said to her, "Daughter, thy FAITH has cured thee; go in Peace."

49 ‡While he was still speaking, some one came from the SYNAGOGUE-RULER's house, who said, "Thy DAUGHTER is dead; trouble *no more the TEACHER."

50 But JESUS having heard it, answered him, "Fear not, only believe, and she will be saved."

51 And coming to the HOUSE, he permitted no one *to go in with him, except Peter, and John, and James, and the FATHER and the MOTHER of the CHILD.

52 And all were weeping and lamenting her. But HE said, "Weep not; *for she is not dead, ‡but sleeps."

53 And they derided him, knowing That she was dead.

54 But he, grasping her HAND called out, saying, "MAIDEN, ‡arise,"

55 And her BREATH returned, and she stood up immediately; and he ordered them to give her food.

56 And her PARENTS were astonished, but ‡HE charged them to tell no one WHAT had been DONE.

* VATICAN MANUSCRIPT.—47. to him—*omit*. 48. Take courage—*omit*. 49. to him—*omit*. 49. no more the TEACHER. 50. saying—*omit*. 51. to go in with him, except. 52. for she. 54. having put them all out, and—*omit*.

‡ 46. Mark v. 30; Luke vi. 19. ‡ 49. Mark v. 35. ‡ 52. John xi. 11, 13. ‡ 54. Luke vii. 14; John xi. 43. ‡ 56. Matt. viii. 4; ix. 30; Mark v. 43.

ΚΕΦ. θ'. 9.

1 Συγκαλεσαμενος δε τους δωδεκα, εδωκεν
Having called together and the twelve, he gave
αυτοις δυναμιν και εξουσιαν επι παντα τα δαι-
to them power and authority over all the de-
μονια, και νοσους θεραπευειν. 2 Και απεστει-
mons, and diseases to cure. And he sent
λεν αυτους κηρυσσειν την βασιλειαν του θεου,
them to publish the kingdom of the God,
και ιασθαι *[τους ασθενουντας.] 3 Και ειπε
and to heal [those being sick.] And said
προς αυτους· Μηδεν αιρετε εις την όδον, μητε
to them; Nothing take you for the journey, neither
ραβδον, μητε πηραν, μητε αρτον, μητε αργυ-
a staff, nor a bag, nor bread, nor sil-
ριον· μητε *[ανα] δυο χιτωνας εχειν. 4 Και
ver; nor [each] two coats to have. And
εις ἥν αν οικιαν εισελθητε, εκει μενετε, και
into whatever house you may enter, there remain, and
εκειθεν εξερχεσθε. 5 Και όσοι αν μη δεξωνται
thence depart. And whoever not may receive
ὑμας, εξερχομενοι απο της πολεως εκεινης, και
you, coming out from the city that, even
τον κονιορτον απο των ποδων ὑμων αποτιναξατε,
the dust from the feet of you shake off,
εις μαρτυριον επ' αυτους. 6 Εξερχομενοι δε
for a testimony against them. Going forth and
διηρχοντο κατα τας κωμας, ευαγγελιζομενοι και
they traveled through the villages, publishing glad tidings and
θεραπευοντες πανταχου.
healing everywhere.
7 Ηκουσε δε Ἡρωδης ὁ τετραρχης τα γινο-
Heard and Herod the tetrarch that being
μενα *[ὑπ' αυτου] παντα· και διηπορει, δια
done [by him] all; and he was perplexed, because
το λεγεσθαι ὑπο τινων, ὁτι Ιωαννης εγηγερται
the to be said by some, that John has been raised
εκ νεκρων· 8 ὑπο τινων δε, ὁτι Ηλιας εφανη·
out of dead; by some and, that Elias had appeared;
αλλων δε, ὁτι προφητης εἱς των αρχαιων ανεσ-
others and, that a prophet one of the ancients has stood
τη. 9 Και ειπεν Ἡρωδης· Ιωαννην εγω απεκε-
up. And said Herod; John I be-
φαλισα· τις δε εστιν οὗτος, περι οὗ εγω
headed; who but is this, concerning whom I
ακουω τοιαυτα; Και εζητει ιδειν αυτον.
hear such things? And he sought to see him.
10 Και ὑποστρεψαντες οἱ αποστολοι διηγησαντο
And having returned the apostles related
αυτῳ ὁσα εποιησαν· και παραλαβων αυτους
to him what things they had done; and taking them
ὑπεχωρησε κατ' ιδιαν εις *[τοπον ερημον]
he withdrew by himself into [a place desert]
πολεως καλουμενης Βηθσαιδα. 11 Οἱ δε οχλοι
of a city being called Bethsaida. The and crowds

CHAPTER IX.

1 ‡ And having convened the TWELVE, he gave them Power and Authority over All DEMONS, and to cure Diseases.

2 And ‡ he sent them forth to proclaim the KINGDOM of GOD, and to cure * the SICK.

3 ‡ And he said to them; "Take Nothing for the JOURNEY, neither Staff, nor Traveling Bag, nor Bread, nor Silver, nor have Two Coats.

4 ‡ And into Whatever House you may enter, there remain, and thence depart.

5 And whoever shall not receive you, when you go out from that CITY, ‡ shake off even the DUST from your FEET, for a Testimony to them."

6 ‡ And going forth, they traveled through the VILLAGES, proclaiming the glad tidings, and performing cures everywhere.

7 ‡ Now Herod, the TETRARCH, heard of ALL that was DONE; and he was perplexed, because it was SAID by some, "John has been raised from the Dead;"

8 and by some, "Elijah has appeared;" and by others, * "A certain Prophet of the ANCIENTS has risen up."

9 * But HEROD said, "John I beheaded; but who is this of whom * I hear such things?" ‡ And he sought to see him.

10 ‡ And the APOSTLES, having returned, related to him what things they had done. ‡ And taking them aside, he withdrew privately into * a desert Place of a City, called Bethsaida.

11 And the CROWDS

* VATICAN MANUSCRIPT.—2. the SICK—*omit.* 3. each—*omit.* 7. by him—*omit.* 8. a certain Prophet of the ANCIENTS was. 9. But HEROD. 9. I hear. 10. a desert place—*omit.*

‡ 1. Matt. x. 1; Mark iii. 13; vi. 7. ‡ 2. Matt. x. 7; Mark vi. 12; Luke x. 1, 9. ‡ 3. Matt. x. 9; Mark vi. 8; Luke x. 4; xxii. 35. ‡ 4. Matt. x. 11; Mark vi. 10. ‡ 5. Acts xiii. 51. ‡ 6. Matt. vi. 12. ‡ 7. Matt. xiv. 1; Mark vi. 14. ‡ 9. Luke xxiii. 8. ‡ 10. Mark vi. 30. ‡ 10. Matt. xiv. 13.

γνοντες, ηκολουθησαν αυτῳ. Και δεξαμενος
having heard, they followed him. And having received
αυτους, ελαλει αυτοις περι της βασιλειας του
them, he spake to them concerning the kingdom of the
θεου, και τους χρειαν εχοντας θεραπειας, ιατο.
God, and those need having of healing, he cured.
12 Ἡ δε ἡμερα ηρξατο κλινειν· προσελθοντες
The now day began to decline; coming
δε οἱ δωδεκα, ειπον αυτῳ· Απολυσον τον οχλον,
and the twelve, said to him; Dismiss the crowd,
ἱνα πορευθεντες εις τας κυκλῳ κωμας και τους
that having gone into the surrounding villages and the
αγρους, καταλυσωσι, και εὑρωσιν επισιτισμον·
farms, they may lodge, and find provisions;
ὁτι ὡδε εν ερημῳ τοπῳ εσμεν. 13 Ειπε δε προς
for here in a desert place we are. He said but to
αυτους· Δοτε αυτοις ὑμεις φαγειν. Οἱ δε
them: Give to them you to eat. They and
ειπον· Ουκ εισιν ἡμιν πλειον η πεντε αρτοι,
said: Not are to us more than five loaves,
και ιχθυες δυο, ει μητι πορευθεντες ἡμεις αγο-
and fishes two, if not going we may
ρασωμεν εις παντα τον λαον τουτον βρωματα.
buy for all the people this food.
14 Ησαν γαρ ὡσει ανδρες πεντακισχιλιοι. Ειπε
They were for about men five thousand. He said
δε προς τους μαθητας αὑτου· Κατακλινατε
and to the disciples of himself: Make recline
αυτους κλισιας ανα πεντηκοντα. 15 Και εποιη-
them in companies each fifty. And they
σαν οὑτω, και ανεκλιναν ἁπαντας. 16 Λαβων
did so, and they made recline all. Taking
δε τους πεντε αρτους και τους δυο ιχθυας,
and the five loaves and the two fishes,
αναβλεψας εις τον ουρανον, ευλογησεν αυτους·
looking up to the heaven, he blessed them;
και κατεκλασε, και εδιδου τοις μαθηταις, παρα-
and broke, and gave to the disciples, to
τιθεναι τῳ οχλῳ. 17 Και εφαγον, και εχορτασ-
set before the crowd. And they ate, and were satis-
θησαν παντες· και ηρθη το περισσευσαν αυ-
fied all: and was taken up that having been left to
τοις κλασματων, κοφινοι δωδεκα.
them of fragments, baskets twelve.
18 Και εγενετο εν τῳ ειναι αυτον προσευχο-
And it happened in the to be him praying
μενον καταμονας, συνησαν αυτῳ οἱ μαθηται·
in private, came to him the disciples:
και επηρωτησεν αυτους, λεγων· Τινα με
and he asked them, saying: Who me
λεγουσιν οἱ οχλοι ειναι; 19 Οἱ δε αποκριθεντες
say the crowds to be? They and answering
ειπον· Ιωαννην τον βαπτιστην· αλλοι δε, Ηλιαν,
said: John the dipper: others but, Elias·
αλλοι δε, ὁτι προφητης τις των αρχαιων ανεστη.
others and, that a prophet one of the ancients has stood up.
20 Ειπε δε αυτοις· Ὑμεις δε τινα με λεγετε
He said and to them: You but who me say you

knowing it, followed him; and having * gladly received them, he spoke to them concerning the KINGDOM of GOD, and healed THOSE who HAD need of Healing.

12 ‡ * The DAY already began to decline, when the TWELVE came and said to him, "Dismiss the CROWD, that they may go into the adjacent VILLAGES and * Farms, to lodge, and find Provisions; For we are here in a Desert Place."

13 But he said to them, "You supply them." And THEY said, "We have no more than Five Loaves and Two Fishes: unless we should go and buy Food for All this PEOPLE;"

14 for they were about five thousand Men. And he said to his DISCIPLES, "Make them recline in Companies of * fifty each."

15 And they did so, and caused them all to recline.

16 Then taking the FIVE Loaves and the TWO Fishes, and looking towards HEAVEN, he blessed and broke them, and gave to the DISCIPLES to set before the CROWD.

17 And they ate and were all satisfied; and there were taken up of the REMAINING FRAGMENTS, twelve Baskets.

18 ‡ And it came to pass, as he WAS praying in private, the DISCIPLES came to him; and he asked them, saying, "Who do the CROWDS say that I am?"

19 And THEY answering said, ‡ "John the IMMERSER; but others, Elijah; and others, that a certain Prophet of the ANCIENTS has risen up."

20 And he said to them, "But who do you say that

* VATICAN MANUSCRIPT.—11. gladly received. 12. The DAY already began to decline, when the TWELVE came. 12. Farms. 14. as it were by.

‡ 12. Matt. xiv. 15; Mark vi. 35; John vi. 1, 5. ‡ 18. Matt. xvi. 13; Mark viii. 27. 19. Matt. xiv. 2; ver. 7, 8.

ειναι; [20] Αποκριθεις δε ὁ Πετρος ειπε· Τον
to be? Answering and the Peter said; The
Χριστον του θεου. [21] Ὁ δε επιτιμησας αυτοις,
Anointed of the God. He and having strictly charged them,
παρηγγειλε μηδενι λεγειν τουτο· [22] ειπων· Ὁτι
commanded to no one to tell this; saying; That
δει τον υἱον του ανθρωπου πολλα παθειν, και
must the son of the man many things to suffer, and
αποδοκιμασθηναι απο των πρεσβυτερων και
to be rejected by the elders and
αρχιερεων και γραμματεων, και αποκτανθηναι,
high-priests and scribes, and to be killed,
και τη τριτη ἡμερᾳ εγερθηναι.
and the third day to be raised.

[23] Ελεγε δε προς παντας· Ει τις θελει οπισω
He said and to all; If any one wishes after
μου ερχεσθαι, αρνησασθω ἑαυτον, και αρατω
me to come, let him deny himself, and let him bear
τον σταυρον αὑτου καθ' ἡμεραν, και ακολου-
the cross of himself every day, and fol-
θειτω μοι. [24] Ὁς γαρ αν θελη την ψυχην
low me. Who for ever may wish the life
αὑτου σωσαι, απολεσει αυτην· ὁς δ' αν απο-
of himself to save, shall lose her; who but ever may
λεση την ψυχην αὑτου ἑνεκεν εμου, οὑτος σωσει
lose the life of himself on account of me, he shall save
αυτην. [25] Τι γαρ ωφελειται ανθρωπος κερδησας
her. What for is profited a man having won
τον κοσμον ὁλον, ἑαυτον δε απολεσας, η ζημιω-
the world whole, himself and having lost, or having for-
θεις; [26] Ὁς γαρ αν επαισχυνθη με και τους
feited? Who for ever may be ashamed me and the
εμους λογους, τουτον ὁ υἱος του ανθρωπου
my words, this the son of the man
επαισχυνθησεται, ὁταν ελθη εν τη δοξη
will be ashamed, when he may come in the glory
αὑτου, και του πατρος, και των ἁγιων αγγελων.
of himself, and of the father, and of the holy messengers.
[27] Λεγω δε ὑμιν αληθως, εισι τινες των ὡδε
I say but to you truly, are some of those here
ἑστωτων, οἱ ου μη γευσωνται θανατου, ἑως αν
standing, who not not shall taste of death, till
ιδωσι την βασιλειαν του θεου.
they may see the royal majesty of the God.

[28] Εγενετο δε μετα τους λογους τουτους,
It happened and after the words these
ὡσει ἡμεραι οκτω, και παραλαβων Πετρον και
about days eight, and having taken Peter and
Ιωαννην και Ιακωβον, ανεβη εις το ορος
John and James, he went up into the mountain
προσευξασθαι. [29] Και εγενετο, εν τῳ προσευ-
to pray. And it occurred, in the to
χεσθαι αυτον, το ειδος του προσωπου αυτου
pray him, the form of the face of him
ἑτερον, και ὁ ἱματισμος αυτου λευκος εξαστραπ-
different, and the raiment of him whiteness flashing

I am?" ‡ "And *Peter an-
swering said, "The CHRIST
of GOD."

21 ‡ And HE having
strictly charged them, ordered them to tell this to
no one;

22 saying, ‡ "The SON
of MAN must suffer many
things, and be rejected by
the ELDERS, and High-
priests, and Scribes, and
be killed, and on the THIRD
Day be raised."

23 ‡ And he said to all,
"If any one wish to come
after me, let him renounce
himself, and take up his
CROSS daily, and follow
me.

24 For whoever would
save his LIFE, shall lose it;
and whoever loses his LIFE
on my account, he shall
save it.

25 ‡ For what is a Man
profited, if he gain the
whole WORLD, and destroy
or forfeit Himself.

26 ‡ For whoever is
ashamed of me, and MY
Words, of him the SON of
MAN will be ashamed,
when he comes in his own
GLORY, and that of the FA-
THER, and of the HOLY
Angels,

27 ‡ But I tell you truly,
There are SOME STANDING
* here, who will not taste
of Death, till they see
GOD'S ROYAL MAJESTY."

28 And it occurred about
eight Days after these
WORDS, taking *Peter,
and John, and James, he
went up into the MOUN-
TAIN to pray.

29 And it happened, as
he PRAYED, the FORM of
his FACE was changed,
and his RAIMENT became
white and dazzling.

* VATICAN MANUSCRIPT.—20. Peter. 27. there, who.

‡ 20. Matt. xvi. 16; John vi. 69. ‡ 21. Matt. xvi. 20. ‡ 22. Matt. xvi. 21; xvii. 22. ‡ 23. Matt. x. 38; xvi. 24; Mark viii. 34; Luke xiv. 27. ‡ 25. Matt. xvi. 26; Mark viii. 36. ‡ 26. Matt. x. 33; Mark viii. 38; 2 Tim. ii. 12. ‡ 27 Matt. xvi. 28; Mark ix. 1.

των. 30 Και ιδου, ανδρες δυο συνελαλουν αυτῳ,
forth. And lo, men two were talking with him,

οἵτινες ησαν Μωσης και Ἡλιας· 31 οἱ οφθεντες
who were Moses and Elias: they appearing

εν δοξῃ, ελεγον την εξοδον αυτου, ἡν εμελλε
in glory, spoke of the departure of him, which he was about

πληρουν εν Ιερουσαλημ. 32 Ὁ δε Πετρος και
to fulfil in Jerusalem. The but Peter and

οἱ συν αυτῳ ησαν βεβαρημενοι ὑπνῳ. Δια-
those with him were having been heavy with sleep. Hav-

γρηγορησαντες δε ειδον την δοξαν αυτου, και
ing awakened but they saw the glory of him, and

τους δυο ανδρας τους συνεστωτας αυτῳ. 33 Και
the two men those standing with him. And

εγενετο εν τῳ διαχωριζεσθαι αυτους απ' αυτου,
it happened in the to depart them from him,

ειπεν ὁ Πετρος προς τον Ιησουν· Επιστατα,
said the Peter to the Jesus: O master,

καλον εστιν ἡμας ὡδε ειναι· και ποιησωμεν
good it is us here to be. and we may make

σκηνας τρεις, μιαν σοι, και μιαν Μωσει, και
tents three, one for thee, and one for Moses, and

μιαν Ηλια· μη ειδως ὁ λεγει. 34 Ταυτα δε αυτου
one for Elias: not knowing what he says. These and of him

λεγοντος, εγενετο νεφελη, και επεσκιασεν
saying, came a cloud, and overshadowed

αυτους, εφοβηθησαν δε εν τῳ εκεινους εισηλθειν
them, they feared and in the those to enter

εις την νεφελην. 35 Και φωνη εγενετο εκ της
into the cloud. And a voice came out of the

νεφελης, λεγουσα· "Οὗτος εστιν ὁ υἱος μου ὁ
cloud, saying: "This is the son of me the

αγαπητος· αυτου ακουετε." 36 Και εν τῳ
beloved: him hear you." And in the

γενεσθαι την φωνην, εὑρεθη ὁ Ιησους μονος.
to have been the voice, was found the Jesus alone.

Και αυτοι εσιγησαν, και ουδενι απηγγειλαν εν
And they were silent, and to no one told in

εκειναις ταις ἡμεραις ουδεν ὡν ἑωρακασιν.
those the days nothing of what they had seen.

37 Εγενετο δε εν τῃ ἑξης ἡμερᾳ, κατελθοντων
It happened and in the next day, having come down

αυτων απο του ορους, συνηντησεν αυτῳ οχλος
them from the mountain, met him a crowd

πολυς. 38 Και ιδου, ανηρ απο του οχλου ανε-
great. And lo, a man from the crowd cried

βοησε, λεγων· Διδασκαλε, δεομαι σου, επιβλε-
loudly, saying: O teacher, I pray thee, to look

ψαι επι τον υἱον μου, ὁτι μονογενης εστι μοι·
on the son of me, for only-born he is to me;

39 και ιδου, πνευμα λαμβανει αυτον, και εξαι-
and lo, a spirit seizes him, and sud-

30 And behold, two Men were conversing with him and these were Moses and Elijah;

31 who appearing in Glory, spoke of his DEPARTURE which was about to be consummated at Jerusalem.

32 Now PETER and THOSE with him ‡were overpowered with Sleep; but having awakened, they saw his GLORY, and THOSE TWO Men STANDING with him.

33 And it occurred, when they were DEPARTING from him, PETER said to JESUS, "Master, it is good for us to be here; and let us make three Booths; One for thee, and One for Moses, and One for Elijah;" not knowing what he said.

34 And as he was thus speaking, a Cloud came and covered them; and they were afraid when *they ENTERED the CLOUD.

35 And a Voice proceeded from the CLOUD, saying, ‡"This is my *SON, the BELOVED; ‡hear him."

36 And when the VOICE had ceased, *Jesus was found alone. ‡And they were †silent, and told no one in Those DAYS what they had seen.

37 ‡Now it happened the NEXT Day, when they came down from the MOUNTAIN, a great Crowd met him.

38 And behold, a Man from the CROWD, cried loudly, saying, "Teacher, I beseech thee, to look on my SON, For he is my Only Child.

39 And behold, a Spirit seizes him, and he suddenly

* VATICAN MANUSCRIPT.—34. they. 35. CHOSEN SON. 36. Jesus.

† 36. Jesus enjoined silence upon the spectators of his transfiguration, (see Matt. xvii. 9), till after his resurrection; and probably one principal reason of this injunction of secrecy to the disciples might be our Lord's unwillingness to force the people into a belief of his divine character by a degree of evidence which would control the mind, and not leave free scope for the exercise of the moral dispositions and the ingenuous workings of the heart. He appears to have consulted this purpose, on all occasions, with particular attention.—*Wakefield.*

‡ 32. Dan. viii. 18; x. 9. ‡ 35. Matt. iii. 17. ‡ 35. Acts iii. 22. ‡ 36. Matt. xvii. 9. ‡ 37. Matt. xvii. 14; Mark ix. 14, 17.

φνης κραζει, και σπαρασσει αυτον μετα αφρου,
denly he cries out, and convulses him with foam,
και μογις αποχωρει απ' αυτου, συντριβον αυτον.
and hardly departs from him, bruising him.
40 Και εδεηθην των μαθητων σου, ἱνα εκβαλωσιν
And I besought the disciples of thee, that they might expel
αυτο· και ουκ ηδυνηθησαν. 41 Αποκριθεις δε ὁ
it; and not they were able. Answering and the
Ιησους ειπεν· Ω γενεα απιστος και διεσ-
Jesus said; O generation without faith and having
τραμμενη· ἑως ποτε εσομαι προς ὑμας, και
been perverted; till when shall I be with you, and
ανεξομαι ὑμων; Προσαγαγε τον υἱον σου ὡδε.
bear with you? Lead the son of thee here.
42 Ετι δε προσερχομενου αυτου, ερρηξεν αυτον
While and coming to him, dashed down him
το δαιμονιον, και συνεσπαραξεν. Επετιμησε δε
the demon, and violently convulsed. Rebuked and
ὁ Ιησους τῳ πνευματι τῳ ακαθαρτῳ, και ιασατο
the Jesus the spirit the unclean, and healed
τον παιδα, και απεδωκεν αυτον τῳ πατρι αυτου.
the child, and delivered him to the father of him.
43 Εξεπλησσοντο δε παντες επι τῃ μεγαλειοτητι
Were amazed and all at the majesty
του θεου.
of the God.

Παντων δε θαυμαζοντων επι πασιν οἱς εποιει
All and were wondering at all which did
ὁ Ιησους, ειπε προς τους μαθητας αὐτου·
the Jesus, he said to the disciples of himself;
44 Θεσθε ὑμεις εις τα ωτα ὑμων τους λογους
Place you into the ears of you the words
τουτους· ὁ γαρ υἱος του ανθρωπου μελλει παρα-
these; the for son of the man is about to be
διδοσθαι εις χειρας ανθρωπων· 45 Οἱ δε ηγνοουν
delivered into hands of men; They but understood not
το ῥημα τουτο, και ην παρακεκαλυμμενον απ'
the word this, and it was having been veiled from
αυτων, ἱνα μη αισθωνται αυτο· και εφοβουντο
them, that not they might perceive it; and they feared
ερωτησαι αυτον περι του ῥηματος τουτου.
to ask him concerning the word this.
46 Εισηλθε δε διαλογισμος εν αυτοις, το, τις αν
Arose and a dispute among them, that, which
ειη μειζων αυτων. 47 Ὁ δε Ιησους ιδων τον
would be greater of them. The and Jesus perceiving the
διαλογισμον της καρδιας αυτων, επιλαβομενος
thought of the heart of them, having taken
παιδιου, εστησεν αυτο παρ' ἑαυτῳ, και ειπεν
a little child, placed it near himself, and said
αυτοις· 48 Ὁς εαν δεξηται τουτο το παιδιον επι
to them; Whoever may receive this the little child in
τῳ ονοματι μου, εμε δεχεται· και ὁς εαν εμε
the name of me, me receives; and whoever me
δεξηται, δεχεται τον αποστειλαντα με. Ὁ γαρ
may receive, receives the having sent me. He for
μικροτερος εν πασιν ὑμιν ὑπαρχων, οὑτος εσται
less among all you being, he shall be

cries out; and it so convulses him that he foams; and after bruising him, with difficulty departs from him.

40 And I entreated thy DISCIPLES to expel it; and they could not."

41 And JESUS answering, said, "O unbelieving and perverse Generation! how long shall I be with you, and endure you? Conduct thy SON here."

42 And while he was approaching, the DEMON dashed him down, and violently convulsed him. And JESUS rebuked the IMPURE SPIRIT, and cured the CHILD, and delivered him to his FATHER.

43 And they were all struck with awe at the MAJESTIC POWER of GOD. But while all were wondering at every thing which JESUS did, he said to his DISCIPLES;

44 ‡"Place you these WORDS in your EARS—The SON of MAN is about to be delivered into the Hands of Men."

45 ‡But THEY did not understand this SAYING; and it was so veiled from them that they might not perceive it; and they were afraid to ask him concerning this SAYING.

46 ‡And a Dispute arose among them, WHICH OF THEM WOULD BE GREATEST.

47 But JESUS, perceiving the THOUGHT of their HEART, having taken a Little child, placed it near himself,

48 and said to them, ‡"Whoever may receive This LITTLE CHILD in my NAME, receives Me; and whoever may receive Me, receives HIM who SENT me; ‡for HE who is LEAST among you all, he *shall be great."

* VATICAN MANUSCRIPT.—48. is great.

‡ 44. Matt. xvii. 22. ‡ 45. Mark ix. 32; Luke ii. 50; xviii. 34. ‡ 46. Matt. xviii. 1; Mark ix. 34. ‡ 48. Matt. x. 40; xviii. 5; Mark ix. 37; John xii. 44; xiii. 20. ‡ 48. Matt. xxiii. 11, 12.

μεγας. 49 Αποκριθεις δε ὁ Ιωαννης ειπεν· Επισ-
great. Answering and the John said; O mas-
τατα, ειδομεν τινα επι τῳ ονοματι σου εκβαλ-
ter. we saw one in the name of thee casting
λοντα τα δαιμονια· και εκωλυσαμεν αυτον, ὁτι
out the demons; and we forbade him, because
ουκ ακολουθει μεθ' ἡμων. 50 Και ειπε προς
not he follows with us. And said to
αυτον ὁ Ιησους· Μη κωλυετε· ὁς γαρ ουκ εστι
him the Jesus; Not forbid you; who for not is
καθ' ὑμων, ὑπερ ὑμων εστιν.
against you, for you is.

51 Εγενετο δε εν τῳ συμπληρουσθαι τας
It came to pass and in the to be completed the
ἡμερας της αναληψεως αυτου, και αυτος το
days of the withdrawing of him, and he the
προσωπον αὑτου εστηριξε του πορευεσθαι εις
face of himself firmly set of the to go to
Ιερουσαλημ. 52 Και απεστειλεν αγγελους
Jerusalem. And he sent messengers
προ προσωπου αὑτου· και πορευθεντες εισηλθον
before face of himself; and having gone they entered
εις κωμην Σαμαρειτων, ὡστε ἑτοιμασαι αυτῳ.
into a village of Samaritans, so as to prepare for him.
53 Και ουκ εδεξαντο αυτον, ὁτι το προσωπον
And not they received him, because the face
αυτου ην πορευομενον εις Ἱερουσαλημ. 54 Ιδον-
of him was going to Jerusalem. See-
τες δε οἱ μαθηται αυτου, Ιακωβος και Ιωαννης,
ing and the disciples of him, James and John,
ειπον· Κυριε, θελεις ειπωμεν πυρ καταβηναι
said; O lord, wilt thou we speak fire to come down
απο του ουρανου, και αναλωσαι αυτους, *[ὡς και
from the heaven, and to consume them, [as even
Ηλιας εποιησε;] 55 Στραφεις δε επετιμησεν
Elias did?] Turning and he rebuked
αυτοις, [και ειπεν· Ουκ οιδατε, οἱου πνευματος
them, [and said; Not you know, of what spirit
εστε ὑμεις;] 56 Και επορευθησαν εις ἑτεραν
are you?] And they went to another
κωμην.
village.

57 *[Εγενετο] δε πορευομενων αυτων εν τῃ
[It happened] and going of them in the
ὁδῳ, ειπε τις προς αυτον· Ακολουθησω σοι,
way, said one to him; I will follow thee,
ὁπου αν απερχῃ, *[κυριε.] 58 Και ειπεν αυτῳ
wherever thou mayest go, [O master.] And said to him
ὁ Ιησους· Αἱ αλωπεκες φωλεους εχουσι, και τα
the Jesus; The foxes dens have, and the

49 ‡And *John answering said, "Master, we saw one expelling *Demons in thy NAME; and we forbade him, Because he does not follow us."

50 But *Jesus said, "Forbid him not; ‡for he who is not against you is for you."

51 Now it occurred, when the DAYS of his †RETIREMENT were COMPLETED, he resolutely set his FACE to GO to Jerusalem.

52 And he sent Messengers before him; and having gone, they went into a Village of the Samaritans, in order to make preparation for him.

53 And ‡they did not receive him, Because he was going towards Jerusalem.

54 And *his DISCIPLES, James and John, observing this, said, "Master, dost thou wish that we command Fire to come down from HEAVEN, to consume them?"

55 But turning he rebuked them;

56 and they went to Another Village.

57 ‡And as they were travelling on the ROAD, one said to him, "I will follow thee wherever thou goest."

58 And *Jesus said to him, "The FOXES have Holes, and the BIRDS of

* VATICAN MANUSCRIPT.—49. John. 49. Demons. 50. Jesus. 54. the DISCIPLES. 54. as even Elias did—*omit*. 55. and said, "Know ye not of what spirit you are"—*omit*. 57. It happened—*omit*. 57. O master—*omit*. 58. Jesus.

† 51. "I think the word *analepseos* must signify, of Jesus's *retiring* or *withdrawing* himself, and not of his being *received up*; because the word *sumpleerousthai* here used before it, denotes a time *completed*, which that of his *ascension* was not then. The sense is, that the time was come, when Jesus was no longer to retire from Judea and the parts about Jerusalem as he had hitherto done; for he had lived altogether in *Galilee*, lest the Jews should have laid hold on him, before the work of his ministry was ended, and full proofs of his divine mission given, and some of the prophecies concerning him accomplished. John says, chap. vii. 1, *Jesus walked in Galilee; for he would not walk in Jewry, because the Jews sought to kill him.* Let it be observed, that all which follows here in Luke to chap. xix. 45, is represented by him, as done by Jesus in his last journey from Galilee to Jerusalem."—*Pearce*.

‡ 49. Mark ix. 38; see Num. xi. 28. ‡ 50. See Matt. xii. 30; Luke xi. 23. ‡ 53. John iv. 4, 9. ‡ 57. Matt. viii. 19.

πετεινα του ουρανου κατασκηνωσεις· ὁ δε υἱος
birds of the heaven roosts; the but son
του ανθρωπου ουκ εχει, που την κεφαλην κλινῃ.
of the man not has, where the head he may rest.
59 Ειπε δε προς ἑτερον· Ακολουθει μοι. Ὁ δε
He said and to another; Follow me. He but
ειπε· Κυριε, επιτρεψον μοι απελθοντι πρωτον
said; O master, permit thou me having gone first
θαψαι τον πατερα μου. 60 Ειπε δε αυτῳ ὁ
to bury the father of me. Said and to him the
Ιησους· Αφες τους νεκρους θαψαι τους ἑαυτων
Jesus; Leave the dead ones to bury the of themselves
νεκρους· συ δε απελθων διαγγελλε την βασι-
dead ones; thou and having gone publish the king-
λειαν του θεου. 61 Ειπε δε και ἑτερος· Ακολου-
dom of the God. Said and also another; I will
θησω σοι, κυριε· πρωτον δε επιτρεψον μοι
follow thee, O master; first but permit thou me
αποταξασθαι τοις εις τον οικον μου. 62 Ειπε δε
to bid farewell to those in the house of me. Said but
*[προς αυτον] ὁ Ιησους· Ουδεις επιβαλων την
[to him] the Jesus; No one having put the
χειρα αὑτου επ' αροτρον, και βλεπων εις τα
hand of himself on a plough, and looking for the things
οπισω, ευθετος εστιν εις την βασιλειαν του θεου.
behind, well-disposed is for the kingdom of the God.

ΚΕΦ. ι'. 10.

1 Μετα δε ταυτα ανεδειξεν ὁ κυριος *[και]
After now these things appointed the lord [also]
ἑτερους εβδομηκοντα, και απεστειλεν αυτους
others seventy, and sent them
ανα δυο προ προσωπου αὑτου εις πασαν πολιν
each two before face of himself into every city
και τοπον, οὑ εμελλεν αυτος ερχεσθαι. 2 Ελε-
and place, where was about he to go. He
γεν ουν προς αυτους· Ὁ μεν θερισμος πολυς,
said then to them; The indeed harvest great,
οἱ δε εργαται ολιγοι· δεηθητε ουν του κυριου
the but laborers few; implore therefore the lord
του θερισμου, ὁπως εκβαλῃ εργατας εις τον
of the harvest, that he would send out laborers into the
θερισμον αὑτου. 3 Ὑπαγετε· ιδου, εγω αποσ-
harvest of himself. Go you; lo, I send
τελλω ὑμας ὡς αρνας εν μεσῳ λυκων. 4 Μη
you as lambs in midst of wolves. Not
βασταζετε βαλαντιον, μη πηραν μηδε ὑποδη-
carry you a purse, nor a bag nor san-
ματα· και μηδενα κατα την ὁδον ασπασησθε.
dals; and no one by the way salute.
5 Εις ἡν δ' αν οικιαν εισερχησθε, πρωτον λεγετε·
Into what and ever house you may enter, first say you.
Ειρηνη τῳ οικῳ τουτῳ. 6 Και εαν ῃ εκει
Peace to the house this. And if may be there
υἱος ειρηνης, επαναπαυσεται επ' αυτον ἡ ειρηνη
a son of peace, shall rest on him the peace

HEAVEN places of shelter; but the SON of MAN has not where he may recline his HEAD."

59 ‡And he said to another, "Follow me." But HE said, "Sir, permit me first to go and bury my FATHER."

60 *And he said to him, "Leave the DEAD ONES to inter THEIR own Dead; but go thou and publish the KINGDOM of GOD."

61 And another also said, "Sir, ‡I will follow thee; but permit me first to set in order my affairs at HOME."

62 But JESUS said, "No one, having put his HAND on the Plough, and looking BEHIND, is properly disposed towards the KINGDOM of GOD."

CHAPTER X.

1 Now after this, the LORD appointed *Seventy Others, and ‡sent them two by two before him into Every City and Place, where he was about to go.

2 *And he said to them, ‡"The HARVEST indeed is plenteous, but the REAPERS are few; beseech, therefore, the LORD of the HARVEST, that he would send out Laborers to REAP it.

3 Go; ‡behold, *I send you forth as Lambs among Wolves.

4 ‡Carry no Purse, nor Bag, nor Shoes, and salute no one by the ROAD.

5 ‡And into Whatever House you enter, say first, 'Peace to this HOUSE.'

6 And if a Son of Peace is there, your PEACE shall

* VATICAN MANUSCRIPT.—60. And he said. 62. to him—omit. 1. Seventy-two, and sent. 1. also—omit. 2. and he said. 3. I send.

‡ 59. Matt. viii. 21. ‡ 61. See 1 Kings xix. 20. ‡ 1. Matt. x. 1; Mark vi. 7. ‡ 2. Matt. ix. 37, 38; John iv. 35. ‡ 3. Matt. x. 16. ‡ 4. Matt. x. 9, 10; Mark vi. 8; Luke ix. 3. ‡ 5. Matt. x. 12.

ὑμων· ει δε μηγε, εφ᾽ ὑμας ανακαμψει. 7 Εν
of you; if but not, on you it shall return. In
αυτῃ δε τῃ οικιᾳ μενετε, εσθιοντες και πινοντες
this and the house remain, eating and drinking
τα παρ᾽ αυτων· αξιος γαρ ὁ εργατης του
the things with them: worthy for the laborer of the
μισθου αὑτου εστι.
reward of himself is.
Μη μεταβαινετε εξ οικιας εις οικιαν. 8 Και
Not go you from house to house. Also
εις ἡν δ᾽ αν πολιν εισερχησθε, και δεχωνται
into what and ever city you may enter, and they may receive
ὑμας, εσθιετε τα παρατιθεμενα ὑμιν, 9 και
you, eat you the things being set before you, and
θεραπευετε τους εν αυτῃ ασθενεις, και λεγετε
cure you those in her sick, and say you
αυτοις· Ηγγικεν εφ᾽ ὑμας ἡ βασιλεια του θεου.
to them; Has come nigh to you the kingdom of the God.
10 Εις ἡν δ᾽ αν πολιν εισερχησθε, και μη
Into what but ever city you may enter, and not
δεχωνται ὑμας, εξελθοντες εις τας πλατειας
they may receive you, going out into the wide places
αυτης, ειπατε· 11 Και τον κονιορτον, τον κολλη-
of her, say you: Even the dust, that clea-
θεντα ἡμιν εκ της πολεως ὑμων, απομασσομεθα
ving to us from the city of you, we wipe off
ὑμιν· πλην τουτο γινωσκετε, ὁτι ηγγικεν ἡ
for you: however this know you, that has approached the
βασιλεια του θεου. 12 Λεγω ὑμιν, ὁτι Σοδομοις
kingdom of the God. I say to you, that for Sodom
εν τῃ ἡμερᾳ εκεινῃ ανεκτοτερον εσται η τῃ
in the day that more tolerable it will be than the
πολει εκεινῃ. 13 Ουαι σοι, Χοραζιν, ουαι σοι,
city that. Woe to thee, Chorasin, woe to thee,
Βηθσαιδα· ὁτι ει εν Τυρῳ και Σιδωνι εγενοντο
Bethsaida: for if in Tyre and Sidon had been done
αἱ δυναμεις, αἱ γενομεναι εν ὑμιν, παλαι αν εν
the miracles, those being done in you, long ago would in
σακκῳ και σποδῳ καθημεναι μετενοησαν.
sackcloth and ashes sitting they have reformed.
14 Πλην Τυρῳ και Σιδωνι ανεκτοτερον εσται εν
But for Tyre and Sidon more tolerable it will be in
τῃ κρισει, η ὑμιν. 15 Και συ, Καπερναουμ, ἡ
the judgment, than for you. And thou, Capernaum, which
ἑως του ουρανου ὑψωθεισα, ἑως ᾁδου κατα-
even to the heaven art being exalted, even to invisibility down
βιβασθησῃ. 16 Ὁ ακουων ὑμων, εμου ακουει·
shalt be brought. He hearing you, me hears:

rest on him; but if not, it shall return to you.

7 ‡ And in That HOUSE remain, eating and drinking the THINGS with them; for the LABORER is worthy of his REWARD. Go not from House to House.

8 And into Whatever City you enter, and they receive you, eat WHAT is PLACED BEFORE you;

9 and ‡ cure the SICK in it, and say to them, 'The KINGDOM of GOD has approached you.'

10 But into Whatever City you enter, and they receive you not, going out into its WIDE PLACES, say,—

11 ‡ 'even THAT DUST of your CITY which adheres * to our FEET, we wipe off for you; however, know this, That the KINGDOM of GOD has approached.'

12 But I tell you, ‡ that it will be more tolerable for Sodom, in that DAY, than for that CITY.

13 ‡ Woe to thee, Chorasin! woe to thee, Bethsaida! For if THOSE MIRACLES which are BEING PERFORMED in you, had been done in Tyre and Sidon, they would have reformed long ago, sitting † in Sackcloth and Ashes.

14 But it will be more tolerable for Tyre and Sidon, in the JUDGMENT, than for you.

15 ‡ And thou, Capernaum, THOU * which art BEING EXALTED to HEAVEN, wilt be brought down to † Hades.

16 ‡ HE who HEARS you, hears Me; and HE who

* VATICAN MANUSCRIPT.—11. to our FEET, we. 15. shalt not be exalted to HEAVEN, thou shalt go down.

† 13. This expression of mourning and sorrow was frequent in the East. Thus Tamar signified her distress when dishonored by Amnon, 2 Sam. xiii. 9. Thus also, "When Mordecai perceived all that was done, Mordecai rent his clothes, and put on sackcloth and ashes," Esther iv. 1. Thus Job expressed his repentance, Job xlii. 6. Thus Daniel "set his face unto the Lord God, to seek by prayer and supplication, with fasting, and sackcloth and ashes," Dan. ix. 3. Other nations adopted the practice, and it became a very common method, whereby to exhibit great grief and misery.—*Burder.* † 15. See note on Matt. xi. 23.

‡ 7. Matt. x. 11. ‡ 9. Luke ix. 2. ‡ 11. Matt. x. 14; Luke ix. 5; Acts xiii. 51; xviii. 6. ‡ 12. Matt. x. 15; Mark vi. 11. ‡ 13. Matt. xi. 21. ‡ 15. Matt. xi. 23. ‡ 16. Matt. x. 40; Mark ix. 37; John xiii. 20.

και ὁ αθετων ὑμας εμε αθετει· ὁ δε εμε αθετων,
and he rejecting you me rejects: he and me rejecting,
αθετει, τον αποστειλαντα με.
rejects, the one sending me.

17 Ὑπεστρεψαν δε οἱ ἑβδομηκοντα μετα χαρας,
Having returned and the seventy with joy,
λεγοντες· Κυριε, και τα δαιμονια ὑποτασσεται
saying: O lord, and the demons are subject
ἡμιν εν τῳ ονοματι σου. 18 Ειπε δε αυτοις· Εθεω-
to us in the name of thee. He said and to them; I be-
ρουν τον σαταναν ὡς αστραπην εκ του ουρανου
held the adversary as lightning out of the heaven
πεσοντα. 19 Ιδου, διδωμι ὑμιν την εξουσιαν
having fallen. Lo, I give to you the authority
του πατειν επανω οφεων και σκορπιων, και επι
of the to tread on serpents and scorpions, and on
πασαν την δυναμιν του εχθρου· και ουδεν ὑμας
all the power of the enemy; and nothing you
ου μη αδικηση. 20 Πλην εν τουτῳ μη χαιρετε,
not not you may hurt. But in this not rejoice,
ὁτι τα πνευματα ὑμιν ὑποτασσεται· χαιρετε δε,
that the spirits to you are subject; rejoice you but,
ὁτι τα ονοματα ὑμων εγραφη εν τοις ουρανοις.
that the names of you are written in the heavens.

21 Εν αυτῃ τῃ ὡρᾳ ηγαλλιασατο τῳ πνευματι
In this the hour exulted the spirit
ὁ Ιησους, και ειπεν· Εξομολογουμαι σοι, πατερ,
the Jesus, and said; I praise thee, O father,
κυριε του ουρανου και της γης, ὁτι απεκρυψας
O lord of the heaven and the earth, that thou hast hid
ταυτα απο σοφων και συνετων, και απεκαλυψας
these things from wise men and discerning men, and thou hast revealed
αυτα νηπιοις· ναι, ὁ πατηρ, ὁτι οὑτως εγενετο
them to babes; yes, the father, for even so it was
ευδοκια εμπροσθεν σου. 22 Παντα μοι παρεδοθη
good in presence of thee. All to me are given
ὑπο του πατρος μου· και ουδεις γινωσκει, τις
by the father of me; and no one knows, who
εστιν ὁ υἱος ει μη ὁ πατηρ· και τις εστιν ὁ
is the son if not the father; and who is the
πατηρ, ει μη ὁ υἱος, και ᾡ εαν βουληται ὁ
father, if not the son, and to whom may be willing the
υἱος αποκαλυψαι. 23 Και στραφεις προς τους
son to reveal. And turning to the
μαθητας, κατ' ιδιαν ειπε· Μακαριοι οἱ οφθαλμοι,
disciples, privately he said; Blessed the eyes,
οἱ βλεποντες, ἁ βλεπετε. 24 Λεγω γαρ ὑμιν,
those seeing, what you see. I say for to you,
ὁτι πολλοι προφηται και βασιλεις ηθελησαν
that many prophets and kings desired
ιδειν, ἁ ὑμεις βλεπετε, και ουκ ειδον· και
to see, what you see, and not saw: and
ακουσαι, ἁ ακουετε, και ουκ ηκουσαν.
to hear, what you hear, and not heard.

REJECTS you, rejects Me; and he who REJECTS Me, rejects HIM who SENT me."

17 And the *SEVENTY returned with Joy, saying, "Lord, even the DEMONS are subject to us by thy NAME."

18 And he said to them, "I saw the ADVERSARY falling from HEAVEN like Lightning.

19 Behold, *I have given you AUTHORITY to TREAD on Serpents and Scorpions, and on All *THAT POWER which is of the ENEMY; and nothing shall by any means injure You;

20 but rejoice not in this, That the SPIRITS are subject to you; but rejoice That ‡your NAMES *have been enrolled in the HEAVENS."

21 ‡In That HOUR *he exulted in the HOLY SPIRIT, and said, "I adore thee, O Father, Lord of HEAVEN and EARTH, Because, having concealed these things from the Wise and Intelligent, thou hast revealed them to Babes; yes, FATHER; For thus it was well-pleasing in thy sight.

22 ‡All things are imparted to me by my FATHER; and no one, knows who the SON is, except the FATHER; and who the FATHER is, except the SON, and he to whom the SON may be disposed to reveal him."

23 And turning to his DISCIPLES, he said privately, ‡"Happy are THOSE EYES which SEE what you see;

24 For I tell you, ‡That Many Prophets and Kings desired to see the things which you see, and saw them not; and to hear the things which you *hear, and heard them not."

* VATICAN MANUSCRIPT.—17. SEVENTY-TWO. 19. I have given. 19. THAT POWER which is of the ENEMY. 20. have been enrolled in. 21. he exulted in the HOLY SPIRIT, and. 24. hear of me, and.

‡ 20. Phil. iv. 3; Heb. xii. 23; Rev. iii. 5; xxi. 27. ‡ 21. Matt. xi. 27. ‡ 22. Matt. xxviii. 18; John iii. 35; v. 27; xvii. 2. ‡ 23. Matt. xiii. 16. ‡ 24. 1 Pet. i. 10.

25 Και ιδου, νομικος τις ανεστη, εκπειραζων
And lo, a lawyer certain stood up, tempting
αυτον, και λεγων· Διδασκαλε, τι ποιησας ζωην
him, and saying; O teacher, what shall I do life
αιωνιον κληρονομησω; 26 Ὁ δε ειπε προς αυτον·
age-lasting I may inherit? He and said to him;
Εν τῳ νομῳ τι γεγραπται; πως αναγινωσκεις;
In the law what has been written? how readest thou?
27 Ὁ δε αποκριθεις ειπεν· "Αγαπησεις κυριον
He and answering said: "Thou shalt love Lord
τον θεον σου εξ ὁλης της καρδιας σου, και εξ
the God of thee out of whole of the heart of thee, and out of
ὁλης της ψυχης σου, και εξ ὁλης της ισχυος
whole of the soul of thee, and out of whole of the strength
σου, και εξ ὁλης της διανοιας σου· και τον
of thee, and out of whole of the mind of thee: and the
πλησιον σου ὡς σεαυτον." 28 Ειπε δε αυτῳ·
neighbor of thee as thyself." He said and to him:
Ορθως απεκριθης· τουτο ποιει, και ζησῃ. 29 Ὁ
Rightly thou hast answered: this do, and thou shalt live. He
δε θελων δικαιουν ἑαυτον, ειπε προς τον Ιησουν·
but choosing to justify himself, said to the Jesus:
Και τις εστι μου πλησιον; 30 Ὑπολαβων *[δε] ὁ
And who is of me a neighbor? Replying and the
Ιησους ειπεν· Ανθρωπος τις κατεβαινεν απο
Jesus said: A man certain was going down from
Ἱερουσαλημ εις Ἱεριχω, και λησταις περιεπεσεν·
Jerusalem to Jericho, and robbers fell among:
οἱ και εκδυσαντες αυτον και πληγας επιθεντες,
who both stripping him and blows having inflicted,
απηλθον, αφεντες ἡμιθανη τυγχανοντα. 31 Κατα
they departed, leaving half-dead being. By
συγκυριαν δε ἱερευς τις κατεβαινεν εν τῃ ὁδῳ
chance and a priest certain was going down in the way
εκεινῃ, και ιδων αυτον, αντιπαρηλθεν. 32 Ὁμοιως
that, and seeing him, passed along. In like manner
δε και Λευιτης, *[γενομενος] κατα τον τοπον,
and also a Levite, [having come] near the place,
ελθων και ιδων, αντιπαρηλθε. 33 Σαμαρειτης δε
coming and seeing, passed along. A Samaritan but
τις ὁδευων, ηλθε κατ' αυτον, και ιδων αυτον,
certain traveling, came near him, and seeing him,
εσπλαγχνισθη. 34 Και προσελθων κατεδησε
he was moved with pity. And having approached he bound
τα τραυματα αυτου, επιχεων ελαιον και οινον·
the wounds of him, pouring on oil and wine:
επιβιβασας δε αυτον επι το ιδιον κτηνος ηγαγεν
having set and him on the own beast led
αυτον εις πανδοχειον, και επεμεληθη αυτου.
him to an inn, and he took care of him.
35 Και επι την αυριον *[εξελθων,] εκβαλων
And on the next day [having come out,] having taken out
δυο δηναρια εδωκε τῳ πανδοχει, και ειπεν
two denarii he gave to the innkeeper. and said
*[αυτῳ·] Επιμεληθητι αυτου· και ὁ, τι αν
[to him:] Take care of him: and whatever

25 And, behold, a certain Lawyer, stood up to try him, saying, ‡"Teacher, what shall I do to inherit aionian Life?"

26 And HE said to him, "What is written in the LAW? How dost thou read?"

27 And HE answering, said, ‡"Thou shalt love "Jehovah thy GOD with "All thy HEART, and with "All thy SOUL, and with "All thy STRENGTH, and "with All thy MIND, and "‡ thy NEIGHBOR as thyself."

28 And HE said to him, "Thou hast answered correctly; ‡ do this, and thou shalt live."

29 But HE, wishing ‡ to justify himself, said to JESUS, "Who is My Neighbor?"

30 JESUS replying, said, "A certain Man was going down from Jerusalem to Jericho, and fell among Robbers, who both having stripped him, and inflicted blows, they departed, leaving him half dead.

31 And by Chance a certain Priest was going down that ROAD, and seeing him, he passed along.

32 And in like manner also a Levite, coming near the PLACE, and seeing, passed along.

33 But a certain ‡ Samaritan traveling, came near him, and seeing him, he was moved with pity;

34 and approaching, he bound up his WOUNDS, pouring on Oil and Wine, and having placed him on his OWN Beast, brought him to an Inn, and took care of him.

35 And on the NEXT DAY, having taken out Two Denarii, he gave them to the INNKEEPER, and said, 'Take care of him, and

* VATICAN MANUSCRIPT.—30. And—*omit.* 32. having come—*omit.* 35. having come out—*omit.* 35. to him—*omit.*

‡ 25. Matt. xix. 16; xxii. 35. ‡ 27. Deut. vi. 5. ‡ 27. Lev. xix. 18. ‡ 28. Lev. xviii. 5; Neh. ix. 29; Ezek. xx. 11; xiii. 21; Rom. x. 5. ‡ 29. Luke xvi. 15. ‡ 33. John iv. 9.

προσδαπανησης, εγω, εν τῳ επανερχεσθαι με,
thou mayest expend more, I, in the return me,
αποδωσω σοι. 36 Τις *[ουν] τουτων των τριων
I will pay to thee. Which [then] of them of the three
πλησιον δοκει σοι γεγονεναι του εμπεσοντος
a neighbor seems to thee to have been to the having fallen
εις τους λῃστας; 37 Ὁ δε ειπεν· Ὁ ποιησας το
among the robbers; He and said; He having shown the
ελεος μετ' αυτου. Ειπεν δε αυτῳ ὁ Ιησους·
pity towards him. Said and to him the Jesus;
Πορευου, και συ ποιει ὁμοιως.
Go, and thou do in like manner.
38 *[Εγενετο] δε εν τῳ πορευεσθαι αυτους,
[It happened] and in the to go them,
*[και] αυτος εισηλθεν εις κωμην τινα· γυνη δε
[and] he entered into a village certain; a woman and
τις ονοματι Μαρθα, ὑπεδεξατο αυτον *[εις τον
certain to a name Martha, received him [into the
οικον αὑτης.] 39 Και τῃδε ην αδελφη καλουμενη
house of herself.] And to her was a sister having been called
Μαρια, η και παρακαθισασα παρα τους ποδας
Mary, who also having sat at the feet
του Ιησου, ηκουε τον λογον αυτου. 40 Ἡ δε
of the Jesus, heard the word of him. The but
Μαρθα περιεσπατο περι πολλην διακονιαν·
Martha was-over-busied about much serving;
επιστασα δε ειπε· Κυριε, ου μελει σοι, ὁτι ἡ
having come near and said; O lord, not concerns thee, that the
αδελφη μου μονην με κατελιπε διακονειν; ειπε
sister of me alone me has left to serve? say
ουν αυτῃ, ἱνα μοι συναντιλαβηται. 41 Αποκρι-
then to her, that to me she may give aid. Answer-
θεις δε ειπεν αυτῃ ὁ Ιησους· Μαρθα, Μαρθα,
ing and said to her the Jesus; Martha, Martha,
μεριμνας και τυρβαζῃ περι πολλα· 42 ἑνος δε
thou art anxious and troubled about many things; of one but
εστι χρεια. Μαρια δε την αγαθην μεριδα
is need. Mary and the good part
εξελεξατο, ἡτις ουκ αφαιρεθησεται απ' αυτης.
has chosen, which not shall be taken away from her.

ΚΕΦ. ια'. 11.

1 Και εγενετο εν τῳ ειναι αυτον εν τοπῳ τινι
And it happened in the to be him in a place certain
προσευχομενον, ὡς επαυσατο, ειπε τις των
praying, when he ceased, said one of the
μαθητων αυτου προς αυτον· Κυριε, διδαξον ἡμας
disciples of him to him: O lord, teach us
προσευχεσθαι, καθως και Ιωαννης εδιδαξε τους
to pray, as even John taught the
μαθητας αυτου. 2 Ειπε δε αυτοις· Ὁταν προσ-
disciples of himself. He said and to them; When you
ευχησθε, λεγετε· Πατηρ, ἁγιασθητω το ονομα
pray, say; O father, be hallowed the name
σου· ελθετω σου ἡ βασιλεια· 3 τον αρτον ἡμων
of thee: let come of thee the kingdom: the bread of us
τον επιουσιον διδου ἡμιν το καθ' ἡμεραν· 4 Και
the necessary give thou to us the every day: and

whatever thou mayest expend more, ‡, at my RETURN, will pay thee.'

36 Now which of These THREE, thinkest thou, was Neighbor to HIM who FELL among the ROBBERS?"

37 And HE said, "HE who MANIFESTED PITY towards him." And JESUS said to him, "Go, and do thou in like manner."

38 Now as they WENT on, he entered a certain Village; and a certain Woman, named ‡ Martha, entertained him.

39 And SHE had a Sister called Mary, who also, ‡ sitting at * the FEET of the LORD, heard his WORD.

40 But MARTHA was perplexed with Much Serving; and coming near, she said, "Master, dost thou not care That my SISTER has left Me to serve alone? Tell her, then, to assist me."

41 And * the LORD answering, said to her, "Martha, Martha, thou art anxious, and troublest thyself about many things;

42 but * of few things, or of one, is there Need; and Mary has chosen the GOOD Part, which shall not be taken away from her."

CHAPTER XI.

1 And it occurred, as he was PRAYING in a certain Place, when he ceased, one of his DISCIPLES said to him, "Master, teach us to pray, even as John taught his DISCIPLES."

2 And he said to them, "When you pray say, ‡ O Father, Revered be thy NAME! let Thy KINGDOM come;

3 give us DAY BY DAY our NECESSARY FOOD;

* VATICAN MANUSCRIPT.—36. then—*omit.* 38. It happened—*omit.* 38. and—*omit.* 38. into her house—*omit.* 39. the FEET of the LORD. 41. the LORD answering. 42. of few things, or of one, is there Need; and.

‡ 38. John. xi. 1; xii. 2, 3. ‡ 39. Luke viii. 35; Acts xxii. 3. ‡ 2. Matt. vi. 9.

αφες ἡμιν τας αμαρτιας ἡμων, και γαρ αυτοι
forgive to us the sins of us, even for ourselves
αφιεμεν παντι οφειλοντι ἡμιν· και μη εισενεγ-
forgive all owing us; and not thou mayest
κης ἡμας εις πειρασμον. 5 Και ειπε προς αυτους·
lead us into temptation. And he said to them,
Τις εξ ὑμων ἑξει φιλον, και πορευσεται προς
Which of you shall have a friend, and shall go to
αυτον μεσονυκτιου, και ειπῃ αυτῳ· Φιλε,
him at midnight, and say to him; O friend,
χρησον μοι τρεις αρτους· 6 επειδη φιλος μου
lend to me three loaves; because a friend of me
παρεγενετο εξ ὁδου προς με, και ουκ εχω ὁ
has come from a way to me, and not I have what
παραθησω αυτῳ· 7 κακεινος εσωθεν αποκριθεις
I shall set for him; And he from within answering
ειπῃ· Μη μοι κοπους παρεχε· ηδη ἡ θυρα
should say; Not to me trouble do thou cause; already the door
κεκλεισται, και τα παιδια μου μετ' εμου εις την
has been shut, and the children of me with me in the
κοιτην εισιν· ου δυναμαι αναστας δουναι σοι.
bed are; not I am able having arisen to give to thee.
8 Λεγω ὑμιν, ει και ου δωσει αυτῳ αναστας,
I say to you, if and not will give to him having arisen,
δια το ειναι αυτου φιλον, δια γε την αναιδειαν
because the to be of him a friend, through indeed the importunity
αυτου εγερθεις δωσει αυτῳ ὁσων χρῃζει. 9 Κα-
of him arising he will give to him as many as he wants. And
γω ὑμιν λεγω· Αιτειτε, και δοθησεται ὑμιν·
I to you say; Ask you, and it shall be given to you;
ζητειτε, και εὑρησετε· κρουετε, και ανοιγησε-
seek you, and you shall find: knock you, and it shall be
ται ὑμιν. 10 Πας γαρ ὁ αιτων λαμβανει· και
opened to you. All for the asking receives: and
ὁ ζητων εὑρισκει· και τῳ κρουοντι ανοιγησεται.
the seeking finds; and to the knocking it shall be opened.
11 Τινα δε ὑμων τον πατερα αιτησει ὁ υἱος αρτον,
Which now of you the father shall ask the son bread,
μη λιθον επιδωσει αυτῳ; η και ιχθυν, μη αντι
not a stone will give to him? or also a fish, not in place of
ιχθυος οφιν επιδωσει αυτῳ; 12 η και εαν αιτησῃ
a fish a serpent will give to him? or also if he may ask
ωον, μη επιδωσει αυτῳ σκορπιον; 13 Ει ουν
an egg, not will give to him a scorpion? If then
ὑμεις, πονηροι ὑπαρχοντες, οιδατε δοματα
you, evil being, know you gifts
αγαθα διδοναι τοις τεκνοις ὑμων, ποσῳ μαλλον
good to give to the children of you, how much more
ὁ πατηρ, ὁ εξ ουρανου, δωσει πνευμα ἁγιον τοις
the father, that of heaven, will give a spirit holy to those
αιτουσιν αυτον;
asking him?

14 Και ην εκβαλλων δαιμονιον, και αυτου ην
And he was casting out a demon, and it was

4 and forgive us our SINS; for we ourselves also forgive every one who is indebted to us; and abandon us not to Trial."

5 And he said to them, "Which of you shall have a Friend, and shall go to him at Midnight, and say to him, 'Friend, lend me Three Loaves;

6 for a Friend of mine has come to me out of his Road, and I have nothing to place before him?'

7 And he answering from within should say, 'Do not trouble me; the DOOR is now closed, and my CHILDREN are with me in BED; I cannot rise to give thee.'

8 I tell you, ‡ Though he will not rise and give him because he IS His Friend, yet because of his IMPORTUNITY indeed, he will rise and give him, as many as he needs.

9 ‡ And I say to you, Ask, and it will be given you; seek, and you will find; knock, and it will be opened to you.

10 For EVERY ONE who ASKS, receives; and HE who SEEKS, finds; and to HIM who KNOCKS, the door * is opened.

11 ‡ * And What FATHER among you, who, if his SON request Bread, will give him a Stone? or if he ask for a Fish, will instead of a Fish give him a Serpent?

12 or also, if he should ask an Egg, will give him a Scorpion?

13 If you, then, being Evil, know how to impart good Gifts to your CHILDREN, how much more will the FATHER, THAT OF HEAVEN, give holy Spirit to THOSE who ASK him?"

14 ‡ And he was casting out * a dumb Demon. And

* VATICAN MANUSCRIPT.—10. is opened. 11. If a SON ask a Fish of any one of you that is a FATHER, will he for a fish give him a Serpent? 12. or also, if he ask an Egg, will he give him a Scorpion? 14. dumb Demon. And it.

‡ 8. Luke xviii. 1. ‡ 9. Matt. vii. 7; xxi. 22; Mark xi. 24; John xv 7; James i. 6; 1 John iii. 22. ‡ 11. Matt. vii. 9. ‡ 14. Matt. ix. 32; xii. 22.

κωφον· εγενετο δε του δαιμονιου εξελθοντος,
dumb: it came to pass and of the demon having come out,
ελαλησεν ὁ κωφος· και εθαυμασαν οἱ οχλοι.
spoke the dumb and wondered the crowds.
15 Τινες δε εξ αυτων ειπον· Εν Βεελζεβουλ,
Some but of them said: By Beelzebul,
αρχοντι των δαιμονιων, εκβαλλει τα δαιμονια·
a ruler of the demons, he cast out the demons:
16 ἑτεροι δε πειραζοντες, σημειον παρ' αυτου
others but tempting, a sign from him
εζητουν εξ ουρανου. 17 Αυτος δε ειδως αυτων
sought from heaven. He but knowing of them
τα διανοηματα, ειπεν αυτοις· Πασα βασιλεια,
the thoughts, said to them: Every kingdom,
εφ' ἑαυτην διαμερισθεισα, ερημουται, και
against herself having been divided, is brought to desolation, and
οικος επι οικον πιπτει. 18 Ει δε και ὁ σατανας
house upon house falls. If and also the adversary
εφ' ἑαυτον διεμερισθη, πως σταθησεται ἡ
gainst himself has been divided, how shall stand the
βασιλεια αυτου; ὁτι λεγετε, εν Βεελζεβουλ
kingdom of him? for you say, by Beelzebul
εκβαλλειν με τα δαιμονια. 19 Ει δε εγω εν
to cast out me the demons. If but I by
Βεελζεβουλ εκβαλλω τα δαιμονια, οἱ υἱοι
Beelzebul cast out the demons, the sons
ὑμων εν τινι εκβαλλουσι; Δια τουτο κριται
of you by whom do they cast out? Through this judges
ὑμων αυτοι εσονται. 20 Ει δε εν δακτυλῳ θεου
of you they shall be. If but by a finger of God
εκβαλλω τα δαιμονια, αρα εφθασεν εφ' ὑμας
I cast out the demons, then has suddenly come upon you
ἡ βασιλεια του θεου. 21 Ὁταν ὁ ισχυρος καθω-
the royal majesty of the God. When the strong one having
πλισμενος φυλασσῃ την ἑαυτου αυλην, εν
been armed should he guard the of himself a palace, in
ειρηνῃ εστι τα ὑπαρχοντα αυτου· 22 επαν δε ὁ
peace are the possessions of him; as soon as but the
ισχυροτερος αυτου επελθων νικησῃ αυτον,
stronger of him having entered should overcome him,
την πανοπλιαν αυτου αιρει, εφ' ᾗ επεποιθει,
the arms of him takes away, in which he had confided,
και τα σκυλα αυτου διαδιδωσιν. 23 Ὁ μη ων
and the spoils of him distributed. He not being
μετ' εμου, κατ' εμου εστι· και ὁ μη συναγων
with me, against me is; and he not gathering
μετ' εμου, σκορπιζει. 24 Ὁταν το ακαθαρτον
with me, scatters. When the unclean
πνευμα εξελθῃ απο του ανθρωπου, διερχεται
spirit may come out from the man, passes
δι' ανυδρων τοπων, ζητουν αναπαυσιν· και
through dry places, seeking a resting place; and
μη εὑρισκον, λεγει· Ὑποστρεψω εις τον οικον
not finding, says; I will return into the house
μου, ὁθεν εξηλθον. 25 Και ελθον εὑρισκει
of me, whence I came out. And having come it finds
σεσαρωμενον και κεκοσμημενον. 26 Τοτε πορευε-
having been swept and having been adorned. Then it goes

it came to pass, when the DEMON had departed, the DUMB man spoke, and the CROWDS wondered.

15 But some of them said, "He expels DEMONS through Beelzebul, * the PRINCE of the DEMONS."

16 And others, ‡ trying him, sought of him a Sign from Heaven.

17 But ‡ he knowing Their THOUGHTS, said to them, "Every Kingdom being divided against itself is desolated; and House falls against House.

18 And if the ADVERSARY also is divided against himself, how shall his KINGDOM stand? Because you say that I expel DEMONS through Beelzebul.

19 Besides, if I through Beelzebul expel DEMONS, by whom do your SONS cast them out? Therefore, they will be your JUDGES.

20 But if ‡ by a Finger of God I cast out the DEMONS, † then God's ROYAL MAJESTY has unexpectedly come to you.

21 ‡ When the STRONG one armed guards HIS Palace, his POSSESSIONS are in Safety;

22 but whenever one * stronger than he, having entered should overcome him, he takes away the ARMS in which he confided, and distributes his SPOILS.

23 HE who IS not with me, is against me; and HE who GATHERS not with me, scatters.

24 ‡ When the IMPURE Spirit is gone out of the MAN, it roves through Parched Deserts, seeking a Place of Rest; and not finding one, * then it says, I will return to my HOUSE, from which I came out.

25 And coming, it finds it * empty, swept, and furnished.

26 Then it goes, and

* VATICAN MSS.—15. the PRINCE. 22. stronger. 25. empty swept, and furnished.

† 20. See Note on Matt. xii. 28.

‡ 16. Matt. xvi. 1. ‡ 17. Matt. xii 25; Mark iii. 24; John ii. 25. ‡ 20. Exod. viii. 19. ‡ 21. Matt. xii. 29; Mark iii. 27. ‡ 24. Matt. xii. 43.

ται και παραλαμβανει ἑπτα ἑτερα πνευματα
and takes with seven other spirits
πονηροτερα ἑαυτου, και εισελθοντα κατοικει
more evil of itself, and they having entered dwell
εκει· και γινεται τα εσχατα του ανθρωπου
there; and becomes the last of the man
εκεινου χειρονα των πρωτων. 27 Εγενετο δε εν
that worse of the first. It happened and in
τῳ λεγειν αυτον ταυτα, επαρασα τις γυνη
to the to speak him these things, having lifted certain woman
φωνην εκ του οχλου, ειπεν αυτῳ· Μακαρια ἡ
a voice out of the crowd, said to him; Blessed the
κοιλια ἡ βαστασασα σε, και μαστοι οὑς εθη-
womb that having carried thee, and breasts those thou
λασας. 28 Αυτος δε ειπε· Μενουνγε μακαριοι
hast sucked. He but said; Yea rather blessed
οἱ ακουοντες τον λογον του θεου, και φυλασ-
those hearing the word of the God, and obser-
σοντες.
ving.
29 Των δε οχλων επαθροιζομενων, ηρξατο
The and crowds gathering together, he began
λεγειν· Ἡ γενεα αὑτη πονηρα εστι· σημειον
to say; The generation this evil is; a sign
επιζητει· και σημειον ου δοθησεται αυτῃ, ει μη
it seeks, and a sign not shall be given to her, except
το σημειον Ιωνα. 30 Καθως γαρ εγενετο Ιωνας
the sign of Jonas. Even as for became Jonas
σημειον τοις Νινευιταις, οὑτως εσται και ὁ
a sign to the Ninevites, so will be also the
υἱος του ανθρωπου τῃ γενεᾳ ταυτῃ. 31 Βασιλ-
son of the man to the generation this. A queen
ισσα Νοτου εγερθησεται εν τῃ κρισει μετα των
of south will be raised in the judgment with the
ανδρων της γενεας ταυτης, και κατακρινει
men of the generation this, and will condemn
αυτους· ὁτι ηλθεν εκ των περατων της γης
them; because she came from the ends of the earth
ακουσαι την σοφιαν Σολομωνος· και ιδου, πλειον
to hear the wisdom of Solomon; and lo, a greater
Σολομωνος ὡδε. 32 Ανδρες Νινευι αναστησονται
of Solomon here. Men of Nineveh will stand up
εν τῃ κρισει μετα της γενεας ταυτης, και
in the judgment with the generation this, and
κατακρινουσιν αυτην· ὁτι μετενοησαν εις το
will condemn her; because they reformed at the
κηρυγμα Ιωνα· και ιδου, πλειον Ιωνα ὡδε.
preaching of Jonas; and lo, a greater of Jonas here.
33 Ουδεις δε λυχνον ἁψας, εις κρυπτην
No one and a lamp having lighted, into a secret place
τιθησιν, ουδε ὑπο τον μοδιον, αλλ' επι την
places, neither under the corn-measure, but on the
λυχνιαν, ἱνα οἱ εισπορευομενοι το φεγγος βλε-
lamp-stand, that those entering the light may

takes with it Seven Other Spirits more wicked than itself, and entering, they abide there; and the LAST state of that MAN becomes worse than the FIRST."

27 And it occurred, while he was speaking these things, a Certain Woman from the CROWD, raising her Voice, said to him, ‡ "Happy is THAT WOMB which BORE thee, and those Breasts which thou hast sucked!"

28 But he said, ‡ "Yes, rather, happy THOSE who HEAR the WORD of GOD, and keep it!"

29 And the CROWDS gathering about him, he began to say, * "This GENERATION is a wicked Generation. It demands a Sign; but no Sign will be given it, except the SIGN of Jonah.

30 ‡ For as * JONAH became a Sign to the NINEVITES, thus also will the SON of MAN be to this GENERATION.

31 ‡ The Queen of the South will rise up at the JUDGMENT with the MEN of this GENERATION, and cause them to be condemned; Because she came from the EXTREMITIES of the LAND to hear the WISDOM of Solomon; and behold, one greater than Solomon is here.

32 The Ninevites will stand up in the JUDGMENT with this GENERATION, and cause it to be condemned; ‡ Because they reformed at the WARNING of Jonah; and behold, one greater than Jonah is here.

33 No one having lighted a LAMP, ‡ places it in a Secret place, neither under the CORN-MEASURE, but on the LAMP-STAND; that THOSE ENTERING may see the LIGHT.

---

* VATICAN MANUSCRIPT.—29. This GENERATION is a wicked Generation. 30. Jonah.

‡ 27. Luke i. 28, 48. ‡ 28. Matt. vii. 21; Luke viii. 21; James i. 25. ‡ 30. Jonah i. 17; ii. 10. ‡ 31. 1 Kings x. 1. ‡ 32. Jonah iii. 5. ‡ 33. Matt. v. 15; Mark iv. 21; Luke viii. 16.

πωσιν. 34 Ὁ λυχνος του σωματος εστιν ὁ
see. The lamp of the body is the
οφθαλμος· ὁταν *[ουν] ὁ οφθαλμος σου ἁπλους
eye; when [therefore] the eye of thee sound
ῃ, και ὁλον το σωμα σου φωτεινον εστιν·
may be, also whole the body of thee enlightened is:
επαν δε πονηρος ῃ, και το σωμα σου σκοτεινον.
when but evil may be, also the body of thee darkened.
35 Σκοπει ουν, μη το φως το εν σοι σκοτος εστιν.
Take heed therefore, not the light that in thee darkness is.
36 Ει ουν το σωμα σου ὁλον φωτεινον, μη εχον
If therefore the body of thee whole is enlightened, not having
τι μερος σκοτεινον, εσται φωτεινον ὁλον, ὡς
any part dark, will be enlightened whole, as
ὁταν ὁ λυχνος τῃ αστραπῃ φωτιζῃ σε.
when the lamp by the brightness may enlighten thee.

37 Εν δε τῳ λαλησαι, ηρωτα αυτον Φαρισαιος
In and the to have spoken, asked him a Pharisee
*[τις] ὁπως αριστηση παρ' αυτῳ. Εισελθων
[certain] that he might dine with him. Having entered
δε ανεπεσεν. 38 Ὁ δε Φαρισαιος ιδων εθαυμα-
and he reclined. The and Pharisee seeing wondered
σεν, ὁτι ου πρωτον εβαπτισθη προ του αριστου.
because not first he was dipped before the dinner.
39 Ειπε δε ὁ κυριος προς αυτον· Νυν ὑμεις οἱ
Said and the Lord to him; Now you the
Φαρισαιοι το εξωθεν του ποτηριου και του πινα-
Pharisees the outside of the cup and of the plat-
κος καθαριζετε· το δε εσωθεν ὑμων γεμει
ter you cleanse: the but inside of you is full
ἁρπαγης και πονηριας. 40 Αφρονες, ουχ ὁ
of extortion and of evil. O unwise, not he
ποιησας το εξωθεν, και το εσωθεν εποιησε;
having made the outside, also the inside made?
41 Πλην τα ενοντα δοτε ελεημοσυνην· και
But the things being within give you alms: and
ιδου, παντα καθαρα ὑμιν εστιν. 42 Αλλ' ουαι
lo, all things clean to you is. But woe
ὑμιν τοις Φαρισαιοις, ὁτι αποδεκατουτε το
to you the Pharisees, for you tithe the
ἡδυοσμον, και το πηγανον, και παν λαχανον·
mint, and the rue, and every pot-herb:
και παρερχεσθε την κρισιν και την αγαπην του
and you pass by the justice and the love of the
θεου. Ταυτα εδει ποιησαι, κακεινα μη
God. These things you ought to have done, and those not
αφιεναι.
to omit.

43 Ουαι ὑμιν τοις Φαρισαιοις, ὁτι αγαπατε
Woe to you the Pharisees, for you love

34 ‡The LAMP of the BODY is * thine EYE; when thine EYE is clear, thy Whole BODY also is enlightened; but when it is dim, thy BODY also is darkened.

35 Take heed therefore, that THAT LIGHT which is in thee be not Darkness.

36 If, therefore, thy whole BODY be enlightened, having no Part dark, the Whole will be enlightened, as when the LAMP by its BRIGHTNESS enlightens thee."

37 And while he was speaking a Pharisee invited him † to dine with him; and he went in, and reclined.

38 And ‡ the PHARISEE noticing it, wondered that he did not first † immerse before the DINNER.

39 ‡ And the LORD said to him, "Now you PHARISEES cleanse the OUTSIDE of the CUP and PLATTER; but ‡ your INSIDE is full of Extortion and Wickedness.

40 Senseless men! did not HE who MADE the OUTSIDE make the INSIDE also?

41 ‡But give in Alms the THINGS WITHIN, and behold, all things are pure to you.

42 ‡But Woe to you, PHARISEES! Because you tithe of MINT, and RUE, and Every Pot-herb, but disregard JUSTICE and the LOVE of GOD; these things you ought to practise, and not to omit those.

43 ‡Woe to you, PHARISEES! Because you love

* VATICAN MANUSCRIPT.—34. thine EYE. 34. therefore—*omit.* 37 certain—*omit.*

† 37. Perhaps, rather, "to *breakfast* with him," as *ariston*, signifies a *morning meal.* The Jews made but two meals in the day: their *ariston*, may be called their *breakfast* or their *dinner*, because it was *both*, and was but a slight meal. Their chief meal was their *deipnon* or *supper*, after the heat of the day was over and the same was the principal meal among the *Greeks* and *Romans*. *Josephus*, in his life, says, sec. 54, *that the legal hour of the ariston on the Sabbath was the sixth hour*, or at twelve o'clock at noon, as we call it. What the hour was on the other days of the week, he does not say; but probably it was much the same.—*Pearce.* † 38. Some critics refer this to the dipping of the hands; others to the immersion of the whole person. From Mark vii. 3, 4, it is evident, that both were practised, as well as various other ablutions.

‡ 34. Matt. vi. 22. ‡ 38. Mark vii. 3. ‡ 39. Matt. xxiii. 25. ‡ 39. Titus i. 15. ‡ 41. Isa. lviii. 7; Dan. iv. 27; Luke xii. 33. ‡ 41. Matt. xxiii. 23. ‡ 43. Matt. xxiii. 6; Mark xii. 38, 39.

την πρωτοκαθεδριαν εν ταις συναγωγαις, και
the first seat in the synagogues, and
τους ασπασμους εν ταις αγοραις. 44 Ουαι ὑμιν,
the salutations in the markets. Woe to you,
ὁτι εστε ὡς τα μνημεια τα αδηλα, και οἱ
for you are like the tombs those unseen, and the
ανθρωποι, οἱ περιπατουντες επανω, ουκ οιδασιν.
men, those walking over, not know.
45 Αποκριθεις δε τις των νομικων λεγει αυτῳ·
Answering and one of the lawyers says to him;
Διδασκαλε, ταυτα λεγων και ἡμας ὑβριζεις.
O teacher, these things saying also us thou reproachest.
46 Ὁ δε ειπε· Και ὑμιν τοις νομικοις ουαι, ὁτι
He and said; Also to you the lawyers woe, for
φορτιζετε τους ανθρωπους φορτια δυσβαστακτα,
you load the men burdens oppressive,
και αυτοι ἑνι των δακτυλων ὑμων ου προσ-
and yourselves with one of the fingers of you not you
ψαυετε τοις φορτιοις.
touch the burdens.

47 Ουαι ὑμιν, ὁτι οικοδομειτε τα μνημεια των
Woe to you, for you build the tombs of the
προφητων, οἱ δε πατερες ὑμων απεκτειναν
prophets, the and fathers of you killed
αυτους. 48 Αρα μαρτυρειτε και συνευδοκειτε
them. Therefore you testify and you consent
τοις εργοις των πατερων ὑμων· ὁτι αυτοι μεν
to the works of the fathers of you; for they indeed
απεκτειναν αυτους, ὑμεις δε οικοδομειτε *[αυ-
killed them, you and build [of
των τα μνημεια.] 49 Δια τουτο και ἡ σοφια
them the tombs.] Because of this and the wisdom
του θεου ειπεν· Αποστελω εις αυτους προφητας
of the God said; I will send to them prophets
και αποστολους, και εξ αυτων αποκτενουσι
and apostles, and out of them they will kill
και εκδιωξουσιν· 50 ἱνα εκζητηθῃ το αἱμα παν-
and persecute, so that may be required the blood of
των των προφητων, το εκχυνομενον απο κατα-
all of the prophets, that being shed from a lay-
βολης κοσμου, απο της γενεας ταυτης· 51 απο
ing down of a world, from the generation this; from
του αἱματος Αβελ ἑως του αἱματος Ζαχαριου,
the blood of Abel to the blood of Zecharias,
του απολομενου μεταξυ του θυσιαστηριου και
that having perished between the altar and
του οικου. Ναι λεγω ὑμιν, εκζητηθησεται απο
the house. Yes I say to you, it will be required from
της γενεας ταυτης.
the generation this.

52 Ουαι ὑμιν τοις νομικοις, ὁτι ηρατε την
Woe to you the lawyers. for you took away the
κλειδα της γνωσεως· αυτοι ουκ εισηλθετε, και
key of the knowledge; yourselves not you entered, and
τους εισερχομενους εκωλυσατε. 53 Λεγοντος δε
those entering you hindered. Saying and

the CHIEF SEAT in the SYNAGOGUES, and SALUTATIONS in the PUBLIC PLACES.

44 ‡ Woe to you! Because you are like those CONCEALED TOMBS, which MEN WALKING over, know not."

45 Then one of the LAWYERS, answering, says to him, "Teacher, in saying these things thou reproachest Us also."

46 And HE said, "Woe to you, LAWYERS! ‡ For you impose oppressive Burdens on MEN, and yet, you yourselves touch not the BURDENS with one of your FINGERS.

47 ‡ Woe to you! For you build the SEPULCHRES of the PROPHETS, and your FATHERS killed them.

48 Thus you testify that you approve the ACTS of your FATHERS; For they, indeed, killed them, and you build.

49 And because of this, the WISDOM of GOD said, ‡ 'I will send them Prophets and Apostles, and some of them they will kill and persecute;'

50 so that the BLOOD of All the PROPHETS being shed from the Formation of the World, may be required of this GENERATION;

51 from the * Blood of Abel to the * Blood of THAT Zechariah, † who will perish between the ALTAR and the HOUSE. Yes, I tell you, it will be required of this GENERATION.

52 ‡ Woe to you, LAWYERS! Because you have taken away the KEY of KNOWLEDGE; you entered not yourselves, and THOSE APPROACHING, you hindered."

* VATICAN MANUSCRIPT—48. Their TOMBS—omit. 51. Blood. 51. Blood.

† 51. See Note on Matt. xxiii. 35.

‡ 44. Matt. xxiii. 27. ‡ 46. Matt. xxiii. 4. ‡ 47. Matt. xxiii. 29. ‡ 49. Matt. xxiii. 34. ‡ 52. Matt. xxiii. 14.

αυτου ταυτα προς αυτους, ηρξαντο οἱ γραμματεις
of him these things to them, began the scribes
και οἱ Φαρισαιοι δεινως ενεχειν, και αποστο-
and the Pharisees greatly to be incensed, and to make
ματιζειν αυτον περι πλειονων· 54 ενεδρευοντες
speak off-hand him about many things; trying to entrap
αυτον, *[ζητουντες] θηρευσαι τι εκ του
him, [seeking] to catch something out of the
στοματος αυτου, ἱνα κατηγορησωσιν αυτου.
mouth of him, that they might accuse him.
ΚΕΦ. ιβ'. 12. 1 Εν οἱς επισυναχθεισων των
In those having assembled of the
μυριαδων του οχλου, ὡστε καταπατειν αλλη-
myriads of the crowd, so as to tread upon one
λους, ηρξατο λεγειν προς τους μαθητας αὑτου·
another, he began to say to the disciples of himself;
Πρωτον προσεχετε ἑαυτοις απο της ζυμης των
First take heed to yourselves of the leaven of the
Φαρισαιων, ἡτις εστιν ὑποκρισις. 2 Ουδεν δε
Pharisees, which is hypocrisy. Nothing and
συγκεκαλυμμενον εστιν, ὁ ουκ αποκαλυφθησε-
having been covered is, which not shall be uncovered:
ται· και κρυπτον, ὁ ου γνωσθησεται. 3 Ανθ'
and secret, which not shall be known. On which
ὡν ὁσα εν τῃ σκοτιᾳ ειπατε, εν τῳ φωτι
account what in the dark you speak, in the light
ακουσθησεται· και ὁ προς το ους ελαλησατε εν
shall be heard: and what to the ear you spoke in
τοις ταμειοις, κηρυχθησεται επι των δωματων.
the closets, shall be published on the house-tops.
4 Λεγω δε ὑμιν τοις φιλοις μου· Μη φοβηθητε
I say and to you the friends of me: Not you be afraid
απο των αποκτεινοντων το σωμα, και μετα ταυτα
of those killing the body, and after these
μη εχοντων περισσοτερον τι ποιησαι. 5 Ὑπο-
not having more anything to have done. I will
δειξω δε ὑμιν, τινα φοβηθητε· φοβηθητε τον
point out and to you, whom you should fear: you should fear the
μετα το αποκτειναι, εξουσιαν εχοντα εμβαλειν
after the to have killed, authority having to cast
εις την γεενναν· ναι λεγω ὑμιν, τουτον φοβη-
into the Gehenna; yes I say to you, this fear
θητε. 6 Ουχι πεντε στρουθια πωλειται ασσαριων
you. Not five sparrows are sold assarii
δυο; και ἑν εξ αυτων ουκ εστιν επιλελησμενον
two? and one out of them not is being forgotten
ενωπιον του θεου. 7 Αλλα και αἱ τριχες της
in presence of the God. But also the hairs of the
κεφαλης ὑμων πασαι ηριθμηνται. Μη *[ουν]
head of you all have been numbered. Not [therefore]
φοβεισθε· πολλων στρουθιων διαφερετε. 8 Λεγω
fear you: many sparrows you are better. I say
δε ὑμιν· Πας ὁς αν ὁμολογησῃ εν εμοι εμπροσ-
and to you: All whoever may confess to me in pres-
θεν των ανθρωπων, και ὁ υἱος του ανθρωπου
ence of the men, also the son of the man

53 And *having gone out thence, the SCRIBES and PHARISEES began to be extremely angry, and to press him to speak unguardedly on many things;

54 trying to entrap him, and ‡to catch something from his MOUTH, that they might accuse him.

CHAPTER XII.

1 At that time, the CROWD having assembled by TENS OF THOUSANDS, so that they trampled on each other, he began to say to his DISCIPLES, "First, ‡guard yourselves against the LEAVEN of the PHARISEES, which is Hypocrisy.

2 ‡And there is nothing concealed, which will not be discovered; and hid, which will not be made known.

3 Therefore, what you speak in the DARK, will be heard in the LIGHT; and what you whispered to the EAR in CLOSETS, will be proclaimed on the HOUSE-TOPS.

4 ‡But I say to you, my FRIENDS, Be not afraid of THOSE who KILL the BODY, and after this can do no more.

5 But I will show you whom you should fear; Fear HIM, who, after having killed, HAS Authority to cast into GEHENNA; yes, I tell you, Fear him.

6 Are not Five Sparrows sold for two †Assarii? and yet not one of them is forgotten before GOD.

7 But even the HAIRS of your HEAD have all been numbered. Fear not; you are of more value than Many Sparrows.

8 ‡And I say to you, Whoever may acknowledge me before MEN, the SON of

* VATICAN MANUSCRIPT.—53. having gone out thence, the SCRIBES. 54. seeking—omit. 7. therefore—omit.

† 6. An assarion was about one cent and five mills in value, or three farthings sterling.

‡ 54. Mark xii. 13. ‡ 1. Matt. xvi. 6; Mark viii. 15. ‡ 2. Matt. x. 26; Mark iv. 22; Luke viii. 17. ‡ 4. Matt. x. 28; Isa. li. 7, 8, 12; Jer. i. 8. ‡ 8. Matt. x. 32; Mark viii. 38; 2 Tim. ii. 12; 1 John ii. 23.

ὁμολογησει εν αυτῳ εμπροσθεν των αγγελων
will confess in him in presence of the messengers
του θεου. 9 Ὁ δε αρνησαμενος με ενωπιον των
of the God. He but having denied me in presence of the
ανθρωπων, απαρνηθησεται ενωπιον των αγγε-
men, will be denied in presence of the messen-
λων του θεου. 10 Και πας ὁς ερει λογον εις τον
gers of the God. And all who shall speak a word against the
υἱον του ανθρωπου, αφεθησεται αυτῳ· τῳ δε
son of the man, it will be forgiven to him; to the but
εις το ἁγιον πνευμα βλασφημησαντι ουκ αφε-
against the holy spirit having spoken evil not will
θησεται. 11 Ὁταν δε προσφερωσιν ὑμας επι
be forgiven. When and they may may you to
τας συναγωγας και τας αρχας και τας εξουσιας,
the synagogues and the rulers and the authorities,
μη μεριμνατε, πως η τι απολογησησθε, η τι
not be you anxious, how or what you may answer, or what
ειπητε· 12 το γαρ ἁγιον πνευμα διδαξει ὑμας εν
you may say; the for holy spirit will teach you in
αυτῃ τῃ ὡρα, ἁ δει ειπειν.
this the hour, what it is proper to say.

13 Ειπε δε τις αυτῳ εκ του οχλου· Διδασ-
Said and one to him out of the crowd; O tea-
καλε, ειπε τῳ αδελφῳ μου μερισασθαι μετ'
cher, speak to the brother of me to divide with
εμου την κληρονομιαν. 14 Ὁ δε ειπεν αυτῳ·
me the inheritance. He and said to him
Ανθρωπε, τις με κατεστησε δικαστην η μεριστ-
O man, who me appointed a judge or a divi-
την εφ' ὑμας; 15 Ειπε δε προς αυτους· Ὁρατε
der over you? He said and to them; See you
και φυλασσεσθε απο της πλεονεξιας· ὁτι ουκ εν
and beware you of the covetousness; because not in
τῳ περισσευειν τινι ἡ ζωη αυτου εστιν εκ των
the to abound any one the life of him is out of the
ὑπαρχοντων αυτου.
possessions of him.

16 Ειπε δε παραβολην προς αυτους, λεγων·
He spoke and a parable to them, saying;
Ανθρωπου τινος πλουσιου ευφορησεν ἡ χωρα.
A man certain rich yielded plentifully the farm.
17 Και διελογιζετο εν ἑαυτῳ, λεγων· Τι ποιησω;
And he reasoned in himself, saying; What shall I do?
ὁτι ουκ εχω, που συναξω τους καρπους μου.
because not I have, where I will gather the fruits of me.
18 Και ειπε· Τουτο ποιησω· καθελω μου τας
And he said; This will do: I will pull down of me the
αποθηκας, και μειζονας οικοδομησω· και συναξω
barns, and greater I will build: and I will collect
εκει παντα τα γεννηματα μου, και τα αγαθα μου·
there all the products of me, and the fruits of me:
19 και ερω τῃ ψυχῃ μου· Ψυχη, εχεις πολλα
and I will say to the soul of me: Soul, thou hast many

MAN will also acknowledge him in the presence of the ANGELS of GOD.

9 But he who has RENOUNCED me before MEN, will be renounced in the presence of the ANGELS of GOD.

10 ‡ And every one who may speak a Word against the SON of MAN, it will be forgiven him; but HE who BLASPHEMES against the HOLY Spirit shall not be forgiven.

11 ‡ And when they may bring you to the SYNAGOGUES, and the RULERS, and the MAGISTRATES, be not anxious how you may defend yourselves, or what you may say;

12 for the HOLY Spirit will instruct you, in that HOUR, what it is proper to say."

13 Then one out of the CROWD said to him, "O Teacher, speak to my BROTHER to divide the INHERITANCE with me."

14 But HE replied to him, ‡ "Man, who appointed Me a Judge or Arbiter over you?"

15 And he said to them, ‡ "See, and beware of * All Covetousness; for one's LIFE is not in the ABUNDANCE of his POSSESSIONS."

16 And he spoke a Parable to them, saying, "The FARM of a certain rich Man produced abundantly;

17 and he reasoned within himself, saying, 'What shall I do? For I have no place where to deposit my FRUITS.'

18 And he said, 'I will do this; I will pull down My STOREHOUSES, and build Greater; and there I will bring together All my * WHEAT and my GOOD things;

19 and I will say to MYSELF, 'Life! thou hast an

* VATICAN MANUSCRIPT.—15. All Covetousness. 18. WHEAT and.

‡ 10. Matt. xii. 31, 32; Mark iii. 28; 1 John v. 16. ‡ 11. Matt. x. 19; Mark xiii. 11; Luke xxi. 14. ‡ 14. Exod. ii. 14. ‡ 15. 1 Tim. vi. 7—19.

αγαθα κειμενα εις ετη πολλα· αναπαυου,
good things being laid up for years many; rest thou,
φαγε, πιε, ευφραινου. 20 Ειπε δε αυτῳ ὁ θεος·
eat, drink, be glad. Said but to him the God;
Αφρον, ταυτῃ τῃ νυκτι την ψυχην σου απαι-
O unwise, this the night the life of thee they
τουσιν απο σου· ἁ δε ητοιμασας, τινι
require from thee; what and thou hast prepared, for whom
εσται; 21 Οὑτως ὁ θησαυριζων ἑαυτῳ, και μη
shall be? Thus he laying up treasure for himself, and not
εις θεον πλουτων. 22 Ειπε δε προς τους μαθητας
for God being rich. He said and to the disciples
αὑτου· Δια τουτο ὑμιν λεγω, μη μεριμνατε
of himself; Through this to you I say, not be you anxious
τῃ ψυχῃ ὑμων, τι φαγητε· μηδε τῳ σωματι,
for the life of you, what you may eat, nor for the body,
τι ενδυσησθε. 23 Ἡ ψυχη πλειον εστι της
what you may put on. The life greater it is of the
τροφης· και το σωμα του ενδυματος. 24 Κατα-
food; and the body of the clothing. Ob-
νοησατε τους κορακας, ὁτι ου σπειρουσιν, ουδε
serve you the ravens, that not they sow, nor
θεριζουσιν· οἱς ουκ εστι ταμειον, ουδε αποθη-
reap; for whom not is a store-house, nor a barn;
κη· και ὁ θεος τρεφει αυτους. Ποσῳ μαλλον
and the God feeds them. How much more
ὑμεις διαφερετε των πετεινων; 25 Τις δε εξ ὑμων
you are valuable of the birds? Which and of you
μεριμνων δυναται προσθειναι επι την ἡλικιαν
being anxious is able to add to the age
αὑτου πηχυν ἑνα; 26 Ει ουν ουτε ελαχιστον
of himself span one? If then not even least
δυνασθε, τι περι των λοιπων μεριμνατε;
you are able, why about the remaining ones are you anxious?
27 Κατανοησατε τα κρινα, πως αυξανει· ου
Observe you the lilies, how it grows; not
κοπιᾳ, ουδε νηθει. Λεγω δε ὑμιν, ουδε Σολο-
it labors, nor it spins. I say but to you, not even Solo-
μων εν πασῃ τῃ δοξῃ αὑτου περιεβαλετο ὡς ἑν
mon in all the glory of himself was clothed like one
τουτων. 28 Ει δε τον χορτον εν τῳ αγρῳ,
of these. If and the grass in the field,
σημερον οντα και αυριον εις κλιβανον βαλλο-
to-day existing and to-morrow into an oven is being
μενον, ὁ θεος οὑτως αμφιεννυσι, ποσῳ μαλλον
cast, the God so clothes, how much more
ὑμας, ολιγοπιστοι; 29 Και ὑμεις μη ζητειτε,
you, O you of weak faith? And you not seek,

Abundance of Good things laid up for many Years; ‡ rest, eat, drink, and enjoy thyself.'

20 But GOD said to him, 'Foolish man! This NIGHT they will demand ‡ thy LIFE from thee; ‡ and who then will possess what thou hast provided?'

21 Thus is HE who AMASSES TREASURE for himself, and is not ‡ rich with respect to God."

22 And he said to * the DISCIPLES, "For this reason I charge you, Be not anxious about * your LIFE, what you shall eat, nor for * the BODY, what you shall put on.

23 * For the LIFE is of more value than FOOD, and the BODY than RAIMENT.

24 Observe the RAVENS; For they neither sow nor reap; have no Storehouse nor Granary; but GOD feeds them. How much more valuable are you than the BIRDS!

25 And which of you, by being anxious, can prolong his LIFE † one Moment?

26 If, then, you are not able to do the least, why are you anxious about the REST?

27 Observe the LILIES! How do they grow? They neither labor nor spin; and yet I say to you, that not even Solomon in All his SPLENDOR, was arrayed like one of these.

28 If, then, GOD so decorate the HERB of the FIELD, (which flourishes To-day, and To-morrow will be cast into a Furnace,) how much more you, O you distrustful!

29 And seek you not what you shall eat, * and

---

* VATICAN MANUSCRIPT.—22. the DISCIPLES. 22. the LIFE. 22. your BODY. 23. For the LIFE. 29. and.

† 25. Literally, to add a *cubit* or *span* to one's life. The phrase of adding a cubit was proverbial, denoting something minute. The Psalmist wrote—"Lord, let me know the *measure* of my days? Thou hast made my days *hand-breadths?*" To add a *cubit* to one's stature would be an extraordinary accession of height.

‡ 19. Eccl. xi. 9; 1 Cor. xv. 32; James v 5. ‡ 20. Job xx. 22; xxvii. 8; Psa. lii 7; James iv. 14 ‡ 20 Psa xxxix 6· Jer. xvii. 11. ‡ 21. Matt. vi. 20; ver 33; 1 Tim. vi 18, 19; James ii. 5.

τι φαγητε η τι πιητε· και μη μετεωριζεσθε.
what you may eat or what you may drink; and not be you in anxiety.
30 Ταυτα γαρ παντα τα εθνη του κοσμου επιζη-
These for all the nations of the world seeks;
τει· ὑμων δε ὁ πατηρ οιδεν, ὁτι χρηζετε τουτων.
of you and the father knows, that you have need of these.
31 Πλην ζητειτε την βασιλειαν του θεου, και
But seek you the kingdom of the God, and
ταυτα *[παντα] προστεθησεται ὑμιν.
these [all] shall be superadded to you.
32 Μη φοβου, το μικρον ποιμνιον· ὁτι ευδο-
Not fear, the little flock; for it has
κησεν ὁ πατηρ ὑμων δουναι ὑμιν την βασιλειαν.
pleased the father of you to give to you the kingdom.
33 Πωλησατε τα ὑπαρχοντα ὑμων, και δοτε
Sell you the possessions of you, and give you
ελεημοσυνην. Ποιησατε ἑαυτοις βαλαντια μη
alms. Make for yourself bags not
παλαιουμενα, θησαυρον ανεκλειπτον εν τοις
growing old, a treasure exhaustless in the
ουρανοις, ὁπου κλεπτης ουκ εγγιζει, ουδε σης
heavens, where a thief not approaches, nor moth
διαφθειρει. 34 Ὁπου γαρ εστιν ὁ θησαυρος
destroys. Where for is the treasure
ὑμων, εκει και ἡ καρδια ὑμων εσται.
of you, there also the heart of you will be.
35 Εστωσαν ὑμων αἱ οσφυες περιεζωσμεναι,
Let be of you the loins having been girded,
και οἱ λυχνοι καιομενοι· 36 και ὑμεις ὁμοιοι
and the lamps burning; and you like
ανθρωποις προσδεχομενοις τον κυριον ἑαυτων,
to men looking for the lord of themselves,
ποτε αναλυσει εκ των γαμων· ἱνα ελθοντος
when he will return from the marriage feasts; that having come
και κρουσαντος, ευθεως ανοιξωσιν αυτῳ.
and having knocked, immediately it may be opened to him.
37 Μακαριοι οἱ δουλοι εκεινοι, οὑς ελθων ὁ
Blessed the slaves those, whom having come the
κυριος εὑρησει γρηγορουντας· αμην λεγω ὑμιν,
lord shall find watching; indeed I say to you,
ὁτι περιζωσεται, και ανακλινει αυτους, και
that he will gird himself, and will make to recline them, and
παρελθων διακονησει αυτοις. 38 Και εαν ελ-
going forth he will minister to them. And if he may
θῃ εν τῃ δευτερᾳ *[φυλακῃ,] και εν τῃ τριτῃ
come in the second [watch,] or in the third
φυλακῃ *[ελθῃ,] και εὑρῃ οὑτως μακαριοι εισιν
watch [may come,] and may find thus; blessed are
οἱ δουλοι εκεινοι. 39 Τουτο δε γινωσκετε, ὁτι,
the slaves those. This and know you, that,
ει ᾐδει ὁ οικοδεσποτης, ποιᾳ ὡρᾳ ὁ κλεπτης
if had known the householder, in what hour the thief
ερχεται, εγρηγορησεν αν, και ουκ αν αφηκε
comes, he would watch, and not would allow
διορυγηναι τον οικον αὑτου. 40 Και ὑμεις *[ουν]
to dig through the house of himself. And you [therefore]

what you shall drink; and be not in restless suspense.

30 For all these things do the NATIONS of the WORLD seek; and Your FATHER knows That you need them.

31 ‡ But seek *his KINGDOM; and these shall be superadded to you.

32 Fear not, LITTLE Flock; ‡ For it has pleased your FATHER to give you the KINGDOM.

33 Sell your POSSESSIONS, and give Alms; ‡ make for yourselves Purses which grow not old, an unfailing Treasure in the HEAVENS, where no Thief approaches, nor Moth destroys.

34 For where your TREASURE is, there your HEART will also be.

35 ‡ Stand with Your LOINS girded, and ‡ and LAMPS burning;

36 and be you like Men waiting for their MASTER, when he will return from the NUPTIAL FEASTS; that when he comes and knocks, they may instantly open to him.

37 ‡ Happy are those SERVANTS, whom, when their MASTER arrives, he shall find watching! I assure you, That he will gird himself, and cause them to recline, and going forth he will serve them.

38 And if he should come in the SECOND, or in the THIRD Watch, and thus find them, happy are they!

39 ‡ Now you know this, That if the HOUSEHOLDER had known at What Hour the THIEF would come, he would have watched, and not have permitted him to break into his HOUSE.

40 ‡ Be you also pre-

* VATICAN MANUSCRIPT.—31. his KINGDOM; and these. 31. all—omit. 38. they. 38. Watch—omit. 38. may come—omit. 40. therefore—omit.

‡ 31. Matt. vi. 33. ‡ 32. Matt. xi. 25, 26. ‡ 33. Matt. vi. 20; Luke xvi. 9; 1 Tim. vi. 19. ‡ 35. Eph. vi. 14; 1 Pet. i. 13. ‡ 36. Matt. xxv. 1, etc. ‡ 37. Matt. xxiv. 46. ‡ 39. Matt. xxiv. 43; 1 Thess. v. 2; Rev. iii. 3; xvi. 15. ‡ 40. Mark xiii 33; Luke xxi. 36.

γινεσθε ετοιμοι· ὁτι, ᾑ ὡρα ου δοκειτε, ὁ
be prepared; because, in the hour not you think. the
υἱος του ανθρωπου ερχεται. 41 Ειπε δε *[αυτῳ]
son of the man comes. Said and [to him]
ὁ Πετρος· Κυριε, προς ἡμας την παραβολην
the Peter; O lord, to us the parable
ταυτην λεγεις, η και προς παντας.
this thou sayest, or also to all?
42 Ειπε δε ὁ κυριος· Τις αρα εστιν ὁ πιστος
Said and the Lord; Who then is the faithful
οικονομος και φρονιμος, ὁν καταστησει ὁ κυριος
steward and wise, whom will appoint the lord
επι της θεραπειας αὑτου του διδοναι εν καιρῳ
over the domestics of himself the to give in season
το σιτομετριον; 43 Μακαριος ὁ δουλος εκεινος,
the measure of food? Blessed the slave that,
ὁν ελθων ὁ κυριος αυτου εὑρησει ποιουντα οὑτως
whom coming the lord of him will find doing thus.
44 Αληθως λεγω ὑμιν, ὁτι επι πασι τοις ὑπαρ-
Truly I say to you, that over all to the be-
χουσιν αὑτου καταστησει αυτον. 45 Εαν δε
longing of himself he will appoint him. If but
ειπῃ ὁ δουλος εκεινος εν τῃ καρδιᾳ αὑτου·
should say the slave that in the heart of himself:
Χρονιζει ὁ κυριος μου ερχεσθαι· και αρξηται
Delays the lord of me to come; and shall begin
τυπτειν τους παιδας και τας παιδισκας, εσθιειν
to strike the servants and the maidens, to eat
τε και πινειν και μεθυσκεσθαι· 46 ἡξει ὁ κυριος
and also to drink and to be drunken; will come the lord
του δουλου εκεινου εν ἡμερᾳ, ᾑ ου προσδοκᾳ,
the slave that in a day, to which not he looks,
και εν ὡρᾳ ᾑ ου γινωσκει· και διχοτομησει
and in an hour which not he knows; and shall cut asunder
αυτον, και το μερος αυτου μετα των απιστων
him, and the part of him with the unbelievers
θησει. 47 Εκεινος δε ὁ δουλος ὁ γνους το
will place. That and the slave who having known the
θελημα του κυριου ἑαυτου, και μη ἑτοιμασας,
will of the lord of himself, and not having prepared,
μηδε ποιησας προς το θελημα αυτου, δαρησε-
neither having done according to the will of him, shall be bea-
ται πολλας· 48 ὁ δε μη γνους, ποιησας δε
ten many; he but not having known, having done and
αξια πληγων δαρησεται ολιγας. Παντι δε ᾡ
deserving of stripes shall be beaten few. To all and to whom
εδοθη πολυ, πολυ ζητηθησεται παρ' αυτου·
is given much, much will be required from him;
και ᾡ παρεθεντο πολυ, περισσοτερον αιτη-
and to whom they have entrusted much, more they
σουσιν αυτον.
will ask him.
49 Πυρ ηλθον βαλειν εις την γην· και τι
Fire I came to throw into the earth; and what
θελω, ει ηδη ανηφθη. 50 Βαπτισμα δε εχω
do I wish, if already it were kindled. A dipping and I have

pared; For at an Hour you think not, the SON of MAN comes."

41 Then PETER said, "Master, dost thou speak this PARABLE to us, or even to all?"

42 And the LORD said, ‡ "Who then is *the FAITHFUL, the WISE Steward, whom the LORD will appoint over his DOMESTICS, to DISPENSE the *proper allowance of food **in its Season.**

43 Happy that SERVANT, whom his MASTER, at his arrival, shall find thus employed!

44 ‡ I tell you truly, That he will appoint him over ALL his PROPERTY.

45 But if that SERVANT should say in his HEART, 'My MASTER delays to come;' and shall begin to beat the SERVANTS and the MAIDENS, and to eat and drink and be drunk;

46 the MASTER of that SERVANT will come in a Day when he does not expect him, and at an Hour of which he is not aware, ‡ and will cut him off, and will appoint his PORTION with the UNBELIEVERS.

47 And ‡ THAT SERVANT, who knew the WILL of his MASTER, and was not prepared, nor did according to his WILL, he shall be beaten with many stripes;

48 ‡ but HE WHO KNEW not, and did things worthy of Stripes, shall be beaten with few. And from any one to whom much is given much will be required; and from him with whom much has been deposited, they will exact the more.

49 I came to throw Fire on the LAND; and what do I wish,—if it were already kindled?

50 But I have an Im-

* VATICAN MANUSCRIPT.—41. to him—*omit.* 42. the FAITHFUL Steward, the WISE, whom. 42. portion of food in.

‡ 42. Matt. xxiv. 45; xxv. 21. ‡ 44. Matt. xxiv. 47. ‡ 46. Num. xv. 30; Matt xxiv. 51. ‡ 47. Deut. xxv. 2; James iv. 17. ‡ 48. Lev. v. 17; 1 Tim. i. 13.

βαπτισθηναι· και πως συνεχομαι, ἑως οὑ
to be dipped; and how I am pressed, till
τελεσθη. 51 Δοκειτε, ὁτι ειρηνην παρεγενομην
may be finished. Do you think, that peace I came
δουναι εν τῃ γῃ; Ουχι, λεγω ὑμιν, αλλ' η
to give in the earth? No, I say to you, but rather
διαμερισμον. 52 Εσονται γαρ απο του νυν
division. Shall be for from the now
πεντε εν οικῳ ἑνι διαμεμερισμενοι, τρεις επι
five in house one having been divided, three against
δυσι, και δυο επι τρισι. 53 Διαμερισθησεται
two, and two against three. Will be divided
πατηρ εφ' υἱῳ, και υἱος επι πατρι· μητηρ επι
a father against a son, and a son against a father: a mother against
θυγατρι, και θυγατηρ επι μητρι· πενθερα
a daughter, and a daughter against a mother: a mother-in-law
επι την νυμφην αὑτης, και νυμφη επι
against the a daughter-in-law of herself, and a daughter-in-law against
την πενθεραν αὑτης.
the mother-in-law of herself.
54 Ελεγε δε και τοις οχλοις· Ὁταν ιδητε την
He said and also to the crowds: When you see the
νεφελην ανατελλουσαν απο δυσμων, ευθεως
cloud rising from west, immediately
λεγετε· Ομβρος ερχεται· και γινεται οὑτω.
you say: A shower comes: and it happens so.
55 Και ὁταν Νοτον πνεοντα, λεγετε· Ὁτι καυ-
And when South wind is blowing, you say: That burning
σων εσται· και γινεται. 56 Ὑποκριται, το
heat shall be: and it happens. O hypocrites, the
προσωπον της γης και του ουρανου οιδατε
face of the earth and of the heaven you know
δοκιμαζειν· τον δε καιρον τουτον πως ου
to discern: the but season this how not
δοκιμαζετε; 57 Τι δε και αφ' ἑαυτων ου κρινετε
do you discern? Why and even of yourselves not judge you
το δικαιον; 58 Ὡς γαρ ὑπαγεις μετα του αντι-
the right? When for thou goest with the oppo-
δικου σου επ' αρχοντα, εν τῃ ὁδῳ δος εργασιαν
nent of thee to a ruler, in the way give thou labor
απηλλαχθαι απ' αυτου· μηποτε κατασυρῃ σε
to be set free from him: lest he may drag thee
προς τον κριτην, και ὁ κριτης σε παραδῳ τῳ
to the judge, and the judge thee may deliver to the
πρακτορι, και ὁ πρακτωρ σε βαλῃ εις φυλα-
officer, and the officer thee may cast into prison.
κην. 59 Λεγω σοι, ου μη εξελθῃς εκειθεν,
I say to thee, not not thou mayest come out thence,
ἑως οὑ και το εσχατον λεπτον αποδῳς.
till even the last lepton thou hast paid.

mersion ‡ to undergo; and
how am I pressed, till it
may be consummated?
51 ‡ Do you imagine
That I am come to give
Peace in the LAND? I tell
you, No; but rather Divi-
sion.
52 For from this TIME,
five in * One House will
be divided; three against
two, and two against
three;—
53 ‡ a Father against a
Son, and a Son against a
Father; a Mother against
* the DAUGHTER, and a
Daughter against * the
MOTHER; a Mother-in-law
against her DAUGHTER-IN-
LAW, and a Daughter-in-
law against her MOTHER-
IN-LAW."
54 And he said also to
the CROWDS, ‡ "When you
see † * a Cloud rising from
the West, you immediately
say, 'A Shower is coming;'
and so it happens.
55 And when † the South
wind is blowing, you say,
'There will be scorching
Heat;' and it occurs.
56 O Hypocrites! you
know how to scan the FACE
of the EARTH and of the
SKY; but how is it, you
*cannot discern this TIME?
57 And why do you not,
even of yourselves, judge
what is RIGHT?
58 ‡ When thou goest
with thy LEGAL OPPONENT
to a Magistrate, on the
ROAD labor to be released
from him, lest he drag
thee to the JUDGE, and the
JUDGE deliver Thee to the
OFFICER, and the OFFICER
cast Thee into Prison.
59 I tell thee, thou wilt
by no means be released,
till thou hast paid even
the LAST † Lepton?"

* VATICAN MANUSCRIPT.—52. One House. 53. the DAUGHTER. 53. the MOTHER. 54. a Cloud. 56. cannot.

† 54. The westerly winds in the Holy Land are still generally attended with rain, whilst the easterly winds are usually dry. † 55. Le Bruyn tells us, there blew when he was at Rama, a south-east wind, which coming from the desert beyond Jordan, caused a great heat, and that it continued some days.—*Harmer.* † 59. *Lepton*, in value about two mills, or half a farthing.

‡ 50. Mark x. 38. ‡ 51. Matt. x. 34. ‡ 53. Micah vii. 6. ‡ 54. Matt. xvi. 2. ‡ 58. Prov. xxv. 8; Matt. v. 25.

ΚΕΦ. ιγ'. 13.

1 Παρησαν δε τινες εν αυτῳ τῳ καιρῳ, απαγ-
Were present and some in to him the season, re-

γελλοντες αυτῳ περι των Γαλιλαιων, ὡν το
porting to him concerning the Galileans, of whom the

αἱμα Πιλατος εμιξε μετα των θυσιων αυτων.
blood Pilate mingled with the sacrifices of them.

2 Και αποκριθεις ὁ Ιησους ειπεν αυτοις· Δοκειτε,
And answering the Jesus said to them; Suppose you,

ὁτι οἱ Γαλιλαιοι οὑτοι ἁμαρτωλοι παρα παντας
that the Galileans these sinners above all

τους Γαλιλαιους εγενοντο, ὁτι τοιαυτα πεπονθα-
the Galileans were, because such things they have

σιν; 3 Ουχι, λεγω ὑμιν· αλλ' εαν μη μετανοητε,
suffered? No, I say to you; but except you reform,

παντες ὡσαυτως απολεισθε. 4 Η εκεινοι οἱ
all in like manner you will perish. Or those the

δεκα και οκτω, εφ' οὑς επεσεν ὁ πυργος εν τῳ
ten and eight, on whom fell the tower in the

Σιλωαμ, και απεκτεινεν αυτους, δοκειτε, ὁτι
Siloam, and killed them, suppose you, that

οὑτοι οφειλεται εγενοντο παρα παντας ανθρω-
they offenders were above all men

πους τους κατοικουντας εν Ἱερουσαλημ; 5 Ουχι,
those dwelling in Jerusalem? No,

λεγω ὑμιν· αλλ' εαν μη μετανοητε, παντες
I say to you; but except you reform, all

ὁμοιως απολεισθε. 6 Ελεγε δε ταυτην την
in like manner you will perish. He spoke and this the

παραβολην· Συκην ειχε τις εν τῳ αμπελωνι
parable; A fig-tree had one in the vineyard

αὑτου πεφυτευμενην· και ηλθε ζητων καρπον
of himself having been planted; and came seeking fruit

εν αυτῃ, και ουκ εὑρεν. 7 Ειπε δε προς τον
on her, and not found. He said and to the

αμπελουργον· Ιδου, τρια ετη ερχομαι ζητων
vine-dresser; Lo, three years came seeking

καρπον εν τῃ συκῃ, ταυτῃ, και ουχ εὑρισκω·
fruit on the fig-tree this, and not to find;

εκκοψον αυτην· ἱνατι και την γην καταργει;
cut down her; why and the earth it renders useless?

8 Ὁ δε αποκριθεις λεγει αυτῳ· Κυριε, αφες
He and answering says to him: O lord, leave

αυτην και τουτο το ετος, ἑως ὁτου σκαψω περι
her also this the year, till I may dig about

αυτην, και βαλω κοπρια· 9 καν μεν ποιησῃ
her, and I may put dung; and if indeed it may bear

καρπον· ει δε μηγε, εις το μελλον εκκοψεις
fruit: if and not, in the future thou mayest cut down

αυτην. 10 Ην δε διδασκων εν μιᾳ των συνα-
her. He was and teaching in one of the syna-

CHAPTER XIII.

1 And some were present at That PERIOD, informing him concerning the GALILEANS, † Whose BLOOD Pilate mingled with their SACRIFICES.

2 And * he answering said to them, "Do you think That those GALILEANS were the greatest Transgressors in All GALILEE, Because they suffered Such things?

3 I tell you, No; but, unless you reform, you will all in like manner be destroyed.

4 Or, Those EIGHTEEN, on whom † the TOWER in SILOAM fell, and killed them, do you imagine they were greater Offenders than All THOSE MEN who DWELL in Jerusalem?

5 I tell you, No; but, unless you reform, you will all in like manner be destroyed."

6 And he spoke This PARABLE; ‡ "A certain man had a Fig-tree planted in his VINEYARD; and he came seeking Fruit on it, but found none.

7 And he said to the VINE-DRESSER, 'Behold, I have come Three Years seeking Fruit on this FIG-TREE, and find none: cut it down, why should it render the GROUND unproductive?'

8 And HE answering, said to him, 'Sir, leave it This YEAR also, till I dig about it, and manure it;

9 and * perhaps it may bear Fruit; but if not, at a FUTURE time thou mayest cut it down.'"

10 And he was teaching

* VATICAN MANUSCRIPT.—2. he answering. 9. AFTER THAT it may bear Fruit; but if not, thou mayest.

† 1. Josephus says, that Archelaus sent his soldiers into the temple, "who suddenly falling upon them, as they were sacrificing, slew about three thousand of them." And Antipater, when he accused Archelaus for this among other crimes before the Emperor Augustus, is reported by Josephus as saying that he had "cruelly cut the throats of those who came up to the feast, and were at their own sacrifices." † 4. A tower near the pool Siloam, which supplied the city with water, and being situated in the midst of Jerusalem, at the foot of Mount Zion, was a place of great resort.—See John ix. 7; Neh. iii. 55.

‡ 6. Isa. v. 2; Matt. xxi. 19.

γωγων εν τοις σαββασι. 11 Και ιδου, γυνη ην
gogues in the sabbaths. And lo, a woman was
πνευμα εχουσα ασθενειας ετη δεκα και οκτω·
a spirit having of infirmity years ten and eight;
και ην συγκυπτουσα, και μη δυναμενη ανακυψαι
and was being bent double, and not being able to raise up
εις το παντελες. 12 Ιδων δε αυτην ὁ Ιησους,
for all time. Seeing and her the Jesus,
προσεφωνησε, και ειπεν αυτῃ· Γυναι, απολε-
he called to, and said to her; O woman, thou hast
λυσαι της ασθενειας σου. 13 Και επεθηκεν
been loosed of the infirmity of thee. And he placed
αυτῃ τας χειρας· και παραχρημα ανωρθωθη,
to her the hands, and immediately she stood erect,
και εδοξαζε τον θεον. 14 Αποκριθεις δε ὁ αρχι-
and glorified the God. Answering and the syna-
συναγωγος, αγανακτων, ὁτι τῳ σαββατῳ εθερα-
gogue-ruler, being angry, because in the sabbath healed
πευσεν ὁ Ιησους, ελεγε τῳ οχλῳ· Ἑξ ἡμεραι
the Jesus, he said to the crowd; Six days
εισιν, εν αἱς δει εργαζεσθαι· εν ταυταις ουν
are, in which it is proper to work; in these therefore
ερχομενοι θεραπευεσθε, και μη τῃ ἡμερᾳ του
coming be you healed, and not in the day of the
σαββατου. 15 Απεκριθη ουν αυτῳ ὁ κυριος, και
sabbath. Answered therefore to him the lord, and
ειπεν· Ὑποκριτα, ἑκαστος ὑμων τῳ σαββατῳ
said; O hypocrites, each one of you in the sabbath
ου λυει τον βουν αὑτου η τον ονον απο της
not loose the ox of himself or the ass from the
φατνης, και απαγαγων ποτιζει; 16 Ταυτην δε,
stall, and having led he drinks? This and,
θυγατερα Αβρααμ ουσαν ἡν εδησεν ὁ σατανας
a daughter of Abraham being, whom bound the adversary
ιδου δεκα και οκτω ετη, ουκ εδει λυθηναι απο
lo ten and eight years, not ought to be loosed from
του δεσμου τουτου τῃ ἡμερᾳ του σαββατου;
the bond this in the day of the sabbath?
17 Και ταυτα λεγοντος αυτου, κατῃσχυνοντο
And these things saying of him, were ashamed
παντες οἱ αντικειμενοι αυτῳ· και πας ὁ οχλος
all the opponents to him; and all the crowd
εχαιρεν επι πασι τοις ενδοξοις τοις γινομενοις
rejoiced for all the glorious things those being done
ὑπ' αυτου.
by him.

18 Ελεγε δε· Τινι ὁμοια εισιν ἡ βασιλεια του
He said and; To what like is the kingdom of the
θεου; και τινι ὁμοιωσω αυτην; 19 Ὁμοια εστι
God; and to what shall I compare her; Like it is
κοκκῳ σιναπεως, ὁν λαβων ανθρωπος εβαλεν
a grain of mustard, which having taken a man he cast
εις κηπον ἑαυτου· και ηυξησε, και εγενετο εις
into a garden of himself; and it grew, and became into
δενδρον *[μεγα,] και τα πετεινα του ουρανου
a tree [great,] and the birds of the heaven

in one of the SYNAGOGUES on the SABBATH.

11 And behold, there was a Woman who had a Spirit of Infirmity for eighteen Years, and was bent down, and was not able to raise herself up at all.

12 And JESUS seeing her, called to her and said, "Woman, thou art released from thine INFIRMITY."

13 ‡ And he placed his HANDS on her; and immediately she stood erect, and praised GOD.

14 And the SYNAGOGUE-RULER, being angry, Because JESUS had healed on the SABBATH, answering, said to the CROWD, ‡ "There are Six Days in which you ought to labor, in these, therefore, come and be cured, ‡ and not on the SABBATH."

15 * But the LORD answered him, and said, "Hypocrites! ‡ does not every one of you, on the SABBATH, loose his OX or his ASS from the STALL, and lead him to DRINK?

16 And was it not proper, that this woman, ‡ being a Daughter of Abraham, whom the ADVERSARY has bound, behold, Eighteen Years, to be released from this BOND on the SABBATH?"

17 And on his saying this, All his OPPOSERS were ashamed; and All the CROWD rejoiced at All THOSE GLORIOUS WORKS which were PERFORMED by him.

18 And he said, ‡ "What is the KINGDOM of GOD like? and to what shall I compare it?

19 It is like a Grain of Mustard, which a Man took, and planted in his Garden; and it grew, and became a Tree; and the BIRDS of the HEAVEN

* VATICAN MANUSCRIPT.—15. But the Lord answered him, and said. 19. great—omit.

‡ 13. Mark xvi. 18; Acts ix. 17. ‡ 14. Exod. xx. 9. ‡ 14. Matt. xii. 10; Mark iii. 2; Luke vi. 7; xiv. 3. ‡ 15. Luke xv. 5. ‡ 16. Luke xix. 9. ‡ 18. Matt. xiii. 31; Mark iv. 30.

κατεσκηνωσεν εν τοις κλαδοις αυτου. 20 Και
lodged in the branches of it. And
παλιν ειπε· Τινι ὁμοιωσω την βασιλειαν του
again he said: To what shall I compare the kingdom of the
θεου; 21 Ὁμοια εστι ζυμῃ, ἡν λαβουσα γυνη
of God? Like it is to leaven, which having taken a woman
ενεκρυψεν εις αλευρου σατα τρια, ἑως οὑ εζυ-
mixed into of meal measures three, till was
μωθη ὁλον. 22 Και διεπορευετο κατα πολεις
leavened whole. And he passed throughout cities
και κωμας, διδασκων, και πορειαν ποιουμενος
and towns, teaching, and went on making
εις Ἱερουσαλημ. 23 Ειπε δε τις αυτῳ· Κυριε,
for Jerusalem. Said and one to him: O lord,
ει ολιγοι οἱ σωζομενοι; Ὁ δε ειπε προς αυτους·
are few those being saved: He and said to them:
24 Αγωνιζεσθε εισελθειν δια της στενης θυρας·
Agonize you to enter through the strait door:
ὁτι πολλοι, λεγω ὑμιν, ζητησουσιν εισελθειν,
for many, I say to you, will seek to enter,
και ουκ ισχυσουσιν. 25 Αφ' οὑ αν εγερθῃ ὁ
and not will be able. From when may be raised the
οικοδεσποτης, και αποκλεισῃ την θυραν, και
householder, and may have shut the door, and
αρξησθε εξω ἑσταναι, και κρουειν την θυραν,
you may begin without to stand, and to knock the door,
λεγοντες· Κυριε, *[κυριε,] ανοιξον ἡμιν· και
saying: O lord, [O lord,] open thou to us: and
αποκριθεις ερει ὑμιν· Ουκ οιδα ὑμας, ποθεν
answering he will say to you: Not I know you, whence
εστε. 26 Τοτε αρξεσθε λεγειν· Εφαγομεν ενω-
you are. Then you will begin to say: We ate in pre-
πιον σου και εν ταις πλατειαις ἡμων εδιδαξας.
sence of thee and in the wide places of us thou hast taught.
27 Και ερει· Λεγω ὑμιν, ουκ οιδα *[ὑμας,]
And he will say: I say to you, not I know [you,]
ποθεν εστε· αποστητε απ' εμου παντες οἱ
whence you are: depart you from me all the
εργαται της αδικιας· 28 Εκει εσται ὁ κλαυθμος
workers of the wrong. There will be the weeping
και ὁ βρυγμος των οδοντων, ὁταν οψησθε Αβρααμ
and the gnashing of the teeth, when you may see Abraam
και Ισαακ και Ἰακωβ και παντας τους προφητας
and Isaac and Jacob and all the prophets
εν τῃ βασιλειᾳ του θεου, ὑμας δε εκβαλομενους
in the kingdom of the God, you and being cast
εξω. 29 Και ἡξουσιν απο ανατολων και δυσμων,
outside. And they will come from east and west,
και απο Βορρα και Νοτου· και ανακλιθησονται
and from North and South: and will recline
εν τῃ βασιλειᾳ του θεου. 30 Και ιδου, εισιν
in the kingdom of the God. And lo, they are

built their nests in its BRANCHES."
20 And again he said, "To what shall I compare the KINGDOM of GOD?
21 It resembles Leaven, which a Woman taking, mingled in three † Measures of Meal, till the whole fermented."
22 ‡ And he passed through Cities and Villages, teaching, and traveling towards Jerusalem.
23 And some one said to him, "Master, are those few who are BEING saved?" And HE said to them,
24 ‡ "Earnestly endeavor to enter through the NARROW Door; For many, I tell you, will seek to enter in, and will not be able.
25 When the HOUSEHOLDER shall rise and close the DOOR, and you shall begin to stand without, and to knock at the DOOR, saying, ‡ 'Master, open to us;' and he shall answer and say to you, 'I do not recognize you; whence are you?'
26 you will then begin to say, 'We have eaten and drank in thy presence, and thou hast taught in our OPEN SQUARES.'
27 ‡ But he will say *to you, 'I do not know from whence you are. Depart from me, all you WORKERS of Wickedness.'
28 There will be the WEEPING and the GNASHING of TEETH, ‡ when you shall see Abraham, and Isaac, and Jacob, and All the PROPHETS in the KINGDOM of GOD, and you cast out.
29 And they will come from the East and West, and from the North and South, and will recline in the KINGDOM of GOD.
30 ‡ And behold, they

* VATICAN MANUSCRIPT.—25. Lord—*omit*. 27. speaking to you, I know not. 27. you—*omit*.

† 21. See Note on Matt. xiii. 33.

‡ 22. Matt. ix. 35; Mark vi. 6. ‡ 24. Matt. vii. 13. ‡ 25. Luke vi. 46. ‡ 27. Matt. vii. 23; xxv. 41. ‡ 28. Matt. viii. 11. ‡ 30. Matt. xix. 30; xx. 16. Mark x. 31.

εσχατοι, οἱ εσονται πρωτοι· και εισι πρωτοι, οἱ
last. who shall be first; and they are first, who
εσονται εσχατοι. 31 Εν αυτῃ τῃ ἡμερᾳ προσηλ-
will be last. In this the day approached
θον τινες Φαρισαιοι, λεγοντες αυτῳ· Εξελθε,
certain of Pharisees, saying to him; Come out,
και πορευου εντευθεν· ὁτι Ἡρωδης θελει σε
and go thou hence; for Herod wishes thee
αποκτειναι. 32 Και ειπεν αυτοις· Πορευθεντες
to kill. And he said to them; Having gone
ειπατε τῃ αλωπεκι ταυτῃ· Ιδου, εκβαλλω δαι-
say you to the fox this; Lo, I cast out de-
μονια και ιασεις επιτελω σημερον και αυριον,
mons and cures perform to-day and to-morrow,
και τῃ τριτῃ τελειουμαι. 33 Πλην δει με
and in the third I shall have ended. But it behoves me
σημερον και αυριον και τῃ ερχομενῃ πορευεσθαι·
to-day and to-morrow and in the coming to go;
ὁτι ουκ ενδεχεται προφητην απολεσθαι εξω
for not it is possible a prophet to perish out
Ἱερουσαλημ. 34 Ἱερουσαλημ, Ἱερουσαλημ, ἡ
of Jerusalem. Jerusalem, Jerusalem, the
αποκτεινουσα τους προφητας, και λιθολουσα
killing the prophets, and stoning
τους απεσταλμενους προς αυτην, ποσακις ηθε-
those having been sent to her, how often I de-
λησα επισυναξαι τα τεκνα σου, ὁν τροπον
sired to gather the children of thee, what manner
ορνις την ἑαυτης νοσσιαν ὑπο τας πτερυγας;
a bird the of herself brood under the wings?
και ουκ ηθελησατε. 35 Ιδου, αφιεται ὑμιν ὁ
and not you were willing. Lo, is left to you the
οικος ὑμων. Λεγω δε ὑμιν, ὁτι ου μη με ιδητε,
house of you. I say and to you, that not not me you may see,
ἑως *[αν ἡξῃ ὁτε] ειπητε· Ευλογημενος ὁ
till [may come when] you may say; Having been blessed he
ερχομενος εν ονοματι κυριου.
coming in name of Lord.

ΚΕΦ. ιδ'. 14.

1 Και εγενετο εν τῳ ελθειν αυτον εις οικον
And it happened in the to come him into a house
τινος των αρχοντων των Φαρισαιων σαββατῳ
of one of the rulers of the Pharisees in a sabbath
φαγειν αρτον, και αυτοι ησαν παρατηρουμενοι
to eat bread, and they were watching
αυτον. 2 Και ιδου, ανθρωπος τις ην ὑδρωπικος
him. And lo, a man certain was dropsical
εμπροσθεν αυτου. 3 Και αποκριθεις ὁ Ιησους
in presence of him. And answering the Jesus
ειπε προς τους νομικους και Φαρισαιους, λεγων·
said to the lawyers and Pharisees, saying;
Ει εξεστι τῳ σαββατῳ θεραπευειν; Οἱ δε
If it is lawful in the sabbath to cure? They but

are last who will be first, and they are first who will be last.

31 On That DAY, certain Pharisees approached, saying, "Go, depart hence; For Herod intends to kill Thee."

32 And he said to them, "Go, and tell that † FOX, Behold, I expel Demons, and perform Cures To-day and To-morrow, and on the THIRD * Day I shall have finished.

33 But I must go on To-day, and To-morrow, and the day FOLLOWING; For it is not possible for a Prophet to perish † out of Jerusalem.

34 ‡ O Jerusalem, Jerusalem! DESTROYING the PROPHETS, and stoning THOSE SENT to thee! how often have I desired to assemble thy CHILDREN, as a Bird collects HER Young under her WINGS, but you would not!

35 Behold, your HABITATION is left to you; and I tell you, That you shall not see me, till you shall say, ‡ 'Blessed be HE who COMES in the Name of Jehovah.'"

CHAPTER XIV.

1 And it occurred, on a Sabbath, as he WENT to eat Bread into the House of one of the RULING PHARISEES, that they were watching him.

2 And behold, there was a certain dropsical Person in his presence.

3 And JESUS answering, spoke to the LAWYERS and Pharisees, saying, ‡ "Is it lawful to cure on the SABBATH * Day, or not?

4 But THEY were silent.

* VATICAN MANUSCRIPT.—32. Day. 35. may come, when—omit. 3. Day, or not? But.

† 32. It is not certain that Jesus meant Herod here; he might have only intended to call that man so, from whom the advice of departing came, (whether from the speaker himself, or from the person who sent him;) for it is probable that the advice was given craftily, and with a design to frighten Jesus, and make him go from that place.—*Pearce*. † 33. Because he was only to be judged by the great Sanhedrim, and they were only to pass judgment on him in that place.—*Lightfoot*.

‡ 34. Matt. xxiii. 37. ‡ 35. Psa. cxviii. 26. ‡ 3. Matt. xii. 10.

ἡσυχασαν. Και επιλαβομενος ιασατο αυτον,
were silent. And having taken hold he cured him,
και απελυσε. 5 Και αποκριθεις προς αυτους
and dismissed. And answering to them
ειπε· Τινος ὑμων ονος η βους εις φρεαρ εμπε-
said; Of any one of you an ass or an ox into a pit shall
σειται, και ουκ ευθεως ανασπασει αυτον εν τῃ
fall, and not immediately will draw out him in the
ἡμερᾳ του σαββατου; 6 Και ουκ ισχυσαν ανταπο-
day of the sabbath? And not they were able to
ποκριθηναι *[αυτῳ] προς ταυτα.
reply [to him] to these things.
7 Ελεγε δε προς τους κεκλημενους παραβολην,
He spoke and to those having been invited a parable,
επεχων πως τας πρωτοκλισιας εξελεγοντο,
observing how the first reclining places they were choosing out,
λεγων προς αυτους· 8 Ὁταν κληθῃς ὑπο
saying to them; When thou mayest be invited by
τινος εις γαμους, μη κατακλιθῃς εις την πρω-
any one to marriage-feasts, not thou mayest recline in the first
τοκλισιαν· μηποτε εντιμοτερος σου ῃ κεκλη-
reclining place; lest a more honorable of thee may be having
μενος ὑπ᾽ αυτου· 9 και ελθων ὁ σε και αυτον
been invited by him; and coming he thee and him
καλεσας, ερει σοι· Δος τουτῳ τοπον· και
having invited, shall say to thee: Give thou to this a place; and
τοτε αρξῃ μετ᾽ αισχυνης τον εσχατον
then thou shouldst begin with shame the farthest
τοπον κατεχειν· 10 Αλλ᾽ ὁταν κληθῃς,
place to occupy; But when thou mayest be invited,
πορευθεις αναπεσαι εις τον εσχατον τοπων, ἱνα
having gone recline thou in the farthest place, that
ὁταν ελθῃ ὁ κεκληκως σε, ειπῃ σοι· Φιλε,
when may come he having invited thee, may say to thee; O friend,
προσαναβηθι ανωτερον. Τοτε εσται σοι δοξα
go thou up to a higher place. Then will be to thee glory
ενωπιον των συνανακειμενων σοι. 11 Ὁτι πας
in presence of those reclining with thee. For every one
ὁ ὑψων ἑαυτον, ταπεινωθησεται· και ὁ ταπει-
the exalting himself, shall be humbled; and the hum-
νων ἑαυτον ὑψωθησεται. 12 Ελεγε δε και τῳ
bling himself shall be exalted. He said and also to the
κεκληκοτι αυτον· Ὁταν ποιῃς αριστον η
(one) having invited him: When thou mayest make a dinner or
δειπνον, μη φωνει τους φιλους σου, μηδε τους
a supper, not call the friends of thee, nor the
αδελφους σου, μηδε τους συγγενεις σου, μηδε
brethren of thee, nor the relations of thee, nor
γειτονας πλουσιους· μηποτε και αυτοι σε
neighbors rich lest also they thee

And taking hold of him, he cured, and dismissed him.

5 And *he said to them, ‡"If a Son or an Ox of any of you shall fall into a Pit, will he not immediately draw him out on the SABBATH DAY?"

6 And they could not reply to this.

7 And he spoke a Parable to THOSE who had been INVITED, observing how they were choosing out the CHIEF PLACES; saying to them,

8 "When thou art invited by any one to a Marriage-feast, do not recline in the †CHIEF PLACE; lest one more honorable than thou may have been invited by him;

9 and HE who INVITED Thee and Him, should come and say to thee, 'Give this man a Place;' and then with shame thou shouldst begin to occupy the LOWEST Place.

10 ‡But when thou art invited, go and recline in the LOWEST Place; that when HE who INVITED thee comes, he may say to thee, 'Friend, go up to a higher place;' then thou wilt have honor in the presence of *All THOSE RECLINING with thee.

11 ‡For EVERY ONE who EXALTS himself will be humbled, and HE who HUMBLES himself will be exalted."

12 And he said also to HIM who had INVITED him, "When thou makest a Dinner or a Supper, call not thy FRIENDS, nor thy BROTHERS, nor thy RELATIVES, *nor rich NEIGHBORS; lest they also should

---

* VATICAN MANUSCRIPT—5. he said to them, If a Son or an Ox. 6. him—*omit*. 10. All THOSE. 12. not rich.

† 8. Rather, to lie down first: to place themselves first on the couches, whereon the Jews were used to lay at their meals. Each couch held three, who sat or rather laid themselves down upon it; and it was esteemed the greatest mark of respect to any man, when the master of the house desired him to place himself first on the couch, in what part of it he pleased. Josephus telling us how craftily Herod treated Hyrcanus, says, that he deceived him by "calling him father, and making him take his place first at feasts."—*Pearce.*

‡ 5. Exod. xxiii. 5; Deut. xxii. 4; Luke xiii. 15. ‡ 10. Prov. xxv. 6, 7. ‡ 11. Job xxii. 29; Psa. xviii 27; Prov. xxix. 23; Matt. xxiii. 12; Luke xviii. 14; James iv. 6; 1 Pet. v. 5.

αντικαλεσωσι, και γενηται σοι ανταποδομα.
should invite again, and be made to thee a recompense.
[13] Αλλ' όταν ποιης δοχην, καλει πτωχους,
But when thou mayest make a feast, invite poor ones,
αναπηρους, χωλους, τυφλους· [14] και μακαριος
maimed ones, lame ones, blind ones: and blessed
εση, ότι ουκ εχουσιν ανταποδουναι σοι·
thou wilt be, because not they have to recompense to thee:
ανταποδοθησεται γαρ σοι εν τη αναστασει των
it will be recompensed for to thee in the resurrection of the
δικαιων. [15] Ακουσας δε τις των συνανακειμενων
just. Hearing and one of those reclining
ταυτα, ειπεν αυτῳ· Μακαριος, ός φαγεται αρτον
these, said to him: Blessed, who shall eat bread
εν τη βασιλεια του θεου. [16] Ὁ δε ειπεν αυτῳ·
in the kingdom of the God. He and said to him:
Ανθρωπος τις εποιησε δειπνον μεγα, και εκαλεσε
A man certain made a supper great, and invited
πολλους. [17] Και απεστειλε τον δουλον αὑτου
many. And he sent the slave of himself
τη ὡρᾳ του δειπνου ειπειν τοις κεκλημενοις·
in the hour of the supper to say to those having been invited
Ερχεσθε, ότι ηδη ἑτοιμα εστι *[παντα.] [18] Και
Come you, for now ready is [all.] And
ηρξαντο απο μιας παραιτεισθαι παντες. Ὁ
they began from one to excuse themselves all. The
πρωτος ειπεν αυτῳ· Αγρον ηγορασα, και εχω
first said to him: A field I bought, and I have
αναγκην εξελθειν και ιδειν αυτον· ερωτω σε,
need to go out and to see him: I beseech thee,
εχε με παρητημενον. [19] Και ἑτερος ειπε· Ζευγη
have me having been excused. And another said: Yokes
βοων ηγορασα πεντε, και πορευομαι δοκιμασαι
of oxen I bought five, and I go to try
αυτα· ερωτω σε, εχε με παρητημενον. [20] Και
them: I beseech thee, have me having been excused. And
ἑτερος ειπε· Γυναικα εγημα, και δια τουτο ου
another said. A wife I married, and because of this not
δυναμαι ελθειν· [21] Και παραγενομενος ὁ δουλος
I am able to come. And having come the slave
εκεινος απηγγειλε τῳ κυριῳ αὑτου ταυτα. Τοτε
that reported to the lord of himself these. Then
οργισθεις ὁ οικοδεσποτης ειπε τῳ δουλῳ αὑτου·
being angry the householder said to the slave of himself:
Εξελθε ταχεως εις τας πλατειας και ῥυμας της
Go out quickly into the wide places and streets of the
πολεως, και τους πτωχους και αναπηρους και
city, and the poor ones and maimed ones and
χωλους και τυφλους εισαγαγε ὡδε. [22] Και ειπεν
lame ones and blind ones bring in hither. And said

invite Thee again, and a Recompense be made thee.

13 But when thou makest a Feast, invite the Poor, the Crippled, the Lame, the Blind;

14 and thou wilt be happy; Because they have no means to repay thee, therefore thou shalt be repaid at the RESURRECTION of the RIGHTEOUS."

15 And one of THOSE RECLINING with him, hearing this, said to him, ‡ "Happy he who shall eat † Bread in the KINGDOM of GOD."

16 ‡ And HE said to him, "A certain Man made a great SUPPER, and invited many.

17 And ‡ he sent his SERVANT, at the HOUR of the SUPPER, to say to THOSE who had been INVITED, 'Come, for it is now ready.'

18 And they all began, with one accord, to excuse themselves. The FIRST said to him, 'I have bought a Field, and I must go out and see it; I beseech thee to have Me excused.'

19 And another said, 'I have bought five Yoke of Oxen, and I am going to try them; I entreat thee to have Me excused.'

20 And another said, 'I have married a Wife, and, therefore, I cannot come.'

21 And that SERVANT having returned, related all to his MASTER. Then the HOUSEHOLDER, being angry, said to his SERVANT, 'Go out quickly into the OPEN SQUARES and Streets of the CITY, and bring in hither † the POOR, and Crippled, and * Blind, and Lame.'

22 And the SERVANT

* VATICAN MANUSCRIPT.—17. All—*omit*. 21. Blind and Lame.

† 15. Instead of *arton*, bread, some one hundred MSS., with some Versions and Fathers, read *ariston*, a dinner. This is probably the best reading, as they were now at dinner.—*Clarke*.
† 21. Faint traces remain of indiscriminate invitations to Oriental entertainments at this day. See Matt. xxii. 9; Prov. ix. 23. Dr. Pococke speaks of the admission of the poor to the tables of the great. "The Arabs never set by any thing that is brought to table, but call in their neighbors and the poor, and finish every thing." An Arab prince will often dine in the street before his door, and call to all that pass, even beggars, who come and sit down.

‡ 15. Rev. xix. 9. ‡ 16. Matt. xxii. 2. ‡ 17. Prov. ix. 2, 5.

ὁ δουλος· Κυριε, γεγονεν ὡς επεταξας, και
the slave; O lord, it is done as thou didst order, and
ετι τοπος εστι. 23 Και ειπεν ὁ κυριος προς τον
still room is. And said the lord to the
δουλον· Εξελθε εις τας ὁδους και φραγμους, και
slave; Go out into the ways and hedges, and
αναγκασον εισελθειν, ἱνα γεμισθῃ ὁ οικος μου.
urge to enter, that may be filled the house of me.
24 Λεγω γαρ ὑμιν, ὁτι ουδεις των ανδρων εκεινων
I say for to you, that no one of the men those
των κεκλημενων γευσεται μου του δειπνου.
the having been invited shall taste of me the supper.
25 Συνεπορευοντο δε αυτῳ οχλοι πολλοι· και
Were going with and him crowds great; and
στραφεις ειπε προς αυτους· 26 Ει τις ερχεται
turning he said to them; If any one comes
προς με, και ου μισει τον πατερα ἑαυτου, και
to me, and not hates the father of himself, and
την μητορα, και την γυναικα, και τα τεκνα, και
the mother, and the wife, and the children, and
τους αδελφους, και τας αδελφας, ετι δε και την
the brothers, and the sisters, still more and even the
ἑαυτου ψυχην, ου δυναται μου μαθητης ειναι.
of himself life, not is able of me a disciple to be.
27 Και ὁστις ου βασταζει τον σταυρον αὑτου,
And whoever not bears the cross of himself,
και ερχεται οπισω μου, ου δυναται μου ειναι
and comes after me, not is able of me to be
μαθητης. 28 Τις γαρ εξ ὑμων, θελων πυργον
a disciple. Who for of you, wishing a tower
οικοδομησαι, ουχι πρωτον καθισας ψηφιζει την
to build, not first having sat down computes the
δαπανην, ει εχει εις απαρτισμον; 29 ἱνα μηποτε
cost, if he has to finish; that lest
θεντος αυτου θεμελιον, και μη ισχυοντος εκτε-
having laid of him a foundation, and not being able to
λεσαι, παντες οἱ θεωρουντες αρξωνται εμπαιζειν
finish, all those beholding should begin to deride
αυτῳ, 30 λεγοντες· Ὁτι οὑτος ὁ ανθρωπος ηρξατο
him, saying; That this the man began
οικοδομειν, και ουκ ισχυσεν εκτελεσαι. 31 Η
to build, and not was able to finish. Or
τις βασιλευς πορευομενος συμβαλειν ἑτερῳ
what king going to engage with another
βασιλει εις πολεμον, ουχι καθισας πρωτον
king in battle, not having sat down first

said, 'Sir, * I have done what thou didst command, and yet there is Room.'

23 And the MASTER said to the SERVANT, 'Go to the ROADS and Hedges, and constrain people to come in, that * the HOUSE may be filled;'

24 for I tell you, ‡ That none of THOSE MEN who have been INVITED shall taste of My SUPPER."

25 And great Crowds were going with him; and turning he said to them,

26 ‡ "If any one comes to me, and † hates not his FATHER, and MOTHER, and WIFE, and CHILDREN, and BROTHERS, and SISTERS, ‡ and still more even * his own LIFE, he cannot be my DISCIPLE.

27 ‡ * Whoever, therefore, does not bear his own CROSS, and come after me, he cannot be My Disciple.

28 For who of you wishing to build a Tower, does not first sit down and estimate the EXPENSE, to know whether he has the means to complete it?

29 lest having laid a Foundation, and not being able to finish, ALL who SEE it begin to deride him,

30 saying, 'This MAN began to build, but was not able to finish.'

31 Or What King, going to encounter Another King in Battle, * will not first

* VATICAN MANUSCRIPT—22. I have done what thou didst command. 23. the HOUSE. 26. his own LIFE. 27. Whoever therefore does not bear his own CROSS. 31. will not first sit down and consult.

† 26. This is one amongst many examples in the sacred writings of Oriental figurative language, where the expression is hyperbolical in order to render the truth meant to be conveyed in it more striking and impressive. Matthew, in chap. x. 37, expresses the literal meaning of this passage, when he says, "loves his father and mother more than me;" and in chap. vi. 24, uses the word *hate* with similar force. So when we read in Rom. ix. 13, "Jacob have I loved, but Esau have I hated," the meaning is, I have loved Jacob more than Esau; and that this is no arbitrary interpretation of the word *hate*, but one agreeable to the Hebrew idiom, appears from what is said in Gen. xxix. 30, 31, where Leah's being *hated* is explained by Rachel's being *loved more than Leah*; see also Deut. xxi. 15—17. Something resembling what Jesus here teaches, is said by Philo (de Monarch, lib. ii. *p.* 230) concerning the duty of a high-priest; that he was to "estrange himself from all his relations, and not, out of love to his parents, his children, or brethren, to omit any part of his duty, or act in any thing contrary to it."—*Pearce.*

‡ 24. Matt. xxi. 43; xxii. 8; Acts xiii. 46. ‡ 26. Deut. xiii. 6; xxxiii. 9; Matt. x. 37; Rom. ix. 13. ‡ 26. Rev. xii. 11. ‡ 27. Matt. xvi. 24; Mark viii. 34; Luke ix. 23; 2 Tim. iii. 12.

βουλευεται, ει δυνατος εστιν εν δεκα χιλιασιν
consult, if able he is with ten thousand
απαντησαι τῳ μετα εικοσι χιλιαδων ερχομενῳ
to meet the (one) with twenty thousand coming
επ' αυτον; 32 Ει δε μηγε, ετι αυτου πορρω
against him? If but not, while of him far off
οντος, πρεσβειαν αποστειλας, ερωτᾳ *[τα] προς
being, an embassy having sent, he asks [the] to
ειρηνην. 33 Ούτως ουν πας εξ ὑμων, ὁς ουκ
peace. So then all of you, who not
αποτασσεται πασι τοις ἑαυτου ὑπαρχουσιν, ου
bids farewell to all the of himself possessions, not
δυναται μου ειναι μαθητης. 34 Καλον το ἁλας
is able of me to be a disciple. Good the salt;
εαν δε το ἁλας μωρανθῃ, εν τινι αρτυθησεται;
if but the salt should be tasteless, by what shall it be salted?
35 Ουτε εις γην, ουτε εις κοπριαν ευθετον εστιν·
Neither for land, nor for manure fit it is;
εξω βαλλουσιν αυτο. Ὁ εχων ωτα ακουειν,
out they cast it. He having ears to hear,
ακουετω.
let him hear.

ΚΕΦ. ιε'. 15.

1 Ησαν δε εγγιζοντες αὐτῳ παντες οἱ τελω-
Were and drawing near to him all the tax-gath-
ναι και οἱ ἁμαρτωλοι, ακουειν αυτου. 2 Και
erers and the sinners, to hear him. And
διεγογγυζον οἱ Φαρισαιοι και οἱ γραμματεις,
murmured the Pharisees and the scribes,
λεγοντες· Ὁτι οὑτος ἁμαρτωλους προσδεχεται,
saying: That this sinners receives,
και συνεσθιει αυτοις. 3 Ειπε δε προς αυτους
and eats with them. He said and to them
την παραβολην ταυτην, λεγων. 4 Τις ανθρωπος
the parable this, saying: What man
εξ ὑμων εχων ἑκατον προβατα, και απολεσας
of you having a hundred sheep, and having lost
ἑν εξ αυτων, ου καταλειπει τα εννενηκονταεννεα
one of them, not leaves behind the ninty-nine
εν τῃ ερημῳ, και πορευεται επι το απολωλος,
in the desert, and goes after that having been lost,
ἑως εὑρῃ αυτο, 5 Και εὑρων, επιτιθησιν επι τους
till he may find it? And having found, he lays on the
ωμους ἑαυτου χαιρων· 6 και ελθων εις τον οικον
shoulders of himself rejoicing: and coming into the house
συγκαλει τους φιλους και τους γειτονας, λεγων
he calls together the friends and the neighbors, saying
αυτους· Συγχαρητε μοι, ὁτι εὑρον το προβατον
to them Rejoice with me, for I found the sheep
μου το απολωλος. 7 Λεγω ὑμιν, ὁτι οὑτω χαρα
of me that having been lost. I say to you, that thus joy

sit down, and consult whether he is able with Ten Thousand, to meet HIM who COMES against him with Twenty Thousand.

32 And if not, while the other is at a distance, he sends an Embassy, and asks for Peace.

33 So, therefore, no one of you who does not forsake ALL his POSSESSIONS, can be My Disciple.

34 ‡SALT is good; †but if *the SALT should become insipid, how shall it recover its savor?

35 It is not fit for Land, nor for Manure; they throw it away. HE who HAS Ears to hear, let him hear."

CHAPTER XV.

1 ‡And All the TRIBUTE-TAKERS and the SINNERS were drawing near to hear him.

2 And *both the PHARISEES and SCRIBES murmured, saying, "This man receives Sinners, ‡and eats with them."

3 Then he spoke this PARABLE to them, saying,

4 ‡"What Man of you, having a Hundred Sheep, and losing one of them, does not leave the NINETY-NINE in the DESERT, and go after THAT which is LOST, till he finds it?

5 And having found it, he lays it on his SHOULDERS, rejoicing.

6 And coming to the HOUSE, he calls together his FRIENDS and NEIGHBORS, saying to them, 'Rejoice with me, For I have found THAT SHEEP of mine ‡which was LOST.'

7 I say to you, That

* VATICAN MANUSCRIPT.—32. the—*omit*. 34. also the SALT. 2. both the.

† 34. That this is possible in Palestine, is proved by what Mr. Maundrell says, in describing the *Valley of Salt*. He remarks, "Along on one side of the valley, towards *Gibul*, there is a small precipice about two men's lengths, occasioned by the continual taking away of the salt; and in this you may see how the veins of it lie. I broke a piece of it, of which that part that was exposed to the rain, sun, and air, though it had the sparks and particles of salt, YET IT HAD PERFECTLY LOST ITS SAVOR; the inner part, which was connected to the rock, retained its savor, as I found by proof."

‡ 34. Matt. v. 13, Mark ix. 50. ‡ 1. Matt ix. 10. ‡ 2. Acts xi. 3; Gal ii. 12.
‡ 4. Matt. xviii. 12. ‡ 6. 1 Pet. ii. 10, 25.

εσται εν τῳ ουρανῳ επι ἑνι αμαρτωλῳ μετανο-
will be in the heaven over one sinner reform-
ουντι, η επι εννενηκονταεννεα δικαιοις, ὁιτινες
ing, than over ninety-nine just ones, who
ου χρειαν εχουσι μετανοιας. 8 Η τις γυνη,
no need have of reformation. Or what woman,
δραχμας εχουσα δεκα, εαν απολεσῃ δραχμην
drachmas having ten, if she may lose drachma
μιαν, ουχι ἁπτει λυχνον, και σαροι την οικιαν,
one, not lights a lamp, and sweeps the house,
και ζητει επιμελως, ἑως ὁτου εὑρῃ; 9 Και
and seeks carefully, till she finds? And
εὑρουσα συγκαλειται τας φιλας και τας γειτο-
having found she calls together the friends and the neigh-
νας, λεγουσα· Συγχαρητε μοι, ὁτι εὑρον την
bors, saying; Rejoice with me, for I found the
δραχμην, ἡν απωλεσα. 10 Οὑτω, λεγω ὑμιν,
drachma, which I lost. Thus, I say to you,
χαρα γινεται ενωπιον των αγγελων του θεου
joy is produced in presence of the messengers of the God
επι ἑνι ἁμαρτωλῳ μετανοουντι.
over one sinner reforming.
11 Ειπε δε· Ανθρωπος τις ειχε δυο υἱους.
He said and; A man certain had two sons.
12 Και ειπεν ὁ νεωτερος αυτων τῳ πατρι· Πατερ,
And said the younger of them to the father: O father,
δος μοι το επιβαλλον μερος της ουσιας. Και
give to me the falling to part of the property. And
διειλεν αυτοις τον βιον. 13 Και μετ' ου πολλας
he divided to them the living. And after not many
ἡμερας συναγαγων ἁπαντα ὁ νεωτερος υἱος,
days having gathered together all the younger son,
απεδημησεν εις χωραν μακραν· και εκει
went abroad into a country distant: and there
διεσκορπισε την ουσιαν αὑτου, ζων ασωτως.
wasted the property of himself, living dissolutely.
14 Δαπανησαντος δε αυτου παντα, εγενετο λιμος
Having expended and of him all, came a famine
ισχυρος κατα την χωραν εκεινην· και αυτος
mighty throughout the country that: and he
ηρξατο ὑστερεισθαι. 15 Και πορευθεις εκολληθη
began to be in want. And having gone he united
ἑνι των πολιτων της χωρος εκεινης· και επεμ-
with one of the citizens of the country that; and he
ψεν αυτον εις τους αγρους αὑτου βοσκειν χοιρους.
sent him into the fields of himself to feed swine.
16 Και επεθυμει γεμισαι την κοιλιαν αὑτου απο
And he longed to fill the belly of himself from
των κερατιων, ὡν ησθιον οἱ χοιροι· και ουδεις
the pods, which were eating the swine; and no one
εδιδου αυτῳ. 17 Εις ἑαυτον δε ελθων, ειπε·
gave to him. To himself and coming, he said;

thus there will be more Joy in HEAVEN over One reforming Sinner, ‡ than for Ninety-nine Righteous persons who need no Reformation.

8 Or, what Woman, having ten † Drachmas, if she loses one of them, does not light a Lamp, and sweep the HOUSE, and search carefully, till she finds it?

9 And having found it, she calls together her FRIENDS and NEIGHBORS saying, 'Rejoice with me, For I have found the DRACHMA which I had lost.'

10 Thus, I say to you, there is Joy in the Presence of the ANGELS of GOD over One reforming Sinner."

11 And he said, "A certain Man had Two Sons.

12 And the YOUNGEST of them said to his FATHER, 'Father, give me the PORTION of the ESTATE FALLING to me. And * HE divided ‡ his LIVING between them.

13 And not Many Days after, the YOUNGEST Son having gathered all together, went abroad into a distant Country, and there wasted his PROPERTY in profligate living.

14 And having spent all, a great Famine occurred in that COUNTRY; and he began to be in want.

15 Then he went and attached himself to one of the CITIZENS of that COUNTRY, and he sent him into his FIELDS † to feed Swine.

16 And he longed * to be fed with the CAROB PODS, which the SWINE were eating; but no one gave to him.

17 And coming to him-

* VATICAN MANUSCRIPT—12. HE divided. 16. to be fed with the.

† 8. The Grecian *Drachma* was about the same value as the Roman *Denarius*, i. e. about 14 cents, or 7d. † 15. This prodigal is supposed to be a Jew; and (if so) as the Jews were forbidden by their law to eat swine's flesh, the care of swine in that distant and heathen country must have been an employment as inconsistent with his religion as he could possibly have had. This circumstance therefore serves to show us to what a very low condition he was reduced.—*Pearce.*

‡ 7. Luke v. 32. ‡ 12. Mark xii. 44.

Ποσοι μισθιοι του πατρος μου περισσευουσιν
How many hired servants of the father of me have an abundance
αρτων; εγω δε ὡδε λιμῳ απολλυμαι. 18 Αναστ-
of bread? I and here with hunger am perishing. Having
ας πορευσομαι προς τον πατερα, μου, και ερω
arisen I will go to the father of me, and will say
αυτῳ· Πατερ, ἡμαρτον εις τον ουρανον και
to him; O father, I sinned against the heaven and
ενωπιον σου· 19 ουκετι ειμι αξιος κληθηναι υἱος
in presence of thee; no longer I am fit to be called a son
σου· ποιησον με ὡς ἑνα των μισθιων σου. 20 Και
of thee; make me as one of the hired servants of thee. And
αναστας ηλθε προς τον πατερα ἑαυτου. Ετι
having arisen he went to the father of himself. While
δε αυτου μακραν απεχοντος, ειδεν αυτον ὁ πα-
but of him at a distance being, saw him the fa-
τηρ αυτου, και εσπλαγχνισθη· και δραμων
ther of him, and was moved with pity; and running
επεπεσεν επι τον τραχηλον αυτου, και κατεφι-
he fell on the neck of him, and repeatedly
λησεν αυτον. 21 Ειπε δε αυτῳ ὁ υἱος· Πατερ,
kissed him. Said and to him the son; O father,
ἡμαρτον εις τον ουρανον και ενωπιον σου· και
I sinned against the heaven and in presence of thee; and
ουκετι ειμι αξιος κληθηναι υἱος σου. 22 Ειπε δε ὁ
no longer I am fit to be called a son of thee. Said but the
πατηρ προς τους δουλους αὑτου· Εξενεγκατε
father to the slaves of himself; Bring you out
την στολην την πρωτην, και ενδυσατε αυτον,
the robe the chief, and clothe you him,
και δοτε δακτυλιον εις την χειρα αυτου, και
and give you a finger-ring into the hand of him, and
ὑποδηματα εις τους ποδας. 23 Και ενεγκαντες
shoes for the feet. And having brought
τον μοσχον τον σιτευτον θυσατε· και φαγοντες
the calf the fatted do you sacrifice; and eating
ευφρανθωμεν· 24 ὁτι οὑτος ὁ υἱος μου νεκρος ην,
we may be joyful: for this the son of me dead was,
και *[αν]εζησε· και απολωλως ην, και εὑρεθη.
and [again] is alive; and having been lost he was, and is found.
Και ηρξαντο ευφραινεσθαι. 25 Ην δε ὁ υἱος
And they began to be merry. Was and the son
αυτου ὁ πρεσβυτερος εν αγρῳ· και ὡς ερχομενος
of him the elder in a field: and as he was coming
ηγγισε τῃ οικιᾳ, ηκουσε συμφωνιας και χορων.
near to the house, he heard a sound of music and dancers.
26 Και προσκαλεσαμενος ἑνα των παιδων, επυν-
And having called to one of the servants, he in-
θανετο τι ειη ταυτα; 27 Ὁ δε ειπεν αυτῳ·
quired what may be these things? He and said to him:
Ὁτι ὁ αδελφος σου ἡκει· και εθυσεν ὁ πατηρ
That the brother of thee is come: and has sacrificed the father
σου τον μοσχον τον σιτευτον, ὁτι ὑγιαινοντα
of thee the calf the fatted, because safe
αυτον απελαβεν. 28 Ωργισθη δε, και ουκ ηθε-
him he received. He was angry and, and not was dis-

self, he said, 'How many of my FATHER's Hired servants have an abundance of Bread, and I am perishing here with Hunger!

18 I will arise and go to my FATHER, and will say to him, Father, I have sinned against HEAVEN, and before thee.

19 I am no longer worthy to be called thy Son; make me as one of thy HIRED SERVANTS.'

20 And he arose, and went to his FATHER. But while he was yet at some distance, his FATHER saw him, and was moved with pity; and running, he fell on his neck, and repeatedly kissed him.

21 And the SON said to him, 'Father, I have sinned against HEAVEN, and before * thee. I am no longer worthy to be called thy Son; make me as one of thy HIRED SERVANTS.'

22 But the FATHER said to his SERVANTS, 'Bring * out quickly that CHIEF ROBE, and clothe him; and attach a Ring to his HAND, and Sandals to his FEET;

23 and bring the FATTED CALF, and kill it; and let us eat, and be joyful;

24 For This my SON was dead, but is restored to life; he was even lost, but is found.' And they began to be joyful.

25 Now his OLDER SON was in the Field, and as he was coming and approached the HOUSE, he heard Music and † Dancing.

26 And summoning one of the SERVANTS, he asked him the reason of this.

27 And HE said to him, 'Thy BROTHER is come; and thy FATHER has killed the FATTED CALF, Because he has received him in health.'

28 And he was enraged,

* VATICAN MANUSCRIPT—21. thee. I am no longer worthy to be called thy Son; make me as one of thy HIRED SERVANTS. But. 22. out quickly. 24. again—*omit.*

† 25. *Choron,* probably ought to be rendered *a choir of singers.* Le Clerc denies that the word means dancing at all. *Symphonia,* translated *music,* may mean the musical instruments, which accompanied the choir of singers.

λεν εισελθειν. 'Ο ουν πατηρ αυτου εξελθων
posed to enter. The therefore father of him going out
παρεκαλει αυτον. [29] 'Ο δε αποκριθεις ειπε τῳ
besought him. He and answering said to the
πατρι· Ιδου, τοσαυτα ετη δουλευω σοι, και
father: Lo, so many years do I slave for thee, and
ουδεποτε εντολην σου παρηλθον· και εμοι ουδε-
never a command of thee I passed by: and to me never
ποτε εδωκας εριφον, ἱνα μετα των φιλων μου
thou gavest a kid, that with the friends of me
ευφρανθω. [30] 'Οτε δε ὁ υἱος σου οὑτος, ὁ κατα-
I might be joyful. When and the son of thee this, the having
φαγων σου τον βιον μετα πορνων, ηλθεν, εθυ-
devoured of thee the living with harlots, came, thou hast
σας αυτῳ τον μοσχον τον σιτευτον. [31] 'Ο δε
sacrificed for him the calf the fatted. He and
ειπεν αυτῳ· Τεκνον, συ παντοτε μετ' εμου ει,
said to him: O child, thou always with me art,
και παντα τα εμα σα εστιν. [32] Ευφρανθηναι δε
and all the mine thine is. To be joyful but
και χαρηναι εδει, ὁτι ὁ αδελφος σου οὑτος
and to be glad it is proper, for the brother of thee this
νεκρος ην, και *[αν]εζησε· και απολωλως ην,
dead was, and [again] is alive: and having been lost was,
και εὑρεθη.
and is found.

and refused to enter. *And his FATHER going out, entreated him.

29 And HE answering, said to his FATHER, 'Behold, so many years have I slaved for thee, and never disobeyed thy command; and yet thou never gavest Me a Kid, that I might be joyful with my FRIENDS;

30 but when THIS SON of thine came, who has CONSUMED Thy LIVING with PROSTITUTES, thou hast killed for him the *FATTED Calf.'

31 And HE said to him, 'Child, thou art always with me, and ALL that is MINE is thine.

32 It was proper to be joyful and be glad; For THIS BROTHER of thine was dead, but is restored to life; he was even lost, but is found.'"

ΚΕΦ. ιϛ'. 16.

[1] Ελεγε δε και προς τους μαθητας αὑτου·
He said and also to the disciples of himself:
Ανθρωπος τις ην πλουσιος, ὁς ειχεν οικονομον·
A man certain was rich, who had a steward;
και οὑτος διεβληθη αυτῳ ὡς διασκορπιζων τα
and this was accused to him as wasting the
ὑπαρχοντα αυτου. [2] Και φωνησας αυτον, ειπεν
possessions of him. And having called him, he said
αυτῳ· Τι τουτο ακουω περι σου; αποδος τον
to him; What this I hear concerning thee? render the
λογον της οικονομιας σου· ου γαρ δυνηση ετι
account of the stewardship of thee: not for thou wilt be able longer
οικονομειν. [3] Ειπε δε εν ἑαυτῳ ὁ οικονομος· Τι
to be steward. Said and in himself the steward: What
ποιησω, ὁτι ὁ κυριος μου αφαιρειται την οικονο-
shall I do, for the lord of me takes the steward-
μιαν απ' εμου; Σκαπτειν ουκ ισχυω, επαιτειν
ship from me? To dig not I have strength, to beg
αισχυνομαι. [4] Εγνων τι ποιησω, ἱνα, ὁταν
I am ashamed. I know what I will do, that, when
μετασταθω της οικονομιας, δεξωνται με εις
I may be put out of the stewardship, they may receive me into
τους οικους αὑτων. [5] Και προσκαλεσαμενος
the houses of themselves. And having summoned
ἑνα ἑκαστον των χρεωφειλετων του κυριου
one each of the debtors of the lord
ἑαυτου, ελεγε τῳ πρωτῳ· Ποσον οφειλεις τῳ
of himself, he said to the first, How much owest thou to the

CHAPTER XVI.

1 And he said also to *the Disciples, "There was a certain rich Man, who had a Steward; and he was accused to him of wasting his POSSESSIONS.

2 And having called him, he said to him, 'What is this that I hear of thee? render an ACCOUNT of thy STEWARDSHIP; for thou canst be a Steward no longer.'

3 And the STEWARD said within himself, 'What shall I do? For my MASTER takes the STEWARDSHIP away from me; I have not strengh to dig: *and I am ashamed to beg.

4 I know what I will do, that when I am deprived of the STEWARDSHIP, they may receive me into their own HOUSES.'

5 And calling each one of his MASTER'S DEBTORS, he said to the FIRST, 'How much dost thou owe my MASTER?'

* VATICAN MANUSCRIPT.—28. And his FATHER. 30. FATTED Calf. 32. again—omit. 1. the Disciples. [illegible]

κυριῳ μου; [6]Ὁ δε ειπεν· Ἑκατον βατους ελαιου.
lord of me? He and said; A hundred baths of oil.

Και ειπεν αυτῳ· Δεξαι σου το γραμμα, και
And he said to him; Receive of thee the bill, and

καθισας ταχεως γραψον πεντηκοντα. [7]Επειτα
sitting down quickly write thou fifty. Then

ἑτερῳ ειπε· Συ δε ποσον οφειλεις; Ὁ δε ειπεν·
to another he said, Thou and how much owest thou? He and said;

Ἑκατον κορους σιτου. *[Και] λεγει αυτῳ·
A hundred cors of wheat. [And] he says to him,

Δεξαι σου το γραμμα, και γραψον ογδοηκοντα.
Receive of thee the bill, and write eighty.

[8]Και επῃνεσεν ὁ κυριος τον οικονομον της
And praised the lord the steward the

αδικιας, ὁτι φρονιμως εποιησεν· ὁτι οἱ υἱοι του
unjust, because prudently he had done: for the sons of the

αιωνος τουτου φρονιμωτεροι ὑπερ τους υἱους του
age this more prudent above the sons of the

φωτος εις την γενεαν την ἑαυτων εισι. [9]Καγω
light for the generation that of themselves are. And I

ὑμιν λεγω· Ποιησατε ἑαυτοις φιλους εκ του
to you say; Make you to yourselves friends out of the

μαμωνα της αδικιας· ἱνα, ὁταν εκλιπητε, δεξων-
mammon of the unjust: that, when you may fail, they may

ται ὑμας εις τας αιωνιους σκηνας. [10]Ὁ πιστος
receive you into the age-lasting tabernacles. He faithful

εν ελαχιστῳ και εν πολλῳ πιστος εστι· και ὁ
in least also in much faithful is: and he

εν ελαχιστῳ αδικος, και εν πολλῳ αδικος εστιν.
in least unjust, also in much unjust is.

[11]Ει ουν εν τῳ αδικῳ μαμωνᾳ πιστοι ουκ
If therefore in the unrighteous mammon faithful not

εγενεσθε, το αληθινον τις ὑμιν πιστευσει; [12]και
you have been, the true who to you will entrust? and

ει εν τῳ αλλοτριῳ πιστοι ουκ εγενεσθε, το
if in the another faithful not you have been, the

ὑμετερον τις ὑμιν δωσει;
yours who to you will give?

[13]Ουδεις οικετης δυναται δυσι κυριοις δουλευ-
No one domestic is able two lords to serve:

ειν· η γαρ τον ἑνα μισησει, και τον ἑτερον
either for the one he will hate, and the other

αγαπησει· η ἑνος ανθεξεται, και του ἑτερου
he will love; or one he will cling to, and the other

καταφρονησει. Ου δυνασθε θεῳ δουλευειν και
he will slight. Not you are able God to serve and

6 And HE said, †'A Hundred Baths of Oil.' And *HE said to him, 'Take back *Thy ACCOUNT, and sit down quickly, and write one for fifty.'

7 Then he said to another, 'And how much dost thou owe?' And HE said, †'A Hundred Cors of Wheat.' He says to him, 'Take back *Thy ACCOUNT, and write one for eighty.'

8 And the MASTER applauded the UNJUST STEWARD, Because he had acted prudently; For the SONS of this AGE are more prudent as to THAT GENERATION which is their own, than ‡the SONS of LIGHT.

9 And I say to you, ‡Make for yourselves Friends with the DECEITFUL WEALTH, that, when *it fails, they may receive you into AIONIAN Mansions.

10 ‡HE who is FAITHFUL in a little, is also faithful in much; and HE who is UNJUST in a little, is also unjust in much.

11 If, therefore, you have not been faithful in the DELUSIVE Riches, who will confide the TRUE to you.

12 And if you have not been faithful in THAT which is ANOTHER'S, who will give you THAT which is *YOUR OWN?

13 ‡No Domestic can serve Two Masters; for he will either hate the ONE, and love the OTHER; or he will attend to one, and neglect the OTHER. You cannot serve God and Mammon.

* VATICAN MANUSCRIPT—6. HE said. 6. Thy LETTERS, and. 7. And—*omit*. 7. Thy LETTERS, and. 9. it fails. 12. OUR OWN.

† 6. The *bath* was the largest measure of capacity among the Hebrews, except the *homer*, of which it was the tenth part. See Ezek. xlv. 11, 14. It is equal to the *ephah*, i. e., to *seven gallons and a half* of our measure.—*Clarke*. Josephus states that it contained seventy-two sextarii, or about thirteen and a half gallons. † 7. The *cor* was the largest measure of capacity among the Hebrews, whether for solids or liquids. As the *bath* was equal to the *ephah*, so the *cor* was equal to the *homer*. It contained about seventy-five gallons and five pints English.

‡ 8. John xii. 36; Eph. v. 8; 1 Thess. v. 5. ‡ 9. Dan. iv. 27; Matt. vi. 19; xix. 21; 1 Tim. vi. 17—19. ‡ 10. Matt. xxv. 21; Luke xix. 17. ‡ 13. Matt. vi. 24.

μαμωνα. [14] Ηκουον δε ταυτα παντα και οἱ
mammon. Heard and these all also the
Φαρισαιοι, φιλαργυροι ὑπαρχοντες· και εξεμυκ-
Pharisees, money-lovers being; and they
τηριζον αυτον. [15] Και ειπεν αυτοις· Ὑμεις
mocked him. And he said to them; You
εστε οἱ διδαιουντες ἑαυτους ενωπιον των
are those justifying yourselves in presence of the
ανθρωπων· ὁ δε θεος γινωσκει τας καρδιας ὑμων·
men: the but God knows the hearts of you;
ὁτι το εν ανθρωποις ὑψηλον, βδελυγμα ενωπιον
for that by men highly prized, an abomination in presence
του θεου.
of the God.
[16] Ὁ νομος και οἱ προφηται ἑως Ιωαννου· απο
The law and the prophets till John: from
τοτε ἡ βασιλεια του θεου ευαγγελιζεται, και
then the kingdom of the God is preached. and
πας εις αυτην βιαζεται. [17] Ευκοπωτερον δε
every one into her presses. Easier but
εστι τον ουρανον και την γην παρελθειν, η του
it is the heaven and the earth to pass away, than of the
νομου μιαν κεραιαν πεσειν. [18] Πας ὁ απολυων
law one fine point to fail. Every one who dismissing
την γυναικα αὑτου, και γαμων ἑτεραν, μοι-
the wife of himself, and marrying another, commits
χευει· και πας ὁ απολελυμενην απο ανδρος
adultery: and every one who her being divorced from an husband
γαμων, μοιχευει.
marrying, commits adultery.
[19] Ανθρωπος δε τις ην πλουσιος, και ενεδι-
A man now certain was rich, and was
δυσκετο πορφυραν και βυσσον, ευφραινομενος
clothed purple and fine linen, feasting
καθ' ἡμεραν λαμπρως. [20] Πτωχος δε τις *[ην]
every day sumptuously. A poor and certain [was]
ονοματι Λαζαρος, *[ὁς] εβεβλητο προς τον
named Lazarus, [who] was laid at the
πυλωνα αυτου ἡλκωμενος, [21] και επιθυμων
gate of him being covered with sores, and longing
χορτασθηναι απο των ψιχιων των πιπτοντων
to be fed from the crumbs those falling
απο της τραπεζης του πλουσιου· αλλα και οἱ
from the table of the rich: but even the
κυνες ερχομενοι απελειχον τα ἑλκη αυτου.
dogs coming licked the sores of him.
[22] Εγενετο δε αποθανειν τον πτωχον, και απε-
It happened and to die the poor, and to
νεχθηναι αυτον ὑπο των αγγελων εις τον κολ-
be borne away him by the messengers into the bo-

14 And the PHARISEES, ‡being money-lovers, also heard all these things, and they ridiculed him.

15 And he said to them, "You are THOSE who ‡JUSTIFY yourselves before MEN; but GOD knows your HEARTS; For THAT which is HIGHLY PRIZED among Men is an Abomination before *GOD.

16 ‡The LAW and the PROPHETS were till John; from that period, the KINGDOM of GOD is proclaimed, and every one presses towards it.

17 ‡And it is easier for HEAVEN and EARTH to pass away, than for one Point of the LAW to fail.

18 ‡EVERY ONE who DISMISSES his WIFE, and marries another, commits adultery; and *HE who MARRIES her being divorced from her Husband, commits adultery.

19 †Now there was a certain rich Man, who was clothed in Purple and Fine linen, and feasted sumptuously every Day.

20 And a certain Poor man, named Lazarus, was laid at his GATE, full of sores,

21 and longing to be fed with *THOSE CRUMBS which FELL from the RICH man's TABLE; but even the DOGS came and licked his sores.

22 And it occurred, that the POOR man died, and was carried away by the ANGELS to ABRAHAM'S

* VATICAN MANUSCRIPT.—15. the Lord. 18. HE who MARRIES. 20. was—omit. 20. who—omit. 21. THINGS which FELL.

† 19. This parable stands in connection with a palpable confusion and interruption of our Savior's discourse, which is broken after the fifteenth verse by three verses neither connected with each other, nor with what precedes them. Neither is it directly said that our Savior did use the parable, but is abruptly introduced, &c. I am unable to learn whether a similar parable has been recognized in the rabbinical writings but the complexion of it certainly accords with their mode of illustration much better than it does with that employed by our Savior.—*McCulloh*. Dr. Lightfoot and others have shown that the Jews in their *Gemara* have a parable much to the same purpose.—*Doddridge*.

‡ 14. Matt. xxiii. 14. ‡ 15. Luke x. 23. ‡ 16. Matt. iv. 17; xi. 12, 13; Luke xii. 20. ‡ 17. Matt. v. 18. ‡ 18. Matt. v. 32; xix. 9; Mark x. 11; 1 Cor. vii. 10, 11

τον Αβρααμ. Απεθανε δε και ὁ πλουσιος, και
som Abraam. Died and also the rich, and
εταφη. 23 Και εν τῳ ᾅδῃ επαρας τους οφθαλ-
was buried. And in the unseen having lifted the eyes
μους αὐτου, ὑπαρχων εν βασανοις, ὁρᾳ τον
of himself, being in torments, sees the
Αβρααμ απο μακροθεν, και Λαζαρον εν τοις κολ-
Abraam from a distance, and Lazarus in the bo-
ποις αυτου. 24 Και αυτος φωνησας ειπε· Πατερ
soms of him. And he crying out he said; O father
Αβρααμ, ελεησον με, και πεμψον Λαζαρον, ἱνα
Abraham, do thou pity me, and send Lazarus, that
βαψῃ το ακρον του δακτυλου αὐτου ὑδατος,
he may dip the tip of the finger of himself of water,
και καταψυξῃ την γλωσσαν μου· ὁτι οδυνωμαι
and may cool the tongue of me; for I am in pain
εν τῃ φλογι ταυτῃ. 25 Ειπε δε Αβρααμ· Τεκνον,
in the flame this. Said and Abraam; O child,
μνησθητι, ὁτι απελαβες τα αγαθα σου εν τῃ
remember, that thou didst receive the things good of thee in the
ζωῃ σου, και Λαζαρος ὁμοιως τα κακα· νυν
life of thee, and Lazarus in like manner the things bad; now
δε ὡδε παρακαλειται, συ δε οδυνασαι. 26 Και
but this is comforted, thou and art in pain. And
επι πασι τουτοις, μεταξυ ἡμων και ὑμων χασμα
besides all these, between of us and of you a chasm
μεγα εστηρικται, ὁπως οἱ θελοντες διαβηναι
great has been fixed, so that those wishing to pass over
ενθεν προς ὑμας, μη δυνωνται, μηδε οἱ εκειθεν
hence to you, not is able, nor those thence
προς ἡμας διαπερωσιν. 27 Ειπε δε· Ερωτω ουν
to us cross over. He said then; I beseech then
σε, πατερ, ἱνα πεμψῃς αυτον εις τον οικον του
thee, O father, that thou wouldst send him to the house of the
πατρος μου· 28 εχω γαρ πεντε αδελφους· ὁπως
father of me; I have for five brothers: that
διαμαρτυρηται αυτοις, ἱνα μη και αυτοι ελθωσιν
he may testify to them, that not also they may come
εις τον τοπον τουτον της βασανου. 29 Λεγει
into the place this of the torment. Says
*[αυτῳ] Αβρααμ· Εχουσι Μωσεα και τους
[to him] Abraam: They have Moses and the
προφητας· ακουσατωσαν αυτων. 30 Ὁ δε ειπεν·
prophets: let them hear them. He and said:
Ουχι, πατερ, Αβρααμ· αλλ' εαν τις απο νεκρων
No, O father, Abraam: but if one from dead ones
πορευθῃ προς αυτους, μετανοησουσιν. 31 Ειπε δε
may go to them, they will reform. He said but

† BOSOM. And the RICH
man also died, and was
buried;
23 and in HADES, being
in Torments, he lifted up
his EYES, and sees * Abraham at a distance, and
Lazarus in † the FOLDS of
his mantle.
24 And crying out he
said, 'Father Abraham,
pity me, and send Lazarus,
that he may dip the TIP of
his FINGER in Water, and
cool my TONGUE; For I
am tortured in this FLAME.'
25 But Abraham said,
'Child, recollect That thou,
during thy LIFE, ‡ didst receive thy GOOD things, and
Lazarus, in like manner,
his EVIL things; but now
* here he is comforted, and
thou art tormented.
26 And besides all this,
a great Chasm is situated
between us and you; so
that THOSE WISHING to
pass over hence to you are
unable; nor can * those
cross over thence to us.'
27 Then he said, 'I en-
treat thee, then, Father, to
send him to my FATHER'S
HOUSE;
28 For I have Five Bro-
thers; that he may testify
fully to them, lest they
also come into this PLACE
of MISERY.'
29 * But Abraham says,
‡ 'They have Moses and
the PROPHETS; let them
hear them.'
30 And HE said, 'No,
Father Abraham, but if
one should go to them from
the Dead, they will reform.'
31 And he said to him,

* VATICAN MANUSCRIPT—23. Abraham. 25. here he is comforted, and. 26. those. 29. But Abraham. 29. to him—*omit.*

† 22. The expression, "Abraham's bosom," alludes to the posture used by the Jews at table. This was reclining on couches after the manner of the Romans, the upper part of the body resting upon the left elbow, and the lower lying at length upon the couch. When two or three reclined on the same couch, some say the worthiest or most honorable person lay first, (Lightfoot says, in the middle;) the next in dignity lay with his head reclining on the breast or bosom of the first, as John is said to have done on the bosom of Jesus at supper; and hence is borrowed the phrase of Abraham's bosom, as denoting the state of celestial happiness. Abraham being esteemed the most honorable person, and the father of the Jewish nation, to be in his bosom signifies (in allusion to the order in which guests were placed at an entertainment) the highest state of felicity next to that of Abraham himself. —*Burder.* † 23. *Tois kolpois,* being plural, the idea seems to be as expressed in the text See Parkhurst.

‡ 25. Job xxi. 13; Luke vi. 24. ‡ 29. Isa. viii. 20; xxxiv. 16; John v. 39, 45; Acts xv 21: xvii. 11.

αυτῳ· Ει Μωσεως και των προφητων ουκ ακου-
to him: If Moses and the prophets not they
ουσιν, ουδε εαν τις εκ νεκρων αναστῃ, πεισ-
hear. neither if one out of dead ones should rise, will
θησονται.
they be convinced.

'If they hear not Moses and the PROPHETS, ‡neither will they be convinced, though one should rise from the Dead.'"

ΚΕΦ. ιζʹ. 17.

¹ Ειπε δε προς τους μαθητας· Ανενδεκτον
He said and to the disciples: Impossible
εστι του μη ελθειν τα σκανδαλα· ουαι δε, δι'
it is of the not to come the snares; woe but, through
οὗ ερχεται. ² Λυσιτελει αυτῳ, ει μυλος ονικος
whom they come. It is profitable for him, if a millstone upper
περικειται περι τον τραχηλον αυτου, και ερριπ-
was hung about the neck of him, and have been
ται εις την θαλασσαν, η ἱνα σκανδαλισῃ ἑνα
thrown into the sea, than that he should ensnare one
των μικρων τουτων. ³ Προσεχετε ἑαυτοις. Εαν
of the little ones these. Take heed to yourselves. If
δε ἁμαρτῃ *[εις σε] ὁ αδελφος σου, επιτιμησον
and should sin [against thee] the brother of thee, rebuke
αυτῳ· και εαν μετανοησῃ, αφες αυτῳ. ⁴ Και
him; and if he should reform, forgive him. And
εαν ἑπτακις της ἡμερας ἁμαρτῃ εις σε, και
if seven times of the day he should sin against thee, and
ἑπτακις *[της ἡμερας] επιστρεψῃ, λεγων·
seven times [of the day] he should turn, saying;
Μετανοω· αφησεις αυτῳ.
I reform; thou shalt forgive him.
⁵ Και ειπον οἱ αποστολοι τῳ κυριῳ· Προσθες
And said the apostles to the lord; Do thou add
ἡμιν πιστιν. ⁶ Ειπε δε ὁ κυριος· Ει ειχετε
to us faith. Said and the lord: If you had
πιστιν ὡς κοκκον σιναπεως, ελεγετε αν τῃ
faith as a grain of mustard, you might say to the
συκαμινῳ ταυτῃ· Εκριζωθητι, και φυτευθητι εν
sycamine-tree this; Be thou uprooted, and be thou planted in
τῃ θαλασσῃ· και ὑπηκουσεν αν ὑμιν. ⁷ Τις δε
the sea, and it would obey you. Which but
εξ ὑμων δουλον εχων αροτριωντα η ποιμαινοντα,
of you a slave having ploughing or feeding cattle,
ὁς εισελθοντι εκ του αγρου ερει· Ευθεως
who having come out of the field will say; Immediately
παρελθων αναπεσαι; ⁸ Αλλ' ουχι ερει αυτῳ
going do thou recline? But not will say to him
Ετοιμασον τι δειπνησω, και περιζωσαμενος
Make ready what I may sup, and having girded
διακονει μοι, ἑως φαγω και πιω· και μετα ταυτα
do thou serve me, till I may eat and drink: and after these
φαγεσαι και πιεσαι συ; ⁹ Μη χαριν εχει τῳ δουλῳ
shalt eat and drink thou? Not favor has the slave
εκεινῳ, ὁτι εποιησε τα διαταχθεντα; *[Ου
that, because he did the things having been commanded? [No
δοκω.] ¹⁰ Οὑτω και ὑμεις, ὁταν ποιησητε ταυτα
I think.] So also you, when you shall have done all

CHAPTER XVII.

1 And he said to *his DISCIPLES, ‡"It is impossible for SNARES not *to come; but Woe to him through whom they come!
2 It would be better for him, if an upper Millstone were hanged about his NECK, and he be thrown into the SEA, than that he should insnare one of these LITTLE ONES.
3 Take heed to yourselves; ‡If thy BROTHER sins, ‡rebuke him; and if he reforms, forgive him.
4 And if seven times in a DAY he sins against thee, and seven times he turns to thee again, saying, 'I reform;' thou shalt forgive him."
5 And the APOSTLES said to the LORD, "Increase our Faith."
6 ‡And the LORD said, "If you had Faith as a Grain of Mustard, you might say to this SYCAMINE-TREE, Be thou uprooted and planted in the SEA; and it would obey you.
7 But which of you having a Servant ploughing or feeding cattle, will say to him as he comes in from the FIELD, 'Come immediately, and recline?'
8 But will he not say to him, 'make ready my supper; gird thyself, and serve me, while I eat and drink; and afterwards thou shalt eat and drink?'
9 Does he thank *that SERVANT 'Because he did what was commanded?
10 So also you, when you shall have done All the

* VATICAN MANUSCRIPT.—1. his disciples. 1. should COME; nevertheless Woe the SERVANT. 3. against thee—*omit.* 4. of the day—*omit.* 9. him. I think not—*omit.*

‡ 31. John xii. 10, 11. ‡ 1. Matt. xviii. 6, 7; Mark ix. 42; 1 Cor. xi. 19. ‡ 3. Matt. xviii. 15, 21. ‡ 3. Lev. xix. 17; Prov. xvii. 10; James v. 19. ‡ 6. Matt. xvii. 20; xxi. 21; Mark ix. 23; xi. 23.

τα διαταχθεντα ὑμιν, λεγετε· Ὁτι δουλοι
the things having been commanded you, say you: That slaves
αχρειοι εσμεν· ὁτι ὁ ωφειλομεν ποιησαι,
unprofitable we are: because what we were bound to do,
πεποιηκαμεν.
we have done.
11 Και εγενετο εν τῳ πορευεσθαι αυτον εις
And it happened in the to go him to
Ἱερουσαλημ, και αυτος διηρχετο δια μεσου
Jerusalem, and he passed through midst
Σαμαρειας και Γαλιλαιας. 12 Και εισερχομενου
of Samaria and Galilee. And entering
αυτου εις τινα κωμην, απηντησαν αυτῳ δεκα
of him into a certain village, met him ten
λεπροι ανδρες, οἱ εστησαν πορρωθεν. 13 Και
leprous men, who stood far off. And
αυτοι ηραν φωνην, λεγοντες· Ιησου επιστατα
they lifted up a voice, saying: Jesus master,
ελεησον ἡμας. 14 Και ιδων ειπεν αυτοις·
pity us. And seeing he said to them:
Πορευθεντες επιδειξατε ἑαυτους τοις ἱερευσι.
Going show you yourselves to the priests.
Και εγενετο εν τῳ ὑπαγειν αυτους, εκαθαρισθη-
And it happened in the to go them, they were cleansed.
σαν. 15 Εἱς δε εξ αυτων, ιδων ὁτι ιαθη, ὑπεσ-
One and of them, seeing that he was cured, turned
τρεψε, μετα φωνης μεγαλης δοξαζων τον θεον·
back, with a voice loud glorifying the God:
16 και επεσεν επι προσωπον παρα τους ποδας
and fell on face at the feet
αυτου, ευχαριστων αυτῳ· και αυτος ην Σαμα-
of him, giving thanks to him: and he was a Sama-
ρειτης. 17 Αποκριθεις δε ὁ Ιησους ειπεν· Ουχι
ritan. Answering and the Jesus said: Not
οἱ δεκα εκαθαρισθησαν; οἱ δε εννεα που; 18 Ουχ
the ten were cleansed? the but nine where? Not
εὑρεθησαν ὑποστρεψαντες δουναι δοξαν τῳ θεῳ,
were found having returned to give glory to the God,
ει μη ὁ αλλογενης οὑτος; 19 Και ειπεν αυτῳ·
except the foreigner this? And he said to him:
Αναστας πορευου· *[ἡ πιστις σου σεσωκε σε.]
Arising go thou: [the faith of thee has saved thee.]
20 Επερωτηθεις δε ὑπο των φαρισαιων, ποτε
Having been asked and by the Pharisees, when
ερχεται ἡ βασιλεια του θεου, απεκριθη αυτοις,
comes the kingdom of the God, he answered them,
και ειπεν· Ουκ ερχεται ἡ βασιλεια του θεου
and said: Not comes the kingdom of the God
μετα παρατηρησεως· 21 ουδε ερουσιν· Ιδου ὡδε,
with careful watching; nor will they say; Lo here,
η, *[ιδου] εκει· ιδου γαρ, ἡ βασιλεια του θεου
or, [lo] there, lo for, the majesty of the God

THINGS COMMANDED you say, 'We are unprofitable Servants; for we have done only what we were bound to do.'"

11 And it occurred, as he was PROCEEDING to Jerusalem, he passed through the Interior of Samaria and Galilee.

12 And as he was about entering a Certain Village, Ten Lepers met him, who stood ‡at a distance;

13 and they lifted up their Voice, saying, "Jesus, Master, pity us."

14 And seeing them, he said to them, ‡"Go, show yourselves to the PRIESTS." And it happened, as they were GOING, they were cleansed.

15 And one of them perceiving That he was cured, returned, praising GOD with a loud Voice;

16 and he fell on his Face at his FEET, thanking him; and he was a Samaritan.

17 And JESUS answering, said, "Were not the TEN cleansed? but where are the NINE?

18 Were none found to return to give Praise to GOD, except this ALIEN?"

19 And he said to him; "Arise, go thy way; *thy FAITH has saved thee."

20 And having been asked by the PHARISEES, when GOD'S KINGDOM was coming, he answered them, and said, "The KINGDOM of GOD comes not with outward show;

21 nor shall they say, 'Behold here! or there!' for, behold, † GOD'S ROYAL MAJESTY is among you."

* VATICAN MANUSCRIPT.—19. thy FAITH has saved thee—*omit.* 21. lo—*omit.*

† 21. In this verse it has been found necessary to depart from the usual signification of *hee basileia tou theou*, the KINGDOM of GOD, and render as in the text. That this rendering is admissible and correct, see Note on Matt. iii. 2. *Basileia* here refers to the *person* to whom the title and honor of king belonged, rather than to his *territory* or *kingdom*. Prof. Whiting, an able Hebrew and Greek scholar, says, this clause in the 21st verse ought to be rendered "the *king* is among you." Dr. A. Clarke in a note on the 21st verse evidently understood it as relating to the Christ. He says, "Perhaps those Pharisees thought, that Messiah was kept secret, in some private place, known only to some of their rulers; and that by and by he should be proclaimed in a similar way to that in which *Joash* was by Jehoiada the priest. See the account, 2 Chron. xxiii. 1—11."

‡ 12. Lev. xiii. 46. ‡ 14. Lev. xiii. 2; xiv. 2; Matt. viii. 4; Luke v. 14.

ἐντος ὑμων εστιν. 22 Ειπε δε προς τους μαθη-
in the midst of you is. He said and to the disci-
τας· Ελευσονται ἡμεραι, ὁτε επιθυμησετε μιαν
ples: Will come days, when you will desire one
των ἡμερων του υἱου του ανθρωπου ιδειν· και
of the days of the son of the man to see; and
ουκ οψεσθε. 23 Και ερουσιν ὑμιν· Ἰδου ὡδε, η,
not you will see. And they will say to you; Lo here, or,
ιδου εκει· μη απελθητε, μηδε διωξητε. 24 Ὡσπερ
lo there; not you may go away, nor may you follow. Even as
γαρ ἡ αστραπη, ἡ αστραπτουσα εκ της ὑπ'
for the lightning, that flashing out of the under
ουρανον, εις την ὑπ' ουρανον λαμπει· οὑτως
heaven, to the under heaven shines; so
εσται ὁ υἱος του ανθρωπου *[εν τῃ ἡμερᾳ αυτου.]
will be the son of the man [in the day of him.]
25 Πρωτον δε δει αυτον πολλα παθειν, και
First but it behoves him many things to suffer, and
αποδοκιμασθηναι απο της γενεας ταυτης. 26 Και
to be rejected from the generation this. And
καθως εγενετο εν ταις ἡμεραις Νωε, οὑτως εσται
as it happened in the days of Noe, so it will be
και εν ταις ἡμεραις του υἱου του ανθρωπου.
also in the days of the son of the man.
27 Ησθιον, επινον, εγαμουν, εξεγαμιζοντο, αχρι
They ate, they drank, they married, they were given in marriage, till
ἡς ἡμερας εισηλθε Νωε εις την κιβωτον· και
of which day entered Noe into the ark; and
ηλθεν ὁ κατακλυσμος, και απωλεσεν ἁπαντας.
came the flood, and destroyed all.
28 Ὁμοιως και ὡς εγενετο εν ταις ἡμεραις Λωτ·
In like manner also as it happened in the days of Lot;
ησθιον, επινον ηγοραζον, επωλουν, εφυτευον,
they ate, they drank, they bought, they sold, they planted,
ᾠκοδομουν· 29 ᾗ δε ἡμερᾳ εξηλθε Λωτ απο
they built: in the but day went out Lot from
Σοδομων, εβρεξε πυρ και θειον απ' ουρανου, και
Sodom, it rained fire and brimstone from heaven, and
απωλεσεν ἁπαντας· 30 κατα ταυτα εσται ᾗ
destroyed all: according to these it will be in the
ἡμερᾳ ὁ υἱος του ανθρωπου αποκαλυπτεται. 31 Εν
day the son of the man is revealed. In
εκεινῃ τῃ ἡμερᾳ, ὁς εσται επι του δωματος, και
that the day, who will be on the roof, and
τα σκευη αυτου εν τῃ οικιᾳ, μη καταβατω αραι
the goods of him in the house, not let him descend to take
αυτα· και ὁ εν τῳ αγρῳ, ὁμοιως μη επιστρε-
them; and he in the field, in like manner not let him
ψατω εις τα οπισω. 32 Μνημονευετε της γυναι-
turn for the things behind. Remember you of the wife
κος Λωτ. 33 Ὁς εαν ζητησῃ την ψυχην αὑτου
of Lot. Whoever may seek the life of himself

22 And he said to the DISCIPLES, ‡ Days will come, when you will desire to see one of the DAYS of the SON of MAN, and you will not see it.

23 ‡ And they will say to you, * 'Behold, there!' or 'behold, here!' follow not.

24 ‡ For as THAT LIGHTNING FLASHING out of ONE part under Heaven, shines to the OTHER part under Heaven; so will the SON of MAN be.

25 ‡ But first he must suffer Much, and be rejected by this GENERATION.

26 ‡ And as it was in the DAYS of Noah, so will it be also in the DAYS of the SON of MAN.

27 They were eating, they were drinking, they were marrying, they were given in marriage, till the DAY that Noah entered the ARK, and the DELUGE came, and destroyed them all.

28 In like manner also as it was in the DAYS of Lot; they were eating, they were drinking, they were buying, they were selling, they were planting, they were building;

29 but ‡ on the DAY that Lot went out from Sodom, it rained Fire and Sulphur from Heaven, and destroyed them all.

30 Thus will it be in the Day when the SON of MAN is revealed.

31 On That DAY, ‡ let not him who shall be on the ROOF, and his FURNITURE in the HOUSE, descend to take it away; and in like manner, let not him who shall be in the * Field turn back.

32 ‡ Remember Lot's WIFE.

33 ‡ Whoever may seek to * save his LIFE, will

* VATICAN MANUSCRIPT.—23. there! or behold here! follow not. For. 24. in his DAY—omit. 31. Field. 33. insure his LIFE.

‡ 22. Matt. ix. 15. ‡ 23. Matt. xxiv. 23; Mark xiii. 21; Luke xxi. 8. ‡ 24. Matt. xxiv. 27. ‡ 25. Mark viii. 31; ix. 31; x. 33; Luke ix. 22. † 26. Gen. vii Matt. xxiv. 37 ‡ 29. Gen. xix. 16, 24. ‡ 31. Matt. xxiv. 17; Mark xiii. 15. ‡ 32. Gen. xix. 26. ‡ 33. Matt. x. 39; xvi. 25; Mark viii. 35; Luke ix. 24; John xii. 25.

σωσαι, απολεσει αυτην· και ὁς εαν απολεση
to save, will lose her; and whoever may lose
αυτην, ζωογονησει αυτην. 34 Λεγω ὑμιν· Ταυτη
her, will preserve her. I say to you: In this
τη νυκτι εσονται δυο επι κλινης μιας· εἱς παρα-
the night will be two on bed one; one will
ληφθησεται, και ὁ ἑτερος αφεθησεται. 35 Δυο
be taken, and the other will be left. Two
εσονται αληθουσαι επι το αυτο· ἡ μια παραληφ-
will be grinding on the same; the one will be
θησεται, και ἡ ἑτερα αφεθησεται. 36 Και αποκ-
taken, and the other will be left. And an-
ριθεντες λεγουσιν αυτω· Που, κυριε; Ὁ δε
swering they said to him; Where, O lord? He and
ειπεν αυτοις· Ὁπου το σωμα, εκει συναχθησον-
said to them: Where the body, there will be gathered
ται οἱ αετοι.
the eagles.

ΚΕΦ. ιη'. 18.

1 Ελεγε δε και παραβολην αυτοις, προς το
He spoke and also a parable to them, in order that
δειν παντοτε προσευχεσθαι, και μη εκκακειν,
ought always to pray, and not to be weary,
2 λεγων· Κριτης τις ην εν τινι πολει, τον θεον
saying: A judge certain was in a certain city, the God
μη φοβουμενος, και ανθρωπον μη εντρεπομενος.
not fearing, and man not regarding.
3 Χηρα δε ην εν τη πολει εκεινη· και ηρχετο
A widow and was in the city that; and she went
προς αυτον, λεγουσα· Εκδικησον με απο του
to him, saying; Do justice me from the
αντιδικου μου. 4 Και ουκ ηθελησεν επι χρονον.
opponent of me. And not he would for a time.
Μετα δε ταυτα ειπεν εν ἑαυτω· Ει και τον θεον
Afterwards but these he said in himself; If even the God
οὐ φοβουμαι, και ανθρωπον ουκ εντρεπομαι·
not I fear, and man not I regard:
5 διαγε το παρεχειν μοι κοπον την χηραν ταυτην,
through the to render to me trouble the widow this,
εκδικησω αυτην· ἱνα μη εις τελος ερχομενη
I will do justice her; that not to end coming
ὑπωπιαζη με. 6 Ειπε δε ὁ κυριος· Ακουσατε,
she should pester me. Said and the lord: Hear you,
τι ὁ κριτης της αδικιας λεγει. 7 Ὁ δε θεος
what the judge the unjust says. The and God
οὐ μη ποιησει την εκδικησιν των εκλεκτων
not not will do the justice for the chosen ones
αὑτου των βοωντων προς αυτον ἡμερας και
of himself those crying to him day and
νυκτος, και μακροθυμων επ' αυτοις; 8 Λεγω
night, and bearing long towards them? I say
ὑμιν, ὁτι ποιησει την εκδικησιν αυτων εν ταχει.
to you, that he will do the justice for them in an instant.
Πλην ὁ υἱος του ανθρωπου ελθων ἀρα εὑρησει
But the son of the man coming indeed will he find
την πιστιν επι της γης;
the faith on the earth?

lose it; and whoever may lose it, will preserve it.

34 ‡ I tell you, in That NIGHT there will be two on *a Bed; One will be taken, and the OTHER left.

35 Two will be grinding together; the ONE will be taken, and the OTHER left."

36 And answering, they said to him, ‡ "Where, Lord?" And HE said to them, "Where the BODY is, there *also the EAGLES will be assembled."

CHAPTER XVIII.

1 And he also spoke a Parable to them, to show that they OUGHT ‡ to pray continually, and not be weary;

2 saying, "There was a certain Judge in a certain City, who feared not GOD nor respected Man.

3 And there was a Widow in that City; and she went to him, saying, 'Obtain justice for me from my OPPONENT.'

4 And he would not for a time; but afterwards he said within himself 'Though I fear not GOD nor regard Man;

5 ‡ yet, because this WIDOW importunes me, I will do her justice, lest at last her coming should weary me!'"

6 And the LORD said, "Hear what the UNJUST JUDGE says;

7 and ‡ will not GOD do justice for THOSE CHOSEN ONES of his, who are CRYING to him Day and Night, and he is compassionate towards them?

8 I tell you, ‡ That he will speedily do them JUSTICE. But when the son of MAN comes, will he find this BELIEF on the LAND?"

* VATICAN MANUSCRIPT.—34. a Bed. 37. also will.

‡ 34. Matt. xxiv. 40, 41; 1 Thes. iv. 17. ‡ 36. Matt. xxiv. 28. ‡ 1. Luke xi. 5 Rom. xii. 12; Eph. vi. 18 ‡ 5. Luke xi. 8. ‡ 7. Rev. vi. 10. ‡ 8. Heb. x 37; 2 Pet iii. 8, 9.

9 Ειπε δε και προς τινας τους πεποιθοτας εφ'
He spoke and also to some those trusting in
ἑαυτοις ὁτι εισι δικαιοι, και εξουθενουντας τους
themselves that they are just ones, and despising the
λοιπους, την παραβολην ταυτην· 10 Ανθρωποι
others, the parable this: Men
δυο ανεβησαν εις το ιερον προσευξασθαι· ὁ εις
two went up into the temple to pray: the one
Φαρισαιος, και ὁ ἑτερος τελωνης. 11 Ὁ Φαρι-
a Pharisee, and the other a tax-gatherer. The Phari-
σαιος, σταθεις προς ἑαυτον, ταυτα προσηυχετο·
see, standing by himself, these he prayed:
Ὁ θεος, ευχαριστω σοι, ὁτι ουκ ειμι ὡσπερ οἱ
The God, I give thanks to thee, that not I am like the
λοιποι των ανθρωπων, ἁρπαγες, αδικοι, μοιχοι,
others of the men, plunderers, unjust ones, adulterers,
η και ὡς οὑτος ὁ τελωνης. 12 Νηστευω δις του
or even like this the tax-gatherer. I fast twice of the
σαββατου, αποδεκατω παντα ὁσα κτωμαι. 13 Και
week, I tithe all what I acquire. And
ὁ τελωνης μακροθεν ἑστως ουκ ηθελεν
the tax-gatherer at a distance having been standing not would
ουδε τους οφθαλμους εις τον ουρανον επαραι·
not even the eyes to the heaven lift up:
αλλ' ετυπτεν *[εις] το στηθος αὑτου, λεγων·
but he smote [on] the breast of himself, saying:
Ὁ θεος, ἱλασθητι μοι τῳ ἁμαρτωλῳ. 14 Λεγω
The God, be propitious to me the sinner. I say
ὑμιν, κατεβη οὑτος δεδικαιωμενος εις τον οικον
to you, went down this having been justified to the house
αὑτου, η γαρ εκεινος· ὁτι πας ὁ ὑψων ἑαυτον,
of himself, or for that: for every one the exalting himself,
ταπεινωθησεται· ὁ δε ταπεινων ἑαυτον, ὑψωθη-
will be humbled; he but humbling himself, will be
σεται.
exalted.

15 Προσεφερον δε αυτῳ και τα βρεφη, ἱνα
They brought and to him also the infants, that
αυτων ἁπτηται· ιδοντες δε οἱ μαθηται επετιμη-
them he might touch; seeing and the disciples rebuked
σαν αυτοις. 16 Ὁ δε Ιησους προσκαλεσαμενος
them. The but Jesus calling to
αυτα, ειπεν· Αφετε τα παιδια ερχεσθαι προς με,
them, he said; Allow the little children to come to me,
και μη κωλυετε αυτα· των γαρ τοιουτων εστιν
and not forbid them; for the because such like is
ἡ βασιλεια του θεου. 17 Αμην λεγω ὑμιν, ὁς
the kingdom of the God. Indeed I say to you, who
εαν μη δεξηται την βασιλειαν του θεου ὡς
ever not may receive the kingdom of the God as
παιδιον, ου μη εισελθῃ εις αυτην.
a little child, not not may enter into her.

9 And he spoke this PARABLE also to SOME, ‡who TRUSTED in themselves That they were righteous, and despised OTHERS.

10 "Two Men went up into the TEMPLE to pray; the ONE a Pharisee, and the OTHER a Tribute-taker.

11 The PHARISEE standing by himself, prayed thus; †'O GOD, I thank thee, That I am not like OTHER MEN,—Rapacious, Unjust, Dissolute, or even like This TRIBUTE-TAKER.

12 I fast twice in the WEEK, I tithe all that I acquire.'

13 *But the TRIBUTE-TAKER, standing at a distance, would not even lift up his EYES to HEAVEN, but smote his BREAST, saying, 'O GOD, be propitious to me a SINNER.'

14 I tell you, this man went down to his HOUSE justified *more than the other; ‡For EVERY ONE who EXALTS himself will be humbled; and HE who HUMBLES himself will be exalted."

15 ‡And they brought to him their INFANTS also, that he might touch them; but the DISCIPLES seeing it, rebuked them.

16 But JESUS calling them to him, said, "Permit the LITTLE CHILDREN to come to me, and forbid them not; for to ‡SUCH LIKE belongs the KINGDOM of GOD.

17 ‡Indeed I say to you, Whoever does not receive the KINGDOM of GOD like a Little child, he will by no means enter it."

* VATICAN MANUSCRIPT.—13. But. 13. on—*omit.* 14. more than the other.

† 11. The following from *Bereshith Rabba,* will illustrate this Pharisaic pride:—"Rabbi Simeon, the son of Jochai, said: The world is not worth thirty righteous persons such as our father Abraham. If there were only thirty righteous persons in the world, I and my son should make two of them; and if there were but twenty, I and my son would be of the number; and if there were but ten, I and my son would be of the number; and if there were but five, I and my son would be of the five; and if there were but two, I and my son would be those two; and if there were but one, myself should be that one."

‡ 9. Luke x. 29; xvi. 15. ‡ 14. Job xxii. 29; Matt. xxiii. 12; Luke xiv. 11; James iv. 6; 1 Pet. v. 5, 3. ‡ 15. Matt. xix. 13, Mark x. 13. ‡ 16. 1 Cor. xiv. 20; 1 Pet. ii. 2. ‡ 17. Mark x. 15.

18 Και επηρωτησε τις αυτον αρχων, λεγων·
And asked certain him ruler, saying;
Διδασκαλε αγαθε, τι ποιησας ζωην αιωνιον
O teacher good, what shall I do life age-lasting
κληρονομησω; 19 Ειπε δε αυτῳ ὁ Ιησους· Τι με
to inherit? Said and to him the Jesus; Why me
λεγεις αγαθον; ουδεις αγαθος, ει μη εἱς, ὁ
callest thou good? no one good, if not one, the
θεος. 20 Τας εντολας οιδας· "Μη μοιχευ-
God. The commandments thou knowest: "Not thou mayest
σῃς· μη φονευσῃς· μη κλεψῃς· μη
commit adultery; not thou mayest kill; not thou mayest steal; not
ψευδομαρτυρησῃς· τιμα τον πατερα σου, και
thou mayest bear false testimony; honor the father of thee, and
την μετερα *[σου."] 21 Ὁ δε ειπε· Ταυτα παντα
the mother of thee."] He and said: These all
εφυλαξαμην εκ νεοτητος μου. 22 Ακουσας δε
I observed from youth of me. Having heard and
*[ταυτα] ὁ Ιησους, ειπεν αυτῳ· Ετι ἑν σοι λει-
[these] the Jesus, said to him; Yet one to thee is
πει· παντα ὁσα εχεις πωλησον, και διαδος πτω-
wanting; all what thou hast sell, and give thou to poor
χοις, και ἑξεις θησαυρον εν ουρανῳ· και δευρο,
ones, and thou shalt have a treasure in heaven: and come,
ακολουθει μοι. 23 Ὁ δε ακουσας ταυτα, περιλυ-
follow me. He and having heard these, greatly
πος εγενετο· ην γαρ πλουσιος σφοδρα. 24 Ιδων δε
grieved became: he was for rich exceedingly. Seeing and
αυτον ὁ Ιησους *[περιλυπον γενομενον,] ειπε·
him the Jesus [greatly grieved becoming,] said:
Πως δυσκολως οἱ τα χρηματα εχοντες εισελευ-
How with difficulty those the riches having shall
σονται εις την βασιλειαν του θεου. 25 Ευκοπωτε-
enter into the kingdom of the God. Easier
ρον γαρ εστι, καμηλον δια τρυμαλιας ῥαφιδος
for it is, a camel through hole of a needle
εισελθειν, η πλουσιον εις την βασιλειαν του
to enter, than a rich man into the kingdom of the
θεου εισελθειν. 26 Ειπον δε οἱ ακουσαντες· Και
God to enter. Said and those having heard: And
τις δυναται σωθηναι; 27 Ὁ δε ειπε· Τα αδυνατα
who is able to be saved? He but said: The things impossible
παρα ανθρωποις, δυνατα εστι παρα τῳ θεῳ.
with men, possible is with the God.
28 Ειπε δε ὁ Πετρος· Ιδου, ἡμεις αφηκαμεν
Said and the Peter: Lo, we left
παντα, και ηκολουθησαμεν σοι. 29 Ὁ δε ειπεν
all, and followed thee. He and said
αυτοις· Αμην λεγω ὑμιν, ὁτι ουδεις εστιν ὁς
to them: Indeed I say to you, that no one is who
αφηκεν οικιαν, η γονεις, η αδελφους, η γυναικα,
left house, or parents, or brethren, or wife,
η τεκνα, ἑνεκεν της βασιλειας του θεου, 30 ὁς
or children, on account of the kingdom of the God, who

18 ‡ And a Certain Ruler asked him, saying, "Good Teacher, what shall I do to inherit aionian Life?"

19 And JESUS said to him, "Why dost thou call Me good? There is none good, except one,—GOD.

20 Thou knowest the COMMANDMENTS; ‡ Do not commit adultery, Do not kill, Do not steal, Do not testify falsely, Honor thy FATHER and MOTHER."

21 And HE said, "All these have I kept from my Youth."

22 And JESUS having heard, said to him, "Yet in One thing thou art wanting; ‡ sell all that thou hast, and give to the Poor, and thou shalt have Treasure in * HEAVEN; and come follow me."

23 And hearing this, HE became very sorrowful; for he was exceedingly rich.

24 And * Jesus seeing him, said, "With what difficulty will THOSE HAVING RICHES enter the KINGDOM of God!

25 It is easier for a Camel to pass through a Needle's Eye, than for a Rich man to enter the KINGDOM of GOD."

26 And THOSE HEARING him, said, "Who then can be saved?"

27 And HE said, ‡ "The THINGS IMPOSSIBLE with Men are possible with GOD."

28 Then PETER said, ‡ "Behold, we have forsaken * our OWN, and followed thee."

29 And HE said to them, "Indeed, I say to you, That no one has forsaken a House, or a * Wife, or Brothers, or Parents, or Children, on account of the KINGDOM of GOD,

* VATICAN MANUSCRIPT.—20. of thee—omit. 22. these—omit. 22. HEAVEN. 24. Jesus seeing him, said. 24. becoming greatly grieved—omit. 28. our OWN, and. 29. Wife, or Brothers, or Parents, or Children.

‡ 18. Matt. xix. 16; Mark x. 17. ‡ 20. Exod. xx. 12, 16; Deut. v. 16—20; Rom. xiii 9. ‡ 22. Matt. vi. 19, 20; xix. 21; 1 Tim. vi. 19. ‡ 27. Jer. xxxii. 17; Zech. viii 6. ‡ 28. Matt. iv. 18—22; xix. 27.

ου μη απολαβη πολλαπλασιονα εν τῳ καιρῳ
not not may receive many times more in the season
τουτῳ, και εν τῳ αιωνι τῳ ερχομενῳ ζωην
this, and in the age the coming life
αιωνιον.
age-lasting.

31 Παραλαβων δε τους δωδεκα, ειπε προς
Having taken and the twelve, he said to
αυτους· Ιδου, αναβαινομεν εις Ἱεροσολυμα, και
them: Lo, we go to Jerusalem, and
τελεσθησεται παντα τα γεγραμμενα δια των
will be finished all the having been written through the
προφητων τῳ υιῳ του ανθρωπου. 32 Παραδοθη-
prophets in the son of the man. He will be deliv-
σεται γαρ τοις εθνεσι, και εμπαιχθησεται, και
ered up for to the Gentiles, and will be derided, and
ὑβρισθησεται, και εμπτυσθησεται· 33 και μασ-
will be shamefully treated, and will be spit on: and having
τιγωσαντες αποκτενουσιν αυτον· και τῃ ἡμερᾳ
been scourged they will kill him: and the day
τῃ τριτῃ αναστησεται. 34 Και αυτοι ουδεν του-
the third he will stand up. And they not one of
των συνηκαν· και ην το ῥημα τουτο κεκρυμμε-
these understood: and was the thing this having been hid-
νον απ' αυτων, και ουκ εγινωσκον τα λεγομενα.
den from them, and not they knew the things being spoken.

35 Εγενετο δε εν τῳ εγγιζειν αυτον εις Ἱεριχω,
It happened and in the to draw nigh him to Jericho,
τυφλος τις εκαθητο παρα την ὁδον προσαιτων.
a blind man certain sat by the way begging.
36 Ακουσας δε οχλου διαπορευομενου, επυνθανετο,
Hearing and a crowd passing along, he asked,
τι ειη τουτο; 37 Απηγγειλαν δε αυτῳ, ὁτι
what may be this? They told and him, that
Ιησους ὁ Ναζαραιος παρερχεται. 38 Και εβοησε,
Jesus the Nazarene passes by. And he shouted,
λεγων· Ιησου, υἱε Δαυιδ, ελεησον με. 39 Και
saying: Jesus, O son of David, pity me. And
οἱ προαγοντες επετιμων αυτῳ, ἱνα σιωπησῃ.
those going before rebuked him, that he might be silent.
Αυτος δε πολλῳ μαλλον εκραζεν· Υἱε Δαυιδ,
He but much more cried out: O son of David,
ελεησον με. 40 Σταθεις δε ὁ Ιησους εκελευσεν
pity me. Stopping and the Jesus commanded
αυτον αχθηναι προς αὑτον. Εγγισαντος δε
him to be led to himself. Having come and
αυτου, επηρωτησεν αυτον, 41 *[λεγων·] Τι σοι
of him, he asked him, [saying:] What for thee
θελεις ποιησω; Ὁ δε ειπε· Κυριε, ἱνα ανα-
thou desirest I should do? He and said: O lord, that I may
βλεψω. 42 Και ὁ Ιησους ειπεν αυτῳ· Αναβλε-
see again. And the Jesus said to him: See thou
ψον· ἡ πιστις σου σεσωκε σε. 43 Και παραχρημα
again: the faith of thee has saved thee. And instantly

30 who will not receive manifold, in this TIME, and in the COMING AGE aionian Life."

31 ‡ And taking the TWELVE aside, he said to them, "Behold, we go up to Jerusalem, and All the THINGS WRITTEN through the PROPHETS, will be accomplished in the SON of MAN.

32 For ‡ he will be delivered to the GENTILES, and will be mocked, and insulted, and spit upon;

33 and having scourged him, they will kill him; and the THIRD DAY he will rise again."

34 ‡ But they understood none of these things; and this MATTER was concealed from them, and they did not recognize WHAT was SPOKEN.

35 ‡ And it occurred, as he APPROACHED Jericho, a certain blind man sat begging by the ROAD.

36 And hearing a Crowd passing along, he inquired what it meant.

37 And they told him, "Jesus the NAZARITE is passing by."

38 And he shouted, saying, "Jesus, Son of David, have pity on me!"

39 And THOSE GOING BEFORE, charged him to be silent; but he cried out much more, "Son of David, have pity on me!"

40 And JESUS stopping, commanded him to be led to him. And having come near, he asked him,

41 "What dost thou wish that I should do to thee?" And HE said, "Master, to restore my sight."

42 And JESUS said to him, "Receive thy sight; ‡ thy FAITH has cured thee."

43 And instantly he saw

* VATICAN MANUSCRIPT.—41. saying—*omit.*

‡ 31. Matt. xvi. 21; xvii. 22; xx. 17; Mark x. 32. ‡ 32. Matt. xxvii. 2; Luke xxiii. 1; John xviii. 28; Acts iii. 13. ‡ 34. Mark ix. 32; Luke ii. 50; ix. 45; John x. 6; xii. 16. ‡ 35. Matt. xx. 29; Mark x. 46. ‡ 42. Luke xvii. 19

ανεβλεψε, και ηκολουθει αυτῳ, δοξαζων τον
he saw again, and followed him, glorifying the
θεον· και πας ὁ λαος ιδων, εδωκεν αινον τῳ θεῳ.
God; and all the people seeing, gave praise to the God.

ΚΕΦ. ιθʹ. 19.

1 Και εισελθων διηρχετο την Ἱεριχω. 2 Και
And having entered he passed through the Jericho. And
ιδου, ανηρ ονοματι καλουμενος Ζακχαιος· και
lo, a man for a name being called Zaccheus; and
αυτος ην αρχιτελωνης, και οὑτος ην πλουσιος.
he was a chief tax-gatherer, and this was rich.
3 Και εζητει ιδειν τον Ιησουν, τις εστι· και ουκ
And he sought to see the Jesus, who he is; and not
ηδυνατο απο του οχλου, ὁτι τῃ ἡλικιᾳ μικρος
was able on account of the crowd, for the stature little
ην. 4 Και προδραμων εμπροσθεν, ανεβη επι
was. And running before, he went up on
συκομορεαν, ἱνα ιδῃ αυτον· ὁτι εκεινης
a sycamore, that he might see him; for that
ημελλε διερχεσθαι. 5 Και ὡς ηλθεν επι τον
he was about to pass by. And as he came to the
τοπον, αναβλεψας ὁ Ιησους *[ειδεν αυτον, και]
place, having looked the Jesus [saw him, and]
ειπε προς αυτον· Ζακχαιε, σπευσας καταβηθι·
said to him; O Zaccheus, having hastened descend thou;
σημερον γαρ εν τῳ οικῳ σου δει με μειναι.
to-day for in the house of thee must me to abide.
6 Και σπευσας κατεβη, και ὑπεδεξατο αυτον
And having hastened he came down, and he received him
χαιρων. 7 Και ιδοντες ἁπαντες διεγογγυζον,
rejoicing. And seeing all murmured,
λεγοντες· Ὁτι παρα ἁμαρτωλῳ ανδρι εισηλθε
saying: That with a sinner a man he went in
καταλυσαι. 8 Σταθεις δε Ζακχαιος ειπε προς
to lodge. Standing up but Zaccheus said to
τον κυριον· Ιδου, τα ἡμιση των ὑπαρχοντων
the lord; Lo, the half of the possessions
μου, κυριε, διδωμι τοις πτωχοις· και ει τινος
of me, O lord, I give to the poor; and if of any one
τι εσυκοφαντησα αποδιδωμι τετραπλουν.
any thing I extorted I give back fourfold.
9 Ειπε δε προς αυτον ὁ Ιησους· Ὁτι σημερον
Said and to him the Jesus; That to-day
σωτηρια τῳ οικῳ τουτῳ εγενετο· καθοτι και
salvation to the house this has come: since also
αυτος υἱος Αβρααμ εστιν· 10 ηλθε γαρ ὁ υιος
he a son of Abraham is: came for the son
του ανθρωπου ζητησαι και σωσαι το απολωλος.
of the man to seek and to save that having been lost.
11 Ακουοντων δε αυτων ταυτα, προσθεις
Hearing and of them these things, proceeding
ειπε παραβολην, δια το εγγυς αυτον ειναι
he spoke a parable, because the near him to be
Ἱερουσαλημ, και δοκειν αυτους, ὁτι παραχρημα
Jerusalem, and to think them, that immediately

again, and followed him, ‡ glorifying GOD; and all the PEOPLE seeing it, gave Praise to GOD.

CHAPTER XIX.

1 And having entered he was passing through JERICHO;

2 and behold, a Man named Zaccheus, (he was rich, and a Chief Tribute-taker,)

3 sought to see who JESUS was, and could not on account of the CROWD, for he was of low STATURE.

4 And running *BEFORE, he climbed a Sycamore to see him; For he was about to pass by it.

5 And when *Jesus came to the PLACE, looking up he said to him, "Zaccheus, hasten down, for To-day I must abide at thy HOUSE."

6 And he hastened down, and received him rejoicing

7 And seeing it, they all murmured, saying, ‡ "He has gone in to lodge with a Sinful man."

8 But Zaccheus standing up, said to the LORD, "Behold, Master, the HALF of * My POSSESSIONS I give to the Poor; and if I have extorted any thing from any one, ‡ I restore fourfold."

9 And * Jesus said to him, "To-day has Salvation come to this HOUSE, since he also is ‡ a Son of Abraham.

10 ‡ For the SON of MAN has come to seek and to save THAT which was LOST."

11 And as they were hearing these things, proceeding he spoke a Parable, because he was near Jerusalem, and they thought that the KINGDOM of GOD

* VATICAN MANUSCRIPT.—4. BEFORE. 5. Jesus. 5. saw him, and—omit. 8. My POSSESSIONS I give to the Poor. 9. Jesus.

‡ 43. Luke v. 26; Acts iv. 21; xi. 18. ‡ 7. Matt. ix. 11; Luke v. 30. ‡ 8. Exod. xxii. 1; 1 Sam. xii. 3; 2 Sam. xii. 6. ‡ 9. Rom. iv. 11, 12, 16; Gal. iii. 7. ‡ 10. Matt. xviii. 11.

μελλει ἡ βασιλεια του θεου αναφαινεσθαι.
is about the kingdom of the God to appear.
12 Ειπεν ουν· Ανθρωπος τις ευγενης επορυθη
He said therefore: A man certain well-born went
εις χωραν μακραν, λαβειν ἑαυτῳ βασιλειαν, και
into a country distant, to receive for himself royal dignity, and
ὑποστρεψαι. 13 Καλεσας δε δεκα δουλους ἑαυ-
to return. Having called and ten slaves of him-
του, εδωκεν αυτοις δεκα μνας, και ειπε προς
self, he gave to them ten minas, and he said to
αυτους· Πραγματευσασθε ἑως ερχομαι. 14 Οἱ
them: Do you business till I come. The
δε πολιται αυτου εμισουν αυτον, και απεστειλαν
but citizens of him hated him, and sent
πρεσβειαν οπισω αυτου, λεγοντες· Ου θελομεν
an embassy after him, saying: Not we are willing
τουτον βασιλευσαι εφ᾽ ἡμας. 15 Και εγενετο
this to reign over us. And it happened
εν τῳ επανελθειν αυτον λαβοντα την βασιλειαν,
in the to return him having received the royal dignity,
και ειπε φωνηθηναι αὐτῳ τους δουλους τουτους,
and he ordered to be called to himself the slaves those,
οἱς εδωκε το αργυριον· ἱνα γνῳ, τις τι
to whom he gave the silver: that he might know, what each
διεπραγματευσατο. 16 Παρεγενετο δε ὁ πρω-
had gained by trading. Came and the first,
τος, λεγων· Κυριε, ἡ μνα σου προσειργασατο
saying: O lord, the mina of thee has gained
δεκα μνας. 17 Και ειπεν αυτῳ· Ευ, αγαθε δουλε·
ten minas. And he said to him: Well, O good slave:
ὁτι εν ελαχιστῳ πιστος εγενου, ισθι εξου-
because in least faithful thou hast been, be thou autho-
σιαν εχων επανω δεκα πολεων. 18 Και ηλθεν
rity having over ten cities. And came
ὁ δευτερος, λεγων· Κυριε, ἡ μνα σου εποιησε
the second, saying; O lord, the mina of thee has made
πεντε μνας. 19 Ειπε δε και τουτῳ· Και συ
five minas. He said and also to this; Also thou
γινου επανω πεντε πολεων. 20 Και ἑτερος
be over five cities. And another
ηλθε, λεγων· Κυριε, ιδου ἡ μνα σου, ἡν ειχον
came, saying: O lord, lo the mina of thee, which I had
αποκειμενην εν σουδαριῳ. 21 Εφοβουμην γαρ
being laid up in a napkin. I feared for
σε, ὁτι ανθρωπος αυστηρος ει· αιρεις, ὁ
thee, because a man harsh thou art; thou takest up, what
ουκ εθηκας, και θεριζεις, ὁ ουκ εσπειρας.
not thou didst lay down, and thou reapest, what not thou didst sow.
22 Λεγει δε αυτῳ· Εκ του στοματος σου κρινω
He says and to him; Out of the mouth of thee I will judge

was about immediately to appear.

12 Therefore he said, † "A certain Man of noble birth went into a distant Country to procure for himself Royalty, and to return

13 And he called Ten of his Servants, and gave them Ten † Minas, and said to them, 'Trade till I come.'

14 But his CITIZENS hated him, and sent an Embassy after him, saying, 'We are not willing for this man to reign over us.'

15 And it occurred, that at his RETURN, having received the ROYALTY, he ordered those SERVANTS to be called to him, to whom he gave the SILVER, that he might know what * they had gained by traffic.

16 Then the FIRST came, saying, 'Sir, thy MINA has gained Ten Minas.'

17 And he said to him, * 'Well done, good Servant' because thou hast been ‡ faithful in a very small matter, possess authority over Ten Cities.'

18 And the SECOND, came, saying, 'Sir, thy MINA has made Five Minas.'

19 And he said also to this, 'Be thou also over Five Cities.'

20 And * the OTHER came, saying, 'Sir, behold thy MINA, which I had laid up in a Napkin;

21 ‡ for I feared thee, because thou art a harsh Man; thou takest up what thou didst not lay down, and reapest what thou didst not sow.'

22 And he said to him, ‡ Out of thine own MOUTH

* VATICAN MANUSCRIPT.—15. they had gained. 17. Well done. 20. the OTHER.

† 12. Our Lord manifestly alludes to the case of Archelaus, who went to Rome to solicit the Emperor that he might be reinstated in his father's kingdom; and the Jews sent an ambassage after him, to petition and plead against him But however he was confirmed in the kingdom of Judea; and when he returned, took ample vengeance of his enemies and opposers.—*Newcome.* † 13. The LXX use the original word *mnaa* for the Hebrew *maneh* from which it is evidently derived, and it appears from Ezek. xiv. 12, to have been equal to sixty shekels. Now allowing the shekel with Dr. Prideaux, to be three shillings, then the mina was equal to nine pounds English.—*A. Clarke* Horne makes the *mnaa* equal to £3. 2s. 6d., or fifteen dollars.

‡ 17. Matt. xxv. 21; Luke xvi. 10. ‡ 21. Matt. xxv. 24. ‡ 22. Matt. xii. 37

σε, πονηρε δουλε· ηδεις, ὁτι εγω ανθρωπος
thee, O evil slave; thou knewest, that I a man

αυστηρος ειμι, αιρων ὁ ουκ εθηκα, και θερι-
harsh am, taking up what not I laid down, and reap-

ζων ὁ ουκ εσπειρα· 23 και διατι ουκ εδωκας το
ing what not I sowed; and why not thou gavest the

αργυριον μου επι την τραπεζαν, και εγω ελθων
silver of me on the table, and I coming

συν τοκῳ αν επραξα αυτο; 24 Και τοις παρεσ-
with interest might have exacted it? And to those having

τωσιν ειπεν· Αρατε απ' αυτου την μναν, και
stood by he said: Take you from him the mina, and

δοτε τῳ τας δεκα μνας εχοντι. 25 (Και ειπον
give you to the the ten minas having. (And they said

αυτῳ· Κυριε, εχει δεκα μνας.) 26 Λεγω *[γαρ]
to him; O lord, he has ten minas.) I say [for]

ὑμιν ὁτι παντι τῳ εχοντι δοθησεται· απο δε
to you that to every one the having will be given; from but

του μη εχοντος, και ὁ εχει, αρθησεται *[απ'
of the not having, even what he has, will be taken [from

αυτου.] 27 Πλην τους εχθρους μου εκεινους,
him.] But the enemies of me those,

τους μη θελησαντας με βασιλευσαι επ' αυτους,
the not willing me to reign over them,

αγαγετε ὡδε, και κατασφαξατε εμπροσθεν μου.
bring you hither, and slay in presence of me.

28 Και ειπων ταυτα, επορευετο εμπροσθεν,
And having said these, he went before,

αναβαινων εις Ἱεροσολυμα. 29 Και εγενετο ὡς
going up to Jerusalem. And it happened as

ηγγισεν εις Βηθφαγη και Βηθανιαν, προς το
he drew near to Bethphage and Bethany, to the

ορος το καλουμενον ελαιων, απεστειλε δυο
mountain that being called of olive-trees, he sent two

των μαθητων αὑτου, 30 ειπων· Ὑπαγετε εις
of the disciples of himself, saying; Go you into

την κατεναντι κωμην· εν ᾗ εισπορευομενοι
the over-against village; in which entering

εὑρησετε πωλον δεδεμενον, εφ' ὁν ουδεις
you will find a colt having been tied, on which no one

πωποτε ανθρωπων εκαθισε· λυσαντες αυτον
ever of men sat; having loosed him

αγαγετε. 31 Και εαν τις ὑμας ερωτᾳ· Διατι
bring you. And if any one you may ask: Why

λυετε; οὑτως ερειτε *[αυτῳ·] Ὁτι ὁ κυριος
do you loose? thus say you [to him:] That the lord

αυτου χρειαν εχει. 32 Απελθοντες δε οἱ απεσ-
of him need has. Having gone and those having

ταλμενοι εὑρον, καθως ειπεν αυτοις. 33 Λυον-
been sent found, as he said to them. Loos-

I will judge thee, Wicked Servant. ‡ Didst thou know that I am a harsh Man taking up what I laid not down, and reaping what I did not sow?

23 Why, then, didst thou not place my MONEY in the BANK, that coming I might have exacted the Same with Interest?'

24 And he said to THOSE STANDING BY, 'Take from him the MINA, and give it to HIM who has † the TEN Minas.'

25 (And they said to him, 'Sir, he has Ten Minas.')

26 'I say to you, ‡ That to EVERY ONE who HAS, more shall be given; and from HIM who HAS not, even what he has shall be taken away.

27 But * THOSE ENEMIES of mine, who were not WILLING that I should reign over them, bring hither, and slaughter them in my presence.'"

28 And having said these things, ‡ he went on before, going up to Jerusalem.

29 ‡ And it occurred, as he drew near to Bethphage and Bethany, at THAT MOUNTAIN which is CALLED the Mount of Olives, he sent two of * the DISCIPLES,

30 saying, "Go to the VILLAGE OVER AGAINST you, in which, having entered, you will find a Colt tied, on which no Man ever sat; loose, and bring him.

31 And if any one asks you, 'Why do you loose him?' you shall thus say, 'Because the MASTER wants him.'"

32 And THOSE who were SENT, went away, and found it even as he had told them.

* VATICAN MANUSCRIPT.—26. For—*omit.* 26. from him—*omit.* 27. THESE. 29. the DISCIPLES. 31. to him—*omit.*

† 24. Perhaps it would be well to supply the word *gained* here—"Give it to him who has *gained* ten Minas; for I say to you, That to every one who has *gained*, shall be given; and from him who has not *gained*, even what he has *received* shall be taken away."—*Clarke.*

‡ 22. Matt. xxv. 26. ‡ 26. Matt xiii. 12; xxv. 29; Mark iv. 25; Luke viii. 18. ‡ 28. Mark x. 32. ‡ 29. Matt. xxi. 1; Mark xi. 1.

των δε αυτων τον πωλον, ειπο οἱ κυριοι αυτου
ing and of them the colt, said the lords of him
προς αυτους· Τι λυετε τον πωλον· 34 Οἱ δε ειπον·
to them; Why loose you the colt: They and said:
Ὁ κυριος αυτου χρειαν εχει. 35 Και ηγαγον
The lord of him need has. And they led
αυτον προς τον Ιησουν· και επιρριψαντες ἑαυ-
him to the Jesus: and having thrown of them-
των τα ἱματια επι τον πωλον, επεβιβασαν τον
selves the mantles on the colt, they set on the
Ιησουν. 36 Πορευομενου δε αυτου, ὑπεστρωννυον
Jesus. Going and of him, they spread under
τα ἱματια αὑτων εν τῃ ὁδῳ. 37 Εγγιζοντες δε
the mantles of them in the way. Drawing near and
αυτου ηδη προς τῃ καταβασει του ορους των
of him now to the descent of the mountain of the
ελαιων, ηρξαντο ἁπαν το πληθος των μαθητων
olive-trees, began all the multitude of the disciples
χαιροντες αινειν τον θεον φωνῃ μεγαλῃ περι
rejoicing to praise the God with a voice loud for
πασων ὡν ειδον δυναμεων, 38 λεγοντες· Ευλογ-
all which they saw mighty works, saying: Worthy
ημενος ὁ ερχομενος βασιλευς εν ονοματι κυριου·
of blessing the coming king in name of Lord:
ειρηνη εν ουρανῳ, και δοξα εν ὑψιστοις. 39 Και
peace in heaven, and glory in highest. And
τινες των Φαρισαιων απο του οχλου ειπον προς
some of the Pharisees from the crowd said to
αυτον· Διδασκαλε, επιτιμησον τοις μαθηταις
him: O teacher, rebuke the disciples
σου. 40 Και αποκριθεις ειπεν *[αυτοις·] Λεγω
of thee. And answering he said [to them:] I say
ὑμιν, ὁτι εαν οὑτοι σιωπησωσιν, οἱ λιθοι κεκ-
to you, that if these should be silent, the stones will
ραξονται.
cry out.

41 Και ὡς ηγγισεν, ιδων την πολιν, εκλαυσεν
And as he drew near, seeing the city, he wept
επ' αυτῃ, λεγων· 42 Ὁτι ει εγνως και συ,
over her, saying; That if thou hadst known even thou,
*[καιγε] εν τῃ ἡμερᾳ *[σου] ταυτῃ, τα προς
[at least] in the day [of thee] this, the things to
ειρηνην σου· νυν δε εκρυβη απο εφθαλμων
peace of thee; now but it is hidden from eyes
σου. 43 Ὁτι ἡξουσιν ἡμεραι επι σε, και περι-
of thee. For will come days on this, and will
βαλουσιν οἱ εχθροι σου χαρακα σοι, και περικυκ-
throw around the enemies of thee a rampart to thee, and will sur-
λωσουσι σε, και συνεξουσι σε παντοθεν· 44 και
round thee, and will press thee on every side; and
εδαφιουσι σε, και τα τεκνα σου εν σοι·
will level with the ground thee and the children of thee in thee.
και ουκ αφησουσιν εν σοι λιθον επι λιθῳ· ανθ'
and not they will leave in thee a stone on a stone; because

33 And as they were loosing the COLT, the OWNERS of it said to them, "Why do you untie the COLT?"

34 And THEY said, *"Because the MASTER wants him,"

35 And they led it to JESUS; ‡and having cast Their own MANTLES on the COLT, they set JESUS on it.

36 ‡And as he was going, they spread their GARMENTS on the ROAD.

37 And when he was now approaching, at the DESCENT of the MOUNT of OLIVES, all the MULTITUDE of the DISCIPLES began to rejoice, and praise God with a loud Voice, for all the Miracles which they had seen,

38 saying, ‡"Blessed be the COMING KING in the Name of Jehovah! Peace in Heaven, and Glory in the highest heaven."

39 And some of the PHARISEES, among the CROWD, said to him, "Teacher, rebuke thy DISCIPLES."

40 But answering he said; "I tell you, That if these should be silent, ‡the STONES would immediately cry out."

41 And as he drew near, beholding the CITY, ‡ he wept over it,

42 saying, "O, that thou hadst known, even thou, at this DAY, the THINGS which are for thy Peace! But now they are hidden from thine Eyes.

43 For the Days will come on thee, when thine ENEMIES shall throw a Rampart around thee, and enclose thee and press thee in on every side,

44 and will lay thee level with the ground, and thy CHILDREN in thee and they will not leave a Stone upon a Stone in thee

* VATICAN MANUSCRIPT.—34. Because the MASTER. 40. to them—*omit.* 42. at least—*omit.* 42. of thee—*omit.*

‡ 35. 2 Kings ix. 13; Matt. xxi. 7; Mark xi. 7; John xii. 14. ‡ 36. Matt. xxi. 8. ‡ 38. Psa. cxviii. 26; Luke xiii. 35. ‡ 40. Hab. ii. 11. ‡ 41. John xi. 35.

ὧν ουκ εγνως τον καιρον της επισκοπης σου.
of which not thou knowest the season of the visitation of thee.
45 Και εισελθων εις το ἱερον, ηρξατο εκβαλλειν
And entering into the temple, he began to cast out
τους πωλουντας *[εν αυτῳ και αγοραζοντας,]
those selling [in it and buying,]
46 λεγων αυτοις· Γεγραπται· "Ὁ οικος μου
saying to them; It is written; "The house of me
οικος προσευχης εστιν· ὑμεις δε αυτον εποιη-
a house of prayer is, you but it made
σατε σπηλαιον ληστων." 47 Και ἠν διδασκων
a den of robbers." And he was teaching
το καθ' ἡμεραν εν τῳ ἱερῳ· οἱ δε αρχιερεις και
the every day in the temple: the and high-priests and
οἱ γραμματεις εζητουν αυτον απολεσαι, και οἱ
the scribes sought him to destroy, and the
πρωτοι του λαου. 48 Και ουχ εὑρισκον το τι
chief ones of the people. And not finding that what
ποιησωσιν· ὁ λαος γαρ ἁπας εξεκρεματο αυτου
they might do: the people for all were very attentive him
ακουων.
hearing.

ΚΕΦ. κ'. 20.

1 Και εγενετο εν μιᾳ των ἡμερων εκεινων
And it happened in one of the days those
διδασκοντος αυτου τον λαον εν τῳ ἱερῳ, και
was teaching of him the people in the temple, and
ευαγγελιζομενου, επεστησαν οἱ αρχιερεις και
preaching glad tidings, stood by the high-priests and
οἱ γραμματεις συν τοις πρεσβυτεροις, 2 και
the scribes with the elders, and
ειπον προς αυτον, λεγοντες· Ειπε ἡμιν, εν
said to him, saying: Say to us, by
ποιᾳ εξουσιᾳ ταυτα ποιεις; η τις εστιν ὁ
what authority these things doest thou? or who is he
δους σοι την εξουσιαν ταυτην; 3 Αποκριθεις
having given to thee the authority this? Answering
δε ειπε προς αυτους· Ερωτησω ὑμας καγω ἑνα
and he said to them: Will ask you also I one
λογον, και ειπατε μοι· 4 Το βαπτισμα Ιωαννου
word, and say you to me: The dipping of John
εξ ουρανου ην, η εξ ανθρωπων; 5 Οἱ δε συνε-
from heaven was, or from men? They and rea-
λογισαντο προς ἑαυτους, λεγοντες· Ὁτι εαν
soned among themselves, saying; That if
ειπωμεν· Εξ ουρανου ερει· Διατι *[ουν] ουκ
we should say, From heaven he will say; Why [then] not
επιστευσατε αυτῳ; 6 Εαν δε ειπωμεν· Εξ
did you believe him? If and we should say; From
ανθρωπων· πας ὁ λαος καταλιθασει ἡμας·
men; all the people will stone us.
πεπεισμενος γαρ εστιν, Ιωαννην προφητην
having been persuaded for it is, John a prophet
ειναι. 7 Και απεκριθησαν μη ειδεναι ποθεν.
to be. And they answered not to have known whence.

because thou didst not know the SEASON of thy VISITATION.

45 ‡And going into the TEMPLE, he began to expel THOSE who SOLD,

46 saying to them, "It is written, ‡'My HOUSE '*shall be a House of 'Prayer;' but you have made it a Den of Robbers."

47 And he was teaching in the TEMPLE EVERY DAY; and ‡the HIGH-PRIESTS and the SCRIBES and the CHIEFS of the PEOPLE, were seeking to destroy him.

48 And they could not find HOW to do it, for all the PEOPLE were very attentive to hear him.

CHAPTER XX.

1 ‡And it occurred on one of *those DAYS, as he was teaching the PEOPLE in the TEMPLE, and proclaiming glad tidings, the HIGH-PRIESTS, and the SCRIBES, with the ELDERS came upon him,

2 and said to him, saying, "Tell us, ‡by What Authority thou doest These things? or who is HE that EMPOWERED thee?"

3 And answering he said to them, "I also will ask you *a Question; and answer me;

4 Was the IMMERSION of John from Heaven, or from Men?"

5 And THEY reasoned among themselves, saying, "If we say, 'From Heaven,' he will retort, 'Why did you not believe him?'

6 But if we say, 'From Men,' all the PEOPLE will STONE us; ‡for they are persuaded that John was a Prophet."

7 And they answered, that they did not know whence it was.

* VATICAN MANUSCRIPT.—45. in it and buying—*omit.* 46. shall be a HOUSE. 1. the DAYS. 3. a Question. 5. then—*omit.*

‡ 45. Matt. xxi. 12; Mark xi. 11. 15. ‡ 46. Isa. lvi. 7. ‡ 47. Mark xi. 18; John vii. 19; viii. 37. ‡ 1. Matt. xxi. 23. ‡ 2. Acts iv. 7; vii. 27. ‡ 6. Matt. xvi. 14; xxi. 26; Luke vii. 29

8 Και ὁ Ιησους ειπεν αυτοις· Ουδε εγω λεγω
And the Jesus said to them: Neither I tell
ὑμιν, εν ποιᾳ εξουσια ταυτα ποιω.
to you, by what authority these I do.
9 Ηρξατο δε προς τον λαον λεγειν την παρα-
He began and to the people to say the para-
βολην ταυτην· Ανθρωπος εφυτευσεν αμπελωνα,
ble this: A man planted a vineyard,
και εξεδοτο αυτον γεωργοις· και απεδημησε
and let out it to husbandmen: and went abroad
χρονους ἱκανους. 10 Και εν καιρῳ απεστειλε
times many. And in season he sent
προς τους γεωργους δουλον, ἱνα απο του καρπου
to the husbandmen a slave, that from of the fruit
του αμπελωνος δωσιν αυτῳ· οἱ δε γεωργοι,
of the vineyard they might give to him: the but husbandmen,
δειραντες αυτον, εξαπεστειλαν κενον. 11 Και
having beaten him, sent away empty. And
προσεθετο πεμψαι ἑτερον δουλον· οἱ δε κακεινον
he proceeded to send another slave: they but also this
δειραντες και ατιμασαντες, εξαπεστειλαν κενον.
having beaten and having dishonored, sent away empty.
12 Και προσεθετο πεμψαι τριτον· οἱ δε και του-
And he proceeded to send a third: they but also this
τον τραυματισαντες εξεβαλον. 13 Ειπε δε ὁ
having wounded cast out. Said and the
κυριος του αμπελωνος· Τι ποιησω; πεμψω τον
lord of the vineyard; What shall I do? I will send the
υἱον μου τον αγαπητον· ἰσως τουτον ιδοντες
son of me the beloved; perhaps this seeing
εντραπησονται. 14 Ιδοντες δε αυτον οἱ γεωργοι,
they will regard. Seeing but him the husbandmen,
διελογιζοντο προς ἑαυτους, λεγοντες· Οὑτος
they reasoned with themselves, saying; This
εστιν ὁ κληρονομος· *[δευτε,] αποκτεινωμεν
is the heir; [come,] we may kill
αυτον, ἱνα ἡμων γενηται ἡ κληρονομια. 15 Και
him, that to us may be the inheritance. And
εκβαλοντες αυτον εξω του αμπελωνος, απεκτει-
casting him out of the vineyard, they
ναν. Τι ουν ποιησει αυτοις ὁ κυριος του αμπε-
killed. What then will do to them the lord of the vine-
λωνος; 16 Ελευσεται και απολεσει τους γεωρ-
yard? He will come and will destroy those husband-
γους τουτους, και δωσει τον αμπελωνα αλλοις.
men those, and give the vineyard to others.
Ακουσαντες δε ειπον· Μη γενοιτο. 17 Ὁ δε,
Having heard and they said; Not let it be. He but,
εμβλεψας αυτοις, ειπε· Τι ουν εστι το γεγραμ-
having looked to them, he said; What then is that having been
μενον τουτο· "Λιθον ὁν απεδοκιμασαν οἱ οικο-
written this; "A stone which rejected the build-
δομουντες, οὑτος εγενηθη εις κεφαλην γωνιας;"
ing, this has been made into a head corner?"
18 Πας ὁ πεσων επ' εκεινον τον λιθον, συνθλασ-
All the falling upon that the stone, will be
θησεται· εφ' ὁν δ' αν πεσῃ, λικμησει αυτον.
bruised; on whom but it may fall, will grind to powder him.

8 And JESUS said to them, "Neither do I tell you by What Authority I perform these things."

9 And he began to speak this PARABLE to the PEOPLE. ‡"A Man planted a Vineyard, and leased it to Cultivators, and left the country for a long time.

10 And at the Season he sent a Servant to the CULTIVATORS, that they should give him of the FRUIT of the VINEYARD. But the CULTIVATORS beat him, and sent him away empty.

11 And again he sent Another Servant; and THEY beat him also, and having shamefully treated him, sent him away empty.

12 And again he sent a third; and THEY wounded him also, and drove him out.

13 Then the OWNER of the VINEYARD said, 'What shall I do? I will send my BELOVED SON; perhaps they will respect him.'

14 But when the CULTIVATORS saw him, they reasoned among themselves, saying, 'This is the HEIR; let us kill him, that the INHERITANCE may become ours.'

15 And having thrust him out of the VINEYARD, they killed him. What, therefore, will the OWNER of the VINEYARD do to them?

16 He will come and destroy those CULTIVATORS, and give the VINEYARD to others." And having heard it, they said, "Let it not be."

17 And looking on them, HE said, "What is THIS then that is WRITTEN, ‡'A 'Stone which the BUILDERS rejected, has become 'the Head of the Corner.'

18 WHOEVER FALLS ON that STONE will be bruised; but on whom it may fall, it will crush him to pieces."

* VATICAN MANUSCRIPT.—14 come—*omit*.

‡ 9. Matt. xxi. 33; Mark xii. 1. ‡ 17. Psa. cxviii. 22; Matt. xxi. 42.

19 Και εζητησαν οἱ αρχιερεις και οἱ γραμματεις
And sought the high-priests and the scribes
επιβαλειν επ' αυτον τας χειρας εν αυτῃ τῃ
to put on him the hands in this the
ὡρᾳ· και εφοβηθησαν τον λαον· εγνωσαν γαρ,
hour; but they feared the people; they knew for,
ὁτι προς αυτους την παραβολην ταυτην ειπε.
that to them the parable this he spoke.
20 Και παρατηρησαντες απεστειλαν εγκαθε-
And having watched they sent spies,
τους, ὑποκρινομενους ἑαυτους δικαιους ειναι·
feigning themselves righteous to be;
ἱνα επιλαβωνται αυτου λογου, εις το παρα-
that they might lay hold of him of a word, in order to the to de-
δουναι αυτον τῃ αρχῃ και τῃ εξουσιᾳ του ἡγε-
liver up him to the rule and to the authority of the gov-
μονος. 21 Και επηρωτησαν αυτον, λεγοντες·
ernor. And they asked him, saying;
Διδασκαλε, οιδαμεν, ὁτι ορθως λεγεις και
O teacher, we know, that rightly thou speakest and
διδασκεις, και ου λαμβανεις προσωπον, αλλ' επ'
thou teachest, and not thou dost accept a countenance, but in
αληθειας την ὁδον του θεου διδασκεις. 22 Εξεσ-
truth the way of the God thou teachest. Is it
τιν ἡμιν Καισαρι φορον δουναι, η ου; 23 Κατα-
lawful for us to Cesar tax to give, or not? Per-
νοησας δε αυτων την πανουργιαν, ειπε προς
ceiving but of them the craftiness, he said to
αυτους· *[Τι με πειραζετε;] 24 Δειξατε μοι
them. [Why me tempt you?] Show you to me
δηναριον· τινος εχει εικονα και επιγραφην;
a denarius; of whom has it a likeness and inscription?
Αποκριθεντες δε ειπον· Καισαρος. 25 Ὁ δε ειπεν
Answering and they said; Of Cesar. He and said
αυτοις· Αποδοτε τοινυν τα Καισαρος, Καισαρι·
to them: Give you back then the things of Cesar, to Cesar:
και τα του θεου, τῳ θεῳ. 26 Και ουκ ισχυσαν
and the things of the God, to the God. And not they were able
επιλαβεσθαι αυτου ῥηματος εναντιον του λαου·
to take hold of him of a word in presence of the people;
και θαυμασαντες επι τῃ αποκρισει αυτου,
and wondering at the answer of him,
εσιγησαν.
they were silent.
27 Προσελθοντες δε τινες των Σαδδουκαιων,
Approaching and some of the Sadducees,
οἱ αντιλεγοντες αναστασιν μη ειναι, επηρωτη-
those denying a resurrection not to be, asked
σαν αυτον, 28 λεγοντες· Διδασκαλε, Μωσης
him, saying; O teacher, Moses
εγραψεν ἡμιν, "εαν τινος αδελφος αποθανῃ
wrote for us, "if any one a brother should die
εχων γυναικα, και οὑτος ατεκνος αποθανῃ, ἱνα
having a wife, and this childless should die, that
λαβῃ ὁ αδελφος αυτου την γυναικα, και εξαν-
should take the brother of him the wife, and should
αστησῃ σπερμα τῳ αδελφῳ αυτου." 29 Ἑπτα
raise up seed to the brother of himself." Seven

19 In that very HOUR the HIGH-PRIESTS and SCRIBES sought to lay HANDS on him, but they feared the PEOPLE; for they knew That he had spoken this PARABLE concerning them.

20 ‡ And watching him, they sent forth Spies, feigning themselves to be righteous men, that they might take hold of His Speech, in order to DELIVER him up to the COMMAND and AUTHORITY of the GOVERNOR.

21 And they asked him, saying, ‡ "Teacher, we know That thou speakest and teachest correctly, and dost not partially respect personal Appearance, but teachest the WAY of GOD in Truth;

22 Is it lawful for us, or not, to pay Tribute to Cesar?"

23 But perceiving Their CUNNING, he said to them,

24 "Show me a Denarius. Whose Likeness and Inscription has it?" And * THEY said, "Cesar's."

25 And HE said to them, "Render, then, the THINGS of Cesar, to Cesar; and the THINGS of GOD, to GOD."

26 And they were not able to take hold of * a WORD before the PEOPLE; and they wondered at his ANSWER, and were silent.

27 ‡ Then SOME of the SADDUCEES, * who SAY there is no Resurrection, approaching, asked him,

28 saying, "Teacher, ‡ Moses wrote for us, 'If a man's brother should die, having a Wife, and * he be without children, that his BROTHER should take his WIFE, and raise up Offspring to his BROTHER.'

* VATICAN MANUSCRIPT.—23. Why tempt you me—*omit.* 24. THEY said, Cesar's. 26. a WORD before. 27. who SAY that there is no Resurrection. 28. he be without.

‡ 20. Matt. xxii. 15. ‡ 21. Matt. xxii. 16; Mark xii. 14. ‡ 27. Matt. xxii. 23; Mark xii. 18. ‡ 28. Deut. xxv. 5.

ουν αδελφοι ησαν· και ὁ πρωτος λαβων γυναικα,
now brothers were; and the first having taken a wife,
απεθανεν ατεκνος. 30 Και *[ελαβεν] ὁ δευτερος
died childless. And [took] the second
*[την γυναικα, και οὑτος απεθαναν ατεκνος.]
[the wife, and this died childless.]
31 Και ὁ τριτος ελαβεν αυτην· ὡσαυτως δε και
And the third took her: in like manner and also
οἱ ἑπτα· ου κατελιπον τεκνα, και απεθανον·
the seven: not they left children, and died:
32 Ὑστερον *[δε παντων] απεθανε και ἡ γυνη.
Last [and of all] died also the woman.
33 Εν τῃ ουν αναστασει, τινος αυτων γινεται
In the therefore resurrection, of which of them will be
γυνη; οἱ γαρ ἑπτα εσχον αυτην γυναικα. 34 Και
a wife? the for seven had her a wife. And
*[αποκριθεις] ειπεν αυτοις ὁ Ιησους· Οι υἱοι
[answering] he said to them the Jesus: The sons
του αιωνος τουτου γαμουσι και εκγαμισκονται·
of the age this marry and are given in marriage
35 οἱ δε καταξιωθεντες του αιωνος εκεινου
those but having been accounted worthy of the age that
τυχειν, και της αναστασεως της εκ νεκρων,
to obtain, and of the resurrection that out of dead ones,
ουτε γαμουσιν, ουτε εκγαμισκονται· 36 ουτε γαρ
neither marry, nor are given in marriage: nor for
αποθανειν ετι δυνανται· ισαγγελοι γαρ εισι,
to die more are able: like angels for they are,
και υἱοι εισι του θεου, της αναστασεως υἱοι
and sons they are of the God, of the resurrection sons
οντες. 37 Οτι δε εγειρονται οἱ νεκροι, και Μω-
being. That but rise the dead ones, even Mo-
σης εμηνυσεν επι της βατου, ὡς λεγει κυριον,
ses declared at the bush, when he calls a Lord,
τον θεον Αβρααμ, και τον θεον Ισαακ, και τον
the God of Abraham, and the God of Isaac, and the
θεον Ιακωβ. 38 Θεος δε ουκ εστι νεκρων, αλλα
God of Jacob. A God now not he is of dead ones, but
ζωντων· παντες γαρ αυτῳ ζωσιν. 39 Αποκριθεντες
of living ones; all for to him live. Answering
δε τινες των γραμματεων ειπον· Διδασκαλε,
and some of the scribes said; O teacher,
καλως ειπας. 40 Ουκετι δε ετολμων επερωταν
well thou hast spoken. No longer and they presumed to ask
αυτον ουδεν.
him nothing.

41 Ειπε δε προς αυτους· Πως λεγουσι τον
He said and to them; How say they the

29 Now there were Seven Brothers; and the FIRST, having taken a Wife, died childless.

30 And the SECOND

31 and the THIRD took her; and in like manner also the SEVEN; they died, and left no Children.

32 And last, the WOMAN died also.

33 At the RESURRECTION, therefore, To which of them does she become a Wife; for the SEVEN had her for a Wife."

34 And JESUS said to them, "The CHILDREN of this AGE marry, and are given in marriage;

35 but THOSE DEEMED WORTHY to obtain that AGE, and THAT RESURRECTION from the Dead, neither marry, nor are given in marriage;

36 for they can die no more; ‡ because they are like angels; and are Sons of * God, being Sons of the RESURRECTION.

37 But That the DEAD rise, even Moses has declared, † at the BUSH, when he calls Jehovah, 'the 'GOD of Abraham, and 'the * God of Isaac, and 'the * God of Jacob.'

38 Now he is not a God of the Dead, but of the Living; † for to him all are alive."

39 Then some of the SCRIBES answering, said, "Teacher, thou hast spoken well."

40 * And they dared not question him any more.

41 And he said to them, ‡ "How do they say, that

* VATICAN MANUSCRIPT.—30. took—omit. 30. the wife, and this died childless—omit. 32. And of all—omit. 34. answering—omit. 36. God. 37. God. 37. God. 40. For after.

† 37. Many modern critics regard the phrase,—at the Bush,—as referring to the section in the book of Exodus, commencing at chap. iii. 2, where it is recorded that the angel of Jehovah appeared to Moses "in a flame of fire out of a bush." In Mark xii 26. we read, Jesus asks, "Have you not read in the BOOK of Moses, at the BUSH, how GOD spoke to him?" evidently alluding to the place or section where it was to be found. So here, he says "That the dead rise, even Moses has declared at the [section of] The Bush, when he calls Jehovah," &c. Now Moses could only be said to declare this by recording what the angel said. See the account in Exodus. † 38. To him who regards the future resurrection of his people as though it was present:—"God, who makes alive the dead, and calls things not in being as though they were." Rom. iv. 17.

‡ 36. 1 Cor. xv. 42, 49, 52; Rom. viii. 23; 1 John iii. 2. ‡ 41. Matt. xxii. 42; Mark xii. 35.

Χριστον υἱον Δαυιδ ειναι; 42 Και αυτος Δαυιδ
Anointed a son of David to be? And yet himself David
λεγει εν βιβλῳ ψαλμων· "Ειπεν ὁ κυριος τῳ
says in a book of psalms; "Said the Lord to the
κυριῳ μου· 43 Καθου εξ δεξιων μου ἑως αν θω
lord of me; Sit thou at right hand of me till I may place
τους εχθρους σου ὑποποδιον των ποδων σου."
the enemies of thee a footstool of the feet of thee."
44 Δαυιδ ουν κυριον αυτον καλει, και πως υἱος
David therefore a lord him calls, and how a son
αυτου εστιν; 45 Ακουοντος δε παντος του λαου,
of him he is? Hearing and all of the people,
ειπε τοις μαθηταις αὑτου· 46 Προσεχετε απο
he said to the disciples of himself; Beware of
των γραμματεων, των θελοντων περιπατειν εν
the scribes, those wishing to walk in
στολαις, και φιλουντων ασπασμους εν ταις
robes, and loving salutations in the
αγοραις, και πρωτοκαθεδριας εν ταις συναγωγαις,
markets, and first seats in the synagogues,
και πρωτοκλισιας εν τοις δειπνοις· 47 οἱ κατεσ-
and first places in the feasts; they de-
θιουσι τας οικιας των χηρων, και προφασει
vour the houses of the widows, and for a show
μακρα προσευχονται· οὑτοι ληψονται περισσο-
long they pray; these will receive greater
τερον κριμα.
judgment.

the MESSIAH is to be a Son of David?

42 * For David himself says in the Book of Psalms, ‡ *'Jehovah said to my 'LORD, sit thou at my 'Right hand,

43 'till I put thine EN-'EMIES underneath thy 'FEET.'

44 David, therefore, calls him Lord, and how then is he * His Son?"

45 ‡ Then in the hearing of All the PEOPLE he said to * the DISCIPLES,

46 "Beware of THOSE SCRIBES who DESIRE to walk about in Long robes, and ‡ love Salutations in the MARKETS, and the Principal seats in the SYNAGOGUES, and the Upper couch at FEASTS;

47 ‡ those PLUNDERING the FAMILIES of WIDOWS, and for a Show make long Prayers; these will receive a Heavier Judgment."

ΚΕΦ. κα'. 21.

1 Αναβλεψας δε ειδε τους βαλλοντας τα δωρα
Looking and he saw those casting the gifts
αὑτων εις το γαζοφυλακιον πλουσιους. 2 Ειδε
of them into the treasury rich ones. He saw
δε *[και] τινα χηραν πενιχραν βαλλουσαν εκει
and [also] a certain widow poor casting there
δυο λεπτα· 3 και ειπεν· Αληθως λεγω ὑμιν, ὁτι
two lepta; and he said: Truly I say to you, that
ἡ χηρα ἡ πτωχη αὑτη πλειον παντων εβαλεν.
the widow that poor this more of all has cast.
4 Ἁπαντες γαρ οὑτοι εκ του περισσευοντος
All for they out of the abundance
αὑτοις εβαλον εις τα δωρα *[του θεου·] αὑτη δε
of them cast into the gifts [of the God;] she but
εκ του ὑστερηματος αὑτης ἁπαντα τον βιον,
out of the want of herself all the living,
ὁν ειχεν, εβαλε. 5 Και τινων λεγοντων περι
which she said, she cast. And some speaking about
του ἱερου ὁτι λιθοις καλοις και αναθημασι
the temple that with stones beautiful and offerings
κεκοσμηται, ειπε· 6 Ταυτα ἁ θεωρειτε, ελευ-
it was adorned, he said; These which you behold, will
σονται ἡμεραι εν αἱς ουκ αφεθησεται λιθος επι
come days in which not will be left a stone upon
λιθῳ, ὁς ου καταλυθησεται. 7 Επηρωτησαν δε
a stone, which not will be thrown down. They asked and

CHAPTER XXI.

1 And looking up, ‡ he saw the RICH CASTING their GIFTS into the TREASURY.

2 And he saw a Certain poor Widow casting in there Two † Lepta.

3 And he said, "I assure you, That this POOR WIDOW cast in more than all;

4 for all these have cast among the GIFTS out of their SUPERFLUITY; but she, out of her POVERTY, cast in All the LIVING that she had.

5 ‡ And some speaking of the TEMPLE, That it was adorned with beautiful Stones and Offerings, he said,

6 "As for these things which you behold, the Days will come, in which ‡ there will not be * left here a Stone upon a Stone, that will not be thrown down."

* VATICAN MANUSCRIPT.—42. For David. 42. Lord. 44. His Son. 45. his DISCIPLES. 2. also—omit. 4. of GOD—omit. 6. left here.

† 2. In value about four mills, or nearly half a farthing.

‡ 42. Psa. cx. 1; Acts ii. 34. ‡ 45. Matt xxiii. 1; Mark xii. 38. ‡ 46. Luke xi. 43. ‡ 47. Matt. xxiii. 14. ‡ 1. Matt. xii. 41. ‡ 5. Matt. xxiv 1; Mark xiii. 1. ‡ 6. Luke xix. 44.

αυτον, λεγοντες· Διδασκαλε, ποτε ουν ταυτα
him, saying; O teacher, when then these
εσται; και τι το σημειον, όταν μελλη ταυτα
will be? and what the sign, when may be about these
γινεσθαι; 8 'Ο δε ειπε· Βλεπετε, μη πλανηθητε.
to be done? He but said; Look you, not you may be deceived.
Πολλοι γαρ ελευσονται επι τῳ ονοματι μου,
Many for will come in the name of me,
λεγοντες· 'Οτι εγω ειμι, και ὁ καιρος ηγγικε.
saying, That I am, and the season has approached.
Μη *[ουν] πορευθητε οπισω αυτων. 9 'Οταν δε
Not [therefore] go you after them. When and
ακουσητε πολεμους και ακαταστασιας, μη πτο-
you may hear of wars and commotions, not you may
ηθητε· δει γαρ ταυτα γενεσθαι πρωτον· αλλ'
be terrified; must for these come to pass first; but
ουκ ευθεως το τελος. 10 Τοτε ελεγεν αυτοις·
not immediately the end. Then he said to them;
Εγερθησεται εθνος επι εθνος, και βασιλεια
Will rise a nation on a nation, and a kingdom
επι βασιλειαν· 11 σεισμοι τε μεγαλοι κατα το-
on a kingdom; earthquakes and great in many
πους, και λιμοι, και λοιμοι εσονται· φοβητρα
places, and famines, and pestilences will be; fearful sights
τε και σημεια απ' ουρανου μεγαλα εσται.
also and signs from heaven great will be.
12 Προ δε τουτων παντων επιβαλουσιν εφ' ὑμας
Before but this all they will lay on you
τας χειρας αὑτων, και διωξουσι, παραδιδοντες
the hands of them, and they will persecute, delivering up
εις συναγωγας και φυλακας, αγομενους επι
to synagogues and prisons, dragging to
βασιλεις και ἡγεμονας, ἑνεκεν του ονοματος
kings and governors, on account of the name
μου. 13 Αποβησεται δε ὑμιν εις μαρτυριον.
of me. It will turn out and to you for a testimony.
14 Θεσθε ουν εις τας καρδιας ὑμων, μη προμε-
Settle you therefore in the hearts of you, not to pre-
λεταν απολογηθηναι. 15 Εγω γαρ δωσω ὑμιν
meditate to make a defence. I for will give to you
στομα και σοφιαν, ᾑ ου δυνησονται αντειπειν η
a mouth and wisdom, which not will be able to gainsay or
αντιστηναι παντες οἱ αντικειμενοι ὑμιν. 16 Παρα-
resist all the opponents to you. You will
δοθησεσθε δε και ὑπο γονεων, και αδελφων,
be delivered up and also by parents, and brothers,
και συγγενων, και φιλων· και θανατωσουσιν εξ
and relatives, and friends; and they will put to death of
ὑμων. 17 Και εσεσθε μισουμενοι ὑπο παντων
you. And you will be being hated by all
δια το ονομα μου. 18 Και θριξ εκ της κεφαλης
through the name of me. And a hair from the head

7 And they asked him, saying, "Teacher, when then will these things be?" and "What will be the SIGN when these things are about to be accomplished?"

8 And HE said, ‡ "See that you be not deceived; for many will come in my NAME, saying, 'I am he, and the TIME draws near;' go not after them.

9 And when you hear of Battles and Insurrections, be not alarmed; for these things must first occur; but the END comes not immediately."

10 ‡ Then he said to them, "Nation will rise against Nation, and Kingdom against Kingdom;

11 *and in various Places there will be great Earthquakes, and Famines, and Pestilences; there will be also Fearful sights and great Signs from Heaven.

12 ‡ But before all these things they will lay their HANDS on you, and persecute you, delivering you up to Synagogues and ‡ Prisons, dragging you before Kings and Governors on account of my NAME.

13 And it will turn out to you for a Testimony.

14 ‡ Settle it in your HEARTS, therefore, not to premeditate on your defence;

15 for I will give you Eloquence and Wisdom, ‡ which All your OPPONENTS will not be able to gainsay, or resist.

16 And you will be delivered up even by Parents, and Brothers, and Relatives, and Friends; and some of you they will put to death.

17 And you will be hated by all on account of my NAME;

18 But not a Hair of your HEAD will perish.

* VATICAN MANUSCRIPT.—8. therefore—omit. 11. there will be great Earthquakes, and in various Places Famines, and.

‡ 8. Matt. xxiv. 4; Mark xiii. 5; Eph. v. 6; 2 Thess. ii. 3. ‡ 10. Matt. xxiv. 7. ‡ 12. Mark xiii. 9. ‡ 12. Acts iv. 3; v. 18; xii. 4; xvi. 24; xxv. 23. ‡ 14. Matt. x. 19; xiii. 11; xii. 11. ‡ 15. Acts vi. 10.

ὑμων ου μη αποληται. [19] Εν τῃ ὑπομονῃ ὑμων
of you not not will perish. In the patient endurance of you
κτησασθε τας ψυχας ὑμων.
preserve you the lives of you.
[20] Ὁταν δε ιδητε κυκλουμενην ὑπο στρατοπε-
When and you may see surrounded by encampments
δων την Ἱερουσαλημ, τοτε γνωτε, ὁτι ηγγικεν
the Jerusalem, then you may know, that has come near
ἡ ερημωσις αυτης. [21] Τοτε οἱ εν τῃ Ιουδαιᾳ,
the desolation of her. Then those in the Judea,
φευγετωσαν εις τα ορη· και οἱ εν μεσῳ αυ-
let them flee to the mountains; and those in midst of
της, εκχωρειτωσαν· και οἱ εν ταις χωραις, μη
her let them go out; and those in the country places, not
εισερχεσθωσαν εις αυτην. [22] Ὁτι ἡμεραι εκδι-
let them enter into her. For days of
κησεως αὑται εισι, του πλησθηναι παντα τα
vengeance these are, of the to be fulfilled all the things
γεγραμμενα. [23] Ουαι *[δε] ταις εν γαστρι εχου-
having been written. Woe [but] to the in womb hold-
σαις και ταις θηλαζουσαις εν εκειναις ταις ἡμε-
ing and to the giving suck in those the days;
ραις· εσται γαρ αναγκη μεγαλη επι της γης,
will be for distress great upon the land,
και οργη τῳ λαῳ τουτῳ· [24] και πεσουνται
and wrath to the people this; and they will fall
στοματι μαχαιρας, και αιχμαλωτισθησονται
by edge of a sword, and they will be led captive
εις παντα τα εθνη· και Ἱερουσαλημ εσται
into all the nations; and Jerusalem will be
πατουμενη ὑπο εθνων, αχρι πληρωθωσι καιροι
trodden down by Gentiles, till may be fulfilled seasons
εθνων. [25] Και εσται σημεια εν ἡλιῳ και σεληνῃ
of Gentiles. And will be signs in sun and moon
και αστροις· και επι της γης συνοχη εθνων εν
and stars; and on the earth anguish of nations in
απορια ηχους θαλασσης και σαλου· [26] αποψυ-
perplexity of a roar of sea and of tossing; faint-
χοντων ανθρωπων απο φοβου και προσδοκιας
ing men from fear and expectation
των επερχομενων τῃ οικουμενῃ· αἱ γαρ δυναμεις
of the things coming on the habitable; the for powers
των ουρανων σαλευθησονται. [27] Και τοτε οψον-
of the heavens will be shaken. And then they will
ται τον υἱον του ανθρωπου ερχομενον εν νεφελῃ,
see the son of the man coming in a cloud,
μετα δυναμεως και δοξης πολλης. [28] Αρχομενων
with power and glory great. Beginning
δε τουτων γινεσθαι, αναψυσατε και επαρατε
and of these to occur, raise yourselves and lift up
τας κεφαλας ὑμων· διοτι εγγιζει ἡ απολυτρωσις
the heads of you; because draws near the deliverance
ὑμων. [29] Και ειπε παραβολην αυτοις· Ιδετε την
of you. And he spoke a parable to them; See you the
συκην και παντα τα δενδρα· [30] ὁταν προβαλωσιν
fig-tree and all the trees; when they shoot forth

19 By your PATIENT ENDURANCE preserve your LIVES.

20 ‡ And when you see JERUSALEM surrounded by Encampments, then know That its DESOLATION has approached.

21 Then let THOSE who are in JUDEA, flee to the MOUNTAINS; let THOSE who are in the city, depart out; and let not THOSE who are in the COUNTRY PLACES enter it.

22 For these are Days of Vengeance, ‡ that All the THINGS WRITTEN may be ACCOMPLISHED.

23 ‡ But alas for the PREGNANT and NURSING WOMEN in Those DAYS! for there will be great Distress on the LAND, and Wrath against this PEOPLE.

24 And they will fall by the Edge of the Sword, and be led captive into All the NATIONS; and Jerusalem will be trodden down by Gentiles, ‡ till * the Times of Gentiles may be accomplished.

25 ‡ And there will be Signs in the Sun and Moon and Stars; and on the EARTH Anguish of Nations in Perplexity; * Roarings of the Sea and Waves;

26 Men fainting from Fear and Apprehension of the THINGS COMING on the HABITABLE; ‡ for the POWERS of the HEAVENS will be shaken.

27 And then they will see the SON of MAN ‡ coming in a Cloud with Power and great Glory.

28 When these things are beginning to occur, raise yourselves, and lift up your HEADS; for your DELIVERANCE is drawing near."

29 And he spoke a Parable to them;—"Behold the FIG-TREE, and All the TREES.

30 When they now put

* VATICAN MANUSCRIPT.—23. But—*omit*. 24. when they should be fulfilled; and the Times shall be those of the Gentiles. And 25. Roarings of the Sea.

‡ 20. Matt. xxiv. 15; Mark xiii. 14. ‡ 22. Dan. ix. 26; Zech. xi. 1. ‡ 24. Dan. xii. 7; Rom. xi. 25. ‡ 25. Matt. xxiv. 29; Mark xiii. 24; 2 Pet. iii. 10, 12. ‡ 26. Matt. xxiv. 29. ‡ 27. Matt. xxiv. 30; Rev. i. 7.

ηδη, βλεποντες, αφ' ἑαυτων γινωσκετε, ὁτι
now, beholding, from of yourselves you know, that
ηδη εγγυς το θερος εστιν. 31 Οὑτω και ὑμεις,
now near the summer is. So also you,
ὁταν ιδητε ταυτα γινομενα, γινωσκετε, ὁτι
when you may see these occurring, know you, that
εγγυς εστιν ἡ βασιλεια του θεου. 32 Αμην λεγω
near is the kingdom of the God. Indeed I say
ὑμιν, ὁτι ου μη παρελθῃ ἡ γενεα αὑτη, ἑως
to you, that not not may pass away the generation this, till
αν παντα γενηται. 33 Ὁ ουρανος και ἡ γη
all may be done. The heaven and the earth
παρελευσονται· οἱ δε λογοι μου ου μη παρελ-
shall pass away; the but words of me not not may pass
θωσι. 34 Προσεχετε δε ἑαυτοις, μηποτε βαρη-
away. Take heed but to yourselves, lest should be
θωσιν ὑμων αἱ καρδιαι εν κραιπαλῃ, και μεθῃ,
burdened of you the hearts with surfeiting, and drunkenness,
και μεριμναις βιωτικαις· και αιφνιδιος εφ' ὑμας
and anxieties of life; and suddenly on you
επιστῃ ἡ ἡμερα εκεινη. 35 Ὡς παγις γαρ επε-
may come the day that. As a snare for it will
λευσεται επι παντας τους καθημενους επι προ-
come on all those dwelling on face
σωπον πασης της γης. 36 Αγρυπνειτε ουν εν
of all of the earth. Watch you then in
παντι καιρῳ, δεομενοι, ἱνα καταξιωθητε εκ-
every season, praying, that you may be accounted worthy to
φυγειν ταυτα παντα τα μελλοντα γινεσθαι,
escape these all the things being about to occur,
και σταθηναι εμπροσθεν του υἱου του ανθρωπου.
and to stand in presence of the son of the man.
37 Ην δε τας ἡμερας εν τῳ ἱερῳ διδασκων·
He was and the days in the temple teaching;
τας δε νυκτας εξερχομενος ηυλιζετο εις το
the and nights going out he lodged in the
ορος το καλουμενον ελαιων. 38 Και πας ὁ
mountain that being called of olive-trees. And all the
λαος ωρθριζε προς αυτον εν τῳ ἱερῳ ακουειν
people came early to him in the temple to hear
αυτου. ΚΕΦ. κβ'. 22. 1 Ηγγιζε δε ἡ ἑορτη
him. Drew near now the feast
των αζυμων, ἡ λεγομενη πασχα· 2 και εζητουν
of the unleavened cakes, that being called passover; and sought
οἱ αρχιερεις και οἱ γραμματεις, το πως ανελωσιν
the high-priests and the scribes, the how they might kill
αυτον· εφοβουντο γαρ τον λαον. 3 Εισηλθε δε
him; they feared for the people. Entered and
σατανας εις Ιουδαν τον επικαλουμενον Ισκαριω-
adversary into Judas that being surnamed Iscariot
την, οντα εκ του αριθμου των δωδεκα. 4 Και
being of the number of the twelve. And

forth, observing it, you know of yourselves That the SUMMER already is near.

31 Thus, also, when you see these events occurring, know That the KINGDOM of GOD is near.

32 Indeed I say to you, This GENERATION will not pass away, till all be accomplished.

33 The HEAVEN and the EARTH will fail; but my WORDS cannot fail.

34 But ‡ take heed to yourselves, lest Your HEARTS be oppressed by Gluttony, and Drunkenness, and Anxieties of life, and that DAY should come unexpectedly upon you.

35 For it will come, like a Snare, on All THOSE DWELLING on the Face of the Whole LAND.

36 ‡* Be you watchful, therefore, at all times, praying that you may be regarded worthy to escape All these THINGS BEING ABOUT to occur, and to stand before the SON of MAN."

37 Now he was teaching ‡ during the DAYS in the TEMPLE, and going out he lodged at NIGHTS in THAT MOUNTAIN which is called the Mount of Olives.

38 And All the PEOPLE came early to him in the TEMPLE to hear him.

CHAPTER XXII.

1 Now ‡ THAT FEAST of UNLEAVENED BREAD, which is CALLED the Passover, was drawing near.

2 And the HIGH-PRIESTS and SCRIBES sought HOW they might kill him; for they feared the PEOPLE.

3 ‡ And the Adversary entered * into THAT Judas, CALLED Iscariot, who was of the NUMBER of the TWELVE.

* VATICAN MANUSCRIPT.—36. But watch you, and pray always, that you may prevail to escape. 3. into THAT Judas, called Iscariot.

‡ 34. Rom xiii. 13; 1 Thess. v. 6; 1 Pet. iv. 7. ‡ 36. Matt. xxiv 42; xxv. 13; Mark xiii. 33. ‡ 37. John viii 1, 2; Luke xxii. 39. ‡ 1. Matt. xxvi. 2; Mark xiv. 1. ‡ 3. Matt. xxvi. 14; Matt. xiv. 10; John xiii. 2, 27.

απελθων συνελαλησε τοις αρχιερευσι και τοις
going he talked with the high-priests and the
στρατηγοις, το πως αυτον παραδῳ αυτοις.
officers, the how him he might deliver up to them.
5 Και εχαρησαν· και συνεθεντο αυτῳ αργυριον
And they were glad, and agreed to him silver
δουναι. 6 Και εξωμολογησε· και εζητει ευκαι-
to give. And he consented; and he sought oppor-
ριαν του παραδουναι αυτον αυτοις ατερ οχλου.
tunity of the to deliver up him to them without of a crowd.
7 Ηλθε δε ἡ ἡμερα των αζυμων, εν ᾑ
Came and the day of the unleavened cakes, in which
εδει θυεσθαι το πασχα· 8 και απεστειλε
it is necessary to sacrifice the paschal lamb; and he sent
Πετρον και Ιωαννην, ειπων· Πορευθεντες ἑτοι-
Peter and John, saying; Going pre-
μασατε ἡμιν το πασχα, ἱνα φαγωμεν. 9 Οἱ δε
pare you for us the passover, that we may eat. They and
ειπον αυτῳ· Που θελεις ατοιμασωμεν; 10 Ὁ δε
said to him; Where wilt thou we make ready? He and
ειπεν αυτοις· Ιδου, εισελθοντων ὑμων εις την
said to them; Lo, having entered of you into the
πολιν, συναντησει ὑμιν ανθρωπος κεραμιον
city, will meet you a man a pitcher
ὑδατος βασταζων· ακολουθησατε αυτῳ εις την
of water carrying; follow you him into the
οικιαν, οὑ εισπορευεται· και ερειτε τῳ οικο-
house. where he enters; and say you to the house
δεσποτῃ της οικιας· 11 Λεγει σοι ὁ διδασκαλος·
master of the house: Says to thee the teacher:
Που εστι το καταλυμα, ὁπου το πασχα μετα
Where is the guest-chamber, where the passover with
των μαθητων μου φαγω; 12 Κακεινος ὑμιν δειξει
the disciples of me I may eat? And he to you will show
αναγιον μεγα εστρωμενον· εκει ἑτοιμασατε.
an upper room large having been furnished: there prepare you.
13 Απελθοντες δε εὑρον καθως ειρηκεν αυτοις·
Having gone and they found even as he had said to them:
και ἡτοιμασαν το πασχα.
and they prepared the passover.
14 Και ὁτε εγενετο ἡ ὡρα, ανεπεσε, και οἱ
And when came the hour, he reclined, and the
δωδεκα αποστολοι συν αυτῳ. 15 Και ειπε προς
twelve apostles with him. And he said to
αυτους· Επιθυμιᾳ επεθυμησα τουτο το πασχα
them: With desire I have desired this the passover
φαγειν μεθ' ὑμων, προ του με παθειν. 16 Λεγω
to eat with you, before the me to suffer. I say
γαρ ὑμιν, ὁτι *[ουκετι] ου μη φαγω εξ αυτου,
for to you, that [no more] not not I may eat of it,
ἑως* ὁτου πληρωθῃ εν τῃ βασιλειᾳ του θεου.
till it may be fulfilled in the kingdom of the God.
17 Και δεξαμενος ποτηριον, ευχαριστησας ειπε·
And having taken a cup, having given thanks he said:

4 And he went and talked with the HIGH-PRIESTS and OFFICERS, HOW he might deliver him up to them.

5 And they were glad, and agreed to give him Money.

6 And he consented, and sought a Convenient time to DELIVER him up to them in the absence of the Crowd.

7 ‡ Now the DAY of UNLEAVENED BREAD came, on which it was necessary to sacrifice the PASCHAL LAMB.

8 And he sent Peter and John, saying, "Go, and prepare the PASSOVER for us, that we may eat."

9 And THEY said to him, "Where dost thou wish that we * prepare for thee to eat the PASSOVER?"

10 And HE said to them, "Behold, as you enter the CITY, a Man carrying a Pitcher of Water will meet you; follow him into the HOUSE where he enters.

11 And you shall say to the MASTER of the HOUSE, 'The TEACHER says to thee, Where is the GUEST-CHAMBER, where I may eat the PASSOVER with my DISCIPLES?'

12 And he will show you a large Upper-room furnished ready; there prepare."

13 And they went, and found all even as he had said to them; and they prepared the PASSOVER.

14 ‡ And when the HOUR came, he reclined, and * the APOSTLES with him.

15 And he said to them, "I have earnestly desired to eat This PASSOVER with you before I SUFFER;

16 for I say to you, I will not eat * of it, till it shall be fulfilled in the KINGDOM of GOD."

17 And taking a Cup, having given thanks, he

* VATICAN MANUSCRIPT.—9. prepare for thee to eat the PASSOVER. 14. the APOSTLES with him. 16. no more—omit. 16. the same, till.

‡ 7 Matt. xxvi. 17; Mark xiv. 12. ‡ 14. Matt. xxvi. 20; Mark xiv. 17.

Λαβετε τουτο, και διαμερισατε ἑαυτοις. 18 Λεγω
Take you this, and divide you among yourselves. I say
γαρ ὑμιν, ὁτι ου μη πιω απο του γεννηματος
for to you, that not not I may drink of the product
της αμπελου, ἑως ὁτου ἡ βασιλεια του θεου
of the vine, till the kingdom of the God
ελθῃ. 19 Και λαβων αρτον, ευχαριστησας
may come. And having taken a loaf, having given thanks
εκλασε, και εδωκεν αυτοις, λεγων· Τουτο εστι
he broke, and gave to them, saying: This is
το σωμα μου, το ὑπερ ὑμων διδομενον· τουτο
the body of me, that in behalf of you being given: this
ποιειτε εις την εμην αναμνησιν. 20 Ὡσαυτως
do you in the my remembrance. In like manner
και το ποτηριον, μετα το δειπνησαι, λεγων·
also the cup, after the supper, saying:
Τουτο το ποτηριον, ἡ καινη διαθηκη εν τῳ
This the cup, the new covenant in the
αἱματι μου, το ὑπερ ὑμων εκχυνομενον. 21 Πλην
blood of me, that in behalf of you being poured out. But
ιδου, ἡ χειρ του παραδιδοντος με μετ᾽ εμου επι
lo, the hand of the delivering up me with mine on
της τραπεζης. 22 Και ὁ μεν υἱος του ανθρωπου
the table. And the indeed son of the man
πορευεται κατα το ὡρισμενον· πλην ουαι
goes away according to that having been appointed, but woe
τῳ ανθρωπῳ εκεινῳ, δι᾽ οὑ παραδιδοται.
to the man that, through whom he is delivered up.
23 Και αυτοι ηρξαντο συζητειν προς ἑαυτους, το,
And they began to inquire among themselves, the,
τις αρα ειη εξ αυτων ὁ τουτο μελλων πρασ-
which then it could be of them the this being about to
σειν.
do.

24 Εγενετο δε και φιλονεικια εν αυτοις,
There had been and also a strife among them,
το, τις αυτων δοκει ειναι μειζων. 25 Ὁ δε
the, which of them thinks to be greater. He but
ειπεν αυτοις· Οἱ βασιλεις των εθνων κυριευου-
said to them; The kings of the nations exercise lordship
σιν αυτων· και οἱ εξουσιαζοντες αυτων, ευερ-
over them; and those having authority of them, bene-
γεται καλουνται. 26 Ὑμεις δε ουχ οὑτως· αλλ᾽
factors are called. You but not so; but
ὁ μειζων εν ὑμιν, γενεσθω ὡς ὁ νεωτερος· και
the greater among you, let him become as the younger; and
ὁ ἡγουμενος, ὡς ὁ διακονων. 27 Τις γαρ μει-
the governor, as he serving. Which for greater?
ζων, ὁ ανακειμενος, η ὁ διακονων, ουχι ὁ
he reclining, or he serving? not he
ανακειμενος; εγω δε ειμι εν μεσῳ ὑμων ὡς ὁ
reclining? I but am in midst of you as he

said, "Take this, and divide it among yourselves;

18 for ‡ I say to you, I will not drink * from HENCEFORTH of the PRODUCT of the VINE, till the KINGDOM of GOD shall come."

19 ‡ And taking a Loaf, and having given thanks, he broke it, and gave to them, saying, "This is THAT BODY of mine which IS GIVEN for you; do this in MY Remembrance."

20 In like manner also the CUP, after the SUPPER, saying, "This CUP is the NEW Covenant in my BLOOD, THAT in your behalf being POURED OUT.

21 ‡ But, behold, the HAND of HIM who DELIVERS me up is with mine on the TABLE.

22 * For indeed the SON of MAN is going away, according to THAT which has been APPOINTED; but Woe to that MAN by whom he is delivered up!"

23 And they began to inquire among themselves, WHICH of them it could be who was about to do this.

24 ‡ And there was also a Contention among them, WHICH of them should be thought the greatest.

25 ‡ And HE said to them, "The KINGS of the NATIONS exercise dominion over them; and THOSE HAVING AUTHORITY over them are styled † Benefactors.

26 But you must not be so; but let the GREATEST among you become as the LEAST, and the GOVERNOR as HE who SERVES.

27 For who is greater, HE who RECLINES, or HE who SERVES? Is not HE who RECLINES? but I am among you as HE who SERVES.

* VATICAN MANUSCRIPT.—18. from HENCEFORTH. 22. for indeed.

† 25. *Euergetes*, Benefactors, was a name borne by several kings in Egypt and Syria, and had become proverbial for a tyrant.—*Sharpe*.

‡ 18. Matt. xxvi. 29; Mark xiv. 25. ‡ 19. 1 Cor. xi. 24. ‡ 21. Psa. xli. 9; Matt. xxvi. 21, 23; Mark xiv 18; John xiii. 21, 26. ‡ 24. Mark ix 34; Luke ix. 46. ‡ 25 Matt. xx. 25; Mark x. 42.

διακονων. 28 Ὑμεις δε εστε οἱ διαμεμενηκοτες
serving. You but are those having continued

μετ' εμου εν τοις πειρασμοις μου. 29 Καγω
with me in the trials of me. And I

διατιθεμαι ὑμιν, καθως διεθετο μοι ὁ πατηρ
covenant for you, even as has covenanted for me the father

μου βασιλειαν, 30 ἱνα εσθιητε και πινητε επι
of me a kingdom, that you may eat and you may drink at

της τραπεζης μου εν τῃ βασιλειᾳ μου· και
the table of me in the kingdom of me; and

καθισεσθε επι θρονων, κρινοντες τας δωδεκα
you may sit on thrones, judging the twelve

φυλας του Ισραηλ.
tribes of the Israel.

31 *[Ειπε δε ὁ κυριος·] Σιμων, Σιμων, ιδου,
[Said and the lord;] Simon, Simon, lo,

ὁ σατανας εξῃτησατο ὑμας, του σινιασαι ὡς
the adversary has asked for you, the to sift as

τον σιτον. 32 Εγω δε εδεηθην περι σου, ἱνα μη
the wheat. I but prayed for thee, that not

εκλειπῃ ἡ πιστις σου. Και συ ποτε επιστρε-
may fail the faith of thee. And thou when having been

ψας, στηριξον τους αδελφους σου. 33 Ὁ δε
turned, strengthen the brethren of thee. He and

ειπεν αυτῳ· Κυριε, μετα σου ἑτοιμος ειμι και
said to him; O lord, with thee ready I am both

εις φυλακην και εις θανατον πορευεσθαι. 34 Ὁ
to prison and to death to go. He

δε ειπε· Λεγω σοι, Πετρε, ου μη φωνησει
but said; I say to thee, O Peter, not not will crow

σημερον αλεκτωρ, πριν η τρις απαρνησῃ μη
to-day a cock, before thrice thou wilt deny not

ειδεναι με. 35 Και ειπεν αυτοις· Ὁτε απεσ-
to have known me. And he said to them; When I

τειλα ὑμας ατερ βαλαντιου, και πηρας, και
sent you without a purse, and a bag, and

ὑποδηματων, μη τινος ὑστερησατε; Οἱ δε ειπον·
shoes, not anything wanted you? They and said;

Ουδενος. 36 Ειπεν ουν αυτοις· Αλλα νυν, ὁ
Nothing. He said then to them; But now, he

εχων βαλαντιον, ἀρατω, ὁμοιως και πηραν·
having a purse, let him take, in like manner and a bag;

και ὁ μη εχων, πωλησατω το ἱματιον αὑτου, και
and he not having, let him sell the mantle of himself, and

αγορασατω μαχαιραν. 37 Λεγω γαρ ὑμιν, ὁτι
let him buy a sword. I say for to you, that

*[ετι] τουτο το γεγραμμενον δει τελεσθηναι εν
[yet] this the having been written must to be finished in

εμοι, το· "Και μετα ανομων ελογισθη." Και
me, that; "And with law-breakers he was counted." Also

γαρ τα περι εμου τελος εχει. 38 Οἱ δε ειπον·
for the things about me an end has. They but said;

Κυριε, ιδου, μαχαιραι ὡδε δυο. Ὁ δε ειπεν
O lord, lo, swords here two. He and said

αυτοις· Ἱκανον εστι.
to them; Enough it is.

28 And you are THEY who have CONTINUED with me in my TRIALS.

29 And I covenant for you, even as my FATHER has covenanted for me, ‡ a Kingdom,

30 that you may eat and drink at my TABLE in my KINGDOM, ‡ and sit on Thrones, Judging the TWELVE Tribes of ISRAEL.

31 Simon, Simon, behold, the ADVERSARY has asked for you, that he may SIFT you like WHEAT;

32 but I have prayed for thee, that thy FAITH may not fail, and when thou hast turned, strengthen thy BRETHREN."

33 And HE said to him, "Master, I am ready to go with thee both to Prison and to Death."

34 ‡ And HE said, "I tell thee, Peter, a Cock will not crow To-day, * till thou shalt thrice deny that thou knowest me."

35 And he said to them, ‡ "When I sent you out without a Purse, and Bag, and Sandals, did you want any thing?" And THEY said, "Nothing."

36 * And he said to them, "But now, HE who HAS a Purse, let him take it, and in like manner, a Bag; and HE who HAS no Sword, let him sell his MANTLE, and buy one.

37 For I tell you, That THIS which has been WRITTEN must be fully accomplished in me, ‡ AND HE 'WAS NUMBERED WITH 'LAW-BREAKERS;' for also the THINGS concerning me have an end."

38 And THEY said, "Master, Behold, here are two Swords." And HE said to them, "It is sufficient."

* VATICAN MANUSCRIPT.—31. And the Lord said—*omit*. 34. till thou shalt. 36. And he said. 37. yet—*omit*.

‡ 29. Matt. xxiv. 47; Luke xii. 32; 2 Cor. i. 7; 2 Tim. ii. 12; Rev. ii. 26, 27. ‡ 30. Matt. xix. 28; 1 Cor. vi. 2; Rev. iii. 21. ‡ 34. Matt. xxvi. 34; Mark xiv. 30; John xiii. 38. ‡ 35. Matt. x. 9; Luke ix. 3; x. 4. ‡ 37. Isa. liii. 12; Mark xv. 28.

39 Και εξελθων επορευθη κατα το εθος εις
And going out he went according to the custom to
το ορος των ελαιων· ηκολουθησαν δε αυτῳ
the mountain of the olive-trees: followed and him
και οἱ μαθηται αυτου. 40 Γενομενος δε επι του
also the disciples of him. Having come and to the
τοπου, ειπεν αυτοις· Προσευχεσθε μη εισελθειν
place. he said to them: Pray you not to enter
εις πειρασμον. 41 Και αυτος απεσπασθη απ'
into temptation. And he was withdrawn from
αυτων ὡσει λιθου βολην, και θεις τα γονατα
them about of a stone throw, and having placed the knees
προσηυχετο, λεγων· 42 Πατερ, ει βουλει παρε-
he prayed, saying: O father, if thou art willing to take
νεγκειν το ποτηριον τουτο απ' εμου· πλην μη
away the cup this from me: but not
το θελημα μου, αλλα το σον γενεσθω. 43*[Ωφθη
the will of me, but the thine be done. [Appeared
δε αυτῳ αγγελος απ' ουρανου, ενισχυων αυτον.
and to him a messenger from heaven, strengthening him.
44 Και γενομενος εν αγωνιᾳ, εκτενεστερον
And being in agony, very earnestly
προσηυχετο. Εγενετο δε ὁ ἱδρως αυτου ὡσει
he prayed. Was and the sweat of him like
θρομβοι αἱματος καταβαινοντες επι την γην.]
clots of blood falling down to the ground.]
45 Και αναστας απο της προσευχης, ελθων προς
And having stood up from the prayer. coming to
τους μαθητας, εὑρεν αυτους κοιμωμενους απο
the disciples, he found them sleeping from
της λυπης· και ειπεν αυτοις· 46 Τι καθευδετε;
the grief: and he said to them: Why sleep you?
αναστατες προσευχεσθε, ἱνα μη εισελθητε εις
having stood up pray you, that not you may enter into
πειρασμον.
temptation.
47 Ετι *[δε] αυτου λαλουντος, ιδου οχλος,
While [and] of him speaking, lo a crowd,
και ὁ λεγομενος Ιουδας, εἱς των δωδεκα, προηρ-
and he being called Judas, one of the twelve, went
χετο αυτους, και ηγγισε τῳ Ιησου φιλησαι
before them, and drew near to the Jesus to kiss
αυτον. 48 Ὁ δε Ιησους ειπεν αυτῳ· Ιουδα,
him. The but Jesus said to him; Judas,
φιληματι τον υἱον του ανθρωπου παραδιδως;
with a kiss the son of the man betrayest thou?
49 Ιδοντες δε οἱ περι αυτον το εσομενον, ειπον
Seeing and those about him the was going to be, said
*[αυτῳ·] Κυριε, ει παταξομεν εν μαχαιρᾳ;
to him;] O lord, if shall we strike with a sword?

39 ‡And going out, he went according to his custom to the MOUNT of OLIVES; and his DISCIPLES also followed him.

40 And having arrived at the PLACE, he said to them, "Pray that you may not enter into Trial."

41 And he retired from them about a stone's throw, and kneeling down, he prayed, saying,

42 "Father, if thou art willing, take away *This Cup from me; yet not my WILL, but THINE be done."

43 †[And there appeared to him an Angel from Heaven, strengthening him.

44 And being in Agony, he prayed very earnestly; and his SWEAT was like Clots of Blood falling down to the GROUND.]

45 And rising from PRAYER, and coming to the DISCIPLES, he found them sleeping from GRIEF,

46 and said to them, "Why do you sleep? Arise, and pray that you may not enter into Trial."

47 And while he was yet speaking, ‡behold a Crowd, and HE who was CALLED Judas, one of the TWELVE, preceded them, and drew near to JESUS to kiss him.

48 But *Jesus said to him, "Judas, dost thou betray the SON of MAN with a Kiss?"

49 And THOSE about him perceiving WHAT was about TRANSPIRING, said, "Master, shall we strike with the Sword?"

* VATICAN MANUSCRIPT.—42. This Cup. 43, 44.—*omit.* 47. And—*omit.* 48. Jesus. 49. to him—*omit.*

† 43. There is no mention of this circumstance in any of the other Evangelists: and it is worthy of remark, that among many of the ancients, the authenticity of these two verses, the 43rd and 44th, has been doubted, and in consequence, they are omitted in several MSS., and in some Versions and Fathers. The Codex Alexandrinus, and the Codex Vaticanus, the two oldest MSS. in the world, omit both verses; in some very ancient MSS. they stand with an asterisk before them, as a mark of dubiousness; and they are both wanting in the Coptic fragments published by Dr. Ford. They are however extant in such a vast number of MSS., Versions and Fathers, as to leave no doubt with most critics, of their authenticity.—*Clarke.* Griesbach notes them as wanting in some authorities, but thinks that they ought not to be omitted.

‡ 39. Matt. xxvi. 36; Mark xiv. 32; John xviii. 1. ‡ 47. Matt. xxvi. 47; Matt. xiv 43; John xviii. 3.

50 Και επαταξεν εἱς τις εξ αυτων τον δουλον του
And struck one a certain of them the slave of the
αρχιερεως, και αφειλεν αυτου το ους το δεξιον.
high-priest, and cut off of him the ear the right.
51 Αποκριθεις δε ὁ Ιησους ειπεν· Εατε ἑως
Answering and the Jesus said; Let you be till
τουτου. Και ἁψαμενος του ωτιου αυτου, ιασατο
this. And touching the ear of him, he healed
αυτον. 52 Ειπε δε ὁ Ιησους προς τους παραγενο-
him. Said and the Jesus to those having
μενους επ' αυτον αρχιερεις, και στρατηγους του
come on him high-priests, and officers of the
ἱερου, και πρεσβυτερους· Ὡς επι ληστην εξελη-
temple, and elders; As on a robber you have
λυθατε μετα μαχαιρων και ξυλων· 53 καθ' ἡμεραν
come out with swords and clubs; every day
οντος μου μεθ' ὑμων εν τῳ ἱερῳ, ουκ εξετεινατε
being of me with you in the temple, not you did stretch out
τας χειρας επ' εμε· αλλ' αὑτη ὑμων εστιν ἡ
the hands on me; but this of you it is the
ὡρα, και ἡ εξουσια του σκοτους.
hour, and the authority of the darkness.
54 Συλλαβοντες δε αυτον ηγαγον, και εισηγα-
Having seized and him they led, and brought
γον αυτον εις τον οικον του αρχιερεως. Ὁ δε
him into the house of the high-priest. The but
Πετρος ηκολουθει μακροθεν. 55 Ἁψαντων δε
Peter followed at a distance. Having kindled and
πυρ εν μεσῳ της αυλης, και συγκαθισαντων
a fire in midst of the court, and having sat down
αυτων, εκαθητο ὁ Πετρος εν μεσῳ αυτων.
of them, sat the Peter in midst of them.
56 Ιδουσα δε αυτον παιδισκη τις καθημενον προς
Seeing and him a maid-servant certain sitting by
το φως, και ατενισασα αυτῳ, ειπε· Και οὑτος
the light, and looking steadily to him, she said: Also this
συν αυτῳ ην. 57 Ὁ δε ηρνησατο *[αυτον,]
with him was. He but denied [him,]
λεγων· Γυναι, ουκ οιδα αυτον. 58 Και μετα
saying; O woman, not I know him. And after
βραχυ ἑτερος ιδων αυτον, εφη· Και συ εξ
a little another seeing him, said; Also thou of
αυτων ει. Ὁ δε Πετρος ειπεν· Ανθρωπε, ουκ
them art. The but Peter said: O man, not
ειμι. 59 Και διαστασης ὡσει ὡρας μιας, αλλος
I am. And having intervened about hour one, another
τις διισχυριζετο, λεγων· Επ' αληθειας και
person confidently affirmed, saying: In truth also
οὑτος μετ' αυτου ην· και γαρ Γαλιλαιος εστιν.
this with him was: also for a Galilean he is.
60 Ειπε δε ὁ Πετρος· Ανθρωπε, ουκ οιδα ὁ λε-
Said but the Peter: O man, not I know what thou
γεις. Και παραχρημα, ετι λαλουντος αυτου,
sayest. And immediately, while speaking of him,

50 And ‡ one of them struck the SERVANT of the HIGH-PRIEST, and cut off His RIGHT EAR.
51 But *Jesus answering said, "Let this suffice." And he touched *his EAR, and healed him.
52 ‡ Then JESUS said to the HIGH-PRIESTS, and Officers of the TEMPLE, and Elders, who were COMING against him, "As in pursuit of a Robber, have you come with Swords and Clubs to take me?
53 When I was with you every day in the TEMPLE, you did not stretch out your HANDS against me; ‡ but this is Your HOUR, and the POWER of DARKNESS."
54 Then having seized him, they led him away, and brought him to the HOUSE of the HIGH-PRIEST. ‡ But PETER followed at a distance.
55 ‡ And they having kindled a Fire in the Midst of the COURT, sat down together, and PETER sat down among them.
56 And a certain Maid-servant seeing him sitting by the LIGHT, and looking steadily at him, she said, "This man also was with him."
57 But HE denied, saying, "Woman, I do not know him."
58 ‡ And after a little, another saw him and said, "Thou also art one of them." And PETER said, "Man, I am not."
59 And about an HOUR having intervened, another confidently affirmed, saying, "In Truth this man was also with him; for he is also a Galilean."
60 And PETER said, "Man, I know not what thou sayest." And immediately, while he was

* VATICAN MANUSCRIPT.—51. Jesus. 51. the EAR. 57. him—omit.

‡ 50. Matt. xxvi. 51; Mark xiv. 47; John xviii. 10. ‡ 52. Matt. xxvi. 55; Mark xiv 48. ‡ 53. John xii. 27. ‡ 54. Matt. xxvi. 58; John xviii. 15. ‡ 55. Matt xxvi. 69; Mark xiv. 66; John xviii. 17, 18. ‡ 58. Matt. xxvi. 71; Mark xiv. 69; John xviii. 25.

εφωνησεν αλεκτωρ. 61 Και στραφεις ὁ κυριος
crew a cock. And having turned the Lord
ενεβλεψε τῳ Πετρῳ· και ὑπεμνησθη ὁ Πετρος
looked to the Peter; and was reminded the Peter
του λογου του κυριου, ὡς ειπεν αυτῳ· Ὁτι πριν
of the word of the Lord, as he said to him; That before
αλεκτορα φωνησαι, απαρνησῃ με τρις. 62 Και
a cock to crow, thou mayest deny me thrice. And
εξελθων εξω, εκλαυσε πικρως. 63 Και οἱ ανδρες
going out, he wept bitterly. And the men
οἱ συνεχοντες τον Ιησουν, ενεπαιζον αυτῳ,
those having in custody the Jesus, mocked him,
δεροντες· 64 και περικαλυψαντες αυτον, *[ετυπ-
scourging; And having blindfolded him, [they
τον αυτου το προσωπον,] και επηρωτων αυτον,
struck of him the face,] and they asked him,
λεγοντες· Προφητευσον, τις εστιν ὁ παισας
saying; Prophesy, who is he striking
σε; 65 Και ἑτερα πολλα βλασφημουντες ελεγον
thee? And other many blaspheming they spoke
εις αυτον.
against him.

66 Και ὡς εγενετο ἡμερα, συνηχθη το πρεσ-
And as it became day, were assembled the elder-
βυτεριον του λαου, αρχιερεις τε και γραμ-
ship of the people, high-priests and and scribes,
ματεις, και ανηγαγον αυτον εις το συνεδριον
and brought him into the sanhedrim
ἑαυτων, 67 λεγοντες· Ει συ ει ὁ Χριστος, ειπε
of themselves, saying; If thou art the Anointed, tell
ἡμιν. Ειπε δε αυτοις· Εαν ὑμιν ειπω, ου μη
us. He said and to them; If to you I tell, not not
πιστευσητε· 68 εαν δε *[και] ερωτησω, ου μη
you will believe; if but [also] I ask, not not
αποκριθητε *[μοι, η απολυσητε.] 69 Απο του
you would answer [me, or would loose.] From of the
νυν εσται ὁ υἱος του ανθρωπου καθημενος εκ
now shall be the son of the man sitting at
δεξιων της δυναμεως του θεου. 70 Ειπον δε
right hand of the power of the God. Said and
παντες· Συ ουν ει ὁ υἱος του θεου; Ὁ δε προς
all; Thou then art the son of the God? He and to
αυτους εφη· Ὑμεις λεγετε· ὁτι εγω ειμι.
them said: You say; that I am.
71 Οἱ δε ειπον· Τι ετι χρειαν εχομεν μαρτυριας;
They and said: What further need have we of testimony?
Αυτοι γαρ ηκουσαμεν απο του στοματος
Ourselves for we have heard from the mouth
αυτου. ΚΕΦ. κγ'. 23. 1 Και ανασταν ἁπαν
of him. And having stood up whole
το πληθος αυτων, ηγαγον αυτον επι τον Πι-
the multitude of them, they led him to the Pi-
λατον.
late.

2 Ηρξαντο δε κατηγορειν αυτου, λεγοντες·
They began and to accuse him, saying:

yet speaking, the cock crew.

61 ‡And the LORD, turning, looked on PETER; and PETER was reminded of the DECLARATION of the LORD, how he said to him, "Before a Cock *crows To-day, thou shalt deny me thrice."

62 And going out, he wept bitterly.

63 And THOSE MEN who had *him in CUSTODY, derided and beat him;

64 and having blindfolded him, they asked him, saying, "Divine who is HE that STRUCK thee?"

65 And many other things they blasphemously spoke against him.

66 ‡And when it was Day, the ELDERSHIP of the PEOPLE, both High-priests and Scribes, were assembled, and they led him into their SANHEDRIM, saying,

67 "If thou art the MESSIAH, tell us." And he said to them, "If I inform you, you will not believe;

68 and if I interrogate, you will not answer.

69 *But from this TIME the ‡SON of MAN will sit on the Right hand of the POWER of GOD."

70 And they all said, "Thou art, then, the SON of GOD?" And HE said to them, "You say; I am."

71 And they said, "What further need have we of Testimony? since we ourselves have heard this from his own MOUTH."

CHAPTER XXIII.

1 And ‡the Whole MULTITUDE of them rising up, led him to PILATE.

2 And they began to accuse him, saying, "We

* VATICAN MANUSCRIPT.—61. crows To-day, thou shalt. 63. him. 64. struck him on the FACE and—*omit.* 68. also—*omit.* 68. me, or would loose—*omit.* 69. But from this TIME.

‡ 61. Matt. xxvi. 75; Mark xiv. 72. ‡ 66. Matt. xxvii. 1. ‡ 69. Matt. xxvi; Mark xiv. 62; Heb. i. 3; viii. 1. ‡ 1. Matt. xxvii. 2; Mark xv. 1; John xviii. 28.

Τουτον εὑρομεν διαστρεφοντα το εθνος, και
This we found misleading the nation, and
κωλυοντα Καισαρι φορυς διδοναι, λεγοντα ἑαυ-
forbidding to Cesar tax to give, saying him-
τον Χριστον βασιλεα ειναι. 3 Ὁ δε Πιλατος
self an anointed king to be. The and Pilate
επηρωτησεν αυτον, λεγων· Συ ει ὁ βασιλευς
asked him, saying: Thou art the king
των Ιουδαιων; Ὁ δε αποκριθεις αυτῳ εφη· Συ
of the Jews? He and answering to him said: Thou
λεγεις. 4 Ὁ δε Πιλατος ειπε προς τους αρχιε-
sayest. The and Pilate said to the high-
ρεις και τους οχλους· Ουδεν εὑρισκω αιτιον εν
priests and the crowds: Nothing I find criminal in
τῳ ανθρωπῳ τουτῳ. 5 Οἱ δε επισχυον, λεγον-
the man this. They but were urgent, saying:
τες· Ὁτι ανασειει τον λαον, διδασκων καθ'
That he stirs up the people, teaching in
ὁλης της Ιουδαιας, αρξαμενος απο της Γαλιλαιας
whole of the Judea, having begun from the Galilee
ἑως ὡδε. 6 Πιλατος δε ακουσας *[Γαλιλαιαν,]
to here. Pilate and having heard [of Galilee,]
επηρωτησεν, ει ὁ ανθρωπος Γαλιλαιος εστι.
he asked, if the man a Galilean is.
7 Και επιγνους, ὁτι εκ της εξουσιας Ἡρωδου
And having learned, that of the authority of Herod
εστιν, ανεπεμψεν αυτον προς Ἡρωδην, οντα
he is, he sent him to Herod, being
και αυτον εν Ἱεροσολυμοις εν ταυταις ταις
also him in Jerusalem in those the
ἡμεραις.
days.

8 Ὁ δε Ἡρωδης ιδων τον Ιησουν, εχαρη λιαν·
The and Herod seeing the Jesus, rejoiced greatly;
ην γαρ θελων εξ ἱκανου ιδειν αυτον, δια το
he was for wishing of a long time to see him, because the
ακουειν *[πολλα] περι αυτου· και ηλπιζε τι
to hear [many things] about him; and hoped some
σημειον ιδειν ὑπ' αυτου γινομενον. 9 Επηρωτα
sign to see by him being done. He asked
δε αυτον εν λογοις ἱκανοις· αυτος δε ουδεν
and him in words many; he and nothing
απεκρινατο αυτῳ. 10 Ειστηκεισαν δε οἱ αρχιε-
answered him. Stood up and the high-
ρεις και οἱ γραμματεις, ευτονως κατηγορουντες
priests and the scribes, vehemently accusing
αυτου. 11 Εξουθενησας δε αυτον ὁ Ἡρωδης συν
him. Having despised and him the Herod with
τοις στρατευμασιν αὑτου, και εμπαιξας, περι-
the soldiers of himself, and having mocked, casting
βαλων αυτον εσθητα λαμπραν, ανεπεμψεν αυτον
around him a robe splendid, sent again him
τῳ Πιλατῳ. 12 Εγενοντο δε φιλοι ὁ, τε Πι-
to the Pilate. Became and friends the, both Pi-
λατος και ὁ Ηρωδης εν αυτῃ τῃ ἡμερᾳ μετ'
late and the Herod in this the day with

found this man misleading * our NATION, and forbidding to pay Tax to Cesar, * and saying, ‡ that he himself is an anointed King.

3 ‡ And PILATE asked him, saying, "Art thou the KING of the JEWS?" And HE answering him, said, "Thou sayest."

4 Then PILATE said to the HIGH-PRIESTS and the CROWDS, ‡ "I find Nothing Criminal in this MAN."

5 But THEY were urgent, saying, "He stirreth up the PEOPLE, teaching in All JUDEA, beginning from GALILEE even to this place."

6 Now Pilate hearing of Galilee, asked if the MAN was a Galilean.

7 And ascertaining That he was of the ‡ PROVINCE of Herod, he sent him to * HEROD, who was also in Jerusalem in Those DAYS.

8 And HEROD ‡ seeing JESUS, was very glad; for he had wished for a long time to see him, because he had HEARD about him; and he hoped to see Some Sign done by him.

9 And he questioned him in many Words; but he answered him nothing.

10 And the HIGH-PRIESTS and the SCRIBES stood up, and vehemently accused him.

11 And HEROD, with his SOLDIERS, treated him with contempt; and having, in derision, arrayed him in a splendid Robe, sent him back to PILATE.

12 And * HEROD and PILATE became Friends to each other on That DAY;

* VATICAN MANUSCRIPT.—2. our NATION. 2. and saying. 6. of Galilee—omit. 7. HEROD. 8. many things—omit. 12. HEROD and PILATE.

‡ 2. John xix. 12. ‡ 3. Matt. xxvii. 11; 1 Tim. vi. 13. ‡ 4. 1 Pet. ii. 22. ‡ 7. Luke iii. 1. ‡ 8. Matt. xiv. 1; Mark vi. 14; Luke ix. 9.

αλληλων· προυπηρχον γαρ εν εχθρα οντες προς
each other; formerly for in hatred being with
ἑαυτους.
themselves.
13 Πιλατος δε συγκαλεσαμενος τους αρχιερεις
Pilate and having summoned the high-priests
και τους αρχοντας και τον λαον, 14 ειπε προς
and the chiefs and the people, said to
αυτους· Προσηνεγκατε μοι τον ανθρωπον του-
them; You have brought to me the man this,
τον, ὡς αποστρεφοντα τον λαον· και ιδου, εγω
as misleading the people; and lo, I
ενωπιον ὑμων ανακρινας, ουδεν εὑρον εν τῳ
in presence of you having examined, nothing I found in the
ανθρωπῳ τουτῳ αιτιον, ὡν κατηγορειτε κατ'
man this a fault, of which you accuse against
αυτου. 15 Αλλ' ουδε Ἡρωδης· ανεπεμψα γαρ
him. But not even Herod; I sent for
ὑμας προς αυτον, και ιδου, ουδεν αξιον θανατου
you to him, and lo, nothing worthy of death
εστι πεπραγμενον αυτῳ. 16 Παιδευσας ουν
is having been done to him. Having scourged therefore
αυτον απολυσω. 17 *[Αναγκην δε ειχεν απο-
him I will release. [Necessary now it was to
λυειν αυτοις κατα ἑορτην ἑνα.] 18 Ανεκραξαν
release to them at a feast one.] Cried out
δε παμπληθει, λεγοντες· Αιρε τουτον, απολυ-
and all together, saying: Take away this, release
σον δε ἡμιν τον Βαραββαν· 19 Ὁστις ην δια
and to us the Barabbas; Who was through
στασιν τινα γενομενην εν τῃ πολει, και φονον,
a sedition certain having occurred in the city, and a murder,
βεβλημενος εις φυλακην.
having been cast into prison.
20 Παλιν ουν ὁ Πιλατος προσεφωνησε, θελων
Again therefore the Pilate spoke to, wishing
απολυσαι τον Ιησουν. 21 Οἱ δε επεφωνουν,
to release the Jesus. They but cried,
λεγοντες· Σταυρωσον, σταυρωσον αυτον. 22 Ὁ
saying; Crucify, crucify him. He
δε τριτον ειπε προς αυτους· Τι γαρ κακον
and third said to them: What for evil
εποιησεν οὑτος; ουδεν αιτιον θανατου εὑρον εν
has done this? nothing a cause of death I found in
αυτῳ· παιδευσας ουν αυτον απολυσω. 23 Οἱ δε
him; having scourged therefore him I will release. They but
επεκειντο φωναις μεγαλαις, αιτουμενοι αυτον
pressed with voices loud, demanding him
σταυρωθηναι· και κατισχυον αἱ φωναι αυτων
to be crucified; and prevailed the voices of them
*[και των αρχιερεων.] 24 Ὁ δε Πιλατος επε-
[and of the high-priests.] The and Pilate de-
κρινε γενεσθαι το αιτημα αυτων. 25 Απελυσε
cided to satisfy the request of them. He released
δε τον δια στασιν και φονον βεβλημενον εις
and the through sedition and murder having been cast into

for before they had been at Enmity with each other.

13 ‡ And Pilate, having called the HIGH-PRIESTS and the RULERS, and the PEOPLE,

14 said to them, "You have brought this MAN to me, as one who misleads the PEOPLE; and behold, having examined him in your presence, I have not found this MAN guilty of the Crimes you bring against him.

15 Nor, indeed, has Herod; for * he sent him back again to you; and behold, nothing worthy of Death has been done by him;

16 having chastised him, therefore, I will release him."

17 ‡* [For it was Necessary to release one to them at the Feast.]

18 Then they all exclaimed with one accord, saying, "Take away this man, and release to us BARABBAS;"

19 (who had been cast into * PRISON for a certain Insurrection made in the CITY, and a Murder.)

20 PILATE, therefore, again addressed them, wishing to release JESUS.

21 But THEY cried, saying, "Crucify, crucify him."

22 And HE said to them, a Third time, "For what? Has this man done Evil? I have found No Cause of Death in him; having chastised him, therefore, I will release him."

23 And THEY were urgent with loud Voices, demanding him to be crucified, and their CRIES prevailed;

24 and * Pilate decided to satisfy their REQUEST.

25 And he released HIM who had been CAST into * Prison for Insurrection

* VATICAN MANUSCRIPT.—15. he sent him back again to you; and, behold, nothing worthy of Death has been done by him. 17.—omit. 19. PRISON. 23. and of the HIGH-PRIESTS—omit. 24. Pilate. 25. Prison.

‡ 13. Matt. xxvii. 23; Mark xv. 14; John xviii. 38; xix. 4. ‡ 17. Matt. xxvii. Mark xv. 6; John xviii. 39.

την φυλακην, ὁν ητουντο· τον δε Ιησουν παρε-
the prison, whom they asked; the but Jesus he de-
δωκε τῳ θεληματι αυτων.
livered to the will of them.
26 Και ὡς απηγαγον αυτον, επιλαβομενοι Σι-
And as they led him, having laid hold of Si-
μωνος τινος Κυρηναιου ερχομενου απ' αγρου,
mon a certain Cyrenian coming from country,
επεθηκαν αυτῳ τον σταυρον, φερειν οπισθεν
they placed to him the cross, to carry after
του Ιησου. 27 Ηκολουθει δε αυτῳ πολυ πληθος
the Jesus. Followed and him a great multitude
του λαου, και γυναικων· αἱ *[και] εκοπτοντο
of the people, and of women: who [also] lamented
και εθρηνουν αυτον. 28 Στραφεις δε προς αυτας
and bewailed him. Turning but to them
ὁ Ιησους, ειπε· Θυγατερες Ἱερουσαλημ, μη
the Jesus, said: Daughters of Jerusalem, not
κλαιετε επ' εμε, πλην εφ' ἑαυτας κλαιετε, και
weep you for me, but for yourselves weep you, and
επι τα τεκνα ὑμων. 29 Ὁτι ιδου, ερχονται ἡμε-
for the children of you. For lo, come days,
ραι, εν αἱς ερουσι· Μακαριαι αἱ στειραι, και
in which they will say; Blessed the barren ones, and
κοιλιαι αἱ ουκ εγεννησαν, και μαστοι οἱ ουκ
wombs which not bore, and breasts which not
εθηλασαν. 30 Τοτε αρξονται λεγειν τοις ορεσι·
suckled. Then they will begin to say to the mountains;
Πεσετε εφ' ἡμας· και τοις βουνοις· Καλυψατε
Fall you on us; and to the hills; Cover you
ἡμας. 31 Ὁτι ει εν τῳ ὑγρῳ ξυλῳ ταυτα ποιου-
us. For if in the green tree these they
σιν, εν τῳ ξηρῳ τι γενηται;
do, in the dry what will be done?
32 Ηγοντο δε και ἑτεροι δυο κακουργοι συν
Were led and also others two malefactors with
αυτῳ αναιρεθηναι. 33 Και ὁτε απηλθον επι τον
him to be put to death. And when they came to the
τοπον, τον καλουμενον Κρανιον εκει εσταυρω-
place, that being called a skull, there they cruci-
σαν αυτον, και τους κακουργους· ὁν μεν εκ
fied him, and the malefactors; one indeed at
δεξιων, ὁν δε εξ αριστερων. 34 *[Ὁ δε Ιησους
right, one and at left. [The and Jesus
ελεγε· Πατερ, αφες αυτοις· ου γαρ οιδασι τι
said; O father, forgive them; not for they know what
ποιουσι.] Διαμεριζομεναι δε τα ἱματια αυτου,
they do.] Having divided and the garments of him,
εβαλον κληρον. 35 Και εἱστηκει ὁ λαος θεωρων·
they cast a lot. And stood the people gazing:
εξεμυκτηριζον δε και οἱ αρχοντες *[συν αυτοις,]
scoffed at and also the rulers [with them,]
λεγοντες· Αλλους εσωσε, σωσατω ἑαυτον, ει
saying: Others he saved, let him save himself, if

and Murder, whom they desired; and delivered up JESUS to their WILL.

26 And as they led him away, having laid hold of Simon, a certain Cyrenian, coming from the Country, they laid the CROSS on him, that he might carry it after JESUS.

27 And there followed him a Great Multitude of the PEOPLE, and of Women who lamented and bewailed him.

28 But * Jesus, turning to them, said, "Daughters of Jerusalem, weep not for me, but weep for yourselves, and for your CHILDREN.

29 For behold, ‡ Days are approaching, in which they will say, 'Happy the BARREN! even the Wombs which never bore, and the Breasts which never suckled.'

30 Then they will begin to say to the MOUNTAINS, 'Fall on us;' and to the HILLS, 'Cover us.'

31 For if these things are done while the Tree is * Green, what will be done when it is DRY."

32 ‡ Now two others, who were Criminals, were also led with him to be put to death.

33 And ‡ when they came to THAT PLACE which is CALLED Skull, they there nailed him to the cross, and the CRIMINALS; one at his Right hand, and the other at his Left.

34 * [Then JESUS said, "Father, forgive them, for they know not what they do."] And having divided his GARMENTS, they cast Lots.

35 And the PEOPLE stood gazing. And the RULERS also scoffed, saying, "He saved others; let him save himself, * if he is the Son,

---

* VATICAN MANUSCRIPT.—27. also—*omit.* 28. Jesus. 31. Green. 34 Then Jesus said, "Father, forgive them, for they know not what they do."—*omit.* 35. with them—*omit.* 35. if he is the Son, the MESSIAH, the CHOSEN of GOD.

‡ 29. Matt. xxvi. 19; Luke xxi. 23. ‡ 32 Isa. liii. 12; Matt. xxvii. 38. ‡ 33. Matt. xxvii. 33; Mark xv. 22; John xix. 17, 18.

οὗτος εστιν ὁ Χριστος, ὁ του θεου εκλεκτος.
this is the Anointed, the of the God chosen.
36 Ενεπαιζον δε αυτῳ και οἱ στρατιωται, προσ-
Mocked and him also the soldiers, com-
ερχομενοι *[και] οξος προσφεροντες αυτῳ,
ing near [and] vinegar offering to him,
37 και λεγοντες· Ει συ ει ὁ βασιλευς των Ιου-
and saying. If thou art the king of the Jews,
δαιων, σωσον σεαυτον. 38 Ην δε και επιγραφη
save thyself. Was and also an inscription
*[γεγραμμενη] επ' αυτῳ *[γραμμασιν Ἑλλη-
[having been written] over him [letters In
νικοις, και Ῥωμαικοις, και Ἑβραικοις·] "Οὗτος
Greek, and Latin, and Hebrew.] This
ἐστιν ὁ βασιλευς των Ιουδαιων."
is the king of the Jews."

39 Εἱς δε των κρεμασθεντων κακουργων εβλασ-
One and of those having been hanged malefactors spoke
φημει αυτον, *[λεγων·] Ει συ ει ὁ Χριστος,
against him, [saying.] If thou art the Christ,
σωσον σεαυτον και ἡμας. 40 Αποκριθεις δε ὁ
save thyself and us. Answering but the
ἑτερος επιτιμα αυτῳ λεγων· Ουδε φοβῃ συ τον
other rebuked him saying; Not even fearest thou the
θεον, ὁτι εν τῳ αυτῳ κριματι ει; 41 Και ἡμεις
God, since in the same condemnation thou art? And we
μεν δικαιως· αξια γαρ ὡν επραξαμεν απολαμβα-
indeed justly; due for which has been done we receive:
νομεν· οὗτος δε ουδεν ατοπον επραξε. 42 Και
this but nothing amiss has done. And
ελεγε τῳ Ιησου· Μνησθητι μου, *[κυριε,]
he said to the Jesus; Do thou remember me, [O lord,]
ὁταν ελθῃς εν τῃ βασιλειᾳ σου. 43 Και ειπεν
when thou mayest come in the kingdom of thee. And said
αυτῳ ὁ Ιησους· Αμην λεγω σοι, σημερον μετ'
to him the Jesus; Indeed I say to thee, to-day with
εμου εσῃ εν τῳ παραδεισῳ.
me thou shalt be in the paradise.

44 Ην δε ὡσει ὡρα ἑκτη, και σκοτος εγενετο
It was and about hour sixth, and darkness came
εφ' ὁλην την γην, ἑως ὡρας εννατης. 45 Και
over whole the land, till hour ninth. And
εσκοτισθη ὁ ἡλιος· και εσχισθη το καταπε-
was darkened the sun; and was rent the veil
τασμα του ναου μεσον. 46 Και φωνησας φωνῃ
of the temple midst. And crying with a voice

the MESSIAH, the CHOSEN of GOD."

36 And the SOLDIERS also derided him, coming near and offering him Vinegar,

37 and saying, "If thou art the KING of the JEWS, save thyself."

38 ‡ And there was also an Inscription over him;—"This is the KING of the JEWS."

39 ‡ And one of the CRIMINALS who were † SUSPENDED, reviled him, saying, * "Art not thou the MESSIAH? save thyself and us."

40 But the OTHER answering rebuked him, saying, "Dost thou not even fear GOD, since thou art under the SAME Sentence?

41 And we, indeed, justly; for we receive what is due for the deeds we have done; but this man has done nothing amiss."

42 And he said to * Jesus, "Remember me when thou comest * in thy KINGDOM."

43 † And * he said to him, "Indeed I say to thee, This day thou shalt be with me in † PARADISE."

44 ‡ * And it was now about the sixth Hour, and there was Darkness over the Whole LAND till the ninth * Hour;

45 the SUN failing, * and ‡ the VEIL of the TEMPLE was rent in the Midst.

46 And JESUS exclaim-

* VATICAN MANUSCRIPT.—36. and—*omit.* 38. written—*omit.* 38. in Letters of Greek, and Latin, and Hebrew—*omit.* 39. saying—*omit.* 39. Art not thou the MESSIAH? save. 42. Jesus. 42. Lord—*omit.* 42. to. 43. he said. 44. It was now about. 44. Hour; the SUN failing, 45. and the VEIL.

† 39. It is likely that the two robbers were not *nailed* to their crosses, but only *tied* to them by cords, and thus they are represented in ancient paintings.—*A. Clarke.* † 43. This verse was wanting in the copies of Marcion and other reputed heretics; and in some of the older copies in the time of Origen; nor is it cited by Justin, Irenæus, or Tertullian; though the two former have quoted almost every text in Luke which relates to the crucifixion; and Tertullian wrote concerning the intermediate state. See Evanson's Diss. p. 28. Im. Ver note. † 43. The word *paradise* is not Greek, but is of Asiatic origin. In Arabic and Persian it signifies a *garden*, a *vineyard*. The Septuagint renders Gen. ii. 8, thus; "God planted a *paradise* in Eden." The word only occurs in two other places in the New Testament—2 Cor. xii. 4; and Rev. ii. 7.

‡ 38. Matt. xxvii. 37; Mark xv. 26; John xix. 19. ‡ 39. Matt. xxvii. 44; Mark xv 32. ‡ 44. Matt. xxvii. 45; Mark xv. 33. ‡ 45. Matt. xxvii. 51; Mark xv. 38.

μεγαλῃ ὁ Ιησους, ειπε· Πατερ, εις χειρας σου
out the Jesus, said; O father, into hands of thee
παραθησομαι το πνευμα μου. Και ταυτα ειπων,
I commit the breath of me. And these having said,
εξεπνευσεν. [47] Ιδων δε ὁ ἑκατονταρχος το γε-
he breathed out. Seeing and the centurion that hav-
νομενον, εδοξασε τον θεον, λεγων· Οντως ὁ
ing occurred, glorified the God, saying; Truly the
ανθρωπος οὗτος δικαιος ην. [48] Και παντες οἱ
man this just was. And all the
συμπαραγενομενοι οχλοι επι την θεωριαν ταυ-
having come together crowds to the sight this,
την, θεωρουντες τα γενομενα, τυπτοντες
beholding the things having occurred, striking
*[ἑαυτων] τα στηθη ὑπεστρεφον. [49] Εἱστη-
[of themselves] the breasts returned. Stood
κεισαν δε παντες οἱ γνωστοι αυτου μακροθεν,
but all the acquaintances of him at a distance,
και γυναικες αἱ συνακολουθησασαι αυτῳ απο
and women those having followed him from
της Γαλιλαιας, ὁρωσαι ταυτα.
the Galilee, beholding these things.
[50] Και ιδου, ανηρ ονοματι Ιωσηφ, βουλευτης
And lo, a man with a name Joseph, a senator
ὑπαρχων, ανηρ αγαθος και δικαιος, [51] (οὗτος
being, a man good and just, (this
ουκ ην συγκατατεθειμενος τῃ βουλῃ και τῃ
not was having assented to the will and the
πραξει αυτων,) απο Αριμαθαιας πολεως των
act of them,) from Arimathea a city of the
Ιουδαιων, ὁς και προσεδεχετο *[και αυτος] την
Jews, who and was looking for [also himself] the
βασιλειαν του θεου· [52] οὗτος προσελθων τῳ
kingdom of the God; this having gone to the
Πιλατῳ, ῃτησατο το σωμα του Ιησου. [53] Και
Pilate, asked the body of the Jesus. And
καθελων αυτο, ενετυλιξεν αυτο σινδονι, και
having taken down it, he wrapped it in linen, and
εθηκεν αυτο, εν μνηματι λαξευτῳ, οὗ ουκ ην
laid it in a tomb hewn in a rock, where not was
ουδεπω ουδεις κειμενος. [54] Και ἡμερα ην παρα-
ever yet no one being laid. And day was prepa-
σκευη, και σαββατον επεφωσκε. [55] Κατακο-
ration, and sabbath approached. Having fol-
λουθησασαι δε *[και] γυναικες, αἱτινες ησαν
lowed after and [also] women, who were
συνεληλυθυιαι αυτῳ εκ της Γαλιλαιας, εθεα-
having been with him out of the Galilee, be-
σαντο το μνημειον, και ὡς ετεθη το σωμα αυτου.
held the tomb, and how they laid the body of him.
[56] Ὑποστρεψασαι δε ἡτοιμασαν αρωματα και
Having returned and they prepared aromatics and
μυρα· και το μεν σαββατον ἡσυχασαν κατα
ointments; and the indeed sabbath they rested according to
την εντολην.
the commandment.

ing with a loud Voice, said, "Father, into thy Hands I commit my † SPIRIT;" and having said this, ‡ he expired.

47 ‡ And the CENTURION seeing WHAT had OCCURRED, he glorified GOD, saying, "Truly This MAN was righteous."

48 And All the CROWDS who had COME TOGETHER to this SPECTACLE, having beheld the THINGS which OCCURRED, returned, beating their BREASTS.

49 And All his ACQUAINTANCE, * and THOSE WOMEN who had FOLLOWED him from GALILEE, stood at a distance, beholding these things.

50 ‡ And behold, a Man named Joseph, a Senator, a good and righteous Man,

51 (he had not consented to their DESIGNS and DEEDS,) from Arimathea, a City of the Jews; and who was waiting for the KINGDOM of GOD.

52 This man coming to PILATE, asked for the BODY of JESUS.

53 And having taken it down, he wrapped it in Linen, and laid it in a Tomb cut out of a rock, in which no one had ever yet been laid.

54 And it was the Day of ‡ Preparation, and the Sabbath approached.

55 And the WOMEN following after, who had accompanied him from GALILEE, saw the TOMB, and how his BODY was laid.

56 And returning, they ‡ prepared Aromatics and Ointments; and rested on the SABBATH, according to the COMMANDMENT.

* VATICAN MANUSCRIPT.—48. of themselves—omit. 49. and THOSE WOMEN who 51. also himself—omit. 55 also—omit.

† 46. My breath or life. Luke viii. 55.

‡ 46. Matt. xxvii. 50; Mark xv. 37; John xix. 30. ‡ 47. Matt. xxvii. 54; Mark xv. 39 ‡ 50. Matt. xxvii. 57; Mark xv. 42; John xix. 38. ‡ 54. Matt. xxvii. 62. ‡ 56. Mark xvi. 1.

ΚΕΦ. κδ'. 24.

[1]Τῃ δε μιᾳ των σαββατων, ορθρου βαθεος,
In the and first of the weeks, of morning very early,
ηλθον επι το μνημα, φερουσαι ἁ ἡτοιμασαν
came to the tomb, bringing what they prepared
αρωματα· *[και τινες συν αυταις.] [2]Ευρον
aromatics: [and some with them.] They found
δε τον λιθον αποκεκυλισμενον απο του μνημειου.
and the stone having been rolled from the tomb.
[3]Και εισελθουσαι ουχ εὑρον το σωμα του κυριου
And having entered not they found the body of the Lord
Ιησου. [4]Και εγενετο εν τῳ διαπορεισθαι αυτας
Jesus. And it happened in the to be perplexed them
περι τουτου, και ιδου, ανδρες δυο επεστησαν
about this, and lo, men two stood
αυταις εν εσθησεσιν αστραπτουσαις. [5]Εμφο-
by them in clothing shining. Afraid
βων δε γενομενων αυτων, και κλινουσων το
and having become of them, and bowing the
προσωπον εις την γην, ειπον προς αυτας· Τι
face to the earth they said to them: Why
ζητειτε τον ζωντα μετα των νεκρων; [6]Ουκ
seek you the living among the dead ones? Not
εστιν ὡδε, αλλ' ηγερθη. Μνησθητε ὡς ελαλη-
he is here, but has been raised. Remember you how he spoke
σεν ὑμιν, ετι ὢν εν τῃ Γαλιλαιᾳ, [7]λεγων· Ὁτι
to you, while being in the Galilee, saying; That
δ.ι τον υἱον του ανθρωπου παραδοθηναι εις
it behoves the son of the man to be delivered into
χειρας ανθρωπων ἁμαρτωλων, και σταυρωθηναι,
hands of men of sinners, and to be crucified,
και τῃ τριτῃ ἡμερα αναστηναι. [8]Και εμνησ-
and the third day to stand up. And they re-
θησαν των ῥηματων αυτου· [9]και ὑποστρεψασαι
membered the words of him: and having returned
απο του μνημειου, απηγγειλαν ταυτα παντα
from the tomb, they related these all
τοις ἑνδεκα και πασι τοις λοιποις. [10]Ησαν δε
to the eleven and to all the others. Were and
η Μαγδαληνη Μαρια, και Ιωαννα, και Μαρια
the Magdalene Mary, and Joanna, and Mary
Ιακωβου και αἱ λοιπαι συν αυταις, αἱ ελεγον
of James, and the others with them, who spoke
προς τους αποστολους ταυτα. [11]Και εφανησαν
to the apostles these. And appeared
ενωπιον αυτων ὡσει ληρος τα ῥηματα αυτων,
in presence of them as an idle tale the words of them.
και ἠπιστουν αυταις. [12]Ὁ δε Πετρος αναστας
and they believed not them. The and Peter arising
εδραμεν επι το μνημειον, και παρακυψας βλεπει
ran to the tomb, and having stooped down he sees
τα οθονια *[κειμενα] μονα· και απηλθε προς
the linen bands [lying] alone: and he departed by
ἑαυτον, θαυμαζων το γεγονος.
himself, wondering that having occurred.

CHAPTER XXIV.

1 ‡ And on the FIRST day of the WEEK, very early in the Morning, they went to the TOMB, carrying the Aromatics which they had prepared.

2 And they found the STONE rolled away from the TOMB;

3 ‡ and having entered, they found not the BODY † of the LORD Jesus.

4 And it occurred, as they were in PERPLEXITY about this, ‡ behold two Men stood by them in shining Clothing.

5 And the women being afraid, and bowing their FACES to the EARTH, these said to them, "Why do you seek the LIVING one among the DEAD?

6 He is not here, but has been raised. ‡ Remember how he spoke to you, while he was yet in GALILEE;

7 saying, 'The SON of MAN must be delivered up into the Hands of Sinners, and be crucified, and the THIRD day rise again.'"

8 And they recollected his WORDS;

9 ‡ and returning from the TOMB, related all these things to the ELEVEN, and to All the REST.

10 Now they were the MAGDALA Mary, and Joanna, and *THAT Mary the mother of James, and the OTHERS with them, who told these things to the APOSTLES.

11 ‡ And * these WORDS appeared to them like idle talk; and they believed them not.

12 † But PETER arising ran to the TOMB, and stooping down he saw only the LINEN BANDS; and he went away by himself, wondering at WHAT had HAPPENED.

* VATICAN MANUSCRIPT.—1. and some with them—*omit.* 10. THAT Mary. 11. these WORDS. 12. lying—*omit.*

† 3. Tischendorf omits the words "of the Lord Jesus." † 12. Tischendorf omits this verse.

‡ 1. Matt. xxviii. 1; Mark xvi. 1; John xx. 2. ‡ 3. Mark xvi. 5. ‡ 4. John xx. 12. ‡ 6. Matt. xvi. 21; xvii. 23; Mark viii. 31; ix 31; Luke ix. 22. ‡ 9. Matt. xxviii. 8; Mark xvi. 10. ‡ 11. Mark xvi. 11.

13 Και ιδου, δυο εξ αυτων ησαν πορευομενοι εν
And lo, two of them were going in
αυτῃ τῃ ἡμερᾳ εις κωμην απεχουσαν σταδιους
this the day into a village being distant furlongs
εξηκοντα απο Ἱερουσαλημ, ᾗ ονομα Εμμαους.
sixty from Jerusalem, to which a name Emmaus.
14 Και αυτοι ὡμιλουν προς αλληλους περι παν-
And they were talking to each other about all
των των συμβεβηκοτων τουτων. 15 Και εγενετο
of the having happened of these. And it occurred
εν τῳ ὁμιλειν αυτους και συζητειν, και αυτος ὁ
in the to talk them and to reason, even he the
Ιησους εγγισας συνεπορευετο αυτοις. 16 Οἱ δε
Jesus having come near went with them. The but
οφθαλμοι αυτων εκρατουντο, του μη επιγνωναι
eyes of them were held, the not to know
αυτον. 17 Ειπε δε προς αυτους· Τινες οἱ λογοι
him. He said and to them; What the words
οὑτοι, οὑς αντιβαλλετε προς αλληλους περιπα-
these, which you throw to one another walk-
τουντες, και εστε σκυθρωποι; 18 Αποκριθεις δε
ing, and are sad? Answering and
ὁ εἱς, ᾡ ονομα Κλεοπας, ειπε προς αυτον·
the one, to whom a name Cleopas, said to him:
Συ μονος παροικεις Ἱερουσαλημ, και ουκ εγ-
Thou alone sojournest Jerusalem, and not thou
νως τα γενομενα εν αυτῃ εν ταις ἡμεραις
knowest the things having been done in her in the days
ταυταις; 19 Και ειπεν αυτοις· Ποια; Οἱ
these? And he said to them: What things? They
δε ειπον αυτῳ· Τα περι Ιησου του Ναζω-
and said to him: The things about Jesus the Naza-
ραιου, ὁς εγενετο ανηρ προφητης, δυνατος εν
rene, who was a man a prophet, powerful in
εργῳ και λογῳ εναντιον του θεου και παντος
work and word in presence of the God and all
του λαου. 20 Ὁπως τε παρεδωκαν αυτον οἱ
the people. How and delivered up him the
αρχιερεις και οἱ αρχοντες ἡμων εις κριμα θανα-
high-priests and the chiefs of us to a sentence of
του, και εσταυρωσαν αυτον. 21 Ἡμεις δε ηλπι-
death, and crucified him. We but hoped,
ζομεν, ὁτι αυτος εστιν ὁ μελλων λυτρουσθαι
that he it is the being about to redeem
τον Ισραηλ· αλλαγε συν πασι τουτοις τριτην
the Israel: but besides all these third
ταυτην ἡμεραν αγει σημερον, αφ᾽ οὑ ταυτα
this day goes away to-day, from of which these
εγενετο· 22 αλλα και γυναικες τινες εξ ἡμων
occurred: but also women some of us
εξεστησαν ἡμας, γενομεναι ορθριαι επι το μνη-
astonished us, having been early at the tomb;
μειον· 23 και μη εὑρουσαι το σωμα αυτου, ηλθον,
and not having found the body of him, came,
λεγουσαι και οπτασιαν αγγελων ἑωρακεναι, οἱ
saying also a vision of messengers to have seen, who

13 ‡ And behold, two of
them were going on the
Same DAY, to a Village
called Emmaus, sixty Fur-
longs from Jerusalem.
14 And they were con-
versing with each other
about All these THINGS
which had HAPPENED.
15 And it occurred, while
they were conversing and
reasoning, * Jesus himself
having approached, went
with them.
16 But ‡ their EYES were
held, so that they did not
RECOGNIZE him.
17 And he said to them,
"What WORDS are these
which you are exchanging
with each other, as you
* walk? and why are you
dejected?"
18 And the ONE ‡ named
Cleopas, answering, said
to him, "Art thou the only
Sojourner in Jerusalem,
who is unacquainted with
the THINGS which have
OCCURRED in it in these
DAYS?"
19 And he said to them,
"What things?" And they
said to him, "The THINGS
concerning Jesus, the NA-
ZARITE, ‡ a Man who was
a Prophet, powerful in
Work and Word before
GOD and All the PEOPLE;
20 † and how the HIGH-
PRIESTS and our RULERS
delivered him up to a Sentence of Death, and crucified him.
21 But we hoped ‡ That
it was HE who WAS ABOUT
to redeem ISRAEL; and
besides all this, * This Day
is the Third since these
things were done.
22 But ‡ some of our
Women also astonished us;
for having been early at
the TOMB,
23 and not finding his
BODY, they came, saying,
that they had even seen a

* VATICAN MANUSCRIPT.—15. Jesus. 17. walk? And they stood still and were sad. 21. This Day is the Third since.

† 13. Mark xvi. 12. ‡ 16. John xx. 14; xxi. 4. ‡ 18. John xix. 25. 19. Matt xxi. 11; Luke vii. 16; John iii. 2; iv. 19; vi. 14; Acts ii. 22; vii. 22. ‡ 20. Luke xxiii 1; Acts xiii. 27, 28. ‡ 21. Luke i. 68; ii. 38; Acts i. 6. ‡ 22. Matt. xxviii. 8; Mark xvi. 10; John xx. 18.

λεγουσιν αυτον ζην. 24 Και απηλθον τινες
say him to be alive. And went some
των συν ἡμιν επι το μνημειον, και εὑρον
of those with us to the tomb, and found
*[οὑτω,] καθως και αἱ γυναικες ειπον· αυτον
[thus,] even as also the woman said; him
δε ουκ ειδον. 25 Και αυτος ειπε προς αυτους·
but not they saw. And he said to them;
Ω ανοητοι και βραδεις τῃ καρδιᾳ του πιστευειν
O thoughtless and slow with the heart of the to believe
επι πασιν, οἱς ελαλησαν οἱ προφηται. 26 Ουχι
in all, which spoke the prophets. Not
ταυτα εδει παθειν τον Χριστον, και εισελ-
these it was binding to have suffered the Anointed, and to
θειν εις την δοξαν αὑτου; 27 Και αρξαμενος απο
enter into the glory of himself? And beginning from
Μωσεως και απο παντων των προφητων, διηρ-
Moses and from all of the prophets, he
μηνευεν αυτοις εν πασαις ταις γραφαις τα
explained to them in all the writings the things
περι αὑτου. 28 Και ηγγισαν εις την κωμην, οὑ
about himself. And they drew near to the village, where
επορευοντο· και αυτος προσεποιειτο πορρωτερω
they were going: and he seemed intending further
πορευεσθαι. 29 Και παρεβιασαντο αυτον,
to go. But they pressed him,
λεγοντες· Μεινον μεθ' ἡμων, ὁτι προς ἑσπεραν
saying: Abide with us, for toward evening
εστι, και κεκλικεν ἡ ἡμερα. Και εισηλθε του
it is, and has declined the day. And he went in the
μειναι συν αυτοις. 30 Και εγενετο εν τῳ κατα-
to abide with them. And it happened in the to
κλιθηναι αυτον μετ' αυτων, λαβων τον αρτον,
recline him with them, having taken the loaf,
ευλογησε, και κλασας επεδιδου αυτοις. 31 Αυ-
he blessed, and having broken he gave to them. Of
των δε διηνοιχθησαν οἱ οφθαλμοι, και επεγνω-
them and were opened the eyes, and they knew
σαν αυτον· και αυτος αφαντος εγενετο απ'
him: and he disappeared from
αυτων. 32 Και ειπον προς αλληλους· Ουχι ἡ
them. And they said to each other: Not the
καρδια ἡμων καιομενη ην *[εν ἡμιν,] ὡς ελαλει
heart of us burning was [in us,] as he was talking
ἡμιν εν τῃ ὁδῳ, *[και] ὡς διηνοιγεν ἡμιν τας
to us in the way, [and] as he was opening to us the
γραφας;
writings?

33 Και ανασταντες αυτῃ τῃ ὡρᾳ, ὑπεστρεψαν
And rising up in this the hour, they returned
εις Ἱερουσαλημ· και εὑρον συνηθροισμενους
to Jerusalem: and found having been assembled
τους ἑνδεκα και τους συν αυτοις, 34 λεγοντας·
the eleven and those with them, saying:
Ὁτι ηγερθη ὁ κυριος οντως, και ωφθη Σι-
That has been raised the Lord indeed, and has appeared to Si-

Vision of Angels, who said that he was alive.

24 And some of THOSE with us went to the TOMB, and found it as the WOMEN had said; but Him they saw not."

25 And he said to them, "O inconsiderate men, and slow of HEART to BELIEVE all which the PROPHETS have spoken!

26 Was it not necessary ‡ for the MESSIAH to have suffered these things, and to enter his GLORY?"

27 And beginning from Moses, and through All the PROPHETS, he explained to them in All the SCRIPTURES the THINGS concerning himself.

28 And they drew near to the VILLAGE where they were going; and he seemed as intending to go further.

29 But they urged him, saying, "Remain with us, for it is towards Evening, and the DAY has *already declined. And he went in to ABIDE with them.

30 And it occurred, as he RECLINED with them, ‡ taking the LOAF, he blessed God, and having broken it, he gave to them.

31 And Their EYES were opened, and they knew him; and he disappeared from them.

32 And they said to each other, "Did not our HEARTS † burn, while he talked to us on the ROAD, and while he unfolded to us the SCRIPTURES?"

33 And rising up the Same HOUR, they returned to Jerusalem, and found the ELEVEN, and THOSE with them, assembled,

34 SAYING, "The LORD has indeed been raised, and has appeared to Simon."

* VATICAN MANUSCRIPT.—24. thus—*omit*. 29. already past. 32. in us—and—*om*.

† 32. The *Codex Bezæ* has a very remarkable reading here; instead of *kaiomenee*, burned, it has *kekalummenee*, veiled, and one of the *Itala*, has *fuit excæcatum*, was blinded. "Was not our hearts veiled (blinded) when he conversed with us on the way, and while he unfolded the Scriptures to us," seeing we did not know him.—*A. Clarke*.

‡ 26. verse 46; Acts xvii. 3; 1 Pet. i. 11. ‡ 30. Matt. xiv. 19.

μονι. 35 Και αυτοι εξηγουντο τα εν τη ὁδῳ,
mon. And they related the things in the way,
και ὡς εγνωσθη αυτοις εν τη κλασει του αρτου.
and how he was known to them in the breaking of the loaf.
36 Ταυτα δε αυτων λαλουντων, αυτος εστη εν
These and of them speaking, he stood in
μεσῳ αυτων, και λεγει αυτοις· Ειρηνη ὑμιν.
midst of them, and says to them; Peace to you.
37 Πτοηθεντες δε και εμφοβοι γενομενοι,
Being terrified but and affrighted having become,
εδοκουν πνευμα θεωρειν. 38 Και ειπεν αυτοις·
they thought a spirit to see. And he said to them;
Τι τεταραγμενοι εστε; και διατι διαλογισμοι
Why having been agitated are you? and why reasonings
αναβαινουσιν εν ταις καρδιαις ὑμων; 39 Ιδετε
rise in the hearts of you? See you
τας χειρας μου και τους ποδας μου, ὁτι αυτος
the hands of me and the feet of me, that he
εγω ειμι· ψηλαφησατε με και ιδετε· ὁτι πνευμα
I am; handle you me and see you; for a spirit
σαρκα και οστεα ουκ εχει, καθως εμε θεωρειτε
flesh and bones not has, as me you perceive
εχοντα. 40 Και τουτο ειπων, επεδειξεν αυτοις
having. And this saying, he showed to them
τας χειρας και τους ποδας. 41 Ετι δε απιστουν-
the hands and the feet. While and not believ-
των αυτων απο της χαρας, και θαυμαζοντων,
ing of them from the joy, and were wondering,
ειπεν αυτοις· Εχετε τι βρωσιμον ενθαδε;
he said to them; Have you anything eatable here?
42 Οἱ δε επεδωκαν αυτῳ ιχθυος οπτου μερος,
They and gave to him of a fish broiled a piece,
*[και απο μελισσιου κηριου.] 43 Και λαβων,
[and from a honey comb.] And having taken,
ενωπιον αυτων εφαγεν. 44 Ειπε δε αυτοις·
in presence of them he ate. He said and to them;
Οὑτοι οἱ λογοι, οὑς ελαλησα προς ὑμας, ετι ων
These the words, which I spoke to you, while being
συν ὑμιν, ὁτι δει πληρωθηναι παντα τα γεγ-
with you, that must to be fulfilled all the things having
ραμμενα εν τῳ νομῳ Μωσεως, και προφηταις,
been written in the law of Moses, and prophets,
και ψαλμοις περι εμου. 45 Τοτε διηνοιξεν
and psalms, concerning me. Then he opened
αυτων τον νουν, του συνιεναι τας γραφας·
of them the mind, of the to understand the writings;
46 και ειπεν αυτοις· Ὁτι οὑτω γεγραπται, και
and he said to them; That thus it is written, and
οὑτως εδει παθειν τον Χριστον, και αναστη-
thus it behoved to have suffered the Anointed, and to stand
ναι εκ νεκρων τῃ τριτῃ ἡμερᾳ, 47 και κηρυχ-
up out of dead ones in the third day, and to be

35 And they related what THINGS happened on the ROAD, and how he was known to them in the BREAKING of the LOAF.

36 ‡ And as they were saying these things, he stood in the Midst of them, † and says to them, "Peace be to you."

37 But they being * troubled and terrified, thought they saw ‡ † a Spirit.

38 And he said to them, "Why are you troubled? and why do Doubts arise in your * HEARTS?

39 ‡ See my HANDS and my FEET, that I am he; handle me, and be convinced; For a Spirit has not * both Flesh and Bones as you perceive me to have."

40 † And having said this, he showed them his HANDS and his FEET.

41 And while from JOY they were unbelieving, and were wondering, he said to them, "Have you any Food here?"

42 And THEY gave him Part of a broiled Fish;

43 and taking it, ‡ he ate in their presence.

44 And he said to them, ‡ "These are the WORDS which I spoke to you, while I was yet with you, That All THINGS WRITTEN in the LAW of Moses, and in the * PROPHETS, and in the Psalms, concerning me, must be fully accomplished."

45 Then he opened Their MINDS to UNDERSTAND the SCRIPTURES,

46 and said to them, "Thus it is written, * that the MESSIAH should suffer, and should rise from the Dead the THIRD Day;

* VATICAN MANUSCRIPT.—37. troubled, and. 38. HEART. 39. both Flesh and 42. and from a Honey comb—*omit*. 44. PROPHETS. 46. that the Messiah should suffer, and should rise.

† 36. Tischendorf omits, "And says to them, 'Peace be to you.'" † 37. Griesbach has *phantasma*, phantom, in the margin, which agrees with Mark vi. 49. † 40. Tischendorf omits this verse.

‡ 36. Mark xvi. 14; John xx. 19; 1 Cor. xv. 5. ‡ 37. Mark vi. 49. ‡ 39. John xx. 20, 27. ‡ 43. Acts x. 41. ‡ 44. Matt. xvi. 21; xvii. 22; xx. 18; Mark viii. 31; Luke ix. 22; xviii. 31.

θηναι επι τῳ ονοματι αυτου μετανοιαν και αφε-
proclaimed in the name of him reformation and forgive-
σιν αμαρτιων εις παντα τα εθνη, αρξαμενον απο
ness of sins to all the nations, beginning from
Ἱερουσαλημ. 48 Ὑμεις δε εστε μαρτυρες τουτων.
Jerusalem. You and are witnesses of these.
49 Και ιδου, εγω αποστελλω την επαγγελιαν
And lo, I send forth the promise
του πατρος μου εφ᾽ ὑμας· ὑμεις δε καθισατε εν
of the father of me on you; you but remain you in
τῃ πολει, ἑως οὑ ενδυσησθε δυναμιν εξ ὑψους.
the city, till you may be clothed power from on high.
50 Εξηγαγε δε αυτους εξω ἑως εις Βηθανιαν· και
He led and them out even to Bethany: and
επαρας τας χειρας αὑτου, ευλογησεν αυτους.
having lifted up the hands of himself, he blessed them.
51 Και εγενετο εν τῳ ευλογειν αυτον αυτους,
And it happened in the to bless him them,
διεστη απ᾽ αυτων, και ανεφερετο εις τον ου-
he stood apart from them, and was carried up into the hea-
ρανον. 52 Και αυτοι προσκυνησαντες αυτον,
ven. And they having prostrated to him,
ὑπεστρεψαν εις Ἱερουσαλημ μετα χαρας μεγα-
returned to Jerusalem with joy great:
λης· 53 και ησαν διαπαντος εν τῳ ἱερῳ, *[αινουν-
and were continually in the temple, [praising
τες και] ευλογουντες τον θεον.
and] blessing the God.

47 and that in his NAME, Reformation * in order to Forgiveness of Sins should be proclaimed to All the NATIONS, beginning at Jerusalem.

48 And ‡ you are Witnesses of these things.

49 And, behold, I send forth ‡ the PROMISE of my FATHER upon you; but remain you in the CITY, till you are invested with Power from on high."

50 And he led them out ‡ to Bethany; and lifting up his HANDS, he blessed them.

51 And it occurred, while he was BLESSING them, he was separated from them, † and carried up into HEAVEN.

52 And they † having prostrated to him, returned to Jerusalem with great Joy;

53 and were constantly in the TEMPLE, blessing GOD.

* ACCORDING TO LUKE.

* VATICAN MANUSCRIPT.—47. in order to Forgiveness. 53. praising and—*omit.* *Subscription*—ACCORDING TO LUKE.

† 51 & 52. Tischendorf omits, "and carried up into HEAVEN," and "having prostrated to him."

‡ 48. John xv. 27; Acts i. 8, 22; ii. 32; iii. 15. ‡ 49. Acts i. 4. ‡ 50. Acts i. 12

*[ΕΥΑΓΓΕΛΙΟΝ] ΚΑΤΑ ΙΩΑΝΝΗΝ.
[GLAD TIDINGS] BY JOHN.

* ACCORDING TO JOHN.

ΚΕΦ. α'. 1.

1 Εν αρχῃ ην ὁ λογος, και ὁ λογος ην προς
In a beginning was the word, and the word was with
τον θεον, και θεος ην ὁ λογος. 2 Οὗτος ην εν
the God, and a god was the word. This was in
αρχῃ προς τον θεον. 3 Παντα δι' αυτου
a beginning with the God. All through it
† εγενετο· και χωρις αυτου εγενετο ουδε ἑν, ὁ
was done: and without it was done not even one, that
γεγονεν. 4 Εν αυτῳ ζωη ην, και ἡ ζωη ην το
has been done. In it life was, and the life was the
φως των ανθρωπων· 5 και το φως εν τῃ σκοτιᾳ
light of the men: and the light in the darkness
φαινει, και ἡ σκοτια αυτο ου καταλαβεν.
shines, and the darkness it not apprehended.

6 Εγενετο ανθρωπος απεσταλμενος παρα θεου,
Was a man having been sent from God,
ονομα αυτῳ Ιωαννης· 7 οὗτος ηλθεν εις μαρτυριαν,
a name to him John; this came for a witness,
ἱνα μαρτυρησῃ περι του φωτος, ἱνα παντες πισ-
that he might testify about the light, that all might
τευσωσι δι' αυτου. 8 Ουκ ην εκεινος το φως,
believe through him. Not was he the light,
αλλ' ἱνα μαρτυρησῃ περι του φωτος. 9 Ην το
but that he might testify about the light. Was the
φως το αληθινον, ὁ φωτιζει παντα ανθρωπον
light, the true, which enlightens every man
ερχομενον εις τον κοσμον. 10 Εν τῳ κοσμῳ ην,
coming into the world. In the world he was,
και ὁ κοσμος δι' αυτου εγενετο, και ὁ κοσμος
and the world through him was, and the world
αυτον ουκ εγνω. 11 Εις τα ιδια ηλθε, και οἱ
him not knew. Into the own he came, and the
ιδιοι αυτον ου παρελαβον. 12 Ὁσοι δε ελαβον
own him not received. As many as but received

CHAPTER I.

1 In the ‡ Beginning was the † LOGOS, and the LOGOS was with GOD, and the LOGOS was God.

2 This was in the Beginning with GOD.

3 ‡ Through it every thing was done; and without it not even one thing was done, which has been done.

4 In it was Life; and the LIFE was the LIGHT of MEN.

5 And the ‡ LIGHT shone in the DARKNESS, and the DARKNESS apprehended it not.

6 ‡ There was a Man, named John, sent by God.

7 He came for a Witness, that he might testify concerning the LIGHT, that all might believe through him.

8 He was not the LIGHT, but to testify concerning the LIGHT.

9 The TRUE LIGHT was that, which, coming into the WORLD, enlightens Every Man.

10 He was in the WORLD, and † the WORLD was (enlightened) through him; and yet the WORLD knew Him not.

11 ‡ He came to his OWN domains, and yet his OWN people received Him not;

12 but to as many as received him, ‡ he gave

---

* VATICAN MANUSCRIPT.—*Title*—ACCORDING TO JOHN.

† 1. In this and the fourteenth verse *logos*, has been transferred, rather than translated. Dr. A. Clarke remarks, "This term should be left untranslated, for the very same reasons why the names *Jesus* and *Christ* are left untranslated. As every appellative of the Savior of the world, was descriptive of some excellence in his *person*, *nature*, or *work*, so the epithet *Logos*, which signifies a word spoken, speech, eloquence, doctrine, reason, or the faculty of reasoning, is very properly applied to him." See 1 John i. 1, for a clear and useful comment by the apostle John on the proem to this Gospel. † 3. *Ginomai* occurs upwards of seven hundred times in the New Testament, but never in the sense of *create*, yet in most versions it is translated, as though the word was *ktizo*. "The word occurs fifty-three times in this Gospel, and signifies to be, to come, to become, to come to pass; also, to be done or transacted. All things in the christian dispensation were done by Christ, i. e. by his authority, and according to his direction; and in the ministry committed to his apostles, nothing has been done without his warrant. See John xv. 4, 5, 'Without me ye can do nothing.' Compare ver. 7, 10, 16; John xvii. 2; Col. i. 16, 17." Cappe's Diss. † 10. *ho kosmos*, the order, arrangement of things, the human race; here it evidently means that *kosmos* of human beings which he came to *enlighten* and to *save*. John viii. 12; iii. 16.

‡ 1. Prov. viii. 22, &c.; 1 John i. 1. ‡ 3. Eph. iii. 9; Col. i. 16. ‡ 5. John viii. 12; ix. 5; xii. 35, 46. ‡ 6. Mal. iii. 1; Matt. iii. 1; Luke iii. 2. ‡ 11. Matt. xxi. 38; Mark xii. 7; Luke xix. 14; xx. 14. ‡ 12. Rom. viii. 15; Gal. iii. 26, 27; 1 John iii. 1

αυτον, εδωκεν αυτοις εξουσιαν τεκνα θεου
him, he gave to them authority children of God
γενεσθαι, τοις πιστευουσιν εις το ονομα αυτου·
to become, to those believing into the name of him;
13 οἱ ουκ εξ αἱματων, ουδε εκ θεληματος σαρκος,
who not from bloods, nor from a will of flesh,
ουδε εκ θεληματος ανδρος, αλλ' εκ θεου εγεννη-
nor from a will of a man, but from God were be-
θησαν. 14 Και ὁ λογος σαρξ εγενετο, και εσκη-
gotten. And the word flesh became, and taber-
νωσεν εν ἡμιν, (και εθεασαμεθα την δοξαν αυτου,
nacled among us, (and we beheld the glory of him,
δοξαν ὡς μονογενους παρα πατρος,) πληρης
a glory as of an only-begotten from a father,) full
χαριτος και αληθειας. 15 Ιωαννης μαρτυρει περι
of favor and truth. John testifies concerning
αυτου, και κεκραγε, λεγων· Οὑτος ην, ὁν
him, and cried, saying; This was, of whom
ειπον· Ὁ οπισω μου ερχομενος, εμπροσθεν μου
I said; He after me coming, before me
γεγονεν· ὁτι πρωτος μου ην. 16 Ὁτι εκ του
has become; for first of me he was. Because out of the
πληρωματος αυτου ἡμεις παντες ελαβομεν, και
fulness of him we all received, and
χαριν αντι χαριτος. 17 Ὁτι ὁ νομος δια Μω-
favor upon favor. For the law through Mo-
σεως εδοθη· ἡ χαρις και ἡ αληθεια δια Ιησου
ses was given; the favor and the truth through Jesus
Χριστου εγενετο.
Christ came.
18 Θεον ουδεις ἑωρακε πωποτε· ὁ μονογενης
God no one has seen ever; the only-begotten
υἱος, ὁ ων εις τον κολπον του πατρος, εκεινος
son, that being in the bosom of the father, he
εξηγησατο. 19 Και αὑτη εστιν ἡ μαρτυρια του
has made known. And this is the testimony of the
Ιωαννου, ὁτε απεστειλαν οἱ Ιουδαιοι εξ Ἱεροσο-
John, when sent the Jews from Jeru-
λυμων ἱερεις και Λευιτας, ἱνα ερωτησωσιν αυτον·
salem priests and Levites, that they might ask him;
Συ τις ει; 20 Και ὡμολογησε, και ουκ ηρνη-
Thou who art? And he confessed, and not denied;
σατο· και ὡμολογησεν· Ὁτι ουκ ειμι εγω ὁ
and confessed; That not am I the
Χριστος 21 Και ηρωτησαν αυτον· Τι ουν;
Anointed. And they asked him. What then?

Authority to become Children of God, to THOSE BELIEVING into his NAME;

13 ‡†who were begotten not of Blood, nor of the Will of the Flesh, nor of the Will of Man, but of God.

14 And the † LOGOS became ‡ Flesh, and dwelt among us,—and ‡ we beheld his GLORY, a Glory as of an Only-begotten from a Father,—full of Favor and Truth.

15 † [John testified concerning him, and cried, saying, "This is he of whom I said, ‡ 'HE who COMES after me is in advance of me; For he is my Superior.'"]

16 For out of his FULNESS we all received; even Favor upon Favor.

17 For the LAW was given through Moses; the FAVOR and the TRUTH came through Jesus Christ.

18 No one has ever seen God; the * Only-begotten Son, who is in the BOSOM of the FATHER, he has made him known.

19 Now this is the TESTIMONY of JOHN. ‡ When the JEWS sent * to him Priests and Levites to ask him, "Who art thou?"

20 he acknowledged, and did not deny, but acknowledged, "I am not the MESSIAH."

21 And they asked him, "Who * then art thou?

* VATICAN MANUSCRIPT.—18. Only-begotten Son, HE who is. 19. to him Priests 21. then art thou? Art thou Elijah?

† 13. Griesbach notes a different reading of this verse. Instead of *hoi......egennetheesan* he has *hos......egenneethee*; the singular pronoun and verb for the plural; which would make the passage read—"Who *was* not begotten of Blood, nor of the Will of the Flesh, nor of the Will of a Man, but of God;" thus referring it directly to the *physical* generation of the Messiah, by the Spirit of God, rather than to the moral regeneration of believers. † 14. *Newcome* in his Translation of the New Testament, remarks, "Jesus, the Son of God, is called the Word, because God revealed himself or *his word* by him." The following singular Eastern custom may perhaps illustrate the phraseology of the first part of this chapter. "In Abyssinia, there is an officer named *Kal Hatze*, the *word* or *voice* of the king, who stands always upon the steps of the throne, at the side of a lattice window, where there is a hole, covered in the inside with a curtain of green taffeta. Behind this curtain the king sits; and speaks through the aperture to the *Kal Hatze*, who communicates his commands to the officers, judges, and attendants.—*Bruce's Travels.* † 15. Some put this verse after the 18th

‡ 13. John iii. 5; James i. 18; 1 Pet. i. 23. ‡ 14. Matt. i. 16, 20; Luke i. 31, 35; ii. 7 1 Tim. iii. 16. ‡ 14. Matt. xvii. 2; 2 Pet. i. 17. ‡ 15. Matt. iii. 11; Mark i. [illegible] Luke iii. 16; ver. 27, 30; John iii. 31. ‡ 19. John v. 33,

Ηλιας ει συ, Και λεγει· Ουκ ειμι. Ὁ προ-
Elias art thou? And he says: Not I am. The pro-
φητης ει συ; Και απεκριθη Ου. 22 Ειπον ουν
phet art thou? And he answered; No. They said then
αυτῳ· Τις ει; ἱνα αποκρισιν δωμεν τοις πεμ-
to him; Who art thou? that an answer we may give to those having
ψασιν ἡμας· τι λεγεις περι σεαυτου; 23 Εφη
sent us; what sayest thou about thyself? He said
Εγω· "φωνη βοωντος εν τῃ ερημῳ· Ευθυνατε
I; "A voice crying in the desert; Make you straight
την ὁδον κυριου," καθως ειπεν Ἡσαιας ὁ προ-
the way of a lord," as said Esaias the pro-
φητης. 24 Και οἱ απεσταλμενοι ησαν εκ των
phet. And those having been sent were of the
Φαρισαιων· 25 και ηρωτησαν αυτον, και ειπον
Pharisees; and they asked him, and said
αυτῳ· Τι ουν βαπτιζεις, ει συ ουκ ει ὁ Χρισ-
to him; Why then dippest thou, if thou not art the Anoin-
τος, ουτε Ηλιας, ουτε προφητης; 26 Απεκριθη
ted, nor Elias, nor a prophet? Answered
αυτοις ὁ Ιωαννης, λεγων· Εγω βαπτιζω εν
them the John, saying; I dip in
ὑδατι· μεσος *[δε] ὑμων ἑστηκεν, ὁν ὑμεις ουκ
water: midst [but] of you stands, whom you not
οιδατε, 27 ὁ οπισω μου ερχομενος, οὗ εγω ουκ
know, he after me coming, of whom I not
ειμι αξιος, ἱνα λυσω αυτου τον ἱμαντα του
am worthy, that I may loose of him the strap of the
ὑποδηματος. 28 Ταυτα εν Βηθανιᾳ εγενετο
sandal. These in Bethany were done
περαν του Ιορδανου, ὁπου ην Ιωαννης βαπ-
beyond the Jordan, where was John dip-
τιζων.
ping.

29 Τῃ επαυριον βλεπει τον Ιησουν ερχομενον
In the morrow he beholds the Jesus coming
προς αυτον, και λεγει· Ιδε ὁ αμνος του θεου, ὁ
to him, and he says: Behold the lamb of the God, he
αιρων την ἁμαρτιαν του κοσμου. 30 Οὗτος
taking away the sin of the world. This
εστι, περι οὗ εγω ειπον· Οπισω μου ερχεται
is he, about whom I said: After me comes
ανηρ, ὁς εμπροσθεν μου γεγονεν· ὁτι πρωτος
a man, who before me has become: because first
μου ην. 31 Καγω ουκ ηδειν αυτον· αλλ' ἱνα
of me he was. And I not knew him: but that
φανερωθη τῳ Ισραηλ, δια τουτο ηλθον
he might be manifested to the Israel, because of this am come
εγω εν τῳ ὑδατι βαπτιζων. 32 Και εμαρτυρη-
I in the water dipping. And bore testi-
σεν Ιωαννης, λεγων· Ὁτι τεθεαμαι το πνευμα
mony John, saying: That I saw the spirit
καταβαινον ὡς περιστεραν εξ ουρανου, και εμει-
coming down like a dove out of heaven, and it

Art thou ‡ Elijah?" And he said, "I am not." "Art thou the PROPHET?" And he answered, "No."

22 * They said to him, "Who art thou? that we may give an Answer to THOSE who SENT us. What dost thou say concerning thyself?"

23 He said, ‡ "I am a Voice proclaiming in the DESERT, 'Make straight 'the WAY for the Lord,' as ‡ Isaiah the PROPHET said."

24 Now * those sent were of the PHARISEES.

25 And they asked him, and said to him, "Why then dost thou immerse, if thou art not the MESSIAH, nor Elijah, nor a Prophet?"

26 John answered them, saying, ‡ "I immerse in Water; * in the Midst of you, stands one coming after me, whom you do not know,

27 the STRAP of Whose SANDAL I am not worthy to untie."

28 These things occurred in Bethany beyond the JORDAN, where * JOHN was immersing.

29 On the NEXT DAY he sees JESUS coming to him, and says, "Behold ‡ the LAMB of GOD, who TAKES AWAY the SIN of the WORLD.

30 This is he of whom I said, 'After me comes a Man who is in advance of of me; for he is my Superior.'

31 And I did not know him; but for this purpose, that he might be manifested to ISRAEL, I am come immersing in * Water."

32 ‡ And John testified, saying, "I saw the SPIRIT coming down like a Dove

* VATICAN MANUSCRIPT.—22. They said to him. 24. they who were sent. 26. but —*omit*. 26. in the Midst of you, coming after me, stands one whom you do not know, the STRAP of Whose SANDAL. 28. JOHN. 31. Water.

‡ 21. Mal. iv. 5; Matt. xvii. 10. ‡ 23. Matt. iii. 3; Mark i. 3; Luke iii. 4; John iii. 28. ‡ 23. Isa. xl. 3. ‡ 26. Matt. iii. 11. ‡ 29. 1 Pet. i. 19; Rev. v. 6. ‡ 32. Matt. iii. 16; Mark i. 10; Luke iii. 22.

νεν επ' αυτον. 33 Καγω ουκ ηδειν αυτον· αλλ'
abode on him. And I not knew him: but

ὁ πεμψας με βαπτιζειν εν ὑδατι, εκεινος μοι
he having sent me to dip in water, he to me

ειπον· Εφ' ὁν αν ιδῃς το πνευμα καταβαινον,
said: On whom thou mayest see the spirit coming down,

και μενον επ' αυτον, οὑτος εστιν ὁ βαπτιζων εν
and abiding on him, this is he dipping in

πνευματι ἁγιῳ. 34 Καγω ἑωρακα, και μεμαρτυ-
spirit holy. And I have seen, and have testi-

ρηκα, ὁτι οὑτος εστιν ὁ υἱος του θεου.
fied, that this is the son of the God.

35 Τῃ επαυριον παλιν εἱστηκει ὁ Ιωαννης, και
The morrow again was standing the John, and

εκ των μαθητων αυτου δυο. 36 Και εμβλεψας
of the disciples of him two. And having looked on

τῳ Ιησου περιπατουντι, λεγει· Ιδε ὁ αμνος του
the Jesus walking, he says: Behold the lamb of the

θεου. 37 Και ηκουσαν αυτου οἱ δυο μαθηται
God. And heard him the two disciples

λαλουντος, και ηκολουθησαν τῳ Ιησου. 38 Στρα-
speaking, and they followed the Jesus. Having

φεις δε ὁ Ιησους, και θεασαμενος αυτους ακο-
turned and the Jesus, and seeing them fol-

λουθουντας, λεγει αυτοις· Τι ζητειτε; Οἱ δε
lowing, he says to them; What seek you? They and

ειπον αυτῳ· Ῥαββι,. (ὁ λεγεται ἑρμηνευομε-
said to him, Rabbi, (which means being interpreted.

ον, διδασκαλε,) που μενεις; 39 Λεγει αυτοις·
O teacher,) where dwellest thou? He says to them.

Ερχεσθε και ιδετε. Ηλθον και ειδον, που μενει·
Come you and see you. They came and saw, where he dwells:

και παρ' αυτῳ εμειναν την ἡμεραν εκεινην.
and with him abode the day that.

Ὡρα ην ὡς δεκατη. 40 Ην Ανδρεας, ὁ αδελφος
Hour it was about tenth. Was Andrew, the brother

Σιμωνος Πετρου, εἱς εκ των δυο των ακουσαν-
of Simon Peter, one of the two of those having heard

των παρα Ιωαννου, και ακολουθησαντων αυτῳ.
from John, and having followed him.

41 Εὑρισκει οὑτος πρωτως τον αδελφον τον
Finds he first the brother that

ιδιον Σιμωνα, και λεγει αυτῳ· Εὑρηκαμεν τον
own Simon, and he says to him; We have found the

Μεσσιαν (ὁ εστι μεθερμηνευομενον, Χριστος.)
Messiah which is being interpreted, Anointed.)

42 *[Και] ηγαγεν αυτον προς τον Ιησουν.
[And] he brought him to the Jesus.

from Heaven, and resting on him.

33 And I did not know him; but HE who SENT me to immerse in Water, he said to me, 'On whom thou shalt see the SPIRIT descending and resting, this is HE who ‡IMMERSES in holy Spirit.'

34 And I have seen and testified, That he is the SON of GOD."

35 On the NEXT DAY *John was again standing, and two of his DISCIPLES;

36 and observing JESUS walking, he says, "Behold the LAMB of GOD!"

37 The TWO Disciples hearing this, followed JESUS.

38 And JESUS turning, and seeing them following, says to them, "What do you seek?" And THEY said to him, "Rabbi, (which signifies, being translated, Teacher,) where dwellest thou?"

39 He says to them, "Come and see." They went, *therefore, and saw where he dwelt, and continued with him that DAY. It was about the †tenth Hour.

40 ‡Andrew, the BROTHER of Simon Peter, was one of THOSE TWO who having heard from John, followed him.

41 He first finds his OWN BROTHER Simon; and says to him, "We have found the MESSIAH," (which is, being translated, Anointed.)

42 He conducted him to JESUS. JESUS looking

* VATICAN MANUSCRIPT.—35. John. 39. therefore, and saw. 42. And—*omit*.

† 39. It was the way of the ancients to divide the day into twelve hours, and the night into as many. The first hour of the day was an hour after the sun rose, and the twelfth was when it set. This was the way in Judea, and to this the other Evangelists adhere. But St. John appears to have reckoned the hours as we do, from midnight to noon, and again from noon to midnight. And it may be observed, that he mentions the hour of the day oftener than any other Evangelist; as if with design to give his readers an opportunity of discerning his method, by comparing one passage with another. If the time here intended was that which we may call Jewish, (to distinguish it, not from the Greek and Roman which were the same with the Jewish, but from the modern) the tenth hour was about four in the afternoon, or two hours before the day ended in Judea; with which time neither the words nor circumstances of the narration seem to agree. For the words, *they abode with him that day*, rather imply, that they spent a good part of the day with him. Therefore the most reasonable account of this tenth hour is, that it was ten in the morning.—*Townson.*

‡ 33. Matt. iii. 11; Acts i. 5; ii. 4; x. 44; xi. 15. ‡ 40. Matt. iv. 18.

Εμβλεψας αυτῳ ὁ Ιησους ειπε· Συ ει Σιμων, ὁ
Having looked to him the Jesus said; Thou art Simon, the
υἱος Ιωνα· συ κληθηση Κηφας· ὁ ἑρμηνευεται
son of Jonas; thou shalt be called Cephas; which means
Πετρος.
Peter.
43 Τῃ επαυριον ηθελησεν εξελθειν εις την
The morrow he desired to go forth into the
Γαλιλαιαν· και εὑρισκει Φιλιππον, και λεγει
Galilee; and he finds Philip, and says
αυτῳ· Ακολουθει μοι. 44 Ην δε ὁ Φιλιππος απο
to him; Follow me. Was and the Philip from
Βηθσαιδα, εκ της πολεως Ανδρεου και Πετρου.
Bethsaida, of the city of Andrew and Peter.
45 Εὑρισκει Φιλιππος τον Ναθαναηλ, και λεγει
Finds Philip the Nathanael, and says
αυτῳ· Ὁν εγραψε Μωσεως εν τῳ νομῳ, και
to him: Whom wrote Moses in the law, and
οἱ προφηται, εὑρηκαμεν, Ιησουν τον υἱον
the prophets, we have found, Jesus the son
του Ιωσηφ, τον απο Ναζαρεθ. 46 Και ειπεν
of the Joseph, that from Nazareth. And said
αυτῳ Ναθαναηλ· Εκ Ναζαρεθ δυναται τι αγαθον
to him Nathanael: Out of Nazareth is able any good
ειναι. Λεγει αυτῳ Φιλιππος· ερχου και ιδε.
to be? Says to him Philip; Come and see.
47 Ειδεν ὁ Ιησους τον Ναθαναηλ ερχομενον προς
Saw the Jesus the Nathanael coming to
αυτον, και λεγει περι αυτου· Ιδε αληθως Ισ-
him, and he says concerning him; Behold indeed an
ραηλιτης, εν ᾡ δολος ουκ εστι. 48 Λεγει αυτῳ
Israelite, in whom guile not is. Says to him
Ναθαναηλ· Ποθεν με γινωσκεις; Απεκριθη
Nathanael; Whence me knowest thou? Answered
Ιησους και ειπεν αυτῳ· Προ του σε Φιλιππον
Jesus and said to him; Before the thee Philip
φωνησαι, οντα ὑπο την συκην, ειδον σε.
to have called, being under the fig-tree, I saw thee.
49 Απεκριθη Ναθαναηλ *[και λεγει αυτῳ·]
Answered Nathanael [and says to him:]
Ῥαββι, συ ει ὁ υἱος του θεου, συ ει ὁ βασι-
Rabbi, thou art the son of the God, thou art the king
λευς του Ισραηλ. 50 Απεκριθη Ιησους και ειπεν
of the Israel. Answered Jesus and said
αυτῳ· Ὁτι ειπον σοι· Ειδον σε ὑποκατω της
to him: Because I said to thee: I saw thee underneath the
συκης, πιστευεις; μειζω τουτων οψῃ. 51 Και
fig-tree, believest thou? greater of these thou shalt see. And
λεγει αυτῳ· Αμην αμην λεγω ὑμιν, *[απ' αρτι]
he says to him: Indeed indeed I say to you, [from now]
οψεσθε τον ουρανον ανεῳγοτα, και τους αγγε-
you shall see the heaven having been opened, and the messen-
λους του θεου αναβαινοντας και καταβαινοντας
gers of the God ascending and descending
επι τον υἱον του ανθρωπου.
on the son of the man.

at him, said, "Thou art Simon, the SON of Jonas; ‡ thou shalt be called Cephas; (which denotes the same as Peter.)

43 On the NEXT DAY he wished to go to GALILEE, and finding Philip, * JESUS says to him, "Follow me."

44 Now ‡ PHILIP was from Bethsaida, the CITY of Andrew and Peter.

45 Philip finds ‡ NATHANAEL, and says to him, "We have found the person described by Moses in the LAW, and by the PROPHETS, THAT JESUS, the * Son of JOSEPH, from Nazareth."

46 And Nathanael said to him, ‡ "Can any † good thing proceed from Nazareth?" * PHILIP says to him, "Come and see."

47 * Jesus saw NATHANAEL coming to him, and said concerning him, "Behold a genuine Israelite; in whom is no deceit."

48 Nathanael says to him, "How dost thou know Me?" Jesus answered and said to him, "Before PHILIP called Thee, when thou wast under the FIG-TREE, I saw thee."

49 Nathanael answered, "Rabbi, thou art the SON of GOD; thou art the ‡ KING of ISRAEL."

50 Jesus answered and said to him; "Because I told thee * That I saw thee under the FIG-TREE, thou believest! Thou shalt see greater things than this."

51 And he says to him, "Truly, indeed, I say to you, you shall see the HEAVENS opened, and the ANGELS of GOD ascending from and descending to the SON of MAN."

* VATICAN MANUSCRIPT.—43. JESUS says. 45. Son. 46. PHILIP. 47. Jesus 49. and says to him—*omit*. 50. That I saw. 51. From now—*omit*.

† 46. Some think allusion is here made to "that good thing promised," Jer. xxxiii. 14; others think this a term of reproach.

‡ 42. Matt. xvi. 18. ‡ 44. John xii. 21. ‡ 45. John xxi. 2. ‡ 46. John vii. 41, 42, 52. ‡ 49. Matt. xxi. 5; xxvii. 11, 42; John xviii. 37; xix. 3.

ΚΕΦ. β'. 2.

1 Και τῃ ἡμερᾳ τῃ τριτῃ γαμος εγενετο
And in the day the third a marriage-feast occurred
εν Κανᾳ της Γαλιλαιας· και ην ἡ μητηρ
in Cana of the Galilee: and was the mother
του Ιησου εκει. 2 Εκληθη δε και ὁ Ιησους
of the Jesus there. Was invited and also the Jesus
και οἱ μαθηται αυτου εις τον γαμον. 3 Και
and the disciples of him to the marriage-feast. And
ὑστερησαντος οινου, λεγει ἡ μητηρ του Ιησου
having fallen short of wine, says the mother of the Jesus
προς αυτον· Οινον ουκ εχουσι. 4 Λεγει αυτῃ ὁ
to him: Wine not they have. Says to her the
Ιησους· Τι εμοι και σοι, γυναι; ουπω ἡκει ἡ
Jesus: What to me and to thee, O woman? Not yet has come the
ὡρα μου. 5 Λεγει ἡ μητηρ αυτου τοις διακονοις·
hour of me. Says the mother of him to the servants;
Ὁ, τι αν λεγῃ ὑμιν, ποιησατε. 6 Ησαν δε
Whatever he may say to you, do you. Were and
εκει ὑδριαι λιθιναι ἑξ κειμεναι κατα τον καθα-
there water-pots of stone six being placed according to the mode
ρισμον των Ιουδαιων, χωρουσαι ανα μετρητας
of cleansing of the Jews. holding each measures
δυο η τρεις. 7 Λεγει αυτοις ὁ Ιησους· Γεμισατε
two or three. Says to them the Jesus; Fill you
τας ὑδριας ὑδατος. Και εγεμισαν αυτας ἑως
the water-pots of water. And they filled them to
ανω. 8 Και λεγει αυτοις· Αντλησατε νυν, και
top. And he says to them: Draw you now, and
φερετε τῳ αρχιτρικλινῳ. Και ηνεγκαν. 9 Ὡς
carry to the ruler of the feast. And they carried. When
δε εγευσατο ὁ αρχιτρικλινος το ὑδωρ οινον
and tasted the ruler of the feast the water wine
γεγενημενον· (και ουκ ᾐδει ποθεν εστιν· οἱ δε
having become; (and not he knew whence it is; the but
διακονοι ᾐδεισαν, οἱ ηντληκοτες το ὑδωρ·)
servants knew, those having drawn the water:)
φωνει τον νυμφιον ὁ αρχιτρικλινος, 10 και λεγει
calls the bridegroom the ruler of the feast, and says
αυτῳ· Πας ανθρωπος πρωτον τον καλον οινον
to him: Every man first the good wine

CHAPTER II.

1 And on the *THIRD Day there was a Marriage-feast in Cana of GALILEE; and the MOTHER of JESUS was there;

2 and JESUS also, and his DISCIPLES, were invited to the MARRIAGE-FEAST.

3 And the Wine falling short, the MOTHER of JESUS says to him, "They have no Wine."

4 JESUS says to her, ‡"O Woman, what hast thou to do with me? My time has not yet arrived."

5 His MOTHER says to the SERVANTS, "Do whatever he may bid you."

6 Now six stone Water-jars were there, placed ‡ according to the JEWISH CUSTOM of PURIFICATION, each containing two or three † Measures.

7 JESUS says them, "Fill the JARS with Water." And they filled them to the top.

8 And he says them, "Draw now, and carry to the † RULER OF THE FEAST." And *they carried some.

9 And when the RULER OF THE FEAST tasted ‡ the WATER made Wine, and knew not whence it was, (but THOSE SERVANTS knew who had DRAWN the WATER,) the RULER OF THE FEAST called the BRIDEGROOM,

10 and says to him, "Every Man First presents GOOD Wine, and when they

---

* VATICAN MANUSCRIPT.—1. THIRD Day. 8. THEY carried.

† 6. The exact capacity of this measure cannot now be determined. The LXX use the word in the original for the *bath*, which contained about seven gallons: and for the *seah*, which contained one-third of the bath. 2 Chron. iv. 5; 1 Kings xviii. 32. † 8. The Greek word here is a compound, denoting the president of the *tridinium*, or guest chamber, so called from its containing three couches placed in the form of a crescent, on which the guests *reclined* during the entertainment. It was the duty of this officer to prepare the feast, arrange the couches, dispose the guests, place the dishes, and taste the wine and viands.—Stockius in Verb. Lightfoot, in his Horæ Heb. Talmud, adds, "That he performed the duty of chaplain also, by saying grace, and pronouncing those benedictions which were accustomed to be given upon occasion of a marriage. He blessed the cup also prepared for the guests; and having first drank of it himself, sent it round to the company. In the Book of Ecclesiasticus (xxxii. 1) we have an account of his duties.

‡ 4. John xix. 26. ‡ 6. Mark vii. 3. ‡ 9. John iv. 46.

τιθησι, και ὁταν μεθυσθωσι, *[τοτε] τον
places; and when they may have drunk freely, [then] the
ελασσω· συ τετηρηκας τον καλον οινον ἑως αρτι.
worse; thou hast kept the good wine till now.
11 Ταυτην εποιησε την αρχην των σημειων ὁ
This did the beginning of the signs the
Ἰησους εν Κανα της Γαλιλαιας, και εφανερωσε
Jesus in Cana of the Galilee, and manifested
την δοξαν αὑτου· και επιστευσαν εις αυτον οἱ
the glory of himself; and believed into him the
μαθηται αυτου.
disciples of him.
12 Μετα τουτο κατεβη εις Καπερναουμ, αυτος
After this he went down into Capernaum, he
και ἡ μητηρ αυτου, και οἱ αδελφοι *[αυτου,] και
and the mother of him, and the brothers [of him,] and
οἱ μαθηται αυτου· και εκει εμειναν ου πολλας
the disciples of him; and there remained not many
ἡμερας. 13 Και εγγυς ην το πασχα των Ἰουδαι-
days. And nigh was the passover of the Jews,
ων, και ανεβη εις Ἱεροσολυμα ὁ Ἰησους. 14 Και
and went up to Jerusalem the Jesus. And
εὑρεν εν τῳ ἱερῳ τους πωλουντας βοας και προ-
he found in the temple those selling oxen and sheep
βατα και περιστερας, και τους κερματιστας
and doves, and the money-changers
καθημενους. 15 Και ποιησας φραγελλιον εκ
sitting. And having made a whip out of
σχοινιων, παντας εξεβαλεν εκ του ἱερου, τα
rushes, all he drove out of the temple, the
τε προβατα και τους βοας· και των κολλυβισ-
and sheep and the oxen; and of the money-chan-
των εξεχεε το κερμα, και τας τραπεζας ανεσ-
gers he poured out the coin, and the tables over-
τρεψε· 16 και τοις τας περιστερας πωλουσιν
turned; and to those the doves selling
ειπεν· Αρατε ταυτα εντευθεν· μη ποιειτε τον
he said: Take these hence; not make you the
οικον του πατρος μου οικον εμποριου. 17 Εμνησ-
house of the father of me a house of merchandise. Remem-
θησαν *[δε] οἱ μαθηται αυτου, ὁτι γεγραμμενον
bered [and] the disciples of him, that having been written
εστιν· "Ὁ ζηλος του οικου σου καταφαγεται
it is: "The zeal of the house of thee will consume
με." 18 Απεκριθησαν ουν οἱ Ἰουδαιοι και ειπον
me." Answered then the Jews and said
αυτῳ· Τι σημειον δεικνυεις ἡμιν, ὁτι ταυτα
to him; What sign showest thou to us, that these

have † drunk freely, the INFERIOR; but thou hast kept the GOOD Wine till now."

11 This * First of SIGNS JESUS performed in Cana of GALILEE, and displayed his GLORY; and his DISCIPLES believed into him.

12 After this he went down to Capernaum, he, and his MOTHER, and his BROTHERS, and his DISCIPLES; but they did not remain there Many Days.

13 ‡ And the PASSOVER of the JEWS was near, and JESUS went up to Jerusalem.

14 ‡ And he found the MONEY-CHANGERS sitting in the TEMPLE, and THOSE who SOLD Oxen, and Sheep, and Doves.

15 † And having made a Whip of Rushes, he drove them all out of the TEMPLE, with the SHEEP and the CATTLE, and he poured out the COIN of the BANKERS, and overturned the TABLES,

16 and said to THOSE who SOLD DOVES, "Take these things hence. Make not my FATHER'S HOUSE a House of Traffic."

17 And his DISCIPLES recollected That it is written, ‡ "My ZEAL for thy HOUSE consumes me."

18 Then the JEWS answered and said to him, ‡ "What Sign dost thou show us, why thou doest these things?"

* VATICAN MANUSCRIPT.—10. then—*omit.* 11. First of. 12. his—*omit.* 17. And—*omit.*

† 10. The Greek expression here does not imply the least degree of intoxication. The verbs *methusko* and *methuo*, from *methu*, wine, which, from *meta thuein*, to drink after sacrificing, signify not only to inebriate, but to take wine, to drink wine, to drink enough, and in this sense the verb is evidently used in the Septuagint. Gen. xliii. 34; Cant. v. 1; 1 Mac. xvi. 16; Ecclus. i. 16. And the prophet Isaiah, chap. lviii. 11, speaking of the abundant blessings of the godly compares them to a well-watered garden, which the LXX translate *os kepos methuon*, by which is certainly understood, not a garden drowned with water, but one sufficiently saturated with it, not having one drop too much, nor too little.—*Clarke.*
† 15. It is probable that this cleansing of the temple occurred at the commencement of our Lord's ministry, and is not to be confounded with *that* mentioned by the other evangelists, which took place at its close.

‡ 13. Exo. xii. 14; John v. 1; vi. 4; xi. 55. ‡ 14. Matt. xxi. 12; Mark xi. 15; Luke xix. 45.
‡ 17. Psa. lxix. 9. ‡ 18. Matt. xii. 38; John vi. 30.

ποιεις; 19 Απεκριθη ὁ Ιησους και ειπεν αυτοις·
thou doest? Answered the Jesus and said to them;
Λυσατε τον ναον τουτον, και εν τρισιν ἡμεραις
Destroy the temple this, and in three days
εγερω αυτον. 20 Ειπον ουν οἱ Ιουδαιοι· Τεσσα-
I will raise it. Said then the Jews; Forty
ρακοντα και ἑξ ετεσιν ᾡκοδομηθη ὁ ναος οὑτος·
and six years was being built the temple this;
και συ εν τρισιν ἡμεραις εγερεις αυτον, 21 Εκει-
and thou in three days wilt raise it? He
νος δε ελεγε περι του ναου του σωματος αὑτου.
but spoke concerning the temple of the body of himself.
22 Ὁτε ουν ηγερθη εκ νεκρων, εμνησθησαν οἱ
When therefore he was raised out of dead ones, remembered the
μαθηται αυτου, ὁτι τουτο ελεγε· και επιστευ-
disciples of him, that this he spoke; and they believed
σαν τη γραφη, και τῳ λογῳ ᾡ ειπεν ὁ
the writing, and the word which said the
Ιησους.
Jesus.

23 Ὡς δε ην εν τοις Ἱεροσολυμοις εν τῳ
When and was in the Jerusalem at the
πασχα εν τη ἑορτη, πολλοι επιστευσαν εις το
passover at the feast, many believed into the
ονομα αυτου, θεωρουντες αυτου τα σημεια ἁ
name of him, beholding of him the signs which
εποιει. 24 Αυτος δε ὁ Ιησους ουκ επιστευεν
he did. He but the Jesus not committed
εαυτον αυτοις, δια το αυτον γινωσκειν παντας·
himself to them, because the him to know all:
25 και ὁτι ου χρειαν ειχεν, ἱνα τις μαρτυρηση
and because not need he had, that any one should testify
περι του ανθρωπου· αυτος γαρ εγινωσκε, τι
concerning the man: he for knew, what
ην εν τῳ ανθρωπῳ.
was in the man.

ΚΕΦ. γ΄. 3.

1 Ην δε ανθρωπος εκ των Φαρισαιων, Νικοδη-
Was and a man of the Pharisees, Nicode-
μος ονομα αυτῳ, αρχων των Ιουδαιων· 2 οὑτος
mus a name to him, a ruler of the Jews: this
ηλθε προς αυτον νυκτος, και ειπεν αυτῳ· Ῥαβ-
came to him by night, and said to him: Rab-
βι, οιδαμεν, ὁτι απο θεου εληλυθας διδασκαλος·
bi, we know, that from God thou hast come a teacher:
ουδεις γαρ ταυτα τα σημεια δυναται ποιειν, ἁ
no one for these the signs is able to do, which
συ ποιεις, εαν μη ᾐ ὁ θεος μετ' αυτου.
thou doest, expect may be the God with him.
3 Απεκριθη ὁ Ιησους και ειπεν αυτῳ· †Αμην αμην
Answered the Jesus and said to him: Indeed indeed

19 *Jesus answered and said to them, ‡ "Destroy this TEMPLE, and in Three Days I will raise it."

20 Then the JEWS said, "Forty and Six Years has this TEMPLE been in building and wilt thou erect it in Three Days?"

21 But he spoke of the TEMPLE of his BODY.

22 When, therefore, he was raised from the Dead, ‡ his DISCIPLES remembered That he had said This; and they believed the SCRIPTURE, and the WORD which JESUS had spoken.

23 Now while he was in JERUSALEM at the FEAST of the PASSOVER, many believed into his NAME, beholding His SIGNS which he performed.

24 But * Jesus did not trust himself to them; because he KNEW them all,

25 and required not that any one should testify concerning MAN; for he knew what was in MAN.

CHAPTER III.

1 And there was a Man of the PHARISEES, whose name was Nicodemus, a Ruler of the JEWS;

2 He came to him by Night, and said to him, "Rabbi, we know That thou art a Teacher come from God; ‡for no one can work These SIGNS that thou workest, unless GOD be with him."

3 * Jesus answered and said to him, "Indeed I

---

* VATICAN MANUSCRIPT.—19. Jesus. 24. Jesus. 3. Jesus.

† 19. Or, *destroy this very* TEMPLE; perhaps pointing to his body at the same time. † 20. Herod began to rebuild the temple in the 18th year of his reign, or sixteen years before Jesus was born. Jesus was at this time about thirty years old, which makes the term exactly 46 years. But although Herod finished the main work in nine years and a half, yet Josephus tells us that the whole of the buildings were not completed till Nero's reign, some 80 years after the 18th of Herod's reign. † 3. The repetition of *Ameen*, among the Jewish writers, was considered of equal import with the most solemn oath—*Clarke.*

‡ 19. Matt. xxvi. 61; xxvii. 40; Mark xiv. 58; xv. 29, ‡ 22. Luke xxiv. 8. ‡ 2. John vii. 50; xix. 39. ‡ 2. John ix. 16, 33; Acts ii. 22; x. 38.

λεγω σοι, εαν μη τις γεννηθῃ ανωθεν, ου δυνα-
I say to thee, if not any one may be born from above, not is able
ται ιδειν την βασιλειαν του θεου. 4 Λεγει προς
to see the kingdom of the God. Says to
αυτον ὁ Νικοδημος· Πως δυναται ανθρωπος
him the Nicodemus; How is able a man
γεννηθηναι γερων ων; μη δυναται εις την κοι-
to be born old being? not is able into the womb
λιαν της μητρος αὑτου δευτερον εισελθειν, και
of the mother of himself a second time to enter, and
γεννηθηναι; 5 Απεκριθη Ιησους· Αμην αμην
to be born? Answered Jesus; Indeed indeed
λεγω σοι, εαν μη τις γεννηθῃ εξ ὑδατος και
I say to thee, if not any one may be born out of water and
πνευματος, ου δυναται εισελθειν εις την βασι-
spirit, not is able to enter into the king-
λειαν του θεου. 6 Το γεγεννημενον εκ της
dom of the God. That having been born out of the
σαρκος, σαρξ εστι· και το γεγεννημενον εκ της
flesh, flesh is; and that having been born out of the
πνευματος, πνευμα εστι. 7 Μη θαυμασῃς, ὁτι
spirit, a spirit is. Not thou mayest wonder, that
ειπον σοι· Δει ὑμας γεννηθηναι ανωθεν. 8 Το
I said to thee; Must you to be born from above. The
πνευμα ὁπου θελει πνει· και την φωνην αυτου
spirit where it wills breathes; and the sound of it
ακουεις, αλλ᾽ ουκ οιδας, ποθεν ερχεται, και
thou hearest, but not thou knowest, whence it comes, and
που ὑπαγει· οὑτως εστι πας ὁ γεγεννημενος εκ
where it goes: thus is every one the having been born out of
του πνευματος. 9 Απεκριθη Νικοδημος και ειπεν
of the spirit. Answered Nicodemus and said
αυτῳ· Πως δυναται ταυτα γενεσθαι; 10 Απεκ-
to him: How is able these to be? An-
ριθη Ιησους και ειπεν αυτῳ· Συ ει ὁ διδασκαλος
swered Jesus and said to him: Thou art the teacher
του Ισραηλ, και ταυτα ου γινωσκεις; 11 Αμην
of the Israel, and these not thou knowest? Indeed
αμην λεγω σοι, ὁτι ὁ οιδαμεν λαλουμεν, και ὁ
indeed I say to thee, that which we know we speak, and what
ἑωρακαμεν μαρτυρουμεν· και την μαρτυριαν
we have seen we testify; and the testimony
ἡμων ου λαμβανετε. 12 Ει τα επιγεια ειπον
of us not you receive. If the things earthly I told
ὑμιν, και ου πιστευετε· πως, εαν ειπω ὑμιν
you, and not you believe; how, if I tell you
τα επουρανια, πιστευσετε; 13 Και ουδεις
the things heavenly, will you believe? And no one
αναβεβηκεν εις τον ουρανον, ει μη ὁ εκ του
has ascended into the heaven, except he out of the
ουρανου καταβας, ὁ υιος του ανθρωπου, *[ὁ ων
heaven having descended, the son of the man, [he being
εν τῳ ουρανῳ.] 14 Και καθως Μωσης ὑψωσε τον
in the heaven.] And even as Moses raised aloft the
οφιν εν τῃ ερημῳ, οὑτως ὑψωθηναι δει τον
serpent in the desert, thus to be raised it behoves the
υἱον του ανθρωπου· 15 ἱνα πας ὁ πιστευων εις
son of the man: that every one who believing into

assure thee, if any one be not born from above, he cannot see the KINGDOM of GOD.

4 NICODEMUS says to him, "How can a Man be born, being old? Can he enter a second time into his MOTHER'S WOMB, and be born?"

5 Jesus replied, "Truly indeed I say to thee, if any one be not ‡ born of Water and Spirit, he cannot enter the KINGDOM of GOD.

6 THAT which has been BORN of the FLESH, is Flesh; and THAT which has been ‡ BORN of the SPIRIT, is Spirit.

7 Do not wonder, Because I said to thee, you must be born from above.

8 The SPIRIT breathes where it will, and thou hearest its VOICE, but thou knowest not whence it comes, or where it goes; thus it is with EVERY ONE who has been BORN of the SPIRIT."

9 Nicodemus answered and said to him, "How can these things be?"

10 JESUS answered and said to him, "Art thou the TEACHER of ISRAEL, and knowest not these things?

11 Most assuredly I tell thee, That what we know, we speak, ‡ and what we have seen, we testify; and you receive not our TESTIMONY.

12 If I told you of EARTHLY things, and you do not believe, how will you believe if I tell you of HEAVENLY things?

13 ‡ And no one has ascended into HEAVEN, except the SON of MAN who DESCENDED from HEAVEN.

14 ‡ And as Moses elevated the SERPENT in the DESERT, so must the SON of MAN be placed on high;

15 that EVERY ONE BE-

* VATICAN MANUSCRIPT.—13. he being in HEAVEN—omit.

‡ 5. Mark xvi. 16; Acts ii. 38. ‡ 6. 1 Cor. xv. 44—48. ‡ 11. Matt. xi. 27; John i. 18; vii. 16; viii. 28; xii. 49; xiv. 24. ‡ 13. John xvi. 28; Acts ii. 34; 1 Cor. xv. 47; Eph. iv. 9, 10. ‡ 14. Num. xxi. 9.

αυτον, *[μη αποληται, αλλ'] εχῃ ζωην αιω-
him, [not may be destroyed, but] may have life age-
νιον. 16 Οὑτω γαρ ηγαπησεν ὁ θεος τον κοσμον,
lasting. Thus for loved the God the world,
ὡστε τον υἱον αὑτου τον μονογενη εδωκεν, ἱνα
so that the son of himself the only-begotten he gave, that
πας ὁ πιστευων εις αυτον, μη αποληται, αλλ'
every one who believing into him, not may be destroyed, but
εχῃ ζωην αιωνιων. 17 Ου γαρ απεστειλεν ὁ
may have life age-lasting. Not for sent the
θεος τον υἱον αὑτου εις τον κοσμον, ἱνα κρινῃ
God the son of himself into the world, that he might judge
τον κοσμον, αλλ' ἱνα σωθῃ ὁ κοσμος δι'
the world, but that might be saved the world through
αυτου. 18 Ὁ πιστευων εις αυτον, ου κρινεται·
him. He believing into him, not is judged:
ὁ *[δε] μη πιστευων, ηδη κεκριται, ὁτι μη πε-
he [but] not believing, already is judged, because not he
πιστευκεν εις το ονομα του μονογενους υἱου του
has believed into the name of the only-begotten son of the
θεου. 19 Αυτη δε εστιν ἡ κρισις, ὁτι το φως
God. This and is the judgment, that the light
εληλυθεν εις τον κοσμον, και ηγαπησαν οἱ
has come into the world, and loved the
ανθρωποι μαλλον το σκοτος, η το φως· ην γαρ
men rather the darkness, than the light; was for
πονηρα αυτων τα εργα. 20 Πας γαρ ὁ φαυλα
evil of them the works. Every one for the vile things
πρασσων, μισει το φως, και ουκ ερχεται προς
doing, hates the light, and not comes to
το φως, ἱνα μη ελεγχθῃ τα εργα αυτου. 21 Ὁ
the light, that not may be detected the works of him. He
δε ποιων την αληθειαν, ερχεται προς το φως,
but doing the truth, comes to the light,
ἱνα φανερωθῃ αυτου τα εργα, ὁτι εν θεῳ
so that may be made manifest of him the works, that in God
εστιν ειργασμενα.
it is having been done.

22 Μετα ταυτα ηλθεν ὁ Ιησους και οἱ μαθηται
After these came the Jesus and the disciples
αυτου εις την Ιουδαιαν γην· και εκει διετριβε
of him into the Judean land; and there remained
μετ' αυτων, και εβαπτιζεν. 23 Ην δε και Ιωαν-
with them, and was dipping. Was and also John
νης βαπτιζων εν Αινων, εγγυς του Σαλειμ, ὁτι
dipping in Enon, near the Salim, because
ὑδατα πολλα ην εκει· και παρεγινοντο, και
waters many was there: and they were coming, and
εβαπτιζοντο. 24 Ουπω γαρ ην βεβλημενος εις
were being dipped. Not yet for was having been cast into
την φυλακην ὁ Ιωαννης. 25 Εγενετο ουν ζητη-
the prison the John. Occurred then a dis-
σις εκ των μαθητων Ιωαννου μετα Ιουδαιου περι
pute of the disciples of John with a Jew about
καθαρισμου. 26 Και ηλθον προς τον Ιωαννην,
cleansing. And they came to the John,

BELIEVING into him may
‡ have aionian Life.
16 ‡ For GOD so loved
the WORLD, that he gave
* his SON, the ONLY-BE-
GOTTEN, that EVERY ONE
BELIEVING into him may
not perish, but obtain aionian Life.
17 ‡ For GOD sent not
his SON into the WORLD
that he might judge the
WORLD, but that the
WORLD through him might
be saved.
18 ‡ HE BELIEVING into
him is not judged; but HE
not BELIEVING has been
judged already, Because
he has not believed into
the NAME of the ONLY-BE-
GOTTEN Son of GOD.
19 And this is the JUDG-
MENT, ‡ That the LIGHT
has come into the WORLD,
and MEN loved the DARK-
NESS rather than the
LIGHT; for Their WORKS
were evil.
20 For ‡ EVERY ONE who
does Vile things hates the
LIGHT, and comes not to
the LIGHT, that his WORKS
may not be detected.
21 But HE who DOES the
TRUTH comes to the LIGHT,
so that His WORKS may be
manifested That they have
been done in God.
22 After this, JESUS and
his DISCIPLES went into
the TERRITORY of JUDEA,
and there he remained with
them, and was immersing.
23 And * JOHN also was
immersing in Enon, near
SALIM, because there were
many Waters there; and
they were coming and be-
ing immersed.
24 ‡ For * John had not
yet been cast into PRISON.
25 A Dispute then oc-
curred among * the DISCI-
PLES of John with a Jew,
about Purification.
26 And they came to

* VATICAN MANUSCRIPT.—15. may not be destroyed, but—*omit*. 16. the SON. 18 but—*om*. 23. JOHN. 24. John. 25. THOSE DISCIPLES who were of John, and a Jew, about.

‡ 15. John vi. 47. ‡ 16. Rom. v. 8; 1 John iv. 9. ‡ 17. Luke ix. 56; John v. 45; viii. 15; xii. 47; 1 John iv. 14. ‡ 18. John v. 24; vi. 40, 47; xx. 31. ‡ 19. John i. 4, 9—11; viii. 12. ‡ 20. Eph. v. 13. ‡ 24. Matt. xiv. 3.

και ειπον αυτῳ· 'Ραββι, ὁς ην μετα σου περαν
and said to him; Rabbi, who was with thee beyond
του Ιορδανου, ᾡ συ μεμαρτυρηκας, ιδε, οὑτος
the Jordan, to whom thou hast testified, behold, he
βαπτιζει, και παντες ερχονται προς αυτον.
dips, and all come to him.
27 Απεκριθη Ιωαννης και ειπεν· Ου δυναται
Answered John and said; Not is able
ανθρωπος λαμβανειν ουδεν, εαν μη ᾑ δεδομε-
a man to receive nothing, except it may be having been
νον αυτῳ εκ του ουρανου. 28 Αυτοι ὑμεις μοι
given to him from the heaven. Yourselves you to me
μαρτυρειτε, ὁτι ειπον· Ουκ ειμι εγω ὁ Χριστος,
bear testimony, that I said; Not am I the Anointed,
αλλ' ὁτι απεσταλμενος ειμι εμπροσθεν εκεινου.
but that having been sent I am in presence of him.
29 'Ο εχων την νυμφην, νυμφιος εστιν· ὁ δε
He having the bride, a bridegroom is; the but
φιλος του νυμφιου, ὁ ἑστηκως και ακουων αυτου,
friend of the bridegroom, that standing and hearing him,
χαρᾳ χαιρει δια την φωνην του νυμφιου. Αὑτη
with joy rejoices through the voice of the bridegroom. This
ουν ἡ χαρα ἡ εμη πεπληρωται. 30 Εκεινον
therefore the joy that of me has been completed. Him
δει αυξανειν, εμε δε ελαττουσθαι. 31 'Ο
it behoves to increase, me but to decrease. He
ανωθεν ερχομενος, επανω παντων εστιν. 'Ο
from above coming, over all is. He
ων εκ της γης, εκ της γης εστι, και εκ της
being from the earth, from the earth is, and from the
γης λαλει· ὁ εκ του ουρανου ερχομενος, επανω
earth speaks; he from the heaven coming, over
παντων εστι, 32 *[και] ὁ ἑωρακε και ηκουσε,
all is, [and] what he has seen and heard,
τουτο μαρτυρει· και την μαρτυριαν αυτου ουδεις
this he testifies; and the testimony of him no one
λαμβανει. 33 'Ο λαβων αυτου την μαρτυριαν,
receives. He receiving of him the testimony,
εσφραγισεν, ὁτι ὁ θεος αληθης εστιν. 34 'Ον
has set his seal, that the God true is. Whom
γαρ απεστειλαν ὁ θεος, τα ῥηματα του θεου
for has sent the God, the words of the God
λαλει· ου γαρ εκ μετρου διδωσιν ὁ θεος το
speaks; not for by measure gives the God the
πνευμα. 35 'Ο πατηρ αγαπᾳ τον υἱον, και παν-
spirit. The father loves the son, and all
τα δεδωκεν εν τῃ χειρι αυτου. 36 'Ο πιστευων
has been given in the hand of him. He believing
εις τον υἱον, εχει ζωην αιωνιον· ὁ δε απειθων
into the son, has life age-lasting: he but disobeying
τῳ υἱῳ, ουκ οψεται ζωην αλλ' ἡ οργη του θεου
the son, not shall see life, but the anger of the God
μενει επ' αυτον.
abides on him.

JOHN, and said to him, "Rabbi, he who was with thee beyond the JORDAN, ‡to whom thou hast testified, behold, HE immerses, and all are coming to him."

27 John answered and said, ‡"A Man can receive nothing unless it be given him from HEAVEN.

28 You yourselves are witnesses for me, That I said, ‡'I am not the MESSIAH,' but That I have been sent before him.

29 The Bridegroom is HE who POSSESSES the BRIDE; but THAT FRIEND of the BRIDEGROOM who stands and hears him, rejoices with joy, because of the BRIDEGROOM'S VOICE; this, therefore, MY JOY has been completed.

30 He must increase, but I must decrease.

31 ‡HE who COMES from above is over all. HE who is from the EARTH, is of the EARTH, and speaks of the EARTH. HE who COMES from HEAVEN is over all.

32 And what he has seen and heard, this he testifies; and no one receives his TESTIMONY.

33 He who RECEIVES His TESTIMONY has set his seal That GOD is true.

34 ‡ For he whom GOD has sent speaks the WORDS of GOD; for *he gives not the SPIRIT by Measure.

35 The FATHER loves the SON, ‡ and has given All things into his HAND.

36 ‡HE BELIEVING into the SON has aionian Life; but HE DISOBEYING the SON, shall not see Life; but the Anger of GOD abides on him."

* VATICAN MANUSCRIPT.—32. And—omit. 34. he gives not.

‡ 26. John i. 7, 15, 27, 34. ‡ 27. 1 Cor. iv. 7; Heb. v. 4; James i. 17. ‡ 28. John i. 20, 27. ‡ 31. Matt. xxviii. 18; John i. 15, 27; Rom. ix. 5. ‡ 34 John viii. 16. ‡ 35. Luke x. 22; John v. 20, 22; xiii. 3; xvii. 2; Heb. ii. 8. ‡ 36. John vi. 47; 1 John v. 10, 11.

ΚΕΦ. δ'. 4.

1 Ὡς ουν εγνω ὁ κυριος, ὁτι ηκουσαν οἱ
When therefore knew the Lord, that heard the
Φαρισαιοι, ὁτι Ιησους πλειονας μαθητας ποιει
Pharisees, that Jesus more disciples made
και βαπτιζει, η Ιωαννης· 2 (καιτοιγε Ιησους
and dipped, than John; (though indeed Jesus
αυτος ουκ εβαπτιζεν, αλλ οἱ μαθηται αυτου·)
himself not dipped, but the disciples of him;)
3 αφηκε την Ιουδαιαν, και απηλθε παλιν εις
he left the Judea, and went again into
την Γαλιλαιαν. 4 Εδει δε αυτον διερχεσθαι δια
the Galilee. It behoved and him to pass through
της Σαμαρειας. 5 Ερχεται ουν εις πολιν της
the Samaria. He comes therefore into a city of the
Σαμαρειας, λεγομενην Συχαρ, πλησιον του
Samaritans, being called Sychar, near by the
χωριου, οὑ εδωκεν Ιακωβ Ιωσηφ τῳ υἱῳ
field, of which gave Jacob Joseph to the son
αὑτου. 6 Ην δε εκει πηγη του Ιακωβ. Ὁ ουν
of himself. Was and there a spring of the Jacob. The then
Ιησους κεκοπιακως εκ της ὁδοιποριας, εκαθεζετο
Jesus having become weary from the journey, sat down
οὑτως επι τῃ πηγῃ· ὡρα ην ὡσει ἑκτη.
thus over the spring: hour was about six.
7 Ερχεται γυνη εκ της Σαμαρειας, αντλησαι
Comes a woman of the Samaria, to draw
ὑδωρ. Λεγει αυτῃ ὁ Ιησους· Δος μοι πιειν.
water. Say to her the Jesus: Give to me to drink.
8 (Οἱ γαρ μαθηται αυτου απεληλυθεισαν εις την
(The for disciples of him had gone into the
πολιν, ἱνα τροφας αγορασωσι.) 9 Λεγει ουν
city, that provisions they might buy.) Says then
αυτῳ ἡ γυνη ἡ Σαμαρειτις· Πως συ, Ιουδαιος
to him the woman that Samaritan: How thou, a Jew
ων, παρ' εμου πιειν αιτεις, ουσης γυναικος
being, from me to drink askest, being a woman
Σαμαρειτιδος; (Ου γαρ συγχρωνται Ιουδαιοι
a Samaritan? (Not for associate with Jews
Σαμαρειταις.) 10 Απεκριθη Ιησους και ειπεν
Samaritans.) Answered Jesus and said
αυτῃ· Ει ηδεις την δωρεαν του θεου, και
to her: If thou hadst known the gift of the God, and
τις εστιν ὁ λεγων σοι· Δος μοι ποιειν· συ
who is he saying to thee: Give to me to drink: thou
αν ητησας αυτον, και εδωκεν αν σοι ὑδωρ ζων.
wouldst ask him, and he would give thee water living.
11 Λεγει αυτῳ ἡ γυνη· Κυριε, ουτε αντλημα
Says to him the woman: O lord, nothing to draw with

CHAPTER IV.

1 When, therefore, the LORD knew, That the PHARISEES had heard, ‡ That Jesus was making and immersing More Disciples than John;

2 (though Jesus himself did not immerse, but his DISCIPLES;)

3 he left JUDEA, and went again into GALILEE.

4 And it was necessary for him to pass through SAMARIA.

5 He comes, therefore, to a City of SAMARIA called † Sychar, near the FIELD which ‡ Jacob gave * to JOSEPH his SON.

6 And JACOB'S Fountain was there. JESUS, therefore, having become weary from the JOURNEY, sat down over the FOUNTAIN. It was about the † sixth Hour.

7 There comes a Woman of SAMARIA to draw Water. JESUS says to her, "Give me to drink."

8 (For his DISCIPLES had gone into the CITY, that they might buy Provisions.)

9 The SAMARITAN WOMAN, therefore, says to him, "How dost thou, being a Jew, ask drink of me, who am a Samaritan Woman?" (‡ For the Jews do not associate with Samaritans.)

10 Jesus answered and said to her, "If thou didst know the GIFT of GOD, and who is HE that says to thee, 'Give me to drink,' thou wouldst ask him, and he would give thee Living Water."

11 * She says to him, "Sir, thou hast nothing to

---

* VATICAN MANUSCRIPT.—5. to JOSEPH his SON. 11. She says.

† 5. Called at first Sichem, or Shechem, and afterwards Sichar. From Judges ix. 7, it seems to have been situated at the foot of Mount Gerizim, on which the Samaritan temple was built. † 6. According to John's computation of time, this would be six o'clock in the afternoon. See Note on John i. 39. The women of the East have stated times for going to draw water—not in the heat of the day, but in the cool of either morning or evening. It was very likely in the evening that this Samaritan woman came to draw water, because it is said, Jesus had become weary with his journey; and because the Samaritans when they came to see him, invited him to remain or lodge with them.

‡ 1. John iii. 22, 26. ‡ 5. Gen. xxxiii. 10; xlviii. 22; Joshua xxvi. 32. ‡ 9. 2 Kings xvii. 24; Luke ix. 52, 53; Acts x. 28.

εχεις, και το φρεαρ εστι βαθυ· ποθεν ουν εχεις
thou hast, and the well is deep: whence then hast thou
το ὑδωρ το ζων; [12] Μη συ μειζων ει του πατρος
the water the living? Not thou greater art the father
ἡμων Ιακωβ; ὁς εδωκεν ἡμιν το φρεαρ, και
of us Jacob? who gave to us the well, and
αυτος εξ αυτου επιε, και οἱ υἱοι αυτου, και τα
he of it drank, and the sons of him, and the
θρεμματα αυτου. [13] Απεκριθη Ιησους και ειπεν
cattle of him. Answered Jesus and said
αυτῃ· Πας ὁ πινων εκ του ὑδατος τουτου, διψη-
to her; All the drinking of the water this, will
σει παλιν· [14] ὁς δ' αν πιῃ εκ του ὑδατος, οὑ
thirst again; who but ever may drink of the water, of which
εγω δωσω αυτῳ, ου μη διψησῃ εις τον αιωνα·
I shall give to him, not not may thirst to the age;
αλλα το ὑδωρ, ὁ δωσω αυτῳ, γενησεται εν
but the water, which I shall give him, shall be in
αυτῳ πηγη ὑδατος ἁλλομενου εις ζωην αιωνιον.
him a well of water springing into life age-lasting.
[15] Λεγει προς αυτον ἡ γυνη· Κυριε, δος μοι
Says to him the woman; O lord, give to me
τουτο το ὑδωρ, ἱνα μη διψω, μηδε ερχωμαι εν-
this the water, that not I may thirst, nor may come to
θαδε αντλειν. [16] Λεγει αυτῃ ὁ Ιησους· Ὑπαγε,
this place to draw. Says to her the Jesus; Go,
φωνησον τον ανδρα σου, και ελθε ενθαδε.
call the husband of thee, and come here.
[17] Απεκριθη ἡ γυνη και ειπεν· Ουκ εχω ανδρα.
Answered the woman and said; Not I have a husband.
Λεγει αυτῃ ὁ Ιησους· Καλως ειπας· Ὁτι ανδρα
Says to her the Jesus; Rightly thou didst say: That a husband
ουκ εχω. [18] Πεντε γαρ ανδρας εσχες· και νυν
not I have. Five for husbands thou hast had; and now
ὁν εχεις, ουκ εστι σου ανηρ· τουτο αληθες
whom thou hast, not is of thee a husband: this truly
ειρηκας. [19] Λεγει αυτῳ ἡ γυνη· Κυριε, θεωρω,
thou hast said. Says to him the woman; O lord, I see,
ὁτι προφητης ει συ. [20] Οἱ πατερες ἡμων εν τῳ
that a prophet art thou. The fathers of us in the
ορει τουτῳ προσεκυνησαν· και ὑμεις λεγετε,
mountain this worshipped: and you say,
ὁτι εν Ἱεροσολυμοις εστιν ὁ τοπος, ὁπου δει
that in Jerusalem is the place, where it is necessary
προσκυνειν. [21] Λεγει αυτῃ ὁ Ιησους· Γυναι, πισ-
to worship. Says to her the Jesus: O woman, believe
τευσον μοι, ὁτι ερχεται ὡρα, ὁτε ουτε εν τῳ ορει
thou me, that comes an hour, when neither in the mountain
τουτῳ, ουτε εν Ιεροσολυμοις προσκυνησετε τῳ
this, nor in Jerusalem you shall worship the
πατρι. [22] Ὑμεις προσκυνειτε ὁ ουκ οιδατε·
father. You worship what not you know;
ἡμεις προσκυνουμεν ὁ οιδαμεν· ὁτι ἡ σωτηρια
we worship what we know: because the salvation
εκ των Ιουδαιων εστιν. [23] Αλλ' ερχεται ὡρα,
from the Jews is. But comes an hour,

draw with, and the WELL is deep; whence, then, hast thou the LIVING WATER.

12 Art thou greater than our FATHER Jacob, who gave us the WELL, and drank of it himself, and his SONS, and his CATTLE?"

13 Jesus answered and said to her, "EVERY ONE DRINKING of this WATER will thirst again;

14 but ‡he, who may drink of the WATER which I will give him, shall not thirst to the AGE; but the WATER which I will give him, shall become in him a Fountain of Water, springing up into aionian Life."

15 ‡ The WOMAN says to him, "Sir, give me This WATER that I may not thirst, nor * come here to draw."

16 * He says to her, "Go, call thy HUSBAND, and come here."

17 The WOMAN answered and said, "I have no Husband." JESUS said to her, "Correctly thou didst say, 'I have no Husband.'

18 For thou hast had Five Husbands, and he whom now thou hast is not Thy Husband; this thou hast truly spoken."

19 The WOMAN says to him, "Sir, ‡ I see That thou art a Prophet.

20 Our FATHERS worshipped in this MOUNTAIN; and you say, That in ‡Jerusalem is the PLACE where it is necessary to worship."

21 JESUS says to her, "Woman, believe me, That an Hour is coming, when neither in this MOUNTAIN, nor in Jerusalem, will you worship the FATHER.

22 You worship what you do not know; we worship what we know; because SALVATION is of the JEWS.

* VATICAN MANUSCRIPT.—15. come over here. 16. He says.

‡ 14. John vi. 35; vii. 38. ‡ 15. John xvii. 2, 3; Rom. vi. 23; 1 John v. 20. ‡ 19. Luke vii. 16; xxiv. 19; John vi. 14; vii. 40. ‡ 20. Deut. xii. 5, 11; 1 Kings ix. 3; 2 Chron. vii. 12

και νυν εστιν, ὁτε οἱ αληθινοι προσκυνηται
and now is, when the true worshippers
προσκυνησουσι τῳ πατρι εν πνευματι και αλη-
shall worship the father in spirit and truth;
θειᾳ· και γαρ ὁ πατηρ τοιουτους ζητει τους
even for the father such like seeks those
προσκυνουντας αυτον. 24 Πνευμα ὁ θεος· και
worshipping him. A spirit the God: and
τους προσκυνουντας αυτον, εν πνευματι και
those worshipping him, in spirit and
αληθειᾳ δει προσκυνειν. 25 Λεγει αυτῳ ἡ
truth it behoves to worship. Says to him the
γυνη· Οιδα, ὁτι Μεσσιας ερχεται· (ὁ λεγομε-
woman: I know, that Messiah comes: (he being called
νος Χριστος·) ὁταν ελθῃ εκεινος, αναγγελει
Anointed:) when may come he, he will relate
ἡμιν παντα. 26 Λεγει αυτῃ ὁ Ιησους· Εγω ειμι,
to us all. Says to her the Jesus: I am,
ὁ λαλων σοι. 27 Και επι τουτῳ ηλθον οἱ μαθη-
he talking to thee. And on this came the disci-
ται αυτου, και εθαυμαζον, ὁτι μετα γυναικος
ples of him, and wondered, that with a woman
ελαλει. Ουδεις μεντοι ειπε· Τι ζητεις; η, τι
he talked. No one nevertheless said; What seekest thou; or, why
λαλεις μετ' αυτης; 28 Αφηκεν ουν την ὑδριαν
talkest thou with her? Left therefore the bucket
αὑτης ἡ γυνη, και απηλθεν εις την πολιν, και
of herself the woman, and went into the city, and
λεγει τοις ανθρωποις· 29 Δευτε, ιδετε ανθρωπον,
says to the men: Come you, see a man,
ὁς ειπε μοι παντα ὁσα εποιησα· μητι οὑτος
who told me all what I did: not this
εστιν ὁ Χριστος; 30 Εξηλθον εκ της πολεως,
is the Anointed? They went out of the city,
και ηρχοντο προς αυτον.
and were coming to him.

31 Εν δε τῳ μεταξυ ηρωτων αυτον οἱ μαθηται
In and the meantime were asking him the disciples
λεγοντες· Ῥαββι, φαγε. 32 Ὁ δε ειπεν αυτοις·
saying; Rabbi, eat. He but said to them;
Εγω βρωσιν εχω φαγειν, ἡν ὑμεις ουκ οιδατε.
I food have to eat, which you not know.
33 Ελεγον ουν οἱ μαθηται προς αλληλους· Μη
Said then the disciples to each other; Not
τις ηνεγκεν αυτῳ φαγειν; 34 Λεγει αυτοις ὁ
any one brought to him food? Says to them the
Ιησους. Εμον βρωμα εστιν, ἱνα ποιω το
Jesus. My food is, that I may do the
θελημα του πεμψαντος με, και τελειωσω αυτου
will of the sending me, and may finish of him
το εργον. 35 Ουχ ὑμεις λεγετε, ὁτι ετι τετρα-
the work. Not you say, that yet four
μηνος εστι, και ὁ θερισμος ερχεται; Ιδου, λεγω
months it is, and the harvest comes? Lo, I say
ὑμιν, επαρατε τους οφθαλμους ὑμων, και θεα-
to you, lift up the eyes of you, and see

23 But an Hour is coming, and now is, when the TRUE Worshippers will worship the FATHER ‡in Spirit and Truth; for the FATHER even seeks SUCH LIKE as his Worshippers.

24 ‡ God is Spirit; and THOSE WORSHIPPING him must worship in Spirit and Truth."

25 The WOMAN says to him, "I know That Messiah is coming, (HE being CALLED Christ;) when he comes he will tell us all things."

26 JESUS says to her, ‡"I, who am TALKING to thee, am he."

27 And upon this his DISCIPLES came, and wondered That he was talking with a Woman; nevertheless no one said, "What dost thou seek?" or, "Why art thou talking with her?"

28 The WOMAN, therefore, left her PITCHER, and and went into the CITY, and says to the MEN,

29 "Come, see a Man, who told me all things which I have done! Is this the MESSIAH?"

30 They went out of the CITY, and were coming to him.

31 And in the MEANTIME, his DISCIPLES entreating him, said, "Rabbi, eat."

32 But he said to them, "I have Food to eat, of which you know not."

33 Then the DISCIPLES said to each other, "Has any one brought him (food) to eat?"

34 JESUS says to them, ‡"My Food is to do the WILL of HIM who SENT me, and to finish HIS WORK.

35 Do you not say, That it is yet four Months, and the HARVEST comes? Behold, I say to you, Lift up your EYES, and see the

‡ 23. Phil. iii. 3. ‡ 24. 2 Cor. iii. 17. ‡ 26. John ix. 37. ‡ 34. Job xxiii. 12; John vi. 38; xvii. 4; xix. 30.

σασθε τας χωρας, ὁτι λευκαι εισι προς θερισμον
you the fields, that white they are to harvest
ηδη. 36 Ὁ θεριζων μισθον λαμβανει, και συνα-
already. He reaping a reward receives, and gathers
γει καρπον εις ζωην αιωνιον· ἱνα και ὁ σπειρων
fruit for life age-lasting, so that both he sowing
ὁμου χαιρῃ, και ὁ θεριζων. 37 Εν γαρ τουτῳ ὁ
together may rejoice, and he reaping. In for this the
λογος εστιν ὁ αληθινος, ὁτι αλλος εστιν ὁ
word is the true, that one is he
σπειρων, και αλλος ὁ θεριζων. 38 Εγω απεσ-
sowing, and another he reaping. I sent
τειλα ὑμας θεριζειν ὁ ουχ ὑμεις κεκοπιακατε·
you to reap what not you have labored:
αλλοι κεκοπιακασι, και ὑμεις εις τον κοπον
others labored, and you into the labor
αυτων εισεληλυθατε. 39 Εκ δε της πολεως
of them are entered. Out of and the city
εκεινης πολλοι επιστευσαν εις αυτον των Σαμα-
that many believed into him of the Sama-
ρειτων, δια τον λογον της γυναικος, μαρτυ-
ritans, through the word of the woman, testi-
ρουσης· Ὁτι ειπε μοι παντα ὁσα εποιησα.
fying: That he told me all what I did.
40 *[Ὡς] ουν ηλθον προς αυτον οἱ Σαμαρειται,
[When] therefore came to him the Samaritans,
ηρωτων αυτον μειναι παρ' αυτοις· και εμεινεν
asking him to abide with them; and he abode
εκει δυο ἡμερας. 41 Και πολλῳ πλειους επιστευ-
there two days. And many more believed
σαν δια τον λογον αυτου. 42 Τῃ τε γυναικι
through the word of him. To the and woman
ελεγον· Ὁτι ουκετι δια την σην λαλιαν
they said; That no longer through the thy saying
πιστευομεν· αυτοι γαρ ακηκοαμεν, και οιδαμεν,
we believe; ourselves for we have heard, and we know,
ὁτι οὑτος εστιν αληθως ὁ σωτηρ του κοσμου
that this is truly the savior of the world
*[ὁ Χριστος.]
[the Anointed.]
43 Μετα δε τας δυο ἡμερας εξηλθεν εκειθεν,
After and the two days he went out thence.
*[και απηλθεν] εις την Γαλιλαιαν. 44 Αυτος
[and went out] into the Galilee. Himself
γαρ Ιησους εμαρτυρησεν, ὁτι προφητης εν τῃ
for Jesus testified, that a prophet in the
ιδιᾳ πατριδι τιμην ουκ εχει. 45 Ὁτε ουν ηλθεν
own country honor not has. When therefore he came
εις την Γαλιλαιαν, εδεξαντο αυτον οἱ Γαλιλαιοι,
into the Galilee, received him the Galileans,

FIELDS; ‡That they are already white for Harvest.

36 ‡ The REAPER receives a Reward, and gathers Fruit for aionian Life; so that the SOWER and the REAPER may rejoice together.

37 For in this is the SAYING TRUE; 'That one is the SOWER, and another is the REAPER.'

38 I sent you to reap that on which you have not labored; others labored, and you have entered into their LABOR."

39 Now many of the SAMARITANS from that CITY believed into him, because of the WORD of the WOMAN, testifying, "He told me all things which I have done."

40 * Then came the SAMARITANS to him, and asked him to remain with them: and he remained there Two Days.

41 And many more believed on account of his WORD;

42 and said to the WOMAN, "We no longer believe because of * THY Report; for we ourselves have heard; and we know That this is truly the SAVIOR of the WORLD."

43 Now after the TWO Days, he went from thence into GALILEE.†

44 For ‡ JESUS himself testified, That a Prophet has no Honor in his OWN Country.

45 When, therefore, he came into GALILEE, the GALILEANS received him,

* VATICAN MANUSCRIPT.—40. When—*omit.* 40. Then came the SAMARITANS to him, and asked him. 42. thy REPORT. 43. the ANOINTED—*omit.* 43. and went—*omit.*

† 43. Pearce thinks that some words have been lost from the end of this verse, which may be supplied thus: "Went into Galilee, but not to Nazareth; for Jesus himself had declared," etc. In Matt. xiii. 57; Mark vi. 4; and Luke iv. 24, which are the only texts where Jesus is said to have declared this, he spoke of Nazareth only, and not Galilee in general, a country where he lived for the most part, and wrought the greatest number of his miracles, and made the most converts.—*Clarke.* There is a probability that something to this purpose has been very early omitted in transcribing. The casual conjunction *gar*, for, which introduces the next verse, shows that it contains the reason of what had immediately preceded.—*Camp.*

‡ 35. Matt. ix. 37; Luke x. 2. ‡ 36. Dan xii. 3. ‡ 44. Matt. xiii. 57; Mark vi. 4; Luke iv. 24.

παντα ἑωρακοτες ἁ εποιησεν εν Ἱεροσολυμοις
all having seen what he did in Jerusalem
εν τῃ ἑορτῃ· και αυτοι γαρ ηλθον εις την ἑορ-
at the feast; also themselves for came to the feast.
την. 46 Ηλθεν ουν παλιν εις την Κανα της
He came then again into the Cana of the
Γαλιλαιας, ὁπου εποιησε το ὑδωρ οινον. Και
Galilee, where he made the water wine. And
ην τις βασιλικος, οὑ ὁ υἱος ησθενει, εν Κα-
was certain courtier, of whom the son was sick, in Ca-
περναουμ. 47 Οὑτος ακουσας ὁτι Ιησους ἡκει
pernaum. This hearing that Jesus was come
εκ της Ιουδαιας εις την Γαλιλαιαν, απηλθε
out of the Judea into the Galilee, went
προς αυτον, και ηρωτα αυτον, ἱνα καταβῃ,
to him, and was asking him, that he would come down
και ιασηται αυτου τον υἱον· ημελλε γαρ απο-
and heal of him the son; he was about for to
θνησκειν. 48 Ειπεν ουν ὁ Ιησους προς αυτον·
die. Said therefore the Jesus to him;
Εαν μη σημεια και τερατα ιδητε, ου μη πιστευ-
If not signs and prodigies you may see, not not you may
σητε. 49 Λεγει προς αυτον ὁ βασιλικος· Κυριε,
believe. Says to him the courtier: O sir,
καταβηθι, πριν αποθανειν το παιδιον μου.
come down, before to die the child of me.
50 Λεγει αυτῳ ὁ Ιησους· Πορευου· ὁ υἱος σου
Says to him the Jesus: Go: the son of thee
ζῃ. *[Και] επιστευσεν ὁ ανθρωπος τῳ λογῳ
lives. [And] believed the man the word
ᾡ ειπεν αυτῳ Ιησους, και επορευετο. 51 Ηδη
which said to him Jesus, and went. Already
δε αυτου καταβαινοντος, οἱ δουλοι αυτου απην-
and of him was going down, the slaves of him met
τησαν αυτῳ, *[και απηγγειλαν,] λεγοντες·
him, [and reported,] saying;
Ὁτι ὁ παις σου ζῃ. 52 Επυθετο ουν *[παρ'
That the child of thee lives. He inquired then [of
αυτων] την ὡραν, εν ᾗ κομψοτερον εσχε.
them] the hour, in which better he was.
Και ειπον αυτῳ· Ὁτι χθες ὡραν ἑβδομην αφη-
And they said to him; That yesterday hour seventh left
κεν αυτον ὁ πυρετος. 53 Εγνω ουν ὁ πατηρ,
him the fever. Knew then the father,
ὁτι εν εκεινῃ τῃ ὡρᾳ, εν ᾗ ειπεν αυτῳ ὁ Ιη-
that in that the hour, in which said to him the Je-
σους· Ὁτι ὁ υἱος σου ζῃ. Και επιστευσεν
sus: That the son of thee lives. And he believed
αυτος, και ἡ οικια αυτου ὁλη. 54 Τουτο παλιν
himself, and the house of him all. This again
δευτερον σημειον εποιησεν ὁ Ιησους, ελθων εκ
a second sign did the Jesus, having come out of
της Ιουδαιας εις την Γαλιλαιαν.
the Judea into the Galilee.

‡ having seen All that he did in Jerusalem, at the FEAST, for they also went to the FEAST.

46 * Then he came again towards Cana of GALILEE, ‡ where he made WATER Wine. And there was a Certain Courtier, Whose SON was sick in Capernaum.

47 He, having heard That Jesus was come out of JUDEA into GALILEE, went to him, and asked him, that he would come down and cure His SON: for he was about to die.

48 JESUS, therefore, said to him, ‡ "If you see not Signs and Prodigies, you will not believe."

49 The COURTIER says to him, "Sir, come down, before my CHILD die."

50 JESUS says to him, "Go, thy SON lives." The MAN believed the WORD which JESUS said to him, and went.

51 And now as he was going down, his SERVANTS met him, saying, * "Thy CHILD lives."

52 He then inquired * that HOUR in which he grew better. * And they said to him, "Yesterday, at the † seventh Hour, the FEVER left him."

53 The FATHER, therefore, knew That it was in That HOUR in which JESUS said to him, "Thy SON lives." And He believed and all his HOUSE.

54 * This again, a Second Sign, did JESUS, having come out of JUDEA into GALILEE.

* VATICAN MANUSCRIPT.—46. Then he came again towards Cana. 50. And—*omit.* 51. and reported—*omit.* 51. That his son lives. 52. of them—*omit.* 52. that HOUR. 53. Then said they to him. 54. And this again is the Second Sign.

† 52. According to John's computation of time this would be seven o'clock in the evening. Macknight thinks the Roman hour is intended, i. e. seven in the evening; and this he thinks is the reason why our Lord did not accompany the courtier: for as Cana was a day's journey from Capernaum, had our Lord gone at *that hour*, he must have traveled in the *night*, from which it might have been inferred, that he could not cure the child without being personally present. *Harmony*, vol. i. p. 52.

‡ 45. John ii. 23; iii 2. ‡ 46. John ii. 1, 11. ‡ 48. 1 Cor. i. 22.

ΚΕΦ. ε'. 5.

1 Μετα ταυτα ην ἑορτη των Ιουδαιων, και
After these things was a feast of the Jews, and
ανεβη ὁ Ιησους εις Ἱεροσολυμα. 2 Εστι δε εν
went up the Jesus to Jerusalem. Is now in
τοις Ἱεροσολυμοις, επι τη προβατικη, κολυμ-
the Jerusalem, by the sheep-gate, a swimming-
βηθρα, ἡ επιλεγομενη Ἑβραιστι Βηθεσδα, πεντε
bath, that being called in Hebrew Bethesda, five
στοας εχουσα. 3 Εν ταυταις κατεκειτο πληθος
porches having. In these were lying a multitude
*[πολυ] των ασθενουντων, τυφλων, χωλων,
[great] of those being sick, blind, lame,
ξηρων *[εκδεχομενων την του ὑδατος κινησιν.
withered waiting the of the water moving.
4 Αγγελος γαρ κατα καιρον κατεβαινεν εν τη
A messenger for at a season went down in the
κολυμβηθρα, και εταρασσε το ὑδωρ· ὁ ουν πρω-
swimming-bath, and agitated the water; he then first
τος εμβας μετα την ταραχην του ὑδατος, ὑγιης
stepping in after the agitation of the water, sound
εγινετο, ᾡ δηποτε κατειχετο νοσηματι.]
became, who indeed was held by disease.]
5 Ην δε τις ανθρωπος εκει, τριακοντα και οκτω
Was and a certain man there, thirty and eight
ετη εχων εν τη ασθενεια. 6 Τουτον ιδων ὁ
years being in the feeble health. This seeing the
Ιησους κατακειμενον, και γνους ὁτι πολυν ηδη
Jesus lying, and knowing that long already
χρονον εχει, λεγει αυτῳ· Θελεις ὑγιης γενεσ-
time he had been, he says to him; Dost thou wish sound to be-
θαι; 7 Απεκριθη αυτῳ ὁ ασθενων· Κυριε, ανθρω-
come? Answered him he sick being; O sir, a man
πον ουκ εχω, ἱνα, ὁταν ταραχθη το ὑδωρ,
not I have, that, when may be agitated the water,
βαλη με εις την κολυμβηθραν· εν ᾡ δε
he may put me into the swimming-bath; in which but
ερχομαι εγω, αλλος προ εμου καταβαινει.
am coming I, another before me goes down.
8 Λεγει αυτῳ ὁ Ιησους· Εγειραι, αρον τον κραβ-
Says to him the Jesus: Rise, take up the bed
βατον σου, και περιπατει. 9 Και ευθεως εγε-
of thee, and walk. And immediately be-
νετο ὑγιης ὁ ανθρωπος, και ηρε τον κραββατον
came sound the man, and took up the bed
αὑτου, και περιεπατει. Ην δε σαββατον εν
of himself, and walked. It was and a sabbath in
εκεινη τη ἡμερα. 10 Ελεγον ουν οἱ Ιουδαιοι τῳ
that the day. Said then the Jews to the
τεθεραπευμενῳ· Σαββατον εστιν· ουκ εξεστι
having been healed: A sabbath it is; not it is lawful
σοι αραι τον κραββατον. 11 Απεκριθη αυτοις·
for thee to carry the bed. He answered them:

CHAPTER V.

1 After these things there was ‡ a Feast of the JEWS; and * Jesus went up to Jerusalem.

2 Now there is in JERUSALEM ‡ near the SHEEP-GATE, a Bath, which is CALLED in Hebrew, *† Bethesda, having Five covered Walks.

3 In these were lying a Multitude of the SICK,—Blind, Lame, Withered,—*† [waiting the MOTION of the WATER.

4 For a Messenger at times went down into the BATH, and agitated the WATER; the FIRST, therefore, stepping in after the AGITATION of the WATER, was cured of Whatever Disease he was held.]

5 Now a certain Man was there, having been Thirty-eight Years in FEEBLE HEATH.

6 JESUS seeing him lying, and knowing That he had now been thus a Long Time, says to him, "Dost thou wish to become well?"

7 The SICK person answered him, "Sir, I have no Man, that, when the WATER is agitated, he may put me into the BATH; but while I am coming, another goes down before me."

8 JESUS says to him, ‡ "Rise, take up thy COUCH, and walk."

9 And immediately the MAN became well, and took up his COUCH, and walked. ‡ Now That DAY was a Sabbath.

10 The JEWS, therefore, said to HIM who had been CURED, "It is a Sabbath; ‡ it is not lawful for thee to carry the COUCH."

* VATICAN MANUSCRIPT.—1. Jesus. 2. Bethsaida. 3. great—*omit.* 3, 4—*omit.*

† 2. Bethesda, signifies *the house of mercy.* † 3, 4. This clause is without doubt the addition of some transcriber. Five of the most ancient MSS., either reject the whole or the principal part of the clause in brackets. Bloomfield says, "the whole narration savors of Jewish fancy." Meyer calls it *a legendary addition.* It is omitted by Mill and Tischendorf, and marked as spurious by Griesbach.

‡ 1. Lev. xxiii. 2; Deut. xvi. 1; John ii. 13. ‡ 2. Neh. iii. 1; xii. 39. ‡ 8. Matt. ix. 6; Mark ii. 11; Luke v. 24. ‡ 9. John ix. 14. ‡ 10. Exod. xx. 10; Neh. xiii. 19; Jer. xvii. 21; Matt. xii. 2; Mark ii. 24; iii. 4; Luke vi. 2; xiii. 14.

῾Ο ποιησας με ὑγιη, εκεινος μοι ειπεν· Αρον τον
He having made me sound, he to me said; Take up the
κραββατον σου, και περιπατει. 12 Ηρωτησαν
bed of thee, and walk. They asked
*[ουν] αυτον· Τις εστιν ὁ ανθρωπος, ὁ ειπων
[then] him; Who is the man, he saying
σοι· Αρον τον κραββατον σου, και περιπατει;
to thee; Take up the bed of thee, and walk?
13 ῾Ο δε ιαθεις ουκ ηδει τις εστιν· ὁ γαρ
He but having been cured not knew who it is; the for
Ιησους εξενευσεν, οχλου οντος εν τῳ τοπῳ.
Jesus slipped out, a crowd being in the place.
14 Μετα ταυτα εὑρισκει αυτον ὁ Ιησους εν τῳ
After these finds him the Jesus in the
ἱερῳ, και ειπεν αυτῳ· Ιδε, ὑγιης γεγονας· μη-
temple, and said to him; See, sound thou hast become: no
κετι ἁμαρτανε, ἱνα μη χειρον σοι τι γενηται.
longer do thou sin, that no worse to thee anything may happen.
15 Απηλθεν ὁ ανθρωπος, και ανηγγειλε τοις
Went away the man, and told to the
Ιουδαιοις, ὁτι Ιησους εστιν, ὁ ποιησας αυτον
Jews, that Jesus it is, he having made him
ὑγιη. 16 Και δια τουτο εδιωκον τον Ιησουν οἱ
sound. And through this persecuted the Jesus the
Ιουδαιοι, ὁτι ταυτα εποιει εν σαββατῳ. 17 ῾Ο
Jews, because these he did in a sabbath. The
δε Ιησους απεκρινατο αυτοις· ῾Ο πατηρ μου
and Jesus answered them: The father of me
ἑως αρτι εργαζεται, καγω εργαζομαι. 18 Δια
till now works, and I work. Through
τουτο ουν μαλλον εζητουν αυτον οἱ Ιουδαιοι
this therefore more sought him the Jews
αποκτειναι, ὁτι ου μονον ελυε το σαββα-
to kill, because not only he was breaking the sabbath
τον, αλλα και πατερα ιδιον ελεγε τον θεον,
but also a father his own said the God.
ισον ἑαυτον ποιων τῳ θεῳ. 19 Απεκρινατο ουν
equal himself making to the God. Answered then
ὁ Ιησους και ειπεν αυτοις· Αμην αμην λεγω
the Jesus and said to them: Indeed indeed I say
ὑμιν, ου δυναται ὁ υἱος ποιειν αφ' ἑαυτου ουδεν,
to you, not is able the son to do of himself nothing,
εαν μη τι βλεπῃ τον πατερα ποιουντα· ἁ
if not anything he may see the father doing: what
γαρ αν εκεινος ποιῃ, ταυτα και ὁ υἱος ὁμοιως
for ever he may do, these also the son in like manner
ποιει· 20 ῾Ο γαρ πατηρ φιλει τον υἱον, και παν-
does: The for father loves the son, and all
τα δεικνυσιν αυτῳ, ἁ αυτος ποιει· και μειζονα
shows to him, what he does: and greater
τουτων δειξει αυτῳ εργα, ἱνα ὑμεις θαυμαζητε.
of these shows to him works, so that you may wonder.
21 ῾Ωσπερ γαρ ὁ πατηρ εγειρει τους νεκρους και
As for the father raises the dead ones and

11 *But he answered
them, "HE who MADE me
well, he said to me, Take
up thy COUCH, and walk."
12 They asked him,
"Who is the MAN THAT
SAID to thee, *"Take up
thy COUCH, and walk?"
13 But HE who had been
CURED knew not who it
was; for JESUS withdrew,
a Crowd being in the
PLACE.
14 After these things,
*Jesus finds him in the
TEMPLE, and said to him,
"Behold, thou hast become
well; ‡sin no more, lest
something worse may hap-
pen to thee."
15 The MAN went away,
and told the Jews That
Jesus was HE who MADE
him well.
16 And on account of
this the JEWS persecuted
JESUS, because he did
These things on a Sabbath.
17 But *HE answered
and said, ‡"My FATHER
works till now, and I
work."
18 For this, then, the
JEWS ‡sought the more to
kill him, because not only
was he breaking the SAB-
BATH, ‡but he also said,
that GOD was his own Fa-
ther, making himself equal
with GOD."
19 Then *he answered
and said, "Indeed, I as-
sure you, The SON can do
nothing of himself, except
what he may see the FA-
THER doing, for whatever
he does, these things also
does the SON in like man-
ner.
20 For ‡the FATHER
loves the SON, and show
him All what he himse
does; and Greater Works
than these will he s!.o
him, that you may wonder.
21 For as the FATHER
raises up and makes alive
the DEAD, ‡so also the

* VATICAN MANUSCRIPT.—11. But he. 12. Then—*omit.* 12. Take up, and.
14. Jesus. 17. HE answered and said, My FATHER. 19. he answered and said.

‡ 14. Matt. xii. 45; John viii. 11. ‡ 17. John ix. 4; xiv. 10. ‡ 18. John vii. 19
‡ 18. John x. 30, 33; Phil. ii. 6. ‡ 20. Matt. iii. 17; John iii. 35; 2 Pet. i. 17. ‡ 21. Luke
vii. 14; viii. 54; John xi. 25, 43.

ζωοποιει· οὑτω και ὁ υἱος, οὑς θελει, ζωοποιει.
makes alive: thus also the son, whom he will, makes alive.
22 Ουδε γαρ ὁ πατηρ κρινει ουδενα· αλλα την
Not even for the father judges any one; but the
κρισιν πασαν δεδωκε τῳ υἱῳ· 23 ἱνα παντες
judgment all has given to the son; so that all
τιμωσι τον υἱον, καθως τιμωσι τον πατερα. Ὁ
may honor the son, even as they honor the father. He
μη τιμων τον υἱον. ου τιμᾳ τον πατερα, τον
not honoring the son, not honors the father, that
πεμψαντα αυτον. 24 Αμην αμην λεγω ὑμιν, ὁτι
having sent him. Indeed indeed I say to you, that
ὁ τον λογον μου ακουων, και πιστευων, τῳ
he the word of me hearing, and believing, the
πεμψαντι με εχει ζωην αιωνιον, και εις κρισιν
having sent me has life age-lasting, and into judgment
ουκ ερχεται, αλλα μεταβεβηκεν εκ του θανα-
not comes, but has passed out of the death
του εις την ζωην. 25 Αμην αμην λεγω ὑμιν,
into the life. Indeed indeed I say to you,
ὁτι ερχεται ὡρα, και νυν εστιν, ὁτε οἱ νεκροι
that comes an hour, and now is, when the dead ones
ακουσονται της φωνης του υἱου του θεου· και
shall hear the voice of the son of the God; and
οἱ ακουσαντες ζησονται. 26 Ὡσπερ γαρ ὁ πα-
those having heard will live. As for the fa-
τηρ εχει ζωην εν ἑαυτῳ· οὑτως εδωκε και τῳ
ther has life in himself; so he gave also to the
υἱῳ ζωην εχειν εν ἑαυτῳ. 27 Και εξουσιαν εδω-
son life to have in himself. And authority he
κεν αυτῳ και κρισιν ποιειν, ὁτι υἱος ανθρωπου
gave to him also judgment to execute, because a son of man
εστι. 28 Μη θαυμαζετε τουτο· ὁτι ερχεται ὡρα,
he is. Not wonder you this: because comes an hour,
εν ᾗ παντες οἱ εν τοις μνημειοις ακουσονται
in which all those in the tombs shall hear
της φωνης αυτου, 29 και εκπορευσονται, οἱ τα
the voice of him, and shall come forth, those the
αγαθα ποιησαντες, εις αναστασιν ζωης· οἱ
good things having done, to a resurrection of life; those
*[δε] τα φαυλα πραξαντες, εις αναστασιν κρι-
[and] the evil things having done, to a resurrection of
σεως. 30 Ου δυναμαι εγω ποιειν απ' εμαυτου
judgment. Not am able I to do of myself
ουδεν. Καθως ακουω, κρινω, και ἡ κρισις ἡ
nothing. Even as I hear, I judge, and the judgment the
εμη δικαια εστιν· ὁτι ου ζητω το θελημα το
mine just is; that not I seek the will the
εμον, αλλα το θελημα του πεμψαντος με.
mine, but the will of the sending me.
31 Εαν εγω μαρτυρω περι εμαυτου, ἡ μαρτυρια
If I testify concerning myself, the testimony
μου ουκ εστιν αληθης. 32 Αλλος εστιν ὁ μαρ-
of me not is true. Another is he testi-
τυρων περι εμου· και οιδα, ὁτι αληθης εστιν
fying concerning me; and I know, that true is

SON makes alive Whom he pleases.

22 For the FATHER does not even judge any one, but ‡ has given all JUDGMENT to the SON;

23 so that all may honor the SON, even as they honor the FATHER. ‡ HE who HONORS not the SON honors not THAT FATHER who sent him.

24 Indeed, I truly say to you, HE who HEARS my WORD, and believes HIM who SENT me, has aionian Life, and comes not into Judgment, but has passed out of DEATH into LIFE.

25 Indeed, I assure you, That an Hour comes, and now is, when the DEAD will hear the VOICE of the SON of GOD, and THOSE HAVING HEARD will live.

26 For as the FATHER has Life in himself, so he gave also to the SON to have Life in himself;

27 and he gave him Authority also to execute Judgment, Because he is a Son of Man.

28 Wonder not at this; Because an Hour comes in which ALL those in the TOMBS will hear his VOICE,

29 and will come forth; ‡ THOSE HAVING DONE GOOD things, to a Resurrection of Life; and THOSE HAVING DONE EVIL things, to a Resurrection of Judgment.

30 ‡ I am not able to do anything of myself; as I hear, I judge; and MY JUDGMENT is just, Because I seek not ‡ MY WILL, but the will of HIM SENDING me.

31 ‡ Though I testify concerning myself, † is not my TESTIMONY true?

32 There is ANOTHER who testifies concerning me; and I know That the

* VATICAN MANUSCRIPT.—29. and—*omit.*

† 31. By translating this interrogatively, this passage is harmonized with John viii. 14.

‡ 22. Matt. xi. 27; xxviii. 18; Luke x. 22; John iii. 35; xvii. 2; Acts xvii. 31; 1 Pet. iv. 5. ‡ 23. 1 John ii. 23. ‡ 29. Dan. xii. 2; Matt. xxv. 32, 33, 46. ‡ 30. Matt. xxvi 39; John iv. 34, vi. 38. ‡ 31. John viii. 14; Rev. iii. 14.

ἡ μαρτυρια, ἡν μαρτυρει περι εμου. 33 Ὑμεις
the testimony, which he testifies concerning me. You
απεσταλκατε προς Ιωαννην, και μεμαρτυρηκε
have sent to John, and he has testified
τῃ αληθειᾳ. 34 Εγω δε ου παρα ανθρωπου την
to the truth. I but not from a man the
μαρτυριαν λαμβανω· αλλα ταυτα λεγω, ἱνα
testimony receive; but these things I say, that
ὑμεις σωθητε. 35 Εκεινος ην ὁ λυχνος ὁ καιο-
you may be saved. He was the lamp the burn-
μενος και φαινων· ὑμεις δε ηθελησατε αγαλλι-
ing and shining: you and were willing to re-
αθηναι προς ὡραν εν τῳ φωτι αυτου. 36 Εγω
joice for an hour in the light of him. I
δε εχω την μαρτυριαν μειζω του Ιωαννου· τα
but have the testimony greater of the John: the
γαρ εργα, ἁ εδωκε μοι ὁ πατηρ, ἱνα τελειωσω
for works, which gave to me the father, that I might finish
αυτα, αυτα τα εργα, ἁ εγω ποιω, μαρτυρει
them, these the works, which I do, testifies
περι εμου, ὁτι ὁ πατηρ με απεσταλκε. 37 Και
concerning me, because the father me has sent. And
ὁ πεμψας με πατηρ αυτος μεμαρτυρηκε περι
he having sent me father himself has testified concerning
εμου. Ουτε φωνην αυτου ακηκοατε πωποτε,
me. Neither a voice of him have you heard at any time,
ουτε ειδος αυτου ἑωρακατε. 38 Και τον λογον
nor form of him have you seen. And the word
αυτου ουκ εχετε μενοντα εν ὑμιν· ὁτι ὁν απεσ-
of him not you have abiding in you; because whom sent
τειλεν εκεινος, τουτῳ ὑμεις ου πιστευετε.
he, this you not believe.
39 Ερευνατε τας γραφας, ὁτι ὑμεις δοκειτε εν
You search the writings, because you think in
αυταις ζωην αιωνιον εχειν· και εκειναι εισιν αἱ
them life age-lasting to have: and they are those
μαρτυρουσαι περι εμου· 40 και ου θελετε ελθειν
testifying concerning me; and not you are willing to come
προς με, ἱνα ζωην εχητε. 41 Δοξαν παρα ανθρω-
to me, so that life you may have. Glory from men
πων ου λαμβανω· 42 αλλ' εγνωκα ὑμας, ὁτι την
not I receive; but I have known you, that the
αγαπην του θεου ουκ εχετε εν ἑαυτοις. 43 Εγω
love of the God not you have in yourselves. I
εληλυθα εν τῳ ονοματι του πατρος μου, και ου
have come in the name of the father of me, and not
λαμβανετε με· εαν αλλος ελθῃ εν τῳ ονοματι
you receive me: if another should come in the name
τῳ ιδιῳ, εκεινον ληψεσθε. 44 Πως δυνασθε
the own, him you will receive. How are able
ὑμεις πιστευσαι, δοξαν παρα αλληλων λαμβανον-
you to believe, glory from one another receiving,
τες, και την δοξαν την παρα του μονου θεου ου
and the glory that from the only God not
ζητειτε; 45 Μη δοκειτε, ὁτι εγω κατηγορησω
you seek? Not think you, that I will accuse

TESTIMONY which he testifies of me is true.

33 ‡You have sent to John, and he has testified to the TRUTH.

34 But I receive not TESTIMONY from a Man (only;) but These things I say, that you may be saved.

35 He was the BURNING and shining LAMP; and you were willing, for a Time, to rejoice in his LIGHT.

36 But I have TESTIMONY greater than JOHN'S; for the WORKS which the FATHER gave me, that I might finish them, ‡These WORKS which * I do, testify concerning me, That the FATHER has sent Me.

37 And the FATHER who SENT me, he has testified concerning me; ‡(though you have not, at any time, either heard his Voice, or seen his Form.)

38 And his WORD you have not remaining in you; Because you believe not him whom he sent.

39 You search the SCRIPTURES, Because you think by them to obtain aionian Life; ‡and they are THOSE TESTIFYING of me;

40 and yet you are not willing to come to me that you may obtain Life.

41 I receive not Glory from Men;

42 but I know you, That you have not the LOVE of GOD in yourselves.

43 I have come in the NAME of my FATHER, and you do not receive me; if another should come in his OWN NAME, him you will receive.

44 ‡ How can you believe, receiving Glory one from another; and THAT GLORY from the ONLY God you do not seek.

45 Do not think That I will accuse you to the

* VATICAN MANUSCRIPT.—36. I do. 44. the ONLY one.

‡ 33. John i. 15, 19, 27, 32. ‡ 36. John iii. 2; x. 25; xv. 24. ‡ 37. Matt iii. 17; xvii. 5; John vi. 27; viii. 18. ‡ 39. Deut. xviii. 15, 18; Luke xxiv. 27; John i. 45. ‡ 44. John xii. 43.

ὑμων προς τον πατερα· εστιν ὁ κατηγορων
you to the father: it is he accusing
ὑμων, Μωσης, εις ὁν ὑμεις ηλπικατε. 46 Ει
you, Moses, into whom you have hoped. If
γαρ επιστευετε Μωσῃ, επιστευετε αν εμοι·
for you believed Moses, you would believe me;
περι γαρ εμου εκεινος εγραψεν. 47 Ει δε τοις
concerning for me he wrote. If but the
εκεινου γραμμασιν ου πιστευετε, πως τοις εμοις
of him writings not you believe, how the my
ῥημασι πιστευσετε.
words will you believe.

ΚΕΦ. ς'. 6.

1 Μετα ταυτα απηλθεν ὁ Ιησους περαν της
After these things went the Jesus over the
θαλασσης της Γαλιλαιας, της Τιβεριαδος.
sea that of Galilee, of the Tiberias.
2 Και ηκολουθει αυτῳ οχλος πολυς, ὁτι ἑωρων
And was following him a crowd great, because they saw
τα σημεια, ἁ εποιει επι των ασθενουντων.
the signs, which he was doing on those being sick.
3 Ανηλθε δε εις το ορος ὁ Ιησους, και εκει
Went and into the mountain the Jesus, and there
εκαθητο μετα των μαθητων αὑτου. 4 Ην δε
he was sitting with the disciples of himself. Was and
εγγυς το πασχα, ἡ ἑορτη των Ιουδαιων. 5 Επα-
near the passover, the feast of the Jews. Lifted
ρας ουν ὁ Ιησους τους οφθαλμους, και θεασαμε-
up then the Jesus the eyes, and seeing
νος ὁτι πολυς οχλος ερχεται προς αυτον, λεγει
that great a crowd was coming to him, says
προς τον Φιλιππον· Ποθεν αγορασομεν αρτους,
to the Philip; Whence shall we buy loaves,
ἱνα φαγωσιν ουτοι; 6 (Τουτο δε ελεγε πειραζων
that may eat these? (This but he said trying
αυτον· αυτος γαρ ηδει, τι εμελλε ποιειν.)
him; he for knew, what he was about to do.)
7 Απεκριθη αυτῳ Φιλιππος· Διακοσιων δηναριων
Answered him Philip; Two hundred denarii
αρτοι ουκ αρκουσιν αυτοις, ἱνα ἑκαστος
of loaves not are enough for them, so that each
*[αυτων] βραχυ τι λαβῃ. 8 Λεγει αυτῳ εἱς εκ
[of them] a little may take. Says to him one of
των μαθητων αυτου, Ανδρεας, ὁ αδελφος Σιμω-
the disciples of him, Andrew, the brother of Si-
νος Πετρου· 9 Εστι παιδαριον ἑν ὡδε, ὁ εχει
mon Peter; Is little boy one here, who has
πεντε αρτους κριθινους, και δυο οψαρια· αλλα
five loaves barley, and two small fishes: but
ταυτα τι εστιν εις τοσουτους; 10 Ειπε *[δε] ὁ
these what are for so many? Said [and] the
Ιησους· Ποιησατε τους ανθρωπους αναπεσειν.
Jesus: Make you the men to recline.
Ην δε χορτος πολυς εν τῳ τοπῳ. Ανεπεσον
Was and grass much in the place. Reclined

FATHER. * HE who ACCUSES you to the FATHER is Moses, in whom you have hoped.

46 For if you believed Moses you would believe me, ‡ for he wrote about me.

47 But if you do not believe HIS Writings, how * can you believe MY Words?"

CHAPTER VI.

1 ‡ After these things JESUS went across THAT LAKE of GALILEE, the TIBERIAS.

2 And a great Crowd were following him, Because they saw the SIGNS which he was performing on the SICK.

3 And * Jesus went up into the MOUNTAIN, and was sitting there with his DISCIPLES.

4 And the PASSOVER, the FEAST of the JEWS, was near.

5 Then JESUS, lifting up his EYES, and seeing that a great Crowd was coming to him, says to * Philip, "Whence * may we buy Loaves that these may eat."

6 (But this he said, trying him; for he knew what he was about to do.)

7 Philip answered him, "Loaves costing † Two Hundred Denarii are not enough for them, that each may take a little."

8 One of his DISCIPLES, Andrew, the BROTHER of Simon Peter, says to him,

9 "Here is a Little boy, who has Five barley Loaves and Two Small fishes; but what are these for so many?"

10 JESUS said, "Make the MEN recline." And there was much Grass in the PLACE. The men,

* VATICAN MANUSCRIPT.—45. HE who ACCUSES you to the FATHER is Moses, in whom. 47. can you believe. 3. Jesus. 5. Philip. 5. may we buy. 7. of them—*omit.* 10. and—*omit.*

† 7. In value about *thirty dollars,* or about £6. 8s. sterling.

‡ 46. Gen. iii. 15; xii. 3; xviii. 18; xxii. 18; xlix. 10; Deut. xviii. 15, 18; John i. 45; Acts xxvi. 22. ‡ 1. Matt. xiv. 15; Mark vi. 35; Luke ix. 10, 12.

ουν οἱ ανδρες τον αριθμον ὡσει πεντακισχιλιοι.
therefore the men the number about five thousand.
11 Ελαβε δε τους αρτους ὁ Ιησους, και ευχαρισ-
Took and the loaves the Jesus, and having given
τησας διεδωκε *[τοις μαθηταις, οἱ δε μαθηται]
thanks distributed [to the disciples, the and disciples]
τοις ανακειμενοις· ὁμοιως και εκ των οψαριων
to those reclining; in like manner also of the fishes
ὁσον ηθελον. 12 Ὡς δε ενεπλησθησαν, λεγει τοις
what they wished. When and they were filled, he says to the
μαθηταις αὑτου· Συναγαγετε τα περισσευσαντα
disciples of himself: Collect the remaining
κλασματα, ἱνα μη τι αποληται. 13 Συνηγαγον
fragments, so that not any may be lost. They collected
ουν, και εγεμισαν δωδεκα κοφινους κλασματων
therefore, and filled twelve baskets of fragments
εκ των πεντε αρτων των κριθινων, ἁ επερισ-
out of the five loaves of the barley, which remained
σευσε τοις βεβρωκοσιν. 14 Οἱ ουν ανθρωποι
to those having eaten. The therefore men
ιδοντες ὁ εποιησε σημειον ὁ Ιησους, ελεγον·
seeing what did a sign the Jesus, said:
Ὁτι οὑτος εστιν αληθως ὁ προφητης, ὁ ερχο-
That this is truly the prophet, he com-
μενος εις τον κοσμον.
ing into the world.
15 Ιησους ουν γνους ὁτι μελλουσιν ερχεσθαι,
Jesus therefore knowing that they were about to come,
και αρπαζειν αυτον, ἱνα ποιησωσιν αυτον βασι-
and to seize him, *that they might make him, a king,
λεα, ανεχωρησε παλιν εις το ορος αυτος
retired again into the mountain himself
μονος. 16 Ὡς δε οψια εγενετο, κατεβησαν οἱ
alone. As and evening it became, went down the
μαθηται αυτου επι την θαλασσαν. 17 Και εμβαν-
disciples of him on the sea. And stepping
τες εις το πλοιον, ηρχοντο περαν της θαλασσης
into the ship, they were going over the sea
εις Καπερναουμ. Και σκοτια ηδε εγεγονει,
to Capernaum. And dark now it had become,
και ουκ εληλυθει προς αυτους ὁ Ιησους. 18 Ἡ
and not had come to them the Jesus. The
τε θαλασσα, ανεμου μεγαλου πνεοντος διηγει-
and sea, a wind great blowing was becoming
ρετο. 19 Εληλακοτες ουν ὡς σταδιους εικοσι-
agitated. Having driven therefore about furlongs twenty-
πεντε η τριακοντα, θεωρουσι τον Ιησουν
five or thirty, they see the Jesus
περιπατουντα επι της θαλασης, και εγγυς του
walking on the sea, and near the
πλοιου γινομενον· και εφοβηθησαν. 20 Ὁ δε
ship was coming; and they were afraid. He but
λεγει αυτοις· Εγω ειμι, μη φοβεισθε. 21 Ηθε-
says to them; I am, not fear you. They were
λον ουν λαβειν αυτον εις το πλοιον· και
willing therefore to receive him into the ship; and

therefore, reclined, in NUMBER about five thousand.

11 *Then JESUS took the LOAVES, and having given thanks, he distributed to THOSE RECLINING; in like manner also of the FISHES, as much as they wished.

12 And when they were filled, he says to the DISCIPLES, "Collect the REMAINING FRAGMENTS, so that nothing may be lost."

13 Then they collected, and filled Twelve Baskets with Fragments, from the FIVE BARLEY Loaves, which remained to THOSE who had EATEN.

14 The MEN, therefore, seeing the *Sign that JESUS did, said, "This is truly ‡THAT PROPHET COMING into the WORLD."

15 Then Jesus seeing That they were about to come and seize him, that they might make him a King, retired again into the MOUNTAIN, himself alone.

16 ‡And as it became Evening, his DISCIPLES went down to the LAKE,

17 and having entered the BOAT, were crossing the LAKE to Capernaum. And it had already become dark, and JESUS had not * yet come to them.

18 And the LAKE was becoming agitated by a great Wind blowing.

19 Having, therefore, driven about twenty-five or thirty Furlongs, they see JESUS walking on the LAKE, and approaching the BOAT; and they were afraid.

20 But HE says to them, "It is I; be not afraid."

21 They were willing, therefore, to receive him into the BOAT. And im-

* VATICAN MANUSCRIPT.—11. Then JESUS. 11. to the DISCIPLES, and the DISCIPLES.—omit. 14. Signs. 17. yet come.

‡ 14. Gen. xlix. 10; Deut. xviii. 15, 18; Matt. xi. 3; John i. 21; iv. 19, 25; vii. 40. ‡ 16. Matt xiv. 23; Mark vi. 47.

ευθεως το πλοιον εγενετο επι της γης, εις ἡν
immediately the ship was at the land, to which
ὑπηγον.
they were going.
22 Τη επαυριον ὁ οχλος, ὁ ἑστηκως περαν της
The next day the crowd, that standing over the
θαλασσης, ιδων, ὁτι πλοιαριον αλλο ουκ ην
sea, seeing, that boat other not was
εκει, ει μη ἑν, και ὁτι ου συνεισηλθε τοις
there, if not one, and that not went with the
μαθηταις αὑτου ὁ Ιησους εις το πλοιον, αλλα
disciples of himself the Jesus into the boat, but
μονοι οἱ μαθηται αυτου απηλθον· 23 (αλλα δε
alone the disciples of him went away; (other but
ηλθε πλοιαρια εκ Τιβεριαδος εγγυς του τοπου,
came boats from Tiberias near the place,
ὁπου εφαγον τον αρτον, ευχαριστησαντος του
where they ate the bread, having given thanks the
κυριου·) 24 ὁτε ουν ειδεν ὁ οχλος, ὁτι Ιησους
Lord;) when therefore saw the crowd, that Jesus
ουκ εστιν εκει, ουδε οἱ μαθηται αυτου, ενεβησαν
not is there, nor the disciples of him, they entered
αυτοι εις τα πλοια, και ηλθον εις Καπερναουμ,
themselves into the boats, and came to Capernaum,
ζητουντες τον Ιησουν. 25 Και εὑροντες αυτον
seeking the Jesus. And finding him
περαν της θαλασσης, ειπον αυτῳ· Ῥαββι, ποτε
beyond the sea, they said to him; Rabbi, when
ὡδε γεγονας; 26 Απεκριθη αυτοις ὁ Ιησους και
here didst thou come? Answered them the Jesus and
ειπεν· Αμην αμην λεγω ὑμιν· Ζητειτε με, ουχ
said; Indeed indeed I say to you: You seek me, not
ὁτι ειδετε σημεια, αλλ' ὁτι εφαγετε εκ των
because you saw signs, but because you ate of the
αρτων, και εχορτασθητε. 27 Εργαζεσθε μη την
loaves, and were filled. Work you not the
βρωσιν την απολλυμενην, αλλα την βρωσιν την
food that perishing, but the food that
μενουσαν εις ζωην αιωνιον, ἡν ὁ υἱος του ανθρω-
abiding into life age-lasting, which the son of the man
που ὑμιν δωσει· τουτον γαρ ὁ πατηρ εσφραγι-
to you will give: him for the father sealed
σεν ὁ θεος. 28 Ειπον ουν προς αυτον· Τι
the God. Said therefore to him: What
ποιωμεν, ἱνα εργαζωμεθα τα εργα του θεου;
shall we do, that we may work the works of the God?
29 Απεκριθη ὁ Ιησους και ειπεν αυτοις· Τουτο
Answered the Jesus and said to them: This
εστι το εργον του θεου, ἱνα πιστευσητε εις ὁν
is the work of the God, that you may believe into whom
απεστειλεν εκεινος. 30 Ειπον ουν αυτῳ· Τι
sent he. They said therefore to him; What
ουν ποιεις συ σημειον, ἱνα ιδωμεν και πιστευ-
then doest thou sign, that we may see and we may be-
σωμεν σοι; τι εργαζῃ; 31 Οἱ πατερες ἡμων το
lieve thee? what dost thou work? The fathers of us the
μαννα εφαγον εν τῃ ερημῳ, καθως εστι γεγραμ-
manna ate in the desert, as it is having been

mediately the BOAT was at the LAND to which they were going.

22 On the NEXT DAY, THAT CROWD STANDING by the side of the LAKE, seeing That there was no other Boat there, except one, and That JESUS went not with his DISCIPLES into the BOAT, but his DISCIPLES went away alone;—

23 (but Other Boats came from Tiberias near the PLACE where they ate the BREAD, when the LORD had given thanks;—)

24 when, therefore, the CROWD saw That Jesus was not there, nor his DISCIPLES, they entered the BOATS, and came to Capernaum, seeking JESUS.

25 And finding him beyond the LAKE, they said to him, "Rabbi, when didst thou arrive here?"

26 JESUS answered them and said, "Indeed, truly I say to you, You do not seek me Because you saw the Signs, but Because you ate of the LOAVES, and were satisfied.

27 Labor not for THAT FOOD which PERISHES, but for THAT FOOD which abides to aionian Life, which the SON of MAN will give you; ‡ for him, the FATHER, GOD, has sealed."

28 They said to him, therefore, "What shall we do, that we may perform the WORKS of God?"

29 JESUS answered and said to them, ‡ "This is the WORK of GOD, that you should believe into him whom he sent."

30 They said to him, therefore, ‡ "What Sign, dost thou perform, that we may see and believe thee? What dost thou work?

31 ‡ Our FATHERS ate the MANNA in the DESERT, as it has been written,

‡ 27. Matt. iii. 17; xvii. 5; Mark i. 11; ix. 7; Luke iii. 22; ix. 35; John i. 33; v. 37; viii. 18; Acts ii. 22; 2 Pet. i. 17. ‡ 29. 1 John iii. 23. ‡ 30. Matt. xii. 38; xvi. 1; Mark viii. 11; 1 Cor. i. 22. ‡ 31. Exod. xvi. 15; Num. xi. 7; Neh. ix. 15; 1 Cor. x. 3.

μενον· "Αρτον εκ του ουρανου εδωκεν αυτοις
written; "Bread from the heaven gave them
φαγειν." 32 Ειπεν ουν αυτοις ὁ Ιησους· Αμην
to eat." Said therefore to them the Jesus; Indeed
αμην λεγω ὑμιν, ου Μωσης δεδωκεν ὑμιν τον
indeed I say to you, not Moses has given to you the
αρτον εκ του ουρανου· αλλ' ὁ πατηρ μου
bread from the heaven; but the father of me
διδωσιν ὑμιν τον αρτον εκ του ουρανου τον
gives to you the bread from the heaven the
αληθινον. 33 Ὁ γαρ αρτος του θεου εστιν ὁ
true. The for bread of the God is he
καταβαινων εκ του ουρανου, και ζωην διδους
coming down from the heaven, and life is giving
τῳ κοσμῳ. 34 Ειπον ουν προς αυτον· Κυριε,
to the world. They said then to him: O sir,
παντοτε δος ἡμιν τον αρτον τουτον. 35 Ειπε
always give to us the bread this. Said
*[δε] αυτοις ὁ Ιησους· Εγω ειμι ὁ αρτος της
[but] to them the Jesus: I am the bread of the
ζωης· ὁ ερχομενος προς με, ου μη πειναση·
life: he coming to me, not not may hunger:
και ὁ πιστευων εις εμε, ου μη διψηση πωποτε.
and he believing into me, not not may thirst ever.
36 Αλλ' ειπον ὑμιν, ὁτι και ἑωρακατε με, και ου
But I said to you, that even you have seen me, and not
πιστευετε. 37 Παν ὁ διδωσι μοι ὁ πατηρ, προς
you believe. All what gives to me the father, to
εμε ἡξει· και τον ερχομενον προς με, ου μη
me will come: and the coming to me, not not
εκβαλω εξω· 38 ὁτι καταβεβηκα εκ του ουρα-
I will cast out; because I have come down from the hea-
νου, ουχ ἱνα ποιω το θελημα το εμον, αλλα
ven, not that I may do the will the mine, but
το θελημα του πεμψαντος με. 39 Τουτο δε εστι
the will of the having sent me. This and is
το θελημα του πεμψαντος με, ἱνα παν ὁ
the will of the having sent me, that every one which
δεδωκε μοι, μη απολεσω εξ αυτου, αλλα ανασ-
he has given to me, not I may lose out of it, but raise
τησω αυτο εν τῃ εσχατῃ ἡμερᾳ. 40 Τουτο γαρ
up it in the last day. This for
εστι το θελημα του πεμψαντος με, ἱνα πας ὁ
is the will of the having sent me, that all who
θεωρων τον υἱον, και πιστευων εις αυτον, εχῃ
seeing the son, and believing into him, may have
ζωην αιωνιον· και αναστησω αυτον εγω τῃ
life age-lasting; and will raise up him I in the
εσχατῃ ἡμερᾳ.
last day.

41 Εγογγυζον ουν οἱ Ιουδαιοι περι αυτου, ὁτι
Were murmuring then the Jews about him, because
ειπεν· Εγω ειμι ὁ αρτος ὁ καταβας εκ του ου-
he said; I am the bread that having come down from the hea-
ρανου· 42 και ελεγον· Ουχ οὑτος εστιν Ιησους ὁ
ven; and they said; Not this is Jesus the

‡ 'He gave them Bread from HEAVEN to eat.'"

32 JESUS then said to them, "Indeed, I assure you, Moses did not give you the BREAD from HEAVEN; but my FATHER gives you the TRUE BREAD from HEAVEN.

33 For the BREAD of GOD is THAT which DESCENDS from HEAVEN, and is giving Life to the WORLD."

34 They, therefore, said to him, "Sir, always give us this BREAD."

35 JESUS said to them, "I am the BREAD of LIFE. ‡ HE who COMES to me will by no means hunger; and HE who BELIEVES into me will never thirst.

36 But I said to you, That you have even seen me, and yet you do not believe.

37 Whatever the FATHER gives me will come to me; and HIM, who COMES to me, I will by no means reject;

38 because I have descended from HEAVEN, ‡ not that I may do MY WILL, but the WILL of HIM who SENT me.

39 And this is the WILL of HIM who SENT me, ‡ that I may lose nothing of all that he HAS GIVEN me, but may raise it up at the LAST Day.

40 For this is the WILL of HIM who SENT me, that EVERY ONE SEEING the SON, ‡ and BELIEVING into him, may have aionian Life; and I will raise him up at the LAST Day."

41 Then the JEWS murmured about him, Because he said, "I am THAT BREAD which DESCENDED from HEAVEN."

42 And they said, ‡ "Is not this Jesus, the SON of

* VATICAN MANUSCRIPT.—35. δε—omit.

‡ 31. Psa. lxxviii. 24, 25. ‡ 35. John iv. 14; vii. 37. ‡ 38. John v. 30 ‡ 39. John x. 28; xvii. 12; xviii. 9. ‡ 40. John iii. 15, 16; iv. 14. ‡ 42. Matt. xiii. 55; Mark vi. 3; Luke iv. 22.

υἱος Ιωσηφ, οὑ ἡμεις οιδαμεν τον πατερα και
son of Joseph, of whom we know the father and
την μητερα; Πως ουν λεγει οὑτος· Ὁτι εκ
the mother? How then he says this; That from
του ουρανου καταβεβηκα; 43 Απεκριθη ὁ Ιησους
the heaven I have come down? Answered the Jesus
και ειπεν αυτοις· Μη γογγυζετε μετ' αλληλων.
and said to them: Not murmur you with one another.
44 Ουδεις δυναται ελθειν προς με, εαν μη ὁ
No one is able to come to me, if not the
πατηρ, ὁ πεμψας με, ἑλκυσῃ αυτον, και εγω
father, that having sent me, may draw him, and I
αναστησω αυτον εν τῃ εσχατῃ ἡμερᾳ. 45 Εστι
will raise up him in the last day. It is
γεγραμμενον εν τοις προφηταις· "Και εσονται
having been written in the prophets: "And they shall be
παντες διδακτοι θεου." Πας ὁ ακουσας παρα
all taught of God." Every one who having heard from
του πατρος και μαθων, ερχεται προς με. 46 Ουχ
the father and having learned, comes to me. Not
ὁτι τον πατερα τις ἑωρακεν, εἰ μη ὁ ων παρα
that the father any one has seen, if not he being from
του θεου· οὑτος ἑωρακε τον πατερα. 47 Αμην
the God: this has seen the father. Indeed
αμην λεγω ὑμιν, ὁ πιστευων *[εις εμε,] εχει
indeed I say to you, he believing [into me,] has
ζωην αιωνιον. 48 Εγω ειμι ὁ αρτος της ζωης.
life age-lasting. I am the bread of the life.
49 Οἱ πατερες ὑμων εφαγον το μαννα εν τῃ ερη-
The fathers of you ate the manna in the desert,
μῳ, και απεθανον· 50 οὑτος εστιν ὁ αρτος, ὁ εκ
and died; this is the bread, that from
του ουρανου καταβαινων, ἱνα τις εξ αυτου
the heaven coming down, so that any one of it
φαγῃ, και μη αποθανῃ. 51 Εγω ειμι ὁ αρτος ὁ
may eat, and not may die. I am the bread that
ζων, ὁ εκ του ουρανου καταβας· εαν τις φαγῃ
living that from the heaven having come down: if any one may eat
εκ τουτου του αρτου, ζησεται εις τον αιωνα. Και
of this the bread, he shall live into the age. And
ὁ αρτος δε, *[ὁν εγω δωσω,] ἡ σαρξ μου εστιν,
the bread also, [which I will give,] the flesh of me is,
ἡν εγω δωσω ὑπερ της του κοσμου ζωης.
which I will give in behalf of the of the world life.
52 Εμαχοντο ουν προς αλληλους οἱ Ιουδαιοι,
Were contending therefore with one another the Jews,
λεγοντες· Πως δυναται οὑτος ἡμιν δουναι την
saying; How is able this to us to give the
σαρκα φαγειν; 53 Ειπεν ουν αυτοις ὁ Ιησους·
flesh to eat? Said then to them the Jesus;
Αμην αμην λεγω ὑμιν, εαν μη φαγητε την
Indeed indeed I say to you, if not you may eat the
σαρκα του υἱου του ανθρωπου, και πιητε αυτου
flesh of the son of the man, and you may drink of him
το αἱμα, ουκ εχετε ζωην εν ἑαυτοις. 54 Ὁ
the blood, not you have life in yourselves. He

Joseph, Whose FATHER and MOTHER we know? How, *then, does he say, 'I have come down from HEAVEN?'"

43 JESUS answered and said to them, "Murmur not one with another.

44 No one can come to me, unless THAT FATHER who SENT me draw him; and I will raise him up at the LAST Day.

45 ‡ It has been written in the PROPHETS, 'And they shall all be taught of God.' Every one HAVING HEARD and having learned of the FATHER, comes to me.

46 Not that any one has seen the FATHER, ‡ except HE who IS from * God; he has seen the FATHER.

47 Indeed, I assure you, ‡ HE BELIEVING into me has aionian Life.

48 I am the BREAD of LIFE.

49 Your FATHERS ate the MANNA in the DESERT, and died.

50 This is THAT BREAD DESCENDING from HEAVEN, so that any one may eat of it, and not die.

51 I am THAT LIVING BREAD who ‡ HAS DESCENDED from HEAVEN. If any one eat of This BREAD, he shall live to the AGE; and the BREAD is my FLESH, which I will give in behalf of the LIFE of the WORLD."

52 The JEWS, therefore, ‡ were contending with each other, saying, "How can he give us his FLESH to eat?"

53 Then JESUS said to them, "Indeed, I assure you, ‡ if you do not eat the FLESH of the SON of MAN, and drink His BLOOD, you have no Life in yourselves.

* VATICAN MANUSCRIPT.—42. now then. 46. God. 47. into me—*omit*.
51. that I will give—*omit*.

‡ 45. Isa. liv. 13; Jer. xxxi. 34; Micah iv. 2; Heb. viii. 10; x. 16. ‡ 46. John i. 18; v. 37.
‡ 47. John iii. 16, 18, 36. ‡ 51. John iii. 13. ‡ 52. John vii. 43; ix. 16; x. 19.
‡ 53. Gal. ii. 20.

τρωγων μου την σαρκα, και πινων μου το αἷμα,
eating of me the flesh, and drinking of me the blood,
εχει ζωην αιωνιον· και εγω αναστησω αυτον τῃ
has life age-lasting; and I will raise up him in the
εσχατῃ ἡμερᾳ. 55 Ἡ γαρ σαρξ μου αληθως
last day. The for flesh of me truly
εστι βρωσις, και το αἷμα μου αληθως εστι
is food, and the blood of me truly is
ποσις. 56 Ὁ τρωγων μου την σαρκα, και πινων
drink. He eating of me the flesh, and drinking
μου το αἷμα, εν εμοι μενει, καγω εν αυτῳ.
of me the blood, in me abides, and I in him.
57 Καθως απεστειλε με ὁ ζων πατηρ, καγω ζω
As sent me the living father, and I live
δια τον πατερα· και ὁ τρωγων με, κακεινος
through the father; also he eating me, even he
ζησεται δι' εμε. 58 Οὗτος εστιν ὁ αρτος, ὁ εκ
shall live through me. This is the bread, that from
του ουρανου καταβας· ου καθως εφαγον οἱ
the heaven having come down; not as ate the
πατερες ὑμων, και απεθανον· ὁ τρωγων τουτον
fathers of you, and died; he eating this
τον αρτον, ζησεται εις τον αιωνα. 59 Ταυτα
the bread, shall live into the age. These things
ειπεν εν συναγωγῃ διδασκων εν Καπερναουμ.
he said in a synagogue teaching in Capernaum.
60 Πολλοι ουν ακουσαντες εκ των μαθητων
Many therefore having heard of the disciples
αυτου, ειπον· Σκληρος εστιν οὗτος ὁ λογος·
of him, said; Hard is this the saying;
τις δυναται αυτου ακουειν; 61 Ειδως δε ὁ Ιησους
who is able it to hear? Knowing but the Jesus
εν ἑαυτῳ, ὁτι γογγυζουσι περι τουτου οἱ μαθη-
in himself, that were murmuring about this the disci-
ται αὑτου, ειπεν αυτοις· Τουτο ὑμας σκανδαλι-
ples of himself, he said to them; This you offends?
ζει; 62 Εαν ουν θεωρητε τον υἱον του ανθρωπου
If then you should see the son of the man
αναβαινοντα, ὁπου ην το προτερον; 63 Το
ascending, where he was the first? The
πνευμα εστι το ζωοποιουν· ἡ σαρξ ουκ ωφελει
spirit is that making alive; the flesh not profits
ουδεν. Τα ῥηματα, ἁ εγω λαλω ὑμιν, πνευμα
nothing. The words, which I speak to you, spirit
εστι και ζωη εστιν. 64 Αλλ' εισιν εξ ὑμων
is and life is. But are of you
τινες, οἱ ου πιστευουσιν· ηδει γαρ εξ αρχης ὁ
some, who not believe; knew for from beginning the
Ιησους, τινες εισιν οἱ μη πιστευοντες, και τις
Jesus, some are who not believing, and who
εστιν ὁ παραδωσων αυτον. 65 Και ελεγε· Δια
is he about betraying him. And he said; Through
τουτο ειρηκα ὑμιν ὁτι ουδεις δυναται ελθειν
this I have said to you that no one is able to come
προς με, εαν μη ᾐ δεδομενον αυτῳ εκ του
to me, if not may be having been given to him from the
πατρος μου. 66 Εκ τουτου πολλοι απηλθον των
father of me. From this many went the

54 HE who EATS My FLESH, and drinks My BLOOD, has aionian Life, and I will raise him up at the LAST Day.

55 For my FLESH is * the True Food, and my BLOOD is * the True Drink.

56 HE who EATS My FLESH, and DRINKS My BLOOD, ‡ abides in me, and I in him.

57 As the LIVING Father sent me, and I live through the FATHER; so HE who EATS me, even he shall live through me.

58 This is THAT BREAD which HAS DESCENDED from * Heaven. Not as * the FATHERS ate, and died; he who EATS This BREAD shall live to the AGE."

59 These things he said, teaching in a Synagogue, in Capernaum.

60 ‡ Many, therefore, of his DISCIPLES, hearing, said, "Hard is This SAYING; who can hear it?"

61 But JESUS, knowing in himself, That his DISCIPLES were murmuring about This, he said to them, "Does this offend You?"

62 ‡ What then, if you should see the SON of MAN ascending where he was BEFORE?

63 ‡ The SPIRIT is THAT which MAKES ALIVE; the FLESH profits nothing; the WORDS which I * have spoken to you are Spirit and are Life.

64 But there are some of you who do not believe." For ‡ JESUS knew from the Beginning WHO those were that did not BELIEVE, and WHO he was that was about to BETRAY him.

65 And he said, "Because of this I have said to you, That no one can come to me, unless it may be given him from the * FATHER."

66 From this time many

* VATICAN MANUSCRIPT.—55. the True Food. 55. the True Drink. 58. Heaven. 58. the FATHERS. 63. have spoken to.

‡ 56. 1 John iii. 24; iv. 15, 16. ‡ 60. Matt. xi. 6. ‡ 62. John iii. 13; Mark xvi 19; Acts i. 9; Eph. iv. 8. ‡ 63. 2 Cor. iii. 6. ‡ 64. John ii. 24, 25; xiii. 11.

μαθητων αυτου εις τα οπισω· και ουκετι μετ'
disciples of him into the things behind; and no longer with
αυτου περιεπατουν. 67 Ειπεν ουν ὁ Ιησους τοις
him were walking. Said therefore the Jesus to the
δωδεκα· Μη και ὑμεις θελετε ὑπαγειν; 68 Απεκ-
twelve; Not and you wish to go? An-
ριθη αυτῳ Σιμων Πετρος· Κυριε, προς τινα απε-
swered him Simon Peter; O lord, to whom shall
λευσομεθα; ῥηματα ζωης αιωνιου εχεις· 69 και
we go? words of life age-lasting thou hast, and
ἡμεις πεπιστευκαμεν και εγνωκαμεν, ὁτι συ ει
we have believed and have known, that thou art
ὁ ἁγιος του θεου. 70 Απεκριθη αυτοις ὁ Ιησους·
the holy one of the God. Answered them the Jesus.
Ουκ εγω ὑμας τους δωδεκα εξελεξαμην; και εξ
Not I you the twelve choose? and of
ὑμων εἱς διαβολος εστιν. 71 Ελεγε δε τον Ιου-
you one an accuser is. He spoke now the Ju-
δαν Σιμωνος Ισκαριωτην· οὑτος γαρ ημελλεν
das of Simon Iscariot, this for was about
αυτον παραδιδοναι, εἱς ων εκ των δωδεκα.
him to deliver up, one being of the twelve.

ΚΕΦ. ς'. 7.

1 Και περιεπατει ὁ Ιησους μετα ταυτα εν τη
And was walking the Jesus after these things in the
Γαλιλαιᾳ· ου γαρ ηθελεν εν τη Ιουδαιᾳ περιπα-
Galilee; not for he wished in the Judea to walk,
τειν, ὁτι εζητουν αυτον οἱ Ιουδαιοι αποκτειναι.
because were seeking him the Jews to kill.
2 Ην δε εγγυς ἡ ἑορτη των Ιουδαιων, ἡ σκηνοπ-
Was and near the feast the Jews, the feast of ta-
ηγια. 3 Ειπον ουν προς αυτον οἱ αδελφοι
bernacles. Said therefore to him the brothers
αυτου· Μεταβηθι εντευθεν, και ὑπαγε εις την
of him; Depart hence, and go into the
Ιουδαιαν, ἱνα και οἱ μαθηται σου θεωρησωσι τα
Judea, so that also the disciples of thee may see the
εργα σου, ἁ ποιεις. 4 Ουδεις γαρ εν κρυπτῳ
works of thee, which thou doest. No one for in secret
τι ποιει, και ζητει αυτος εν παρρησιᾳ ειναι.
anything does, and he seeks himself in public to be.
Ει ταυτα ποιεις, φανερωσον σεαυτον τῳ κοσμῳ.
If these things thou doest, manifest thyself to the world.
5 Ουδε γαρ οἱ αδελφοι αυτου επιστευον εις αυτον.
Not even for the brothers of him believed into him.
6 Λεγει ουν αυτοις ὁ Ιησους· Ὁ καιρος ὁ εμος
Says then to them the Jesus; The season the mine

of his DISCIPLES withdrew, and walked no longer with him.

67 JESUS, therefore, said to the TWELVE, "Do you also wish to go away?"

68 Simon Peter answered him, "Master, to whom shall we go? Thou hast the ‡ Words of aionian Life;

69 and we have believed and known, ‡ That thou art the HOLY one of GOD."

70 JESUS answered them, ‡ "Did I not choose you, the TWELVE, and of you one is an Accuser?"

71 Now he spoke of JUDAS, the son of Simon iscariot; for he, being one of the TWELVE, was about to betray him.

CHAPTER VII.

1 And after these things * Jesus walked about in GALILEE; for he did not wish to walk in JUDEA, ‡ Because the JEWS were seeking to kill him.

2 ‡ And the FEAST of the JEWS was near,—the † FEAST of TABERNACLES.

3 His BROTHERS, therefore, said to him, "Remove hence, and go into JUDEA, so that thy DISCIPLES also may see thy WORKS which thou doest.

4 For no one does Anything in secret, and * seeks himself to be in public. If thou doest These things, manifest thyself to the WORLD."

5 (For ‡ not even his BROTHERS believed into him.)

6 JESUS then said to them. "My TIME is not

* VATICAN MANUSCRIPT.—1. Jesus. 4. seeks that the same be known.

† 2. The Feast of Tabernacles continued for a week, and was to commemorate the dwelling of the Israelites in tents. It is sometimes called the *feast of ingatherings.* Ex. xxiii. 16, and xxxiv. 22. The following are the principal ceremonies. (1.) During the entire week of its continuance, the people dwelt in booths or tents, erected in the fields or streets, or on the flat, terrace-like roofs of their houses. (2.) Extraordinary offerings were made. See Num. xxix. (3.) During the feast, branches of palm, olive, citron, myrtle, and willow, were carried in the hands, singing "*Hosanna,*" that is, *Save now;* or, *Save, I beseech thee.* Psa. cxviii. 25. It was meant as a prayer for the coming of the Messiah. Thus was Jesus conducted into Jerusalem, by the multitude, who believed him to be the promised Savior. (4.) The libation of water upon and around the altar, which was an emblem of the effusion of the Holy Sprit. To this Christ alluded, when, in the last day of the feast, he cried, "If any man thirst, let him come unto me and drink." During the whole festival, music, feasting, rejoicings, and illuminations, gladdened the city.—*Malcom.*

‡ 68. Acts v. 20. ‡ 69. Matt xvi. 16; Mark viii. 29; Luke ix. 20; John i. 49; xi. 27. ‡ 70. Luke vi. 13. ‡ 1 John v. 16. 18. ‡ 2. Lev. xxiii. 34. ‡ 3. Matt. xii. 46; Mark iii. 31; Acts i. 14. ‡ 5. Mark iii. 21.

ουπω παρεστιν· ὁ δε καιρος ὁ ὑμετερος παντοτε
not yet is present; the and season the yours always
εστιν ἑτοιμος. 7 Ου δυναται ὁ κοσμος μισειν
is ready. Not is able the world to hate
ὑμας· εμε δε μισει, ὁτι εγω μαρτυρω περι
you; me but it hates, because I testify concerning
αυτου, ὁτι τα εργα αυτου πονηρα εστιν. 8 Ὑμεις
it, that the works of it evil is. You
αναβητε εις την ἑορτην ταυτην· εγω ουκ ανα-
go up to the feast this; I not go
βαινω εις την ἑορτην ταυτην, ὁτι ὁ καιρος ὁ
up to the feast this, because the season the
εμος ουπω πεπληρωται. 9 Ταυτα ειπων αυτοις,
mine not yet has fully come. These things saying to them,
εμεινεν εν τῃ Γαλιλαιᾳ.
he remained in the Galilee.

10 Ὡς δε ανεβησαν οἱ αδελφοι αυτου, τοτε
When but had gone up the brothers of him, then
και αυτος ανεβη εις την ἑορτην, ου φανερως,
also he went up to the feast, not openly,
αλλ' ὡς εν κρυπτῳ. 11 Οἱ ουν Ιουδαιοι εζητουν
but as in secret. The then Jews sought
αυτον εν τῃ ἑορτῃ, και ελεγον· Που εστιν
him in the feast, and said; Where is
εκεινος; 12 Και γογγυσμος πολυς περι αυτου ην
he? And murmuring much about him was
εν τοις οχλοις. Οἱ μεν ελεγον· Ὁτι αγαθος
among the crowds. The some said; That good
εστιν· αλλοι ελεγον· Ου· αλλα πλανᾳ τον
he is; others said; No; but he deceives the
οχλον. 13 Ουδεις μεντοι παρρησιᾳ ελαλει περι
crowd. No one however with freedom spoke about
αυτου, δια τον φοβον των Ιουδαιων.
him, because of the fear of the Jews.

14 Ηδη δε της ἑορτης μεσουσης, ανεβη ὁ
Now and of the feast being half out, went up the
Ιησους εις το ἱερον, και εδιδασκε. 15 Και εθαυ-
Jesus into the temple, and taught. And won-
μαζον οἱ Ιουδαιοι, λεγοντες· Πως οὑτος γραμ-
dered the Jews, saying; How this let-
ματα οιδε, μη μεμαθηκως; 16 Απεκριθη αυτοις ὁ
ters knows, not having learned? Answered them the
Ιησους και ειπεν· Ἡ εμη διδαχη ουκ εστιν
Jesus and said; The my teaching not is
εμη, αλλα του πεμψαντος με. 17 Εαν τις θελῃ
mine, but of the sending me. If any one may wish
το θελημα αυτου ποιειν, γνωσεται περι της
the will of him to do, he shall know concerning the
διδαχης, ποτερον εκ του θεου εστιν, η εγω απ'
teaching, whether from the God it is, or I from
εμαυτου λαλω. 18 Ὁ αφ' ἑαυτου λαλων, την
myself speak. He from himself speaking, the
δοξαν την ιδιαν ζητει· ὁ δε ζητων την δοξαν
glory the own seeks; he but seeking the glory
του πεμψαντος αυτον, οὑτος αληθης εστι, και
of the sending him, this true is, and

yet arrived; but YOUR TIME is always ready.
7 ‡ The WORLD cannot hate you; but it hates Me, ‡ because I testify concerning it, That its WORKS are evil.
8 Go you up to *the FEAST; I am not going up to this FEAST, because *MY Time has not yet fully arrived."
9 And saying These Things to them he remained in GALILEE.
10 But when his BROTHERS, had gone up, then he also went up to the FEAST, not openly, but rather in a private manner.
11 ‡ The JEWS therefore, kept seeking him during the FEAST, and said, "Where is he?"
12 ‡ And there was much murmuring about him among the CROWDS; SOME said, "He is good;" OTHERS said, "No, but he is misleading the PEOPLE."
13 No one, however, spoke with freedom concerning him, ‡ because of the FEAR of the JEWS.
14 And now, the FEAST being advanced midway, *Jesus went up into the TEMPLE, and taught.
15 ‡ * Then the JEWS were astonished, saying, "How does this person know Letters, not having learned?"
16 *Jesus then answered them, and said, ‡ "MY Teaching is not mine, but HIS who SENT me.
17 ‡ If any one wish to perform his WILL, he shall know of the TEACHING, whether it is from GOD, or I am speaking from myself.
18 ‡ HE who SPEAKS from himself seeks his OWN GLORY; but HE who SEEKS the GLORY of HIM who SENT him, he is true, and

* VATICAN MANUSCRIPT.—8. the FEAST. 8. MY Time. 14. Jesus. 15. Then the JEWS. 16. Jesus then.

‡ 7. John xv. 19. ‡ 7. John iii. 19. ‡ 11. John xi. 56. ‡ 12. John ix. 16; x. 19. ‡ John. ix. 22; xii. 42; xix. 38. ‡ 15. Matt. xiii. 54; Mark vi. 2; Luke iv, 22; Acts ii. 7. ‡ 16. John iii. 11; viii. 28; xii. 49; xiv. 10, 24. ‡ 17. John viii. 40. ‡ 18. John v. 41; viii. 50.

αδικια εν αυτῳ ουκ εστιν. 19 Ου Μωσης
unrighteousness in him not is. Not Moses
δεδωκεν ὑμιν τον νομον; και ουδεις εξ ὑμων
has given to you the law? and no one of you
ποιει τον νομον· τι με ζητειτε αποκτειναι;
does the law: why me do you seek to kill?
20 Απεκριθη ὁ οχλος *[και ειπε·] Δαιμονιον
Answered the crowd [and said;] A demon
εχεις· τις σε ζητει αποκτειναι; 21 Απεκριθη ὁ
thou hast; who thee seeks to kill? Answered the
Ιησους και ειπεν αυτοις· Ἑν εργον εποιησα,
Jesus and said to them, One work I did,
και παντες θαυμαζητε δια τουτο. 22 Μωσης
and all you wonder because of this. Moses
δεδωκεν ὑμιν την περιτομην· (ουχ ὁτι εκ του
has given to you the circumcision; (not that of the
Μωσεως εστιν, αλλ' εκ των πατερων,) και εν
Moses it is, but of the fathers,) and in
σαββατῳ περιτεμνετε ανθρωπον. 23 Ει περι-
a sabbath you circumcise a man. If circum-
τομην λαμβανει ανθρωπος εν σαββατῳ, ἱνα μη
cision receives a man in a sabbath, that not
λυθῃ ὁ νομος Μωσεως, εμοι χολατε, ὁτι
may be loosed the law of Moses, with me are you angry, because
ὁλον ανθρωπον ὑγιη εποιησα εν σαββατῳ;
whole a man sound I made in a sabbath?
24 Μη κρινετε κατ' οψιν, αλλα την δικαιαν
Not judge you according to appearance, but the righteous
κρισιν κρινατε. 25 Ελεγον ουν τινες εκ των
judgment judge you. Said then some of the
Ἱεροσολυμιτων· Ουχ οὑτος εστιν, ὁν ζητουσιν
Jerusalemites; Not this is he, whom they seek
αποκτειναι; 26 και ιδε, παρρησια λαλει, και
to kill? and lo, boldly he is talking, and
ουδεν αυτῳ λεγουσι· μηποτε αληθως εγνωσαν
nothing to him they say; not truly did know
οἱ αρχοντες, ὁτι οὑτος εστιν ὁ Χριστος; 27 Αλλα
the rulers, that this is the Anointed? But
τουτον οιδαμεν, ποθεν εστιν· ὁ δε Χριστος ὁταν
this we know, whence he is; the but Anointed when
ερχηται, ουδεις γινωσκει, ποθεν εστιν. 28 Εκρα-
he comes, no one knows, whence he is. Cried
ξεν ουν εν τῳ ἱερῳ διδασκων ὁ Ιησους, και
then in the temple teaching the Jesus, and
λεγων· Καμε οιδατε, και οιδατε ποθεν ειμι· και
saying; And me you know, and you know whence I am; and
απ' εμαυτου ουκ εληλυθα, αλλ' εστιν αληθινος
of myself not I have come, but is true
ὁ πεμψας με, ὁν ὑμεις ουκ οιδατε. 29 Εγω οιδα
he having sent me, whom you not know. I know
αυτον, ὁτι παρ' αυτου ειμι, κακεινος με απεσ-
him, because from him I am, and he me sent.
τειλεν. 30 Εζητουν ουν αυτον πιασαι· και
They sought therefore him to seize; and
ουδεις επεβαλεν επ' αυτον την χειρα, ὁτι ουπω
no one put on him the hands, because not yet
εληλυθει ἡ ὡρα αυτου.
had come the hour of him.

there is no Unrighteousness in him.

19 Has not Moses given you the LAW, and not one of you performs the LAW? Why are you seeking to kill me?"

20 The CROWD answered, ‡ "Thou hast a Demon; who is seeking to kill thee?"

21 *Jesus answered and said to them, "I have done One Work, and you are all astonished because of this.

22 ‡ Moses has given you CIRCUMCISION; (not that it is of MOSES, but of ‡ the FATHERS;) and you circumcise a Man on a Sabbath.

23 If a * Man on a Sabbath receive Circumcision, so that the LAW of Moses may not be violated, are you angry with me ‡ Because I made a Man entirely well on a Sabbath?

24 ‡ Judge not according to Appearance, but judge RIGHTEOUS Judgment."

25 Then some inhabitants of Jerusalem said, "Is not this he whom they are seeking to kill?

26 And, behold, he is talking boldly, and they say nothing to him. Do the RULERS really acknowledge That this is the MESSIAH?

27 ‡ But we know Him, whence he is, but when the MESSIAH comes, no one knows whence he is."

28 JESUS, therefore, exclaimed, teaching in the TEMPLE, and saying, "You both know Me, and you know whence I am, and I have not come of myself, but HE who SENT me is true, whom you know not.

29 ‡ I know him Because I am from him, and He sent Me."

30 Then they sought to take him; and no one laid HANDS on him, Because his HOUR had not yet arrived.

* VATICAN MANUSCRIPT.—20. and said—*omit.* 21. Jesus. 23. MAN.

‡ 20. John viii. 48, 52; x. 20. ‡ 22. Lev xii. 3. ‡ 22. Gen. xvii. 10. ‡ 23. John v. 8, 9, 16. ‡ 24. Deut. i. 16, 17; Prov. xxiv. 23; viii. 15; James ii. 1. ‡ 27. Matt xiii. 55; Mark vi. 3; Luke iv. 22. ‡ 29. Matt. xi. 27; John x. 15.

31 Πολλοι δε εκ του οχλου επιστευσαν εις
Many, and out of the crowd believed into
αυτον, και ελεγον· Ότι ὁ Χριστος ὁταν ελθῃ,
him, and said; That the Anointed when he may come,
μητι πλειονα σημεια *[τουτων] ποιησει, ὡν
not more signs [of these] will do, which
οὑτος εποιησεν; 32 Ηκουσαν οἱ Φαρισαιοι του
he did? Heard the Pharisees of the
οχλου γογγυζοντος περι αυτου ταυτα· και
crowd murmuring about him these things; and
απεστειλαν οἱ Φαρισαιοι και οἱ αρχιερεις ὑπηρε-
sent the Pharisees and the high-priests officers,
τας, ἱνα πιασωσιν αυτον. 33 Ειπεν ουν ὁ Ιησους·
that they might seize him. Said then the Jesus;
Ετι μικρον χρονον μεθ' ὑμων ειμι, και ὑπαγω
Yet a little time with you I am, and I go
προς τον πεμψαντα με. 34 Ζητησετε με, και
to the sending me. You will seek me, and
ουχ εὑρησετε· και ὁπου ειμι εγω ὑμεις ου
not will find; and where am I you not
δυνασθε ελθειν. 35 Ειπον ουν οἱ Ιουδαιοι προς
are able to come. Said therefore the Jews to
ἑαυτους· Που οὑτος μελλει πορευεσθαι, ὁτι
themselves; Where this he is about to go, that
ἡμεις ουχ εὑρησομεν αυτον; μη εις την διασ-
we not shall find him? not into the dis-
πoραν των Ἑλληνων μελλει πορευεσθαι, και
persion of the Greeks is about to go, and
διδασκειν τους Ἑλληνας; 36 Τις εστιν οὑτος ὁ
to teach the Greeks? What is this the
λογος, ὁν ειπε· Ζητησετε με, και ουχ εὑρησετε·
word, which he said: You will seek me, and not you will find;
και ὁπου ειμι εγω ὑμεις ου δυνασθε ελθειν:
and where am I you not are able to come?

37 Ἐν δε τῃ εσχατῃ ἡμερᾳ τῃ μεγαλῃ της ἑορ-
In and the last day the great of the feast
της εἱστηκει ὁ Ιησους, και εκραξε, λεγων· Εαν
stood the Jesus, and cried, saying; If
τις διψᾳ, ερχεσθω προς με, και πινετω.
any one may thirst, let him come to me, and let him drink.
38 Ὁ πιστευων εις εμε, καθως ειπεν ἡ γραφη,
He believing into me, as said the scripture,
ποταμοι εκ της κοιλιας αυτου ῥευσουσιν ὑδατος
rivers out of the belly of him shall flow of water
ζωντος. 39 Τουτο δε ειπε περι του πνευματος,
living. This but said concerning the spirit,

31 But ‡ many of the CROWD believed into him, and said, "When the MESSIAH comes, will he do More Signs than what this person did?"

32 The PHARISEES heard the CROWD murmuring these things about him; and the * HIGH-PRIESTS and the PHARISEES sent Officers that they might seize him.

33 JESUS therefore said, ‡ "Yet a Little Time am I with you; then I am going to HIM who SENT me.

34 ‡ You will seek me, and will not find * me; and where I am, * there you cannot come."

35 The JEWS then said among themselves, "Where is he about to go, that we shall not find him? Is he about to go to ‡ the DISPERSION of † the GREEKS, and to teach the GREEKS?

36 What is This WORD that he said, 'You will seek me, and will not find * me; and where I am you cannot come?'"

37 ‡ Now in † the LAST, the GREAT Day of the FEAST, JESUS stood and cried, saying, ‡ "If any one thirst, let him come to me and drink.

38 HE BELIEVING into me, as the SCRIPTURE says, ‡ out of HIM shall flow Rivers of living Water."

39 ‡ But this he said concerning the SPIRIT,

* VATICAN MANUSCRIPT.—31. of these—*omit.* 32. HIGH-PRIESTS and the PHARISEES sent. 34. me; and. 34. there. 36. me; and.

† 35. Probably the Hellenists, or Grecian Jews, are here intended. These spoke the Greek language, and are thus distinguished from the Hebrews, who spoke the Hebrew language at that time. † 37. The last day grew into high esteem with the Jews, because on the preceding seven days they held that sacrifices were offered, not so much for themselves, as for the whole world. They offered, in the course of them, seventy bullocks, for the seventy nations of the world; but the eighth was wholly on their own behalf. They had then this solemn offering of water, the reason of which is this:—At the passover the Jews offered an omer to obtain from God his blessing on their harvest; at Pentecost, their first-fruits, to request his blessing on the fruits of the trees; and in the feast of tabernacles they offered water to God, partly referring to the water from the rock in the wilderness, (1 Cor. x. 4,) but chiefly to solicit the blessing of rain on the approaching seedtime.—*Lightfoot.* At the feast of tabernacles the Jews drew water from Siloam, with the sound of trumpets and of songs, to derive a blessing on the rains of the year; this season or September being the beginning of the year. There was therefore a pertinency in the images of thirsting, drinking, and rivers of water.—*Newcome.*

‡ 31. Matt. xii. 23; John iii. 2; viii. 30. ‡ 33. John xiii. 33; xvi. 16. ‡ 34. Hoshea v. 6; John viii. 21. ‡ 35. James i. 1; 1 Pet. i. 1. ‡ 37. Lev. xxiii. 36. ‡ 37. Isa. lv. 1; John vi. 35; Rev. xxii. 17. ‡ 38. Isa. xii. 3; John iv. 14. ‡ 39. John xvi. 7.

οὗ εμελλον λαμβανειν οἱ πιστευοντες εις
of which was about to receive the believing into
αυτον· ουπω γαρ ην πνευμα ἁγιον, ὁτι ὁ Ιησους
him; not yet for was spirit holy, because the Jesus
ουδεπω εδοξασθη. 40 Πολλοι ουν εκ του οχλου
not yet was glorified. Many therefore out of the crowd
ακουσαντες τον λογον, ελεγον· Οὑτος εστιν
having heard the word, said; This is
αληθως ὁ προφητης. 41 Αλλοι ελεγον· Οὑτος
truly the prophet. Others said; This
εστιν ὁ Χριστος. Αλλοι δε ελεγον· Μη γαρ
is the Anointed. Others but said; Not for
εκ της Γαλιλαιας ὁ Χριστος ερχεται; 42 Ουχι ἡ
out of the Galilee the Anointed comes? Not the
γραφη ειπεν, ὁτι εκ του σπερματος Δαυιδ, και
writing said, that of the seed of David, and
απο Βηθλεεμ της κωμης, ὁπου ην Δαυιδ, ὁ
from Bethlehem the village, where was David, the
Χριστος ερχεται; 43 Σχισμα ουν εν τῳ οχλῳ
Anointed comes? A division then in the crowd
εγενετο δι' αυτον. 44 Τινες δε ηθελον εξ αυτων
occurred through him. Some and wished of them
πιασαι αυτον· αλλ' ουδεις επεβαλεν επ' αυτον
to seize him; but no one put on him
τας χειρας.
the hands.

45 Ηλθον ουν οἱ ὑπηρεται προς τους αρχιερεις
Came therefore the officers to the high-priests
και Φαρισαιους. Και ειπον αυτοις εκεινοι·
and Pharisees. And said to them these;
Διατι ουκ ηγαγετε αυτον; 46 Απεκριθησαν οἱ
Why not did you bring him? Answered the
ὑπηρεται· Ουδεποτε οὑτως ελαλησεν ανθρωπος,
officers; Never thus spoke a man,
*[ὡς οὑτος ὁ ανθρωπος.] 47 Απεκριθησαν ουν
[as this the man.] Answered then
*[αυτοις] οἱ Φαρισαιοι· Μη και ὑμεις πεπλαν-
[them] the Pharisees; Not also you have been
ησθε; 48 μη τις εκ των αρχοντων επιστευσεν
deceived? not any one of the rulers believed
εις αυτον, η εκ των Φαρισαιων; 49 αλλ' ὁ οχλος
into him, or of the Pharisees? but the crowd
οὑτος ὁ μη γινωσκων τον νομον· επικαταρατοι
this the not knowing the law, accursed
εισι. 50 Λεγει Νικοδημος προς αυτους, ὁ ελθων
are. Says Nicodemus to them, he coming
νυκτος προς αυτον, εἱς ων εξ αυτων· 51 Μη ὁ
of night to him, one being of them; Not the
νομος ἡμων κρινει τον ανθρωπον, εαν μη ακου-
law of us judges the man, if not it may
σῃ παρ' αυτου προτερον, και γνῳ τι ποιει;
hear from him first, and may know what he does?
52 Απεκριθησαν και ειπον αυτῳ· Μη και συ εκ
They answered and said to him; Not also thou of

which THOSE BELIEVING into him were about to receive; for the Holy Spirit * had not yet been given, because JESUS was not yet glorified.

40 Many, therefore, of the CROWD, having heard * these WORDS, said, "This is truly ‡ the PROPHET."

41 * SOME said, "This is the MESSIAH." But others said, "Does the MESSIAH, then, come from GALILEE?

42 ‡ Does not the SCRIPTURE say, That of the SEED of David, and from Bethlehem, ‡ the VILLAGE where David was, the MESSIAH comes?"

43 A Division then occurred, among the CROWD because of him;

44 and some of them wished to seize him, but no one laid HANDS on him.

45 The OFFICERS then came to the HIGH-PRIESTS and Pharisees, and they said to them, "Why did you not bring him?"

46 The OFFICERS answered, ‡ "A Man never spoke thus."

47 Then the PHARISEES answered, "Have you also been deceived?

48 ‡ Did any of the RULERS believe into him, or of the PHARISEES?

49 But † THIS CROWD, who do not KNOW the LAW, are accursed."

50 Nicodemus says to them, (‡ HE who CAME * to him before, being one of them,)

51 "Does our LAW judge the MAN, unless it first hear from him, and know what he does?"

52 They answered and said to him, "Art thou also

---

* VATICAN MANUSCRIPT.—39. had not yet been given. 40. these WORDS, said. 41. SOME said. 46. as this the MAN—*omit*. 47. them—*omit*. 50. to him before.

† 49. The common people were treated by the Pharisees with the most sovereign contempt. They were termed *am ha-arets, people of the earth;* and were not thought worthy to have a resurrection to eternal life.—*Clarke.*

‡ 40. Deut. xviii. 15, 18; John i. 21; vi. 14. ‡ 42. Psa. cxxxii. 11; Jer. xxiii. 5; Micah v. 2; Matt. ii. 5; Luke ii. 4. ‡ 43. 1 Sam. xvi. 1, 4. ‡ 46. Matt. vii. 29. ‡ 48. John xii. 42; Acts vi. 7; 1 Cor. i. 20, 26; ii. 8. ‡ 50. John iii. 2.

της Γαλιλαιας ει; ερευνησον και ιδε, ὁτι προ-
the Galilee art? search and see, that a pro-
φητης εκ της Γαλιλαιας ουκ εγηγερται.
phet out of the Galilee not has been raised.
53 *[Και επορευθη ἑκαστος εις τον οικον
[And went every one into the house
αὑτου. ΚΕΦ. η'. 8. 1 Ιησους δε επορευθη εις
of himself. Jesus but went into
το ορος των ελαιων. 2 ορθρου δε παλιν παρε-
the mountain of the olive-trees. early morn and again he
γενετο εις το ἱερον, και πας ὁ λαος ηρχετο προς
came into the temple, and all the people came to
αυτον· και καθισας εδιδασκεν αυτους. 3 Αγουσι
him; and having sat down he taught them. Bring
δε οἱ γραμματεις και οἱ Φαρισαιοι προς αυτον
and the scribes and the Pharisees to him
γυναικα εν μοιχειᾳ κατειλημμενην, και στη-
a woman in adultery having been taken, and plac-
σαντες αυτην εν μεσῳ, 4 λεγουσιν αυτῳ·
ing her in middle, they say to him;
Διδασκαλε, αὑτη ἡ γυνη κατειληφθη επαυτοφω-
O teacher, this the woman was taken in the very act
ρῳ μοιχευομενη. 5 Εν δε τῳ νομῳ Μωσης ἡμιν
committing adultery. In now the law Moses to us
ενετειλατο τας τοιαυτας λιθοβολεισθαι· συ
commanded the such like to be stoned? thou
ουν τι λεγεις; 6 Τουτο δε ελεγον πειραζον-
therefore what sayest thou; This but they said tempting
τες αυτον, ἱνα εχωσι κατηγορειν αυτου. Ὁ δε
him, that they might have to accuse him. The-but
Ιησους κατω κυψας, τῳ δακτυλῳ εγραφεν εις
Jesus down stooping, with the finger wrote on
την γην. 7 Ὡς δε επεμενον ερωτωντες αυτον,
the ground. When but they continued asking him,
ανακυψας ειπε προς αυτους· Ὁ αναμαρτητος
having raised up he said to them; He without sin
ὑμων, πρωτος τον λιθον επ' αυτῃ βαλετω.
of you, first the stone on her let him cast.
8 Και παλιν κατω κυψας, εγραφεν εις την γην.
And again down stooping, wrote on the ground.
9 Οἱ δε ακουσαντες, και ὑπο της συνειδησεως
They and having heard, and by the conscience
ελεγχομενοι, εξηρχοντο εἱς καθ' εἱς, αρξαμενοι
being convinced, went out one by one, beginning
απο των πρεσβυτερων ἑως των εσχατων· και
from the elders even to the last ones; and
κατελειφθη μονος ὁ Ιησους, και ἡ γυνη εν μεσῳ
left alone the Jesus, and the woman in middle

from GALILEE? Search, and see, that no Prophet has been raised † out of GALILEE."

53 *[[And every one went to his own HOUSE;

CHAPTER VIII.

1 but Jesus went to the MOUNT of OLIVES.

2 And in the Morning he came again to the TEMPLE, and All the PEOPLE came to him, and having sat down, he taught them.

3 And the SCRIBES and the PHARISEES bring to him a Woman having been taken in Adultery; and placing her in the Midst,

4 they say to him, "Teacher, This WOMAN was taken in the very act, committing adultery.

5 ‡ Now, in the LAW, Moses commanded us to stone SUCH LIKE women; therefore, what dost thou say?"

6 But this they said, trying him, that they might have something of which to accuse him. But JESUS stooping down, wrote on the GROUND with his FINGER.

7 And when they continued asking him, rising up, he said to them, "HE who is WITHOUT SIN of you, ‡ let him first cast the STONE at her."

8 And again, stooping down, he wrote on the GROUND.

9 And THEY, HAVING HEARD, and being convicted by their CONSCIENCES, went out, one by one, beginning from the ELDERS, even to the LAST; and JESUS was left alone, and the WOMAN standing in the Midst.

* VATICAN MANUSCRIPT.—53. to viii. 11—*omit*.

† 52. This conclusion, according to Calmut, was incorrect. *Jonah* was of *Gathheper*, in Galilee; see 2 Kings xiv. 25, compared with Josh. xix. 13. *Nahum* was a *Galilean*, for he was of the tribe of Simeon, and some suppose *Malachi* was of the same place. † 53. This paragraph concerning the woman taken in adultery is wanting in the Alexandrian (see Woide's Preface,). Vatican, Ephrem, and other manuscripts of great authority, and in the oldest copies of the Syraic version; and is not cited by Origen, Chrysostom, and other ancient ecclesiastical writers. It is found in the Cambridge manuscript, though with some variations from the received text. Griesbach keeps it in his text; but with great hesitation. *Improved Version*.

‡ 5. Lev. xx. 10; Deut. xxii. 22. ‡ 7. Deut. xvii. 7; Rom. ii. 1.

ἑστωσα. 10 Ανακυψας δε ὁ Ιησους, και μηδενα
standing. Having raised up and the Jesus, and no one
θεασαμενος πλην της γυναικος, ειπεν αυτῃ· Ἡ
seeing but the woman, said to her; The
γυνη, που εισιν εκεινοι οἱ κατηγοροι σου;
woman, where are those the accusers of thee?
ουδεις σε κατεκρινεν; 11 Ἡ δε ειπεν· Ουδεις,
no one thee condemned? She and said; No one,
κυριε. Ειπε δε αυτῃ ὁ Ιησους· Ουδε εγω σε
O lord. Said and to her the Jesus; Neither I thee
κατακρινω· πορευου, και μηκετι ἁμαρτανε.]
condemn; go, and no longer do thou sin.]
12 Παλιν ουν ὁ Ιησους αυτοις ελαλησε, λεγων·
Again therefore the Jesus to them spoke, saying;
Εγω ειμι το φως του κοσμου· ὁ ακολουθων εμοι,
I am the light of the world; he following me,
ου μη περιπατησει εν τῃ σκοτιᾳ, αλλ' ἑξει το
not not shall walk in the darkness, but shall have the
φως της ζωης. 13 Ειπον ουν αυτῳ οἱ Φαρισαιοι·
light of the life. Said therefore to him the Pharisees;
Συ περι σεαυτου μαρτυρεις· ἡ μαρτυρια σου
Thou concerning thyself dost testify; the testimony of thee
ουκ εστιν αληθης. 14 Απεκριθη Ιησους και
not is true. Answered Jesus and
ειπεν αυτοις· Καν εγω μαρτυρω περι εμαυτου,
said to them; Even if I testify concerning myself,
αληθης εστιν ἡ μαρτυρια μου· ὁτι οιδα, ποθεν
true is the testimony of me; because I know, whence
ηλθον, και που ὑπαγω· ὑμεις δε ουκ οιδατε,
I came, and where I go; you but not know,
ποθεν ερχομαι, η που ὑπαγω. 15 Ὑμεις κατα
whence I came, or where I go. You according to
την σαρκα κρινετε, εγω ου κρινω ουδενα. 16 Και
the flesh judge, I not judge no one. Even
εαν κρινω δε εγω, ἡ κρισις ἡ εμη αληθης εστιν·
if judge but I, the judgment the my true is;
ὁτι μονος ουκ ειμι, αλλ' εγω και ὁ πεμψας με
because alone not I am, but I and the having sent me
πατηρ. 17 Και εν τῳ νομῳ δε τῳ ὑμετερῳ γεγ-
father. Also in the law and the your it has
ραπται· "Ὁτι δυο ανθρωπων ἡ μαρτυρια
been written; "That two of men the testimony
αληθης εστιν." 18 Εγω ειμι ὁ μαρτυρων περι
true is." I am he testifying concerning
εμαυτου, και μαρτυρει περι εμου ὁ πεμψας με
myself, and testifies concerning me the having sent me
πατηρ. 19 Ελεγον ουν αυτῳ· που εστιν ὁ πατηρ
father. They said then to him; where is the father

10 And JESUS raising up and seeing no one but the WOMAN, said to her, "WOMAN, where are those, thine ACCUSERS? Did no one condemn Thee?"
11 And she said, "No one, sir." And JESUS said to her, ‡ "Neither do I condemn Thee; ‡ go, and sin no more."]]
12 Again, therefore, JESUS spoke to them, saying, † ‡ "I am the LIGHT of the WORLD; HE who FOLLOWS me shall not walk in the DARKNESS, but shall have the LIGHT of LIFE."
13 Then the PHARISEES said to him, ‡ "Thou dost testify of thyself; thy TESTIMONY is not true."
14 Jesus answered and said to them, "Even if I testify concerning myself, my TESTIMONY is true; Because I know whence I came and where I go; but you know not whence I came, or where I go.
15 ‡ You judge according to the FLESH; ‡ I judge no one.
16 But even if I judge, MY JUDGMENT is true; Because I am not alone, but I and the FATHER who SENT me.
17 And it has also been written in YOUR LAW, ‡ That the TESTIMONY of Two Men is true.
18 I am ONE who TESTIFIES concerning myself, and the FATHER who SENT me testifies concerning me."
19 Then they said to him, "Where is thy FA-

† 12. The Rabbins denominated the Supreme Being *the light of the world*, and this title being assumed by our Lord was a cause of offence to the Jews. The Messiah was also frequently spoken of by the prophets under the emblem of *light*. See Isa. lx. 1; xlix. 6; ix. 2. Therefore, by applying this symbol to himself, the Pharisees must at once have perceived that he claimed the Messiahship. Buxtorf in Synag. Jud. c. xxii. tells us, that the 9th day, or day after the expiration of the 8th, which belonged to "the feast of the tabernacles," is a solemn day likewise, and is called "the feast of joy for the law;" because on that day (says he,) the last section of the law was read, the rest having been read weekly in the course of the preceding sabbaths. He adds, that on this 9th day the custom of the Jews is to take all the books of the law out of the chest and to put a candle into it, in allusion to Prov. vi. 23, or rather Psa. cxix. 105. But perhaps, after all, it was to the *light* which their understanding received from the reading of the law, that Jesus here alluded to, when he said, "I am the light of the world."

‡ 11. Luke ix. 56; xii. 14; John iii. 17. ‡ 11. John v. 14. ‡ 12. John i. 4, 5, 9; iii. 19; ix. 5; xii. 35, 36, 46. ‡ 13. John v. 31. ‡ 15. John vii. 24. ‡ 15. John iii. 17; xii. 47; xviii. 36. ‡ 17. Deut. xvii. 6; xix. 15; Matt. xviii. 16; 2 Cor. xiii. 1; Heb x. 28.

σου; Απεκριθη Ιησους· Ουτε εμε οιδατε, ουτε
of thee? Answered Jesus; Neither me you know, nor
τον πατερα μου. Ει εμε ηδειτε, και τον πατερα
the father of me. If me you knew, also the father
μου ηδειτε αν. 20 Ταυτα τα ῥηματα ελαλησεν
of me you would know. These the words he spoke
εν τῳ γαζοφυλακιῳ, διδασκων εν τῳ ἱερῳ· και
in the treasury, teaching in the temple; and
ουδεις επιασεν αυτον, ὁτι ουπω εληλυθει ἡ ὡρα
no one seized him, because not yet had come the hour
αυτου.
of him.

21 Ειπεν ουν παλιν αυτοις ὁ Ιησους· Εγω
Said therefore again to them the Jesus; I
ὑπαγω, και ζητησετε με, και εν τῃ ἁμαρτιᾳ
go away, and you will seek me, and in the sin
ὑμων αποθανεισθε· ὁπου εγω ὑπαγω, ὑμεις ου
of you you will die; where I go, you not
δυνασθε ελθειν. 22 Ελεγον ουν οἱ Ιουδαιοι·
are able to come. Said then the Jews;
Μητι αποκτενει ἑαυτον, ὁτι λεγει· Ὁπου εγω
Not will he kill himself, because he says; Where I
ὑπαγω, ὑμεις ου δυνασθε ελθειν; 23 Και ειπεν
go, you not are able to come? And he said
αυτοις· Ὑμεις εκ των κατω εστε, εγω εκ των
to them; You from the beneath are, I from the
ανω ειμι· ὑμεις εκ του κοσμου τουτου εστε,
above am; you from the world this are,
εγω ουκ ειμι εκ του κοσμου τουτου. 24 Ειπον
I not am from the world this. I said
ουν ὑμιν, ὁτι αποθανεισθε εν ταις ἁμαρτιαις
therefore to you, that you will die in the sins
ὑμων· εαν γαρ μη πιστευσητε, ὁτι εγω ειμι,
of you; if for not you may believe, that I am,
αποθανεισθε εν ταις ἁμαρτιαις ὑμων. 25 Ελεγον
you will die in the sins of you. They said
ουν αυτῳ· Συ τις ει; Και ειπεν αυτοις ὁ
therefore to him; Thou who art? And said to them the
Ιησους· Την αρχην ὁ, τι και λαλω ὑμιν.
Jesus; The beginning what, what even I say to you.
26 Πολλα εχω περι ὑμων λαλειν, και κρινειν·
Many things I have about you to say, and to judge;
αλλ' ὁ πεμψας με αληθης εστι· καγω ἁ ηκουσα
but he having sent me true is; and I what I heard
παρ' αυτου, ταυτα λεγω εις τον κοσμον. 27 Ουκ
from him, these things I say to the world Not
εγνωσαν, ὁτι τον πατερα αυτοις ελεγεν. 28 Ειπεν
they knew, that the father to them he spoke. Said
ουν *[αυτοις] ὁ Ιησους· Ὁταν ὑψωσητε τον υἱον
then [to them] the Jesus; When you may lift up the son
του ανθρωπου, τοτε γνωσεσθε ὁτι εγω ειμι· και
of the man, then you will know that I am; and
απ' εμαυτου ποιω ουδεν, αλλα καθως εδιδαξε με
from myself I do nothing, but as taught me
ὁ πατηρ μου ταυτα λαλω· 29 και ὁ πεμψας με,
the father of me these things I say; and he having sent me,
μετ' εμου εστιν· ουκ αφηκε με μονον ὁ πατηρ,
with me is; not left me alone the father,

THER?" Jesus answered, "You neither know Me, nor my FATHER; if you knew Me, you would also know my FATHER."

20 ‡ These WORDS he spoke in the TREASURY, teaching in the TEMPLE; and no one seized him, Because his HOUR had not yet come.

21 Then *he said to them again, ‡ "I am going away, and you will seek me, and will die in your SIN; where I go, you cannot come."

22 The JEWS therefore said, "Will he kill himself, that he says, Where I go, you cannot come?"

23 And he said to them, "You are from BELOW; I am from ABOVE. ‡ You are of *This WORLD; I am not of this WORLD.

24 Therefore I said to you, That you will die in your SINS; for if you believe not That I am he, you will die in your SINS."

25 Then they said to him, "Who art thou?" *JESUS says to them, Even what I said to you at the BEGINNING.

26 I have many things to say and to judge concerning you; but HE who SENT me is true; ‡ and what I heard from him, These things I say to the WORLD."

27 They knew not That he spoke to them of the FATHER.

28 Jesus therefore said, ‡ "When you shall lift up the SON of MAN, then you will know That I am he; and I do nothing of myself; but as my FATHER taught me, I say These things.

29 And HE who SENT me is with me; *he has not left me alone; ‡ Because I

* VATICAN MANUSCRIPT.—21. he said. 23. of This WORLD. 25. Jesus says. 28. to them—*omit*. 29. he has not left me.

‡ 20. Mark xii. 41. ‡ 21. John vii. 34; xiii. 33. ‡ 23. John xv. 19; xvii. 16; 1 John iv. 5. ‡ 26. John iii. 32; xv. 15. ‡ 28. John xii. 32. ‡ 29. John iv. 34; v. 30; vi. 38.

ὁτι εγω τα αρεστα αυτῳ ποιω παντοτε.
because I the things pleasing to him do always.
30 Ταυτα αυτου λαλουντος, πολλοι επιστευσαν
These of him speaking, many believed
εις αυτον.
into him.
31 Ελεγεν ουν ὁ Ιησους προς τους πεπιστευ-
Said then the Jesus to those having believed
κοτας αυτῳ Ιουδαιους· Εαν ὑμεις μεινητε εν τῳ
him Jews; If you may abide in the
λογῳ τῳ εμῳ, αληθως μαθηται μου εστε, 32 και
word the my, truly disciples of me you are, and
γνωσεσθε την αληθειαν, και ἡ αληθεια ελευθε-
you shall know the truth, and the truth shall make
ρωσει ὑμας. 33 Απεκριθησαν αυτῳ· Σπερμα
free you. They answered him: Seed
Αβρααμ εσμεν, και ουδενι δεδουλευκαμεν πω-
of Abraam we are, and to no one have we been slaves at
ποτε· πως συ λεγεις· Ὁτι ελευθεροι γενησεσθε;
any time; how thou sayest; That free you shall become?
34 Απεκριθη αυτοις ὁ Ιησους· Αμην αμην λεγω
Answered them the Jesus; Indeed indeed I say
ὑμιν, ὁτι πας ὁ ποιων την ἁμαρτιαν, δουλος
to you, that every one who is doing the sin, a slave
εστι της ἁμαρτιας. 35 Ὁ δε δουλος ου μενει εν
is of the sin. The but slave not abides in
τῃ οικιᾳ εις τον αιωνα· ὁ υἱος μενει εις τον αιωνα.
the house to the age; the son abides to the age.
36 Εαν ουν ὁ υἱος ὑμας ελευθερωσῃ, οντως ελευ-
If then the son you may make free, really free
θεροι εσεσθε. 37 Οιδα, ὁτι σπερμα Αβρααμ εστε·
you shall be. I know, that seed of Abraam you are;
αλλα ζητειτε με αποκτειναι, ὁτι ὁ λογος ὁ εμος
but you seek me to kill, because the word the mine
ου χωρει εν ὑμιν. 38 Εγω ὁ ἑωρακα παρα τῳ
not has place in you. I what have seen from the
πατρι μου, λαλω· και ὑμεις ουν ὁ εωρακατε
father of me, I speak; and you therefore what you have seen
παρα τῳ πατρι ὑμων, ποιειτε. 39 Απεριθησαν
from the father of you, do. They answered
και ειπον αυτῳ· Ὁ πατηρ ἡμων Αβρααμ εστι.
and said to him: The father of us Abraam is.
Λεγει αυτοις ὁ Ιησους· Ει τεκνα του Αβρααμ
Says to them the Jesus; If children of the Abraam
εστε, τα εργα του Αβρααμ εποιειτε· 40 Νυν δε
you are, the works of the Abraam you would do: Now but
ζητειτε με αποκτειναι, ανθρωπον, ὁς την αλη-
you seek me to kill, a man, who the truth
θειαν ὑμιν λελαληκα, ἡν ηκουσα παρα του θεου·
to you has spoken, which I have heard from the God;
τουτο Αβρααμ ουκ εποιησεν. Ὑμεις ποιειτε τα
this Abraam not did. You do the
εργα του πατρος ὑμων. 41 Ειπον ουν αυτῳ·
works of the father of you. They said then to him,

always do the things pleasing to him."
30 As he was speaking These things, many believed into him.
31 JESUS therefore said to the Jews who had BELIEVED him, "If you abide in MY WORD, you are certainly my Disciples.
32 And you shall know the TRUTH, and ‡ the TRUTH shall make you free."
33 They answered him, "We are Abraham's Offspring, and have never been in slavery to any one. How dost thou say, 'You shall become free?'"
34 * Jesus answered them, "Indeed, I assure you, ‡ that EVERY ONE DOING SIN is a Slave of SIN.
35 ‡ But the SLAVE does not abide in the HOUSE to the AGE, the son abides to the AGE.
36 If, therefore, the SON make you free, you will indeed be free.
37 I know That you are ABRAHAM'S Offspring; but you are seeking to kill Me, Because MY WORD has no place in you.
38 ‡ I speak what I have seen with my FATHER; and you, therefore, do what you have * heard from your FATHER."
39 They answered and said to him, "Our FATHER is Abraham." JESUS says to them, ‡ "If you were Children of ABRAHAM, you would do the WORKS of ABRAHAM.
40 But now you are seeking to kill Me, a Man who has spoken to you the TRUTH, which I heard from GOD; This Abraham did not.
41 You do the WORKS of your FATHER." * They said to him, 'We have not

* VATICAN MANUSCRIPT.—34. Jesus said to him. 38. heard from your FATHER. 41. They

‡ 32. Rom. vi. 14, 18, 22; viii. 2; Gal. v. 1; James i. 25; ii. 12. ‡ 34. Rom. vi. 16, 20; 2 Pet. ii. 19. * 35. Gal. iv. 30. ‡ 38. John iii. 32; v. 19, 30; xiv. 10, 24. ‡ 39. Rom. ii. 28; ix. 7; Gal. iii. 7, 29.

Ἡμεις εκ πορνειας ου γεγεννημεθα· ἑνα πατε-
We from fornication not have been born; one father
ρα εχομεν, τον θεον. 42 Ειπεν αυτοις ὁ Ιησους·
we have, the God. Said to them the Jesus;
Ει ὁ θεος πατηρ ὑμων ην, ηγαπατε αν εμε· εγω
If the God a father of you was, you would love me; I
γαρ εκ του θεου εξηλθον και ἡκω· ουδε γαρ απ'
for from the God came out and am come; not even for of
εμαυτου εληλυθα, αλλ' εκεινος με απεστειλε.
myself I have come, but he me sent.
43 Διατι την λαλιαν την εμην ου γινωσκετε;
Why the speech the mine not know you?
Ὁτι ου δυνασθε ακουειν τον λογον τον εμον.
Because not you are able to hear the word the mine.
44 Ὑμεις εκ του πατρος του διαβολου εστε, και
You from the father the accuser are, and
τας επιθυμιας του πατρος ὑμων θελετε ποιειν·
the lusts of the father of you you wish to do;
Εκεινος ανθρωποκτονος ην απ' αρχης, και εν τῃ
He a manslayer was from a beginning, and in the
αληθειᾳ ουχ ἑστηκεν· ὁτι ουκ εστιν αληθεια εν
truth not has stood; because not is truth in
αυτῳ. Ὁταν λαλῃ το ψευδος, εκ των ιδιων
him. When may speak the falsehood, from the own
λαλει· ὁτι ψευστης εστι, και ὁ πατηρ αυτου.
he speaks; because a liar is, also the father of him.
45 Εγω δε ὁτι την αληθειαν λεγω, ου πιστευετε
I but because the truth I speak, not you believe
μοι. 46 Τις εξ ὑμων ελεγχει με περι αμαρτιας;
me. Who of you convicts me concerning sin?
ει αληθειαν λεγω, διατι ὑμεις ου πιστευετε μοι;
if truth I speak, why you not believe me?
47 Ὁ ων εκ του θεου, τα ῥηματα του θεου ακουει·
He being from the God, the words of the God hears;
δια τουτο ὑμεις ουκ ακουετε, ὁτι εκ του θεου
through this you not hear, because from the God
ουκ εστε. 48 Απεκριθησαν οἱ Ιουδαιοι και ειπον
not you are. Answered the Jews and said
αυτῳ· Ου καλως λεγομεν ἡμεις, ὁτι Σαμαρειτης
to him; Not well say we, that a Samaritan
ει συ, και δαιμονιον εχεις; 49 Απεκριθη Ιησους·
art thou, and a demon thou hast? Answered Jesus;
Εγω δαιμονιον ουκ εχω, αλλα τιμω τον πατερα
I a demon not have, but I honor the father
μου, και ὑμεις ατιμαζετε με. 50 Εγω δε ου ζητω
of me, and you dishonor me. I but not seek
την δοξαν μου· εστιν ὁ ζητων και κρινων.
the glory of me; it is he seeking and judging.
51 Αμην αμην λεγω ὑμιν, εαν τις τον λογον τον
Indeed indeed I say to you, if any one the word the
εμον τηρησῃ, θανατον ου μη θεωρησῃ εις τον
mine may keep, death not not he may see to the
αιωνα. 52 Ειπον ουν αυτῳ οἱ Ιουδαιοι· Νυν
age. Said then to him the Jews; Now
εγνωκαμεν, ὁτι δαιμονιον εχεις· Αβρααμ απε-
we know, that a demon thou hast; Abraam died

been born of Fornication we have One Father, God."

42 * Jesus said to them, ‡ "If GOD were your * FATHER, you would love me; for I came forth from GOD, and am come; for I am not even come of myself, but He sent Me.

43 Why do you not know MY SPEECH? Because you can not hear MY WORD.

44 ‡ You are from the FATHER, the ACCUSER, and the LUSTS of your FATHER you wish to do. He was a Manslayer from the Beginning, and has not stood in the TRUTH, Because there is no Truth in him. When [any one] speaks a FALSEHOOD, he speaks from his OWN; Because his FATHER also is a Liar.

45 But because I speak the TRUTH, you do not believe me.

46 Who of you convicts me of Sin? If I speak the Truth, why do you not believe me?

47 ‡ HE who is from GOD hears the WORDS of God; on this account you hear not, because you are not from GOD."

48 The JEWS answered and said to him, "Do we not say well That thou art a Samaritan, and ‡ hast a Demon?"

49 Jesus answered, "I have not a Demon; but I honor my FATHER, and you dishonor me.

50 But ‡ I seek not my GLORY; there is ONE who SEEKS it, and judges.

51 Indeed, I assure you, ‡ If any one keep * MY Word, he will by no means see Death to the AGE"

52 * The JEWS said to him, "Now we know That thou hast a Demon. ‡ Abra-

* VATICAN MANUSCRIPT.—42. Jesus. 42. FATHER. 51. MY Word. 52. The JEWS said.

‡ 42. John v. 43; vii. 28, 29. ‡ 44. 1 John iii. 8. ‡ 47. John x. 26, 27; 1 John iv. 6. ‡ 48. John vii. 20; x. 20. ‡ 50. John v. 41; vii. 18. ‡ 51. John v. 24; xi. 26. ‡ 52. Zech. i. 5; Heb. xi. 13.

θανε και οἱ προφηται, και συ λεγεις· Εαν τις
and the prophets, and thou sayest, If any one
τον λογον μου τηρησῃ, ου μη γευσηται θανατου
the word of me may keep, not not may taste of death
εις τον αιωνα. 53 Μη συ μειζων ει του πατρος
to the age. Not thou greater art of the father
ἡμων Αβρααμ, ὁστις απεθανε; και οἱ προφηται
of us Abraam, who died? and the prophets
απεθανον· τινα σεαυτον ποιεις; 54 Απεκριθη
died; whom thyself makest thou? Answered
Ιησους· Εαν εγω δοξαζω εμαυτον, ἡ δοξα μου
Jesus; If I glorify myself, the glory of me
ουδεν εστιν. Εστιν ὁ πατηρ μου ὁ δοξαζων με,
nothing is. He is the father of me he glorifying me,
ὁν ὑμεις λεγετε, ὁτι θεος ὑμων εστι, 55 και ουκ
whom you say, that a God of you he is, and not
εγνωκατε αυτον· εγω δε οιδα αυτον. Και εαν
you know him; I but know him. And if
ειπω, ὁτι ουκ οιδα αυτον, εσομαι ὁμοιος ὑμων,
I say, that not I know him, I shall be like you,
ψευστης. Αλλ' οιδα αυτον, και τον λογον
a liar. But I know him, and the word
αυτου τηρω. 56 Αβρααμ ὁ πατηρ ὑμων ηγαλλι-
of him I keep. Abraam the father of you ardently
ασατο, ἱνα ιδῃ την ἡμεραν την εμην· και ειδε,
desired, that he might see the day the my; and he saw,
και εχαρη. 57 Ειπον ουν οἱ Ιουδαιοι προς
and was glad. Said then the Jews to
αυτον· Πεντηκοντα ετη ουπω εχεις, και Αβρααμ
him; Fifty years not yet thou art, and Abraam
ἑωρακας; 58 Ειπεν αυτοις ὁ Ιησους· Αμην αμην
hast thou seen? Said to them the Jesus, Indeed indeed
λεγω ὑμιν, πριν Αβρααμ γενεσθαι, εγω ειμι.
I say to you, before Abraam to have been born, I am.
59 Ηραν ουν λιθους, ἱνα βαλωσιν επ' αυτον·
They took up therefore stones, that they might cast on him;
Ιησους *[δε] εκρυβη, και εξηλθεν εκ του ἱερου.
Jesus [but] hid himself, and went out of the temple.

ΚΕΦ. θ'. 9.

1 Και παραγων, ειδεν ανθρωπον τυφλον εκ
And passing by, he saw a man blind from
γενετης. 2 Και ηρωτησαν αυτον οἱ μαθηται
birth. And asked him the disciples
αυτου, λεγοντες· Ραββι, τις ἡμαρτεν; οὑτος,
of him, saying; Rabbi, who sinned? this,
η οἱ γονεις αυτου, ἱνα τυφλος γεννηθῃ; 3 Απεκ-
or the parents of him, that blind he should be born? An-
ριθη Ιησους· Ουτε οὑτος ἡμαρτεν, ουτε οἱ
swered Jesus; Neither this sinned, nor the
γονεις αυτου· αλλ' ἱνα φανερωθῃ τα εργα του
parents of him; but that may be manifested the works of the
θεου εν αυτῳ. 4 Εμε δει εργαζεσθαι τα εργα
God in him. Me it behoves to work the works

ham died, and the PROPHETS; and thou sayest, If any one keep my WORD, he will by no means *see Death to the AGE.

53 Art thou greater than our FATHER Abraham, who died, and the PROPHETS died? Whom dost *thou make thyself?"

54 Jesus answered, "If *I should glorify myself, my GLORY is nothing? ‡HE who GLORIFIES me is my FATHER, of whom you say, That he is your God.

55 And you have not known him, but I know him; and if I say, that I do not know him, I shall be like you a Liar; but I know him, and keep his WORD.

56 Abraham, your FATHER, ardently desired that he might see MY DAY: and ‡he saw, and was glad."

57 Then the JEWS said to him, "Thou art not yet Fifty Years old, and hast thou seen Abraham?"

58 *JESUS said to them, "Indeed, I assure you, Before Abraham was born, I am he."

59 ‡Then they took up Stones that they might cast at him; but Jesus hid himself, and went forth out of the TEMPLE.

CHAPTER IX.

1 And passing along, he saw a Man blind from Birth.

2 And his DISCIPLES asked him, saying, "Rabbi, ‡who sinned, he, or his PARENTS, so that he was born blind?"

3 Jesus answered, "Neither did he sin, nor his PARENTS, but that the WORKS of GOD might be displayed in him.

4 ‡*I must perform the

* VATICAN MANUSCRIPT.—52. see Death to the Age. 54. I should glorify. 58. Jesus. 59. but—omit. 4. We must.

‡ 54. John v. 41; xvi. 14; xvii. 1; Acts iii. 13; 2 Pet. i. 17. † 56. Heb. xi. 13. ‡ 59. John x. 31, 39; xi. 8. ‡ 2. ver. 34. ‡ 4. John iv. 34; v. 19, 36; xi. 9; xii. 35; xvii 4.

του πεμψαντος με, ἑως ἡμερα εστιν· ερχεται
of the sending me, while day it is; comes
νυξ, ὁτε ουδεις δυναται εργαζεσθαι. 5 Ὁταν εν
night, when no one is able to work. While in
τῳ κοσμῳ ω, φως ειμι του κοσμου. 6 Ταυτα
the world I may be, light I am of the world. These things
ειπων, επτυσε χαμαι, και εποιησε πηλον εκ του
saying, he spit on the ground, and made clay of the
πτυσματος, και επεχρισε τον πηλον επι τους
spittle, and rubbed the clay on the
οφθαλμους του τυφλου, 7 και ειπεν αυτῳ·
eyes of the blind, and said to him;
Ὑπαγε, νιψαι εις την κολυμβηθραν του Σιλωαμ·
Go, wash thyself in the pool of the Siloam;
(ὁ ἑρμηνευεται, απεσταλμενος.) Απηλθεν
(which is interpreted, having been sent.) He went away
*[ουν, και ενιψατο, και ηλθε] βλεπων. 8 Οἱ
[therefore, and washed himself, and came] seeing. The
ουν γειτονες, και οἱ θεωρουντες αυτον το προ-
then neighbors, and those seeing him the be-
τερον, ὁτι προσαιτης ην, ελεγον· Ουχ οὑτος
fore, because a beggar he was, said; Not this
εστιν ὁ καθημενος και προσαιτων; 9 Αλλοι
is he sitting and begging? Others
ελεγον· Ὁτι οὑτος εστιν. Αλλοι δε· Ὁτι
said; That this is, Others but, That
ὁμοιος αυτῳ εστιν· Εκεινος ελεγεν· Ὁτι εγω
like him it is; He said; That I
ειμι. 10 Ελεγον ουν αυτῳ· Πως ανεῳχθησαν
am. They said then to him· How were opened
σου οἱ οφθαλμοι 11 Απεκριθη εκεινος *[και
of thee the eyes? Answered he [and
ειπεν·] Ανθρωπος, λεγομενος Ιησους, πηλον
said,] A man, being named Jesus, clay
εποιησε, και επεχρισε μου τους οφθαλμους, και
made, and rubbed of me the eyes, and
ειπε μοι· Ὑπαγε εις τον Σιλωαμ, και νιψαι.
said to me; Go into the Siloam, and wash thyself.
Απελθων δε και νιψαμενος, ανεβλεψα. 12 Ειπον
Going and and washing myself, I obtained sight. They said
ουν αυτῳ· Που εστιν εκεινος; Λεγει· Ουκ οιδα.
then to him; Where is he; He says; Not I know.
13 Αγουσιν αυτον προς τους Φαρισαιους, τον
They bring him to the Pharisees. that
ποτε τυφλον. 14 Ην δε σαββατον, ὁτε τον
once blind. It was and a sabbath, when the
πηλον εποιησεν ὁ Ιησους, και ανεῳξεν αυτου
clay made the Jesus, and opened of him
τους οφθαλμους. 15 Παλιν ουν ηρωτων αυτον
the eyes. Again therefore asked him
και οἱ Φαρισαιοι, πως ανεβλεψεν. Ὁ δε ειπεν
also the Pharisees, how he obtained sight. He and said
αυτοις· Πηλον επεθηκε μου επι τους οφθαλμους,
to them; Clay he put of me on the eyes,

WORKS of HIM who SENT
me while it is Day; Night
comes, when no one can
work.
5 While I am in the
WORLD, ‡ I am the Light
of the WORLD."
6 Saying these things.
‡ he spit on the Ground,
and made Clay of the SPIT-
TLE, and * he put the CLAY
on his EYES,
7 and said to him, "Go
wash thyself in † the POOL
of SILOAM," (which signi-
fies, Sent) He went away,
therefore, and washed
himself, and came seeing.
8 Then the NEIGHBORS,
and THOSE who had PRE-
VIOUSLY seen him, because
he was a Beggar, said, "Is
not this HE who was SIT-
TING and begging?"
9 Some said, "This is
he;" others * said, "No;
but he is like him." He
said, "I am he."
10 They then said to
him, "How were Thine
EYES opened?"
11 He answered, * "The
MAN called Jesus made
Clay, and rubbed my EYES,
and said to me, "Go to the
SILOAM, and wash thy-
self;" * I went, therefore,
and washed myself, and
obtained sight.
12 * And they said to
him, "Where is He?" He
says, "I do not know."
13 They bring HIM that
was formerly BLIND to
the PHARISEES.
14 And it was a * Sab-
bath when JESUS made the
CLAY, and opened His
EYES.
15 Then the PHARISEES
also asked him again how
he obtained his sight. And
he said to them, "He put
Clay on Mine EYES, and I
washed myself, and see."

* VATICAN MANUSCRIPT.—6. He put the CLAY thereof on his eyes, and said. 7. therefore, and washed, and came—omit. 9 said; "No; but he is." 11. and said—omit. 11. The MAN called. 11. I went therefore and. 12. And they said to him. 14. a Sabbath, on which Day JESUS.

† 7. The Pool of Siloam is described by recent travellers to have been "a well built oblong tank, some fifty feet long, nearly twenty deep, and somewhat less than this wide." It has now only about two feet of water in it. It is supplied from an upper fountain through a well-cut conduit more than a quater of a mile long.

‡ 5. John i. 5, 9; iii. 19; viii. 12; xii. 35, 46 ‡ 6. Mark vii. 33; viii. 23.

και ενιψαμην, και βλεπω. 16 Ελεγον ουν εκ
and I washed myself, and see. Said therefore of
των Φαρισαιων τινες· Ούτος ὁ ανθρωπος ουκ
the Pharisees some; This the man not
εστι παρα του θεου, ὁτι το σαββατον ου τηρει.
is from the God, because the sabbath not he keeps.
Αλλοι ελεγον· Πως δυναται ανθρωπος ἁμαρ-
Others said; How is able a man a
τωλος τοιαυτα σημεια ποιειν; Και σχισμα ην
sinner such signs to do? And a division was
εν αυτοις. 17 Λεγουσι τῳ τυφλῳ παλιν· Συ τι
among them. They say to the blind again; Thou what
λεγεις περι αυτου, ὁτι ηνοιξε σου τους οφθαλ-
sayest concerning him, seeing that he opened of thee the eyes?
μους; Ὁ δε ειπεν· Ὁτι προφητης εστιν. 18 Ουκ
He and said; That a prophet he is. Not
επιστευσαν ουν οἱ Ιουδαιοι περι αυτου, ὁτι τυφ-
believed therefore the Jews concerning him, that blind
λος ην, και ανεβλεψεν, ἑως ὁτου εφωνησαν
he was, and obtained sight, till when they called
τους γονεις αυτου του αναβλεψαντος. 19 Και
the parents of him the having obtained sight. And
ηρωτησαν αυτους, λεγοντες· Ούτος εστιν ὁ υἱος
they asked them, saying; This is the son
ὑμων, ὁν ὑμεις λεγετε, ὁτι τυφλος εγεννηθη;
of you, whom you say, that blind he was born?
πως ουν αρτι βλεπει; 20 Απεκριθησαν *[αυτοις]
how then now he sees? Answered [them]
οἱ γονεις αυτου και ειπον· Οιδαμεν, ὁτι ούτος
the parents of him and said; We know, that this
εστιν ὁ υἱος ἡμων, και ὁτι τυφλος εγεννηθη·
is the son of us, and that blind he was born;
21 πως δε νυν βλεπει, ουκ οιδαμεν· η τις ηνοιξεν
how but now he sees, not we know; or who opened
αυτου τους οφθαλμους, ἡμεις ουκ οιδαμεν,
of him the eyes, we not know.
αυτος ἡλικιαν εχει, αυτον ερωτησατε· αυτος
he full age has, him ask you; he
περι αὑτου λαλησει. 22 Ταυτα ειπον οἱ
concerning himself shall speak. These things said the
γονεις αυτου, ὁτι εφοβουντο τους Ιουδαιους.
parents of him, because they feared the Jews.
Ηδη γαρ συνετεθειντο οἱ Ιουδαιοι, ἱνα εαν τις
Already for had agreed the Jews, that if any one
αυτον ὁμολογηση Χριστον, αποσυναγωγος
him should confess Anointed, from a synagogue
γενηται. 23 Δια τουτο οἱ γονεις αυτου ειπον·
should be Through this the parents of him said;
Ὁτι ἡλικιαν εχει, αυτον ερωτησατε. 24 Εφω-
That full age he has, him ask you. They
νησαν ουν εκ δευτερου τον ανθρωπον, ὁς ην
called therefore a second time the man, who was
τυφλος, και ειπον αυτῳ· Δος δοξαν τῳ θεῳ·
blind, and said to him; Give glory to the God,
ἡμεις οιδαμεν, ὁτι ὁ ανθρωπος ούτος ἁμαρτωλος
we know, that the man this a sinner

16 Then some of the PHARISEES said, "This MAN is not from * God, Because he keeps not the SABBATH." Others said, ‡ "How can a sinful Man perform such Signs?" And there was ‡ a Division among them.

17 * They say to the BLIND man again, "What dost thou say concerning him, Seeing that he opened Thine EYES?" And he said, ‡ "He is a Prophet."

18 The JEWS, therefore, did not believe of him, That he was blind and obtained sight, till they called the PARENTS of HIM who RECEIVED SIGHT.

19 And they asked them, saying, "Is this your SON, of whom you say, 'That he was born blind?' How then does he now see?"

20 * Then his PARENTS answered and said, "We know That this is our SON, and That he was born blind;

21 but how he now sees, we know not; or who opened His EYES, we know not; * ask Him, he is of mature Age; he will speak concerning himself."

22 His PARENTS said this, ‡ Because they were afraid of the JEWS; for the JEWS had already determined, that if any one should acknowledge him to be the Messiah, ‡ he should be expelled from the synagogue.

23 On this account his PARENTS said, "He is of mature Age, ask him."

24 They called, therefore, a second time, the MAN who had been blind, and said to him, "Give Glory to GOD; we know * That This Man is a Sinner."

* VATICAN MANUSCRIPT.—16. God. 17. Then they say. 20. Then his PARENTS. 20. them—omit. 21. ask Him; he is of mature Age; he will. 24. That This Man is.

‡ 16. ver. 33; John iii. 2. ‡ 16. John vii. 12, 43; x. 19. ‡ 17. John iv. 19; vi. 14. ‡ 22. John vii. 13; xii. 42; xix. 38; Acts v. 13. ‡ 22. ver. 34; John xvi. 2.

εστιν. 25 Απεκριθη ουν εκεινος *[και ειπεν·]
is. Answered then he [and said,]
Ει αμαρτωλος εστιν, ουκ οιδα· ἑν οιδα, ὁτι
If a sinner he is, not I know; one I know, that
τυφλος ων, αρτι βλεπω. 26 Ειπον δε αυτω
blind being, now I see. They said and to him
*[παλιν·] Τι εποιησε σοι; πως ηνοιξε σου
[again;] What did he to thee? how opened of thee
τους οφθαλμους; Απεκριθη αυτοις· Ειπον ὑμιν
the eyes; He answered them; I said to you
ηδη, και ουκ ηκουσατε· τι παλιν θελετε
already, and not you did hear; why again do you wish
ακουειν; μη και ὑμεις θελετε αυτου μαθηται
to hear? not also you wish of him disciples
γενεσθαι; 28 Ελοιδορησαν αυτον, και ειπον· Συ
to be? They reviled him, and said; Thou
ει μαθητης εκεινου· ἡμεις δε του Μωσης εσμεν
art a disciple of him; we but of the Moses are
μαθηται. 29 Ἡμεις οιδαμεν, ὁτι Μωσῃ λελα-
disciples. We know, that to Moses has
ληκεν ὁ θεος· τουτον δε ουκ οιδαμεν ποθεν
spoken the God; this but not we know whence
εστιν. 30 Απεκριθη ὁ ανθρωπος και ειπεν
is. Answered the man and said
αυτοις· Εν γαρ τουτῳ θαυμαστον εστιν, ὁτι
to them; In for this a wonder is, that
ὑμεις ουκ οιδατε ποθεν εστι, και ανεῳξε μου
you not know whence he is, and he has opened of me
τους οφθαλμους. 31 Οιδαμεν *[δε,] ὁτι ἁμαρ-
the eyes. We know [but,] that sin-
τωλων ὁ θεος ουκ ακουει· αλλ' εαν τις θεοσε-
ners the God not hears; but if any one a worshipper
βης ᾐ, και το θελημα αυτου ποιῃ, τουτου
of God may be, and the will of him may do, this
ακουει. 32 Εκ του αιωνος ουκ ηκουσθη, ὁτι
he hears. From the age not it was heard, that
ηνοιξε τις οφθαλμους τυφλου γεγεννημενου.
opened any one eyes of blind having been born.
33 Ει μη ην οὗτος παρα θεου, ουκ ηδυνατο ποιειν
If not was this from God, not were able to do
ουδεν. 34 Απεκριθησαν και ειπον αυτῳ· Εν
nothing. They answered and said to him; In
ἁμαρτιαις συ εγεννηθης ὁλος· και συ διδασκεις
sins thou wast born wholly; and thou teachest
ἡμας; Και εξεβαλον αυτον εξω. 35 Ηκουσεν ὁ
us? And they cast him out. Heard the
Ιησους, ὁτι εξεβαλον αυτον εξω· και εὑρων
Jesus, that they cast him out; and having found
αυτον, ειπεν *[αυτῳ·] Συ πιστευεις εις τον
him, said [to him;] Thou believest into the
υἱον του θεου; 36 Απεκριθη εκεινος και ειπε·
son of the God? Answered he and said:
Και τις εστι, κυριε, ἱνα πιστευσω εις αυτον;
And who is he, O sir, that I may believe into him?
37 Ειπε *[δε] αυτῳ ὁ Ιησους· Και ἑωρακας
Said [and] to him the Jesus; Even thou hast seen

25 Then he answered, "If he is a Sinner, I know not; One thing I do know, That having been blind, now I see."

26 And they said to him, "What did he do to thee? How did he open Thine EYES?

27 He answered them, "I told you just now, and did you not hear? * Why then do you wish to hear again? are you also willing to become His Disciples?"

28 * And they reviled him, and said, "Thou art his Disciple; but we are Disciples of MOSES.

29 We know That GOD has spoken to Moses; but This person,—we ‡ know not whence he is."

30 The MAN answered and said to them, "Why, in this is a wonder, That you know not whence he is, and he opened My EYES!

31 We know ‡ That GOD does not hear Sinners; but if any one be a Worshipper of God, and performs his WILL, him he hears.

32 From the (earliest) AGE it was not heard, that any one opened the Eyes of one having been born blind.

33 If he were not from God, he could do nothing."

34 They answered and said to him, "Thou wast entirely born in Sins, and dost thou teach us?" And they cast him out.

35 JESUS heard That they had cast him out; and having found him, he said to him, "Dost thou believe into ‡ the * SON of GOD?"

36 He answered and said, "Who is he, Sir, that I may believe into him?"

37 JESUS said to him, "Thou hast even seen him,

* VATICAN MANUSCRIPT.—25. and said—*omit*. 26. again—*omit*. 27. Why then do you wish. 28. and they reviled. 31. But—*omit*. 35. to him—*omit*. 35. SON of MAN? and he said, Who. 37. and—*omit*.

‡ 29. John viii. 14. ‡ 30. John iii. 10. ‡ 31. Job xxvii. 9; Psa. lxvi. 18; Prov. xv. 8, 29; xxviii. 9. ‡ 35. Matt. xvi. 16; John x. 36; 1 John v. 13.

αυτον, και ὁ λαλων μετα σου, εκεινος εστιν.
him, and he talking with thee, he is.
38 Ὁ δε εφη· Πιστευω, κυριε· και προσεκυνησεν
He and said; I believe, O sir; and he prostrated
αυτῳ. 39 Και ειπεν ὁ Ιησους· Εις κριμα εγω εις
to him. And said the Jesus; For judgment I into
τον κοσμον τουτον ηλθον, ἱνα οἱ μη βλεποντες
the world this came, that those not seeing
βλεπωσι, και οἱ βλεποντες τυφλοι γενωνται.
might see, and those seeing blind might become.
40 *[Και] ηκουσαν εκ των Φαρισαιων ταυτα οἱ
[And] heard of the Pharisees these things those
οντες μετ' αυτου, και ειπον αυτῳ· Μη και ἡμεις
being with him, and said to him; Not also we
τυφλοι εσμεν; 41 Ειπεν αυτοις ὁ Ιησους· Ει
blind are? Said to them the Jesus; If
τυφλοι ητε, ουκ αν ειχετε ἁμαρτιαν· νυν δε
blind you were, not you would have sin; now but
λεγετε· Ὁτι βλεπομεν· ἡ *[ουν] ἁμαρτια
you say; That we see; the [therefore] sin
ὑμων μενει.
of you remains.

and HE who is TALKING with thee is he."

38 And HE said, "Lord, I believe;" and he threw himself prostrate before him.

39 And JESUS said, ‡ "For Judgment came I into this WORLD; ‡ so that THOSE not SEEING may see, and THOSE SEEING may become blind."

40 THOSE of the PHARISEES BEING with him heard these things, ‡ and said to him, "Are we blind also?"

41 * Jesus said to them, ‡ "If you were blind, you would not have Sin; but now you say, 'We see;' your SIN remains.

ΚΕΦ. θ'. 10.

1 Αμην αμην λεγω ὑμιν, ὁ μη εισερχομενος
Indeed indeed I say to you, he not entering
δια της θυρας εις την αυλην των προβατων,
through the door into the fold of the sheep,
αλλα αναβαινων αλλαχοθεν, εκεινος κλεπτης
but going up another way, he a thief
εστι και ληστης· 2 ὁ δε εισερχομενος δια της
is and a robber; he but entering through the
θυρας, ποιμην εστι των προβατων. 3 Τουτῳ ὁ
door, a shepherd is of the sheep. To him the
θυρωρος ανοιγει· και τα προβατα της φωνης
doorkeeper opens; and the sheep the voice
αυτου ακουει· και τα ιδια προβατα καλει κατ'
of him hears, and the own sheep he calls by
ονομα, και εξαγει αυτα. 4 *[Και] ὁταν τα ιδια
name, and he leads out them. [And] when the own
προβατα εκβαλῃ, εμπροσθεν αυτων πορευεται·
sheep he puts forth, before them he goes;
και τα προβατα αυτῳ ακολουθει, ὁτι οιδασι την
and the sheep him follows, because they know the
φωνην αυτου. 5 Αλλοτριῳ δε ου μη ακολου-
voice of him. A stranger but not not they may
θησωσιν, αλλα φευξονται απ' αυτου· ὁτι ουκ
follow, but will flee from him; because not
οιδασι των αλλοτριων την φωνην. 6 Ταυτην
they know of the strangers the voice This

CHAPTER X.

1 Indeed, I truly say to you, HE who ENTERS not by the DOOR into the FOLD of the SHEEP, but climbs up another way, he is a Thief and a Robber;

2 but HE who COMES IN by the DOOR, is the Shepherd of the SHEEP

3 The DOOR-KEEPER opens to him; and the SHEEP hear his VOICE; and he calls his OWN Sheep by Name, and leads them out.

4 When he puts forth *all his OWN, † he goes before them, and the SHEEP follow him, Because they know his VOICE.

5 But a Stranger they will not follow, but will flee from him; Because they know not the VOICE of STRANGERS."

* VATICAN MANUSCRIPT.—40. And—*omit*. 41. Jesus. 41. therefore—*omit*. 4. And—*omit*. 4. all his OWN, he goes.

† 4. "We see a flock of perhaps threescore black and white sheep returning from the hillside where they have been grazing, or from the caves in which they have been sheltered from the noon-heat. Before them slowly walks the shepherd, staff in hand, not once looking behind him. The flock follows quietly, not scattering nor needing the rod or the angry shout. He and they seem to know each other well, and to have mutual confidence. He who wrote the twenty-third Psalm must have known scenes like this; and still more He who said, "when he putteth forth his own sheep, *he goeth before them, and the sheep follow him*, for they know his voice."—*H. Bonar*.

‡ 39. John v. 22, 27. See John iii. 17; xii. 47. ‡ 39. Matt. xiii. 13. ‡ 40. Rom. ii. 19
‡ 41. John xv. 22, 24.

την παροιμιαν ειπεν αυτοις ὁ Ιησους· εκεινοι
the parable said to them the Jesus; they
δε ουκ εγνωσαν, τινα ην, ἁ ελαλε αυτοις.
but not knew, what was, which he spoke to them.
7 Ειπεν ουν παλιν *[αυτοις] ὁ Ιησους· Αμην
Said then again [to them] the Jesus, Indeed
αμην λεγω ὑμιν, ὁτι εγω ειμι ἡ θυρα των προ-
indeed I say to you, that I am the door of the sheep.
βατων. 8 Παντες ὁσοι ηλθον προ εμου, κλεπται
All as many as came before me, thieves
εισι και λησται· αλλ' ουκ ηκουσαν αυτων τα
are and robbers; but not heard them the
προβατα. 9 Εγω ειμι ἡ θυρα· δι' εμου εαν τις
sheep. I am the door; through me if any one
εισελθῃ, σωθησεται, και εισελευσεται και
may come in, he shall be saved, and shall come in and
εξελευσηται, και νομην εὑρησει. 10 Ὁ κλεπτης
go out and pasture shall find. The thief
ουκ ερχεται, ει μη ἱνα κλεψῃ, και θυσῃ, και
not comes, if not that he may steal, and may kill, and
απολεσῃ· εγω ηλθον, ἱνα ζωην εχωσι, και
may destroy; I came, that life they may have, and
περισσον εχωσιν. 11 Εγω ειμι ὁ ποιμην ὁ καλος
abundance may have. I am the shepherd the good
ὁ ποιμην ὁ καλος την ψυχην αυτου τιθησιν ὑπερ
the shepherd the good the life of himself lays down in behalf
των προβατων. 12 Ὁ μισθωτος δε, και ουκ ων
of the sheep. The hireling but, and not being
ποιμην, οὑ ουκ εισι τα προβατα ιδια, θεωρει
a shepherd, of whom not are the sheep own, sees
τον λυκον ερχομενον, και αφιησι τα προβατα,
the wolf coming, and leaves the sheep,
και φευγει· και ὁ λυκος αρπαζει αυτα, και
and flees; and the wolf seizes them, and
σκορπιζει τα προβατα. 13 Ὁ δε μισθωτος
scatters the sheep. The but hireling
φευγει, ὁτι μισθωτος εστι, και ου μελει αυτῳ
flees, because an hireling he is, and not it concerns him
περι των προβατων.
about the sheep.
14 Εγω ειμι ὁ ποιμην ὁ καλος· και γινωσκω
I am the shepherd the good; and know
το εμα, και γινωσκομαι ὑπο των εμων, 15 καθως
the mine, and am known by the mine, as
γινωσκει με ὁ πατηρ, καγω γινωσκω τον
knows me the father, and I know the
πατερα· και την ψυχην μου τιθημι ὑπερ των
father; and the life of me I lay down in behalf of the
προβατων. 16 Και αλλα προβατα εχω, ἁ ουκ
sheep. And other sheep I have, which not
εστιν εκ της αυλης ταυτης· κακεινα με δει
is of the fold this; also them me it behoves

6 This PARABLE spoke JESUS to them; but they knew not what things they were which he spoke to them.

7 Then said *Jesus again, "Indeed, I truly say to you, ‡ I am the DOOR of the SHEEP.

8 † All who came before me are Thieves and Robbers; but the SHEEP heard them not.

9 ‡ I am the DOOR; if any one come in by me, he shall be saved, and shall come in, and go out, and find Pasture.

10 The THIEF comes not, except that he may steal, and kill, and destroy; I came, that they may have Life, and may have abundance.

11 ‡ I am the GOOD SHEPHERD; the GOOD SHEPHERD lays down his LIFE in behalf of the SHEEP.

12 But the HIRED SERVANT, not being a Shepherd, whose own the SHEEP are not, sees the WOLF coming, and leaves the SHEEP, and flees; and the WOLF seizes and scatters * them;

13 Because he is a Hired Servant, and cares not for the SHEEP.

14 I am the GOOD SHEPHERD; ‡ and I know * MINE, and MINE know me;

15 even as the FATHER knows me, and I know the FATHER; ‡ and I lay down my LIFE in behalf of the SHEEP.

16 And Other Sheep I have, which are not of this FOLD; them also I must

* VATICAN MANUSCRIPT.—7. Jesus. 7. to them—*omit*. 12. them; Because he is a Hireling, and. 14. MINE, and MINE know me; even as.

† 8. *Panta, all,* may be taken in the sense of *pollos, many;* thus, "Many who came before me," &c. Our Savior cannot here mean Moses and the prophets, who were commissioned to speak in the name of Jehovah; but rather those religious leaders who "shut up the kingdom of the heavens against men," by taking away the "key of knowledge." See Matt. xxiii. 13; Luke xi. 52. Such were the priests, scribes, and Pharisees.

‡ 9. John xiv. 6; Eph. ii. 18. ‡ 11. Isa. xl. 11; Ezek. xxxiv. 12, 23; xxxvii. 24; Heb xiii. 20; 1 Pet. ii. 25; v. 4. ‡ 14. 2 Tim. ii. 19. ‡ 15. John xv. 13.

αγαγειν· και της φωνης μου ακουσουσι, και
to lead; and the voice of me they will hear, and
γενεσεται μια ποιμνη, εἱς ποιμην. 17 Δια τουτο
there will be one flock, one shepherd. Through this
ὁ πατηρ με αγαπᾳ, ὁτι εγω τιθημι την ψυχην
the father me loves, because I lay down the life
μου, ἱνα παλιν λαβω αυτην· 18 ουδεις αιρει αυτην
of me, that again I may receive her; no one takes her
απ᾽ εμου, αλλ᾽ εγω τιθημι αυτην απ᾽ εμαυτου·
from me, but I lay down her of myself;
εξουσιαν εχω θειναι αυτην, και εξουσιαν εχω
authority I have to lay down her, and authority I have
παλιν λαβειν αυτην· ταυτην την εντολην ελα-
again to receive her; this the command I re-
βον παρα του πατρος μου. 19 Σχισμα *[ουν]
ceived from the father of me. A division [then]
παλιν εγενετο εν τοις Ιουδαιοις δια τους λογους
again occurred among the Jews through the words
τουτους. 20 Ελεγον δε πολλοι εξ αυτων· Δαι-
these. Said and many of them; A
μονιον εχει, και μαινεται· τι αυτου ακουετε;
demon he has, and is mad; why him hear you?
21 Αλλοι ελεγον· Ταυτα τα ῥηματα ουκ εστι
Others said; These the words not are
δαιμονιζομενου· μη δαιμονιον δυναται τυφλων
of one being demonized; not a demon is able blind
οφθαλμους ανοιγειν;
eyes to open?

22 Εγενετο δε τα εγκαινια εν τοις Ἱεροσολυ-
Occurred now the feast of dedication in the Jerusa-
μοις, και χειμων ην· 23 και περιεπατει ὁ Ιησους
lem, and winter it was; and was walking the Jesus
εν τῳ ἱερῳ, εν τῃ στοᾳ Σολομωνος. 24 Εκυκ-
in the temple, in the porch of Solomon. Sur-
λωσαν ουν αυτον οἱ Ιουδαιοι, και ελεγον αυτῳ·
rounded therefore him the Jews, and said to him;
Ἑως ποτε την ψυχην ἡμων αιρεις; Ει συ ει ὁ
Till when the life of us dost thou take? If thou art the
Χριστος, ειπε ἡμιν παῤῥησιᾳ. 25 Απεκριθη αυτοις
Anointed, tell us plainly. Answered them
ὁ Ιησους· Ειπον ὑμιν, και ου πιστευετε. Τα
the Jesus; I told you, and not you believe. The
εργα, ἁ εγω ποιω εν τῳ ονοματι του πατρος μου,
works, which I do in the name of the father of me,
ταυτα μαρτυρει περι εμου. 26 Αλλ᾽ ὑμεις ου πισ-
these testify concerning me. But you not be-
τευετε· ου γαρ εστε εκ των προβατων των εμων.
lieve; not for you are of the sheep the mine.
*[Καθως ειπον ὑμιν,] 27 τα προβατα τα εμα
As I said to you,] the sheep the mine
της φωνης μου ακουει, καγω γινωσκω αυτα, και
the voice of me hears, and I know them, and
ακολουθουσι μοι· 28 καγω ζωην αιωνιον διδωμι
they follow me; and I life age-lasting give
αυτοις, και ου μη απολωνται εις τον αιωνα, και
to them, and not not they will perish into the age, and

lead, and they will hear my VOICE, ‡and there shall be one Flock, One Shepherd.

17 On account of this the FATHER loves ME, ‡Because I lay down my LIFE, that I may receive it again.

18 No one takes it from me, but I lay it down of myself. I have Authority to lay it down, and I have Authority to receive it again. ‡This COMMANDMENT I received from my FATHER."

19 ‡There was a Division again among the JEWS because of these WORDS.

20 And many of them said, ‡"He has a Demon, and is mad, why do you hear him?"

21 Others said, "These are not the WORDS of a Demoniac; can a Demon open the Eyes of the blind?"

22 *It was then the FEAST OF DEDICATION at JERUSALEM; it was Winter;

23 and *Jesus was walking in the TEMPLE, ‡in SOLOMON'S PORTICO.

24 The JEWS, therefore, surrounded him, and said to him, "How long dost thou hold us in suspense? If thou art the MESSIAH, tell us plainly."

25 JESUS answered them, "I told you, and you did not believe; the WORKS which I do in my FATHER'S NAME, they testify of me.

26 ‡But you believe not, because you are not of MY SHEEP.

27 MY SHEEP hear my VOICE, and I know them, and they follow me;

28 and I give them aionian Life; ‡and they shall by no means perish to the

* VATICAN MANUSCRIPT.—19. then—*omit.* 22. It was then the FEAST OF DEDICATION at JERUSALEM; it was Winter. 23. Jesus. 26. As I said to you—*omit.*

‡ 16. Ezek. xxxvii. 22; Eph. ii 14. ‡ 17. Isa. liii. 7. 8. 12; Heb. ii. 9. ‡ 18. John vi. 38; xv. 10; Acts ii. 24, 32. ‡ 19. John vii. 43; ix. 16. ‡ 20. John vii. 20; viii. 48, 52. ‡ 23. Acts iii. 11; v. 12. ‡ 26. John viii. 47; 1 John iv. 6. ‡ 28. John vi. 37; xvii. 11, 12.

ουχ αρπασει τις αυτα εκ της χειρος μου. 29 Ὁ
not will wrest any one them out of the hand of me. The

πατηρ μου, ὃς δεδωκε μοι, μειζων παντων εστι·
father of me, who has given to me, greater of all is;

και ουδεις δυναται ἁρπαζειν εκ της χειρος
and no one is able to wrest out of the hand

του πατρος μου· 30 εγω και ὁ πατηρ ἑν εσμεν.
of the father of me; I and the father one are.

31 Εβαστασαν ουν παλιν λιθους οἱ Ιουδαιοι, ἱνα
Took up then again stones the Jews, that

λιθασωσιν αυτον. 32 Απεκριθη αυτοις ὁ Ιησους·
they might stone him. Answered them the Jesus;

Πολλα καλα εργα εδειξα ὑμιν εκ του πατρος
Many good works I showed you from the father

μου· δια ποιον αυτων εργον λιθαζετε με;
of me: because of which of them work do you stone me?

33 Απεκριθησαν αυτῳ οἱ Ιουδαιοι *[λεγοντες·]
Answered him the Jews [saying;]

Περι καλου εργου ου λιθαζομεν σε, αλλα
Concerning a good work not we stone thee, but

περι βλασφημιας, και ὁτι συ, ανθρωπος ων,
concerning blasphemy, and that thou, a man being,

ποιεις, σεαυτον θεον. 34 Απεκριθη αυτοις ὁ
makest thyself a god. Answered them the

Ιησους· Ουκ εστι γεγραμμενον εν τῳ νομῳ
Jesus; Not is it having been written in the law

ὑμων· "Εγω ειπα, θεοι εστε;" 35 Ει εκεινους
of you: "I said. gods you are?" If them

ειπε θεους, προς οὑς ὁ λογος του θεου εγενετο,
he called gods, to whom the word of the God came,

και ου δυναται λυθηναι ἡ γραφη· 36 ὁν ὁ πατηρ
and not is able to be broken the writing; whom the father

ἡγιασε, και απεστειλεν εις τον κοσμον, ὑμεις
set apart, and sent into the world, you

λεγετε· Ὁτι βλασφημεις, ὁτι ειπον, υἱος του
say That thou blasphemest, because I said, a son of the

θεου ειμι; 37 Ει ου ποιω τα εργα του πατρος
God I am? If not I do the works of the father

μου, μη πιστευετε μοι. 38 Ει δε ποιω, καν εμοι
of me, not you believe me. If but I do, and if me

μη πιστευητε, τοις εργοις πιστευσατε· ἱνα
not you believe, the works believe you; that

γνωτε και πιστευσητε, ὁτι εν εμοι ὁ πατηρ,
you may know and you may believe, that in me the father,

καγω εν αυτῳ. 39 Εζητουν ουν παλιν αυτον
and I in him. They sought therefore again him

πιασαι· και εξηλθεν εκ της χειρος αυτων.
to seize; and he went forth out of the hand of them.

40 Και απηλθε παλιν περαν του Ιορδανου, εις τον
And he went again beyond the Jordan, to the

AGE, and no one shall wrest them out of my HAND.

29 ‡ My FATHER, who has given them to me, is greater than all; and no one is able to wrest them out of * the FATHER'S HAND.

30 ‡ I and the FATHER are One."

31 Then the JEWS took up Stones again, that they might stone him.

32 JESUS said to them, "Many * good Works did I show you from * the FATHER; on account of which of these Works do you stone * Me?"

33 The JEWS answered him, "We do not stone thee for a Good Work, but for Blasphemy; and Because thou, being a Man, makest thyself God."

34 * Jesus answered them, ‡ "Is it not written in your LAW, 'I said, You are Gods?'

35 If he called them Gods, to whom the WORD of GOD came, and the SCRIPTURE cannot be broken,

36 of him whom the FATHER set apart and sent into the WORLD, do you say, 'Thou blasphemest;' Because I said, 'I am a Son of GOD?'

37 If I do not the WORKS of my FATHER, believe me not.

38 But if I do, and if you believe not me, believe the WORKS, so that you may know and * believe, ‡ That the FATHER is in me, and * I am in the FATHER."

39 Therefore, they were seeking again to seize Him; but he went forth out of their HAND.

40 And he went away again beyond the JORDAN, into the PLACE where

---

* VATICAN MANUSCRIPT.—29. the FATHER'S HAND. 32. good Works. 32. the FATHER. 32. Me. 33. saying—*omit*. 34. Jesus 38. understand, That. 38. I am in the FATHER.

‡ 29. John xiv. 28. ‡ 30 John xvii. 11, 22 ‡ 34. Psa. lxxxii 6. ‡ 38. John xiv. 10, 11; xvii. 21.

τοπον, ὁπου ην Ιωαννης το πρωτον βαπτιζων·
place where was John the first dipping;
και εμεινεν εκει. [41] Και πολλοι ηλθον προς
and he abode there. And many came to
αυτον, και ελεγον· Ὁτι Ιωαννης μεν σημειον
him, and said; That John indeed a sign
εποιησεν ουδεν· παντα δε ὁσα ειπεν Ιωαννης
did not one; all but what things said John
περι τουτου, αληθη ην. [42] Και επιστευσαν
concerning this, true was. And believed
πολλοι εκει εις αυτον.
many there into him.

ΚΕΦ. ια'. 11.

[1] Ην δε τις ασθενων, Λαζαρος, απο Βηθανιας,
Was and a certain sick one, Lazarus, from Bethany,
εκ της κωμης Μαριας και Μαρθας της αδελφης
out of the village of Mary and Martha the sister
αυτης. [2] (Ην δε Μαρια ἡ αλειψασα τον κυριον
of her. (Was and Mary the having anointed the lord
μυρῳ, και εκμαξασα τους ποδας αυτου ταις
with balsam, and wiped the feet of him with the
θριξιν αὑτης· ἡς ὁ αδελφος Λαζαρος ησθε-
hairs of herself; of whom the brother Lazarus was
ναι.) [3] Απεστειλαν ουν αἱ αδελφαι προς αυτον,
sick.) Sent therefore the sisters to him,
λεγουσαι· Κυριε, ιδε, ὁν φιλεις, ασθενει.
saying; O lord, lo, whom thou lovest, is sick.
[4] Ακουσας δε ὁ Ιησους ειπεν· Αὑτη ἡ ασθενεια
Having heard and the Jesus said, This the sickness
ουκ εστι προς θανατον, αλλ' ὑπερ της δοξης
not is to death, but on account of the glory
του θεου, ἱνα δοξασθῃ ὁ υἱος του θεου δι' αυτης.
of the God, that may be glorified the son of the God through her.
[5] Ηγαπα δε ὁ Ιησους την Μαρθαν, και την
Loved now the Jesus the Martha, and the
αδελφην αυτης, και τον Λαζαρον. [6] Ὡς ουν
sister of her, and the Lazarus. When then
ηκουσεν, ὁτι ασθενει, τοτε μεν εμεινεν εν ᾡ
he heard, that he was sick, then indeed he abode in which
ην τοπῳ δυο ἡμερας. [7] Επειτα μετα τουτο
he was place two days. Then after this
λεγει τοις μαθηταις· Αγωμεν εις την Ιουδαιαν
he says to the disciples: Let us go into the Judea
παλιν. [8] Λεγουσιν αυτῳ οἱ μαθηται· Ῥαββι,
again. Say to him the disciples; Rabbi,
νυν εζητουν σε λιθασαι οἱ Ιουδαιοι, και παλιν
now sought thee to stone the Jews, and again
ὑπαγεις εκει; [9] Απεκριθη Ιησους· Ουχι δωδεκα
goest thou there? Answered Jesus; Not twelve
εισιν ὡραι της ἡμερας; εαν τις περιπατῃ εν τῃ
are hours of the day? if any one may walk in the
ἡμερᾳ, ου προσκοπτει, ὁτι το φως του κοσμου
day, not he stumbles, because the light of the world
τουτου βλεπει· [10] εαν δε τις περιπατῃ εν τῃ
this he sees? if but any one may walk in the
νυκτι, προσκοπτει, ὁτι το φως ουκ εστιν εν
night, he stumbles, because the light not is in

John was immersing at the FIRST; and he abode there.

41 And many came to him, and said, "John, indeed, performed no Sign; ‡but Whatever John said concerning him was true."

42 And many believed into him there.

CHAPTER XI.

1 Now there was a certain sick man, Lazarus of Bethany, from the VILLAGE of ‡Mary, and Martha, her SISTER.

2 (‡It was THAT Mary who ANOINTED the LORD, and wiped his FEET with her HAIR, whose BROTHER Lazarus was sick.)

3 The SISTERS, therefore, sent to him, saying, "Lord, behold, he whom thou lovest is sick."

4 But JESUS, having heard, said, "This SICKNESS is not to Death, ‡but for the GLORY of GOD, that the SON of GOD may be glorified by it."

5 Now JESUS loved MARTHA, and her SISTER, and LAZARUS.

6 When, therefore, he heard That he was sick, then, indeed, ‡he abode in the Place where he was Two Days.

7 Then, after this, he says to the DISCIPLES, "Let us go into JUDEA again."

8 The DISCIPLES say to him, "Rabbi, ‡the JEWS recently sought to stone thee; and art thou going there again?"

9 Jesus answered, "Are there not Twelve Hours of the DAY? ‡If any one walk in the DAY, he stumbles not, Because he sees the LIGHT of this WORLD.

10 But if any one walk in the NIGHT, he stumbles. Because the LIGHT is not in him."

‡ 41 John iii. 30. ‡ 1. Luke x. 38, 39. ‡ 2. Matt. xxvi. 7; Mark xiv. 3. John xii 3. ‡ 4. John ix. 3; ver. 40. ‡ 6. John x. 40. ‡ 8. John x. 31 ‡ 9. John ix. 4.

αυτῳ. 11 Ταυτα ειπε· και μετα τουτο λεγει
him. These things he said; and after this he says
αυτοις· Λαζαρος ὁ φιλος ἡμων κεκοιμηται·
to them; Lazarus the friend of us is fallen asleep;
αλλα πορευομαι, ἱνα εξυπνισω αυτον. 12 Ειπον
but I go, that I may awake him Said
ουν οἱ μαθηται αυτου· Κυριε, ει κεκοιμηται,
then the disciples of him; O lord, if he is fallen asleep,
σωθησεται. 13 Ειρηκει δε ὁ Ιησους περι του
he shall be saved. Had spoken but the Jesus about the
θανατου αυτου· εκεινοι δε εδοξαν, ὁτι περι της
death of him; they but thought, that concerning the
κοιμησεως του ὑπνου λεγει. 14 Τοτε ουν ειπεν
repose of the sleep he speaks. Then therefore said
αυτοις ὁ Ιησους παρρησιᾳ· Λαζαρος απεθανε·
to them the Jesus plainly; Lazarus died;
15 και χαιρω δι' ὑμας, ἱνα πιστευσητε, ὁτι ουκ
and I rejoice because of you, that you may believe, that not
ημην εκει· αλλ' αγωμεν προς αυτον. 16 Ειπεν
I was there; but we may go to him. Said
ουν Θωμας, ὁ λεγομενος Διδυμος, τοις συμμαθη-
then Thomas, that being called a twin, to the fellow-disci-
ταις· Αγωμεν και ἡμεις, ἱνα αποθανωμεν μετ'
ples; May go also we, that we may die with
αυτου. 17 Ελθων ουν ὁ Ιησους εὑρεν αυτον τεσ-
him. Coming therefore the Jesus found him four
σαρας ἡμερας ηδη εχοντα εν τῳ μνημειῳ. 18 Ην
days already having been in the tomb. Was
δε ἡ Βηθανια εγγυς των Ἱεροσολυμων, ὡς απο
now the Bethany near the Jerusalem, about from
σταδιων δεκαπεντε.
furlongs fifteen.

19 Και πολλοι εκ των Ιουδαιων εληλυθεισαν
And many of the Jews had come
προς τας περι Μαρθαν και Μαριαν, ἱνα παραμυ-
to those about Martha and Mary, that they might
θησωνται αυτας περι του αδελφου αυτων. 20 Ἡ
comfort them concerning the brother of them. The
ουν Μαρθα ὡς ηκουσεν, ὁτι Ιησους ερχεται,
then Martha when she heard, that Jesus was coming,
ὑπηντησεν αυτῳ· Μαρια δε εν τῳ οικῳ εκαθε-
met him; Mary but in the house was sit-
ζετο. 21 Ειπεν ουν ἡ Μαρθα προς τον Ιησουν·
ting. Said then the Martha to the Jesus;
Κυριε, ει ης ὡδε, ὁ αδελφος μου ουκ αν
O lord, if thou hadst been here, the brother of me not would
ετεθνηκει· 22 αλλα και νυν οιδα, ὁτι ὁσα
have died; But and now I know, that whatever things
αν αιτηση τον θεον, δωσει σοι ὁ θεος. 23 Λεγει
thou mayest ask the God, will give to thee the God. Says
αυτῃ ὁ Ιησους· Αναστησεται ὁ αδελφος σου.
to her the Jesus; Will rise again the brother of thee.
24 Λεγει αυτῳ Μαρθα· Οιδα, ὁτι αναστησεται,
Says to him Martha; I know, that he will rise again,

11 These things he said; and after this he says to them, ‡ "Lazarus, our FRIEND, has fallen asleep; but I am going, that I may awake him."

12 * The DISCIPLES, therefore, said to him, "Lord, if he has fallen asleep, he will recover."

13 But JESUS had spoken concerning his DEATH; but they thought That he was speaking of the REPOSE of SLEEP.

14 Then, therefore, JESUS said plainly, "Lazarus is dead;

15 and I rejoice, on your account, That I was not there, so that you may believe; but let us go to him."

16 Then THAT Thomas, who is CALLED Didymus, said to the FELLOW-DISCIPLES, "Let us also go, that we may die with him."

17 JESUS, therefore, coming, found that he had been already Four Days in the TOMB.

18 Now BETHANY was near JERUSALEM, about fifteen Furlongs distant.

19 And many of the JEWS had come to those with Martha and Mary, that they might console them concerning their BROTHER.

20 MARTHA, therefore, when she heard That * Jesus was coming, went to meet him; but Mary was sitting in the HOUSE.

21 Then MARTHA said to * Jesus, "Lord, if thou hadst been here, my BROTHER would not have died.

22 * And even now I know, ‡ That whatever things thou wilt ask of GOD, GOD will give thee."

23 JESUS said to her, "Thy BROTHER will rise again."

24 * MARTHA said to him, ‡ "I know that he will

* VATICAN MANUSCRIPT.—12. The DISCIPLES, therefore, said to him. 20. Jesus. 21. Jesus. 22. And. 24. MARTHA.

‡ 11. Deut. xxxi. 16; Dan. xii. 2; Matt. ix. 24; Acts vii. 60; 1 Cor. xv. 18, 51. ‡ 22. John ix. 31. ‡ 24. Luke xiv. 14; John v. 29.

εν τη αναστασει εν τη εσχατη ἡμερᾳ. 25 Ειπεν
in the resurrection in the last day. Said
αυτη ὁ Ιησους· Εγω ειμι ἡ αναστασις και ἡ
to her the Jesus; I am the resurrection and the
ζωη· ὁ πιστευων εις εμε, καν αποθανη, ζησεται·
life; he believing into me, even if he may die, he shall live;
26 και πας ὁ ζων και πιστευων εις εμε, ου μη
and all the living and believing into me, not not
αποθανη εις τον αιωνα. Πιστευεις τουτο;
may die into the age. Believest thou this?
27 Λεγει αυτω· Ναι, κυριε· εγω πεπιστευκα, ὁτι
She says to him; Yes, O lord; I have believed, that
συ ει ὁ Χριστος, ὁ υἱος του θεου, ὁ εις τον κοσ-
thou art the Anointed, the son of the God, he into the world
μον ερχομενος. 28 Και ταυτα ειπουσα, απηλθε,
coming. And these things saying, she went,
και εφωνησε Μαριαν την αδελφην αὑτης λαθρα,
and called Mary the sister of her privately,
ειπουσα· Ὁ διδασκαλος παρεστι, και φωνει σε.
saying; The teacher is present, and calls thee.
29 Εκεινη ὡς ηκουσεν, εγειρεται ταχυ, και ερχε-
She when she heard, rises up quickly, and comes
ται προς αυτον. 30 (Ουπω δε εληλυθει ὁ Ιη-
to him. (Not yet now had come the Je-
σους εις την κωμην· αλλ' ην εν τῳ τοπῳ, ὁπου
sus into the village; but was in the place, where
ὑπηντησεν αὑτῳ ἡ Μαρθα.) 31 Οἱ ουν Ιουδαιοι,
met him the Martha.) The therefore Jews,
οἱ οντες μετ' αυτης εν τη οικιᾳ και παραμυθου-
those being with her in the house and were comfort-
μενοι αυτην, ιδοντες την Μαριαν, ὁτι ταχεως
ing her, seeing the Mary, that quickly
ανεστη και εξηλθεν, ηκολουθησαν αυτη, λεγον-
she rose up and went out, followed her, saying;
τες· Ὁτι ὑπαγει εις το μνημειον, ἱνα κλαυση
That she goes into the tomb, that she may weep
εκει. 32 Ἡ ουν Μαρια ὡς ηλθεν ὁπου ην ὁ Ιη-
there. The therefore Mary when came where was the Je-
σους, ιδουσα αυτον, επεσεν αυτου εις τους
sus, seeing him, she fell of him to the
ποδας, λεγουσα αυτῳ· Κυριε, ει ης ὡδε,
feet saying to him; O lord, if thou hadst been here,
ουκ αν απεθανε μου ὁ αδελφος. 33 Ιησους ουν
not would have died of me the brother. Jesus therefore
ὡς ειδεν αυτην κλαιουσαν, και τους συνελθον-
when he saw her weeping, and those having come
τας αυτῃ Ιουδαιους κλαιοντας, ενεβριμησατο τῳ
with her Jews weeping, he was agitated in the
πνευματι, και εταραξεν ἑαυτον, 34 και ειπε·
spirit, and troubled himself, and said;
Που τεθεικατε αυτον; Λεγουσιν αυτῳ· Κυριε,
Where have you laid him? They say to him; O lord,
ερχου, και ιδε. 35 Εδακρυσεν ὁ Ιησους.
come, and see. Wept the Jesus.

rise again, in the RESURRECTION, in the LAST day."

25 JESUS said to her, "I am ‡ the RESURRECTION, and ‡ the LIFE; HE BELIEVING into me, even though he die, shall live;

26 and no one LIVING and believing into me, shall die to the AGE. Dost thou believe this?"

27 She says to him, "Yes, Lord, ‡ I have believed that thou art the MESSIAH, THAT SON of GOD COMING into the WORLD."

28 And saying these things, she went and called Mary, her SISTER, privately, saying, "The TEACHER is come, and calls thee."

29 *And she, when she heard, rose up quickly, and came to him.

30 Now JESUS had not yet come into the VILLAGE, but was *still in the PLACE where Martha met him.

31 THOSE JEWS, therefore, who WERE with her in the HOUSE, and were consoling her, seeing MARY, That she rose up suddenly and went out, followed her, * saying, "She is going to the TOMB, that she may weep there."

32 MARY, therefore, when she came where * Jesus was, seeing him, fell at his FEET, saying to him, "Lord, if thou hadst been here, My BROTHER would not have died."

33 When Jesus, therefore, saw her weeping, and the JEWS having come with her weeping, he was greatly agitated in his SPIRIT, and affected,

34 and said, "Where have you laid him?" They say to him, "Lord, come and see."

35 ‡ JESUS wept.

* VATICAN MANUSCRIPT.—29. And she, when she heard, rose up. 30. still in the PLACE. 31. thinking. 32. Jesus.

‡ 25. John v. 21; vi. 39, 40, 44. ‡ 25. John i. 4; vi. 35; xiv. 6; Col. iii. 4; 1 John i. 1, 2; v. 11. ‡ 27. Matt. xvi. 16; John i. 49; iv. 42; vi. 14, 69. ‡ 35. Luke xix. 41.

36 Ελεγον ουν οἱ Ιουδαιοι· Ιδε, πως εφιλει αυτον.
Said then the Jews; See, how he loved him.
37 Τινες δε εξ αυτων ειπον· Ουκ ηδυνατο οὑτος,
Some but of them said; Not was able this,
ὁ ανοιξας τους οφθαλμους του τυφλου ποιησαι,
he having opened the eyes of the blind to have caused,
ἱνα και οὑτος μη αποθνη; 38 Ιησους ουν παλιν
that even this not should die? Jesus therefore again
εμβριμωμενος εν ἑαυτῳ, ερχεται εις το μνη-
being agitated in himself, comes to the tomb.
μειον. Ην δε σπηλαιον, και λιθος επεκειτο επ'
It was now a cave, and a stone was lying on
αυτῳ. 39 Λεγει ὁ Ιησους· Αρατε τον λιθον.
it. Says the Jesus; Take away the stone.
Λεγει αυτῳ ἡ αδελφη του τεθνηκοτος, Μαρθα·
Says to him the sister of the having died, Martha;
Κυριε, ηδη οζει· τεταρταιος γαρ εστι. 40 Λεγει
O lord, now he smells; fourth day for it is. Says
αυτῃ ὁ Ιησους· Ουκ ειπον σοι, ὁτι εαν πιστευ-
to her the Jesus; Not I said to thee, that if thou wouldst
σῃς, οψει την δοξαν του θεου; 41 Ηραν ουν
believe, thou shalt see the glory of the God? They took away then
τον λιθον. Ὁ δε Ιησους ηρε τους οφθαλμους
the stone.. The but Jesus lifted up the eyes
ανω, και ειπε· Πατερ, ευχαριστω σοι, ὁτι
above, and said; O father, I give thanks to thee, that
ηκουσας μου. 42 Εγω δε ηδειν, ὁτι παντοτε μου
thou didst hear me I and knew, that always me
ακουεις· αλλα δια τον οχλον τον περιεστωτα
thou hearest; but on account of the crowd that standing-by
ειπον, ἱνα πιστευσωσιν, ὁτι συ με απεστειλας.
I spoke, so that they may believe, that thou me hast sent.
43 Και ταυτα ειπων, φωνῃ μεγαλῃ εκραυγασε.
And these things saying, with a voice loud he cried out.
Λαζαρε, δευρο εξω. 44 Εξηλθεν ὁ τεθνηκως.
O Lazarus, come out. Came out he having been dead,
δεδεμενος τους ποδας και τας χειρας κειριαις,
having been bound the feet and the hands with bandages,
και ἡ οψις αυτου σουδαριῳ περιεδεδετο. Λεγει
and the face of him with a napkin bound about. Says
αυτοις ὁ Ιησους· Λυσατε αυτον, και αφετε ὑπα-
to them the Jesus; Loose you him, and allow to
γειν. 45 Πολλοι ουν εκ των Ιουδαιων, οἱ
go Many therefore of the Jews, those
ελθοντες προς την Μαριαν, και θεασαμενοι ἁ
having come to the Mary, and having gazed upon what
εποιησεν, επιστευσαν εις αυτον. 46 Τινες δε
he did, believed into him. Some but
εξ αυτων απηλθον προς τους Φαρισαιους, και
of them went to the Pharisees, and
ειπεν αυτοις ἁ εποιησεν ὁ Ιησους.
told them what did the Jesus.
47 Συνηγαγον ουν οἱ αρχιερεις και οἱ Φαρι-
Assembled then the high-priests and the Phari-

36 The JEWS, therefore, said, "Behold, how he loved him!"

37 But some of them said, "Could not HE, who OPENED the EYES of ‡ the BLIND man, have even prevented this man's death?"

38 JESUS, therefore, again being agitated within himself, comes to the TOMB. Now it was a Cave, and a Stone was lying upon it.

39 JESUS said, "Take away the STONE." Martha, the SISTER of HIM who *had died, says to him, "Lord, he smells now; for it is the fourth day."

40 JESUS says to her, "Did I not tell thee, That if thou wouldst believe, thou shalt ‡ see the GLORY of GOD?"

41 Then they took away the STONE. And JESUS lifted his EYES above, and said, "Father, I give thanks to thee That thou didst hear me.

42 And I knew That thou hearest Me always; ‡ but on account of THAT CROWD STANDING BY I spoke, so that they may believe That thou didst send Me."

43 And having said these words, he cried out with a loud Voice, "Lazarus, come forth!"

44 HE who had been DEAD came forth, having his HANDS and FEET bound with Bandages, and ‡ his FACE bound about with a Napkin. * Jesus says to them, "Loose him, and let him go."

45 MANY, therefore, of the JEWS who CAME to MARY, ‡ and beheld * that which he had done, believed into him.

46 But some of them went to the PHARISEES, and told them what things JESUS did.

47 Then the HIGH-PRIESTS and the PHARI-

* VATICAN MANUSCRIPT.—39. had died, says. 44. Jesus. 45. that which he had done, believed.

‡ 37. John ix. 6. ‡ 40. ver. 4, 23. ‡ 42. John xii. 30. ‡ 44. John xx. 7. ‡ 45. John ii. 23; x. 42; xii. 11, 18.

σαιοι συνεδριον, και ελεγον· Τι ποιουμεν; ὁτι
sees a high council, and said; What are we doing? because
οὑτος ὁ ανθρωπος πολλα σημεια ποιει. 48 Εαν αφ-
this the man many signs does. If we
ωμεν αυτον οὑτω, παντες πιστευσουσιν εις αυτον·
allow him thus, all will believe into him;
και ελευσονται οἱ Ῥωμαιοι, και αρουσιν ἡμων και
and will come the Romans, and will take away of us both
τον τοπον και το εθνος. 49 Εἱς δε τις αυτων,
the place and the nation. One and a certain of them
Καιαφας, αρχιερευς ων του ενιαυτου εκεινου,
Caiaphas, high-priest being of the year that,
ειπεν αυτοις· Ὑμεις ουκ οιδατε ουδεν. 50 Ουδε
said to them; You not know nothing. Neither
διαλογιζεσθε, ὁτι συμφερει ἡμιν, ἱνα εἱς ανθρω-
do you consider, that it is better for us, that one man
πος αποθανῃ ὑπερ του λαου, και μη ὁλον το
should die in behalf of the people, and not whole the
εθνος αποληται. 51 Τουτο δε αφ' ἑαυτου ουκ
nation should perish. This but from himself not
ειπεν· αλλα αρχιερευς ων του ενιαυτου εκεινου,
he said, but high-priest being of the year that,
προεφητευσεν, ὁτι εμελλεν Ιησους αποθνησκειν
he prophesied, that was about Jesus to die
ὑπερ του εθνους· 52 και ουχ ὑπερ του εθνους
in behalf of the nation; and not in behalf of the nation
μονον, αλλ' ἱνα και τα τεκνα του θεου τα
alone, but that also the children of the God those
διεσκορπισμενα συναγαγῃ εις ἑν.
having been scattered he should gather into one.
53 Απ' εκεινης ουν της ἡμερας συνεβουλευ-
From that therefore the day they took counsel
σαντο, ἱνα αποκτεινωσιν αυτον. 54 Ιησους ουν
together, that they might kill him. Jesus therefore
ουκετι παρρησιᾳ περιεπατει εν τοις Ιουδαιοις,
no longer publicly walked among the Jews,
αλλα απηλθεν εκειθεν εις την χωραν εγγυς της
but went away thence into the country near the
ερημου, εις Εφραιμ λεγομενην πολιν· κακει
desert, into Ephraim being called a city; and there
διετριβε μετα των μαθητων αὑτου. 55 Ην δε
remained with the disciples of himself. Was and
εγγυς το πασχα των Ιουδαιων· και ανεβησαν
near the passover of the Jews; and went up
πολλοι εις Ἱεροσολυμα εκ της χωρας προ του
many into Jerusalem out of the country before the
πασχα, ἱνα αγνισωσιν ἑαυτους. 56 Εζητουν ουν
passover, that they might purify themselves. They sought then

SEES convened the Sanhedrim, and said, ‡ "What are we doing? Because This MAN performs Many Signs.

48 If we suffer him thus, all will believe into him; and the ROMANS will come and take away both our PLACE and NATION."

49 And a certain one of them, ‡ Caiaphas, † being High-priest that YEAR, said to them, "You know nothing;

50 ‡ neither do you consider That it is expedient for us that One Man should die in behalf of the PEOPLE, than that the Whole NATION should perish."

51 But he said this not from himself; but being High-priest that YEAR, he predicted That Jesus was about to die in behalf of the NATION;

52 and not only in behalf of the NATION, ‡ but that he should also assemble into one, THOSE CHILDREN of GOD who have been SCATTERED ABROAD.

53 Therefore from That DAY, * they took counsel that they might kill him.

54 * JESUS, ‡ therefore, walked no longer publicly among the JEWS, but went away thence into the COUNTRY near the DESERT, into a City called † Ephraim, and there * abode with the DISCIPLES.

55 ‡ And the PASSOVER of the JEWS was near; and many went up to Jerusalem out of the COUNTRY, before the PASSOVER, that they might purify themselves.

56 Then they sought for

* VATICAN MANUSCRIPT.—53. they took counsel. 54. JESUS. 54. abode with the DISCIPLES.

† 49. By the law of Moses, Exod. xl. 15, the office of high-priest was *for life*, and the son of Aaron's race always succeeded his father. But at this time the high-priesthood was almost *annual*; the Romans and Herod put down and raised up *whom* they pleased, and *when* they pleased, without alluding to any other rule than merely that the person put in this office should be of the *sacerdotal* race. Caiaphas held this office eight or nine years.—*Clarke*. † 54. A little village in the neighborhood of Bethel. Eusebius and Jerome say it was about twenty miles north of Jerusalem.

‡ 47. John xii. 10; Acts iv. 16. ‡ 49. Luke iii. 3; John xviii. 14; Acts iv. 6. ‡ 50. John xviii. 14. ‡ 52. Isa. xlix. 6; John x. 16. Eph. i. 10; ii. 14—17. ‡ 54. John iv. 1, 3; viii. 1. ‡ 55. John ii. 13; v. 1; vi. 4.

τον Ιησουν, και ελεγον μετ' αλληλων εν τῳ
the Jesus, and said with each other in the
ἱερῳ ἑστηκοτες· Τι δοκει ὑμιν; ὁτι ου μη
temple standing; What think you? that not not
ελθῃ εις την ἑορτην; 57 Δεδωκεισαν δε
he may come to the feast? Had given now
*[και] οἱ αρχιερεις και οἱ Φαρισαιοι εντολην,
[both] the high-priests and the Pharisees a commandment,
ἱνα εαν τις γνῳ που εστι, μηνυσῃ, ὁπως
that if any one should know where he is, he should show, how
πιασωσιν αυτον.
they might seize him.

ΚΕΦ. ιβ'. 12.

1 Ὁ ουν Ιησους προ ἑξ ἡμερων του πασχα
The therefore Jesus before six days the passover
ηλθεν εις Βηθανιαν, ὁπου ην Λαζαρος *[ὁ τεθ-
came into Bethany, where was Lazarus [he having
νηκως,] ὁν ηγειρεν εκ νεκρων. 2 Εποιησαν ουν
been dead,] whom he raised out of dead ones. They made therefore
αυτῳ δειπνον εκει, και ἡ Μαρθα διηκονει· ὁ δε
him a supper there, and the Martha served; the but
Λαζαρος εἱς ην των ανακειμενων συν αυτῳ.
Lazarus one was of those reclining with him.
3 Ἡ ουν Μαρια λαβουσα λιτραν μυρου ναρδου
The then Mary having taken a pound of balsam of spikenard
πιστικης πολυτιμου, ηλειψε τους ποδας του
genuine of great price, anointed the feet of the
Ιησου, και εξεμαξε ταις θριξιν αὑτης τους ποδας
Jesus, and wiped with the hairs of herself the feet
αυτου· ἡ δε οικια επληρωθη εκ της οσμης του
of him; the and house was filled with the odor of the
μυρου. 4 Λεγει ουν εις εκ των μαθητων αυτου,
balsam. Says therefore one of the disciples of him,
Ιουδας Σιμωνος Ισκαριωτης, ὁ μελλων αυτον
Judas of Simon Iscariot, he being about him
παραδιδοναι· 5 Διατι τουτο το μυρον ουκ επραθη
to deliver up; Why this the balsam not sold
τριακοσιων δηναριων, και εδοθη πτωχοις; 6 Ειπε
three hundred denarii, and given to poor ones? He said
δε τουτο, ουχ ὁτι περι των πτωχων εμελεν
now this, not because about the poor it concerned
αυτῳ, αλλ' ὁτι κλεπτης ην, και το γλωσσοκο-
him, but because a thief he was, and the box
μον ειχε, και τα βαλλομενα εβασταζεν.
he had, and the things being put in he carried off.
7 Ειπεν ουν ὁ Ιησους· Αφες αυτην· εις την
Said therefore the Jesus; Let alone her, for the
ἡμεραν του ενταφιασμου μου τετηρηκεν αυτο.
day of the embalming of me she has kept it.
8 Τους πτωχους γαρ παντοτε εχετε μεθ' ἑαυ-
The poor for always you have with your-
των, εμε δε ου παντοτε εχετε. 9 Εγνω ουν
selves, me but not always you have. Knew therefore
οχλος πολυς εκ των Ιουδαιων, ὁτι εκει εστι·
a crowd great of the Jews, that there he is,

JESUS, and said to one another, standing in the TEMPLE, "What think you? Will he not come to the FEAST?"

57 Now the HIGH-PRIESTS and the PHARISEES had given * a Command, that if any one knew where he was, he should show how they might apprehend him.

CHAPTER XII.

1 Then JESUS Six Days before the PASSOVER came to Bethany, ‡ where THAT Lazarus was whom * Jesus raised from the Dead.

2 ‡ They made him, therefore, a Supper there, and MARTHA served; but LAZARUS was one of THOSE RECLINING with him.

3 Then ‡ MARY having taken a Pound of Balsam of genuine Spikenard, very costly, anointed the FEET of * Jesus, and wiped his FEET with her HAIR; and the HOUSE was filled with the ODOR of the BALSAM.

4 * And one of his DISCIPLES, THAT ISCARIOT who was ABOUT to betray him, says,

5 "Why was not This BALSAM sold for Three hundred Denarii, and given to the Poor?"

6 Now he said this, not Because he cared for the POOR; but because he was a Thief, and ‡ had the BOX, and stole what THINGS were DEPOSITED in it.

7 JESUS, therefore, said, * "Suffer her, that she may keep it for the DAY of my EMBALMING.

8 For ‡ the POOR you have always with yourselves; but Me you have not always."

9 A great Crowd of the JEWS, therefore, knew That he was there; and they

* VATICAN MANUSCRIPT.—57. Commandments that. 57. both—*omit*. 1. he having been dead—*omit*. 1. Jesus raised. 3. Jesus. 4. And one of his DISCIPLES, that ISCARIOT who was ABOUT to betray him, says. 7. Suffer her, that she may keep it for the DAY of my EMBALMING.

‡ 1. John xi. 1, 43. ‡ 2. Matt. xxvi. 6; Mark xiv. 3. ‡ 3. John xi. 2. ‡ 6. John xiii. 29. ‡ 8. Matt. xxvi. 11; Mark xiv. 7.

και ηλθον ου δια τον Ιησουν μονον, αλλ' ἱνα
and they came not on account of the Jesus alone, but that
και τον Λαζαρον ιδωσιν, ὁν ηγειρεν εκ νεκρων.
also the Lazarus they might see, whom he raised out of dead ones.
10 Εβουλευσαντο δε οἱ αρχιερεις, ἱνα και τον
Took counsel but the high-priests, that also the
Λαζαρον αποκτεινωσιν· 11 ὁτι πολλοι δι' αυτον
Lazarus they might kill; because many on account of him
ὑπηγον των Ιουδαιων, και επιστευον εις τον Ιη-
went away of the Jews, and believed into the Je-
σουν.
sus.

12 Τη επαυριον οχλος πολυς, ὁ ελθων εις την
On the morrow a crowd great, who having come to the
ἑορτην, ακουσαντες, ὁτι ερχεται Ιησους εις
feast, having heard that was coming Jesus into
Ἱεροσολυμα, 13 ελαβον τα βαια των φοινικων,
Jerusalem, they took the branches of the palm-trees,
και εξηλθον εις ὑπαντησιν αυτῳ, και εκραζον·
and went out to a meeting with him, and cried out;
Ὡσαννα, ευλογημενος ὁ ερχομενος εν ονοματι
Hosanna, worthy of blessing he coming in name
κυριου, ὁ βασιλευς του Ισραηλ. 14 Εὑρων δε ὁ
of Lord, the king of the Israel. Finding and the
Ιησους οναριον, εκαθισεν επ' αυτο, καθως εστι
Jesus a young ass, he sat on it, as it is
γεγραμμενον· 15 "Μη φοβου, θυγατερ Σιων·
having been written; "Not fear, O daughter of Sion;
ιδου, ὁ βασιλευς σου ερχεται καθημενος επι
lo, the king of thee comes sitting on
πωλον ονου." 16 Ταυτα δε ουκ εγνωσαν οἱ
a foal of an ass." These things now not knew the
μαθηται αυτου το πρωτον· αλλ' ὁτε εδοξασθη
disciples of him the first; but when was glorified
ὁ Ιησους, τοτε εμνησθησαν, ὁτι ταυτα ην επ'
the Jesus, then they remembered, that these things was about
αυτῳ γεγραμμενα, και ταυτα εποιησαν αυτῳ.
him having been written, and these things they did to him.
17 Εμαρτυρει ουν ὁ οχλος, ὁ ων μετ' αυτου, ὁτι
Testified then the crowd, that being with him, that
τον Λαζαρον εφωνησεν εκ του μνημειου, και
the Lazarus he called out of the tomb, and
ηγειρεν αυτον εκ νεκρων. 18 Δια τουτο και
raised him out of dead ones. On account of this also
ὑπηντησεν αυτῳ ὁ οχλος, ὁτι ηκουσαν τουτο
met him the crowd, because they heard this
αυτον πεποιηκεναι το σημειον. 19 Οἱ ουν Φαρι-
him to have done the sign. The then Phari-
σαιοι ειπον προς ἑαυτους· Θεωρειτε ὁτι ουκ
sees said to themselves; You see that not
ωφελειτε ουδεν· ιδε, ὁ κοσμος οπισω αυτου
you gain nothing; see, the world after him
απηλθεν.
is going away.

20 Ησαν δε τινες Ἑλληνες εκ των αναβαινον-
Were and some Greeks of those going
των, ἱνα προσκυνησωσιν εν τῃ ἑορτῃ. 21 Οὑτοι
up, that they might worship in the feast. These

came, not on account of JESUS only, but also that they might see LAZARUS, whom he raised from the DEAD.

10 ‡ * And even the HIGH-PRIESTS took counsel, that they might kill LAZARUS also;

11 ‡ Because, on account of him, many of the JEWS went away, and believed into JESUS.

12 ‡ The NEXT DAY, a great Crowd HAVING COME to the FEAST, having heard That JESUS was coming to Jerusalem,

13 took BRANCHES of PALM-TREES, and went out to meet him, and cried out, ‡ "Hosanna, Blessed is HE who COMES in the Name of Jehovah, the KING of ISRAEL!"

14 And JESUS having found a Young ass, sat on it, as it has been written,

15 ‡ "Fear not, * daughter of Zion; behold, thy "KING comes, sitting on "the Colt of an Ass."

16 Now these things his DISCIPLES knew not at FIRST; but when JESUS was glorified, ‡ then they remembered That These things had been written about him, and they did these things to him.

17 Then THAT CROWD which was with him, testified that he called LAZARUS out of the TOMB, and raised him from the dead.

18 On this account also the CROWD met him, Because they heard that he had done This SIGN.

19 Therefore the PHARISEES, said among themselves, ‡ "You see that you are gaining nothing; behold, the WORLD is gone away after him."

20 And there were ‡ some Greeks of THOSE HAVING GONE UP, that they might worship during the FEAST.

* VATICAN MANUSCRIPT.—10. But even the HIGH-PRIESTS. 15. DAUGHTER of Zion.

‡ 10. Luke xvi. 31. ‡ 11. John xi. 45. ‡ 12. Matt. xxi. 8; Mark xi. 8; Luke xix. 35, &c. ‡ 13. Psa. cxviii. 25, 26. ‡ 15. Zech. ix. 9. ‡ 16. John xiv. 26. ‡ 19. John xi. 47, 48. ‡ 20. Acts xvii. 4.

ουν προσηλθον Φιλιππῳ, τῳ απο Βηθσαιδα της
therefore came to Philip, that from Bethsaida of the
Γαλιλαιας, και ηρωτων αυτον, λεγοντες· Κυριε,
Galilee, and were asking him, saying; O sir,
θελομεν τον Ιησουν ιδειν. 22 Ερχεται Φιλιπ-
we wish the Jesus to see. Comes Philip,
πος, και λεγει τῳ Ανδρεᾳ· *[και παλιν] Αν-
and says to the Andrew; [and again] An-
δρεας και Φιλιππος λεγουσι τῳ Ιησου. 23 Ὁ δε
drew and Philip say to the Jesus. The but
Ιησους απεκρινατο αυτοις, λεγων· Εληλυθεν ἡ
Jesus answered them, saying; Has come the
ὡρα, ἱνα δοξασθῃ ὁ υἱος του ανθρωπου. 24 Αμην
hour, that may be glorified the son of the man. Indeed
αμην λεγω ὑμιν, εαν μη ὁ κοκκος του σιτου
indeed I say to you, if not the grain of the wheat
πεσων εις την γην αποθανῃ, αυτος μονος μενει·
falling into the ground should die, he alone abides;
εαν δε αποθανῃ, πολυν καρπον φερει. 25 Ὁ
if but it may die. much fruit it bears. He
φιλων την ψυχην αὑτου, απολεσει αυτην· και
loving the life of himself, shall lose her; and
ὁ μισων την ψυχην αὑτου εν τῳ κοσμῳ τουτῳ,
he hating the life of himself in the world this,
εις ζωην αιωνιον φυλαξει αυτην.
into life age-lasting shall keep her.
26 Εαν εμοι διακονῃ τις, εμοι ακολουθειτω·
If me may serve any one, me let him follow;
και ὁπου ειμι εγω, εκει και ὁ διακονος ὁ εμος
and where am I, there also the servant the mine
εσται· εαν τις εμοι διακονῃ, τιμησει αυτον ὁ
shall be; if any one me may serve, will serve him the
πατηρ. 27 Νυν ἡ ψυχη μου τεταρακται· και τι
father. Now the soul of me is troubled; and what
ειπω· Πατερ, σωσον με εκ της ὡρας ταυτης;
shall I say? O father, save me from the hour this?
Αλλα δια τουτο ηλθον εις την ὡραν ταυτην.
But on account of this I came to the hour this.
28 Πατερ, δοξασον σου το ονομα. Ηλθεν ουν
O father, glorify of thee the name. Came then
φωνη εκ του ουρανου· "Και εδοξασα, και
a voice out of the heaven; "Both I glorified, and
παλιν δοξασω." 29 Ὁ *[ουν] οχλος ὁ ἑστως
again will glorify." The [therefore] crowd that standing
και ακουσας, ελεγε βροντην γεγονεναι. Αλλοι
and hearing, said thunder to have been. Others
ελεγον· Αγγελος αυτῳ λελαληκεν. 30 Απεκριθη
said; A messenger to him has spoken. Answered
ὁ Ιησους και ειπεν· Ου δι εμε αυτη ἡ φωνη
the Jesus and said; Not on account of me this the voice
γεγονεν, αλλα δι' ὑμας. 31 Νυν κρισις εστι
had come, but on account of you. Now a judgment is
του κοσμου τουτου· νυν ὁ αρχων του κοσμου
the world this; now the ruler of the world
τουτου· νυν ὁ αρχων του κοσμου τουτου εκβλη-
this; now the ruler of the world this will be

21 These, therefore, came
to THAT Philip who was of
Bethsaida of GALILEE, and
asked him, saying, "Sir,
we wish to see JESUS."

22 * PHILIP comes and
tells ANDREW; Andrew
and Philip * come and tell
JESUS.

23 And JESUS * answers
them, saying, ‡ "The HOUR
has come that the SON of
MAN may be glorified.

24 Indeed, I assure you,
‡ If the GRAIN of WHEAT
falling into the GROUND
should not die, it remains
alone; but if it should die,
it bears Much Fruit.

25 ‡ HE LOVING his
LIFE shall lose it, and HE
HATING his LIFE in this
WORLD shall preserve it to
aionian Life.

26 If any one serve me,
let him follow me; ‡ and
where I am, there also shall
MY SERVANT be. If any
one serve me, him will the
FATHER honor.

27 ‡ Now is my SOUL
troubled; and what shall I
say? Father, save me from
this HOUR? But on this
account I came to this
HOUR.

28 Father, glorify * Thy
NAME." ‡ Then a Voice
came from HEAVEN, "I
both glorified and will
glorify again."

29 THAT CROWD STAND-
ING and hearing, said, "It
was Thunder;" others said,
"An Angel has spoken to
him."

30 * Jesus answered and
said, "This VOICE has not
come on account of me, but
on your account.

31 There is now a Judg-
ment of this WORLD; ‡ the
RULER of this WORLD shall
now be cast out.

* VATICAN MANUSCRIPT.—22. PHILIP. 22. and again—*omit*. 22. come and tell. 23. answers. 28. My NAME. 29. therefore—*omit*. 30. Jesus.

‡ 23. John xiii. 32; xvii. 1. ‡ 24. 1 Cor. xv. 36. ‡ 25. Matt. x. 39; xvi. 25; Mark viii 35: Luke ix. 24; xvii. 33. ‡ 26. John xiv. 3; xvii. 24; 1 Thess. iv 17. ‡ 27. Matt xxvi. 38, 39; Luke xii. 50; John xiii. 21. ‡ 28. Matt. iii. 17. ‡ 31. John xiv. 30; xvi. 11.

θησεται εξω. 32 Καγω εαν ὑψωθω εκ της
cast out. And I if I should be lifted up from the
γης, παντας ἑλκυσω προς εμαυτον. 33 Τουτο
earth, all will draw to myself. This
δε ελεγε, σημαινων ποιῳ θανατῳ ημελλεν απο-
but he said, signifying by what death he was about to
θνησκειν. 34 Απεκριθη αυτῳ ὁ οχλος· Ἡμεις
die. Answered him the crowd; We
ηκουσαμεν εκ του νομου, ὁτι ὁ Χριστος μενει
heard out of the law, that the Anointed abides
εις τον αιωνα· και πως συ λεγεις, ὁτι δει
into the age; and how thou sayest, that it behoves
ὑψωθηναι τον υἱον του ανθρωπου; τις εστιν
to be lifted up the son of the man? who is
οὑτος ὁ υἱος του ανθρωπου; 35 Ειπεν ουν αυτοις
this the son of the man? Said then to them
ὁ Ιησους· Ετι μικρον χρονον το φως εν ὑμιν
the Jesus; Yet a little time the light among you
εστι. Περιπατειτε, ἑως το φως εχετε, ἱνα μη
is. Walk you, while the light you have, that not
σκοτια ὑμας καταλαβῃ· και ὁ περιπατων εν τῃ
darkness you may overtake; and he walking in the
σκοτιᾳ ουκ οιδε που ὑπαγει. 36 Ἑως το φως
darkness not knows where he goes. While the light
εχετε, πιστευετε εις το φως, ἱνα υἱοι φωτος
you have, believe into the light, that sons of light
γενησθε. Ταυτα ελαλησεν ὁ Ιησους, και
you may become. These things spoke the Jesus, and
απελθων εκρυβη απ' αυτων.
going away he was hid from them.

37 Τοσαυτα δε αυτου σημεια πεποιηκοτος
So many but of him signs having been done
εμπροσθεν αυτων ουκ επιστευον εις αυτον· 38 ἱνα
in presence of them not they did believe into him; that
ὁ λογος Ησαιου του προφητου πληρωθῃ, ὁν
the word of Esaias the prophet might be fulfilled, which
ειπε· "Κυριε, τις επιστευσε τῃ ακοῃ ἡμων;
he said; "O lord, who believed the report of us?
και ὁ βραχιων κυριου τινι απεκαλυφθη;" 39 Δια
and the arm of lord to whom was it revealed?" On account of
τουτο ουκ ηδυναντο πιστευειν· ὁτι παλιν ειπεν
this not they were able to believe; because again said
Ἡσαιας· 40 "Τετυφλωκεν αυτων τους οφθαλ-
Esaias; He has blinded of them the eyes,
μους, και πεπωρωκεν αυτων την καρδιαν· ἱνα
and has hardened of them the heart; so that
μη ιδωσι τοις οφθαλμοις, και νοησωσι τῃ
not they might see with the eyes, and understand with the
καρδιᾳ, και επιστραφωσι, και ιασωμαι αυτους."
heart, and should turn back, and I should heal them."
41 Ταυτα ειπεν Ἡσαιας, ὁτι ειδε την δοξαν
These things said Esaias, because he saw the glory
αυτου, και ελαλησε περι αυτου. 42 Ὁμως
of him, and spoke concerning him. Nevertheless

32 And I, ‡ if I be raised on high from the EARTH, will draw All to myself."

33 ‡ Now this he said, signifying by What Death he was about to die.

34 * Then the CROWD answered him, ‡ "We heard out of the LAW, That the MESSIAH continues to the AGE; and how sayest thou, 'That the SON of MAN must be raised on high?' Who is This SON of MAN?"

35 JESUS, therefore said to them, ‡ "Yet a Little Time the LIGHT is among you. Walk while you have the LIGHT, so that Darkness may not overtake You; and ‡ HE who WALKS in DARKNESS knows not where he is going.

36 While you have the LIGHT, believe into the LIGHT, that you may become ‡ the SONS of LIGHT." These things spoke *Jesus, and going away he was concealed from them.

37 But though he had performed so Many Signs in their presence, they did not believe into him;

38 that the WORD of Isaiah, the PROPHET, might be verified, which he said, ‡ "Lord, who believed our "REPORT? and the ARM of "the Lord, to whom was it "revealed?"

39 On account of this they could not believe, Because Isaiah said again,

40 ‡ "He has blinded "Their EYES, and hardened "Their HEART, so that they "should not see with the "EYES, and understand "with the HEART, and "should turn, and I should "heal them."

41 Isaiah said these things, because he saw his ‡ GLORY, and spoke of him.

42 Nevertheless, many

* VATICAN MANUSCRIPT.—34. Then the CROWD. 36. Jesus.

‡ 32. John iii. 14; viii. 28. ‡ 33. John xviii. 32. ‡ 34. Psa. lxxxix. 36, 37; cx. 4. Isa. ix. 7, &c. ‡ 35. John i. 9; viii. 12; ix. 5; ver. 46. ‡ 35. John xi. 10; 1 John ii. 11. ‡ 36. Luke xvi. 8; Eph. v. 8; 1 Thess. v. 5; 1 John ii. 9—11. ‡ 38. Isa. liii. 1; Rom. x. 16. ‡ 40. Isa. vi. 9, 10; Matt. xiii. 14. ‡ 41. Isa. vi. 1.

μεντοι και εκ των αρχοντων πολλοι επιστευσαν
truly and of the rulers many believed
εις αυτον· αλλα δια τους Φαρισαιους ουχ
into him; but on account of the Pharisees not
ὡμολογουν, ἱνα μη αποσυναγωγοι γενωνται·
did confess, so that not from synagogues they might be;
43 ηγαπησαν γαρ την δοξαν των ανθρωπων
they loved for the glory of the men
μαλλον, ηπερ την δοξαν του θεου.
more, than the glory of the God.
44 Ιησους δε εκραξε και ειπεν· Ὁ πιστευων
Jesus and cried and said; He believing
εις εμε, ου πιστευει εις εμε,, αλλ' εις τον πεμ-
into me, not believes into me, but into him having
ψαντα με· 45 και ὁ θεωρων εμε, θεωρει τον πεμ-
sent me; and he seeing me, sees him having
ψαντα με. 46 Εγω φως εις τον κοσμον εληλυ-
sent me. I a light into the world have come,
θα, ἱνα πας ὁ πιστευων εις εμε, εν τη σκοτια
that all the believing into me, in the darkness
μη μεινη. 47 Και εαν τις μου ακουση των
not may abide. And if any one of me may hear the
ῥηματων, και μη πιστευση, εγω ου κρινω αυτον·
words, and not may believe, I not judge him;
(ου γαρ ηλθον, ἱνα κρινω τον κοσμον, αλλ' ἱνα
(not for I came, that I might judge the world, but that
σωσω τον κοσμον·) 48 ὁ αθετων εμε, και
I might save the world;) he rejecting me, and
μη λαμβανων τα ῥηματα μου εχει τον κρινοντα
not receiving the words of me has that judging
αυτον· ὁ λογος ὁν ελαλησα, εκεινος κρινει
him; the word which I spoke, that shall judge
αυτον εν τη εσχατη ἡμερᾳ. 49 Ὁτι εγω εξ
him in the last day. Because I from
εμαυτου ουκ ελαλησα· αλλ' ὁ πεμψας με πατηρ
myself not spoke; but the having sent me father
αυτος μοι εντολην εδωκε, τι ειπω και τι
he me a commandment gave, what I should say and what
λαλησω· 50 και οιδα, ὁτι ἡ εντολη αυτου ζωη
I should speak; and I know, that the commandment of him life
αιωνιος εστιν. Ἁ ουν λαλω εγω, καθως ειρη-
age-lasting is. What therefore say I, as has spo-
κε μοι ὁ πατηρ, οὑτω λαλω.
ken to me the father, so I speak.

of the RULERS also believed into him, ‡ but because of the PHARISEES they did not confess him, so that they might not be put out of the synagogues.

43 ‡ For they loved the GLORY of MEN more than the GLORY of GOD.

44 But Jesus cried out and said, ‡"HE BELIEVING into me, believes not into me, but into HIM who SENT me;

45 and ‡ HE BEHOLDING me, beholds HIM who SENT me.

46 ‡ I have come a Light into the WORLD, so that * HE BELIEVING into me may not abide in DARKNESS.

47 And if any one hear, and * keep not My WORDS, I do not judge him; ‡ for I came not that I might judge the WORLD, but that I might save the WORLD.

48 HE REJECTING me, and receiving not my WORDS, has THAT which JUDGES him; ‡ the WORD which I spoke, that will judge him in the LAST Day.

49 Because ‡ I spoke not from myself; but the FATHER who SENT me, he *has given me a Commandment, what I should enjoin, and what I should speak;

50 and I know That his COMMANDMENT is aionian Life. What things I speak, therefore, as the FATHER has told me, so I speak."

ΚΕΦ. ιγ'. 13.

1 Προ δε της ἑορτης του πασχα, ειδως ὁ Ιη-
Before and the feast of the passover, knowing the Je-
σους, ὁτι εληλυθεν αὑτου ἡ ὡρα, ἱνα μεταβῃ
sus, that was come of himself the hour, that he should depart
εκ του κοσμου τουτου προς τον πατερα,
out of the world this to the father,
αγαπησας τους ιδιους τους εν τῳ κοσμῳ, εις
having loved the own those in the world, to
τελος ηγαπησεν αυτους. 2 Και δειπνου γενο-
an end he loved them. And supper being

CHAPTER XIII.

1 Now JESUS knowing before the FEAST of the PASSOVER, That His HOUR was come, that he should depart out of this WORLD to the FATHER, having loved THOSE his OWN who were in the WORLD, he loved them to the End.

2 And as Supper was pre-

* VATICAN MANUSCRIPT.—46. HE BELIEVING. 47. keep not. 49. has given me.

‡ 42. John vii. 13; ix. 22. ‡ 43. John v. 44. ‡ 44. Mark ix. 37; 1 Pet. i. 21. ‡ 45. John xiv. 9. ‡ 46. ver. 35, 36; John iii. 19; viii. 12; ix. 5, 39. ‡ 47. John iii. 17. ‡ 48. Deut. xviii. 19; Mark xvi. 16. ‡ 49. John viii. 38; xiv. 10.

μενου, (του διαβολου ηδη βεβληκοτος εις την
done, (the accuser already having put into the
καρδιαν Ιουδα Σιμωνος Ισκαριωτου, ἱνα αυτον
heart Judas of Simon Iscariot, that him
παραδῳ,) 3 ειδως ὁ Ιησους, ὁτι παντα δεδωκεν
he might betray,) knowing the Jesus, that all things had given
αυτῳ ὁ πατηρ εις τας χειρας, και ὁτι απο θεου
him the father into the hands, and that from God
εξηλθε, και προς τον θεον ὑπαγει· 4 εγειρεται
he came out, and to the God he goes; rises
εκ του δειπνου, και τιθησι τα ἱματια, και λα-
from the supper, and puts off the mantles, and having
βων λεντιον, διεζωσεν ἑαυτον. 5 Ειτα βαλλει
taken a towel, girded himself. Afterward he puts
ὑδωρ εις τον νιπτηρα, και ηρξατο νιπτειν τους
water into the wash-basin, and began to wash the
ποδας των μαθητων, και εκμασσειν τῳ λεντιῳ
feet of the disciples, and to wipe with the towel
ᾡ ην διεζωσμενος. 6 Ερχεται ουν προς
with which he was having been girded. He comes then to
Σιμωνα Πετρον· και λεγει αυτῳ εκεινος· Κυριε,
Simon Peter; and says to him he; O lord,
συ μου νιπτεις τους ποδας; 7 Απεκριθη Ιησους
thou of me washest the feet? Answered Jesus
και ειπεν αυτῳ. Ὁ εγω ποιω, συ ουκ οιδας
and said to him. What I do, thou not knowest
αρτι, γνωσῃ δε μετα ταυτα. 8 Λεγει αυτῳ
now, thou shalt know but after these things. Says to him
Πετρος. Ου μη νιψῃς τους ποδας μου εις
Peter. Not not thou mayest wash the feet of me into
τον αιωνα. Απεκριθη αυτῳ ὁ Ιησους· Εαν μη
the age. Answered him the Jesus: If not
νιψω σε, ουκ εχεις μερος μετ᾽ εμου. 9 Λεγει
I may wash thee, not thou hast a part with me. Says
αυτῳ Σιμων Πετρος· Κυριε, μη τους ποδας μου
to him Simon Peter; O lord, not the feet of me
μονον, αλλα και τας χειρας, και την κεφαλην.
alone, but also the hands, and the head.
10 Λεγει αυτῳ ὁ Ιησους· Ὁ λελουμενος ου
Says to him the Jesus; He having been bathed not
χρειαν εχει η τους ποδας νιψασθαι, αλλ᾽ εστι
need has than the feet to wash, but is
καθαρος ὁλος· και ὑμεις καθαροι εστε, αλλ᾽
clean wholly; and you clean are, but
ουχι παντες. 11 Ηδει γαρ τον παραδιδοντα
not all. He knew for the betraying
αυτον· δια τουτο ειπεν· Ουχι παντες καθαροι
him; on account of this he said: Not all clean
εστε.
you are.

paring, the ENEMY having already put into the HEART of Judas Iscariot, son of Simon, that he should betray him,
3 * he knowing ‡ That the FATHER had given him All things into his HANDS, and That he came out ‡ from God, and was going to GOD,
4 rises from the SUPPER, and puts off his MANTLE, and taking a Towel girded himself.
5 † Afterward he puts Water into the WASH-BASIN, and began to wash the FEET of the DISCIPLES, and to wipe them with the TOWEL with which he was girded.
6 Then he comes to Simon Peter; * he says to him, "Lord, dost thou wash My FEET?"
7 Jesus answered and said to him, "What I am doing, thou knowest not now, but ‡ after this thou wilt know."
8 Simon Peter says to him, "Thou shalt not wash my FEET to the AGE." *He answered him; "Unless I wash thee, thou hast no PART with me."
9 Simon Peter says to him, "Lord, not my FEET only, but also my HANDS and my HEAD."
10 * Jesus says to him, †"HE who has been BATHING, has no need unless to wash his FEET, but is wholly clean; and ‡ you are clean, but not all."
11 For ‡ he knew WHO was BETRAYING him; on this account he said, "You are not all clean."

* VATICAN MANUSCRIPT.—3. he knowing. 6. he says. 8. He answered. 10. Jesus.

† 5. The washing of the feet in times of primitive simplicity was performed by the host or hostess to the guest, but afterwards it was committed to the servants, and therefore was accounted a servile employment. When David sent to Abigail, to inform her that he had chosen her for a wife, she arose and said,—"Behold, let thy handmaid be a *servant*, to *wash* the *feet* of the *servants* of my lord," 1 Sam. xxv. 41. At the time when our Lord performed this office, it was esteemed the office of the meanest slaves. This act plainly showed the humility and condescension of Jesus, and emphatically taught the same to his disciples.
† 10. It was customary for the Jews to bathe themselves (*twice*, according to some,) before eating the paschal supper.

‡ 3. Matt. xi. 27; xxviii. 18; John iii. 35; xvii. 2. ‡ 3. John xiii. 42; xvi. 28. ‡ 7. ver. 12—17. ‡ 10. John xv. 3. ‡ 11. John vi. 64.

12 Ὁτε ουν ενιψε τους ποδας αυτων, και
When therefore he had washed the feet of them, and
ελαβε τα ἱματια αὑτου, αναπεσων παλιν, ειπεν
taken the mantles of himself, falling down again, he said
αυτοις· Γινωσκετε τι πεποιηκα ὑμιν; 13 Ὑμεις
to them; Know you what I have done to you? You
φωνειτε με· Ὁ διδασκαλος και ὁ κυριος· και
call me; The teacher and the lord; and
καλως λεγετε· ειμι γαρ. 14 Ει ουν εγω ενιψα
well you say; I am for. If then I washed
ὑμων τους ποδας, ὁ κυριος και ὁ διδασκαλος,
of you the feet, the lord and the teacher,
και ὑμεις οφειλετε αλληλων νιπτειν τους
also you are bound of one another to wash the
ποδας. 15 Ὑποδειγμα γαρ εδωκα ὑμιν, ἱνα
feet. An example for I gave to you, that
καθως εγω εποιησα ὑμιν, και ὑμεις ποιητε.
as I did to you, also you should do.
16 Αμην αμην λεγω ὑμιν, ουκ εστι δουλος μειζων
Indeed indeed I say to you, not is a slave greater
του κυριου αὑτου, ουδε αποστολος μειζων του
of the lord of himself, nor a messenger greater of the
πεμψαντος αυτον. 17 Ει ταυτα οιδατε, μακαριοι
sending him. If these things you know, blessed
εστε, εαν ποιητε αυτα. 18 Ου περι παντων
are you, if you should do them. Not about all
ὑμων λεγω· εγω οιδα οὑς εξελεξαμην· αλλ',
of you I speak; I know whom I chose; but,
ἱνα ἡ γραφη πληρωθη· "Ὁ τρωγων μετ' εμου
that the writing may be fulfilled; "He eating with me
τον αρτον, επηρεν επ' εμε την πτερναν αὑτου."
the loaf, lifted up against me the heel of himself."
19 Απ' αρτι λεγω ὑμιν, προ του γενεσθαι, ἱνα
From now I say to you, before the to happen, that
ὁταν γενηται, πιστευσητε, ὁτι εγω ειμι.
when it may happen, you may believe, that I am.
20 Αμην αμην λεγω ὑμιν· Ὁ λαμβανων εαν τινα
Indeed indeed I say to you; He receiving if any one
πεμψω, εμε λαμβανει· ὁ δε εμε λαμβανων,
I may send, me receives; he and me receiving,
λαμβανει τον πεμψαντα με.
receives him having sent me.

21 Ταυτα ειπων ὁ Ιησους εταραχθη τῳ πνευμα-
These things saying the Jesus was troubled in the spirit,
τι, και εμαρτυρησε, και ειπεν· Αμην αμην λεγω
and testified, and said; Indeed indeed I say
ὑμιν, ὁτι εις εξ ὑμων παραδωσει με. 22 Εβλε-
to you, that one of you will betray me. Looked
πον *[ουν] εις αλληλους οἱ μαθηται, απορου-
[then] to each other the disciples, doubt-
μενοι περι τινος λεγει. 23 Ην δε ανακειμενος
ing about whom he was speaking. Was now reclining

12 When, therefore, he had washed their FEET, and taken his MANTLE, reclining again he said to them, "Do you know what I have done to you?

13 ‡ You call me The TEACHER, and The LORD; and you say well; for I am.

14 If I then, the LORD and the TEACHER, have washed Your FEET, you ought also to wash One another's FEET.

15 For ‡ I have given you an Example, that, as I have done to you, so you should do.

16 Indeed, I assure you, ‡ a Servant is not greater than his LORD, nor an Apostle greater than HE who SENT him.

17 ‡ If you know These things, happy are you if you do them.

18 I am not speaking about all of you; I know * whom I chose; but that the SCRIPTURE may be fulfilled, ‡ 'HE that EATS * 'My BREAD, lifted up his 'HEEL against me.'

19 I tell you now, before it OCCURS, that when it occurs you may believe That I am he.

20 Indeed, I assure you, ‡ HE who RECEIVES one whom I send receives Me; and HE who RECEIVES Me receives HIM who SENT me."

21 Having said these things *Jesus was troubled in his SPIRIT, and testified, and said, "Indeed I assure you, That one of you will deliver me up."

22 The DISCIPLES looked one on another, doubting of whom he spoke.

23 † Now there was re-

* VATICAN MANUSCRIPT.—18. same I chose. 18. My BREAD. 21. Jesus. 22. Then—*omit.*

† 23. As two or more lay on one couch, each resting on his left elbow, with his feet sloping away from the table towards the back of the couch, he that turned his back on his next neighbor was said to be lying in his bosom. This position made it easy for John to speak to Jesus in a whisper which could not be heard by the other disciples.—*S. Sharpe.*

‡ 13. Matt. xxiii. 8, 10; Luke vi. 46; 1 Cor. viii. 6; xii. 3; Phil. ii. 11. ‡ 15. Matt. xi. 29; Phil. ii. 5; 1 Pet. ii. 21; 1 John ii. 5. ‡ 16. Matt. v. 24; Luke vi. 40; John xv. 20. ‡ 17. James i. 25. ‡ 18. Psa. xli 9, Matt. xxvi. 23. ‡ 20. Matt. x. 40; xxv. 40; Luke x. 16.

εις εκ των μαθητων αυτου εν τῳ κολπῳ του
one of the disciples of him in the bosom of the
Ιησου, ὁν ηγαπα ὁ Ιησους. 24 Νευει ουν τουτῳ
Jesus, whom loved the Jesus. Nods then to him
Σιμων Πετρος, πυθεσθαι τις αν ειη περι οὑ
Simon Peter, to ask who it might be concerning of whom
λεγει. 25 Επιπεσων δε εκεινος επι το στηθος
he speaks. Falling and he on the breast
του Ιησου, λεγει αυτῳ· Κυριε, τις εστιν;
of the Jesus, he says to him; O lord, who is it?
26 Αποκρινεται ὁ Ιησους· Εκεινος εστιν, ᾡ
Answers the Jesus; He it is, to whom
εγω βαψας το ψωμιον επιδωσω. Και εμβαψας
I having dipped the little piece shall give. And having dipped
το ψωμιον, διδωσιν Ιουδᾳ Σιμωνος Ισκαριωτῃ.
the little piece, he gives to Judas of Simon Iscariot.
27 Και μετα το ψωμιον, τοτε εισηλθεν εις εκει-
And after the little piece, then entered into him
νον ὁ σατανας. Λεγει ουν αυτῳ ὁ Ιησους· Ὁ
the adversary. Says then to him the Jesus: What
ποιεις, ποιησον ταχιον. 28 Τουτο *[δε] ουδεις
thou doest, do thou quickly. This [now] no one
εγνω των ανακειμενων προς τι ειπεν αυτῳ.
knew of those reclining with why he said to him.
29 Τινες γαρ εδοκουν, επει το γλωσσοκομον
Some for thought, seeing that the box
ειχεν ὁ Ιουδας, ὁτι λεγει αυτῳ ὁ Ιησους· Αγο-
had the Judas, that says to him the Jesus; Buy
ρασον ὡν χρειαν εχομεν εις την ἑορτην· η τοις
what things need we have for the feast; or to the
πτωχοις ἱνα τι δῳ. 30 Λαβων ουν το
poor that something he should give Having taken then the
ψωμιον εκεινος, ευθεως εξηλθεν· ην δε νυξ.
little piece he, immediately went out; it was and night.
31 Ὁτε εξηλθε, λεγει ὁ Ιησους· Νυν εδοξασθη
When he went out, says the Jesus; Just now was glorified
ὁ υἱος του ανθρωπου, και ὁ θεος, εδοξασθη εν
the son of the man. and the God. was glorified in
αυτῳ. 32 *[Ει ὁ θεος εδοξασθη εν αυτῳ,] και
him. [If the God was glorified in him,] also
ὁ θεος δοξασει αυτον εν ἑαυτῳ, και ευθυς
the God will glorify him in himself, and immediately
δοξασει αυτον. 33 Τεκνια, ετι μικρον μεθ'
will glorify him. O little children, yet a little with
ὑμων ειμι. Ζητησετε με· και καθως ειπον τοις
you I am. You will seek me; and as I said to the
Ιουδαιοις· Ὁτι ὁπου εγω ὑπαγω, ὑμεις ου
Jews, That where I go, you not

clining on the BOSOM of JESUS ‡ one of his DISCIPLES, whom * Jesus loved.

24 To him, therefore, Simon Peter nods, * and says to him, "Inquire who it is of whom he is speaking."

25 And he, * leaning back on the BREAST of Jesus, says to him, "Lord, who is it?"

26 * Then JESUS answers, "He it is, * for whom I shall dip a LITTLE PIECE and give it to him." Then having dipped the LITTLE PIECE, he took and gave it to * Judas, the son of Simon Iscariot.

27 ‡ And after the LITTLE PIECE, then the ADVERSARY entered into him. * Jesus, therefore, says to him "What thou doest, do quickly."

28 No one of THOSE RECLINING knew for what he said this to him.

29 For some thought, seeing ‡ that * Judas had the BOX, That * Jesus said to him, "Buy what things we need for the FEAST;" or, that he should give something to the POOR.

30 He, therefore, having taken the LITTLE PIECE, immediately went out. And it was Night.

31 When, therefore, he went out, * Jesus says, ‡ "Just now was the SON of MAN glorified, and ‡ GOD was glorified by him.

32 * ‡ [If GOD be glorified by him,] GOD will also glorify him by himself, and he will immediately glorify him.

33 My Children, yet a little while I am with you. You will seek me, and ‡ as I said to the JEWS, 'That where I am going, you

* VATICAN MANUSCRIPT.—23. Jesus. 24. and says to him, "Inquire who it is of whom. 25. leaning back on the BREAST of Jesus. 26 Then JESUS. 26. for whom I shall dip a LITTLE PIECE and give it to him. Then having dipped the LITTLE PIECE, he took and gave. 27. Jesus. 28. now—*omit.* 29. Judas. 29. Jesus says to him. 31. Jesus. 32. If GOD be glorified by him.—*omit.*

‡ 23. John xix. 26; xx. 2; xxi. 7. 20, 24. ‡ 27 Luke xxii. 3; John vi. 70. ‡ 29. John xii. 6. ‡ 31 John xii. 23. ‡ 31. John xiv 13; 1 Pet. iv. 11. ‡ 33. John xvii. 1 4—6. ‡ 33. John vii. 34; viii. 21

δυνασθε ελθειν· και ὑμιν λεγω αρτι. [34] Εντο-
are able to come; even to you I say now. A com-
λην καινην διδωμι ὑμιν, ἱνα αγαπατε αλλη-
mandment new I give to you, that you may love each
λους· καθως ηγαπησα ὑμας, ἱνα και ὑμεις
other; as I loved you, that also you
αγαπατε αλληλους. [35] Εν τουτῳ γνωσονται
might love each other. By this will know
παντες, ὁτι εμοι μαθηται εστε, εαν αγαπην
all, that to me disciples you are, if love
εχητε εν αλληλοις. [36] Λεγει αυτῳ Σιμων Πε-
you have in each other. Says to him Simon Pe-
τρος· Κυριε, που ὑπαγεις; Απεκριθη *[αυτῳ] ὁ
ter; O lord, where goest thou? Answered [him] the
Ιησους· Ὁπου ὑπαγω, ου δυνασαι μοι νυν ακο-
Jesus; Where I go, not thou art able me now to
λουθησαι· ὑστερον δε ακολουθησεις *[μοι.]
follow; afterwards but thou shalt follow [me.]
[37] Λεγει αυτῳ Πετρος· Κυριε, διατι ου δυναμαι
Says to him Peter; O lord, why not I am able
σοι ακολουθησαι αρτι; την ψυχην μου ὑπερ
thee to follow now? the life of me in behalf
σου θησω. [38] Απεκριθη αυτῳ ὁ Ιησους· Την
of thee I will lay down. Answered him the Jesus; The
ψυχην σου ὑπερ εμου θησεις; Αμην αμην λεγω
life of thee in behalf of me wilt thou lay down? Indeed indeed I say
σοι ου μη αλεκτωρ φωνησει, ἑως οὑ απαρνησῃ
to thee not not a cock will crow, till not thou wilt deny
με τρις.
me thrice.

ΚΕΦ. ιδ'. 14.

[1] Μη ταρασσεσθω ὑμων ἡ καρδια· πιστευετε
Not let be troubled of you the heart; believe you
εις τον θεον, και εις εμε πιστευετε. [2] Εν τῃ
into the God, and into me believe you. In the
οικιᾳ του πατρος μου μοναι πολλαι εισιν· ει δε
house of the father of me dwellings many are; if but
μη, ειπον αν ὑμιν. Πορευομαι ἑτοιμασαι
not, I would have told you. I am going to prepare
τοπον ὑμιν· [3] και εαν πορευθω, και ἑτοιμασω
a place for you; and if I should go, and should prepare
ὑμιν τοπον, παλιν ερχομαι, και παραληψομαι
for you a place, again I am coming, and will receive
ὑμας προς εμαυτον· ἱνα ὁπου ειμι εγω, και
you to myself; so that where am I, also
ὑμεις ητε. [4] Και ὁπου εγω ὑπαγω οιδατε,
you may be. And where I am going you know,
*[και] την ὁδον † οιδατε· [5] Λεγει αυτῳ Θω-
[and] the way you know. Says to him Tho-
μας· Κυριε, ουκ οιδαμεν που ὑπαγεις; *[και]
mas; O lord, not we know where thou art going? [and]

cannot come,' I now also say to you.

34 ‡ A new Commandment I give to you, That you love each other; as I loved you, that you also should love each other.

35 ‡ By this, all will know That you are My Disciples, if you have Love for each other."

36 Simon Peter says to him, "Lord, where art thou going?" * Jesus answered, "Where I am going, thou canst not follow me now; but ‡ thou shalt follow afterwards."

37 Peter says to him, "Lord, why cannot I follow thee now? ‡ I will lay down my LIFE in behalf of thee."

38 * Jesus answers him, "Wilt thou lay down thy LIFE in my behalf? Indeed, I assure thee, † The Cock will not crow till thou wilt disown me three times.

CHAPTER XIV.

1 ‡ Let not your HEART be troubled; believe into GOD, and believe into Me.

2 In my FATHER'S HOUSE are many Dwellings; but if not, I would have told * you; Because I am going to prepare a Place for you.

3 And if I go and prepare a Place for you, ‡ I am coming again, and will receive you to myself, so that ‡ where I am you also may be.

4 And where I am going you know the WAY."

5 Thomas says to him, "Lord, we know not where thou art going; * how do we know the WAY?"

* VATICAN MANUSCRIPT.—36. Jesus. 36. him—*omit.* 36. me—*omit.* 38. Jesus answers. 2. you; Because I. 4. and—*omit.* 5. and—*omit.* 5. how do we know the WAY.

† 38. See Note on Matt. xxvi. 34. † 4. Tischendorf omits the second *oidate*, on the authority of several ancient MSS. and versions. The connection seems to indicate that it ought to be excluded from the text.

‡ 34. John xv. 12, 17; Eph. v. 2; 1 Thess. iv. 9; James ii. 8; 1 Pet. i. 22; 1 John ii. 7, 8; iii. 11, 23; iv. 21. ‡ 35. 1 John ii. 5; iv. 20. ‡ 36. John xxi. 18; 2 Pet. i. 14. ‡ 37. Matt. xxvi. 33—35; Mark xiv. 29—31; Luke xxii. 33, 34. ‡ 1. ver. 27. ‡ 3. ver. 18, 28. ‡ 3. John xii. 26; xvii. 24; 1 Thess. iv. 17.

πως δυναμεθα την ὁδον ειδεναι; 6 Λεγει αυτῳ ὁ
how are we able the way to know? Says to him the
Ιησους· Εγω ειμι ἡ ὁδος, και ἡ αληθεια, και ἡ
Jesus; I am the way, and the truth, and the
ζωη· ουδεις ερχεται προς τον πατερα, ει μη δι'
life; no one comes to the father, if not through
εμου. 7 Ει εγνωκειτε με, και τον πατερα μου
me. If you had known me, also the father of me
εγνωκειτε αν· *[και] απ' αρτι γινωσκετε
you would have known; [and] from now you know
αυτον, και ἑωρακατε αυτον. 8 Λεγει αυτῳ
him, and have seen him. Says to him
Φιλιππος· Κυριε, δειξον ἡμιν τον πατερα, και
Philip; O lord, show to us the father, and
αρκει ἡμιν. 9 Λεγει αυτῳ ὁ Ιησους· Τοσουτον
it is enough for us. Says to him the Jesus; So long
χρονον μεθ' ὑμων ειμι, και ουκ εγνωκας με,
a time with you am I, and not knowest thou me,
Φιλιππε; Ὁ ἑωρακως εμε, ἑωρακε τον πατερα·
O Philip? He having seen me, has seen the father;
*[και] πως συ λεγεις· Δειξον ἡμιν τον πατερα;
[and] how thou sayest; Show to us the father?
10 Ου πιστευεις, ὁτι εγω εν τῳ πατρι, και ὁ
Not believest thou, that I in the father, and the
πατηρ εν εμοι εστι; Τα ῥηματα ἁ εγω λαλω
father in me is? The words which I speak
ὑμιν, απ' εμαυτου ου λαλω· ὁ δε πατηρ, ὁ εν
to you, from myself, not I speak; the but father, he in
εμοι μενων, αυτος ποιει τα εργα. 11 Πιστευετε
me abiding, he does the works. You believe
μοι, ὁτι εγω εν τῳ πατρι, και ὁ πατηρ εν εμοι,
me, because I in the father, and the father in me,
ει δε μη, δια τα εργα αυτα πιστευετε μοι.
if but not, on account of the works themselves believe me.
12 Αμην αμην λεγω ὑμιν, ὁ πιστευων εις εμε,
Indeed indeed I speak to you, he believing into me,
τα εργα ἁ εγω ποιω, κακεινος ποιησει, και
the works which I do, also he shall do, and
μειζονα τουτων ποιησει· ὁτι εγω προς τον
greater of these shall he do; because I to the
πατερα μου πορευομαι, 13 και ὁ, τι αν αιτησητε
father of me am going, and what, any thing you may ask
τε εν τῳ ονοματι μου, τουτο ποιησω· ἱνα
in the name of me, this I will do; that
δοξασθῃ ὁ πατηρ εν τῳ υἱῳ. 14 Εαν τι αιτη-
may be glorified the father in the son. If anything you
σητε εν τῳ ονοματι μου, εγω ποιησω. 15 Εαν
may ask in the name of me, I will do. If
αγαπατε με, τας εντολας τας εμας τηρησατε·
you love me, the commandments the mine keep you;
16 και εγω ερωτησω τον πατερα, και αλλον
and I will ask the father, and another

6 JESUS says to him, "‡ I am ‡ the WAY, and ‡ the TRUTH, and ‡ the LIFE No one comes to the FATHER, except by me.

7 If you had known me, you would have known my FATHER; and from this time you know him, and have seen him."

8 Philip says to him, "Lord, show us the FATHER, and it is enough for us."

9 JESUS says to him, "So long a Time am I with you, and dost thou not know me, Philip? HE HAVING SEEN me has seen the FATHER; how sayest thou, Show us the FATHER?

10 Dost thou not believe That I am in the FATHER, and the FATHER is in me? The words which I speak to you, ‡ I speak not from myself; and THAT FATHER * abiding in me, he does the WORKS.

11 Believe me, because I am in the FATHER, and the FATHER in me; but if not, on account of * his WORKS believe me.

12 ‡ Indeed, I assure you, HE BELIEVING into me, the WORKS which I do shall he do also; and greater than these shall he do, Because I am going to * the FATHER;

13 ‡ and whatever you may ask in my NAME, this I will do; so that the FATHER may be glorified in the SON.

14 If you ask * anything in my name, this I will do.

15 ‡ If you love me, * you will keep MY COMMANDMENTS;

16 and I will ask the FATHER, and ‡ he will give

* VATICAN MANUSCRIPT.—7. and—*omit*. 9. and—*omit*. 10. dwells in me, does his WORKS. 12. the FATHER. 14. ask me anything in my name, this I will do. 15. you will keep.

‡ 6. Heb. ix. 8. ‡ 6. John i. 17; viii. 32. ‡ 6. John i. 4; xi. 25. ‡ 10. John v. 19; vii. 16; viii. 28; xii. 49. ‡ 12. Matt. xxi. 21; Mark xvi. 17; Luke x. 17. ‡ 13. Matt vii. 7; xxi. 22; Mark xi. 24; Luke xi. 9; John xv. 7, 16; xvi. 23, 24; James i. 5; 1 John iii. 22; v. 14. ‡ 15. ver. 21, 23; xv. 10, 14; 1 John v. 3. ‡ 16. John xv. 26; xvi. 7; Rom. viii. 15, 26.

παρακλητον δωσει ὑμιν, ἱνα μενῃ μεθ' ὑμων
helper' he will give to you, that he may abide with you
εις τον αἰῶνα· [17] το πνευμα της αληθειας, ὁ ὁ
into the age; the spirit of the truth, which the
κοσμος ου δυναται λαβειν, ὁτι ου θεωρει αυτο,
world not is able to receive, because not it beholds it,
ουδε γινωσκει αυτο· ὑμεις *[δε] γινωσκετε αυτο,
nor knows it; you [but] know it,
ὁτι παρ' ὑμιν μενει, και εν ὑμιν εσται.
because with you it abides, and in you it will be.
[18] Ουκ αφησω ὑμας ορφανους· ερχομαι προς
Not I will leave you orphans; I am coming to
ὑμας. [19] Ετι μικρον, και ὁ κοσμος με ουκετι
you. Yet a little, and the world me no more
θεωρει· ὑμεις δε θεωρειτε με· ὁτι εγω ζω, και
beholds; you but behold me; because I live, also
ὑμεις ζησεσθε. [20] Εν εκεινῃ τῃ ἡμερᾳ γνωσεσθε
you shall live. In that the day shall know
ὑμεις, ὁτι εγω εν τῳ πατρι μου, και ὑμεις εν
you, because I in the father of me, and you in
εμοι, καγω εν ὑμιν. [21] Ὁ εχων τας εντολας
me, and I in you. He having the commandments
μου, και τηρων αυτας, εκεινος εστιν ὁ αγαπων
of me, and keeping them, that is he loving
με· ὁ δε αγαπων με, αγαπηθησεται ὑπο του
me; he and loving me, shall be loved by the
πατρος μου· και εγω αγαπησω αυτον, και
father of me; and I will love him, and
εμφανισω αυτῳ εμαυτον.
will manifest to him myself.

[22] Λεγει αυτῳ Ιουδας (ουκ ὁ Ισκαριωτης·)
Says to him Judas (not the Iscariot;)
Κυριε, και τι γεγονεν, ὁτι ἡμιν μελλεις εμφα-
O lord, and how has it happened, that to us thou art about to mani-
νιζειν σεαυτον, και ουχι τῳ κοσμῳ; [23] Απεκριθη
fest thyself, and not to the world? Answered
Ιησους και ειπεν αυτῳ· Εαν τις αγαπᾳ με,
Jesus and said to him; If any one love me,
τον λογον μου τηρησει· και ὁ πατηρ μου
the word of me he will keep; and the father of me
αγαπησει αυτον, και προς αυτον ελευσομεθα,
will love him, and to him we will come,
και μονην παρ' αυτῳ ποιησομεν. [24] Ὁ μη
and a dwelling with him we will make. He not
αγαπων με, τους λογους μου ου τηρει· και ὁ
loving me, the words of me not will keep; and the
λογος ὁν ακουετε, ουκ εστιν εμος, αλλα του
word which you hear, not is mine, but of the
πεμψαντος με πατρος. [25] Ταυτα λελαληκα
sending me father. These things I have spoken
ὑμιν, παρ' ὑμιν μενων· [26] ὁ δε παρακλητος, το
to you, with you abiding; the but helper, the
πνευμα το αγιον, ὁ πεμψει ὁ πατηρ εν τῳ
spirit the holy, which will send the father in the

you Another Helper, that he may *be with you to the AGE;

17 the SPIRIT of TRUTH, ‡ which the WORLD cannot receive, Because it beholds it not, nor knows it; but you know it; Because it abides with you, ‡ and * will be in you.

18 I will not leave you Orphans; I am coming to you.

19 Yet a little while, and the WORLD beholds me no more? but you behold me; ‡ Because I live you also shall live.

20 In That DAY you shall know That I am in my FATHER, and you in me, and I in you.

21 ‡ HE who HAS my COMMANDMENTS, and observes them, that is HE who LOVES me; and HE who LOVES me shall be loved by my FATHER; and I will love him, and will manifest myself to him."

22 Judas says to him, (not the ISCARIOT,) "Lord, what has occurred, That thou art about to manifest thyself to us, and not to the WORLD?"

23 Jesus answered and said to him, ‡ "If any one love me, he will observe my WORD; and my FATHER will love him; and we will come to him, and make an Abode with him.

24 HE who LOVES me not, observes not my WORDS; and ‡ the WORD which you hear is not mine, but that of the FATHER who sent me.

25 These things I have spoken to you, while abiding with you.

26 But ‡ the HELPER, the HOLY SPIRIT, which the FATHER will send in my NAME, ‡ shall teach

---

* VATICAN MANUSCRIPT.—16. be with you. 17. but—omit. 17. is in you.

‡ 17. John xv. 26; xvi. 13; 1 John iv. 6. ‡ 17. 1 Cor. ii. 14. ‡ 19. 1 Cor. xv. 20. ‡ 21. ver. 15, 23; 1 John ii. 5; v. 3. ‡ 23. 1 John ii. 24; Rev. iii. 20. ‡ 24. ver. 10; John v. 19, 38; vii. 16; viii. 28; xii. 49. ‡ 26. ver. 16; Luke xxiv. 49; John xv. 26; xvi. 7. ‡ 26. John ii. 22; xii. 16; xvi. 13; 1 John ii. 20, 27.

ονοματι μου, εκεινος ὑμας διδαξει παντα, και
name of me, that you will teach all things, and
ὑπομνησει ὑμας παντα ἁ ειπον ὑμιν.
will remind you all things which I told you.
27 Ειρηνην αφιημι ὑμιν, ειρηνην την εμην
Peace I leave to you, peace the mine
διδωμι ὑμιν· ου καθως ὁ κοσμος διδωσιν, εγω
I give to you; not as the world gives, I
διδωμι ὑμιν. Μη ταρασσεσθω ὑμων ἡ καρδια
give to you. Not let be troubled of you the heart
μηδε δειλιατω. 28 Ηκουσατε, ὁτι εγω ειπον
nor let it be afraid. You heard, that I said
ὑμιν· Ὑπαγω, και ερχομαι προς ὑμας. Ει
to you; I am going away, and I am coming to you. If
ηγαπατε με, εχαρητε αν, ὁτι πορευομαι προς
you loved me, you would rejoice, that I am going to
τον πατερα· ὁτι ὁ πατηρ μου μειζων μου εστι.
the father; because the father of me greater of me is.
29 Και νυν ειρηκα ὑμιν πριν γενεσθαι, ἱνα ὁταν
And now I have told you before it happens, so that when
γενηται, πιστευσητε. 30 Ουκετι πολλα λαλησω
it happens, you may believe. No more much I will speak
μεθ' ὑμων. Ερχεται γαρ ὁ του κοσμου αρχων,
with you. Is coming for he of the world ruling,
και εν εμοι ουκ εχει ουδεν. 31 Αλλ' ἱνα γνῳ
and in me not has nothing. But that may know
ὁ κοσμος, ὁτι αγαπω τον πατερα, και καθως
the world, that I love the father, and as
ενετειλατο μοι ὁ πατηρ, οὑτω ποιω·
commanded me the father, so I do;
εγειρεσθε, αγωμεν εντευθεν. ΚΕΦ. ιε'. 15.
arise you, let us go from this place.
1 Εγω ειμι ἡ αμπελος ἡ αληθινη, και ὁ πατηρ μου
I am the vine the true, and the father of me
ὁ γεωργος εστι. 2 Παν κλημα εν εμοι μη
the vine-dresser is. Every branch in me not
φερον καρπον, αιρει αυτο· και παν το καρπον
bearing fruit, he takes away it; and every one the fruit
φερον, καθαιρει αυτο, ἱνα πλειονα καρπον φερῃ.
bearing he cleanses it, that more fruit it may bear.
3 Ηδη ὑμεις καθαροι εστε, δια τον λογον, ὁν
Already you clean are, through the word, which
λελαληκα ὑμιν. 4 Μεινατε εν εμοι, καγω εν
I have spoken to you. Abide you in me, and I in
ὑμιν. Καθως το κλημα ου δυναται καρπον
you. As the branch not is able fruit
φερειν αφ' ἑαυτου, εαν μη μεινῃ εν τῃ αμπελῳ·
to bear of itself, if not it may abide in the vine;
οὑτως ουδε ὑμεις, εαν μη εν εμοι μεινητε.
so neither you, if not in me you abide.
5 Εγω ειμι ἡ αμπελος, ὑμεις τα κληματα. Ὁ
I am the vine, you the branches. He

You all things, and remind you of all things which I said to you.

27 Peace * I leave to you; MY Peace I give to you; not as the WORLD gives, do I give to you. Let not Your HEART be troubled, nor let it be afraid.

28 You heard That I said to you, I am going away and I am coming to you. If you loved me, you would rejoice, That I am going to the FATHER; Because ‡ my FATHER is greater than I.

29 And now I have told you before it occurs, so that when it occurs, you may believe.

30 I will not speak much more with you; ‡ for the † RULER of the WORLD is coming, and has nothing in me.

31 But that the WORLD may know That I love the FATHER, and that as ‡ the FATHER commanded me, even so I do; arise, let us go hence.

CHAPTER XV.

1 I am the TRUE VINE, and my FATHER is the VINE-DRESSER.

2 Every Branch in me not bearing Fruit, he takes away; and every one bearing FRUIT, he prunes it, that it may bear More Fruit.

3 ‡ You are already clean through the WORD which I have spoken to you.

4 ‡ Abide in me, and I in you. As the BRANCH cannot bear fruit of itself, if it abide not in the VINE, so neither can you, unless you abide in me.

5 I am the VINE, you are the BRANCHES. He

* VATICAN MANUSCRIPT.—27. I leave.

† 30. Some say the *ruler of this world* means *Satan*; some, the *Roman government*; others, the *Jewish hierarchy* and *magistracy*; but *Wakefield*, in his translation, thinks that Christ here speaks of himself; (as he does in chap. xii. 30, and xvi. 11,) not of what he *then* was, but of what he *shall be*, when he *comes again*. He translates this clause as follows:—"For the ruler of this world is coming; and I have nothing now to do, but to convince the world that I love the Father, and do as he commanded me."

‡ 28. John v. 18; x. 30; Phil. ii. 6. ‡ 30. John xii. 30; xvi. 11. ‡ 31. John x. 18; Phil. ii. 8; Heb. v. 8. ‡ 3. John xiii. 10; xvii. 17; Eph. v. 26; 1 Pet. i. 22. ‡ 4. Col. i. 23; 1 John ii. 6.

μενων εν εμοι, καγω εν αυτῳ, οὑτος φερει καρ-
abiding in me, and I in him, this bears fruit
πον πολυν· ὁτι χωρις εμου ου δυνασθε ποιειν
much; because apart from me not you are able to do
ουδεν. 6 Εαν μη τις μεινῃ εν εμοι, εβληθη
nothing. If not any one may abide in me, he is cast
εξω, ὡς το κλημα, και εξηρανθη· και συναγου-
out, like the branch, and is withered; and they gather
σιν αυτα, και εις πυρ βαλλουσι, και καιεται.
them, and into a fire they cast, and it is burned.
7 Εαν μεινητε εν εμοι και τα ῥηματα μου εν
If you abide in me and the words of me in
ὑμιν μεινῃ, ὁ εαν θελητε † αιτησεσθε, και
you may abide, whatever you may wish you shall ask, and
γενησεται ὑμιν. 8 Εν τουτῳ εδοξασθη ὁ πατηρ
it shall be for you. In this was glorified the father
μου, ἱνα καρπον πολυν φερητε, και γενησεσθε
of me, that fruit much you might bear, and you shall be
εμοι μαθηται. 9 Καθως ηγαπησε με ὁ πατηρ,
to me disciples. As loved me the father,
καγω ηγαπησα ὑμας· μεινατε εν τῃ αγαπῃ τῃ
and I loved you; abide you in the love the
εμῃ. 10 Εαν τας εντολας μου τηρησητε, με-
mine. If the commandments of me you may keep, you
νειτε εν τῃ αγαπῃ μου· καθως εγω τας εντολας
will abide in the love of me, as I the commandments
του πατρος μου τετηρηκα, και μενω αυτου εν
of the father of me have kept, and abide of him in
τῃ αγαπῃ.
the love.
11 Ταυτα λελαληκα ὑμιν, ἱνα ἡ χαρα ἡ εμη εν
These things I have spoken to you, that the joy the mine in
ὑμιν μεινῃ, και ἡ χαρα ὑμων πληρωθῃ. 12 Αυτη
you may abide, and the joy of you may be fulfilled. This
εστιν ἡ εντολη ἡ εμη, ἱνα αγαπατε αλληλους,
is the commandment the mine, that you love each other,
καθως ηγαπησα ὑμας. 13 Μειζονα ταυτης
as I loved you. Greater of this
αγαπην ουδεις εχει, ἱνα τις την ψυχην αὑτου
love no one has, that any one the life of himself
θῃ ὑπερ των φιλων αὑτου. 14 Ὑμεις
may lay down in behalf of the friends of himself. You
φιλοι μου εστε, εαν ποιητε ὁσα εγω εντελ-
friends of me are, if you may do what things I com-
λομαι ὑμιν. 15 Ουκετι ὑμας λεγω δουλους·
mand you. No more you I call slaves,
ὁτι ὁ δουλος ουκ οιδε τι ποιει αυτου ὁ κυριος·
because the slave not knows what does of him the lord;
ὑμας δε ειρηκα φιλους, ὁτι παντα ἁ ηκουσα
you but I have called friends, because all things which I heard
παρα του πατρος μου, εγνωρισα ὑμιν. 16 Ουχ
from the father of me, I made known to you. Not
ὑμεις με εξελεξασθε, αλλ' εγω εξελεξαμην
you me did choose, but I chose

who ABIDES in me, and I in him, He ‡ bears much Fruit; Because severed from me you can do nothing.

6 If any one abide not in me, he is cast out like the BRANCH, and is withered; and such are gathered, and cast into a Fire, and are burned.

7 ‡ If you abide in me, and my WORDS abide in you, ask whatever you wish, and it shall be given you.

8 ‡ In this is my FATHER glorified, that you bear much Fruit, and you shall be My Disciples.

9 As the FATHER loved me, and I loved you, abide in MY LOVE.

10 ‡ If you observe my COMMANDMENTS, you shall abide in my LOVE; as I have observed * the FATHER'S COMMANDMENTS, and abide in His LOVE.

11 These things I have spoken to you, that MY JOY * may be in you, and ‡ your JOY may be completed.

12 ‡ This is MY COMMANDMENT, That you love each other, as I loved you.

13 ‡ No one has greater Love than this, that one should lay down his LIFE in behalf of his FRIENDS.

14 ‡ You are my Friends if you do what things I command you.

15 No more I call you Servants; Because the SERVANT knows not what His MASTER does; but I have called You Friends, Because all things which I heard from my FATHER I made known to you.

16 You did not choose Me, but I chose you, and

* VATICAN MANUSCRIPT.—10. the FATHER'S. 11. be in you.

† 7. Griesbach favors the reading, *aiteesasthe* instead of *aiteesesthe;* which is adopted by Lachmann and Tischendorf.

‡ 5. Phil. i. 11; iv. 13. ‡ 7. ver. 16; John xiv. 13, 14; xvi. 23. ‡ 8. Matt. v. 16; Phil. i. 11. ‡ 10. John xiv. 15, 21, 23. ‡ 11. John xvi. 24; xvii. 13; 1 John i. 4 ‡ 12. John xiii. 34; 1 Thess. iv. 9; 1 Pet. iv 8; 1 John iii. 11; iv. 21. ‡ 13. John x. 11, 15; Rom. v. 7, 8; Eph. v. 2; 1 John iii. 16. ‡ 14. John xiv. 15, 23; Matt. xii. 50.

ὑμας, και εθηκα ὑμας, ἱνα ὑμεις ὑπαγητε και
you, and appointed you, that you might go and
καρπον φερητε, και ὁ καρπος ὑμων μενῃ· ἱνα
fruit might bear, and the fruit of you might abide; so that
ὁ, τι αν αιτησητε τον πατερα εν τῳ ονοματι
whatever you may ask the father in the name
μου, δῳ ὑμιν.
of me, he may give to you.
17 Ταυτα εντελλομαι ὑμιν, ἱνα αγαπατε
These things I command you, that you may love
αλληλους. 18 Ει ὁ κοσμος ὑμας μισει, γινωσ-
each other. If the world you hates, you
κετε, ὁτι εμε πρωτον ὑμων μεμισηκεν. 19 Ει
know, that me before you it has hated. If
εκ του κοσμου ητε, ὁ κοσμος αν το ιδιον εφι-
of the world you were, the world would the own kiss,
λει· ὁτι δε εκ του κοσμου ουκ εστε, αλλ' εγω
because but of the world not you are, but I
εξελεξαμην ὑμας εκ του κοσμου, δια τουτο
chose you out of the world, on account of this
μισει ὑμας ὁ κοσμος. 20 Μνημονευετε του
hates you the world. Remember you the
λογου, οὑ εγω ειπον ὑμιν· Ουκ εστι δουλος
word, of which I said to you; Not is a slave
μειζων του κυριου αὑτου. Ει εμε εδιωξαν, και
greater of the lord of himself. If me they persecuted, also
ὑμας διωξουσιν· ει τον λογον μου ετηρησαν,
you they will persecute; if the word of me they kept,
και τον ὑμετερον τηρησουσιν. 21 Αλλα ταυτα
also the yours they will keep. But these things
παντα ποιησουσιν ὑμιν δια το ονομα μου,
all they will do to you on account of the name of me,
ὁτι ουκ οιδασι τον πεμψαντα με. 22 Ει μη
because not they know him sending me. If not
ηλθον και ελαλησα αυτοις, ἁμαρτιαν ουκ ειχον·
I had came and spoken to them, sin not they had;
νυν δε προφασιν ουκ εχουσι περι της ἁμαρτιας
now but an excuse not they have about the sin
αυτων. 23 Ὁ εμε μισων, και τον πατερα μου
of them. He me hating, also the father of me
μισει. 24 Ει τα εργα, μη εποιησα εν αυτοις, ἁ
hates. If the works, not I had done among them, which
ουδεις αλλος πεποιηκεν, ἁμαρτιαν ουκ ειχον·
no one other has done, sin not they had;
νυν δε και ἑωρακασι, και μεμισηκασι και εμε
now but even they have seen, and have hated both me
και τον πατερα μου. 25 Αλλ', ἱνα πληρωθῃ ὁ
and the father of me. But, that may be fulfilled the
λογος ὁ γεγραμμενος εν τῳ νομῳ αυτων· "Ὁτι
word the having been written in the law of them; "That
εμισησαν με δωρεαν."
they hated me without cause."
26 Ὁταν δε ελθῃ ὁ παρακλητος, ὁν εγω
When but may come the helper, whom I
πεμψω ὑμιν παρα του πατρος, (το πνευμα της
will send to you from the father, (the spirit of the

appointed you, that you may go and bear Fruit, and that your FRUIT may abide; so that whatever * you ask of the FATHER in my NAME, he may give you.

17 These things I command you, so that you may love each other.

18 ‡ If the WORLD hate You, you know That it has hated Me before you.

19 ‡ If you were of the WORLD, the WORLD would love its OWN; but Because you are not of the WORLD, but I chose you out of the WORLD, on this account the WORLD hates you.

20 Remember the WORD which I said to you, ‡ 'A Servant is not greater than his Master.' If they persecuted Me, they will also persecute You; if they observed my WORD they will also observe YOURS.

21 But ‡ all These things they will do to you, on account of my NAME, Because they know not HIM who SENT me.

22 If I had not come and spoken to them, they would not have had Sin; but now they have no Excuse for their SIN.

23 HE who HATES Me, hates my FATHER also.

24 If I had not done among them ‡ the WORKS which no other one had done, they would not have had Sin; but now they have even seen them, and yet have hated both me and my FATHER.

25 Thus they verify THAT WORD which was WRITTEN in their LAW, ‡ 'They hated 'me without cause.'

26 ‡ But when the HELPER comes, whom I will send to you from the FATHER, the SPIRIT of

* VATICAN MANUSCRIPT.—16. you ask.

‡ 18. 1 John iii. 1, 13. ‡ 19. John iv. 5; xvii. 14. ‡ 20. Matt. x. 24; Luke vi. 40; John xiii. 16. ‡ 21. Matt. x. 22; xxiv. 9; John xvi. 3. ‡ 24. John iii. 2; vii. 31; ix. 32. ‡ 25. Psa. xxxv. 19. ‡ 26. Luke xxiv. 49; John xiv. 17, 26; xvi. 7, 13; Acts ii. 33.

αληθειας, ὁ παρα του πατρος εκπορευεται,)
truth, which from the father shall come out,)

εκεινος μαρτυρησει περι εμου. 27 Και ὑμεις δε
that will testify concerning me. Also you and

μαρτυρειτε, ὁτι απ' αρχης μετ' εμου εστε.
shall testify, because from a beginning with me you are.

ΚΕΦ. ιϛ'. 16. 1 Ταυτα λελαληκα ὑμιν, ἱνα μη
These things I have spoken to you, that not

σκανδαλισθητε. 2 Αποσυναγωγους ποιησουσιν
you may be ensnared. From synagogues they will put

ὑμας· αλλ' ερχεται ὡρα, ἱνα πας ὁ αποκτεινας
you; but comes an hour, that every one the killing

ὑμας, δοξῃ λατρειαν προσφερειν τῳ θεῳ.
you, may think a service to offer to the God.

3 Και ταυτα ποιησουσιν, ὁτι ουκ εγνωσαν τον
And these things they will do, because not they know the

πατερα, ουδε εμε. 4 Αλλα ταυτα λελαληκα
father, nor me. But these things I have spoken

ὑμιν, ἱνα ὁταν ελθῃ ἡ ὡρα, μνημονευητε
to you, that when may come the hour, you may remember

αυτων, ὁτι εγω ειπον ὑμιν. Ταυτα δε ὑμιν εξ
them, that I said to you. These things but to you from

αρχης ουκ ειπον, ὁτι μεθ' ὑμων ημην. 5 Νυν
a beginning not I said, because with you I was. Now

δε ὑπαγω προς τον πεμψαντα με, και ουδεις εξ
but I go to him having sent me, and no one of

ὑμων ερωτᾳ με· Που ὑπαγεις; 6 Αλλ' ὁτι
you asks me; Where goest thou? But because

ταυτα λελαληκα ὑμιν, ἡ λυπη πεπληρωκεν
these things I have spoken to you, the sorrow has filled

ὑμων την καρδιαν. 7 Αλλ' εγω την αληθειαν
of you the heart. But I the truth

λεγω ὑμιν· συμφερει ὑμιν, ἱνα εγω απελθω.
say to you; it is better for you, that I should go away.

Εαν γαρ μη απελθω, ὁ παρακλητος ουκ ελευ-
If for not I should go away, the helper not will

σεται προς ὑμας· εαν δε πορευθω, πεμψω αυτον
come to you; if but I go, I will send him

προς ὑμας. 8 Και ελθων εκεινος ελεγξει τον
to you. And having come he will convict the

κοσμον περι ἁμαρτιας, και περι δικαιοσυνης,
world concerning sin, and concerning righteousness,

και περι κρισεως. 9 Περι ἁμαρτιας μεν, ὁτι
and concerning judgment. Concerning sin indeed, because

ου πιστευουσιν εις εμε· 10 περι δικαιοσυνης δε,
not they believe into me; concerning righteousness but,

ὁτι προς τον πατερα μου ὑπαγω, και ουκετι
because to the father of me I go away, and no more

θεωρειτε με· 11 περι δε κρισεως, ὁτι ὁ αρχων
you behold me; concerning and judgment, because the ruling

TRUTH which comes forth from the FATHER, he will testify of me.

27 And ‡ you also will testify, Because you are with me from the Beginning.

CHAPTER XVI.

1 These things I have spoken to you, that you may not be ensnared.

2 ‡ They will expel you from the synagogues; but an Hour is coming, when EVERY ONE who KILLS you will think to offer Service to GOD.

3 And ‡ these things they will do Because they know not the FATHER, nor me.

4 But These things I have spoken to you, so that when * their HOUR comes you may remember them, That I told you. And these things I said not to you from the Beginning, Because I was with you.

5 And now ‡ I am going away to HIM who SENT me; and no one of you asks me, 'Where art thou going?'

6 But Because I have said These things to you, SORROW has filled Your HEART.

7 But I tell you the TRUTH; It is better for you That I should go away; for if I go not away; ‡ the HELPER will not come to you; but if I go I will send him to you.

8 And having come, he will convict the WORLD concerning Sin, and concerning Righteousness, and concerning Judgment;

9 concerning Sin, indeed, Because they believe not into me;

10 but concerning Righteousness, Because I am going to my FATHER, and you behold me no more;

11 and concerning Judg-

* VATICAN MANUSCRIPT.—4. their HOUR.

‡ 27. Luke xxiv. 48; Acts i. 8, 21, 22; ii. 32; iii. 15; iv. 20, 33; v. 32; x. 39; xiii. 31; 1 Pet. v. 1; 2 Pet. i. 16. ‡ 2. John ix. 22, 34; xii. 42; viii. 1; ix. 1; xxvi. 9—11. ‡ 3. John xv. 21; Rom. x. 2; 1 Cor. ii. 8; 1 Tim. i. 13. ‡ 5. ver. 10, 16; John vii. 33; xiii. 3; xiv. 28. ‡ 7. John vii. 39; xiv. 16, 26; xv. 26.

του κοσμου τουτου κεκριται. 12 Ετι πολλα εχω
of the world this has been judged. Yet many things I have
λεγειν ὑμιν, αλλ' ου δυνασθε βασταζειν αρτι.
to say to you, but not you are able to bear now.
13 Ὁταν δε ελθῃ εκεινος, το πνευμα της
When but may come he, the spirit of the
αληθειας, ὁδηγησει ὑμας εις πασαν την αλη-
truth, he will lead you into all the truth.
θειαν. Ου γαρ λαλησει αφ' ἑαυτου, αλλ' ὁσα αν
Not for he will speak from himself, but whatever
ακουσῃ, λαλησει, και τα ερχομενα αναγγελει
he may hear, he will speak, and the things coming he will declare
ὑμιν. 14 Εκεινος εμε δοξασει, ὁτι εκ του εμου
to you. He me will glorify, because out of the mine
ληψεται, και αναγγελει ὑμιν. 15 Παντα ὁσα
he will take, and will declare to you. All things what
εχει ὁ πατηρ, εμα εστι. Δια τουτο ειπον, ὁτι
has the father, mine is. On account of this I said, that
εκ του εμου λαμβανει, και αναγγελει ὑμιν.
out of the mine he takes, and declares to you.
16 Μικρον, και ου θεωρειτε με· και παλιν μικρον,
A little while, and not you see me; and again a little while,
και οψεσθε με, *[ὁτι ὑπαγω προς τον πατερα.]
and you shall see me, [because I am going to the father.]
17 Ειπον ουν εκ των μαθητων αυτου προς
Said then of the disciples of him to
αλληλους· Τι εστι τουτο ὁ λεγει ἡμιν· Μικρον,
each other; What is this which he says to us; A little while,
και ου θεωρειτε με· και παλιν μικρον, και
and not you see me; and again a little while, and
οψεσθε με· και· Ὁτι εγω ὑπαγω προς τον
you shall see me; and; Because I am going to the
πατερα; 18 Ελεγον ουν· Τουτο τι εστιν ὁ
father? They said therefore; This what is which
λεγει, το μικρον; Ουκ οιδαμεν *[τι λαλει.]
he says, the little while? Not we know [what he says.]
19 Εγνω ὁ Ιησους, ὁτι ηθελον αυτον ερωταν,
Knew the Jesus, that they wished him to ask,
και ειπεν αυτοις· Περι τουτου ζητειτε μετ'
and said to them; Concerning this inquire you with
αλληλων, ὁτι ειπον· Μικρον, και ου θεωρειτε
each other, because I said; A little while, and not you see
με· και παλιν μικρον, και οψεσθε με; 20 Αμην
me; and again a little while, and you shall see me? Indeed
αμην λεγω ὑμιν, ὁτι κλαυσετε και θρηνησετε
indeed I say to you, that will weep and will lament
ὑμεις, ὁ δε κοσμος χαρησεται· ὑμεις *[δε]
you, the but world will rejoice; you [and]
λυπηθησεσθε, αλλ' ἡ λυπη ὑμων εις χαραν
will be sorrowful, but the sorrow of you into joy
γενησεται. 21 Ἡ γυνη ὁταν τικτῃ, λυπην εχει,
shall become. The woman when she may bear, sorrow has,

ment, Because †the RULER of this WORLD has been judged.

12 I have yet Many things to tell you, ‡but you cannot bear them now.

13 But when He may come, ‡ the SPIRIT of TRUTH, he will lead you into * all the TRUTH; for he will not speak from himself; he will speak whatever he may hear; and declare to you the COMING THINGS.

14 He will glorify Me; Because he will take of MINE, and declare to you.

15 ‡ All things that the FATHER has are mine; on account of this I said, That out of MINE he takes, and will declare to you.

16 ‡ A little while, and you see me * no more, and again a little while, and you will see me."

17 Then some of his DISCIPLES said to each other, "What is this he is saying to us, 'A little while, and you will see me not; and again a little while, and you will see me;' and, 'Because I am going to the FATHER?'"

18 They said, therefore, "What is this that he is saying, 'A * little while?' We know not."

19 * Jesus knew That they wished to ask Him, and said to them, "Do you inquire one with another concerning this, Because I said, 'A little while, and you see me not, and again a little while, and you will see me?'

20 Indeed, I assure you, That you will weep and lament, but the WORLD will rejoice; you will be sorrowful, but your SORROW shall become Joy.

21 ‡ The WOMAN when she is in labor has Sorrow,

* VATICAN MANUSCRIPT.—13. all the TRUTH. 16. no more. 16. Because I am going to the FATHER—*omit*. 18. little while. 18. what he says—*omit*. 19. Jesus. 20 and—*omit*.

† 11. See Note on chap. xiv. 30.

‡ 12. Mark iv. 33; 1 Cor. iii. 2; Heb. v. 12. ‡ 13. John xiv. 17, 26; xv. 26; 1 John ii. 20, 27. ‡ 15. Matt. xi. 27; John iii. 35; xiii. 3; xvii. 10. ‡ 16. ver. 10; John vii 33; xiii. 33; xiv. 19. ‡ 21. Isa. xxvi. 17.

ὁτι ηλθεν ἡ ὡρα αυτης· ὁταν δε γεννηση
because has come the hour of her; when but she may have borne
το παιδιον, ουκετι μνημονευει της θλιψεως,
the child, no more she remembers of the distress,
δια την χαραν, ὁτι εγεννηθη ανθρωπος εις
on account of the joy, that was born a man into
τον κοσμον. 22 Και ὑμεις ουν λυπην μεν νυν
the world. And you therefore sorrow indeed now
εχετε· παλιν δε οψομαι ὑμας, και χαρησεται
have; again but I will see you, and will be rejoiced
ὑμων ἡ καρδια, και την χαραν ὑμων ουδεις
of you the heart, and the joy of you no one
αιρει αφ᾽ ὑμων· 23 και εν εκεινῃ τῃ ἡμερᾳ εμε
takes from you; and in that the day me
ουκ ερωτησετε ουδεν· Αμην αμην λεγω ὑμιν,
not you will ask nothing; Indeed indeed I say to you,
ὁτι ὁσα αν αιτησητε τον πατερα εν τῳ ονοματι
that whatever you may ask the father in the name
μου, δωσει ὑμιν. 24 Ἑως αρτι ουκ ῃτησατε
of me, he will give to you. Till now not you asked
ουδεν εν τῳ ονοματι μου· αιτειτε, και ληψεσθε,
nothing in the name of me; ask you. and you shall receive,
ἱνα ἡ χαρα ὑμων ῃ πεπληρωμενη.
so that the joy of you may be completed.

25 Ταυτα εν παροιμιαις λελαληκα ὑμιν·
These things in figures I have spoken to you;
ερχεται ὡρα, ὁτε ουκετι εν παροιμιαις λαλησω
comes an hour, when no more in figures I will speak
ὑμιν, αλλα παρρησιᾳ περι του πατρος αναγ-
to you, but plainly concerning the father I will
γελω ὑμιν. 26 Εν εκεινῃ τῃ ἡμερᾳ εν τῳ ονο-
tell you. In that the day in the name
ματι μου αιτησεσθε· και ου λεγω ὑμιν, ὁτι εγω
of me you will ask; and not I say to you, that I
ερωτησω τον πατερα περι ὑμων· 27 αυτος γαρ
will entreat the father concerning you; himself for
ὁ πατηρ φιλει ὑμας, ὁτι ὑμεις εμε πεφιληκατε,
the father loves you, because you me have loved,
και πεπιστευκατε, ὁτι εγω παρα του θεου
and have believed, that I from the God
εξηλθον. 28 Εξηλθον παρα του πατρος, και
came out. I came out from the father, and
εληλυθα εις τον κοσμον· παλιν αφιημι τον
have come into the world; again I leave the
κοσμον, και πορευομαι προς τον πατερα.
world, and am going to the father.

29 Λεγουσιν *[αυτῳ] οἱ μαθηται αυτου· Ιδε,
Say [to him] the disciples of him; Lo,
νυν παρρησιᾳ λαλεις, και παροιμιαν ουδεμιαν
now plainly thou speakest, and a figure not one
λεγεις. 30 Νυν οιδαμεν, ὁτι οιδας παντα, και
thou sayest. Now we know, that thou knowest all things, and
ου χρειαν εχεις, ἱνα τις σε ερωτᾳ· εν τουτῳ
no need has, that any one thee should ask; in this
πιστευομεν, ὁτι απο θεου εξηλθες. 31 Απεκ-
we believe, that from God thou didst come out. An-

Because her TIME has
come; but when she has
borne the CHILD, she re-
members the DISTRESS no
more, on account of the JOY
That a Man was born into
WORLD.

22 And you, therefore,
now indeed have Sorrow;
but I will see you again,
and ‡ Your HEART shall
rejoice; and your JOY no
one takes from you.

23 And in That DAY you
will ask Me nothing. ‡ Indeed, I assure you, What-
ever you may ask the FA-
THER in my NAME, he will
give you.

24 Till now you asked
nothing in my NAME; ask,
and you shall receive, so
‡ that your JOY may be
completed.

25 These things I have
spoken to you in Figures;
an Hour is coming, when
I will no more speak to you
in Figures, but I will tell
you plainly about the FA-
THER.

26 In That DAY you will
ask in my NAME, and I do
not say to you, That I will
entreat the FATHER for
you;

27 ‡ for the FATHER
himself loves you, Because
you have loved me, and
have believed that I came
out from * GOD.

28 ‡ I came out from the
FATHER, and have come
into the WORLD; again I
leave the WORLD, and am
going to my FATHER."

29 His DISCIPLES said
to him, "Behold, now thou
art speaking plainly, and
without a Figure.

30 Now we know That
thou knowest all things,
and hast no need that any
one should ask Thee; by
this we believe That thou
didst come out from God."

31 * Jesus answered,

---

* VATICAN MANUSCRIPT.—27. the FATHER. 29. to him—*omit.* 31. Jesus.

‡ 22. Luke xxiv. 41, 52; John xx. 20. ‡ 23. Matt. vii. 7; John xiv. 13; xv. 16. ‡ 24. John xv. 11. ‡ 27. John xiv. 21, 23. ‡ 27. ver. 30; John iii. 13; xvii. 8. ‡ 28. John xiii. 3.

ρiθη αυτοις ὁ Ιησους· Αρτι πιστευετε· 32 ἰδου,
swered them the Jesus Now do you believe? Lo.
ερχεται ὡρα, και νυν εληλυθεν, ἱνα σκορπισθητε
comes an hour, and now is come, that you will be scattered
ἑκαστος εις τα ιδια, και εμε μονον αφητε· και
every one to the own, and me alone you may leave; and
ουκ ειμι μονος, ὁτι ὁ πατηρ μετ' εμου εστι.
not I am alone, because the father with me is.
33 Ταυτα λελαληκα ὑμιν, ἱνα εν εμοι ειρηνην
These things I have spoken to you, that in me peace
εχητε. Εν τῳ κοσμῳ θλιψιν εχετε· αλλα θαρ-
you may have. In the world affliction you have; but be you of
σειτε, εγω νενικηκα τον κοσμον.
good courage, I have overcome the world.

ΚΕΦ. ιζ'. 17.

1 Ταυτα ελαλησεν ὁ Ιησους, και επηρε τους
These things spoke the Jesus, and lifted up the
οφθαλμους αυτου εις τον ουρανον, και ειπε·
eyes of him to the heaven, and said:
Πατερ, εληλυθεν ἡ ὡρα· δοξασον σου τον υἱον,
O father, is come the hour; glorify of thee the son,
ἱνα *[και] ὁ υἱος σου δοξασθῃ σε· 2 καθως εδω-
that [also] the son of thee may glorify thee; as thou
κας αυτῳ εξουσιαν πασης σαρκος, ἱνα παν ὁ
gavest to him authority over all flesh, so that all which
δεδωκας αυτῳ, δωσῃ αυτοις ζωην αιωνιον.
thou hast given to him, he may give to them life age-lasting.
3 Αυτη δε εστιν ἡ αιωνιος ζωη, ἱνα γενωσκωσι
This and is the age-lasting life, that they might know
σε τον μονον αληθινον θεον, και ὁν απεστειλας
thee the only true God, and whom thou hast sent
Ιησουν Χριστον. 4 Εγω σε εδοξασα επι της
Jesus Christ. I thee glorified on the
γης· το εργον ετελειωσα, ὁ δεδωκας μοι, ἱνα
earth; the work I finished, which thou hast given me, that
ποιησω. 5 Και νυν δοξασον με, συ πατερ, παρα
I might do. And now glorify me, thou O father, with
σεαυτῳ, τῃ δοξῃ, ᾑ ειχον, προ του τον
thyself, with the glory, which I had, before of the the
κοσμον ειναι, παρα σοι. 6 Εφανερωσα σου το
world to be, with thee. I manifested of thee the
ονομα τοις ανθρωποις, οὑς δεδωκας μοι εκ του
name to the men, whom thou hast given to me out of the
κοσμου· σοι ἠσαν, και εμοι αυτους δεδωκας·
world; thine they were, and to me them thou hast given;
και τον λογον σου τετηρηκασι. 7 Νυν εγνω-
and the word of thee they have kept. Now they
καν, ὁτι παντα ὁσα δεδωκας μοι, παρα σου
know, that all things whatever thou hast given me, from thee

them, "Do you now believe?"

32 Behold, an HOUR is coming, and is come, that you will be scattered every one to his OWN home, and will leave Me alone; and yet I am not alone, Because the FATHER is with me.

33 These things I have spoken to you, that in me you may have Peace. ‡ In the WORLD you have Affliction; but be of good courage; ‡ I have conquered the WORLD."

CHAPTER XVII.

1 JESUS spoke these things, and lifted up his EYES to HEAVEN, and said, "Father, the HOUR is come; glorify Thy SON, that * the SON may glorify thee;

2 ‡ as thou didst give him Authority over All Flesh, so that every thing which thou hast given to him, he may give to them, even aionian Life.

3 And this is the AIONIAN Life, that they may know thee, the ONLY TRUE God, and him whom thou didst send, Jesus Christ.

4 I glorified thee on the EARTH, ‡ * having finished the WORK which thou hast given me, that I might do it.

5 And now, O Father, glorify thou me with thyself, with the GLORY which I had with thee before the WORLD WAS.

6 I manifested Thy NAME to the MEN whom thou hast given me out of the WORLD; thine they were, and thou hast given them to me; and they have kept thy WORD.

7 Now they know That all things whatever thou gavest me are from thee.

* VATICAN MANUSCRIPT.—1. the SON. 1. also—*omit.* 4. having finished.

‡ 33. John xv. 19—21; 2 Tim. iii. 12. ‡ 33. Rom. viii. 37; 1 John iv. 4; v. 4. ‡ 2. Matt. xi. 27; xxviii. 18; John iii. 35; v. 27; 1 Cor. xv. 25, 27; Phil. ii. 10. ‡ 4. John iv. 34; v. 36; ix. 3; xix. 30.

εστιν· 8 ὁτι τα ῥηματα ἁ δεδωκας μοι, δεδωκα
is; because the words which thou hast given me, I have given

αυτοις· και αυτοι ελαβον, και εγνωσαν αληθως,
to them; and they received, and knew truly,

ὁτι παρα σου εξηλθον, και επιστευσαν, ὁτι συ
that fr m thee I came out, and believed that thou

με απεστειλας. 9 Εγω περι αυτων ερωτω· ου
me didst send. I concerning them ask; not

περι του κοσμου ερωτω, αλλα περι ὡν
concerning the world I ask, but concerning whom

δεδωκας μοι, ὁτι σοι εισι· 10 και τα εμα παντα
thou hast given me, because thine they are; and the mine all

σα εστι, και τα σα εμε, και δεδοξασμαι εν
thine is, and the thine mine, and I have been glorified in

αυτοις. 11 Και ουκετι ειμι εν τῳ κοσμῳ, και
them. And no more I am in the world, and

ουτοι εν τῳ κοσμῳ εισι, και εγω προς σε ερχο-
these in the world are, and I to thee am

μαι. Πατερ αγιε, τηρησον αυτους εν τῳ ονο-
coming. O father holy, keep them in the name

ματι σου, ᾧ δεδωκας μοι· ἱνα ωσιν ἑν,
of thee, by which thou hast given to me; that they may be one,

καθως ἡμεις. 12 Ὁτε ημην μετ' αυτων *[εν τῳ
as we. When I was with them in the

κοσμῳ,] εγω ετηρουν αυτους εν τῳ ονοματι
world,] I kept them in the name

σου· οὑς δεδωκας μοι εφυλαξα, και ουδεις εξ
of thee; whom thou hast given to me I guarded, and no one of

αυτων απωλετο, ει μη ὁ υἱος της απωλειας, ἱνα
them was destroyed, if not the son of the destruction, that

ἡ γραφη πληρωθῃ. 13 Νυν δε προς σε ερχομαι,
the writing may be fulfilled. Now and to thee I am coming,

και ταυτα λαλω εν τῳ κοσμῳ, ἱνα εχωσι την
and these things I say in the world, that they may have the

χαραν την εμην πεπληρωμενην εν αυτοις.
joy the mine fulfilled in them.

14 Εγω δεδωκα αυτοις τον λογον σου· και ὁ
I have given to them the word of thee; and the

κοσμος εμισησεν αυτους, ὁτι ουκ εισιν εκ του
world hated them, because not they are of the

κοσμου, καθως εγω ουκ ειμι εκ του κοσμου.
world, as I not am of the world.

15 Ουκ ερωτω, ἱνα αρῃς αυτους εκ του κοσ-
Not I ask, that thou wouldst take them out of the world,

μου, αλλ' ἱνα τηρησῃς αυτους εκ του πονηρου.
but that thou wouldst keep them from the evil one.

16 Εκ του κοσμου ουκ εισι, καθως εγω εκ του
Of the world not they are, as I of the

κοσμου ουκ ειμι. 17 Αγιασον αυτους εν τῃ
world not am. Sanctify them in the

8 Because I have given to them the WORDS which ‡ thou hast given to me; and they received and knew truly that I came out from thee, and believed That thou didst send Me.

9 I entreat for them; not for the WORLD I entreat, but for those whom thou hast given me; Because they are thine.

10 And all MINE are thine, and ‡ THINE are mine; and I have been glorified in them.

11 And I am no more in the WORLD, but they are in the WORLD, and I am coming to thee. Holy Father, keep them in thy NAME, by which thou hast given them me, that they may be one, as we * also are.

12 When I was with them, I kept them in thy * NAME, by which thou hast given them me; and I guarded them, and no one of them was destroyed, except the ‡ SON of DESTRUCTION; ‡ that the SCRIPTURE might be verified.

13 But now I am coming to thee; and These things I speak in the WORLD, that they may have MY JOY completed in them.

14 I have given thy WORD to them, ‡ and the WORLD hated them; Because they are not of the WORLD, as I am not of the WORLD.

15 I entreat not that thou wouldst take them out of the WORLD, but ‡ that thou wouldst keep them from EVIL.

16 They are not of the WORLD, as I am not of the WORLD.

17 ‡ Sanctify them in

---

* VATICAN MANUSCRIPT.—11. also. 12. in the WORLD—omit. 12. NAME, by which thou hast given them me; and I guarded them.

‡ 8. John viii. 28; xii. 49; xiv. 10. ‡ 10. John xvi. 15. ‡ 12. John vi. 70; xiii. 18. ‡ 12. Psa. cix. 8; Acts i. 20. ‡ 14. John xv. 18, 19; 1 John iii. 13. ‡ 15. Matt. vi 13; 2 Thess. iii. 3; 1 John v 18. ‡ 17. John xv. 3; Acts xv. 9; Eph. v. 26; 1 Pet. i. 22

αληθεια σου· ὁ λογος ὁ σος αληθεια εστι.
truth of thee; the word the thine truth is.
18 Καθως εμε απεστειλας εις τον κοσμον, καγω
As me thou didst send into the world, also I
απεστειλα αυτους εις τον κοσμον. 19 Και ὑπερ
sent them into the world. And in behalf
αυτων εγω αγιαζω ἑμαυτον, ἱνα και αυτοι ωσιν
of them I sanctify myself, so that also they may be
ἡγιασμενοι εν αληθειᾳ. 20 Ου περι τουτων δε
sanctified in truth. Not concerning these and
ερωτω μονον, αλλα και περι των πιστευοντων
I ask alone, but also concerning those believing
δια του λογου αυτων εις εμε. 21 Ἱνα παντες
through the word of them into me. That all
ἑν ὡσι· καθως συ, πατερ, εν εμοι, καγω εν σοι,
one may be; as thou, father, in me, and I in thee,
ἱνα και αυτοι εν ἡμιν *[ἑν] ὡσιν· ἱνα ὁ κοσ-
that also they in us [one] may be, that the world
μος πιστευσῃ, ὁτι συ με απεστειλας. 22 Και
may believe, that thou me didst send. And
εγω την δοξαν ην δεδωκας μοι, δεδωκα αυτοις·
I the glory which thou hast given to me, have given to them;
ἱνα ὡσιν ἑν, καθως ἡμεις ἑν εσμεν· 23 (εγω εν
that they may be one, as we one are; (I in
αυτοις, και συ εν εμοι·) ἱνα ὡσι τετελειωμε-
them, and thou in me;) that they may be perfected
νοι εις ἑν, *[και] ἱνα γινωσκῃ ὁ κοσμος, ὁτι συ
into one, [and] that may know the world, that thou
με απεστειλας, και ηγαπησας αυτους, καθως
me didst send, and thou didst love them, as
εμε ηγαπησας. 24 Πατερ, οὑς δεδωκας μοι,
me thou didst love. O father, whom thou hast given to me,
θελω, ἱνα ὁπου ειμι εγω, κακεινοι ὡσι μετ'
I wish, that where am I, also they may be with
εμου· ἱνα θεωρωσι την δοξαν την εμην, ην
me; that they may behold the glory the mine, which
ἑδωκας μοι, ὁτι ηγαπησας με προ καταβολης
thou didst give to me, because thou didst love me before a laying down
κοσμου. 25 Πατερ δικαιε, και ὁ κοσμος σε ουκ
of a world. O father righteous, and the world thee not
εγνω· εγω δε σε εγνων, και οὑτοι εγνωσαν ὁτι
knew; I but thee knew, and these knew that
συ με απεστειλας. 26 Και εγνωρισα αυτοις το
thou me didst send. And I made known to them the
ονομα σου, και γνωρισω· ἱνα ἡ αγαπη ην
name of thee, and will make known; that the love which
ηγαπησας με, εν αυτοις ᾐ, καγω εν αυτοις.
thou didst love me, in them may be, and I in them.

*Truth; ‡ THY WORD is the TRUTH.

18 ‡ As thou didst send Me into the WORLD, so I sent them into the WORLD;

19 ‡ and in their behalf I sanctify myself, so that they also may be sanctified in Truth.

20 Nor do I entreat for these only, but also for THOSE BELIEVING into me through their WORD;

21 ‡ so that all may be one; as ‡ thou, Father, art in me, and I in thee, that they also may be in us; so that the WORLD may believe That thou didst send Me.

22 And the GLORY which thou hast given me, I have given them; ‡ that they may be one, as we are one;

23 I in them, and thou in me, that they may be perfected into one; so that the WORLD may know That thou didst send me, and didst love them, as thou didst love me.

24 ‡ Father, those whom thou hast given me, I wish that where I am, they also may be with me; so that they may behold MY GLORY, which thou didst give me, because thou didst love me before the Formation of the World.

25 O righteous Father, the WORLD did not know Thee, but I knew Thee, and these knew That thou didst send Me.

26 And I made known, and will make known to them thy NAME; so that ‡ the LOVE with which thou didst love me may be in them, and I in them.

* VATICAN MANUSCRIPT.—17. Truth; THY WORD is the TRUTH. 21. one—*omit.* and—*omit.*

‡ 17. 2 Sam. vii. 28; Psa. cxix. 142, 151; John viii. 40. ‡ 18. John xx. 21. ‡ 19. 1 Cor. i. 30; Heb. x. 10. ‡ 21. ver. 11, 22, 23; John x. 16; Rom. xii. 5; Gal. iii. 28. ‡ 21. John x. 38; xiv. 11. ‡ 22. John xiv. 20; 1 John i. 3; iii. 24. ‡ 24. John xii. 26; xiv. 3; 1 Thess. iv. 17. ‡ 26. John xv. 9.

ΚΕΦ. ιη'. 18.

[1] Ταυτα ειπων ὁ Ιησους εξηλθε συν τοις
These things saying the Jesus went out with the
μαθηταις αὑτου περαν του χειμαρρου του
disciples of himself beyond the brook of the
Κεδρων, ὁπου ην κηπος, εις ὁν εισηλθεν αυτος
Kedron, where was a garden, into which entered himself
και οἱ μαθηται αυτου. [2] Ηδει δε και Ιουδας, ὁ
and the disciples of him. Knew and also Judas, he
παραδιδους αυτον, τον τοπον· ὁτι πολλακις
delivering up him, the place; because often
συνηχθη ὁ Ιησους εκει μετα των μαθητων
met the Jesus there with the disciples
αὑτου. [3] Ὁ ουν Ιουδας λαβων την σπειραν,
of himself. The then Judas having taken the band,
και εκ των αρχιερεων και Φαρισαιων ὑπηρετας,
and from the high-priests and Pharisees officers,
ερχεται εκει μετα φανων και λαμπαδων και
comes there with torches and lamps and
ὁπλων. [4] Ιησους ουν ειδως παντα τα ερχο-
weapons. Jesus therefore knowing all the things com-
μενα επ' αυτον, εξελθων ειπεν αυτοις· Τινα ζη-
ing on him, going out said to them; Whom seek
τειτε; [5] Απεκριθησαν αυτῳ· Ιησουν τον Να-
you; They answered him; Jesus the Na-
ζωραιον. Λεγει αυτοις ὁ Ιησους· Εγω ειμι.
zarene. Says to them the Jesus; I am.
(Εἱστηκει δε και Ιουδας, ὁ παραδιδους αυτον,
(Was standing and also Judas, the delivering up him,
μετ' αυτων.) [6] Ὡς ουν ειπεν αυτοις· Ὁτι
with them.) When therefore he said to them; That
εγω ειμι· απηλθον εις τα οπισω, και επεσον
I am; they went into the behind, and fell
χαμαι. [7] Παλιν ουν αυτους επηρωτησε· Τινα
on the ground. Again then them he asked; Whom
ζητειτε; Οἱ δε ειπον· Ιησουν τον Ναζωραιον.
seek you? They and said; Jesus the Nazarene.
[8] Απεκριθη Ιησους· Ειπον ὑμιν, ὁτι εγω ειμι·
Answered Jesus; I said to you, that I am;
ει ουν εμε ζητειτε, αφετε τουτους ὑπαγειν.
if therefore me you seek, suffer these to go.
[9] Ἱνα πληρωθη ὁ λογος, ὁν ειπεν· "Ὁτι οὑς
So that might be fulfilled the word, which he said; "That whom
δεδωκας μοι, ουκ απολεσα εξ αυτων ουδενα."
thou hast given to me, not I lost of them no one."
[10] Σιμων ουν Πετρος εχων μαχαιραν, εἱλκυσεν
Simon then Peter having a sword, drew
αυτην, και επαισε τον του αρχιερεως δουλον,
her, and struck the of the high-priest slave,
και απεκοψεν αυτου το ωτιον το δεξιον. Ην δε
and cut off of him the ear the right. Was now
ονομα τῳ δουλῳ Μαλχος. [11] Ειπεν ουν ὁ Ιη-
a name to the slave Malchus. Said therefore the Je-

CHAPTER XVIII.

1 * Jesus, saying These things, ‡ went out with his DISCIPLES beyond the † BROOK KEDRON, where was † a Garden, into which he entered, and his DISCIPLES.

2 Now THAT JUDAS also, who DELIVERED him up, knew the PLACE; Because * Jesus often met there with his DISCIPLES.

3 ‡ Then JUDAS, having obtained the BAND and Officers from the HIGH-PRIESTS and * PHARISEES, comes there with Torches, and Lamps, and Weapons.

4 Jesus, therefore, knowing All THINGS that were COMING upon him, going out, * says to them, "Whom do you seek?"

5 They answered him, "Jesus the NAZARENE." * He says to them, "I am JESUS." And THAT JUDAS also, who DELIVERED him up, was standing with them.

6 When therefore, he said to them, "I am he," they went back, and fell on the Ground.

7 Then he asked them again, "Whom do you seek?" And THEY said, "Jesus, the NAZARENE."

8 Jesus answered, "I told you That I am he; if, therefore, you seek Me, permit these to go."

9 That the WORD might be fulfilled which he said, ‡ "Of those whom thou hast given me, I lost no one."

10 ‡ Then Simon Peter having a Sword, drew it, and struck the SERVANT of the HIGH-PRIEST, and cut off his RIGHT * EAR-TIP. Now the SERVANT's Name was Malchus.

11 JESUS, therefore,

* VATICAN MANUSCRIPT.—1. Jesus. 2. Jesus. 3. PHARISEES. 4. says. 5. He says to them, "I am JESUS." 10. EAR-TIP.

† 1. The name of a small rivulet, and of a valley towards the east of Jerusalem; probably derived from an Hebrew root signifying to be darkened, the valley being shaded with wood. † 1. Gethsemane.

‡ 1. Matt. xxvi. 36; Mark xiv. 32; Luke xxii. 39. ‡ 3. Matt. xxvi. 47; Mark xiv. 43; Luke xxii. 47; Acts i. 16. ‡ 9. John xvii. 12. ‡ 10. Matt. xxvi. 51; Mark xiv. 47; Luke xxii. 49, 50.

σους τῳ Πετρῳ· Βαλε την μαχαιραν εις την
sus to the Peter; Put up the sword into the
θηκην· το ποτηριον ὁ δεδωκε μοι ὁ πατηρ, ου
sheath: the cup which has given to me the father, not
μη πιω αυτο;
not should I drink it?
12 Ἡ ουν σπειρα και ὁ χιλιαρχος και οἱ ὑπη-
The then band and the commander and the offi-
ρεται των Ιουδαιων συνελαβον τον Ιησουν, και
cers of the Jews apprehended the Jesus, and
εδησαν αυτον, 13 και απηγαγον αυτον προς
bound him, and led him to
Ανναν πρωτον· ην γαρ πενθερος του Καιαφα,
Annas first; he was for father-in-law of the Caiaphas,
ὁς ην αρχιερευς του ενιαυτου εκεινου. 14 Ην
who was high-priest of the year that. Was
δε Καιαφας ὁ συμβουλευσας τοις Ιουδαιοις, ὁτι
now Caiaphas he having advised the Jews, that
συμφερει ἑνα ανθρωπον απολεσθαι ὑπερ του
it is better one man to be destroyed in behalf of the
λαου. 15 Ηκολουθει δε τῳ Ιησου Σιμων Πετρος,
people. Followed and the Jesus Simon Peter,
και ὁ αλλος μαθητης. Ὁ δε μαθητης εκεινος
and the other disciple. The and disciple that
ην γνωστος τῳ αρχιερει, και συνεισηλθε τῳ
was known to the high-priest, and went in with the
Ιησου εις την αυλην του αρχιερεως. 16 Ὁ δε
Jesus into the palace of the high-priest. The but
Πετρος εἱστηκει προς τῃ θυρῃ εξω. Εξηλθεν
Peter stood at the door without. Went out
ουν ὁ μαθητης ὁ αλλος, ὁς ην γνωστος τῳ
therefore the disciple the other, who was known to the
αρχιερει, και ειπε τῃ θυρωρῳ, και εισηγαγε τον
high-priest, and spoke to the door-keeper, and brought in the
Πετρον. 17 Λεγει ουν ἡ παιδισκη ἡ θυρωρος
Peter. Says then the female-servant the door-keeper
τῳ Πετρῳ· Μη και συ εκ των μαθητων ει του
to the Peter; Not also thou of the disciples art the
ανθρωπου τουτου; Λεγει εκεινος· Ουκ ειμι.
man this? Says he; Not I am.
18 Εἱστηκεισαν δε οἱ δουλοι και οἱ ὑπηρεται αν-
Stood and the slaves and the officers a
θρακιαν πεποιηκοτες, ὁτι ψυχος ην, και εθερ-
coal fire having made, because cold it was, and warmed
μαινοντο· ην δε μετ' αυτων ὁ Πετρος ἑστως
themselves; was and with them the Peter standing
και θερμαινομενος. 19 Ὁ ουν αρχιερευς ηρω-
and warming himself. The therefore high-priest asked
τησε τον Ιησουν περι των μαθητων αυτου,
the Jesus concerning the disciples of him,
και περι της διδαχης αυτου. 20 Απεκριθη
and concerning the teaching of him. Answered
αυτῳ ὁ Ιησους· Εγω παρρησιᾳ ελαλησα τῳ
him the Jesus; I publicly spoke to the

said to PETER, "Put the SWORD into the SCABBARD; ‡ the CUP which the FATHER has given me, shall I not drink it?"

12 Then the BAND, and the COMMANDER, and the OFFICERS of the JEWS apprehended JESUS, and bound him,

13 and led him first to Annas, for he was Father-in-law of CAIAPHAS, who was High-Priest that YEAR.

14 ‡ Now Caiaphas was the one HAVING ADVISED the JEWS, "That it is expedient that One Man be destroyed in behalf of the PEOPLE."

15 ‡ And Simon Peter followed JESUS; also the OTHER Disciple. And that DISCIPLE was known to the HIGH-PRIEST, and went in with JESUS into the PALACE of the HIGH-PRIEST;

16 ‡ but PETER stood at the DOOR without. Therefore, * THAT OTHER DISCIPLE who was the ACQUAINTANCE of the HIGH-PRIEST, went out, and spoke to the DOOR-KEEPER, and brought in PETER.

17 Then THAT FEMALE SERVANT, the DOOR KEEPER, says to PETER, "Art thou also of this MAN'S DISCIPLES?" He says, "I am not."

18 And the SERVANTS and OFFICERS having made a Fire of coals, Because it was cold, stood and warmed themselves. And PETER * also was standing with them, and warming himself.

19 Then the HIGH-PRIEST asked JESUS about his DISCIPLES, and about his TEACHING.

20 JESUS answered him, "‡ * have spoken publicly

* VATICAN MANUSCRIPT.—16. THAT OTHER DISCIPLE who was the ACQUAINTANCE of the HIGH PRIEST, and. 18. also. 20. have spoken.

‡ 11. Matt. xx. 22; xxvii. 39, 42. ‡ 14. John xi. 50. ‡ 15. Matt. xxvi. 58; Mark xiv. 54; Luke xxii. 54. ‡ 16. Matt. xxvi. 69; Mark xiv. 66; Luke xxii. 54.

κοσμῳ· εγω παντοτε εδιδαξα εν συναγωγῃ και
world; I always taught in a synagogue and
εν τῳ ἱερῳ, ὁπου παντες οἱ Ιουδαιοι συνερχον-
in the temple, where all the Jews come together,
ται, και εν κρυπτῳ ελαλησα ουδεν. 21 Τι με
and in secret I said nothing. Why me
επερωτᾳς; επερωτησον τους ακηκοοτας, τι
dost thou ask? ask those having heard, what
ελαλησα αυτοις· ιδε, οὑτοι οιδασιν ἁ ειπον
I said to them; lo, they know what things said
εγω. 22 Ταυτα δε αυτου ειποντος, εις των
I. These things and of him having said, one of the
ὑπηρετων παρεστηκως εδωκε ῥαπισμα τῳ
officer having stood by gave a blow to the
Ιησου, ειπων· Οὑτως αποκρινῃ τῳ αρχιερει;
Jesus, saying; Thus dost thou answer the high-priest?
23 Απεκριθη αυτῳ ὁ Ιησους· Ει κακως ελαλη-
Answered him the Jesus; If evil I spoke,
σα, ματυρρησον περι του κακου· ει δε καλως,
testify concerning the evil; if but well;
τι με δερεις;
why me dost thou beat?

24 Απεστειλαν αυτον ὁ Αννας δεδεμενον προς
Sent him the Annas having been bound to
Καιαφαν τον αρχιερεα. 25 Ην δε Σιμων Πετρος
Caiaphas the high-priest. Was and Simon Peter
ἑστως και θερμαινομενος. Ειπον ουν αυτῳ·
standing and warming himself. They said therefore to him;
Μη και συ εκ των μαθητων αυτου ει; Ηρνη-
Not also thou of the disciples of him thou art? Denied
σατο εκεινος, και ειπεν· Ουκ ειμι. 26 Λεγει
he, and said; Not I am. Says
εἱς εκ των δουλων του αρχιερεως, συγγενης ὠν
one of the slaves of the high-priest, a relative being
οὑ απεκοψε Πετρος το ωτιον· Ουκ εγω σε
of whom cut off Peter the ear; Not I thee
ειδον εν τῳ κηπῳ μετ' αυτου; 27 Παλιν ουν
saw in the garden with him? Again therefore
ηρνησατο ὁ Πετρος· και ευθεως αλεκτωρ εφω-
denied the Peter; and immediately a cock crew.
νησεν.

28 Αγουσιν ουν τον Ιησουν απο του Καιαφα
They lead then the Jesus from of the Caiaphas
εις το πραιτωριον· ην δε πρωια. Και αὐτοι
into the judgment hall; it was and morning. And they
ουκ εισηλθον εις το πραιτωριον, ἱνα μη μιαν-
not went into the judgment hall, that not they might
θωσιν, αλλ' ἱνα φαγωσι το πασχα. 29 Εξηλ-
be defiled, but that they might eat the passover. Went
θεν ουν ὁ Πιλατος προς αυτους, και ειπε· Τινα
out therefore the Pilate to them, and said; What

to the WORLD; I always taught in a Synagogue and in the TEMPLE, where All the JEWS come together; and in secret I said nothing.

21 Why dost thou ask Me? Ask those HAVING HEARD what I said to them; behold, they know what things I said."

22 And he having said these things, ‡one of the OFFICERS standing by gave JESUS a Blow, saying, "Dost thou thus answer the HIGH-PRIEST?"

23 *Jesus answered him, "If I spoke evil, testify concerning the EVIL; but if well, why dost thou beat Me?"

24 ‡†(ANNAS sent him, having been bound, to Caiaphas, the HIGH-PRIEST.)

25 And Simon Peter was standing and warming himself. ‡Then they said to him, "Art not thou also of his DISCIPLES?" He denied, and said, "I am not."

26 One of the SERVANTS of the HIGH-PRIEST, being a relative of him Whose EAR Peter cut off, says, "Did not I see Thee in the GARDEN with him?"

27 Then *Peter again denied, ‡and immediately †a Cock crew.

28 ‡Then they lead JESUS from CAIAPHAS into the †PRÆTORIUM. It was now morning; and they went not into the PRÆTORIUM so that they might not be defiled, but †that they might eat the PASSOVER.

29 PILATE, therefore, went out to them, and *said, "What Accusation

* VATICAN MANUSCRIPT.—23. Jesus. 27. Peter. 29. says.

† 24. This clause by some is added to the end of the 13th verse where it seems more properly to belong. † 27. The trumpet, called the cock-crowing, sounded at the beginning of the third watch; this was at midnight. See Note on Matt. xxvi. 34. † 28. See Note on Matt. xxvii. 27. † 28. It was probably then thought lawful for the Jews to eat the paschal lamb at any hour between the two evenings, though Exod. xii. 6, 8, seems to require it to be eaten at the time when Jesus ate it.

‡ 22. Jer. xx. 2; Acts xxiii. 2. ‡ 24. Matt. xxvi. 57. ‡ 25. Matt. xxvi. 69, 71; Mark xiv. 69; Luke xxii. 58. ‡ 27. Matt. xxvi. 74; Mark xiv. 72; Luke xxii. 60; John xiii. 38. ‡ 28. Matt. xxvii. 2; Mark xv. 1; Luke xxiii. 1; Acts iii. 13.

κατηγοριαν φερετε κατα του ανθρωπου τουτο;
accusation bring you against the man this?
30 Απεκριθησαν και ειπον αυτῳ· Ει μη ην οὑτος
They answered and said to him, If not was this
κακοποιος, ουκ αν σοι παρεδωκαμεν αυτον.
an evil-doer, not would to thee we delivered up him.
31 Ειπεν ουν αυτοις ὁ Πιλατος· Λαβετε αυτον
Said then to them the Pilate; Take him
ὑμεις, και κατα τον νομον ὑμων κρινατε αυτον.
you, and according to the law of you judge him.
Ειπον *[ουν] αυτῳ οἱ Ιουδαιοι· Ἡμιν ουκ
Said [therefore] to him the Jews; To us not
εξεστιν αποκτειναι ουδενα. 32 Ἱνα ὁ λογος του
it is lawful to kill no one. So that the word of the
Ιησου πληρωθῃ, ὁν ειπε, σημαινων ποιῳ θανα-
Jesus might be fulfilled, which he said, pointing out by what death
τῳ ημελλεν αποθνησκειν.
he was about to die.
33 Εισηλθεν ουν εις το πραιτωριον παλιν ὁ
Went then into the judgment-hall again the
Πιλατος, και εφωνησε τον Ιησουν, και ειπεν
Pilate, and called the Jesus, and said
αυτῳ· Συ ει ὁ βασιλευς των Ιουδαιων; 34 Απεκ-
to him; Thou art the king of the Jews? An-
ριθη *[αυτῳ] ὁ Ιησους· Αφ᾽ ἑαυτου συ τουτο
swered [him] the Jesus; From thyself thou this
λεγεις, η αλλοι σοι ειπον περι εμου; 35 Απεκ-
sayest, or others to thee told concerning me? An-
ριθη ὁ Πιλατος· Μητι εγω Ιουδαιος ειμι; το
swered the Pilate; Not I a Jew am? the
εθνος το σον και οἱ αρχιερεις παρεδωκαν σε
nation the thine and the high-priests delivered up thee
εμοι· τι εποιησας; 36 Απεκριθη Ιησους· Ἡ
to me; what didst thou do? Answered Jesus; The
βασιλεια ἡ εμη ουκ εστιν εκ του κοσμου τουτου·
kingdom the mine not is of the world this;
ει εκ του κοσμου τουτου ην ἡ βασιλεια ἡ εμη,
if of the world this was the kingdom the mine,
οἱ ὑπηρεται αν οἱ εμοι ηγωνιζοντο, ἱνα μη
the officers would those for me contend, that not
παραδοθω τοις Ιουδαιοις, νυν δε ἡ
I might be delivered up to the Jews, now but the
βασιλεια ἡ εμη ουκ εστιν εντευθεν. 37 Ειπεν
kingdom the mine not is from this place. Said
ουν αυτῳ ὁ Πιλατος· Ουκουν βασιλευς ει συ;
then to him the Pilate; Not then a king art thou?
Απεκριθη ὁ Ιησους· Συ λεγεις· ὁτι βασιλευς
Answered the Jesus; Thou sayest; that a king
ειμι εγω. Εγω εις τουτο γεγεννημαι, και
am I. I for this have been born, and
εις τουτο εληλυθα εις τον κοσμον, ἱνα μαρτυ-
for this I have come into the world, that I may tes-
ρησω τῃ αληθειᾳ. Πας ὁ ων εκ της αλη-
tify to the truth. Every one who being of the truth,
θειας, ακουει μου της φωνης. 38 Λεγει αυτῳ
hears of me the voice. Says to him
ὁ Πιλατος· Τι εστιν αληθεια; Και τουτο ειπων,
the Pilate; What is truth? And this saying,

do you bring * against this MAN?"

30 They answered and said to him, "If he was not * one who does evil, we would not have delivered him up to thee."

31 Then * Pilate said to them, "Take you him, and judge him according to your LAW." The JEWS said to him, "It is not lawful for us to kill any one;"

32 ‡ that the WORD of JESUS might be verified, which he spoke, intimating by What Death he was about to die.

33 ‡ PILATE, therefore, went into the PRÆTORIUM again, and called JESUS, and said to him, "Art thou the KING of the JEWS?"

34 Jesus answered, "Dost thou say this from thyself, or did others tell thee concerning me?"

35 PILATE answered, "Am I a Jew? THINE OWN NATION, even the HIGH-PRIESTS have delivered thee to me. What didst thou do?"

36 ‡ Jesus answered, "My KINGDOM is not of this WORLD. If MY KINGDOM were of this WORLD, MY OFFICERS would fight, so that I might not be delivered up to the JEWS; but now MY KINGDOM is not from hence."

37 PILATE, therefore, said to him, "Art thou not a King then?" JESUS answered, "Thou sayest; * I am a King. For this I have been born; and for this I have come into the WORLD, that I may testify to the TRUTH. ‡ EVERY ONE WHO IS of the TRUTH, hears My VOICE."

38 PILATE says to him, "What is Truth?" ‡ And saying This, he went out

* VATICAN MANUSCRIPT.—29. of this MAN. 30. one who does evil, we would. 31. Pilate. 31. therefore—omit. 34. him—omit. 37. I am.

‡ 32. Matt. xx. 19; John xii. 32, 33. ‡ 33. Matt. xxvii. 11. ‡ 36. 1 Tim. vi. 13. ‡ 37. John viii. 47; 1 John iii. 19; iv. 6. ‡ 38. Matt. xxvii. 24; Luke xxiii. 4; John xix. 4, 6.

παλιν εξηλθε προς τους Ιουδαιους, και λεγει
again he went out to the Jews, and says
αυτοις· Εγω ουδεμιαν αιτιαν εὑρισκω εν αυτῳ.
to them; I not one fault find in him.
39 Εστι δε συνηθεια ὑμιν, ἱνα ἑνα ὑμιν απολυσω
It is but a custom for you, that one to you I release
εν τῳ πασχα· βουλεσθε ουν, ὑμιν απολυσω
in the passover; are you willing therefore, to you I release
τον βασιλεα των Ιουδαιων; 40 Εκραυγασαν ουν
the king of the Jews?. They cried out then
παλιν *[παντες,] λεγοντες· Μη τουτον, αλλα
again [all,] saying; Not this, but
τον Βαραββαν. Ην δε ὁ Βαραββας ληστης.
the Barabbas. Was now the Barabbas a robber.

ΚΕΦ. ιθ'. 19.

1 Τοτε ουν ελαβεν ὁ Πιλατος τον Ιησουν, και
Then therefore took the Pilate the Jesus, and
εμαστιγωσε. 2 Και οἱ στρατιωται πλεξαντες
scourged. And the soldiers braiding
στεφανον εξ ακανθων, επεθηκαν αυτου τῃ κεφα-
a crown of thorns, placed of him to the head,
λῃ, και ἱματιον πορφυρουν περιεβαλον αυτον,
and a mantle purple threw about him,
3 και ελεγον· Χαιρε ὁ βασιλευς των Ιουδαιων·
and said; Hail the king of the Jews;
και εδιδουν αυτῳ ῥαπισματα. 4 Εξηλθεν παλιν
and they gave him blows. Went again
εξω ὁ Πιλατος, και λεγει αυτοις· Ιδε, αγω ὑμιν
out the Pilate, and says to them; Lo, I bring to you
αυτον εξω, ἱνα γνωτε, ὁτι εν αυτῳ ουδεμιαν
him out, that you may know, that in him not one
αιτιαν εὑρισκω. 5 (Εξηλθεν ουν ὁ Ιησους εξω,
fault I find. (Came then the Jesus out,
φορων τον ακανθινον στεφανον, και το πορφυ-
wearing the thorny crown, and the purple
ρουν ἱματιον.) Και λεγει αυτοις· Ιδε, ὁ ανθρω-
mantle,) And he says to them; See, the man.
πος. 6 Ὁτε ουν ειδον αυτον οἱ αρχιερεις και οἱ
When therefore saw him the high-priest and the
ὑπηρεται, εκραυγασαν λεγοντες· Σταυρωσον,
officers, they cried out saying; Crucify,
σταυρωσον αυτον. Λεγει αυτοις ὁ Πιλατος·
crucify him. Says to them the Pilate;
Λαβετε αυτον ὑμεις, και σταυρωσατε· εγω γαρ
Take him you, and crucify; I for
ουχ εὑρισκω εν αυτῳ αιτιαν. 7 Απεκριθησαν
not find in him a fault. Answered
αυτῳ οἱ Ιουδαιοι· Ἡμεις νομον εχωμεν, και
him the Jews; We a law have, and
κατα τον νομον ἡμων οφειλει αποθανειν,
according to the law of us he ought to die,
ὁτι ἑαυτον, υἱον θεου εποιησεν. 8 Ὁτε ουν
because himself, a son of God he made. When therefore
ηκουσεν ὁ Πιλατος τουτον τον λογον, μαλλον
heard the Pilate this the word, more

again to the JEWS, and says to them, "I find No Fault in him."

39 ‡ But it is customary for you that I release to you One during the PASSOVER; are you willing, therefore, that I release to you the KING of the JEWS?"

40 Then they cried out again, saying, ‡ "Not him, but BARABBAS." ‡ Now BARABBAS was a Robber.

CHAPTER XIX.

1 ‡ Then PILATE, therefore took and scourged JESUS.

2 And the SOLDIERS, wreathing a Crown of Acanthus, placed it on His HEAD; and they threw around him a purple Mantle,

3 * and they came to him and said, "Hail, KING of the JEWS!" And they gave him Blows.

4 * And PILATE went out again, and says to them, "Behold, I bring him out to you, That you may know that I find ‡ No Fault in him."

5 Then * Jesus came out, wearing the ACANTHINE Crown, and the PURPLE Mantle. And he says to them, "Behold, the MAN!"

6 ‡ When, therefore, the HIGH-PRIESTS and the OFFICERS saw him, they cried out, saying, "Crucify, crucify him!" PILATE says to them, "Take him yourselves, and crucify him; for I find no Fault in him."

7 The JEWS answered him, ‡ "We have a Law, and by * the LAW he ought to die, because ‡ he made himself a Son of God."

8 When PILATE, therefore, heard This WORD, he was more afraid,

* VATICAN MANUSCRIPT.—40. all—*omit*. 3. they came to him and said. 4. And PILATE went. 5. Jesus. 7. the LAW.

‡ 39. Matt. xxvii. 15; Mark. xv. 6; Luke xxiii. 17. ‡ 40. Acts iii. 14. ‡ 40. Luke xxiii. 19. ‡ 1. Matt. xx. 19; xxvii. 26; Mark xv. 15; Luke xviii. 33. ‡ 4. John xviii. 38; ver. 6. ‡ 6. Acts iii. 13. ‡ 7. Lev. xxiv. 16. ‡ 7. Matt. xxvi. 65; John v. 18; x. 33.

εφοβηθη· 9 και εισηλθεν εις το πραιτωριον παλιν,
he was afraid; and went into the judgment-hall again,
και λεγει τῳ Ιησους· Ποθεν ει συ; Ὁ δε Ιη-
and says to the Jesus; Whence art thou? The but Je-
σους αποκρισιν ουκ εδωκεν αυτῳ. 10 Λεγει ουν
sus an answer not gave to him. Says then
αυτῳ ὁ Πιλατος· Εμοι ου λαλεις; ουκ οιδας,
to him the Pilate; To me not thou dost speak? not knowest thou,
ὁτι εξουσιαν εχω σταυρωσαι σε, και εξουσιαν
that authority I have to crucify thee, and authority
εχω απολυσαι σε; 11 Απεκριθη Ιησους· Ουκ
I have to release thee? Answered Jesus; Not
ειχες εξουσιαν ουδεμιαν κατ' εμου, ει μη
thou couldst have authority not any against me, if not
ην σοι δεδομενον ανωθεν· δια τουτο ὁ
it was to thee having been given from above; on account of this he
παραδιδους με σοι, μειζονα ἁμαρτιαν εχει. 12 Εκ
delivering up me to thee, greater sin has. From
τουτου εζητει ὁ Πιλατος απολυσαι αυτον. Οἱ
this seeks the Pilate to release him. The
δε Ιουδαιοι εκραζον, λεγοντες· Εαν τουτον
but Jews cried out, saying; If this
απολυσης, ουκ ει φιλος του Καισαρος· πας ὁ
thou release, not thou art a friend of the Cesar; every one the
βασιλεια ἑαυτον ποιων, αντιλεγει τῳ Καισαρι.
king himself making, speaks against the Cesar.
13 Ὁ ουν Πιλατος ακουσας τουτον τον λογον,
The therefore Pilate having heard this the word,
ηγαγεν εξω τον Ιησουν, και εκαθισεν επι του
brought out the Jesus, and sat down on the
βηματος εις τοπον λεγομενον Λιθοστρωτον,
tribunal into a place being called Pavement,
Εβραιστι δε Γαββαθα· 14 (ην δε παρασκευη του
in Hebrew but Gabbatha; (it was and a preparation of the
πασχα, ὡρα δε ὡσει εκτη·) και λεγει τοις Ιου-
passover, hour and about sixth;) and he says to the Jews;
δαιοις· Ιδε ὁ βασιλευς ὑμων. 15 Οἱ δε εκραυγα-
See the king of you. They but cried out;
σαν· Αρον, αρον· σταυρωσον αυτον. Λεγει
Away, away; crucify him. Says
αυτοις ὁ Πιλατος· Τον βασιλεα ὑμων σταυρωσω;
to them the Pilate; The king of you shall I crucify?
Απεκριθησαν οἱ αρχιερεις· Ουκ εχομεν βασιλεα
Answered the high-priests; Not we have a king,
ει μη Καισαρα.
if not Cesar.
16 Τοτε ουν παρεδωκεν αυτον αυτοις, ἱνα
Then therefore he delivered up him to them, that

9 and went again into
the PRÆTORIUM, and
says to JESUS, "Whence
art thou?" ‡ But JESUS
gave him no Answer.
10 PILATE then says to
him, "Dost thou not speak
to me? Dost thou not
know That I have Autho-
rity * to release thee, and
I have Authority to crucify
thee?"
11 * Jesus answered
him, ‡ "Thou wouldst
have no Authority against
me, if it had not been given
thee from above. On this
account HE who DELIV-
ERED me to thee has a
Greater Sin."
12 From this time, PI-
LATE sought to release
him; but the JEWS cried
out, saying, ‡ "If thou release him, thou art not a
Friend of CESAR; ‡ EVERY
ONE who MAKES Himself
a King speaks against CE-
SAR."
13 PILATE, therefore,
having heard * these
WORDS, brought JESUS
out, and sat down on † the
* Tribunal, in a Place called
† The Pavement, but in
Hebrew, Gabbatha.
14 ‡ (Now it was the
Preparation of the PASS-
OVER, and the Hour was
about the † Sixth;) and he
says to the JEWS, "Be-
hold your KING!"
15 * Then they cried out,
"Away, away, crucify
him!" PILATE says to
them, "Shall I crucify your
KING?" The HIGH-PRIESTS
answered, ‡ "We have no
king, except Cesar."
16 ‡ Then, therefore, he
delivered him to them that
he might be crucified.

* VATICAN MANUSCRIPT.—10. to release thee, and I have Authority to crucify thee? 11. Jesus answered him, Thou. 13. These WORDS, brought. 13. Tribunal, in a Place. 15. Then they.

† 13. The Tribunal seems to have been placed in the open air, agreeably to what Josephus says of Herod, when he tried his two sons; "He came to the tribunal, and that was placed in the stadium, (the circus, or place for races,) behind which his soldiers kept guard unseen."—*Pearce.* † 13. A spot paved with stones, enclosed and elevated, where the judge sat in his chair of state. † 14. Six o'clock in the morning. See Note on John i. 39.

‡ 9. Isa. liii. 7; Matt. xxvii, 12, 14. ‡ 11. Luke xxii. 53; John vii. 30. ‡ 12. Luke xxiii. 2. ‡ 12. Acts xvii. 7. ‡ 14. Matt. xxvii. 62. ‡ 15. Gen. xlix. 10. ‡ 16. Matt. xxvii. 26, 31; Mark xv. 15; Luke xxiii. 24.

σταυρωθη. Παρελαβον δε τον Ιησουν *[και
he might be crucified. They took and the Jesus [and
ηγαγον.] 17 Και βασταζων τον σταυρον αυτου,
led.] And carrying the cross of himself,
εξηλθεν εις τον λεγομενον κρανιου τοπον, ὁς
he went out into the being called of a skull a place, which
λεγεται Εβραιστι Γολγοθα. 18 Ὁπου αυτον
is called in Hebrew Golgotha. Where him
εσταυρωσαν, και μετ' αυτου αλλους δυο, εντευ-
they crucified, and with him others two, hence
θεν και εντευθεν, μεσον δε τον Ιησουν. 19 Εγ-
and hence, in middle and the Jesus. Wrote
ραψε δε και τιτλον ὁ Πιλατος, και εθηκεν επι του
and also a title the Pilate, and placed upon the
σταυρου. Ην δε γεγραμμενον· "Ιησους ὁ Να-
cross. It was and having been written; "Jesus the Na-
ζωραιος, ὁ βασιλευς των Ιουδαιων." 20 Τουτον
zarene, the king o the Jews." This
ουν τον τιτλον πολλοι ανεγνωσαν των Ιου-
therefore the title many read of the Jews."
δαιων, ὁτι εγγυς ην ὁ τοπος της πολεως, ὁπου
because near was the place of the city, where
εσταυρωθη ὁ Ιησους· και ην γεγραμμενον Ἑβ-
was crucified the Jesus; and it was having been writen in
ραιστι Ἑλληνιστι, Ῥωμαιστι. 21 Ελεγον ουν
Hebrew in Greek, in Latin. Said therefore
τῳ Πιλατῳ οἱ αρχιερεις των Ιουδαιων· Μη
to the Pilate the high-priests of the Jews; Not
γραφε· Ὁ βασιλευς των Ιουδαιων· αλλ' ὁτι
write thou; The king of the Jews; but that
εκεινος ειπε· Βασιλευς ειμι των Ιουδαιων.
he said; A king I am of the Jews.
22 Απεκριθη ὁ Πιλατος· Ὁ γεγραφα, γεγραφα.
Answered the Pilate; What I have written, I have written.
23 Οἱ ουν στρατιωται, ὁτε εσταυρωσαν τον
The then soldiers, when they crucified the
Ιησουν, ελαβον τα ἱματια, αυτου, (και εποιησαν
Jesus, took the mantles o him, (and made
τεσσαρα μερη, ἑκαστῳ στρατιωτῃ μερος,) και
four parts, to each soldier a part,) and
τον χιτωνα. Ην δε ὁ χιτων αρραφος, εκ των
the coat. Was but the coat without seam, from the
ανωθεν ὑφαντος δι' ὁλου· 24 ειπον ουν προς
top woven throughout whole; they said then to
αλληλους· Μη σχισωμεν αυτον, αλλα λαχωμεν
each other; Not let us tear him, but we may cast lots
περι αυτου, τινος εσται. Ἱνα ἡ γραφη πλη-
about him, of whom it shall be. That the writing might
ρωθη *[ἡ λεγουσα·] "Διεμερισαντο τα
be fulfilled [that saying;] They divided the
ἱματια μου ἑαυτοις, και επι τον ἱματισμον μου
mantles of me for themselves, and on the raiment of me
εβαλον κληρον."
they cast a lot."

Οἱ μεν ουν στρατιωται ταυτα εποιησαν.
The indeed therefore soldiers these things did.

17 ‡* Then they took JESUS, and putting the CROSS on him, he went out into WHAT IS CALLED a Place of a Skull, which signifies in Hebrew Golgotha;

18 where they crucified Him, and two others with him, one on each side, and JESUS in the Middle.

19 ‡ And PILATE wrote a Title, and placed it on the CROSS. Now that having been written was, "Jesus, the NAZARENE, the KING of the JEWS."

20 This TITLE, therefore, many of the JEWS read because the PLACE was near the CITY, where JESUS was crucified; and it had been written in Hebrew, * Latin, and Greek.

21 Then the HIGH-PRIESTS of the JEWS said to PILATE, "Do not write, The KING of the JEWS, but That he said, I am King of the JEWS."

22 PILATE answered, "What I have written, I have written."

23 ‡ Then the SOLDIERS, when they had nailed JESUS to the CROSS, took his GARMENTS, and made Four Parts, to Each Soldier a Part. But his COAT was without seam, woven from the top through the whole.

24 They said, therefore, to each other, "Let us not tear it, but cast lots for it, whose it shall be;" that the SCRIPTURE might be verified, ‡ "They divided my GARMENTS among themselves, and upon my RAIMENT they cast a Lot." The SOLDIERS, therefore, did these things.

* VATICAN MANUSCRIPT.—16. And led—*omit*. 17. Then they took JESUS, and putting the CROSS on him. 20. Latin and Greek. 24. that saying—*omit*.

‡ 17. Matt. xxvii. 31 33; Mark xv. 21, 22; Luke xxiii. 26, 33. ‡ 19. Matt. xxvii. 37; Mark xv. 26; Luke xxiii. 38 ‡ 23. Matt xxvii. 35; Mark xv. 24; Luke xxiii. 34. ‡ 24. Psa. xxii. 18.

25 Εἱστηκεισαν δε παρα τῳ σταυρῳ του Ἰησου, ἡ
Stood now by the cross of the Jesus the
μητηρ αυτου, και ἡ αδελφη της μητρος αυτου,
mother of him, and the sister of the mother of him,
Μαρια ἡ του Κλωπα, και Μαρια ἡ Μαγδαληνη.
Mary that of the Klopas, and Mary the Magdalene.
26 Ιησους ουν ιδων την μητερα, και τον μαθη-
Jesus therefore seeing the mother, and the disci-
την παρεστωτα, ὁν ηγαπα, λεγει τῃ μητρι
ple standing by, whom he loved, he says to the mother
αὑτου· Γυναι, ιδε, ὁ υιος σου. 27 Ειτα λεγει τῳ
of himself; O woman, Lo, the son of thee. Then he says to the
μαθητῃ· Ιδου ἡ μητηρ σου. Και απ' εκεινης
disciple, Lo the mother of thee. And from that
της ὡρας ελαβεν ὁ μαθητης αυτην εις τα ιδια.
the hour took the disciple her into the own.
28 Μετα τουτον ειδως ὁ Ιησους, ὁτι παντα ηδη
After this knowing the Jesus, that all things already
τετελεσται ἱνα τελειωθῃ ἡ γραφη, λεγει·
had been finished that might be finished the writing, says;
Διψω. 29 Σκευος *[ουν] εκειτο οξους μεστον·
I thirst. A vessel [therefore] stood of vinegar full;
οἱ δε πλησαντες σπογγον οξους, και ὑσσω-
they and filling a sponge of vinegar, and to a hyssop stalk
πῳ περιθεντες, προσηνεγκαν αυτου τῳ στοματι.
putting round, brought of him to the mouth.
30 Ὁτε ουν ελαβε το οξος ὁ Ιησους, ειπε·
When therefore took the vinegar the Jesus, he said;
Τετελεσται· και κλινας την κεφαλην, παρε-
It has been finished; and having inclined the head, he gave
δωκε το πνευμα.
up the spirit.
31 Οἱ ουν Ιουδαιοι (ἱνα μη μεινῃ επι του
The then Jews (that not might remain on the
σταυρου τα σωματα εν τῳ σαββατῳ· επει
cross the bodies in the sabbath; since
παρασκευη ην· ην γαρ μεγαλη ἡ ἡμερα εκεινου
a preparation it was; was for great the day that
του σαββατου) ηρωτησαν τον Πιλατον, ἱνα
of the sabbath) asked the Pilate, that
κατεαγωσιν αυτων τα σκελη, και αρθω-
might be broken of them the legs, and they might be taken
σιν. 32 Ηλθον ουν οἱ στρατιωται, και του μεν
away. Came therefore the soldiers, and of the indeed
πρωτου, κατεαξαν τα σκελη, και του αλλου
first, they brake the legs, and of the other
του συσταυρωθεντος αυτῳ. 33 Επι δε τον Ιη-
that having been crucified with him. To but the Je-

25 ‡ And there were standing by the CROSS of JESUS his MOTHER, and his MOTHER'S SISTER, † Mary, the MOTHER of ‡ CLOPAS, and Mary of MAGDALA.

26 Jesus, therefore, seeing his MOTHER, and ‡ the DISCIPLE whom he loved standing near, says to his MOTHER, "Woman, behold thy SON!"

27 He then says to the DISCIPLE, "Behold thy MOTHER!" And from that HOUR the DISCIPLE took her to his OWN [house.]

28 After this, * Jesus knowing That all things had already been finished, ‡ that the SCRIPTURE might be fully accomplished, says, "I thirst."

29 A Vessel was placed full of Vinegar; ‡ * then a Sponge full of the VINEGAR, having been attached to a Hyssop-stalk, they brought to his MOUTH.

30 When therefore, * Jesus took the VINEGAR, he said, "It has been finished!" And inclining his HEAD, he expired.

31 Then the JEWS, (‡ that the BODIES might not remain upon the CROSS during the SABBATH, since it was the Preparation; for the DAY of That SABBATH was a great one;) asked PILATE that their LEGS might be broken. and they might be taken away.

32 The SOLDIERS therefore came, and did, indeed, break the LEGS of the FIRST, and of THAT OTHER who was CRUCIFIED with him;

33 but having come to

* VATICAN MANUSCRIPT.—28. Jesus. 29. Then—*omit.* 29. then a Sponge full of the VINEGAR having been attached to a Hyssop-stalk, they brought to His MOUTH. 30 Jesus.

† 25. The Greek does not state the relationship between Mary and Clopas, and we must supply it by conjecture. In other gospels she is called James's Mary, and Mary the mother of James; and Clopas was probably another name for James, being a Greek translation of the Hebrew Jacob or James, *a thief*. Paul tells us that the Savior after his resurrection was seen by James (1 Cor. xv. 7,) which is not mentioned in the gospels or Acts, unless we suppose that Cleopas, who walked with him to Emmaus, was James. See Luke xxiv. 18.—*Sharpe*

‡ 25. Matt. xxvii. 56; Mark xv. 40; Luke xxiii. 49. ‡ 25. Luke xxiv. 18. ‡ 26 John xiii. 23. xx. 2; xxi 7, 20, 24. ‡ 28. Psa. lxix. 21. ‡ 29. Matt. xxvii. 48. ‡ 31. Deut. xxi. 23.

σουν ελθοντες, ὡς ειδον αυτον ηδη τεθνηκοτα,
sus having come, when they saw him already having died,
ου κατεαξαν αυτου τα σκελη· 34 αλλ' εἱς των
not they broke of him the legs; but one of the
στρατιωτων λογχῃ αυτου την πλευραν ενυξε,
soldiers with a spear of him the side pierced,
και ευθυς εξηλθεν αιμα και ὑδωρ. 35 Και
and immediately came out blood and water. And
ὁ ἑωρακως μεμαρτυρηκε, και αληθινη αυτου
he having seen has testified, and true of him
εστιν ἡ μαρτυρια· κακεινος οιδεν, ὁτι αληθη
is the testimony; and he knows, that true things
λεγει, ἱνα και ὑμεις πιστευσητε. 36 Εγενετο
he says, so that also you may believe. Occurred
γαρ ταυτα, ἱνα ἡ γραφη πληρωθη· "Οστουν
for these things, that the writing might be fulfilled; "A bone
ου συντριβησεται αυτου." 37 Και παλιν ἑτερα
not shall be broken of him." And again another
γραφη λεγει· "Οψονται εις ὁν εξεκεντησαν."
writing says; 'They shall look into whom they pierced."
38 Μετα δε ταυτα ηρωτησε τον Πιλατον ὁ
After and these things asked the Pilate the
Ιωσηφ ὁ απο Αριμαθαιας, (ων μαθητης του Ιη-
Joseph that from Arimathea, (being a disciple of the Je-
σου, κεκρυμμενος δε δια τον φοβον των Ιου-
sus, having been hid but through the fear of the Jews,)
δαιων,) ἱνα αρη το σωμα του Ιησου·
that he might take away the body of the Jesus;
και επετρεψεν ὁ Πιλατος. Ηλθεν ουν και
and permitted the Pilate. He came therefore and
ηρε το σωμα του Ιησου. 39 Ηλθε δε και
took away the body of the Jesus. Came and also
Νικοδημος, (ὁ ελθων προς τον Ιησουν νυκτος
Nicodemus, (he having come to the Jesus by night
το πρωτον,) φερων μιγμα σμυρνης και αλοης
the first,) bringing a mixture of myrrh and aloes
ὡς λιτρας ἑκατον. 40 Ελαβον ουν το σωμα
about pounds a hundred. They took therefore the body
του Ιησου, και εδησαν αυτο οθονιοις μετα των
of the Jesus, and bound it with linen cloths with the
αρωματων, καθως εθος εστι τοις Ιουδαιοις εντα-
spices, as customary it is with the Jews to
φιαζειν. 41 Ην δε εν τῳ τοπῳ, ὁπου εσταυρωθη,
embalm. Was and in the place, where he was crucified,
κηπος, και εν τῳ κηπῳ μνημειον καινον, εν ᾡ
a garden, and in the garden a tomb new, in which
ουδεπω ουδεις ετεθη. 42 Εκει ουν δια την
not yet no one was laid. There therefore on account of the
παρεσκευην των Ιουδαιων, ὁτι εγγυς ην το
preparation of the Jews, because near was the
μνημειον, εθηκαν τον Ιησουν.
tomb, they laid the Jesus.

JESUS, when they saw that he had already died, they did not break His LEGS,

34 but one of the SOLDIERS pierced His SIDE with a Spear, and immediately there came out Blood and Water.

35 And HE HAVING SEEN has testified, and His TESTIMONY is true; and he knows That he is saying true things, so that you also may believe.

36 For these things occurred, that the SCRIPTURE might be verified, ‡"A Bone of him shall not be broken."

37 And again Another SCRIPTURE says, ‡"They shall look on him whom they pierced."

38 ‡ And after these things, *Joseph, from Arimathea, (being a Disciple of *Jesus, but a concealed one through FEAR of the JEWS,) asked Pilate, that he might take away the BODY of JESUS; and PILATE permitted him. He came therefore, and took away *his Body.

39 And ‡ Nicodemus came also, (he having come to *him by Night at the FIRST,) bringing a Mixture of Myrrh and Aloes, about a hundred Pounds.

40 Then they took the BODY of JESUS, and ‡bound it with Linen cloths, with the AROMATICS, as it is a Custom with the JEWS to embalm.

41 And there was in the PLACE where he was crucified a Garden, and in the GARDEN a new TOMB, in which no one was yet laid.

42 There, therefore, on account of the PREPARATION of the JEWS, Because the TOMB was near, they laid JESUS.

* VATICAN MANUSCRIPT.—38. Joseph. 38. Jesus. 38. his Body. 39. him by Night.

‡ 36. Exod. xii. 46; Num. ix. 12; Psa. xxxiv. 20. ‡ 37. Psa. xxii. 16; Zech. xii. 10; Rev. i. 7. ‡ 38. Matt. xxvii. 57; Mark xv. 42; Luke xxiii. 50. ‡ 39. John iii. 1, 2; vii. 50. ‡ 40. Acts v. 6.

ΚΕΦ. κ'. 20.

1 Τῃ δε μιᾳ των σαββατων Μαρια ἡ Μαγδα-
The and first of the week Mary the Magda-
ληνη ερχεται πρωι, σκοτιας ετι ουσης, εις το
lene comes early, dark yet being, into the
μνημειον· και βλεπει τον λιθον ηρμενον
tomb; and sees the stone having been taken away
εκ του μνημειου, 2 τρεχει ουν και ερχεται
out of the tomb, she runs therefore and comes
προς Σιμωνα Πετρον, και προς τον αλλον μαθη-
to Simon Peter, and to the other disci-
την, ὁν εφιλει ὁ Ιησους, και λεγει αυτοις·
ple, whom loved the Jesus, and says to them;
Ηραν τον κυριον εκ του μνημειου, και ουκ
They took away the lord out of the tomb, and not
οιδαμεν, που εθηκαν αυτον. 3 Εξηλθεν ουν ὁ
we know, where they laid him. Went out then the
Πετρος και ὁ αλλος μαθητης, και ηρχοντο εις
Peter and the other disciple, and they came into
το μνημειον. 4 Ετρεχον δε οἱ δυο ὁμου· και ὁ
the tomb. Ran andthey two together; and the
αλλος μαθητης προεδραμε ταχιον του Πετρου,
other disciple ran before more quickly of the Peter,
και ηλθε πρωτος εις το μνημειον· 5 και παρακυ-
and came first into the tomb; and stooping
ψας βλεπει κειμενα τα οθονια· ου μεντοι εισηλ-
down he sees lying the linen cloths; not however he went
θεν. 6 Ερχεται ουν Σιμων Πετρος ακολουθων
in. Comes then Simon Peter following
αυτῳ, και εισηλθεν εις το μνημειον, και θεωρει
him, and entered into the tomb, and sees
τα οθονια καιμενα, 7 και το σουδαριον ὁ ην επι
the linen cloths lying, and the napkin which was on
της κεφαλης αυτου, ου μετα των οθονιων κει-
the head of him, not with the linen cloths ly-
μενον, αλλα χωρις εντετυλιγμενον εις ἑνα
ing, but apart having been folded up into one
τοπον. 8 Τοτε ουν εισηλθε και ὁ αλλος μαθη-
place. Then therefore went in also the other disci-
της, ὁ ελθων πρωτος εις το μνημειον, και
ple, he coming first into the tomb, and
ειδε, και επιστευσεν. 9 Ουδεπω γαρ ηδεισαν
saw, and believed. Not yet for they knew
την γραφην, ὁτι δει αυτον εκ νεκρων αναστ-
the writing, that it behoved him out of dead ones to have
τηναι. 10 Απηλθον ουν παλιν προς ἑαυτους οἱ
been raised. Went then again to themselves the
μαθηται.
disciples.

CHAPTER XX.

1 ‡ And on the FIRST of the WEEK, Mary of MAGDALA comes early, it being yet dark, † into the TOMB, and sees the STONE, having been removed out of the TOMB.

2 She runs, therefore, and comes to Simon Peter, and to the ‡ OTHER Disciple whom JESUS loved, and says to them, "They have taken away the LORD out of the TOMB and we know not where they have laid him."

3 ‡ PETER then went out, and the OTHER Disciple; and they came into the TOMB.

4 And the TWO ran together; and the OTHER Disciple outran PETER, and came first into the TOMB.

5 And stooping down, he sees ‡ the LINEN CLOTHS lying; however, he went not in.

6 Then Simon Peter * also comes following him, and entered into the TOMB, and beheld the LINEN CLOTHS lying,

7 and ‡ the NAPKIN, which was on his HEAD, not lying with the LINEN CLOTHS, but having been folded up in a separate Place.

8 Then, therefore, THAT OTHER Disciple, who CAME first into the TOMB, also went in, and he saw, and believed [her.]

9 For they did not yet know ‡ the SCRIPTURE, That he must rise from the Dead.

10 Then the DISCIPLES went away by themselves.

* VATICAN MANUSCRIPT.—6. also Simon Peter.

† 1. The very definite manner in which John expresses himself in this narrative, with reference to going (*eis*) into and coming (*ek*) out of the tomb, makes it very probable that this tomb, had two chambers, an *outer* and *inner* one. The body was placed in the inner one, to the door of which the stone was placed. Hence when they entered the first apartment they were said to go into the tomb, though they might not enter or see what was in the inner chamber. Such tombs are not uncommon in the East. That which is now called the "Holy Sepulchre" is one of this class.

‡ 1. Matt. xxviii. 1; Mark xvi. 1, Luke xxiv. 1. ‡ 2. John xiii. 23; xix. 26; xxii. 7 20, 24. ‡ 3. Luke xxiv. 12. ‡ 5. John xix. 40. ‡ 7. John xi. 44. ‡ 9. Psa. xvi. 10; Acts ii. 25—31; xiii. 34, 35.

11 Μαρια δε ειστηκει προς τῳ μνημειῳ κλαι-
Mary but stands by the tomb weep-
ουσα εξω. Ὡς ουν εκλαιε, παρεκυψεν εις το
ing outside. As therefore she wept, she stooped down into the
μνημειον, 12 και θεωρει δυο αγγελους εν λευκοις
tomb, and sees two messengers in white
καθεζομενους, ἑνα προς τῃ κεφαλῃ, και ἑνα
sitting, one at the head, and one
προς τοις ποσιν, ὁπου εκειτο το σωμα του Ιη-
at the feet, where was laid the body of the Je-
σου. 13 Και λεγουσιν αυτῃ εκεινοι· Γυναι, τι
sus. And say to her they; O woman, why
κλαιεις; Λεγει αυτοις· Ὁτι ηραν τον
weepest thou? She says to them; Because they took away the
κυριον μου, και ουκ οιδα που εθηκαν αυτον.
lord of me, and not I know where they laid him.
14 Ταυτα ειπουσα, εστραφη εις τα οπισω, και
These things having said, she turned into the behind, and
θεωρει τον Ιησουν ἑστωτα· και ουκ ῃδει, ὁτι
sees the Jesus standing; and not knew, that
Ιησους εστι. 15 Λεγει αυτῃ ὁ Ιησους· Γυναι, τι
Jesus it is. Says to her the Jesus; O woman, why
κλαιεις; τινα ζητεις; Εκεινη, δοκουσα ὁτι ὁ
weepest thou? whom seekest thou? She, supposing that the
κηπουρος εστι, λεγει αυτῳ· Κυριε, ει συ εβασ-
gardener it is, says to him; O sir, if thou didst
τασας αυτον, ειπε μοι που εθηκας αυτον, καγω
carry off him, tell me where thou didst lay him, and I
αυτον αρω. 16 Λεγει αυτῃ ὁ Ιησους· Μαρια.
him will take away. Says to her the Jesus; Mary.
Στραφεισα εκεινη λεγει αυτῳ· Ῥαββουνι, ὁ
Turning round she says to him; Rabboni, which
λεγεται, διδασκαλε. 17 Λεγει αυτῃ ὁ Ιησους·
means, O teacher. Says to her the Jesus;
Μη μου ἁπτου· ουπω γαρ αναβεβηκα προς τον
Not me touch; not yet for I have gone up to the
πατερα μου· πορευου δε προς τους αδελφους
father of me; go but to the brethren
μου, και ειπε αυτοις· Αναβαινω προς τον πατε-
of me, and say to them; I go up to the father
ρα μου και πατερα ὑμων, και θεον μου και θεον
of me and father of you, even God of me and God
ὑμων. 18 Ερχεται Μαρια ἡ Μαγδαληνη απαγ-
of you. Comes Mary the Magdalene tel-
γελλουσα τοις μαθηταις, ὁτι ἑωρακε τον κυριον,
ling the disciples, that she had seen the lord,
και ταυτα ειπεν αυτῃ.
and these things he said to her.

19 Ουσης ουν οψιας τῃ ἡμερᾳ εκεινῃ τῃ μιᾳ
Being then evening in the day that the first
των σαββατων, και των θυρων κεκλεισμενων,
of the week, and the doors having been shut,
ὁπου ησαν οἱ μαθηται *[συνηγμενοι,] δια τον
where were the disciples [having been assembled,] through the
φοβον των Ιουδαιων, ηλθεν ὁ Ιησους, και εστη
fear of the Jews, came the Jesus, and stood

11 But Mary was standing near the TOMB outside, weeping. As she was weeping, therefore, she stooped down into the TOMB,

12 and sees Two Angels in white sitting, one at the HEAD, and one at the FEET, where the BODY of JESUS had been laid.

13 And they say to her, "Woman, why dost thou weep?" * And she says to them, "Because they took away my LORD, and I know not where they laid him."

14 ‡ Having said these things, she turned BACKWARD, and beholds JESUS standing, and ‡ knew not That it was Jesus.

15 * Jesus says to her, "Woman, why dost thou weep? Whom dost thou seek?" She, supposing that he was the GARDENER, says to him, "Sir, if thou didst carry him off, tell me where thou didst lay him, and I will take Him away."

16 * Jesus says to her, "Mary!" She, having turned, says to him * in Hebrew, "Rabboni!" which signifies, Teacher.

17 * Jesus says to her, "Touch me not; for I have not yet ascended to my FATHER; but go to ‡ my BRETHREN, and tell them, I ascend to my FATHER, and your Father; even my God, and your God."

18 ‡ Mary of MAGDALA comes, telling the DISCIPLES That she had seen the LORD, and he said These things to her.

19 ‡ Then being Evening of that DAY, the FIRST of the * Week, and the DOORS having been closed where the DISCIPLES were, through FEAR of the JEWS, JESUS came into the MIDST,

* VATICAN MANUSCRIPT.—13. And she says. 15. Jesus. 16. Jesus. 16. in Hebrew, Rabboni. 17. Jesus. 19. Week. 19. having been assembled—*omit.*

‡ 14. Matt. xxviii. 9; Mark xvi. 9. ‡ 14. Luke xxiv. 16, 31; John xxi. 4. ‡ 17. Psa. xxii. 22; Matt. xxviii. 10; Rom. viii. 29; Heb. ii. 11. ‡ 18. Matt. xxviii. 10; Luke xxiv. 10. ‡ 19. Mark xvi. 14; Luke xxiv. 36; 1 Cor xv. 5.

εις το μεσον, και λεγει αυτοις· Ειρηνη ὑμιν.
into the midst, and says to them; Peace to you.
20 Και τουτο ειπων, εδειξεν αυτοις τας χειρας
And this having said, he showed to them the hands
και την πλευραν αὑτου. Εχαρησαν ουν οἱ
and the side of himself. Were glad therefore the
μαθηται, ιδοντες τον κυριον. 21 Ειπεν ουν
disciples, seeing the lord. Said then
αυτοις ὁ Ιησους παλιν· Ειρηνη ὑμιν· καθως
to them the Jesus again; Peace to you; as
απεσταλκε με ὁ πατηρ, καγω πεμπω ὑμας.
sent me the father, also I send you.
22 Και τουτο ειπων, ενεφυσησε, και λεγει
And this having said, he breathed on, and says
αυτοις· Λαβετε πνευμα ἁγιον. 23 Αν τινων
to them; Receive you a spirit holy. If of whom
αφητε τας ἁμαρτιας, αφιενται αυτοις· αν
you may forgive the sins, they are forgiven them, if
τινων κρατητε, κεκρατηνται.
of whom you may retain, they have been retained.
24 Θωμας δε, εἱς εκ των δεδωκα, ὁ λεγομενος
Thomas but, one of the twelve, he being called
Διδυμος, ουκ ην μετ' αυτων ὁτε ηλθεν ὁ Ιη-
a twin, not was with them when came the Je-
σους. 25 Ελεγον ουν αυτῳ οἱ αλλοι μαθηται·
sus. Said then to him the other disciples;
Ἑωρακαμεν τον κυριον. Ὁ δε ειπεν αυτοις·
We have seen the lord. He but said to them;
Εαν μη ιδω εν ταις χερσιν αυτου τον τυπον
If not I may see in the hands of him the mark
των ἡλων, και βαλω τον δακτυλον μου εις τον
of the nails, and may put the finger of me into the
τυπον των ἡλων, και βαλω την χειρα μου εις
mark of the nails, and may put the hand of me into
την πλευραν αυτου, ου μη πιστευσω.
the side of him, not not I will believe.
26 Και μεθ' ἡμερας οκτω παλιν ησαν εσω οἱ
And after days eight again were within the
μαθηται αυτου, και Θωμας μετ' αυτων. Ερχε-
disciples of him, and Thomas with them. Comes
ται ὁ Ιησους, των θυρων κεκλεισμενων, και
the Jesus, the doors having been shut, and
εστη εις το μεσον, και ειπεν· Ειρηνη ὑμιν.
stood into the midst, and said; Peace to you.
27 Ειτα λεγει τῳ Θωμᾳ· Φερε τον δακτυλον σου
Afterwards he says to the Thomas; Bring the finger of thee
ὡδε, και ιδε τας χειρας μου, και φερε την
here, and see the hands of me, and bring the
χειρα σου, και βαλε εις την πλευραν μου· και
hand of thee, and put into the side of me; and
μη γινου απιστος, αλλα πιστος. 28 Απεκριθη
not be thou unbelieving, but believing. Answered
Θωμας και ειπεν αυτῳ· Ὁ κυριος μου και ὁ θεος
Thomas and said to him; The lord of me and the God
μου. 29 Λεγει αυτῳ ὁ Ιησους· Ὁτι ἑωρακας με,
of me. Says to him the Jesus; Because thou hast seen me,

and stood, and says to them, "Peace be with you!"

20 And having said this, he showed them * his HANDS and his SIDE. The DISCIPLES, therefore, ‡ rejoiced, seeing the LORD.

21 Then JESUS said to them again, "Peace be with you; ‡ as the FATHER has sent me, I also send you."

22 And having said this, he breathed on and says to them, "Receive the Holy Spirit.

23 ‡ If the SINS * of any one you may forgive, they are forgiven them; if those * of any you may retain, they have been retained."

24 But Thomas, THAT one of the TWELVE, ‡ BEING CALLED Didymus, was not with them, when * Jesus came.

25 The OTHER Disciples, therefore, said to him, "We have seen the LORD." But HE said to them, "If I do not see in his HANDS the IMPRESSION of the NAILS, and put my FINGER into the IMPRESSION of the NAILS, and put * My HAND into his SIDE, I will by no means believe."

26 And after eight Days his DISCIPLES were again within, and Thomas with them. The DOORS having been closed, JESUS comes into the MIDST, and stood, and said, "Peace be with you!"

27 Afterwards he says to THOMAS, "Reach here thy FINGER, and behold my HANDS, and ‡ reach here thy HAND, and put it into my SIDE; and be not unbelieving, but believing."

28 Thomas answered and said to him, "My LORD and my GOD!"

29 JESUS says to him, "Because thou hast seen

* VATICAN MANUSCRIPT.—20. both the HANDS and the SIDE. 23. of any one. 24. Jesus. 25. My HAND.

‡ 20. John xvi. 22. ‡ 21. Matt xxviii. 18; John xvii. 17—19. ‡ 23. Matt. x, 19: xviii. 18. ‡ 24. John xi. 16. ‡ 27. 1 John i. 1.

πεπιστευκας· μακαριοι οἱ μη ἰδοντες, και πισ-
thou hast believed; blessed they not having seen, and having
τευσαντες. 30 Πολλα μεν ουν και αλλα σημεια
believed. Many indeed then and other signs
εποιησεν ὁ Ιησους ενωπιον των μαθητων αὐτου,
did the Jesus in presence of the disciples of him,
ἁ ουκ εστι γεγραμμενα εν τῳ βιβλιῳ τουτῳ.
which not it is having been written in the book this.
31 Ταυτα δε γεγραπται, ἱνα πιστευσητε, ὁτι
These things but have been written, that you may believe, that
Ιησους εστιν ὁ Χριστος, ὁ υἱος του θεου, και
Jesus is the Anointed, the son of the God, and
ἱνα πιστευοντες ζωην εχητε εν τῳ ονοματι
that believing life you may have in the name
αυτου.
of him.

ΚΕΦ. κα'. 21.

1 Μετα ταυτα εφανερωσεν ἑαυτον παλιν ὁ
After these things manifested himself again the
Ιησους τοις μαθηταις επι της θαλασσης της
Jesus to the disciples on the sea of the
Τιβεριαδος. Εφανερωσε δε οὑτως. 2 Ησαν
Tiberias. He manifested and thus. Were
ὁμου Σιμων Πετρος, και Θωμας ὁ λεγομενος
together Simon Peter, and Thomas he being called
Διδυμος, και Ναθαναηλ ὁ απο Κανα της Γαλι-
a twin, and Nathanael he from Cana of the Gali-
λαιας, και οἱ του Ζεβεδαιου, και αλλοι εκ των
lee, and they of the Zebedee, and others of the
μαθητων αυτου δυο. 3 Λεγει αυτοις Σιμων Πε-
disciples of him two. Says to them Simon Pe-
τρος· Ὑπαγω ἁλιευειν. Λεγουσιν αυτῳ· Ερ-
ter; I am going to fish. They say to him; Are
χομεθα και ἡμεις συν σοι. Εξηλθον, και ενε-
going also we with thee. They went out, and en-
βησαν εις το πλοιον *[ευθυς,] και εν εκεινῃ
tered into the ship [immediately,] and in that
τῃ νυκτι επιασαν ουδεν. 4 Πρωιας δε ηδη
the night they caught nothing. Morning but now
γενομενης, εστη ὁ Ιησους εις τον αιγιαλον· ου
being come, stood the Jesus on the shore; not
μεντοι ῃδεισαν οἱ μαθηται, ὁτι Ιησους εστι.
however knew the disciples, that Jesus it is.
5 Λεγει ουν αυτοις ὁ Ιησους· Παιδια, μη τι
Says therefore to them the Jesus; Children, not any
προσφαγιον εχετε; Απεκριθησαν αυτῳ· Ου.
food have you? They answered him; No.
6 Ὁ δε ειπεν αυτοις· Βαλετε εις τα δεξια μερη
He and said to them; Cast you into the right parts
του πλοιου το δικτυον, και εὑρησετε. Εβαλον
of the ship the net, and you will find. They cast
ουν, και ουκετι αυτο ἑλκυσαι ισχυσαν απο του
then, and no longer it to draw were able from the
πληθους των ιχθυων. 7 Λεγει ουν ὁ μαθητης
multitude of the fishes. Says therefore the disciple
εκεινος ὁν ηγαπα ὁ Ιησους, τῳ Πετρῳ· Ὁ
that whom loved the Jesus, to the Peter; The

me, thou hast believed: ‡ happy those who see not and believe!"

30 ‡ Then, indeed, many Other Signs JESUS performed in the presence of * the DISCIPLES, which have not been written in this BOOK.

31 ‡ But these have been written, that you may believe That JESUS is the MESSIAH, the SON of GOD; and that, believing, you may have Life in his NAME.

CHAPTER XXI.

1 After these things * Jesus manifested himself again to the DISCIPLES, at the LAKE of TIBERIAS; and in this manner he appeared.

2 Simon Peter, and THAT Thomas CALLED Didymus, and ‡ THAT Nathanael of Cana in GALILEE, and ‡ the SONS of Zebedee, and two others of his DISCIPLES, were together.

3 Simon Peter says to them, "I am going a fishing." They say to him, "We also go with thee." They went out, and entered into the BOAT, and during That NIGHT they caught nothing.

4 But now Morning being come, * Jesus stood on the SHORE. The DISCIPLES, however, ‡ knew not That it was Jesus.

5 Then ‡ * Jesus says to them, "Children, have you any food?" They answered him, "No."

6 And HE said to them, ‡ "Throw the NET on the RIGHT side of the BOAT, and you will find." Then they threw it, and were no longer able to draw it, from the MULTITUDE of FISHES.

7 ‡ That DISCIPLE therefore, whom Jesus loved, says to PETER, "It is the

* VATICAN MANUSCRIPT.—30. the DISCIPLES. 1. Jesus. 3. immediately—omit. 4. Jesus. 5. Jesus.

‡ 29. 2 Cor. v. 7; 1 Pet. i. 8. ‡ 30. John xxi. 25. ‡ 31. Luke i. 4. ‡ 31. John iii. 15, 16; v. 24; 1 Pet. i. 9. ‡ 2. John i. 45. ‡ 2. Matt. iv. 21. ‡ 4. John xx. 14. ‡ 5. Luke xxiv. 41. ‡ 6. Luke v. 4, 6, 7. ‡ 7. John xiii. 23; xx. 2.

κυριος εστι· Σιμων ουν Πετρος, ακουσας ὁτι ὁ
lord it is. Simon then Peter, having heard that the
κυριος εστι, τον επενδυτην διεζωσατο· ην γαρ
Lord it is, the upper garment he girded, he was for
γυμνος· και εβαλεν ἑαυτον εις την θαλασσαν
naked; and threw himself into the sea.
8 Οἱ δε αλλοι μαθηται τῳ πλοιαριῳ ηλθον (ου
The but other disciples by the little ship came (not
γαρ ησαν μακραν απο της γης, αλλ' ὡς απο
for they were far from the land, but about from
πηχων διακοσιων,) συροντες το δικτυον των
cubits two hundred,) dragging the net of the
ιχθυων. 9 Ὡς ουν απεβησαν εις την γην, βλε-
fishes. When therefore they went up to the land, they
πουσιν ανθρακιαν κειμενην, και οψαριον επικει-
see a fire of coals lying, and a fish lying
μενον, και αρτον. 10 Λεγει αυτοις ὁ Ιησους·
on, and bread. Says to them the Jesus;
Ενεγκατε απο των οψαριων, ὡν επιασατε νυν.
Bring you from the fishes, which you caught just now.
11 Ανεβη Σιμων Πετρος, και εἱλκυσε το δικτυον
Went up Simon Peter, and drew the net
επι της γης, μεστον ιχθυων μεγαλων ἑκατον
to the land, full of fishes great a hundred
πεντηκοντατριων· και τοσουτων οντων, ουκ
fifty-three; and so many being, not
εσχισθη το δικτυον. 12 Λεγει αυτοις ὁ Ιησους·
was torn the net. Says to them the Jesus,
Δευτε, αριστησατε. Ουδεις *[δε] ετολμα
Come, breakfast you. No one [and] presumed
των μαθητων εξετασαι αυτον· Συ τις ει;
of the disciples to ask him, Thou who art?
ειδοτες, ὁτι ὁ κυριος εστιν. 13 Ερχεται ὁ Ιη-
knowing, that the Lord it is. Comes the Je-
σους, και λαμβανει τον αρτον, και διδωσιν
sus, and takes the bread, and gives
αυτοις, και το οψαριον ὁμοιως. 14 Τουτο ηδη
to them, and the fish in like manner This already
τριτον εφανερωθη ὁ Ιησους τοις μαθηταις αυτου,
third was manifested the Jesus to the disciples of himself,
εγερθεις εκ νεκρων.
having been raised out of dead ones
15 Ὁτε ουν ηριστησαν, λεγει τῳ Σιμωνι
When therefore they had breakfasted, says to the Simon
Πετρῳ ὁ Ιησους· Σιμων Ιωνα, αγαπᾳς με πλειον
Peter the Jesus; Simon of Jona, lovest thou me more
τουτων; Λεγει αυτῳ· Ναι, κυριε, συ οιδας, ὁτι
of these? He says to him; Yes, O lord, thou knowest, that
φιλω σε. Λεγει αυτῳ· Βοσκε τα αρνια μου.
I dearly love thee. He says to him; Feed the lambs of me.
16 Λεγει αυτῳ παλιν δευτερον· Σιμων Ιωνα,
He says to him again a second time; Simon of Jona,
αγαπᾳς με; Λεγει αυτῳ· Ναι, κυριε, συ οιδας,
lovest thou me? He says to him; Yes. O lord, thou knowest,
ὁτι φιλω σε· Λεγει αυτῳ· Ποιμαινε τα προ-
that I dearly love thee; He says to him; Tend thou the sheep

LORD." Then Simon Peter having heard that it was the LORD, girded on his UPPER GARMENT, (for he was † naked,) and threw himself into the LAKE.

8 But the OTHER Disciples came by the BOAT; (for they were not far from the LAND, but about two hundred Cubits off,) dragging the NET with the FISHES.

9 When, therefore, they went out to the LAND, they see a Fire of coals lying, and a Fish lying on it, and Bread.

10 * Jesus says to them, "Bring of the FISHES which you just now caught."

11 * Simon Peter went on board and drew the NET to the LAND, full of great Fishes, a hundred and fifty-three; and though there were so many, the NET was not torn.

12 * Jesus says to them, ‡ "Come and breakfast." No one of the DISCIPLES presumed to ask him, "Who art thou?"

13 * Jesus comes, and takes the BREAD, and gives to them, and the FISH in like manner.

14 This ‡ third time now was * Jesus manifested to * the DISCIPLES, having been raised from the Dead.

15 When, therefore, they had breakfasted, JESUS says to SIMON Peter, "Simon, son of Jonas, lovest thou me more than these?" He says to him, "Yes, Lord; thou knowest That I affectionately love thee." He says to him, "Feed my LAMBS."

16 He says to him again, a second time, "Simon, son of Jonas, lovest thou me?" He says to him, "Yes, Lord; thou knowest That I affectionately love thee."

* VATICAN MANUSCRIPT.—10. Jesus. 11. Then Simon Peter. 12. Jesus. 12. and—omit. 13. Jesus. 14. Jesus. 14. the DISCIPLES.

† 7. So the Jews called those who were clothed in their under garments only.—*Newcome*

‡ 12. Acts x. 41. ‡ 14. See John xx. 19, 26.

βατα μου. [17]Λεγει αυτῳ το τριτον· Σιμων
of me. He says to him the third; Simon
Ιωνα, φιλεις με; Ελυπηθη ὁ Πετρος, ὁτι
of Jonas, dearly lovest thou me? Was grieved the Peter, because
ειπεν αυτῳ το τριτον, Φιλεις με; και ειπεν
he said to him the third, Dearly lovest thou me? and he said
*[αυτῳ·] Κυριε, συ παντα οιδας· συ γινωσκεις,
[to him;] O lord, thou all things knowest; thou knowest,
ὁτι φιλω σε· Λεγει αυτῳ ὁ Ιησους· Βοσκε
that I dearly love thee; Says to him the Jesus; Feed
τα προβατα μου. [18]Αμην αμην λεγω σοι, ὁτε
the sheep of me. Indeed indeed I say to thee, when
ης νεωτερος, εζωννυες σεαυτον, και περιεπατεις
thou wast younger, thou didst gird thyself, and didst walk
ὁπου ηθελες· ὁταν δε γηρασῃς, εκτενεις
where thou didst wish; when but thou art old, thou wilt stretch out
τας χειρας σου, και αλλος σε ζωσει, και
the hands of thee, and another thee will gird, and
οισει ὁπου ου θελεις. [19]Τουτο δε ειπε, ση-
will carry where not thou wishest. This now he said, sig-
μαινων, ποιῳ θανατῳ δοξασει τον θεον. Και
nifying, by what death he will glorify the God. And
τουτο ειπων, λεγει αυτῳ· ακολουθει μοι.
this having said, he says to him; Follow me.
[20]Επιστραφεις *[δε] ὁ Πετρος βλεπει τον
Having turned about [and] the Peter sees the
μαθητην, ὁν ηγαπα ὁ Ιησους, ακολουθουντα·
disciple, whom loved the Jesus, following;
(ὁς και ανεπεσεν εν τῳ δειπνῳ επι το στηθος
(who also reclined at the supper on the breast
αυτου, και ειπε· Κυριε, τις εστιν ὁ παραδιδους
of him, and said; O lord, who is he betraying
σε;) [21]Τουτον ιδων ὁ Πετρος λεγει τῳ Ιησου·
thee?) Him seeing the Peter says to the Jesus;
Κυριε, ουτος δε τι; [22]Λεγει αυτῳ ὁ Ιησους·
O lord, this and what? Says to him the Jesus;
Εαν αυτον θελω μενειν ἑως ερχομαι, τι προς
If him I wish to abide till I come, what to
σε; συ ακολουθει μοι. [23]Εξηλθεν ουν ὁ λογος
thee? thou follow me. Went out therefore the word
ουτος εις τους αδελφους, ὁτι ὁ μαθητης εκεινος
this among the brethren, that the disciple that
ουκ αποθνησκει. Και ουκ ειπεν αυτῳ ὁ Ιησους,
not dies. And not said to him the Jesus,
ὁτι ουκ αποθνησκει· αλλ'· Εαν αυτον θελω
that not he dies; but; If him I wish
μενειν ἑως ερχομαι, τι προς σε; [24]Ουτος εστιν
to abide till I come, what to thee? This is

He says to him, ‡ "Tend my SHEEP.
17 He says to him the THIRD time, "Simon, son of Jonas, dost thou affectionately love me?" Peter was grieved, Because he said to him the THIRD time, "Dost thou affectionately love me?" And he said, "Lord, thou knowest All things; ‡ thou knowest That I affectionately love thee." * Jesus says to him, "Feed my SHEEP.
18 ‡ Indeed, I truly say to thee, When thou wast younger, thou didst gird thyself, and walk where thou didst wish; but when, thou art old, † thou wilt extend thy HANDS, and another will gird thee, and carry thee where thou dost not wish."
19 Now this he said, intimating, by † What Death he would glorify GOD. And having said this, he says to him, "Follow me."
20 PETER, having turned about, sees the DISCIPLE, following, ‡ whom JESUS loved; (who also reclined at the SUPPER on his BREAST, and said, "Lord, who is HE BETRAYING thee?"
21 * PETER, therefore, seeing him, says to JESUS, "Lord, and what of this man?"
22 JESUS says to him, "If I wish him to abide ‡ till I come, what is it to thee? follow thou me."
23 * This REPORT, therefore, went out among the BRETHREN, That that DISCIPLE would not die; * but JESUS did not say to him, "That he shall not die;" but, "If I wish him to abide till I come, what is it to thee?"

* VATICAN MANUSCRIPT.—17. to him—*omit.* 17. Jesus. 20. and—*omit.* 21. PETER therefore. 23. This. 23. but.

† 18. Wetstein observes, that it was a custom in Rome, to put the necks of those who were to be crucified, into a yoke, and *to stretch out their hands*, and fasten them to the end of it, and having thus led them through the city, they were carried out to be crucified.—*Clarke.*
† 19. Many ancient writers say that Peter was crucified with his head downwards, a short time before the destruction of Jerusalem.

‡ 16. Acts xx. 28; Heb. xiii. 20; 1 Pet. ii. 25; v. 2, 4. ‡ 17. John ii. 24, 25; xvi. 30. ‡ 18. John xiii. 36; Acts xii. 3, 4. ‡ 19. 2 Pet. i. 14. ‡ 20. John xiii. 23, 25; xx. 2. ‡ 23. Matt. xvi. 27, 28; xxv. 31; 1 Cor. iv. 5; xi. 26; Rev. ii. 25; iii. 11; xxii. 7, 20.

ὁ μαθητης, ὁ μαρτυρων περι τουτων, και
the disciple, he testifying concerning these things, and
γραψας ταυτα· και οιδαμεν, ὁτι αληθης
having written these things; and we know, that true
εστιν ἡ μαρτυρια αυτου. 25 Εστι δε και αλλα
is the testimony of him. Is and also other
πολλα ὁσα εποιησεν ὁ Ιησους, ἁτινα εαν γρα-
many things did the Jesus, which if they should
φηται καθ' ἑν, ουδε αυτον οιμαι τον κοσμον
be written every one, not even him I suppose the world
χωρησαι τα γραφομενα βιβλια.
to contain the being written books.

24 This is THAT DISCIPLE, who *both TESTIFIES of these things and WROTE these things; and ‡ we know That * His TESTIMONY is true.
25 ‡And there are many other things which JESUS performed, which, if they should be written, every one, † I suppose that not even the WORLD itself would contain the WRITTEN BOOKS.

* ACCORDING TO JOHN.

VATICAN MANUSCRIPT.—24. both. 24. His. *Subscription*—ACCORDING TO JOHN.

† 25. This is a very strong eastern expression, to represent the great number of miracles which Jesus wrought. But however strong and strange this expression may seem to us of the western world, we find sacred and other authors using hyperboles of the like kind and signification; some instances of which it may be proper to lay before the reader. In Num. xiii. 33, the spies, who returned from the search of the land of Canaan, say they saw giants there of such a prodigious size, that they were "in their own sight as grasshoppers." In Deut. i. 28, cities with high walls round about them are said to be "walled up to heaven." In Dan. iv. 11, mention is made of a tree, whereof "the height reached unto the heaven," and the sight thereof unto the end of all the earth;" and the author of Ecclesiasticus, in chap. xlvii. 15, speaking of Solomon's wisdom, says, "Thy soul covered the whole earth, and thou filledst it with parables;" as the world is there said to be filled with Solomon's parables, so here, by one degree more of hyperbole, it is said that the world would not contain all the books which should be written concerning Jesus' miracles, if the particular account of every one of them were given.—*Pearce.*

‡ 24. John xix. 35; 3 John 12. ‡ 25. John xx. 30.

ΠΡΑΞΕΙΣ ΤΩΝ ΑΠΟΣΤΟΛΩΝ.
ACTS OF THE APOSTLES.

* ACTS OF APOSTLES.

ΚΕΦ. α΄. 1.

1 Τον μεν πρωτον λογον εποιησαμεν περι
The indeed first account I made concerning
παντων, ω Θεοφιλε, ὡν ηρξατο ὁ Ιησους
all things, O Theophilus, which began the Jesus
ποιειν τε και διδασκειν, 2 αχρι ης ἡμερας, εν-
to do and also to teach, even to which day, hav-
τειλαμενος τοις αποστολοις, δια πνευματος
ing given charge to the apostles, through spirit
ἁγιου οὑς εξελεξατο, ανεληφθη. 3 Οἱς και
holy whom he chose, he was taken up. To whom also
παρεστησεν ἑαυτον ζωντα μετα το παθειν
he presented himself living after the to suffer
αυτον, εν πολλοις τεκμηριοις, δι' ἡμερων τεσ-
him, in many clear proofs, through days forty
σαρακοντα οπτανομενος αυτοις, και λεγων τα
being seen by them, and saying the things
περι της βασιλειας του θεου. 4 Και συναλι-
concerning the kingdom of the God. And assem-
ζομενος παρηγγειλεν αυτοις, απο Ἱεροσολυμων
bling them he commanded them, from Jerusalem
μη χωριζεσθαι, αλλα περιμενειν την επαγγελιαν
not to depart, but to wait for the promise
του πατρος, ην ηκουσατε μου· 5 ὁτι Ιωαννης
of the father, which you heard from me; that John
μεν εβαπτισεν ὑδατι, ὑμεις δε βαπτισθησεσθε
indeed dipped in water, you but shall be dipped
εν πνευματι ἁγιῳ, ου μετα πολλας ταυτας ἡμε-
in spirit holy, not after many these days.
ρας. 6 Οἱ μεν ουν συνελθοντες επηρωτων
They indeed therefore having come together, asked
αυτον· λεγοντες· Κυριε, ει εν τῳ χρονῳ τουτῳ
him; saying; O lord, if in the time this
αποκαθιστανεις την βασιλειαν τῳ Ισραηλ;
thou restorest the kingdom to the Israel?
7 Ειπε δε προς αυτους· Ουχ ὑμων εστι γνωναι
He said and to them; Not for you it is to know
χρονους η καιρους, οὑς ὁ πατηρ εθετο εν τῃ
times or seasons, which the father placed in the
ιδιᾳ εξουσιᾳ. 8 Αλλα ληψεσθε δυναμιν επελ-
own authority. But you shall receive power hav-
θοντες του ἁγιου πνευματος εφ' ὑμας· και
ing come the holy spirit upon you; and
εσεσθε μοι μαρτυρες εν τε Ἱερουσαλημ, και
you shall be to me witnesses in both Jerusalem, and
εν πασῃ τῃ Ιουδαιᾳ και Σαμαρειᾳ, και ἑως εσχα-
in all the Judea and in Samaria, and even to farthest

CHAPTER I.

1 The FORMER History[1] compiled, ‡ O Theophilus, concerning all things which * Jesus began both to do and to teach,

2 ‡ even to the Day in which, ‡ having given commandment, through the holy Spirit, to the APOSTLES whom he had chosen, he was taken up;

3 ‡ to whom also he presented himself living, after his SUFFERING, by Many Infallible proofs; being seen of them forty Days, and speaking the THINGS concerning the KINGDOM of GOD.

4 ‡ And assembling them, he charged them "not to depart from Jerusalem, but to wait for the PROMISE of the FATHER, ‡ which you heard from me;

5 ‡ that John, indeed, immersed in Water, but you will be immersed in holy Spirit, after a few Days."

6 THEY, therefore, having come together, asked him, saying, "Lord, wilt thou, at this TIME, ‡ restore the KINGDOM to ISRAEL?"

7 * Then he said to them, "It is not for you to know the Times or Seasons, which the FATHER appointed by his OWN Authority.

8 But you shall receive Power by the HOLY Spirit coming upon you; and ‡ you shall be My Witnesses both in Jerusalem, and in All JUDEA, and in Samaria, and even to the

* VATICAN MANUSCRIPT.—*Title*—ACTS OF APOSTLES. 1. Jesus. 7. Then he said.

‡ 1. Luke i. 31. ‡ 2. Mark xvi. 19; Luke xxiv. 51; ver. 9; 1 Tim. iii. 16. ‡ 2. Matt. xxviii. 19; Mark xvi. 15; John xx. 21; Acts x. 41, 42. ‡ 3. Mark xvi. 14; Luke xxiv. 36; John xx. 19, 26; xxi. 1, 14; 1 Cor. xv. 5. ‡ 4. Luke xxiv. 43, 49. ‡ 4. Luke xxiv. 49; John xiv. 16, 26, 27; xv. 26; xvi. 7; Acts ii. 33. ‡ 5. Matt. iii. 11; Acts xi. 16; xix. 4. ‡ 6. Isa. i. 26; Amos ix. 11; Micah iv. 8; Acts iii. 21. ‡ 8. Luke xxiv. 48; John xv. 27; Acts ii. 32.

του της γης. [9] Και ταυτα ειπων, βλεποντων
art of the land. And these things having said, beholding
αυτων επηρθη· και νεφελη ὑπελαβεν αυτον απο
of them he was lifted up; and a cloud withdrew him from
των οφθαλμων αυτων. [10] Και ὡς ατενιζοντες
the eyes of them. And as fixedly gazing
ησαν εις τον ουρανον, πορευομενου αυτου, και
they were into the heaven, going away of him, and
ιδου, ανδρες δυο παρειστηκεισαν αυτοις εν εσθη-
lo, men two were standing by them in rai-
τι λευκῃ, [11] οἱ και ειπον· Ανδρες Γαλιλαιοι, τι
ment white, they and said; Men of Galilee, why
εστηκατε εμβλεποντες εις τον ουρανον; ουτος
stand you looking into the heaven? this
ὁ Ιησους, ὁ αναληφθεις αφ' ὑμων εις τον ουρα-
the Jesus, he being taken up from you into the heaven,
νον, οὑτως ελευσεται, ὁν τροπον εθεασασθε
thus will come, which manner you saw
αυτον πορευομενον εις τον ουρανον. [12] Τοτε
him going into the heaven. Then
ὑπεστρεψαν εις Ἱερουσαλημ απο ορους του
they returned into Jerusalem from a mountain that
καλουμενου Ελαιωνος, ὁ εστιν εγγυς Ἱερουσα-
being called of olive trees, which is near Jerusalem.
λημ, σαββατου εχον ὁδον. [13] Και ὁτε εισηλ-
a sabbath being distant journey. And when they came
θον, ανεβησαν εις το ὑπερῳον, οὑ ησαν κατα-
into, they went up into the upper room, where were re-
μενοντες, ὁ, τε Πετρος και Ιακωβος, και Ιωαν-
maining, the, both Peter and James, and John
νης και Ανδρεας, Φιλιππος και Θωμας,
and Andrew, Philip and Thomas,
Βαρθολομαιος και Ματθαιος, Ιακωβου Αλφαι-
Bartholomew and Matthew, James of Alphe-
ου και Σιμων ὁ ζηλωτης και Ιουδας Ιακωβου.
us also Simon the zealot and Judas of James.
[14] Ουτοι παντες ησαν προσκαρτερουντες ὁμοθυ-
These all were being constantly engaged with one
μαδον τῃ προσευχῃ, συν γυναιξι, και Μαριᾳ τῃ
mind in the prayer, with women, and Mary the
μητρι του Ιησου, και συν τοις αδελφοις αυτου.
mother of the Jesus, and with the brother of him.
[15] Και εν ταις ἡμεραις ταυταις αναστας Πε-
And in the days these having stood up Pe-
τρος εν μεσῳ των μαθητων, ειπεν· (ην τε
ter in middle of the disciples, he said; (was and
οχλος ονοματων, επι το αυτο ὡς ἑκατον εικοσιν·)
a crowd of names, in the same about a hundred twenty;)
[16] Ανδρες αδελφοι, εδει πληρωθηναι την
Men brethren, it was necessary to be fulfilled the
γραφην ταυτην, ην προειπε το πνευμα το ἁγιον
writing this, which spoke before the spirit the holy
δια στοματος Δαυιδ, περι Ιουδα του γενομενου
through mouth of David, about Judas that having become

remotest parts of the EARTH."

9 And having said These things, as they were looking on he was lifted up; and a Cloud carried him away from their SIGHT.

10 And while they were fixedly gazing towards the HEAVENS, as he was going up, behold, two Men were standing by them in white Raiment;

11 who also said, "Men of Galilee, why do you stand looking towards the HEAVENS? This JESUS, who is taken up from you into the HEAVENS, ‡shall so come in the manner in which you saw him go into the HEAVENS."

12 ‡Then they returned to Jerusalem, from THAT Mountain CALLED the Mount of Olives, which is near Jerusalem, being distant a Sabbath-day's Journey.

13 And when they came into the city, they went up into the UPPER ROOM, where were remaining both PETER and * John, and James and Andrew, Philip and Thomas, Bartholomew and Matthew, James the son of Alpheus, and Simon the ZEALOT, and Judas the brother of James.

14 All these were constantly engaged with one mind in PRAYER, with the Women, and with Mary the MOTHER of *Jesus, and with his BROTHERS.

15 And in these DAYS, Peter standing up in the Midst of the *BRETHREN, (the Number of Persons assembled were about a hundred and twenty,) said,

16 "Brethren, it was necessary for * the SCRIPTURE to be fulfilled, ‡which the HOLY SPIRIT, through the mouth of David, foretold concerning THAT Judas ‡who BECAME a Guide

* VATICAN MANUSCRIPT.—13. John, and James and Andrew. 14. Jesus. 15. BRETHREN, said. 16. The SCRIPTURE.

‡ 11. Dan. vii. 13; Matt. xxiv. 30; Mark xiii. 26; Luke xxi. 27; John xiv. 3; 1 Thess. i. 10; iv. 16; 2 Thess. i. 10; Rev. i. 7. ‡ 12. Luke xxiv. 52. ‡ 16. Psa. xli. 9; John xiii. 18. ‡ 16. Luke xxii. 47; John xviii. 3.

ὁδηγου τοις συλλαβουσι τον Ιησουν· 17 ὁτι
a guide to those having seized the Jesus; because
κατηριθμημενος ην εν ἡμιν, και ελαχε τον
having been numbered he was among us, and obtained the
κληρον της κιακονιας ταυτης. 18 Ουτος μεν
lot of the service this. This indeed
ουν εκτησατο χωριον εκ μισθου της αδικιας·
therefore bought a field out of a reward of the wickedness,
και πρηνης γενομενος, ελακησε μεσος, και εξε-
and head-foremost having fallen, he burst in middle, and were
χυθη παντα τα σπλαγχνα αυτου· 19 και γνωσ-
poured out all the bowels of him; and known
τον εγενετο πασι τοις κατοικουσιν Ἱερουσαλημ,
became to all those dwelling in Jerusalem,
ὡστε κληθηναι το χωριον εκεινο τη ιδιᾳ δια-
so as to be called the field that in the own lan-
λεκτῳ αυτων, Ακελδαμα, τουτ᾽ εστι, χωριον
guage of them, Aceldama, this is, a field
αἱματος. 20 Γεγραπται γαρ εν βιβλῳ ψαλμων·
of blood. It is written for in book of Psalms:
Γενηθητω ἡ επαυλις αυτου ερημος, και μη εστω
Let be the dwelling of him desolate, and not let be
ὁ κατοικων εν αυτῃ· και· Την επισκοπην αυτου
the dwelling in her; and, The charge of him
λαβοι ἑτερος. 21 Δει ουν των συνελθον-
let take another. It is necessary therefore of those having associ-
των ἡμιν ανδρων εν παντι χρονῳ, εν ᾡ εισ-
ated with us men in all time, in which went
ηλθε και εξηλθεν εφ᾽ ἡμας ὁ κυριος Ιησους,
in and went out among us the lord Jesus,
22 αρξαμενος απο του βαπτισματος Ιωαννου ἑως
beginning from the dipping of John to
της ἡμερας ης ανεληφθη αφ᾽ ἡμων, μαρτυρα της
the day which he was taken up from us, a witness of the
αναστασεως αυτου γενεσθαι συν ἡμιν ἑνα του-
resurrection of him to become with us one of
των. 23 Και εστησαν δυο, Ιωσηφ τον καλου-
these. And they set forth two, Joseph that being
μενον Βαρσαβαν, ὁς επεκληθη Ιουστος, και
called Barsabas, who was surnamed Justus, and
Ματθιαν. 24 Και προσευξαμενοι ειπον· Συ,
Matthias. And praying they said; Thou,
κυριε, καρδιογνωστα παντων, αναδειξον ὁν εξε-
O lord, heart-knower of all, show which thou
λεξω εκ τουτων των δυο ἑνα, 25 λαβειν τον
didst select out of these the two one, to take the
κληρον της διακονιας ταυτης και αποστολης,
lot of the service this and apostleship,
εξ ης παρεβη Ιουδας, πορευθηναι εις τον τοπον
from which stepped aside Judas, to go into the place
τον ιδιον. 26 Και εδωκαν κληρους αυτων· και
the own. And they gave lots of them; and

to THOSE who APPREHENDED * Jesus.

17 For ‡ he was numbered among us, and obtained the LOT of this SERVICE."

18 (‡ This man, therefore, purchased a Field with the WAGES of the WICKEDNESS, and falling head foremost, he burst in the middle, and All his BOWELS were poured out;

19 and it was known to all those DWELLING at Jerusalem; so that that FIELD is called in their OWN Language, * Aceldamach, which is, a Field of Blood.)

20 "For it is written in the Book of Psalms, ‡ 'Let 'his DWELLING be deso-'late, and let no one 'DWELL in it;' and ‡ 'Let 'another take his OF-'FICE.'

21 It is necessary, therefore, that from those MEN HAVING ASSOCIATED with us all the Time in which the LORD Jesus went in and out among us,

22 ‡ beginning from the IMMERSION of John, to the DAY on which he was taken up from us, one of these BECOME with us a Witness of his RESURRECTION."

23 And they set forth two, THAT Joseph, CALLED ‡* Barsabbas, who was surnamed Justus, and Matthias.

24 And praying, they said, "Thou, Lord, ‡ who knowest the hearts of all, show which one of These TWO thou didst select

25 to take * the PLACE of this SERVICE and Apostleship, from which Judas stepped aside, to go into his OWN PLACE."

26 And they gave * the Lots to them; and the LOT

* VATICAN MANUSCRIPT.—16. Jesus. 19. Aceldamach. 23. Barsabbas. 25. the PLACE of this. 26. the Lots to them; and.

‡ 17. Matt. x. 4; Luke vi. 16. ‡ 18. Matt. xxvii. 5, 7, 8. ‡ 20. Psa. lxix. 25. ‡ 20. Psa. cix. 8. ‡ 22. John xv. 27; ver. 8; Acts iv. 33. ‡ 23. Acts xv. 22. ‡ 24. 1 Sam. xvi. 7; 1 Chron. xxviii. 9; xxix. 17; Jer. xi. 20; xvii. 10; Acts xv. 8; Rev. ii. 23.

επεσεν ὁ κληρος επι Ματθιαν, και συγκατεψη-
fell the lot on Matthias, and he was counted
φισθη μετα των ἑνδεκα αποστολων.
with the eleven apostles.

ΚΕΦ. β'. 2.

1 Και εν τῳ συμπληρουσθαι την ἡμεραν της
And in the to be fully come the day of the
πεντηκοστης, ησαν ἁπαντες ὁμοθυμαδον επι το
Pentecost, were all with one mind in the
αυτο. 2 Και εγενετο αφνω εκ του ουρανου
same. And were suddenly from the heaven
ηχος ὡσπερ φερομενης πνοης βιαιας, και επλη-
a sound as of a rushing wind violent, and it
ρωσεν ὁλον τον οικον οὑ ησαν καθημενοι·
filled whole the house, where they were sitting;
3 και ωφθησαν αυτοις διαμεριζομεναι γλωσσαι
and they saw with them being divided tongues
ὡσει πυρος· εκαθισε τε εφ' ἑνα ἑκαστον αυτων,
like fire, sat and on one each one of them,
4 και επλησθησαν ἁπαντες πνευματος ἁγιου,
and they were filled all spirit holy,
και ηρξαντο λαλειν ἑτεραις γλωσσαις, καθως
and they began to speak with other tongues, as
το πνευμα εδιδου αυτοις αποφθεγγεσθαι. 5 Ησαν
the spirit gave to them to speak. Were
δε εν Ἱερουσαλημ κατοικουντες Ιουδαιοι, ανδρες
now in Jerusalem dwelling Jews, men
ευλαβεις, απο παντος εθνους των ὑπο τον ουρανον.
pious, from every nation of those under the heaven.
6 Γενομενης δε της φωνης ταυτης, συνηλθε το
Having happened and the sound this, came together the
πληθος, και συνεχυθη· ὁτι ηκουον εις ἑκαστος
multitude, and were perplexed. because heard one each
τῃ ιδιᾳ διαλεκτῳ λαλουντων αυτων. 7 Ε[illegible]σ-
in the own language speaking of them. Were as-
ταντο δε *[παντες] και εθαυμαζον, λεγοντες
tonished and [all] and wondered, saying
*[προς αλληλους·] Ουκ ιδου παντες οὑτοι
[to each other;] Not lo all these
εισιν οἱ λαλουντες Γαλιλαιοι; 8 Και πως ἡμεις
are who are speaking Galileans? And how we
ακουομεν εκαστος τῃ ιδιᾳ διαλεκτῳ ἡμων, εν ᾑ
hear each one in the own language of us, in which
εγεννηθημεν, 9 Παρθοι και Μηδοι και Ελαμιται,
we were born, Parthians and Medes and Elamites,
και οἱ κατοικουντες την Μεσοποταμιαν, Ιουδαιαν,
and those dwelling the Mesopotamia, Judea,
τε και Καππαδοκιαν, Ποντον και την Ασιαν,
both and Cappadocia, Pontus and the Asia,
10 Φρυγιαν τε και Παμφυλιαν, Αιγυπτον και τα
Phrygia both and Pamphylia, Egypt and the
μερη της Λιβυης της κατα Κυρηνην, και οἱ
parts of the Lybia that upon Cyrene, and those

fell on Matthias, and he was counted with the ELEVEN Apostles.

CHAPTER II.

1 And when the ‡DAY of PENTECOST was FULLY COME, ‡they were all with one mind in the same place.

2 And suddenly there came a Sound from HEAVEN, like a violent Wind rushing; and it filled the Whole HOUSE where they were sitting.

3 And Divided Tongues appeared to them, like Fire, and one rested on each one of them.

4 And they were ‡all filled with holy Spirit, and began to speak ‡in Other Languages, as the SPIRIT gave them utterance.

5 Now there were sojourning in Jerusalem, Jews, pious Men, from Every Nation under HEAVEN.

6 And †this REPORT having been circulated, the MULTITUDE came together, and were perplexed, Because e[illegible]y one heard them speaking in his OWN Language.

7 And they were astonished and wondered, saying, "Behold, are not all THESE, who are SPEAKING, ‡Galileans?

8 And how do we hear each one in our OWN Language, in which we were born;—

9 Parthians and Medes and Elamites, and those DWELLING in MESOPOTAMIA, both in †Judea and Cappadocia, in Pontus and ASIA,

10 both in Phrygia and Pamphylia, in Egypt and the PARTS of THAT Lybia about Cyrene, and the

* VATICAN MANUSCRIPT.—7. all—*omit*. 7. to each other—*omit*.

† 6. It is difficult to determine whether it was the *voice* of those speaking in foreign languages; the *report* or *rumor* of the transaction; or the supernatural "rushing *sound*," which is indicated here. † 9. Pearce renders Judea as an adjective, thus; "DWELLERS in Jewish Mesopotamia." Bloomfield thinks there may have been a corruption of the text, changing *Idoumiou*, Idumea, to *Ioudian*, Judea.

‡ 1. Lev. xxiii. 15; Deut. xvi. 9; Acts xx. 16. ‡ 1. Acts i. 14. ‡ 4. Acts i. 4.
‡ 4. Mark xvi. 17; Acts x. 46; xix. 6; 1 Cor. xii. 10, 28, 30; xiii. 1; xiv. 2. ‡ 7. Acts i. 11.

επιδημουντες Ῥωμαιοι, Ιουδαιοι τε και προση-
sojourning Romans, Jews both and prose-
λυτοι, 11 Κρητες και Αραβες, ακουομεν λαλουν-
lytes, Cretans and Arabians, we hear speaking
των αυτων ταις ἡμετεραις γλωσσαις τα μεγα-
them in the our tongues the great
λεια του θεου; 12 Εξισταντο δε παντες και διη-
things of the God? Were astonished and all and per-
πορουν, αλλος προς αλλον λεγοντες· Τι αν
plexed, one to another saying; What
θελοι τουτο ειναι; 13 Ετεροι δε διαχλευαζοντες
will this to be? Others but deriding
ελεγον· Ὁτι γλευκους μεμεστωμενοι εισι.
said; That sweet wine having been filled they are.
14 Σταθεις δε Πετρος συν τοις ἑνδεκα, επηρε
Standing up but Peter with the eleven, lifted up
την φωνην αὑτου, και απεφθεγξατο αυτοις.
the voice of himself, and said to them.
Ανδρες Ιουδαιοι, και οἱ κατοικουντες Ἱερουσα-
Men Jews, and those dwelling in Jerusa-
λημ ἁπαντες, τουτο ὑμιν γνωστον εστω, και
lem all, this to you known let be, and
ενωτισασθε τα ῥηματα μου. 15 Ου γαρ, ὡς
listen you the words of me. Not for, as
ὑμεις ὑπολαμβανετε, οὑτοι μεθυουσιν· εστι γαρ
you suppose, these are drunk; it is for
ὡρα τριτη της ἡμερας· 16 αλλα τουτο εστι το
hour third of the day; but this is that
ειρημενον δια του προφητου Ιωηλ· 17 και
having been spoken through the prophet Joel; and
εσται εν ταις εσχαταις ταις ἡμεραις, λεγει ὁ
it shall be in the last the days, says the
θεος, εκχεω απο του πνευματος μου επι πασαν
God, I will pour out from of the spirit of me upon all
σαρκα· και προφητευσουσιν οἱ υἱοι ὑμων και αἱ
flesh; and shall prophesy the sons of you and the
θυγατερες ὑμων, και οἱ νεανισκοι ὑμων ὁρασεις
daughters of you, and the young men of you visions
οψονται, και οἱ πρεσβυτεροι ὑμων ενυπνιοις
shall see, and the old men of you dreams
ενυπνιασθησονται· 18 καιγε επι τους δουλους μου
shall dream; and even on the male-slaves of me
και επι τας δουλας μου εν ταις ἡμεραις εκειναις
and on the female slaves of me in the days those
εκχεω απο του πνευματος μου, και προφη-
I will pour out from of the spirit of me, and they
τευσουσι. 19 Και δωσω τερατα εν τῳ ουρανῳ
shall prophesy. And I will give prodigies in the heaven
ανω, και σημεια επι της γης κατω, αιμα και
above, and signs on the earth below, blood and
πυρ και ατμιδα καπνου· 20 ὁ ἡλιος μεταστραφη-
fire and a cloud of smoke; the sun shall be turned
σεται εις σκοτος, και ἡ σεληνη εις αιμα, πριν
into darkness, and the moon into blood, sooner
η ελθειν την ἡμεραν κυριου την μεγαλην και
than to come the day of lord the great and
επιφανη. 21 Και εσται, πας ὁς αν επικαλεση-
illustrious. And it shall be, every one who may call upon
ται το ονομα κυριου, σωθησεται.
the name of lord, shall be saved.

Roman STRANGERS, both
Jews and Proselytes,
11 Cretans and Arabi-
ans; we hear them speak-
ing in OUR Tongues the
GREAT THINGS of GOD."
12 And they were all
astonished and perplexed,
saying one to another,
"What can this be?"
13 But others scoffing,
said, "They are full of
Sweet wine."
14 But Peter standing
with the ELEVEN, lifted
up his VOICE, and said to
them, "Jews! and all who
are SOJOURNING in Jeru-
salem! let this be known
to you, and listen to my
WORDS.
15 For these are not
drunk as you suppose, ‡for
it is the third Hour of the
DAY;
16 but this is WHAT was
SPOKEN through the PRO-
PHET Joel;
17 ‡'And it shall be *in
'the LAST Days, says GOD,
'I will pour out of my
'Spirit upon All Flesh;
'and your SONS and your
'DAUGHTERS shall pro-
'phesy; and your YOUNG
'MEN shall see Visions,
'and your OLD MEN shall
'dream Dreams.
18 'And indeed on my
'MEN-SERVANTS and ‡ on
'my WOMEN-SERVANTS in
'those DAYS I will pour
'out of my SPIRIT, and
'they shall prophesy.
19 'And I will give Pro-
'digies in the HEAVENS
'above, and Signs on the
'EARTH below; Blood, and
'Fire, and a Cloud of
'Smoke.
20 ‡'The SUN shall be
'turned into Darkness, and
'the MOON into Blood, be-
'fore THAT great and illus-
'trious Day of the Lord
'come.
21 'And it shall be, ‡ev-
'ery one who may invoke
'the NAME of the Lord,
'shall be saved.'

* VATICAN MANUSCRIPT.—17. after these things, says GOD.

‡ 15. 1 Thess. v. 7. ‡ 17. Joel ii. 28, 29. ‡ 18. Acts xxi. 4, 9, 10; 1 Cor. xii. 10, 28; xvi. 1. ‡ 20. Matt. xxiv. 29; Mark xiii. 24; Luke xxi. 25. ‡ 21. Rom. x. 13.

22 Ανδρες Ισραηλιται, ακουσατε τους λογους
Men Israelites, hear you the words
τουτους· Ιησουν τον Ναζωραιον, ανδρα απο του
these; Jesus the Nazarene, a man from the
θεου αποδεδειγμενον εις ὑμας δυναμεσι και
God having been pointed out to you by mighty works and
τερασι και σημειοις, (οἱς εποιησε δι' αυτου ὁ
prodigies and signs, (which did through him the
θεος εν μεσῳ ὑμων, καθως *[και] αυτοι οιδατε,)
God in midst of you, as [also] yourselves you know,)
23 τουτον τῃ ὡρισμενῃ βουλῃ και προγνωσει
this by the having been fixed purpose and foreknowledge
του θεου εκδοτον λαβοντες, δια χειρων ανο-
of the God given up having been taken, by hands of law-
μων προσπηξαντες ανειλατε. 24 Ὁν ὁ θεος
less ones having affixed to you killed. Whom the God
ανεστησε· λυσας τας ωδινας του θανατου,
raised up; having loosed the pains of the death,
καθοτι ουκ ην δυνατον κρατεισθαι αυτου ὑπ'
inasmuch as not was possible to be held him under
αυτου.
it.

25 Δαυιδ γαρ λεγει εις αυτον· Προωρωμην
David for says concerning him; I saw
τον κυριον ενωπιον μου διαπαντας, ὁτι εκ δεξιων
the lord in presence of me always, because at right hand
μου εστιν, ἱνα μη σαλευθω. 26 Δια τουτο
of me he is, so that not I may be shaken. Through this
ευφρανθη ἡ καρδια μου, και ηγαλλιασατο ἡ
rejoiced the heart of me, and exulted the
γλωσσα μου· ετι δε και ἡ σαρξ μου κατασκη-
tongue of me; moreover and also the flesh of me will repose
νωσει επ' ελπιδι· 27 ὁτι ουκ εγκαταλειψεις
in hope; because not thou wilt abandon
την ψυχην μου εις ᾁδου, ουδε δωσεις
the life of me to invisibility, nor thou wilt abandon
τον ὁσιον σου ιδειν διαφθοραν. 28 Εγνωρισας
the holy one of thee to see corruption. Thou didst make known
μοι ὁδους ζωης· πληρωσεις με ευφροσυνης μετα
to me ways of life; thou wilt fill me of joy with
του προσωπου σου.
the face of thee.

29 Ανδρες αδελφοι, εξον ειπειν μετα παρρη-
Men brethren, it is lawful to speak with freedom
σιας προς ὑμας περι του πατριαρχου Δαυιδ,
to you concerning the patriarch David,
ὁτι και ετελευτησε και εταφη, και το μνημα
that both he died and was buried, and the tomb
αυτου εστιν εν ἡμιν αχρι της ἡμερας ταυτης.
of him is among us till of the day this.
30 Προφητης ουν ὑπαρχων, και ειδως ὁτι ὁρκῳ
A prophet therefore being, and knowing that with an oath
ωμοσεν αυτῳ ὁ θεος, εκ καρπου της οσφυος
swore to him the God, out of fruit of the loins
αυτου καθισαι επι του θρονου αυτου. 31 Προι-
of him to cause to sit on the throne of him. foresee-

22 Israelites! hear these WORDS. Jesus, the NAZARENE, a Man from GOD, celebrated among you ‡ by Miracles, and Prodigies, and Signs, which GOD wrought through him in the Midst of you, as you yourselves know;

23 him, ‡ given up by the FIXED Counsel and Foreknowledge of God, * by the Hand of Lawless ones, ‡ you nailed to the cross, and killed;

24 ‡ whom GOD raised up, having loosed the PAINS of DEATH; as it was impossible to hold him under it.

25 For David says concerning him, ‡ 'I saw the 'LORD always before me, 'Because he is at my Right 'hand, so that I may not 'be moved.

26 'On account of this '* My heart rejoiced, and 'my TONGUE exulted; and 'moreover, my FLESH also 'shall repose in Hope;

27 'because thou wilt 'not abandon my SOUL in 'Hades, nor give up thine 'HOLY ONE to see Corrup'tion.

28 'Thou didst make 'known to me the Ways of 'Life; thou wilt make me 'full of Joy with thy 'COUNTENANCE.'

29 Brethren! I may speak to you, with freedom, concerning the PATRIARCH David, that he both died and was buried, and his TOMB is among us to this DAY.

30 Being, therefore, a Prophet, ‡ and knowing That GOD swore to him with an Oath, that of the Fruit of his LOINS he would cause one to sit upon his THRONE;

* VATICAN MANUSCRIPT.—22. also—*omit*. 23. by the Hand of Lawless ones, you nailed to the cross and killed. 26. My HEART.

‡ 22. John iii. 2; xiv. 10, 11; Acts x. 38. ‡ 23. Matt. xxvi. 24; Luke xxii. 22; xxiv. 44; Acts iii. 18; iv. 28. ‡ 23. Acts v. 30. ‡ 24. ver. 32. ‡ 25. Psa. xvi. 8. ‡ 30. 2 Sam. vii. 12, 13; Psa. cxxxii. 11; Luke i. 32, 69; Rom. i. 3; 2 Tim. ii. 8.

ἰδων ελαλησε περι της αναστασεως του Χριστου,
ing he spoke concerning the resurrection of the Anointed,
ὁτι ου κατελειφθη εις ᾁδου, ουδε ἡ σαρξ
that not he was abandoned into invisibility, nor the flesh
αυτου ειδε διαφθοραν. 32 Τουτον τον Ιησουν
of him saw corruption. This the Jesus
ανεστησεν ὁ θεος, οὑ παντες ἡμεις εσμεν
raised up the God, of which all we are
μαρτυρες. 33 Τῃ δεξιᾳ ουν του θεου ὑψω-
witnesses. To the right hand therefore of the God having been
θεις, την τε επαγγελιαν του ἁγιου πνευματος
exalted, the and promise of the holy spirit
λαβων παρα του πατρος, εξεχεε τουτο, ὁ
having received from the father, he poured out this, which
ὑμεις βλεπετε και ακουετε. 34 Ου γαρ Δαυιδ
you see and hear. Not for David
ανεβη εις τους ουρανους· λεγει δε αυτος· Ειπεν
ascended into the heavens; he says but himself; Said
ὁ κυριος τῳ κυριῳ μου· Καθου εκ δεξιων μου,
the lord to the lord of me; Sit thou at right hand of me,
35 ἑως αν θω τους εχθρους σου ὑποποδιον των
till I may place the enemies of thee a footstool for the
ποδων σου. 36 Ασφαλως ουν γινωσκετω πας
feet of thee. Certainly therefore let know all
οικος Ισραηλ, ὁτι και κυριον αυτον και Χριστον
house of Israel, that both lord him and Anointed
ὁ θεος εποιησε, τουτον τον Ιησουν, ὁν ὑμεις
the God made, this the Jesus, whom you
εσταυρωσατε. 37 Ακουσαντες δε κατενυγησαν
crucified. Having heard and they were pierced
τῃ καρδιᾳ, ειπον τε προς τον Πετρον και τους
to the heart, said and to the Peter and the
λοιπους αποστολους· Τι ποιησομεν, ανδρες
other apostles; What shall we do, men
αδελφοι; 38 Πετρος δε *[εφη] προς αυτους·
brethren? Peter and [said] to them;
Μετανοησατε, και βαπτισθητω ἑκαστος ὑμων
Reform you, and be dipped each one of you
επι τῳ ονοματι Ιησου Χριστου, εις αφεσιν ἁμαρ-
in the name of Jesus Anointed, for forgiveness of
τιων, και ληψεσθε την δωρεαν του ἁγιου πνευ-
sins, and you shall receive the gift of the holy spirit.
ματος. 39 Ὑμιν γαρ εστιν ἡ επαγγελια και
To you for is the promise and
τοις τεκνοις ὑμων, και πασι τοις εις μακραν,
to the children of you, and to all those at a distance,
ὁσους αν προσκαλεσηται κυριος ὁ θεος ἡμων.
as many as may call lord the God of us.
40 Ἑτεροις τε λογοις πλειοσι διεμαρτυρετο,
Other and words with many he testified.
και παρεκαλει, λεγων· Σωθητε απο της γενεας
and exhorted, saying; Be saved from the generation
της σκολιας ταυτης. 41 Οἱ μεν ουν *[ασμενως]
of the perverse this. They indeed therefore [gladly]

31 foreseeing he spoke
concerning the RESURREC-
TION of the MESSIAH,
'that he was not left in
'Hades, nor did his FLESH
'see Corruption.'
32 GOD raised up this
JESUS, ‡ of which we all
are Witnesses.
33 Having been, there-
fore, exalted to the RIGHT
HAND of God, ‡ and hav-
ing received from the FA-
THER the PROMISE of the
* HOLY SPIRIT, ‡ he poured
out this which you * both
see and hear.
34 For David ascended
not to HEAVEN, but he
says himself, ‡ 'JEHOVAH
'said to my LORD, Sit thou
'at my Right hand,
35 'till I put thine EN-
'EMIES underneath thy
'FEET.'
36 Therefore, let all the
House of Israel certainly
know, that This JESUS,
whom you crucified, ‡ GOD
made him both Lord and
Messiah."
37 And having heard
this, they were pierced to
the HEART, and said to
PETER and the OTHER
Apostles, "Brethren! what
shall we do?"
38 And Peter said to
them; ‡ "Reform, and let
each of you be immersed
in the NAME of Jesus
Christ, for the Forgiveness
* of your SINS; and you
will receive the GIFT of
the HOLY Spirit.
39 For the PROMISE is
to you and ‡ to your
CHILDREN, and ‡ to ALL
who are far off, as many
as the Lord our GOD may
call."
40 And with many Oth-
er Words he testified and
* exhorted them, saying,
"Be you saved from this
PERVERSE GENERATION."
41 Then THOSE who RE-

VATICAN MANUSCRIPT.—33. HOLY SPIRIT. 33. both see. 38. said—*omit.*
38. of the SINS. 40. exhorted them, saying.

‡ 32. Acts i. 8. ‡ 33. Acts v. 31; Phil. ii. 9; Heb. x. 12. ‡ 33. John xiv. 26; xv. 26; xvi. 7, 13; Acts i. 4. ‡ 34. Psa. cx. 1; Matt. xxii. 24; 1 Cor. xv. 25; Eph. i. 20—22; Heb. i. 13; x. 12, 13. ‡ 36. Acts v. 31. ‡ 38. Luke xxiv. 47; Acts iii. 19. ‡ 39. Acts iii. 25. ‡ 39. Acts x. 45; xi. 15, 18; xiv. 27; xv. 3, 8, 14; Eph. ii. 13, 17.

αποδεξαμενοι τον λογον αυτου, εβαπτισθησαν·
having received the word of him, were dipped;
και προσετεθησαν τη ἡμερᾳ εκεινῃ ψυχαι ὡσει
and were added the day that souls about
τρισχιλιαι. 42 Ησαν δε προσκαρτερουντες τῃ
three thousand. Were and constantly attending to the
διδαχῃ των αποστολων, και τῃ κοινωνιᾳ, *[και]
teaching of the apostles, and to the distribution, [and]
τῃ κλασει του αρτου, και ταις προσευχαις.
to the breaking of the loaf, and to the prayers.
43 Εγενετο δε πασῃ ψυχῃ φοβος, πολλα τε
Came and to every soul fear, many and
τερατα και σημεια δια των αποστολων εγι-
prodigies and signs through the apostles were
νετο. 44 Παντες δε οἱ πιστευοντες ησαν επι
done. All and those believing were in
το αυτο, και ειχον ἁπαντα κοινα, 45 και τα
the same, and had all things common, and the
κτηματα και τας ὑπαρξεις επιπρασκον, και διε-
possessions and the goods they were selling, and they
μεριζον αυτα πασι, καθοτι αν τις χρειαν ειχε.
were dividing them to all, as any one need had.
46 Καθ' ἡμεραν τε προσκαρτερουντες ὁμοθυμαδον
Every day and constantly attending with one mind
εν τῳ ἱερῳ, κλωντες τε κατ' οικον αρτον, μετε-
in the temple, breaking and at home bread, they
λαμβανον τροφης εν αγαλλιασει και αφελοτητι
were partaking of food in gladness and singleness
καρδιας, 47 αινουντες τον θεον, και εχοντες
of heart, praising the God, and having
χαριν προς ὁλον τον λαον. Ὁ δε κυριος προσε-
favor with whole the people. The and lord was
τιθει τους σωζομενους καθ' ἡμεραν *[τῃ εκκλη-
adding those being saved every day [to the congre-
σιᾳ.]
gation.]

42 ‡ And they were constantly attending to the TEACHING of the APOSTLES, and to the † CONTRIBUTION, and to the BREAKING of the LOAF, and to the PRAYERS.

43 And Fear came upon Every Soul; and ‡ Many Prodigies and Signs were done through the APOSTLES.

44 And ALL the BELIEVERS ‡ * had all things common together;

45 and sold their POSSESSIONS and GOODS, and divided them to all, as any one had Need.

46 And constantly attending with one mind ‡ in the TEMPLE every day, and breaking Bread at Home, they partook of Food in Joyfulness and Simplicity of Heart;

47 praising God, and having Favor with all the PEOPLE. And ‡ the LORD daily added THOSE BEING SAVED to the CONGREGATION.

ΚΕΦ. γ'. 3.

1 Επι το αυτο δε Πετρος και Ιωαννης ανεβαι-
In the same now Peter and John were going
νον εις το ἱερον επι την ὡραν της προσευχης
up into the temple at the hour of the prayer
την εννατην. 2 Και τις ανηρ χωλος εκ κοι-
the ninth. And a certain man lame from womb
λιας μητρος αὑτου ὑπαρχων, εβασταζετο· ὁν
of mother of himself being, was being carried; whom
ετιθουν κατ' ἡμεραν προς την θυραν του ἱερου
they placed every day at the door of the temple
την λεγομενην ὡραιαν, του αιτειν ελεημοσυνην
that being called beautiful, the to ask alms
παρα των εισπορευομενων εις το ἱερον. 3 Ὁς
from those entering into the temple. Who

CHAPTER III

1 Now Peter and John were going up TOGETHER into the TEMPLE, at the HOUR of PRAYER, being the NINTH hour.

2 And a Certain Man, lame from his Birth, was being carried, whom they placed daily at † THAT GATE of the TEMPLE which is CALLED Beautiful, to ASK Alms of THOSE ENTERING into the TEMPLE;

* VATICAN MANUSCRIPT.—42. and—omit. 44. had all things common together; and sold. 47. to the congregation—omit.

† 42. See the following passages where the same original word is used:—Rom. xv. 26; 2 Cor. viii. 4; ix. 13; Phil. i. 5; Heb. xiii. 16. Also Appendix. † 2. This gate is said to have led from the court of the Gentiles into the court of the Israelites on the eastern side of the temple. It was built by Herod the Great, almost or quite wholly of Corinthian brass. The folds of this gate were fifty cubits high and forty broad, and covered with plates of gold and silver.

‡ 42. Heb. x. 25. ‡ 43. Mark xvi. 17; Acts iv. 33; v. 12. ‡ 44. Acts iv. 32. ‡ 46. Luke xxiv. 53; Acts v. 42. ‡ 47. Acts v. 14; xi. 24.

ιδων Πετρον και Ιωαννην μελλοντας εισιεναι
seeing Peter and John being about to go

εις το ἱερον, ηρωτα ελεημοσυνην λαβειν. 4 Ατε-
into the temple, asked alms to receive. Looking

νισας δε Πετρος εις αυτον συν τῳ Ιωαννῃ, ειπε·
steadily and Peter on him with the John, said;

βλεψον εις ἡμας. 5 Ὁ δε επειχεν αυτοις, προσ-
Look on us. He and gave heed to them, ex-

δοκων τι παρ' αυτων λαβειν. 6 Ειπε δε Πε-
pecting something from them to receive. Said and Pe-

τρος· Αργυριον και χρυσιον ουχ ὑπαρχει μοι·
ter; Silver and gold not are possessed by me;

ὁ δε εχω, τουτο σοι διδωμι· Εν τῳ ονοματι
what but I have, this to thee I give; In the name

Ιησου Χριστου του Ναζωραιου *[εγειραι και]
of Jesus Anointed the Nazarene [do thou arise and]

περιπατει. 7 Και πιασας αυτον της δεξιας
walk. And having taken him the right

χειρος ηγειρε· παραχρημα δε εστερεωθησαν
hand he rose up, immediately and were strengthened

αυτου αἱ βασεις και τα σφυρα. 8 Και εξαλλο-
of him the feet and the ankle-bones. And leaping

μενος, εστη, και περιεπατει· και εισηλθε συν
up, he stood, and walked; and entered with

αυτοις εις το ἱερον, περιπατων και αλλομενος,
them into the temple, walking and leaping,

και αινων τον θεον. 9 Και ειδεν αυτον πας ὁ
and praising the God. And saw him all the

λαος περιπατουντα και αινουντα τον θεον·
people walking and praising the God;

10 επεγινωσκον τε αυτον, ὁτι ουτος ην ὁ προς
they knew and him, that he was who for

την ελεημοσυνην καθημενος επι τῃ ὡραιᾳ πυλῃ
the alms sitting at the beautiful gate

του ἱερου· και επλησθησαν θαμβους και εκτα-
of the temple; and they were filled with wonder and amaze-

σεως επι τῳ συμβεβηκοτι αυτῳ. 11 Κρατουντος
ment at that having happened to him. Holding fast

δε αυτου τον Πετρον και Ιωαννην, συνεδραμε
and of him the Peter and John, ran together

προς αυτους πας ὁ λαος επι τῃ στοᾳ τῃ καλου-
to them all the people to the porch that being

μενῃ Σολομωνος, εκθαμβοι. 12 Ιδων δε Πετρος
called of Solomon, awe-struck. Seeing and Peter

απεκρινατο προς τον λαον· Ανδρες Ισραηλιται,
answered to the people; Men Israelites,

τι θαυμαζετε επι τουτῳ; η ἡμιν τι ατενιζετε,
why do you wonder at this? or to us why look you earnestly,

ὡς ιδιᾳ δυναμει η ευσεβειᾳ πεποιηκοσι του
as by own power or piety having been made of the

περιπατειν αυτον; 13 Ὁ θεος Αβρααμ και Ισαακ
to walk him? The God of Abraam and Isaac

και Ιακωβ, ὁ θεος των πατερων ἡμων, εδοξασε
and Jacob, the God of the fathers of us, glorified

τον παιδα αυτου Ιησουν, ὁν ὑμεις μεν παρεδω-
the servant of himself Jesus, whom you indeed delivered

3 who seeing Peter and John being about to go into the TEMPLE, asked Alms.

4 And Peter, with John, having earnestly fixed his eyes on him, said, "Look on us."

5 And HE gave heed to them, expecting to receive Something from them.

6 But Peter said, "Silver and Gold I have not; but what I have, This I give thee; ‡ in the NAME of Jesus Christ, the NAZARENE, walk."

7 And having taken him by the RIGHT Hand he raised *him up; and immediately *his FEET and ANKLES were strengthened;

8 and leaping up, he stood, and walked about, and entered with them into the TEMPLE, walking, and leaping, and praising GOD.

9 ‡ And All the PEOPLE saw him walking and praising GOD;

10 and they knew him, That HE was the ONE who SAT for ALMS at the BEAUTIFUL Gate of the TEMPLE; and they were filled with Wonder and Amazement at WHAT had HAPPENED to him.

11 And while he held fast to PETER and John, All the PEOPLE ran together to them, into THAT PORTICO ‡ which is CALLED Solomon's, greatly astonished.

12 And *PETER seeing it, answered the PEOPLE, "Israelites! why do you wonder at this? or why do you look intently at Us, as though by Our Power or Piety we had caused him to walk.

13 ‡ The GOD of Abraham, and of Isaac, and of Jacob, the GOD of our FATHERS, glorified his SERVANT Jesus, whom you

VATICAN MANUSCRIPT.—6. rise up and—*omit*. 7. him. 7. his FEET. 12. PETER.

‡ 6. Acts iv. 10. ‡ 9. Acts iv. 16, 21. ‡ 11. John x. 23; Acts v. 12. ‡ 13. Acts v. 30.

κατε, και ηρνησασθε *[αυτον] κατα προσωπον
up, and denied [him] in face
Πιλατου, κριναντος εκεινου απολευειν. 14 Ὑμεις
of Pilate, having judged he to release. You
δε τον ἁγιον και δικαιον ηρνησασθε, και ητη-
but the holy and righteous denied, and asked
σασθε ανδρα φονεα καρισθηναι ὑμιν, 15 τον δε
a man a murderer to be granted to you, the and
αρχηγον της ζωης απεκτεινατε· ὁν ὁ θεος ηγει-
prince of the life you killed; whom the God raised
ρεν εκ νεκρων, οὑ ἡμεις μαρτυρες εσμεν·
out of dead ones, of whom we witnesses are;
16 και επι τη πιστει του ονοματος αυτου, τουτον
and by the faith of the name of him, this
ὁν θεωρειτε και οιδατε, εστερεωσε το ονομα
whom you behold and know, strengthened the name
αυτου· και ἡ πιστις ἡ δι' αυτου εδωκεν αυτῳ
of him; and the faith that through him gave to him
την ὁλοκληριαν ταυτην απεναντι παντ[ων] ὑμων.
the perfect soundness this in presence of all of you.
17 Και νυν, αδελφοι, οιδα ὁτι κατα αγνοιαν
And now, brethren, I know that in ignorance
επραξετε, ὡσπερ και οἱ αρχοντες ὑμων. 18 Ὁ
you did, as also the rulers of you. The
δε θεος ἁ προκατηγγειλε δια στοματος παντων
but God what he foretold through mouth of all
των προφητων αὑτου, παθειν τον Χριστον,
of the prophets of himself, to suffer the Anointed,
επληρωσεν οὑτω. 19 Μετανοησατε ουν και
he fulfilled thus. Reform you therefore and
επιστρεψατε, εις το εξαλειφθηναι ὑμων τας
turn you, in order that the to be wiped out of you the
ἁμαρτιας, ὁπως αν ελθωσι καιροι αναψυξεως απο
sins, that may come seasons of refreshing from
προσωπου του κυριου, 20 και αποστειλῃ τον
face of the lord, and he may send him
προκεχειρισμενον ὑμιν Ιησουν Χριστον· 21 ὁν
having been before destined for you Jesus Anointed; whom
δει ουρανον μεν δεξασθαι αχρι χρονων αποκα-
must heaven indeed to receive till times of restora-
ταστασεως παντων, ὡν ελαλησεν ὁ θεος δια
tion of all things, which spoke the God through
στοματος των ἁγιων αυτου προφητων απ' αιω-
mouth of the holy of himself prophets from an
νος. 22 Μωυσης μεν *[προς τους πατερας]
age. Moses indeed [to the fathers]
ειπεν· Ὁτι προφητην ὑμιν αναστησει κυριος ὁ
said; That a prophet to you shall raise up lord the
θεος ὑμων, εκ των αδελφων ὑμων· ὡς εμε·
God of you, from of the brethren of you; like me;
αυτου ακουσεσθε κατα παντα, ὁσα αν λαλησῃ
of him you shall hear in all things, which he may speak
προς ὑμας. 23 Εσται δε, πασα ψυχη ἡτις αν μη
to you. It shall be and, every soul whatever not
ακουσῃ του προφητου εκεινου, εξολοθρευθησε-
may hear the prophet that, shall be destroyed

indeed delivered up, and ‡rejected in the Presence of Pilate, when he resolved to release him.

14 But you rejected the HOLY and Righteous one, and asked a Murderer to be given you,

15 and killed the PRINCE of LIFE; whom GOD raised from the Dead, of which we are Witnesses.

16 And by the FAITH of his NAME, ‡this NAME strengthened This Man, whom you behold and know; and THAT FAITH, through him, gave him this PERFECT SOUNDNESS in the presence of you all.

17 And now, Brethren, I know That in ‡Ignorance you did it, as also your RULERS.

18 But GOD thus fulfilled ‡what he foretold by the Mouth of All *the PROPHETS, ‡that his ANOINTED should suffer.

19 ‡Reform, therefore, and turn, that Your SINS may be BLOTTED OUT; so that Seasons of Refreshment may come from the Presence of the LORD,

20 and he may send him HAVING BEEN BEFORE DESTINED for you, Jesus Christ;

21 whom, indeed, Heaven must retain till the Times of Restoration of all things which GOD spoke by the Mouth of HIS HOLY Prophets, from of Old.

22 Moses indeed said, ‡'The Lord your God shall 'raise up to you, from your 'BRETHREN, a Prophet, 'like me; Him you shall 'hear in all things which 'he may speak to you;

23 'and it shall be, Every Soul which may not 'hear that PROPHET, shall 'be destroyed from among 'the PEOPLE.'

* VATICAN MANUSCRIPT.—13. him—*omit.* 18. the PROPHETS his ANOINTED. 21. of HIS HOLY. 22. to the FATHERS—*omit.*

‡ 13. Matt. xxvii. 20; Mark xv. 11; Luke xxiii. 18, 20, 21; John xviii. 40; xix. 15; Acts xiii. 28. ‡ 16. Acts iv. 10. ‡ 17. Luke xxiii. 34; John xvi. 3; Acts xiii. 27; 1 Cor. ii. 8; 1 Tim. i. 13. ‡ 18. Luke xxiv. 44; Acts xxvi. 22. ‡ 18. Psa. xxii.; Isa. liii.; Dan. ix. 26; 1 Pet. i. 10, 11. ‡ 19. Acts ii. 38. ‡ 22. Deut. xviii. 15, 18, 19; Acts vii. 37.

ται εκ του λαου. 24 Και παντες δε οἱ προφη-
out of the people. Also all and the prophets
ται απο Σαμουηλ και των καθεξης ὁσοι ελαλη-
from Samuel and those succeeding as many as spoke,
σαν. και κατηγγειλαν τας ἡμερας ταυτας.
also told of the days these.
25 Ὑμεις εστε οἱ υἱοι των προφητων, και της
You are the sons of the prophets, and of the
διαθηκης, ἡς διεθετο ὁ θεος προς τους πατερας
covenant, which ratified the God to the fathers
ἡμων, λεγων προς Αβρααμ· Και εν τῳ σπερματι
of us, saying to Abraham; And in the seed
σου ενευλογηθησονται πασαι αἱ πατριαι της
of thee shall be blessed all the families of the
γης. 26 Ὑμιν πρωτον ὁ θεος, αναστησας τον
earth. To you first the God, having raised up the
παιδα αὑτου, απεστειλεν αυτον ευλογουντα
servant of himself, sent him blessing
ὑμας, εν τῳ αποστρεφειν ἑκαστον απο των
you, in the to turn each one from the
πονηριων *[ὑμων.]
evil deeds [of you.]

ΚΕΦ. δ'. 4.

1 Λαλουντων δε αυτων προς τον λαον, και
Speaking and of them to the people, and
επεστησαν αυτοις οἱ ἱερεις και ὁ στρατηγος του
came upon them the priests and the captain of the
ἱερου και οἱ Σαδδουκαιοι, 2 διαπονουμενοι δια
temple and the Sadducees, being grieved through
το διδασκειν αυτους τον λαον, και καταγγελλειν
the to teach them the people, and to announce
εν τῳ Ιησου την αναστασιν την εκ νεκρων.
in the Jesus the resurrection that out of dead ones.
3 Και επεβαλον αυτοις τας χειρας, και εθεντο
And they laid on them the hands, and put
εις τηρησιν εις την αυριον· ην γαρ εσπερα ηδη.
into keeping to the morrow; it was for evening now.
4 Πολλοι δε των ακουσαντων τον λογον επισ-
Many but of those having heard the word be-
τευσαν· και εγενηθη ὁ αριθμος των ανδρων ὡσει
lieved; and became the number of the men about
χιλιαδες πεντε. 5 Εγενετο δε επι την αυριον συν-
thousand five. It happened and on the morrow to be
αχθηναι αυτων τους αρχοντας και πρεσβυτερους
assembled of them the rulers and elders
και γραμματεις εις Ἱερουσαλημ· 6 και Ανναν τον
and scribes at Jerusalem; also Annas the
αρχιερεα, και Καιαφαν και Ιωαννην και Αλεξαν-
high-priest, and Caiaphas and John and Alexan-
δρον, και ὁσοι ησαν εκ γενους αρχιερατικου.
der, and as many as were of a family of highpriesthood.
7 Και στησαντες αυτους εν μεσῳ, επυνθανοντο·
And having placed them in middle, they asked;
Εν ποιᾳ δυναμει, η εν ποιῳ ονοματι εποιησατε
By what power, or in what name did

24 And also All the PROPHETS from Samuel, and THOSE succeeding in order, as many as spoke, also announced these DAYS.

25 ‡ You are * Sons of the PROPHETS, and of the COVENANT which GOD ratified with our FATHERS, saying to Abraham, ‡ 'And 'in thy SEED shall all the 'FAMILIES of the EARTH 'be blessed.'

26 GOD having raised up his SERVANT, sent him ‡ first to you, to bless each one who shall TURN from his EVIL WAYS."

CHAPTER IV.

1 And while they were speaking to the PEOPLE, the * HIGH-PRIESTS, and the COMMANDER of the TEMPLE, and the SADDUCEES, came upon them,

2 ‡ being grieved because they TAUGHT the PEOPLE, and announced THAT RESURRECTION from the Dead in JESUS.

3 And they laid HANDS on them, and placed them in Custody till the NEXT DAY; for it was now Evening.

4 But many of THOSE HAVING HEARD the WORD believed; and the NUMBER of the MEN became about five Thousand.

5 And it occurred on the NEXT DAY, that Their RULERS, and * the ELDERS, and the SCRIBES assembled at Jerusalem;

6 and ‡ Annas, the HIGH-PRIEST, and Caiaphas, and John, and Alexander, and as many as were of the family of the High-Priesthood;

7 and having placed them in the Midst, they asked, ‡ "By What Power, or in What Name, have you done this?"

* VATICAN MANUSCRIPT.—25. the Sons of. 26. of you—*omit.* 1. HIGH-PRIESTS and. 5. and the ELDERS and the SCRIBES.

‡ 25. Acts ii. 39; Rom. ix. 4, 8; xv. 8. ‡ 25. Gen. xii. 3; xxii. 18; Gal. iii. 8. ‡ 26. Matt. x. 5; xv. 24; Luke xxiv. 47; Acts xiii. 32, 33, 46. ‡ 2. Matt. xxii. 23; Acts xxiii. 8. ‡ 6. Luke iii. 2; John xi. 49; xviii. 13. ‡ 7. Matt. xxi. 23.

τουτο ὑμεις; [8] Τοτε Πετρος πλησθεις πνευμα-
this you? Then Peter being filled with spirit
τος ἁγιου, ειπε προς αυτους· Αρχοντες του
holy, said to them; Rulers of the
λαου, και πρεσβυτεροι *[του Ισραηλ,] [9] ει ἡμεις
people, and elders [of the Israel,] if we
σημερον ανακρινομεθα επι ευεργεσιᾳ ανθρωπου
to-day be examined to for kindness a man
ασθενους, εν τινι οὑτος σεσωσται· [10] Γνωστον
sick, by what he has been saved Known
εστω πασιν ὑμιν και παντι τῳ λαῳ Ισραηλ, ὁτι
be it all to you and to all the people of Israel, that
εν τῳ ονοματι Ιησου Χριστου του Ναζωραιου,
in the name of Jesus Anointed the Nazarene,
ὁν ὑμεις εσταυρωσατε ὁν ὁ θεος ηγειρεν εκ
whom you crucified whom the God raised out of
νεκρων, εν τουτῳ οὑτος παρεστηκεν ενωπιον
dead ones, by him this has stood in presence
ὑμων ὑγιης. [11] Οὑτος εστιν ὁ λιθος ὁ εξουθενη-
of you sound. This is the stone that having been
θεις ὑφ' ὑμων των οικοδομουντων, ὁ γενομε-
despised by you the builders, the having been
νος εις κεφαλην γωνιας. [12] Και ουκ εστιν εν
made into a head of a corner. And not is in
αλλῳ ουδενι ἡ σωτηρια· ουδε γαρ ονομα εστιν
another to any one the salvation; not even for a name is
ἑτερον ὑπο τον ουρανον, τον δεδομενον εν
another under the heaven, that having been given among
ανθρωποις, εν ᾡ δει σωθηναι ἡμας.
men, in which must to be saved us.
[13] Θεωρουντες δε την του Πετρου παρῥησιαν
Seeing and the of the Peter boldness
και Ιωαννου, και καταλαβομενοι, ὁτι ανθρωποι
and of John, and having perceived, that men
αγραμματοι εισι και ιδιωται, εθαυμαζον, επεγι-
unlearned they are and ungifted, they wondered. they
νωσκον τε αυτους, ὁτι συν τῳ Ιησου ησαν·
knew and them, that with the Jesus they were;
[14] τον δε ανθρωπον βλεποντες συν αυτοις εστω-
the and man beholding with them stand-
τα τον τεθεραπευμενον, ουδεν ειχον αντειπειν.
ing that having been healed, nothing they had to say against.
[15] Κελευσαντες δε αυτους εξω του συνεδριου
Having ordered and them outside of the high-council
απελθειν, συνεβαλον προς αλληλους, [16] λεγον-
to go, they consulted with each other. saying;
τες· Τι ποιησομεν τοις ανθρωποις τουτοις; ὁτι
What shall we do to the men these? that
μεν γαρ γνωστον σημειον γεγονε δι' αυτων,
indeed for known a sign has been done by them,
πασι τοις κατοικουσιν Ἱερουσαλημ φανερον, και
to all those dwelling in Jerusalem manifest, and
ου δυναμεθα αρνησασθαι. [17] Αλλ' ἱνα μη επι
not we were able to deny. But that not to
πλειον διανεμηθῃ εις τον λαον, *[απειλῃ] απει-
more it may spread among the people, [with a threat] let us

8 ‡ Then Peter being filled with holy Spirit, said to them, "Rulers of the PEOPLE, and Elders of ISRAEL!

9 if we are to-day examined about a Good Deed conferred on the sick Man, by what means he has been cured;

10 be it known to you all, and to All the PEOPLE of Israel, ‡ That by the NAME of Jesus Christ, the NAZARENE, whom you crucified, ‡ whom GOD raised from the Dead, by him has this man stood before you whole.

11 ‡ This is 'THAT STONE which HAS BEEN REJECTED by You, the BUILDERS, THAT which HAS BECOME the Head of the Corner.'

12 And there is no SALVATION in any other; for there is no other Name under HEAVEN, which HAS BEEN GIVEN among Men, by which we can be saved."

13 And seeing the BOLDNESS of PETER and John, ‡ and perceiving that they were illiterate and ungifted Men, they wondered, and recognized them That they had been with JESUS.

14 And beholding THAT MAN who had been CURED standing with them, they had nothing to say against it.

15 But having ordered them to withdraw from the SANHEDRIM, they conferred with each other,

16 saying, ‡ "What shall we do to these MEN? for that, indeed, a Signal Sign has been wrought by them, is manifest to All THOSE DWELLING in Jerusalem; and we cannot deny it.

17 But that it may spread no further among the PEOPLE, let us threat-

---

VATICAN MANUSCRIPT.—8. of ISRAEL—*omit*. 17. with a threat—*omit*.

‡ 8. Luke xii. 11, 12. ‡ 10. Acts iii. 6. 16. ‡ 10. Acts ii. 24. ‡ 11. Psa. cxviii. 22; Isa. xxviii. 16; Matt. xxi. 42. ‡ 13. Matt. xi. 25; 1 Cor. i. 27. ‡ 16. John xi. 47.

λησωμεθα αυτοις, μηκετι λαλειν επι τῳ ονοματι
threaten them, no longer to speak in the name
τουτῳ μηδενι ανθρωπον. 18 Και καλεσαντες
this to any man. And having called
αυτους, παρηγγειλαν αυτοις το καθολου μη
them, they charged them not at all not
φθεγγεσται μηδε διδασκειν επι τῳ ονοματι του
to speak nor to teach in the name of the
Ιησου. 19 Ὁ δε Πετρος και Ιωαννης αποκριθεν-
Jesus. The but Peter and John answering
τες προς αυτους ειπον· Ει δικαιον εστιν ενωπιον
to them said; If just it is in presence
του θεου, ὑμων ακουειν μαλλον η του θεου, κρι-
of the God, you to hearken rather than the God, judge
νατε. 20 Ου δυναμεθα γαρ ἡμεις, ἁ ειδομεν και
you. Not are able for we, what we saw and
ηκουσαμεν, μη λαλειν. 21 Οἱ δε προσαπειλη-
heard, not to speak. They and having again threat-
σαμενοι απελυσαν αυτους, μηδεν εὑρισκοντες
ened them dismissed them, nothing finding
το πως κολασωνται αυτους, δια τον λαον· ὁτι
the how they might punish them, on account of the people; because
παντες εδοξαζον τον θεον επι τῳ γεγονοτι.
all glorified the God on account of that having been done.
22 Ετων γαρ ην πλειονων τεσσαρακοντα ὁ ανθρω-
Years for was more forty the man,
πος, εφ' ὁν εγεγονει το σημειον τουτο της
on whom was wrought the sign this of the
ιασεως.
cure.
23 Απολυθεντες δε ηλθον προς τους ιδιους,
Having been dismissed and they came to the own friends,
και απηγγειλεν ὁσα προς αυτους οἱ αρχιερεις
and related what things to them the high-priests
και οἱ πρεσβυτεροι ειπον. 24 Οἱ δε ακουσαντες,
and the elders said. They and having heard,
ὁμοθυμαδον ηραν φωνην προς τον θεον, και
with one mind lifted up a voice to the God, and
ειπον· Δεσποτα, συ *[ὁ θεος,] ὁ ποιησας τον
said; O sovereign, thou [the God,] that having made the
ουρανον και την γην και την θαλασσαν, και
heaven and the earth and the sea, and
παντα τα εν αυτοις· 25 ὁ δια στοματος
all the things in them; who through mouth
Δαυιδ παιδος σου ειπων· Ινατι εφρυαξεν εθνη,
of David a servant of thee having said; Why raged nations,
και λαοι εμελετησαν κενα; 26 Παρεστησαν οἱ
and peoples devised vain things? Stood up the
βασιλεις της γης, και οἱ αρχοντες συνηχθησαν
kings of the earth, and the rulers were assembled
επι το αυτο, κατα του κυριου, και κατα του
in the same, against the lord, and against the
Χριστου αυτου. 27 Συνηχθησαν γαρ επ' αλη-
Anointed of him. Were gathered for in truth,
θειας εν τῃ πολει ταυτῃ επι τον ἁγιον παιδα
in the city this against the holy servant

on them, to speak no more to any Man in this NAME."

18 And having called them, they commanded *that they should not speak at all nor teach in the NAME of JESUS.

19 But PETER and John answering, said to them, ‡"Whether it is righteous in the sight of GOD to obey you rather than GOD, judge you;

20 ‡for we cannot forbear to speak of the things we ‡have seen and heard."

21 And THEY, having again threatened them, dismissed them, finding Nothing HOW they might punish them, ‡on account of the PEOPLE; because all glorified GOD for WHAT was DONE;

22 for the MAN on whom this SIGN of HEALING had been performed, was more than forty Years old.

23 And being dismissed, they went to their OWN friends, and related all that the HIGH-PRIESTS and ELDERS had said to them.

24 And THEY, having heard it, lifted up their Voice to GOD with one mind, and said, "O Sovereign Lord, thou who didst make the HEAVENS, and the EARTH, and the SEA, and ALL things in them;

25 who didst say *by the Mouth of thy SERVANT David, ‡'Why did 'the Nations rage, and 'the Peoples devise vain 'things?

26 'The KINGS of the 'EARTH stood up, and 'the RULERS assembled to-'gether, against the LORD, 'and against his ANOINT-'ED.'

27 For truly, in this CITY, both Herod, and Pontius Pilate, with the Gentiles and People of Is-

---

* VATICAN MANUSCRIPT.—18. that they should not speak at all nor. 24. the God—omit. 25. through the holy Spirit, by the mouth of our FATHER David thy Servant hast SAID.

‡ 19. Acts v. 29. ‡ 20. Acts [illegible] ‡ 20. Acts ii. 32. ‡ 21. Matt. xxi. 26; Luke xx. 6, 19; xxii. 2; Acts v. 26. ‡ 25. Psa. ii. 1.

σου Ιησουν, ὃν εχρισας, Ἡρωδης τε και Πον-
of thee Jesus, whom thou didst anoint, Herod both and Pon-
τιος Πιλατος, συν εθνεσι και λαοις Ισραηλ,
tius Pilate, with Gentiles and peoples of Israel,
28 ποιησαι ὁσα ἡ χειρ σου και ἡ βουλη *[σου]
to do what things the hand of thee and the will [of thee]
προωρισε γενεσθαι. 29 Και τανυν, κυριε, επιδε
before marked out to be done. And now, O lord, look thou
επι τας απειλας αυτων, και δος τοις δουλοις
upon the threats of them, and grant to the slaves
σου μετα παρρησιας πασης λαλειν τον λογον
of thee with freedom all to speak the word
σου, 30 εν τῳ την χειρα σου εκτεινειν σε εις
of thee, in the the hand of thee to stretch out thee for
ιασιν, και σημεια και τερατα γινεσθαι δια του
healing, and signs and prodigies to do through the
ονοματος του ἁγιου παιδος σου Ιησου. 31 Και
name of the holy child of thee Jesus. And
δεηθεντων αυτων εσαλευθη ὁ τοπος, εν ᾡ ησαν
having prayed of them was shaken the place, in which they were
συνηγμενοι· και επλησθησαν ἁπαντες πνευμα-
assembled; and they were filled all of a spirit
τος ἁγιου, και ελαλουν τον λογον του θεου μετα
holy, and spoke the word of the God with
παρρησιας.
freedom.
32 Του δε πληθους των πιστευσαντων ην ἡ
Of the and multitude of those having believed was the
καρδια και ἡ ψυχη μια· και ουδε εἱς τι των
heart and the soul one; and not even one any of the
ὑπαρχοντων αυτῳ ελεγεν ιδιον ειναι, αλλ' ην
possessions to him said his own to be, but was
αυτοις ἁπαντα κοινα. 33 Και μεγαλῃ δυναμει
to them all things common. And with great power
απεδιδουν το μαρτυριον οἱ αποστολοι της αναστ-
gave the testimony the apostles of the resur-
ασεως του κυριου Ιησου· χαρις τε μεγαλη ην
rection of the lord Jesus; favor and great was
επι παντας αυτους. 34 Ουδε γαρ ενδεης τις
on all them. Not even for poor any one
ὑπηρχεν εν αυτοις· ὁσοι γαρ κτητορες χωριων
was among them; such as for owners of lands
η οικιων ὑπηρχον, πωλουντες εφερον τας τιμας
or houses were, were selling bringing the prices
των πιπρασκομενων, 35 και ετιθουν παρα τους
of those being sold, and were placing at the
ποδας των αποστολων· διεδιδοτο δε ἑκαστῳ,
feet of the apostles; it was divided and to each one,
καθοτι αν τις χρειαν ειχεν. 36 Ιωσης δε, ὁ
according as might one need have. Joses and, he
επικληθεις Βαρναβας ὑπο των αποστολων, (ὁ
being surnamed Barnabas by the apostles, (which
εστι μεθερμηνευομενον, υἱος παρακλησεως,)
is being translated, a son of exhortation,)
Λευιτης, Κυπριος τῳ γενει, 37 ὑπαρχοντος αυτῳ
a Levite, a Cyprian by the birth, having to him

rael were gathered toge-
ther against thy HOLY Servant Jesus, whom thou
hast anointed,
28 ‡ to do what thy
HAND and COUNSEL before
appointed to be done.
29 And NOW, O Lord,
look upon their THREATS;
and grant to thy SERVANTS
to speak thy WORD with all
Freedom,
30 while thou art EX-
TENDING thy HAND for
healing; ‡ and while per-
forming Signs and Prodi-
gies through the NAME of
thy HOLY Servant Jesus."
31 And while they were
praying, ‡ the PLACE was
shaken where they were
assembled; and they were
all filled with *the HOLY
Spirit, and they spoke the
WORD of GOD with Free-
dom.
32 And of the MULTI-
TUDE of those HAVING BE-
LIEVED ‡ the HEART and
the SOUL was one; and no
one said that any thing of
his POSSESSIONS was his
own; ‡ but all things were
common among them.
33 And with * great
Power the APOSTLES de-
livered the TESTIMONY of
the RESURRECTION of the
LORD Jesus; and great
Favor was upon them all.
34 For no one among
them was in want; ‡ for
such as were Owners of
Lands or Houses were con-
stantly selling and bringing
the VALUE of WHAT was
SOLD,
35 and placing it at the
FEET of the APOSTLES;
and it was distributed to
each as any one might have
Necessity.
36 And THAT Joses, who
by the APOSTLES was SUR-
NAMED Barnabas, (which
signifies, being translated,
a Son of Exhortation,) a
Levite, a Cyprian by birth,
37 having a Field, sold

* VATICAN MANUSCRIPT.—28. of thee—omit. 31. the HOLY Spirit. 33. great Power.

‡ 28. Acts ii. 23; iii. 18. ‡ 30. Acts ii. 43; v. 12. ‡ 31. Acts ii. 2, 4; xvi. 26. ‡ 31. ver. 29. ‡ 32. Acts v. 12; Rom. xv. 5, 6; 2 Cor. xiii. 11; Phil. i. 27; ii. 2. 1 Pet iii. 8. ‡ 32. Acts ii. 44. ‡ 34. Acts ii. 45.

αργου, πωλησας ηνεγκε το χρημα, και εθηκε
a field, having sold brought the price, and placed
παρα τους ποδας των αποστολων.
at the feet of the apostles.

ΚΕΦ. ε'. 5.

1 Ανηρ δε τις Ανανιας ονοματι, συν Σαπφει-
A man but certain Ananias by name, with Sapphira
ρη τη γυναικι αὐτου, επωλησε κτημα· 2 και
the wife of himself, sold a possession; and
ενοσφισατο απο της τιμης, συνειδυιας και της
kept back from the price, being privy also the
γυναικος αυτου· και ενεγκας μερος τι, παρα
wife of him; and having brought a part certain, at
τους ποδας των αποστολων εθηκεν. 3 Ειπε δε
the feet of the apostles placed. Said and
Πετρος· Ανανια, διατι επληρωσεν ὁ σατανας
Peter; Ananias, why has filled the adversary
την καρδιαν σου, ψευσασθαι σε το πνευμα το
the heart of thee, to deceive thee the spirit the
αγιον, και νοσφισασθαι απο της τιμης του χω-
holy, and to keep back from the price of the land?
ριου; 4 Ουχι μενον, σοι εμενε, και πρα-
Not remaining, to thee it remained, and having been
θεν, εν τη ση εξουσιᾳ ὑπηρχε; τι ὁτι
sold, in the thine authority it was? why that
εθου. εν τη καρδιᾳ σου το πραγμα τουτο;
hast thou placed in the heart of thee the thing this?
ουκ εψευσω ανθρωποις, αλλα τῳ θεῳ.
not thou hast lied to men, but to the God.
5 Ακουων δε ὁ Ανανιας τους λογους τουτους,
Having heard and the Ananias the words these,
πεσων εξεψυξε. Και εγενετο φοβος μεγας επι
falling down breathed out. And came a fear great on
παντας τους ακουοντας ταυτα. 6 Αναστaντες δε
all those having heard these. Having arisen and
οἱ νεωτεροι συνεστειλαν αυτον, και εξενεγκαν-
the younger ones wrapped up him, and having carried
τες εθαψαν. 7 Εγενετο δε ὡς ὡρων τριων δια-
out they buried. It happened and about hours three apart,
στημα, και ἡ γυνη αυτου μη ειδυια το γεγο-
and the wife of him not having known that having
νος εισηλθεν. 8 Απεκριθη δε αυτη ὁ Πετρος·
been done came in. Answered and to her the Peter;
Ειπε μοι, ει τοσουτου το χωριον απεδοσθε; Ἡ
Tell me, if for so much the land you sold? She
δε ειπε· Ναι τοσουτου. 9 Ὁ δε Πετρος ειπε
and said; Yes for so much. The and Peter said
προς αυτην· Τι ὁτι συνεφωνηθη ὑμιν πειρασαι
to her; Why that it has been agreed upon by you to tempt
το πνευμα κυριου; Ιδου οἱ ποδες των θαψαντων
the spirit of lord? Lo the feet of those having buried
τον ανδρα σου, επι τη θυρᾳ, και εξοισουσι σε.
the husband of thee, at the door, and they will carry out thee.

it, and brought the MONEY, and laid it at the FEET of the APOSTLES.

CHAPTER V.

1 And a certain Man, Ananias by name with Sapphira his WIFE, sold an Estate,

2 and appropriated a part of the PRICE, * his WIFE also knowing of it; and having brought a certain part, ‡ laid it at the FEET of the APOSTLES.

3 ‡ But Peter said, "Ananias, why has the ‡ ADVERSARY filled thine HEART to deceive the HOLY SPIRIT, and to appropriate a part of the PRICE of the LAND?

4 While remaining unsold was it not thine? and when sold, was it not at thine own disposal? Why is it that thou hast admitted this thing into thine HEART? Thou hast not lied to Men, but to GOD."

5 And ANANIAS, having heard these WORDS, ‡ fell down, and expired. And great Fear came on all THOSE who HEARD these things.

6 Then the YOUNGER disciples arising, ‡ wrapped him up, and carrying him out, buried him.

7 And it occurred after an interval of about three Hours, his WIFE also came in, not knowing WHAT had been DONE.

8 And * Peter answered her, "Tell me whether you sold the LAND for so much?" and SHE said, "Yes, for so much."

9 And Peter said to her, "Why have you agreed together ‡ to try the SPIRIT of the Lord? Behold, the FEET of THOSE who have been BURYING thy HUSBAND are at the DOOR, and they will carry thee out."

* VATICAN MANUSCRIPT.—2. the WIFE. 8. Peter.

‡ 2. Acts iv. 37. ‡ 3. Num. xxx. 2; Deut. xxiii. 21; Eccl. v. 4. ‡ 3. Luke xxii. 3. ‡ 5. ver. 10, 11. ‡ 6. Judges xix. 40. ‡ 9. Matt. iv. 7.

[10] Επεσε δε παραχρημα παρα τους ποδας αυτου,
She fell and immediately at the feet of him,
και εξεψυξεν· εισελθοντες δε οἱ νεανισκοι ευρον
and breathed out; having come in and the younger ones found
αυτην νεκραν, και εξενεγκαντες εθαψαν προς
her dead, and having carried out they buried with
τον ανδρα αυτης. [11] Και εγενετο φοβος μεγας
the husband of her. And came a fear great
εφ' ὁλην την εκκλησιαν, και επι παντας τους
on whole the assembly, and on all those
ακουοντας ταυτα.
having heard these things.
[12] Δια δε των χειρων των αποστολων εγινετ
Through and the hands of the apostles were done
σημεια και τερατα εν τῳ λαῳ πολλα· και ησαν
signs and prodigies among the people many; and they were
ὁμοθυμαδον ἁπαντες εν τῃ στοᾳ Σολομωνος
with one mind all in the porch of Solomon;
[13] των δε λοιπων ουδεις ετολμα κολλασθαι
of the and others no one presumed to join himself
αυτοις. Αλλ' εμεγαλυνεν αυτους ὁ λαος·
to them. But magnified them the people;
[14] (μαλλον δε προσετιθεντο πιστευοντες τῳ
(more and were added believing to the
κυριῳ πληθη ανδρων τε και γυναικων·) [15] Ὡστε
Lord multitudes of men both and women;) so that
κατα τας πλατειας εκφερειν τους ασθενεις, και
in the open squares to bring out the sick ones, and
τιθενει επι κλινων και κραββατων, ἱνα ερχομενου
to place on beds and couches, that coming
Πετρου καν ἡ σκια επισκιαση τινι αυτων.
of Peter if even the shadow might overshadow some of them.
[16] Συνηρχετο δε και το πληθος των περιξ πολ-
Came together and also the multitude from the surrounding cities
εων εις Ἱερουσαλημ, φεροντες ασθενεις και
into Jerusalem, bringing sick ones and
οχλουμενους ὑπο πνευματων ακαθαρτων· οἱτινες
those being troubled by spirits impure; whom
εθεραπευοντο ἁπαντες. [17] Αναστας δε ὁ αρχιε-
were healed all. Having arisen and the high-
ρευς και παντες οἱ συν αυτῳ, ἡ ουσα αἱρεσις
priest and all those with him, the being sect
των Σαδδουκαιων, επλησθησαν ζηλου. [18] Και
of the Sadducees, were filled of anger. And
επεβαλον τας χειρας *[αὐτων] επι τους αποστο-
laid the hands [of them] on the apostles,
λους, και εθεντο αυτους εν τηρησει δημοσιᾳ.
and placed them in prison public.
[19] Αγγελος δε κυριου δια της νυκτος ηνοιξε τας
A messenger but of a lord by the night opened the
θυρας της φυλακης, εξαγαγων τε αυτους ειπε·
doors of the prison, having brought out and them said;
[20] πορευεσθε, και σταθεντες λαλειτε εν τῳ ἱερῳ
go, and standing speak you in the temple
τῳ λαῳ παντα τα ῥηματα της ζωης ταυτης.
to the people all the words of the life this.

10 And she fell down immediately at his FEET, and expired; and the YOUNG MEN coming in, found her dead, and having carried her out, buried her by her HUSBAND.

11 ‡ And great Fear came on the Whole ASSEMBLY, and on all THOSE who HEARD these things.

12 ‡ And many Signs and Prodigies were performed among the PEOPLE by the HANDS of the APOSTLES – (and they were all with one mind in Solomon's PORTICO;

13 and of the REST, no one presumed to unite himself to them; ‡ but the PEOPLE magnified them;

14 and Believers were added the more to the LORD, Multitudes both of Men and Women;)—

15 so that they brought out the SICK *even into the OPEN SQUARES, and laid them on Beds and Couchs, that at least the SHADOW of Peter, coming along, might overshadow some of them.

16 And the MULTITUDE came together even from the CITIES surrounding Jerusalem, bringing Sick persons, and those troubled by impure Spirits; all of whom were cured.

17 And the HIGH-PRIEST arising, and All THOSE who were with him, —being the SECT of the SADDUCEES,—were filled with Anger.

18 and laid HANDS on the APOSTLES, and put them into the public Prison.

19 ‡ But an Angel of the Lord, in the NIGHT, opened the DOORS of the PRISON, and bringing them out said,

20 "Go, stand and speak in the TEMPLE to the PEOPLE All the words of this LIFE."

* VATICAN MANUSCRIPT.—15. even into. 18. of them—*omit.*

‡ 11. Acts ii. 43; xix. 17. ‡ 12. Acts xiv. 3; xix. 11; Rom. xv. 19; 2 Cor. xii. 12; Heb. ii. 4. ‡ 13. Acts ii. 47; iv. 21. ‡ 19. Acts xii. 7; xvi. 26.

21 Ακουσαντες δε εισηλθον ὑπο τον ορθρον εις το
Having heard and they entered at the dawn into the
ἱερον, και εδιδασκον.
temple, and taught.
Παραγενομενος δε ὁ αρχιερευς και οἱ συν
Having come and the high-priest and those with
αυτῳ, συνεκαλεσαν το συνεδριον και πασαν την
him, they called together the high council even all the
γερουσιαν των υἱων Ισραηλ, και επεστειλαν εις
senate of the sons Israel, and sent into
το δεσμωτηριον, αχθηναι αυτους. 22 Οι δε ὑπη-
the prison, to have brought them. The but offi-
ρεται παραγενομενοι ουχ ευρον αυτους εν τη
cers having gone not found them in the
φυλακῃ· αναστρεψαντες δε απηγγειλαν, 23 λεγ-
prison; having returned and reported, say-
οντες· Ὁτι το *[μεν] δεσμωτηριον εὑρομεν κε-
ing; That the [indeed] prison we found hav-
κλεισμενον εν παση ασφαλειᾳ, και τους φυλα-
ing been closed with all safety, and the guards
κας εστωτας προ των θυρων· ανοιξαντες δε, εσω
standing before the doors; having opened but, within
ουδενα εὑρομεν. 24 Ὡς δε ηκουσαν τους λογους
no one we found. When and they heard the words
τουτους *[ὁ, τε ἱερευς και] ὁ στρατηγος του
these [the, both priest and] the commander of the
ἱερου και οἱ αρχιερεις, διηπορουν περι αυτων, τι
temple and the high-priests, they doubted concerning them, what
αν γενοιτο τουτο. 25 Παραγενομενος δε τις απηγ-
might be this. Having come but one told
γειλεν αυτοις· Ὁτι ιδου, οἱ ανδρες οὑς εθεσθε
them; That lo, the men whom you put
εν τη φυλακη, εισιν εν τῳ ἱερῳ εστωτες και
in the prison, are in the temple standing and
διδασκοντες τον λαον. 26 Τοτε απελθων ὁ
teaching the people. Then having gone the
στρατηγος συν τοις ὑπηρεταις, ηγαγεν αυτους,
commander with the officers, they brought them,
ου μετα βιας· εφοβουντο γαρ τον λαον, ἱνα μη
not with violence; they feared for the people, that not
λιθασθωσιν. 27 Αγαγοντες δε αυτους εστησαν εν
they might be stoned. Having brought and them they stood in
τῳ συνεδριῳ. Και επηρωτησεν αυτους ὁ αρχιε-
the sanhedrim. And asked them the high-
ρευς, 28 λεγων· Ου παραγγελιᾳ παρηγγειλαμεν
priest, saying; Not with a charge we charged
ὑμιν, μη διδασκειν επι τῳ ονοματι τουτῳ; και
you, not to teach in the name this? and
ιδου, πεπληρωκατε την Ἱερουσαλημ της διδα-
lo, you have filled the Jerusalem of the teach-
χης ὑμων, και βουλεσθε επαγαγειν εφ' ἡμας το
ing of you, and you wish to bring on us the
αιμα του ανθρωπου τουτου. 29 Αποκριθεις δε ὁ
blood of the man this. Answering and the
Πετρος και οἱ αποστολοι, ειπον· Πειθαρχειν
Peter and the apostles, said; To obey
δει θεῳ μαλλον η ανθρωποις. 30 Ὁ θεος
it is necessary God rather than men. The God

21 And having heard this, they entered into the TEMPLE, early in the MORNING, and taught. ‡ And the HIGH-PRIEST coming, and THOSE with him, called the SANHEDRIM together, even All the SENATE of the SONS of Israel, and sent to the PRISON to have them brought.

22 But the OFFICERS going did not find them in the PRISON; and having returned, they reported,

23 saying, "We found the PRISON closed with All Safety, and the GUARDS standing *at the DOORS; but having opened them, we found no one within."

24 And when they heard these WORDS, ‡ both the COMMANDER of the TEMPLE, and the HIGH-PRIESTS were perplexed concerning them, how this thing could be.

25 But some one having come, told them, "Behold, the MEN whom you put in the PRISON are standing in the TEMPLE, and teaching the PEOPLE."

26 Then the COMMANDER going away with the OFFICERS, brought them without Violence; ‡ for they feared the PEOPLE, lest they should be stoned.

27 And having brought them, they stood before the SANHEDRIM; and the HIGH-PRIEST asked them, saying,

28 *‡ "We charged you strictly not to teach in this NAME, and behold, you have filled JERUSALEM with your TEACHING, and ‡ wish to bring this MAN'S BLOOD on us."

29 And PETER answering, and the APOSTLES, said, ‡ "It is necessary to obey God, rather than Men.

* VATICAN MANUSCRIPT.—23. indeed—*omit*. 23. at the DOORS. 24. both the PRIEST, and—*omit*. 28. We charged you strictly not.

‡ 21. Acts iv. 5, 6. ‡ 24. Luke xxii. 4; Acts iv. 1. ‡ 26. Matt. xxi. 26. ‡ 28. Acts iv. 18. ‡ 28. Acts ii. 23. 36; iii. 15; vii. 52. ‡ 29. Acts iv. 19.

των πατερων ἡμων ηγειρεν Ιησουν, ὁν ὑμεις
of the fathers of us raised up Jesus, whom you
διεχειρισασθε, κρεμασαντες επι ξυλου· 31 τουτον
laid violent hands upon, having hanged on a cross; him
ὁ θεος αρχηγον και σωτηρα ὑψωσε τῃ δεξιᾳ
the God a prince and a savior has lifted up to the right hand
αὑτου, δουναι μετανοιαν τῳ Ισραηλ, και αφεσιν
of himself, to give reformation to the Israel, and forgiveness
ἁμαρτιων. 32 Και ἡμεις εσμεν αυτου μαρτυρες
of sins. And we are of him witnesses
των ῥηματων τουτων, και το πνευμα δε το
of the matters these, and the spirit also the
ἁγιον, ὁ εδωκεν ὁ θεος τοις πειθαρχουσιν αυτῳ.
holy, which gave the God to those submitting to him.
33 Οἱ δε ακουσαντες διεπριοντο, και εβουλευοντο
They and having heard were sawn through, and took counsel
ανελειν αυτους.
to kill them.
34 Αναστας δε τις εν τῳ συνεδριῳ Φαρισαιος,
Having arisen and one in the high counsel a Pharisee,
ονοματι Γαμαλιηλ νομοδιδασκαλος, τιμιος παν-
by name Gamaliel a teacher of law, honored by
τι τῳ λαῳ, εκελευσεν εξω βραχυ τι τους
all the people, ordered without a little while the
αποστολους ποιησαι. 35 Ειπε τε προς αυτους·
apostles to be put. He said and to them;
Ανδρες Ισραηλιται, προσεχετε ἑαυτοις, επι τοις
Men Israelites, take heed to yourselves, to the
ανθρωποις τουτοις τι μελλετε πρασσειν.
men these what you are about to do.
36 Προ γαρ τουτων των ἡμερων ανεστη Θευδας,
Before for these the days stood up Theudas,
λεγων ειναι τινα ἑαυτον, ᾡ προσεκολληθη
saying to be some one himself, to whom adhered
αριθμος ανδρων ὡσει τετρακοσιων· ὁς ανηρεθη,
a number of men about four hundred; who was put to death,
και παντες ὁσοι επειθοντο αυτῳ, διελυθησαν
and all as many as listened to him, were dispersed
και εγενοντο εις ουδεν. 37 Μετα τουτον ανεστη
and came to nothing. After this stood up
Ιουδας ὁ Γαλιλαιος, εν ταις ἡμεραις της απο-
Judas the Galilean, in the days of the regis-
γραφης, και απεστησε λαον *[ἱκανον] οπισω
tering, and drew away people [much] behind
αὑτου· κακεινος απωλετο, και παντες ὁσοι επει-
himself; and he was destroyed, and all as many as lis-
θοντο αυτῳ, διεσκορπισθησαν. 38 Και τανυν
tened to him, were dispersed. And now
λεγω ὑμιν, αποστητε απο των ανθρωπων του-
I say to you, withdraw from the men these
των, και εασατε αυτους, ὁτι εαν ῃ εξ ανθρω-
and let alone them, because if may be from men
πων ἡ βουλη αὑτη η το εργον τουτο, καταλυ-
the counsel this or the work this, it will be
θησεται· 39 ει δε εκ θεου εστιν, ου δυνασθε
overthrown; if but from God it is, not you are able
καταλυσαι αυτους, μηποτε και θεομαχοι εὑρε-
to overthrow them, not and fighters against God you

30 ‡The GOD of our FATHERS raised up *JESUS, whom, having hanged on a Cross, you killed.
31 Him, a Prince and a Savior, GOD has lifted up to his own RIGHT-HAND, ‡*to GIVE Reformation to ISRAEL, and Forgiveness of Sins.
32 And we are Witnesses *in him of these THINGS; ‡and GOD gave the HOLY SPIRIT to THOSE who SUBMIT to him."
33 And THEY, having heard this, were enraged, and took counsel to kill them.
34 But a certain Pharisee in the SANHEDRIM, named Gamaliel, a teacher of the law, honored by All the PEOPLE, standing up ordered *the MEN to be put out for a little time.
35 And he said to them, "Israelites! take heed to yourselves what you are about to do to these MEN.
36 For before These DAYS Theudas stood up, saying that he was somebody; to whom a Number of Men, about four hundred, adhered; who was put to death, and all, as many as obeyed him, were dispersed, and came to nothing.
37 After him stood up Judas the Galilean, in the DAYS of the REGISTERING, and drew away PEOPLE after him; and he was destroyed, and all, as many as obeyed him, were dispersed.
38 And NOW I say to you, Keep away from these MEN, and let them alone; ‡Because if this COUNSEL or this WORK be from Men, it will be overthrown;
39 but if it be from God, you are not able to overthrow them; be not you found fighters against God."

* VATICAN MANUSCRIPT.—31. to GIVE. 32. in him of these THINGS; and GOD gave the HOLY SPIRIT to THOSE who SUBMIT to him. 34. the MEN. 37. much—omit.

‡ 30. Acts iii. 13, 15; xxii. 14. ‡ 31. Luke xxiv. 47; Acts iii. 26; xiii. 38. ‡ 32. Acts ii. 4; x. 44. ‡ 38. Prov. xxi. 30; Isa. viii. 10; Matt. xv. 13.

θητε. 40 Επεισθησαν δε αυτῳ· και προσκα-
should be found. They were persuaded and by him; and having
λεσαμενοι τους αποστολους, δειραντες παραγ-
called the apostles, having beaten they com-
γειλαν μη λαλειν επι τῳ ονοματι του Ιησου, και
manded not to speak in the name of the Jesus, and
απελυσαν αυτους. 41 Οἱ μεν ουν επορευοντο
released them. They indeed therefore went
χαιροντες απο προσωπου του συνεδριου, ὁτι
rejoicing from presence of the high council, because
ὑπερ του ονοματος κατηξιωθησαν ατιμασθηναι.
in behalf of the name they were accounted worthy to be dishonored.
42 Πασαν τε ἡμεραν εν τῳ ἱερου και κατ' οικον
Every and day in the temple and at home
ουκ επαυοντο διδασκοντες και ευαγγελιζομενοι
not they ceased teaching and announcing glad tidings of
Ιησουν τον Χριστον.
Jesus the Anointed.

ΚΕΦ. ς'. 6.

1 Εν δε ταις ἡμεραις ταυταις πληθυνοντων
In and the days those increasing
των μαθητων, εγενετο γογγυσμος των Ἑλλη-
the disciples, came a murmuring of the Helle-
νιστων προς τους Ἑβραιους, ὁτι παρεθεωρουντο
nists to the Hebrews, because were overlooked
εν τῃ διακονιᾳ τῃ καθημερινῃ αἱ χηραι αυτων.
in the service the daily the widows of them.
2 Προσκαλεσαμενοι δε οἱ δωδεκα το πληθος
Having called and the twelve the multitude
των μαθητων, ειπον· Ουκ αρεστον εστιν ἡμας
of the disciples, said; Not proper it is us
καταλειψαντας τον λογον του θεου, διακονειν
having left the word of the God, to serve
τραπεζαις. 3 Επισκεψασθε ουν, αδελφοι,
tables. Look you out therefore, brethren,
ανδρας εξ ὑμων μαρτυρουμενους ἑπτα, πληρεις
men from of you being attested seven, full
πνευματος και σοφιας, οὑς καταστησομεν επι
of spirit and wisdom, whom we will appoint to
της χρειας ταυτης· 4 ἡμεις δε τῃ προσευχῃ και
the need this; we but to the prayer and
τῃ διακονιᾳ του λογου προσκαρτερησομεν.
to the service of the word will constantly attend.
5 Και ηρεσεν ὁ λογος ενωπιον παντος του πλη-
And pleased the word in presence of all of the multi-
θους· και εξελεξαντο Στεφανον, ανδρα πληρη
tude; and they choose Stephen, a man full
πιστεως και πνευματος ἁγιου, και Φιλιππον,
of faith and spirit holy, and Philip,
και Προχορον, και Νικανορα, και Τιμωνα, και
and Prochorus, and Nicanor, and Timon, and
Παρμεναν, και Νικολαον προσηλυτον Αντιοχεα·
Parmenas, and Nicolaus a proselyte of Antioch;

40 And they were persuaded by him; and having summoned the APOSTLES and ‡ scourged them, they charged them not to speak in the NAME of JESUS, and dismissed them.
41 Then indeed THEY went ‡ rejoicing from the Presence of the SANHEDRIM, Because they were deemed worthy to be dishonored on account of the NAME.
42 ‡ And every Day, in the TEMPLE and at Home, they ceased not teaching and preaching the glad tidings * of the ANOINTED Jesus.

CHAPTER VI.

1 And in those DAYS, the DISCIPLES increasing, there arose a Complaint of the † ‡ HELLENISTS against the HEBREWS, Because their WIDOWS were neglected in the ‡ DAILY SERVICE.
2 And the TWELVE, having summoned the MULTITUDE of the DISCIPLES, said, "It is not proper for us to leave the WORD of GOD and serve Tables.
3 * Therefore, Brethren, look out from among yourselves, seven Men of good reputation, full of Spirit and Wisdom, whom we may set over this BUSINESS;
4 but we will constantly attend to PRAYER, and to the MINISTRY of the WORD."
5 And the PROPOSITION was pleasing to All the MULTITUDE; and they selected Stephen, a man full of Faith and holy Spirit, and ‡ Philip, and Prochorus, Nicanor, and Timon, and Parmenas, and Nicolaus, a Proselyte of Antioch;

* VATICAN MANUSCRIPT.—42. of the ANOINTED Jesus. 3. But, Brethren, we will look out among you.

† 1. Proselytes to the Jewish religion, or foreign Jews who spoke the Greek language.

‡ 40. Matt. x. 17; xxiii. 34; Mark xiii. 9. ‡ 41. Matt. v. 12; Rom. v. 3; James i. 2; 1 Pet. iv. 13, 16. ‡ 42. Acts ii. 46. ‡ 1 Acts ix. 29. ‡ 1. Acts iv. 35. ‡ 5. Acts viii. 5, 26: xxi. 8.

6 οὓς εστησαν ενωπιον των αποστολων· και
whom they placed in presence of the apostles; and
προσευξαμενοι επεθηκαν αυτοις τας χειρας.
having prayed they put to them the hands.
7 Και ὁ λογος του θεου ηυξανε, και επληθυνετο
And the word of the God grew, and was multiplied
ὁ αριθμος των μαθητων εν Ἱερουσαλημ σφοδρα·
the number of the disciples in Jerusalem greatly;
πολυς τε οχλος των ἱερεων ὑπηκουον τη πιστει.
great and a crowd of the priests were obedient to the faith.
8 Στεφανος δε πληρης χαριτος και δυναμεως
Stephen and full of favor and of power
εποιει τερατα και σημεια μεγαλα εν τῳ λαῳ.
performed prodigies and signs great among the people.
9 Ανεστησαν δε τινες των εκ της συναγω-
Stood up and some of those from the syna-
γης της λεγομενης Λιβερτινων, και Κυρηναιων,
gogue of that being called of Libertines, and of Cyrenians,
και Αλεξανδρεων, και των απο Κιλικιας και
and of Alexandrians, and of those from Cilicia and
Ασιας, συζητουντες τῳ Στεφανῳ· 10 και ουκ
Asia, disputing with the Stephen; and not
ισχυον αντιστηναι τη σοφιᾳ και τῳ πνευματι
were able to resist the wisdom and the spirit
ᾡ ελαλει. 11 Τοτε ὑπεβαλον ανδρας,
with which he spoke. Then they thrust under men,
λεγοντας· Ὁτι ακηκοαμεν αυτου λαλουντος
saying; That we have heard him speaking
ῥηματα βλασφημα εις Μωυσην και τον θεον.
words blasphemous against Moses and the God.
12 Συνεκινησαν τε τον λαον και τους πρεσβυτε-
They stirred up and the people and the elders
ρους και τους γραμματεις, και επισταντες
and the scribes, and having come upon
συνηρπασαν αυτον, και ηγαγον εις το συνεδριον,
they seized him, and led into the high council,
13 εστησαν τε μαρτυρας ψευδεις, λεγοντας· Ὁ
stood up and witnesses false, saying; The
ανθρωπος οὗτος ου παυεται ῥηματα λαλων κατα
man this not ceases words speaking against
του τοπου του ἁγιου και του νομου. 14 Ακηκοα-
the place of the holy and the law. We have heard
μεν γαρ αυτου λεγοντος· Ὁτι Ἰησους ὁ Ναζω-
for him saying; That Jesus the Naza-
ραιος οὗτος καταλυσει τον τοπον τουτον, και
rene this will destroy the place this, and
αλλαξει τα εθη, ἁ παρεδωκεν ἡμιν Μωυσης.
will change the customs, which delivered to us Moses.
15 Και ατενισαντες εις αυτον ἁπαντες οἱ καθε-
And having gazed on him all those being
ζομενοι εν τῳ συνεδριῳ, ειδον το προσωπον
seated in the high-council, saw the face
αυτου ὡσει προσωπον αγγελου.
of him like a face of a messenger.

6 whom they set before the APOSTLES; ‡ and they, having prayed, ‡ laid HANDS on them.

7 ‡ And the WORD of GOD grew; and the NUMBER of the DISCIPLES was greatly multiplied in Jerusalem; and a great Crowd of the † PRIESTS obeyed the FAITH.

8 And Stephen, full of Favor and Power, performed Prodigies and great Signs among the PEOPLE.

9 And there arose some of THAT SYNAGOGUE which is CALLED of the † Libertines, and of the Cyrenians and Alexandrians, and of THOSE from Cilicia and Asia, disputing with STEPHEN;

10 and ‡ they were not able to resist the WISDOM and the SPIRIT with which he spoke.

11 Then they bribed Men to say, "We have heard him speak blasphemous Words against Moses and GOD."

12 And they excited the PEOPLE, and the ELDERS, and the SCRIBES; and coming suddenly, they seized him, and led him into the SANHEDRIM;

13 and introduced false Witnesses, saying, "This MAN is incessantly speaking against the HOLY PLACE, and the LAW;

14 ‡ for we have heard him say, That this Jesus, the NAZARENE, ‡ will destroy this PLACE, and will change the CUSTOMS which Moses delivered to us."

15 And ALL those BEING SEATED in the SANHEDRIM, looking steadily at him, saw his FACE like the Face of an Angel.

† 7. The number of the priests must have been quite large about this time, as it appears from Ezra ii. 36—39, that 4280 priests returned from the captivity. † 9. These persons seem to have been Jews, who having been carried captive to Rome, were freed by their masters, and thus became *freed-men*. Some think they received their name from the place where they lived.—*Owen*.

‡ 6. Acts i. 24. ‡ 6. Acts xiii. 3; 1 Tim. iv. 14; v. 22; 2 Tim. i. 6. ‡ 7. Acts xii. 24; xix. 20. ‡ 10. Luke xxi. 15; v. 39. ‡ 14. Acts xxv. 8. ‡ 14. Dan ix. 26; Matt. xxii. 7.

ΚΕΦ. ϛ'. 7.

1 Ειπε δε ὁ αρχιερευς, Ει *[αρα] ταυτα οὑτως
Said and the high-priest, If [then] these things thus
εχει; 2 Ὁ δε εφη· Ανδρες αδελφοι και πατερες,
are? He and said; Men brethren and fathers,
ακουσατε. Ὁ θεος της δοξης ωφθη τῳ πατρι
hear you. The God of the glory appeared to the father
ἡμων Αβρααμ οντι εν τῃ Μεσοποταμια, πριν η
of us Abraham being in the Mesopotamia, before
κατοικησαι αυτον εν Χαρραν· 3 Και ειπε προς
to dwell him in Charran; and said to
αυτον· Εξελθε εκ της γης σου, και εκ της
him; Go out from the land of thee, and from the
συγγενειας σου, και δευρο εις γην, ἡν αν σοι
kindred of thee, and come into a land, which to thee
δειξω. 4 Τοτε εξελθων εκ γης Χαλδαιων, κατῳ-
I may show. Then going out from land of Chaldeans, he dwelt
κησεν εν Χαρραν· κἀκειθεν, μετα το αποθανειν
in Charran; and thence, after the to have died
τον πατερα αυτου, μετῳκισεν αυτον εις την
the father of him, he caused to remove him into the
γην ταυτην, εις ἡν ὑμεις νυν κατοικειτε· 5 και
land this, in which you now dwell; and
ουκ εδωκεν αυτῳ κληρονομιαν εν αυτῃ, ουδε
not he gave to him inheritance in her, not even
βημα ποδος· και επηγγειλατο αυτῳ δουναι εις
a foot-breadth; and he promised to him to give for
κατασχεσιν αυτην, και τῳ σπερματι αυτου μετ'
a possession her, and to the seed of him after
αυτον, ουκ οντος αυτῳ τεκνου. 6 Ελαλησε δε
him, not being to him a child. Spoke and
οὑτως ὁ θεος· Ὁτι εσται το σπερμα αυτου
thus the God; That shall be the seed of him
παροικον εν γῃ αλλοτριᾳ, και δουλωσουσιν
a stranger in a land foreign, and they will enslave
αυτο και κακωσουσιν ετη τετρακοσια· 7 και το
it and they will oppress years four hundred; and the
εθνος, ᾡ εαν δουλευσωσι, κρινω εγω, ειπεν
nation, to which they may be enslaved, will judge I, said
ὁ θεος· και μετα ταυτα εξελευσονται, και
the God; and after these things they shall come out, and
λατρευσουσι μοι εν τῳ τοπῳ τουτῳ. 8 (Και
shall render service to me in the place this. (And
εδωκεν αυτῳ διαθηκην περιτομης· και οὑτως
he gave to him a covenant of circumcision; and this
εγεννησε τον Ισαακ, και περιετεμεν αυτον τῃ
he begot of the Isaac, and circumcised him the

CHAPTER VII.

1 Then the HIGH-PRIEST
said, "Are these things
so?"

2 And HE said, ‡ "Breth-
ren and Fathers, hearken!
The GLORIOUS GOD ap-
peared † to our FATHER
Abraham, when in MESO-
POTAMIA, before he resided
in Haran,

3 and said to him, ‡ 'De-
part from thy COUNTRY,
and from thy KINDRED,
and come into * the LAND
which I will show thee.'

4 Then ‡ going out from
the Land of the Chaldeans,
he dwelt in Haran; from
thence also, † after the
DEATH of his FATHER, he
removed him into this
LAND in which you now
dwell;

5 and gave him ‡ no IN-
HERITANCE in it, not even
the breadth of his Foot;
‡ but he promised to give
it to him for a Possession,
and to his SEED after him,
though he had no Child.

6 And GOD spoke thus,
‡ 'That his SEED should be
a Stranger in a foreign
Land; and that they will
enslave and oppress it
‡ four hundred years;

7 and the NATION to
which they shall be en-
slaved ‡ I will judge,' said
GOD, 'and after that, they
shall come out and serve
me in this PLACE.'

8 ‡ And he gave him a
Covenant of Circumcision;
‡ and thus he begot ISAAC,
and circumcised him the

---

* VATICAN MANUSCRIPT.—1. then—*omit*. 3. the LAND.

† 2. It seems probable that Stephen here followed the Jewish tradition, (adopted by Philo,) that God appeared *twice* to Abraham,—1st, when living in Chaldea, and 2dly, when resident in Haran. He left *Ur* at the first call, and came to *Haran* with his father Terah, (Gen. xi. 31;) he left Haran at the second call, and came into the promised land. In this way the account harmonizes with the call as narrated in Gen. xii. 1: "Now the Lord *had said* unto Abraham," &c. † 4. By recurring to Gen xi. 26, 32, and xii. 4, it will appear that Terah lived 60 years after the removal of Abraham, and yet here he is said to have died before Abraham left Haran. Unless with some we suppose Abraham to have been the youngest of Terah's sons, and born when his father was 130 years old we must presume that Stephen followed some traditionary account of the transaction.—*Owen*. The Samaritan copy makes the age of Terah at his death to be 145, or 60 years less than the Hebrew text.

‡ 2. Acts xxii. 1. ‡ 3. Gen xii. 1. ‡ 4. Gen. xi. 31; xii. 4, 5. ‡ 5. Heb. xi. 13. ‡ 5. Gen. xii. 7; xiii. 15; xv. 3, 18; xvii. 8; xxvi. 3; Heb. xi. 8, 9. ‡ 6. Gen. xv. 13, 16. ‡ 6. Exod. xii. 40; Gal. iii. 17. ‡ 7. See Exod. vii—xi. ‡ 8. Gen. xvii. 9—11. ‡ 8. Gen. xxi. 2—4.

ἡμερᾳ τῃ ογδοῃ· και ὁ Ισαακ τον Ιακωβ, και ὁ
day the eighth; and the Isaac the Jacob, and the
Ιακωβ τους δωδεκα πατριαρχας. 9 Και οἱ
Jacob the twelve patriarchs. And the
πατριαρχαι ζηλωσαντες τον Ιωσηφ απεδοντο
patriarchs envying the Joseph sold
εις Αιγυπτον· και ην ὁ θεος μετ' αυτου, 10 και
into Egypt; and was the God with him, and
εξειλετο αυτον εκ πασων των θλιψεων αυτου,
delivered him out of all of the afflictions of him,
και εδωκεν αυτῳ χαριν και σοφιαν εναντιων
and gave to him favor and wisdom in presence
Φαραω βασιλεως Αιγυπτου, και κατεστησεν
of Pharaoh king of Egypt, and placed
αυτον ἡγουμενον επ' Αιγυπτον και ὁλον τον
him ruling over Egypt and whole the
οικον αὑτου.
house of himself.
11 Ηλθε δε λιμος εφ' ὁλην την γην Αιγυπτου
Came and a famine on whole the land of Egypt
και Χαναaν, και θλιψις μεγαλη· και ουκ εὑρισκον
and Canaan, and affliction great; and not found
χορτασματα οἱ πατερες ἡμων. 12 Ακουσας δε
provisions the fathers of us. Having heard and
Ιακωβ οντα σιτα εν Αιγυπτῳ, εξαπεστειλε τους
Jacob being grain in Egypt, he sent the
πατερας ἡμων πρωτον. 13 Και εν τῳ δευτερῳ
fathers of us first. And in the second
ανεγνωρισθη Ιωσηφ τοις αδελφοις αὑτου, και
was made known Joseph to the brothers of himself, and
φανερον εγενετο τῳ Φαραω το γενος του Ιωσηφ.
shown became to the Pharaoh the family of the Joseph.
14 Αποστειλας δε Ιωσηφ μετεκαλεσατο τον
Having sent and Joseph called for the
πατερα αὑτου Ιακωβ, και πασαν την συγγενειαν,
father of himself Jacob, and all the kindred,
εν ψυχαις εβδομηκοντα πεντε. 15 Κατεβη δε
in souls seventy five. Went down and
Ιακωβ *[εις Αιγυπτον,] και ετελευτησεν αυτος
Jacob [into Egypt,] and died he
και οἱ πατερες ἡμων. 16 Και μετετεθησαν εις
and the fathers of us. And they were carried into
Συχεμ, και ετεθησαν εν τῳ μνηματι, ᾡ ωνη-
Sychem, and were placed in the tomb, which bought
σατο Αβρααμ τιμης αργυριου παρα των υἱων
Abraam for a price of silver from the sons
Εμμορ του Συχεμ.) 17 Καθως δε ηγγιζεν ὁ
of Emmor of the Sychem.) When but drew near the
χρονος της επαγγελιας, ἡς ωμοσεν ὁ θεος τῳ
time of the promise, which swore the God to the

EIGHTH DAY; and ISAAC, JACOB, and JACOB the TWELVE Patriarchs.

9 ‡ And the PATRIARCHS envying JOSEPH, sold him into Egypt; ‡ but God was with him,

10 and delivered him from All his AFFLICTIONS, and gave him Favor and Wisdom in the sight of Pharaoh, King of Egypt, who constituted him Ruler over Egypt, and All his HOUSE.

11 ‡ And a Famine came upon All the LAND of Egypt and Canaan, and great Distress; and our FATHERS found no Provisions.

12 ‡ But Jacob, having heard that there was Grain * in Egypt, sent our FATHERS the first time;

13 ‡ and at the SECOND time, Joseph was made known to his BROTHERS; and * Joseph's FAMILY was shown to PHARAOH.

14 ‡ And Joseph sent and invited his FATHER Jacob to him, and ‡ All his KINDRED, † seventy-five Souls.

15 And Jacob went down into Egypt, and died, he, and our FATHERS;

16 and † they were carried to Shechem, and laid in the TOMB which † Jacob bought for Money of the SONS of Hamor * in SHECHEM.

17 But when ‡ the TIME of the PROMISE drew near, which God ‡ * solemnly

* VATICAN MANUSCRIPT.—12. for Egypt. 13. Joseph's FAMILY. 15. into Egypt—*omit*. 16. in Shechem. 17. solemnly made to ABRAHAM.

† 14. It states in Gen. xlvi. 26, "All the souls that came with Jacob into Egypt, which came out of his loins, *besides Jacob's sons' wives*, all the souls were three score and six." Stephen adds to this number nine of Jacob's sons' wives, which makes the number of seventy-five. These though not of his blood, were of his *kindred*, as Stephen expresses it, being related to him by marriage. † 16. In Gen. l. 13, it is stated, "that *Jacob* was buried in the cave of the field of Machpelah, before Mamre;" and in Josh. xxiv. 32, that *Joseph* was buried in Shechem; and here we have the authority of Stephen that the rest of the twelve patriarchs were interred in the same place. † 10. The best critics are of the opinion that *Abraham*, as found in the text, is spurius, and has been inserted by some officious transcriber. The word *Jacob* ought to be supplied.

‡ 9. Gen. xxxvi. 4, 11, 28; Psa. cv. 17. ‡ 9. Gen. xxxix. 2, 21, 23. ‡ 10. Gen. xli. 37; xlii. 6. ‡ 11. Gen. xli. 54. ‡ 12. Gen. xlii. 1. ‡ 13. Gen. xlv. 4, 16. ‡ 14. Gen. xlv. 9, 27. ‡ 14. Gen. xlvi. 27; Deut. x. 22. ‡ 17. Gen. xv. 13. ‡ 17. Exod. i. 7—9

Αβρααμ, ηυξησεν ὁ λαος και επληθυνθη εν
Abraam, grew the people and were multiplied in
Αιγυπτῳ· 18 αχρις οὗ ανεστη βασιλευς ἑτερος,
Egypt; till for whom stood up a king another,
ὃς ουκ ᾐδει τον Ιωσηφ. 19 Οὗτος κατασοφι-
who not knew the Joseph. This having dealt
σαμενος το γενος ἡμων, εκακωσε τους πατερας
deceitfully the family of us, ill-treated the fathers
ἡμων, του ποιειν εκθετα τα βρεφη αυτων, εις
of us, of the to cause to be exposed the babes of them, in order
το μη ζωογονεισθαι. 20 Εν ᾧ καιρῳ εγεννη-
that not they might be preserved. In which season was born
θη Μωυσης, και ην αστειος τῳ θεῳ· ὃς ανετρα-
Moses, and was beautiful to the God; who was nursed
φη μηνας τρεις εν τῳ οικῳ του πατρος.
months three in the house of the father.
21 Εκτεθεντα δε αυτον, ανειλετο αυτον ἡ θυγα-
Having exposed and him, took up him the daugh-
τηρ Φαραω, και ανεθρεψατο αυτον ἑαυτῃ εις υἱον.
ter of Pharaoh, and nursed him herself for a son.
22 Και επαιδευθη Μωυσης πασῃ σοφιᾳ Αιγυπ-
And was taught Moses in all wisdom of Egyp-
τιων· ην δε δυνατος εν λογοις και εν εργοις
tians; was and powerful in words and in works
αὑτου. 23 Ὡς δε επληρουτο αυτῳ τεσσαρακον-
of himself. When but was completed to him forty
ταετης χρονος, ανεβη επι την καρδιαν αυτου
years of time, it came up in the heart of him
επισκεψασθαι τους αδελφους αὑτου, τους υἱους
to visit the brethren of himself, the sons
Ισραηλ. 24 Και ιδων τινα αδικουμενον, ημυνατο,
of Israel. And seeing one being wronged, he defended,
και εποιησεν εκδικησιν τῳ καταπονουμενῳ,
and did justice to him being oppressed,
παταξας τον Αιγυπτιον. 25 Ενομιζε δε συνιεναι
having smitten the Egyptian. He thought and to understand
τους αδελφους αὑτου, ὁτι ὁ θεος δια χειρος
the brethren of himself, that the God by hands
αυτου διδωσιν αυτοις σωτηριαν· οἱ δε ου συνη-
of him gives to them salvation; they but not under-
καν. 26 Τῃ δε επιουσῃ ἡμερᾳ ωφθη αυτοις
stood. In the but next day he appeared to those
μαχομενοις, και συνηλασεν αυτους εις ειρηνην,
contending, and urged them to peace,
ειπων· Ανδρες, αδελφοι, εστε ὑμεις· ἱνατι
saying; Men, brethren, are you; why
αδικειτε αλληλους; 27 Ὁ δε αδικων τον πλησιον,
wrong you each other? He but wronging the neighbor,
απωσατω αυτον, ειπων· Τις σε κατεστησεν
thrust away him, saying; Who thee has appointed
αρχοντα και δικαστην εφ' ἡμας; 28 Μη ανελειν
a ruler and a judge over us; Not to kill

made to ABRAHAM, the PEOPLE grew and were multiplied in Egypt,

18 till another King *arose, who did not acknowledge Joseph.

19 He, having outwitted our RACE, ill-treated *our FATHERS, causing their INFANTS to be EXPOSED in order that they might not LIVE.

20 ‡At which period Moses was born, and ‡was DIVINELY beautiful; and he was nursed in his FATHER'S HOUSE three Months;

21 ‡but having exposed him, the DAUGHTER of Pharaoh took him up, and cherished him for her own Son.

22 And Moses was educated in All the Wisdom of the Egyptians, and was ‡Powerful in his Words and Works.

23 ‡And when he was full †forty years of age, it came into his HEART to visit his BRETHREN, the Sons of Israel.

24 And observing one wronged, he defended and executed judgment for HIM who was OPPRESSED, smiting the EGYPTIAN.

25 Now he thought that his BRETHREN understood That GOD by his Hand would give them Deliverance; but they did not understand.

26 ‡And on the FOLLOWING Day, he presented himself to them as they were contending, and urged them to peace, saying, 'Men, *you are brethren; why do you injure each other?'

27 But HE INJURING his NEIGHBOR, thrust him away, saying, ‡'Who made Thee a Ruler and a Judge over us?

* VATICAN MANUSCRIPT.—18. rose up in Egypt, who knew. 19. the FATHERS 26. you are.

† 23. This was a general tradition among the Jews; "Moses was 40 years in Pharaoh's court, 40 years in Midian, and 40 years he served Israel."—*Clarke.*

‡ 20. Exod. ii. 2. ‡ 20. Heb. xi. 23. ‡ 21. Exod. ii. 3—10. ‡ 22. Luke ii. 19. ‡ 23. Exod. ii. 11, 12. ‡ 26. Exod. ii. 13. ‡ 27. See Luke xii. 14 Acts iv. 7.

με συ θελεις, ὁν τροπον ανειλες χθες τον
me thou wishest, in which manner thou didst kill yesterday the
Αιγυπτιον; 29 *Εφυγε δε Μωυσης εν τῳ λογῳ*
Egyptian? Fled and Moses at the word
τουτῳ, και εγενετο παροικος εν γῃ Μαδιαμ, οὑ
this, and became a sojourner in land of Midian, where
εγεννησεν υἱους δυο. 30 *Και πληρωθεντων ετων*
he begot sons two. And being completed years
τεσσαρακοντα, ωφθη αυτῳ εν τῃ ερημῳ του
forty, appeared to him in the desert of the
ορους Σινα αγγελος *[*κυριου*] *εν φλογι πυρος*
mountain Sinai a messenger [of Lord] in a flame of fire
βατου. 31 *Ὁ δε Μωυσης ιδων εθαυμαζε το*
of a bush. The but Moses having seen admired the
ὁραμα· προσερχομενου δε αυτου κατανοησαι,
sight; coming near and of him to observe,
εγενετο φωνη κυριου *[*προς αυτον·*] 32 *εγω ὁ*
came a voice of lord [to him;] I the
θεος των πατερων σου, ὁ θεος Αβρααμ, και *[*ὁ*
God of the fathers of thee, the God of Abraam, and [the
θεος] *Ισαακ, και* *[*ὁ θεος*] *Ιακωβ. Εντρομος*
God] of Isaac, and [the God] of Jacob. Terrified
δε γενομενος Μωυσης ουκ ετολμα κατανοησαι.
and being Moses not dared to look.
33 *Ειπε δε αυτῳ ὁ κυριος· Λυσον το ὑποδημα*
Said and to him the Lord; Loose the sandals
των ποδων σου· ὁ γαρ τοπος εν ᾡ ἑστηκας,
of the feet of thee; the for place in which thou standest,
γη ἁγια εστιν. 34 *Ιδων ειδον την κακωσιν*
ground holy is. Having seen I saw the evil treatment
του λαου μου του εν Αιγυπτῳ, και του στεναγ-
of the people of me of that in Egypt, and the groaning
μου αυτων ηκουσα, και κατεβην εξελεσθαι
of them I have heard, and am come down to deliver
αυτους· και νυν δευρο, αποστελω σε εις Αιγυπ-
them; and now come, I will send thee into Egypt.
τον.

35 *Τουτον τον Μωυσην ὁν ηρνησατο, ειπον-*
This the Moses whom they denied, say-
τες· Τις σε κατεστησεν αρχοντα και δικαστην;
ing. Who thee appointed a ruler and a judge?
τουτον ὁ θεος αρχοντα και λυτρωτην απεσ-
this the God a ruler and a redeemer sent
τειλεν εν χειρι αγγελου του οφθεντος αυτῳ
by hand of a messenger of that having appeared to him
εν τῃ βατῳ. 36 *Οὑτος εξηγαγεν αυτους, ποιη-*
in the bush. This led out them, having
σας τερατα και σημεια εν γῃ Αιγυπτῳ, και εν
done prodigies and signs in the Egypt, and in
ερυθρᾳ θαλασσῃ, και εν τῃ ερημῳ, ετη τεσσα-
red sea, and in the desert, years forty.
ρακοντα. 37 *Οὑτος εστιν ὁ Μωυσης, ὁ ειπων*
This is the Moses, he saying
τοις υἱοις Ισραηλ· Προφητην ὑμιν αναστησει
to the sons of Israel; A prophet for you will raise up

28 Wilt thou kill me as thou didst the Egyptian yesterday?'

29 ‡ And Moses fled at that SAYING, and became a Sojourner in the Land of Midian, where he begot two Sons.

30 ‡ And forty Years being completed, there appeared to him in the DESERT of MOUNT Sinai, an Angel in a Flame of Fire, in a Bush.

31 And MOSES having seen, admired the SIGHT; and coming near to look at it, a Voice came from the Lord, saying,

32 ‡ 'I am the GOD of thy FATHERS,—the GOD of Abraham, and Isaac, and Jacob.' And Moses being afraid dared not look at it.

33 ‡ And the LORD said to him, 'Loose thy SANDALS from * Thy FEET; for the PLACE on which thou standest is holy Ground.

34 ‡ I have surely seen the EVIL TREATMENT of THAT PEOPLE of mine in Egypt, and I have heard their GROANING, and am come down to deliver them; and now, come, I will send thee into Egypt.'

35 This is the MOSES whom they renounced, saying, 'Who made Thee a Ruler and a Judge?' * even Him GOD sent to be a Ruler and a Redeemer, * with the Hand of ‡ THAT Angel which appeared to him in the BUSH.

36 ‡ He led them out, having ‡ performed Prodigies and Signs in EGYPT, ‡ and in the Red Sea, ‡ and in the DESERT forty years.

37 This is THAT MOSES, who SAID to the SONS of Israel, ‡ 'A Prophet will GOD raise up for you from

* VATICAN MANUSCRIPT.—30. of the Lord—*omit.* 31. to him—*omit.* 32. the GOD—*omit.* 32. the GOD—*omit.* 33. Thy FEET. 35. even. 35. with the Hand.

‡ 29. Exod. ii. 15, 22; iv. 20; xviii. 3, 4. ‡ 30. Exod. iii. 2. ‡ 32. Matt. xxii. 32; Heb. xi. 16. ‡ 33. Exod. iii. 5; Josh. v. 15. ‡ 34. Exod. iii. 7. ‡ 35. Exod. xiv. 19; Num. xx. 16. ‡ 36. Exod. xii. 41; xxxiii. 1. ‡ 36. Exod. vii—xi, xiv. Psa. cv. 27. ‡ 36. Exod. xiv. 21, 27—29. ‡ 36. Exod. xvi. 1, 35. ‡ 37. Deut. xviii. 15.

*[κυριος] ὁ θεος εκ των αδελφων ὑμων, ὡς εμε·
[lord] the God from of the brethren of you, like me;
*[αυτον ακουσεσθε.] 38 Οὑτος εστιν ὁ γενομε-
[him you shall hear.] This is he being,
νος, εν τῃ εκκλησιᾳ εν τῃ ερημῳ, μετα του
in the congregation in the desert, with the
αγγελου του λαλουντος αυτῳ εν τῳ ορει Σινα
messenger that speaking to him in the mountain Sinai,
και των πατερων ἡμων, ὁς εδεξατο λογια ζωντα
and of the fathers of us, who received oracles living
δουναι ἡμιν· 39 ᾡ ουκ ηθελησαν ὑπηκοοι γενεσ-
to give to us; to whom not were willing obedient to become
θαι οἱ πατερες ἡμων, αλλ' απωσαντο, και εστρα-
the fathers of us, but thrust away, and turned
φησαν ταις καρδιαις αὑτων εις Αιγυπτον,
back in the hearts of them into Egypt,
40 ειποντες τῳ Ααρων· Ποιησον ἡμιν θεους, οἱ
saying to the Aaron; Make for us gods, who
προπορευσονται ἡμων· ὁ γαρ Μωυσης οὑτος ὁς
shall go before us; the for Moses this who
εξηγαγεν ἡμας εκ γης Αιγυπτου, ουκ οιδαμεν
led out us from land Egypt, not we know
τι γεγονεν αυτῳ. 41 Και εμοσχοποιησαν εν
what has happened to him. And they made a calf in
ταις ἡμεραις εκειναις, και ανηγαγον θυσιαν τῳ
the days those, and offered a sacrifice to the
ειδωλῳ, και ευφραινοντο εν τοις εργοις των
idol, and rejoiced in the works of the
χειρων αὑτων. 42 Εστρεψε δε ὁ θεος, και
hands of them. Turned and the God, and
παρεδωκεν αυτους λατρευειν τῃ στρατιᾳ του
gave up them to serve the host of the
ουρανου· καθως γεγραπται εν βιβλῳ των προ-
heaven; as it is written in book of the pro-
φητων· Μη σφαγια και θυσιας προσηνεγκατε
phets; Not victims and sacrifices did you offer
μοι ετη τεσσαρακοντα εν τῃ ερημῳ, οικος
to me years forty in the desert, house
Ισραηλ; 43 Και ανελαβετε την σκηνην του
of Israel? And you took up the tabernacle of the
Μολοχ και αστρον του θεου ὑμων Ῥεμφαν, τους
Moloch and star of the god of you Remphan, the
τυπους, οὑς εποιησατε προσκυνειν αυτοις· και
images, which you made to worship them; and
μετοικιω ὑμας επεκεινα Βαβυλωνος. 44 Ἡ
I will cause to remove you beyond Babylon. The
σκηνη του μαρτυριου ην εν τοις πατρασιν ἡμων
tabernacle of the testimony was with the fathers of us
εν τῃ ερημῳ, καθως διεταξατο ὁ λαλων τῳ Μωυ-
in the desert, as directed he speaking to the Mo-
σῃ, ποιησαι αυτην κατα τον τυπον ὁν ἑωρακει·
ses, to make her according to the form which he had seen;

among your BRETHREN, like me.'

38 ‡ This is HE who WAS in the CONGREGATION in the DESERT, with ‡ THAT ANGEL who SPOKE to him on MOUNT Sinai, and with our FATHERS; ‡ who received the living ‡ Oracles to give to us;

39 to whom our FATHERS would not become obedient, but thrust away, and in their HEARTS turned back into Egypt,

40 ‡ saying to AARON, 'Make us Gods to go before us; for this MOSES, who led us out of the Land of Egypt, we know not what has happened to him.'

41 ‡ And they made a Calf in those DAYS, and offered a Sacrifice to the IDOL, and rejoiced in the WORKS of their own HANDS.

42 ‡ But GOD turned, and gave them up to serve ‡ the HOST of HEAVEN; as it is written in the Book of the PROPHETS, ‡ 'Did you not offer Victims and Sacrifices to me forty Years in the DESERT, O House of Israel?

43 And yet you took up the TABERNACLE of MOLOCH, and the STAR of the GOD † Remphan, the FIGURES which you made to worship them; I will even cause you to remove beyond † Babylon.'

44 Our FATHERS had the TABERNACLE of the TESTIMONY in the DESERT, as HE who SPOKE to Moses directed him ‡ to make it according to the PATTERN which he had seen;

* VATICAN MANUSCRIPT.—37. Lord—*omit*. 37. him you shall hear—*omit*. 43. the GOD.

† 43. *Remphan* or *Raiphan* was the name of the same idol in Egypt, which was called *Chiun* in Syria, and represented the planet Saturn. † 43. Both the Septuagint, from which this appears to be a quotation, and the Hebrew, read *Damascus*, instead of *Babylon*. Bloomfield thinks it is a marginal reading which has crept into the text.

‡ 38. Exod. xix. 3, 17. ‡ 38. Isa. lxiii. 9; Gal. iii. 19; Heb. ii. 2. ‡ 38. Exod. xxi. 1; Deut. v. 27, 31; xxxiii. 4; John i. 17. ‡ 38. Rom. iii. 2. ‡ 40. Exod. xxxii. 1. ‡ 41. Deut. ix. 16; Psa. cvi. 19. ‡ 42. Psa. lxxxi. 12; Ezek. xx. 25, 39; Rom. i. 24; 2 Thess. ii. 11. ‡ 42. Deut. iv. 19; xvii. 3; 2 Kings xvii. 16; xxi. 3; Jer. xix. 13. ‡ 42. Amos v. 25, 26. ‡ 44. Exod. xxv. 40; xxvi. 30; Heb. viii. 5.

45 ἣν και εισηγαγον διαδεξαμενοι οἱ πατερες
which also brought having received by succession the fathers
ἡμων μετα Ιησου εν τη κατασχεσει των εθνων,
of us with Jesus in to the possession of the nations,
ὧν εξωσεν ὁ θεος απο προσωπου των πατερων
which drove out the God from face of the fathers
ἡμων, ἑως των ἡμερων Δαυιδ· 46 ὃς εὑρε χαριν
of us, till the days of David; who found favor
ενωπιον του θεου, και ητησατο εὑρειν σκηνωμα
in presence of the God, and asked to find a dwelling
τῳ θεῳ Ιακωβ. 47 Σολομων δε ῳκοδομησεν
for the God of Jacob. Solomon but built
αυτῳ οικον. 48 Αλλ' ουχ ὁ ὑψιστος εν χειρο-
for him a house. But not the Most High in hand
ποιητοις κατοικει, καθως ὁ προφητης λεγει·
made things dwells, as the prophet says;
49 ὁ ουρανος μοι θρονος, ἡ δε γη ὑποποδιον των
the heaven to me a throne, the and earth a footstool of the
ποδων μου. Ποιον οικον οικοδομησετε μοι;
feet of me. What house will you build for me?
λεγει κυριος· η τις τοπος της καταπαυσεως
says Lord; or what place of the dwelling
μου; 50 Ουχι ἡ χειρ μου εποιησε ταυτα παντα;
of me? Not the hand of me made these things all?
51 Σκληροτραχηλοι, και απεριτμητοι τη καρδιᾳ
O stiff-necked, and uncircumcised in the heart
και τοις ωσιν· ὑμεις αει τῳ πνευματι τῳ ἁγιῳ
and the ears; you always the spirit the holy
αντιπιπτετε, ὡς οἱ πατερες ὑμων και ὑμεις.
fight against, like the fathers of you also you.
52 Τινα των προφητων ουκ εδιωξαν οἱ πατερες
Which of the prophets not persecuted the fathers
ὑμων; και απεκτειναν τους προκαταγγειλαντας
of you? and they killed those having foretold
περι της ελευσεως του δικαιου, οὗ νυν ὑμεις
concerning the coming of the righteous, of whom now you
προδοται και φονεις γεγενησθε· 53 οἵτινες ελα-
betrayers and murderers have become; who re-
βετε τον νομον εις διαταγας αγγελων, και ουκ
ceived the law by injunctions of messengers, and not
εφυλαξατε. 54 Ακουοντες δε ταυτα, διεπριον-
you kept. Having heard and these things, they were sawn
το ταις καρδιας αὐτων, και εβρυχον τους οδον-
through the hearts of them, and gnashed the teeth
τας επ' αυτον. 55 Ὑπαρχων δε πληρης πνευματος
on him. Being but full of spirit
ἁγιου, ατενισας εις τον ουρανον, ειδε δοξαν
holy, having gazed intently into the heaven, he saw glory
θεου, και Ιησουν ἑστωτα εκ δεξιων του θεου,
of God, and Jesus having stood at right of the God,

45 ‡ Which also our FATHERS, having received it by succession, brought in with Joshua into the POSSESSION of the NATIONS, ‡ whom GOD drove out before the Face of our FATHERS, to the DAYS of David;
46 ‡ who found Favor in the sight of GOD, and ‡ requested to find a Dwelling for the * GOD of Jacob.
47 ‡ But Solomon built for him a House.
48 Yet ‡ the MOST HIGH dwells not in things made with hands; as the PROPHET says,
49 ‡ 'HEAVEN is My Throne, and the EARTH my FOOTSTOOL; What House will you build for me? says the Lord; or what is the PLACE of my REST?
50 Has not my HAND made all these things?'
51 O stiff-necked and uncircumcised in HEART and EARS! you always fight against the HOLY SPIRIT; as your FATHERS did you also do.
52 ‡ Which of the PROPHETS did not your FATHERS persecute? And they killed THOSE who FORETOLD the COMING of the RIGHTEOUS ONE; of whom you now have become Betrayers and Murderers:—
53 ‡ you who received the LAW by Injunctions of Angels, and kept it not."
54 And having heard these things, they were enraged in their HEARTS, and gnashed their TEETH upon him.
55 But being full of holy Spirit, and looking steadily towards HEAVEN, he saw the Glory of God, and Jesus standing at the right hand of GOD,

* VATICAN MANUSCRIPT.—46. HOUSE of Jacob.

‡ 45. Josh. iii. 14. ‡ 45. Neh. ix. 24; Psa. xliv. 2; lxxviii. 55; Acts xiii. 19. ‡ 46. 1 Sam. xvi. 1; 2 Sam. vii. 1; Acts xiii. 22. ‡ 46. 1 Kings viii. 17; 1 Chron. xxii. 7; Psa. cxxxii. 4, 5. ‡ 47. 1 Kings vi. 1; viii. 20. ‡ 48. 1 Kings viii. 27; Acts xvii. 24. ‡ 49. Matt. v. 34, 35. ‡ 52. Matt. xxi. 35; xxiii. 34, 37. ‡ 53. Exod xx. 1; Gal. iii. 19; Heb. ii. 2.

56 και ειπεν· Ιδου, θεωρω τους ουρανους ανεωγ-
and said; Lo, I see the heavens having been
μενους, και τον υἱον του ανθρωπου εκ δεξιων
opened, and the son of the man at right
ἑστωτα του θεου. 57 Κραξαντες δε φωνη μεγα-
having stood of the God. Having cried and with a voice loud,
λη, συνεσχον τα ὠτα αὑτων, και ὡρμησαν
they shut up the ears of them, and they ran
ὁμοθυμαδον επ' αυτον· 58 και εκβαλοντες εξω
with one mind on him; and having cast outside
της πολεως, ελιθοβολουν. Και οἱ μαρτυρες
the city, they stoned. And the witnesses
απεθεντο τα ἱματια αὑτων παρα τους ποδας
laid down the mantles of them at the feet
νεανιου καλουμενου Σαυλου, 59 και ελιθοβολουν
of a young man being called Saul, and they stoned
τον Στεφανον, επικαλουμενον και λεγοντα·
the Stephen, calling upon and saying;
Κυριε Ιησου, δεξαι το πνευμα μου. 60 Θεις
O lord Jesus, do thou receive the breath of me. Having placed
δε τα γονατα εκραξε φωνη μεγαλη· Κυριε, μη
and the knees he cried out with a voice loud; O lord, not
στησης αυτοις την ἁμαρτιαν ταυτην. Και
thou mayest place to them the sin this. And
τουτο ειπων, εκοιμηθη.
this having said, he fell asleep.

ΚΕΦ. η'. 8.

1 Σαυλος δε ην συνευδοκων τη αναιρεσει
Saul and was consenting to the death
αυτου. Εγενετο δε εν εκεινη τη ἡμερα διωγμος
of him. Was and in that the day a persecution
μεγας επι την εκκλησιαν την εν Ἱεροσολυμοις·
great against the congregation that in Jerusalem;
παντες τε διεσπαρησαν κατα τας χωρας της
all and were scattered in the regions of the
Ιουδαιας και Σαμαρειας, πλην των αποστολων.
Judea and Samaria, except the apostles.
2 Συνεκομισαν δε τον Στεφανον ανδρες ευλαβεις,
Buried and the Stephen men pious,
και εποιησαντο κοπετον μεγαν επ' αυτῳ.
and they made lamentation great for him.
3 Σαυλος δε ελυμαινετο την εκκλησιαν, κατα
Saul but was outraging the congregation, into
τους οικους εισπορευομενος, συρων τε ανδρας
the houses entering, dragging and men
και γυναικας, παρεδιδου εις φυλακην· 4 οἱ μεν
and women, was delivering up into prison; they indeed
ουν διασπαρεντες διηλθον, ευαγγελιζομενοι
therefore having been scattered wandered about, preaching glad tidings
τον λογον. 5 Φιλιππος δε κατελθων εις πολιν
the word. Philip and going down into a city
της Σαμαρειας, εκηρυσσεν αυτοις τον Χριστον.
of the Samaria, proclaimed to them the Anointed.

56 and said, ‡ "Behold, I see the HEAVENS opened, and the SON of MAN standing on the right hand of God."

57 And crying out with a loud Voice, they stopped their EARS, and rushed upon him with one accord;

58 and ‡ having cast him out of the CITY, they stoned him. And ‡ the WITNESSES laid down their MANTLES at the FEET of a Young man, named Saul,

59 and they stoned STEPHEN, as he was invoking and saying, "Lord Jesus, ‡ † receive my SPIRIT."

60 And bending his KNEES he cried with a loud Voice, ‡ "Lord, place not * This Sin against them." And having said This, he fell asleep.

CHAPTER VIII.

1 Now ‡ Saul was consenting to his DEATH. And in That DAY there was a great Persecution against THAT CONGREGATION in Jerusalem; and ‡ they were all dispersed through the REGIONS of JUDEA and Samaria, except the APOSTLES.

2 And pious Men buried Stephen, and made great Lamentation over him.

3 ‡ But Saul ravaged the CONGREGATION, entering HOUSES, and violently seizing Men and Women, he committed them to Prison.

4 Then THOSE HAVING BEEN DISPERSED, went about preaching the glad tidings of the WORD.

5 And Philip going down to * the CITY of SAMARIA, proclaimed to them the MESSIAH.

---

* VATICAN MANUSCRIPT.—60. This SIN. 5. the CITY.

† 59. *Dexai* may also be rendered *sustain* or *support*. Booth, in his Lexicon of Primitive Greek words, gives this as one of the significations of the word. The prayer of Stephen then would read, "Lord Jesus, *sustain* my spirit," or "*assist me* to suffer."

‡ 56. Ezek. i. 1; Matt. iii. 16; Acts x. 11. ‡ 58. 1 Kings xxi. 13; Luke iv. 29; Heb. xiii. 12. ‡ 58. Deut. xiii. 9, 10; xvii. 7. ‡ 59. Luke xxiii. 46. ‡ 60. Matt. v. 44; Luke vi. 28; xxiii. 34. ‡ 1. Acts vii. 58; xxii. 20. ‡ 1. Acts xi. 19. ‡ 3. Acts vii. 58; ix. 1, 13, 21; xxii. 4; xxvi. 10, 11; 1 Cor. xv. 9; Gal. i. 13; Phil. iii. 6; 1 Tim. i. 13.

[6] Προσειχον τε οἱ οχλοι τοις λεγομενοις ὑπο
Assented and the crowds to the things being spoken by
του Φιλιππου ὁμοθυμαδον, εν τῳ ακουειν αυτους
the Philip with one mind, in the to hear them
και βλεπειν τα σημεια ἁ εποιει. 7 Πολλων γαρ
and to see the signs which he did. Many for
των εχοντων πνευματα ακαθαρτα, βοωντα φωνῃ
of those possessing spirits unclean, crying with a voice
μεγαλῃ εξηρχετο· πολλοι δε παραλελυμενοι
loud came out; many and having been palsied
και χωλοι εθεραπευθησαν. 8 Και εγενετο χαρα
and lame were cured. And was joy
μεγαλη εν τῃ πολει εκεινῃ.
great in the city that.
9 Ανηρ δε τις, ονοματι Σιμων, προυπηρχεν
A man but certain, by name Simon, formerly
εν τῃ πολει, μαγευων, και εξιστων το εθνος
in the city, practising magic, and amazing the nation
της Σαμαρειας, λεγων ειναι τινα ἑαυτον μεγαν·
of the Samaria, saying to be somebody himself great;
10 ᾡ προσειχον παντες απο μικρου ἑως μεγα-
to whom they assented all from least to great-
λου, λεγοντες· Οὑτος εστιν ἡ δυναμις του θεου
est, saying; This is the power of the God
ἡ καλουμενη μεγαλη. 11 Προσειχον δε αυτῳ,
which is being called great. They attended and to him,
δια το ἱκανῳ χρονῳ ταις μαγειαις εξεστακεναι
because that for a long time with the magic arts to have amazed
αυτους. 12 Ὁτε δε επιστευσαν τῳ Φιλιππῳ
them. When but they believed the Philip
ευαγγελιζομενῳ *[τα] περι της βασιλειας
announcing glad tidings [the things] concerning the kingdom
του θεου και του ονοματος Ιησου Χριστου,
of the God and the name of Jesus Anointed,
εβαπτιζοντο ανδρες τε και γυναικες. 13 Ὁ δε
they were dipped men both and women. The and
Σιμων και αυτος επιστευσε, και βαπτισθεις ην
Simon and himself believed, and having been dipped he was
προσκαρτερων τῳ Φιλιππῳ· θεωρων τε δυναμεις
constantly attending to the Philip; beholding and miracles
και σημεια μεγαλα γινομενα, εξιστατο.
and signs great being done, he was amazed.
14 Ακουσαντες δε οἱ εν Ἱεροσολυμοις αποστολοι,
Having heard and the in Jerusalem apostles,
ὁτι δεδεκται ἡ Σαμαρεια τον λογον του θεου,
that had received the Samaria the word of the God,
απεστειλαν προς αυτους τον Πετρον και Ιωαν-
they sent to them the Peter and John;
νην· 15 οἱτινες καταβαντες προσηυξαντο περι
who having gone down offered prayer concerning
αυτων, ὁπως λαβωσι πνευμα ἁγιον. 16 (Ουπω
them, so that they might receive spirit holy. (Not yet
γαρ ην επ᾽ ουδενι αυτων επιπεπτωκος, μονον
for it was on any one of them having fallen, only

6 And the CROWDS with
one mind attended to the
THINGS SPOKEN by PHI-
LIP, as they HEARD and
saw the SIGNS which he
performed.
7 ‡ For many of THOSE
POSSESSING impure Spi-
rits, crying with a loud
Voice, were dispossessed;
and many paralytic and
lame persons were cured.
8 And there was * Much
Joy in that CITY.
9 Now a certain man,
named Simon, came be-
fore into the CITY ‡ using
magic, and astonishing the
NATION of SAMARIA, ‡ say-
ing that he himself was
somebody great;
10 to whom all attended,
from the least to the greatest, saying, "This is THAT
which is CALLED the
GREAT POWER of GOD."
11 And to him they gave
heed, because that for a
Long Time he had aston-
ished them with his MAGIC
ARTS.
12 But when they be-
lieved PHILIP announcing
glad tidings ‡ concerning
the KINGDOM of GOD, and
the NAME of Jesus Christ,
they were immersed, both
Men and Women.
13 And SIMON himself
also believed; and having
been immersed, he was
constantly attending to
PHILIP; and beholding the
* SIGNS and great Mira-
cles which were performed,
he was astonished.
14 And the APOSTLES
in Jerusalem having heard
That SAMARIA had re-
ceived the WORD of GOD,
sent to them PETER and
John;
15 who, having gone
down, prayed for them
that they might receive the
holy Spirit;
16 ‡ for it was not yet
fallen on any of them; but
they had only ‡ been im-

* VATICAN MANUSCRIPT.—8. Much Joy. 12. the things—*omit.* 13. SIGNS and great Miracles.

‡ 7. Mark xvi. 17. ‡ 9. Acts xiii. 6. ‡ 9. Acts v. 36. ‡ 12. Acts i. 3
‡ 16. Acts xix. 2. ‡ 16. Matt. xxviii. 19; Acts ii. 38.

δε βεβαπτισμενοι ὑπηρχον εις το ονομα του
but having been dipped they were into the name of the
κυριου Ιησου.) 17 Τοτε επετιθουν τας χειρας
Lord Jesus.) Then they placed the hands
επ' αυτους, και ελαμβανον πνευμα ἁγιον.
on them, and they received spirit holy.
18 Ιδων δε ὁ Σιμων, ὁτι δια της επιθεσεως
Having seen and the Simon, that through the placing on
των χειρων των αποστολων διδοται το πνευμα
of the hands of the apostles was given the spirit
το ἁγιον, προσηνεγκεν αυτοις χρηματα, 19 λε-
the holy, he offered to them money, say-
γων· Δοτε καμοι την εξουσιαν ταυτην, ἱνα ᾧ
ing; Give you also to me the authority this, that to whom-
εαν επιθω τας χειρας, λαμβανη πνευμα ἁγιον.
ever I may place the hands, they may receive spirit holy.
20 Πετρος δε ειπε προς αυτον· Το αργυριον σου
Peter but said to him; The silver of thee
συν σοι ειη εις απωλειαν· ὁτι την δωρεαν του
with thee may be into destruction; because the gift of the
θεου ενομισας δια χρηματων κτασθαι. 21 Ουκ
God thou hast thought with money to buy. Not
εστι σοι μερις ουδε κληρος εν τῳ λογῳ τουτῳ·
is to thee a part nor lot in the word this;
ἡ γαρ καρδια σου ουκ εστιν ευθεια εναντι του
the for heart of thee not is right before the
θεου. 22 Μετανοησον ουν απο της κακιας σου
God. Do thou reform therefore from the wickedness of thee
ταυτης, και δεηθητι του θεου, ει αρα αφεθη-
this, and entreat of the God, if indeed may be
σεται σοι ἡ επινοια της καρδιας σου. 23 Εις
forgiven to thee the thought of the heart of thee. In
γαρ χολην πικριας και συνδεσμον αδικιας ὁρω
for a gall of bitterness and a bond of wickedness I see
σε οντα. 24 Αποκριθεις δε ὁ Σιμων ειπε· Δεη-
thee being. Answering and the Simon said; Entreat
θητε ὑμεις ὑπερ εμου προς τον κυριον, ὁπως
you in behalf of me to the lord, that
μηδεν επελθη επ' εμε ὡν ειρηκατε. 25 Οἱ μεν
nothing may come on me of which you have spoken. They indeed
ουν διαμαρτυραμενοι και λαλησαντες τον
therefore having earnestly testified and having spoken the
λογον του κυριου, ὑπεστρεψαν εις Ἱερουσαλημ,
word of the lord, turned back for Jerusalem,
πολλας τε κωμας των Σαμαρειτων ευηγγελι-
many and villages of the Samaritans announced
σαντο.
glad tidings.
26 Αγγελος δε κυριου ελαλησε προς Φιλιππον,
A messenger and of a lord spoke to Philip,
λεγων· Αναστηθι, και πορευου κατα μεσημ-
saying; Do thou arise, and go towards south,
βριαν, επι την ὁδον την καταβαινουσαν απο
in the way that leading down from
Ἱερουσαλημ εις Γαζαν· αὑτη εστιν ερημος.
Jerusalem to Gaza, this is desert.
27 Και αναστας επορευθη· και ιδου, ανηρ Αιθιοψ
And having arisen he went; and lo, a man of Ethiopia

mersed into the ‡ NAME of
the LORD Jesus.
17 Then they ‡placed
their HANDS on them, and
they received the holy
Spirit.
18 And SIMON seeing
That through the IMPOSI-
TION of the HANDS of the
APOSTLES, the * SPIRIT
was given, he offered them
Money,
19 saying, "Give me
also this AUTHORITY, that
on whom I place my
HANDS, he may receive the
holy Spirit."
20 But PETER said to
him, "May thy SILVER go
to Destruction with thee,
Because thou hast thought
to buy ‡ the GIFT of GOD
with Money.
21 Thou hast no Part
nor Lot in this THING;
for thy HEART is not right
before GOD.
22 Reform, therefore,
from this thy WICKED-
NESS, and entreat * the
LORD, if perhaps the
THOUGHT of thine HEART
may be forgiven thee;
23 for I see that thou
art in ‡ the Gall of Bitterness, and in the Bond of
Wickedness."
24 And SIMON answer-
ing, said, ‡ "Entreat you
the LORD in my behalf,
that nothing of which you
have spoken may come on
me."
25 Then THEY, having
fully testified and spoken
the WORD of the LORD,
turned back for Jerusalem,
and announced the glad
tidings in Many Villages
of the SAMARITANS.
26 And an Angel of the
Lord spoke to Philip, saying, "Arise, and go to-
wards the South, by THAT
ROAD LEADING DOWN
from Jerusalem to Gaza;"
this is a Desert.
27 And having arisen,
he went; and behold, an
Ethiopian Eunuch, a Gran-

* VATICAN MANUSCRIPT.—18. SPIRIT was given. 22. the Lord, if.

‡ 16. Acts x. 48; xix. 5. ‡ 17. Acts xix. 6. ‡ 20. Acts x. 45; xi. 17. ‡ 23. Heb. xii. 15. ‡ 24. Gen. xx. 7, 17; Exod. viii. 8; Num. xxi. 7; 1 Kings xiii. 6

ευνουχος, δυναστης Κανδακης της βασιλισσης
a eunuch, a grandee of Candace of the queen
Αιθιοπων, ὁς ην επι πασης της γαζης αυτης· ὁς
of Ethiopians, who was over all the treasure of her; who
εληλυθει προσκυνησων εις Ἱερουσαλημ, 28 ην
had come worshipping to Jerusalem, was
τε ὑποστρεφων και καθημενος επι του ἁρματος
and returning and sitting in the chariot
αὑτου, και ανεγινωσκε τον προφητην Ἡσαιαν.
of himself, and was reading the prophet Isaiah.
29 Ειπε δε το πνευμα τῳ Φιλιππῳ· Προσελθε,
Said and the spirit to the Philip; Go thou near,
και κολληθητι τῳ ἁρματι τουτῳ. 30 Προσδρα-
and be joined to the chariot this. Running
μων δε ὁ Φιλιππος ηκουσεν αυτου αναγινωσκον-
to and the Philip heard him reading
τος τον προφητην Ἡσαιαν, και ειπεν· Αραγε
the prophet Isaiah, and said; Truly
γινωσκεις, ἁ αναγινωσκεις; 31 Ὁ δε ειπε· Πως
understandest thou, what thou readest? He but said; How
γαρ αν δυναιμην, εαν μη τις ὁδηγηση με;
for should I be able, if not some one should guide me?
Παρεκαλεσε τε τον Φιλιππον, αναβαντα καθι-
He called and the Philip, having gone up to sit
σαι συν αυτῳ. 32 Ἡ δε περιοχη της γραφης,
with him. The and portion of the writing,
ἡν ανεγινωσκεν, ην αὑτη· Ὡς προβατον επι
which he was reading, was this: As a sheep to
σφαγην ηχθη, και ὡς αμνος εναντιον του κει-
slaughter was led, and as a lamb before the one
ροντος αυτον αφωνος, οὑτως ουκ ανοιγει το
shearing him is dumb, so not he opens the
στομα αὑτου. 33 Εν τῃ ταπεινωσει αυτου ἡ
mouth of himself. In the low estate of him the
κρισις αὑτου ηρθη· την δε γενεαν αυτου τις
judgment of himself was taken away; the and generation of him who
διηγησεται; ὁτι αιρεται απο της γης ἡ ζωη
shall declare? because is taken away from the earth the life
αυτου. 34 Αποκριθεις δε ὁ ευνουχος τῳ Φιλιπ-
of him. Answering but the eunuch to the Philip
πῳ ειπε· Δεομαι σου, περι τινος ὁ προφητης
said; I beseech thee, concerning whom the prophet
λεγει τουτο; περι εαυτου, η περι ἑτερου
says this? concerning himself, or concerning another
τινος; 35 Ανοιξας δε ὁ Φιλιππος το στομα
one? Having opened and the Philip the mouth
αὑτου, και αρξαμενος απο της γραφης ταυτης,
of himself, and having begun from the writing this,
ευηγγελισατο αυτῳ τον Ιησουν. 36 Ὡς δε επο-
announced glad tidings to him the Jesus. As and they
ρευοντο κατα την ὁδον, ηλθον επι τι ὑδωρ· και
were going in the way, they came to a certain water; and
φησιν ὁ ευνουχος· Ιδου ὑδωρ· τι κωλυει με
said the eunuch; Lo water; what hinders me

dee of Candace, * Queen
of the Ethiopians, who was
over All her TREASURE,
and who had come to wor-
ship at Jerusalem,
28 was returning, and
sitting in his CHARIOT he
was reading the PROPHET
Isaiah.
29 And the SPIRIT said
to PHILIP, "Approach,
and join thyself to this
CHARIOT."
30 And PHILIP running
forward heard him read-
ing * Isaiah the PROPHET,
and he said, "Dost thou
indeed understand what
thou art reading?"
31 And HE said, "How
can I, unless some one
should guide me?" And
he requested PHILIP to
come up and sit with him.
32 Now the PORTION
of the SCRIPTURE which
he was reading was this,
‡ "As a Sheep he was led
"to Slaughter, and like a
"Lamb before the SHEAR-
"ER is dumb, so he opens
"not his MOUTH.
33 "In * his HUMILIA-
"TION his JUDGMENT was
"taken away; and who
"will tell of his GENERA-
"TION? Because his
"LIFE is taken from the
"EARTH."
34 And the EUNUCH
answering PHILIP, said,
"I beseech thee, of whom
speaks the PROPHET this
—of himself, or of some
other person."
35 Then PHILIP open-
ing his MOUTH, ‡ and be-
ginning from this SCRIP-
TURE, announced the glad
tidings of JESUS to him.
36 And as they were
going on the ROAD, they
came to a Certain Water;
and the EUNUCH said,
"Behold, Water! ‡ what
hinders my being immer-
sed?" †

* VATICAN MANUSCRIPT.—27. Queen. 30. Isaiah the PROPHET, and said. 33. the HUMILIATION.

† 36. Verse 37 of the common version is spurious. It is not found in the Vatican MS., nor in the ancient Syriac. Griesbach rejects it; and it is cancelled or rejected by Grotius, Mill, Wetstein, Pearce, Tittman, Knapp, Lachmann, Tischendorf, and others.

‡ 32. Isa. liii. 7, 8. ‡ 35. Luke xxiv. 27; Acts xviii. 28. ‡ 36. Acts x. 47.

βαπτισθηναι; 38 Και εκελευσε στηναι το ἁρμα·
to be dipped? And he ordered to stand the chariot;
και κατεβησαν αμφοτεροι εις το ὑδωρ ὁ, τε
and they went down both into the water the, both
Φιλιππος και ὁ ευνουχος· και εβαπτισεν αυτον.
Philip and the eunuch; and he dipped him.
39 Ὁτε δε ανεβησαν εκ του ὑδατος, πνευμα
When and they came up out of the water, spirit
κυριου ἡρπασε τον Φιλιππον· και ουκ ειδεν
of lord seized the Philip; and not saw
αυτον ουκετι ὁ ευνουχος· επορευετο γαρ την
him no longer the eunuch; he went for the
ὁδον αὑτου χαιρων. 40 Φιλιππος δε εὑρεθη εις
way of himself rejoicing. Philip but was found into
Αζωτον· και διερχομενος ευηγγελιζετο τας
Azotus; and passing through he announced glad tidings the
πολεις πασας, ἑως του ελθειν αυτον εις Καισα-
cities all, till of the to come him into Cesa-
ρειαν.
rea.

KEΦ. θ'. 9.

1 Ὁ δε Σαυλος ετι εμπνεων απειλης και
The and Saul still breathing of threatening and
φονου εις τους μαθητας του κυριου, προσελθων
slaughter towards the disciples of the Lord, coming
τῳ αρχιερει, 2 ῃτησατο παρ' αυτου επιστολας
to the high-priest, he desired from him letters
εις Δαμασκον προς τας συναγωγας, ὁπως εαν
to Damascus to the synagogues, that if
τινας εὑρῃ της ὁδου οντας, ανδρας τε και
any he might find of the way being, men both and
γυναικας, δεδεμενους αγαγῃ εις Ἱερουσαλημ.
women, having been bound he might lead into Jerusalem.
3 Εν δε τῳ πορευεσθαι, εγενετο αυτον εγγιζειν
In and the to go, came him to draw near
τῃ Δαμασκῳ· και εξαιφνης περιηστραψεν αυτον
to the Damascus; and suddenly flashed around him
φως απο του ουρανου· 4 και πεσων επι την γην,
a light from the heaven; and having fallen to the earth
ηκουσε φωνην λεγουσαν αυτῳ· Σαουλ, Σαουλ·
he heard a voice saying to him: Saul, Saul;
τι με διωκεις; 5 Ειπε δε· τις ει, κυριε; Ὁ
why me dost thou persecute? He said and; who art thou, O lord. The
δε κυριος ειπεν· Εγω ειμι Ιησους ὁν συ διω-
and Lord said; I am Jesus whom thou persecu-
κεις· 6 αλλα αναστηθι και εισελθε εις την πολιν,
test; but stand thou up and enter into the city,
και λαληθησεται σοι τι σε δει ποιειν.
and it shall be told to thee what thee it is necessary to do.
7 Οἱ δε ανδρες οἱ συνοδευοντες αυτῳ, ειστηκει-
The and men those traveling with him, stood
σαν ενεοι, ακουοντες μεν της φωνης, μηδενα
dumb, hearing indeed the voice, no one
δε θεωρουντες. 8 Ηγερθη δε ὁ Σαυλος απο της
but seeing. Arose and the Saul from the
γης· ανεῳγμενων δε των οφθαλμων αυτου,
earth; having been opened and the eyes of him,

38 And he ordered the CHARIOT to stop; and they both went down into the WATER, both PHILIP and the EUNUCH, and he immersed him.

39 And when they came up out of the WATER, ‡the Spirit of the Lord seized PHILIP; and the EUNUCH saw him no more, for he went *His WAY rejoicing.

40 Philip, however, was found at Azotus; and passing through, he announced the glad tidings in all the CITIES, till he CAME to Cesarea.

CHAPTER IX.

1 And ‡Saul, still breathing out Threatenings and Slaughter against the DISCIPLES of the LORD, proceeding to the HIGH-PRIEST,

2 asked from him Letters to the SYNAGOGUES at Damascus, that if he should find Any of ‡ that RELIGION, whether Men or Women, he might bring them bound to Jerusalem.

3 ‡And as he was GOING ALONG, he came near to DAMASCUS; and suddenly a Light from HEAVEN flashed around him;

4 and having fallen to the EARTH, he heard a Voice saying to him, "Saul, Saul, why dost thou ‡persecute Me?"

5 And he said, "Who art thou, Sir?" And *HE said, "I am Jesus whom thou persecutest.

6 But arise, and go into the CITY, and it shall be told thee what thou must do."

7 ‡And THOSE MEN traveling with him, stood speechless, hearing indeed the VOICE, but seeing no one.

8 And Saul arose from the EARTH; and his EYES having been opened, he

* VATICAN MANUSCRIPT.—39. His WAY. 5. HE.

‡ 39. 1 Kings xviii. 12; 2 Kings ii. 16; Ezek. iii. 12, 14. ‡ 1. Acts viii. 3; Gal. i. 13; 1 Tim. i. 13. ‡ 2. Acts xix. 9, 23. ‡ 3. Acts xxii. 6; xxvi. 12. ‡ 4. Matt. xxv. 40. ‡ 7. Dan. x. 7; Acts xxii. 9; xxvi. 13.

ουδενα εβλεπε· χειραγωγουντες δε αυτον ειση-
no one he saw; leading by the hand and him they
γαγον εις Δαμασκον· 9 και ην ἡμερας τρεις μη
led into Damascus; and he was days three not
βλεπων· και ουκ εφαγεν, ουδε επιεν.
seeing; and not ate, not drank.
10 Ην δε τις μαθητης εν Δαμασκῳ ονοματι
Was and a certain disciple in Damascus by name
Ανανιας, και ειπε προς αυτον ὁ κυριος εν ὁρα-
Ananias, and said to him the Lord in a
ματι· Ανανια. Ὁ δε ειπεν· Ιδου εγω, κυριε.
vision; Ananias. He and said; Lo I, O lord.
11 Ὁ δε κυριος προς αυτον· Αναστας πορευθητι
The and Lord to him; Having arisen go thou
επι την ῥυμην την καλουμενην ευθειαν, και
to the street that being called Straight, and
ζητησον εν οικιᾳ Ιουδα Σαυλον ονοματι, Ταρ-
seek for in house of Judas Saul by name, of Tar-
σεα· ιδου γαρ προσευχεται, 12 και ειδεν εν ὁρα-
sus; lo for he prays, and saw in a
ματι ανδρα ονοματι Ανανιαν, εισελθοντα και
vision a man by name Ananias, having come in and
επιθεντα αυτῳ χειρα, ὁπως αναβλεψῃ. 13 Απεκ-
having placed to him a hand, that he might receive sight. An-
ριθη δε Ανανιας· Κυριε, ακηκοα απο πολλων
swered and Ananias; O lord, I have heard from many
περι του ανδρος τουτου, ὁσα κακα εποιη-
concerning the man this, what things bad he did
σε τοις ἁγιοις σου εν Ἱερουσαλημ. 14 Και ὡδε
to the saints of thee in Jerusalem. And here
εχει εξουσιαν παρα των αρχιερεων, δησαι παν-
he has authority from the high-priests, to bind all
τας τους επικαλουμενους το ονομα σου. 15 Ειπε
those calling upon the name of thee. Said
δε προς αυτον ὁ κυριος· Πορευου, ὁτι σκευος
and to him the Lord; Go thou, because a vessel
εκλογης μοι εστιν οὑτος, του βαστασαι το ονο-
chosen to me is this, of the to bear the name
μα μου ενωπιον εθνων, και βασιλεων, υἱων τε
of me before nations, and kings, sons and
Ισραηλ. 16 Εγω γαρ ὑποδειξω αυτῳ, ὁσα
of Israel. I for will point out to him, what things
δει αυτον ὑπερ του ονοματος μου παθειν.
it behoves him in behalf of the name of me to suffer.
17 Απηλθε δε Ανανιας και εισηλθεν εις την
Went away and Ananias and entered into the
οικιαν· και επιθεις επ' αυτον τας χειρας, ειπε·
house; and having placed on him the hands, he said;
Σαουλ αδελφε, ὁ κυριος απεσταλκε με, (Ιησους
Saul O brother, the Lord has sent me, (Jesus

saw No one; but leading him by the hand they conducted him to Damascus.

9 And he was three Days without sight, and neither ate nor drank.

10 Now there was in Damascus a certain Disciple, ‡ named Ananias; and the LORD said to him in a Vision, "Ananias." And HE said, "Behold, I am here, Lord."

11 And the LORD said to him, "Arise, and go into † THAT STREET which is CALLED Straight, and inquire in the house of Judas, for ‡ a man of † Tarsus, named Saul; for behold, he is praying,

12 and has seen in a Vision a Man, named Ananias, entering, and laying his * HANDS on him, that he might recover his sight."

13 And Ananias answered, "Lord, I have heard from many concerning this MAN, how much Evil he has done to thy SAINTS in Jerusalem;

14 and here, he has Authority from the HIGH-PRIESTS to bind ALL who ‡ INVOKE thy NAME."

15 But the LORD said to him, "Go; Because he is to me ‡ a chosen Vessel, to BEAR my NAME before Nations, and * Kings, and Sons of Israel;

16 for ‡ I will point out to him what things he must suffer in behalf of my NAME."

17 And Ananias departed, and entered the HOUSE, and placing his HANDS on him, said, "Brother Saul, the LORD sent me, even THAT Jesus who

* VATICAN MANUSCRIPT.—12. HANDS on him. 15. also Kings.

† 11. This street has continued under the same name to the present day. It runs in a direct line from the eastern to the western gate, a distance of three miles. † 11. Tarsus, was the capital of Cilicia, situated on the banks of the *Cnidus*, which flowed through the midst of it. It is now called *Tarasso*. As a seat of learning, it ranked with Athens and Alexandria. Its inhabitants, in the time of Julius Cesar, were endowed with all the privileges of Roman citizens.

‡ 10. Acts xxii. 12. ‡ 11. Acts xxi. 39; xxii. 3. ‡ 14. Acts vii. 59; verse 21; xxii. 16; 1 Cor. i. 2; 2 Tim. ii. 22. ‡ 15. Acts xiii. 2; xxii. 21; xxvi. 17; Rom. i. 1; Eph. iii. 7, 8. ‡ 16. 2 Cor. xi. 23.

ὁ οφθεις σοι εν τῃ οδῳ ᾗ ηρχου,) ὁπως ανα-
he having appeared to thee in the way in which thou camest, that thou
βλεψῃς, και πλησθῃς πνευματος ἁγιου. 18 Και
mayest receive sight, and mayest be filled of spirit holy. And
ευθεως απεπεσον απο των οφθαλμων αυτου
immediately fell from the eyes of him
ὡσει λεπιδες, ανεβλεψε τε· και αναστας εβαπ-
as it were scales, he recovered sight and; and having arisen he was
τισθη. 19 Και λαβων τροφην ενισχυσεν. Εγεν-
dipped. And having taken food he was strengthened. He
ετο δε μετα των εν Δαμασκῳ μαθητων ἡμερας
was and with the in Damascus disciples days
τινας. 20 Και ευθεως εν ταις συναγωγαις
several. And immediately in the synagogues
εκηρυσσε τον Ιησουν, ὁτι οὑτος εστιν ὁ υἱος
he proclaimed the Jesus, that this is the son
του θεου. 21 Εξισταντο δε παντες οἱ ακουοντες,
of the God. Were amazed and all those having heard,
και ελεγον· Ουχ οὑτος εστιν ὁ πορθησας εν
and said; Not this is the one having wasted in
Ἱερουσαλημ τους επικαλουμενους το ονομα
Jerusalem those calling upon the name
τουτο; και ὡδε εις τουτο εληλυθει, ἱνα δεδε-
this? and here for this had come, that having
μενους αυτους αγαγῃ επι τους αρχιερεις.
bound them he might lead to the high-priests.
22 Σαυλος δε μαλλον ενεδυναμουτο, και συνε-
Saul but more was strenghtened. and perplexed
χυνε τους Ιουδαιους τους κατοικουντας εν Δα-
the Jews those dwelling in Da-
μασκῳ, συμβιβαζων, ὁτι οὑτος εστιν ὁ Χριστος.
mascus, proving, that this is the Anointed.
23 Ὡς δε επληρουντο ἡμεραι ἱκαναι, συνεβου-
When and were fulfilled days many, consulted
λευσαντο οἱ Ιουδαιοι ανελειν αυτον· 24 εγνωσθη
together the Jews to kill him; was made known
δε τῳ Σαυλῳ ἡ επιβουλη αυτων· παρετηρουν
but to the Saul the plot of them; they were watching
τε τας πυλας ἡμερας τε και νυκτος, ὁπως αυτον
and the gates day both and night, that him
ανελωσι. 25 Λαβοντες δε αυτον οἱ μαθηται
they might kill. Having taken but him the disciples
νυκτος, κατηκαν δια του τειχους, χαλασαντες
by night, they let down through the wall, lowering
εν σπυριδι. 26 Παραγενομενος δε εις Ἱερουσα-
in a basket. Having come and into Jerusalem,
λημ, επειρατο κολλασθαι τοις μαθηταις· και
he tried to unite himself to the disciples; and
παντες εφοβουντο αυτον, μη πιστευοντες ὁτι
all feared him, not believing that
εστι μαθητης. 27 Βαρναβας δε επιλαβομενος
he is a disciple. Barnabas but having taken

APPEARED to thee on the
the ROAD in which thou
camest, in order that thou
mayest receive sight, and
be filled with holy Spirit.
18 And immediately
something fell from * His
EYES, like Scales, and he
recovered sight; and rising
up, he was immersed.
19 And having received
Food he was strenghtened;
and was with the DISCIPLES
in Damascus several
Days.
20 And immediately in
the SYNAGOGUES he proclaimed
JESUS, That he
is the SON of GOD.
21 But ALL who heard
him were astonished, and
said, ‡ "Is not this HE
who in Jerusalem spread
DESOLATION among THEM
who CALL on this NAME,
and had come here for this
purpose, that he might lead
them bound to the HIGH-PRIESTS?"
22 But Saul increased
more in power, ‡ and * perplexed
THOSE Jews DWELLING
in Damascus, demonstrating
That this is the
MESSIAH.
23 And when † many
Days were fulfilled, ‡ the
JEWS conspired to kill
him;
24 but their PLOT was
made known to Saul. And
they * also watched the
GATES both Day and Night,
that they might murder
him.
25 But the DISCIPLES
took him by Night, and
‡ through the WALL lowered
him down in a Basket.
26 ‡ And having come
to Jerusalem he attempted
to associate with the DISCIPLES;
but they all feared
him, not believing That he
was a Disciple.
27 But Barnabas taking

* VATICAN MANUSCRIPT.—18. His EYES. 22. perplexed THOSE Jews DWELLING. 24. also watched the GATES.

† 23. The *many days* here alluded to, probably included the *three years* mentioned by Paul in Gal. i. 18, during which he preached in Damascus and visited Arabia.

‡ 21. Acts viii. 3; verse 1; Gal. i. 13, 23. ‡ 22. Acts xviii. 28. ‡ 23. Acts xxiii. 12; xxv. 3. 2 Cor. xi. 26. ‡ 25. Josh. ii. 15; 1 Sam. xix. 12; 2 Cor. xi. 33. ‡ 26. Acts xxii. 17; Gal. i. 17, 16.

αυτον, ηγαγε προς τους αποστολους, και διη-
him, brought to the apostles, and re-
γησατο αυτοις, πως εν τη ὁδῳ ειδε τον κυριον,
lated to them, how in the way he saw the Lord,
και ὁτι ελαλησεν αυτῳ, και πως εν Δαμασκῳ
and that he spoke to him, and how in Damascus
επαρρησιασατο εν τῳ ονοματι του Ιησου. 28 Και
he spoke boldly in the name of the Jesus. And
ην μετ᾽ αυτων εισπορευομενος και εκπορευομενος
he was with them coming in and going out
εν Ιερουσαλημ, *[και] παρρησιαζομενος εν τῳ
in Jerusalem, [and] speaking boldly in the
ονοματι του κυριου *[Ιησου.] 29 Ελαλει τε
name of the Lord [Jesus.] He spoke and
και συνεζητει προς τους Ἑλληνιστας· οἱ δε
and contended with the Hellenists; they but
επεχειρουν αυτον ανελειν. 30 Επιγνοντες δε οἱ
took in hand him to kill. Having known but the
αδελφοι κατηγαγον αυτον εις Καισαρειαν, και
brethren they brought down him to Cesarea, and
εξαπεστειλαν αυτον εις Ταρσον. 31 Αἱ μεν ουν
sent away him into Tarsus. The indeed then
εκκλησιαι καθ᾽ ὁλης της Ιουδαιας και Γαλιλαιας
congregations in whole of the Judea and Galilee
και Σαμαρειας ειχον ειρηνην, οικοδεμουμεναι
and Samaria had peace, being built up
και πορευομεναι τῳ φοβῳ του κυριου και τῃ
and proceeding in the fear of the Lord and the
παρακλησει του ἁγιου πνευματος, επληθυνοντο.
consolation of the holy spirit, were multiplied.
32 Εγενετο δε Πετρον, διερχομενον δια παν-
It happened and Peter, passing through all,
των, κατελθειν και προς τους ἁγιους τους
to have gone down also to the saints those
κατοικουντας Λυδδαν. 33 Εὑρε δε εκει ανθρω-
dwelling Lydda. He found and there a man
πον τινα Αινεαν ονοματι, εξ ετων οκτω κατα-
certain Eneas by name, from years eight being
κειμενον επι κραββατῳ, ὁς ην παραλελυμενος.
laid in bed, who was a paralytic.
34 Και ειπεν αυτῳ ὁ Πετρος· Αινεα, ιαται σε
And said to him the Peter; Eneas, cures thee
Ιησους ὁ Χριστος· αναστηθι, και στρωσον σε-
Jesus the Anointed; arise thou, and make the bed for
αυτῳ. Και ευθεως ανεστη. 35 Και ειδον αυτον
thyself. And immediately he arose. And saw him
παντες οἱ κατοικουντες Λυδδαν και τον Σαρωνα,
all those dwelling Lydda and the Saron,
οἱτινες επεστρεψαν επι τον κυριον. 36 Εν Ιοπ-
who turned to the Lord. In Jop-
πῃ δε τις ην μαθητρια ονοματι Ταβιθα, ἡ διερ-
pa and certain was a female disciple by name Tabitha, which being
μηνευομενη λεγεται Δορκας· αὑτη ην πληρης
translated is called Dorcas; she was full
αγαθων εργων και ελεημοσυνων ὡν εποιει.
of good works and of alms which she did.

him, conducted him to the APOSTLES, and related to them how he saw the LORD on the ROAD, and That he spoke to him, and how he ‡ spoke publicly in Damascus in the NAME of JESUS.

28 ‡ And he was with them coming in and going out at Jerusalem, speaking publicly in the NAME of the LORD.

29 And he spoke and disputed with the Hellenists; ‡ they however undertook to kill him.

30 But the BRETHREN having been informed of it, conducted him to Cesarea, and sent him to Tarsus.

31 Then the * CHURCH had Peace in All JUDEA, and Galilee, and Samaria; and being built up, and walking in the FEAR of the Lord, and in the admonition of the HOLY Spirit, was increased.*

32 And Peter, passing through all places, happened to go down also to those SAINTS DWELLING at Lydda.

33 And he found a certain Man named Eneas, who, being palsied, had lain on a bed for eight Years.

34 And PETER said to him, "Eneas, ‡ Jesus the MESSIAH, restores thee; arise, and make the bed for thyself." And he instantly arose.

35 And ALL THOSE DWELLING in Lydda and SHARON saw him; ‡ and they turned to the LORD.

36 And there was in Joppa a Certain female Disciple named † Tabitha, (which being translated signifies Dorcas;) she was full of good Works and Charities which she did.

* VATICAN MANUSCRIPT.—28. and—*omit*. 28. Jesus—*omit*. 31. the CHURCH. 31. was increased.

† 36. *Tabitha*, is a Syria word, and *Dorcas* a Greek word, both signifying *an antelope*. The name here is expressive of beauty; as "*antelopes* are particularly remarkable for their *beautiful eyes*." See Parkhurst.

‡ 27. verse 20, 22. ‡ 28. Gal. i. 18. ‡ 29. verse 23; 2 Cor. xi. 26. ‡ 34. Acts iii. 6, 16; iv. 10. ‡ 35. Acts xi. 21.

37 Εγενετο δε εν ταις ἡμεραις εκειναις ασθενη-
It happened and in the days those having
σασαν αυτην αποθανειν· λουσαντες δε *[αυτην]
been sick her to have died; having washed and [her]
εθηκαν εν ὑπερῳῳ. 38 Εγγυς δε ουσης Λυδδης
they laid in an upper room. Near and being Lydda
τῃ Ιοππῃ, ὁι μαθηται ακουσαντες ὁτι Πετρος
to the Joppa, the disciples having heard that Peter
εστιν εν αυτῃ, απεστειλεν δυο ανδρας προς
is in her, sent two men to
αυτον, παρακαλουντες μη οκνησαι διελθειν ἑως
him, entreating not to delay to come over to
αυτων. 39 Αναστας δε Πετρος συνηλθεν αυτοις·
them. Having arisen and Peter came with them;
ὁν παραγενομενον ανηγαγον εις το ὑπερῳον,
whom having come they led into the upper room,
και παρεστησαν αυτῳ πασαι ἁι χηραι κλαιου-
and stood beside him all the widows weeping,
σαι, και επιδεικνυμεναι χιτωνας και ἱματια,
and showing tunics and mantles,
ὁσα εποιει μετ' αυτων ουσα ἡ Δορκας.
as many as she made with them being the Dorcas.
40 Εκβαλων δε εξω παντας ὁ Πετρος, θεις
Having put and out all the Peter, having placed
τα γονατα προσηυξατο· και επιστρεψας προς
the knees he prayed; and having turned to
το σωμα, ειπε· Ταβιθα, αναστηθι. Ἡ δε
the body, said; Tabitha, do thou arise. She and
ηνοιξε τους οφθαλμους αὑτης· και ιδουσα τον
opened the eyes of herself; and seeing the
Πετρον, ανεκαθισε. 41 Δους δε αυτῃ χειρα,
Peter, sat up. Having given and to her a hand,
ανεστησεν αυτην· φωνησας δε τους ἁγιους και
he raised her; having called and the saints and
τας χηρας, παρεστησεν αυτην ζωσαν. 42 Γνωσ-
the widows, he presented her living. Known
τον δε εγενετο καθ' ὁλης της Ιοππης· και
and it became in whole of the Joppa; and
πολλοι επιστευσαν επι τον κυριον. 43 Εγενετο
many believed in the Lord. It happened
δε ἡμερας ἱκανας μειναι αυτον εν Ιοππῃ, παρα
and days many to remain him in Joppa, with
τινι Σιμωνι βυρσει.
one Simon a tanner.

ΚΕΦ. ι'. 10.

1 Ανηρ δε τις εν Καισαρειᾳ, ονοματι Κορνη-
A man and certain in Cesarea, by name Corne-
λιος, εκατονταρχης εκ σπειρης της καλουμενης
lius, a centurion of a cohort that being called
Ιταλικης, 2 ευσεβης και φοβουμενος τον θεον
Italian, pious and fearing the God
συν παντι τῳ οικῳ αὑτου, ποιων *[τε] ελεημο-
with all the house of himself, doing [and] alms
συνας πολλας τῳ λαῳ, και δεομενος του θεου
many to the people, and praying of the God
διαπαντος· 3 ειδεν εν ὁραματι φανερως, ὡσει
always; he saw in a vision clearly, about

37 And it happened in
those DAYS, that she was
sick and died; and having
washed they placed her in
an upper room.

38 Now Lydda being
near to JOPPA, and the
DISCIPLES having heard
That Peter was there, sent
Two Men to him entreat-
ing, * "Do not delay to
come over to us."

39 And Peter arose and
went with them; and hav-
ing arrived they conducted
him to the UPPER ROOM;
and All the WIDOWS stood
beside him weeping, and
showing the Tunics and
Mantles which DORCAS
made, while she was with
them.

40 But PETER ‡ putting
them all out, kneeled down
and prayed; and turning
to the BODY, ‡ he said,
"Tabitha, arise!" And
SHE opened her EYES; and
beholding PETER, she sat
up.

41 And giving her his
Hand, he raised her; and
having called the SAINTS
and WIDOWS, he presented
her living.

42 And it became known
through All * Joppa; and
‡ many believed in the
LORD.

43 And it occurred, he
continued many DAYS in
Joppa, with One ‡ Simon a
Tanner.

CHAPTER X.

1 And a certain Man in
Cesarea, named Cornelius,
a Centurion of THAT Co-
hort CALLED the Italian,

2 ‡ a pious man, and one
fearing GOD with All his
HOUSE, doing many Chari-
ties for the PEOPLE, and
praying to GOD always,

3 ‡ saw distinctly in a
Vision, * about the ninth

* VATICAN MANUSCRIPT.—37. her—*omit*. 38. Do not delay to come over to us. 42. Joppa. 2. and—*omit*. 3. as if about.

‡ 40. Matt. ix. 25. ‡ 40. Mark v. 41, 42; John xi. 43. ‡ 42. John xi. 45; xii. 11. ‡ 43. Acts x. 6. ‡ 2. verse 22. ‡ 3. verse 30; xi. 13.

ὡραν εννατην της ἡμερας, αγγελον του θεου
hour ninth of the day, a messenger of the God
εισελθοντα προς αυτον, και ειποντα αυτῳ·
having come to him, and saying to him;
Κορνηλιε. [4] Ὁ δε ατενισας αυτῳ και
O Cornelius. He and having looked steadily to him and
εμφοβος γενομενος, ειπε· Τι εστι, κυριε;
afraid becoming, he said; What is it, O sir?
Ειπε δε αυτῳ· Αἱ προσευχαι σου και αἱ ελεη-
He said and to him; The prayers of thee and the alms
μοσυναι σου ανεβησαν εις μνημοσυνον ενωπιον
of thee went up for a memorial before
του θεου. [5] Και νυν πεμψον εις Ιοππην ανδρας,
the God. And now send into Joppa men,
και μεταπεμψαι Σιμωνα, ὁς επικαλειται Πετρος·
and send after Simon, who is surnamed Peter;
[6] οὑτος ξενιζεται παρα τινι Σιμωνι βυρσει, ᾧ
he lodges with one Simon a tanner, to whom
εστιν οικια παρα θαλασσαν. [7] Ὡς δε απηλθεν
is a house by sea. When and went away
ὁ αγγελος, ὁ λαλων αυτῳ, φωνησας δυο των
the messenger, that speaking to him, having called two of the
οικετων αὑτου, και στρατιωτην ευσεβη των
house servants of himself, and a soldier pious of those
προσκαρτερουντων αυτῳ, [8] και εξηγησαμενος
constantly attending him, and having related
αυτοις ἁπαντα, απεστειλεν αυτους εις την
to them all things, he sent them into the
Ιοππην. [9] Τῃ δε επαυριον, ὁδοιπορουντων
Joppa On the and morrow, pursuing the journey
εκεινων, και τῃ πολει εγγιζοντων, ανεβη Πετ-
of them, and to the city drawing near, went up Pe-
ρος επι το δωμα προσευξασθαι, περι ὡραν
ter to the roof to pray, about hour
ἑκτην. [10] Εγενετο δε προσπεινος, και ηθελε
sixth He became and very hungry, and wished
γευσασθαι· παρασκευαζοντων δε εκεινων, επε-
to eat; making ready and of them, fell
πεσεν επ' αυτον εκστασις, [11] και θεωρει τον ουρα-
on him a trance, and he beholds the heaven
νον ανεῳγμενον, και καταβαινον σκευος τι ὡς
having been opened, and coming down a vessel certain like
οθονην μεγαλην, τεσσαρσιν αρχαις δεδεμενον,
a sheet great, four ends having been bound,
και καθιεμενον επι της γης· [12] εν ᾧ ὑπηρχε
and being lowered down to the earth; in which were
παντα τα τετραποδα της γης και τα θηρια και
all the four-footed beasts of the earth and the wild beasts and
τα ερπετα και τα πετεινα του ουρανου· [13] και
the creeping things and the birds of the heaven; and
εγενετο φωνη προς αυτον· Αναστας, Πετρε,
came a voice to him; Having arisen, O Peter,
θυσον και φαγε. [14] Ὁ δε Πετρος ειπε· Μηδα-
sacrifice and eat. The but Peter said; By no

Hour of the DAY, an Angel of GOD coming in to him, and saying to him, "Cornelius!"

4 And steadily gazing at him, and becoming afraid, he said, "What is it, Sir!" And he said to him, "Thy PRAYERS and thine ALMS went up as a Memorial before GOD.

5 And now send Men to Joppa, and invite one Simon, who is surnamed Peter;

6 he lodges with ‡One Simon a Tanner, whose House is by the Sea.

7 And when THAT ANGEL which SPOKE to him was gone away, he called two of *the HOUSE SERVANTS, and a pious Soldier of THOSE who ATTENDED constantly on him;

8 and having related to them all things, he sent them to JOPPA.

9 And on the NEXT DAY, †while they were pursuing their journey, and drawing near to the CITY, ‡Peter went upon †the ROOF to pray, about the sixth Hour.

10 And he became very hungry, and wished to eat; but while they were making ready, a Trance fell on him,

11 and he beheld ‡HEAVEN opened, and a certain Vessel like a great Sheet descending, *being let down by the Four Ends to the EARTH;

12 in which were *All the QUADRUPEDS and REPTILES of the EARTH, and BIRDS of HEAVEN.

13 And a Voice came to him, "Rise, Peter, kill and eat."

14 But PETER said "By no means, Lord;

* VATICAN MANUSCRIPT.—7. the HOUSE SERVANTS. 11. being let down by the Four Ends to the EARTH. 12. All the QUADRUPEDS and REPTILES of the EARTH.

† 9. It was about forty miles from *Joppa* to *Cesarea*, therefore the messengers must have travelled a part of the night to reach *Joppa* towards noon on the next day. † 9. It has been remarked before, that the houses in Palestine had flat roofs, on which people walked, conversed, meditated and prayed.

‡ 6 Acts ix. 43 ‡ Acts xi. 5. ‡ [illegible] vii. 56.

μως, κυριε· ὁτι ουδεποτε εφαγον παν κοινον η
means, O lord; because never I ate any thing common or
ακαθαρτον. 15 Και φωνη παλιν εκ δευτερου
unclean. And a voice again a second time
προς αυτον. Ἁ ὁ θεος εκαθαρισε, συ μη κοινου.
to him. What the God has cleansed, thou not pollute.
16 Τουτο δε εγενετο επι τρις· και παλιν ανελη-
This and was done for three times; and again was taken
φθη το σκευος εις τον ουρανον. 17 Ὡς δε εν
up the vessel into the heaven As and in
ἑαυτῳ διηπορει ὁ Πετρος, τι αν ειη το ὁραμα
himself was pondering the Peter, what might be the vision
ὁ ειδε, και ιδου, οἱ ανδρες οἱ απεσταλμενοι
which he saw, even lo, the men those being sent
απο του Κορνηλιου, διερωτησαντες την οικιαν
from the Cornelius, having inquired for the house
Σιμωνος, επεστησαν επι τον πυλωνα· 18 και
of Simon, stood at the gate; and
φωνησαντες επυνθανοντο, ει Σιμων ὁ επικαλου-
having called aloud they asked, if Simon he being called
μενος Πετρος ενθαδε ξενιζεται.
Peter here lodges.

19 Του δε Πετρου διενθυμουμενου περι του
The and Peter reflecting concerning the
ὁραματος, ειπεν *[αυτῳ] το πνευμα· Ιδου, ανδρες
vision, said [to him] the spirit; Lo, men
τρεις ζητουσι σε· 20 αλλα αναστας κατα-
three are seeking thee; but having arisen do thou
βηθι, και πορευου συν αυτοις, μηδεν δια-
go down, and go with them, nothing doubt-
κρινομενος ὁτι εγω απεσταλκα αυτους. 21 Κατα-
ing because I have sent them. Having gone
βας δε Πετρος προς τους ανδρας, ειπεν· Ιδου,
down but Peter to the men, said, Lo,
εγω ειμι, ὁν ζητειτε· τις ἡ αιτια, δι' ἡν
I am, whom you seek; what the cause, on account of which
παρεστε; 22 Οἱ δε ειπον· Κορνηλιος εκατονταρ-
you are present? They and said; Cornelius a centurion,
χης, ανηρ δικαιος και φοβουμενος τον θεον,
a man just and fearing the God,
μαρτυρουμενος τε ὑπο ὁλου του ἐθνους των Ιου-
being testified of and by whole of the nation of the Jews,
δαιων, εχρηματισθη ὑπο αγγελου ἁγιου, μετα-
was divinely instructed by a messenger holy, to
πεμψασθαι σε εις τον οικον αὑτου, και ακουσαι
send after thee to the house of himself, and to hear
ῥηματα παρα σου. 23 Εισκαλεσαμενος ουν
words from thee. Having called in then
αυτους εξενισε. Τῃ δε επαυριον αναστας
them he lodged. On the and morrow having arisen
εξηλθε συν αυτοις, και τινες των αδελφων, των
he went out with them, and some of the brethren, those
απο Ιοππης, συνηλθον αυτῳ. 24 Και τῃ επαυ-
from Joppa, went with him. And on the mor-

‡ For never did I eat any thing common and impure."

15 And a Voice came to him again a second time, ‡ "What GOD has cleansed, do not thou regard as common.

16 And this was done three times; and * immediately the VESSEL was taken up into HEAVEN.

17 And as PETER was pondering in himself, what the VISION which he saw might mean, behold, even THOSE MEN who were SENT * by CORNELIUS, having inquired for the HOUSE of * Simon, stood at the GATE;

18 and calling aloud, they asked, "Is THAT Simon who was SURNAMED Peter lodging here?"

19 Now while PETER was reflecting concerning the VISION, ‡ the SPIRIT said, "Behold, * three Men are seeking thee;

20 ‡ arise and go down, and go with them, without any hesitation, Because I have sent them."

21 Then Peter having gone down to the MEN, said, "Behold, I am he whom you seek; what is * the Cause of your coming?"

22 And THEY said, ‡ "Cornelius, a Centurion, a righteous Man, and one fearing GOD, ‡ and esteemed by all the NATION of the JEWS, was divinely instructed by a holy Angel to send after thee to his HOUSE, and to hear WORDS from thee."

23 Having, therefore, invited them in, he entertained them. And on the NEXT DAY he arose and went with them, and some of THOSE BRETHREN from Joppa accompanied him.

24 And on the DAY FOL-

* VATICAN MANUSCRIPT.—16. immediately the VESSEL. 17. by CORNELIUS. 17. SIMON. 19. to him—*omit*. 19. two Men. 21. the Cause.

‡ 14. Lev. xi. 4; xx. 25; Deut. xiv. 3, 7; Ezek. iv. 14. ‡ 15. verse 28. ‡ 19. Acts xi. 12. ‡ 20. Acts xv. 7. ‡ 22. verses 1, 2. ‡ 22. Acts xxii. 12.

ριον εισηλθον εις την Καισαρειαν. 'Ο δε Κορ-
low they entered into the Cesarea. The and Cor-
νηλιος ην προσδοκων αυτους, συγκαλεσαμενος
nelius was expecting them, having assembled
τους συγγενεις αὑτου και τους αναγκαιους
the relatives of himself and the intimate
φιλους. 25 'Ως δε εγενετο του εισελθειν τον
friends. When and came the to enter the
Πετρον, συναντησας αυτῳ ὁ Κορνηλιος, πεσων
Peter, having met him the Cornelius, having fallen
επι τους ποδας, προσεκυνησεν. 26 'Ο δε Πετρος
to the feet, he worshipped. The but Peter
αυτον ηγειρε, λεγων· Αναστηθι· καγω αυτος
him raised up, saying; Do thou arise; also I myself
ανθρωπος ειμι. 26 Και συνομιλων αυτῳ, εισηλθε,
a man am. And talking with him, he went in,
και ευρισκει συνεληλυθοτας πολλους. 28 Εφη
and finds having been assembled many. He said
τε προς αυτους· 'Υμεις επιστασθε, ὡς αθεμιτον
and to them; You know, how unlawful
εστιν ανδρι Ιουδαιῳ, κολλασθαι η προσερχεσθαι
it is for a man a Jew, to unite or come near
αλλοφυλῳ· και εμοι ὁ θεος εδειξε, μηδενα
to a foreigner; and to me the God has shown, not
κοινον η ακαθαρτον λεγειν ανθρωπον. 29 Διο
common or unclean to say a man. Therefore
και αναντιρρητως ηλθον μεταπεμφθεις. Πυνθα-
also without hesitation I came having been sent after. I ask
νομαι ουν, τινι λογῳ μετεπεμψασθε με;
therefore, for what reason you sent after me?
30 Και ὁ Κορνηλιος εφη· Απο τεταρτης ἡμερας
And the Cornelius said; From four days
μεχρι ταυτης της ὡρας, ημην νηστευων, και
till this the hour, I was fasting, and
την εννατην ὡραν προσευχομενος εν τῳ οικῳ
the ninth hour praying in the house
μου· και ιδου, ανηρ, εστη ενωπιον μου εν εσθη-
of me; and lo, a man, stood before me in cloth-
τι λαμπρᾳ, 31 και φησι· Κορνηλιε, εισηκουσθη
ing shining, and he said, O Cornelius, heard
σου ἡ προσευχη, και αἱ ελεημοσυναι σου εμνησ-
of thee the prayer, and the alms of thee are re-
θησαν ενωπιον του θεου. 32 Πεμψον ουν εις
membered before the God. Send therefore into
Ιοππην, και μετακαλεσαι Σιμωνα ὁς επικαλειται
Joppa, and call for Simon who is surnamed
Πετρος· οὑτος ξενιζεται εν οικιᾳ Σιμωνος βυρ-
Peter; he lodges in a house of Simon a tan-
σεως παρα θαλασσαν· *[ὁς παραγενομενος
ner by sea; [who having come
λαλησει σοι.] 33 Εξαυτης ουν επεμψα προς
will speak to thee.] Immediately therefore I sent to
σε· συ τε καλως εποιησας παραγενομενος.
thee; thou and well didst having come.
Νυν ουν παντες ἡμεις ενωπιον του θεου παρεσ-
Now therefore all we before the God are pre-
μεν, ακουσαι παντα τα προστεταγμενα σοι ὑπο
sent, to hear all the things having been commanded thee by

LOWING they entered CÆSAREA. And CORNELIUS was expecting them, having assembled his RELATIVES and INTIMATE Friends.

25 And as PETER was COMING IN, CORNELIUS met him, and falling down at his FEET he worshipped him.

26 But PETER raised him up, saying, ‡ "Arise; I also am a Man."

27 And conversing with him, he went in, and found many gathered together.

28 And he said to them, ‡ "You know that it is unlawful for a Jew to associate with a Foreigner; ‡ but GOD has showed Me not to call any man common or impure.

29 Therefore, being sent for, I also came without hesitation. I ask, therefore, for what reason you sent for me?"

30 And CORNELIUS said, "Four days ago * I was fasting till This HOUR; and at the NINTH Hour I was praying in my HOUSE, and behold, ‡ a Man stood before me in ‡ splendid Clothing,

31 and said, 'Cornelius! thy PRAYER is heard, and thine ALMS are remembered before GOD.

32 Send therefore to Joppa, and invite Simon, whose surname is Peter; he lodges in the HOUSE of Simon, a Tanner, by the Sea; who, when he is come, will speak to thee.'

33 Immediately, therefore I sent to thee, and thou hast done well in having come. Now therefore we are all present before God to hear ALL THINGS which * the LORD has COMMANDED thee."

* VATICAN MANUSCRIPT.—30. till This Hour, I was at the NINTH praying in my HOUSE. 32. who having come will speak to thee—*omit*. 33. the LORD.

‡ 26. Acts xiv. 14, 15; Rev. xix. 10; xxii. 9. ‡ 28. Josh. iv. 9; xviii. 28; Acts xi. 3; Gal. ii. 12, 14. ‡ 28. Acts xv. 8; Eph. iii. 6. ‡ 30. Acts i. 10. ‡ 30. Matt. xxviii. 3; Mark xvi. 5; Luke xxiv. 4.

του θεου. 34 Ανοιξας δε Πετρος το στομα, ειπεν·
the God. Having opened and Peter the mouth, said,
Επ' αληθειας καταλαμβανομαι, ότι ουκ εστι
In truth I perceive, that not is
προσωποληπτης ὁ θεος· 35 αλλ' εν παντι εθνει
a respecter of persons the God; but in every nation
ὁ φοβουμενος αυτον, και εργαζομενος δικαιο-
he fearing him, and working righteous-
συνην, δεκτος αυτῳ εστι. 36 Τον λογον ὁν
ness, acceptable to him is. The word which
απεστειλε τοις υίοις Ισραηλ, ευαγγελιζομενος
he sent to the sons of Israel, proclaiming glad tidings of
ειρηνην δια Ιησου Χριστου· οὑτος εστι παντων
peace through Jesus Anointed; this is of all
κυριος. 37 Ὑμεις οιδατε το γενομενον ῥημα
a lord. You know that having been a spoken word
καθ ὁλης της Ιουδαιας αρξαμενον απο της Γαλι-
in whole of the Judea beginning from the Gali-
λαιας, μετα το βαπτισμα ὁ εκηρυξεν Ιωαννης·
lee, after the dipping which was preached of John;
38 Ιησουν τον απο Ναζαρετ, ὡς εχρισεν αυτον ὁ
Jesus that from Nazareth, how anointed him the
θεος πνευματι ἁγιῳ και δυναμει, ὁς διηλθεν ευερ-
God with spirit holy and power, who went about doing
γετων και ιωμενος παντας τους καταδυναστευ-
good and curing all those being oppressed
ομενους ὑπο του διαβολου, ότι ὁ θεος ην μετ'
by the accuser, because the God was with
αυτου· 39 και ἡμεις μαρτυρες παντων, ὡν εποιη-
him; and we witnesses of all, which he did
σεν εν τε τῃ χωρᾳ των Ιουδαιων και εν Ἱερου-
in both the country of the Jews and in Jerusa-
σαλημ· ὁν και ανειλον κρεμασαντες επι ξυλου.
lem; whom also they killed having hanged on a cross.
40 Τουτον ὁ θεος ηγειρε τῃ τριτῃ ἡμερᾳ, και
This the God raised up the third day, and
εδωκεν αυτον εμφανη γενεσθαι, 41 ου παντι τῳ
gave him manifest to become, not to all the
λαῳ, αλλα μαρτυσι τοις προκεχειροτονημενοις
people, but to witnesses to those having been chosen before
ὑπο του θεου, ἡμιν, οίτινες συνεφαγομεν και
by the God, to us, who ate with and
συνεπιομεν αυτῳ μετα το αναστηναι αυτον εκ
drank with him after that to have raised him out of
νεκρων. 42 Και παρηγγειλεν ἡμιν, κηρυξαι τῳ
dead ones. And he commanded us, to publish to the
λαῳ και διαμαρτυρασθαι, ότι αυτος εστιν ὁ
people and to fully testify, that he is the
ὡρισμενος ὑπο του θεου κριτης ζωντων και
having been appointed by the God a judge of living ones and
νεκρων. 43 Τουτῳ παντες οἱ προφηται μαρτυ-
dead ones. To him all the prophets bear testi-

34 And Peter opening his MOUTH, said, ‡ "I perceive in Truth That GOD is not a Respecter of persons,

35 but in Every Nation, he who FEARS him and works Righteousness is acceptable to him.

36 * He sent the WORD to the SONS of Israel, ‡ announcing glad tidings of Peace, through Jesus Christ—He is Lord of all—

37 (* you know that WORD which was SPOKEN through All JUDEA, ‡ beginning from GALILEE, after the IMMERSION which John preached;)

38 even THAT Jesus from Nazareth, how ‡ GOD anointed him with holy Spirit and Power; who went about doing good, and curing ALL who were OPPRESSED by the ENEMY; ‡ Because GOD was with him.

39 And We are Witnesses of all things which he did, both in the COUNTRY of the JEWS, and in Jerusalem; whom also, having hanged on a Cross, they killed.

40 Him GOD raised up the THIRD Day, and permitted him to become manifest,

41 not to All the PEOPLE, but to THOSE Witnesses PREVIOUSLY CHOSEN by GOD, to us, ‡ who did eat and drink with him after he ROSE from the Dead.

42 And ‡ he commanded us to proclaim to the PEOPLE, and to fully testify * That this is HE ‡ who has been APPOINTED by GOD the Judge of the Living and the Dead.

43 To Him All the PRO-

* VATICAN MANUSCRIPT.—36. He sent the WORD to the SONS of Israel. 37. You know. 42. That this is HE.

‡ 34. Deut. x. 17; 2 Chron. xix. 7; Job xxxiv. 19; Rom. ii. 11; Eph. vi. 9; Col. vi. 25; 1 Pet. i. 17. ‡ 36. Matt. xxviii. 18; Rom. x. 12; 1 Cor. xv. 27; Eph. i. 20—22; 1 Pet. iii. 22; Rev. xvii. 14; xix. 16. ‡ 37. Luke iv. 14. ‡ 38. Luke iv. 18; Acts ii. 22; iv. 27; Heb. i. 9. ‡ 38. John iii. 2. ‡ 41. Luke xxiv. 30, 43; John xxi. 13. ‡ 42. Matt. xxviii. 19, 20; Acts i. 8. ‡ 42. John v. 22, 27; Acts xvii. 31; Rom. xiv. 9; 2 Cor. v. 10; 2 Tim. iv. 1; 1 Pet. iv. 5.

φουσιν, αφεσιν ἁμαρτιων λαβειν δια του ονο-
mony, forgiveness of sins to receive through the name
ματος αυτου παντα τον πιστευοντα εις αυτον.
of him every one the believing into him.
44 Ετι λαλουντος του Πετρου τα ῥηματα ταυτα,
While speaking the Peter the words these,
επεπεσε το πνευμα το ἁγιον επι παντας τους
fell the spirit the holy on all those
ακουοντας τον λογον. 45 Και εξεστησαν οἱ εκ
hearing the word. And were astonished those of
περιτομης πιστοι ὁσοι συνηλθον τῳ Πετρῳ,
circumcision believers as many as came with the Peter,
ὁτι και επι τα εθνη ἡ δωρεα του ἁγιου πνευμα-
because also on the gentiles the gift of the holy spirit
τος εκκεχυται· 46 ηκουον γαρ αυτων λαλουντων
has been poured out; they heard for them speaking
γλωσσαις, και μεγαλυνοντων τον θεον. Τοτε
with tongues, and magnifying the God. Then
απεκριθη ὁ Πετρος· 47 μητι το ὑδωρ κωλυσαι
answered the Peter; not the water to forbid
δυναται τις, του μη βαπτισθηναι τουτους,
is able any- that not to be dipped these,
οἱτινες το πνευμα το ἁγιον ελαβον καθως και
who the spirit the holy received as even
ἡμεις; 48 Προσεταξε τε αυτους βαπτισθηναι εν
we? He directed and them to be dipped in
τῳ ονοματι του κυριου. Τοτε ηρωτησαν αυτον
the name of the Lord. Then they asked him
επιμειναι ἡμερας τινας.
to remain days some.

ΚΕΦ. ια'. 11.

1 Ηκουσαν δε οἱ αποστολοι και οἱ αδελφοι οἱ
Heard and the apostles and the brethren those
οντες κατα την Ιουδαιαν, ὁτι και τα εθνη εδεξ-
being in the Judea, that also the gentiles re-
αντο τον λογον του θεου. 2 Και ὁτε ανεβη
ceived the word of the God. And when went up
Πετρος εις Ἱεροσολυμα, διεκρινοντο προς αυτον
Peter into Jerusalem, disputed with him
οἱ εκ περιτομης, 3 λεγοντες· Ὁτι προς ανδρας
those of circumcision, saying; That to men
ακροβυστιαν εχοντας εισηλθες, και συνεφαγης
uncircumcision having thou wentest in, and thou didst eat
αυτοις. 4 Αρξαμενος δε ὁ Πετρος εξετιθετο
with them. Having begun and the Peter set forth
αυτοις καθεξης, λεγων· 5 εγω ημην εν πολει
to them in order, saying; I was in city
Ιοππῃ προσευχομενος· και ειδον εν εκστασει
of Joppa praying; and I saw in a trance
ὁραμα, καταβαινον σκευος τι ὡς οθονην μεγα-
a vision, coming down a vessel certain like a sheet great,
λην, τεσσαρσιν αρχαις καθιεμενην εκ του ουρα-
four ends being lowered out of the hea-

PHETS bear testimony; and EVERY ONE BELIEVING into him shall receive Forgiveness of Sins, through his NAME.

44 While PETER was yet speaking these WORDS,
‡ the HOLY SPIRIT fell on all THOSE HAVING HEARD the WORD.

45 And THOSE BELIEVERS of the Circumcision,
* who came with Peter, were astonished, ‡ Because the GIFT of the HOLY Spirit was even poured out upon the GENTILES;

46 for they heard them speaking with Tongues, and magnifying GOD. Then answered PETER,

47 "Can any one forbid WATER, that these should not be IMMERSED, who received the HOLY SPIRIT, even as we did?"

48 ‡ And he ordered them to be immersed in the name of * the LORD. Then they desired him to remain some Days.

CHAPTER XI.

1 And the APOSTLES and THOSE BRETHREN who WERE in JUDEA heard That the Gentiles also had received the WORD of GOD.

2 And when Peter went up to Jerusalem, THOSE of the Circumcision contended with him,

3 saying, ‡ * That he went in to Men uncircumcised, and did eat with them.

4 But * Peter, having begun, set it forth in order to them, saying,

5 "‡ I was in the City of Joppa praying, ‡ and in a Trance I saw a Vision, a certain Vessel like a great Sheet descending, being let down by the Four Ends out of HEAVEN, and it came to me.

* VATICAN MANUSCRIPT.—45. who came with. 48. Jesus Christ. 3. That he went in to Men uncircumcised, and did eat with them. 4. Peter.

‡ 44. Acts ii. 2; xi. 15. ‡ 45. Acts xi. 18; Gal. iii. 14. ‡ 48. Acts ii. 38; viii. 16.
‡ 3. Acts x. 28. ‡ 5. Acts x. 9, &c.

νου, και ηλθεν αρχις εμου· 6 εις ην ατενισας
ven, and came as far as me; into which having looked
κατενοουν και ειδον τα τετραποδα της γης και
I observed and saw the four-footed beasts of the earth and
τα θηρια και τα ἑρπετα και τα πετεινα του ου-
the wild beasts and the reptiles and the birds of the hea-
ρανου. 7 Ηκουσα δε φωνης λεγουσης μοι·
ven. I heard and a voice saying to me;
Αναστας, Πετρε, θυσον και φαγε. 8 Ειπον δε
Having arisen, O Peter, sacrifice and eat. I said but;
Μηδαμως, κυριε· ὁτι κοινον η ακαθαρτον ουδε-
By no means, O lord; because common or unclean never
ποτε εισηλθεν εις το στομα μου. 9 Απεκριθη
entered into the mouth of me. Answered
δε μοι φωνη εκ δευτερου εκ του ουρανου· Ἁ ὁ
but to me a voice a second time out of the heaven; What the
θεος εκαθαρισε, συ μη κοινου. 10 Τουτο δε
God cleansed, thou not pollute. This and
εγενετο επι τρις· και παλιν ανεσπασθη ἁπαν-
was done for three times; and again was drawn up all
τα εις τον ουρανον. 11 Και ιδου, εξαυτης τρεις
into the heaven. And lo, immediately three
ανδρες επεστησαν επι την οικιαν εν ᾗ ημην,
men stood at the house in which I was,
απεσταλμενοι απο Καισαρειας προς με. 12 Ειπε
having been sent from Cesarea to me. Said
δε μοι το πνευμα, συνελθειν αυτοις, μηδεν δια-
and to me the spirit, to go with them, nothing doubt-
κρινομενον· ηλθον δε συν εμοι και οἱ εξ αδελ-
ing; went and with me also the six breth-
φοι οὑτοι, και εισηλθομεν εις τον οικον του
ren these, and we entered into the house of the
ανδρος. 13 Απηγγειλε τε ἡμιν, πως ειδε τον
man. He related and to us, how he saw the
αγγελον εν τῳ οικῳ αὑτου σταθεντα και ειποντα
messenger in the house of himself standing and saying
τα *[αυτῳ·] Αποστειλον εις Ιοππην, και μετα-
[to him;] Send into Joppa, and send
πεμψαι Σιμωνα τον επικαλουμενον Πετρον·
after Simon that having been surnamed Peter;
14 ὁς λαλησαι ῥηματα προς σε, εν οἱς σωθησῃ
who will speak words to thee, by which mayest be saved
συ και πας ὁ οικος σου. 15 Εν δε τῳ αρξασθαι
thou and all the house of thee. In and the to have begun
με λαλειν, επεπεσε το πνευμα το ἁγιον επ'
me to speak, fell the spirit the holy on
αυτους, ὡσπερ και εφ' ἡμας εν αρχῃ. 16 Εμ-
them, as also on us in beginning. I
νησθην δε του ῥηματος του κυριου, ὡς ελεγεν·
remembered and the words of the Lord, how he said;
Ιωαννης μεν εβαπτισεν ὑδατι, ὑμεις δε βαπτισ-
John indeed dipped in water, you but shall be
θησεσθε εν πνευματι ἁγιῳ. 17 Ει ουν την
dipped in spirit holy. If then the
ισην δωρεαν εδωκεν αυτοις ὁ θεος ὡς και ἡμιν,
like gift gave to them the God as even to us,
πιστευσασιν επι τον κυριον Ιησουν Χριστον,
having believed on the Lord Jesus Anointed,

6 And looking attentively into it, I observed and saw QUADRUPEDS of the EARTH and WILD BEASTS, and REPTILES, and BIRDS of HEAVEN.

7 And * I also heard a Voice saying to me, 'Arise, kill and eat.'

8 But I said, 'By no means, Lord; For a common or impure thing never entered into my MOUTH.'

9 And a Voice answered me a second time from HEAVEN, 'What GOD has cleansed, do not thou regard as common.'

10 And this was done three times; and again all were drawn up into HEAVEN.

11 And behold, immediately Three Men stood at the HOUSE in which I was, having been sent to me from Cesarea.

12 And ‡ the SPIRIT commanded me to go with them, without any hesitation. And ‡ these SIX Brethren also went with me, and we entered the MAN'S HOUSE.

13 ‡ And he told us how he saw the ANGEL in his HOUSE, standing and saying, 'Send into Joppa, and invite THAT Simon, surnamed Peter;

14 who will speak Words to thee, by which thou mayest be saved, and All thy HOUSE.

15 And as I BEGAN to speak, the HOLY SPIRIT fell on them, ‡ even as on us in the Beginning.

16 And I remembered the WORD of the LORD, how he said, ‡ 'John indeed immersed in Water; but you shall be immersed in holy Spirit.'

17 Since, then, GOD imparted the SAME Gift to them, who believed on the LORD Jesus Christ, as

* VATICAN MANUSCRIPT.—7. I also heard. 13. to him—*omit*.

‡ 12. John xvi. 13; Acts x. 19; xv. 7. ‡ 12. Acts x. 23. ‡ 13. Acts x. 30.
‡ 15. Acts ii. 2; x. 44, 47. ‡ 16. Matt. iii. 11; John i. 26, 33; Acts i. 5; xix. 4.

εγω δε τις ημην, δυνατος κωλυσαι τον θεον;
I and who was, having power to restrain the God?
18 Ακουσαντες δε ταυτα, ησυχασαν, και εδοξα-
Having heard and these, they were silent, and glori-
ζον τον θεον, λεγοντες· Αραγε και τοις εθνεσιν
fied the God, saying; Then also to the gentiles
ὁ θεος την μετανοιαν εδωκεν εις ζωην. 19 Οἱ
the God the reformation gave into life. Those
μεν ουν διασπαρεντες απο της θλιψεως της
indeed therefore having been scattered from the affliction that
γενομενης επι Στεφανῳ, διηλθον ἑως Φοινικης
having happened about Stephen. went through to Phenicia
και Κυπρου και Αντιοχειας, μηδενι λαλουντες
and Cyprus and Antioch, not speaking
τον λογον ει μη μονον Ιουδαιοις. 20 Ησαν δε
the word if not alone to Jews. Were and
τινες εξ αυτων ανδρες Κυπριοι και Κυρηναιοι,
some of them men Cyprians and Cyrenians,
οἱτινες, ελθοντες εις Αντιοχειαν ελαλουν προς
who. having come into Antioch spoke to
τους Ἑλληνας, ευαγγελιζομενοι τον κυριον
the Greeks, announcing glad tidings of the Lord
Ιησουν. 21 Και ην χειρ κυριου μετ' αυτων,
Jesus. And was hand of Lord with them,
πολυς τε αριθμος πιστευσας επεστρεψεν επι
great and number having believed turned to
τον κυριον. 22 Ηκουσθη δε ὁ λογος εις τα ωτα
the Lord. Was reported and the word into the ears
της εκκλησιας της εν Ἱεροσολυμοις περι αυτων·
of the congregation that in Jerusalem concerning them;
και εξαπεστειλαν Βαρναβαν διελθειν ἑως Αντιο-
and they sent out Barnabas to go through to Anti-
χειας. 23 Ὁς παραγενομενος και ιδων την
och. Who having come and having seen the
χαριν του θεου, εχαρη, και παρεκαλει παντας,
favor of the God, rejoiced, and called on all,
τῃ προθεσει της καρδιας προσμενειν τῳ κυριῳ·
with the purpose of the heart to adhere to the Lord;
24 ὁτι ην ανηρ αγαθος, και πληρης πνευματος
for he was a man good, and full of spirit
ἁγιου και πιστεως. Και προσετεθη οχλος ἱκα-
holy and faith. And was added a crowd great
νος τῳ κυριῳ. 25 Εξηλθε δε εις Ταρσον *[ὁ
to the Lord. Went out and into Tarsus [the
Βαρναβας,] αναζητησαι Σαυλον· και εὑρων
Barnabas,] to seek Saul: and having found
*[αυτον,] ηγαγεν *[αυτον] εις Αντιοχειαν.
[him,] he brought [him] to Antioch.
26 Εγενετο δε αυτους ενιαυτον ὁλον συναχθηναι
It happened and them a year whole to assemble
εν τῃ εκκλησιᾳ, και διδαξαι οχλον ἱκανον,
in the congregation, and to teach a crowd great,

even to us, who was I, that
I should be able to restrain
GOD?"‡

18 And having heard
these things, they were
silent, and glorified GOD,
saying, ‡ "Then to the
GENTILES also has GOD
given REFORMATION to
Life."

19 ‡ Then THOSE indeed
HAVING BEEN DISPERSED
on account of THAT AF-
FLICTION which AROSE
about Stephen, traveled to
Phenicia, and Cyprus, and
Antioch, speaking the WORD
to no one, except to Jews
only.

20 But some of them
were Cyprians and Cyre-
nians, who, having come
to Antioch, spoke * also to
the GREEKS, announcing
the glad tidings of the
LORD Jesus.

21 ‡ And the Hand of
the LORD was with them,
* and a Great Number hav-
ing believed, turned to the
LORD.

22 And the REPORT con-
cerning them came to the
EARS of * THAT CONGRE-
GATION which WAS in
Jerusalem; and they sent
forth Barnabas to An-
tioch;

23 who having come
and seen * THAT FAVOR of
GOD, rejoiced, and called
on all to * continue in the
LORD with PURPOSE of
HEART;

24 for he was a good
Man, and full of holy Spirit
and Faith. And a considerable Number were added
to the LORD.

25 And * he went to
‡ Tarsus to seek Saul; and
having found him he
brought him to Antioch.

26 And it occurred that
during a whole Year they
associated with the CON-
GREGATION, and taught a

* VATICAN MANUSCRIPT.—20. also to the. 21. and THAT Great Number. 22. THAT CONGREGATION which WAS. 23. THAT FAVOR. 23. continue in the LORD. 25. Barnabas—*omit.* 25. him—*omit.* 25. him—*omit.*

‡ 18. Rom. x. 12; xv. 9, 16. ‡ 19. Acts viii. 1. ‡ 21. Acts ix. 35. ‡ 25. Acts ix. 30.

χρματισαι τε πρωτον εν Αντιοχειᾳ τους μαθη-
to have been styled and first in Antioch the disci-
τας Χριστιανους.
ples Christians.

[27] Εν ταυταις δε ταις ἡμεραις κατηλθον απο
In these and the days came down from
Ιεροσολυμων προφηται εις Αντιοχειαν. [28] Αναστ-
Jerusalem prophets into Antioch. Having
τας δε εἱς εξ αυτων, ονοματι Αγαβος, εσημανε
arisen and one of them, by name Agabus, signified
δια του πνευματος, λιμον μεγαν μελλειν εσεσ-
through the spirit, a famine great about is going
θαι εφ᾽ ὁλην την οικουμενην· ὁστις και εγενετο
to be over whole the habitable? which also occurred
επι Κλαυδιου. [29] Των δε μαθητων καθως ηυπο-
under Claudius. The and disciples as was
ρειτο τις, ὡρισαν ἑκαστος αυτων εις διακονιαν
able each, determined each one of them for a relief
πεμψαι τοις κατοικουσιν εν τῃ Ιουδαιᾳ αδελφοις·
to send to the dwelling in the Judea brethren;
[30] ὁ και εποιησαν, αποστειλαντες προς τους
which also they did, sending to the
πρεσβυτερους δια χειρος Βαρναβα και Σαυλου.
elders through hand of Barnabas and Saul.

ΚΕΦ. ιβ΄. 12.

[1] Και εκεινον δε τον καιρον επεβαλεν Ἡρωδης
In that and the season put forth Herod
ὁ βασιλευς τας χειρας, κακωσαι τινας των απο
the king the hands, to afflict some of the from
της εκκλησιας, [2] ανειλε δε Ιακωβον, τον αδελ-
of the congregation, he killed and James, the bro-
φον Ιωαννου, μαχαιρᾳ. [3] Και ιδων, ὁτι αρεστον
ther of John, with a sword. And having seen, that pleasing
εστι τοις Ιουδαιοις, προσεθετο συλλαβειν και
it is to the Jews, he proceeded to take also
Πετρον· (ησαν δε αἱ ἡμεραι των αζυμων·) [4] ὁν
Peter; (they were and the days of the unleavened cakes;) whom
και πιασας εθετο εις φυλακην, παραδους τεσ-
also having seized he placed into a prison, having delivered to
σαρσι τετραδιοις στρατιωτων φυλλασειν αυτον,
four sets of four soldiers to watch him,
βουλομενος μετα το πασχα αναγαγειν αυτον
intending after the passover to lead out him
τῳ λαῳ. [5] Ὁ μεν ουν Πετρος ετηρειτο εν τῃ
to the people. The indeed therefore Peter was watched by the
φυλακῃ· προσευχη δε ην εκτενης γινομενη ὑπο
guard; prayer but was earnest was made by
της εκκλησιας *[προς τον θεον] ὑπερ αυτου.
the congregation [to the God] in behalf of him.
[6] Ὁτε δε εμελλεν αυτον προαγειν ὁ Ηρωδης,
When but was about him to bring before the Herod,

great Crowd. And the DISCIPLES were styled † Christians first in Antioch.

27 And in Those DAYS ‡ Prophets came down from Jerusalem to Antioch;

28 And one of them, named ‡ Agabus, standing up signified by the SPIRIT that a great Famine was about to come on the Whole HABITABLE; which also happened under Claudius.

29 And the DISCIPLES, according to the ability of each, determined to send ‡ Relief to the BRETHREN DWELLING in JUDEA;

30 ‡ which also they did, sending to the ELDERS by the Hand of Barnabas and Saul.

CHAPTER XII.

1 Now at That TIME Herod the KING put forth his HANDS to injure SOME of the CHURCH.

2 And he killed ‡ James the BROTHER of John with the Sword.

3 And seeing that it pleased the JEWS, he proceeded to arrest Peter also; (and it was during the DAYS of UNLEAVENED BREAD;)

4 and having seized he put him in Prison, delivering him to Four Quarternions of Soldiers to guard him, intending after the PASSOVER to lead him out to the PEOPLE.

5 Therefore, indeed, PETER was watched by the GUARD; ‡ but earnest Prayer was made * in his behalf by the CHURCH.

6 But when HEROD was about to bring him forward,

---

* VATICAN MANUSCRIPT.—5. to GOD—*omit*. 5. concerning him.

† 26. This name is only found in two other places in the New Testament, viz. Acts xxvi. 28, and 1 Pet. iv. 16. Some understand it to have been given by Divine authority and so translate it; some think that it was a term of reproach applied to the followers of Christ, by their enemies; while others with much more probability suppose it was adopted by themselves, both for convenience, and to keep out a term of reproach. † 1. Herod Agrippa, grandson of Herod the Great.

‡ 27. Acts ii. 17; xiii. 1; xv. 32; xxi. 9; 1 Cor. xii. 28; Eph. iv. 11. ‡ 28. Acts xxi. 10. ‡ 29. Rom. xv. 26; 1 Cor. xvi. 1; 2 Cor. ix. 1. ‡ 30. Acts xii. 25. ‡ 2. Matt. iv. 21; xx. 23. ‡ 5. 2 Cor. i. 10; Eph. vi. 18; 1 Thess. v. 17.

τῃ νυκτι εκεινῃ ην ὁ Πετρος κοιμωμενος μεταξυ
in the night that was the Peter sleeping between
δυο στρατιωτων, δεδεμενος αλυσεσι δυσι,
two soldiers, having been bound with chains two,
φυλακες τε προ της θυρας ετηρουν την φυλα-
guards and before the door watching the prison.
κην. 7 Και ιδου, αγγελος κυριου επεστη, και
And lo, a messenger of Lord stood by, and
φως ελαμψεν εν τῳ οικηματι· παταξας δε την
a light shone in the building; having struck and the
πλευραν του Πετρου, ηγειρεν αυτον, λεγων·
side of the Peter, aroused him, saying,
Αναστα εν ταχει. Και εξεπεσον αυτου αἱ αλυ-
Arise in haste. And fell off of him the chains
σεις εκ των χειρων. 8 Ειπε τε ὁ αγγελος προς
from the hands. Said and the messenger to
αυτον· Περιζωσαι, και ὑποδησαι τα σανδαλια
him, Gird thyself, and bind under the sandals
σου. Εποιησε δε οὑτω. Και λεγει αυτῳ·
of thee. He did and so, And he says to him;
Περιβαλου το ἱματιον σου, και ακολουθει μοι.
Throw around the mantle of thee, and follow me.
9 Και εξελθων ηκολουθει *[αυτῳ·] και ουκ ηδει,
And having gone out he followed [him;] and not knew,
ὁτι αληθες εστι το γινομενον δια του αγγελου,
that real it is that being done through the messenger,
εδοκει δε ὁραμα βλεπειν. 10 Διελθοντες δε
thought but a vision to see. Passing through and
πρωτην φυλακην και δευτεραν, ηλθον επι την
first guard and second, they came to the
πυλην την σιδηραν την φερουσαν εις την πολιν,
gate the iron that leading into the city,
ἡτις αυτοματη ηνοιχθη αυτοις· και εξελθοντες
which self-moved opened to them; and having gone out
προηλθον ῥυμην μιαν, και ευθεως απεστη ὁ
went forward street one, and immediately stood the
αγγελος απ᾽ αυτου. 11 Και ὁ Πετρος γενομενος
messenger from him. And the Peter having come
εν ἑαυτῳ, ειπε· Νυν οιδα αληθως, ὁτι εξαπεσ-
in to himself, said; Now I know really, that sent forth
τειλε κυριος τον αγγελον αὑτου, και εξειλατο
Lord the messenger of himself, and delivered
με εκ χειρος Ἡρωδου, και πασης της προσ-
me out of hand of Herod, and all the expec-
δοκιας του λαου των Ιουδαιων. 12 Συνιδων τε
tation of the people of the Jews. Considering and
ηλθεν επι την οικιαν Μαριας της μητρος Ιωαν-
he came to the house of Mary the mother of John,
νου, του επικαλουμενου Μαρκου, οὑ ησαν ἱκα-
that being surnamed Mark, where were many
νοι συνηθροισμενοι και προσευχομενοι. 13 Κρου-
assembled and were praying. Having
σαντος δε αυτου την θυραν του πυλωνος, προσ-
knocked and him the door of the gateway, came

on that NIGHT PETER was sleeping † between Two Soldiers, bound with two Chains; and the Guards before the DOOR were watching the PRISON.

7 And behold, ‡ an Angel of the Lord stood by him, and a Light shone in the Building; and striking PETER on the SIDE, he awoke him, saying, "Arise quickly." And HIS CHAINS fell from his HANDS.

8 And the ANGEL said to him, "Gird thyself, and tie on thy SANDALS." And he did so. And he says to him, "Throw thy MANTLE around thee, and follow me."

9 And going out he followed him; and knew not That WHAT was DONE by the ANGEL was real, but thought ‡ he saw a Vision.

10 And having passed through the First and second Guard, they came to THAT IRON GATE that LEADS into the CITY, ‡ which opened to them of itself; and going out they went forward one Street; and immediately the ANGEL withdrew from him.

11 And PETER becoming self-possessed, said, "Now I know truly, ‡ That the Lord sent his ANGEL and ‡ delivered me from the Hand of Herod, and All the EXPECTATION of the JEWISH PEOPLE."

12 And reflecting, ‡ he came to the HOUSE of Mary, the MOTHER of ‡ THAT John, surnamed MARK; where many were assembled, and were praying.

13 And as he was knocking at the DOOR of the

* VATICAN MANUSCRIPT.—9. him—*omit.*

† 6. Peter was bound to each of the soldiers, so that the least movement on his part to free himself from the chains, would awaken his guard. Two keepers were also stationed at the doors to prevent any ingress of his friends, or any egress on his part.

‡ 7. Acts v. 19. ‡ 9. Acts x. 3, 17; xi. 5. ‡ 10. Acts xvi. 26. ‡ 11. Psa. xxxiv. 7; Dan. iii. 28; vi. 22; Heb. i. 14. ‡ 11. Job v. 19; Psa. xxxiii. 18, 19; xxxiv. 22; xli. 2: xcvii. 10; 2 Cor. i. 10; 2 Pet. ii. 9. ‡ 12. Acts iv. 23. ‡ 12. Acts xv. 37.

ηλθε παιδισκη ὑπακουσαι, ονοματι Ῥοδη· 14 και
a female servant to listen, by name Rhoda; and
επιγνουσα την φωνην του Πετρου, απο της
knowing the voice of the Peter, from the
χαρας ουκ ηνοιξε τον πυλωνα· εισδραμουσα δε
joy not she opened the gate; having run in and
απηγγειλεν, ἑσταναι τον Πετρον προ του πυλω-
told, to have stood the Peter before the gate.
νος. 15 Οἱ δε προς αυτην ειπον· Μαινη. Ἡ δε
The but to her said; Thou art mad She but
διισχυριζετο οὑτως εχειν. 16 Οἱ δε ελεγον· Ὁ
confidently affirmed thus to be. They and said; The
αγγελος αυτου εστιν. Ὁ δε Πετρος επεμενε
messenger of him it is. The but Peter continued
κρουων· ανοιξαντες δε ειδον αυτον, και εξεστη-
knocking; having opened and they saw him, and were amazed.
σαν. 17 Κατασεισας δε αυτοις τῃ χειρι σιγαν,
Having waved but to them the hand to be silent,
διηγησατο αυτοις, πως ὁ κυριος αυτον εξηγαγεν
he related to them, how the Lord him led
εκ της φυλακης. Ειπε δε· Απαγγειλατε Ιακω-
out of the prison. Said and; Report you to James
βῳ και τοις αδελφοις ταυτα. Και εξελθων
and to the brethren these things. And going out
επορευθη εις ἑτερον τοπον.
he went into another place.

18 Γενομενης δε ἡμερας, ην ταραχος ουκ ὀλι-
Having become and day, was a stir not small
γος εν τοις στρατιωταις, τι αρα ὁ Πετρος εγε-
among the soldiers, what then the Peter was
νετο. 19 Ἡρωδης δε επιζητησας αυτον, και μη
become. Herod and having sought him, and not
εὑρων, ανακρινας τους φυλακας, εκελευσεν
having found, having examined the guards, commanded
απαχθηναι· και κατελθων απο της Ιουδαιας εις
to be led off; and going down from the Judea into
την Καισαρειαν διετριβεν. 20 Ην δε θυμομαχων
the Cesarea he remained. He was and being enraged
Τυριοις και Σιδωνιοις· ὁμοθυμαδον δε παρησαν
with Tyrians and Sidonians; with one mind but was present
προς αυτον, και πεισαντες Βλαστον, τον επι
with him, and having persuaded Blastus, that over
του κοιτωνος του βασιλεως, ῃτουντο ειρηνην·
the bed-chamber of the king, desired peace;
δια το τρεφεσθαι αυτων την χωραν απο της
because that to be nourished of them the country from of the
βασιλικης. 21 Τακτῃ δε ἡμερᾳ ὁ Ἡρωδης ενδυ-
king. On a set and day the Herod having
σαμενος εσθητα βασιλικην, και καθισας επι του
put on apparel royal, and having sat down on the
βηματος, εδημηγορει προς αυτους. 22 Ὁ δε
throne, made a speech to them. The but

GATE, a female servant named Rhoda, came to listen.

14 And having recognised PETER'S VOICE, she opened not the GATE from JOY, but running in, told them that Peter was standing at the GATE.

15 And THEY said to her, "Thou art mad." But SHE strongly asserted that it was so. And THEY said, "It is his ANGEL."

16 But PETER continued knocking; and having opened they saw him, and were astonished.

17 ‡ And waving his hand for them to be silent, he related to them how the LORD conducted Him out of the PRISON. And he said, "Tell these things to James and to the BRETHREN." And going out, he went into Another Place.

18 Now when it was Day, there was no small Commotion among the SOLDIERS, as to what had become of PETER.

19 And Herod having sought for him, and not finding him, examined the GUARDS, and commanded them to be led away to execution. And going down from JUDEA to CESAREA, he abode there.

20 And he was highly displeased with the Tyrians and Sidonians; but they came with one accord to him, and having persuaded THAT Blastus who was over the KING'S CHAMBER, they desired Peace; because ‡ their COUNTRY was NOURISHED from that of the KING'S.

21 And on † an appointed Day, * Herod, having put on his regal Robes, and sitting upon the THRONE, made an oration to them.

* VATICAN MANUSCRIPT.—21. Herod.

† 21. This appointed day appears to have been the second day of the Games then celebrating in honor of Cesar. This history is remarkably confirmed by Josephus. See Ant. xix. 7, 2.

‡ 17. Acts xiii 16; xix. 13; xxi 40. ‡ 20. 1 Kings v. 9, 11.

δημος επεφωνει· Θεου φωνη, και ουκ ανθρωπου.
people shouted; Of a god a voice, and not of a man.
23 Παραχρημα δε επαταξεν αυτον αγγελος
Immediately and struck him a messenger
κυριου, ανθ' ὡν ουκ εδωκε δοξαν τῳ θεῳ· και
of Lord, because not he gave glory to the God; and
γενομενος σκωληκοβρωτος, εξεψυξεν. 24 Ὁ δε
being eaten of worms, he breathed out. The and
λογος του θεου ηυξανε και επληθυνετο. 25 Βαρ-
word of the God grew and was multiplied. Bar-
ναβας δε και Σαυλος ὑπεστρεψαν εξ Ἱερουσα-
nabas and and Saul returned from Jerusa-
λημ, πληρωσαντες την διακονιαν, συμπαραλα-
lem, having fulfilled the service, having brought
βοντες και Ιωαννην τον επικληθεντα Μαρκον.
along also John that having been surnamed Mark.

ΚΕΦ. ιγ'. 13.

1 Ησαν δε *[τινες] εν Αντιοχειᾳ κατα την
Were and [some] in Antioch in the
ουσαν εκκλησιαν προφηται και διδασκαλοι, ὁ,
being congregation prophets and teachers, the,
τε Βαρναβας και Συμεων ὁ καλουμενος Νιγερ,
both Barnabas and Simeon that being called Black,
και Λουκιος ὁ Κυρηναιος, Μαναην τε, Ἡρωδου
and Lucius the Cyrenian, Manaen also, of Herod
του τετραρχου συντροφος, και Σαυλος. 2 Λει-
the tetrarch a foster brother, and Saul. Serv-
τουργουντων δε αυτων τῳ κυριῳ και νηστευον-
ing and of them the Lord and fasting,
των, ειπε το πνευμα το ἁγιον· Αφορισατε δη
said the spirit the holy; Separate you indeed
μοι τον Βαρναβαν και *[τον] Σαυλον εις το
for me the Barnabas and [the] Saul for the
εργον, ὁ προσκεκλημαι αυτους. 3 Τοτε νηστευ-
work, which I have called them. Then having
σαντες και προσευξαμενοι, και επιθεντες τας
fasted and having prayed, and having laid the
χειρας αυτοις, απελυσαν. 4 Οὑτοι μεν ουν
hands to them, they sent forth. These indeed then
εκπεμφθεντες ὑπο του πνευματος του ἁγιου,
having been sent forth by the spirit the holy,
κατηλθον εις την Σελευκειαν, εκειθεν τε απε-
went down into the Seleucia, thence and sailed
πλευσαν εις την Κυπρον. 5 Και γενομενοι εν
into the Cyprus. And having arrived in
Σαλαμινι, κατηγγελον τον λογον του θεου εν
Salamis, they announced the word of the God in
ταις συναγωγαις των Ιουδαιων· ειχον δε και
the synagogues of the Jews; they had and also
Ιωαννην ὑπηρετην. 6 Διελθοντες δε ὁλην την
John an attendant. Having gone through and whole the
νησον αχρι Παφου, εὑρον τινα μαγον, ψευδο-
island to Paphos, they found a certain magian, a false
προφητην Ιουδαιον, ᾡ ονομα Βαριησους, 7 ὁς
prophet a Jew, to whom a name Barjesus, who

22 And the PEOPLE shouted, "It is the Voice of a God, and not of a Man."

23 And instantly an Angel of the Lord smote him, because he gave not Glory to GOD; and being eaten with worms, he expired.

24 But the WORD of * God grew and multiplied.

25 And Barnabas and Saul returned from Jerusalem, having fulfilled the SERVICE, ‡ taking with them also THAT John who was SURNAMED MARK.

CHAPTER XIII.

1 And there were Prophets and Teachers in the CONGREGATION at Antioch;—BARNABAS, and THAT Simeon CALLED Niger, and Lucius, the CYRENIAN, and Manaen, a foster-brother of Herod the TETRARCH, and Saul.

2 And while they were serving the LORD and fasting, the HOLY SPIRIT said, "Separate to me BARNABAS and SAUL for the WORK to which I called them."

3 Then ‡ having fasted and prayed, and laid their HANDS on them, they sent them forth.

4 They, therefore, having been sent out by the * HOLY SPIRIT, went down to * Seleucia; and from thence they sailed to * Cyprus.

5 And having arrived at Salamis, they announced the WORD of GOD in the SYNAGOGUES of the JEWS; and they also had John for an Attendant.

6 And having gone through the Whole ISLAND to Paphos, they found ‡ * a Certain Magian, a False-prophet, a Jew, whose Name was Bar-Jesus,

* VATICAN MANUSCRIPT.—24. the LORD grew. 1. some—*omit.* 2. the—*omit.* 4. HOLY Spirit. 4. Seleucia. 4. Cyprus. 6. a Certain Man, a Magian, a False-Prophet.

‡ 25. Acts xiii. 5, 13; xv. 37. ‡ 3. Acts vi. 6. ‡ 6. Acts viii. 9.

ην συν τῳ ανθυπατῳ Σεργιῳ Παυλῳ, ανδρι
was with the proconsul Sergius Paulus, a man

συνετῳ. Οὗτος προσκαλεσαμενος Βαρναβαν και
intelligent. This having summoned Barnabas and

Σαυλον, επεζητησεν ακουσαι τον λογον του
Saul, desired to hear the word of the

θεου. 8 Ανθιστατο δε αυτοις Ελυμας ὁ μαγος,
God. Stood against but them Elymas the magian,

(οὕτω γαρ μεθερμηνευεται το ονομα αυτου,)
(thus for is translated the name of him,)

ζητων διαστρεψαι τον ανθυπατον απο της πισ-
seeking to turn away the proconsul from the faith.

τεως. 9 Σαυλος δε (ὁ και Παυλος) πλησθεις
Saul but (he also Paul) being filled

πνευματος ἁγιου, *[και] ατενισας εις αυτον,
of spirit holy, [and] having looked earnestly on him,

10 ειπεν· Ω πληρης παντος δολου και πασης
said; O full of all deceit and of all

ῥᾳδιουργιας, υιε διαβολου, εχθρε πασης δικαιοσυ-
ready working, O son of an accuser, enemy of all righteous-

νης, ου παυσῃ διαστρεφων τας οδους κυριου τας
ness, not wilt thou cease perverting the ways of Lord the

ευθειας; 11 Και νυν ιδου, χειρ κυριου επι σε,
straight? And now lo, a hand of Lord on thee,

και εσῃ τυφλος, μη βλεπων τον ἡλιον αχρι
and thou shalt be blind, not seeing the sun till

καιρου. Παραχρημα δε επεπεσεν επ' αυτον
a season. Immediately and fell on him

αχλυς και σκοτος· και περιαγων εζητει χειρα-
a mist and darkness; and going about he sought guides.

γωγους. 12 Τοτε ιδων ὁ ανθυπατος το γεγονος,
Then seeing the proconsul that having been done,

επιστευσεν, εκπλησσομενος επι τῃ διδαχῃ του
believed, being astonished at the teaching of the

κυριου.
Lord.

13 Αναχθεντες δε απο της Παφου οἱ περι τον
Having set sail and from the Paphos those about the

Παυλον, ηλθον εις Περγην της Παμφυλιας.
Paul, came into Perga of the Pamphylia.

Ιωαννης δε, αποχωρησας απ' αυτων, ὑπεστρε-
John but, having gone away from them, returned

ψεν εις Ἱεροσολυμα. 14 Αυτοι δε διελθοντες
into Jerusalem. They and having passed through

απο της Περγης παρεγενοντο εις Αντιοχειαν
from the Perga went to Antioch

της Πισιδιας, και εισελθοντες εις την συναγω-
of the Pisidia, and having entered into the synagogue

γην τῃ ἡμερᾳ των σαββατων, εκαθισαν. 15 Μετα
in the day of the sabbaths, they sat down. After

δε την αναγνωσιν του νομου και των προφητων,
and the reading of the law and the prophets,

απεστειλαν οἱ αρχισυναγωγοι προς αυτους,
sent the synagogue-rulers to them,

λεγοντες· Ανδρες αδελφοι, ει εστι λογος εν
saying; Men brethren, if is a word in

ὑμιν παρακλησεως προς τον λαον, λεγετε.
you of consolation to the people, say you.

7 who was with the PROCONSUL, Sergius Paulus, an intelligent Man. This man having called for Barnabas and Saul desired to hear the WORD of GOD.

8 But Elymas, the MAGIAN, (for so his NAME is translated,) opposed them, seeking to turn away the PROCONSUL from the FAITH.

9 Then THAT Saul, also called Paul, being filled with holy Spirit, looking intently on him, said,

10 "O full of All Deceit, and of All Imposture! Son of an Accuser! Enemy of all Righteousness! wilt thou not cease to pervert the STRAIGHT WAYS of the Lord?

11 And now, behold, the Hand of the Lord is upon thee; and thou shalt be blind, not seeing the SUN for a Season." And immediately a Mist and darkness fell *on him, and going about he sought Guides.

12 Then the PROCONSUL seeing THAT HAVING BEEN DONE, believed, being astonished at the TEACHING of the LORD.

13 And sailing from PAPHOS, THOSE with * Paul came to Perga in Pamphylia; ‡ but John having withdrawn from them, returned to Jerusalem.

14 And these, having passed through from PERGA, came to Antioch in PISIDIA, and ‡ went into the SYNAGOGUE on the DAY of the SABBATHS, and sat down.

15 And ‡ after the READING of the LAW and the PROPHETS, the SYNAGOGUE-RULERS sent to them, saying, "Brethren, if * any one among you have a Word of Exhortation for the PEOPLE, speak."

* VATICAN MANUSCRIPT.—9. and—*omit.* 11. on him—*omit.* 13. Paul. 15. any one among you have a Word of.

‡ 13. Acts xv. 38. ‡ 14. Acts xvi. 13; xvii. 2; xviii. 4. ‡ 15. Luke iv. 16; ver. 27.

16 Αναστας δε Παυλος, και κατασεισας τη χειρι,
Having stood up and Paul, and having waved the hand,
ειπεν· Ανδρες Ισραηλιται, και οἱ φοβουμενοι
said; Men Israelites, and those fearing
τον θεον, ακουσατε. 17 Ὁ θεος του λαου του-
the God, hear you. The God of the people this
του εξελεξατο τους πατερας ἡμων· και τον
chose the fathers of you; and the
λαον ὑψωσεν εν τῃ παροικιᾳ εν γῃ Αιγυπτῳ,
people exalted in the sojourning in land of Egypt,
και μετα βραχιονος ὑψηλου εξηγαγεν αυτους εξ
and with an arm lifted up he brought them out of
αυτης· 18 και ὡς τεσσαρακονταετη χρονον ετρο-
her; and about forty years time he
φοφορησεν αυτους εν τῃ ερημῳ· 19 *[και] καθε-
nourished them in the desert; [and] having
λων εθνη ἑπτα εν γῃ Χανααν, κατεκληρονο-
cast out nations seven in land of Canaan, he distributed
μησεν αυτοις την γην αυτων. 20 Και μετα
by lot to them the land of them. And after
ταυτα ὡς ετεσι τετρακοσιοις και πεντηκοντα
these things about years four hundred and fifty
εδωκε κριτας, ἑως Σαμουηλ του προφητου.
he gave judges, till Samuel the prophet.
21 Κακειθεν ᾐτησαντο βασιλεα, και εδωκεν
And then they asked for a king, and gave
αυτοις ὁ θεος τον Σαουλ υἱον Κις, ανδρα εκ
to them the God the Saul son of Kis, a man of
φυλης Βενιαμιν, ετη τεσσαρακοντα. 22 Και
tribe of Benjamin, years forty. And
μεταστησας αυτον, ηγειρεν αυτοις τον Δαυιδ
having removed him, he raised up to them the David
εις βασιλεα, ᾡ και ειπε μαρτυρησας· Εὑρον
for a king, to whom also he said having testified; I found
Δαυιδ, τον του Ιεσσαι, *[ανδρα] κατα την
David, that of the Jesse, [a man] according to the
καρδιαν μου, ὁς ποιησει παντα τα θεληματα
heart of me, who will do all the will
μου. 23 Τουτου ὁ θεος απο του σπερματος κατ'
of me. This the God from the seed according to
επαγγελιαν ηγαγε τῳ Ισραηλ σωτηρα Ιησουν,
promise brought forth to the Israel a Savior Jesus,
24 προκηρυξαντος Ιωαννου προ προσωπου της
having announced before of John before face of the

16 Then Paul standing up, and waving his HAND, said, "Israelites! and YOU who fear GOD, listen!
17 The GOD of * the PEOPLE of ISRAEL ‡ chose our FATHERS, and elevated the PEOPLE ‡ during their EXILE in the Land of Egypt, ‡ and brought them out of it with an uplifted Arm.
18 And ‡ for a period of Forty Years he nourished them in the DESERT;
19 and ‡ having cast out seven Nations in the Land of Canaan, ‡ he * distributed their LAND to them by Lot.
20 And after these things, ‡ he gave Judges about † four hundred and fifty Years, ‡ till Samuel the PROPHET.
21 ‡ And then they asked for a King; and GOD gave them SAUL, the Son of Kish, a Man of the Tribe of Benjamin, for forty Years.
22 And ‡ having removed him, ‡ he raised up to them DAVID for a King; to whom also giving testimony, he said, ‡ 'I have 'found David, the son of 'JESSE, ‡ a Man according 'to my HEART, who will 'perform All my WILL.'
23 ‡ From This man's POSTERITY, ‡ according to Promise, God brought forth to ISRAEL ‡ a Savior, Jesus;
24 ‡ John having previously proclaimed, before his APPEARANCE, an Im-

* VATICAN MANUSCRIPT.—17. the PEOPLE of ISRAEL. 19. And—*omit*. 19. gave their LAND for an inheritance, about four hundred and fifty Years. And after that he gave them Judges till Samuel the Prophet. 22. a man—*omit*.

† 20. A difficulty occurs here which has very much puzzled Biblical chronologists. The date given here is at variance with the statement found in 1 Kings vi. 1. There have been many solutions offered, but only one which seems entirely satisfactory, i. e., that the text in 1 Kings vi. 1, has been corrupted, by substituting the Hebrew character *daleth* (4) for *hay* (5,) which is very similar in form. This would make 580 years (instead of 480) from the exode to the building of the temple, and exactly agree with Paul's chronology.

‡ 17. Deut. vii. 6, 7. ‡ 17. Psa. cv. 23, 24; Acts vii. 17. ‡ 17. Exod. xiii. 14, 16. ‡ 18. Num. xiv. 33, 34; Psa. xcv. 9, 10; Acts vii. 36. ‡ 19. Deut. vii. 1. ‡ 19. Josh. xiv. 1, 2; Psa. lxxviii. 55. ‡ 20. Judges ii. 16. ‡ 20. 1 Sam. iii. 20. ‡ 21. 1 Sam. viii. 5; x. 1. ‡ 22. 1 Sam. xv. 23, 26, 28; xvi. 1; Hosea xiii. 11. ‡ 22. 1 Sam. xvi. 13; 2 Sam. ii. 4; v. 3. ‡ 22. Psa. lxxxix. 20. ‡ 22. 1 Sam. xiii. 14; Acts vii. 46. ‡ 23. Isa. xi. 1; Luke i. 32, 69; Acts ii. 30; Rom. i. 3. ‡ 23. 2 Sam. vii. 12; Psa. cxxxii. 11. ‡ 23. Matt. i. 21. ‡ 24. Matt. iii. 1; Luke iii. 3.

εισοδου αυτου βαπτισμα μετανοιας παντι τῳ
entrance of him a dipping of reformation to all the
λαῳ Ισραηλ. 25 Ὡς δε επληρου ὁ Ιωαννης τον
people Israel. As and was fulfilling the John the
δρομον, ελεγε· Τινα με ὑπονοειτε ειναι; ουκ
race, he said; Who me do you suppose to be? not
ειμι εγω, αλλ' ιδου, ερχεται μετ' εμε, οὑ ουκ
am I, but lo, comes after me, of whom not
ειμι αξιος το ὑποδημα των ποδων λυσαι.
I am worthy the sandal of the feet to loose.
26 Ανδρες αδελφοι, υἱοι γενους Αβρααμ, και
Men brethren, sons race of Abraham, and
οἱ εν ὑμιν φοβουμενοι τον θεον, ὑμιν ὁ λογος
those among you fearing the God, to you the word
της σωτηριας ταυτης απεσταλη. 27 Οἱ γαρ
of the salvation this is sent. Those for
κατοικουντες εν Ἱερουσαλημ, και οἱ αρχοντες
dwelling in Jerusalem, and the rulers
αυτων, τουτον αγνοησαντες, και τας φωνας
of them, him not knowing, and the voices
των προφητων τας κατα παν σαββατον αναγι-
of the prophets those in every sabbath being
νωσκομενας, κριναντες επληρωσαν. 28 Και μη-
read, judging fulfilled. And no
δεμιαν αιτιαν θανατου εὑροντες, ητησαντο
one cause of death having found, they asked
Πιλατον αναιρεθηναι αυτον. 29 Ὡς δε ετελεσαν
Pilate to kill him. When and they finished
παντα τα περι αυτου γεγραμμενα, καθελον-
all the things concerning him having been written, having taken
τες απο του ξυλου, εθηκαν εις μνημειον. 30 Ὁ
down from the cross, they placed in a tomb. The
δε θεος ηγειρεν αυτον εκ νεκρων, 31 ὁς ωφθη
but God raised him out of dead ones, who appeared
επι ἡμερας πλειους τοις συναναβασιν αυτῳ απο
on days many to those having gone up with him from
της Γαλιλαιας εις Ἱερουσαλημ, οἱτινες εισι
of the Galilee into Jerusalem, who are
μαρτυρες αυτου προς τον λαον. 32 Και ἡμεις
witnesses of him to the people. And we
ὑμας ευαγγελιζομεθα την προς τους πατερας
you address with glad tidings that to the fathers
επαγγελιαν γενομενην, ὁτι ταυτην ὁ θεος εκ-
promise having been made, that this the God has
πεπληρωκε τοις τεκνοις αυτων ἡμιν, αναστησας
fulfilled to the children of them to us, having raised up
Ιησουν· 33 ὡς και εν τῳ πρωτῳ ψαλμῳ γεγραπ-
Jesus; as also in the first psalm it is written,
ται· Υἱος μου ει συ, εγω σημερον γεγεννηκα
A son of me art thou, I to-day have begotten

mersion of Reformation to All the PEOPLE of ISRAEL.
25 And as John was fulfilling his RACE, he said,
‡ * 'Whom do you suppose me to be? I am not he; but behold, one comes after me, the SANDALS of Whose FEET I am not worthy to untie.'
26 Brethren, sons of the Family of Abraham, and THOSE among you who FEAR GOD, ‡ to you is the WORD of this SALVATION * sent.
27 For THOSE DWELLING in Jerusalem, and their RULERS, ‡ not knowing him, nor the DECLARATIONS of the PROPHETS ‡ which are READ Every Sabbath, ‡ have fulfilled them in judging him.
28 ‡ And without having found any Cause of Death they desired Pilate to kill him.
29 And when they had finished ALL things WRITTEN concerning him, ‡ having taken him down from the CROSS, they laid him in a Tomb.
30 ‡ But GOD raised him from the Dead;
31 ‡ and he appeared for several Days to THOSE who went up with him from GALILEE to Jerusalem, who are his Witnesses to the PEOPLE.
32 And we announce glad tidings to you, ‡ the PROMISE which was made to the FATHERS; because GOD has fulfilled this to * us their CHILDREN, having raised up Jesus;
33 as it is written also in the † * SECOND Psalm, ‡ 'Thou art my Son; this 'day I have begotten thee.'

* VATICAN MANUSCRIPT.—25. What think you that. 26. sent forth. For. 32. our CHILDREN, having. 33. SECOND Psalm.

† 33. The two first Psalms as they stand in our editions, were anciently joined together. See *Wetstein*. *Griesbach* has followed some MSS which have *first* instead of *second*. So also Tischendorf. The common reading, however, has been adopted, which agrees with the Vat. MS.

‡ 25. Matt. iii. 11; Mark i. 7; Luke iii. 16; John i. 20, 27. ‡ 26. Matt. x. 6; Luke xxiv. 47; Acts iii. 26; ver. 46. ‡ 27. Luke xxiii. 34; Acts iii. 17; 1 Cor. ii. 8. ‡ 27. Acts xv. 21. ‡ 27. Luke xxiv. 20, 44; Acts xxviii. 23. ‡ 28. Matt. xxvii. 22, &c.; Acts iii. 13, 14. ‡ 29. Matt. xxvii. 59, &c. ‡ 30. Matt. xxviii. 6; Acts ii. 24; iii. 13. 15. 26; v. 30. ‡ 31. Acts i. 3; 1 Cor. xv. 5—7. ‡ 32. Gen. xii. 3; xxii. 18; Acts xxvi. 6; Gal. iii. 16. ‡ 33. Psa. ii. 7; Heb. i. 5; v. 5.

σε. 34 Ὁτι δε ανεστησεν αυτον εκ νεκρων,
thee. Because and he raised him out of dead ones,
μηκετι μελλοντα ὑποστρεφειν εις διαφθοραν,
no more being about to return to corruption,
οὑτως ειρηκεν· Ὁτι δωσω ὑμιν τα ὁσια Δαυιδ
thus he said; That I will give to you the holy things of David
τα πιστα. 35 Διο και εν ἑτερῳ λεγει· Ου
the faithful. Therefore also in another he says; Not
δωσεις τον ὁσιον σου ιδειν διαφθοραν.
thou wilt permit the holy one of thee to see corruption.
36 Δαυιδ μεν γαρ ιδιᾳ γενεᾳ ὑπηρετησας τῃ
David indeed for own generation having served by the
του θεου βουλῃ εκοιμηθη, και προσετεθη προς
of the God will fell asleep, and was laid with
τους πατερας αὑτου και ειδε διαφθοραν· 37 ὁν δε
the fathers of himself and saw corruption; whom but
ὁ θεος ηγειρεν, ουκ ειδε διαφθοραν. 38 Γνωσ-
the God raised up, not saw corruption. Known
τον ουν εστω ὑμιν, ανδρες αδελφοι, ὁτι δια
therefore let it be to you, men brethren, that through
τουτου ὑμιν αφεσις ἁμαρτιων καταγγελλεται·
this to you forgiveness of sins is announced;
39 και απο παντων, ὡν ουκ ηδυνηθητε εν τῳ
and from all things, which not you are able by the
νομῳ Μωσεως δικαιωθηναι, εν τουτῳ πας ὁ
law of Moses to be justified, in him every one the
πιστευων δικαιουται. 40 Βλεπετε ουν, μη
believing is justified. See then, not
επελθῃ εφ' ὑμας το ειρημενον εν τοις προφη-
may come upon you that having been spoken by the prophets;
ταις· 41 ιδετε οἱ καταφρονηται, και θαυμασατε,
behold you the despisers, and wonder you,
και αφανισθητε· ὁτι εργον εγω εργαζομαι εν
and disappear you, because a work I work in
ταις ἡμεραις ὑμων, εργον, ᾡ ου μη πιστευ-
the days of you, a work, which not not you would
σητε, εαν τις εκδιηγηται ὑμιν. 42 Εξιοντων δε
believe, if one should narrate to you. Having gone out and
αυτων, παρεκαλουν εις το μεταξυ σαββατων
of them, they desired on the next sabbath
λαληθηναι αυτοις τα ῥηματα ταυτα. 43 Λυθει-
to be spoken to them the words these. Being broken
σης δε της συναγωγης, ηκολουθησαν πολλοι
up and the synagogue, followed many
των Ιουδαιων και των σεβομενων προσηλυτων
of the Jews and of the worshipping proselytes
τῳ Παυλῳ και τῳ Βαρναβᾳ· οἱτινες προσλα-
the Paul and the Barnabas; who speaking
λουντες αυτοις, επειθον αυτους προσμενειν τῃ
to them, persuaded them to continue in the

34 And because he raised him from the Dead, no more to return to Corruption, he has spoken thus, ‡ 'I will give you 'the SURE MERCIES of Da- 'vid.'

35 Therefore also in another place he says, ‡ 'Thou wilt not permit 'thy HOLY ONE to see Cor- 'ruption.'

36 For David, indeed, having in his Own Generation served the WILL of GOD, ‡ fell asleep, and was laid with his FATHERS, and saw Corruption;

37 but he whom GOD raised up saw not Corruption.

38 Be it therefore known to you, Brethren, ‡ That through him Forgiveness of Sins is proclaimed to you;

39 ‡ and by him EVERY ONE who BELIEVES is justified from all things, from which you could not be justified by the LAW of Moses.

40 See then that WHAT is SPOKEN in ‡ the PROPHETS may not come upon you;

41 'Behold, DESPISERS, 'and wonder, and 'dis- 'appear; For I perform a 'Work in your DAYS, a 'Work which you will by 'no means believe, though 'one should declare it to 'you.'"

42 And they having gone out, * it was thought proper that these WORDS should be spoken to them on the NEXT Sabbath.

43 And when the SYNAGOGUE was broken up, many of the JEWS and RELIGIOUS Proselytes followed PAUL and BARNABAS, who, speaking to them, persuaded them to

---

* VATICAN MANUSCRIPT.—42. it was thought proper that these WORDS should be spoken.

‡ 34. Isa. lv. 3. ‡ 35. Psa. xvi. 10; Acts ii. 31. ‡ 36. 1 Kings ii. 10; Acts ii. 29. ‡ 38. Luke xxiv. 47. ‡ 39. Rom. iii. 28; viii. 3; 1 John ii. 12. ‡ 40. Isa. xxix. 14; Hab. i. 5.

χαριτι του θεου. 44 Τῳ τε ἐχομενῳ σαββατῳ
favor of the God. On the and coming sabbath,
σχεδον πασα ἡ πολις συνηχθη ακουσαι τον
almost all the city came together to hear the
λογον του θεου. 45 Ιδοντες δε οἱ Ιουδαιοι τους
word of the God. Seeing and the Jews the
οχλους, επλησθησαν ζηλου, και αντελεγόν
crowds, they were filled of zeal, and spoke against
τοις ὑπο του Παυλου λεγομενοις, *[αντιλε-
the things by the Paul being spoken, [contra-
γοντες και] βλασφημουντες. 46 Παρρησιασα-
dicting and] blaspheming. Speaking
μενοι δε ὁ Παυλος και ὁ Βαρναβας ειπον·
freely and the Paul and the Barnabas said;
Ὑμιν ην αναγκαιον πρωτον λαληθηναι τον
To you it was necessary first to be spoken the
λογον του θεου· επειδη *[δε] απωθεισθε αυτον,
word of the God: since [but] you thrust away him,
και ουκ αξιους κρινετε ἑαυτους της αιωνιου
and not worthy judge yourselves of the age-lasting
ζωης, ιδου, στρεφομεθα εις τα εθνη. 47 Οὑτω
life, lo, we turn to the gentiles. Thus
γαρ εντεταλται ἡμιν ὁ κυριος· Τεθεικα σε εις
for has commanded us the Lord. I have set thee for
φως εθνων, του ειναι σε εις σωτηριαν ἑως εσχα-
a light of nations, the to be thee for salvation to end
του της γης. 48 Ακουοντα δε τα εθνη εχαιρον,
of the earth. Having heard and the Gentiles rejoiced,
και εδοξαζον τον λογον του κυριου· και επισ-
and glorified the word of the Lord; and be-
τευσαν ὁσοι ησαν τεταγμενοι εις ζωην αιωνιον.
lieved as many as were having been disposed for life age-lasting.
49 Διεφερετο δε ὁ λογος του κυριου δι' ὁλης
Was published and the word of the Lord through whole
της χωρας. 50 Οἱ δε Ιουδαιοι παρωτρυναν τας
of the country. The but Jews stirred up the
σεβομενας γυναικας τας ευσχημονας, και τους
religious women the honorable, and the
πρωτους της πολεως, και επηγειραν διωγμον
chiefs of the city, and raised a persecution
επι τον Παυλον και τον Βαρναβαν, και εξεβαλον
against the Paul and the Barnabas, and cast out
αυτους απο των ὁριων αυτων. 51 Οἱ δε εκτινα-
them from the borders of them. They but having
ξαμενοι τον κονιορτον των ποδων αὑτων επ'
shaken off the dust of the feet of them against
αυτους, ηλθον εις Ικονιον.
them, came into Iconium.

52 Οἱ δε μαθηται επληρουντο χαρας και πνευ-
The and disciples were filled joy and spirit
ματος ἁγιου. ΚΕΦ. ιδ'. 14. 1 Εγενετο δε εν
holy. It happened and in
Ικονιῳ, κατα το αυτο εισελθειν αυτοις εις την
Iconium, at the same to enter them into the

continue in the FAVOR of GOD.

44 And on the FOLLOWING Sabbath, almost the Whole CITY assembled to hear the WORD of GOD.

45 And the JEWS seeing the CROWDS, were filled with Envy, and opposed the things spoken by *Paul, blaspheming.

46 And both PAUL and BARNABAS speaking freely, said, ‡"It was necessary for the WORD of GOD first to be spoken to you; ‡ but since you thrust it away from you, and judge yourselves unworthy of AIONIAN Life, behold, ‡ we turn to the GENTILES.

47 For thus the LORD has commanded us; ‡'I 'have set thee for a Light 'of Nations, that thou 'shouldst BE for Salva'tion to the Extremity of 'the EARTH.'"

48 And the GENTILES having heard this, rejoiced, and glorified the WORD of * the LORD; and as many as were disposed for aionian Life, believed.

49 And the WORD of the LORD was published through the Whole of the COUNTRY.

50 But the JEWS excited the RELIGIOUS and HONORABLE Women, and the FIRST MEN of the CITY, and raised a Persecution against PAUL and * Barnabas, and expelled them from * their BORDERS.

51 ‡ And THEY, shaking off the DUST of * their feet against them, went to Iconium.

52 And the DISCIPLES ‡ were filled with Joy and holy Spirit.

CHAPTER XIV.

1 And it occurred at Iconium, that they went TOGETHER into the SYNA-

* VATICAN MANUSCRIPT.—45. Paul, blaspheming. And Paul and. 45. contradicting and—omit. 46. but—omit. 48. GOD; and as many. 50. Barnabas. 50. the BORDERS. 51. the FEET.

‡ 46. Matt. x. 6; Acts iii. 26; v. 26; Rom. i. 16. ‡ 46. Matt. xxi. 43; Rom. x. 19. ‡ 46. Acts xviii. 6; xxviii. 28. ‡ 47. Isa. xlii. 6; xlix. 6; Luke ii. 32. ‡ 51. Matt. x. 14; Mark vi. 11; Luke ix. 5; Acts xviii. 6. ‡ 52. Matt. v. 12; John xvi. 22; Acts ii. 46.

σuναγωγην των Ιουδαιων, και λαλησαι οὑτως,
synagogue of the Jews, and to speak so,
ὡστε πιστευσαι Ιουδαιων τε και Ἑλληνων πολυ
that to believe of Jews and also Greeks a great
πληθος. 2 Οἱ δε απειθουντες Ιουδαιοι επηγει-
multitude. The but unbelieving Jews stirred up
ραν και εκακωσαν τας ψυχας των εθνων κατα
and imbittered the souls of the Gentiles against
των αδελφων. 3 Ἱκανον μεν ουν χρονον διετρι-
the brethren. Considerable indeed then time they re-
ψαν παῤῥησιαζομενοι επι τῳ κυριῳ, τῳ μαρτυ-
mained speaking freely about the Lord, that testifying
ρουντι τῳ λογῳ της χαριτος αὑτου, διδοντι
to the word of the favor of himself, granting
σημεια και τερατα γινεσθαι δια των χειρων
signs and prodigies to be done through the hands
αυτων. 4 Εσχισθη δε το πληθος της πολεως
of them. Was divided and the multitude of the city
και οἱ μεν ησαν συν τοις Ιουδαιοις, οἱ δε
and these indeed were with the Jews, those and
συν τοις αποστολοις. 5 Ὡς δε εγενετο ὁρμη
with the apostles. As and was a rush
των εθνων τε και Ιουδαιων συν τοις αρχουσιν
of the gentiles and also of Jews with the rulers
αυτων, ὑβρισαι και λιθοβολησαι αυτους,
of them, to insult and to stone them,
6 συνιδοντες κατεφυγον εις τας πολεις της
seeing they fled into the city of the
Λυκαονιας, Λυστραν και Δερβην, και την
Lyconium, Lystra and Derbe, and the
περιχωρον· 7 κακει ησαν ευαγγελιζομενοι.
surrounding country; and there they were preaching glad tidings.

8 Και τις ανηρ εν Λυστροις αδυνατος τοις
And a certain man in Lystra unable in the
ποσιν εκαθητο, χωλος εκ κοιλιας μητρος αὑτου,
feet was sitting, lame from womb of mother of himself,
ὁς ουδεποτε περιεπεπατηκει. 9 Οὑτος ηκουε
who never had walked about. This heard
του Παυλου λαλουντος· ὁς ατενισας αυτῳ,
the Paul speaking; who having looked intently to him,
και ιδων ὁτι πιστιν εχει του σωθηναι, 10 ειπε
and seeing that faith he has of the to be saved. said
μεγαλῃ τῃ φωνῃ· Αναστηθι επι τους ποδας σου
loud with the voice; Do thou stand upon the feet of thee
ορθος. Και ἡλατο, και περιεπατει. 11 Οἱ δε
erect. And he leaped up, and walked about. The and
οχλοι, ιδοντες ὁ εποιησεν ὁ Παυλος, επηραν
crowds, seeing what did the Paul, lifted up
την φωνην αὑτων, Λυκαονιστι λεγοντες· Οἱ
the voice of them, in Lycaonian language saying; The
θεοι ὁμοιωθεντες ανθρωποις κατεβησαν προς
gods being like men came down to
ἡμας. 12 Εκαλουν τε τον μεν Βαρναβαν, Δια·
us. They called and the indeed Barnabas, Jupiter;

GOGUE of the JEWS, and spoke in such a manner, that a Great Multitude both of the Jews and Greeks believed.

2 But the UNBELIEVING Jews excited and embittered the MINDS of the GENTILES against the BRETHREN.

3 For a considerable Time however, they continued there, speaking boldly in the LORD, ‡ who TESTIFIED to the WORD of his FAVOR, by granting Signs and Prodigies to be performed by their HANDS.

4 But the MULTITUDE of the CITY was divided; and SOME were with the JEWS, and SOME with the APOSTLES.

5 And as a violent attempt was made, both by the GENTILES and Jews, with their RULERS, ‡ to wantonly disgrace and stone them,

6 knowing it, ‡ they fled to the CITIES of LYCAONIA, Lystra and Derbe, and the SURROUNDING COUNTRY;

7 and there they proclaimed glad tidings.

8 ‡ And there was sitting a certain Man at Lystra, disabled in his FEET, lame from his Birth, who had never walked.

9 This man heard PAUL speaking; who, looking intently on him, and ‡ seeing That he had Faith to be RESTORED,

10 said with a * Loud Voice, "Stand erect on thy FEET." And he leaped up, and walked about.

11 And the CROWDS seeing what PAUL did, they lifted up their VOICE in the Lycaonian language, saying, ‡ "The GODS, resembling men, have come down to us."

12 And they, indeed, called BARNABAS, Jupiter;

* VATICAN MANUSCRIPT.—10. Loud Voice.

‡ 3. Mark xvi. 20: Heb. ii. 4. ‡ 5. 2 Tim. iii. 11. ‡ 6. Matt. x. 23. ‡ 8. Acts iii. 2. ‡ 9. Matt. viii. 10; x. 28, 29. ‡ 11. Acts viii. 10; xxviii. 6.

τον δε Παυλον, Ἑρμην· επειδη αυτος ην ὁ
the and Paul, Mercury; because he was the
ἡγουμενος του λογου. [13] Ὁ δε ἱερευς του Διος
leader of the word. The and priest of the Jupiter
του οντος προ της πολεως, ταυρους και στεμ-
of that being before the city, bulls and gar-
ματα επι τους πυλωνας ενεγκας, συν τοις
lands to the gates having brought, with the
οχλοις ηθελε θυειν. [14] Ακουσαντες δε οἱ αποσ-
crowds wished to sacrifice. Having heard and the apostles
τολοι Βαρναβας και Παυλος, διαρρηξαντες τα
Barnabas and Paul, having rent the
ἱματια αὑτων, εξεπηδησαν εις τον οχλον, κρα-
mantles of them, rushed out into the crowd, crying
ζοντες [15] και λεγοντες· Ανδρες, τι ταυτα ποι-
out and saying; Men, why these things do
ειτε; και ἡμεις ὁμοιοπαθεις εσμεν ὑμιν ανθρω-
you? also we being like are to you men,
ποι, ευαγγελιζομενοι ὑμας απο τουτων των
announcing glad tidings you from these the
ματαιων επιστρεφειν επι τον θεον τον ζωντα,
superstitions to turn to the God the living,
ὁς εποιησε τον ουρανον και την γην και την
who made the heaven and the earth and the
θαλασσαν, και παντα τα εν αυτοις· [16] ὁς εν
sea, and all the things in them; who in
ταις παρῳχημεναις γενεαις ειασε παντα τα
the having gone by generations permitted all the
εθνη πορευεσθαι ταις ὁδοις αὑτων. [17] Καιτοιγε
nations to go in the ways of themselves. Although indeed
ουκ αμαρτυρον ἑαυτον αφηκεν, αγαθοποιων,
not without witness himself left, doing good,
ουρανοθεν ὑμιν ὑετους διδους και καιρους καρ-
from heaven to you rains giving and seasons fruit-
ποφορους, εμπιπλων τροφης και ευφροσυνης
ful, being full of food and of joy
τας καρδιας ὑμων. [18] Και ταυτα λεγοντες,
the hearts of you. And these things saying,
μολις κατεπαυσαν τους οχλους του μη θυειν
hardly they restrained the crowds the not to sacrifice
αυτοις. [19] Επηλθον δε απο Αντιοχειας και Ικο-
to them. Came and from Antioch and Ico-
νιου Ιουδαιοι· και πεισαντες τους οχλους, και
nium Jews; and having persuaded the crowds, and
λιθασαντες τον Παυλον, εσυρον εξω της
having stoned the Paul, they dragged outside of the
πολεως, νομισαντες αυτον τεθναναι. [20] Κυκ-
city, supposing him to be dead. Sur-
λωσαντων δε αυτον των μαθητων, αναστας
rounding and him the disciples, having arisen
εισηλθεν εις την πολιν. Και τῃ επαυριον
he entered into the city. And on the morrow
εξηλθε συν τῳ Βαρναβᾳ εις Δερβην. [21] Ευαγ-
he went with the Barnabas into Derbe. Having

and PAUL, Mercury, because he was the CHIEF SPEAKER.

13 And the PRIEST of THAT [image of] JUPITER which WAS † before the CITY, brought Bulls and Garlands to the GATES, and wished to sacrifice with the CROWDS.

14 But the APOSTLES, Barnabas and Paul, having heard of it, rent their MANTLES, and rushing out among the CROWD, exclaiming

15 and saying, "Men, why do you These things? ‡ We are also Men, subject to frailty with you, proclaiming glad tidings to turn you from These VANITIES to the LIVING GOD, ‡ who made the HEAVEN, and the EARTH, and the SEA, and all THINGS in them;

16 ‡ who, in PRECEDING Generations permitted All the GENTILES to walk in their own WAYS;

17 ‡ though indeed he left not Himself without testimony, doing good, ‡ giving you Rains from heaven, and fruitful Seasons, and filling your HEARTS with Food and Gladness."

18 And saying These things, they with difficulty restrained the CROWDS from SACRIFICING to them.

19 But ‡ Jews came from Antioch and Iconium, and having persuaded the CROWDS, and ‡ having stoned PAUL, they dragged him out of the CITY, supposing him to be dead.

20 But the DISCIPLES having surrounded him, he rose up and entered the CITY. And on the NEXT DAY he departed with BARNABAS to Derbe.

† 13. As was common in that day, cities were placed under the protection of heathen deities. The city of Lystra had the image of *Jupiter*, before its gates.

‡ 15. James v. 17; Rev. xix. 10. ‡ 15. 1 Thess. 1. 9. ‡ 16. Psa. lxxxi. 12; Acts xvii. 30; 1 Pet. iv. 3. ‡ 17. Acts xvii. 27; Rom. x. 20. ‡ 17. Lev. xxvi. 4; Deut. xi. 14; xxviii. 12; Job v. 10; Psa. lxv. 10; lxviii. 9; cxlvii. 8; Jer. xiv. 22; Matt. v 45. ‡ 19. Acts xiii. 45 ‡ 19. 2 Cor xi. 25; 2 Tim. iii. 11.

γελισαμενοι τε την πολιν εκεινην, και μαθη-
preached glad tidings and the city that, and having
τευσαντες ἱκανους, ὑπεστρεψαν εις την Λυστραν
made disciples many, they returned to the Lystra
και Ικονιον και Αντιοχειαν· 22 επιστηριζοντες
and Iconium and Antioch; confirming
τας ψυχας των μαθητων, παρακαλουντες εμμενειν
the souls of the disciples, exhorting to abide
τῃ πιστει, και ὁτι δια πολλων θλιψεων δει
in the faith, and that through many afflictions it behoves
ἡμας εισηλθειν εις την βασιλειαν του θεου.
us to enter into the kingdom of the God.
23 Χειροτονησαντες δε αυτοις πρεσβυτερους κατ'
Having appointed and for them elders in every
εκκλησιαν, προσευξαμενοι μετα νηστειων παρε-
congregation, having prayed with fasting they
θεντο αυτους τῳ κυριῳ, εις ὁν πεπιστευκει-
commended them to the Lord, into whom they had believed.
σαν. 24 Και διελθοντες την Πισιδιαν, ηλθον
And having passed through the Pisidia, they came
εις Παμφυλιαν· 25 και λαλησαντες εν Περγῃ
into Pamphylia; and having spoken in Perga
τον λογον, κατεβησαν εις Ατταλειαν· 26 κακει-
the word, they went down into Attalia; and thence
θεν απεπλευσαν εις Αντιοχειαν, ὁθεν ησαν
they sailed into Antioch, whence they were
παραδεδομενοι τῃ χαριτι του θεου εις το εργον,
having been commended to the favor of the God for the work,
ὁ επληρωσαν. 27 Παραγενομενοι δε και συνα-
which they fulfilled. Having arrived and and having
γαγοντες την εκκλησιαν, ανηγγειλαν ὁσα
assembled the congregation, they related what things
εποιησεν ὁ θεος μετ' αυτων, και ὁτι ηνοιξε τοις
did the God with them, and that he opened to the
εθνεσι θυραν πιστεως. 28 Διετριβον δε χρονον
Gentiles a door of faith. They remained and a time
ουκ ολιγον συν τοις μαθηταις. ΚΕΦ. ιε'. 15.
not a little with the disciples.
1 Και τινες κατελθοντες απο της Ιουδαιας,
And some having come down from the Judea,
εδιδασκον τους αδελφους· Ὁτι εαν μη περιτεμ-
were teaching the brethren; That if not you are cir-
νησθε τῳ εθει Μωυσεως, ου δυνασθε σωθηναι.
cumcised with the rite of Moses, not you are able to be saved.
2 Γενομενης ουν στασεως και ζητησεως ουκ
Being therefore a dispute and discussion no
ολιγης τῳ Παυλῳ και τῳ Βαρναβᾳ προς αυτους,
a little the Paul and the Barnabas with them,
εταξαν αναβαινειν Παυλον και Βαρναβαν και
they decided to send up Paul and Barnabas and

21 And having preached the glad tidings in that CITY, and ‡made many disciples, they returned to LYSTRA, and Iconium, and Antioch,
22 confirming the SOULS of the DISCIPLES, and ‡ exhorting them to continue in the FAITH, ‡ and That through Many Afflictions we must enter the KINGDOM of GOD.
23 And ‡ having appointed ELDERS for them in every Congregation, and having prayed with Fasting, they commended them to the LORD, into whom they had believed.
24 And passing through PISIDIA, they came to * PAMPHYLIA;
25 and having spoken the WORD in Perga, they went to Attalia;
26 ‡ and thence they sailed to Antioch, whence they were ‡ recommended to the FAVOR of GOD for the WORK which they fulfilled.
27 And having arrived, and assembled the CONGREGATION, ‡they related what things GOD did by them, and that he had ‡ opened a Door of Faith to the GENTILES.
28 And they remained not a little Time with the DISCIPLES.

CHAPTER XV.

1 And ‡ some having come down from JUDEA taught the BRETHREN, ‡ "If you are not circumcised according to the CUSTOM of * Moses, you cannot be saved."
2 There being, therefore, a Contention, and PAUL and BARNABAS had no little Debate with them, they decided ‡ to send up Paul and Barnabas, and some

* VATICAN MANUSCRIPT.—24. PAMPHYLIA. 1. MOSES.

‡ 21. Matt. xxviii. 19. ‡ 22. Acts xi. 23; xiii. 43. ‡ 22. Matt. x. 38; xvi. 24; Luke xxii. 28, 29; Rom. viii. 17; 2 Tim. ii. 11, 12, iii. 12. ‡ 23. Titus i. 5. ‡ 26. Acts xiii. 1, 3. ‡ 26. Acts xv. 40. ‡ 27. Acts xv. 4, 12; xxi. 19. ‡ 27. 1 Cor. xvi. 9; 2 Cor. ii. 12; Col. iv. 3; Rev. iii. 4. ‡ 1. Gal. ii. 12. ‡ 1. John vii. 22; ver. 5; Gal. v. 2; Phil. iii. 2; Col. ii. 8, 11, 16. ‡ 2. Gal. ii. 1.

τινας αλλους εξ αυτων προς τους αποστολους
some others of them to the apostles

και πρεσβυτερους εις Ἱερουσαλημ, περι του
and elders at Jerusalem, about the

ζητηματος τουτου. 3 Οἱ μεν ουν προπεμφθεν-
question this. They indeed therefore having been sent

τες ὑπο της εκκλησιας, διηρχοντο την Φοινι-
forward by the congregation, passed through the Pheni-

κην και Σαμαρειαν, εκδιηγουμενοι την επιστρο-
cia and Samaria, narrating the turning

φην των εθνων· και εποιουν χαραν μεγαλην
of the Gentiles; and caused joy great

πασι τοις αδελφοις. 4 Παραγενομενοι δε εις
to all the brethren. Having come and into

Ἱερουσαλημ, απεδεχθησαν ὑπο της εκκλησιας
Jerusalem, they were received by the congregation

και των αποστολων και των πρεσβυτερων, ανηγ-
and the apostles and the elders, they

γειλαν τε ὁσα ὁ θεος εποιησε μετ' αυτων.
related and what things the God did with them.

5 Εξανεστησαν δε τινες των απο της αἱρεσεως
Stood up and some of those from the sect

των Φαρισαιων πεπιστευκοτες, λεγοντες· Ὁτι
of the Pharisees having believed, saying; That

δει περιτεμνειν αυτους, παραγγελλειν τε
it is necessary to circumcise them, to command and

τηρειν τον νομον Μωυσεως. 6 Συνηχθησαν δε
to keep the law of Moses. Assembled and

οἱ αποστολοι και οἱ πρεσβυτεροι ιδειν περι του
the apostles and the elders to see concerning the

λογου τουτου. 7 Πολλης δε συζητησεως γενο-
word this. Much and debate being,

μενης, αναστας Πετρος ειπε προς αυτους·
having arisen Peter said to them:

Ανδρες αδελφοι, ὑμεις επιστασθε, ὁτι αφ' ἡμε-
Men brethren, you know, that from days

ρων αρχαιων ὁ θεος εν ἡμιν εξελεξατο δια του
former the God among us chose through the

στοματος μου ακουσαι τα εθνη τον λογον του
mouth of me to hear the Gentiles the word of the

ευαγγελιου, και πιστευσαι. 8 Και ὁ καρδιογ-
glad tidings, and to believe. And the heart-

νωστης θεος εμαρτυρησεν αυτοις, δους αυτοις
knowing God testified to them, giving to them

το πνευμα το ἁγιον, καθως και ἡμιν· 9 και
the spirit the holy, as even to us, and

ουδεν διεκρινε μεταξυ ἡμων τε και αυτων, τῃ
nothing judged between us and also them, by the

πιστει καθαρισας τας καρδιας αυτων. 10 Νυν
faith having purified the hearts of them. Now

ουν τι πειραζετε τον θεον, επιθειναι ζυγον
therefore why do you tempt the God, to place a yoke

επι τον τραχηλον των μαθητων, ὁν ουτε οἱ
on the neck of the disciples, which neither the

πατερες ἡμων ουτε ἡμεις ισχυσαμεν βαστασαι;
fathers of us nor we were able to bear?

11 Αλλα δια της χαριτος του κυριου Ιησου πισ-
But through the favor of the Lord Jesus we be-

others of them, to the APOSTLES and Elders at Jerusalem, about this QUESTION.

3 THEY, therefore, having been sent forward by the CONGREGATION, went through PHENICIA and Samaria, ‡ relating the CONVERSION of the GENTILES, and caused great Joy to All the BRETHREN.

4 And having arrived at Jerusalem, they were received by the CONGREGATION, and the APOSTLES, and the ELDERS, and ‡ related what things GOD performed with them.

5 But SOME of those having BELIEVED, from the SECT of the PHARISEES, stood up, saying, "It is necessary to circumcise them, and to command them to keep the LAW of Moses.

6 And the APOSTLES and ELDERS were gathered together to see about this MATTER.

7 And there being much Debate, Peter arising said to them, ‡ "Brethren, you know That in former Days GOD chose among us, that by my MOUTH the GENTILES should hear the WORD of the GLAD TIDINGS, and believe.

8 And God, the HEART-SEARCHER, testified to them, ‡ giving to them the HOLY SPIRIT, even as to us;

9 ‡ And made no distinction between us and them, ‡ having purified their HEARTS through the FAITH.

10 Now, therefore, why do you try GOD, ‡ to put a Yoke on the NECK of the DISCIPLES, which neither our FATHERS nor we were able to bear?

11 But through the FAVOR of the Lord Jesus

* VATICAN MANUSCRIPT.—8. to them—omit.

‡ 3. Acts xiv. 27. ‡ 4. ver 12; xxi. 19 ‡ 7. Acts x. 20; xi. 12. ‡ 8. Acts x. 44. ‡ 9. Rom. x 11. ‡ 9. Acts x. 15, 28, 43; 1 Cor. i. 2; 1 Pet. i. 22. ‡ 10. Matt. xxiii 4; Gal v. 1

τευομεν σωθηναι, καθ' ὁν τροπον κακεινοι.
lieve to be saved, in which manner also they.
12 Εσιγησε δε παν το πληθος, και ηκουον Βαρ-
Was silent and all the multitude. and heard Bar-
ναβα και Παυλου εξηγουμενων, ὁσα εποιησεν
nabas and Paul narrating, what did
ὁ θεος σημεια και τερατα εν τοις εθνεσι δι'
the God signs and prodigies among the Gentiles through
αυτων. 13 Μετα δε το σιγησαι αυτους, απεκ-
them. After and the to be silent them, an-
ριθη Ιακωβος, λεγων· Ανδρες αδελφοι, ακουσατε
swered James, saying; Men brethren, hear you
μου. 14 Συμεων εξηγησατο, καθως πρωτον ὁ
of me. Simeon related, how first the
θεος επεσκεψατο λαβειν εξ εθνων λαον επι τῳ
God looked to take out of Gentiles a people for the
ονοματι αὑτου. 15 Και τουτῳ συμφωνουσιν οἱ
name of himself. And with this harmonize the
λογοι των προφητων, καθως γεγραπται· 16 μετα
words of the prophets, as it is written; after
ταυτα αναστρεψω και ανοικοδομησω την σκη-
these things I will return and I will build again the taber-
νην Δαυιδ την πεπτωκυιαν· και τα κατεσκαμ-
nacle of David that having fallen down; and the ruins
μενα αυτης ανοικοδομησω, και ανορθωσω αυτην·
of her I will build again, and I will set up her;
17 ὁπως αν εκζητησωσιν οἱ καταλοιποι των
so that may seek the rest of the
ανθρωπων τον κυριον, και παντα τα εθνη, εφ'
men the Lord, and all the nations, on
οὑς επικεκληται το ονομα μου επ' αυτους, 18 λε-
whom has been called the name of me over them, says
γει κυριος *[ὁ] ποιων ταυτα γνωστα απ' αιωνος.
Lord [he] doing these things known from an age.
19 Διο εγω κρινω μη παρενοχλειν τοις απο των
Therefore I judge not to trouble those from the
εθνων επιστρεφουσιν επι τον θεον· 20 αλλα
Gentiles turning to the God; but
επιστειλαι αυτοις του απεχεσθαι απο των
to send word to them the to abstain from the
αλισγηματων των ειδωλων και της πορνειας και
pollutions of the idols and the fornication and
του πνικτου και του αἱματος. 21 Μωυσης γαρ
the strangled and the blood. Moses for
εκ γενεων αρχαιων κατα πολιν τους κηρυσ-
from generations of old in every city those preach-
σοντας αυτον εχει, εν ταις συναγωγαις κατα
ing him has, in the synagogues in
παν σαββατον αναγινωσκομενος. 22 Τοτε εδοξε
every sabbath being read. Then it seemed good
τοις αποστολοις και τοις πρεσβυτεροις συν ὁλῃ
to the apostles and the elders with whole
τῃ εκκλησιᾳ, εκλεξαμενους ανδρας εξ αὑτων
the congregation, having chosen men out of themselves

we trust to be saved; in
like manner they also.
12 And All the MULTI-
TUDE was silent, and heard
Barnabas and Paul relate
What Signs and Prodigies
GOD ‡ performed among
the GENTILES through
them.
13 And after they were
SILENT, ‡ James answered,
saying, "Brethren, hear
me!
14 ‡ Simon has related
how GOD first looked to
take out of the Gentiles
a People for his NAME.
15 And with this the
WORDS of the PROPHETS
harmonize; as it is writ-
ten,
16 ‡ 'After these things
'I will return; and I will
'rebuild THAT TABERNA-
'CLE of David which has
'FALLEN DOWN; and I
'will rebuild its RUINS,
'and will re-establish it;
17 'in order that the
'REMAINDER of MEN may
'seek the LORD, even All
'the GENTILES upon
'whom my NAME has been
'invoked,
18 'says the Lord, who
'does these things,' which
were known from the Age.
19 Therefore ‡ I judge
that we should not trouble
THOSE, who from among
the GENTILES are TURN-
ING to GOD,
20 but write to them
to ABSTAIN from the POL-
LUTED ‡ OFFERINGS to
IDOLS, and ‡ FORNICA-
TION, and THAT which is
STRANGLED, and ‡ BLOOD.
21 For from ancient Gen-
erations Moses has, in every
City, THOSE who PREACH
him, being read in the
SYNAGOGUES Every Sab-
bath."
22 Then it seemed good
to the APOSTLES and EL-
DERS, with the Whole CON-
GREGATION, to send Men

* VATICAN MANUSCRIPT.—18. he—*omit.*

‡ 12. Acts xiv. 27. ‡ 13. Acts xii 17. ‡ 14. ver. 7 ‡ 16. Amos ix. 11, 12. ‡ 19. ver 28. ‡ 20. ver. 29; Acts xxi. 25; 1 Cor. viii. 1; Rev. ii. 14, 20 ‡ 20. 1 Cor. vi. 9, 18; Gal. v. 19; Eph. v. 3, Col. iii. 5, 1 Thess. iv. 3; 1 Pet. iv. 3. ‡ 20. Gen ix. 4; Lev. iii. 17; Deut. xii. 16, 23.

πεμψαι εις Αντιοχειαν συν τῳ Παυλῳ και Βαρ-
to send to Antioch with the Paul and Bar-
ναβᾳ, Ιουδαν τον επικαλουμενον Βαρσαβαν, και
nabas, Judas that being called Barsabas, and
Σιλαν, ανδρας ἡγουμενους εν τοις αδελφοις·
Silas, men leading among the brethren;
23 γραψαντες δια χειρος αυτων *[ταδε·]
having written by hand of them [thus;]
Οἱ αποστολοι και οἱ πρεσβυτεροι και οἱ
The apostles and the elders and the
αδελφοι, τοις κατα την Αντιοχειαν και Συριαν
brethren, to those in the Antioch and Syria
και Κιλικιαν αδελφοις, τοις εξ εθνων, χαιρειν.
and Cilicia brethren, those from Gentiles, health.
24 Επειδη ηκουσαμεν, ὁτι τινες εξ ἡμων *[εξελ-
Since we have heard, that some from us [having
θοντες] εταραξαν ὑμας λογοις, ανασκευαζοντες
gone out] troubled you with words, unsettling
τας ψυχας ὑμων, *[λεγοντες περιτεμνεσθαι
the souls of you, [saying to be circumcised
και τηρειν τον νομον,] οἱς ου διεστειλαμεθα·
and to keep the law,] to whom not we gave commands;
25 εδοξεν ἡμιν γενομενοις ὁμοθυμαδον, εκλεξα-
it seemed good to us being of one mind, having
μενους ανδρας πεμψαι προς ὑμας, συν τοις αγα-
chosen out men to send to you, with the be-
πητοις ἡμων Βαρναβᾳ και Παυλῳ, 26 ανθρωποις
loved of us Barnabas and Paul, men
παραδεδωκοσι τας ψυχας αὐτων ὑπερ του ονο-
having given up the lives of them in behalf of the name
ματος του κυριου ἡμιν Ιησου Χριστου. 27 Απεσ-
of the Lord of us Jesus Anointed. We
ταλκαμεν ουν Ιουδαν και Σιλαν, και αυτους
have sent therefore Judas and Silas, and them
δια λογου απαγγελλοντας τα αυτα. 28 Εδοξε
through word announcing the same things. It seemed good
γαρ τῳ αγιῳ πνευματι και ἡμιν, μηδεν πλεον
for to the holy spirit and to us, no more
επιτιθεσθαι ὑμιν βαρος, πλην των επαναγκες
to lay to you a burden, besides the necessary things
τουτων, 29 απεχεσθαι ειδωλοθυτων και αἱματος
these, to abstain from things offered to idols and blood
και πνικτου και πορνειας· εξ ὡν διατηρουντες
and strangled and fornication; from which keeping
ἑαυτους, ἑυ πραξετε. Ερρωσθε. 30 Οἱ μεν
yourselves, well you will do. Farewell They indeed
ουν απολυθεντες ηλθον εις Αντιοχειαν· και
therefore being dismissed went to Antioch; and
συναγαγοντες το πληθος, επεδωκαν την επισ-
having assembled the multitude, delivered the let-
τολην. 31 Αναγνοντες δε, εχαρησαν επι τη
ter. Having read and, they rejoiced at the
παρακλησει. 32 Ιουδας τε και Σιλας, και αυτοι
exhortation. Judas and and Silas, also themselves

chosen from among themselves to Antioch with PAUL and Barnabas;—THAT Judas * being called Barsabbas, and Silas, leading Men among the BRETHREN;

23 having written by their Hand, thus:—"The APOSTLES and * ELDERS and BRETHREN, to THOSE BRETHREN in ANTIOCH and Syria and Cilicia, who are of the Gentiles, greeting.

24 Since we have heard That ‡ some having gone out from us troubled you with Words, unsettling your MINDS, to whom we gave no commands;

25 it seemed good to us, being of one mind, to chose out men to send to you, with your BELOVED Barnabas and Paul,

26 ‡ Men who have given up their LIVES in behalf of the NAME of our LORD Jesus Christ.

27 We have therefore sent Judas and Silas, who will also tell you the SAME things by Word.

28 For it seemed good to the * HOLY SPIRIT, and to us, to lay on you no Additional Burden besides * These NECESSARY things,

29 To abstain from things offered to Idols, and Blood, and That which is Strangled, and Fornication; from which if you keep yourselves you will do well. Farewell."

30 THEY, therefore, being dismissed, * went down to Antioch, and having assembled the MULTITUDE, delivered the LETTER.

31 And when they had read it, they rejoiced at the EXHORTATION.

32 And Judas and Silas, also themselves being ready

* VATICAN MANUSCRIPT.—22. being called Barsabbas. 23. thus—*omit*. 23. ELDER BRETHREN. 24. having gone out—*omit*. 24. saying, to be circumcised, and to keep the LAW—*omit*. 28. HOLY SPIRIT. 28. These. 30. went down

‡ 24. ver. 1; Gal. ii. 4, 5, 12; Titus i, 10, 11. ‡ 26. Acts xiii. 50; xiv. 19; 1 Cor. xv 30; 2 Cor. xi. 23, 26.

προφηται οντες, δια λογου πολλου παρεκαλε-
prophets being, through a word great exhorted
σαν τους αδελφους, και επεστηριξαν. 33 Ποιη-
the brethren, and confirmed. Having
σαντες δε χρονον, απελυθησαν μετ' ειρηνης
spent and a time, they were dismissed with peace
απο των αδελφων προς τους αποστειλαντας
from the brethren to those having sent
αυτους. 34 *[Εδοξε δε τω Σιλα επιμειναι
them. [It seemed good but to the Silas to remain
αυτου.] 35 Παυλος δε και Βαρναβας διετριβον
there.] Paul but and Barnabas remained
εν Αντιοχεια, διδασκοντες και ευαγγελιζομενοι,
in Antioch, teaching and announcing glad tidings,
μετα και ἑτερων πολλων, τον λογον του κυριου.
with also others many, the word of the Lord.
36 Μετα δε τινας ἡμερας ειπε Παυλος προς Βαρ-
After and some days said Paul to Bar-
ναβαν· Επιστρεψαντες δη επισκεψωμεθα τους
nabas; Having returned indeed we may visit the
αδελφους κατα πασαν πολιν, εν αἱς κατηγγει-
brethren in every city, in which we have
λαμεν τον λογον του κυριου, πως εχουσι.
preached the word of the Lord, how they are.
37 Βαρναβας δε εβουλευσατο συμπαραλαβειν και
Barnabas and counselled to take with also
Ιωαννην τον καλουμενον Μαρκον. 38 Παυλος
John that being called Mark. Paul
δε ηξιου, τον αποσταντα απ' αυτων απο
out deemed fitting, the having gone away from them from
Παμφυλιας, και μη συνελθοντα αυτοις εις το
Pamphylia, and not having gone with them to the
εργον, μη συμπαραλαβειν τουτον. 39 Εγενετο
work, not to take him. Occurred
ουν παροξυσμος, ὡστε αποχωρισθηναι αυτους
therefore a sharp contention, so as to separate them
απ' αλληλων, τον τε Βαρναβαν παραλαβοντα
from one another, the and Barnabas having taken
τον Μαρκον εκπλευσαι εις Κυπρον.
the Mark sailed to Cyprus.
40 Παυλος δε επιλεξαμενος Σιλαν εξηλθε,
Paul but having selected Silas went out,
παραδοθεις τῃ χαριτι του θεου ὑπο των
having been commended to the favor of the God by the
αδελφων. 41 Διηρχετο δε την Συριαν και Κιλι-
brethren. He passed through and the Syria and Cili-
κιαν, επιστηριζων τας εκκλησιας. ΚΕΦ. ις'.
cia, confirming the congregations.
16. 1 Κατηντησε δε εις Δερβην και Λυστραν·
He came and to Derbe and Lystra;
και ιδου, μαθητης τις ην εκει, ονοματι Τιμο-
and lo, a disciple certain was there, by name Timo-

speakers, exhorted the BRETHREN in a long Discourse and confirmed them.

33 And having spent some Time, they were dismissed with Peace from the BRETHREN to those HAVING SENT them.

34 *†[But it seemed good to SILAS to remain there.]

35 ‡And Paul and Barnabas remained at Antioch, teaching and proclaiming the glad tidings of the WORD of the LORD, with many others also.

36 And after Some Days Paul said to Barnabas, "Let us return and visit the BRETHREN ‡in *Every City in which we proclaimed the WORD of the LORD, and see how they are."

37 And Barnabas wished to take also with them ‡THAT John, who was SURNAMED Mark.

38 But Paul deemed it improper to take HIM with them, ‡who DESERTED them from Pamphylia, and did not go with them to the WORK.

39 A sharp Contention therefore ensued, so as to separate them from each other; and BARNABAS having taken MARK sailed to Cyprus.

40 But Paul having selected Silas, departed, ‡being commended to the FAVOR of * the Lord by the BRETHREN.

41 And he went through SYRIA and Cilicia, ‡establishing the CONGREGATIONS.

CHAPTER XVI.

1 And he came * both to ‡Derbe and to Lystra. And behold a certain Disciple was there, ‡named Timo-

* VATICAN MANUSCRIPT.—34. *omit.* 36. every City. 40. the LORD. 1. both to Derbe and to Lystra.

† 34. This sentence is omitted by the *Vatican*, and a great number of other MSS; also by the Syriac, Arabic, Coptic, Slavonic, and Vulgate. Griesbach marks it as doubtful, and to be expunged.

‡ 35. Acts xiii. 1. ‡ 36. Acts xiii. 4, 13, 14, 51; xiv. 1, 6, 24, 25. ‡ 37. Acts xii. 12. 25; xiii. 5; Col. iv. 10; 2 Tim. iv. 11; Philemon 24. ‡ 38. Acts xiii. 13. ‡ 40. Acts xiv. 26. ‡ 41. Acts xvi. 5. ‡ 1. Acts xiv. 6. ‡ 1. Acts xix. 22; Rom. xvi. 21; 1 Cor. iv. 17; Phil. ii. 19; 1 Thess. iii. 2; 1 Tim. i. 2; 2 Tim. i. 2.

θεος, υἱος γυναικος Ιουδαιας πιστης, πατρος δε
thy, a son of a woman Jew believing, father but
Ἑλληνος· 2 ὁς εμαρτυρειτο ὑπο των εν Λυσ-
a Greek; who was testified to by those in Lys-
τροις και Ικονιῳ αδελφων. 3 Τουτον ηθελησεν
tra and Iconium brethren. This wished
ὁ Παυλος συν αὐτῳ εξελθειν· και λαβων περι-
the Paul with him to go out; and having taken he cir-
ετεμεν αυτον, δια τους Ιουδαιους τους οντας
cumcised him, on account of the Jews those being
εν τοις τοποις εκεινοις· ηδεισαν γαρ ἁπαντες
in the places those; they knew for all
τον πατερα αυτου, ὁτι Ἑλλην ὑπηρχην. 4 Ὡς
the father of him, that a Greek he was. As
δε διεπορευοντο τας πολεις, παρεδιδουν αυτοις
and they went through the cities, they delivered to them
φυλασσειν τα δογματα, τα κεκριμενα ὑπο
to keep the decrees, those having been determined by
των αποστολων και των πρεσβυτερων των εν
the apostles and the elders those in
Ἱερουσαλημ. 5 Αἱ μεν ουν εκκλησιαι εστερ-
Jerusalem. The indeed then congregations were es-
εουντο τη πιστει, και επερισσευον τῳ αριθμῳ
tablished in the faith, and were increased in the number
καθ' ἡμεραν. 6 Διελθοντες δε την Φρυγιαν και
every day. Going through and the Phrygia and
την Γαλατικην χωραν, κωλυθεντες ὑπο του
the Galatia country, being forbidden by the
ἁγιου πνευματος λαλησαι τον λογον εν τη Ασιᾳ,
holy spirit to speak the word in the Asia,
7 ελθοντες κατα την Μυσιαν, επιραζον εις την
coming by the Mysia, they attempted into the
Βιθυνιαν πορευεσθαι· και ουκ ειασεν αυτους το
Bithynia to go; and not permitted them the
πνευμα Ιησου. 8 Παρελθοντες δε την Μυσιαν,
spirit of Jesus. Having passed by and the Mysia,
κατεβησαν εις Τρωαδα. 9 Και ὁραμα δια της
they came down to Troas. And a vision in the
νυκτος ωφθη τῳ Παυλῳ· ανηρ τις ην Μακε-
night was seen by the Paul; a man certain was of Mace-
δων εστως, παρακαλων αυτον, και λεγων· Δια-
donia had been standing, beseeching him, and saying; Having
βας εις Μακεδονιαν, βοηθησον ἡμιν. 10 Ὡς δε
passed over into Macedonia, help thou us. When and
το ὁραμα ειδεν, ευθεως εζητησαμεν εξελθειν εις
the vision he saw, immediately we sought to go out into
την Μακεδονιαν, συμβιβαζοντες, ὁτι προσκεκ-
the Macedonia, inferring, that had called
ληται ἡμας ὁ κυριος ευαγγελισασθαι αυτους.
to us the Lord to announce glad tidings to them.
11 Αναχθεντες ουν απο της Τρωαδος, ευθυδρο-
Having sailed therefore from the Troas, we run a

thy, (a ‡ Son of a believing Jewess, but of a Greek Father;)

2 to whom the BRETHREN in Lystra and Iconium, gave ‡ good testimony.

3 Him PAUL wished to go forth with him; and ‡ he took and circumcised him on account of THOSE JEWS who were in those PLACES; for they all knew That his FATHER was a Greek.

4 And as they went through the CITIES, they delivered for their observance THOSE DECREES ‡ which had been made by * THOSE APOSTLES and Elders in Jerusalem.

5 Then, indeed, the CONGREGATIONS ‡ were established in the FAITH, and were increased in NUMBER every Day.

6 * And they went through the Country of PHRYGIA and Galatia, being forbidden by the HOLY Spirit to speak the WORD in ASIA;

7 and coming by MYSIA, they attempted to go into BITHYNIA; and the SPIRIT of Jesus did not permit them.

8 And having passed by MYSIA, ‡ they came down to Troas.

9 And a Vision was seen by PAUL in the * Night; a certain ‡ Man of Macedonia was standing, and entreating him, and saying, "Come over into Macedonia, and help us."

10 And when he saw the VISION, we immediately sought to go ‡ into MACEDONIA, inferring that * the LORD had called us to announce glad tidings to them.

11 Having sailed, therefore, from TROAS, we run

---

* VATICAN MANUSCRIPT.—4. of THOSE APOSTLES and Elders. 6. And they went through the Country of PHRYGIA and Galatia. 9. Night. 10. GOD called us.

‡ 1. 2 Tim. i. 5. ‡ 2. Acts vi. 3. ‡ 3. 1 Cor. ix. 20. Gal. ii. 3. ‡ 4. Acts xv. 28, 29. ‡ 5. Acts xv. 41. ‡ 8. 2 Cor. ii. 12. 2 Tim. iv. 13. ‡ 9. Acts x. 30. ‡ 10. 2 Cor. ii. 12.

μησαμην εις Σαμοθρακην, τη τε επιουση εις
direct course to Samothracia, the and succeeding to
Νεαπολιν· [12] εκειθεν τε εις Φιλιππους, ἡτις εστι
Neapolis; thence and to Philippi, which is
πρωτη της μεριδος της Μακεδονιας πολις, κο-
first of the part that Macedonia city, a
λωνια. Ημεν δε εν ταυτῃ τῃ πολει διατριβον-
colony. We were and in this the city abiding
τες ἡμερας τινας. [13] Τῃ τε ἡμερᾳ των σαββα-
days some. On the and day of the sab-
των εξηλθομεν εξω της πολεως παρα ποταμον,
baths we went out of the city by a river,
οὑ ενομιζετο προσευχη ειναι, και καθισαντες
where was allowed a place of prayer to be, and having sat down
ελαλουμεν ταις συνελθουσαις γυναιξι.
we spoke to the having come together women.
[14] Και τις γυνη ονοματι Λυδια, πορφυροπω-
And a certain woman by name Lydia, a seller of pur-
λις πολεως Θυατειρων σεβομενη τον θεον,
ple of a city of Thyatira worshipping the God,
ηκουεν· ἡς ὁ κυριος διηνοιξε την καρδιαν,
heard; for whom the Lord opened the heart,
προσεχειν τοις λαλουμενοις ὑπο του Παυλου.
to attend to those being spoken by the Paul.
[15] Ὡς δε εβαπτισθη, και ὁ οικος αυτης, παρε-
When and she was dipped, and the house of her, she en-
καλεσε, λεγουσα· Ει κεκρικατε με πιστην τῳ
treated us, saying; If you have judged me faithful to the
κυριῳ ειναι, εισελθοντες εις τον οικον μου,
Lord to be, having entered into the house of me,
μεινατε. Και παρεβιασατο ἡμας. [16] Εγενετο
abide you And she forced us. It happened
δε πορευομενων ἡμων εις προσευχην, παιδισκην
and going of us to a place of prayer, a female-servant
τινα εχουσαν πνευμα πυθωνος απαντησαι ἡμιν,
certain having a spirit of Python to meet us,
ἡτις εργασιαν πολλην παρειχε τοις κυριοις
who gain much brought the lords
αὑτης, μαντευομενη. [17] Αὑτη κατακολουθησασα
of herself, divining. She having followed closely
τῳ Παυλῳ και ἡμιν, εκραζε λεγουσα· Οὑτοι οἱ
the Paul and us, cried saying; These the
ανθρωποι δουλοι του θεου του ὑψιστου εισιν,
men bond-servants of the God the most high are,
οἱτινες καταγγελλουσιν ἡμιν ὁδον σωτηριας.
who are proclaiming to us a way of salvation.
[18] Τουτο δε εποιει επι πολλας ἡμερας. Διαπο-
This and she did for many days. Being
νηθεις δε ὁ Παυλος, και επιστρεψας, τῳ πνευ-
grieved but the Paul, and having turned, to the spirit
ματι ειπε· Παραγγελλω σοι εν τῳ ονοματι Ιη-
he said; I command thee in the name of Je-

a direct course to Samothracia, and the NEXT day to Neapolis;

12 and thence to ‡ Philippi, which is the Chief of its * District, a City of MACEDONIA, a Colony. And we remained several Days in That CITY.

13 And on the SABBATH DAY we went out of the * CITY by a River, where there was allowed to be an † Oratory; and having sat down, we spoke to the WOMEN who were ASSEMBLED.

14 And a Certain Woman named Lydia, a Seller of purple, of the City of Thyatira, a worshipper of GOD, heard; ‡ Whose HEART the LORD opened, to attend to THOSE things SPOKEN by * Paul.

15 And when she was immersed, and her FAMILY, she entreated, saying, "If you have judged me to be faithful to the LORD, enter my HOUSE, and remain." ‡ And she compelled us.

16 And it occurred, as we were going to the * ORATORY, a certain Female-servant, ‡ having a Spirit of † Python, met us, who brought her MASTERS much Gain by divining.

17 She having closely followed * Paul and us, cried saying, "These MEN are the Servants of the MOST HIGH GOD, who are proclaiming to us the Way of Salvation."

18 And she did this for Several Days. But PAUL, being grieved, turned and said to the SPIRIT, "I command thee in the * Name of Jesus Christ to

* VATICAN MANUSCRIPT.—12. District. 13. GATE. 14. Paul. 16. ORATORY. 17. Paul. 18. Name.

† 13. A place of prayer. See Note on Luke vi. 12. † 16. Or of *Apollo*. Pytho was, according to fable, a huge serpent, that had an oracle at Mount Parnassus, famous for predicting future events; that Apollo slew this serpent, and hence he was called *Pythius*, and became celebrated as the foreteller of future events; and that all those who either could, or pretended to predict future events, were influenced by the spirit of *Apollo Pythius*.—*Clarke*.

‡ 12. Phil. i. 1. ‡ 14. Luke xxiv. 45. ‡ 15. Luke xxiv. 29; Heb. xiii. 2. ‡ 16. 1 Sam. xxviii. 7.

σου Χριστου, εξελθειν απ᾽ αυτης. Και
sus Anointed, to come out from her. And
εξηλθεν αυτῃ τῃ ὡρᾳ. 19 Ιδοντες δε οἱ κυριοι
it came out in that the hour. Seeing and the lords
αυτης, ὁτι εξηλθεν ἡ ελπις της εργασιας
of her, that came out the hope of the gain
αὑτων, επιλαβομενοι τον Παυλον και τον
of them, having taken hold of the Paul and the
Σιλαν, εἱλκυσαν εις την αγοραν επι τους
Silas, they dragged into the market to the
αρχοντας· 20 και προσαγαγοντες αυτους
rulers; and they having led them
τοις στρατηγοις, ειπον· Οὑτοι οἱ ανθρωποι
to the commanders, said, These the men
εκταρασσουσιν ἡμων την πολιν, Ιουδαιοι ὑπαρ-
greatly disturb of us the city, Jews being,
χοντες, 21 και καταγγελλουσιν εθη, ἁ ουκ
and preach customs, which not
εξεστιν ἡμιν παραδεχεσθαι, ουδε ποιειν, Ῥω-
it is lawful for us to receive, or to do, Ro-
μαιοις ουσι. 22 Και συνεπεστη ὁ οχλος κατ᾽
mans being. And rose up together the crowd against
αυτων, και οἱ στρατηγοι περιρῥηξαντες αυτων
them, and the commanders having torn off of them
τα ἱματια, εκελευον ῥαβδιζειν· 23 πολλας τε
the mantles, they ordered to beat with rods; many and
επιθεντες αυτοις πληγας, εβαλον εις φυλακην,
having laid on them blows, they cast into prison,
παραγγειλαντες τῳ δεσμοφυλακι, ασφαλως
having charged the jailor, securely
τηρειν αυτους· 24 ὁς παραγγελιαν τοιαυτην
to keep them; who a charge such
ειληφως, εβαλην αυτους εις την εσωτεραν
having received, cast them into the inner
φυλακην, και τους ποδας αυτων ησφαλισατο
prison, and the feet of them were made fast
εις το ξυλον.
into the stocks.

25 Κατα δε το μεσονυκτιον Παυλος και Σιλας
At and the midnight Paul and Silas
προσευχομενοι ὑμνουν τον θεον· επηκροωντο δε
praying sung a hymn to the God; listened to and
αυτων οἱ δεσμιοι. 26 Αφνω δε σεισμος εγενετο
them the prisoners. Suddenly and a shaking occurred
μεγας, ὡστε σαλευθηναι τα θεμελια του δεσμω-
great, so as to shake the foundations of the pri-
τηριου· ανεῳχθησαν τε *[παραχρημα] αἱ θυραι
son; were opened and [immediately] the doors
πασαι, και παντων τα δεσμα ανεθη. 27 Εξυπνος
all, and all the bonds were loosed. Out of sleep
δε γενομενος ὁ δεσμοφυλαξ, και ιδων ανεῳγ-
and having arisen the jailor, and seeing having been
μενας τας θυρας της φυλακης, σπασαμενος
opened the doors of the prison, having drawn
μαχαιραν, εμελλεν ἑαυτον αναιρειν, νομιζων
a sword, was about himself to kill, supposing
εκπεφευγεναι τους δεσμιους. 28 Εφωνησε δε
to have been fled the prisoners. Cried out and

come out of her." ‡ And
it came out in That Hour.
19 And her MASTERS
seeing That the HOPE of
their GAIN was gone,
‡ seizing PAUL and SI-
LAS, ‡ they dragged them
into the MARKET, to the
RULERS;
20 and they having con-
ducted them before the
COMMANDERS, said, "These
MEN, being Jews, ‡ greatly
disturb our CITY,
21 and preach Customs,
which it is not lawful for
us to receive or observe,
being Romans."
22 And the CROWD rose
up together against them;
and the COMMANDERS
having torn off their MAN-
TLES, ‡ gave orders to beat
them with rods.
23 And having laid
Many Stripes on them,
they cast them into Pri-
son, charging the jailor to
keep them safely;
24 who, having received
such a Charge, cast them
into the INNER prison, and
made their FEET fast in
the STOCKS.
25 And at MIDNIGHT,
Paul and Silas praying,
sung a hymn to GOD; and
the PRISONERS listened to
them.
26 ‡ And suddenly there
was a great Concussion,
so as to shake the FOUN-
DATIONS of the PRISON,
and ‡ all the DOORS were
opened, and the FETTERS
of All were loosed.
27 And the JAILOR,
awaking from sleep, and
seeing the DOORS of the
PRISON opened, drew a
SWORD, and was about to
kill Himself, supposing
that the PRISONERS had
escaped.
28 But PAUL cried with

* VATICAN MANUSCRIPT.—26. immediately—omit.

‡ 18. Mark xvi. 17. ‡ 19. 2 Cor. vi. 5. ‡ 19. Matt. x. 18. ‡ 20. Acts xvii. 6. ‡ 22. 2 Cor. vi. 5; xi. 23, 25; 1 Thess. ii. 2. ‡ 26. Acts iv. 31. ‡ 26. Acts v. 19, xii. 7, 10.

φωνη μεγαλη ὁ Παυλος, λεγων· Μηδεν πραξῃς
with a voice loud the Paul, saying; Not thou mayest do

σεαυτῳ κακον, ἁπαντες γαρ εσμεν ενθαδε.
to thyself harm, all for we are here.

29 Αιτησας δε φωτα εισεπηδησε, και εντρομος
Having asked and lights he rushed in, and terrified

γενομενος προσεπεσε τῳ Παυλῳ και τῳ Σιλᾳ.
having become he fell before the Paul and the Silas.

30 Και προαγαγων αυτους εξω, εφη· Κυριοι,
And having led them out, he said; O sirs,

τι με δει ποιειν, ἱνα σωθω; 31 Οἱ δε ειπον·
what me it behoves to do, that I may be saved? They and said;

Πιστευσον επι τον κυριον Ιησουν Χριστον, και
Believe thou in the Lord Jesus Anointed, and

σωθηση συ και ὁ οικος σου. 32 Και ελαλησαν
shalt be saved thou and the house of thee. And they spoke

αυτῳ τον λογον του κυριου, συν πασι τοις εν
to him the word of the Lord, with all those in

τῃ οικιᾳ αυτου. 33 Και παραλαβων αυτους εν
the house of him. And having taken them in

εκεινῃ τῃ ὡρᾳ της νυκτος, ελουσεν απο των
that the hour of the night, he washed from the

πληγων· και εβαπτισθη αυτος και οἱ αυτου
stripes; and was dipped he and those of him

παντες παραχρημα. 34 Αναγαγων τε αυτους εις
all immediately. Having led up and them into

τον οικον αὑτου, παρεθηκε τραπεζαν, και ηγαλ-
the house of himself, he set a table, and re-

λιασατο πανοικι πεπιστευκως τῳ θεῳ.
joiced with all his house, having believed in the God.

35 Ἡμερας δε γενομενης, απεστειλαν οἱ στρα-
Day and having become, sent the com-

τηγοι τους ῥαβδουχους, λεγοντες· Απολυσον
manders the rod bearers, saying; Release thou

τους ανθρωπους εκεινους. 36 Απηγγειλε δε ὁ
the men those. Told and the

δεσμοφυλαξ τους λογους τουτους προς τον Παυ-
jailor the words these to the Paul;

λον· Ὁτι απεσταλκασιν οἱ στρατηγοι, ἱνα απο-
That has sent the commanders, that you

λυθητε· νυν ουν εξελθοντες, πορευεσθε εν
may be released; now therefore going out, do you go in

ειρηνῃ. 37 Ὁ δε Παυλος εφη προς αυτους·
peace. The but Paul said to them;

Δειραντες ἡμας δημοσιᾳ, ακατακριτους, ανθρω-
Having beaten us publicly, uncondemned, men

πους Ῥωμαιους ὑπαρχοντας, εβαλον εις φυλα-
Romans being, they cast into prison,

κην, και νυν λαθρα ἡμας εκβαλλουσιν; Ου
and now privately us do they cast out? No

γαρ· αλλα ελθοντες αυτοι ἡμας εξαγαγετωσαν.
indeed; but having come themselves us let them lead out.

38 Ανηγγειλαν δε τοις στρατηγοις οἱ ῥαβδουχοι
Told and to the commanders the rod-bearers

τα ῥηματα ταυτα· και εφοβηθησαν, ακουσαντες
the words these; and they were afraid, having heard

ὁτι Ῥωμαιοι εισι. 39 Και ελθοντες παρακαλε-
that Romans they are. And having come they entreated

a loud Voice, saying, "Do thyself no harm; for we are All here."

29 And having asked for Lights, he rushed in, and being in a tremor, fell down before PAUL and * SILAS.

30 And conducting them out, he said, ‡ "Sirs, what must I do that I may be saved?"

31 And THEY said, ‡ "Believe in the LORD Jesus Christ, and thou shalt be saved, and thy FAMILY.

32 And they spoke to him the WORD of * the LORD, and to ALL those in his HOUSE.

33 And taking them in That HOUR of the NIGHT, he washed them from their STRIPES, and was immediately immersed, he and all HIS.

34 And having brought them into * his HOUSE, ‡ he set a Table, and rejoiced with all his household, believing in GOD.

35 And when it was Day, the COMMANDERS sent the OFFICERS, saying, "Let those men go."

36 And the JAILOR told * these WORDS to PAUL, "The COMMANDERS have sent to release you; now therefore depart, and go in Peace."

37 But PAUL said to them, "They have beaten us publicly uncondemned, ‡ being Romans, and cast us into Prison; and now do they privately cast Us out? No, indeed; but let them come themselves and conduct Us out."

38 And the OFFICERS related these words to the COMMANDERS; and they were afraid when they heard that they were Romans.

39 And they came and

* VATICAN MANUSCRIPT.—29. Silas. 32. GOD, with ALL that were. 34. the HOUSE. 36. the WORDS.

‡ 30. Luke iii. 10; Acts ii. 37; ix. 6. ‡ 31. John iii. 16, 36; vi. 47; 1 John v. 10. ‡ 34. Luke v. 29; xix. 6. ‡ 37. Acts xxii. 25.

σαν αυτους, και εξαγαγοντες ηρωτων εξηλθειν
them, and having led out they asked to go out
της πολεως. 40 Εξελθοντες δε εκ της φυλα-
of the city. Having gone and out of the prison
κης εισηλθον προς την Λυδιαν· και ιδοντες τους
they came in to the Lydia; and having seen the
αδελφους, παρεκαλεσαν αυτους, και εξηλθον.
brethren, they exhorted them, and went out.
ΚΕΦ. ιζ'. 17. 1 Διοδευσαντες δε την Αμφι-
Having passed through and the Amphi-
πολιν και Απολλωνιαν, ηλθον εις Θεσσαλονι-
polis and Apollonia, they came into Thessalonica,
κην, όπου ην ἡ συναγωγη των Ιουδαιων.
where was the synagogue of the Jews.
2 Κατα δε το ειωθος τῳ Παυλῳ εισηλθε προς
According to and the custom the Paul went in to
αυτους, και επι σαββατα τρια διελεγετο αυ-
them, and for sabbaths three reasoned with
τοις απο των γραφων· 3 Διανοιγων και παρατι-
them from the writings; opening and setting
θεμενος, ότι τον Χριστον εδει παθειν και
forth, that the Anointed it was necessary to have suffered and
αναστηναι εκ νεκρων, και ότι ούτος εστιν ὁ
to have been raised out of dead ones, and that this is the
Χριστος Ιησους, ὁν εγω καταγγελλω ὑμιν.
Anointed Jesus, whom I announce to you.
4 Και τινες εξ αυτων επεισθησαν, και προσε-
And some of them were convinced, and joined
κληρωθησαν τῳ Παυλῳ και τῳ Σιλᾳ, των τε
themselves to the Paul and to the Silas, of the and
σεβομενων Ἑλληνων πολυ πληθος, γυναικων
pious Greeks a great number, women
τε των πρωτων ουκ ολιγαι.
and of the chief not a few.
5 Προσλαβομενοι δε οἱ Ιουδαιοι των αγοραιων
Having taken to themselves and the Jews of the market-loungers
τινας ανδρας πονηρους, και οχλοποιησαντες,
some men of evil, and having gathered a crowd,
εθορυβουν την πολιν· επισταντες τε τῃ οικιᾳ
they disturbed the city; having assaulted and the house
Ιασονος, εζητουν αυτους αγαγειν εις τον δημον·
of Jason, they sought them to lead out into the people;
6 μη εὑροντες δε αυτους, εσυρον τον Ιασονα
not having found and them, they dragged the Jason
και τινας αδελφους επι τους πολιταρχης, βοων-
and some brethren to the city-rulers, crying;
τες· Ὁτι οἱ την οικουμενην αναστατωσαντες,
That they the habitable having disturbed,
ούτοι και ενθαδε παρεισιν· 7 οὓς ὑποδεδεκται
these also here are present; whom has received
Ιασων· και ούτοι παντες απεναντι των δογμα-
Jason; and these all against the decrees

entreated them; and conducting them out, asked them ‡ to depart * from the CITY.

40 And going out of the PRISON, ‡ they entered into the house of LYDIA, and having seen the BRETHREN, they exhorted them, and departed.

CHAPTER XVII.

1 And traveling through Amphipolis and Apollonia they came to * THESSALONICA, where was * a Synagogue of the JEWS.

2 And according to his CUSTOM, PAUL ‡ went in to them, and on three Sabbaths reasoned with them from the SCRIPTURES,

3 opening and setting forth, ‡ That the MESSIAH ought to suffer and to rise from the dead, and That "This is the ANOINTED Jesus whom I announce to you."

4 ‡ And some of them believed and adhered to PAUL and ‡ * Silas, and of the PIOUS Greeks a * great Multitude, and of the CHIEF Women not a few.

5 But the JEWS taking some evil-disposed MEN from the MARKET-LOUNGERS, and gathering a crowd, alarmed the CITY; and having assailed the HOUSE of ‡ Jason sought to bring them * forth into the assembly of the PEOPLE;

6 but not finding them, they dragged * Jason and some of the Brethren to the RULERS of the CITY, crying out, ‡ "THESE men who have disturbed the EMPIRE, are come here also;

7 whom Jason has received; and all these oppose the ‡ DECREES of Ce-

* VATICAN MANUSCRIPT.—39. from the CITY. 1. THESSALONICA. 1. a Synagogue of. 4. Silas. 4. great Multitude. 5. forth to the PEOPLE. 6. Jason.

‡ 39. Matt. viii. 31. ‡ 40. ver. 14. ‡ 2. Acts ix. 20; xiii. 5, 14; xiv. 1; xvi. 13; xix. 8. ‡ 3. Luke xxiv. 26, 46; Acts xviii. 28; Gal. iii. 1. ‡ 4. Acts xxviii. 24. ‡ 4. Acts xv. 22, 27, 32, 40. ‡ 5. Rom. xvi. 21. ‡ 6. Acts xvi. 20. ‡ 7. Luke xxiii. 2; John xix. 12.

των Καισαρος πραττουσι, βασιλεα λεγοντες
of Cesar do, a king saying
ἑτερον ειναι, Ιησουν. 8 Εταραξεν δε τον οχλον
another to be, Jesus. Troubled and the crowd
και τους πολιταρχας ακουοντας ταυτα. 9 Και
and the city-rulers having heard these things. And
λαβοντες το ἱκανον παρα του Ιασονος και των
having taken the security from the Jason and the
λοιπων, απελυσαν αυτους. 10 Οἱ δε αδελφοι
rest. they let go them. The and brethren
ευθεως δια της νυκτος εξεπεμψαν τον τε
immediately by the night sent away the both
Παυλον και τον Σιλαν εις Βεροιαν· οἱτινες παρα-
Paul and the Silas into Berea; who hav-
γενομενοι, εις την συναγωγην των Ιουδαιων
ing arrived, into the synagogue of the Jews
απηεσαν. 11 Οὗτοι δε ησαν ευγενεστεροι των
went. These and were more candid of those
εν Θεσσαλονικῃ, οἱτινες εδεξαντο τον λογον
in Thessalonica, who received the word
μετα πασης προθυμιας, το καθ' ἡμεραν ανακρι-
with all promptness, that every day closely
νοντες τας γραφας, ει εχοι ταυτα οὑτως.
scrutinizing the writings, if was these things thus.
12 Πολλοι μεν ουν εξ αυτων επιστευσαν, και
Many indeed therefore out of them believed, and
των Ἑλληνιδων γυναικων των ευσχημονων και
of the Greek women of the honorable and
ανδρων ουκ ολιγοι. 13 Ὡς δε εγνωσαν οἱ απο
men not a few. When but knew those from
της Θεσσαλονικης Ιουδαιοι, ὁτι και εν τῃ Βεροιᾳ
the Thessalonica Jews, that also in the Berea
κατηγγελη ὑπο του Παυλου ὁ λογος του θεου,
was preached by the Paul the word of the God,
ηλθον κακει σαλευοντες τους οχλους. 14 Ευθεως
they came also there stirring up the crowds. Immediately
δε τοτε τον Παυλον εξαπεστειλαν οἱ αδελφοι
and then the Paul sent out the brethren
πορευεσθαι ὡς επι την θαλασσαν· ὑπεμενον δε
to go as to the sea; remained and
ὁ, τε Σιλας και ὁ Τιμοθεος εκει. 15 Οἱ δε καθισ-
the, both Silas and the Timothy there. They but conduct-
τωντες τον Παυλον ηγαγον *[αυτον] ἑως Αθη-
ing the Paul led [him] to Ath-
νων· και λαβοντες εντολην προς τον Σιλαν και
ens; and having received a charge to the Silas and
Τιμοθεον, ἱνα ὡς ταχιστα ελθωσι προς αυτον,
Timothy, that as soon as possible they should come to him,
εξῃεσαν. 16 Εν δε ταις Αθηναις εκδεχομενου
they departed. In and the Athens waiting
αυτους του Παυλου, παρωξυνετο το πνευμα
them of the Paul, was stirred up the spirit
αυτου εν αυτῳ, θεωρουντι κατειδωλον οὖσαν
of him in him, beholding full of idols being

sar, saying that there is another King, Jesus."

8 And they alarmed the CROWD and the RULERS of the CITY, when they heard these things.

9 And having taken SECURITY from Jason, and the REST, they let them go.

10 But the BRETHREN immediately, by * Night, ‡ sent away PAUL and SILAS, to Berea; who, having arrived, went into the SYNAGOGUE of the JEWS.

11 And These were of a more noble disposition than THOSE in Thessalonica, for they received the WORD with All Readiness, DAILY ‡ examining the SCRIPTURES whether these things were so.

12 Many of them, therefore, believed; and of the HONORABLE GREEK WOMEN, and Men not a few.

13 But when the JEWS of THESSALONICA knew That the WORD of GOD was preached by PAUL at BEREA, they came there also exciting * and troubling the CROWDS.

14 ‡ And then the BRETHREN immediately sent PAUL away, as if he were to go towards the SEA; but SILAS and TIMOTHY remained there.

15 And THOSE CONDUCTING PAUL led him to Athens; and having received a charge for SILAS and * TIMOTHY to come to him as soon as possible, they departed.

16 Now while PAUL was waiting for them at ATHENS, ‡ his SPIRIT was stirred within him, on beholding the CITY was † full of idols.

* VATICAN MANUSCRIPT.—10. Night. 13. and troubling the CROWDS. 15. him—omit. 15. TIMOTHY.

† 16. This expression denotes the appearance of Athens to the eye of a stranger. "A person could hardly take his position any where in ancient Athens, where the eye did not range over temples, altars, and statues of the gods almost without number." Bib. Sac. Vol. vi. p. 339

‡ 10. Acts ix. 25; ver. 14. ‡ 11. Luke xvi. 29; John v. 39. ‡ 14. Matt. x 23. ‡ 16. 2 Pet. ii. 8.

την πολιν. 17 Διελεγετο μεν ουν εν τη συνα-
the city. He reasoned indeed then in the syna-
γωγη τοις Ιουδαιοις και τοις σεβομενοις, και
gogue with the Jews and with those being pious, and
εν τη αγορᾳ κατα πασαν ἡμεραν προς τους
in the market during every day with those
παρατυγχανοντας. 18 Τινες δε των Επικουρειων
happening to meet. Some but of the Epicureans
και των Στωικων φιλοσοφων συνεβαλλον αυτῳ·
and of the Stoics philosophers encountered him;
και τινες ελεγον· Τι αν θελοι ὁ σπερμολογος
and some said; What may intend the seed-picker
οὑτος λεγειν; Οἱ δε· Ξενων δαιμονιων δοκει
this to say? They and; Of strange demons he seems
καταγγελευς ειναι· ὁτι τον Ιησουν και την
a proclaimer to be; because the Jesus and the
αναστασιν *[αυτοις] ευηγγελιζετο. 19 Επιλα-
resurrection [to them] he announced glad tidings. Having
βομενοι τε αυτου, επι τον Αρειον παγον ηγα-
taken hold and of him, to the Mars hill they
γον, λεγοντες· Δυναμεθα γνωναι, τις ἡ καινη
led, saying; Are we able to know, what the new
αὑτη ἡ ὑπο σου λαλουμενη διδαχη; 20 Ξενιζον-
this that by thee being spoken teaching? Strange things
τα γαρ τινα εισφερεις εις τας ακοας ἡμων.
for certain thou bringest to the ears of us.
Βουλομεθα ουν γνωναι, τι αν θελοι ταυτα
We desire therefore to know, what may intend these things
ειναι. 21 Αθηναιοι δε παντες και οἱ επιδημουν-
to be. Athenians and all and the sojourning
τες ξενοι, εις ουδεν ἑτερον ευκαιρουν, η λεγειν
strangers, in nothing else spend leisure, than to tell
τι και ακουειν καινοτερον.
something and to hear newer.
22 Σταθεις δε ὁ Παυλος εν μεσῳ του Αρειου
Having stood up and the Paul in midst of the Mars
παγου, εφη· Ανδρες Αθηναιοι, κατα παντα
hill, said; Men Athenians, in all things
ὡς δεισιδαιμονεστερους ὑμας θεωρω· 23 διερ-
as it were worshippers of demons you I perceive; pass-
χομενος γαρ και αναθεωρων τα σεβασματα
ing through for and beholding the objects of worship
ὑμων, εὑρον και βωμον, εν ᾡ επεγεγραπτο·
of you, I found also an altar, in which had been written,
Αγνωστῳ θεῳ. Ὁν ουν αγνοουντες ευσεβειτε,
To an unknown God. Whom therefore not knowing you worship,
τουτον εγω καταγγελλω ὑμιν. 24 Ὁ θεος ὁ
this I announce to you. The God that
ποιησας τον κοσμον και παντα τα εν αυτῳ,
having made the world and all the things in it,

17 He reasoned therefore in the SYNAGOGUE with the JEWS, and with the PIOUS persons; and in the MARKET every Day with THOSE he happened to MEET.

18 But some of the EPICUREAN and * STOIC PHILOSOPHERS encountered him. And some said, "What does this † BABBLER wish to say?" And OTHERS, "He seems to be a Proclaimer of Strange Demons;" Because he announced glad tidings concerning JESUS and the RESURRECTION.

19 And laying hold of him, they led him to the † AREOPAGUS, saying, "Can we know what This NEW Doctrine is, which is spoken by thee?

20 For thou bringest certain strange things to our EARS; we desire, therefore, to know what these things mean."

21 Now all the Athenians, and the RESIDENT STRANGERS among them, spent their time in nothing else but to tell and hear something new.

22 And PAUL standing in the midst of the AREOPAGUS, said, "Athenians, I perceive that in all things you are † extremely devoted to the worship of Demons.

23 For as I passed through, and beheld the OBJECTS of your worship, I found also an Altar on which was an inscription, 'To an Unknown God.' * What therefore you worship without knowing, This I announce to you.

24 That ‡ GOD who made the WORLD and All THINGS in it, he being

* VATICAN MANUSCRIPT.—18. Stoics. 18. to them—*omit*. 23. What therefore you worship without knowing.

† 18. Literally, a *seed-picker*, a name given to crows, etc., and applied to a person who picks up scraps of knowledge, which he imparts to others without sense or purpose, and upon any and every occasion.—*Owen*. † 19. The supreme court of Athens. † 22. Or, more religiously inclined than others.

‡ 24. Acts xiv. 15.

οὑτος ουρανου και γης κυριος ὑπαρχων, ουκ
this of heaven and earth Lord being, not
εν χειροποιητοις ναοις κατοικει, 25 ουδε ὑπο
in hand-made temples dwells. nor by
χειρων ανθρωπων θεραπευεται, προσδεομενος
hands of men is served, wanting
τινος, αυτος διδους πασι ζωην και πνοην και
anything, he giving to all life and breath and
τα παντα· 26 εποιησε τε εξ ἑνος *[αἱματος]
the things all, made and out of one [blood]
παν εθνος ανθρωπων κατοικειν επι παν το προ-
every nation of men to dwell on all the face
σωπον της γης, ὁρισας προστεταγμενους και-
of the earth, having fixed having been appointed sea-
ρους και τας ὁροθεσιας της κατοικιας αυτων·
sons and the fixed limits of the habitation of them;
27 ζητειν τον θεον, ει αραγε ψηλαφησειαν αυτον
to seek the God, if indeed they might feel him
και εὑροιεν, καιτοιγε ου μακραν απο ἑνος ἑκασ-
and might find, and indeed not far from one each
του ἡμων ὑπαρχοντα. 28 Εν αυτῳ γαρ ζωμεν
of us being. In him for we live
και κινουμεθα και εσμεν· ὡς και τινες των καθ'
and are moved and we are: as also some of those with
ὑμας ποιητων ειρηκασι· Του γαρ και γενος
you poets have said; Of the for also offspring
εσμεν. 29 Γενος ουν ὑπαρχοντες του θεου,
we are. Offspring therefore being of the God,
ουκ οφειλομεν νομιζειν, χρυσῳ η αργυρῳ η
not we are bound to suppose, gold or silver or
λιθῳ, χαραγματι τεχνης και ενθυμησεως ανθρω-
stone, a sculpture of art and device of man,
που, το θειον ειναι ὁμοιον. 30 Τους μεν ουν
the Deity to be like. The indeed therefore
χρονους της αγνοιας ὑπεριδων ὁ θεος, τανυν
times of the ignorance overlooking the God, now
παραγγελλει τοις ανθρωποις πασι πανταχου
he commands to the men all in all places
μετανοειν· 31 διοτι εστησεν ἡμεραν, εν ᾑ
to reform; because he established a day, in which
μελλει κρινειν την οικουμενην εν δικαιοσυνῃ,
he is about to judge the habitable in righteousness,
εν ανδρι ᾡ ὡρισε, πιστιν παρασχων πασιν,
by a man whom he appointed, a guarantee having furnished to all,
αναστησας αυτον εκ νεκρων. . . . . 32 Ακουσαν-
having raised him out of dead ones. Having heard
τες δε αναστασιν νεκρων, οἱ μεν εχλευαζον·
and a resurrection of dead ones, these indeed mocked;
οἱ δε ειπον· Ακουσομεθα σου παλιν περι του-
those but said: We will hear thee again about this.

‡ Lord of Heaven and
Earth, ‡ dwells not in
Temples made with hands;
25 nor is he served by
the HANDS of MEN, ‡ as
needing anything; ‡ he
having given to all Life,
and Breath, and all things;
26 and made from One,
Every Nation of Men to
dwell on * the Whole Face
of the EARTH; having de-
termined the appointed
Seasons, and ‡ the FIXED
LIMITS of their HABITA-
TION;
27 ‡ to seek GOD, if per-
haps they might feel after
and find him; ‡ and in-
deed he is not far from
every one of us;
28 for in him we live,
and move, and exist; as
even some of † YOUR OWN
Poets have said, 'For also
we HIS Offspring are.'
29 Being, therefore, the
Offspring of GOD, ‡ we
ought not to imagine a
Gold or Silver or Stone
Sculpture,—a work of Art
and human Skill,—to be
like the DEITY.
30 Therefore, indeed,
overlooking ‡ the TIMES of
IGNORANCE, GOD ‡ now
commands all MEN, in
every place, to reform;
31 because he has es-
tablished a DAY ‡ in which
he is about to judge the
HABITABLE in Righteous-
ness, by a Man whom
he has appointed, having
furnished a Proof to all by
‡ raising him from the
Dead."
32 And when they heard
of the Resurrection of the
Dead, SOME derided, but
OTHERS said, "We will
hear thee * again about
this.

* VATICAN MANUSCRIPT.—26. Blood—omit. 26. The Whole Face of. 32. also again.

† 28. The *Phænomena* of Aratus, and *Cleanthes'* Hymn to Jupiter, contain this quotation. Aratus was a Cilician, one of Paul's countrymen, with whose writings Paul was probably well acquainted.

‡ 24. Matt. xi. 25. ‡ 24. Acts vii. 48. ‡ 25. Psa. l. 8. ‡ 25 Gen. ii. 7; Num. xvi. 22; Job xii. 10; xxvii. 3; xxxiii. 4; Isa. xlii. 5; lvii. 16; Zech. xii. 1. ‡ 26. Deut. xxxii. 8. ‡ 27. Rom. i. 20. ‡ 27. Acts xiv. 17. ‡ 29. Isa. xl. 18. ‡ 30. Acts xiv. 16; Rom. iii. 25. ‡ 30. Luke xxiv. 47; Titus ii. 11, 12, 1 Pet. i. 14; iv. 3 ‡ 31. Acts x. 42; Rom. ii. 16; xiv. 10. ‡ 31. Acts ii. 24.

του. 33 Και οὑτως ὁ Παυλος εξηλθεν εκ μεσου
And thus the Paul went out from midst
αυτων.
of them.
34 Τινες δε ανδρες κολληθεντες αυτῳ, επισ-
Some but men having associated with him, be-
τευσαν· εν οἱς και Διονυσιος ὁ Αρεοπαγιτης,
lieved; among whom also Dionysius the Areopagite,
και γυνη ονοματι Δαμαρις, και ἑτεροι συν
and a woman by name Damaris, and others with
αυτοις. ΚΕΦ. ιη'. 18. 1 Μετα δε ταυτα
them. After and these things
χωρισθεις ὁ Παυλος εκ των Αθηνων, ηλθεν εις
having withdrawn the Paul from the Athens, came into
Κορινθον. 2 Και εὑρων τινα Ιουδαιον ονοματι
Corinth. And having found a certain Jew by name
Ακυλαν, Ποντικον τῳ γενει, προσφατως εληλυ-
Aquila, Pontus by the race, recently having
θοτα απο της Ιταλιας, και Πρισκιλλαν γυναικα
come from the Italy, and Priscilla wife
αυτου, (δια το διατεταχεναι Κλαυδιον χωρι-
of him, (because the to have commanded Claudius to with-
ζεσθαι παντας τους Ιουδαιους εκ της Ῥωμης,)
draw all the Jews from the Rome,)
προσηλθεν αυτοις· 3 και δια το ὁμοτεχνον
he went to them; and because the same trade
ειναι, εμενε παρ' αυτοις· και ειργαζετο· ησαν
to be, he remained with them; and worked; they were
γαρ σκηνοποιοι την τεχνην. 4 Διελεγετο δε εν
for tent-makers the trade. He reasoned and in
τῃ συναγωγῃ κατα παν σαββατον, επειθε τε
the synagogue during every sabbath, persuaded and
Ιουδαιους και Ἑλληνας. 5 Ὡς δε κατηλθον
Jews and Greeks. When but came down
απο της Μακεδονιας ὁ, τε Σιλας και ὁ Τιμοθεος,
from the Macedonia the, both Silas and the Timothy,
συνειχετο τῳ λογῳ ὁ Παυλος, διαμαρτυρομενος
was confined to the word the Paul, earnestly testifying
τοις Ιουδαιοις τον Χριστον Ιησουν. 6 Αντιτασ-
to the Jews the Anointed Jesus. Resisting
σομενων δε αὐτων και βλασφημουντων, εκτινα-
but them and blaspheming, having
ξαμενος τα ἱματια, ειπε προς αυτους· Το αἱμα
shaken the mantles, he said to them; The blood
ὑμων επι την κεφαλην ὑμων, καθαρος εγω,
of you on the head of you, pure I,
απο του νυν εις τα εθνη πορευσομαι. 7 Και
from the now to the Gentiles I will go. And
μεταβας εκειθεν, ηλθεν εις οικιαν τινος ονο-
having removed thence, he went into a house of one by
ματι Ιουστου, σεβομενου τον θεον, οὑ ἡ οικια
name Justus, worshipping the God, of whom the house
ην συνομορουσα τῃ συναγωγῃ. 8 Κρισπος δε ὁ
was adjoining to the synagogue. Crispus but the
αρχισυναγωγος επιστευσε τῳ κυριῳ συν ὁλῳ
synagogue-ruler believed in the Lord with whole
τῳ οικῳ αὐτου· και πολλοι των Κορινθιων ακου-
the house of himself; and many of the Corinthians hear-

33 And thus Paul went
out from the midst of
them.
34 But Some Men ad-
hering to him, believed;
among whom were Diony-
sius the *Areopagite, and
a Woman named Demaris,
and others with them.

CHAPTER XVIII.

1 And after these things
* PAUL withdrawing from
ATHENS, came to Corinth;
2 and having found a
Certain Jew named
‡ Aquila, a native of Pontus, recently come from
ITALY, and his wife Pris-
cilla, (because * Claudius
had COMMANDED All JEWS
to withdraw from ROME,)
he went to them.
3 And because he WAS
of the same trade, he re-
mained with them, ‡ and
* labored; for they were
Tent makers by trade.
4 ‡ And he reasoned in
the SYNAGOGUE Every
Sabbath, and persuaded
Jews and Greeks.
5 ‡ And when SILAS and
TIMOTHY came from MA-
CEDONIA, PAUL was con-
fined to the WORD, ear-
nestly testifying to the
JEWS the ANOINTED Je-
sus.
6 ‡ But when they re-
sisted and blasphemed,
shaking his CLOTHES, he
said to them, "Your
BLOOD be upon your head!
I am pure; from this TIME
I will go to the GENTILES."
7 And having removed
thence he went into the
House of one named Jus-
tus, a worshipper of GOD,
Whose HOUSE was adjoin-
ing the SYNAGOGUE.
8 And ‡ Crispus, the
RULER of the SYNAGOGUE,
believed in the LORD, with
All his HOUSE; and many
of the CORINTHIANS hear-

* VATICAN MANUSCRIPT.—34. Areopagite. 1. he departed from. 2. All JEWS were COMMANDED to withdraw from ROME. 3. they labored.

‡ 2. Rom. xvi. 3; 1 Cor. xvi. 19; 2 Tim. iv. 19. ‡ 3. Acts xx. 34; 1 Cor. iv. 12; 1 Thess. ii. 9; 2 Thess. iii. 8. ‡ 4. Acts xvii. 2. ‡ 5. Acts xvii. 14, 15. ‡ 6. Acts xiii. 45, 46; xxviii. 28. ‡ 8. 1 Cor. i. 14.

οντες επιστευον, και εβαπτιζοντο· 9 ειπε δε ὁ
ing believed, and were dipped; said and the
κυριος δι' ὁραματος εν νυκτι τῳ Παυλῳ· Μη
Lord through a vision by night to the Paul; Not
φοβου, αλλα λαλει και μη σιωπησης· 10 διοτι
fear, but speak and no be silent; because
εγω ειμι μετα σου, και ουδεις επιθησεται σοι
I am with thee, and no one shall attack thee
του κακωσαι σε· διοτι λαος εστι μοι πολυς εν
of the to hurt thee; because people is for me much in
τη πολει ταυτῃ. 11 Εκαθισε τε ενιαυτον και
the city this. He continued and a year and
μηνας ἑξ, διδασκων εν αυτοις τον λογον του
months six, teaching among them the word of the
θεου.
God.

12 Γαλλιωνος δε ανθυπατευοντες της Αχαιας,
Gallio and being proconsul of the Achaia,
κατεπεστησαν ὁμοθυμαδον οἱ Ιουδαιοι τῳ Παυ-
rushed with one mind the Jews to the Paul,
λῳ, και ηγαγον αυτον επι το βημα, 13 λεγοντες·
and led him to the tribunal, saying;
Ὁτι παρα τον νομον οὑτος αναπειθει τους
That from the law this persuades the
ανθρωπους σεβεσθαι τον θεον. 14 Μελλοντος
men to worship the God. Being about
δε του Παυλου ανοιγειν το στομα, ειπεν ὁ
but the Paul to open the mouth, said the
Γαλλιων προς τους Ιουδαιους· Ει μεν ουν ην
Gallio to the Jews; If indeed therefore it was
αδικημα τι, η ῥᾳδιουργημα πονηρον, ω Ιου-
injustice any, or reckless evil, O Jews,
δαιοι, κατα λογον αν ηνεσχομην ὑμων· 15 ει
according to reason I would bear with you; if
δε ζητημα εστι περι λογου και ονοματων και
but a question it is about a word and names and
νομου του καθ' ὑμας, οψεσθε αυτοι· κριτης
of a law of that with you, you will see yourselves; a judge
*[γαρ] εγω τουτων ου βουλομαι ειναι. 16 Και
[for] I of these not choose to be. And
απηλασεν αυτους απο του βηματος. 17 Επιλα-
he drove them from the tribunal. Having
βομενοι δε παντες *[οἱ Ἑλληνες] Σωσθενην
taken hold and all [the Greeks] of Sosthenes
τον αρχισυναγωγον, ετυπτον εμπροσθεν του
the synagogue-ruler, they struck before the
βηματος· και ουδεν τουτων τῳ Γαλλιωνι εμε-
tribunal, and nothing of these the Gallio cared.
λεν. 18 Ὁ δε Παυλος ετι προσμεινας ἡμερας
The and Paul yet having remained days
ἱκανας, τοις αδελφοις αποταξαμενος, εξεπλει
many, to the brethren having bid farewell, sailed out
εις την Συριαν, και συν αυτῳ Πρισκιλλα και
into the Syria, and with him Priscilla and
Ακυλας, κειραμενος την κεφαλην εν Κεγχρεαις·
Aquila, having shaved the head in Cenchrea;
ειχε γαρ ευχην. 19 Κατηντησε δε εις Εφεσον,
he had for a vow. He came and to Ephesus,

ing, believed, and were immersed.

9 ‡ And the LORD said to PAUL, in a Vision by Night, "Fear not, but speak, and be not silent;

10 ‡ for I am with thee; and no one shall attack thee, to HURT thee; for there are many People for me in this CITY.

11 And he remained there a Year and six Months, teaching among them the WORD of GOD.

12 But when Gallio was Proconsul of ACHAIA, the JEWS with one mind assaulted PAUL, and brought him to the TRIBUNAL,

13 saying, "This man persuades MEN to worship GOD contrary to the LAW."

14 And PAUL being about to SPEAK, GALLIO said to the JEWS, ‡ "If indeed it was an act of Injustice or reckless Evil, O Jews! according to Reason I would bear with you;

15 but if it be a Question concerning Doctrine, and Names, and THAT Law which is among you, see you to it, for I will not be a Judge of these things."

16 And he drove them from the TRIBUNAL.

17 And they All took ‡ Sosthenes, the RULER of the SYNAGOGUE, and beat him before the TRIBUNAL. But GALLIO cared for none of these things.

18 And PAUL having remained yet many Days, bidding farewell to the BRETHREN, sailed thence for SYRIA, in company with Priscilla and Aquila; ‡ having shaved his HEAD in ‡ Cenchrea, for he had a Vow.

19 And he came to

* VATICAN MANUSCRIPT.—15. for—*omit.* 17. the GREEKS—*omit.*

‡ 9. Acts xxiii. 11. ‡ 10. Jer. i. 18, 19; Matt. xxviii. 20. ‡ 14. Acts xxiii. 29; xxv. 11, 19. ‡ 17. 1 Cor. i. 1. ‡ 18. Num. vi. 12; Acts xxi. 24. ‡ 18. Rom. xvi. 1.

κακεινους κατελιπεν αυτου· αυτος δε εισελ-
and them he left there; he but having en-
θων εις την συναγωγην, διελεχθη τοις
tered into the synagogue, reasoned with the
Ιουδαιοις. 20 Ερωτωντων δε αυτων επι πλειονα
Jews. Asking and them for longer
χρονον μειναι *[παρ᾽ αυτοις,] ουκ επενευσεν·
a time to remain [with them,] not he consented;
21 αλλ᾽ απεταξατο *[αυτοις,] ειπων· *[Δει με
but he bade farewell [to them,] saying; [It behoves me
παντως την ἑορτην την ερχομενην ποιησαι εις
by all means the feast that coming to keep into
Ἱεροσολυμα·] παλιν *[δε] ανακαμψω προς
Jerusalem;] again [but] I will return to
ὑμας, του θεου θελοντος. *[Και] ανηχθη απο
you, the God willing. [And] he sailed from
της Εφεσου· 22 και κατελθων εις Καισαρειαν,
the Ephesus, and having gone down to Cesarea,
αναβας, και ασπασαμενος την εκκλησιαν,
having gone up, and having saluted the congregation,
κατεβη εις Αντιοχειαν. 23 Και ποιησας χρονον
he went down to Antioch. And having spent time
τινα, εξηλθε, διερχομενος καθεξης, την Γαλα-
some, he went out, passing through in order, the Gala-
τικην χωραν και Φρυγιαν, επιστηριζων παντας
tia country and Phrygia, establishing all
τους μαθητας. 24 Ιουδαιος δε τις Απολλως
the disciples. A Jew and certain Apollos
ονοματι, Αλεξανδρευς τῳ γενει, ανηρ λογιος,
by name, an Alexandrian by the birth, a man eloquent,
κατηντησεν εις Εφεσον δυνατος ων εν ταις
came to Ephesus powerful being in the
γραφαις. 25 Οὑτος ην κατηχημενος την ὁδον
writings. This was having been instructed the way
του κυριου· και ζεων τῳ πνευματι, ελαλει και
of the Lord; and being fervent in the spirit, he spoke and
εδιδασκεν ακριβως τα περι του κυριου,
taught accurately the things concerning the Lord,
επισταμενος μονον το βαπτισμα Ιωαννου.
being acquainted with only the dipping of John.
26 Οὑτος τε ηρξατο παρρησιαζεσθαι εν τῃ συνα-
This and began to speak boldly in the syna-
γωγῃ. Ακουσαντες δε αυτου Ακυλας και
gogue. Having heard and of him Aquila and
Πρισκιλλα, προσελαβοντο αυτον, και ακριβεσ-
Priscilla, took him, and more accu-
τερον αυτῳ εξεθεντο την του θεου ὁδον. 27 Βου-
rately to him explained the of the God way. Wish-
λομενου δε αυτου διελθειν εις την Αχαιαν, προ-
ing and of him to pass through into the Achaia, hav-
τρεψαμενοι οἱ αδελφοι εγραψαν τοις μαθηταις
ing exhorted the brethren they wrote to the disciples
αποδεξασθαι αυτον· ὁς παραγενομενος, συνε-
to receive him; who having arrived, he
βαλετο πολυ τοις πεπιστευκοσι δια της χαρι-
helped much those having believed through the grace.

Ephesus, and left them there; as he entered into the SYNAGOGUE, and reasoned with the JEWS.

20 And when they requested him to remain a longer Time, he did not consent;

21 but bade them farewell, saying, "I will return to you again, ‡GOD willing." And he sailed from EPHESUS;

22 and coming down to Cesarea, and going up, and saluting the CONGREGATION, he went down to Antioch.

23 And having spent some Time there, he departed; going through the COUNTRY of ‡GALATIA and Phrygia, in order, ‡establishing All the DISCIPLES.

24 ‡And a certain Jew named Apollos, a Native of Alexandria, an eloquent Man, being powerful in the SCRIPTURES, came to Ephesus.

25 This person was being instructed in the WAY of the LORD, and being fervent in SPIRIT, he spoke and *also taught accurately the THINGS *concerning JESUS, ‡being acquainted only with the IMMERSION of John.

26 And he began to speak boldly in the SYNAGOGUE. And *Aquila and Priscilla explained to him more accurately the WAY of GOD.

27 And when he was wishing to pass over into ACHAIA, the BRETHREN wrote exhorting the DISCIPLES to receive him; who, having arrived, ‡he greatly assisted THOSE BELIEVERS, by his GIFT;

* VATICAN MANUSCRIPT.—20. with them—*omit*. 21. to them—*omit*. 21. It behoves me to keep the COMING FEAST in Jerusalem—*omit*. 21. but—*omit*. 21. And—*omit*. 25. also taught. 25. concerning JESUS. 26. Priscilla and Aquila.

‡ 21. 1 Cor. iv. 19; Heb. vi. 3; James iv. 15. ‡ 23. Gal. i. 2; iv. 14. ‡ 23. Acts xiv. 22. xv. 32, 41. ‡ 24. 1 Cor. i. 12. iii. 5, 6; iv. 6; Titus iii. 13. ‡ 25. Acts xix. 3. ‡ 27. 1 Cor. iii. 6.

τος. [28] Ευτονως γαρ τοις Ιουδαιοις διακατη-
Strenuously for with the Jews he was discus-
λεγχετο δημοσια, επιδεικνυς δια των γραφων,
sing publicly, proving by the writings,
ειναι τον Χριστον Ιησουν.
to be the Anointed Jesus.

ΚΕΦ. ιθ'. 19.

[1] Εγενετο δε εν τῳ τον Απολλω ειναι εν
It happened and in the the Apollos to be in
Κορινθῳ, Παυλον διελθοντα τα ανωτερικα μερη,
Corinth, Paul having passed through the upper parts,
ελθειν εις Εφεσον. Και εὑρων τινας μαθητας,
to come to Ephesus. And having found some disciples,
[2] ειπε προς αυτους· Ει πνευμα ἁγιον ελαβετε
he said to them; If a spirit holy you received
πιστευσαντες; Οἱ δε ειπον προς αυτον· Αλλ'
having believed; They and said to him; But
ουδε ει πνευμα ἁγιον εστιν, ηκουσαμεν. [3] Ειπε
not even if a spirit holy is, we have heard. He said
τε *[προς αυτους·] Εις τι ουν εβαπτισθητε;
and [to them,] Into what then were you dipped?
Οἱ δε ειπον· Εις το Ιωαννου βαπτισμα. [4] Ειπε
They and said; Into the of John dipping. Said
δε Παυλος· Ιωαννης εβαπτισε βαπτισμα μετα-
and Paul, John dipped a dipping of refor-
νοιας, τῳ λαῳ λεγων, εις τον ερχομενον μετ'
mation, to the people saying, into him coming after
αυτον ἱνα πιστευσωσι· τουτ' εστιν, εις τον
him that they should believe; that is, into the
Ιησουν. [5] Ακουσαντες δε εβαπτισθησαν εις το
Jesus. Having heard and they were dipped into the
ονομα του κυριου Ιησου. [6] Και επιθεντος
name of the Lord Jesus. And having placed
αυτοις του Παυλου τας χειρας, ηλθε το πνευμα
to them the Paul the hands, came the spirit
το ἁγιον επ' αυτους, ελαλουν τε γλωσσαις και
the holy upon them, they spoke and with tongues and
προεφητευον. [7] Ησαν δε οἱ παντες ανδρες ὡσει
prophesied. Were and the all men about
δεκαδυο. [8] Εισελθων δε εις την συναγωγην,
twelve. Having entered and into the synagogue,
επαρρησιαζετο, επι μηνας τρεις διαλεγομενος
he spoke freely, for months three reasoning
και πειθων *[τα] περι της βασιλειας του
and persuading [the things] concerning the kingdom of the
θεου. [9] Ὡς δε τινες εσκληρυνοντο και ηπει-
God. When and some were hardened and disbe-
θουν, κακολογουντες την ὁδον ενωπιον του
lieved, speaking evil of the way in presence of the

28 for he strenuously discussed with the JEWS in public, ‡ proving by the SCRIPTURES that Jesus is the MESSIAH.

CHAPTER XIX.

1 And it happened, while ‡ APOLLOS was in Corinth, Paul, having passed through the UPPER Parts, came to *Ephesus; and having found Some Disciples,

2 he said to them, "Have you received the holy Spirit since you believed?" And THEY said to him, ‡ "We have not even heard whether there be any holy Spirit."

3 And he said, "Into what then were you immersed?" And THEY said, ‡ "Into JOHN'S IMMERSION?"

4 And Paul said, ‡ "John administered the Immersion of Reformation, saying to the PEOPLE, that they should believe into HIM that was COMING after him, that is, into Jesus."

5 And having heard this, they were immersed ‡ into the NAME of the LORD Jesus.

6 And Paul ‡ putting his *Hands on them, the HOLY SPIRIT came on them, and ‡ they spoke with Tongues and prophesied.

7 And ALL the Men were about twelve.

8 And having entered the SYNAGOGUE, he spoke boldly for three Months, reasoning and persuading ‡ about the KINGDOM of GOD.

9 But when some were hardened, and disbelieved, speaking evil of the WAY

* VATICAN MANUSCRIPT.—1. Ephesus, and found Certain Disciples; and he said to them. 3. to them—*omit.* 6. Hands. 8. the things—*omit.*

‡ 28. Acts ix. 22; xvii. 3; ver. 5. ‡ 1. 1 Cor. i. 12; iii. 5, 6. ‡ 2. Acts viii. 16. ‡ 3. Acts xviii. 25. ‡ 4. Matt. iii. 11; John i. 15, 27, 30; Acts i. 5; xi. 16; xiii. 24, 25. ‡ 5. Acts viii. 16. ‡ 6. Acts vi. 6; viii. 17. ‡ 6. Acts ii. 4; x. 46. ‡ 8. Acts xvii. 2; xviii. 4. ‡ 8. Acts i. 3; xxviii. 23.

πληθους, αποστας απ' αυτων, αφωρισε τους
multitude, having departed from them, he separated the
μαθητας, καθ' ἡμεραν διαλεγομενος εν τη
disciples, every day reasoning in the
σχολη Τυραννου *[τινος.] 10 Τουτο δε εγενετο
school of Tyrannus [one.] This and was done
επι ετη δυο, ὡστε παντας τους κατοικουντες
for years two, so that all the dwellers
την Ασιαν ακουσαι τον λογον του κυριου, Ιου-
the Asia to hear the word of the Lord, Jews
δαιους τε και Ἑλληνας. 11 Δυναμεις τε ου τας
both and Greeks. Miracles and not the
τυχουσας εποιει ὁ θεος δια των χειρων
common ones did the God through the hands
Παυλου· 12 ὡστε και επι τους ασθενουντας
of Paul; so that even to those being sick
επιφερεσθαι απο του χρωτος αυτου σουδαρια η
to be brought from the skin of him napkins or
σιμικινθια, και απαλλασσεσθη απ' αυτων τας
aprons, and to be set free from them the
νοσους, τα τε πνευματα τα πονηρα εκπορευεσ-
diseases, the and spirits the evil to be cast
θαι.
out.
13 Επεχειρησαν δε τινες απο των περιερχο-
Took in hand and some from of those going
μενων Ιουδαιων εξορκιστων ονομαζειν επι τους
about Jews exorcists to name on those
εχοντας τα πνευματα τα πονηρα το ονομα του
having the spirits the evil the name of the
κυριου Ιησου, λεγοντες· Ὁρκιζω ὑμας τον
Lord Jesus, saying; I adjure you the
Ιησουν, ὁν ὁ Παυλος κηρυσσει. 14 Ησαν δε
Jesus, whom the Paul preaches. Were and
τινες υἱοι Σκευα Ιουδαιου αρχιερεως επτα, οἱ
some sons of Sceva a Jew a high-priest seven, who
τουτο ποιουντες. 15 Αποκριθεν δε το πνευμα το
this were doing. Answering and the spirit the
πονηρον ειπε· Τον Ιησουν γινωσκω, και τον
evil said; The Jesus I know, and the
Παυλον επισταμαι· ὑμεις δε τινες εστε; 16 και
Paul I am acquainted with; you but who are? and
εφαλλομενος επ' αυτους ὁ ανθρωπος, εν 'ῳ ην
leaping on them the man, in which was
το πνευμα το πονηρον, και κατακυριευσας
the spirit the evil. and having overcome
αυτων, ισχυσε κατ' αυτων, ὡστε γυμνους και
them, prevailed against them, so that naked and
τετραυματισμενους εκφυγειν εκ του οικου
having been wounded to have fled out of the house
εκεινου. 17 Τουτο δε εγενετο γνωστον πασιν
that. This and became known to all
Ιουδαιοις τε και Ἑλλησι τοις κατοικουσι την
Jews both and Greeks those dwelling the
Εφεσον· και επεπεσε φοβος επι παντας αυτους,
Ephesus; and fell a fear on all them,

before the PEOPLE, having departed from them, he separated the DISCIPLES, reasoning daily in the SCHOOL of Tyrannus.

10 ‡ And this was done for two Years, so that All the INHABITANTS of ASIA, heard the WORD of the LORD, both Jews and Greeks.

11 And ‡ God performed EXTRAORDINARY Miracles by the HANDS of Paul;

12 ‡ so that Napkins or Aprons were brought from him to the SICK, and the DISEASES departed from them, and the EVIL SPIRITS were cast out.

13 ‡ And some of the TRAVELING Jewish exorcists ‡ undertook to name the NAME of the LORD Jesus over THOSE HAVING EVIL SPIRITS, saying, "I adjure you by JESUS whom PAUL preaches."

14 And there were some * Seven Sons of One Sceva, a Jewish High-priest, who did so.

15 But the EVIL SPIRIT answering, * said to them, "Jesus indeed I know, and Paul I know, but who are you?"

16 And the MAN in whom the EVIL SPIRIT was leaped on them, and having overcome * them, prevailed against them, so that they fled out of that HOUSE naked and wounded.

17 And this became known to ALL, both Jews and GREEKS, dwelling in Ephesus; ‡ and fear fell

* VATICAN MANUSCRIPT.—9. one—*omit*. 14. Seven Sons of One Sceva. 15. said to them, JESUS indeed I know, and. 16. them both, and prevailed.

‡ 10. Acts xx. 31. ‡ 11 Mark xvi. 20; Acts xiv. 3. ‡ 12. Acts v. 15; See 2 Kings iv. 29. ‡ 13. Matt. xii. 27. ‡ 13. See Matt. ix. 38; Luke ix. 49. ‡ 17. Luke i. 65; vii. 16; Acts ii. 43; v. 5, 11.

και εμεγαλυνετο το ονομα του κυριου Ιησου.
and was magnified the name of the Lord Jesus.
18 Πολλοι τε των πεπιστευκοτων ηρχοντο εξο-
Many and of those having believed came con-
μολογουμενοι και αναγγελλοντες τας πραξεις
fessing and declaring the deeds
αὐτων. 19 Ἱκανοι δε των τα περιεργα πραξαν-
of them. Many and of those the magical arts practis-
των, συνενεγκαντες τας βιβλους, κατεκαιον
ing, having brought together the books, burned
ενωπιον παντων· και συνεψηφισαν τας τιμας
in presence of all; and they computed the prices
αυτων, και εὗρον αργυριου μυριαδας πεντε.
of them, and found pieces of silver myriads five.
20 Οὕτω κατα κρατος ὁ λογος του κυριου
Thus according to power the word of the Lord
ηυξανε και ισχυεν. 21 Ὡς δε επληρωθη ταυτα,
grew and prevailed. When and was fulfilled these things,
εθετο ὁ Παυλος εν τῳ πνευματι, διελθων
was disposed the Paul in the spirit, having passed through
την Μακεδονιαν και Αχαιαν, πορευεσθαι εις
the Macedonia and Achaia, to go into
Ἱερουσαλημ, ειπων· Ὁτι μετα το γενεσθαι με
Jerusalem, saying; That after the to be come me
εκει, δει με και Ῥωμην ιδειν. 22 Αποστειλας
there, it behoves me also Rome to see. Having sent
δε εις την Μακεδονιαν δυο των διακονουντων
and into the Macedonia two of those ministering
αυτῳ, Τιμοθεον και Εραστον, αυτος επεσχε
to him, Timothy and Erastus, he remained
χρονον εις την Ασιαν. 23 Εγενετο δε κατα τον
a time in the Asia. It happened and during the
καιρον εκεινον ταραχος ουκ ολιγος περι της
season that a tumult not small concerning the
ὁδου.
way.
24 Δημητριος γαρ τις ονοματι, αργυροκοπος,
Demetrius for a certain by name, a silversmith,
ποιων ναους *[αργυρους] Αρτεμιδος, παρειχετο
making temples [of silver] for Diana, brought
τοις τεχνιταις εργασιαν ουκ ολιγην. 25 Οὓς
to the workmen gain not a little. Whom
συναθροισας, και τους περι τα τοιαυτα εργα-
having brought together, and those about the such like work-
τας, ειπεν· Ανδρες, επιστασθε, ὁτι εκ ταυ-
men, said; Men. you know, that out of this
της της εργασιας ἡ ευπορια ἡμων εστι· 26 και
the work the wealth of us is; and
θεωρειτε και ακουετε, ὁτι ου μονον Εφεσου,
you see and you hear, that not only of Ephesus,

on them all, and the NAME
of the LORD Jesus was
magnified.
18 And MANY of those
who BELIEVED, came,
confessing and declaring
their DEEDS.
19 And many of THOSE
PRACTISING MAGICAL
ARTS, having brought to-
gether their BOOKS, burnt
them before all; and they
computed the value of
them, and found it to be
fifty thousand pieces of
Silver.
20 Thus the WORD of
* the LORD powerfully in-
creased and prevailed.
21 ‡ And when these
things were accomplished,
‡ PAUL was disposed by
the SPIRIT, having passed
through Macedonia and
Achaia, to go to Jerusalem,
saying, "After I have
BEEN there, ‡ I must also
see Rome."
22 And having sent two
of ‡ THOSE who MINIS-
TERED to him, Timothy
and Erastus, into Macedo-
nia, he remained for a
Time in ASIA.
23 And ‡ there occurred,
during that PERIOD, no
small Tumult concerning
‡ that WAY.
24 For a certain man,
named Demetrius, a Sil-
versmith, making † silver
Temples of Diana afforded
‡ no * Small Gain to the
WORKMEN.
25 whom he having as-
sembled, with THOSE em-
ployed about the LIKE BU-
SINESS, said, "Men, you
know That from This WORK
is our WEALTH;
26 and you see and hear,
That not only at Ephesus

* VATICAN MANUSCRIPT.—20. the LORD. 24. silver—*omit.* 24. Small Gain.

† 24. Portable representations of this temple, which were bought by strangers as matters of curiosity, and probably of devotion. The temple of Diana was raised at the expense of all Asia Minor, and yet was 220 years in building, before it was brought to its sum of perfection. It was in length 425 feet, by 228 in breadth, and was beautified by 127 columns, which were made at the expense of so many kings; and was adorned with the most beautiful statues.—*Clarke.*

‡ 21. Rom. xv. 25; Gal. ii. 1. ‡ 21. Acts xx. 22. ‡ 21. Acts xviii. 21; xxiii. 11. Rom. xv. 24—28. ‡ 22. Acts xiii. 5. ‡ 23. 2 Cor. i. 8. ‡ 23. See Acts ix. 2. ‡ 24. Acts xvi. 16, 19.

αλλα σχεδον πασης της Ασιας ὁ Παυλος οὑτος
but almost all the Asia the Paul this
πεισας μετεστησεν ἱκανον οχλον, λεγων,
having persuaded misled large a crowd, saying,
ὁτι ουκ εισι θεοι οἱ δια χειρων γινομενοι. 27 Ου
that not are gods those by hands being made. Not
μονον δε τουτο κινδυνευει ἡμιν το μερος εις
only and this in danger to us the craft into
απελεγμον ελθειν· αλλα και το της μεγαλης
contempt to come; but also that the great
θεας Αρτεμιδος ἱερον εις ουδεν λογισθηναι,
goddess Diana temple into nothing to be despised,
μελλειν τε και καθαιρεισθαι την μεγαλειοτητα
to be about and also to be destroyed the magnificence
αυτης, ἡν ὁλη ἡ Ασια και ἡ οικουμενη σεβεται.
of her, which whole the Asia and the habitable worships.
28 Ακουσαντες δε, και γενομενοι πληρεις θυμου,
Having heard and, and having become full of wrath,
εκραζον, λεγοντες· Μεγαλη ἡ Αρτεμις Εφεσιων.
they cried out, saying; Great the Diana of Ephesians.
29 Και επλησθη ἡ πολις *[ὁλη] της συγχυσεως·
And was filled the city [whole] the confusion;
ὡρμησαν τε ὁμοθυμαδον εις το θεατρον, συναρ-
they rushed and with one mind into the theatre, having
πασαντες Γαιον και Αρισταρχον Μακεδονας,
seized Gaius and Aristarchus Macedonians,
συνεκδημους Παυλου. 30 Του δε Παυλου βου-
fellow-travelers of Paul. The and Paul wish-
λομενου εισελθειν εις τον δημον, ουκ ειων
ing to enter into the assembly of the people, not suffered
αυτον οἱ μαθηται. 31 Τινες δε και των Ασιαρ-
him the disciples. Some and even of the rulers of
χων οντες αυτῳ φιλοι, πεμψαντες προς αυτον,
Asia being to him friends, having sent to him,
παρεκαλουν μη δουναι ἑαυτον εις το θεατρον.
besought not to venture himself into the theatre.
32 Αλλοι μεν ουν αλλο τι εκραζον· ην γαρ ἡ
Some indeed therefore some thing cried; was for the
εκκλησια συγκεχυμενη, και οἱ πλειους ουκ
assembly having been confused, and the greater not
ηδεισαν, τινος ἑνεκεν συνεληλυθεισαν. 33 Εκ
knew, for what purpose they were come together. Out of
δε του οχλου προεβιβασαν Αλεξανδρον, προ-
and the crowd they pushed forward Alexander, thrust-
βαλοντων αυτον των Ιουδαιων· ὁ δε Αλεξαν-
ing forward him the Jews; the and Alexan-
δρος κατασεισας την χειρα, ηθελεν απολογεισ-
der having waved the hand, wished to defend himself
θαι τῳ δημῳ. 34 Επιγνοντες δε ὁτι Ιου-
in the assembly of the people. Knowing but that a

but almost All ASIA, this PAUL has persuaded and turned aside Many People, saying, That ‡ THEY are not Gods which are MADE by Hands.

27 And not only This WORK of ours is in danger of being brought into contempt, but also that the TEMPLE of the GREAT Goddess Diana should be despised, and her GRANDEUR destroyed, whom All ASIA and the HABITABLE worships."

28 And having heard this, they were full of Wrath, and cried out, saying, "Great is the DIANA of the Ephesians."

29 And the CITY was filled with Confusion; and having seized ‡ Gaius and ‡ Aristarchus, Macedonians, Paul's Fellow-travelers, they rushed with one mind into the THEATRE.

30 And * PAUL desiring to enter the THEATRE, the DISCIPLES did not permit him.

31 And some even of the † ASIARCHS, who were his Friends, sent to him, advising him not to venture into the THEATRE.

32 Some therefore cried one thing, and some another; for the ASSEMBLY was confused, and the GREATER part did not know why they were come together.

33 And they pushed Alexander out of the CROWD, the JEWS thrusting him forward. And ‡ ALEXANDER ‡ having waved the HAND wished to defend himself in the ASSEMBLY OF THE PEOPLE.

34 But knowing that he

* VATICAN MANUSCRIPT.—29. Whole—*omit*. 30. Paul.

† 31. These persons presided over religious observances and the public games. They were ten in number, chosen by the cities from persons of wealth and influence, and approved by the proconsul. One of them styled the chief Asiarch resided at Ephesus; the others were his associates and advisers.

‡ 26. Psa. cxv. 4; Isa. xliv. 10—20; Jer. x. 3. ‡ 29. Rom. xvi. 23; 1 Cor. i. 14. ‡ 29. Acts xx. 4; xxvii. 2; Col. iv. 10; Philemon 24. ‡ 33. 1 Tim. i. 20; 2 Tim. iv. 14. ‡ 33. Acts xii. 17.

δαιος εστι, φωνη εγενετο μια εκ παντων, ὡς
Jew he is, voice came one from all, about
επι ὡρας δυο κραζοντων· Μεγαλη ἡ Αρτεμις
for hours two crying; Great the Diana
Εφεσιων. [35] Κατασειλας δε ὁ γραμματευς τον
of Ephesians. Having stilled and the scribe the
οχλον, φησιν· Ανδρες Εφεσιοι, τις γαρ εστιν
crowd, he said; Men Ephesians, what for is
ανθρωπος, ὁς ου γινωσκει την Εφεσιων πολιν
man, who not knows the Ephesians city
νεωκορον ουσαν της μεγαλης Αρτεμιδος και
temple-keeper being of the great Diana and
του Διοπετους; [36] Αναντιῤῥητων ουν οντων
of that fallen from Jupiter? Cannot be denied therefore being
τουτων, δεον εστιν ὑμας κατεσταλμενους
these things, necessary it is you having been quiet
ὑπαρχειν, και μηδεν προπετες πραττειν.
to be, and nothing rashly to do.
[37] Ηγαγετε γαρ τους ανδρας τουτους, ουτε
You brought for the men these, neither
ἱεροσυλους, ουτε βλασφημουντας την θεον
temple-robbers, nor blasphemers of the goddess
ὑμων· [38] Ει μεν ουν Δημητριος και οἱ συν
of you; If indeed therefore Demetrius and those with
αυτῳ τεχνιται εχουσι προς τινα λογον, αγοραιοι
him workmen have against any a word, courts
αγονται, και ανθυπατοι εισιν· εγκαλειτωσαν
are held, and proconsuls are; let them accuse
αλληλοις. [39] Ει δε τι περι ἑτερων επιζη-
each other. If but anything about other things you in-
τειτε, εν τῃ εννομῳ εκκλησιᾳ επιλυθησεται.
quire, in the lawful assembly it shall be settled.
[40] Και γαρ κινδυνευομεν εγκαλεισθαι στασεως
Even for we are in danger to be accused of tumult
περι της σημερον, μηδενος αιτιου ὑπαρχον-
concerning the day, not one cause being,
τος, περι οὑ δυνησομεθα αποδουναι λογον της
about which we are able to give a reason for the
συστροφης ταυτης. [41] Και ταυτα ειπων, απε-
gathering this. And these having said, he dis-
λυσε την εκκλησιαν.
missed the assembly.

ΚΕΦ. κ'. 20.

[1] Μετα δε το παυσασθαι τον θορυβον, προσ-
After and the to be restrained the tumult, having
καλεσαμενος ὁ Παυλος τους μαθητας, και ασπα-
called to the Paul the disciples, and having
σαμενος, εξηλθε πορευθηναι εις την Μακεδονιαν.
embraced, he went out to go into the Macedonia.
[2] Διελθων δε τα μερη εκεινα, και παρακα-
Having passed through and the parts those, and having ex-
λεσας αυτους λογῳ πολλῳ, ηλθεν εις την
horted them with a word great, he went into the

was a Jew, one Voice came from all for about two Hours, crying, "Great is the DIANA of the * Ephesians!"

35 And the RECORDER having quieted the CROWD, said, "Ephesians! What Man is there who does not know that the CITY of the EPHESIANS is Temple-keeper of the GREAT Diana, and of that which FELL FROM JUPITER?

36 These things, therefore, being indisputable, it is necessary for you to be quiet, and to do nothing rashly;

37 for you have brought these MEN, which are neither Temple-robbers, nor Blasphemers of your GODDESS.

38 If, therefore, Demetrius and the ARTIFICERS with him have a Charge against any one, Courts are held, and there are Proconsuls; let them accuse each other.

39 But if you seek anything * further, it shall be settled in the LAWFUL Assembly.

40 For we are even in danger of being accused about the Tumult of TO-DAY; there being no cause by which we can excuse this CONCOURSE."

41 And having said this, he dismissed the ASSEMBLY.

CHAPTER XX.

1 Now after the TUMULT was allayed, PAUL, * having summoned the DISCIPLES, and embracing them, ‡ departed to go into MACEDONIA.

2 And passing through those PARTS, and exhorting them with many Words, he went into GREECE.

* VATICAN MANUSCRIPT.—34. Ephesians! Great is the DIANA of the Ephesians! And, the. 39. further, it shall be. 1. sent for the DISCIPLES, and exhorting and embracing them, he departed for.

‡ 1. 1 Cor. xvi. 5; 1 Tim. i. 3.

Ἑλλαδα· 3 ποιησας τε μηνας τρεις, γενομενης
Greece; having continued and months three, being formed
αυτῳ επιβουλης ὑπο των Ιουδαιων, μελλοντι
him a plot against by the Jews, being about
αναγεσθαι εις την Συριαν, εγενετο γνωμη του
to sail into the Syria, came a resolution of the
ὑποστρεφειν δια Μακεδονιας. 4 Συνειπετο δε
to return through Macedonia. Went with and
αυτῳ *[αχρι της Ασιας] Σωπατρος Πυῤῥου Βε-
him [as far as the Asia] Sopater of Pyrrhus a Be-
ροιαιος. Θεσσαλονικεων δε, Αρισταρχος και
rean. Of Thessalonians and, Aristarchus and
Σεκουνδος, και Γαιος Δερβαιος και Τιμοθεος·
Secundus, and Gaius of Derbe and Timothy;
Ασιανοι δε, Τυχικος και Τροφιμος. 5 Οὑτοι
Asiatics and, Tychicus and Trophimus. These
προελθοντες εμενον ἡμας εν Τρωαδι· 6 ἡμεις δε
going before awaited us in Troas; we but
εξεπλευσαμεν μετα τας ἡμερας των αζυμων
sailed out after the days of the unleavened cakes
απο Φιλιππων, και ηλθομεν προς αυτους εις την
from Philippi, and came to them into the
Τρωαδα αχρις ἡμερων πεντε, οὑ διετριψαμεν
Troas in days five, where we remained
ἡμερας ἑπτα. 7 Εν δε τῃ μιᾳ των σαββατων,
days seven. In and the first of the sabbaths,
συνηγμενων ἡμων κλασαι αρτον, ὁ Παυλος
having been assembled of us to break bread, the Paul
διελεγετο αυτοις, μελλων εξιεναι τῃ επαυριον·
discoursed to them, being about to depart on the morrow;
παρετεινε τε τον λογον μεχρι μεσονυκτιου.
continued and the discourse till midnight.
8 Ησαν δε λαμπαδες ἱκαναι εν τῳ ὑπερῳῳ, οὑ
Were and lamps many in the upper room, where
ημεν συνηγμενοι. 9 Καθημενος δε τις νεανιας,
we were assembled. Was sitting and a certain youth,
ονοματι Ευτυχος, επι της θυριδος, καταφερο-
by name Eutychus, in the window, * being over-
μενος ὑπνῳ βαθει, διαλεγομενου του Παυλου
powered with sleep deep, discoursing the Paul
επι πλειον, κατενεχθεις απο του ὑπνου, επεσεν
for a longer time, having been overcome from the sleep, fell
απο του τριστεγου κατω, και ηρθη νεκρος.
from the third story down, and was taken up dead.
10 Καταβας δε ὁ Παυλος επεπεσεν αυτῳ, και
Having gone down and the Paul fell upon him, and
συμπεριλαβων ειπε· Μη θορυβεισθε· ἡ γαρ
having embraced said; Not be you troubled; the for
ψυχη αυτου εν αυτῳ εστιν. 11 Αναβας δε, και
life of him in him is. Having come up and, and
κλασας αρτον και γευσαμενος, εφ' ἱκανον τε
having broken bread and having tasted, for a longer time and

3 And having remained three Months, ‡ a Plot being laid for him by the JEWS, as he was about to sail into SYRIA, he resolved to RETURN through Macedonia.

4 And there went with him into ASIA, Sopater, the son of Pyrrhus, a Berean; but ‡ Aristarchus and Secundus of the Thessalonians; and Gaius of Derbe, and ‡ Timothy: and ‡ Tychicus and ‡ Trophimus, Asiatics;

5 *these going before waited for us at Troas.

6 And we sailed out from Philippi, after the ‡ DAYS of UNLEAVENED BREAD, and came to them at ‡ TROAS in five Days; where we continued seven Days.

7 And on ‡ the FIRST day of the WEEK, we having assembled ‡ to break Bread, Paul, intending to depart on the NEXT day, discoursed to them, and continued his SPEECH till Midnight.

8 And there were many Lamps in the ‡ UPPER ROOM where we were assembled.

9 And there was a Certain Youth, named Eutychus, sitting in a WINDOW, being overpowered with deep Sleep; and as PAUL prolonged his discourse, having been overcome by SLEEP, he fell from the THIRD STORY down, and was taken up dead.

10 And PAUL going down, ‡ fell on him, and embracing him, said, ‡ "Be not troubled; for his LIFE is in him."

11 And having come up and broken * Bread, and tasting it, and con-

* VATICAN MANUSCRIPT.—4. as far as ASIA—omit. 5. And these going. 11. BREAD.

‡ 3. Acts ix. 23; xxiii. 12; xxv. 3; 2 Cor. xi. 26. ‡ 4. Acts xix. 29; xxvii. 2; Col. iv. 10. ‡ 4. Acts xvi. 1. ‡ 4. Eph. vi. 21; Col. iv. 7; 2 Tim. iv. 12; Tit. iii. 12. ‡ 4. Acts xxi. 29; 2 Tim. iv. 20. ‡ 6. Exod. xii. 14, 15; xxiii. 15. ‡ 6. Acts xvi. 8; 2 Cor. ii. 12; 2 Tim. iv. 13. ‡ 7. 1 Cor. xvi. 2; Rev. i. 10. ‡ 7. 1 Cor. ii. 42; 1 Cor. x 16; xi. 20. ‡ 8. Acts i. 13. ‡ 10. 1 Kings xvii. 21; 2 Kings iv. 34. ‡ 10. Matt. ix. 24

ὁμιλησας αχρις αυγης, οὑτως εξηλθεν. 12 Ηγα-
having conversed till day-break, so he departed. They
γον δε τον παιδα ζωντα, και παρεκληθησαν ου
brought and the youth living, and were comforted not
μετριως. 13 Ἡμεις δε προελθοντες επι το
a little. We but going before to the
πλοιον, ανηχθημεν εις το Ασσον, εκειθεν μελ-
ship, sailed to the Assos, there in-
λοντες αναλαμβανειν τον Παυλον· οὑτω γαρ ην
tending to take in again the Paul; so for it was
διατεταγμενος, μελλων αυτος πεζευειν. 14 Ὡς
having been arranged, being about himself to go on foot. When
δε συνεβαλεν ἡμιν εις την Ασσον, αναλαβοντες
and he met with us at the Assos, having again received
αυτον ηλθομεν εις Μιτυληνην· 15 κακειθεν απο-
him we came to Mitylene; and thence hav-
πλευσαντες, τῃ επιουσῃ κατηντησαμεν αντικρυ
ing sailed away, on the morrow we came opposite
Χιου. Τῃ δε ἑτερα παρεβαλομεν εις Σαμον·
Chios. In the and another we touched at Samos;
*[και μειναντες εν Τρωγυλλιῳ,] τῃ εχομενῃ
[and having remained in Trogyllium,] in the following
ηλθομεν εις Μιλητον. 16 Κεκρικει γαρ ὁ Παυ-
we came to Miletus. Had determined for the Paul
λος παραπλευσαι την Εφεσον, ὁπως μη γενηται
to sail by the Ephesus, so that not it might be
αυτῳ χρονοτριβησαι εν τῃ Ασιᾳ· εσπευδε γαρ,
for him to spend time in the Asia; he was hastening for,
ει δυνατον ην αυτῳ, την ἡμεραν της πεντηκοσ-
if possible it was for him, the day of the pentecost
της γενεσθαι εις Ἱεροσολυμα. 17 Απο δε της
to be in Jerusalem. From and the
Μιλητου πεμψας εις Εφεσον, μετεκαλεσατο
Miletus having sent to Ephesus, he called for
τους πρεσβυτερους της εκκλησιας. 18 Ὡς δε
the elders of the congregation. When and
παρεγενοντο προς αυτον, ειπεν αυτοις· Ὑμεις
they were come to him, he said to them; You
επιστασθε, απο πρωτης ἡμερας αφ᾽ ἡς επεβην
know, from first day in which I entered
εις την Ασιαν, πως μεθ᾽ ὑμων τον παντα χρονον
into the Asia, how with you the whole time
εγενομην, 19 δουλευων τῳ κυριῳ μετα πασης
I was, serving the Lord with all
ταπεινοφροσυνης και δακρυων και πειρασμων,
lowliness and tears and temptations,
των συμβαντων μοι εν ταις επιβουλαις των
of those having happened to me by the plots of the
Ιουδαιων· 20 ὡς ουδεν ὑπεστειλαμην των συμ-
Jews; how nothing I kept back of that being
φεροντων, του μη αναγγειλαι ὑμιν και διδαξαι
profitable, the not to declare to you and to teach
ὑμας δημοσιᾳ και κατ᾽ οικους· 21 διαμαρτυρομε-
you publicly and in houses; earnestly testifying

versed for a long time, even till Day-break, he so departed.
12 And they brought the YOUTH alive, and were not a little comforted.
13 But we, having gone before to the SHIP, sailed to Assos, there intending to take PAUL in again; for it was so arranged, he being about to go by land.
14 And when he met us at Assos, we received him, and came to Mitylene.
15 And sailing thence, on the NEXT day we came opposite to Chios; and on *the NEXT we arrived at Samos; and having remained at Trogyllium, on the FOLLOWING we came to Miletus.
16 For PAUL had determined to sail by EPHESUS, that it might not be necessary for him to spend time in ASIA; ‡ for he was hastening, if it were possible for him, ‡ to be at Jerusalem on ‡ the DAY of PENTECOST.
17 But sending from MILETUS to Ephesus, he called to him the ELDERS of the CONGREGATION.
18 And when they were come to him, he said to them, "You know, ‡ from the First Day in which I came into ASIA, how I was the WHOLE Time with you,
19 serving the LORD with all humility, and with Tears, and THOSE Trials which happened to me ‡ by the PLOTS of the JEWS;
20 how ‡ I kept back NOTHING that was PROFITABLE; neglecting not to declare to you and to teach you publicly, and at your Houses;
21 earnestly testifying

* VATICAN MANUSCRIPT.—15. in the EVENING we arrived. 15. and remained at Trogyllium—omit.

‡ 16. Acts xviii. 21; xix. 21; xxi. 4, 12. ‡ 16. Acts xxiv. 17. ‡ 16. Acts ii. 1; 1 Cor. xvi. 8. ‡ 18. Acts xviii. 19; xix. 1, 10. ‡ 19. verse 3. ‡ 20. verse 27.

νος Ιουδαιοις τε και Ἑλλησι την εις τον θεον
to Jews both and Greeks the towards the God
μετανοιαν, και πιστιν την εις τον κυριον ἡμων
reformation, and faith that towards the Lord of us
Ιησουν Χριστον. 22 Και νυν ιδου, δεδεμενος
Jesus Anointed. And now lo, having been bound
εγω τῳ πνευματι, πορευομαι εις Ἱερουσαλημ,
I in the spirit, to go to Jerusalem,
τα εν αυτῃ συναντησοντα μοι μη ειδως,
the things in her shall be happening to me not knowing.
23 πλην ὁτι το πνευμα το ἁγιον κατα πολιν
except that the spirit the holy every city
διαμαρτυρεται μοι, λεγον, ὁτι δεσμα με και
witnesses to me, saying, that bonds me and
θλιψεις μενουσιν. 24 Αλλ᾽ ουδενος λογον ποιου-
afflictions await. But of no account I make,
μαι, ουδε εχω την ψυχην μου τιμιαν εμαυτῳ,
nor I the life of me valuable to myself,
ὡς τελειωσαι τον δρομον μου *[μετα χαρας,]
so that to finish the course of me [with joy,]
και την διακονιαν ἡν ελαβον παρα του κυριου
and the service which I received from the Lord
Ιησου, διαμαρτυρασθαι τα ευαγγελιον της
Jesus, to earnestly declare the glad tidings of the
χαριτος του θεου. 25 Και νυν ιδου, εγω οιδα,
favor of the God. And now lo, I know,
ὁτι ουκετι οψεσθε το προσωπον μου ὑμεις παν-
that no longer will see the face of me you all,
τες, εν οἱς διηλθον κηρυσσων την βασιλειαν
among whom I have gone about proclaiming the kingdom
*[του θεου.] 26 Διο μαρτυρομαι ὑμιν εν τῃ
[of the God.] Therefore I testify to you in the
σημερον ἡμερᾳ, ὁτι καθαρος εγω απο του
this day, that clean I from the
αἱματος παντων· 27 ου γαρ ὑπεστειλαμην του
blood of all; not for I kept back of the
μη αναγγειλαι ὑμιν πασαν την βουλην του
not to declare to you all the will of the
θεου. 28 Προσεχετε *[ουν] ἑαυτοις και παντι
God. Take heed [therefore] to yourselves and to all
τῳ ποιμνιῳ, εν ᾡ ὑμας το πνευμα το ἁγιον
the flock, in which you the spirit the holy
εθετο επισκοπους, ποιμαινειν την εκκλησιαν
placed overseers, to feed the congregation
του κυριου, ἡν περιεποιησατο δια του αἱματος
of the Lord, which he purchased through the blood
του ιδιου. 29 Εγω γαρ οιδα *[τουτο,] ὁτι εισ-
of the own. I for know [this,] that shall

both to Jews and Greeks, ‡of REFORMATION towards GOD, and THAT Faith which is towards our LORD Jesus Christ.

22 And now behold, ‡being constrained by the SPIRIT, I go to Jerusalem, not knowing the things which will happen to me there;

23 except That ‡the HOLY SPIRIT testifies to me in every City, saying That Bonds and Afflictions await Me.

24 ‡But * of No Account make I LIFE precious to myself, so that I may finish my COURSE, even the SERVICE which I received from the LORD Jesus, earnestly to declare the GLAD TIDINGS of the FAVOR of GOD.

25 And now, behold, ‡I know That you all, among whom I have gone proclaiming the KINGDOM of GOD, will see my FACE no more.

26 Therefore I testify to you THIS Day, That * I am pure from the BLOOD of All;

27 for I kept not back from announcing * All the WILL of GOD to you.

28 ‡Take heed to yourselves, therefore, and to All the FLOCK among whom the HOLY SPIRIT made you Overseers, to feed † the CHURCH of GOD, ‡ which he acquired by the BLOOD of his OWN.

29 For I know, That

* VATICAN MANUSCRIPT.—24. of No Account make I LIFE precious to myself. 24. with Joy—*omit.* 25. of GOD—*omit.* 26. I am pure. 27. All the WILL of GOD to you. 28. therefore—*omit.* 28. the CHURCH of GOD. 29. this—*omit.*

† 28. The Common Version and Vatican MS. have been followed in the above rendering. Griesbach, and nearly all modern editors, read "Church of the Lord." The phrase *ecclesia tou Kuriou* nowhere occurs in the New Testament, while *ecclesia tou theou* occurs about ten times in Paul's epistles. There are no less than six different readings of this phrase in the MSS., which have probably arisen from a presumed difficulty in understanding it in connection with the latter part of the sentence—"purchased with his own blood." But read it as it stands in the original, and it still makes good sense, without rejecting the reading of the most ancient MS., and some of the oldest Peshito Syriac copies. The reader can supply the elliptical word after *own*, whether it be *Son*, or *Lamb*, or *Sacrifice*. Thus, "feed the CHURCH of GOD, which he acquired by the BLOOD of his OWN [Son.]

‡ 21. Luke xxiv. 47; Acts ii. 38. ‡ 22. Acts xix. 21. ‡ 23. Acts xxi. 4, 11; 1 Thess. iii. 3. ‡ 24. Acts xxi. 13; Rom viii. 35; 2 Cor. iv. 16. ‡ 25. ver. 38; Rom. xv. 23. ‡ 28. 1 Pet. v. 2. ‡ 28. Eph. i. 7, 14; Col. i. 14; Heb. ix. 12; 1 Pet. i. 19; Rev. v. 9.

ελευσονται μετα την αφιξιν μου λυκοι βαρεις
enter after the departure of me wolves rapacious
εις ὑμας, μη φειδομενοι του ποιμνιου· 30 και
among you, not sparing the flock; and
εξ ὑμων αυτων αναστησονται ανδρες λαλουν-
from yourselves will arise men speaking
τες διεστραμμενα, του αποσπαν τους μαθητας
perverse things, the to draw away the disciples
οπισω αὑτων. 31 Διο γρηγορειτε, μνημονευ-
after them. Therefore watch you, remember-
οντες, ὁτι τριετιαν νυκτα και ἡμεραν ουκ επαυ-
ing, that three years night and day not I
σαμην μετα δακρυων νουθετων ἑνα ἑκαστον.
ceased with tears admonishing one each.
32 Και τανυν παρατιθεμαι ὑμας, *[αδελφοι,] τῳ
And now I commend you, [brethren,] to the
Θεῳ και τῳ λογῳ της χαριτος αυτου, τῳ δυνα-
God and to the word of the favor of him, to that being
μενῳ εποικοδομησαι, και δουναι ὑμιν κληρονο-
able to build up, and to give you an inheri-
μιαν εν τοις ἡγιασμενοις πασιν. 33 Αργυριου η
tance among those having been sanctified all. Silver or
χρυσιου η ἱματισμου ουδενος επεθυμησα·
gold or raiment of no one I coveted,
34 αυτοι γινωσκετε, ὁτι ταις χρειαις μου και
yourselves you know, that the necessities of me and
τοις ουσι μετ᾽ εμου ὑπηρετησαν αἱ χειρες αὑται.
those being with me supplied the hands these.
35 Παντα ὑπεδειξα ὑμιν, ὁτι οὑτω κοπιωντας
All things I pointed out to you, that so laboring
δει αντιλαμβανεσθαι των ασθενουντων,
it is necessary to aid those being weak,
μνημονευειν τε των λογων του κυριου Ιησου,
to remember and the words of the Lord Jesus,
ὁτι αυτος ειπε· Μακαριον εστι μαλλον διδοναι,
that he said; Blessed it is more to give,
η λαμβανειν. 36 Και ταυτα ειπων, θεις
than to receive. And these things having said, having placed
τα γονατα αὑτου, συν πασιν αυτοις προσηυξατο.
the knees of himself, with all those he prayed.
37 Ἱκανος δε εγενετο κλαυθμος παντων· και
Much and was weeping of all; and
επιπεσοντες επι τον τραχηλον του Παυλου,
having fallen on the neck of the Paul,
κατεφιλουν αυτον· 38 οδυνωμενοι μαλιστα
they affectionately kissed him; sorrowing most of all
επι τῳ λογῳ ᾡ ειρηκει, ὁτι ουκετι, μελλουσι
for the word which he spoke, that no more, they are about
το προσωπον αυτου θεωρειν. Προεπεμπον δε
the face of him to see. They accompanied and
αυτον εις το πλοιον.
him to the ship.

after my DEPARTURE ‡ rapacious Wolves will come in among you, not sparing the FLOCK;

30 ‡ and * of you will Men arise speaking perverse things, to DRAW AWAY DISCIPLES after them.

31 Therefore watch, remembering That for three years, by Night and by Day, I ceased not to admonish every one with Tears.

32 And NOW I commend you * to GOD, and to THAT WORD of his FAVOR, which is able to edify, and to give you ‡ an Inheritance among all THOSE who were SANCTIFIED.

33 I have coveted no man's Silver, or Gold, or Apparel;

34 you yourselves know ‡ That these HANDS have served my NECESSITIES, and THOSE who WERE with me.

35 I have showed you in All things, ‡ That by thus laboring you ought to assist the WEAK, and to remember the WORDS of the LORD Jesus, That he said, 'It is more blessed to give than to receive.'''

36 And having said these WORDS, he kneeled, and prayed with them all.

37 And there was much weeping among them all; and falling on PAUL'S NECK, they affectionately kissed him.

38 grieving chiefly for the WORDS which he spoke, That they should see his FACE no more. And they accompanied him to the SHIP.

* VATICAN MANUSCRIPT.—30. of you will men arise. 32. brethren—*omit*. 32. to the LORD, and to THAT WORD.

‡ 29. Matt. vii. 15; 2 Pet. ii. 1. ‡ 30. 1 Tim. i. 20; 1 John ii. 19. ‡ 32. Acts xxvi. 18; Eph. i. 18; Col. i. 12; iii. 24; Heb. ix. 15; 1 Pet. i. 4. ‡ 34. Acts xviii. 3; 1 Cor. iv. 12; 1 Thess. ii. 9; 2 Thess. iii. 8. ‡ 35. Rom. xv. 1; 1 Cor. ix. 12; 2 Cor. xi. 9, 12; xii. 13; Eph. iv. 28; 1 Thess. iv. 11; v. 14; 2 Thess. iii. 8.

ΚΕΦ. κα'. 21.

1 Ὡς δε εγενετο αναχθηναι ἡμας αποσπασθεν-
When and it happened to have sailed us having separated
τας απ' αυτων, ευθυδρομησαντες ηλθομεν εις
from them, having run a straight course we came to
την Κω, τῃ δε ἑξης εις την Ῥοδον, κἀκειθεν εις
the Coos, the and next to the Rhodes, and thence to
Παταρα. 2 Και εὑροντες πλοιον διαπερων εις
Patara. And having found a ship passing over to
Φοινικην, επιβαντες ανηχθημεν. 3 Αναφανεν-
Phenicia, going on board we set sail. Having come in
τες δε την Κυπρον, και καταλιποντες αυτην
view and the Cyprus, and having left behind her
ευωνυμον, επλεομεν εις Συριαν, και κατηχθη-
on the left, we sailed into Syria, and were brought
μεν εις Τυρον· εκεισε γαρ ην το πλοιον απο-
to Tyre; there for was the ship un-
φορτιζομενον τον γομον. 4 Και ανευροντες
loading the freight. And having found
τους μαθητας, επεμειναμεν αυτου ἡμερας ἑπτα·
the disciples, we remained there days seven;
οἱτινες τῳ Παυλῳ ελεγον δια του πνευματος,
these to the Paul said through the spirit,
μη αναβαινειν εις Ἱεροσολυμα. 5 Ὁτε δε εγε-
not to go up to Jerusalem. When and it
νετο ἡμας εξαρτισαι τας ἡμερας, εξελθοντες
happened us to have completed the days, having gone out
επορευομεθα, προπεμποντων ἡμας παντων συν
we went our way, accompanying us all with
γυναιξι και τεκνοις, ἑως εξω της πολεως· και
wives and children, till outside of the city; and
θεντες το γονατα επι τον αιγιαλον, προσηυ-
having placed the knees on the shore, we prayed.
ξαμεθα. 6 Και ασπασαμενοι αλληλους, επεβη-
And having embraced each other, en-
μεν εις το πλοιον· εκεινοι δε ὑπεστρεψαν εις
tered into the ship, they and returned into
τα ιδια. 7 Ἡμεις δε τον πλουν διανυσαντες,
the own. We and the voyage having finished,
απο Τυρου κατηντησαμεν εις Πτολεμαιδα· και
from Tyre we came down to Ptolemais; and
ασπασαμενοι τους αδελφους, εμειναμεν ἡμεραν
having embraced the brethren, we remained day
μιαν παρ' αυτοις. 8 Τῃ δε επαυριον εξελθοντες
one with them. On the and morrow having gone out
ηλθομεν εις Καισαρειαν· και εισελθοντες εις
we came into Cesarea; and having entered into
τον οικον Φιλιππου του ευαγγελιστου, οντος
the house of Philip the Evangelist, being
εκ των ἑπτα, εμειναμεν παρ' αυτῳ. 9 Τουτῳ
out of the seven. we remained with him. To this
δε ησαν θυγατερες παρθενοι τεσσαρες προφη-
and were daughters virgins four being
τευουσαι. 10 Επιμενοντων δε ἡμων ἡμερας
gifted with prophecy. Continuing and of us days

CHAPTER XXI.

1 Now it occurred, when we had separated from them, and had sailed, having run a straight course we came to Coos; and on the FOLLOWING day to RHODES, and thence to Patara.

2 And having found a Ship passing over to Phenicia, going on board we sailed.

3 And arriving in view of CYPRUS, and leaving it on the left, we sailed into Syria, and landed at Tyre; for there the SHIP was to unload its FREIGHT.

4 And having found the DISCIPLES we remained there seven Days; ‡ and these told PAUL, through the SPIRIT, not to go up to Jerusalem.

5 And it happened when we had completed the DAYS, we went our way; they all accompanying us with Wives and Children, till out of the CITY; and ‡ kneeling down on the SHORE, we prayed.

6 And having embraced each other, we entered the SHIP; and they returned to ‡ their OWN homes.

7 And having finished the VOYAGE, from Tyre we went down to Ptolemais, and having embraced the BRETHREN, we remained one Day with them.

8 And departing on the NEXT day we came to Cesarea; and having entered the house of THAT PHILIP ‡ the EVANGELIST, ‡ who WAS one of the SEVEN, we lodged with him.

9 And this man had four Virgin Daughters, ‡ who prophesied.

10 And as we continued there many Days, a Cer-

‡ 4. ver. 12; Acts xx. 23. ‡ 5. Acts xx. 36. ‡ 6. John i. 11. ‡ 8. Eph. iv. 11; 2 Tim. iv. 5. ‡ 8. Acts vi. 5; viii. 26, 40. ‡ 9. Joel ii. 28; Acts ii. 17.

πλειους, κατηλθε τις απο της Ιουδαιας προφη-
many, came down a certain from the Judea a pro-

της ονοματι Αγαβος· 11 και ελθων προς ἡμας,
phet by name Agabus; and having come to us,

και αρας την ζωνην του Παυλου, δησας τε
and having taken the girdle of the Paul, having bound and

αὑτου τας χειρας και τους ποδας, ειπε· Ταδε
of himself the hands and the feet, said; Thus

λεγει το πνευμα το ἁγιον· Τον ανδρα, οὗ
says the spirit the holy; The man, of whom

εστιν ἡ ζωνη αὑτη, οὑτω δησουσιν εν Ἱερουσα-
is the girdle this, so shall bind in Jerusa-

λημ οἱ Ιουδαιοι, και παραδωσουσιν εις χειρας
lem the Jews, and deliver into hands

εθνων. 12 Ὡς δε ηκουσαμεν ταυτα, παρεκα-
of Gentiles. When and they heard these things, entreated

λουμεν ἡμεις τε και οἱ εντοπιοι, του μη ανα-
we both and those of the place, of the not to

βαινειν αυτον εις Ἱερουσαλημ. 13 Απεκριθη δε
go up him to Jerusalem. Answered and

ὁ Παυλος· Τι ποιειτε, κλαιοντες και συνθρυπ-
the Paul; What do you, weeping and breaking

τοντες μου την καρδιαν; εγω γαρ ου μονον
of me the heart? I for not only

δεθηναι, αλλα και αποθανειν εις Ἱερουσαλημ
to be bound, but also to die in Jerusalem

ἑτοιμως εχω ὑπερ του ονοματος του κυριου
in readiness I in behalf of the name of the Lord

Ιησου. 14 Μη πειθομενου δε αυτου, ἡσυχασα-
Jesus. Not being persuaded and of him, we were silent,

μεν, ειποντες· Το θελημα του κυριου γενεσθω.
saying; The will of the Lord let it be done.

15 Μετα δε τας ἡμερας ταυτας αποσκευασα-
After and the days these packing up bag-

μενοι ανεβαινομεν εις Ἱερουσαλημ. 16 Συνηλ-
gage we went up to Jerusalem. Went with

θον δε και των μαθητων απο Καισαρειας συν
and also of the disciples from Cesarea with

ἡμιν, αγοντες παρ' ᾡ ξενισθωμεν, Μνασωνι
us, leading with whom we might lodge, to Mnason

τινι Κυπριῳ, αρχαιῳ μαθητῃ. 17 Γενομενων δε
one a Cyprian, an old disciple. Having arrived and

ἡμων εις Ἱεροσολυμα, ασμενως εδεξαντο ἡμας
of us to Jerusalem, gladly received us

οἱ αδελφοι. 18 Τῃ δε επιουσῃ εισῃει ὁ Παυλος
the brethren. On the and next had entered the Paul

συν ἡμιν προς Ιακωβον· παντες τε παρεγενον-
with us to James; all and were present

το οἱ πρεσβυτεροι. 19 Και ασπασαμενος αυτους,
the elders. And having saluted them,

εξηγειτο καθ' ἑν ἑκαστον, ὡν εποιησεν ὁ θεος
he related one by one, which did the God

εν τοις εθνεσι δια της διακονιας αυτου. 20 Οἱ
among the Gentiles through the service of him. They

tain Prophet, named ‡ Agabus, came down from JUDEA.

11 And coming to us, taking PAUL'S GIRDLE and having bound his * FEET and HANDS, he said, "Thus says the HOLY SPIRIT, ‡ So will the JEWS at Jerusalem bind the MAN who owns this GIRDLE, and deliver him into the Hands of the Gentiles."

12 And when we heard these things, both we and THOSE of that place, entreated him not to GO UP to Jerusalem.

13 But PAUL answered, ‡ "What do you, weeping and breaking My HEART? for I am ready not only to be bound, but also to die at Jerusalem in behalf of the NAME of the LORD Jesus."

14 And he not being persuaded, we were silent, saying, ‡ "Let the WILL of the LORD be done."

15 And after these DAYS, packing up our baggage, we went up to Jerusalem.

16 And some of the DISCIPLES also from Cesarea accompanied us, conducting us to one Mnason, a Cyprian, an Old Disciple, with whom we might lodge.

17 ‡ And on our arriving at Jerusalem, the BRETHREN received us gladly.

18 And on the FOLLOWING day, PAUL went in with us to ‡ James; and all the ELDERS were present.

19 And having saluted them, ‡ he particularly related what things GOD did among the GENTILES by ‡ his MINISTRY.

* VATICAN MANUSCRIPT.—11. FEET and HANDS. he said.

‡ 10. Acts xi. 28. ‡ 11. ver. 33; Acts xx. 23. ‡ 13. Acts xx. 24. ‡ 14. Matt. vi. 10; xxvi. 42; Luke xi. 2; xxii. 42. ‡ 17. Acts xv. 4. ‡ 18. Acts xv. 13 Gal. i. 19; ii. 9. ‡ 19. Acts xv. 4, 12; Rom. xv. 18, 19. ‡ 19. Acts xx. 24.

δε ακουσαντες εδοξαζον τον θεον· ειπον τε
and having heard glorified the God; they said and
αυτῳ· Θεωρεις, αδελφε, ποσαι μυριαδας εισιν
to him, Thou seest, O brother, how many myriads are
Ιουδαιων των πεπιστευκοτων· και παντες ζηλω-
of Jews of those having believed; and all zealots
ται του νομου ὑπαρχουσι. 21 Κατηχηθησαν δε
of the law being. They were informed and
περι σου, ὁτι αποστασιαν διδασκεις απο
concerning thee, that apostacy thou teachest from
Μωυσεως τους κατα τα εθνη παντας Ιουδαιους,
Moses those among the Gentiles all Jews,
λεγων, μη περιτεμνειν αυτους τα τεκνα, μηδε
saying, not to circumcise them the children, nor
τοις εθεσι περιπατειν. 22 Τι ουν εστι; παντως
the customs to walk. What then is it? certainly
*[δει πληθος συνελθειν·] ακουσονται *[γαρ,]
[must a multitude to assemble;] they will hear [for,]
ὁτι εληλυθας. 23 Τουτο ουν ποιησον, ὁ σοι
that thou hast come. This therefore do thou, what to thee
λεγομεν· Εισιν ἡμιν ανδρες τεσσαρες ευχην
we say; Are to us men four a vow
εχοντες εφ' ἑαυτων. 24 Τουτους παραλαβων,
having upon themselves. These having taken,
ἁγνισθητι συν αυτοις, και δαπανησον επ'
be thou purified with them, and be at expense for
αυτοις, ἱνα ξυρησωνται την κεφαλην, και γνω-
them, that they may shave the head, and will
σονται παντες, ὁτι ὡν κατηχηνται περι
know all, that the things they have been informed concerning
σου ουδεν εστιν, αλλα στοιχεις και αυτος τον
thee nothing is, but walkest orderly also himself the
νομον φυλασσων. 25 Περι δε των πεπιστευκο-
law keeping. Concerning but those having be-
των εθνων ἡμεις επεστειλαμεν, κριναντες
lieved of Gentiles we sent word, judging
*[μηδεν τοιουτον τηρειν αυτους, ει μη] φυ-
[nothing such like to observe them, if not] to
λασσεσθαι αυτους το, τε ειδωλοθυτον και το
keep themselves the, both things offered to idols and the
αἱμα και πνικτον και πορνειαν.
blood and strangled and fornication.

26 Τοτε ὁ Παυλος παραλαβων τους ανδρας,
Then the Paul having taken the men,
τῃ εχομενῃ ἡμερᾳ συν αυτοις αγνισθεις εισῃει
on the following day with them being purified entered
εις το ἱερον, διαγγελλων την εκπληρωσιν των
into the temple, announcing the completion of the
ἡμερων του ἁγνισμου, ἑως οὑ προσηνεχθη
days of the purification, till of which they offered
ὑπερ ἑνος ἑκαστου αυτων ἡ προσφορα. 27 Ὡς
in behalf of one of each of them the offering. When
δε εμελλον αἱ ἑπτα ἡμεραι συντελεισθαι, οἱ απο
and were about the seven days to be completed, those from
της Ασιας Ιουδαιοι θεασαμενοι αυτον εν τῳ ἱερῳ,
the Asia Jews having seen him in the temple,

20 And THEY, having heard, glorified GOD, and said to him, "Thou seest, brother, how Many Myriads *there are, among the JEWS, of THOSE who who BELIEVE, and all are ‡ Zealots for the LAW.

21 And they have been informed concerning thee, That thou teachest ALL the JEWS among the GENTILES to apostatize from Moses, telling them not to circumcise their CHILDREN, nor to follow the CUSTOMS.

22 What is it then? They will certainly hear That thou hast come.

23 Do this, therefore, which we say to thee. We have four Men who have a Vow on them;

24 take them, and be purified with them, and be at expense for them, that they may ‡ shave the HEAD; and all will know That those things of which they were informed concerning thee are not correct; but that thou thyself walkest orderly, keeping the LAW.

25 But concerning the BELIEVING GENTILES ‡ we have sent word, judging that they avoid WHAT IS OFFERED TO IDOLS, and BLOOD, and what is Strangled, and Fornication."

26 Then PAUL took the MEN, and on the FOLLOWING Day being purified with them, ‡ entered the TEMPLE, ‡ announcing the COMPLETION of the DAYS of PURIFICATION; till the OFFERING should be offered in behalf of each one of them.

27 But when the SEVEN DAYS were about to be completed, the Jews from Asia seeing him in the

* VATICAN MANUSCRIPT.—20. there are among the JEWS, of THOSE who BELIEVE. 22. the Multitude must assemble—*omit.* 22. for—*omit.* 25. that they observe no such thing, except—*omit.*

‡ 20. Acts xxii. 3; Rom. x. 2; Gal. i. 14. ‡ 24. Num. vi. 2, 13, 18; Acts xviii. 18. ‡ 25. Acts xv. 20, 29. ‡ 26. Acts xxiv. 18. ‡ 26. Num. vi. 13.

συνεχεον παντα τον οχλον, και επεβαλον επ'
stirred up all the crowd, and put on
αυτον τας χειρας, [28] κραζοντες· Ανδρες Ισραηλι-
him the hands, crying; Men Israel-
ται, βοηθειτε· ὑυτος εστιν ὁ ανθρωπος, ὁ κατα
ites, help you, this is the man, who against
του λαου και του νομου και του τοπου τουτου
the people and the law and the place this
παντας πανταχου διδασκων· ετι τε και Ἑλλη-
all everywhere is teaching; besides and also Greeks
νας εισηγαγεν εις το ἱερον, και κεκοινωκε τον
he led into the temple, and has made common the
ἁγιον τοπον τουτον. [29] (Ησαν γαρ προεωρακο-
holy place this. (Were for having seen before
τες Τροφιμον τον Εφεσιον εν τῃ πολει συν
Trophimus the Ephesian in the city with
αυτῳ, ὁν ενομιζον ὁτι εις το ἱερον εισηγαγεν ὁ
him, whom they supposed that into the temple led the
Παυλος.) [30] Εκινηθη τε ἡ πολις ὁλη, και εγενε-
Paul.) Was moved and the city whole, and was
το συνδρομη του λαου· και επιλαβομενοι του
a running together of the people; and having taken hold of the
Παυλου, εἱλκον αυτον εξω του ἱερου· και
Paul, they were dragging him outside of the temple; and
ευθεως εκλεισθησαν αἱ θυραι. [31] Ζητουντων
immediately were closed the gates. Seeking
δε αυτον αποκτειναι, ανεβη φασις τῳ χιλιαρχῳ
and him to kill, went up a report to the commander
της σπειρης, ὁτι ὁλη συγκεχυται Ἱερουσαλημ·
of the band, that whole was in confusion Jerusalem;
[32] ὁς εξαυτης παραλαβων στρατιωτας και ἑκα-
who immediately having taken soldiers and cen-
τονταρχους, κατεδραμεν επ' αυτους. Οἱ δε
turions, ran down upon them. They and
ἱδοντες τον χιλιαρχον και τους στρατιωτας,
seeing the commander and the soldiers,
επαυσαντες τυπτοντες τον Παυλον. [33] Τοτε
ceased beating the Paul. Then
εγγισας ὁ χιλιαρχος επελαβετο αυτου, και
having approached the commander laid hold of him, and
εκελευσε δεθηναι ἁλυσεσι δυσι· και επυνθα-
ordered to be bound with chains two; and inquired,
νετο, τις αν ειη, και τι εστι πεποιηκως.
who it might be, and what it is having been done.
[34] Αλλοι δε αλλο τι εβοων εν τῳ οχλῳ. Μη
Others and another thing were crying in the crowd. Not
δυναμενος δε γνωναι το ασφαλες δια τον θορυ-
being able and to know the certainty through the tumult,
βον, εκελευσεν αγεσθαι αυτον εις την παρεμ-
he ordered to be brought him into the castle.
βολην. [35] Ὁτε δε εγενετο επι τους αναβαθμους,
When and he came on the steps,
συνεβη βασταζεσθαι αυτον ὑπο των στρατιω-
it happened to he carried him by the soldiers
των δια την βιαν του οχλου· [36] ηκολουθει γαρ
through the violence of the crowd; followed for

TEMPLE, stirred up All the CROWD, ‡and laid HANDS on him,

28 exclaiming, "Israelites, help! This is THAT MAN ‡ who TEACHES all men everywhere against the PEOPLE, and the LAW, and this PLACE; and besides he brought Greeks into the TEMPLE, and made this HOLY Place common."

29 (For they had previously seen ‡ Trophimus the EPHESIAN, in the CITY with him, whom they imagined That PAUL had brought into the TEMPLE.)

30 ‡ And all the CITY was moved, and there was a running together of the PEOPLE; and having seized PAUL they dragged him out of the TEMPLE; and the GATES were instantly closed.

31 And while they were seeking to kill HIM, a Report went up to the COMMANDER of the COHORT, That All Jerusalem was in confusion;

32 ‡ who immediately having taken Soldiers and Centurions, rushed down upon them, and THEY, seeing the COMMANDER and the SOLDIERS, ceased beating PAUL.

33 Then the COMMANDER coming near, seized him, and ‡ ordered him to be bound with two Chains; and inquired who he was, and what he has done.

34 And some among the CROWD shouted one thing, and some another; and not being able to ascertain the TRUTH on account of the TUMULT, he ordered him to be led into the CASTLE.

35 But when he was upon the STEPS, it happened that he was borne away by the SOLDIERS, because of the VIOLENCE of the CROWD.

‡ 27. Acts xxvi. 21. ‡ 28. Acts xxiv. 5, 6. ‡ 29. Acts xx. 4. ‡ 30. Acts xxvi 21. ‡ 32. Acts xxiii. 27; xxiv. 7. ‡ 33. ver. 11; Acts xx. 23.

το πληθος του λαου, κραζον· Αιρε αυτον.
the multitude of the people, crying; Lift up him.
37 Μελλων τε εισαγεσθαι εις την παρεμβολην ὁ
Being about and to be led into the castle the
Παυλος, λεγει τῳ χιλιαρχῳ· Ει εξεστι μοι
Paul, he says to the commander; If it is permitted for me
ειπειν τι προς σε; Ὁ δε εφη· Ἑλληνιστι
to say anything to thee? He and said; Greek
γινωσκεις; 38 Ουκ αρα συ ει ὁ Αιγυπτιος, ὁ
understandest thou? Not then thou art the Egyptian who
προ τουτων των ἡμερων αναστατωσας και
before these the days having raised an insurrection and
εξαγαγων εις την ερημον τους τετρακισχιλιους
having led out into the desert the four thousand
ανδρας των σικαριων; Ειπε δε ὁ Παυλος· 39 εγω
men of the Sicarii? Said and the Paul; I
ανθρωπος μεν ειμι Ιουδαιος Ταρσευς, της Κιλι-
a man indeed am a Jew of Tarsus, of the Cili-
κιας ουκ ασημου πολεως πολιτης· δεομαι δε
cia not of a mean city a citizen; I beseech and
σου, επιτρεψον μοι λαλησαι προς τον λαον.
of thee, permit me to speak to the people.
40 Επιτρεψαντες δε αυτου, ὁ Παυλος ἑστως επι
Having permitted and him, the Paul having been set on
των αναβαθμων κατεσεισε τη χειρι τῳ λαῳ·
the steps waved with the hand to the people;
πολλης δε σιγης γενομενης, προσεφωνησε τη
great and silence occurring, he spoke in the
Ἑβραιδι διαλεκτῳ, λεγων·
Hebrew dialect, saying;

ΚΕΦ. κβ'. 22.

1 Ανδρες αδελφοι και πατερες, ακουσατε μου
Men brethren and fathers, hear you of me
της προς ὑμας νυνι απολογιας. 2 Ακουσαντες
the to you now apology. Hearing
δε ὁτι τη Εβραιδι διαλεκτῳ προσεφωνει αυτοις,
and that in the Hebrew dialect he was speaking to them,
μαλλον παρεσχον ἡσυχιαν. Και φησιν· 3 εγω
more they kept silence. And he said; I
μεν ειμι ανηρ Ιουδαιος, γεγεννημενος εν Ταρσῳ
indeed am a man a Jew, having been born in Tarsus
της Κιλικιας; ανατεθραμμενος δε εν τη πολει
of the Cilicia? having been brought up and in the city
ταυτη, παρα τους ποδας Γαμαλιηλ πεπαιδευμε-
this, at the feet of Gamaliel having been taught
νος κατα ακριβειαν του πατρῳου νομου, ζηλω-
with accuracy the ancestral law, a zea-
της ὑπαρχων του θεου, καθως παντες ὑμεις εστε
lot being of the God, even as all you are
σημερον· 4 ὁς ταυτην την ὁδον εδιωξα αχρι
to-day; who this the way I persecuted till

36 for the MULTITUDE
of the PEOPLE followed,
crying, ‡ "Take him
away!"
37 And PAUL being
about to be led into the
CASTLE, he says to the
COMMANDER, "May I be
allowed to say something
to thee?" And HE said,
"Dost thou understand
Greek?
38 Art thou not then
THAT † Egyptian, who
didst before These DAYS,
excite a Sedition, and lead
out into the DESERT FOUR
THOUSAND Men of the
† SICARII?"
39 But PAUL said, ‡ "I
am a Jew, of Tarsus in CI-
LICIA, a Citizen of no In-
considerable City; and I
entreat thee, permit me
to speak to the PEOPLE."
40 And having given
him permission, PAUL,
standing on the STEPS,
‡ waved the HAND to the
PEOPLE; and when there
was Great Silence, he ad-
dressed them in the HE-
BREW Dialect, saying,

CHAPTER XXII.

1 "Men, ‡ Brethren,
and Fathers, hear now
My APOLOGY before you."
2 (And hearing that he
spoke to them in the HE-
BREW Dialect, they kept
greater silence; and he
said,)
3 ‡ "I am a Jew, born
in Tarsus, of CILICIA, but
having been brought up in
this CITY, at the FEET of
‡ Gamaliel, and accurately
instructed in the ANCES-
TRAL LAW; ‡ being a Zea-
lot for GOD, ‡ as you all
are To-day.
4 And I persecuted
This WAY to Death,

† 38. Josephus mentions this Egyptian as having raised a mob of 30,000 men, (or as some think it originally read 4,000.) which he led against Jerusalem, as far as Mount Olivet, but was suddenly dispersed by Felix. † 38. The Sicarii were a body of rebels mentioned by Josephus, Wars b. vii, c. 10, § 1.

‡ 36. Luke xxiii. 18; John xix. 15; xxii. 22. ‡ 38. See Acts v. 36. ‡ 39. Acts ix. 11; xxii. 3. ‡ 40. Acts xii. 17. ‡ 1. Acts vii. 2. ‡ 3. Acts xxi. 39; 2 Cor. xi. 22; Phil. iii. 5. ‡ 3. Acts v. 34. ‡ 3. Acts xxi. 20; Gal. i. 14. ‡ 3. Rom. x. 2.

θανατου, δεσμευων και παραδιδους εις φυλακας
death, binding and delivering into prisons

ανδρας τε και γυναικας, 5 ὡς και ὁ αρχιερευς
men both and women, as also the high-priest

μαρτυρει μοι, και παν το πρεσβυτεριον· παρ'
testifies to me, and all the eldership; from

ὡν και επιστολας δεξαμενος προς τους αδελ-
whom also letters having received to the breth-

φους, εις Δαμασκον επορευομην, αξων και
ren, to Damascus I went, going to lead and

τους εκεισε οντας, δεδεμενους εις Ἱερουσαλημ,
those there being, having been bound into Jerusalem,

ἱνα τιμωρηθωσιν. 6 Εγενετο δε μοι πορευομενῳ
that they might be punished. It happened and to me traveling

και εγγιζοντι τῃ Δαμασκῳ, περι μεσημβριαν
and drawing near to the Damascus, about noon

εξαιφνης εκ του ουρανου περιαστραψαι φως ἱκα-
suddenly out of the heaven to shine round a light great

νον περι εμε· 7 επεσον τε εις το εδαφος, και
about me; fell and on the ground, and

ηκουσα φωνης λεγουσης μοι· Σαουλ, Σαουλ, τι
heard a voice saying to me; Saul, Saul, why

με διωκεις; 8 Εγω δε απεκριθην· Τις ει,
me persecutest thou? I and answered; Who art thou,

κυριε; Ειπε τε προς με· Εγω ειμι Ιησους ὁ
O sir? He said and to me; I am Jesus the

Ναζωραιος, ὁν συ διωκεις. 9 Οἱ δε συν εμοι
Nazarene, whom thou persecutest. Those and with me

οντες το μεν φως εθεασαντο, *[και εμφοβοι
being the indeed light saw, [and terrified

εγενοντο·] την δε φωνην ουκ ηκουσαν του
they were,] the but voice not they heard of the

λαλουντος μοι. 10 Ειπον δε· Τι ποιησω, κυριε;
speaking to me. I said and; What shall I do, O Lord?

Ὁ δε κυριος ειπε προς με· Αναστας πορευου
The and Lord said to me, Having arisen go thou

εις Δαμασκον· κακει σοι λαληθησεται περι
into Damascus; and there to thee it shall be told concerning

παντων, ὡν τετακται σοι ποιησαι. 11 Ὡς δε
all things, which have been appointed for thee to do. As and

ουκ ενεβλεπον απο της δοξης του φωτος εκει-
not I saw from the glory of the light of that,

νου, χειραγωγουμενος ὑπο των συνοντων μοι,
being led by the hand by those being with me,

ηλθον εις Δαμασκον.
I came into Damascus

12 Ανανιας δε τις, ανηρ ευσεβης κατα τον
Ananias and one, a man pious according to the

νομον, μαρτυρουμενος ὑπο παντων των κατοι-
law, being testified to by all the resi-

κουντων Ιουδαιων, 13 ελθων προς με και επισ-
ding Jews, having come to me and having

τας ειπε μοι· Σαουλ αδελφε, αναβλεψον.
stood said to me; Saul O brother, look up.

binding and delivering into Prisons both Men and Women;

5 as the HIGH-PRIEST also *is my witness, ‡ and All the ELDERSHIP, ‡ from whom also receiving Letters to the BRETHREN, I went to Damascus to bring THOSE who WERE there bound to Jerusalem, that they might be punished.

6 ‡ And it occurred, as I was traveling and drawing near to Damascus, about noon, suddenly a great Light from HEAVEN shone around me;

7 and I fell to the GROUND, and heard a Voice saying to me, 'Saul, Saul, why dost thou persecute Me?'

8 And I answered; 'Who art thou, Sir?' And he said to me, 'I am Jesus the NAZARENE, whom thou persecutest.'

9 And ‡ THOSE who WERE with me saw indeed the LIGHT, but they understood not the VOICE of HIM who SPOKE to me.

10 And I said, 'What shall I do, Lord?' And the LORD said to me, 'Arise, and go into Damascus, and there it shall be told thee of all things which are appointed for thee to do.'

11 And as I could not see from the GLORY of that LIGHT, being led by the hand of THOSE who WERE with me, I came into Damascus.

12 And ‡ one Ananias, a pious Man according to the LAW, ‡ having a good tesimony from All the JEWS RESIDING there.

13 coming to me, and standing by, said to me, 'Brother Saul, look up.'

* VATICAN MANUSCRIPT.—5. did bear me witness. 9. and they were terrified—*omit*.

‡ 5. Luke xxii. 66; Acts iv. 5. ‡ 5. Acts ix. 2; xxvi. 10, 12. ‡ 6. Acts ix. 3; xxvi. 12, 13. ‡ 9. Acts ix. 7; Dan. x. 7. ‡ 12. Acts ix. 17. ‡ 12. Acts x. 22. ‡ 12. 1 Tim. iii. 7.

Καγω αυτῃ τῃ ὡρᾳ ανεβλεψα εις αυτον. 14 Ὁ
And I in this the hour looked on him. He
δε ειπεν· Ὁ θεος των πατερων ἡμων προεχειρι-
and said; The God of the fathers of us destined
σατο σε γνωναι το θελημα αὑτου, και ιδειν τον
thee to know the will of himself, and to see the
δικαιον, και ακουσαι φωνην εκ του στοματος
righteous one, and to hear a voice out of the mouth
αυτου· 15 ὁτι εσῃ μαρτυς αυτῳ προς παντας
of him; because thou shalt be a witness for him to all
ανθρωπους ὡν ἑωρακας και ηκουσας. 16 Και
men of what thou hast seen and thou hast heard. And
νυν τι μελλεις; αναστας βαπτισαι, και απο-
now why dost thou delay? having arisen be thou dipped, and wash
λουσαι τας ἁμαρτιας σου, επικαλεσαμενος το
thyself from the sins of thee, having invoked the
ονομα αυτου. 17 Εγενετο δε μοι ὑποστρεψαντι
name of him. It happened and to me having returned
εις Ἱερουσαλημ, και προσευχομενου μου εν τῳ
to Jerusalem, and praying of me in the
ἱερῳ, γενεσθαι με εν εκστασει, 18 και ιδειν
temple, to have been me in an ecstacy, and to see
αυτον λεγοντα μοι· Σπευσον, και εξελθε εν
him saying to me; Do thou hasten, and come out with
ταχει εξ Ἱερουσαλημ· διοτι ου παραδεξονται
speed from Jerusalem; because not they will receive
σου την μαρτυριαν περι εμου. 19 Καγω ειπον·
of thee the testimony concerning me. And I said;
Κυριε, αυτοι επιστανται, ὁτι εγω ημην φυλα-
O Lord, they know, that I was impris-
κιζων και δερων κατα τας συναγωγας τους πισ-
oning and beating in the synagogues those be-
τευοντας επι σε· 20 και ὁτε εξεχειτο το αἱμα
lieving on thee; and when was poured out the blood
Στεφανου του μαρτυρος σου, και αυτος ημην
of Stephen the martyr of thee, and myself was
εφεστως, και συνευδοκων, και φυλασσων τα
having been standing, and approving, and keeping the
ἱματια των αναιρουντων αυτον. 21 Και ειπε
mantles of those killing him. And he said
προς με· Πορευου· ὁτι εγω εις εθνη μακραν
to me; Go thou; for I to nations at a distance
εξαποστελω σε. . . . 22 Ηκουον δε αυτου αχρι
will send thee. They heard and him till
τουτου του λογου, και επηραν την φωνην
this the word, and they raised the voice
αὑτων, λεγοντες· Αιρε απο της γης τον τοιου-
of them, saying; Lift up from the earth the such a
τον· ου γαρ καθηκεν αυτον ζην. 23 Κραυγα-
person; not for it is fit him to live. Crying
ζοντων δε αυτων και ῥιπτουντων τα ἱματια, και
out and of them and tossing up the mantles, and
κονιορτον βαλλοντων εις τον αερα, 24 εκελευσεν
dust throwing into the air, ordered

And in That HOUR I looked
upon him.
14 And HE said, ‡ 'The
GOD of our FATHERS ‡ ap-
pointed thee to know his
WILL, and to ‡ see that
‡ RIGHTEOUS ONE, and ‡ to
hear a Voice from his
MOUTH;
15 ‡ for thou shalt be a
Witness for him to All
Men of ‡ what thou hast
seen and heard.
16 And now, why dost
thou delay? Arising, be
immersed, ‡ and wash thy-
self from thy SINS, ‡ having invoked his NAME.'
17 ‡ And it happened,
when I returned to Jeru-
salem, and was praying in
the TEMPLE, I was in a
Trance,
18 and saw him saying
to me, 'Make haste, and
go quickly out from Jeru-
salem; because they will
not receive * Thy TESTI-
MONY concerning me.'
19 And I said, 'Lord,
they know That I was im-
prisoning and beating in
the SYNAGOGUES THOSE
BELIEVING on thee;
20 ‡ and when the
BLOOD of Stephen, thy
WITNESS, was poured out,
I also was standing by
and consenting, and hav-
ing in charge the MANTLES
of THOSE who KILLED
him.'
21 And he said to me,
‡ 'Go; for I will send thee
to NATIONS far away.'" . .
22 And they heard him
to This WORD, and then
raised their VOICE, saying,
‡ "Take away SUCH a man
from the EARTH, for it is
not fit that he should live."
23 And as they were
crying out, and tossing up
their MANTLES, and throw-
ing Dust into the AIR,

* VATICAN MANUSCRIPT.—18. Thy Testimony concerning me.

‡ 14. Acts iii. 13; v. 30. ‡ 14. Acts ix. 15; xxvi. 16. ‡ 14. 1 Cor. ix. 1; xv. 8. ‡ 14. Acts iii. 14; vii. 52. ‡ 14. 1 Cor. xi. 23; Gal. i. 12. ‡ 15. Acts xxiii. 11. ‡ 15. Acts iv. 20; xxvi. 16. ‡ 16. Acts ii. 38; Titus iii. 5; Heb. x. 22. ‡ 16. Acts ix. 14; Rom. x. 13; 1 Cor. i. 2; 2 Tim. ii. 22. ‡ 17. Acts ix. 26; 1 Cor. xii. 2. ‡ 20. Acts vii. 58. ‡ 21. Acts ix. 15; xiii. 2. 46, 47; xviii. 6; xxvi. 17; Rom. i. 5; xi. 13; xv. 16; Gal. i. 15, 16; ii. 7, 8; Eph. iii. 7, 8; 1 Tim. ii. 7; 2 Tim. i. 11. ‡ 22. Acts xxi. 36; xxv. 24.

ὁ χιλιαρχος εισαγεσθαι αυτον εις την παρεμ-
the commander to lead him into the castle,
βολην, ειπων μαστιξιν ανεταζεσθαι αυτον·
saying with scourges to examine him;
ἱνα επιγνῳ δι' ἡν αιτιαν οὑτως επεφω-
that he might know, on account of what cause thus they were
νουν αυτῳ. 25 Ὡς δε προετειναν αυτον τοις
crying against him. As and they stretched out him with the
ἱμασιν, ειπε προς τον ἑστωτα ἑκατονταρχον ὁ
thongs, said to the standing by centurion the
Παυλος· Ει ανθρωπον Ρωμαιον και ακατακριτον
Paul; If a man a Roman and uncondemned
εξεστιν ὑμιν μαστιζειν; 26 Ακουσας δε ὁ ἑκα-
it is lawful for you to scourge? Having heard and the centu-
τονταρχος, προσελθων τῳ χιλιαρχῳ απηγ-
rion, having gone to the commander reported,
γειλε, λεγων· τι μελλεις ποιειν; ὁ γαρ ανθρω-
saying; what art thou about to do? the for man
πος οὑτος Ῥωμαιος εστι. 27 Προσελθων δε ὁ
this a Roman is. Having come to and the
χιλιαρχος ειπεν αυτῳ· Λεγε μοι, συ Ῥωμαιος
commander said to him; Tell me, thou a Roman
ει; Ὁ δε εφη· Ναι. 28 Απεκριθη τε ὁ χιλιαρ-
art? He and said; Yes. Answered and the comman-
χος· Εγω πολλου κεφαλαιου την πολιτειαν
der; I of a great sum of money the citizenship
ταυτην εκτησαμην. Ὁ δε Παυλος εφη· Εγω
this purchased. The and Paul said; I
δε και γεγεννημαι. 29 Ευθεως ουν απεστησαν
but even have been born. Immediately then went away
απ' αυτου οἱ μελλοντες αυτον ανεταζειν. Και
from him those being about him to examine. And
ὁ χιλιαρχος δε εφοβηθη, επιγνους ὁτι Ῥωμαιος
the commander also was afraid, having ascertained that a Roman
εστι, και ὁτι ην αυτον δεδεκως. 30 Τῃ δε επαυ-
he is, and that he was him having been bound. On the and morrow
ριον βουλομενος γνωναι το ασφαλες, το τι κα-
wishing to know the certainty, that what he
τηγορειται παρα των Ιουδαιων, ελυσεν αυτον,
was accused of by the Jews, he loosed him,
και εκελευσεν συνελθειν τους αρχιερεις και παν
and ordered to come together the high-priests and all
το συνεδριον· και καταγαγων τον Παυλον, εσ-
the sanhedrim; and having led down the Paul, he
τησεν εις αυτους.
stood among them.

ΚΕΦ. κγ'. 23.

1 Ατενισας δε ὁ Παυλος τῳ συνεδριῳ,
Having looked intently and the Paul to the sanhedrim,
ειπεν· Ανδρες, αδελφοι, εγω πασῃ συνειδησει
said; Men, brethren, I in all conscience
αγαθῃ πεπολιτευμαι τῳ θεῳ αχρι ταυτης της
good have been as a citizen to the God till this the
ἡμερας. . . . . 2 Ὁ δε αρχιερευς Ανανιας επε-
day. The and high-priest Ananias gave

24 the COMMANDER ordered him to be led into the CASTLE, and to be examined with Scourges, so that he might know for what reason they thus cried against him.

25 And as they extended him with the THONGS, PAUL said to the CENTURION STANDING BY, ‡ "Is it lawful to scourge a Man, a Roman, and uncondemned?"

26 And the CENTURION having heard, went and told the COMMANDER, saying, "What art thou about to do? for this MAN is a Roman."

27 And the COMMANDER coming near said to him, "Tell me, art thou a Roman?" And HE said, "Yes."

28 And the COMMANDER answered, "I purchased this CITIZENSHIP with a Great Sum of money." And PAUL said, "But I have even been born so."

29 Then THOSE being about to examine him, immediately departed from him; and the COMMANDER also was afraid, having ascertained That he was a Roman, and Because he had bound him.

30 And on the NEXT DAY, desiring to know the CERTAINTY of WHAT he was accused by the JEWS, he loosed him; and ordered the HIGH-PRIESTS and all the SANHEDRIM to come together, and having led PAUL down, placed him before them.

CHAPTER XXIII.

1 And PAUL earnestly looking on the SANHEDRIM, said, "Brethren! ‡ I have lived before GOD in All good Conscience to This DAY."......

2 And the HIGH-PRIEST, Ananias, ordered THOSE

‡ 25. Acts xvi. 37.

‡ 1. Acts xxiv. 16; 1 Cor. iv. 4; 2 Cor. i. 12; iv. 2; 2 Tim. i. 3. Heb. xiii. 18.

ταξε τοις παρεστωσιν αυτῳ, τυπτειν αυτου
a charge to those having been standing by him, to strike of him
το στομα. 3 Τοτε ὁ Παυλος προς αυτον ειπε·
the mouth. Then the Paul to him said;
Τυπτειν σε μελλει ὁ θεος, τοιχε κεκονιαμενε·
To strike thee is about the God, O wall having been whitewashed;
και συ καθῃ κρινων με κατα τον νομον, και
and thou sittest judging me according to the law, and
παρανομων κελευεις με τυπτεσθαι; 4 Οἱ δε
violating the law thou orderest me to be struck? Those and
παρεστωτες ειπον· Τον αρχιερεα του θεου
having been standing by said; The high-priest of the God
λοιδορεις; 5 Εφη τε ὁ Παυλος· Ουκ ῃδειν,
revilest thou? Said and the Paul, Not I had known,
αδελφοι, ὁτι εστιν αρχιερευς· γεγραπται γαρ·
brethren, that it is a high-priest; it is written for;
Αρχοντα του λαου σου ουκ ερεις κακως.
A ruler of the people of thee not thou shalt speak evil.
6 Γνους δε ὁ Παυλος, ὁτι το ἑν μερος εστι Σαδ-
Knowing and the Paul, that the one part is of Sad-
δουκαιων, το δε ἑτερον Φαρισαιων, εκραξεν εν
ducees, the and other of Pharisees, he cried out in
τῳ συνεδριῳ· Ανδρες αδελφοι, εγω Φαρισαιος
the sanhedrim; Men brethren, I a Pharisee
ειμι, υἱος Φαρισαιου· περι ελπιδος και αναστ-
am, a son of a Pharisee; concerning hope and a resur-
τασεως νεκρων εγω κρινομαι. 7 Τουτο δε αυτου
rection of dead ones I being judged. This and of him
λαλησαντος, εγενετο στασις των Φαρισαιων
having spoken, was a dispute of the Pharisees
και των Σαδδουκαιων, και εσχισθη το πληθος.
and the Sadducees, and was divided the multitude.
8 Σαδδουκαιοι μεν γαρ λεγουσι μη ειναι αναστα-
Sadducees indeed for say not to be a resurrec-
σιν, μηδε αγγελον μητε πνευμα· Φαρισαιοι δε
tion, nor a messenger nor a spirit; Pharisees but
ὁμολογουσι τα αμφοτερα. 9 Εγενετο δε κραυγη
confess the both. Was and an outcry
μεγαλη· και αναστατες οἱ γραμματεις του
great; and having arisen the scribes of the
μερους των Φαρισαιων διεμαχοντο, λεγοντες·
party of the Pharisees contended, saying;
Ουδεν κακον εὑρισκομεν εν τῳ ανθρωπῳ τουτῳ·
Nothing evil we find in the man this;
ει δε πνευμα ελαλησεν αυτῳ, η αγγελος. . . .
if but a spirit spoke to him, or a messenger.
10 Πολλης δε γενομενης στασεως, ευλαβηθεις ὁ
Great and becoming dispute, fearing the
χιλιαρχος μη διασπασθῃ ὁ Παυλος ὑπ᾽ αυτων,
commander lest would be torn to pieces the Paul by them,
εκελευσε το στρατευμα καταβαν ἁρπασαι αυτον
he ordered the armed force having gone down to take him

STANDING BY him, ‡ to strike him on the MOUTH.
3 Then PAUL said to him, "GOD is about to strike thee, O whitened Wall! and dost thou sit judging me according to the LAW, ‡ and yet, violating the law, commandest me to be struck?"
4 And THOSE STANDING BY said, "Dost thou revile the HIGH-PRIEST of GOD?"
5 And PAUL said, "I did not know, Brethren, That he was a High-priest; for it is written, ‡ 'Thou 'shalt not speak evil of the 'Ruler of thy PEOPLE.'"
6 And PAUL perceiving That the ONE Part were of the Sadducees, and the OTHER of the Pharisees, he exclaimed in the SANHEDRIM, "Brethren, ‡ I am a Pharisee, † a Son * of PHARISEES; concerning ‡ the Hope and the Resurrection of the Dead * I am being judged."
7 And having said this, there was a Dispute between the PHARISEES and the SADDUCEES; and the MULTITUDE was divided.
8 ‡ For indeed the Sadducees say, there is no Resurrection, nor Angel, nor Spirit; but the Pharisees confess BOTH.
9 And there was a great Clamor; and * some of the SCRIBES of the PARTY of the PHARISEES arising contended, saying, ‡ "We find no Evil in this MAN; ‡ and what if a Spirit or an Angel spoke to him?"......
10 And the Dispute becoming vehement, the COMMANDER, fearing that Paul would be torn in pieces by them, ordered the Troops to go down and take him by force from the

* VATICAN MANUSCRIPT.—6. of PHARISEES. 6. I am being judged. 9. some of the SCRIBES.

† 6. Or, a Disciple of the Pharisees.

‡ 2. 1 Kings xxii. 24; Jer. xx. 2; John xviii. 22. ‡ 3. Lev. xix. 35; Deut. xxv. 1, 2; John vii. 51. ‡ 5. Exod. xxii. 28; Eccl. x. 10; 2 Pet. ii. 10; Jude 8. ‡ 6. Acts xxvi. 5; Phil. iii. 5. ‡ 6. Acts xxiv. 15, 21; xxvi. 6; xxviii. 20. ‡ 8. Matt. xxii. 23; Mark xii. 18; Luke xx. 27. ‡ 9. Acts xxv. 25, 31. ‡ 9. Acts xxiii. 7, 17, 18.

εκ μεσου αυτων, αγειν *[τε] εις την παρεμβολην.
from midst of them, to lead [and] into the castle.
11 Τῃ δε επιουσῃ νυκτι επιστας αυτῳ ὁ κυριος
On the and next night having stood by him the Lord
ειπε· Θαρσει· ὡς γαρ διεμαρτυρω τα περι
said: Take courage: as for thou didst testify the things concerning
εμου εις Ἱερουσαλημ, οὑτω σε δει και εις Ῥω-
me in Jerusalem, so thee it behoves also in Rome
μην μαρτυρησαι.
to testify.
12 Γενομενης δε ἡμερας, ποιησαντες συστρο-
Becoming and day, having formed a conspir-
φην οἱ Ιουδαιοι, ανεθεματισαν ἑαυτους, λεγον-
acy the Jews, they bound with a curse themselves, saying
τες μητε φαγειν μητε πιειν ἑως οὑ αποκτεινωσι
neither to eat nor drink till they might kill
τον Παυλον· 13 ησαν δε πλειους τεσσαρακοντα
the Paul; were and more forty
οἱ ταυτην την συνωμοσιαν πεποιηκοτες· 14 οἱτι-
those this the conspiracy having been engaged; who
νες προσελθοντες τοις αρχιερευσι και τοις πρεσ-
having come to the high-priests and the elders,
βυτεροις, ειπον· Αναθεματι ανεθεματισαμεν
said; With a curse we have cursed
ἑαυτους, μηδενος γευσασθαι ἑως οὑ αποκτεινω-
ourselves, of nothing to taste till we have killed
μεν τον Παυλον. 15 Νυν ουν ὑμεις εμφανισατε τῳ
the Paul. Now therefore you make known to the
χιλιαρχῳ συν τῳ συνεδριῳ, ὁπως αυτον κατα-
commander with the sanhedrim, in order that him he may
γαγῃ προς ὑμας, ὡς μελλοντας διαγινωσκειν
lead down to you, as being about to examine
ακριβεστερον τα περι αυτου· ἡμεις δε, προ
more accurately the things concerning him; we and, before
του εγγισαι αυτον, ἑτοιμοι εσμεν του ανελειν
of the to have come nigh him, ready we are of the to kill
αυτον. 16 Ακουσας δε ὁ υἱος της αδελφης Παυ-
him. Having heard but the son of the sister of Paul
λου την ενεδραν, παραγενομενος και εισελθων
the lying in wait, having come near and having gone
εις την παρεμβολην, απηγγειλε τῳ Παυλῳ.
into the castle, he related to the Paul.
17 Προσκαλεσαμενος δε ὁ Παυλος ἑνα των ἑκα-
Having summoned and the Paul one of the cen-
τονταρχων, εφη· Τον νεανιαν τουτον απαγαγε
turions, he said; The young man this lead thou
προς τον χιλιαρχον· εχει γαρ τι απαγγειλαι
to the commander; he has for something to relate
αυτῳ. 18 Ὁ μεν ουν παραλαβων αυτον ηγαγε
to him. He indeed then having taken him led
προς τον χιλιαρχον, και φησιν· Ὁ δεσμιος
to the commander, and said; The prisoner
Παυλος προσκαλεσαμενος με, ηρωτησε τουτον
Paul having summoned me, asked this
τον νεανιαν αγαγειν προς σε, εχοντα τι λαλη-
the young man to lead to thee, having something to say
σαι σοι. 19 Επιλαβομενος δε της χειρος αυτου
to thee. Having taken and the hand of him

midst of them, and to lead him into the CASTLE.

11 ‡And on the FOLLOWING Night the LORD standing by him, said, "Take courage; for as thou didst testify the things concerning me in Jerusalem, so thou must also testify at Rome."

12 And when it was Day, ‡the JEWS, forming a Conspiracy, bound themselves with a Curse, declaring that they would neither eat nor drink till they had killed Paul.

13 And THOSE HAVING FORMED This CONSPIRACY, were more than forty;

14 who having come to the HIGH-PRIESTS and the ELDERS, said, "We have cursed ourselves with a Curse to taste nothing till we have killed PAUL.

15 Now therefore, do you, with the SANHEDRIM, intimate to the COMMANDER, that he may bring him down to you, as if you were about to examine more accurately the things concerning him; and we, before he COMES NEAR, are ready to KILL him."

16 But the SON of Paul's SISTER having heard the PLOT, came up, and going into the CASTLE, told PAUL.

17 And PAUL, having called one of the CENTURIONS to him, said, "Conduct This YOUNG MAN to the COMMANDER, for he has something to tell him."

18 Then HE took him and led him to the COMMANDER, and said, "Paul the PRISONER calling me to him, asked me to conduct This YOUNG MAN to thee, who has something to tell thee."

19 And the COMMANDER, taking him by the

* VATICAN MANUSCRIPT.—10. and—omit.

‡ 11. Acts xviii. 9; xxvii. 23, 24. ‡ 12. ver 21, 30; xxv. 3.

ὁ χιλιαρχος, και αναχωρησας κατ᾽ ιδιαν, επυν-
the commander, and having retired by one's self, he in-
θανετο· Τι εστιν ὁ εχεις απαγγειλαι μοι;
quired; What is it which thou hast to relate to me?
20 ειπε δε· Ὁτι οἱ Ιουδαιοι συνεθεντο του ερω-
he said and; That the Jews agreed together of the to ask
τησαι σε, ὁπως αυριον εις το συνεδριον καταγα-
thee, that to-morrow into the sanhedrim thou mayest lead
γης τον Παυλον, ὡς μελλοντες τι ακριβεστε-
down the Paul, as being about something more accu-
ρον πυνθανεσθαι περι αυτου. 21 Συ ουν μη
rately to investigate concerning him. Thou therefore not
πεισθῃς αυτοις· ενεδρευουσι γαρ αυτον εξ
shouldst be persuaded by them; lie in wait for him of
αυτων ανδρες πλειους τεσσαρκοντα, οἱτινες ανε-
them men more forty, who bound
θεματισαν ἑαυτους, μητε φαγειν μητε πιειν
with a curse themselves, neither to eat nor to drink
ἑως οὑ ανελωσιν αυτον· και νυν ἑτοιμοι εισι
till they killed him; and now ready they are
προσδεχομενοι την απο σου επαγγελιαν.
looking for the from thee promise.
22 Ὁ μεν ουν χιλιαρχος απελυσε τον νεα-
The indeed then commander dismissed the young
νιαν, παραγγειλας μηδενι εκλαλησαι, ὁτι ταυτα
man, having charged to no one to speak out, that these things
ενεφανισας προς με. 23 Και προσκαλεσαμενος
thou didst report to me. And having summoned
δυο τινας των ἑκατονταρχων, ειπεν· Ἑτοιμα-
two certain of the centurions, he said; Make
σατε στρατιωτας διακοσιους, ὁπως πορευθωσιν
ready soldiers two hundred, that they may go
ἑως Καισαρειας, και ἱππεις εβδομηκοντα, και
to Cesarea, and horsemen seventy, and
δεξιολαβους διακοσιους, απο τριτης ὡρας της
spearmen two hundred, from third hour of the
νυκτος· 24 κτηνη τε παραστησαι, ἱνα επιβιβα-
night; animals and to have provided, that having
σαντες τον Παυλον διασωσωσι προς Φηλικα
mounted the Paul they might convey safely to Felix
τον ἡγεμονα· 25 γραψας επιστολην περιεχουσαν
the governor; having written a letter containing
τον τυπον τουτον· 26 Κλαυδιος Λυσιας τῳ
the form this; Claudius Lysias to the
κρατιστῳ ἡγεμονι Φηλικι χαιρειν. 27 Τον
most excellent governor Felix health. The
ανδρα τουτον συλληφθεντα ὑπο των Ιουδαιων,
man this having been seized by the Jews,
και μελλοντα αναιρεισθαι ὑπ᾽ αυτων, επισ-
and being about to be killed by them, having come
τας συν τῳ στρατευματι εξειλομην *[αυτον,]
suddenly with the armed force I rescued [him,]
μαθων ὁτι Ῥωμαιος εστι. 28 Βουλομενος δε
having learned that a Roman he is. Wishing and

HAND, and having retired by himself, he inquired, "What is it that thou hast to tell me?"

20 And he said, ‡ "The JEWS have agreed together to ASK thee that thou wouldst bring down PAUL To-morrow into the SANHEDRIM, as if about to investigate something more accurately concerning him.

21 Therefore, be not thou persuaded by them; for more than forty Men of them lie in wait for him, who have bound themselves with a curse, neither to eat nor drink till they have killed him; and now they are ready, looking for the PROMISE from thee."

22 Then the COMMANDER dismissed the YOUNG MAN, charging him, "Inform No one That thou hast told me these things."

23 And having summoned * Certain Two of the CENTURIONS, he said, "Prepare two hundred Soldiers to go to Cesarea, and seventy Horsemen, and two hundred Spearmen, after the Third Hour of the NIGHT;

24 and provide Animals on which to place PAUL, that they may convey him safely to † Felix, the GOVERNOR."

25 And he wrote a Letter having this FORM:—

26 "Claudius Lysias to the MOST-EXCELLENT Governor Felix, greeting:

27 ‡ This MAN having been seized by the JEWS, and being about to be killed by them, I rescued, having come suddenly upon them with an ARMED FORCE. Having learned that he is a Roman,

* VATICAN MANUSCRIPT.—27. him—*omit.*

† 24. Felix was a freed man of the emperor Claudius, and brother of Pallas, chief favorite of the emperor. Tacitus gives us to understand that he governed with all the authority of a king, and the baseness and insolence of a quondam slave. He was an unrighteous governor, a base, mercenary, and bad man.

‡ 20. ver. 12. ‡ 27. Acts xxi. 33; xxiv. 7.

γνωναι την αιτιαν δι' ἡν ενεκαλουν αυτῳ,
to know the cause on account of which they were accusing him,

κατηγαγον αυτον εις το συνεδριον αυτων· 29 ὁν
I led down him into the sanhedrim of them: whom

εὑρον εγκαλουμενον περι ζητηματων του νομου
I found being accused concerning questions of the law

αυτων, μηδεν δε αξιον θανατου η δεσμων εγκλη-
of them, nothing but worthy of death or bonds an accu-

μα εχοντα. 30 Μηνυθεισης δε μοι επιβουλης εις
sation having. Having been disclosed but to me a plot against

τον ανδρα μελλειν εσεσθαι ὑπο των Ιουδαιων,
the man to be about to be by the Jews,

εξαυτης επεμψα προς σε, παραγγειλας και τοις
instantly I sent to thee, having commanded also the

κατηγοροις λεγειν τα προς αυτον επι σου.
accusers to say the things against him before thee.

*[Ερρωσο.] 31 Οἱ μεν ουν στρατιωται, κατα
[Farewell.] The indeed therefore soldiers, according to

το διατεταγμενον αυτοις, αναλαβοντες τον
that having been commanded them, having taken the

Παυλον, ηγαγον δια της νυκτος εις την Αντι-
Paul, they led through the night into the Anti-

πατριδα. 32 Τῃ δε επαυριον εασαντες τους ἱπ-
patris. On the and morrow having left the horse-

πεις πορευεσθαι συν αυτῳ, ὑπεστρεψαν εις την
men to go with him, they returned to the

παρεμβολην. 33 Οἱτινες εισελθοντες εις την
castle. Who having come into the

Καισαρειαν, και αναδοντες την επιστολην τῳ
Cesarea, and having delivered the letter to the

ἡγεμονι, παρεστησαν και τον Παυλον αυτῳ.
governor, presented also the Paul to him.

34 Αναγνους δε, και επερωτησας εκ ποιας επαρ-
Having read and, and having asked from what province

χιας εστι, και πυθομενος ὁτι απο Κιλικιας·
he is, and having understood that from Cilicia;

35 διακουσομαι σου, εφη, ὁταν και οἱ κατηγοροι
I will fully hear thee, he said, when also the accusers

σου παραγενωνται. Εκελευσε τε αυτον εν τῳ
of thee may arrive. He commanded and him in the

πραιτωριῳ του Ἡρωδου φυλασσεσθαι.
judgment-hall of the Herod to be kept.

ΚΕΦ. κδ'. 24.

1 Μετα δε πεντε ἡμερας κατεβη ὁ αρχιερευς
After and five days went down the high-priest

Ανανιας μετα των πρεσβυτερων και ῥητορος
Ananias with the elders and an orator

Τερτυλλου τινος, οἱτινες ενεφανισαν τῳ ἡγε-
Tertullus certain, who appeared before the gov-

μονι κατα του Παυλου. 2 Κληθεντος δε αυτου,
ernor against the Paul. Having been called and of him,

ηρξατο κατηγορειν ὁ Τερτυλλος, λεγων· 3 πολ-
began to accuse the Tertullus, saying; great

28 ‡ and desiring to know the CRIME of which they accused him, I led him down into their SANHEDRIM;

29 whom I found being accused ‡ concerning Questions of their LAW, ‡ but having no Accusation worthy of Death or Bonds.

30 ‡ But it having been disclosed to me that a Plot was about to be formed against the MAN by the JEWS, I instantly sent to thee, ‡ having commanded his ACCUSERS also * to speak against him before thee."

31 The SOLDIERS, therefore, according to THAT which was COMMANDED them, took Paul, and conveyed him by * Night to ANTIPATRIS.

32 And on the NEXT DAY they returned to the CASTLE, having left the HORSEMEN to proceed with him;

33 who, having entered CESAREA, and delivered the LETTER to the GOVERNOR, they also presented PAUL to him.

34 And having read it, he asked of What Province he was; and being informed That he was from ‡ Cilicia,

35 he said, ‡ "I will fully hear thee, when thine ACCUSERS are also come." And he commanded him to be kept in ‡ HEROD'S PRETORIUM.

CHAPTER XXIV.

1 And after ‡ Five Days the HIGH-PRIEST, ‡ Ananias, went down with * the ELDERS, and a certain Orator named Tertullus, and appeared before the GOVERNOR against PAUL.

2 And he being called, TERTULLUS began to accuse him, saying;

* VATICAN MANUSCRIPT.—30. to speak against him before thee. 30. Farewell—*omit.* 31. Night. 1. certain Elders.

‡ 28. Acts xxii. 30. ‡ 29. Acts xviii. 15; xxv. 19. ‡ 29. Acts xxvi. 31. ‡ 30. ver. 20. ‡ 30. Acts xxiv. 8; xxv. 6. ‡ 34. Acts xxi. 39. ‡ 35. Acts xxiv. 1, 10; xxv. 16. ‡ 35. Matt. xxvii. 27. ‡ 1. Acts xxi. 27. ‡ 1. Acts xxiii. 2, 30, 35; xxv. 2.

λης ειρηνης τυγχανοντες δια σου, και κατορ-
peace enjoying through thee, and worthy

θωματων γινομενων τῳ εθνει τουτῳ δια της σης
deeds being done to the nation this through of the of thy

προνοιας, παντῃ τε και πανταχου αποδεχομεθα,
foresight, in every thing and and everywhere we accept,

κρατιστε Φηλιξ, μετα πασης ευχαριστιας.
O most excellent Felix, with all thankfulness.

4 Ἱνα δε μη επι πλειον σε εγκοπτω, παρακαλω
That and not to longer thee I may detain, I beseech

ακουσαι σε ἡμων συντομως τῃ σῃ επιεικειᾳ.
to hear thee of us briefly in the thy clemency.

5 Εὑροντες γαρ τον ανδρα τουτον λοιμον, και
We have found for the man this a pestilence, and

κινουντα στασιν πασι τοις Ιουδαιοις τοις κατα
exciting a sedition in all the Jews those in

την οικουμενην, πρωτοστατην τε της των Να-
the habitable, a leader and of the of the Na-

ζωραιων αἱρεσεως, 6 ὁς και το ἱερον επειρασε
zarenes sect, who also the temple attempted

βεβηλωσαι· ὁν και εκρατησαμεν, *[και κατα
to profane; whom also we apprehended, [and according to

τον ἡμετερον νομον ηθελησαμεν κρινειν. 7 Παρ-
the our law we wished to judge. Having

ελθων δε Λυσιας ὁ χιλιαρχος, μετα πολλης
come but Lysias the commander, with a great

βιας εκ των χειρων ἡμων απηγαγε, 8 κελευσας
force out of the hands of us led away, having commanded

τους κατηγορους αυτου ερχεσθαι επι σε·] παρ'
the accusers of him to come to thee;] from

οὑ δυνησῃ αυτος, ανακρινας περι
whom thou wilt be able thyself, having examined closely, concerning

παντων τουτων επιγνωναι, ὡν ἡμεις κατη-
all of these things to have knowledge, of which we ac-

γορουμεν αυτου. 9 Συνεπεθεντο δε και οἱ Ιου-
cuse him. United in impeaching and also the Jews,

δαιοι, φασκοντες ταυτα οὑτως εχειν. 10 Απεκ-
asserting these things thus to be. Answered

ριθη δε ὁ Παυλος, νευσαντος αυτῳ του ἡγεμο-
and the Paul, nodding to him the governor

νος λεγειν· Εκ πολλων ετων οντα σε κριτην τῳ
to speak; From many years being thee a judge to the

εθνει τουτῳ επισταμενος, ευθυμοτερον τα
nation this knowing, more cheerfully the things

περι εμαυτου απολογουμαι· 11 δυναμενου σου
concerning myself I defend; being able of thee

γνωναι, ὁτι ου πλειους εισι μοι ἡμεραι δεκαδυο,
to know, that not more are to me days twelve,

αφ' ἡς ανεβην προσκυνησων εν Ἱερουσαλημ.
from which I went up to worship in Jerusalem.

12 Και ουτε εν τῳ ἱερῳ εὑρον με προς τινα δια-
And neither in the temple they found me with any one dis-

λεγομενον, η επισυστασιν ποιουντα οχλου,
puting, or a tumult making of a crowd,

3 "Having obtained Great Peace through thee, and * worthy Deeds being done for this NATION by THY Forethought, and in every thing and everywhere, we accept it, Most excellent Felix, with all Thankfulness.

4 But that I may not further detain thee, I beseech thee to hear us briefly, with THY usual Candor.

5 ‡For we found this MAN a Pestilence, and exciting * Seditions among ALL THOSE JEWS throughout the EMPIRE, and a Chief of the SECT of the NAZARENES;

6 ‡who even attempted to profane the TEMPLE, and whom we apprehended, *[and wished ‡to judge according to OUR Law;

7 ‡but Lysias, the COMMANDER, having come with a Great Force, took him away out of our HANDS,

8 ‡commanding his ACCUSERS to come to thee;] from whom thou wilt be able to learn for thyself, on examination, of all these things of which we accuse him."

9 And the JEWS also jointly impeached him, asserting that these things were so.

10 And the GOVERNOR having made a sign for him to speak, PAUL answered, "Knowing that thou hast been for Several Years a Judge of this NATION, *I cheerfully defend myself;

11 it also being in thy power to ascertain, That it is not more than twelve Days since ‡I went up to worship at Jerusalem.

12 ‡And they did not find me disputing with any one in the TEMPLE, or making an Insurrection of

* VATICAN MANUSCRIPT.—3. Reformations are going on in this NATION. 5. Seditions among. 6—8. *omit.* 10. I cheerfully.

‡ 5. Luke xxiii. 2; Acts vi. 13; xvi. 20; xvii. 6; xxi. 28; 1 Pet. ii. 12, 15. ‡ 6. Acts xxi. 28. ‡ 6. John xviii. 31. ‡ 7. Acts xxi. 33. ‡ 8. Acts xxiii. 30. ‡ 11. ver. 17; Acts xxi. 26. ‡ 12. Acts xxv. 8; xxviii. 17.

ουτε εν ταις συναγωγαις, ουτε κατα την πολιν·
nor in the synagogues, nor in the city;
13 ουτε παραστησαι δυνανται, περι ὧν νυν
nor to prove are they able, concerning which now
κατηγορουσι μου. 14 Ὁμολογω δε τουτο σοι,
they accuse me. I confess but this to thee,
ὁτι κατα την ὁδον, ἡν λεγουσιν αἱρεσιν, οὑτω
that according to the way, which they called a sect, so
λατρευω τῳ πατρῳῳ θεῳ, πιστευων πασι τοις
I serve the patriarchal God, believing all things those
κατα τον νομον και τοις εν τοις προφηταις
according to the law and those in the prophets
γεγραμμενοις· 15 ελπιδα εχων εις τον θεον, ἡν
having been written; a hope having in the God, which
και αυτοι οὑτοι προσδεχονται, αναστασιν μελ-
even they themselves are looking for, a resurrection about
λειν εσεσθαι *[νεκρων,] δικαιων τε και αδι-
to be [of dead ones,] of just ones and also unjust
κων. 16 Εν τουτῳ δε αυτος ασκω, απροσκοπον
ones. In this and myself I exercise, a clear
συνειδησιν εχειν προς τον θεον και τους ανθρω-
conscience to have towards the God and the men
πους διαπαντος. 17 Δι' ετων δε πλειονων
always. In the course of years and many
παρεγενομην ελεημοσυνας ποιησων εις το εθνος
I came alms bringing to the nation
μου, και προσφορας. 18 Εν οἱς εὑρον με ἡγ-
of me, and offerings. In which they found me having
νισμενον εν τῳ ἱερῳ, ου μετα οχλου, ουδε μετα
been purified in the temple, not with a crowd, nor with
θορυβου. Τινες δε απο της Ασιας Ιουδαιοι,
a tumult. Some and from the Asia Jews,
19 οὑς εδει επι σου παρειναι, και κατηγορειν ει
who ought before thee to be present, and to accuse if
τι εχοιεν προς με. 20 Η αυτοι οὑτοι ειπα-
anything they may have against me Or these themselves let
τωσαν, τι εὑρον εν εμοι αδικημα, σταντος
them say, what they found in me crime, having stood
μου επι του συνεδριου· 21 η περι μιας ταυ-
of me before the sanhedrim; or concerning one this
της φωνης, ἡς εκραξα ἑστως εν αυτοις· Ὁτι
voice, which I cried out standing among them; That
περι αναστασεως νεκρων εγω κρινομαι σημε-
concerning a resurrection of dead ones I am judged to-day
ρον ὑφ' ὑμων. 22 Ανεβαλετο δε αυτους ὁ Φηλιξ,
by you. Put off but them the Felix,
ακριβεστερον ειδως τα περι της ὁδου,
more accurately knowing the things concerning the way,
ειπων· Ὁταν Λυσιας ὁ χιλιαρχος καταβῃ,
saying; When Lysias the commander may come down,

the Crowd, either in the SYNAGOGUES, or in the CITY;
13 nor are they able to prove the things concerning which they now accuse me.
14 But this I confess to thee, that according to the WAY which they call a Sect, so serve I the GOD of my FATHERS, believing * the THINGS which are according to the LAW, and THOSE which have been written in the PROPHETS;
15 having a Hope in GOD, which even they themselves are looking for,—‡that there is to be a Resurrection both of the Righteous and Unrighteous.
16 And in this I exercise myself, always to have ‡a clear Conscience towards GOD and MEN.
17 But in the course of several Years ‡I came bringing Alms to my NATION, and Offerings;
18 at which time they found me purified in the TEMPLE, neither with a Crowd, nor with Tumult. ‡But there are some Jews from ASIA,
19 ‡who ought to be present before thee, and to accuse, if they may have anything against me.
20 Or let these themselves say, What Crime they found in me while I stood before the SANHEDRIM;
21 unless it be for This One Declaration which I made while I was standing among them,—‡'That concerning the Resurrection of the Dead I am judged by you This day.'"
22 But FELIX knowing more accurately about that WAY, put them off, saying, "When Lysias, the COMMANDER, comes down, I

* VATICAN MANUSCRIPT.—14. the THINGS according to Law. 15. of the dead—*omit*.

‡ 15. Dan. xii. 2; John v. 28, 29. ‡ 16. Acts xxiii. 1. ‡ 17. Acts xi. 29, 30; xx. 16; Rom. xv. 25; 2 Cor. viii. 4; Gal. ii. 10. ‡ 18. Acts xxi. 26, 27; xxvi. 21. ‡ 19. Acts xxiii. 30; xxv. 16. ‡ 21. Acts xxiii. 6; xxviii. 20.

διαγνωσομαι τα καθ' ὑμας. [23] Διαταξαμενος
I will inquire into the things about you. Having given orders
τε τῳ ἑκατονταρχῃ τηρεισθαι αυτον, εχειν τε
and to the centurion to keep him, to have and
ανεσιν, και μηδενα κωλυειν των ιδιων αυτου
liberty, and no one to forbid of the own friends of him
ὑπηρετειν, *[η προσερχεσθαι] αυτῳ.
to assist, [or to come] to him.
[24] Μετα δε ἡμερας τινας παραγενομενος ὁ Φη-
After and days some having come the Fe-
λιξ συν Δρουσιλλῃ τῃ γυναικι, ουσῃ Ιουδαιᾳ,
lix with Drusilla the wife, being a Jewess,
μετεπεμψατο τον Παυλον, και ηκουσεν αυτου
he sent for the Paul, and heard him
περι της εις Χριστον πιστεως. [25] Διαλεγο-
concerning the into Anointed faith. Discours-
μενου δε αυτου περι δικαιοσυνης και εγκρα-
ing and of him concerning justice and self-con-
τειας και του κριματος του μελλοντος, εμφο-
trol and of the judgment that being about to come, terri-
βος γενομενος ὁ Φηλιξ απεκριθη· Το νυν εχον
fied being the Felix answered; The present being
πορευου· καιρον δε μεταλαβων μετακαλεσομαι
go thou; a season and having found I will call
σε. [26] Ἁμα και ελπιζων, ὁτι χρηματα δοθη-
thee. At the same time also hoping, that money will be
σεται *[αυτῳ] ὑπο του Παυλου, *[ὁπως λυσῃ
given [to him] by the Paul, [so that he might loose
αυτον·] διο και πυκνοτερον αυτον μεταπεμ-
him;] therefore and oftener him sending
πομενος ὡμιλει αυτῳ. [27] Διετιας δε πληρωθει-
for talked with him. Two years but being ended
σης ελαβη διαδοχον ὁ Φηλιξ Πορκιον Φηστον·
received a successor the Felix Porcius Festus;
θελων τε χαριτας καταθεσθαι τοις Ιουδαιοις ὁ
wishing and favors to lay in store for himself with the Jews the
Φηλιξ, κατελιπε τον Παυλον δεδεμενον.
Felix, left the Paul having been bound.

ΚΕΦ. κε'. 25.

[1] Φηστος ουν επιβας τῃ επαρχιᾳ, μετα
Festus therefore having entered upon the perfecture, after
τρεις ἡμερας ανεβη εις Ἱεροσολυμα απο Καισα-
three days went up to Jerusalem from Cesa-
ρειας. [2] Ενεφανισαν δε αυτῳ ὁ αρχιερευς και
rea. Appeared before and him the high-priest and
οἱ πρωτοι των Ιουδαιων κατα του Παυλου, και
the chiefs of the Jews against the Paul, and
παρεκαλουν αυτον, [3] αιτουμενοι χαριν κατ'
entreated him, asking a favor against
αυτου, ὁπως μεταπεμψηται αυτον εις Ἱερουσα-
him, that he would send for him to Jerusa-
λημ· ενεδραν ποιουντες ανελειν αυτον κατα
lem; an ambush forming to kill him in

will inquire about your MATTERS."

23 And he commanded the CENTURION to keep him, and let him have Liberty, ‡ and to forbid none of his FRIENDS to assist him.

24 And after some Days, FELIX coming with † Drusilla, * his WIFE, who was a Jewess, sent for PAUL, and heard him concerning the FAITH in * Christ Jesus.

25 And as he was discoursing concerning Justice, Self-government, and THAT JUDGMENT about to COME, FELIX, being terrified, answered, "Go for the PRESENT; and when I find an Opportunity I will call for thee."

26 At the same time also hoping that Money would be given him by PAUL; and therefore he more frequently sent for Him, and conversed with him.

27 But when two Years were ended, FELIX had a Successor, Porcius Festus; and FELIX, ‡ wishing to be favorably regarded by the JEWS, left PAUL a prisoner.

CHAPTER XXV.

1 Festus, therefore, having entered upon his GOVERNMENT, after Three Days went up from Cesarea to Jerusalem.

2 ‡ And * the HIGH-PRIESTS and the CHIEFS of the JEWS appeared against PAUL, and entreated him,

3 asking a Favor against him, that he would send for him to Jerusalem, ‡ forming an Ambuscade to kill him on the ROAD.

* VATICAN MANUSCRIPT.—23. or to come—*omit.* 24. HIS OWN Wife. 24. Christ Jesus. 26. to him—*omit.* 26. so that he might loose him—*omit.* 2. the HIGH-PRIESTS.

† 24. Drusilla was the youngest daughter of Herod Agrippa, and had been married to Azizus, king of Emessa, whom Felix had persuaded her to abandon, in order to an adulterous marriage with himself.

‡ 23. Acts xxvii. 3; xxviii. 16. ‡ 27. Acts xii. 3; xxv. 9, 14. ‡ 2. Acts xxiv, 1; ver. 15. ‡ 3. Acts xxiii. 12, 15.

την ὁδον. [4] Ὁ μεν ουν Φηστος απεκριθη,
the way. The indeed then Festus answered,
τηρεισθαι τον Παυλον εν Καισαρεια, ἑαυτον δε
to be kept the Paul in Cesarea, himself but
μελλειν εν ταχει εκπορευεσθαι. [5] Οἱ ουν εν
to be about with speed to go out. Those therefore among
ὑμιν, φησι, δυνατοι, συγκαταβαντες, ει τι
you, he says, being able, having gone down with, if anything
εστιν εν τῳ ανδρι, κατηγορειτωσαν αυτου.
is in the man, let them accuse him.
[6] Διατριψας δε εν αυτοις ἡμερας ου πλειους οκτω
Having remained and among them days not more eight
η δεκα, καταβας εις Καισαρειαν, τῃ επαυριον
or ten, having gone down into Cesarea, on the morrow
καθισας επι του βηματος, εκελευσε τον
having sat down on the judgment-seat, he commanded the
Παυλον αχθηναι. [7] Παραγενομενου δε αυτου,
Paul to be led forth. Having approached and of him,
περιεστησαν οἱ απο Ἱεροσολυμων καταβεβηκο-
stood around the from Jerusalem having been come
τες Ιουδαιοι, πολλα και βαρεα αιτιαματα φερον-
down Jews, many and heavy accusations bring-
τες *[κατα του Παυλου,] ἁ ουκ ισχυον αποδειξαι·
ing [against the Paul,] which not they were able to point out;
[8] απολογουμενου αυτου· Ὁτι ουτε εις τον νομον
saying in defence of him; That neither against the law
των Ιουδαιων, ουτε εις το ἱερον, ουτε εις Και-
of the Jews, nor against the temple, nor against Ce-
σαρα τι ημαρτον. [9] Ὁ Φηστος δε, τοις Ιουδαι-
sar anything did I wrong. The Festus but, with the Jews
οις θελων χαριν καταθεσθαι, αποκριθεις τῳ
wishing a favor to lay up for himself answering to the
Παυλῳ ειπε· Θελεις εις Ἱεροσολυμα αναβας,
Paul said; Art thou willing to Jerusalem having gone up,
εκει περι τουτων κρινεσθαι επ' εμου; [10] Ειπε
there concerning these things to be judged before me? Said
δε ὁ Παυλος· Επι του βηματος Καισαρος εστως
but the Paul; At the judgment-seat of Cesar standing
ειμι, οὑ με δει κρινεσθαι. Ιουδαιους ουδεν
I am, where me it behoves to be judged. Jews nothing
ηδικησα, ὡς και συ καλλιον επιγινωσκεις.
I have done wrong, as also thou full well hast ascertained.
[11] Ει μεν γαρ αδικω, και αξιον θανατου πεπρα-
If indeed for I am unjust, and worthy of death I have
χα τι, ου παραιτουμαι το αποθανειν· ει δε
done anthing, not I refuse the to die; if but
ουδεν εστιν ὡν οὑτοι κατηγορουσι μου, ουδεις
nothing is of which these accuse me, no one
με δυναται αυτοις χαρισασθαι. Καισαρα επι-
me is able to them to give as a favor. Cesar I call
καλουμαι. [12] Τοτε ὁ Φηστος συλλαλησας μετα
upon. Then the Festus having conferred with

4 But FESTUS answered that PAUL should be kept at Cesarea, and that he himself would go down there shortly.

5 "Therefore," said he, "let THOSE among you who are ABLE go down with me, ‡ and * if there is anything amiss in the MAN, accuse him.

6 And having continued among them eight or ten Days, he went down to Cesarea; and on the NEXT DAY, sitting down on the TRIBUNAL, commanded PAUL to be brought.

7 And he having come, the JEWS who had COME DOWN from Jerusalem stood * round him, ‡ bringing down Many and Heavy Accusations, which they were not able to prove,

8 * while PAUL maintained in his defence, ‡ "Neither against the LAW of the JEWS, nor against the TEMPLE, nor against Cesar, have I sinned in anything."

9 But FESTUS, ‡ wishing to gratify the JEWS, answering PAUL, said, ‡ "Art thou willing to go up to Jerusalem, and there be judged before me concerning these things?"

10 And PAUL said, "I am standing at Cesar's TRIBUNAL, where I ought to be judged. I have done no wrong to the Jews, as thou also very well knowest.

11 ‡ * For if, indeed, I do wrong, or have done anything deserving of Death, I refuse not to die; but if there be nothing of which they accuse me, no one can give Me up to gratify Them. ‡ I appeal to Cesar."

12 Then FESTUS, having conferred with the

* VATICAN MANUSCRIPT.—5. if there is anything amiss in the man, accuse him. 7. round him, bringing down Many. 7. against Paul—*omit.* 8. PAUL answering. 11. If, then, indeed.

‡ 5. Acts xviii. 14; ver. 18. ‡ 7. Mark xv. 3; Luke xxiii. 2, 10; Acts xxiv. 5, 13. ‡ 8. Acts vi. 13; xxiv. 12; xxviii. 17. ‡ 9. Acts xxiv. 27. ‡ 9. ver. 20. ‡ 11. ver. 25; Acts xviii. 14; xxiii. 29; xxvi. 31. ‡ 11. Acts xxvi. 32; xxviii. 19.

του συμβουλιου, απεκριθη· Καισαρα επικεκλη-
the council, answered; Cesar thou hast called
σαι· επι Καισαρα πορευση.
upon; to Cesar thou shalt go.
13 Ἡμερων δε διαγενομενων τινων, Αγριππας
Days and having intervened some, Agrippa
ὁ βασιλευς και Βερνικη κατηντησαν εις Καισα-
the king and Bernice came down to Cesarea,
ρειαν, ασπασομενοι τον Φηστον. 14 Ὡς δε
paying their respects to the Festus. When and
πλειους ἡμερας διετριβον εκει, ὁ Φηστος τῳ
many days they remained there, the Festus to the
βασιλει ανεθετο τα κατα τον Παυλον, λεγων·
king submitted the things against the Paul, saying;
Ανηρ τις εστι καταλελειμμενος ὑπο Φηλικος
A man certain is having been left behind by Felix
δεσμιος· 15 περι οὑ, γενομενου μου εις Ἱερο-
a prisoner; concerning whom, being of me in Jeru-
σολυμα, ενεφανισαν οἱ αρχιερεις και οἱ πρεσβυ-
salem, gave information the high-priests and the elders
τεροι των Ιουδαιων, αιτουμενοι κατ᾽ αυτου
of the Jews, asking against him
δικην. 16 Προς οὑς απεκριθην, ὁτι ουκ εστιν
a judgment. To whom I answered, that not it is
εθος Ῥωμαιοις χαριζεσθαι τινα ανθρωπον, πριν η
a custom for Romans to give as a favor any man, before
ὁ κατηγορουμενος κατα προσωπον εχοι τους
he being accused face to face may have the
κατηγορους, τοπον τε απολογιας λαβοι περι
accusers, an opportunity and of defence he may take concerning
του εγκληματος. 17 Συνελθοντων ουν *[αυτων]
the accusation. Having come therefore [of them]
ενθαδε, αναβολην μηδεμιαν ποιησαμενος, τῃ
here, delay none having made, on the
ἑξης καθισας επι του βηματος, εκελευσα αχ-
next day having sat down on the judgment-seat, I commanded to be
θηναι τον ανδρα. 18 Περι οὑ σταθεντες οἱ
brought the man. Concerning whom having stood up the
κατηγοροι ουδεμιαν αιτιαν επεφερον, ὡν ὑπε-
accusers no one accusation brought, of things sup-
νοουν εγω· 19 ζητηματα δε τινα περι της
posed I; questions but certain concerning of the
ιδιας δεισιδαιμονιας ειχον προς αυτον, και
own religion they had with him, and
περι τινος Ιησου τεθνηκοτος, ὁν εφασκεν ὁ
concerning one Jesus having been dead, whom affirmed the
Παυλος ζην. 20 Απορουμενος δε εγω εις την
Paul to be alive. Being in doubt but I on that
περι τουτου ζητησιν, ελεγον, ει βουλοιτο
concerning this question, I said, if he would be willing
πορευεσθαι εις Ἱερουσαλημ, κᾳκει κρινεσθαι
to go to Jerusalem, and there to be judged
περι τουτων. 21 Του δε Παυλου επικαλεσα-
concerning these things. The but Paul having appealed

COUNSEL, answered, "To Cesar thou hast appealed; to Cesar thou shalt go."

13 And after some Days, † Agrippa the KING and Bernice came down to Cesarea, to pay their respects to FESTUS.

14 And when they had spent Many Days there, FESTUS submitted PAUL'S CASE to the KING, saying, ‡ "There is a certain Man left a Prisoner by Felix;

15 ‡ concerning whom, when I was in Jerusalem, the HIGH-PRIESTS and the ELDERS of the JEWS * appeared; asking a Sentence of judgment against him;

16 ‡ to whom I answered, That it is not a Custom for Romans to make a present of Any Man, before the ACCUSED has the ACCUSERS Face to Face, and an Opportunity is allowed for defence concerning the ACCUSATION.

17 Therefore, when they arrived here, ‡ making no Delay, the NEXT DAY, sitting down on the TRIBUNAL, I commanded the MAN to be brought;

18 concerning whom the ACCUSERS having stood up, brought No Charge of * such Evil things as I supposed;

19 ‡ but had certain Questions with him about their OWN Religion, and about One Jesus who died, whom PAUL affirmed to be alive.

20 And I being in doubt on that concerning this QUESTION, I inquired if he would be willing to go to Jerusalem, and there be judged concerning these things.

21 But PAUL having ap-

* VATICAN MANUSCRIPT.—15. appeared, asking a Sentence of judgment. 17. of them—*omit*. 18. such Evil things.

† 13. This was the son of Agrippa, whose miserable death is recorded in Acts xii. 23. In A. D. 53, he was transferred from the kingdom of Chalcis, which he had received from Claudius, when only 17 years old, to the provinces possessed by his father, viz., Batanea, Trachonitis, Auranitis, and Abilene, which he governed with the title of king. He died A. D. 100, after a reign including that over Chalcis, of 51 years.—*Owen*.

‡ 14. Acts xxiv. 27. ‡ 15. ver. 2, 3. ‡ 16. ver. 4, 5. ‡ 17. ver. 6. ‡ 19. Acts xviii. 15; xxiii. 29.

μενου τηρηθηναι αὐτον εις την του Σεβαστου
to be kept himself for the of the Augustus
διαγνωσιν, εκελευσα τηρεισθαι αυτον, ἑως οὑ
decision, I commanded to be kept him, till
πεμψω. αυτον προς Καισαρα. 22 Αγριππας δε
I could send him to Cesar. Agrippa but
προς τον Φηστον *[εφη·] Εβουλομην και
to the Festus [said;] I was wishing also
αυτος του ανθρωπου ακουσαι. Ὁ δε αυριον,
myself the man to hear. The and morrow;
φησιν, ακουσῃ αυτου. 23 Τῃ ουν επαυριον
he said, thou shalt hear him. On the therefore morrow
ελθοντος του Αγριππα και της Βερνικης μετα
having come the Agrippa and the Bernice with
πολλης φαντασιας, και εισελθοντων εις το
great display, and having entered into the
ακροατηριον, συν τε τοις χιλιαρχοις και ανδρασι
place of hearing, with both the commanders and men
τοις κατ' εξοχην *[ουσι] της πολεως, και κε-
those principal [being] of the city, and hav-
λευσαντος του Φηστου, ηχθη ὁ Παυλος. 24 Και
ing commanded the Festus, was brought the Paul. And
φησιν ὁ Φηστος· Αγριππα βασιλευ, και παντες
said the Festus; Agrippa O king, and all
οἱ συμπαροντες ἡμιν ανδρες, θεωρειτε τουτον,
those being present with us men, you see this,
περι οὑ παν το πληθος των Ιουδαιων ενετυ-
concerning whom all the multitude of the Jews applied
χον μοι εν τε Ἱεροσολυμοις και ενθαδε, επι-
to me in both Jerusalem and here, cry-
βοωντες μη δειν ζῃν αυτον μηκετι. 25 Εγω
ing out not to be right to live him longer. I
δε καταλαβομενος μηδεν αξιον θανατου αυτον
but having detected nothing worthy of death him
πεπραχεναι, και αυτου δε τουτου επικαλεσα-
to have done, also of him and of this having appealed
μενου τον Σεβαστον, εκρινα πεμπειν *[αυτον.]
to the Augustus, I resolved to send [him.]
26 Περι οὑ ασφαλες τι γραψαι τῳ κυριῳ
Concerning whom certain anything to write to the Lord
ουκ εχω, διο προηγαγον αυτον εφ' ὑμων, και
not I have, therefore I led forth him before you, and
μαλιστα επι σου, βασιλευ Αγριππα, ὁπως της
especially before thee, O king Agrippa, so that the
ανακρισεως γενομενης σχω τι γραψαι.
examination having taken place I may have something to write.
27 Αλογον γαρ μοι δοκει πεμποντα δεσμιον, μη
Absurd for to me it seems sending a prisoner, not
και τας κατ' αυτου αιτιας σημαναι.
and the against him charges to signify.

pealed to be kept for the DECISION of † AUGUSTUS, I ordered him to be kept till I could send him * to Cesar.

22 And Agrippa said to FESTUS, "I myself also desire to hear this MAN." And he said, "To-morrow, thou shalt hear him."

23 On the NEXT DAY, therefore, AGRIPPA and BERNICE having arrived with Great Pomp, and having entered into the PLACE OF HEARING, with the * Commanders and THOSE Men who were of Distinction in the CITY, at the COMMAND of FESTUS, PAUL was brought.

24 And FESTUS said, "King Agrippa, and All the MEN PRESENT with us! you see this man, about whom ‡ All the MULTITUDE of the JEWS applied to me, both in Jerusalem and here, crying out that he ought ‡ not to live any longer.

25 But when I detected Nothing which ‡ he had done deserving Death, ‡ and he also having appealed to † AUGUSTUS, I determined to send him;

26 concerning whom I have nothing definite to write to the † SOVEREIGN. Therefore I have brought him before you, and especially before thee, King Agrippa! that on EXAMINATION, I may have something to write.

27 For it appears to Me unreasonable to send a Prisoner, and not to signify the CHARGES alleged against him."

* VATICAN MANUSCRIPT.—21. up to Cesar. 22. said—*omit.* 23. Commanders and. 23. being—*omit.* 25. him—*omit.*

† 21 & 25. Although *Sebastos,* is usually translated *Augustus,* and the Roman emperors generally assumed this epithet, which signifies no more than the *venerable, the august;* yet here it seems to be used merely to express the *emperor,* without any reference to any of his attributes or titles. † 26. The title *Kurios, Lord,* both *Augustus* and *Tiberius* had absolutely refused; and forbad, even by public edicts, the application of it to themselves. Tiberius himself was accustomed to say, that he was *lord* of his *slaves, emperor* of the *troops,* and *prince* of the *senate.* See *Suetonius,* in his life of this prince. The succeeding emperors were not so modest; they affected the title. Nero, the emperor, *would* have it; and Pliny the younger is continually giving it to Trajan, in his letters.—*Clarke.*

‡ 24. ver. 2, 3, 7. ‡ 24. Acts xxii. 22. ‡ 25 Acts xxiii. 9, 29; xxvi. 31. ‡ 25. ver. 11, 12.

ΚΕΦ. κϛʹ. 26.

[1] Αγριππας δε προς τον Παυλον εφη· Επι-
Agrippa and to the Paul said; It is
τρεπεται σοι ὑπερ σεαυτου λεγειν. Τοτε ὁ
permitted for thee in behalf of thyself to speak. Then the
Παυλος απελογειτο, εκτεινας την χειρα·
Paul made a defence, having stretched out the hand;
[2] περι παντων ὡν εγκαλουμαι ὑπο Ιου-
concerning all things of which I am accused by Jews,
δαιων, βασιλευ Αγριππα, ἡγημαι εμαυτον μακα-
O king Agrippa, I esteem myself happy,
ριον, επι σου μελλων σημερον απολογεισθαι·
before thee being about to-day to make a defence;
[3] μαλιστα γνωστην οντα σε παντων των κατα
especially acquainted being thee of all of the among
Ιουδαιους εθων τε και ζητηματων. Διο δεο-
Jews customs and also questions. Therefore I en-
μαι *[σου,] μακροθυμως ακουσαι μου. [4] Την
treat [thee,] patiently to hear of me. The
μεν ουν βιωσιν μου την εκ νεοτητος, την
indeed therefore mode of life of me that from youth, that
απ᾽ αρχης γενομενην εν τῳ εθνει μου εν Ἱερο-
from beginning being among the nation of me in Jeru-
σολυμοις, ισασι παντες οἱ Ιουδαιοι· [5] προγινωσ-
salem, know all the Jews; previously know-
κοντες με ανωθεν, (εαν θελωσι μαρτυρειν,) ὁτι
ing me from the first, (if they would be willing to testify,) that
κατα την ακριβεστατην αἱρεσιν της ἡμετε-
according to the most rigid sect of the our
ρας θρησκειας εζησα Φαρισαιος. [6] Και νυν επ᾽
religion I lived a Pharisee. And now for
ελπιδι της προς τους πατερας επαγγελιας γενο-
hope of that to the fathers promise being
μενης ὑπο του θεου, ἑστηκα κρινομενος· [7] εις
made by the God, I have stood being judged; to
ἡν το δωδεκαφυλον ἡμων, εν εκτενειᾳ νυκτα
which the twelve tribes of us, in intently night
και ἡμεραν λατρευον, ελπιζει καταντησαι·
and day serving, hopes to attain;
περι ἡς ελπιδος εγκαλουμαι, βασιλευ
concerning which hope I am accused, O king
*[Αγριππα,] ὑπο Ιουδαιων. [8] Τι; απιστον
[Agrippa,] by Jews. What? incredible
κρινεται παρ᾽ ὑμιν, ει ὁ θεος νεκρους εγειρει;
is it judged by you, if the God dead ones raises?
[9] Εγω *[μεν] ουν εδοξα εμαυτῳ προς το
I [indeed] therefore thought in myself to the
ονομα Ιησου του Ναζωραιου δειν πολλα εναντια
name of Jesus the Nazarene ought many things against
πραξαι. [10] Ὁ και εποιησα εν Ἱεροσολυμοις·
to practise, Which also I did in Jerusalem;
και πολλους των αγιων εγω εν φυλακαις κατε-
and many of the saints I in prisons shut
κλεισα, την παρα των αρχιερεων εξουσιαν λα-
up, the from of the high-priests authority having

CHAPTER XXVI.

1 And Agrippa said to
PAUL, "It is permitted
thee to speak in behalf of
thyself." Then PAUL ex-
tending his HAND, spoke
his defence.
2 "Concerning all things
of which I am accused by
the Jews, I esteem myself
happy, King Agrippa! that
I am about This day to
speak my defence before
thee;
3 especially as thou art
acquainted with all the
CUSTOMS and Questions
among the Jews, therefore,
I entreat thee, to hear me
patiently.
4 My MODE OF LIFE,
from my Youth, THAT
which WAS from the Be-
ginning among my own
NATION, * and in Jerusa-
lem, is known to All the
* Jews;
5 who, knowing me from
the first, if they would,
might testify, That according to ‡ the MOST RIGID
Sect of our Religion, I lived
a Pharisee.
6 ‡ And now I stand on
trial for the Hope of that
PROMISE made by GOD to
our FATHERS;
7 to which our ‡ TWELVE
TRIBES, earnestly serving
Night and Day, hope to
attain; concerning Which
Hope, O King, I am ac-
cused by the Jews.
8 What! is it judged by
you as an incredible thing,
that God should raise the
Dead?
9 ‡ Therefore, indeed, I
thought within myself that
I ought to do Many things
against the NAME of Jesus
the NAZARENE;
10 ‡ * which even I did
in Jerusalem; and Many
of the SAINTS I shut up in
Prisons, having received
AUTHORITY ‡ from the

* VATICAN MANUSCRIPT.—3. thee—*omit*. 4. and in Jerusalem. 4. the Jews. 7. Agrippa—*omit*. 9. Indeed—*omit*. 10. Therefore also I did.

‡ 5. Acts xxii. 3; xxiii. 6; xxiv. 15, 22; Phil. iii. 5. ‡ 6. Gen. xii. 3; xxii. 18; xxvi. 4; Psa. cxxxii. 11. ‡ 7. James i. 1. ‡ 9. 1 Tim. i. 13. ‡ 10. Gal. i. 3. ‡ 10. Acts ix. 14, 21; xxii. 5.

βων· αναιρουμενων τε αυτων, κατηνεγκα ψηφον·
received; being killed and of them, I brought against a vote;
[11] και κατα πασας τας συναγωγας πολλακις τι-
and in all the synagogues often pun-
μωρων αυτους, ηναγκαζον βλασφημειν· περισ-
ishing them. I was compelling to blaspheme; exceed-
σως *[τε] εμμαινομενος αυτοις, εδιωκον ἑως
ingly [and] being furious towards them, I pursued till
και εις τας εξω πολεις. [12] Εν οἱς *[και] πορευ-
even into the foreign cities. In which [also] going
ομενος εις την Δαμασκον μετ' εξουσιας και επι-
to the Damascus with authority and a com-
τροπης της *[παρα] των αρχιερεων, [13] ἡμερας
mission of that [from] the high-priests, of a day
μεσης, κατα την ὁδον ειδον, βασιλευ, ουρανο-
middle, in the way I saw, O king, from heaven
θεν, ὑπερ την λαμπροτητα του ἡλιου,
above the brightness of the sun,
περιλαμψαν με φως και τους συν εμοι πορευο-
having shone round me a light and those with me going.
μενους. [14] Παντων δε καταπεσοντων *[ἡμων] εις
All and having fallen down [of us] on
την γην, ηκουσα φωνην λαλουσαν προς με,
the earth, I heard a voice speaking to me,
*[και λεγουσαν] τη ῾Εβραιδι διαλεκτῳ· Σαουλ,
[and saying] in the Hebrew dialect; Saul,
Σαουλ, τι με διωκεις; σκληρον σοι προς
Saul, why me persecutest thou? hard for thee against
κεντρα λακτιζειν. [15] Εγω δε ειπον· Τις ει,
sharp points to kick. I and said; Who art thou,
κυριε; ῾Ο δε ειπεν· Εγω ειμι Ιησους, ὁν συ
O sir? He and said; I am Jesus, whom thou
διωκεις. [16] Αλλα αναστηθι, και στηθι επι
persecutest. But arise thou, and stand up on
τους ποδας σου· εις τουτο γαρ ωφθην σοι,
the feet of thee; for this for I appeared to thee,
προχειρισασθαι σε ὑπηρετην και μαρτυρα, ὡν
to constitute thee a minister and a witness, of what
τε ειδες, ὡν τε οφθησομαι σοι· [17] εξαιρου-
both thou didst see, of what and I will appear to thee; deliver-
μενος σε εξ του λαου και των εθνων, εις οὑς
ing thee from the people and the Gentiles, to whom
εγω σε αποστελλω, [18] ανοιξαι οφθαλμους αυτων,
I thee send, to open eyes of them,
του επιστρεψαι απο σκοτους εις φως, και της
of the to have turned from darkness to light, and of the
εξουσιας του σατανα επι τον θεον, του λαβειν
authority of the adversary to the God, of the to receive
αυτους αφεσιν ἁμαρτιων, και κληρον εν τοις
them forgiveness of sins, and inheritance among those
ἡγιασμενοις, πιστει τη εις εμε. [19] ῾Οθεν, βασι-
having been sanctified, faith by the into me. Thereupon, O king

HIGH-PRIESTS; and when they were killed I gave my vote against them.

11 ‡And punishing them often in All the SYNAGOGUES, I compelled them to blaspheme; and being exceedingly furious towards them, I pursued them even to FOREIGN Cities.

12 ‡At which time, as I was going to DAMASCUS with Authority, and a Commission from the HIGH-PRIESTS,

13 at Mid-day—I saw on the ROAD, O King—from heaven—exceeding the BRIGHTNESS of the SUN—a Light shining round me, and THOSE GOING with me.

14 And all of us having fallen to the EARTH, I heard a Voice speaking to me in the HEBREW Language, 'Saul, Saul, why dost thou persecute Me? It is hard for thee to kick against the Goads.'

15 And I said, 'who art thou, Sir?' And *HE said, 'I am Jesus whom thou persecutest?

16 But arise, and stand on thy FEET; since for this purpose I have appeared to thee, ‡to constitute thee a Minister and a Witness, both *of what thou hast seen, and of those things in which I will appear to thee;

17 delivering thee from the PEOPLE and the GENTILES, ‡to whom I send thee,

18 to open their Eyes, ‡to TURN them from Darkness to Light, and from the DOMINION of the ADVERSARY to GOD; ‡that they may RECEIVE Forgiveness of Sins, and an Inheritance among THOSE HAVING BEEN ‡SANCTIFIED through THAT Faith which leads into me.

* VATICAN MANUSCRIPT.—11. and—*omit.* 12. also—*omit.* 13. from—*omit.* 14. of us—*omit.* 14. and saying—*omit.* 15. the LORD said. 16. in the which thou hast seen me, and of those things.

‡ 11. Acts xxii. 19. ‡ 12. Acts ix. 3; xxii. 6. ‡ 16. Acts xxii. 15. ‡ 17. Acts xxii. 21. ‡ 18. 2 Cor. vi. 14; Eph. iv. 28; v. 8; Col. i. 23; 1 Pet. ii. 7, 25. ‡ 18. Eph. i. 11; Col. i. 12. ‡ 18. Acts xx. 32.

λευ Αγριππα, ουκ εγενομην απειθης τῃ ουρανιῳ
Agrippa, not I was disobedient to the heavenly
οπτασιᾳ· 20 αλλα τοις εν Δαμασκῳ πρωτον και
vision; but to those in Damascus first and
Ἱεροσολυμοις, εις πασαν τε την χωραν της
in Jerusalem, in all and the country of the
Ιουδαιας, και τοις εθνεσιν, απηγγελλον μετα-
Judea, and to the Gentiles, I declared to re-
νοειν, και επιστρεφειν επι τον θεον, αξια της
form, and to turn to the God, worthy of the
μετανοιας εργα πρασσοντας. 21 Ἑνεκα τουτων
reformation works doing. On account of these
με οἱ Ιουδαιοι συλλαβομενοι εν τῳ ἱερῳ επει-
me the Jews having seized in the temple at-
ρωντο διαχειρισασθαι. 22 Επικουριας ουν τυ-
tempted with violent hands to have killed. Help therefore hav-
χων της παρα του θεου, αχρι της ἡμερας
ing obtained of that from of the God, till the day
ταυτης ἑστηκα, μαρτυρουμενος μικρῳ τε και
this I have stood, testifying to small both and
μεγαλῳ, ουδεν εκτος λεγων, ὡν τε οἱ προφηται
to great, nothing beyond saying, of what both the prophets
ελαλησαν μελλοντων γινεσθαι, και Μωυσης·
spoke being about to take place, and Moses;
23 ει παθητος ὁ Χριστος, ει πρωτος εξ αναστα-
that liable to suffer the Anointed, that first from a resurrec-
σεως νεκρων φως μελλει καταγγελλειν τῳ
tion of dead ones a light he is about to announce to the
λαῳ και τοις εθνεσι.
people and to the Gentiles.
24 Ταυτα δε αυτου απολογουμενου, ὁ Φηστος
These things and of him saying in defence, the Festus
μεγαλῃ τῃ φωνῃ εφη· Μαινῃ, Παυλε· τα πολ-
loud with the voice said; Thou art mad, O Paul; the much
λα σε γραμματα εις μανιαν περιτρεπει. 25 Ὁ
thee learning into madness turns about. He
δε· Ου μαινομαι, φησι, κρατιστε Φηστε, αλλ᾽
but; Not I am mad, he says, O most noble Festus, but
αληθειας και σωφροσυνης ῥηματα αποφθεγγο-
of truth and of sanity words I utter.
μαι. 26 Επισταται γαρ περι τουτων ὁ βασι-
Is acquainted for concerning these things the king,
λευς, προς ὁν *[και] παρρησιαζομενος λαλω·
to whom [also] being confident I may speak;
λανθανειν γαρ αυτον τι τουτων ου πειθο-
unobserved by for him any of these things not I am
μαι ουδεν· ου γαρ εστιν εν γωνιᾳ πεπραγμε-
persuaded nothing; not for it is in a corner having been
νον τουτο. 27 Πιστευεις, βασιλευ Αγριππα,
done this. Believest thou, O king Agrippa,
τοις προφηταις; Οιδα, ὁτι πιστευεις. 28 Ὁ δε
in the prophets? I know, that thou believest. The and

19 Wherefore, O King Agrippa, I was not disobedient to the HEAVENLY Vision;

20 but ‡ declared first to THOSE * in Damascus and in Jerusalem, and in All the COUNTRY of JUDEA, and to the GENTILES, that they should reform, and turn to GOD, performing ‡ Works worthy of REFORMATION.

21 On account of these things, ‡ the JEWS, having seized Me in the TEMPLE, attempted with violent hands to kill me.

22 Having obtained, therefore, THAT Assistance which is from GOD, I have continued to this DAY, testifying both to small and great, saying nothing beyond what ‡ the PROPHETS and ‡ Moses spoke as being about to transpire;

23 ‡ That the MESSIAH would be a sufferer—would be ‡ the first from the Resurrection of the Dead—and would communicate ‡ * Light both to the PEOPLE and to the GENTILES."

24 And while saying these things in his defence, FESTUS said with a Loud VOICE, "‡ Thou art mad, Paul; thy GREAT Learning has turned Thee into a Madman."

25 But * PAUL replied, "I am not mad, Most excellent Festus, but utter Words of Truth and Sanity.

26 For the KING knows about these things, to whom I speak with freedom; for I am persuaded that none of these things have escaped his notice; for this was not done in a Corner.

27 King Agrippa! dost thou believe the PROPHETS? I know That thou believest."

---

* VATICAN MANUSCRIPT.—20. in Damascus, and also in Jerusalem, and All the COUNTRY of JUDEA. 23. Light both to the PEOPLE. 25. Paul. 26. also—omit.

‡ 20. Acts ix. 20; xxii. 29; xi. 26; xiii.; xiv.; xvi.—xxi. ‡ 20. Matt. iii. 8. ‡ 21. Acts xxi. 30, 31. ‡ 22. Luke xxiv. 27, 44; Acts xxiv. 14; xxviii. 23; Rom. iii. 21. ‡ 22. John v. 46. ‡ 23. Luke xxiv. 26, 46. ‡ 23. 1 Cor. xv. 20; Col. i. 18; Rev. i. 5. ‡ 23. Luke ii. 32. ‡ 24. 2 Kings ix. 11; John x. 20; 1 Cor. i. 23; ii. 13, 14; iv. 10.

Αγριππας προς τον Παυλον *[εφη·] Εν ολιγῳ
Agrippa to the Paul [said;] Within a little
με πειθεις Χριστιανον γενεσθαι. 29 Ὁ δε
me thou persuadest a Christian to become. The and
Παυλος *[ειπεν·] Ευξαιμην αν τῳ θεῳ, και
Paul [said;] I would pray to the God, and
εν ολιγῳ και εν πολλῳ, ου μονον σε, αλλα
within a little and within much, not only thee, but
και παντας τους ακουοντας μου σημερον, γενεσ-
also all those hearing me to-day, to be
θαι τοιουτους, ὁποιος καγω ειμι, παρεκτος των
come such, as even I am, except the
δεσμων τουτων. 30 Ανεστη τε ὁ βασιλευς και
chains these. Arose and the king and
ὁ ἡγεμων, ἡ τε Βερνικη, και οἱ συγκαθημενοι
the governor, the and Bernice, and those being seated with
αυτοις· 31 και αναχωρησαντες ελαλουν προς
them; and having retired they spoke to
αλληλους, λεγοντες· Ὁτι ουδεν θανατου αξιον
each other, saying; That nothing of death worthy
η δεσμων πρασσει ὁ ανθρωπος οὑτος. 32 Αγριπ-
or of bonds does the man this. Agrippa
πας δε τῳ Φηστῳ εφη· Απολελυσθαι εδυνατο ὁ
and to the Festus said; To have been released might the
ανθρωπος οὑτος, ει μη επεκεκλητο Καισαρα.
man this, if not he had called on Cesar.

ΚΕΦ. κζ'. 27.

1 Ὡς δε εκριθη του αποπλειν ἡμας εις την
When and it was determined of the to sail us to the
Ιταλιαν, παρεδιδουν τον τε Παυλον και τινας
Italy, they delivered the both Paul and some
ἑτερους δεσμωτας ἑκατονταρχῃ, ονοματι Ιου-
other prisoners to a centurion, by name Julius,
λιῳ, σπειρης Σεβαστης. 2 Επιβαντες δε πλοιῳ
of a cohort of Augustus. Having gone on board and a ship
Αδραμυττηνῳ, μελλοντες πλειν τους κατα την
Adramyttium, being about to sail the in the
Ασιαν τοπους, ανηχθημεν, οντος συν ἡμιν
Asia places, we were put to sea, being with us
Αρισταρχου Μακεδονος Θεσσαλονικεως. 3 Τῃ
Aristarchus a Macedonian of Thessalonica. On the
τε ἑτερᾳ κατηχθημεν εις Σιδωνα· φιλανθρωπως
and next day we were brought to Sidon; humanely
τε ὁ Ιουλιος τῳ Παυλῳ χρησαμενος, επετρεψε
and the Julius to the Paul having treated, permitted
προς τους φιλους πορευθεντες επιμελειας
to the friends having gone care
τυχειν. 4 Κακειθεν αναχθεντες ὑπεπλευσα-
to have obtained. And from thence having put to sea we sailed under
μεν την Κυπρον, δια το τους ανεμους ειναι
the Cyprus, because the the winds to be
εναντιους. 5 Το, τε πελαγος το κατα την
contrary. The, and deep that by the
Κιλικιαν και Παμφυλιαν διαπλευσαντες, κατηλ-
Cilicia and Pamphylia having sailed through, we came
θομεν εις Μυρα της Λυκιας. 6 Κακει εὑρων ὁ
down to Myra of the Lycia. And there having found the

28 And AGRIPPA said to PAUL, * "Thou almost persuadest Me to become a Christian."

29 And PAUL said, ‡ "I would to GOD, that not only thou, but also All who HEAR me This day, were both almost and altogether such as I am, except these CHAINS."

30 And the KING arose, and the GOVERNOR, and BERNICE, and THOSE who SAT with them;

31 and having retired, they spoke to each other, saying, ‡ "This Man does nothing deserving Death or Bonds."

32 And Agrippa said to FESTUS, "This MAN might have been released, ‡ if he had not appealed to Cesar."

CHAPTER XXVII.

1 And when it was determined for us to SAIL to ITALY, they delivered PAUL, and some Other Prisoners, to a Centurion of the Cohort of Augustus, named Julius,

2 And embarking in an Adramyttian Ship, which was about to sail to PLACES in ASIA, we were put to sea, ‡ Aristarchus, a Macedonian of Thessalonica, being with us.

3 And on the NEXT day we were brought to Sidon; and JULIUS ‡ treating PAUL with much kindness, permitted him to go to his Friends to receive attention.

4 And having put to sea from thence, we sailed under CYPRUS, because the WINDS WERE contrary;

5 and having sailed through the SEA by CILICIA and Pamphylia, we came to * Myrrha, of LYCIA.

6 And there the CENTU-

* VATICAN MANUSCRIPT.—28. said—*omit.* 28. Almost thou persuadest to make Me a Christian. 29. said—*omit.* 5. Myrrha.

‡ 29. 1 Cor. vii. 7. ‡ 31. Acts xxiii. 9, 29; xxv. 25. ‡ 32. Acts xxv. 11. ‡ 2. Acts xix. 29. ‡ 3. Acts xxiv. 23; xxvii. 10.

ἑκατονταρχος πλοιον Αλεξανδρινον πλεον εις
centurion a ship Alexandrian sailing for
την Ιταλιαν, ενεβιβασεν ἡμας εις αυτο. 7 Εν
the Italy, put us into it. In
ἱκαναις δε ἡμεραις βραδυπλοουντες, και μολις
many and days sailing slowly, and scarcely
γενομενοι κατα την Κνιδον, μη προσεωντος
being by the Cnidus, not permitting an approach
ἡμας του ανεμου, ὑπεπλευσαμεν την Κρητην
us of the wind, we sailed under the Crete
κατα Σαλμωνην· 8 μολις τε παραλεγομενοι αυ-
by Salmone; with difficulty and sailing by her,
την, ηλθομεν εις τοπον τινα καλουμενον Καλους
we came to a place certain being called Fair
λιμενας, ᾡ εγγυς ην πολις Λασαια. 9 Ἱκανου
havens, to which near was a city Lasea. Along
δε χρονου διαγενομενου, και οντος ηδη επισφα-
and time having elapsed, and being already hazard
λους του πλοος, δια το και την νηστειαν ηδη
ous of the sailing, because the even the fast already
παρεληλυθεναι, παρῃνει ὁ Παυλος, 10 λεγων
to have been past, advised the Paul, saying
αυτοις· Ανδρες, θεωρω, ὁτι μετα ὑβρεως και
to them: Men, I perceive, that with damage and
πολλης ζημιας ου μονον του φορτιου και του
much loss not only of the freight and of the
πλοιου, αλλα και των ψυχων ἡμων μελλειν
ship but also of the lives of us to be about
εσεσθαι τον πλουν. 11 Ὁ δε εκατονταρχης τῳ
to be the voyage. The but centurion by the
κυβερνητῃ και τῳ ναυκληρῳ επειθετο μαλλον,
pilot and by the owner of the ship was persuaded rather,
η τοις ὑπο του Παυλου λεγομενοις. 12 Ανευθε-
than by those by the Paul being spoken. Inconve-
του δε του λιμενος ὑπαρχοντος προς παραχειμα-
nient and of the harbor being to winter in,
σιαν, οἱ πλειους εθεντο βουλην αναχθηναι
the greater part placed a wish to be led out
κακειθεν, ειπως δυναιντο καταντησαντες εις
from thence also, if possibly they might be able having come to
Φοινικα παραχειμασαι, λιμενα της Κρητης βλε-
Phenice to winter, a harbor of the Crete look-
ποντα κατα Λιβα και κατα Χωρον. 13 Ὑπο-
ing towards south-west and towards north-west. Hav-
πνευσαντος δε Νοτου, δοξαντες της προθεσεως
ing blown gently and South wind, supposing the purpose
κεκρατηκεναι, αραντες, ασσον παρελεγοντο
to have been attained, having raised up, close passed by
την Κρητην. 14 Μετ' ου πολυ δε εβαλε κατ'
the Crete. After not much but beat against
αυτης ανεμος τυφωνικος, ὁ καλουμενος Ευρο-
her a wind tempestuous, that being called Euro-
κλυδων. 15 Συναρπασθεντος δε του πλοιου, και
clydon. Having been caught and the ship, and

TURION having found an Alexandrian Ship bound for ITALY, put us into it.

7 And having sailed slowly for Several Days, and scarcely being by † CNIDUS, the WIND not permitting us, we sailed under CRETE, by Salmone;

8 and with difficulty passing by it, we came to a certain Place called † Fair Havens, near which is the City Lasea.

9 But Much Time having been spent, and SAILING being now hazardous, (because even the † FAST had already passed by,) PAUL advised,

10 saying to them, "Men, I perceive That the VOYAGE is about to be attended with Injury and Much Loss, not only of the CARGO and the SHIP, but also of our LIVES."

11 But the CENTURION was persuaded by the PILOT and the OWNER OF THE SHIP, rather than by the WORDS SPOKEN by PAUL.

12 And the HARBOR being inconvenient to winter in, the greater part expressed a desire to sail from thence also, and, if possibly, they might be able to reach Phenice, a Harbor of CRETE, looking towards the South west and North west, to winter there.

13 And the South wind blowing gently, supposing that they had attained their PURPOSE, weighing anchor, they passed close by CRETE.

14 But not long after, THAT Tempestuous Wind CALLED Euroclydon, beat against it;

15 and the SHIP, having been caught, and not being able to bear up against the

† 7 This was a city of Caria, situated on the extremity or tongue of land lying between Rhodes and Cos. The distance from Myra to Cnidus is about 130 geographical miles. Salome was the eastern promontory of Crete, or the present Candia, and is now called Cape Salomon. † 8. Fair Havens, near Cape Matala, midway between the eastern and western extremities of the island. Lasea, a city lying between the harbor and the cape, a short distance inland. † 9. The day of expiation, the great Fast on the tenth of the month Tisri, about the tenth of October.

μη δυναμενου αντοφθαλμειν τῳ ανεμῳ, επιδοντες
not being able to bear up against the wind, having given up
εφερομεθα. 16 Νησιον δε τι ὑποδραμοντες
we were driven. A small island and certain having run under
καλουμενον Κλαυδην, μολις ισχυσαμεν περι-
being called Clauda, scarcely we were able mas-
κρατεις γενεσθαι της σκαφης· 17 ἡν αραντες,
ters to become of the boat; which having taken up,
βοηθειαις εχρωντο, ὑποζωννυντες το πλοιον·
helps they used, undergirding the ship;
φοβουμενοι τε μη εις την Συρτιν εκπεσωσι,
fearing and lest into the quicksand they should fall,
χαλασαντες το σκευος, οὑτως εφεροντο.
having lowered the mast, thus were driven.
18 Σφοδρως δε χειμαζομενων ἡμων, τη ἑξης
Exceedingly and being storm-tossed of us, on the next
εκβολην εποιουντο· 19 και τη τριτη αυτοχειρες
a throwing out they began, and on the third with their own hands
την σκευην του πλοιου ερριψαν. 20 Μητε δε
the furniture of the ship they threw out. Neither and
ἡλιου, μητε αστρων επιφαινοντων επι πλειονας
sun, nor stars appearing for many
ἡμερας, χειμωνος τε ουκ ολιγου επικειμενου,
days, a tempest and not small pressing,
λοιπον περιηρειτο πασα ελπις του σωζεσθαι
remaining was taken away all hope of the to be saved
ἡμας. 21 Πολλης δε ασιτιας ὑπαρχουσης, τοτε
us. Long but abstinence existing, then
σταθεις ὁ Παυλος εν μεσῳ αυτων, ειπεν· Εδει
standing the Paul in midst of them, said; It was proper
μεν, ω ανδρες, πειθαρχησαντας μοι μη αναγεσ-
indeed, O men, having taken advice to me not to have
θαι απο της Κρητης, κερδησαι τε την ὑβριν
loosed from the Crete, to have gained and the damage
ταυτην και την ζημιαν. 22 Και τανυν παραινω
this and the loss. And now I exhort
ὑμας ευθυμειν· αποβολη γαρ ψυχης ουδεμια
you to take courage; loss for of a life not one
εσται εξ ὑμων, πλην του πλοιου. 23 Παρεστη
shall be from of you, except the ship. Stood by
γαρ μοι ταυτη τη νυκτι αγγελος του θεου, οὗ
for me this the night a messenger of the God, of whom
ειμι ᾡ και λατρευω, 24 λεγων· Μη φοβου,
I am to whom also I offer service, saying, Not fear,
Παυλε· Καισαρι σε δει παραστηναι· και ιδου,
O Paul, To Cesar thee it behoves to be presented; and lo,
κεχαρισται σοι ὁ θεος παντας τους πλεοντας
has graciously given to thee the God all those sailing
μετα σου. 25 Διο ευθυμειτε, ανδρες· πιστευω
with thee. Therefore take you courage, men; I believe
γαρ τῳ θεῳ ὁτι οὑτως εσται καθ' ὁν τροπον
for in the God that thus it shall be in which manner

WIND, we surrendered, and were driven.

16 And as we ran under a certain little Island, called * Clauda, with difficulty we were able to become masters of the BOAT;

17 which having hoisted up, they used Helps, † undergirding the SHIP; and fearing lest they should fall into the QUICKSAND, lowering the MAST, they were thus driven.

18 And we being exceedingly storm-tossed, on the NEXT day they began to throw overboard;

19 and on the THIRD day ‡ they threw out with their own hands the FURNITURE of the SHIP.

20 And neither Sun nor Stars appearing for Several Days, and no small Tempest pressing on us, * all remaining Hope of our being saved was taken away.

21 But there having been a Great Want of food, then PAUL standing in the Midst of them, said, "O Men! you ought, indeed, having taken my advice, not to have loosed from CRETE, but have avoided this INJURY and LOSS.

22 And now ‡ I exhort you to take courage; for there will be no Loss of Life among you; but only of the SHIP.

23 ‡ For there stood by me This NIGHT, an Angel of the GOD whose I am, and ‡ whom I serve,

24 saying, 'Fear not, Paul; thou must be presented to Cesar; and behold, GOD has graciously given thee All THOSE SAILING with thee.'

25 Therefore, take courage, Men; ‡ for I believe GOD, That it will be so, even as it was told me;

* VATICAN MANUSCRIPT.—16. Cauda. 20. all Hope.

† 17. Dr. Schmitz says, "the *hupozoomata* were thick and broad ropes, which ran in a horizontal direction around the ship from the stern to the prow, and were intended to keep the whole fabric together." Such also is the opinion of Pres. Woolsey, who well remarks that if ropes had passed under the keel, the boat would have been needed in the operation, and yet the boat was first lifted on the deck.—*Owen.*

‡ 19. Jonah i. 5. ‡ 23. Acts xxiii. 11. ‡ 23. Dan. vi. 16; Rom. i. 9; 2 Tim. i. 3.
‡ 25. Luke i. 45; Rom. iv. 20, 21; 2 Tim. i. 12.

λελαληται μοι. [26] Εις νησον δε τινα δει
it has been told to me. On an island but certain it is necessary
ἡμας εκπεσειν.
us to be cast.
[27] Ὡς δε τεσσαρεσκαιδεκατη νυξ εγενετο,
When and fourteenth night was come,
διαφερομενων ἡμων εν τω Αδρια, κατα μεσον
being driven along of us in the Adriatic, about middle
της νυκτος ὑπενοουν οἱ ναυται προσαγειν τινα
of the night suspected the sailors to draw near some
αὑτοις χωραν· [28] και βολισαντες, εὑρον οργυιας
to them country; and having heaved the lead, they found fathoms
εικοσι· βραχυ δε διαστησαντες, και παλιν
twenty; a little and having intervened, and again
βολισαντες, εὑρον οργυιας δεκαπεντε· [29] φο-
having heaved the lead, they found fathoms fifteen; fear-
βουμενοι τε, μηπως εις τραχεις τοπους εκπε-
ing and, lest on rough places we
σωμεν, εκ πρυμνης ῥιψαντας αγκυρας τεσσα-
should fall, out of stern having thrown anchors four,
ρας, ηυχοντο ἡμεραν γενεσθαι. [30] Των δε
they were wishing day to be. The and
ναυτων ζητουντων φυγειν εκ του πλοιου, και
sailors seeking to flee out of the ship, and
χαλασαντων την σκαφην εις την θαλασσαν,
having lowered the boat into the sea,
προφασει ὡς εκ πρωρας μελλοντων αγκυρας
for an excuse as out of prow being about anchors
εκτεινειν, [31] ειπεν ὁ Παυλος τω ἑκατονταρχη
to let down, said the Paul to the centurion
και τοις στρατιωταις· Εαν μη οὑτοι μεινωσιν
and to the soldiers; If not these remain
εν τω πλοιω, ὑμεις σωθηναι ου δυνασθε.
in the ship, you to be saved not are able.
[32] Τοτε οἱ στρατιωται απεκοψαν τα σχοινια της
Then the soldiers cut off the ropes of the
σκαφης, και ειασαν αυτην εκπεσειν. [33] Αχρι δε
boat, and allowed her to fall. Till and
οὑ εμελλεν ἡμερα γινεσθαι, παρεκαλει ὁ Παυ-
while about day to be, called upon the Paul
λος ἁπαντας μεταλαβειν τροφης, λεγων· Τεσ-
all to partake of food, saying; Four-
σαρεσκαιδεκατην σημερον ἡμεραν προσδοκων-
teenth to-day day looking for,
τες, ασιτοι διατελειτε, μηδεν προσλαβομενοι.
without food you continue, nothing having taken.
[34] Διο παρακαλω ὑμας μεταλαβειν τροφης·
Therefore I entreat you to partake of food;
τουτο γαρ προς της ὑμετερας σωτηριας ὑπαρχει·
this for to the your salvation is;
ουδενος γαρ ὑμων θριξ εκ της κεφαλης απο-
of not one for of you a hair from of the head will
λειται. [35] Ειπων δε ταυτα, και λαβων αρτον,
perish. Having said and these, and having taken bread,

26 but we must be cast upon ‡ a certain Island."

27 And on the Fourteenth Night, when we were driven along in the † ADRIATIC, about MIDNIGHT, the SAILORS suspected † that Some Country drew near to them;

28 and having sounded, they found twenty Fathoms; and a short space having intervened, and sounding again, they found fifteen Fathoms;

29 and fearing lest we should fall on rocky Places, they cast out four Anchors from the Stern, and were wishing for Day to break.

30 And the SAILORS seeking to flee from the SHIP, and having lowered the BOAT into the SEA, under Pretence of being about to carry forth Anchors from the Bow,

31 PAUL said to the CENTURION and the SOLDIERS, "Unless these men remain in the SHIP, you cannot be saved."

32 Then the SOLDIERS cut off the ROPES of the BOAT, and allowed her to drift away.

33 And when Day was about to dawn, PAUL urged them all to partake of Food, saying, "This Day, the Fourteenth Day that you have watched, you continue fasting, having taken Nothing.

34 Therefore, I entreat you to partake of Food; for this concerns YOUR Safety; ‡ for † not a Hair shall perish from the HEAD of any one of you."

35 And having said these words, he took Bread, ‡ and

† 27. Not the Gulf of Venice, but the portion of the Mediterranean south of Italy and west of Greece. † 27. A *nautical hypallage*, originating in the optical deception, by which, on approaching a coast, the land seems to approach to the ship, not the ship to the land.—*Bloomfield*. † 34. A proverbial expression, for you shall neither lose your lives, nor suffer any hurt in your bodies, if you follow my advice.—*Clarke*.

‡ 26. Acts xxviii. 1. ‡ 34. 1 Sam. xiv. 45; 2 Sam. xiv. 11; 1 Kings i. 52; Matt. x. 30; Luke xii. 7; xxi. 18. ‡ 35. Matt. xv. 36; Mark viii. 6; John vi. 11; 1 Tim. iv. 3, 4.

ευχαριστησε τῳ θεῳ ενωπιον παντων, και κλα-
he gave thanks to the God in presence of all, and having
σας ηρξατο εσθιειν. 36 Ευθυμοι δε γενομενοι
broken began to eat. Encouraged and becoming
παντες, και αυτοι προσελαβοντο τροφης.
all also they received food.
37 Ημεν δε εν τῳ πλοιῳ αἱ πασαι ψυχαι, *[δια-
We were and in the ship the all souls, [two
κοσιαι] ἑβδομηκοντα ἑξ. 38 Κορεσθεντες δε
hundred] seventy six. Being satisfied and
τροφης, εκουφιζον το πλοιον, εκβαλλομενοι τον
of food, they lightened the ship, throwing the
σιτον εις την θαλασσαν. 39 Ὁτε δε ἡμερα
wheat into the sea. When and day
εγενετο, την γην ουκ επεγινωσκον· κολπον δε
it was, the land not they knew; a bay but
τινα κατενοουν εχοντα αιγιαλον, εις ὁν εβου-
they perceived having a shore, into which they
λευσαντο, ει δυναιντο, εξωσαι το πλοιον. 40 Και
wished, if they were able, to force the ship. And
τας αγκυρας περιελοντες ειων εις την θαλασσαν,
the anchors having cut off left in the sea,
ἁμα ανεντες τας ζευκτηριας των πηδα-
at the same time having loosed the bands of the rud-
λιων· και επαραντες τον αρτεμονα τῃ πνεουσῃ,
ders; and having hoisted the foresail to the wind,
κατειχον εις τον αιγιαλον. 41 Περιπεσοντες δε
they pressed towards the shore. Having fallen and
εις τοπον διθαλασσον, επωκειλαν την ναυν·
into a place with a sea on both sides, they ran aground the vessel;
και ἡ μεν πρωρα ερεισασα εμεινεν ασαλευτος,
and the indeed prow having stuck fast remained immoveable,
ἡ δε πρυμνα ελυετο ὑπο της βιας *[των κυμ-
the but stern was broken by the violence [of the waves.]
ατων.] 42 Των δε στρατιωτων βουλη εγενετο,
The and soldiers design was,
ἱνα τους δεσμωτας αποκτεινωσι, μη τις εκκολυμ-
that the prisoners they should kill, lest any one having
βησας διαφυγῃ. 43 Ὁ δε ἑκατονταρχος βουλο-
swum out should escape. The but centurion wishing
μενος διασωσαι τον Παυλον, εκωλυσεν αυτους
to save the Paul, restrained them
του βουληματος, εκελευσε τε τους δυναμενους
from the purpose, ordered and those being able
κολυμβαν, απορριψαντας πρωτους επι την γην
to swim, having thrown off first to the land
εξιεναι· 44 και τους λοιπους, οὑς μεν επι σανι-
to go out; and the remaining ones, some indeed on boards,
σιν, οὑς δε επι τινων των απο του πλοιου.
some and on things of the from of the ship.
Και οὑτως εγενετο παντας διασωθηναι επι την
And thus it happened all to be safely on the

gave thanks to GOD in the presence of all; and having broken, he began to eat.

36 And being encouraged, they also received Food.

37 And ALL the Souls in the SHIP were two hundred and seventy-six.

38 And being satisfied with Food, they lightened the SHIP, throwing out the WHEAT into the SEA.

39 And when it was Day, they did not know the LAND; but they perceived a certain Bay, having a Shore, into which they wished, if they were able, to force the ship.

40 And having cut off the ANCHORS, they left them in the SEA; having, at the same time, loosed the †BANDS of the RUDDERS, and hoisted the FORESAIL to the WIND, they pressed towards the SHORE.

41 But having fallen into a Place with two currents, they ran the VESSEL aground; and the BOW sticking fast, remained immoveable, but the STERN was broken by the VIOLENCE.

42 Now it was the Design of † the SOLDIERS to kill the PRISONERS, lest any one by swimming out should escape.

43 But the CENTURION wishing to save PAUL, restrained them from their PURPOSE, and ordered THOSE ABLE *to swim out to plunge in first, and get to LAND;

44 and the REMAINDER, SOME on Boards, and SOME on things from the SHIP. And thus it happened that all reached the LAND in safety.

* VATICAN MANUSCRIPT.—37. two hundred—*omit.* 41. of the WAVES—*omit.* 43. to swim out.

† 40. The ships of the ancients usually had two rudders, one on either side of the ship. As one helmsman managed both, they were joined by a pole, so that both rudders would be parallel. The *seukteeriai* were the ropes by which these rudders were fastened to the sides of the ship, and by which they were moved by the helmsman. † 42. The military discipline of the Romans was such, that had the prisoners escaped, the soldiers would have been answerable with their lives.—*Owen.*

γην. ΚΕΦ. κη'. 28. [1] Και διασωθεντες, τοτε
land. And having safely escaped, then
επεγνωσαν ὁτι Μελιτη ἡ νησος καλειται.
they knew that Melita the island is called.
[2] Οἱ δε βαρβαροι παρειχον ου την τυχουσαν
The and barbarians rendered not the ordinary
φιλανθρωπιαν ἡμιν· αναψαντες γαρ πυραν,
kindness to us, having kindled for a fire,
προσελαβοντο παντας ἡμας, δια τον ὑετον τον
they brought to all of us, because of the rain that
εφεστωτα, και δια το ψυχος. [3] Συστρε
having been present, and because of the cold. Having
ψαντος δε του Παυλου φρυγανων πληθος, και
gathered and the Paul of sticks a bundle, and
επιθεντος επι την πυραν, εχιδνα εκ της θερμης
having placed on the fire, a viper from the heat
εξελθουσα καθηψε της χειρος αυτου. [4] Ὡς δε
having come out fastened on the hand of him. When and
ειδον οἱ βαρβαροι κρεμαμενον το θηριον εκ της
saw the barbarians hanging the wild beast from the
χειρος αυτου, ελεγον προς αλληλους· Παντως
hand of him, they said to each other; Certainly
φονευς εστιν ὁ ανθρωπος οὑτος, ὁν διασωθεντα
a murderer is the man this, whom having been saved
εκ της θαλασσης ἡ Δικη ζην ουκ ειασεν. [5] Ὁ
from the sea the Justice to live not permitted. He
μεν ουν αποτιναξας το θηριον εις το πυρ, επα-
indeed then having shaken off the wild beast into the fire, suf-
θεν ουδεν κακον· [6] οἱ δε προσεδοκων αυτον
fered nothing bad; they but were expecting him
μελλειν πιμπρασθαι, η καταπιπτειν αφνω νεκ-
to be about to swell, or to fall down suddenly dead.
ρον. Επι πολυ δε αυτων, προσδοκωντων, και
For a long and of them, expecting, and
θεωρουντων μηδεν ατοπον εις αυτον γινομενον,
seeing nothing out of place to him happening,
μεταβαλλομενοι ελεγον, θεον αυτον ειναι. [7] Εν
changing their minds they said, a god him to be. In
δε τοις περι τον τοπον εκεινον ὑπηρχε χωρια
and to those about the place that were farms
τῳ πρωτῳ της νησου, ονοματι Ποπλιῳ· ὁς ανα-
to the chief of the island, by name Poplius; who having
δεξαμενος ἡμας, τρεις ἡμερας φιλοφρονως εξε-
received us, three days kindly enter-
νισεν. [8] Εγενετο δε τον πατερα του Ποπλιου
tained. It happened and the father of the Poplius
πυρετοις και δυσεντεριᾳ συνεχομενον κατακεισ-
with fevers and desentery being seized was lying
θαι· προς ὁν ὁ Παυλος εισελθων, και προσευ-
down; to whom the Paul going in, and having

CHAPTER XXVIII.

1 And having safely escaped, *we then ascertained ‡That the ISLAND was called †Melita.

2 And the ‡†BARBARIANS treated us with no ORDINARY Philanthropy; for having kindled a Fire, they brought us all to it, on account of the FALLING RAIN, and the COLD.

3 And as PAUL was collecting a Bundle of Sticks, and placing them on the FIRE, a Viper having come out from the HEAT, fastened on his HAND.

4 And when the BARBARIANS saw the SERPENT hanging from his HAND, they said, to each other, "This MAN is certainly a Murderer, whom, though saved from the SEA, †JUSTICE has not permitted to live."

5 Then, indeed, he shook off the SERPENT into the FIRE, and ‡suffered no injury.

6 But THEY were expecting him about to swell up, or to fall down suddenly dead; and waiting a long time, and seeing nothing extraordinary happen to him, changing their minds ‡they said, "He is a God."

7 And in the VICINITY of that PLACE were the LANDS of the CHIEF of the ISLAND, whose Name was †Poplius; who having received us, for *three Days benevolently entertained us.

8 Now it happened, that the FATHER of POPLIUS, being seized with Fevers and Dysentery, was lying in bed; to whom PAUL having entered ‡and

* VATICAN MANUSCRIPT.—1. we then. 7. three Days.

† 1. The recent investigations of Smith show conclusively, that the island now called *Malta*, was the scene of the shipwreck. See *Biblioth. Sacra.* † 2. A name applied by the Greeks and Romans indiscriminately to all foreigners. † 4. *Hee Dikee* was the proper name of the heathen goddess of justice. She was the daughter of Jupiter, and was called also Nemesis. † 8. Poplius is thought to have been the deputy of the prætor of Sicily, as in the time of Cicero, Malta was under the jurisdiction of the Sicilian prætor.

‡ 1. Acts xxvii. 26. ‡ 2. Rom. i. 14; 1 Cor. xiv. 11; Col. iii. 11. ‡ 5. Mark xvi. 18; Luke x. 19. ‡ 6. Acts xiv. 11. ‡ 8. James v. 14, 15.

ξαμενος, επιθεις τας χειρας αυτῳ, ιασατο αυτον.
prayed, having placed the hand to him, healed him.
9 Τουτου ουν γενομενου, και οἱ λοιποι οἱ εχον-
This therefore being done. and the others those hav-
τες ασθενειας εν τῃ νησῳ, προσηρχοντο, και
ing sicknesses in the island, came, and
εθεραπευοντο· 10 οἱ και πολλαις τιμαις ετιμησαν
were healed; who also with many rewards rewarded
ἡμας, και αναγομενοις επεθεντο τα προς την
us, and leading out they placed on the things for the
χρειαν.
need.

11 Μετα δε τρεις μηνας ανηχθημεν εν πλοιῳ
After and three months we sailed in a ship
παρακεχειμακοτι εν τῃ νησῳ, Αλεξανδρινῳ,
having been wintered in the island. Alexandrian.
παρασημῳ Διοσκουροις. 12 Και καταχθεντες εις
with an ensign Dioscuri. And having been led down to
Συρακουσας, επεμειναμεν ἡμερας τρεις· 13 ὁθεν
Syracuse, we remained days three; whence
περιελθοντες κατηντησαμεν εις Ῥηγιον· και
having gone round we came to Rhegium: and
μετα μιαν ἡμεραν επιγενομενου Νοτου, δευτε-
after one day having sprung up a south wind, second
ραιοι ηλθομεν εις Ποτιολους· 14 οὑ εὑροντες
day we came to Puteoli, where having found
αδελφους παρεκληθημεν επ' αυτοις επιμειναι
brethren we were invited by them to remain
ἡμερας επτα· και οὑτως εις την Ῥωμην ηλθο-
days seven; and thus towards the Rome we
μεν. 15 Κακειθεν οἱ αδελφοι ακουσαντες τα
went. And thence the brethren having heard the things
περι ἡμων, εξηλθον εις απαντησιν ἡμιν αχρις
concerning us, came out to a meeting with us as far as
Αππιου φορου, και Τριων ταβερνων· οὑς ιδων ὁ
Appii forum, and Three taverns; whom seeing the
Παυλος, ευχαριστησας τῳ θεῳ, ελαβε θαρσος.
Paul, having given thanks to the God, he took courage.
16 Ὁτε δε ηλθομεν εις Ῥωμην, *[ὁ ἑκατονταρ-
When and we came to Rome, [the centurion
χος παρεδωκε τους δεσμιους τῳ στρατοπεδαρ-
delivered the prisoners to the prefect of the Preto-
χῃ·] τῳ *[δε] Παυλῳ επετραπη μενειν καθ'
rium camp;] the [but] Paul was permitted to abide by
ἑαυτον, συν τῳ φυλασσοντι αυτον στρατιω-
himself, with the watching him soldier.

prayed, ‡ put his HANDS
on him, and cured him.
9 This, therefore, hav-
ing been done, the OTHERS
also in the ISLAND, HAV-
ING Diseases, came, and
were cured;
10 and THEY presented
us with Many ‡ Presents;
and when we left, put on
board THINGS for our
WANTS.
11 And after Three
Months we set sail in an
Alexandrian Ship, which
had wintered in the IS-
LAND, with the Sign of
the † Dioscuri.
12 And having landed
at † Syracuse, we remained
three Days;
13 whence, coasting
round, we came to † Rhe-
gium; and after One Day, a
South wind having sprung
up, we came in Two days
to † Puteoli;
14 where we found
Brethren, and were invited
by them to remain seven
Days; and thus we went
towards Rome.
15 And thence, the
BRETHREN having heard
about our AFFAIRS, came
out to meet us as far as
† Appii Forum, and the
† Three Taverns; whom,
when PAUL saw, he
thanked GOD, and took
Courage.
16 And when we * came
to Rome, the CENTURION
delivered the PRISONERS
to the † PREFECT OF THE
PRETORIUM CAMP; but
‡ PAUL was permitted to
dwell by himself, with the
SOLDIER who GUARDED
him.

* VATICAN MANUSCRIPT.—16. were entered Rome. 16. the CENTURION delivered the PRISONERS to the PREFECT OF THE PRETORIUM CAMP—*omit*. 16. but—*omit*.

† 11. Castor and Pollux, children of Jupiter, the tutelary deities of sailors. † 12. The port of this celebrated city was directly in the course from Malta to Italy. † 13. A maritime city of lower Italy, opposite Messina in Sicily. Its present name is Reggio. † 13. Puteoli is now called Puzzuoli, and lies six miles south-west from Naples. † 15. About 52 miles from Rome, a town on the Appian way, a road paved from Rome to Campania. † 15. Another place on the same road, some 33 miles from Rome. † 16. The usual title given to the chief of the fortress. He commanded the garrison of Rome, a body of 10,000 men, who were lodged in the Pretorium camp, an enclosed fortress of about 40 acres, outside of the city, and about a mile and a half from the emperor's palace.

‡ 8. Mark vi. 5; vii. 32; xvi. 18; Luke iv. 40; Acts xix. 11, 12; 1 Cor. xii. 9, 28. ‡ 10. Matt. xv. 6; 1 Tim. v. 17. ‡ 16. Acts xxiv. 25; xxvii. 3.

τῃ. [17] Εγενετο δε μετα ἡμερας τρεις συγκαλε-
It happened and after days three to have called
σασθαι αυτον τους οντας των Ιουδαιων πρωτους.
together to him those being of the Jews chiefs.
Συνελθοντων δε αυτων, ελεγε προς αυτους·
Having come together and of them, he said to them;
Ανδρες αδελφοι, εγω ουδεν εναντιον ποιησας
Men brethren, I nothing against having done
τῳ λαῳ η τοις εθεσι τοις πατρῳοις, δεσμιος
to the people or to the customs those paternal, a prisoner
εξ Ἱεροσολυμων παρεδοθην εις τας χειρας των
from Jerusalem I was delivered into the hands of the
Ῥωμαιων· [18] οἱτινες ανακριναντες με εβουλοντο
Romans; who having examined me wished
απολυσαι, δια το μηδεμιαν αιτιαν θανατου
to release, because that no one cause of death
ὑπαρχειν εν εμοι. [19] Αντιλεγοντων δε των
to be in me. Speaking against and the
Ιουδαιων, ηναγκασθην επικαλεσασθαι Καισαρα·
Jews, I was forced to call upon Cesar;
ουχ ὡς του εθνους μου εχων τι κατηγορησαι.
not as of the nation of me having anything to accuse.
[20] Δια ταυτην ουν την αιτιαν παρεκαλεσα
Because of this therefore the cause I called
ὑμας ιδειν και προσλαλησαι· ἑνεκεν γαρ της
you to see and to speak with; on account for of the
ελπιδος του Ισραηλ την ἁλυσιν ταυτην περι-
hope of the Israel the chain this I wear
κειμαι. [21] Οἱ δε προς αυτον ειπον· Ἡμεις ουτε
around. They and to him said; We neither
γραμματα περι σου εδεξαμεθα απο της Ιου-
letters concerning thee received from the Ju-
δαιας, ουτε παραγενομενος τις των αδελφων
dea, neither having come any one of the brethren
απηγγειλεν η ελαλησε τι περι σου πονηρον.
related or spoken anything concerning thee evil.
[22] Αξιουμεν δε παρα σου ακουσαι, ἁ φρονεις·
We deem proper but from thee to hear, what thou thinkest;
περι μεν γαρ της αἱρεσεως ταυτης γνωστον
concerning indeed for of the sect this known
εστιν ἡμιν, ὁτι πανταχου αντιλεγεται. [23] Τα-
is to us, that everywhere it is spoken against. Hav-
ξαμενοι δε αυτῳ ἡμεραν, ἡκον προς αυτον εις
ing appointed and to him a day, came to him to
την ξενιαν πλειονες· οἱς εξετιθετο διαμαρτυρο-
the lodging many; to whom he set forth testifying earnestly
μενος την βασιλειαν του θεου, πειθων τε
the kingdom of the God, persuading and
αυτους *[τα] περι του Ιησου, απο τε του
them [the things] concerning the Jesus, from both the
νομου Μωυσεως και των προφητων, απο πρωι
law of Moses and of the prophets, from morning
ἑως εσπερας. [24] Και οἱ μεν επειθοντο τοις
till evening. And these indeed were persuaded by the
λεγομενοις, οἱ δε ηπιστουν. [25] Ασυμφωνοι δε
words being spoken, those but believed not. Not agreed and

17 And it occurred, after
three Days, he called together the CHIEF men of the
JEWS. And they having
convened, he said to them,
"Brethren, ‡ though I
have done nothing con-
trary to the PEOPLE, or to
the PATERNAL CUSTOMS,
yet ‡ I was delivered a
Prisoner from Jerusalem
into the HANDS of the Ro-
MANS;

18 who, ‡ having ex-
amined me, wished to re-
lease me, because there
WAS No Cause of Death in
me.

19 But the JEWS speak-
ing against it, ‡ I was compelled to appeal to Cesar;
not as having anything of
which to accuse my NA-
TION.

20 For This REASON,
therefore, I called you, to
see and speak with you;
‡ for on account of the
HOPE of ISRAEL I wear
‡ this CHAIN."

21 And THEY said to
him, "We neither re-
ceived Letters from JU-
DEA about thee, nor did
any one of the BRETHREN
who came relate or speak
Any Evil concerning thee.

22 But we deem it pro-
per to hear from thee what
thou thinkest; for indeed
it is known to us concerning this SECT, ‡ That it
is every where spoken
against."

23 And having appointed
him a Day, many came to
him into his LODGING;
‡ to whom he set forth,
earnestly testifying the
KINGDOM of GOD, and per-
suading them concerning
JESUS, both from the LAW
of Moses and the PROPH-
ETS, from Morning till
Evening.

24 And ‡ SOME were
persuaded by the WORDS
BEING SPOKEN; but SOME
believed not.

‡ 17. Acts xxiv. 12, 14; xxv. 8. ‡ 17. Acts xxi. 33. ‡ 18. Acts xxii. 24; xxiv. 10; xxv. 8; xxvi. 31. ‡ 19. Acts xxv. 11. ‡ 20. Acts xxvi. 6, 7. ‡ 20. Acts xxvi. 20; Eph. iii. 1; iv. 1; vi. 20; 2 Tim. i. 16; ii. 9; Philemon 10, 13. ‡ 22. Acts xxiv. 5, 14; 1 Pet. ii. 12; iv. 14. ‡ 23. Luke xxiv. 27; Acts xvii. 3; xix. 8. ‡ 24. Acts xiv. 4; xvii. 4; xix. 9.

οντες προς αλληλους, απελυοντο, ειποντος του
being with each other, they were dismissed, saying of the
Παυλου ῥημα ἑν· Ὁτι καλως το πνευμα το
Paul word one; That well the spirit the
ἁγιον ελαλησε δια Ἡσαιου του προφητου προς
holy spoke through Esaias the prophet to
τους πατερας ἡμων, 26 λεγον· Πορευθητι προς
the fathers of us, saying; Go thou to
τον λαον τουτον, και ειπον· Ακοη ακουσετε,
the people this, and say thou; With ears you will hear,
και ου μη συνητε· και βλεποντες βλεψετε,
and not not you may understand; and seeing you will see,
και ου μη ιδητε. 27 Επαχυνθη γαρ ἡ καρδια
and not not you may perceive. Unfeeling for the heart
του λαου τουτου, και τοις ωσι βαρεως ηκουσαν,
of the people this, and with the ears heavily they hear,
και τους οφθαλμους αὑτων εκαμμυσαν· μηποτε
and the eyes of them they closed; lest at any time
ιδωσι τοις οφθαλμοις, και τοις ωσιν ακου-
they should see with the eyes, and with the ears they
σωσι, και τῃ καρδιᾳ συνωσι, και επισ-
should hear, and with the heart they should understand, and should
τρεψωσι, και ιασωμαι αυτους. 28 Γνωστον ουν
return, and I should heal them. Known therefore
εστω ὑμιν, ὁτι τοις εθνεσιν απεσταλη το σωτη-
let it be to you, that to the Gentiles is sent the salva-
ριον του θεου· αυτοι και ακουσονται. 29 *[Και
tion of the God; they and will hear. [And
ταυτα αυτου ειποντος, απηλθον οἱ Ιουδαιοι,
these things of him saying, went the Jews,
πολλην εχοντες εν ἑαυτοις συζητησιν.] 30 Εμει-
much having among themselves discussion.] He abode
νε δε διετιαν ὁλην εν ιδιῳ μισθωματι· και απε-
and two years whole in own hired dwelling; and received
δεχετο παντας τους εισπορευομενους προς
all those coming in to
αυτον, 31 κηρυσσων την βασιλειαν του θεου,
him, publishing the kingdom of the God,
και διδασκων τα περι του κυριου Ιησου
and teaching the things concerning the Lord Jesus
Χριστου μετα πασης παρρησιας, ακωλυτως.
Anointed with all freedom of speech, unrestrained.

25 And not being agreed with each other, they were dismissed, PAUL saying one Word, "Well did the HOLY SPIRIT speak through Isaiah the PROPHET to our FATHERS,
26 saying, ‡ 'Go to this 'PEOPLE, and say, Hear-'ing you will hear, though 'you may not understand; 'and seeing, you will see, 'though you may not per-'ceive.
27 'For the HEART of 'this PEOPLE is stupified; 'they hear heavily with 'their EARS, and their 'EYES they have closed; 'lest at any time they 'should see with their 'EYES, and hear with their 'EARS, and understand 'with their HEART, and 'should retrace their steps, 'and I should heal them.'
28 Be it known to you, therefore, That * This SALVATION of GOD is sent ‡ to the GENTILES, and they will hear it."
29 *[And when he said these things, the JEWS departed, having Much Discussion among themselves.]
30 And he dwelt two whole Years in his Own Hired house, and received ALL those COMING IN to him;
31 ‡ proclaiming the KINGDOM of GOD, and teaching the THINGS concerning the LORD Jesus Christ, with Entire Freedom of speech, and without restraint.

*ACTS OF APOSTLES.

* VATICAN MANUSCRIPT.—28. This SALVATION. 29. *omit*. *Subscription*—ACTS OF APOSTLES.

‡ 26. Isa. vi. 9; Jer. v. 21; Ezek. xii. 2; Matt. xiii. 14, 15; Mark iv. 12; Luke viii. 10; John xii. 40; Rom. xi. 8. ‡ 28. Matt. xxi. 41, 43; Acts xiii. 46, 47; xviii. 6; xxii. 21; xxvi. 17, 18; Rom. xi. 11. ‡ 31. Acts iv. 31; Eph. vi. 19.

9 781425 48642